BIOETHICS AND PUBLIC HEALTH LAW

BIOETHICS AND PUBLIC HEALTH LAW

Third Edition

David Orentlicher
Samuel R. Rosen Professor of Law
Co-director, Hall Center for Law and Health
Indiana University Robert H. McKinney School of Law

Mary Anne Bobinski
Dean and Professor
University of British Columbia Faculty of Law

Mark A. Hall
Fred D. and Elizabeth L. Turnage Professor of Law and Public Health
Wake Forest University

Wolters Kluwer
Law & Business

Printed in the United States of America.

3 4 5 6 7 8 9 0

ISBN 978-1-4548-0535-9

Library of Congress Cataloging-in-Publication Data

Orentlicher, David, 1955-
   Bioethics and public health law / David Orentlicher, Samuel R. Rosen Professor of Law, Co-director, Hall Center for Law and Health, Indiana University Robert H. McKinney School of Law; Mary Anne Bobinski, Dean and Professor, University of British Columbia Faculty of Law; Mark A. Hall, Fred D. and Elizabeth L. Turnage Professor of Law and Public Health, Wake Forest University. — Third Edition.
      pages cm. — (Aspen casebook series)
   ISBN 978-1-4548-0535-9
   1. Public health laws—Moral and ethical aspects—United States. 2. Bioethics—United States. I. Bobinski, Mary Anne. II. Hall, Mark A., 1955- III. Title.
   KF3775.O74 2013
   344.7304—dc23

                                                                            2013014497

SUSTAINABLE FORESTRY INITIATIVE

Certified Chain of Custody
Promoting Sustainable Forestry

www.sfiprogram.org
SFI-01347

About Wolters Kluwer Law & Business

Wolters Kluwer Law & Business is a leading global provider of intelligent information and digital solutions for legal and business professionals in key specialty areas, and respected educational resources for professors and law students. Wolters Kluwer Law & Business connects legal and business professionals as well as those in the education market with timely, specialized authoritative content and information-enabled solutions to support success through productivity, accuracy and mobility.

Serving customers worldwide, Wolters Kluwer Law & Business products include those under the Aspen Publishers, CCH, Kluwer Law International, Loislaw, Best Case, ftwilliam.com and MediRegs family of products.

CCH products have been a trusted resource since 1913, and are highly regarded resources for legal, securities, antitrust and trade regulation, government contracting, banking, pension, payroll, employment and labor, and healthcare reimbursement and compliance professionals.

Aspen Publishers products provide essential information to attorneys, business professionals and law students. Written by preeminent authorities, the product line offers analytical and practical information in a range of specialty practice areas from securities law and intellectual property to mergers and acquisitions and pension/benefits. Aspen's trusted legal education resources provide professors and students with high-quality, up-to-date and effective resources for successful instruction and study in all areas of the law.

Kluwer Law International products provide the global business community with reliable international legal information in English. Legal practitioners, corporate counsel and business executives around the world rely on Kluwer Law journals, looseleafs, books, and electronic products for comprehensive information in many areas of international legal practice.

Loislaw is a comprehensive online legal research product providing legal content to law firm practitioners of various specializations. Loislaw provides attorneys with the ability to quickly and efficiently find the necessary legal information they need, when and where they need it, by facilitating access to primary law as well as state-specific law, records, forms and treatises.

Best Case Solutions is the leading bankruptcy software product to the bankruptcy industry. It provides software and workflow tools to flawlessly streamline petition preparation and the electronic filing process, while timely incorporating ever-changing court requirements.

ftwilliam.com offers employee benefits professionals the highest quality plan documents (retirement, welfare and non-qualified) and government forms (5500/PBGC, 1099 and IRS) software at highly competitive prices.

MediRegs products provide integrated health care compliance content and software solutions for professionals in healthcare, higher education and life sciences, including professionals in accounting, law and consulting.

Wolters Kluwer Law & Business, a division of Wolters Kluwer, is headquartered in New York. Wolters Kluwer is a market-leading global information services company focused on professionals.

To the memory of Prof. Herman I. Orentlicher, for his commitment to "neutral skepticism," rigorous standards, and, above all, decency.
—*D.O.*

To my partner Holly and our daughter Anna, and to my parents, for their encouragement.
—*M.A.B.*

To Larry C. Hall, Ph.D., for showing me the joys of an academic life.
—*M.A.H.*

To Bill Curran, for his guiding light.

Summary of Contents

Summary of Contents

Contents

2

The Treatment Relationship   97

3

The Right and "Duty" to Die

5
■

Reproductive Rights and Genetic Technologies 461

6

■

Public Health Law

Preface

The Content and Organization of This Book

This book contains the materials from *Health Care Law and Ethics* (8th ed., 2013) that are focused on bioethics and public health law. As the larger case-book nears its half-century anniversary, we pause to reflect on the remarkable metamorphosis of health care law from a subspecialty of tort law, to a mush-rooming academic and practice field whose tentacles reach into myriad schol-arly disciplines and areas of substantive law. This book's seven prior editions reflect important stages in this evolutionary growth. Health care law originated as a separate field of professional practice and academic inquiry during the 1960s, when this book was first published. Under the somewhat grandiose label of "medical jurisprudence," the primary focus at first was on medical proof in all kinds of criminal and civil litigation, on medical malpractice actions against physicians, and on public health regulation. The principal concern was how traditional bodies of legal doctrine and practice—such as criminal, tort, and evidence law—should apply in medical settings.

During the 1970s, bioethics became a major additional area of concern as a consequence of the right to die movement spawned by the *Quinlan* case, and the focus on individual autonomy contained in the informed consent doctrine and the landmark decision on reproductive decisionmaking in Roe v. Wade. Law courses during this and earlier periods were taught under the heading of "law and medicine."

In the 1980s, economic and regulatory topics formed the third component of health care law, as exemplified by the increasing application of antitrust laws to the health care industry and the growing body of legal disputes under Medicare and Medicaid. This newer dimension accelerated its growth into the 1990s with the spread of HMOs and other managed care organizations, which propelled various corporate and contractual restructurings. These newer topics found their way into courses described as "health law."

New developments present continuing challenges to each of these areas of health care law and ethics. In the new millennium, biotechnology, consumer-driven health care, medical confidentiality, and bioterrorism are examples of emerging issues that receive increased attention in the previous edition. This decade is witnessing an explosion of interest in health care public policy, coinciding with Congress' massive health care reform law enacted in 2010, whose importance reverberates throughout the field.

This path of development has resulted in an academic discipline defined more by an accretion of topics drawn from historical events than by a systematic conceptual organization of issues. Each of the four major branches—malpractice, bioethics, public health, and financing/regulation—stands apart from the others and is thought to be dominated by a distinct theme. The principal concern of malpractice law is quality of care; bioethics is concerned with individual autonomy; public health poses the rights of patients against the state; and the primary focus of financing and regulatory law is access to care and the cost of care. As a consequence, health care law has yet to become a truly integrated and cohesive discipline.[1] It is too much the creature of history and not of systematic and conceptual organization.

Our major ambition in this book is to improve this state of disarray. This field has reached a stage of maturity that calls for stepping back and rethinking how all of its parts best fit together as a conceptual whole. In our view that conceptual whole is best organized according to the fundamental structural relationships that give rise to health care law. These relationships are:

1. The patient/physician relationship, which encompasses the duty to treat, confidentiality, informed consent, and malpractice
2. State oversight of doctors and patients, which encompasses the right to die, reproductive rights, physician licensure, and public health
3. The institutions that surround the treatment relationship, encompassing public and private insurance, hospitals and HMOs, and more complex transactions and organizational forms

We develop the traditional themes of quality, ethics, access, and cost throughout each of these three divisions. We also address cutting-edge and controversial topics such as health care reform, genetics, managed care, and ration-

---

1. This disarray is reflected by the ongoing confusion over competing names for the field. Although "law and medicine" and "health care law" appear to signify the same topic, the first term is understood to mean older style malpractice subject matter, and the second term is used to refer to newer economic and regulatory issues. Paradoxically, whereas "health care law" and "health law" might be thought to signify somewhat different fields—the latter not restricted to medical treatment and therefore encompassing public health issues—in fact they are taken to mean the same thing.

ing, but not as discrete topics; instead, we integrate these developments within a more permanent, overarching organizational structure, which is capable of absorbing unanticipated new developments as they occur.

In deciding which topics to present in each section and in what depth, our basic guide has been to focus on the essential attributes of the medical enterprise that make it uniquely important or difficult in the legal domain. Health care law is about the delivery of an extremely important, very expensive, and highly specialized professional service. If it were otherwise, this book would likely not exist. Some lawyers and scholars maintain that there is no unifying concept or set of ideas for health care law; instead, it is merely a disparate collection of legal doctrines and public policy responses, connected only by the happenstance that they involve doctors and hospitals in some way—much as if one had a course on the law of green things or the law of Tuesdays. It would be far more satisfying to find one or more organizing principles that explain not only what makes the disparate parts of health care law cohere, but also why that coherence distinguishes health care law from other bodies of integrated legal thought and professional practice.

We believe those organizing principles can, in part, be found in the phenomenology of what it is to be ill and to be a healer of illness. These two human realities are permanent and essential features that distinguish this field from all other commercial and social arenas. They permeate all parts of health care law, giving it its distinctive quality and altering how generic legal doctrine and conventional theories of government respond to its problems and issues. Health care law might still be worth studying even without these unique attributes of medical encounters, but it is much more engaging and coherent because of them. It is these attributes that give rise to an interrelated set of principles that justify classifying health care law as a coherent and integrated academic and professional discipline. Elaborating this perspective, see Mark A. Hall, The History and Future of Health Care Law: An Essentialist View, 41 Wake Forest L. Rev. 347 (2006).[2]

Accordingly, we stress the essential attributes of medical encounters throughout these materials by incorporating insights from other academic disciplines and theoretical perspectives. Behavioral disciplines such as psychology, sociology, and anthropology help to illuminate the nature of medical knowledge and the lived experience of illness, dependency, and trust as they occur in

2. For additional discussion of the overall content of health care law and approaches to teaching and understanding it, see Clark Havighurst, American Health Care and the Law: We Need to Talk!, 19(4) Health Aff. 84 (July 2000); William M. Sage, Relational Duties, Regulatory Duties, and the Widening Gap Between Individual Health Law and Collective Health Policy, 96 Geo. L.J. 497-522 (2008); Theodore W. Ruger, Health Law's Coherence Anxiety, 96 Geo. L.J. 625-648 (2008); Wendy Mariner, Toward an Architecture of Health Law, 35 Am. J.L. & Med. 67 (2009); M. Gregg Bloche, the Emergent Logic of Health Law, 82 S. Cal. L. Rev. 389-480 (2009); Andrew Fichter, The Law of Doctoring: A Study of the Codification of Medical Professionalism, 19 Health Matrix 317-385 (2009); Sandra Johnson, Regulating Physician Behavior: Taking Doctors' "Bad Law" Claims Seriously, 53 St. Louis U. L.J. 973 (2009); Charity Scott, Teaching Health Law, J.L. Med. & Ethics (recurring column); Symposium, 19 Ann. Health L. 1 (2010); Symposium, Patient-Centered Law and Ethics, 45 Wake Forest L. Rev. 1429 (2010); Symposium, Rethinking Health Law, 41 Wake Forest L. Rev. 341 (2006); Symposium, The Field of Health Law: Its Past and Future, 14 Health Matrix 1 (2004); William J. Curran, Titles in the Medicolegal Field: A Proposal for Reform, 1 Am. J.L. & Med. 1 (1975).

real-life medical encounters. Findings from health services research published in the health policy literature create a stronger empirical and theoretical base for exploring health care law, one that better exposes its broad social impact. Analytical disciplines, such as economics and moral and political theory, create the foundation for understanding developments in financing, regulation, and bioethics. And, the perspectives of feminist, communitarian, and critical race theory demonstrate the limitations of conventional analytical models and help us understand how health care law must evolve to accommodate viewpoints and concerns that have been excluded in the past.

The 1992 death of Bill Curran, the original author of this casebook, left us with a considerable burden to shoulder. Although Prof. Curran was involved in the conceptual reorganization of these materials, he was unable to contribute to their selection and editing. Still, his presence is felt in every part of these materials through the inspiration of his mentoring, his friendship, and his vast body of work.

We intend that this book will continue to serve as both a teaching tool and an ongoing resource for conducting research in health care law. To that end, we provide substantial bibliographic notes in each section. Also, we have created a dedicated Web site to serve this book: www.health-law.org. It extends the book's content with interesting background materials, updates of important events since publication, additional relevant topics that were excluded due to space constraints, and links to other resources on the internet.

The following is a bibliography of resources and readings that relate to research in health care law generally. Additional bibliographic references that relate to particular parts of health care law can be found at pages 77 and 648, and on the casebook Web site.

Treatises and Texts: Barry Furrow et al., Health Law (2d ed. 2001); Mark A. Hall, David Orentlicher, and Ira Mark Ellman, Health Care Law and Ethics in a Nutshell (3d ed. 2011); Hooper, Lundy & Bookman, Treatise on Health Care Law; John H. Robinson, Roberta M. Berry & Kevin McDonnell, eds., A Health Law Reader: An Interdisciplinary Approach (1999); World Health Organization, International Digest of Health Legislation, http://apps.who.int/idhl-rils/.

Health Care Law Journals and Recurring Symposia: American Journal of Law and Medicine (Boston Univ.); Annals of Health Law (Loyola-Chicago); DePaul Journal of Health Care Law; Food, Drug and Cosmetic Law Journal; Health Law & Policy Abstracts and Public Health Law Abstracts (SSRN online journals); Health Matrix (Case Western Univ.); Houston Journal of Health Law & Policy; Indiana Health Law Review (Indiana Univ.-Indianapolis); Journal of Contemporary Health Law and Policy (Catholic Univ.); Journal of Health & Biomedical Law (Suffolk), Journal of Health and Life Sciences Law (St. Louis Univ., AHLA); Journal of Health Care Law & Policy (Univ. of Maryland); Journal of Law and Health (Cleveland-Marshall); Journal of Law, Medicine and Ethics (ASLME); Journal of Legal Medicine (So. Illinois Univ.); Medical Trial Technique Quarterly; Journal of Medicine and Law; St. Louis Univ. Law Journal; Seton Hall Law Review; Quinnipiac Health Law Journal; Whittier Law Review; Yale Journal of Health Policy, Law and Ethics.

Leading Medical, Industry, and Health Policy Journals: American Journal of Public Health; American Medical News (AMA); Health Affairs (published by

Project Hope); Health Care Financing and Delivery (SSRN online journal), Medicare & Medicaid Research Review (formerly the Health Care Financing Review) (DHHS/CMS); Health Economics, Policy and Law (Cambridge Press); Health Services Research; Inquiry (published by Excellus, a Blue Cross plan in Rochester, NY); Hospitals and Health Networks (AHA); Journal of the American Medical Association; Journal of Health Politics, Policy and Law; Medical Care; Milbank Quarterly; Modern Healthcare; New England Journal of Medicine.

Health Law Societies, Digests, and Newsletters: ABA Forum on Health Law (newsletter); American College of Legal Medicine (journal); American Society of Law, Medicine, and Ethics (two journals); BNA Health Law Reporter (weekly); American Health Lawyers Association (monthly digest and newsletter, bimonthly journal).

Acknowledgments

This manuscript could not have been prepared without the thoughtful advice of our colleagues who commented on drafts and gave us suggestions for revision (especially Bill Brewbaker, Seth Chandler, Judy Failer, Hank Greely, David Hyman, Eleanor Kinney, Jack Nelson, Mark Pescovitz, Phil Peters, and Dan Strouse), without the diligent help of those students and staff who assisted us over the past few years (Debbie Allen, Rachel Barsky, Lisa Bonine, Kelley Chan, Bobby Courtney, Kelly Dietz, Regiane Garcia, Lisa Jørgensen, Faith Long, James Martin, Britney McMahan, Jacob Perrin, Zöe Prebble, Kathryn Raliski, Brenda Sargent, Aminollah Sabzevari, Rachel Schechter, and Taylor Wright), and without the superhuman patience of our families (who, curiously, wish to remain anonymous). Finally, we thank the authors and publishers who granted permission to use each of the excerpts of copyrighted material in these readings.

David Orentlicher
Mary Anne Bobinski
Mark A. Hall

May 2013

BIOETHICS AND PUBLIC HEALTH LAW

BIOETHICS AND PUBLIC HEALTH LAW

1

Introduction

These readings introduce background information and overarching perspectives that are important for understanding the legal issues developed throughout this book. The readings are diverse and introduce a wide range of challenging ideas and important information, which we present at the outset because they raise cross-cutting themes that cannot be cabined within a single chapter. Therefore, it will be necessary to revisit some of these readings from time to time throughout the course as they become relevant to the discussion of particular legal topics.

A. THE NATURE OF MEDICAL PRACTICE

We begin with a description of the human condition of illness and the professional practice of medicine, since these are what distinguish health care law from other fields of legal study. It is essential throughout this book to have some appreciation of the impact that illness has on how people function, the intricacies of medical decisionmaking, and how doctors and patients interact. To focus your thoughts on these issues, reflect on your own experiences with medical care, and consider the following list of popular "misconceptions" (developed by Alain Enthoven). What observations and evidence emerge from these readings to rebut or qualify each of these commonly held notions?

1. The doctor should be able to know what conditions the patient has, to answer the patient's questions precisely, and to prescribe the right treatment. If the doctor doesn't, that is incompetence or even malpractice.

1

2. For each medical condition, there is a "best" treatment. It is up to the doctor to know about that treatment and to use it. Anything else is unnecessary surgery, waste, fraud, or underservice.

3. Medicine is an exact science. Unlike 50 or 100 years ago, there is now a firm scientific base for what the doctor does. Standard treatments are supported by scientific proof of efficiency.

4. Medical care consists of standard products that can be described precisely and measured meaningfully in standard units such as "inpatient days," "outpatient visits," or "doctor office visits."

5. Much of medical care is a matter of life and death or serious pain or disability.

6. More medical care is better than less care.

7. People have no control over the timing of their need for medical care. Whatever care is needed is needed right away.

1. Patients, Doctors, and Hospitals

■ HEALTH CARE PAST AND PRESENT
Robert Rhodes
Health Care Politics, Policy, and Distributive Justice:
The Ironic Triumph*

Death before the nineteenth century was an ever-looming presence in our ancestors' thoughts and a frequent visitor to their families. They feared it and had little control over it. Sudden death was as central to attitudes prior to the twentieth century as the cemetery was to every village and town. . . .

Resignation and fatalism toward natural occurrences characterize preindustrial societies, just as a sense of self-direction and control characterize modern society. . . . Modern societies have faith that they can control the future. A futurist orientation allows for savings, capital formation, long periods of education, and lifestyles that deny instant gratification for future health. Preindustrial conditions do not reward such faith. . . . Uncontrollable natural or supernatural forces took away life, and one needed to reconcile one's fate to the four horsemen of the apocalypse: disease, famine, pestilence, and drought.

The twentieth century represents perhaps the clearest triumph of science over fatalism. . . . The modern hospital, the professionalism of physicians and nurses, and effective pharmaceuticals have dramatically altered mortality rates and improved the quality of life in postindustrial states.

For those entering a hospital prior to 1900, the probability of treatment helping, rather than harming, would be less than fifty-fifty, and the odds would be considerably poorer prior to 1870. Today, we identify hospitals as technologic citadels of sophisticated medical practice. But their preindustrial origins were as religious and charitable institutions for the hopelessly sick and poor. They were places to comfort the indigent dying.

For the first three quarters of the nineteenth century, medical personnel were not in charge of hospitals. . . . In the main, hospitals at that time were places for the homeless poor and insane to die. The affluent classes were treated at home. For a variety of reasons, however, hospitals became central to medical practice and education between 1870 and 1910.[1] . . .

[T]he development of the medical profession parallels particular developments of the hospital. This is especially true of surgery, which enjoyed a dramatic increase of prestige and precision during this time. Technological advances played a major role in changing surgery. Before painkilling drugs, surgical methods in the first half of the nineteenth century depended upon powerful and swift physicians whose craft and tools were closer to the corner butcher. Mortality rates of about 40 percent followed amputation.

Three developments altered the brutality and mortality rates and allowed abdominal surgery, which was rarely performed prior to 1890. Dentist William Morton's demonstration of ether at Massachusetts General Hospital in 1846 ushered in a means of eliminating pain and allowed more careful and delicate surgery. Joseph Lister's discovery of antisepsis in 1867 gradually led to new procedures during surgery to prevent infection. However, antisepsis was poorly understood. Lister's technique was based on the use of carbolic acid spray, but his methods were adopted only over a long period of time. Fatal infections continued even after using the spray because antiseptic procedures were not followed carefully until after 1880. Soon, sterile procedures were properly followed and surgery rapidly expanded. Finally, the development of the X-ray in 1895, along with other diagnostic tools, opened the way for abdominal surgery for appendicitis, gallbladder, and stomach ulcers. Thoracic surgery and surgery of the nervous and cardiovascular systems developed in the early 1900s.

TRIUMPH AND TRAGEDY

By 1950, the cliché a "medical miracle" had rich meaning. Infant mortality rates in the United States were fewer than 15 per 100,000 births, down from 300 or so per 100,000 at the turn of the century. Pneumonia, once whispered by medical staff who witnessed the suffering of the dying to be the "old man's relief," now was easily controlled with penicillin. Infectious diseases in particular dramatically declined in the first half of the twentieth century. Improvement in health was a triumph of modernity, and part of that triumph was a consequence of modern medicine. There is, however, much debate about the weight of medicine's contribution, compared to other modern factors. . . .

Our dramatic advances in health are also related to improved nutrition, lifestyle, and education, as well as to medical advancements. The literature of health care points, in particular, to . . . proper diet, minimal tension, absence of smoking or heavy drinking, daily exercise, and a life-style that provides low-risk factors for accidents. Advances in health and longevity are more closely tied to higher income, better diets, and especially greater education than to advances in medicine. . . .

Yet, American perception of well-being is closely identified with medicine. Paradoxically, much of the public's present disenchantment with medicine is the

1. Paul Starr, The Social Transformation of American Medicine 151 (1982).

consequence of this identification. Modern medicine has advanced to the frontiers of preserving life, but only by increasingly more expensive therapies and diagnoses to preserve life "on its margins." That is, additional expenditures and efforts to treat disease produce diminishing results in proportion to the effort. We are just beginning to learn that our scientific capacity to triumph over illness, physical anomalies, and death, on many occasions with medical miracles, brings with it a special brand of tragedy.

We have become totally modern. No more can we explain death and suffering as a consequence of fate. It is our medicine, or lack of it, that denies death and suffering. We know we must choose who receives scarce resources and who does not. No longer can we attribute to fate or to God the responsibility for making life-and-death decisions. Yet, these life-and-death decisions involve very expensive procedures and technologies and often contribute only marginally to extending life. Examples are well known and regularly make front-page newspaper drama: organ transplants, aggressive treatment of terminal patients, neonates under 750 grams, or long-term comatose patients.

These new choices challenge our basic values and frequently produce conflict. . . . Conflict is father to politics and law, and politics determines who gets what, when, and how. Conflict also forces moral reassessment of traditional attitudes and postures, including the justice question: "Who *should* get what, when and how."

How do we distribute health care? How should we? How does political power within the present economic system determine the distribution of health care? These questions obviously spill over the boundaries of economics, politics, sociology, law, medicine, history, and philosophy. In particular, looming over the politics of health care is a sense of the tragic, as well as the majestic. Tragedy points to human endeavors that are virtuous and honorable, yet carry the seeds of their own downfall. Our efforts to lessen the suffering and lengthen the lives of Americans through accessible, affordable, quality health care represent the best of our traditions and have been, on balance, an American success story. Sometimes we fall short in that effort because some group is unreasonably left behind in the political shuffle. The [45] million Americans who [have] no health coverage represent[] such a group. At other times, our very success leads to exasperating dilemmas of bioethics and distributive justice that would cross the eyes of a Solomon. Our dilemma over public financing for costly organ transplants at the expense of other badly needed programs or continued aggressive treatment of comatose or terminally ill loved ones are poignant, modern examples. It is here where triumph merges with tragedy.

■ END-OF-LIFE WARNING AT $618,616 MAKES ME WONDER WAS IT WORTH IT
Amanda Bennett
Bloomberg News, Mar. 4, 2010*

It was some time after midnight on Dec. 8, 2007, when [the doctor] told me my husband might not live till morning. The kidney cancer that had metastasized

---

*Excerpted with permission. For a fuller account, see Amanda Bennett, The Cost of Hope (2012).

almost six years earlier was growing in his lungs. He was in intensive care at the Hospital of the University of Pennsylvania in Philadelphia, and had begun to spit blood.

Terence Bryan Foley, 67 years old, my husband of 20 years, father of our two teenagers, a Chinese historian who earned his Ph.D. in his 60s, a man who played more than 15 musical instruments and spoke six languages, a San Francisco cable car conductor and sports photographer, an expert on dairy cattle and swine nutrition, film noir and Dixieland jazz, was confused. He knew his name, but not the year. He wanted a Coke.

Should Terence begin to hemorrhage, the doctor asked, what should he do? This was our third end-of-life warning in seven years. We fought off the others. Perhaps we could dodge this one too. [Terence's oncologist] and I both believed that a new medicine he had just begun to take would buy him more time. Keep him alive if you can, I said. Let's see what the drug, Pfizer Inc.'s Sutent, can do.

Terence died six days later, on Friday, Dec. 14, 2007. What I couldn't know then was that the thinking behind my request—along with hundreds of decisions we made over seven years—was a window on the impossible calculus at the core of the U.S. health-care debate.

EXPENSIVE LAST CHANCES

Terence and I didn't have to think about money, allocation of medical resources, the struggles of [millions of] uninsured Americans, or the impact on corporate bottom lines. Backed by medical insurance provided by my employers, we were able to fight his cancer with a series of expensive last chances like the one I asked for that night.

How expensive? The bills totaled $618,616, almost two-thirds of it for the final 24 months, much of it for treatments that no one can say for sure helped extend his life. In just the last four days of trying to keep him alive—two in intensive care, two in a cancer ward—our insurance was charged $43,711 for doctors, medicines, monitors, X-rays and scans. Two years later, the only thing I know for certain that money bought was confirmation that he was dying.

Some of the drugs probably did Terence no good at all. At least one helped fewer than 10 percent of all those who took it. Pharmaceutical companies and insurers will have to sort out the economics of treatments that end up working for only a small subset. Should everyone have the right to try them? Terence and I answered yes. Each drug potentially added life. Yet that too led me to a question I can't answer. When is it time to quit?

SCIENCE, EMOTION, COSTS

Congress didn't touch the issue in [the Patient Protection and Affordable Care Act of 2010]. The mere hint of somehow limiting the ability to choose care as aggressively as Terence and I did created a whirlwind of accusations that the ill, aged and infirm would be forced before government "death panels."

As the debate heated up, I remembered the fat sheaf of insurance statements that arrived after Terence's death . . . . [from] six hospitals, four insurers, Medicare, three oncologists, and a surgeon. Those papers tell the story of a system filled with people doing their best. And they raise complex questions about a health-care system that consumes 17 percent of the economy. As I leafed through the stack of documents, it was easy to see why 31 percent of the money spent on health care goes to paperwork and administration. . . .

The documents revealed an economic system in which the sellers don't set and the buyers don't know the prices. The University of Pennsylvania hospital charged more than 12 times what Medicare at the time reimbursed for a chest scan. One insurer paid a hospital for 80 percent of the $3,232 price of a scan, while another covered 24 percent. Insurance companies negotiated their own rates, and neither my employers nor I paid the difference between the sticker and discounted prices.

'IT'S COMPLETELY INSANE'

In this economic system, prices of goods and services bear little relation to the demand for them or their cost to make — or, as it turns out, the good or harm they do. "No other nation would allow a health system to be run the way we do it. It's completely insane," said Uwe E. Reinhardt, a political economy professor at Princeton University. . . . Taking it all into account, the data showed we had made a bargain that hardly any economist looking solely at the numbers would say made sense. Why did we do it?

I was one big reason. Not me alone, of course. The medical system has a strong bias toward action. My husband, too, was unusual . . . in his passionate willingness to endure discomfort for a chance to see his daughter grow from a child to a young woman, and his son graduate from high school.

After Terence died, [his doctor] drew me a picture of a bell curve, showing the range of survival times for kidney cancer sufferers. Terence was way off in the tail on the right-hand side, an indication he had indeed beaten the odds. An explosion of research had made it possible to extend lives for years — enough to keep our quest from having been total madness.

Terence used to tell a story, almost certainly apocryphal, about his Uncle Bob. Climbing aboard a landing craft before the invasion of Normandy, so the story went, Bob's sergeant told the men that by the end of the day, nine out of 10 would be dead. Said Bob, on hearing that news: "Each one of us looked around and felt so sorry for those other nine poor sonsabitches."

For me, it was about pushing the bell curve. Knowing that if there was something to be done, we couldn't not do it. Believing beyond logic that we were going to escape the fate of those other poor sonsabitches. It is very hard to put a price on that kind of hope.

PRICING HOPE

We found the cancer by accident [a decade ago]. . . . Within a month, Terence was in surgery, and [another doctor] had taken out the diseased kidney. . . . "We got it all," he said. Terence was visibly moved. "Thank you for saving my life," he said. . . . The statistics looked good. By the traditional method of staging — a 7 centimeter tumor with no sign of having spread — Terence had an 85 percent chance of surviving five years.

The bills from Regence Blue Cross & Blue Shield of Oregon show the operation was relatively inexpensive, too, just over $25,000, or only about 4 percent of the total [eventually] charged to keep Terence alive. Insurance paid a discounted $14,084. Terence and I paid $209.87. The lab soon cast a chill on our optimism.

Terence had "collecting duct" cancer, the rarest and most aggressive form. . . . If that was correct, Terence had almost no chance of making it to the end of the year. . . . "Watchful waiting" was the recommended path. Waiting for him to die was what we feared. He didn't die. He got better. We didn't know why. We tried not to think about it. . . .

Then, on May 6, 2002, I was at work when [our son] Terry called, panic in his voice. "Mom, come home. Dad is very sick." . . . His father was in bed, his face flaming with fever, shaking with chills under a pile of blankets. He could barely speak. "The cancer is in my lungs," he said. "I've got six to nine months left."

A scan had spotted the cancer's spread. Not wanting to worry us, Terence had secretly begun taking Interleukin-2. If he recovered, he figured, we would never know how close he came; if he died, he would have spared us months of anguish. . . . What he didn't reckon on was that the drug would make him violently ill. But it was the only possible therapy at that time. Injections of the protein—at $735 a dose—were intended to stimulate the immune response to help fight off the cancer's invasion. The overall response rate was about 10 percent. For most, it did nothing.

That evening, for the one and only time, I felt pure terror. I spent the night awake in our dark living room. . . . Knowing the long odds, [the oncologist later] told me he had prescribed Interleukin-2 simply because it was all there was. Terence stopped taking it after just a few weeks, unable to stand the side effects.

I shook off my fear and plunged into the Internet. If there was something out there that could save him, I was going to find it. One colleague had been snatched from dying of AIDS by a chance introduction to a doctor who prescribed an experimental antiviral cocktail. Another had beaten leukemia with a cutting-edge bone marrow transplant. We could defeat this, too. . . .

The entire medical bill for seven years . . . was steeply discounted. The $618,616 became $254,176 when the insurers paid their share and imposed their discounts. Of that, Terence and I were responsible for $9,468—less than 4 percent. . . .

[A]s summer in Philadelphia turned to autumn. Terence resumed [another treatment which he had ceased earlier due to side effects]. Because he wasn't in a clinical trial, our insurance company was billed: $27,360 a dose, for four treatments. [But that also failed to stop the cancer's spread.] . . .

READING THEIR GOODBYES

[A few months later] I signed the papers transferring Terence to hospice. The next day, Tuesday, the hospital staff took away the machines and the monitors. The oncologists and radiologists and lab technicians disappeared. Another group of people—hospice nurses, social workers, chaplains and counselors for me and the children—began to arrive one by one, as the focus shifted from treating Terence to easing our transition.

For the next three days, with Terence in the same hospital bed, we spent $14,022 on [pain and anxiety medications], and on monitoring for him and counseling for a different kind of pain management for the children and me. The cost was less than a third of the previous four days' $43,711.

Terence drifted into a coma on Tuesday. I e-mailed his friends and read their goodbyes aloud, hoping he could hear and understand. I slept in a chair. At about 2:30 A.M. Friday, a noise in the hall startled me. I awoke just in time to hold his hand as he died. They gave me back his wedding ring the next day.

Looking back, memories of my zeal to treat are tinged with sadness. Since I didn't believe my husband was going to die, I never let us have the chance to say goodbye. . . .

Would I do it all again? Absolutely. I couldn't not do it again. But I think had he known the costs, Terence would have fought the insurers spending enough, at roughly $200,000, to vaccinate almost a quarter-million children in developing countries. That's how he would have thought about it. . . .

Did we help Terence? Or harm him? . . . [His doctor] and I looked at the numbers. The average patient in his [clinical] trial got 14 months of extra life. Without any treatment, [his doctor] estimates that for someone at Terence's stage of the disease it was three months. Terence got 17 months—still within the realm of chance, but way, way up on the bell curve.

There's another bell curve that starts about where Terence's left off. It charts the survival times for patients treated not just with [the dugs Terence received] but also Novartis's Afinitor and GlaxoSmithKline's Votrient, made available within the past three years. Doctors and patients now are doing what we dreamed of, staggering one drug after another and buying years more of life. . . .

[Terence's] 17 months included an afternoon looking down at the Mediterranean with Georgia from a sunny balcony in Southern Spain. Moving Terry into his college dorm. Celebrating our 20th anniversary with a carriage ride through Philadelphia's cobbled streets. A final Thanksgiving game of charades with cousins Margo and Glenn.

And one last chance for Terence to pave the way for all those other poor sonsabitches.

■ DOCTORS, PATIENTS, AND HEALTH INSURANCE: THE ORGANIZATION AND FINANCING OF MEDICAL CARE
Herman Miles Somers & Anne Ramsay Somers
1961

. . . The popular conception of the doctor-patient relationship is a mixture of fact and fancy. Until World War II the general practitioner family doctor was still in the majority. The one-to-one relationship of a personally chosen physician—where economic and other factors permitted any choice—with his patient was the most common form of medical practice. In big cities the doctor had an office, usually mahogany and leather, sparsely equipped with simple diagnostic aids, a few surgical tools, and some antiseptic drugs. But, especially in rural areas and suburbs, he was more often found in the homes of his patients doing his rounds, working at the bedside of the sick and injured. His black bag held almost all his equipment. His records were kept partly in a small notebook, mostly in his mind and heart. He appeared indefatigable, compassionate, and available wherever and whenever needed. . . .

This doctor of the past has been idealized in story, picture, and legend. . . . Despite its apparent anachronisms, the picture still appeals to people's sentiments—even to those fully aware of its use as a public relations device. It has the warmth and intimate concern that no hypodermic needle—no complex of steel and tubing—can replace, however effective they may be. Although medical miracles are now performed successfully between strangers, doctors and patients both believe that the absence of continuity, personal concern, and individual attention are detrimental to the best medical care. This is not without foundation.

The origin of the "traditional" doctor-patient relationship reaches deep into the past. From the beginning of medical history, the practicing physician has been part priest, part technician, part personal or family counselor. In early days, when medicine had very little in the way of scientific knowledge to rely on, it was inevitable that the subjective priestly element should be dominant. . . .

In modern times medicine has become more scientific. But the traditional reliance on mystical forces and a highly authoritarian doctor-patient relationship persists to a degree unknown in other contemporary human relations. . . . The relationship of citizen and state, of employer and employee, of teacher and pupil, parent and child, even of husband and wife, have undergone profound and acknowledged changes as a result of the technological and socio-economic trends of the past few centuries. But there is no general acknowledgment or acceptance of the significant change that has, in fact, been taking place in the doctor-patient relationship. Of the manifold and complex reasons, only a few of the more important can be noted here.

First and basic is the persistence—in spite of scientific progress—of large elements of uncertainty and fear regarding illness and medical care which are conducive to continued reliance on hope, faith, confidence and other subjective factors on the part of both doctor and patient. "Honor thy physician because of the need thou hast of him." So said apocryphal Ecclesiastes to the Hebrews thousands of years ago. And still, today, patients yearn to have confidence in their doctors, to idealize them, to endow them with superhuman powers. Talcott Parsons, the Harvard sociologist, reconciles the use of such subjective factors—the use of "modern magic"—with the scientific basis of modern medicine by calling it a "functional bias."

> The basic function of magic is to bolster the self-confidence of actors in situations where energy and skill *do* make a difference but where, because of uncertainty factors, outcomes cannot be guaranteed. This fits the situation of the doctor, but in addition on the side of the patient it may be argued the *belief* in the possibility of recovery is an important factor in it. If from purely a technical point of view both the individual doctor and the general tradition are optimistically biased it ought to help. . . . Of course this argument must not be pressed too far.

As the boundaries of medical ignorance and uncertainty are pushed back, one would expect this resort to supra-scientific factors to decline, and, indeed, it has in the case of bacterial and other diseases where the cause and cure are clearly established. But the reduced role of subjective factors in the treatment of specific cases has been more than offset by an increasing interest in the role of the emotions in illness. A widespread increase in psychotherapy and psychosomatic medicine has renewed the emphasis on a personal doctor and a personal doctor-patient relation-ship of a type that permits knowledge of the "whole [person]." . . .

Moreover it is now widely believed that illness, *per se*, tends to create—even in the most intellectual of patients—an attitude of dependence, of "regression" to helplessness, and perhaps to childlike behavior. . . . In this state, confidence in the authority and benevolence of the doctor, as well as in his scientific knowledge and technical skill—the now-familiar "father-image"—is generally desired and often desirable.

Finally, there is the impenetrable mystery of death. The physician's relation to this event—however helpless he in fact may be—has endowed him, in the eyes of centuries of patients, with an aura of the mystery. To the extent that the physician identifies himself with this priestly role and takes on himself the burden associated therewith, or at least appears to do so through the gravity of his personal demeanor and behavior, his supra-scientific role continues to be respected and perpetuated, reinforcing in the eyes of individual patients and society at large his status as a dis-penser of increasingly scientific medicine.

■ COMPETING SOLUTIONS: AMERICAN HEALTH CARE PROPOSALS AND INTERNATIONAL EXPERIENCE
Joseph White
1995

America's systems for delivering and paying for medical care are notably more complex than those of most other countries. Many doctors work in more than one hospital, making governance of medical staffs difficult; specialists are harder to coordinate because there are more of them; and the proliferation of forms of man-aged care means rapid change in patterns of gatekeeping and referral.

PHYSICIANS

American doctors go through extensive training to work long hours for high pay. The typical medical school program requires, after four years of college, four more years of "undergraduate" medical education. During the final two years, stu-dents receive some clinical training. Virtually all graduates then must complete some graduate medical education in order to be licensed to practice medicine. This education is obtained in residency programs, mainly in hospitals affiliated with medical schools. Normally only one year of residency (as an intern) is needed for licensure, but up to eight years (for neurosurgeons) may be required for certifica-tion as a specialist.

. . . Given the length of their training and the size of their debts, it is under-standable that most physicians feel entitled to incomes that are much higher than those of most other Americans. . . . [The median physician salary is about $200,000, roughly five times that of the average American worker. The range across specialties is broad. Pediatricians and general practitioners typically earn around $175,000, common medical specialists (cardiology, dermatology, anesthesiology) are in the $250,000-$350,000 range, while heart surgeons and brain surgeons can earn well over $500,000. Some doctors earn substantially more from entrepreneurial activities such as medical patents and investments in various health care organizations.]

An unusually high proportion of American doctors are trained to specialize. Fewer than 10 percent of American doctors [call] themselves general practitioners (GPs), the standard term for primary care physicians. But because a specialist such as a family practitioner, internist, pediatrician, or obstetrician-gynecologist may be a person's regular physician, between 33 and 40 percent of physicians (depending on who is counting) are mainly primary care providers. [Specialists who receive several years of extra training and pass additional exams are designated as "Board Certified," meaning that they comply with voluntary, private standards set by the American Specialty Boards, which operate under the auspices of the AMA. At one time, board certification was relatively rare, but now the vast majority of new doctors obtain certification. About two dozen boards now exist, covering not only standard specialties but also areas of general practice such as family medicine and internal medicine.] . . .

Two-thirds of physicians practice in offices, the vast majority with admitting privileges to a hospital. Many practice in more [than one hospital] (for example, a nice suburban hospital for simple cases, and a high-tech academic medical center for difficult ones). Hospitals therefore must compete for admissions by making those physicians happy, such as by having the fanciest equipment. . . .

INSTITUTIONAL CARE

Long-term or chronic care, especially for the aged, is a complicated system on its own, and the potential expenses of long-term care are so great that it is highly unlikely that any reform will do much about it. [Therefore, the focus here is] on the costs of the current American health care system, of which one major component is hospital services for acute care.

The American supply of hospitals is dominated by private nonprofit hospitals—many owned by religious organizations. [About two-thirds] of hospital beds [are] provided by the nonprofits, 10 percent by the for-profit sector. The rest, just over a quarter of the beds, [are] in federal, state, or local facilities. It is hard to identify much difference between the behavior and efficiency of the for-profit and private nonprofits. If private institutions are more efficient, the savings go largely or entirely to investors.

Americans spend a great deal of money on hospitals: [about 40 percent] of all spending on patient care. But . . . the hospital is not as dominant a provider as it once was or still is in other countries. Hospitals and doctors tried to avoid regulation by moving care to ostensibly freestanding ambulatory care facilities. Examples include kidney dialysis units, and radiology group practices with close relations with hospitals. Some payers encouraged the shift, believing those facilities would be cheaper. . . .

Back in the traditional hospitals, the nature of care depends greatly on hospitals' relationships with doctors and medical schools, and on hospitals' catchment areas—the areas from which they get most of their patients. . . .

A suburban hospital can generally provide sophisticated care, such as cardiac bypass surgery, but it is not as likely to have clinical professors who are able to provide extremely specialized care for "interesting" cases. All hospitals want the most advanced equipment, but the academic medical centers must have it for research and training. These centers rely heavily on residents and interns for delivery of care and, most important, are likely to have a much lower-class population of patients.

Many of the [academic medical centers] are in inner cities. They are likely to have large outpatient departments to train the students (residents) and serve the local population, which feeds into the inpatient wards; the emergency room not only gets emergencies but also serves as an outpatient clinic for some of the population. All of this is the good news: If a major teaching hospital is in the inner city, then either a large and endowed institution or a state government pays for some care for the inner-city poor.

When local hospitals receive little funding for education, poor populations must frequently rely on a hospital financed by a strapped city or county budget. Such hospitals—for example, Cook County in Chicago, Boston City, and Charity in New Orleans—have interns and residents to do the work because of their relationship with a training program, but nowhere near the resources of a freestanding university hospital. All hospitals in the inner city try to convince Medicare that they deserve an extra subsidy for treating a poorer, less-insured, and often sicker population. The federal government calls these disproportionate share payments. One of the huge issues for American health care reform is what will happen to the academic medical centers and the remaining urban public hospitals if payment systems allow competing insurers to favor hospitals that are less expensive because they have lesser teaching and subsidy burdens.

Another major issue is how a bias toward specialized, high-technology medicine, created in part by how medical education is financed and how physicians are paid, is reinforced by arrangements for capital investment in American medicine. There are hardly any measures in place to prevent a "medical arms race" among hospitals that seek the most advanced technology in order to attract physicians and generate revenue. . . .

Because for years insurers would pay whatever physicians and hospitals billed, and hospitals relied on physicians to provide patients, hospitals competed for patients by having the best equipment, and insurers ended up paying for excess treatments and higher charges per treatment. At one time also physicians could refer patients to any specialist they wished, and patients could go directly to a specialist without referral.

The rise of managed care and of more aggressive bargaining by insurers has change[d] this basic pattern. Insurers have become more likely to refuse to approve a given service or to insist on a lower price. Hospitals still need to attract physicians by offering the best equipment, however, so they are caught between the demands of doctors and payers. Meanwhile insurers are limiting choice of and access to specialists by building closed panels, in which a person covered by a plan either cannot use or must pay a surcharge to use any provider who is not on special contract to the plan. A patient might find that her doctor of 20 years' standing is no longer part of her insurance plan; a physician might find that many of his patients can afford referral only to three nephrologists whom he does not know. One of the key issues in reform is whether these . . . restrictions on choice of physician are necessary.

■ DOCTORS, PATIENTS, AND HEALTH INSURANCE: THE ORGANIZATION AND FINANCING OF MEDICAL CARE
Herman Miles Somers & Anne Ramsay Somers
1961

[T]he conflict between [hospital] medical staff and [hospital] management has become both sharper and more open in recent years. The roots of this conflict—the basic dichotomy in hospital organization—go back to eighteenth century Britain and the establishment of the Anglo-American tradition of voluntary hospitals. There was no such dichotomy in medieval days when hospitals were operated, with little medical assistance, by monastic orders for the sick poor. There is generally no such duality in the major Continental hospitals which are usually run, with unquestioned authority, by full-time chiefs of medical services. The distinguishing feature of the Anglo-American voluntary hospital, however, has been its use by private physicians for private patients with little or no accompanying administrative or financial responsibility. . . .

Recent developments—the hospital's changing role, its increase in size, complexity, utilization, cost, and its greatly altered financial base—have intensified the inherent instability of this administrative structure. . . . Lay influences on hospital administration and policy are clearly increasing. Ultimate policy responsibility has always rested with lay trustees. Traditionally, they limited their oversight to balancing the books. With the tremendous increase in hospital costs, however, this single concern has led to increasing surveillance over the hospital's total functioning, including the organization of the medical staff. The hospital administrator, traditionally an untrained individual content to play a fairly subservient role and socially outranked by doctor and trustee alike, is being transformed into a professional with increasing self-confidence and authority. . . .

At the same time the hospital has become an indispensable workshop for the modern physician, who finds it virtually impossible to practice good medicine without hospital affiliation. The hospital is the center of his professional world, and he is acknowledged to be its key figure. Fully 40 percent of private physician income is now earned in the hospital. Naturally he wants "his" institution equipped with the latest scientific and technological facilities. But the doctor's relationship to the hospital is peculiarly ambiguous. As a rule he assumes neither administrative nor financial responsibility. Yet, in practice, his is the most powerful voice in the organization. He alone admits and discharges patients; he alone can diagnose, prescribe, and treat patients—still the chief purpose for which the hospital exists. With his high professional status, he may, in most hospitals, countermand administrative orders and defy lay authority with relative impunity. The result is the confusing duality that prevails today throughout the hospital system, public and private. . . .

It is sometimes proposed that hiring the medical staff on a salary or contract basis would increase the doctors' sense of responsibility for hospital administration and help clarify lines of accountability. It could integrate the administrative structure without restricting professional integrity. This is the general pattern in a few of the nation's best hospitals, such as the Henry Ford in Detroit and the Cleveland Clinic Hospital. Most of the profession is, however, vigorously opposed to such practice, alleging "hospital domination," "lay control," or the "corporate practice of medicine." Some hospitals have taken a middle road—employing full-time medical directors (this is frequently the practice in government hospitals) and in a few instances, full-time chiefs of medical services. This too is generally frowned on by physicians in private practice. . . .

Many hospital spokesmen, however, content themselves with pleading for physician cooperation in assuring some responsibility for hospital operations and costs. . . . But such recommendations are usually set in a purely hortatory context. It is not clear how such preachments are to influence the individual doctor. The "medical staff" of which he is a member is in most instances simply a term for the collectivity of physicians authorized to practice in a particular hospital. The staff can be as disciplinary an instrument as it chooses to be, but in most places it has chosen minimal responsibility. . . . By and large the staff still prefers not to interfere with the practices of the individual physician.

■ CLINICAL DECISION MAKING: FROM THEORY TO PRACTICE
David M. Eddy
1996

Medical practice is in the middle of a profound transition. Most physicians can remember the day when, armed with a degree, a mission, and confidence, they could set forth to heal the sick. Like Solomon, physicians could receive patients, hear their complaints, and determine the best course of action. While not every patient could be cured, everyone could be confident that whatever was done was the best possible. Most important, each physician was free, trusted, and left alone to determine what was in the best interest of each patient.

All of that is changing. . . . Now physicians must deal with second opinions, precertification, skeptical medical directors, variable coverage, outright denials, utilization review, threats of cookbook medicine, and letters out of the blue chiding that Mrs. Smith is on two incompatible drugs. Solomon did not have to call anyone to get permission for his decisions. What is going on?

What is going on is that one of the basic assumptions underlying the practice of medicine is being challenged. This assumption is not just a theory about cholesterol, antiarrhythmia, or estrogens. This assumption concerns the intellectual foundation of medical care. Simply put, the assumption is that whatever a physician decides is, by definition, correct. The challenge says that while many decisions no doubt *are* correct, many are not, and elaborate mechanisms are needed to determine which are which. Physicians are slowly being stripped of their decisionmaking power.

Notes: Doctors and Hospitals

1. *History and Description.* For general histories and descriptions of the health care delivery system, see David Smith & Arnold Kaluzny, The White Labyrinth: A Guide to the Health Care System (2d ed. 2000); Harry A. Sultz & Kristina M. Young, Health Care USA: Understanding Its Organization and Delivery (6th ed. 2008); David Johnson & Nancy Kane, The U.S. Health Care System: A Product of

American History and Values, *in* E. Elhauge ed., The Fragmentation of U.S. Health Care (2010). For more extensive historical accounts of the transformation of hospitals and their role in modern medicine, see Guenter B. Risse, Mending Bodies, Saving Souls: A History of Hospitals (1999); Charles Rosenberg, The Care of Strangers (1987); David Rosner, A Once Charitable Enterprise (1982); Rosemary Stevens, In Sickness and in Wealth: American Hospitals in the Twentieth Century (1989).

2. *The Two-Headed Monster.* The unique structure of American hospitals, in which doctors are independent but essential to their financial well-being, has been described as "attractive as a two-headed monster" and as "stable as a three-legged stool." See H. L. Smith, Two Lines of Authority Are One Too Many, 84 Modern Hosp. 59 (Mar. 1955). This division of authority is mirrored throughout the organizational structure of the health care system. For instance, hospitals, unlike any other business organization, are required by state licensure laws and private accreditation standards to have *two* sets of corporate bylaws, one for the hospital administration and a second for the medical staff. Similarly, health insurance traditionally pays hospitals separately from doctors, as reflected in the distinctions between Blue Cross (hospital insurance) vs. Blue Shield (physician insurance) and between Medicare Part A vs. Part B.

3. *Power Relationships in Medicine.* Medical sociologists and organizational theorists have produced a rich literature discussing the role of physicians within medical institutions. Leading examples are Eliot Freidson, Doctoring Together (1975); Eliot Freidson, Profession of Medicine (1970); Paul Starr, The Social Transformation of American Medicine (1982); Jeffrey Harris, The Internal Organization of Hospitals: Some Economic Implications, 8 Bell J. Econ. 467 (1977). For an exploration of how these insights illuminate a variety of legal doctrines and public policy debates, see Mark A. Hall, Institutional Control of Physician Behavior: Legal Barriers to Health Care Cost Containment, 137 U. Pa. L. Rev. 431 (1988) ("Because the law absorbs and reflects the values and relationships of traditional medicine, it has codified the ethic of professional dominance, effectively shielding physicians from the institutional influence contemplated by revolutionary changes in health care policy."); Sara Rosenbaum, The Impact of United States Law on Medicine as a Profession, 289 JAMA 1546 (2003); Symposium, 29 J. Health Pol. Pol'y & L. 557 (2004); Symposium, 4 Ind. Health L. Rev. 205-286 (2007).

2. Medicine, Illness, and Healing

■ MAGIC OR MEDICINE? AN INVESTIGATION OF HEALING AND HEALERS*
Robert Buckman & Karl Sabbagh
1995

Despite the enormous variety of their forms and formats and their lack of any apparent common ingredient, every interaction between a patient and a healer

*Copyright © 1995, Prometheus Books. Reprinted by permission.

shares a common structure. In each consultation, (1) the patient comes to the healer with an idea that something is wrong. (2) The healer then tries to find out what the cause of the problem is and (3) makes some intervention—a drug, a spell, a recommendation or something else. After the consultation, (4) the patient (or society on the patient's behalf) rewards the healer for his or her time and trouble. Finally, (5) there is some measure of the outcome of the consultation, something that wouldn't have happened if the consultation hadn't taken place. This might be a measurable improvement (or deterioration) in some physical parameter of the illness or a subjective sense of feeling better (or worse).

And that is all there is to it. In all its guises, in all cultures and in all languages, those are the basic steps in what appears to be a complex and varied first dance between patient and healer which forms the basis of the relationship between them. As a means of analyzing the patient-doctor/healer relationship in greater detail, we propose to start by examining . . . [the first] component of the consultation. . . . This leads to a . . . conclusion that some may find surprising, namely that the exact definition of what constitutes a disease or an illness is determined not by biology but by society. Certainly, there is a class of health problems that are seen in a similar way in all societies. For instance, if a previously fit man suddenly clutches his chest, looks white and sweaty and is acutely short of breath even at rest, then in Western society we would say that this man has probably had a heart attack, and we would prove it with ECGs and blood tests. It might be that in another society that episode is regarded as a visitation from a malevolent spirit, but even so it would be recognized as a serious, acute and unheralded problem—albeit a visitation, not a myocardial infarct.

However, not all diseases are as clear-cut as a heart attack. Some are far more difficult to define and pigeon-hole and are classified differently in different societies. In Germany, for example, doctors prescribe six times the amount of heart drugs per person than in England or France. This is not because of a greater incidence of coronary artery disease in Germany—in fact, there is less of it than in France—and it clearly has no effect on death rates since the mortality from all forms of heart disease is the same in all countries. One of the major reasons is that the German language doesn't have a way of distinguishing heart problems from any other kind of chest pain. . . .

[T]he English and the Americans don't attribute vague chest pains to the heart unless there's some solid evidence for genuine heart disease. Thus *Herzinsuffizienz* is an illness-label that is almost exclusive to Germany—hence, perhaps, the excessive prescription of heart drugs. In the same way, in France, a large number of nonspecific symptoms are attributed to a *crise de foie*—a "crisis of the liver." In fact, approximately 80 percent of problems attributed to a crisis of the liver are actually migraine. And most of the rest are minor gastrointestinal conditions. . . , Similarly, in the American medical view, minor illnesses are much more likely to be ascribed to (unspecified) viral illnesses. This is in line with the prevailing mood of the times in America in which disease is seen as an external invasive threat and there is a predilection for diagnosing infections since they can often be dealt with actively and quickly. . . .

Now consider a common event (in many lives)—a hangover. We all expect a hangover if we drink excessively; so is a hangover an expected consequence of ordinary life or is it a disease? Whether or not it is a disease, is it an illness? What about bereavement? We expect to be sad after the death of someone we love—if the bereaved person cries continuously for a week, is that an illness? If he or she cries for six months, is that an illness? And what about adolescence? In Montana, a change in financing of private hospitals led to many general hospitals quickly changing themselves into psychiatric hospitals. Unfortunately, there were not enough patients to fill them, so there was a sudden epidemic of new diagnoses. Teenagers who had falling grades at school were now diagnosed as psychiatrically disturbed (with a major advertising campaign to get the point across to the parents) and were admitted to a hospital—at four times the rate that occurred in neighboring Utah. . . .

These [examples] again emphasize the partly arbitrary—and rather parochial—definitions of disease and illness. Each society decides for itself at the time what are legitimately regarded as diseases or illnesses. Those definitions vary from culture to culture. Furthermore, those conditions that we regard as normal today may be diagnosed as illnesses tomorrow.

■ THE TYRANNY OF HEALTH*
Faith T. Fitzgerald
331 New Eng. J. Med. 196 (1994)

There has recently been much in both lay and medical literature on the promotion of healthy lifestyles. Once upon a time people did not have lifestyles; they had lives. Those lives were filled with work and play, battle and respite, excitement and boredom, but principally with the day-to-day struggle for existence, centered largely around the family, birth, death, disease, and health. What is the difference between a lifestyle and a life? Central to it, I believe, is the concept that lifestyle is something one chooses, and life is something that happens to one. This distinction will affect the future of medicine, and certainly health care reform, in this country. The emphasis on healthy lifestyles, although salutary in many ways, has a very dark side to it and has led to the increasing peril of a tyranny of health in the United States. To explain the potential dangers of the emphasis on healthy lifestyles, I here review the concept of health and its role in the fabric of our society.

A healthy lifestyle is said to be essential to the promotion of wellness. What is wellness? In 1946, the World Health Organization, largely in revulsion against the activities of Nazi physicians and the creatures who worked with them, redefined health as "a state of complete physical, mental, and social well being, and not merely the absence of disease or infirmity." This has become known as "wellness," a highly desirable state. A well or healthy person is one who is not only physically whole and vigorous, but also happy and socially content. What a good idea! . . .

Concurrently, and perhaps naively, both the lay public and the medical profession began to confuse the ideal of health with the norm for health. That is, we went from "Wouldn't it be great to have this be the definition of health" to "This *is* the definition of health." Having accepted the view that health should be a perfect state of wellness, we went on to declare that it was. But if one accepts the idea that physical vigor and emotional and social contentment are not only desirable, but

---

also expected, there is a problem. If health is normal, then sickness and accidents are faults. Who or what is at fault varies: environmental pollution, for example, or government plots, doctors themselves, diet, radon, or political bias. We now act as if we really believe that disease, aging, and death are unnatural acts and all things are remediable. All we have to do, we think, is know enough (or spend enough), and disease and death can be prevented or fixed. . . .

In his paper "Medical Nemesis," [Lancet 1974;1:918-21,] Illich wrote in 1974 that classifying all the troubles of humanity as medical problems is actually antithetical to true health, in that it limits the ability of people to learn to cope with pain, sickness, and death as integral parts of life. Health, he maintained, is not freedom from the inevitability of death, disease, unhappiness and stress, but rather the ability to cope with them in a competent way. If this is true, then the more medicine and society direct individual behavior, the less autonomous, and therefore the less healthy, the individual may become.

We must beware of developing a zealotry about health, in which we take ourselves too seriously and believe that we know enough to dictate human behavior, penalize people for disagreeing with us, and even deny people charity, empathy, and understanding because they act in a way of which we disapprove. Perhaps the health care crisis could be resolved, in part, if we [health care professionals realized that] . . . we cannot fix everything (though we do some things marvelously well), nor can our patients—no matter how intelligent or attentive—prevent all disease and death. We may be trying to do too much and thus diluting an awareness and application of what we can do well.

■ THE MACHINE AT THE BEDSIDE*
Stanley Joel Reiser & Michael Anbar
1984

Technology has altered significantly the form and meaning of the medical relationship. It allows us to direct our vision and attention to variables singled out by it as significant. Thus, stethoscopes increase the significance of chest sounds, X-rays of anatomic shadows, electrocardiograms of waves on a graph, computers of printouts, dialysis machines of chemical balances, and so forth. Such evidence is important for diagnosis and therapy, and the more precisely it can be stated, the more valuable it becomes. In comparison, evidence given by patients, and altered by its passage through the prism of their experience and personality, has seemed to the technological age of the past two centuries less substantive, accurate, and meaningful as a basis for clinical decisionmaking and actions. Increasingly, practitioners encounter patients for relatively brief and intermittent periods—such as the consultant visiting a hospitalized patient whom he or she has never before met. In such visits the technical aspects often dominate, for there is no time or prior relationship to determine much about who the patient is, or what the patient thinks about the illness or the needs it engenders. And even in medical relationships that are not so discontinuous, technological measurements and measures tend to crowd out other dimensions of evaluation and therapeutics. To speak so of the attention focused on the technological features of practice does not diminish their great significance and benefit. Rather, it points out that they do not encompass all critical aspects of diagnosis or treatment. . . .

From the beginning of their introduction in the mid-nineteenth century, automated machines that generated results in objective formats such as graphs and numbers were thought capable of purging from health care the distortions of subjective human opinion. They were supposed to produce facts free of personal bias, and thus to reduce the uncertainty associated with human choice. This view, held by both practitioners and patients, stimulated the intense use of these devices, sometimes to excess. This excess has been characterized by overreliance on techno-logically depicted features of illness, inadequate understanding of the capabilities and limits of machines and the information they generate, and relative inattention to those aspects of medicine learned by inquiry into the patient's experiences and views. Machines can seem so accurate, so right. They can make us forget who made them, and who designed into them—with all the possibilities of human frailty and error—the programs that dictate their function. They can make us forget the hands and minds behind their creation; they can make us forget ourselves.

Notes: The Social Construction of Disease

1. *Is Anyone Healthy?* Students, especially younger ones, often fail to appreciate the extent to which health issues pervade society. According to one survey, in a typi-cal *month* 80 percent of adults report some type of medical symptom, 20 percent visit a doctor, 6 percent visit an alternative (nontraditional) health care provider, and 4 percent go to a hospital. Larry Green et al., The Ecology of Medical Care Revisited, 344 New Eng. J. Med. 2021 (2001). See also H. Gilbert Welch et al., Overdiagnosed: Making People Sick in the Pursuit of Health (2011); Nortin M. Hadler, Worried Sick (2008); Otis Brawley & Paul Goldberg, How We Do Harm: A Doctor Breaks Ranks About Being Sick in America (2012); Nortin M. Hadler, The Last Well Person (2004); Clifton Meador, The Last Well Person, 330 New Eng. J. Med. 440 (1994).

2. For additional views on the meaning of health and illness and the impact of medical technology, see Peter Conrad, The Medicalization of Society (2007); Nancy King et al. eds., The Social Medicine Reader (2d ed. 2005); R. A. Deyo & D. L. Patrick, Hope or Hype: The Obsession with Medical Advances and the High Cost of False Promises (2005); Robert A. Aronowitz, Making Sense of Illness: Sci-ence, Society, and Disease (1998); Daniel Callahan, False Hopes: Why America's Quest for Perfect Health Is a Recipe for Failure (1998); Rene Dubos, Man, Medi-cine, and Environment (1968); Michel Foucault, The Birth of the Clinic (1963); David Mechanic, Symptoms, Illness Behavior, and Help Seeking (1982); Roy Porter, The Greatest Benefit to Mankind (1998); David Rothman, Beginnings Count: The Technological Imperative in American Health Care (1997); Wm. B. Schwartz, Life Without Disease: The Pursuit of Medical Utopia (1998); Susan Sontag, Illness as Metaphor (1988); Richard A. Miller, Extending Life: Scientific Prospects and Politi-cal Obstacles, 80(2) Milbank Q. (2002); Lars Noah, Pigeonholing Illness: Medical Diagnosis as a Legal Construct, 50 Hastings L. Rev. 241 (1999); Talcott Parsons, The Sick Role and the Role of the Physician Reconsidered, 53 Health & Soc'y 257 (1975); Symposium, The Price of Medical Technology, 27(6) Health Aff. (Nov.

2008); Symposium, 21(2) Health Aff. (Mar. 2002); Symposium, 20(5) Health Aff. (Sept. 2001); Symposium, 25 J. Med. & Phil. 519 (2000); Developments, Medical Technology and the Law, 103 Harv. L. Rev. 1519 (1990).

■ MAKING MEDICAL SPENDING DECISIONS*
Mark A. Hall
1997

THE ONTOLOGICAL ASSAULT OF ILLNESS

Illness is frequently described as an "ontological assault." It undermines one's personal identity by attacking the fundamental unity of mind and body. In a state of health, our body is part of an integrated sense of self that responds instinctively to our will and serves our inner purposes almost effortlessly. When illness strikes, our body becomes an enemy of self. It does not respond as we wish and its frailties dominate our conscious thoughts. Illness strikes at one of our most fundamental assumptions in everyday life—that we will continue to exist and function much as we have in the past. Serious illness shatters our "primordial sense of invulnerability" (Silberman 1991).

The profound incapacitating effect of this assault on our very being is much more debilitating than any of life's other major disruptions, whether they be divorce, incarceration or impoverishment. Physician and philosopher Edmund Pellegrino observes correctly that:

> In no other deprivation is the dissolution of the person so intimate that it impairs the capacity to deal with all other deprivations. The poor man can still hope for a change of fortune, the prisoner for a reprieve, the lonely for a friend. But the ill person remains impaired even when freed of these other constraints on the free exercise of his humanity. (Pellegrino 1982, at 159)

Consider also this account by a philosopher and patient who herself suffers from a severe chronic illness, multiple sclerosis:

> The most deeply held assumption of daily life is the assumption that I, personally, will continue to be alive and it is in light of this assumption that one engages in daily activities. The onset of illness, however, brings one concretely face-to-face with personal vulnerability. . . . Thus, the person who is ill . . . is unable readily to fit illness into the typified schema used to organize and interpret experience. . . . One finds oneself preoccupied with the demands of the here and now, confined to the present moment, unable effectively to project into the future. (Toombs 1992, at 21, 69)

In addition to these profound internal effects, . . . when ill we are often immobilized and confined to bed in a prone position and subjected to mind-altering medications. This compromises our physical ability to act and deliberate and places us in a psychological state of dependency. Treatment also compromises physical integrity and exposes us to singular vulnerability by giving physicians unprecedented access to our bodies and personal histories. Treatment requires us to expose every part of our-selves, down to our very blood and guts, while we remain prostrate or unconscious.

Typically, when ill, we do not resist what would otherwise be viewed as utterly repugnant invasions and vulnerabilities. Sickness returns us to an infantile state where our strongest desire is usually to be cared for and to be relieved of the respon-sibility and anxiety of deciding and acting. "Such sick people . . . may plausibly pre-fer not to take on any kind of work, much less the fierce, foreign, and forbidding labor of medical decisions" (Schneider 1997). This is true even for the most knowl-edgeable of patients—physicians themselves. Franz Ingelfinger, M.D., long time editor of the eminently prestigious New England Journal of Medicine and an expert in diseases of the esophagus, found himself in a dilemma of how best to treat his own difficult case of cancer of the esophagus. His doctors, respecting their patient's world renowned expertise, were leaving this vexing decision to him:

> As a result, not only I but my wife, my son and daughter-in-law (both doctors), and other family members became increasingly confused and emotionally distraught. Finally, when the pangs of indecision had become nearly intolerable, one wise phy-sician friend said, "What you need is a doctor." . . . When that excellent advice was followed, my family and I sensed immediate and immense relief. . . .

[M]y description of the real experience of illness applies to simple and serious con-ditions alike. Sickness does not have to be life threatening for it to profoundly affect thinking and functioning. A bad flu bug, a relentless shooting pain, a case of food poisoning, an inconsolable child, or even an unexplained lump or a persistent bad cough can have these menacing and incapacitating effects at least to some degree. Even if this state of mind is the exception in medical treatment encounters, it nev-ertheless is the dominant explanation of why the medical system exists. . . . Medical ethics and health care policy should have its primary focus on the quintessential features of the treatment relationship even if those features account for only a frac-tion of [medical] decisions.

THE MYSTICAL POWER OF HEALING

[The condition of illness is only half of the story in a medical encounter. We must also understand something about the experience of healing. Modern medi-cine thinks of healing as occurring mainly through biochemical processes activated by medical interventions chosen based on diagnostic analysis and professional expe-rience.] . . . Much of medicine is of this rational quality, but [this account ignores] an essential nonrational component of medicine. . . . This essential component is the mystical power of healing. By this, I mean the hidden elements of the treatment encounter that result in healing through what might be termed charismatic or self-healing means. The power of healing I refer to is the dimension of doctoring that enables physicians to confer relief through spiritual or emotional means akin to those used by parents or priests.[2]

Before alienating the skeptical reader entirely, let me illustrate with an every-day example from my own experience. Last year when my six-year-old daughter was suffering from a common ear ache, her distress brought her to inconsolable tears

2. On the prevalence of the image of physician as parent or priest, see May 1983.

while waiting more than an hour to be seen by the doctor. I convinced a nurse to take her temperature, give her an aspirin, and say a few kind words of reassurance. Instantaneously, my daughter felt much better, far quicker than any possible pharmacological effect could have taken hold. I was puzzled by this abrupt improvement until I had my own excruciating ear ache a few weeks later and experienced exactly the same sort of instantaneous relief as soon as the doctor examined me and wrote a prescription. Knowing that I was in the good hands of a trained professional who offered the prospect of relief produced in me a sense of exhilaration and a release of anxiety accompanied by a pronounced improvement of my symptoms. This instantaneous recovery might be attributed simply to excessive nerves or to a more complex type of placebo effect but, however labeled or explained, it was effective. The pain was not just more bearable; it went away.

Researchers and physicians have documented countless similar examples of mundane and miraculous relief caused by a largely nonscientific or "nonspecific" process of healing. This placebo effect is not limited to purely psychological states, bizarre conditions, especially susceptible patients, or to manipulative physicians. This effect has been documented in the treatment of diabetes, cancer, and heart disease, for instance, and without the physicians even intending to cause the effect. In one scientific study, two sets of patients were subjected to different surgical operations to treat angina (chest pain), one that performed the standard chest operation, and the other that only pretended to do so by cutting the skin under anesthesia. Both the sham and the real procedure produced equal relief of physical symptoms (Beecher 1961). A review of other surgical and medical procedures once firmly believed to be effective but later discarded as entirely unfounded led one author to speculate that placebo healing effects may be present to a significant extent in 70 percent of clinical encounters (Roberts 1993).

Those who have studied this nonspecific healing effect conclude that it pervades medicine, both in modern times and in prescientific and primitive cultures. This is because the effect is connected more to the intervention of the healer than it is to the particular therapeutic agent used. Put another way, the doctor himself is a therapeutic agent, regardless of the actual effectiveness of the particular drug or procedure (Suchman & Matthews 1988; Houston 1938). In each culture and each era, there has been a prevailing theory of medical treatment, many of which are pure fantasy if not dangerous, yet remarkably few have been proven to be wholly without benefit. Doctors and healers have been universally respected throughout the ages and across primitive and advanced societies; we can only assume that most of them have offered some form of relief despite the now apparent quackery they once practiced. Indeed, it has often been commented that the history of medicine until this century has been the history of the placebo effect. Now that medicine has a firm scientific foundation, this mystical or charismatic element has been surpassed by technological skill, but it will never be entirely displaced. One of the prominent trends in modern medicine is the revival of both popular and scientific interest in these poorly understood domains of caring for patients through alternative or holistic schools of medicine (Frohoch 1992; Cousins 1979).

The best scientific explanation for this charismatic healing effect is that the process of treatment, and not its specific content, has universal benefit for many or most illnesses, regardless of the specific physiological effects of the treatment.

The treatment process has this universal healing power by virtue of the archetypal characteristics that activate the patient's own healing mechanisms—mechanisms that are still largely undiscovered and unexplained. This is best demonstrated by the fact that the basic structure of the treatment encounter is remarkably the same across all systems of medicine, including Western, Eastern, religious, herbal, and primitive. In each of these belief systems, society recognizes the healing powers of a professional elite (physicians or shamans), who administer personally to the patient with physical touching and healing agents (drugs or herbs), often in a dramatic and cathartic ritualistic setting (surgery or exorcism) specially designed for the purpose (hospital or bonfire). In the process, patients feel cared for (nurses or mystics), they are given an explanation for their condition (diagnosis or demonization) that is consistent with their prevailing belief system (scientific medicine or spirit worship), and they are assigned tasks of self care in which they take responsibility in part for their own improvement (dietary regimen or prayer).[3]

These many symbolic structural elements are thought to activate patients' internal healing powers through a variety of psychological channels. A patient who knows someone is devoted to caring for him is able to release the dread and anxiety that may be heightening discomfort and weakening the body's resistance. Believing in the power of the healer may enable the patient to regress to an earlier, more infantile state of mind that enhances this release and the resulting comfort. This confidence in the healer is elevated by the healer's status in society, his invocation of methods consistent with that society's belief system, and his offering an explanation of the otherwise troubling and disorienting disease that makes sense to the patient. And, this belief is further cemented by the ritualistic and dramatic elements of laying on of hands, taking of medication, climactic performance, and hallowed setting. . . .

Critical to this healing power is the patient's confidence and trust in the healer. "The image of omnipotence is an essential component of the healer" (see Cassell 1991). The healer appears able to activate the patient's own healing mechanisms because the patient turns himself over both in mind and body to the healer. "A patient's hope and trust lead to a 'letting go' that counteracts stress and is often the key to getting well" (Siegel 1986). Psychiatrists, starting with Freud, have described this phenomenon as "transference," in which patients foist on their healers qualities they formerly attributed to their parents in infancy when parents were viewed as all powerful and all knowing. "Deep in patients' unconscious, physicians are viewed as miracle workers, patterned after the fantasied all-caring parents of infancy. Medicine, after all, was born in magic and religion, and the doctor-priest-magician-parent unity that persists in patients' unconscious cannot be broken" (Katz 1984, at 142-47, 192). . . .

I hasten to concede that none of these assertions are known with any degree of empirical confidence. We are forced into this highly speculative reading of anecdotal accounts from physicians, anthropologists, and enthnographic researchers since empirical testing of this nonspecific healing power is very difficult and has not

3. The leading work developing this explanation is Frank 1973. See also Brody 1992; Novack 1987.

been widely attempted.[4] Nevertheless, many informed observers and patients view the charismatic dimension of healing as fundamental to the treatment relationship (e.g., Brody 1992; Schenck & Churchill 2011).

[PARTIAL BIBLIOGRAPHY, UPDATED]

Beecher, H. (1961). "Surgery as Placebo," 176 JAMA 1102.

Brody, H. (1992). The Healer's Power (New Haven, CT: Yale Univ. Press).

Cassell, E.J. (1991). The Nature of Suffering and the Goals of Medicine (Oxford Univ. Press).

Cousins, N. (1979). Anatomy of an Illness as Perceived by the Patient: Reflections on Healing and Regeneration (New York: W.W. Norton).

Frank, J.D. (1973). Persuasion and Healing: A Comparative Study of Psychotherapy (Baltimore: Johns Hopkins Univ. Press).

Frohoch, F.M. (1992). Healing Powers: Alternative Medicine, Spiritual Communities, and the State (Univ. Chicago Press).

Houston, R. (1938). "The Doctor Himself as a Therapeutic Agent," 11 Annals Int. Med. 1415.

Katz, J. (1984). The Silent World of Doctor and Patient (New York: The Free Press).

Kleinman, A. (1988). The Illness Narratives: Suffering, Healing, and the Human Condition (Basic Books).

Novack, D.H. (1987). "Therapeutic Aspects of the Clinical Encounter," 2 J. Gen. Intern. Med. 346.

Pellegrino, E.D. (1979). "Toward a Reconstruction of Medical Morality: The Primacy of the Act of Profession and the Fact of Illness," 4 J. Med. & Philo. 32.

Pellegrino, E.D. and Thomasma, D.C. (1981). A Philosophical Basis of Medical Practice (Oxford Univ. Press).

Roberts, A.H., et al. (1993). "The Power of Nonspecific Effects in Healing," 12 Clin. Psychol. Rev. 375.

Schenck, D. & Churchill, L. (2011). Healers: Extraordinary Clinicians at Work.

Schneider, C.E. (1997). The Practice of Autonomy: Patients, Doctors, and Medical Decisions (Oxford Univ. Press).

Spiro, H.M. (1986). Doctors, Patients, and Placebos (New Haven, CT: Yale Univ. Press).

Suchman, A.L., and Matthews, D.A. (1988). "What Makes the Doctor-Patient Relationship Therapeutic? Exploring the Connexional Dimension of Medical Care," 108 Ann. Intern. Med. 125.

Toombs, S.K. (1992). The Meaning of Illness, A Phenomenological Account of the Different Perspectives of Physician and Patient (Boston: Kluwer Academic Publishers).

Notes: The Phenomenology of Sickness and Healing

1. *Illness.* Does your own experience with illness confirm or rebut the incapacitating and dehumanizing effects described by Mark Hall? Consider the additional accounts, both analytical and narrative, on the Web site for this book, www.health -law.org. For additional descriptions and analyses of the phenomenology of illness, see Howard Brody, Stories of Sickness (1987); Kathy Charmaz, Good Days, Bad Days:

4. There are some scattered scientific studies demonstrating the placebo effect and the effect of certain of these healing rituals, but no scientific studies exploring what ingredients make this process work . . . [or are counterproductive].

The Self in Chronic Illness and Time (1991); Norman Cousins, The Healing Heart (1983); Michael C. Dohan, Reflections on a Bone Marrow Transplant, 132 Annals Intern. Med. 587 (2000). Discussing how issues of trust and vulnerability affect a number of issues in health care law, see Mark A. Hall, Law, Medicine, and Trust, 55 Stan. L. Rev. 463 (2002); Robert Gatter, Faith, Confidence, and Health Care: Fostering Trust in Medicine Through Law, 39 Wake Forest L. Rev. 395 (2004).

2. *Doctors, Patients, and Placebos.* These readings explain that the placebo effect is not isolated to a few psychologically susceptible individuals or conditions. It permeates medical encounters and typifies the doctor-patient relationship in ways that scientific medicine tends to ignore or deny. The mere encounter with a doctor appears to activate internal, self-healing mechanisms across a wide range of medical conditions, regardless of the actual treatments rendered. In short, doctors do not just administer placebos; they *are* placebos. Considering this, should the FDA deny approval for a drug because it acts "only" as a placebo? How does a doctor obtain informed consent from a patient when he knows the treatment is partially or totally intended to invoke a placebo effect?

In 2006, the AMA issued an ethics opinion that it is unprofessional to use placebos deceptively. Taking issue with this position, see Adam J. Kolber, A Limited Defense of Clinical Placebo Deception, 26 Yale L. & Pol'y Rev. 75-134 (2007); Rachel Sherman & John Hickner, Academic Physicians Use Placebos in Clinical Practice and Believe in the Mind-Body Connection, 23 J. Gen. Intern. Med. 7 (2007). For additional discussion of the placebo effect, see Anup Malani, Regulation with Placebo Effects, 58 Duke L.J. 411 (2008); Kathleen M. Boozang, The Therapeutic Placebo: The Case for Patient Deception, 54 Fla. L. Rev. 687 (2002); Anne Harrington, The Placebo Effect: An Interdisciplinary Exploration (1997); The Science of the Placebo (Harry A. Guess et al. eds., 2002). See generally Amitai Aviram, The Placebo Effect of Law: Law's Role in Manipulating Perceptions, 75 Geo. Wash. L. Rev. 54 (2006) (discussing how, "like the placebo effect of medicine, a law may impact social welfare beyond its objective effects by manipulating the public's subjective perception of the law's effectiveness").

3. *Alternative and Conventional Healers.* There is now widespread social interest in alternative healing, both as a separate area of professional practice and as a component of conventional scientific practice. For further exploration, see the casebook Web site, www.health-law.org; Anne Harrington, The Cure Within: A History of Mind-Body Medicine (2007); Michael H. Cohen, Complementary and Alternative Medicine: Legal Boundaries and Regulatory Perspectives (1998); Michael Ruggio & Lauren DeSantis-Then, Complementary and Alternative Medicine: Longstanding Legal Obstacles to Cutting Edge Treatment, 2 J. Health & Life Sci. L. 137 (2009); Barbara L. Atwell, Mainstreaming Complementary and Alternative Medicine in the Face of Uncertainty, 72 UMKC L. Rev. 593 (2004); Symposium, 31 J.L. Med. Ethics 183 (2003); Michael H. Cohen & Mary C. Ruggie, Integrating Complementary and Alternative Medical Therapies in Conventional Medical Settings, 72 U. Cin. L. Rev. 671-729 (2003); Joseph A. Barrette, The Alternative Medical Practice Act, 77 St. John's L. Rev. 75 (2003); James A. Bulen, Complementary and Alternative Medicine: Ethical and Legal Aspects of Informed Consent to Treatment, 24 J. Leg. Med. 331 (2003); Kathleen M. Boozang, Is the Alternative Medicine? Managed Care Apparently Thinks So, 32 Conn. L. Rev. 567 (2000).

4. *Therapeutic Jurisprudence.* Consider the various implications these provocative readings have for law and public policy. Do they alter conventional legal notions about who should control decisionmaking in the treatment encounter? Do they suggest that health insurance should more freely cover untested or unorthodox therapies? When disputes arise over treatment decisions or insurance coverage, are patients capable of aggressively pursuing their legal rights? Are patients capable of acting as informed consumers in a medical marketplace in which they evaluate the costs and benefits of different treatment options? Questions like these are addressed by a branch of legal thought known as "therapeutic jurisprudence," which views law as a therapeutic agent. This perspective asks whether normal social and behavioral assumptions realistically fit the medical arena, and whether legal rules do a good job of fostering the therapeutic goals of medicine. For leading examples, focused mainly on mental health and criminal law, see Law in a Therapeutic Key (David B. Wexler & Bruce J. Winnick eds., 1996); Marshall B. Kapp, The Law and Older Persons: Is Geriatric Jurisprudence Therapeutic? (2003). For an attempt to further develop this perspective in health care law, see Hall, supra, 55 Stan. L. Rev. 463 (2002).

3. *The Nature of Medical Judgment*

■ CLINICAL DECISION MAKING: FROM THEORY TO PRACTICE
David M. Eddy*
1996

. . . Why do physicians vary so much in the way they practice medicine? At first view, there should be no problem. There are diseases—neatly named and categorized by textbooks, journal articles, and medical specialty societies. There are various procedures physicians can use to diagnose and treat these diseases. It should be possible to determine the value of any particular procedure by applying it to patients who have a disease and observing the outcome. And the rest should be easy—if the outcome is good, the procedure should be used for patients with that disease; if the outcome is bad, it should not. Some variation in practice patterns can be expected due to differences in the incidence of various diseases, patients' preferences, and the available resources, but these variations should be small and explainable.

The problem of course is that nothing is this simple. Uncertainty, biases, errors, and differences of opinions, motives, and values weaken every link in the chain that connects a patient's actual condition to the selection of a diagnostic test or treatment. . . . Uncertainty creeps into medical practice through every pore. Whether a physician is defining a disease, making a diagnosis, selecting a procedure, observing outcomes, assessing probabilities, assigning preference, or putting it all together, he is walking on very slippery terrain. It is difficult for nonphysicians, and for many physicians, to appreciate how complex these tasks are, how poorly we understand them, and how easy it is for honest people to come to different conclusions.

*Reprinted with permission. Dr. Eddy is a physician researcher, formerly on the faculty of Duke University, and now a consultant in Jackson Hole, Wyoming.

DEFINING A DISEASE

If one looks at patients who are obviously ill, it is fairly easy to identify the physical and chemical disorders that characterize that illness. On the other hand, a large part of medicine is practiced on people who do not have obvious illnesses, but rather have signs, symptoms, or findings that may or may not represent an illness that should be treated. Three closely related problems make it difficult to determine whether or not a patient actually has a disease that needs to be diagnosed or treated.

One problem is that the dividing line between "normal" and "abnormal" is not nearly as sharp as a cursory reading of a textbook would suggest. . . . A second problem is that many "diseases," at least at the time they are diagnosed, do not by themselves cause pain, suffering, disability, or threat to life. They are considered diseases only because they increase the probability that something else that is truly bad will happen in the future. . . .

The difficulty of defining a disease is compounded by the fact that many of the signs, symptoms, findings, and conditions that might suggest a disease are extremely common. If a breast biopsy were performed on a random sample of senior citizens, fully 90 percent of them could have fibrocystic disease. If obesity is a disease, the average American is diseased. . . . Morbid obesity is defined as 100 percent above the ideal weight. But what is "ideal," and why 100 percent? The lesson is that for many conditions a clinician faces, there is no clear definition of disease that provides an unequivocal guide to action, and there is wide room for differences of opinion and variations in practice. . . .

[E]ven when sharp criteria are created, physicians vary widely in their application of these criteria—in their ability to ask about symptoms, observe signs, interpret test results, and record the answers. The literature on "observer variation" has been growing for a long time. . . . Thirteen pathologists were asked to read 1,001 specimens obtained from biopsies of the cervix, and then to repeat the readings at a later time. On average, each pathologist agreed with himself only 89 percent of the time (intraobserver agreement), and with a panel of "senior" pathologists only 87 percent of the time (interobserver agreement). Looking only at the patients who actually had cervical pathology, the intraobserver agreement was only 68 percent and the interobserver agreement was only 51 percent. The pathologists were best at reading more advanced disease and normal tissue, but were labeled "unsatisfactory" in their ability to read the precancerous and preinvasive stages.

Similar studies have been reported for . . . many other signs, symptoms, and procedures. Even if there were no uncertainty about what constitutes a disease and how to define it, there would still be considerable uncertainty about whether or not a patient has the signs, symptoms, and findings needed to fit the definition.

SELECTING A PROCEDURE

The task of selecting a procedure is no less difficult. There are two main issues. First, for any patient condition there are dozens of procedures that can be ordered, in any combination, at any time. The list of procedures that might be included in a workup of chest pain or hypertension would take more than a page, spanning the spectrum from simply asking questions, to blood studies, to X-rays. Even for highly specific diagnostic problems, there can be a large choice of procedures. For example, if a woman presents with a breast mass and her physician wants to know its approximate size and architecture, the physician might contemplate an imaging procedure. The choice could include mammography, ultra-sonography, thermography, diaphanography, computed tomography, lymphography, Mammoscan, and magnetic resonance imaging. . . . And why should a diagnostic workup be limited to one test? Why not follow a negative mammogram with a computed tomogram (or vice versa)? For the detection of colorectal cancer, a physician can choose any combination of fecal occult blood tests (and there are more than a dozen brands), digital examination, rigid sigmoidoscopy, flexible 30 cm sigmoidoscopy, flexible 60 cm sigmoidoscopy, barium enema (either plain or air contrast), and colonoscopy. These choices are not trivial. Most procedures have different mechanisms of action and a long list of pros and cons. . . . These procedures are for relatively well-defined diseases; imagine the problems of selecting procedures to evaluate symptoms like fatigue, headache, or fever that can have about a dozen causes. . . .

In theory, much of the uncertainty just described could be managed if it were possible to conduct enough experiments under enough conditions, and observe the outcomes. Unfortunately, measuring the outcomes of medical procedures is one of the most difficult problems we face. The goal is to predict how the use of a procedure in a particular case will affect that patient's health and welfare. Standing in the way are at least a half dozen major obstacles. The central problem is that there is a natural variation in the way people respond to a medical procedure. Take two people who, to the best of our ability to define such things, are identical in all important respects, submit them to the same operative procedure, and one will die on the operating table while the other will not. Because of this natural variation, we can only talk about the probabilities of various outcomes—the probability that a diagnostic test will be positive if the disease is present (sensitivity), the probability that a test will be negative if the disease is absent (specificity), the probability that a treatment will yield a certain result, and so forth.

One consequence of this natural variation is that to study the outcomes of any procedure it is necessary to conduct the procedure on many different people, who are thought to represent the particular patients we want to know about, and then average the results. . . . Some diseases are so rare that, in order to conduct the ideal clinical trials, it would be necessary to collect tens of thousands, if not hundreds of thousands, of participants. A good example concerns the frequency of the Pap smear. One might wonder why the merits of a three-year versus one-year frequency cannot be settled by a randomized controlled trial. Because of the low frequency of cervical cancer, and the small difference in outcomes expected for the two frequencies, almost one million women would be required for such a study. . . .

Finally, even when the best trials are conducted, we still might not get an answer. Consider the value of mammography in women under fifty, and consider just one outcome—the effect on breast cancer mortality. Ignore for the time being the radiation hazard, false-positive test results, inconvenience, financial costs, and other issues. This is one of the best-studied problems in cancer prevention, benefiting from the largest (60,000 women) and longest (more than 15 years) completed randomized controlled trial, and an even larger uncontrolled study involving 270,000 women screened for five years in 29 centers around the country. Yet we still do not know the value of mammography in women under 50. . . .

Unable to turn to a definitive body of clinical and epidemiological research, a clinician or research scientist who wants to know the value of a procedure is left with a mixture of randomized controlled trials, nonrandomized trials, uncontrolled trials, and clinical observations. The evidence from different sources can easily go in different directions, and it is virtually impossible for anyone to sort things out in his or her head. Unfortunately, the individual physician may be most impressed by observations made in his or her individual practice. This source of evidence is notoriously vulnerable to bias and error. What a physician sees and remembers is biased by the types of patients who come in; by the decisions of the patients to accept a treatment and return for follow-up; by a natural desire to see good things; and by a whole series of emotions that charge one's memory. On top of these biases, the observations are vulnerable to large statistical errors because of the small number of patients a physician sees in a personal practice. . . .

Now assume that a physician can know the outcomes of recommending a particular procedure for a particular patient. Is it possible to declare whether those outcomes are good or bad? Unfortunately, no. The basic problem is that any procedure has multiple outcomes, some good and some bad. The expected reduction in chest pain that some people will get from coronary artery bypass surgery is accompanied by a splitting of the chest, a chance of an operative mortality, days in the hospital, pain, anxiety, and financial expense. Because the outcomes are multiple and move in different directions, tradeoffs have to be made. And making tradeoffs involves values. . . . Imagine the variation in how different people value pain, disability, operative mortality, life expectancy, a day in a hospital, and who is going to feed the dogs. . . .

PUTTING IT ALL TOGETHER

The final decision about how to manage a patient requires synthesizing all the information about a disease, the patient, signs and symptoms, the effectiveness of dozens of tests and treatments, outcomes and values. All of this must be done without knowing precisely what the patient has, with uncertainty about signs and symptoms, with imperfect knowledge of the sensitivity and specificity of tests, with no training in manipulating probabilities, with incomplete and biased information about outcomes, and with no language for communicating or assessing values. If each piece of this puzzle is difficult, it is even more difficult for anyone to synthesize all the information and be certain of the answer. It would be an extremely hard task for a research team; there is no hope that it could occur with any precision in the head of a busy clinician. Hence the wide variability in the estimates physicians place on the values of procedures.

[A] final example document[s] how difficult it is to combine information from many sources to estimate the value of a particular procedure. . . . A survey of 1,000 11-year-old schoolchildren in New York City found that 65 percent had undergone tonsillectomy. The remaining children were sent for examinations to a group of physicians and 45 percent were selected for tonsillectomy. Those rejected were examined by another group of physicians and 46 percent were selected for surgery. When the remaining children were examined again by another group of physicians, a similar percent were recommended for tonsillectomy, leaving only 65 students. At that point, the study was halted for lack of physicians.

CONSEQUENCES

The view of anyone who wants a close look at the consequences of different medical procedures is, at best, smoky. Some procedures may present a clear picture, and their value, or lack of it, may be obvious; putting a finger on a bleeding carotid artery is an extreme example. But for many, if not most medical procedures, we can only see shadows and gross movements. . . . We certainly do not know how a particular individual will respond. Words like "rare," "common," and "a lot" must be used instead of "one out of 1,000," or "seven on a scale of one to ten." . . .

In the end, given all the uncertainties, incentives, and heuristics, a physician will have to do what is comfortable. If it is admitted that the uncertainty surrounding the use of a procedure is great, and that there is no way to identify for certain what is best, or to prove that any particular action is right or wrong, the safest and most comfortable position is to do what others are doing. The applicable maxim is "safety in numbers." A physician who follows the practices of his or her colleagues is safe from criticism, free from having to explain his or her actions, and defended by the concurrence of colleagues.

▪ COMPLICATIONS: A SURGEON'S NOTES ON AN IMPERFECT SCIENCE
Atul Gawande*
2002

THE CASE OF THE RED LEG

Seeing patients with one of the surgery professors in his clinic one afternoon, I was struck by how often he had to answer his patients' questions, "I do not know." These are four little words a doctor tends to be reluctant to utter. We're supposed to have the answers. We want to have the answers. But there was not a single person he did not have to say those four little words to that day. . . . The core predicament of medicine—the thing that makes being a patient so wrenching, being a doctor so difficult, and being a part of a society that pays the bills they run up so vexing—is uncertainty. With all that we know nowadays about people and diseases and how to diagnose and treat them, it can be hard to see this, hard to grasp how deeply the uncertainty runs. As a doctor, you come to find, however, that the struggle in caring for people is more often with what you do not know than what you do. Medicine's ground state is uncertainty. And wisdom—for both patients and doctors—is defined by how one copes with it.

This is the story of one decision under uncertainty.

It was two o'clock on a Tuesday afternoon in June. . . . I had just finished admitting someone with a gallbladder infection and was attempting to sneak out for a bite to eat when one of the emergency room physicians stopped me with yet another patient to see: a twenty-three-year-old, Eleanor Bratton, with a red and swollen

*Excerpted with permission, Henry Holt and Company. The author is a physician on the faculty of Harvard's Schools of Medicine and of Public Health. This true story uses fictionalized names.

leg. . . . "It's probably only a cellulitis" [he said]—a simple skin infection. . . . But he wanted me to make sure there wasn't anything "surgical" going on—an abscess that needed draining or some such. "Would you mind taking a quick look?" Groan. No. Of course not. . . .

She looked fit, athletic, and almost teenage, with blond hair tight in a ponytail, nails painted gold, and her eyes fixed on a television. There did not seem anything seriously ill about her. . . . That weekend she had gone back home to Hartford, Connecticut, to attend a wedding . . . and she had kicked off her shoes and danced the whole night. The morning after, however, she woke up with her left foot feeling sore. She had a week-old blister on the top of her foot from some cruddy sandals she had worn, and now the skin surrounding the blister was red and puffy. . . . The redness spread, and during the night she got chills and sweats and a fever of one hundred and three degrees. . . . I asked Eleanor if she had had any pus or drainage from her leg.

No. Any ulcers open up in her skin? No. A foul smell or blackening of her skin? No. Any more fevers? Not since two days ago. I let the data roll around in my head. . . . Objectively, the rash had the exact appearance of a cellulitis, something antibiotics would take care of. But another possibility lodged in my mind now, one that scared the hell out of me. . . .

Decisions in medicine are supposed to rest on concrete observations and hard evidence. But just a few weeks before, I had taken care of a patient I could not erase from my mind. . . . He was found to have a small and very ordinary skin rash on his chest and was sent home with antibiotic pills for cellulitis. That night the rash spread eight inches. The following morning he spiked a fever of one hundred and two degrees. By the time he returned to the emergency room, the skin involved had become numb and widely blistered. Shortly after, he went into shock. He was transferred to my hospital and we quickly took him to the OR.

He didn't have a cellulitis but instead an extremely rare and horrendously lethal type of infection known as necrotizing fasciitis (fah-shee-EYE-tiss). The tabloids have called it a disease of "flesh-eating bacteria" and the term is not an exaggeration. Opening the skin, we found a massive infection, far worse than what appeared from the outside. All the muscles of the left side of his chest, going around to his back, up to his shoulder, and down to his abdomen, had turned gray and soft and foul with invading bacteria and had to be removed. . . . The next day we had to remove his arm. For a while, we actually thought we had saved him. . . . One by one, however, his kidneys, lungs, liver, and heart went into failure, and then he died. It was among the most awful cases I have ever been involved in.

What we know about necrotizing fasciitis is this: it is highly aggressive and rapidly invasive. It kills up to 70 percent of the people who get it. No known antibiotic will stop it. . . . It is an organism that usually causes little more than a strep throat, but in certain strains it has evolved the ability to do far worse. No one knows where these strains come from. As with a cellulitis, they are understood to enter through breaks in the skin. The break can be as large as a surgical incision or as slight as an abrasion. . . . Survival is possible only with early and radical excisional surgery, often requiring amputation. To succeed, however, it must be done early. By the time signs of deep invasion are obvious—such as shock, loss of sensation, widespread blistering of the skin—the person is usually unsalvageable.

Standing at Eleanor's bedside, bent over examining her leg, I felt a little foolish considering the diagnosis. . . . True, in the early stages, a necrotizing fasciitis can look just like a cellulitis, presenting with the same redness, swelling, fever, and high white blood cell count. But . . . [o]nly about a thousand cases of necrotizing fasciitis occur in the entire United States each year, mainly in the elderly and chronically ill—and well over *three million* cases of cellulitis.

What's more, Eleanor's fever had gone away; she didn't look unusually ill; and I knew I was letting myself be swayed by a single, recent, anecdotal case. If there were a simple test to tell the two diagnoses apart, that would have been one thing. But there is none. The only way is to go to the operating room, open the skin, and look—not something you want to propose arbitrarily. . . .

Eleanor and her father looked on with new dread when [the general surgeon, Dr.] Studdert arrived in his scrubs and operating hat to see her. He had her tell her story again and then uncovered her leg to examine it. He didn't seem too impressed. Talking by ourselves, he told me that the rash looked to him only "like a bad cellulitis." But could he say for sure that it was not necrotizing fasciitis? He could not. It is a reality of medicine that choosing to *not* do something—to not order a test, to not give an antibiotic, to not take a patient to the operating room—is far harder than choosing to do it. . . .

Studdert sat down on the edge of her bed . . . and, in a quiet and gentle voice, he went on to explain the unquiet and ungentle effects of necrotizing fasciitis. . . . "I think it is unlikely you have it," he told Eleanor. "I'd put the chances"—he was guessing here—"at well under five percent." But, he went on, "without a biopsy, we cannot rule it out." He paused for a moment to let her and her father absorb this. Then he started to explain what the procedure involved. . . .

Eleanor went rigid. "This is crazy," she said. "This doesn't make any sense." She looked frantic, like someone drowning. "Why don't we just wait and see how the antibiotics go?" Studdert explained that this was a disease that you cannot sit on, that you had to catch it early to have any chance of treating it. Eleanor just shook her head and looked down at her covers.

Studdert and I both turned to her father to see what he might have to say. He . . . asked what would happen if the biopsy were positive for the disease. Studdert . . . hesitated before going on. "This can mean an amputation," he said. Eleanor began to cry. "I don't want to do this, Dad." Mr. Bratton swallowed hard, his gaze fixed somewhere miles beyond us.

In recent years, we in medicine have discovered how discouragingly often . . . medicine still lacks the basic organization and commitment to make sure we do what we know to do. But spend almost any amount of time with doctors and patients, and you will find that the larger, starker, and more painful difficulty is the still abundant uncertainty that exists over what should be done in many situations. The gray zones in medicine are considerable, and every day we confront situations like Eleanor's—ones in which clear scientific evidence of what to do is missing and yet choices must be made.

Exactly which patients with pneumonia, for example, should be hospitalized and which ones sent home? Which back pains treated by surgery and which by conservative measures alone? Which patients with a rash taken to surgery and which just observed on antibiotics? For many cases, the answers can be obvious. But for many others, we simply do not know. . . . In the absence of algorithms and evidence about what to do, you learn in medicine to make decisions by feel. You count on experience and judgment. And it is hard not to be troubled by this. . . . But in the face of uncertainty, what other than judgment does a physician have—or a patient have, for that matter? . . .

Eleanor and her dad now agreed to go ahead. "Let's get it over with," she said. But then I brought her the surgical consent form to sign. On it, I had written not only that the procedure was a "biopsy of the left lower extremity" but also that the risks included a "possible need for amputation." She cried out when she saw the words. It took her several minutes alone with her father before she could sign. . . .

There is, in fact, another approach to decision making, one advocated by a small and struggling coterie in medicine. The strategy, long used in business and the military, is called decision analysis, and the principles are straightforward. On a piece of paper (or a computer), you lay out all your options, and all the possible outcomes of those options, in a decision tree. You make a numeric estimate of the probability of each outcome, using hard data when you have it and a rough prediction when you don't. You weigh each outcome according to its relative desirability (or "utility") to the patient. Then you multiply out the numbers for each option and choose the one with the highest calculated "expected utility." The goal is to use explicit, logical, statistical thinking instead of just your gut. The decision to recommend annual mammograms for all women over age fifty was made this way and so was the U.S. decision to bail out Mexico when its economy tanked. Why not, the advocates ask, individual patient decisions?

Recently, I tried "treeing out" (as the decision buffs put it) the choice Eleanor faced. The options were simple: to biopsy or not biopsy. The outcomes quickly got complicated, however. There was: not being biopsied and doing fine; not being biopsied, getting diagnosed late, going through surgery, and surviving anyway; not being biopsied and dying; being biopsied and getting only a scar; being biopsied and getting a scar plus bleeding from it; being biopsied, having the disease and an amputation, but dying anyway; and so on. When all the possibilities and consequences were penciled out, my decision tree looked more like a bush. Assigning the probabilities for each potential twist of fate seemed iffy. I found what data I could from the medical literature and then had to extrapolate a good deal. And determining the relative desirability of the outcomes seemed impossible after talking to Eleanor about them. Is dying a hundred times worse than doing fine, a thousand times worse, a million? Where does a scar with bleeding fit in? Nonetheless, these are the crucial considerations, the decision experts argue, and when we decide by instinct, they say, we are only papering this reality over.

Producing a formal analysis in any practical time frame proved to be out of the question, though. It took a couple of days—not the minutes that we had actually had—and a lot of back and forths with two decision experts. But it did provide an answer. According to the final decision tree, we should *not* have gone to the OR for a biopsy. The likelihood of my initial hunch being right was too low, and the likelihood that catching the disease early would make no difference anyway was too high. Biopsy could not be justified, the logic said. I don't know what we would have made of this information at the time. We didn't have the decision tree, however. And we went to the OR. . . .

At first glance beneath her skin, there was nothing apparent to alarm us. . . . When we probed with the tip of a clamp inside the calf incision, however, it slid unnaturally easily along the muscle, as if bacteria had paved a path. This is not a definitive finding, but enough of one that Studdert let out a sudden, disbelieving, "Oh shit." . . . . The features he saw were "consistent with necrotizing fasciitis[.]" . . . "She's got it," he finally announced grimly. . . .

Decisions compound themselves, in medicine like in anything else. No sooner have you taken one fork in the road than another and another come upon you. The critical question now was what to do. . . . "I thought about a BKA," a below-knee amputation, Studdert says, "even an AKA," an above-knee amputation. No one would have faulted him for doing either. But he found himself balking. "She was such a young girl," he explains. "It may seem harsh to say, but if it was a sixty-year-old man I would've taken the leg without question." This was partly, I think, a purely emotional unwillingness to cut off the limb of a pretty twenty-three-year-old — the kind of sentimentalism that can get you in trouble. But it was also partly instinct again, an instinct that her youth and fundamentally good health might allow him to get by with just removing the most infested tissue (a "debridement") and washing out her foot and leg. Was this a good risk to take, with one of the deadliest bacteria known to man loose in her leg? Who knows? But take it he did. . . . We ended up operating on her leg four times in four days. . . . Only then was Studdert confident that not only had Eleanor survived, but her foot and leg had, too. . . .

For close to thirty years, Dartmouth physician Jack Wennberg has studied decision making in medicine, . . . [a]nd what he has found is a stubborn, overwhelming, and embarrassing degree of inconsistency in what we do. His research has shown, for example, that the likelihood of a doctor sending you for a gallbladder-removal operation varies 270 percent depending on what city you live in; for a hip replacement, 450 percent; for care in an intensive care unit during the last six months of your life, 880 percent. A patient in Santa Barbara, California, is five times more likely to be recommended back surgery for a back pain than one in Bronx, New York. This is, in the main, uncertainty at work, with the varying experience, habits, and intuitions of individual doctors leading to massively different care for people.

How can this be justified? The people who pay for the care certainly do not see how. (That is why insurers bug doctors so constantly to explain our decisions.) Nor might the people who receive it. Eleanor Bratton, without question, would have been treated completely differently depending on where she went, who she saw, or even just when she saw me (before or after that previous necrotizing fasciitis case I'd seen; at 2 A.M. or 2 P.M.; on a quiet or a busy shift). She'd have gotten merely antibiotics at one place, an amputation at another, a debridement at a third. This result seems unconscionable.

People have proposed two strategies for change. One is to shrink the amount of uncertainty in medicine — with research, not on new drugs or operations (which already attracts massive amounts of funding) but on the small but critical everyday decisions that patients and doctors make (which gets shockingly little funding). Everyone understands, though, that a great deal of uncertainty about what to do for people will always remain. (Human disease and lives are too complicated for reality to be otherwise.) So it has also been argued, not unreasonably, that doctors must agree in advance on what should be done in the uncertain situations that arise — spell out our actions ahead of time to take the guesswork out and get some advantage of group decision. This last goes almost nowhere, though. For it runs counter to everything we doctors believe about ourselves as individuals, about our personal ability to reason out with patients what the best course of action for them is. . . .

The possibilities and probabilities are all we have to work with in medicine, though. What we are drawn to in this imperfect science, what we in fact covet in our way, is the alterable moment—the fragile but crystalline opportunity for one's know-how, ability, or just gut instinct to change the course of another's life for the better. In the actual situations that present themselves, however—a despondent woman arrives to see you about a newly diagnosed cancer, a victim bleeding from a terrible injury is brought pale and short of breath from the scene, a fellow physician asks for your opinion about a twenty-three-year-old with a red leg—we can never be sure whether we have such a moment or not. Even less clear is whether the actions we choose will prove either wise or helpful. That our efforts succeed at all is still sometimes a shock to me. But they do. . . .

Notes: Medical Decisionmaking

1. *The Nature of Medical Judgment.* Medical decisionmaking is best appreciated by examining a range of particular medical cases. One example of a full-length case discussion, which illustrates many of the dimensions of uncertainty of judgment described by Doctors Gawande and Eddy is linked on the Web site for this book, www.health-law.org. For additional readings on the nature of medical judgment, see Kathryn Montgomery, How Doctors Think (2006); Jerome Groopman, How Doctors Think (2007); Kathryn Hunter, Doctors' Stories: The Narrative Structure of Medical Knowledge (1991).

Dr. Gawande mentions the work of Dartmouth researchers documenting dramatic variations in physicians' practice styles in different communities. Dr. Gawande brought this research to widespread attention in The Cost Conundrum: What a Texas Town Can Teach Us About Health Care, The New Yorker, June 1, 2009.

2. *Medical Terminology.* Prior editions of this book contained information about medical terminology, medical science, and anatomy. Lawyers who practice in this field must eventually acquire a fair amount of medical knowledge, and many law students enjoy learning something about a different profession's specialized vocabulary. Others see medical terminology as an obstacle to understanding what's really happening in these cases. We have chosen to cater to the latter group; our feeling is that if you end up working in this field, you will have plenty of opportunity to learn the terminology later. Here, when cases contain uncommon medical terms, we will define them for you. If we fail to do so, most terms used in this book are contained in better-quality general dictionaries. For those who want more specialized information, here is a sampling of various medical texts and treatises, some written especially for lawyers and others for medical professionals or for the lay public. **Medical Dictionaries:** Dorland's Illustrated Medical Dictionary; Stedman's Medical Dictionary; Taber's Cyclopedic Medical Dictionary. Links to the online versions of these can be found on this casebook's Web site, www.health-law.org. A comprehensive guide to medical research for legal purposes is Caroline Young, Medico-Legal Research Using Evidence-Based Medicine, 102 L. Libr. J. 449 (2010).

■ LAW AND MEDICINE
William J. Curran
1st ed. 1960

There may have been a time when doctors and lawyers had much in common, but today their environments are radically divergent and the problem of mutual understanding is a real one. The doctor is trained in a dynamic and experimental science, he is seeking truth in a physical world. He is steeped in the practical judgment, though he avoids generalization. The lawyer, on the other hand, lives within the generalities of the law. The courts apply justice through the advocacy system and seek truth through the burden of proof. When the doctor or other medical person comes into contact with the courts and lawyers, he is often mystified and is generally impatient with the conservatism of the courts in accepting the advances of science. The lawyer often does not seem to the doctor to be seeking truth, but only to place blame.

Most lawyers are Aristotelian in method, if not in philosophy. So are law students by the time they are seniors. That is to say, they work from settled principles on stated fact situations. While they are seeking the results of their deductive logic, their facts remain unchanged. This is not the case in science and in medicine. The scientist seeks truth within the scientific method. The physician is also an experimentalist, an empiricist. At times, however, he does not like being called a scientist, particularly when he is treating a patient. Then he may prefer the title of artisan—but still an empirical artisan.

The failure to understand the basic difference in method between doctors and lawyers is often a stumbling block to greater cooperation between the two professions. It often leads the lawyer into error in presenting the medical issues in a legal action. It may seem obvious that a lawyer should understand the physician's methods as well as his conclusions. Yet, when the attorney accepts a case and prepares it for trial, he tends not to do this. If his client has a back injury, he is interested only in the doctor's conclusions in regard to that injury. He may study the basis for the physician's conclusions in regard to this case, but he rarely does anything more until the next case comes along when again he is interested only in *that* injury. . . .

■ PHYSICIANS VERSUS LAWYERS: A CONFLICT OF CULTURES
Daniel M. Fox*
AIDS and the Law (H. Dalton & S. Burris eds., 1987)

If we are to move in the direction of cooperation rather than conflict, we must understand the roots of the antagonism between the professions and the contemporary forces that threaten to deepen it.

I emphasize physicians' antagonism to lawyers, because I suspect that most lawyers are not normally antagonistic toward physicians. Physicians, on the other

*Daniel Fox is widely known and published in the health care public policy field. He was the long-term president of the Milbank Memorial Fund, before which he held various positions in academics and government.

hand, believe they are being taken advantage of by lawyers who do not understand medicine or value it properly. They are, moreover, mortified because the conflict is usually displayed in public settings controlled by lawyers—court proceedings and legislative hearings.

The conflict between physicians and lawyers, though it is rooted in the modern history of the two professions, has become more intense in recent years as the authority most people accord to physicians has diminished. Some physicians accuse lawyers of helping to undermine public confidence in them by mindlessly pursuing malpractice litigation. Many attribute their rising premiums for malpractice insurance to the work of greedy and unscrupulous lawyers. Physicians often blame lawyers for the mass of regulations that burden them. In an astonishing display of professional bigotry, the new president of the Association of American Medical Colleges told a medical school graduating class in June 1986, "We're swimming in shark-infested w aters where the sharks are lawyers."

To most physicians, adversarial proceedings are an ineffective and irrational method for resolving conflict. Where Anglo-American lawyers presume that a person accused of a crime is innocent until proven guilty in a court of law, physicians believe it is dangerous to make any presumption before examining evidence. Similarly, most physicians do not understand the history or the logic of lawyers' claim that formalized conflict between plaintiffs and defendants in a courtroom or around a table resolves disagreements with reasonable equity and preserves social peace.

Physicians are trained to rely on two methods of addressing conflicts about data and their interpretation. The first method is the assertion of authority from the top of a hierarchy in which power is derived from knowledge. The second method is peer review-discussion to consensus among experts of roughly equal standing and attainment. Both methods, the hierarchical and the consensual, rest on the assumption that truth is best determined by experts. . . .

Note: Law vs. Medicine: A Culture Clash

For additional books and articles that illustrate differences of professional approach, ethical principles, and cultural values between lawyers and physicians (not necessarily with that intention in mind), see J. Katz, The Silent World of Doctor and Patient (1984); Peter Jacobson & Gregg Bloche, Improving Relations Between Attorneys and Physicians, 294 JAMA 2083 (2005); William M. Sage, The Lawyerization of Medicine, 26 J. Health Pol. Pol'y & L. 1179 (2001); Andrew McClurg, Fight Club: Doctors vs. Lawyers—A Peace Plan Grounded in Self-Interest, 83 Temple L. Rev. 309 (2011). Comparing medical education and legal education, see Christine Coughlin et al., See One, Do One, Teach One: Dissecting the Use of Medical Education's Signature Pedagogy in the Law School Curriculum, 26 Ga. St. U. L. Rev. 361 (2010).

B. THE HEALTH CARE FINANCING AND DELIVERY SYSTEM

The readings in this section describe the economic and regulatory forces that shape how health care is delivered in the United States. All of us have some exposure to the world of medicine but few law students have reason to understand the intricacies of this financing and delivery system and how it has developed. This understanding is essential in a course that focuses on the full range of legal and public policy issues pertaining to the delivery and payment for medical care. Those issues have naturally taken shape according to the structural components and historical growth of the health care sector and its various institutions.

We begin with a rudimentary overview of the history of health insurance and of the principal events that have shaped its development. Included in this is a discussion of whether there is a "crisis" in American medicine. We finish with an introduction to more recent developments such as the Affordable Care Act of 2010. As you read through this alphabet soup of actors, institutions, and acronyms, rather than memorizing all the details, try to construct a coherent story line of how the health care sector took shape over time and how its various pieces interconnect at present. You don't need to master all the details now, for they will reemerge throughout the course, but it will be easier to remember them at the end if you have an initial framework to attach them to.

1. The Crises in Access, Cost, and Quality

■ HEALTH AND MEDICAL CARE REFORM IN THE UNITED STATES: ETHICAL QUESTIONS AND CONCERNS
Thomas W. Merrill, David G. Miller, Joseph A. Raho & Ginger Gruters
President's Council on Bioethics, Staff Background Paper, 2008

The reform of health and medical care in the United States has been a topic on our national agenda for decades now. . . . [A]t present, we seem to be witnessing a remarkable coalescence—of the public, health professionals and organizations, and policymakers—around the conclusion that the American "system" of health and medical care is ailing. Three problems—of access and coverage, of quality, and of cost—are usually cited as the signs and symptoms of this increasingly worrisome state. . . . [W]e offer a purely descriptive account of the problems of access, quality, and cost, in order to illustrate their complexity and to draw out their implications for ethical questioning. . . .

I. THE PROBLEM OF ACCESS TO HEALTH AND MEDICAL CARE

In [2010], according to the Current Population Survey of the U.S. Census Bureau, [50] million Americans were uninsured. This statistic is often cited in ways that suggest that it—and it alone—constitutes the whole of the problem of access to health and medical care in the United States. . . . There are other dimensions to the problem of access. The underinsured, who have some coverage but are inadequately protected against high out-of-pocket costs, are the subjects of a growing literature. Difficulties with the supply and geographical distribution of health care professionals, along with some types of health care facilities (for example, emergency rooms), are also constituents of the problem of access. Our focus here, however, is on the uninsured. . . .

According to one estimate, some 18,000 premature deaths per year in the United States (as well as a number of other serious health conditions) could have been prevented by better access to health care.[3] To be sure, the uninsured do have access to emergency room care . . . , but care through this source tends to be less than optimal. Conditions are often treated only when they have become very serious. Moreover, the use of emergency care by the uninsured exacerbates the burdens placed on often strained emergency rooms and centers. . . . Those hospitals and professionals incur costs that eventually lead to higher charges for the insured or to increasing outlays of federal and state funds for uncompensated care. . . .

The preceding review of statistical data underscore[s] one conclusion: the situation of the uninsured in the United States is a complicated one, far more so than the oft-cited figure of [50] million reveals. As this review has shown, that number does not capture how long the uninsured lack this essential component of access to care, nor does it provide important information on who the uninsured are. The number of individuals who lack insurance for a year or more is lower than [50] million—probably somewhere between 30 and 40 million. Nor is it the case that the uninsured are all poor and thus unable to purchase insurance. More than one-third have household incomes above the median national income. Moreover, about a fifth are not citizens. . . . It is also noteworthy that the rates of uninsurance are higher among the poor and among African-American and Hispanic communities. . . .

II. THE PROBLEM OF HEALTH CARE COSTS AND FINANCING

Just as few, if any, would dispute the fact that there are many millions of uninsured Americans, so too would few take issue with the claims that health care costs in the United States are high compared to other industrialized nations and that these costs are increasing in seemingly unconstrained ways. These facts are cause for concern on a number of fronts. Such broad measures of population health as infant mortality and life expectancy, for example, indicate that the U.S. does no better, and in some cases does far worse, than similar countries that spend less on health care: we may not be getting good value for our money. . . . [T]he current situation is made more worrying still by the historical trends in the growth of health care spending. . . . According to some estimates made by the Congressional Budget Office, if current trends continue, health care spending could rise to almost 50 percent of total Gross Domestic Product (GDP) by 2082. . . .

There is much controversy, of course, over the causes of those increases and the ways we might address those causes. Here, we simply lay out some well-known facts about health care spending in the United States: as a portion of GDP and per capita; as it affects employees and employers; and as it affects federal and state budgets.

Today [as of 2011], the United States spends about [$2.7] trillion per year on health care, which amounts to [18] percent of GDP and about [$8,700] per person. Of course, compared with the poorer nations of the world, all of the wealthier nations spend a greater proportion of their income on health care. The United States, however, spends more on health care—both on a per capita basis and as a percentage of its GDP—than *any* other nation in the world. . . . National

---

3. See the Institute of Medicine report *Hidden Costs, Value Lost: Uninsurance in America* (2003). Other scholars point out, however, that it is difficult to establish clear evidence of causation (as opposed to correlation) between insurance status and health status. . . .

spending on health care as a share of GDP increased from about 5 percent in 1960 to our current level of [18] percent today and is projected to continue to grow. . . . The cumulative effect of those growth rates is this: The United States has experienced a *twenty-fold increase* in health care expenditures—a four-fold increase over the consumer price index over the same period. . . .

Of course, the rising share of health care as a portion of GDP may not necessarily be cause for concern. As mentioned above, as countries become wealthier, their citizens tend to spend more money on health care, and there is no way to determine *a priori* what the "appropriate" level of spending on health care may be. Moreover, the percentage of GDP representing health care also depends on the size and character of what happens in other sectors of the economy. Above all, the costs by themselves do not tell us anything about the quality or value of the care being provided. . . . Nevertheless, as the cost of health care rises so quickly relative to growth in GDP, it cannot fail to strain private and public budgets and to make it ever more difficult to solve or ameliorate other problems. . . .

For individuals, rising health care costs lead to increased premiums and to insurance plans that attempt to restrain *their* costs by using higher deductibles, co-pays, and the like. Because individuals and families in the United States tend to get their insurance through their employers, who choose and purchase coverage from an insurer, those employers are often in the middle between the insurance companies and their employees who actually use the insurance. For this reason, employers are often the parties that complain most loudly about rising costs. They also tend to look to devices for holding down costs through cost sharing and the like. In [2012] the average cost of [group] insurance (including both the part of the premium paid by the employer and the employee) was [over $5,000] per year for an individual and [over $15,000] per year for a family. . . .

Most economists argue that, despite appearances, employers are not really paying the insurance premiums of their employees. Rather, the insurance premium is simply part of the total compensation package for the employee. Because of the tax exemption for health insurance, it makes sense for an employee to take part of their compensation as (untaxed) health benefits. For most Americans, our employer picks the insurance company, chooses the plan, and sends in the check, but the employer does not bear the final cost of the insurance premiums. That comes out of whatever the total amount of compensation the employer is willing to pay to the employee. In times of rising health care costs, that means that more of the total compensation has to go to insurance and less can go to increased wages. . . . Rather than coming out of corporate profits, the increasing cost of health care has resulted in relatively flat real wages for 30 years. That is the real health care cost-wage trade-off. . . .

Increased health care costs also put a burden on federal and state governments, primarily through Medicare and Medicaid. . . . [P]ublic funds, including Medicare, Medicaid, Veterans health care, and other programs account for about 45 percent of total health spending in any given year. For the governments that pay for these programs, rising health care costs mean some hard choices: reducing benefits, restricting eligibility, cutting other public programs, raising taxes.

For the states, health care costs are already the single largest part of state budgets. . . . Not surprisingly, states have tended to respond by cutting other programs, most commonly funding for public higher education. . . . For the federal government, rising health care costs . . . could threaten to swamp the budget. . . .

III. The Problem of Health Care Quality

In light of the fact that the United States spends much more on health care than other countries, it is reasonable to ask: are we getting good value for the money? But with respect to the question of the quality of our health care, we find significant division between, on the one hand, those who cite the technological marvels produced in America and the outcomes in the treatment of complex diseases and, on the other hand, those who look to various aggregate measures of population health and find significant defects. . . . Of course, these seemingly opposed arguments are not mutually incompatible: America could produce the world's best technologies while also failing to provide the right care in many routine instances, not to mention the problems of the uninsured. And so we ask: what do we know about the quality of American health care?

On the one hand, it is true that by many measures of population health, the United States does quite poorly: infant mortality rates are higher in the United States than in many other comparable nations, and life expectancy rates are also low compared to other industrialized nations. A study by the World Health Organization (WHO) found that the United States ranked 37th . . . behind many other industrialized nations, all of which, as we have seen, spend far less per capita on health care than the U.S. does. . . .

Yet there is controversy over these facts. Some scholars argue, for example, that the cross-national comparisons fail to take into account differences in the underlying populations in different countries. They suggest that if we control for factors like homicide rates and car accidents—both of which are higher in the United States than in other countries—the measures of population health begin to look more similar to other nations. They also point out that rates of survival after the diagnosis of various serious ailments like cancer tend to be higher in the U.S. than elsewhere. Moreover, defenders of health care in United States point to the medical technologies and innovations developed here: the United States has produced more winners of the Nobel Prize in medicine than any other country. . . . Additionally, the U.S. spends far more of its public and private monies on biomedical research and development than does the European Union. Thus, defenders of U.S. health care argue that we cannot evaluate the level of quality of health care in the United States without keeping in mind the increased quality of the technologies used in health care.

As is often noted, Americans tend to be strongly attached to medical innovation and new medical technologies, more so than citizens of other countries. And there is a respectable body of literature which argues that the benefits of new technologies far outweigh their costs (as heavy as the latter may be). The [Harvard] economist David Cutler . . . and colleagues find that the cost of treating a heart attack has increased by some $10,000 in the 1990s, but that life expectancy after heart attack also rose by about one year. The treatment for low-birth weight infants presents a similarly positive picture. Cutler and colleagues conclude that "technological changes have proved to be worth far more than their costs."[35] . . .

---

35. David Cutler, *Your Money or Your Life: Strong Medicine for America's Healthcare System* (New York: Oxford University Press, 2004).

Of course . . . even the best technology cannot help very much if a particular patient does not have access to it—or does not have *timely* access. [Moreover], with respect to three different indicators—patient safety, receipt of recommended care, and variations in the intensity and outcomes of treatment—evidence suggests troublesome inadequacies in the quality of health care in America.

Patient Safety: Marked and seemingly widespread deficiencies in patient safety were the focus of the Institute of Medicine's *To Err Is Human,* a report published in 2000. According to the IOM, as many as 98,000 deaths are the result of medical error each year in the United States. That is more deaths from medical error than from motor vehicle accidents (around 45,000 deaths annually), from breast cancer (also around 45,000 deaths annually), or from AIDS (around 16,000 deaths annually). . . .

Receipt of Recommended Care: In the last few decades, professional societies along with such government agencies as the Agency for Healthcare Research and Quality have sought to develop and promulgate clinical practice guidelines and clinical pathways that stipulate the evidence-based recommendations for the most effective diagnosis and treatment of a wide range of diseases and disorders, from childhood asthma to adult hypertension. Nonetheless, [the] first national, comprehensive study on quality of care for adults in the U.S. . . . found that patients received the recommended care only 54.9 percent of the time.[41] . . . As [the author] testified before the U.S. Senate, "We spend nearly $2 trillion annually on health care and we get it right about half the time. That may be the best in the world, but I think you would agree that we can and should do better."

Variations in Intensity and Outcomes of Treatment: A substantial body of evidence also supports the finding of wide variations of the amount of money spent and of treatments performed between different areas of the country, but without any corresponding variations in health outcomes. In fact, the evidence seems to suggest that geographical areas that spend more actually have lower levels of quality of care. Researchers at Dartmouth led by Jack Wennberg and Elliott Fisher have shown, for example, that the amount of money spent per capita on Medicare recipients varies widely between different areas of the country, by almost as much as a threefold difference, even after controlling for differences in age, race, and sex. But, . . . the correlation with quality is low.

Many researchers have concluded that increased spending does not translate into better outcomes—in fact it may translate into worse outcomes. Wennberg and Fisher contend that much of the health care spending in Medicare, perhaps as much as 20 percent to 30 percent, does not bring added health benefits and that there may well be a similar proportion of private spending on health care that does not bring better outcomes. Economists suggest that in many cases Americans may be at the "flat of the curve," that is, at that place in a cost-benefit analysis when further resources may not only bring added benefit but may, in fact, bring less benefit. . . . Peter Orszag, director of the Congressional Budget Office, has

41. McGlynn, Asch, Adams, et al., "The Quality of Health Care Delivered to Adults in the United States," *New England Journal of Medicine,* vol. 328: 2635-2645, June 26, 2003.

recently written: "With health care spending currently representing 16 percent of gross domestic product (GDP), [Wennberg and Fisher's results] would suggest that nearly 5 percent of GDP—or roughly $700 billion each year—goes to health care spending that can't be shown to improve health outcomes." Of course, as Orszag observes, trying to figure out how to reduce inappropriate or unnecessary care is no easy task....

Leaving aside the difficult problems of designing the right policies to make American health care more efficient, however, there is a more fundamental question about what we—as patients and as citizens—expect from modern medical technology. Do we have extravagant expectations from medical science? Are we so accustomed to having someone else pay the bill that we no longer question whether a particular intervention is worth its cost? While evaluating the cost-effectiveness of various interventions or organizing the health care system to be more cost effective will not solve all of our health care problems, it may be a necessary condition of a more sustainable system that we come to see that more is not always better.

A variety of problems—access, cost, and quality—make health care in the United States an unavoidably complicated affair, and this is not the place to elaborate specific policy proposals. But we should remember that the health care system is one in which each of us will find ourselves in various capacities at various points in our lives, and the decisions we make about the various aspects of health care reflect our identity as a nation and the type of social union we wish to create and advance....

International Comparison of Spending on Health, 1980-2008

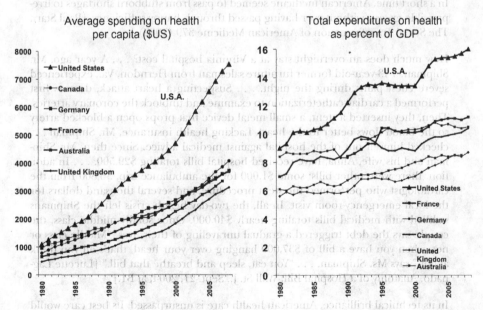

Source: OECD Health Data 2010.

Notes: The Crisis in American Medicine

1. *The Perpetual Crisis.* American medicine has been declared to be in a "crisis" since at least the early 1960s. See Marion Sanders, The Crisis in American Medicine (1961). Can things really be all that bad if they've been like this so long? Note the competing viewpoint of Harvard economist David Cutler, cited above, that major increases in medical spending can be traced to substantial gains in health that, at least in certain areas, are clearly worth their costs. See also Robert E. Hall & Charles I. Jones, The Value of Life and the Rise in Health Spending, 122 Q. J. Econ. 39 (2007); Kevin Murphy & Robert Topel eds., Measuring the Gains from Medical Research (2003). For a counterargument and evidence, see Elliott S. Fisher, Medical Care: Is More Always Better? 349 New Eng. J. Med. 1665 (2003); Nortin M. Hadler, The Last Well Person (2004). See generally Henry Aaron & Paul Ginsburg, Is Health Spending Excessive? If So, What Can We Do About It? 28(5) Health Aff. 1260 (Oct. 2009).

Even if there is not a "crisis," there is still clearly a serious problem in American medicine. In case you're still not convinced, consider the following additional facts, opinions, and anecdotes.

Medicine, like many other American institutions, suffered a stunning loss of confidence in the 1970s. Previously, two premises had guided government health policy: first, that Americans needed more medical care—more than the market alone would provide; and second, that medical professionals and private voluntary institutions were best equipped to decide how to organize those services. . . . In the 1970s this mandate ran out. The economic and moral problems of medicine displaced scientific progress at the center of public attention. Enormous increases in cost seemed ever more certain; corresponding improvements in health ever more doubtful. The prevailing assumptions about the need to expand medical care were reversed: The need now was to curb its apparently insatiable appetite for resources. In a short time, American medicine seemed to pass from stubborn shortages to irrepressible excess, without ever having passed through happy sufficiency. [Paul Starr, The Social Transformation of American Medicine 379 (1982).]

How much does an overnight stay at a Virginia hospital cost? . . . A year ago, Mr. Shipman, a 43-year-old former furniture salesman from Herndon, Va., experienced severe chest pains during the night. . . . Suspecting a heart attack, doctors first performed a cardiac catheterization to examine and unblock the coronary arteries. Then, they inserted a stent, a small metal device that props open a blocked artery so the blood flows better to the heart. Lacking health insurance, Mr. Shipman . . . checked himself out of the hospital against medical advice. Since then, Mr. Shipman and his wife, Alina, have received hospital bills totaling $29,500. . . . In addition, there were other bills: some $1,000 for the ambulance trip, $6,800 from the cardiologist who performed the stent procedure, and several thousand dollars for the local emergency-room visit. In all, the two-day health crisis left the Shipmans saddled with medical bills totaling nearly $40,000. Once solidly middle class, the couple says the debt triggered a gradual unraveling of their lives. "Middle class or not, when you have a bill of $37,000 hanging over your head, that's all you think about," says Ms. Shipman. . . . "You eat, sleep and breathe that bill." [Lucette Lagnado, Anatomy of a Hospital Bill, Wall St. J., Sept. 21, 2004, at B1.]

In its technical brilliance, American health care is unsurpassed. Its best care would have seemed miraculous just a few years ago. But the bad side of American health care is very bad, and there is reason to think that it will get worse before it gets better. For one thing, the coming years will see a further increase in both the number of the elderly in the population and their percentage of the population. The growth will be particularly great among those over 85, the people most likely to make heavy use of the medical system. New technology, for which one can almost always read "expensive" new technology, continues to invade medicine. [Henry T. Greely, The Future of the American Health Care System, 3 Stan. L. & Pol'y Rev. 16 (1991).]

There are few other areas of the U.S. economy where waste is so apparent and the possibility of savings is so tangible. . . . Perhaps the most troubling . . . [fact] is the amount spent on administration. For every office-based physician in the United States, there are 2.2 administrative workers. That exceeds the number of nurses, clinical assistants, and technical staff put together. One large physician group in the United States estimates that it spends 12 percent of revenue just collecting revenue. . . . The situation is no better in hospitals. . . . Duke University Hospital, for example, has 900 hospital beds and 1,300 billing clerks. On top of this are the administrative workers in health insurance. [David Cutler & Dan P. Ly, The (Paper) Work of Medicine, 25 J. Econ. Perspect. 3 (2011).]

There is no U.S. health care system. What we call our health care system is, in daily practice, a hodgepodge of historic legacies, philosophical conflicts, and competing economic schemes. Health care in America combines the tortured, politicized complexity of the U.S. tax code with a cacophony of intractable political, cultural, and religious debates about personal rights and responsibilities. Every time policymakers, corporate health benefits purchasers, or entrepreneurs try to fix something in our health care system, they run smack into its central reality: the primary producers and consumers of medical care are uniquely, stubbornly self-serving as they chew through vast sums of other people's money. Doctors and hospitals stumble their way through irresolvable conflicts between personal gain and ethical responsibilities; patients struggle with the acrimony and anguish that accompany life-and-death medical decisions; consumers, paying for the most part with everybody's money but their own, demand that the system serve them with the immediacy and flexibility of other industries; and health insurers are trapped in the middle, trying to keep everybody happy. A group of highly imaginative, energetic people armed with the world's largest Mark-n-Wipe board could not purposefully design a more complex, dysfunctional system if they tried. It is a $1.3 trillion per year fiasco narrated with moral shrillness and played out one competing anecdote after another. [J. D. Kleinke, Oxymorons: The Myth of a U.S. Health Care System 1 (2001).]

2. *More Facts and Figures.* There is seemingly an endless appetite for facts and figures about the U.S. health care delivery system. Those who wish more, or more recent, numbers can find them in the annual reports of the Medicare Payment Advisory Commission (MedPac), in periodic issues of Health Affairs and on the Web pages for the U.S. Census Bureau and the Centers for Medicare and Medicaid Services (CMS), which are linked to the Web page for this book, www.health-law.org.

For more readings that describe the evolution of the health care financing and delivery system and the various public policy problems it currently faces, see Jonathan Cohn, Sick: The Untold Story of America's Health Care Crisis (2007); Shannon Brownlee, Overtreated: Why Too Much Medicine Is Making Us Sicker and Poorer (2007); David Goldhill, How American Health Care Killed My Father, The Atlantic, Sept. 2009; Tom Daschle, Critical: What We Can Do About the Health-Care Crisis (2008); Einer Elhauge ed., The Fragmentation of U.S. Health Care (2010); Julius B. Richmond & Rashi Fein, The Health Care Mess: How We Got into It and What It Will Take to Get Out (2005); Paul Krugman & Robin Wells, The Health Care Crisis and What to Do About It, 53 N.Y. Review of Books No. 5 (Mar. 23, 2006); Jonathan Gruber & Helen

Levy, The Evolution of Medical Spending Risk, 23 J. Econ. Perspec. 25 (2009); Eleanor D. Kinney, For-Profit Enterprise in Health Care: Can It Contribute to Health Reform?, 36 Am. J.L. & Med. 405 (2010); Symposium, 39 J.L. Med. & Ethics 111 (2011); President's Council of Economic Advisors, The Economic Case for Health Care Reform (2009); Thomas Bodenheimer, High and Rising Health Care Costs, 142 Annals Intern. Med. 847, 932 (2005); Symposium, 28 Health Aff. 1250 (Oct. 2009); Symposium, 362 New Eng. J. Med. 1 (2010); Symposium, 22(1) Health Aff. 1 (Jan. 2003).

3. *International Comparisons.* According to one analysis, the poor U.S. performance on aggregate health statistics noted above (life expectancy, infant death rate) is not due to major differences in health habits or lifestyles, since the United States is similar in many ways to the comparison European countries. Instead, this author argues that the lower U.S. rankings are due in large part to the relatively inadequate system of primary care physicians and the overuse of high-risk procedures. Barbara Starfield, Is U.S. Health Really the Best in the World?, 284 JAMA 483 (2000). Another prominent study found that the British are much healthier than Americans in all major disease areas, such as diabetes, heart disease, stroke, lung disease, and cancer, even after controlling for all relevant sociodemographic factors. J. Banks, M. Marmot, et al., Disease and Disadvantage in the United States and England, 295 JAMA 2037 (2006). See also Cathy Schoen et al., U.S. Health System Performance: A National Scorecard, 25 Health Aff. w457 (Sept. 2006); David Squires, Explaining High Health Care Spending in the United States: An International Comparison (Commonwealth Fund 2012); S. H. Woolf, U.S. Health in International Perspective: Shorter Lives, Poorer Health (Institute of Medicine, 2013).

4. *Medical Tourism.* One sign of better medical value elsewhere is the extent to which Americans who are footing the bill are willing to receive care in other countries, even lesser-developed ones such as India, Mexico, or the Caribbean. Discussing this growing phenomenon of "medical tourism" and its host of legal issues, see Glenn Cohen, Protecting Patients with Passports: Medical Tourism and the Patient Protective Argument, 95 Iowa L. Rev. 1467 (2010); Glenn Cohen, Medical Tourism, Access to Health Care, and Global Justice, 52 Va. J. Int'l L. 1 (2011); Nathan Cortez, Cross-Border Health Care and the Hydraulics of Health Reform (2012); Nathan Cortez, Recalibrating the Legal Risks of Cross-Border Health Care, 10 Yale J. Health Pol'y L. & Ethics 1 (Winter 2010); Nicolas P. Terry, Under-Regulated Health Care Phenomena in a Flat World: Medical Tourism and Outsourcing, 29 W. New Eng. L. Rev. 421 (2007); Kerrie S. Howze, Medical Tourism: Symptom or Cure?, 41 Ga. L. Rev. 1013 (2007); Thomas R. McLean, The Offshoring of American Medicine, 14 Annals Health L. 205 (2005); Note, 18 Kennedy Inst. Ethics J. 193 (2008) (bibliography); Symposium, 26 Wis. Int'l L.J. 591-964 (2008).

2. History and Structure of Financing and Delivery Systems

■ THE MARKET STRUCTURE OF THE HEALTH INSURANCE INDUSTRY

D. Andrew Austin & Thomas L. Hungerford
Congressional Research Service, 2009

The market structure of the modern U.S. health insurance industry not only reflects the complexities and uncertainties of health care, but also its origins in the

1930s and its evolution in succeeding decades. . . . As population shifted from rural agricultural regions to industrialized urban centers, . . . [m]any workers obtained accident or sickness policies through fraternal organizations, labor unions, or private insurers. These policies were usually indemnity plans, that would pay a set cash amount in the event of a serious accident or health emergency. . . .

HOW THE "BLUES" BEGAN

The modern health insurance industry in the United States was spurred by the onset of the Great Depression. In 1929, the Baylor University Hospital in Dallas created a pre-paid hospitalization benefit plan for school teachers after a hospital executive discovered that unpaid bills accumulated by local educators were a large burden on hospital finances as well as on the teachers themselves. Unlike earlier health insurance policies, subscribers were entitled to hospital care and services rather than a cash indemnity. . . . Other hospitals in Dallas quickly followed suit with their own group hospitalization plans as a means of ensuring a steady revenue source in difficult economic times.[11] . . . Community-based plans in St. Paul, Minnesota, Washington, D.C., and Cleveland were created soon afterwards. The Blue Cross emblem, first used by the St. Paul plan, was widely adopted by other prepaid hospital benefit plans adhering to American Hospital Association (AHA) guidelines. . . .

The health insurance market in the United States, according to many historians, was originally structured to avoid competition among providers.[15] . . . Hospital and professional groups . . . soon pushed for joint plans that required "free choice of physicians and hospital," rather than plans offered by individual hospitals. Joint plans dampened incentives for local hospitals to compete on the basis of price or generosity of plan benefits. The American Hospital Association strongly favored joint plans that allowed a subscriber to obtain care from any licensed local hospital and viewed single-hospital plans as a threat to the economic stability of community hospitals. . . .

Insurance coverage of physician services lagged behind the growth of Blue Cross hospital plans due to opposition from the American Medical Association (AMA) and restrictive state laws.[19] In several states, however, medical societies set up prepaid service plans to preempt proposed state or federal plans, which evolved into Blue Shield plans. . . . Blue Cross plans accelerated their growth during World War II and extended to almost all states by 1946. Wartime wage and price controls authorized in October 1942 excluded "reasonable" insurance and pension benefits. As industries struggled to expand war production, many employers used health insurance and other fringe benefits to attract new workers. In the late 1940s, the National Labor Relations Board (NLRB) successfully sued employers that refused to bargain collectively over fringe benefits, opening the way for unions to negotiate with employers over health insurance, which further helped boost enrollments in health insurance plans. . . .

11. Robert Cunningham III and Robert M. Cunningham Jr., *The Blues: A History of the Blue Cross and Blue Shield System* (Dekalb, IL: Northern Illinois University Press, 1997).

15. Rosemary Stevens, *In Sickness and In Wealth: American Hospitals in the 20th Century* (New York: Basic Books, 1989), p. 156.

19. Paul Starr, *The Social Transformation of American Medicine* (New York: Basic Books, 1983), pp. 296-297.

[Today, most] private health insurance is offered through employers. With employer-sponsored plans, employers may simply offer health benefit plans through an insurance company for a negotiated price and bear no insurance risk. At the other extreme, the employer may self-insure and handle the plan itself, thus bearing all of the insurance risk and the administrative burden of the plan. Often the extent of employer involvement depends on the number of employees. Research has found that 80% of large employers (500 or more employees) choose to self-insure rather than purchase coverage from a health insurer. . . .

TAX ADVANTAGES FOR EMPLOYER-PROVIDED HEALTH INSURANCE BENEFITS

. . . Health insurance is subsidized through the tax system in several ways. First, . . . [the] Internal Revenue Code of 1954 included section 106, which explicitly allowed the exclusion of employer contributions for health insurance. . . . The Joint Committee on Taxation (JCT) estimates the federal government forgoes [over $250 billion] annually in tax revenue because of this exclusion. . . . The tax exemption for employer-provided health care made health insurance cheaper than non-exempt forms of consumption for individuals. One study found that health insurance coverage following the 1954 tax changes expanded more rapidly among employees with higher incomes, who generally had marginal tax rates, which could indicate that the tax exclusion led workers to demand more extensive or generous plans. Other factors, such as rising income levels, competition for workers, and rising medical costs, also spurred growth in employer-provided health benefits. . . .

COMMERCIAL INSURERS ENTER

Before World War II, many commercial insurers doubted that hospital or medical costs were an insurable risk. Insurers traditionally considered a risk insurable only if the potential losses were definite, measurable and not subject to control by the insured. The financial risks linked to illness or injury, however, could vary depending on the judgment of medical personnel, and behavior of the insured could affect the probability of ill health in many ways. After the rapid spread of Blue Cross plans in the mid-1930s, however, several commercial insurers began to offer similar health coverage. By the 1950s, commercial health insurers had become potent competitors and began to cut into Blue Cross's market share in many parts of the country. The large-scale entry of commercial insurers into the health insurance market changed the competitive environment. . . .

[T]he commercial health insurers were not bound to set premiums using the Blue Cross community rating principle, which linked premiums to average claims costs across a geographic area rather than to the claims experience of particular groups or individuals. Therefore, commercial insurers using an "experience rating" approach were able to underbid Blue Cross for firms that employed healthier-than-average individuals, which on average were cheaper to insure.

The loss of healthier groups then raised average costs among remaining groups, which . . . compelled Blue Cross to adopt experience rating. . . . The shift toward experience rating changed the nature of competition in the health insurance market. Insurers could cut costs by shifting risks to others, by recruiting firms whose employees and their families were healthier than average, rather than finding more efficient ways of managing risks for a given pool of subscribers. . . .

By the 1980s, health researchers and policymakers had begun to view the differences between Blue Cross/Blue Shield insurers, which were organized as non-profit organizations, and for-profit commercial health insurers as having narrowed. . . . In 1994, Blue Cross/Blue Shield guidelines were amended to let affiliates reorganize as for-profit insurers, leading the way for more than a dozen Blue Cross/Blue Shield affiliates to convert to for-profit status. Other Blue Cross/Blue Shield insurers bought other insurers, merged, or restructured in other ways. At the same time, private insurers acquired HMOs and other managed care organizations. Consolidations reduced both the number of commercial and Blue Cross/Blue Shield organizations, leading to the emergence of a small number of very large insurers with strong market positions across the country. . . .

INTRODUCTION OF MEDICARE AND MEDICAID

. . . While Blue Cross/Blue Shield and commercial insurance plans covered a large portion of employees and their dependents at the end of the 1950s, many low-income and elderly people had trouble obtaining affordable health insurance or paying for health care. . . . Social Security was extended to pay providers to cover certain medical costs incurred by aged, blind, and disabled beneficiaries starting in 1950. . . . State governments, subject to certain federal requirements, retained substantial discretion over benefit levels and income limits, which were typically linked to welfare assistance programs. . . .

In 1965, the Johnson Administration worked with Ways and Means Committee Chairman Wilbur Mills to create the Medicare program, which provided health insurance for nearly all Americans over age 65. Medicare combined a compulsory hospital insurance program (Part A) with a voluntary physician services plan (Part B). While some had worried that Medicare would displace private insurers, Blue Cross organizations became fiscal intermediaries for Medicare, responsible for issuing payments to providers and other back office operations. Medicaid, created in the same 1965 act, is a means-tested program financed by federal and state funds. Each state designs and administers its own program under federal rules. Over time, Medicaid eligibility standards and federal requirements have become more complex. . . .

THE RISE OF MANAGED CARE [AND "CONSUMER-DIRECTED" CARE]

In some parts of the country, plans combining insurance with the direct provision of health care evolved into important players in local markets despite the strong opposition of the AHA and AMA. A health plan designed for southern California construction workers in the mid-1930s eventually became the Kaiser Health Plan. . . . While some of these plans prospered locally or regionally, they did not achieve national reach until the 1970s.

In 1971, President Nixon announced a program to encourage prepaid group plans that joined insurance and care functions as a way to constrain the growth of medical care costs, which had risen sharply in the years following the startup of the Medicare and Medicaid programs, and to enhance competition in the health insurance market. Advocates claimed that health maintenance organizations (HMOs), which integrate health care and health insurance functions, would have a financial motive to promote wellness and would lack incentives to overprovide care. . . .

While this ambitious goal was not reached in the 1970s, by the late 1980s policymakers and businesses began to view greater use of managed care organizations such as HMOs and similar organizations as a key strategy for controlling health care costs. In the mid-1990s, the broader use of more restrictive forms of managed care (such as stringent gatekeeper, second medical opinion, and pre-approval requirements) sparked strong consumer resistance, which forced an industry retreat from some of those strategies. Networks of providers, known as preferred provider organizations (PPOs), grew rapidly in the late 1980s and early 1990s. PPOs, often owned by hospital systems and other providers, typically contract with insurers or self-insured firms and offer discounted fee-for-service (FFS) rates. PPO enrollees who receive care outside of the network typically must obtain plan approval or pay more. Thus, PPO plans provided patients with more flexibility than staff-model HMOs, which generally did not cover care provided outside of the HMO. As various types of managed care plans such as HMOs and PPOs became widespread, more employers offered choices among competing health plans to let workers willing to pay higher premiums avoid restrictive plans. . . .

The predominant type of health insurance plan has changed dramatically over the past 25 years. Over 90% of the privately insured were covered by an indemnity or traditional "unmanaged" health insurance plan in 1980; now the share is less than 10%. Today, most people covered by private insurance are covered by some kind of managed care plan ranging from a managed indemnity plan (e.g., PPOs, where the insurers negotiate fees with providers) to a staff HMO (the insurer and the provider are the same, and patients see physicians who are on salary). . . .

In the 1990s, proponents of "consumer-directed" health care proposed measures intended to make consumers more sensitive to medical care costs. In . . . 2003 . . . Congress passed legislation to allow consumers with high-deductible health insurance plans to set up Health Savings Accounts (HSAs) that allow people to pay for out-of-pocket expenses through a tax-advantaged medical savings account. . . .

DESCRIPTION OF THE HEALTH INSURANCE MARKET

Individuals and families typically buy insurance to avoid risks by paying a known premium in order to receive benefits if an adverse event were to occur during the insurance policy's term. Most individuals are willing to pay an insurer to assume the bulk of financial risks associated with unpredictable health outcomes of uncertain severity. . . . Some insured people will become sick or injured and incur significant medical expenses. Most people, however, will remain relatively healthy, thus incurring little or no medical expenses.[54] . . . In essence, money is shifted from those who remain healthy to those who become sick or injured.

The health insurance market is tightly interrelated with other parts of the health care system. . . . Health insurers not only reimburse providers, but also typically have some control over the number and types of services covered and negotiate contracts with providers on the payments for health services. . . .

54. A analysis of 2002 Medical Expenditure Panel Survey data found that "[h]alf of the population spends little or nothing on health care, while 5 percent of the population spends almost half of the total amount." . . . [See also National Institute for Health Care Management, The Concentration of Health Care Spending (2012).]

The health insurance market has many features that push it far from the economic benchmark of perfect competition. . . . How insurers design health care networks influences how consumers use health care. Consumers typically choose a primary physician who selects tests and treatments and makes referrals to medical specialists. Employers negotiate with insurers on behalf of their workers, and labor unions negotiate with employers over health benefits on behalf of their members. Health insurers, in turn, negotiate contracts with providers and handle payments for individual services. A primary physician's admitting privileges typically determine where his patient goes for non-emergency hospital care. Patients must go through a physician to obtain most medical tests and pharmaceuticals. Health care consumers typically rely on these intermediaries instead of interacting directly with other parts of the health care system. This heavy reliance on intermediaries is a key characteristic of the current health care market. . . .

Using intermediaries such as health insurers protects consumers from financial risks linked to serious medical problems, but also insulates consumers from information about costs and prices for specific health care goods and services. When a third-party, such as a private insurer or a government, pays for the bulk of health care costs, consumers may demand more care and providers may wish to supply more care. Links among intermediaries and providers can also limit consumers' choices. For example, a person's job may limit her health insurance choices, and another person's choice of physician may limit choices among hospitals. Some families and individuals lacking these intermediaries must navigate the health insurance and health care system themselves, which may be a serious challenge. . . .

Finally, how intermediaries interact has important consequences in the health care market. For instance, employers and health insurers, which both intermediate on behalf of individuals, interact through negotiations over insurance benefits packages. Politicians can also act as intermediaries for their constituents by helping determine reimbursement rates for public insurance programs and by changing the regulatory environment facing health insurers. . . .

MORAL HAZARD

Moral hazard, which occurs when insurance status changes behavior, is another problem in the health insurance market. Moral hazard occurs if an insured individual consumes more medical services than she would have had she been uninsured. For example, having health insurance could induce someone to seek medical care for minor conditions (e.g., a sore throat), choose a high-amenity health care setting (e.g., a more hotel-like hospital), or neglect his health (e.g., by eating fatty foods). Consequently, moral hazard leads the insurer to pay providers more for an insured person's medical services than that person would have paid out of his own pocket had he not been insured. Of course, non-monetary costs, such as the pain and inconvenience of obtaining unnecessary medical care, may help limit moral hazard among patients.

Insurers typically react to moral hazard by raising premiums to cover the costs of additional services and by limiting care, either directly (e.g., through prior approval requirements) or through cost-sharing measures such as copayments and deductibles. . . . The lack of transparency in the pricing of medical services contributes to this problem—most people do not know the cost of medical services (both what the provider normally charges and what the insurance company reimburses the provider).

THE PRINCIPAL-AGENT PROBLEM

A patient (here, a *principal*), as noted above, typically relies on a physician (an *agent*) for care and advice. The physician, or other intermediary, might face incentives to act to further their own interests, rather than those of the patient, by providing a higher quantity or lower quality of care than would be appropriate for a patient. . . . [P]ayment and incentive systems may mitigate conflicts of interests. Professional standards and professional organizations may also help mitigate those conflicts. . . .

While that arrangement may avoid some problems, it may not solve others. In fee-for-service (FFS) arrangements, physicians and other providers may face financial incentives to provide more care than would best suit the patient's interests. When insurance pays most of the costs associated with health care, providers have little financial incentive to control costs and may overprovide health care services. One study randomly selected doctors into a salary group and a fee-for-service group during a nine-month study. The results show that doctors in the fee-for-service group scheduled more office visits than salaried doctors and almost all of the difference was due to the fee-for-service doctors seeing well patients rather than sick patients. Defensive medicine, in which physicians or other providers order tests that may reduce the probability of medical malpractice litigation but which provide limited therapeutic benefits to the patient, presents a similar problem. . . .

Responses to . . . moral hazard and principal-agent problems affect the structure of the health financing system. Health insurers, as noted above, use coinsurance and pre-approval requirements to limit potential moral hazard among patients. Health insurers concerned about moral hazard and principal-agent problems among providers design incentive systems to limit overprovision of care. For example, the rapid transition to managed care in the 1990s might be seen as an attempt to control costs due to moral hazard. In addition, research and development (R&D) decisions made by medical technology and pharmaceutical firms may be indirectly guided by how health insurance coverage affects choices of providers and patients. Reforms that change the health financing system without taking into account potential moral hazards that previous structures and practices were designed to mitigate could encounter unanticipated problems. . . .

■ MEDICARE AND THE AMERICAN HEALTH CARE SYSTEM: 1996 REPORT TO CONGRESS
Prospective Payment Assessment Commission

The most common managed care models are health maintenance organizations (HMOs), preferred provider organizations (PPOs), and point-of-service (POS) plans. In a traditional HMO plan, subscribers must receive their care from a limited group of providers. PPO and POS subscribers may not be subject to the same level of plan oversight as in HMOs: Generally they may go to any provider, but their out-of-pocket payments are lower if they choose participating providers that give the insurer discounted rates. . . .

Managed care plans use a variety of techniques to control their costs. First, they actively seek providers with lower-cost practice patterns and offer them a defined patient base in exchange for favorable payment rates. By limiting the number of providers or by creating strong financial incentives to choose certain ones, managed care plans influence which providers subscribers will use. Through this selective contracting, managed care plans can substantially affect providers' revenues. Plans' bargaining positions are strongest in areas with excess provider capacity. Providers that choose not to participate or that are not selected by the managed care plan may experience a decline in their patient volume.

In addition, managed care plans often use discounted fee-for-service rates to control their costs. They also use per case, per day, or per person payments to shift some of the financial risk of treating patients to providers. Per case or per day payments are generally made to hospitals, whereas per person payments are more often made to physicians, predominately primary care practitioners. These payment methods reward providers for delivering care efficiently, discouraging unnecessary service use.

A per person, or capitation, payment system is the most comprehensive way to shift financial risk to providers. Under capitation, providers receive a prepaid sum to furnish a defined set of services to a plan's enrollees. This creates a monetary incentive for physicians to limit patients' use of services (or encourage preventive services) because the physician receives the same payment regardless of the volume or intensity of care, or even if no care is provided at all. Many managed care plans also require primary care physicians to act as "gatekeepers" to specialty care or hospital services. Under these arrangements, the primary care physician must preauthorize any services a patient receives. While these physicians usually do not bear the full financial risk for the additional services, delegating the gatekeeping function enables managed care plans to use financial incentives to limit referrals. . . .

Hospitals are seeking alternative revenue streams by broadening the scope of services they offer and competing for patients with other types of providers, [such as outpatient departments]. . . . Similarly, a growing number of hospitals are . . . developing skilled nursing facilities (SNFs) or are using acute care beds as swing beds to provide skilled nursing services. In addition, they are establishing their own rehabilitation units and home health agencies. . . .

Along with controlling their costs and seeking alternative revenue sources, hospitals are attempting to broaden (or maintain) their market share by securing a patient base through arrangements with other providers or managed care plans. Such arrangements have the potential to make overall service delivery more efficient and provide patients with a continuum of care. . . . Anecdotal evidence suggests that most hospitals have some type of arrangement, such as joint ventures or informal alliances, with other providers. Entering into arrangements with physicians is an increasingly popular strategy for hospitals. Such relationships can bolster a hospital's ability to secure managed care contracts. . . .

The long-term effects of the changing environment on hospitals are still unclear. . . . Hospitals traditionally have been viewed as the hub of the health care system and often have the capital reserves necessary to finance collaborations with other providers. Those that aggressively pursue such arrangements not only can improve their chances of being the hospital of choice for inpatient services, but also can exert more influence over medical practice decisions. In areas where managed care systems exert more control, however, hospitals may be viewed as cost centers with little input into delivery decisions.

PHYSICIANS

Historically, physicians determined not only which services would be provided, but where those services would be delivered. These decisions generally were made with little accountability for costs. Managed care is changing this.... One indication of the level of financial pressure physicians are facing is the [reduced growth] in physician income.... Some physicians are responding to the intensified pressures by selling their practices to hospitals or managed care organizations, and becoming employees of those entities....

Because physicians generate the demand for hospital services, they have leverage to assume a leadership role in arrangements with other providers. As health care funds become more and more limited, physicians—especially those who deliver primary care services—have an opportunity to play a larger part in deciding how those dollars will be distributed....

■ TRANSCRIPT OF INTERVIEW WITH JAMIE ROBINSON, Ph.D.*
Lehman Brothers Industry Expert Conference Call Series
May 17, 2002

As we go into the new decade, the insurance industry is reevaluating whether it wants to be America's method of health care cost control. It's found that this is a very difficult and very unappreciated job. It appears to the public that there is a tradeoff between corporate profits and individual health care, which is a very, very bad image for the industry. The insurers now want to have a completely different image, which is helping the consumer make health care choices....

I think the battle is over and the providers won. The health plans don't really want to get in there and second-guess doctor decision-making. That just proved to be a turf where the providers were very strong, and had the support of the patients and the regulators.... There is a lot of lousy medicine being practiced out there that the insurance companies could detect, and could clean up, but they could never convince anybody that they're doing it for the right reasons rather than simply for their own profits.

They've essentially abandoned that role. Increasingly they want to see themselves as a financial services company, like a Fidelity, [which manages investment funds for retirement accounts.] . . . Fidelity offer[s] a stock fund and a bond fund and a mixed fund and employees can allocate their savings across these however they want [with the help of] some decision support tools.... The health plans want to do that on the health plan side. "We have our PPO product and our HMO product and our Medical Savings Account product and we're not going to try to force people to pick one or the other. We're going to give them choices. We're going to give them information about the different products, about their prices, about access and about quality. We're going to give them Internet based decision support and tools, and we're going to let them choose. After that, what happens is between the

*Prof. Robinson is a health economist at the University of California at Berkeley. Reprinted with the permission of Prof. Robinson and the former Lehman Brothers.

patient and their doctor and their hospital. We, the insurance company, are not going to be responsible for that." . . .

One of the reasons that the insurance industry wants to get out of managed care and go back to being like the financial services industry is that it wants to stop being continually compared to the tobacco industry. It doesn't want to be the second most hated industry in America. The industry needs to re-brand itself as a consumer friendly decision support and information industry rather than something that's trying to save money for corporations.

Notes: Managed Care vs. Consumer-Driven Care

1. *Managed Care Is Here to Stay.* Despite fierce resistance by many doctors and some patients, managed care remains the dominant form of insurance. However, enrollment has shifted rather dramatically in recent years from tightly managed HMO plans to PPO and other open network plans that give patients more options. Regardless of the form managed care takes, it raises a host of legal, ethical, and regulatory issues that are explored throughout this book. For now, consider these broad inquiries: Are you concerned that insurers are interfering with medical judgment by deciding what treatments to pay for? Would you be more comfortable with a regime that let physicians and patients decide for themselves, but rewarded physicians for saving money or punished them for being excessive? Or, is the answer to make patients pay much more out of pocket so that they regulate their own spending decisions?

2. *Accountable Care Organizations.* The latest trend (and newest buzz term) in health care organization and finance are accountable care organizations (or ACOs). ACOs are a loosely defined concept that consists of doctors and hospitals organizing themselves in a fashion that receives and distributes bundled payment for a broader range of services and that claims some joint responsibility for the quality of care across an array of treatment settings. Many skeptics question how this idea differs from the mostly failed attempt in the 1990s to form provider-led HMOs. The typical response is that we've learned from those mistakes and that we'll do it differently this time.

3. *Consumer-Driven Care.* For a fuller account of Prof. Robinson's views, see The End of Managed Care, 285 JAMA 2622 (2001), where he observes:

> [The following] problems will plague a consumer-driven health care system. First, despite the widespread dissemination of information, . . . even the most sophisticated and Internet-enabled consumer . . . will face significant obstacles in understanding the quality and even the true price of health insurance and health care services. . . . [C]onsumers vary enormously in their financial, cognitive, and cultural preparedness to navigate the complex health care system. The new paradigm fits most comfortably the educated, assertive, and prosperous and least comfortably the impoverished, meek, and poorly educated. . . . Finally, the emerging era will make transparent and render difficult the redistribution of income from rich to poor that otherwise results from the collective purchasing and administration of health insurance.

The consumer-driven movement is occurring in several different ways. One is simply to *increase co-payments and deductibles* significantly, even for HMOs, which traditionally have imposed only minimal cost-sharing obligations on patients. The second is for employers to contribute only a fixed amount toward the cost of health insurance (*defined contribution*) and let employees shop for whatever coverage they want, rather than pay for all or most of the cost of a group policy that the employer selects. A complementary approach is for the government to subsidize insurance through a *tax credit* that operates like a voucher. Third, insurers are adopting more tiered forms of coverage, known as "value-based" insurance design, which require patients to pay increased portions of the bill if they opt to use providers or treatment methods that are considered to be less cost-effective.

Other examples of increased consumerism are prescription drug manufacturers' much more aggressively advertising directly to consumers rather than only to physicians, and the wealth of medical and health insurance information now available on the Internet. Consumer-driven ideas are being applied even to the Medicaid program for the poor. Jeb Bush, Market Principles: The Right Prescription for Medicaid, 17 Stan. L. & Pol'y Rev. 33 (2006).

4. *Literature.* The pros, cons, and legal implications of consumer-driven health care have been extensively debated and analyzed. For a sampling of the literature, see Regina Herzlinger ed., Consumer-Driven Health Care: Implications for Providers, Payers, and Policymakers (2004); Timothy S. Jost, Health Care at Risk: A Critique of the Consumer-Driven Movement (2007); James C. Robinson, Reinvention of Health Insurance in the Consumer Era, 291 JAMA 1880 (2004); John V. Jacobi, Consumer-Driven Health Care and the Chronically Ill, 38 U. Mich. J.L. Reform 531 (2005); Amy B. Monahan, The Promise and Peril of Ownership Society Health Care Policy, 80 Tul. L. Rev. 777 (2006); Marshall B. Kapp, Patient Autonomy in the Age of Consumer-Driven Health Care, 2 J. Health & Biomed. L. 1 (2006); Mark A. Hall, Paying for What You Get, and Getting What You Pay For, 69 Law & Contemp. Probs. 159 (Autumn 2006); Peter D. Jacobson & Michael R. Tunick, Consumer-Directed Health Care and the Courts: Let the Buyer (and Seller) Beware, 26(3) Health Aff. 704 (June 2007); Carl Schneider & Mark Hall, The Patient Life: Can Consumers Direct Health Care? 35 Am. J.L. & Med. 7 (2009); John A. Nyman, Consumer-Driven Health Care: Moral Hazard, The Efficiency of Income Transfers, and Market Power, 13 Conn. Ins. L.J. 1-17 (2006-2007); James Robinson & Paul Ginsburg, Consumer-Driven Health Care: Promise and Performance, 28(2) Health Aff. w272 (Jan. 2009); Thomas Buchmueller, Consumer-Oriented Health Care Reform Strategies: A Review of the Evidence, 87 Milbank Q. 820 (2009); Sarah Goodall & Katherine Swartz, Cost-Sharing: Effects on Spending and Outcomes (2010); Symposium, 66 Med. Care Res. & Rev. 3S (Feb. 2009); Symposium, 39 Health Serv. Res. 1049 (2004); Symposium, 24(6) Health Aff. (Dec. 2005); Symposium, 25(6) Health Aff. w516 (2006); Symposium, 28 J. Leg. Med. 1 (2007).

For a good overview of managed care generally, see Peter Kongstvedt, Managed Care: What It Is and How It Works (2d ed. 2002); Jacob S. Hacker & Theodore R. Marmor, How Not to Think About "Managed Care," 32 U. Mich. J.L. Reform 661 (1999). For additional discussion of broad changes in the health care system, see the ongoing publications from the Center for Studying Health System Change.

5. *The Onslaught of Acronyms.* Regrettably, the health care field is overrun with acronyms. Since 1970 or so, no new institution or phenomenon seemingly can exist in medicine without being known primarily by its three-to-five-letter abbreviation. Most of the specialized organizational terms and acronyms you will encounter in

these readings are collected and defined in the glossary at page 741 for convenient reference throughout the semester.

3. Health Care Reform

■ BAD MEDICINE: A GUIDE TO THE REAL COSTS AND CONSEQUENCES OF THE NEW HEALTH CARE LAW
Michael D. Tanner
Cato Institute, July 2010*

On March 21, 2010, in an extraordinary Sunday night session, the House of Representatives gave final approval to President Obama's long-sought health insurance plan in a partisan 219-212 vote. The bill had earlier passed the Senate on Christmas Eve 2009. Not a single Republican in either chamber voted for the bill. . . . More than 2,500 pages and 500,000 words long, the Patient Protection and Affordable Care Act (PPACA) [also known as the Affordable Care Act or ACA] represents the most significant transformation of the American health care system since Medicare and Medicaid. It will fundamentally change nearly every aspect of health care from insurance to the final delivery of care.

The final legislation is, in some ways, an improvement over earlier versions. It is not the single-payer system sought by many liberals. Nor did it include the interim step of a so called "public option" that would likely have led to a single-payer system in the long run. . . . But that does not mean that this is, as the president has claimed, a "moderate" bill. It mandates that every American purchase a government-designed insurance package, while fundamentally reordering the insurance market and turning insurers into something resembling public utilities. . . .

Insurance coverage will be extended to millions more Americans as government subsidies are expanded deep into the middle class. Costs will be shifted between groups, though ultimately not reduced. And a new entitlement will be created, with the threat of higher taxes and new debt for future generations. In many ways, it has rewritten the relationship between the government and the people, moving this country closer to European-style social democracy. . . .

INDIVIDUAL AND EMPLOYER MANDATES

Perhaps the single most important piece of this legislation is its individual mandate, a legal requirement that every American obtain health insurance coverage that meets the government's definition of "minimum essential coverage." Those who don't receive such coverage through government programs, their employer, or some other group would be required to purchase individual coverage on their own. This individual mandate is unprecedented in U.S. governance. . . .

Under the new law, beginning in 2014, those who fail to obtain insurance would be subject to a tax penalty. That penalty would be quite mild at first, either $95 or one percent of annual income in 2014, whichever is greater. But it ramps up

*© The Cato Institute. Reprinted with permission.

quickly after that, ... [to] the greater of $695 or 2.5 percent of annual income. ... Individuals will be exempt from the penalties if they ... are unable to obtain insurance that costs less than 8 percent of their gross incomes. ... While the law imposes penalties for failure to comply, ... it does not contain any criminal penalties for failing to comply, and it forbids the use of liens or levies to collect the penalties. However, the IRS ... may withhold tax refunds to individuals who fail to comply with the mandate. ...

The new law also contains an employer mandate, although it is watered down from the proposal that passed the House last year. ... [B]eginning in 2014, if a company with 50 or more full-time employees (or the equivalent) does not provide health insurance to its workers, ... the company must pay a tax penalty of $2,000 for every person they employ full time (minus 30 workers). ... [A]s with the individual mandate, the penalty may be low enough that many businesses may find it less costly to "pay" than to "play." ...

INSURANCE REGULATIONS

The Patient Protection and Affordable Care Act imposes a host of new federal insurance regulations that will significantly change the way the health insurance industry does business. Some of these regulatory changes are likely to be among the law's most initially popular provisions. But many are likely to have unintended consequences. Perhaps the most frequently discussed regulatory measure is the ban on insurers denying coverage because of preexisting conditions. ... Specifically, ... insurers would be prohibited from making any underwriting decisions based on health status, mental or physical medical conditions, claims experience, medical history, genetic information, disability, [or] other evidence of insurability. ...

Finally, there will be limits on the ability of insurers to vary premiums on the basis of an individual's health. That is, insurers must charge the same premium for someone who is sick as for someone who is in perfect health. Insurers may consider age in setting premiums, but those premiums cannot be more than three times higher for their oldest than their youngest customers. Smokers may also be charged up to 50 percent more than nonsmokers. ... While the ban on medical underwriting may make health insurance more available and affordable for those with preexisting conditions and reduce premiums for older and sicker individuals, it will also increase premiums for younger and healthier individuals. ...

Perhaps the most fundamental reordering of the current insurance market is the creation of "exchanges" in each state. ... The exchanges would function as a clearinghouse, a sort of wholesaler or middleman, matching customers with providers and products. Exchanges would also allow individuals and workers in small companies to take advantage of the economies of scale, both in terms of administration and risk pooling, which are currently enjoyed by large employers. ... Exactly how significant the exchanges will prove to be remains to be seen. ... However, one should be skeptical of claims that the exchange will reduce premiums. ...

SUBSIDIES

The number one reason that people give for not purchasing insurance is that they cannot afford it. Therefore, the legislation's principal mechanism for expanding coverage (aside from the individual and employer mandates) is to pay for it, either through government-run programs such as Medicaid . . . or through subsidizing the purchase of private health insurance.

Starting in 2011, states are required to expand their Medicaid programs to cover all U.S. citizens with incomes below 133 percent of the poverty level [which is roughly $15,000 for an individual or $30,000 for a family of four]. . . . [T]he primary result of the law's Medicaid expansion would be to extend coverage to the parents in low-income families and to childless adults. In particular, single, childless men will now be eligible for Medicaid. . . .

Individuals with incomes too high to qualify for Medicaid but below 400 percent of the poverty level ($88,000 per year [currently, for family of four]) will be eligible for subsidies . . . in the form of refundable tax credits. . . . The credit is calculated on a sliding scale according to income in such a way as to limit the total proportion of income that an individual would have to pay for insurance. Thus, individuals with incomes between 133 and 200 percent of the poverty level will receive a credit covering the cost of premiums up to four percent of their income, while those earning 300-400 percent of the poverty level will receive a credit for costs in excess of 9.5 percent of their income. . . . As with many tax credits, the phase-out of these benefits creates a high marginal tax penalty as wages increase. In some cases, workers who increase their wages could actually see their after-tax income decline as the subsidies are reduced. . . .

All together, this law represents a massive increase in the welfare state, adding millions of Americans to the roll of those dependent, at least to some extent, on government largess. Yet for all the new spending, the Patient Protection and Affordable Care Act falls short of its goal of achieving universal coverage. . . . According to the Congressional Budget Office, the legislation would reduce the number of uninsured Americans by about [25] million people by 2019. . . . Supporters of the legislation point out that that would decrease the number of uninsured Americans to roughly [8] percent of non-elderly Americans, a far cry from universal coverage, but undoubtedly better than today's 15 percent. . . .

OTHER PROVISIONS

The legislation includes a number of pilot programs designed to increase quality of health care or control costs. Most are well intentioned but unlikely to have significant impact, especially in the short term. These would include programs such as bundled payments, global payments, accountable-care organizations and medical homes through multiple payers and settings. It would also create a new Center for Innovation within the Centers for Medicare and Medicaid Services (CMS) to evaluate innovative models of care. . . . Of greater concern is a provision to establish a private, nonprofit institute to conduct comparative effectiveness research. . . . Critics fear that comparative effectiveness research will not simply be used to provide information, but to impose a government-dictated method of practicing medicine. . . .

INCREASED SPENDING, INCREASED DEBT

Health-care costs are rising faster than GDP growth and now total more than $[2.5] trillion—more than Americans spend on housing, food, national defense, or automobiles. However, the Patient Protection and Affordable Care Act fails to do anything to reduce or even restrain the growth in those costs. . . . This should not come as a big surprise. The primary focus of the legislation was to expand insurance coverage. Giving more people access to more insurance, not to mention mandating that current insurance cover more services, will undoubtedly result in more spending. . . .

It is also worth noting that cost estimates for government programs have been wildly optimistic over the years, especially for health care programs. . . . There is certainly reason to believe that the costs of this law will exceed projections. For example, as discussed above, increased insurance coverage could lead to increased utilization and higher subsidy costs. At the same time, if companies choose to drop their current insurance and dump employees into subsidized coverage or Medicaid, it could substantially increase the program's costs. . . .

This is all taking place at a time when the government is facing an unprecedented budgetary crisis. The U.S. budget deficit hit $1.4 trillion in 2009, and we are expected to add as much as $9 trillion to the national debt over the next 10 years, a debt that is already in excess of $12 trillion and rising at a rate of nearly $4 billion per day. Under current projections, government spending will rise from its traditional 20-21 percent of our gross domestic product to 40 percent by 2050. That would require a doubling of the tax burden just to keep up. . . .

CONCLUSION

Health care reform was designed to accomplish three goals: (1) provide health insurance coverage for all Americans, (2) reduce insurance costs for individuals, businesses, and government, and (3) increase the quality of health care and the value received for each dollar of health care spending. . . . The legislation comes closest to success on the issue of expanding the number of Americans with insurance. . . . The law also makes some modest insurance reforms that will prohibit some of the industry's more unpopular practices. However, those changes will come at the price of increased insurance costs, especially for younger and healthier individuals, and reduced consumer choice.

At the same time, the legislation is a major failure when it comes to controlling costs. While we were once promised that health care reform would "bend the cost curve down," this law will actually *increase* U.S. health care spending. . . . Clearly the trajectory of U.S. health care spending under this law is unsustainable. Therefore, it raises the inevitable question of whether it will lead to rationing down the road.

We should be clear, however. With a few minor exceptions governing Medicare reimbursements, the law would not directly ration care or allow the government to dictate how doctors practice medicine. There is no "death board" as Sarah Palin once wrote about in her Facebook posting. Even so, . . . this law represents a fundamental shift in the debate over how to reform health care. It rejects consumer-oriented reforms in favor of a top-down, "command and control," government-imposed solution. As such, it sets the stage for potentially increased government involvement. . . . One thing is certain—the debate over health care reform is far from over. . . .

THE HEALTH BILL EXPLAINED AT LAST
Theodore R. Marmor & Jonathan Oberlander*
New York Review of Books, August 2010

. . . Republicans have sought to make health care reform Barack Obama's "Waterloo" . . . by scaring the public. Ominous and utterly false warnings about "death panels," a government "takeover" of American medicine, and "pulling the plug on grandma" followed. . . . The irony is that for all the apocalyptic rhetoric, the new health reform law is anything but radical. In fact, it closely resembles the 2006 reform in Massachusetts supported by then-governor Republican Mitt Romney. And most strikingly, it does not replace the current mix of US health insurance schemes with a single public health insurance program like Medicare. Instead, the 2010 reform legislation introduces a complex system of subsidies, mandates, regulations, and programs that build on our present patchwork arrangements. . . .

The bill, known as the Patient Protection and Affordable Care Act, begins to take effect [in 2010] but many of its provisions will be carried out during the coming decade. As of now, a majority of working-age adults and their children—some 157 million people—obtain private health insurance through their employers, while virtually all Americans over age sixty-five, as well as younger adults with permanent disabilities, are covered by Medicare. Low-income Americans who fit certain demographic categories, such as pregnant women and children, have access to Medicaid. . . . Still others depend on a loose health care safety net, including community health centers that provide subsidized care, as well as on hospital emergency rooms that must by law see all patients, which of course doesn't mean they will get timely or adequate care.

There are sizable gaps in US health insurance coverage. . . . A high percentage of workers in small businesses are not covered by their employers and find purchasing their own insurance prohibitively expensive. Those with preexisting conditions like diabetes or asthma face particularly serious obstacles since insurers vary premium rates by health status and regularly deny coverage to those they regard as expensive risks. . . . Low-income adults without dependent children are generally not eligible for Medicaid, leaving many of the nation's poor uninsured. . . .

Despite such deep flaws in the US health care system, the central assumption of both the Obama administration and the Democratic leadership in Congress was that only legislation that did not seek to radically change it had a chance of success. That political calculation, in turn, was based on the view that the Clinton administration's health reform effort failed during 1993-1994 because it tried to change too much and provoked too much opposition from insurance companies and other powerful interests.

This time around, reformers hoped to reassure the large number of insured Americans who say they are satisfied with their current coverage that they had nothing to fear from change. Democrats also wanted to work with rather than fight against the health care industry. They hoped to gain support from the insurance, hospital, and pharmaceutical industries, which stood to gain financially from expanded

*The authors are political science professors in the public health departments of Yale University and the University of North Carolina, respectively.

insurance coverage and had the financial resources and political influence to undercut reforms they opposed. As a consequence, the creation of a Canadian-style health program, in which universal insurance—Medicare for all—is provided by the government, was never seriously considered. Such a reform would have caused, in the administration's view, too much disruption of prevailing arrangements and led to an inflammatory and unwinnable debate over "socialized medicine." . . .

How Will the New Law Work?

First, all Americans who earn less than 133 percent of the federal poverty level [amounting to roughly $15,000 for an individual or $30,000 for a family of four] will become eligible for Medicaid [in states that opt to expand Medicaid]. For the first time, Medicaid will offer coverage solely on the basis of income and regardless of family circumstance—including the single adults without children who are now excluded. . . .

Most Americans under age sixty-five will continue to receive employer-sponsored coverage. As a new feature, children can stay on their parents' insurance plans until age twenty-six. New regulations banning insurers from imposing caps on both annual and lifetime payments will also benefit policyholders. Larger employers will have to offer health coverage to their workers or pay a penalty ($2,000 per worker) to the federal government. Smaller employers with fewer than fifty workers will be exempt from this requirement, and, depending on their average wage, businesses with twenty-five or fewer workers are eligible for tax credits to help them buy health insurance for their workers.

The law also expands coverage by offering subsidies to uninsured Americans to purchase insurance in newly formed health benefit exchanges. Each state is expected to set up and administer these exchanges as a regulated market for health insurance. If a state chooses not to do so, its residents can join a federally sponsored exchange. In either case, people will choose from a variety of private insurance plans within each exchange, with federal subsidies available on a sliding scale to help them pay their premiums. Those with incomes up to 400 percent of the federal poverty level (i.e., now up to about $43,000 [for singles or $88,400 for a family of four]) will be eligible for subsidies. In all, 29 million Americans are expected to obtain insurance through the exchanges by 2019. . . .

The insurance exchanges will be regulated extensively. Starting in 2014, insurers will not be able to deny coverage to would-be policyholders or charge them higher premiums because of their health status (though insurers can vary premiums by age). Insurers will also be prohibited from retroactively canceling coverage for sick policyholders. Most Americans will be required to obtain health insurance or pay a federal tax penalty—starting in 2014 at $95 per person or 1 percent of taxable income, whichever is greater, and then increasing to $695 or 2.5 percent of taxable income by 2016.

The CBO estimates that [about 25] million Americans will gain coverage through the expansion of Medicaid, subsidies, and insurance exchanges. This will make an enormous difference to the financial circumstances of many Americans with modest means and large medical expenses. Contrary to what conservative critics have claimed, the reform will undoubtedly mean less, not more, rationing of medical care as tens of millions of uninsured persons gain access to health insurance.

By broadening health insurance coverage, the law moves the United States closer to the principle that no one should go without access to medical care. In regulating the health insurance industry, with provisions to end discrimination on the basis of preexisting conditions, it brings about a long-overdue expansion of federal authority. In these ways and more, the Affordable Care Act is a substantial achievement.

At the same time, large gaps remain between the problems of American medicine and the remedies that Congress has adopted. Even if the Affordable Care Act were fully implemented, an estimated [30] million people would still lack insurance [by 2020]. We cannot know precisely who will be without coverage a decade from now. But analysts expect that the uninsured will be made up of three groups: undocumented immigrants who are ineligible for federal subsidies or Medicaid; Americans who still find coverage, even with subsidies, too expensive to purchase on their own but aren't poor enough to qualify for Medicaid; and healthy people who can afford to buy coverage but will instead choose the cheaper option of paying the penalty for not having insurance. In any case, the United States, alone among industrialized democracies, will likely continue to have a large uninsured population for years to come. . . .

In fact, the expansion of insurance coverage and regulation described in the law is hardly straightforward. . . . [I]nsurers whose profits are at stake can be expected to seek loopholes to evade the new regulations. According to the law, the secretary of health and human services must write the thousands of pages of regulations necessary to implement it, and these will be subject to congressional scrutiny and intense lobbying by the health care industry. . . . One consequence, then, of building on the existing system is that the new law will require coordination of a great many disparate policies if coverage goals are to be met and if the health insurance marketplace is to be transformed.

Perhaps the largest shortcoming of the reform, though, is the absence of reliable, system-wide controls on medical costs. The law takes steps to slow down the rate of increase in Medicare spending, such as cutting projected payments to hospitals. . . . Outside of Medicare, the measures to slow health care spending are far less impressive. . . . The law's strategy to contain costs additionally rests on a series of reforms aimed at improving medical care delivery and health outcomes: paying hospitals on the basis of quality; bundling payments together for inpatient and outpatient care; funding research that compares the clinical effectiveness of medical treatment options; and providing greater coverage of preventive services. It also encourages the formation of so-called accountable care organizations that create networks of primary care doctors, specialists, and hospitals to care (and receive payments) for a defined set of patients. Many of these reforms will be implemented initially in Medicare—a newly established Medicare innovations center is charged with testing payment reform—with the hope that successful policies will then spread through the private sector.

Health and Human Services Secretary Kathleen Sebelius says that "every cost-cutting idea that every health economist has brought to the table is in this bill." That is probably true—but it also shows that American health policy researchers pay scant attention to international experience. . . . The new law seems based on the hope that if a large variety of reforms are tested, at least some will succeed; but nobody knows how many will work in practice or whether they will save money at all.

We do know that other rich democracies that spend much less than the US on medical care do so largely by adopting budgetary targets for health expenditures and by tightly regulating what the governments and insurers pay hospitals, doctors, and other medical care providers. Outside of Medicare, the current reform contains no such measures.

The Obama administration, confronting enormous opposition over proposals to expand coverage, chose mostly to defer addressing the political problems of cost control. But the . . . issue cannot be avoided for long. . . . The expansion of coverage and the requirement that individuals purchase insurance, alongside rising premium costs, . . . will increase [pressure] on the federal government to moderate the growth in health care costs—especially in view of sizable budget deficits. . . . As a result, there is enormous uncertainty about how well and how long the patchwork of health reforms adopted in 2010 will hold together.

Notes: Health Care Reform—A Work in Progress

1. *What's in a Name?* The legislation's full name is too lengthy to catch on, and its full abbreviation (PPACA) is so unpleasant sounding that there isn't even agreement on how to pronounce it. "ObamaCare" is one common shorthand, but some people use that in a derogatory fashion that wrongly suggests government takeover or blame for anything that's not right in U.S. health care. The emerging short descriptor is the "Affordable Care Act" (ACA), but it's too early to know whether that will stick.

2. *Who Pays for All of This?* The ACA is projected to cost the federal government almost $1 trillion over the first ten years. Over half of this financing is from a variety of earmarked taxes, such as an excise tax on "Cadillac" insurance plans that contain very rich benefits, taxes on medical devices and prescription drugs, increased Medicare payroll taxes for high-wage earners, and, oddly, a tax on tanning beds. Most of the remainder of the ACA's price tag is financed by reductions in Medicare payments to providers and insurers. On balance, the Congressional Budget Office projected that these revenue provisions will exceed the ACA's costs by roughly $100 billion over ten years, and thus will slightly reduce the federal deficit. However, the cuts to Medicare and the increase in Medicare payroll taxes used to finance the ACA make it more difficult to enact reforms needed to keep Medicare solvent for the next generation.

3. *Agreeing to Disagree.* These two selections come from policy analysts at different positions in the political spectrum. On which points do they agree? On which do they fundamentally disagree—more than simply a choice of emphasis (glass half full vs. half empty)? Among the full range of views, consider also those of liberal physicians who favor a "single-payer" national health insurance system:

As much as we would like to join the celebration . . . , in good conscience we cannot. We take no comfort in seeing aspirin dispensed for the treatment of cancer. Instead of eliminating the root of the problem—the profit-driven, private health insurance industry—this costly new legislation will enrich and further entrench these firms. . . .

Millions of middle-income people will be pressured to buy commercial health insurance policies costing up to 9.5 percent of their income but covering an average of only 70 percent of their medical expenses, potentially leaving them vulnerable to financial ruin if they become seriously ill. Many will find such policies too expensive to afford or, if they do buy them, too expensive to use because of the high co-pays and deductibles.

Insurance firms will be handed at least $447 billion in taxpayer money to subsidize the purchase of their shoddy products. This money will enhance their financial and political power, and with it their ability to block future reform. . . .

The much-vaunted insurance regulations—e.g., ending denials on the basis of pre-existing conditions—are riddled with loopholes, thanks to the central role that insurers played in crafting the legislation. Older people can be charged up to three times more than their younger counterparts. . . .

Congress and the Obama administration have saddled Americans with an expensive package of onerous individual mandates, new taxes on workers' health plans, countless sweetheart deals with the insurers and Big Pharma, and a perpetuation of the fragmented, dysfunctional, and unsustainable system that is taking such a heavy toll on our health and economy today. This bill's passage reflects political considerations, not sound health policy. . . . We pledge to continue our work for the only equitable, financially responsible and humane remedy for our health care mess: single-payer national health insurance, an expanded and improved Medicare for All.

Physicians for a National Health Program, Health Bill Leaves 23 Million Uninsured: A False Promise of Reform (Mar. 22, 2010). For additional contrasting views, see Grace-Marie Turner et al., Why ObamaCare Is Wrong for America (2011); Tom Daschle & David Nather, Getting It Done: How Obama and Congress Finally Broke the Stalemate to Make Way for Health Care Reform (2010).

For accounts of the law's enactment and general descriptions of its contents, see Washington Post, Landmark: The Inside Story of America's New Health Care Law (2010); Jonathan Gruber, Health Care Reform: What It Is, Why It's Necessary, How It Works (2011); Paul Starr, Remedy and Reaction: The Peculiar American Struggle over Health Care Reform (2011); Stuart Altman, Power, Politics and Universal Health Care (2011); John McDonough, Inside National Health Reform (2011); Lawrence Jacobs & Theda Skocpol, Health Care Reform and American Politics (2010); Janet Dolgin & Katherine Dieterich, Social and Legal Debate About the Affordable Care Act, 80 UMKC L. Rev. 45 (2011); Wilton B. Hyman, An Explanation of the Patient Protection and Affordable Care Act, 38 Ohio N.U. L. Rev. 579 (2012); Note, 29 Yale L. & Pol'y Rev. 559 (2011); Symposium, 29 Health Aff. 1087 (2010); Symposium, 29 Health Aff. 1284 (2010); Symposium, 36 J. Health Pol. Pol'y & L. 367 (2011); Symposium, 44 Conn. L. Rev. 1057 (2012).

4. *Keeping Up with the Times.* The Web site for this casebook, www.health-law .org, links to an array of resources that explain different provisions of the law and update its implementation. For initial legal perspectives, with much more certainly to come, see the symposia in the following law reviews: 65 Tax L. Rev. 619 (2012); 55 How. L.J. 679 (2012); 38 Am. J.L. & Med. 243 (2012); 50 Duq. L. Rev. 231 (2012); 159 U. Penn. L. Rev. 1577 (2011); 11 Yale J. Health Pol'y L. & Ethics 1 (2011); 25 Notre Dame J.L. Ethics & Pub. Pol'y 325 (2011); 5 St. Louis U. J. Health L. & Pol'y 1 (2011); 42 Ariz. St. L.J. 1203 (2010-2011); 4 J. Health & Life Sci. L. 1 (2010); 44 Clearinghouse Rev. 330 (2010).

5. *"The More Things Change, ..."* The following pie charts nicely illustrate what is, and is not, likely to change following implementation of the ACA. These reflect approximate estimates for the year 2019, assuming no reform vs. reform.

Sources of Health Insurance

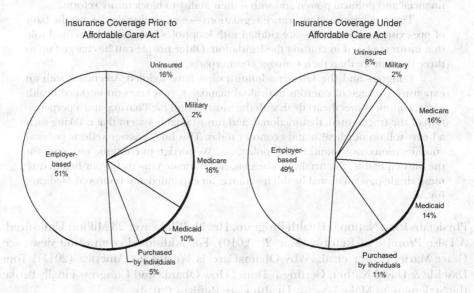

C. MORAL, ECONOMIC, AND POLITICAL THEMES

The remainder of this chapter addresses various analytical theories that give greater depth to our understanding of health care law and public policy. Most of these analytical frameworks spring from some branch of moral and political theory that addresses fundamental questions of social justice, such as how best to distribute scarce medical resources, and whose decision over medical treatment should govern when there is conflict. Necessarily, this must be a grab bag of somewhat disconnected lines of thought drawn from many different intellectual disciplines—primarily philosophy, economics, and political science. This is due to what Einer Elhauge below calls the "paradigm pathology" of health care law: Although this field may have a core set of concerns, it lacks a dominant analytical mode. In classic fields of law such as contracts or torts, most people seem at least to be asking the same sorts of questions, even if they don't arrive at the same answers. Health care law has so many interdisciplinary, intellectual currents that courts and scholars sound at times like the mythical builders of the Tower of Babel. Some order can be brought to this mélange of ideologies by categorizing different and competing "paradigms" of thought. As Clark Havighurst explains in the second reading in this section, the dominant paradigm in past decades has been professionalism, and this is the one to which all the contenders respond. Rather than attempt any neat packaging of the contenders, for they are still very untidy, try to identify which currents of thought are consistent with or opposed to the professionalism paradigm, and in what ways. Then, try to articulate how different paradigms would answer the fundamental questions of social justice mentioned above (who gets which resources, and who decides).

1. *Competing Paradigms*

▇ALLOCATING HEALTH CARE MORALLY*
Einer Elhauge**
82 Cal. L. Rev. 1449 (1994)

Health law policy suffers from an identifiable pathology. . . . [I]t employs four different paradigms for how decisions to allocate resources should be made: the market paradigm, the professional paradigm, the moral paradigm, and the political paradigm. . . . [R]ather than coordinate these decisionmaking paradigms, health law policy employs them inconsistently, such that the combination operates at cross-purposes.

This inconsistency results in part because, intellectually, health care law borrows haphazardly from other fields of law, each of which has its own internally coherent conceptual logic, but which in combination results in an incoherent legal framework and perverse incentive structures. In other words, health care law has not—at least not yet—established itself to be a field of law with its own coherent conceptual logic, as opposed to a collection of issues and cases from other legal fields connected only by the happenstance that they all involve patients and health care providers.

In other part, the pathology results because the various scholarly disciplines focus excessively on their favorite paradigms. Scholars operating in the disciplines of economics, medicine, political science, and philosophy each tend to assume that their discipline offers a privileged perspective. This leads them either to press their favored paradigm too far or to conceptualize policy issues solely in terms of what their paradigm can and cannot solve.

Instead, health law policy issues should be conceived in terms of comparative paradigm analysis. Such analysis focuses on the strengths and weaknesses of the various decisionmaking paradigms, determining which is *relatively* better suited to resolving various decisions, and then assigning each paradigm to the roles for which it is best suited. . . .

Luckily, this is a mode of analysis in which legal scholars, as cross-disciplinary generalists, have some plausible claim to comparative scholarly advantage. Unluckily, it is hard and arduous. Nevertheless, it offers the promise that health law scholars will provide insights into health policy that so far have been missed. In a field as intellectually new as modern health law, it should hardly be surprising that this task has only begun.

**Professor of Law, Harvard University. [The author's name is pronounced "EL-hague."]

■ THE PROFESSIONAL PARADIGM OF MEDICAL CARE: OBSTACLE TO DECENTRALIZATION*
Clark C. Havighurst**
30 Jurimetrics J. 415 (1990)

The thesis of this article is that, despite all the organizational and financial changes that occurred in the health care sector in the 1980s, we still cannot fight the battle for efficiency effectively because we are saddled as a society with a particular paradigmatic conception of the medical care enterprise. The source of this paradigm is a deep-seated belief, long fostered by the medical profession, that medical care is not a commodity, that its characteristics are scientifically determined, and that decisions concerning it must be entrusted exclusively to professionals. That this paradigm is ideologically attractive and contains some significant kernels of truth simply complicates the problem of adapting it to accord with current economic realities.

The professional paradigm of the medical enterprise is a venerable one, stemming from the days early in this century when the medical profession rose to what sociologist Paul Starr has called a position of "cultural authority, economic power, and political influence."[5] Although its tenets are nowhere officially set down, some of them can be deduced from the profession's performance during the era when it exercised rather complete hegemony over health care and its financing. Judging from that experience, the profession's ideology has included the following themes:

- medical care should be evaluated only on the basis of safety and efficacy;
- cost considerations should not enter into medical decisionmaking because counting costs implies both a willingness to trade off a patient's welfare against other societal needs and a tolerance for differences based on ability to pay;
- decisions on the appropriate utilization of medical services should be based exclusively on scientific evidence and expert opinion;
- although patient preferences should be honored under the principle of informed consent, there is no similar urgency about giving people opportunities to express their preferences qua consumers, with cost differences in view; and
- professional norms alone should set the limits of a physician's judgment.

Under these general principles, the role of payers was long limited to ensuring that professional norms were followed, so that only care that was virtually useless or positively harmful was excluded. . . .

The professional paradigm derives much of its force from the egalitarian ideal in medicine—the belief that every citizen is entitled to medical care of the same quality and that "two-tier" medicine is unthinkable. Even though society has not seen fit to adopt an egalitarian policy by accepting either the heavy tax burden or

**Professor of Law Emeritus, Duke University.

5. P. STARR, THE SOCIAL TRANSFORMATION OF AMERICAN MEDICINE 5 (1982).

the stringent rationing necessary to achieve it, the egalitarian ideal colors much thinking about medical care. Indeed, even in the absence of any actual legal or contractual entitlement, a powerful entitlement mentality must be confronted by anyone seeking to economize in the provision of health services. The professional paradigm generally supports this view of things, while the profession as a whole resists most of the measures that would be necessary to create an affordable, truly egalitarian system. There is here a marriage of convenience—between physicians' desires to resist infringements on their clinical freedom and a particularly extreme view of the requirements of social justice.

The scientific character of medicine has also provided vital support for the professional paradigm. Indeed, the success of the medical profession in establishing its scientific character in the early part of the century—in the Flexner Report,[6] for example—laid the groundwork for its claim of exemption from market forces and for its autonomy as a profession. Once medical care was viewed as the application of science to human problems rather than as a commercial service to be bought and sold in market transactions, the profession was able to resist most of the pressures that naturally arose and to head off, by effective lobbying or collective action, market developments that might have threatened its hegemony. . . .

Residues of the professional paradigm can be found in many places but are particularly significant in the legal system. Not only does the law tend to defer to the medical profession's presumed scientific authority on many points, but it is often administered with an egalitarian mentality that tends to define issues in terms of abstract rights. Indeed, the law frequently goes to great lengths to avoid appearing to concede that some persons might ever have a legal or even a contractual right to better medical care than someone else. This refusal to recognize the reality that some consumers might choose, or wish to choose, to purchase more or better health care than others—or have a lesser entitlement because of inability or unwillingness to pay—greatly complicates efforts to economize in the private sector. It also raises, perhaps inappropriately, the cost to government of providing for those who cannot support themselves. As long as the legal system does not acknowledge inequality or recognize efforts to escape the costly standards implicit in the professional/scientific/egalitarian paradigm, neither self-supporting consumers nor taxpayers are in a good position to economize on health care by refusing to buy too much of a good thing.

2. Ethics and Empiricism

■ THE PRACTICE OF AUTONOMY: PATIENTS, DOCTORS, AND MEDICAL DECISIONS
Carl E. Schneider*
1998

Bioethicists, like lawyers, live in danger of what I once called "hyper-rationalism." Hyper-rationalism has both a methodological and a substantive aspect. As a

6. A. Flexner, *Medical Education in the United States and Canada* (Carnegie Foundation for the Advancement of Technology, Bull. No. 4, 1910).
*Professor of Law, University of Michigan.

method, [h]yper-rationalism is essentially the substitution of reason for information and analysis. It has two components: First, the belief that reason can reliably be used to infer facts where evidence is unavailable or incomplete, and second, the practice of interpreting facts through a narrow set of artificial analytic categories. Hyper-rationalism, in other words, tempts us to believe that we can understand how people think and act merely by reasoning, and not by investigating. Hyper-rationalism seductively justifies discussing human behavior without investigating how people actually behave. Hyper-rationalism is the conceptualist's revenge for the world's complexity. . . .

In bioethics, as in many other areas of human thought, these assumptions see people as operating in remarkably rational ways. They hold that people deliberate explicitly about their situations, that they do so in predominantly rational terms, that they are autonomy maximizers, and that they have well-worked-out agendas which they need autonomy to fulfill. They see people primarily as makers of decisions reaching out for control over their lives. . . .

For one thing, the assumptions of hyper-rationalism can lead us into a tendency to see human nature and conduct as verging on the uniform. . . . As empiricists in fields ranging from sociology to psychology to anthropology have been at pains to show, this view exaggerates human rationality and understates the role of social and cultural factors in patient's lives. . . .

Hyper-rationalists' . . . picture of human nature is too simple, too disembodied, to be convincing. They present a bloodless, flat, distant, abstract, depersonalized, impoverished view of the way people think, feel, and act, of the social circumstances in which people live, of the ethical lives they lead. And hyper-rationalism's simplifications are particularly injurious in bioethics, a field that treats people in their least rational moments, in their most emotional travails, in their most contextual complexity.

Hyper-rationalism, of course, has its uses. It promotes the kind of generalization that frees courts and commentators to reason logically about the normative problems that are, after all, one of their central concerns. And some simplification of life's complexity is necessary if human problems are to be dealt with practically and promptly, if comprehensible rules are to be devised, if useful precedent is to be developed, if institutions are to function smoothly. But we should want to insinuate as much of that complexity as possible into normative discourse. A failure to do so perilously distances norms from the people and circumstances they seek to govern.

This is a peril with which law is all too familiar. Indeed, one of the most illuminating bodies of modern legal writing is the scholarship which makes sport of the idea (that seems so natural and right to lawyers and law professors) that the law makes rules and that people know about them, accept them, and respond to them in a considered, rational, and even acquiescent way.[7] . . .

One of the great truths about law is that with unnerving frequency, it fails to achieve the effects intended for it, and sometimes quite fails to have any effect at all. Some of the most fascinating modern legal scholarship reminds lawyers how

---

7. The next five paragraphs constitute an interpolation excerpted from another publication by the same author, Bioethics in the Language of the Law, 24(4) Hastings Center Rep. (July 1994).

removed their talk is from the world's ken. That literature reveals that, to the lawyer's chagrin, businesses resist using contracts, ranchers do not know what rules of liability govern damage done by wandering cattle, suburbanites do not summon the law to resolve neighborhood disputes, engaged couples do not know the law governing how they will own property when they marry, citizens repeatedly reject the due process protections proffered them, and, what is worse, all these people simply don't care what the law says.

Much the same can be said of many of the law's recent bioethical reforms. There is evidence that as few as 10 percent of us have made an advance directive, that only a quarter of us have signed an organ donor card (despite the swarms of us who say we want to be donors), that even competent patients are not widely consulted about do-not-resuscitate orders, that doctors have reduced informed consent to one more bureaucratic chore, and that plaintiffs rarely win informed consent suits.

What is going on here? Well, of course, lots of things. But central among them is society's enormous complexity and the narrow relevance of the law to it. People are enticed by many pressures beyond those the law creates. They have their own agendas and, more important, their own normative systems. The law writes rules, but the governed—when they know the rules—often have the incentives, time, and energy to avoid them.

Consider advance directives. They offer an apparently irresistible way of speaking in one of life's greatest crises. Yet people spurn them. They do so because they have their own lives to lead. Momentous as the crisis may be, it will generally not seem urgent until it arrives. People resist contemplating their own mortality. They heartily dislike and don't easily understand legal forms; they find them obscure and darkly imagine how they might be misused. For that matter, people may doubt that they will be used at all. Further, many people have trouble envisioning their circumstances years into the future or how they would respond to those hypothetical circumstances. And I suspect that people expect that decisions about their welfare would in any case fall to people they trust—to their families. In short, advance directives were formulated and promoted by people—bioethicists, lawyers, and doctors, for instance—who know what they want to do through them and keenly want to do it. But many of us are not clear about what we want and about whether getting it is worth the costs.

In short, while the language of the law may have penetrated into the bosom of society, it must still, in quotidian life, compete with the many other languages that people speak more comfortably, more fluently, and with much more conviction. These are languages of religion and morality, of love and friendship, of pragmatism and social accommodation, of custom and compromise. The danger for bioethicists, then, is believing too deeply that law can pierce the Babel, can speak with precision, can be heard. . . .

This literature, then, should alert us to the dangers of hyper-rationalism, to the perils of believing pure ratiocination can allow us to understand how people will conceive of their problems, organize their lives, resolve their disputes, and respond to legal norms. But what is the antidote to hyper-rationalism? There are several. For instance, [Howard] Brody writes that philosophy of medicine "can indeed advance by . . . abstract discussions; but it can advance only so far. At some point we will require a richer context for the discussion to proceed fruitfully. This context can be provided by stories of sickness." . . .

We need, then, to inhabit all the mansions available in the house of bioethics. And among the least inhabited of those mansions is that of empirical research. Such research offers a breadth, rigor, and precision of understanding that is available in no other way. It provides a disciplined way of reviewing our assumptions and a systematic means of identifying neglected issues. In sum, empirical research provides a fruitful means of obtaining a more detailed, complex, and acute understanding of what patients want, think, and do which can deepen—and darken—our understanding of bioethical problems.

■ MEDICAL LAW AND ETHICS IN THE POST-AUTONOMY AGE
Roger B. Dworkin*
68 Ind. L.J. 727 (1993)

Patient autonomy has long been the dominant rhetorical value in American medical law and medical ethics. It has been far less dominant in fact. Now, developments in genetics raise serious questions about the scientific validity of the assumptions on which autonomy-based law and ethics rest, and new attention to the values of civic republicanism, community, and inclusiveness raises questions about the extent to which the dominance of autonomy is desirable. Yet a move away from autonomy is frightening, especially when no one can be sure what will take its place. In this essay, I shall examine in a preliminary way the extent to which autonomy really dominates our medical law and ethics, the extent to which reformulation seems desirable in light of scientific developments and changing values, and the direction medical law and ethics might safely move in a post-autonomy age.

RHETORIC AND REALITY

Autonomy can mean a number of different things. To the liberal individualist (that is, the typical American), it means the ability and the opportunity to choose one's course of action and to act to effectuate one's choice. It means freedom from constraint as long as one's behavior does not injure others. It tends not to recognize the extent to which most actions, even the most apparently private ones, have an impact on others,[8] and the more apparently private an activity is, the more liberal individual autonomy insists that it not be regulated.

Concern for patient autonomy in the liberal individualist sense dominates the rhetoric of American medical law and medical ethics. Cardozo's dictum that "[e]very human being of adult years and sound mind has a right to determine what shall be done with his own body"[9] is ubiquitous. The entire law of informed consent is premised on the dominance of patient autonomy over competing values, including the value of good medical care. Abortion law, right-to-die law, and even some wrongful birth and life opinions are explained textually as reflecting respect for patient autonomy. . . .

*Professor of Law, Indiana University School of Law—Bloomington.
8. *See generally* MARY ANN GLENDON, RIGHTS TALK (1991).
9. Schloendorff v. Society of N.Y. Hosp., 105 N.E. 92, 93 (N.Y. 1914).

Yet, in reality, autonomy does not seem to be as dominant a value as rhetoric would suggest.

. . . Of course, the law allows autonomy to be sacrificed when important public needs are at stake. Thus, compulsory vaccination laws are plainly valid. However, their existence does not really challenge autonomy's dominant position. It simply demonstrates that even a dominant value must sometimes be sacrificed for the public good.

Often, however, autonomy yields in the face of less clearly public concerns. The most obvious rejections of autonomy are professional licensure statutes and the regulation of drugs and medical devices by Congress and the Food and Drug Administration. Licensure and the control of allegedly beneficial medicines and devices are designed to protect persons from themselves, that is, to paternalistically prevent individuals from autonomously making bad choices. . . .

The law does not honor the freely entered into agreements of doctors and patients. The law of tort, not contract, determines the quality of medical care to which a person is entitled, and a patient may not contract away the right to receive reasonable care. A patient's informed consent to receive medical care does not exempt a health care provider from liability if a consented to risk occurs through negligence. . . .

At first blush, autonomy may seem to be the primary value underlying the Supreme Court's abortion jurisprudence. However, . . . under *Roe*, abortion may be regulated after the end of the first trimester to the extent necessary to protect maternal health. Further, the Court allowed states to prohibit anybody other than doctors from performing abortions even during the first trimester, a restriction that can only be understood as reflecting a paternalistic concern for maternal well-being. . . .

To some extent, right-to-die law reflects a real concern for individual autonomy, yet here too the law remains unwilling to go where the autonomy principle would push it. . . . A patient may effectively ask not to be resuscitated and perhaps not to be fed, but a request for a lethal injection will not be honored. Refusal to honor such a request is inconsistent with a law based on patient autonomy. Patient autonomy has even less to do with right-to-die cases about patients who have never been competent and once-competent patients who did not express their treatment desires before becoming incompetent. . . .

New drug regulation, injury compensation law, informed consent cases, abortion decisions, right-to-die law, and organ transplantation decisions all demonstrate that American medical law, even as it has developed in the heyday of liberal individualism, is not nearly as autonomy-centered as it claims to be. If that is true, what can we expect as liberalism loses its lustre and science challenges its foundations? . . .

Unlike liberal individualism, a second possible meaning of autonomy is rooted not so much in choice as in being let alone. It is a physical concept rather than an intellectual one. If you touch me or eavesdrop on me, you have injured my autonomy by invading my space. If you actually do something to change my body, you have injured my autonomy by changing the very constitution of what I am. This view might be called physical essentialist autonomy. . . .

[E]xtreme cases, like those involving incompetent persons, make plain the insufficiency of that approach. However, the approach is also inadequate for competent persons. Choice making is a characteristic of healthy persons, but it is not their only characteristic. We must be cautious not to factually overrate even healthy persons' abilities to choose and not to ethically overvalue that capacity. Overvaluation risks dehumanizing incompetent persons and creating an ethical vacuum if and when we learn that healthy persons' abilities to choose are more constrained than we like to think. . . .

Liberal individualist autonomy and physical essentialist autonomy thus seem to impale us on the horns of a dilemma. A third approach to autonomy would treat the individual as dominant, but attempt to avoid the failings of both liberal individualism and physical essentialism. This approach would be rooted in respect for the individual as a complete being. It would deviate from common linguistic meanings of the word *autonomy* by focusing neither on the freedom to choose and act nor on the freedom from physical intrusion. It would simply be an approach that put the interests of the person most affected by an action or proposed action first. It would be a highly realistic approach because it would examine what really happens to a person. Thus, it could avoid resort to rhetorical fictions (like liberal individualism) and sacrifice of a person's well-being to someone else's principles (like physical essentialism). Such an approach might be called respectful paternalism. It would be paternalistic because it would involve someone making decisions for somebody else, presumably in that person's best interest. It would be respectful because it would consider the real impact of an action on the person affected, thus avoiding the imposition of one's principles on another to her detriment, and because it would consider the preferences and choices of the affected person, to the extent they can be ascertained, as part of the decisionmaking process. . . .

This weak version of autonomy seems an improvement over either of the other two approaches. Yet it is not without its shortcomings. By focusing solely on the individual, respectful paternalism, like all forms of autonomy, ignores both reality and important personal and social interests. All autonomy-centered approaches ignore the fact that nobody is autonomous. Everybody lives in groups—families, workplaces, clubs, labor unions, towns, states, countries—and almost everything that affects one person affects others as well.

Insights offered by feminist,[10] republican,[11] and communitarian[12] scholars have demonstrated the impoverishment of an exclusively individual rights based approach to social issues, and developments in genetics cast doubt on the factual underpinnings of such an approach. . . .

The same point can be made in every area of bioethics: Pregnant women have fetuses, mates, and parents. . . . Persons with healthy organs may have siblings with unhealthy ones. Potential surrogate mothers may have husbands, preexisting children, the new child, men with whom they have contracted and those men's wives, all of whom are affected by the surrogate mother's behavior. Dying persons have families with both emotional and financial needs.

10. *E.g.*, Leslie Bender, *A Lawyer's Primer on Feminist Theory and Tort*, 38 J. LEGAL ED. 3 (1988).

11. *E.g.*, MICHAEL J. SANDEL, LIBERALISM AND THE LIMITS OF JUSTICE (1982).

12. *E.g.*, MARY ANN GLENDON, RIGHTS TALK (1991).

Autonomy-based systems undervalue those other persons' needs. They assume that it is possible to ascertain who is most affected by an action or condition and then allow that person's interests to trump all others. The factual assumption is true sometimes, but only sometimes. Who is most affected by a decision about whether to use a kidney from an incompetent "donor" to save a dying competent sibling with end stage renal disease? Who is most affected by a decision whether to perform a Caesarian section delivery that may shorten the life of a terminally ill, episodically competent pregnant woman by a few days in order to run an x percent chance of saving her fetus? . . .

[M]odern genetics compounds the difficulties by simultaneously reemphasizing the poverty of autonomy-based approaches and highlighting the risks in surrendering the focus on individuals. . . . Genetic medical practice challenges the conventional notion of the individually based doctor-patient relationship. Genetic medicine only makes sense if it is understood as a family-centered, rather than an individually focused form of medical practice. Typically, physicians and other genetic counselors are consulted by couples who want to learn their risk of having a child with a genetic disease, by couples and their already affected children, or by persons who seek information about their own health based on the condition of their relatives. Each of these situations requires learning about one person to help another. Each may present the diagnostician with information about persons whom he has never seen and may raise serious questions about his obligations. To what individual does the doctor owe a duty when tests of husband, wife, and child reveal that the husband is not the child's father? What are the doctor's duties when diagnosis of a person present in the doctor's office necessarily informs him that relatives of that person are at risk for developing avoidable colon cancer or having a child with hemophilia? In a profession whose raison d'être is doing family studies to reveal family information, these questions cannot be answered by thoughtless recitation of tired slogans about the doctor owing an exclusive obligation to his patient. Indeed, often it is not even clear who the patient is.

Modern genetic research compounds the inadequacy of the individual autonomy model by rekindling the debates between free will and determinism and between nature and nurture. As scientists map the human genome, they increasingly discover not only the genes for well-known genetic diseases, but also uncover the genetic roots of a wide variety of diseases and behaviors that are often not thought of as genetic. What does it mean to talk of an autonomous individual if the individual's genotype predisposes him to alcoholism, schizophrenia, crime, cancer, or heart disease? To the extent that most American law and ethics are based on assumptions about personal moral accountability, modern genetics throws those legal and ethical positions into question.

However, . . . [r]ecognizing that there are limits to what individuals can do or control is not a concession to total determinism. The danger of modern genetics, like the danger of the old eugenics, is that society will mistakenly believe it proves more than it does and use it as an excuse to injure further those who are already disadvantaged. Thus, again, the challenge is to incorporate new understandings in a way that moves away from the excesses of individual autonomy and its frequent inability to help solve problems, without legitimating imposition on underdogs. How is that to be done?

RESPECT FOR ALL INDIVIDUALS

I suggest that a useful way to begin would be (1) to refocus our rhetoric and our rules away from concern for individual choice and toward respect for individuals, while (2) recognizing that individuals live in groups whose individual members deserve respect too. In other words, we should combine what I have called respectful paternalism with respect for all affected members of society. Respect for individuals requires valuing their apparently freely made choices, even if we do not always follow them. Respect for individual affected members of society recognizes the reality of the social condition but reduces risks of imposition by insisting on finding real impacts on real persons before those interests may be weighed against others. Respect for all individuals rejects as unacceptably dangerous a focus on the alleged interests of society as a whole. . . .

In determining an individual's interests, his ability to choose and the negative impact of taking that away from him are relevant. . . . To put it differently, the choices of competent persons are worth points in the legal and ethical calculus. However, choices do not end the inquiry. They may be illusory; the person may no longer be aware of them; and other people count too. Therefore, the way to make a decision is to consider what is best for everyone concerned, while specifically assigning a value to choices in order to avoid running roughshod over affected persons. . . .

Perhaps the approach suggested here can be made clearer by applying it to a few examples. . . .

Respect for all affected individuals would require that before consenting to treatment patients be given the amount of information that a person who cared about their well-being (including their psychological and dignitary well-being) would give them—not the amount a hypothetical reasonable doctor would provide or a reasonable patient would want. Conversation with close family members of the patient and some attention to their desires would be relevant as well. Failure to provide adequate information under such a vague standard should be viewed as an ethical lapse. Whether it makes sense also to treat it as a tort is beyond the scope of this essay.

Terminally ill patients who are incompetent and have expressed no choices about withholding or withdrawing medical care deserve respect. They retain an interest in dignity and in avoiding unnecessary suffering. However, their loved ones' interests are also strong and should be accorded great weight. Suffering from watching a close relative die a prolonged death is real. On the other hand, the anguish of believing one was premature in letting the loved one die is real as well. Respect for relatives requires that they be accorded significant discretion in deciding whether to allow the patient to die. The doctor's sense that he is wasting his time in a futile exercise is probably worth something, especially if the patient is past suffering and the family is split. An identified salvable patient's need for the dying person's hospital bed is also relevant. A generalized concern about not wasting resources is not. Society cannot be allowed to solve its health care cost crisis by running roughshod over its sickest members.

Medical law and ethics based on individual autonomy are rooted in fiction and ignore important values. The salutary role of the autonomy focus is that it avoids state imposition and abuse of the weak. As the illustrations here suggest, an approach rooted in respect for all individuals would avoid fiction and increase the chance of sound results by considering all relevant persons and values in each case, while keeping the door to state imposition and abuse of the powerless tightly closed.

Notes: Medical Ethics and Professionalism

1. *Competing Paradigms*. Recent scholarship has forcefully defended the important role that professionalism plays in medicine and analyzed how law should promote or accommodate desirable features of professionalism. See, e.g., Andrew Fitcher, The Law of Doctoring: A Study of the Codification of Medical Professionalism, 19 Health Matrix 317 (2009); Gail Agrawal, Resuscitating Professionalism: Self-Regulation in the Medical Marketplace, 66 Mo. L. Rev. 341 (2001). On professionalism generally, see Eliot Freidson, Professionalism: The Third Logic (2001). For additional discussion of competing paradigms in health law, see sources cited in note 2 in the Preface, page xxiii.

2. *Bioethics and Law*. For additional insightful discussions of the individual rights paradigm and the proper role of law in deciding issues of medical ethics, see George Annas, Standard of Care: The Law of American Bioethics (1993); Roger Dworkin, Limits: The Role of Law in Bioethical Decision Making (1996); Jerry Menikoff, Law and Bioethics: An Introduction (2001); David Rothman, Strangers at the Bedside: A History of How Law and Bioethics Transformed Medical Decisionmaking (1992); Charity Scott, Why Law Pervades Medicine: An Essay on Ethics in Health Care, 14 Notre Dame J.L. Ethics & Pub. Pol'y, 245 (2000); Michael H. Shapiro, Is Bioethics Broke? On the Idea of Ethics and Law "Catching Up" with Technology, 33 Ind. L. Rev. 17 (1999); Rebecca Kukla, Conscientious Autonomy: Displacing Decisions in Health Care, 35(2) Hastings Center Rep. 34 (Mar. 2005).

Bioethics has spawned an immense multidisciplinary literature, much of which is cited in the portions of this book where it is relevant. These are the leading general and comprehensive sources: **Journals:** Bioethics Reporter; Bioethics; Cambridge Quarterly of Health Care Ethics; Kennedy Institute of Ethics Journal; Hastings Center Report; Issues in Law and Medicine; Journal of Clinical Ethics; Journal of Medical Ethics; Journal of Medical Humanities and Bioethics; Journal of Medicine and Philosophy; and the general medical and legal journals listed in the Preface. **Treatises and Monographs:** T. Beauchamp & J. Childress, Principles of Biomedical Ethics (6th ed. 2008); Baruch A. Brody et al., Medical Ethics: Analysis of the Issues Raised by the Codes, Opinions & Statements (2001); J. Childress & R. Gaare, BioLaw: A Legal and Ethical Reporter on Medicine, Health Care, and Bioengineering; H. Tristram Englehardt, The Foundations of Biomedical Ethics (2d ed. 1996); Bernard Gert et al., Bioethics: A Return to Fundamentals (1997); Nancy Jecker et al., Bioethics: An Introduction to the History, Methods, and Practice (1997); A. Jonsen et al., Clinical Ethics: A Practical Approach to Ethical Decisions in Clinical Medicine (5th ed. 2002); David Orentlicher, Matters of Life and Death: Making Moral Theory Work in Medical Ethics and the Law (2002); W. Reich, Encyclopedia of Bioethics; Robert Veatch, A Theory of Medical Ethics (1981).

3. *The Attack on "Principlism."* The conventional way to frame issues of medical ethics is in terms of autonomy vs. beneficence and to ask which of these two principles is more appropriate and to what degree in particular cases. This

approach grew primarily out of the foundational work of Tom Beauchamp and James Childress at Georgetown University's Kennedy Institute of Ethics and at the University of Virginia, and is presented in their now classic *Principles of Biomedical Ethics.* This framework has become so dominant that it is sometimes referred to as the "Georgetown mantra." But this approach's ordering of discussion according to mid-level principles has come under attack in recent years from several directions.

Some argue that principles are too abstract and so the focus should be on a more intuitive or pragmatic analysis of individual cases. This is known as "casuistry." Others argue that resort to primarily these two principles is too arbitrary or ad hoc and not sufficiently founded in rigorous philosophical analysis. Still others advance a "virtue ethics," which holds that we must look not only at the rightness or goodness of an action but also the character of the actor, in order to identify and cultivate good moral traits such as honesty and compassion.

Beauchamp and Childress respond that their principles framework is more malleable than their critics recognize and so is capable of adapting to all of these competing positions. For more insight into this debate, see Nancy S. Jecker et al., Bioethics: An Introduction to the History, Methods, and Practice (1997); Edmund D. Pellegrino & David C. Thomasma, The Virtues in Medical Practice (1993); Symposium: Emerging Paradigms in Bioethics, 69 Ind. L.J. 945 (1994); Edmund Pellegrino, The Metamorphosis of Medical Ethics, 269 JAMA 1158 (1993).

4. *Empiricism and Narratives.* Whichever philosophical or analytical camp one hails from, all agree that ethical debate is greatly enhanced with good empirical information. So are legal and public policy debates. That is why we try to provide as much insightful empirical data as we can throughout the notes in this book. For other general overviews of empirical work relevant to health care law and ethics, see Michelle M. Mello & Kathryn Zeiler, Empirical Health Law Scholarship: The State of the Field, 96 Geo. L.J. 649-702 (2008); Jeremy Sugarman et al., A Quarter Century of Empirical Research in Biomedical Ethics, *in* Methods in Medical Ethics (2d ed. 2010); Symposium, 31 Ind. L. Rev. 1 (1998).

Empiricism can also take a more anecdotal form. There is growing interest in understanding legal and public policy problems through the rhetorical device of narrative. Telling personal stories can be a powerful way to demonstrate how law actually affects people in real lives. Several compelling examples are contained in these materials, see pages 5 and 30, and others are cited in the bibliography at page 24 and are discussed in Carl Schneider's book. For a gripping account by a law professor who underwent a heart transplant, of why advance directives should not be conclusive, see Louis J. Sirico, Jr., Life and Death: Stories of a Heart Transplant Patient, Real Prop. Prob. & Trust J. 554 (2002). For additional narratives, see Elizabeth A. Pendo, Images of Health Insurance in Popular Film: The Dissolving Critique, 37 J. Health L. 267 (2004); Stacey A. Tovino, Incorporating Literature into a Health Law Curriculum, 9 J. Med. & L. 213 (2005); Kathryn Hunter, Doctors' Stories: The Narrative Structure of Medical Knowledge (1991); Dena Davis, Tell Me a Story: Using Short Fiction in Teaching Law, 47 J. Leg. Educ. 240 (1997). Narrative approaches have also been criticized as excessively anecdotal and tending to be misrepresentative. See David A. Hyman, Patient Dumping: Lies, Damned Lies, and Narrative, 73 Ind. L.J. 797 (1998).

3. Postmodern Critical Theory

■ SLAVERY, SEGREGATION AND RACISM: TRUSTING THE HEALTH CARE SYSTEM AIN'T ALWAYS EASY! AN AFRICAN AMERICAN PERSPECTIVE ON BIOETHICS*
Vernellia R. Randall**
15 St. Louis U. Pub. L. Rev. 191 (1996)

. . . Just like the rest of America, the African American community is facing a number of bioethical issues including: abortion, disparate health status, racial barriers to access to health care, racial disparities in medical treatment, the Human Genome Project and genetic testing, organ transplantation, AIDS, physician assisted suicide and right to die, reproductive technology, and violence. Unlike the dominant American group, African Americans view these issues through an additional screen of fear and distrust. It is this fear and distrust that causes us to believe that the principles of bioethics: autonomy, beneficence, nonmaleficence, and justice, won't protect our community from mistreatment and abuse. . . .

African Americans have been experimented on without consent, thus violating the principle of autonomy. We have been treated and experimented on in ways which have caused us harm, thus violating the principles of nonmaleficence and beneficence. We have been given different treatment and provided different access to health care, thus violating the principle of justice. At best, the judgment in applying the articulated principles has been exercised fairly consistently in a manner which disadvantages and harms African Americans. . . .

Eurocentric bioethics focuses on the individual, ignoring the interests of others who are intimately affected, such as the family and the community. This focus on the individual is based on a philosophy that regards the self, and only the self, as the end per se. However, the African American perspective views this reliance on ethical egoism to be misplaced. African Americans believe that "it takes a whole village" to raise a child, and thus, at a minimum, African Americans view ethical egoism to be contradictory to the raising of healthy children. Furthermore, even as adults, none of us function as islands; we all must rely on others for, at a minimum, reaffirmation of our self-assessment.

Second, Eurocentric bioethics embraces Kantian ethics, which are antithetical to Afrocentric bioethics. Kantian ethics require universal norms and an impartial perspective, which is inattentive to relationships and community. Kantianism privileges abstract reasoning over virtue, character, and moral emotions. Kantian ethics maintain that the only way we can morally constitute ourselves is by free and rational choice. It is the exclusivity of that claim that is troubling. African Americans believe that we morally constitute ourselves not only through free and rational choice but also through our parents and our community.

Third, Eurocentric bioethics tends to view the patient or research subject generically, without attention to race, gender, or insurance status. As a result, the

*This article is reprinted with permission, copyright © 1996, St. Louis University.
**Professor of Law, University of Dayton School of Law. In addition to her legal training, Professor Randall worked for over a decade as a nurse.

development of laws and bioethical principles, discourse, and practices are informed by the values and beliefs of one group: white, middle-class, males.

Eurocentric bioethical principles such as autonomy, beneficence, and informed consent do not have the same force when viewed through the African American bio-ethical perspective of distrust. These principles leave considerable room for individual judgment by health care practitioners. The flaw of a principle-based paradigm is that very judgment. The application of the principles will be subject to other values held by the society. In a racist society (such as ours), the judgment is often exercised in a racist manner.

Thus, Eurocentric bioethics has adopted rules and has applied them with little, if any, concern for how race or other characteristics affect the working of the rules. In fact, numerous studies have documented a disparity between traditional bioethical practice and the needs of minority populations. For instance, African Americans notably differ from European Americans, both in their unwillingness to complete advance directives and in the desires expressed regarding life-sustaining treatment. Substantially more African Americans and Hispanics "wanted their doctors to keep them alive regardless of how ill they were, while more . . . whites agreed to stop life-prolonging treatment under some circumstances. . . ."

The implication for the African American community is the failure of bioethical problem-solving to take into consideration those factors important to solving problems in the African American community. Most of the problem-solving has been at odds with the affirmation of the African American individual and the African American community. In fact, for the most part, mainstream bioethicists have consistently neglected to comment on the social ills or injustices such as "the [African Americans'] enslavement, the injustices and discrimination they have suffered, the stereotyping of their language and culture, and their disadvantaged economic, political, educational, and health status." As a result of this lack of affirmation, or, this oppression, we are in danger of losing our own perspectives—our own gifts. . . .

African Americans face the health care system with anxiety, fear, and disaffection. Such anxiety, fear, and distrust will not be alleviated until bioethics constructs a practical, ethical approach to the anxiety and fear which would lead to community empowerment. Such a practical approach would require behaviors such as: reinstatement of community hospitals; assuring urban perinatal health care; encouraging traditional lay-midwifery; and reestablishing the extended family. However, such practical approach must be based on not only the traditional Eurocentric principles but also on:

- recognizing the needs of the community and not just the individual self;
- formulating bioethical and legal solutions involving both the family and the community;
- aggressively training health care providers and institutions about the African American perspective, thus making the barrier of distrust easier to overcome;
- eliminating the disparities in health status;
- aggressively reducing the existing disparities in health care delivery in the African American community.

THE COLONIZATION OF THE WOMB
Nancy Ehrenreich*
43 Duke L.J. 492 (1993)

Science has been called the religion of modern times, and probably only a fool would attempt to convince a reader, in the course of a law review article no less, that medicine, the form of science most widely used by the consuming public, is not "scientific." Yet that is what I must do here, for central to my argument is the notion that medicine is a hegemonic discourse—that it is laden with value choices and beliefs that masquerade as truth, nature, and biological "fact." My argument will be limited, however, to that part of medicine that deals with women and their reproductive processes, and I will not attempt to prove my point—a rather misguided effort anyway in an argument premised on profound skepticism about the notion of empirical proof itself—so much as to present a substantial amount of material suggestive of it. . . .

The scientific world view is accepted by scientists and laypeople alike. It is a belief system that denies its own reality as a world view, believing instead that it is a series of truths about knowing and controlling the unpredictable world we live in. . . . Through the use of the scientific method, it is thought, science can continually test and perfect the knowledge it acquires, moving ever closer to a "true" understanding of the world and the individuals who occupy it. . . . In the area of medicine, this theme of controlling nature is particularly evident. Technological advances have totally transformed what we mean by life and death, allowing tiny babies to survive and prosper after premature births and the elderly or those with permanent brain damage to exist (if not exactly "live") far beyond anything previously thought possible. Technology is extolled for enabling physicians to overcome "imperfections" in a woman's reproductive organs by removing eggs from ovaries, fertilizing them in petri dishes, and then returning them to the uterus. Physicians correct bad eyesight, replace torn ligaments, set broken bones, refashion hearts. Central to our notion of medicine is its role in controlling and transforming our bodies.

Upon examination, it can be seen that this view strongly associates science with many of the same terms that are traditionally associated with men; whereas, the opposite of science (anything that is unscientific) is associated with opposed and feminized terms. Science is thought to be an objective, neutral, rational, fact-based method of controlling nature, whereas non-"scientific" forms of knowledge are usually stigmatized as superstition and ignorance and thought to be based on subjective, biased, and emotional assessments of reality. Non-science is also clearly associated with women: the phrase "old wives' tale," for example, makes quite explicit the cultural equation between bad health care and women, simultaneously defining women's knowledge as nonscientific and dismissing it as erroneous. Moreover, women are seen not only as the source of dangerous medical advice but also as the sites of dangerous disease and decay. In short, . . . women are often treated as the prototypical embodiment of the natural world that science exists to control.

I can imagine many readers arriving at this point only to say, "So what? Medicine and science are, generally, objective and rational. Of course they are imperfect

*Professor of Law, University of Denver.

and will continually improve, but they are nevertheless as close as we can get to a neutral and accurate understanding of the world." Many recent writings, however, have fundamentally challenged that confidence in medical knowledge. . . .

[T]hings are actually much more complicated. I will start from the fundamental assumption, long accepted in the social sciences, that biological science is a product of culture, rather than an entity existing separate and apart from the world it attempts to know. In other words, the very categories through which medical scientists comprehend the world are themselves the product of the culture in which they live. Medicine is a social construct, rather than a set of "truths" about the world. To accept this premise is not to say that medicine is "wrong" or that it never works but that its understanding is partial, its truths contingent.

Applying this insight to the reproductive context, I will contend, therefore, that the field of obstetrics is not a domain in which experts use generally unchallengeable "facts" about human reproduction to facilitate the birthing process, but rather that it is an arena of struggle over the role(s) of women in society and indeed over the meaning of the word *woman*. Before turning to that broader point, however, I must first add one last piece of the picture of how Western dualisms operate in the realm of medicine by discussing how the reproductive process itself is perceived. . . .

As many writers have pointed out, medicine (as practiced in the United States) conceives of female reproductive processes, from menstruation to childbirth to menopause, as pathological, disease-like conditions that need to be controlled to prevent them from harming the women in whose bodies they occur (or, in the case of childbirth, the fetuses those women are carrying). . . . Childbirth itself is also seen as a dangerous, pathological, and unpredictable medical event. The role of the physician during labor is conceptualized, therefore, as imposing control and predictability on this process (and, hence, on the women through whom it is played out). Physicians "manage" the labor, performing various interventions to ensure that it proceeds along the lines of "normal" births, lines that are derived by averaging the wide range of patterns that labor actually follows among different women into a standardized set of "stages" with their own prescribed durations and symptomatology. In addition, successful childbirth has increasingly become equated with only the production of a "perfect" product, a child free of infection or disabilities. . . .

Protecting a fetus often entails imposing certain risks on the woman carrying it; a cesarean section, for example, is at least twice as likely as a vaginal birth to result in the death of the mother. Yet this risk becomes irrelevant if the cultural norm already prescribes that she be willing to sacrifice anything and everything for her children (born or unborn). Given that norm, it is easy for the doctor to either (1) assume that she is a good mother and therefore not consider her preferences very much during labor, on the assumption that she would want to sacrifice for her child, or (2) assume that she is a bad mother and therefore not consider her preferences very much during labor, on the assumption that she has no right to have them respected. . . .

In recent years, however, the medical model of reproduction has come under sustained attack by a burgeoning (at the beginning, primarily white) women's health movement. . . . [T]here are essentially three ways in which such sets of opposing terms are usually criticized. First, one can argue that the dualisms unfairly stereotype members of the low status group. That is, they are inaccurate: most white women are not passive, most African-Americans are not lazy, and so on. Those presenting a parallel challenge to the medical model claim that it unfairly stigmatizes alternative birthing approaches as less scientific or successful than traditional medicine. Second, one can argue that the dualisms elevate traits that are actually unenviable and socially destructive and disparage traits that are good and valuable. Thus, for example, relational feminists have contended that pure logic is not necessarily superior to intuitive understanding and that striving for self-sufficiency may be less laudable than recognizing human interdependence, and race theorists have suggested that contextual facts and narrative are as powerful conceptual tools as abstract analytics. In the reproductive context, this criticism takes the form of an effort to elevate alternative birthing strategies, arguing that they are actually better—both in terms of quality of care and in terms of human fulfillment—than the traditional approach.

The third critique of Western dualisms, and the one that is most important to my argument, alleges that the distinctions the dualisms draw are themselves incoherent. That is, in any particular instance, it will not be readily apparent whether an individual's reaction to her circumstances is rational or emotional, active or passive. What seems absolutely illogical to one person, for example, might indeed seem perfectly rational to another. Because of this indeterminacy of meaning, the act of labeling conduct as one or the other is facilitated by unstated (and perhaps unconscious) assumptions that reflect and reinforce power disparities in society. In other words, the dualisms do not represent or identify "real" differences in the world but rather serve as vehicles for the deployment of social power.

I mean two things by this assertion. First, the power to decide what is rational (or whatever) and what is not devolves upon those with power in the society at large. Because their visions of the world are those most often conveyed through societal institutions such as law, the media, and schools, it is their interpretations of a particular incident that will seem most "true." Second, that power to name, to interpret the world, legitimates the position of the dominant group to which it belongs as well as that group's oppression of others. The consistent application of the dominant terms of the dualisms to those in power and the devalued terms to a variety of "others" reinforces negative images of those others that then seem to justify their subordination. Relying on these insights, much of the critical feminist and critical race theory scholarship in the last several years has been directed at revealing the ways in which the dominant belief system's interpretation of the world prevents judges from seeing the behavior and concerns of women (of all colors) or people of color (of both sexes) as rational, responsible, and legitimate. . . .

II. Law and Medicine as Mutually Legitimating Discourses and Practices

. . . Legal authorities in general pay great deference to medical expertise. The most obvious example of this deference, of course, is the retention of a custom standard to define medical malpractice. . . . In the area of reproduction, this judicial deference to medical authority is particularly marked. . . . This judicial tendency to subsume women's interest in controlling their reproductive capacities within physicians' right to practice medicine reflects a similar attitude in the society at large. . . .

When considered in light of the sets of associations previously described, law's great deference to medicine is perhaps not surprising. . . . [L]aw is associated with many of the same traits as medicine. Both are thought to be neutral and objective pursuits, devoid of personal bias or subjective self-interest. Both are seen as coldly rational—as based on facts and rules, rather than opinions and values. Moreover, both are seen as controlling people: Whereas medicine controls their physical bodies, law controls the body politic, providing a peaceful means for resolving disputes that otherwise might dissolve into warfare. Put another way, medicine controls physical nature, whereas law avoids a social "state of nature." Finally, both fields are populated by elite white men who enjoy very comfortable incomes and high status. Given these affinities, judicial trust in the medical profession to make dispassionate and value-free decisions in individual cases is not surprising. . . .

Notes: Feminist and Critical Race Theory

1. *Constructive or Confrontational?* Some readers will find this style of analysis disturbing and threatening. Leslie Bender explains, however, that the aim of much critical analytical writing is to enlighten and sensitize:

> [T]here are many feminist analyses and perspectives, of which my arguments are only one. . . . Because many readers are unaware of the extensive writing and theorizing within feminism and from feminist premises about every kind of subject, they think feminist is a label meaning "political struggles for women's rights." Certainly feminist means that but it also means more. Some themes in feminist ethics are challenges to the values and conceptions of human natures and human interactions that dominate our current discourses in law, medicine, and ethics. Some feminist theorizing emphasizes the need to value and focus on care, compassion, responsiveness, responsibility, conversation, and communication, as well as learning to listen closely to others and to pay attention to others' needs, regardless of their differences from our own. I write in that tradition. Feminist ethics also challenges power structures and systemic biases in law and ethics that undervalue or disregard the perspectives and experiences of all women in differing ways and of men of subordinated statuses, whether subordinated by structures of race, class, sexual identity, some other identity-based classification, or some combination thereof. Feminism seeks to reconstruct our understandings and practices in ways that more closely respond to the needs of those people in their daily lives . . . [and] dying processes.

A Feminist Analysis of Physician-Assisted Dying and Active Euthanasia, 59 Tenn. L. Rev. 519 (1992).

2. *Discrimination in Treatment.* Radical critiques of the medical establishment have considerable empirical as well as philosophical and political support. Researchers have demonstrated disturbing ethnic, gender, and socio-economic disparities in treatment patterns for patients with similar conditions. This discrimination can sometimes take the form of the absolute denial of care. More often, treatments are not pursued aggressively for some patients as for others. See Institute of Medicine, Unequal Treatment: Confronting Racial and Ethnic Disparities in Health Care (2002); J. Escarce & S. Goodell, Racial and Ethnic Disparities in Access to and Quality of Health Care, RWJF Synthesis Report (Sept. 2007); Symposium, 55 How. L.J.

679 (2012); Symposium, 9 DePaul J. Health Care L. 667-884 (2005); Symposium, 27(2) Health Aff. 318 (Apr. 2008); Symposium, 9 J. Health Care L. & Pol'y 1-135 (2006); Symposium, 48 St. Louis U. L.J. 1 (2003); Symposium, 29 Am. J.L. & Med. 151-421 (2003); Symposium, 353 New Eng. J. Med. 727 (2005); Symposium, 1 Yale J. Health Pol'y L. & Ethics (2001); Symposium, 40(1) Med. Care 1 (Supp. 2002). For a provocative challenge to this large body of evidence, claiming that it fails to account for legitimate factors that might explain patterns of disparate treatment, such as differing patient preferences, medical conditions, or prognoses, see Sally Satel, PC, M.D.: How Political Correctness Is Corrupting Medicine (2001); Jonathan Klick & Sally Satel, The Health Disparities Myth (2006). See also Kimani Paul-Emile, Patient Racial Preferences and the Medical Culture of Accommodation, 60 UCLA L. Rev. 462 (2012).

Several articles analyze what legal actions might result from the documented pattern of differential treatment of minorities. See Mary A. Crossley, Infected Judgment: Legal Responses to Physician Bias, 48 Vill. L. Rev. 195 (2003); Michael Shin, Redressing Wounds: Finding a Legal Framework to Remedy Racial Disparities in Medical Care, 90 Calif. L. Rev. 2047 (2002); Larry J. Pittman, A Thirteenth Amendment Challenge to Both Racial Disparities in Medical Treatments and Improper Physicians' Informed Consent Disclosures, 48 St. Louis U. L.J. 131 (2003); Symposium, 9 DePaul J. Health Care L. 667 (2005); Symposium, 9 DePaul J. Health Care L. 905 (2006).

Should doctors take race into account at all in deciding how best to treat patients? Critics argue that skin color is an imperfect proxy for genetic or environmental factors that are relevant to choosing the best treatment for each patient. Defenders say that ethnic heritage is a reasonably accurate indicator of a variety of medical risk factors that physicians should and do take into account. For policy and legal analysis, see Symposium, 34 J.L. Med. & Ethics 483 (2006); Symposium, 36 J.L. Med. & Ethics 443 (2008); Michael J. Malinowski, Dealing with the Realities of Race and Ethnicity, 45 Hous. L. Rev. 1415 (2009); D. Wasserman, The Justifiability of Racial Classification and Generalizations in Contemporary Clinical and Research Practice, 9 Law, Probability & Risk 215 (2010); Erik Lillquist & Charles A. Sullivan, The Law and Genetics of Racial Profiling in Medicine, 39 Harv. C.R.-C.L. L. Rev. 393 (2004); Sharona Hoffman, "Racially-Tailored" Medicine Unraveled, 55 Am. U. L. Rev. 395-456 (2005) ("'race-based' medicine might violate numerous antidiscrimination provisions contained in federal law, state law, and federal research regulations and guidelines"); and articles by Jonathan Kahn in 4 Yale J. Health Pol'y L. & Ethics 1 (2004); and 92 Iowa L. Rev. 353 (2007).

3. *Discrimination in Research.* The history of medical research reveals a disturbing pattern of discrimination against racial and ethnic minorities, women, and the poor. See page 262. In this country, the Tuskegee experiments—in which researchers studied the long-term effects of infection with syphilis by withholding treatment from a group of African American males—provide a particularly vivid example of unethical conduct. See James H. Jones, Bad Blood (1993). Medical researchers also have discriminated against women. Researchers argued that excluding women was justified by the potential risks their research might present in the event of pregnancy, even if the women used birth control or were beyond childbearing years. Researchers also argued that women did not make good research subjects because their biological differences might cloud the research findings.

Unfortunately, the routine exclusion of women from research trials meant that women with life-threatening illnesses might be denied access to potentially helpful experimental treatments. It also resulted in flawed research: If one believes the contention that female biology might alter research results, then excluding women from research must produce incomplete results. Finally, the exclusion of pregnant, or potentially pregnant, women from research (1) denies many women access to potentially helpful experimental treatments, (2) values fetal interests over maternal interests, and (3) means that new treatments will not have been proven to be safe for pregnant women or their fetuses. Widespread criticism of these practices has led to some significant congressional reforms, including a presumption that federally funded research would include subjects who were women and members of racial or ethnic minorities. See Rothenberg, supra.

4. *Outsider Jurisprudence.* Feminist critique, critical race theory, and critical legal studies are flourishing in health care law, as they are elsewhere in legal analysis. See, e.g., Symposium, Deconstructing Traditional Paradigms in Bioethics: Race, Gender, Class, and Culture, 15 St. Louis U. Pub. L. Rev. 183 (1996). Leading **critical legal scholars** are David Frankford and Gregg Bloche. Examples of their work include their Measuring Health Care: Political Fate and Technocratic Reform, 19 J. Health Pol. Pol'y & L. 647 (1994) (Frankford); Privatizing Health Care: Economic Magic to Cure Legal Medicine, 66 S. Cal. L. Rev. 1 (1992) (Frankford); The Invention of Health Law, 91 Cal. L. Rev. 247 (2003) (Bloche); Beyond Autonomy: Coercion and Morality in Clinical Relationships, 6 Health Matrix 229 (1996) (Bloche). Professors Dorothy Roberts and Lisa Ikemoto have been especially prominent scholars on **critical race theory**. Examples of their work include Killing the Black Body: Race, Reproduction, and the Meaning of Liberty (1997) (Roberts); The Genetic Tie, 62 U. Chi. L. Rev. 209 (1995) (Roberts); The Fuzzy Logic of Race and Gender in the Mismeasure of Asian Women's Health Needs, 65 U. Cin. L. Rev. 799 (1997) (Ikemoto); In the Shadow of Race: Women of Color in Health Disparities Policy, 39 U.C. Davis L. Rev. 1023 (2006) (Ikemoto). See also Michele Goodwin, Black Markets: The Supply and Demand of Body Parts (2006); Frank M. McClellan, Is Managed Care Good for What Ails You? Ruminations on Race, Age and Class, 44 Vill. L. Rev. 227 (1999); David B. Smith, Health Care Divided: Race and Healing a Nation (1999); Vernellia Randall, Racist Health Care: Reforming an Unjust Health Care System to Meet the Needs of African-Americans, 3 Health Matrix 127 (1993). **Feminist critique** is multidisciplinary, but is especially rich with respect to reproductive issues. For a broad introduction, see articles published in Symposium, Feminist Bioethics, 26 J. Med. & Phil. 339 (2001); Symposium, New Perspectives on Women, Health & Law, 3 Tex. J. Women & L. 1-402 (1994). See also Susan M. Wolf, Feminism & Bioethics: Beyond Reproduction (1996); Leslie Bender, Teaching Feminist Perspectives on Health Care Ethics and Law: A Review Essay, 61 U. Cin. L. Rev. 1251 (1993); Mary Anne Bobinski & Phyllis Griffin Epps, Women, Poverty, Access to Health Care, and the Perils of Symbolic Reform, 5 J. Gender, Race & Just. 233 (2002); Karen H. Rothenberg, New Perspectives for Teaching and Scholarship: The Role of Gender in Law and Health Care, 54 Md. L. Rev. 473 (1995); Symposium, 9 Duke J. Gender L. & Pol'y 1 (2002).

4. *Distributive Justice*

■UNCOMPENSATED HOSPITAL CARE: RIGHTS AND RESPONSIBILITIES*
Uwe Reinhardt**
1986

While honest economists long ago despaired of developing an overarching theory of distributive justice, political philosophers continue to hammer away at the problem. The several distinct theories of distributive justice emerging from these efforts are elegant in their internal logic, and eminently stimulating even to a skeptic. In the end, however, that literature fails as a guide towards a universally acceptable principle of justice. On the contrary, it persuades one that there cannot possibly be such a principle. For however tight the internal logic of any particular philosopher's theory of justice may be, that logic is ultimately anchored on some overarching value for which that author claims primacy on purely subjective grounds. Collectively, the political philosophers writing on the subject teach us that justice, like beauty, rests in the eye of the beholder.

Libertarian philosophers, for example, elevate individual liberty to the status of the single, overriding social value to which all other values are subordinate, and which can never justly be traded off against any subordinate value. Implicit in the libertarian's concept of "liberty" is the tenet that the individual is entitled to dispose of his or her possessions as he or she sees fit. Extreme versions of the theory—articulated, for example, in Robert Nozick's Anarchy, State, and Utopia (1974)—hold that any governmental infringement on this presumed property right is ipso facto unjust. Thus, to tax one person's wealth in order to finance another person's health care is unjust, as is a policy that compels physicians or privately owned facilities to render health care to designated individuals. In the libertarian's credo, it is the health care provider's right to determine whom to serve and whom not to serve, and also what price to exact for health services rendered. Health care providers must find this a comforting credo.

Diametrically opposed to the libertarian credo are the various theories of distributive justice espoused by egalitarian philosophers. Egalitarian philosophers elevate "equal respect for all individuals" or "equality of opportunity" to the overriding value of a just society to which all other values—among them individual liberty—are deemed subordinate. Equality of opportunity, argue these philosophers, requires as a minimum that all members of society have equal access to certain basic commodities, access to which determines an individual's range of opportunities and measure of self-respect. Health care, along with food, shelter, and education, is among these basic commodities.

---

*This reading is excerpted from the first chapter of a book by this title edited by F. Sloan, J. Blumstein & J. Perrin (1986). Reprinted with permission of Johns Hopkins University Press.

**The author, a professor of economics at Princeton University, is a prominent writer and speaker on health care public policy. His first name has the German pronunciation, "OO-vuh."

The entitlements implicit in the egalitarian tenet seem rather open-ended, and as recent history in this country has shown, they certainly are. Egalitarians, however, do not glibly ignore resource constraints. They merely argue that, in the face of such constraints, need, rather than ability to pay, should be the basis for rationing. Clearly this theory of justice implies redistribution of the sort libertarians consider coercive and hence unjust.

One's own predilections aside, it is certainly no more logically compelling to let equal opportunity triumph completely over individual liberty than it is to do the reverse. Indeed, outside the ivory tower any prevailing sense of justice is apt to be an amalgam in which each of the pure theories is somewhat compromised. While purist philosophers may deplore such compromises, policymakers must not only countenance them but actively lead in forging the amalgam.

A remarkable and unique feature of American health policy has been its attempt to accommodate simultaneously both the egalitarian and the libertarian theories of justice in their extreme purity. No other nation in the industrialized West has been quite so bold, or quite so naive, as to attempt that feat. Ironically, no other nation finds itself, in the mid-1980s, with the unsolved problem of uncompensated indigent care at the center stage of its health policy debate. There appears to be a casual link between schizoid thinking on the ethical plane and impotence at the level of policy.

Throughout the postwar period, and possibly even earlier, our policies on the distribution of health care have been firmly rooted in the egalitarian credo: It has been a widely shared notion that health care in the United States should be distributed on the basis of medical need rather than ability to pay. Furthermore, with appeal to the overarching principle of "equal respect for all individuals," it has generally been held (at least in public debate) that the nation should aim for equality in the process of health care—that there should be equity in the so-called amenities accompanying the delivery of health care, including the travel and wait time during access and the degree of free choice among providers. Politicians of all ideological stripes have supported these tenets (at least none has openly questioned them), and health care providers have endorsed them as well.

Cynics may argue that no one seriously entertained these lofty maxims and that they were recited by politicians mainly for public consumption. Some glaring remaining inequalities in access to health care may be cited to buttress that case. But a fair reading of health legislation during the 1960s and 1970s should persuade even a skeptic that public policy in those years was motivated by a genuine desire to move the country closer to an egalitarian distribution of health care. By the end of the 1970s, few policy analysts and even fewer public officials still questioned the proposition that access to all medically necessary and technically feasible health care on equal (process) terms is one of an American citizen's basic rights.

The pursuit of an egalitarian health care system is, of course, not a uniquely American phenomenon. Most other industrialized nations have shared that goal, and some of them seem to have been rather more successful than have we in approaching it. A uniquely American phenomenon, however, has been the endeavor to extract an egalitarian distribution of health care from a delivery system still firmly grounded in libertarian principles.

To be sure, our health care delivery system does not measure up in all respects to a libertarian's dream. Some individual liberties are being compromised by government for the sake of quality control, and even the staunchest defenders of the libertarian credo, America's physicians, have from time to time enlisted the government's coercive power to protect their economic turf through occupational licensing. We share such infringements with other modern societies. But in no other modern society espousing egalitarian principles for the distribution of health care have physicians and hospitals been quite so free as they have in the United States to organize their facilities as they see fit, to practice medicine as they see fit, and to price their services as they see fit. In these realms, libertarian principles have prevailed, and every legislative attempt to compromise them for the sake of cost control or greater equity in distribution has, until very recently, been beaten back successfully, with overt appeals to the libertarian credo. "If you want an egalitarian distribution of health care," providers have said, "we endorse it heartily, and we shall do our best to bring it about—but for a fee, and we want that fee to be reasonable as we define that term."

Libertarian and egalitarian purists wrestle with one another in any democratic society. The politician's task, as noted earlier, is to fashion from this struggle a sustainable social compromise. It is on that count that American health policy has performed poorly relative to other democracies. For, in seeking to cater to both extremes among notions of distributive justice, American policymakers have bestowed upon the nation a maze of public health programs that make a Rube Goldberg contraption appear streamlined by comparison.

There has been extraordinarily generous public health insurance coverage for some services and for some individuals—replete with completely free choice of providers by patients and with virtually open-ended reimbursement formulas for providers, . . . entitlements that have, on occasion, bordered on handing providers the key to the public treasury. . . , Yet, attempts to curb that flow of public funds into private treasuries have always been decried and, until very recently, rejected as an intolerable, regulatory infringement on private liberties.

Congressional respect for this peculiar conception of "liberty" naturally carried the danger of turning any federal health program into a fiscal hemorrhage. Too timid to prevent that outcome through controls on providers, our politicians have pursued the next logical policy to contain public health budgets: They simply have left glaring gaps in health insurance coverage, particularly for the near poor and the unemployed (whose health insurance coverage typically ceases with employment). . . . [O]ne would be hard put to identify any other industrialized society today that would still visit upon an unemployed worker's family, already down on its luck in so many material and emotional ways, the added anxiety and potential real hardship of going without health insurance coverage. It happens only in America.

It has become fashionable to attribute our long-standing failures in this area to a streak of meanness in the American character. Having lived both outside and inside this nation, I do not accept that interpretation. The special genius of nations who have long settled these problems lies not in their citizens' superior character, but lies, as noted, in a political process capable of forging a more stable ethical foundation for their health care systems. In all of these nations, the providers of health care enjoy fewer liberties than do their American counterparts. But in addition, a good many of these countries—for example, the United Kingdom, West Germany, France, Switzerland, and Holland—have been rather more tolerant of some degree of tiering in their health systems than have the champions of egalitarianism in the United States. Perhaps the time has come for Americans, too, to debate more openly—and without the customary rancor and slander—just what are the essential ingredients of a just health care system.

Note: Social Justice

For additional readings, see Madison Powers & Ruth Raden, Social Justice: The Moral Foundations of Public Health and Health Policy (2006); Norman Daniels et al., Benchmarks of Fairness for Health Care Reform (1996); Larry Palmer, Law, Medicine and Social Justice (1989); Kevin P. Quinn, Viewing Health Care as a Common Good: Looking Beyond Political Liberalism, 73 S. Cal. L. Rev. 277 (2000); Jennifer Prah Ruger, Health and Social Justice (2009).

For extensive analysis of the distributive aspects of health care law, finance, and policy, see Clark C. Havighurst & Barak D. Richman, Symposium, Health Policy's Fourth Dimension, 69(4) Law & Contemp. Probs. 1 (Autumn 2006), in which the lead authors argue that:

> [because] the legal and regulatory environment of U.S. health care has been structured according to the perceptions and preferences of [social and political] elites, . . . significant social-justice issues are raised by the American legal system's many ways of making families of modest means, if they want health coverage, pay for especially costly versions of it. . . . [T]he health care system's systematic exploitation of the many for the benefit of the privileged few has been either overlooked, underestimated, or conveniently ignored by analysts and policymakers. . . . Specifically, we see a seemingly well-meant but essentially destructive policy bias—assiduously cultivated by the health care industry and shared by many commentators and policy analysts—in favor of more and better health care for all with only nominal regard for how much it costs or who bears the burden, . . . thereby maintaining a system that is rigged against the true interests of the political majority.

Clark C. Havighurst & Barak D. Richman, Distributive Injustice(s) in American Health Care, 69(4) Law & Contemp. Probs. 7 (Autumn 2006).

■ PATIENT POWER: SOLVING AMERICA'S HEALTH CARE CRISIS
John C. Goodman & Gerald L. Musgrave
1992

The potential demand for health care is virtually unlimited. Even if there were a limit to what medical service can do (which, over time, there isn't), there is an almost endless list of ailments that can motivate our desire to spend. About 83 million people suffer from insomnia, 70 million have severe headaches, 32 million have arthritis, 23 million have allergies, and 16 million have bad backs. Even when the illnesses are not real, our minds have incredible power to convince us that they are.

Consider the case of an 80-year-old man who suffered from the condition of "slowing down." Despite the physician's counsel that the condition was perfectly normal at age 80, the patient and his wife went on a literal shopping spree in the medical marketplace. As the physician explained to the *New York Times*:

A few days ago the couple came in for a follow-up visit. They were upset. At their daughter's insistence they had gone to an out-of-town neurologist. She had wanted the "best" for her father and would spare no (Medicare) expense to get it. The patient had undergone a CAT scan, a magnetic resonance imaging, a spinal tap, a brain-stem evoke potential and a carotid duplex ultrasound. No remediable problems were discovered. The Medicare billing was more than $4,000 so far; . . . they were emotionally exhausted by the experience and anxious over what portion of the expenses might not be covered by insurance. I have seen this Medicare madness happen too often. It is caused by many factors, but contrary to public opinion, physician greed is not high on the list. I tried to stop the crime, but found I was just a pawn in a ruthless game, whose rules are excess and waste. Who will stop the madness? . . .

■ MAKING MEDICAL SPENDING DECISIONS: THE LAW, ETHICS, AND ECONOMICS OF RATIONING MECHANISMS*
Mark A. Hall

When we are ill, we desperately want our doctors to do everything within their power to heal us, regardless of the costs. Medical technology has advanced so far, however, that literal adherence to this credo for every human frailty would consume much more than our country's entire economic output,[13] and, in the process, cause economic collapse. . . . Any workable system for financing and delivering health care must face the fundamental problem of how best to allocate limited medical resources among competing beneficial uses. Someone, somewhere must decide which items of potential medical benefit are not worth the cost. . . .

It is sometimes thought that medical advances will eventually reduce medical spending by making people fundamentally healthier, but this assumption is equally flawed. Medical needs are inherently limitless because aging and illness are a permanent feature of the human condition. Much beneficial medical care results in people living to an older age where they are more frail and succumb to more chronic and expensive diseases. This does not mean we should suppress these innovations, only that the drive to conquer all forms of illness is ultimately doomed to failure. The course of history over this century demonstrates that, as medicine advances, so do both medical needs and medical spending.

For these various reasons, most policy analysts recognize that rationing in some form is desirable and inevitable. Every spending decision is necessarily a

13. The U.S. gross domestic product per capita is about $23,000. To see how easy it would be to spend this amount each year on maximal health care, consider that it costs about this same amount on average simply to incarcerate a prisoner (not counting the costs of building new prison space). See also Lamm, R.D., "Rationing of Health Care: Inevitable and Desirable," 140 U. Pa. L. Rev. 1511, 1512 (1992) ("[A] French study asked how much it would cost to give all the health care that is 'beneficial' to each citizen. The answer was five-and-one-half times the French gross national product.").

rationing decision simply because resources devoted to one person or one use are not available for someone or something else. If wants are limitless and resources are finite, it is impossible to maintain that rationing is avoidable in all its forms.

We have always rationed health care resources on a massive scale, only according to irrational and unjust principles.[14] Presently, we ration health care by denying it to those unfortunate individuals who lack insurance either because their employer does not provide it or because their level of poverty has not yet fallen to the desperate level required for Medicaid eligibility. At the same time, we heavily subsidize health insurance for the upper and middle classes through a regressive tax policy that excludes from an employee's income the value of insurance premiums contributed by employers. Moreover, for those who are fully insured, we devote vast resources to save lives and restore health once an illness or accident occurs, but we spend only microscopic amounts in comparison on basic safety, health education, and health prevention measures. . . .

The haphazard and unprincipled basis on which rationing presently occurs effectively rebuts another argument raised by critics of rationing, namely, that rationing should occur only under numerous, morally demanding conditions that presently do not exist. These critics impose unattainably Utopian prerequisites to rationing, such as developing ethically unassailable and scientifically valid rationing criteria, insisting on their strict egalitarian application throughout all strata of society, and first eliminating all wasteful spending, both within medicine and elsewhere in society. These demands ignore the fact that any systematically thought-out rationing scheme, however flawed, is far superior to the thoughtless and inhumane way in which many uninsured people are now treated. A more considered form of resource allocation is the first step, not the last, toward social equity and broad-based reform. Only with some better approach to rationing will minimally acceptable access to health care become affordable for everyone.

Despite these many powerful arguments, it is still controversial to speak in terms of rationing health care. In order to avoid drawing the fire of those who oppose any use of this term, I will instead lean towards the more neutral terminology of resource allocation or spending decisions. I will not entirely refrain from the "R" word, however. Its emotional baggage can help to dramatize the pervasive necessity of making medical spending decisions. Despite their differing emotional content, both rationing and allocation can fairly be used in the generic sense that refers to either implicit or explicit denial of marginally beneficial medical treatment out of consideration for its cost. . . .

[R]egardless of the overall structure of a health care financing and delivery system, [w]hether it is regulatory or competitive, public or private, we are plagued by two basic issues: (1) Who should decide what care is not worth the costs, and (2) what criteria of benefit should be used to make this determination? The second of these problems is the one that has received more attention to date. Numerous volumes have been written on questions such as whether the short supply of transplantable organs should be distributed based simply on random draw or who has

14. Fuchs, V.R., "The 'Rationing' of Medical Care," 311 New Eng. J. Med. 1572 (1984); Rosenblatt, R.E., "Rationing 'Normal' Health Care: The Hidden Legal Issues," 59 Texas L. Rev. 1401-1420 (1981).

been waiting the longest, or instead based on elaborate concepts of medical need or medical benefit.[15] This literature also gives extensive thought to routine medical technologies. It explores whether medical resources generally should be rationed according to age or instead according to some more quantitative formula for effectiveness or value. Others before me have debated at length whether medical benefit should be defined by the number of lives saved, the length of life, the quality of life, or some more intermediate goal such as diagnostic certainty, and whether judgments about people's social worth can be prevented from tainting these concepts.

These are tremendously fascinating and important questions deserving of continuing inquiry, but they avoid what I see as a more fundamental question: Who should be the rationing decisionmaker? . . . [M]edical sociologist David Mechanic [f]irst articulated that health care spending decisions can be made through three fundamentally different mechanisms. Cost-sensitive treatment decisions can be made by patients, by physicians, or by third parties—primarily private and governmental insurers but also various regulatory or review organizations. Elsewhere in our economy, cost/benefit trade-offs are usually made through the purchasing decisions of individual consumers. For example, nutrition resources are allocated at both the macro and micro levels through the aggregation of countless individual decisions of how much food to buy, of what quality, and from what source. This simple market mechanism is not generally available or desirable for health care because of the unpredictability of illness and the complexities of medical judgment. . . . [W]e purchase insurance rather than pay out of pocket because we want to protect ourselves from the uncertain costs of health care and the anxiety of making spending decisions under the strain of serious illness. Moreover, even without insurance, patients make few of their medical decisions themselves because the complexity of treatment compels us to delegate extensive authority to our doctors. . . .

Insurers, either private or governmental, can make medical spending decisions through cost-sensitive rules about what treatment they will pay for. Until recently, this has seldom happened, but in 1994 Oregon became the first state to attempt explicit rule-based rationing for all of medicine. Oregon ranked over 600 condition-treatment pairings (e.g., surgery for appendicitis) according to their medical effectiveness, for purposes of allocating limited Medicaid funding. Elsewhere in this country, efforts are under way to develop a host of much more detailed and nuanced clinical practice guidelines, which could also serve as rule-based tools for third-party resource allocation. In addition to insurers' payment rules, spending decisions can be imposed by other parties who are similarly outside the doctor-patient

15. Leading general discussions are found in AMA Council in Ethical and Judicial Affairs, "Ethical Considerations in the Allocation of Organs and Other Scarce Medical Resources Among Patients," 155 Archives Internal Med. 29 (1995); Blank, R.H., Rationing Medicine (1988); Churchill, L.R., Rationing Health Care in America: Perceptions and Principles of Justice (1987); Kilner, J.F., Who Lives? Who Dies?: Ethical Criteria in Patient Selection (1990); Winslow, G.R., Triage and Justice (1982). An early general discussion is contained in Note, "Scarce Medical Resources," 69 Colum. L. Rev. 620 (1969). A more recent treatment is the cogent and comprehensive analysis by Elhauge, E., "Allocating Health Care Morally," 82 Cal. L. Rev. 1449 (1994). For a thorough discussion of rationing criteria used commonly throughout society, see generally Elster, J., Local Justice: How Institutions Allocate Scarce Goods and Necessary Burdens (1992).

relationship. Courts, citizen groups or other ideal democratic processes, and physician administrators who review the work of treating doctors are each able to set limits or give directions on how medical resources are spent. . . .

The third fundamental alternative for allocating medical spending authority is for physicians to incorporate cost considerations into their clinical judgment. Authorizing physicians to make cost/benefit trade-off decisions at the bedside differs from centralized, rule-based rationing because it individualizes spending decisions to the circumstances of each patient, and it operates through professional incentives rather than bureaucratic authority. Bedside rationing, however, fundamentally compromises physicians' role-based ethic, which . . . traditionally requires doctors to provide all care that offers any benefit, regardless of its cost. Physician bedside rationing is rendered even more controversial by the use of financial incentives to motivate doctors' performance. . . .

As can be seen from this summary, most of this book is taken up with what Edward Rubin [infra] terms a "microanalysis of social institutions," one that seeks to assess the relative strengths, weaknesses, and characteristics of alternative mechanisms for allocating health care resources, drawing from both political economics and social theory. . . . Accordingly, I will not be wedded to a particular analytical framework or ideological perspective. I will undertake a pragmatic analytical critique, one that seeks to clarify for each rationing mechanism its basic rationale, its inherent limits, the evidence supporting both views, the potential for harm or manipulation, and the accommodations needed to make it work.

Notes: Health Care Rationing; Institutional Analysis

1. Other aspects of rationing, which is perhaps the most important health care policy issue of our times, are explored in Chapter 4.C. See the footnotes above for cites to several multidisciplinary sources. See also Henry J. Aaron & Wm. B. Schwartz, Can We Say No? The Challenge of Rationing Health Care (2005); Norman Daniels & James Sabin, Setting Limits Fairly: Can We Learn to Share Medical Resources? (2002); Gregg Bloche, The Hippocratic Myth: Why Doctors Are Under Pressure to Ration Care, Practice Politics, and Compromise Their Promise to Heal (2011); Symposium, 32 J. Leg. Med. 1 (2011); Symposium, 59 Tex. L. Rev. 1345 (1981); 60 Tex. L. Rev. 899 (1982); Symposium, 82 Va. L. Rev. 1525 (1996).

2. *Comparative Institutional Analysis.* The approach Mark Hall takes to analyzing health care rationing is known as "comparative institutional analysis" or as "legal process theory." It is an approach that is well suited to analyzing numerous legal and public policy issues, in health care and elsewhere, and so it is employed throughout this book. Its focus is not so much on what the correct answer is, but on what are the best (or least worst) institutions and processes for arriving at an answer. This approach compares the strengths and weakness of various institutions and processes within the judicial system, the private sector, the public sector, the nonprofit sector, and professional groups, among others. An excellent example of institutional choice analysis applied to problems in health policy is Russell Korobkin, The Efficiency of Managed Care "Patient Protection" Laws: Incomplete Contracts, Bounded Rationality, and Market Failure, 85 Cornell L. Rev. 1 (1999). See also Einer Elhauge, Can Health Law Become a Coherent Field of Law? 41 Wake Forest L. Rev. 365 (2006); William M. Sage, Unfinished Business: How Litigation

Relates to Health Care Regulation, 28 J. Health Pol. Pol'y & L. 387 (2003); Ezekiel Emanuel, Choice and Representation in Health Care, 56 Med. Care Res. & Rev. 1 (1999). See generally Neil Komesar, Imperfect Alternatives: Choosing Institutions in Law, Economics, and Public Policy (1995); Edward Rubin, The New Legal Process, The Synthesis of Discourse, and the Microanalysis of Institutions, 109 Harv. L. Rev. 1393 (1996).

2

The Treatment Relationship

Ordinarily, the patient-provider relationship is a consensual one to which both parties must agree. Therefore, an individual physician may, generally speaking, refuse to accept patients for any reason or for no reason. The same is true to a lesser extent for hospitals and other institutions. But this general freedom of contract is limited in several important ways. Hospitals may not turn patients away in emergencies until they have at least stabilized the patient's condition. Neither may doctors or hospitals refuse patients for certain discriminatory reasons, such as the patient's race, sex, or HIV status. While historically a physician's freedom to turn away patients found its limitations primarily in the law, the growth of formal arrangements between managed care health plans and physicians means that a provider's obligation to treat is being increasingly defined by the private agreements among the patient, insurance plan, and provider. The following materials explore the origins of, and limits on, this freedom of contract between providers and patients.

A. THE DUTY TO TREAT

1. *The Duty to Accept Patients*

■ **HURLEY v. EDDINGFIELD**
 59 N.E. 1058 (Ind. 1901)

BAKER, Justice.
 The appellant sued appellee for $10,000 damages for wrongfully causing the death of his intestate. The court sustained appellee's demurrer to the complaint, and this ruling is assigned as error.

The material facts may be summarized thus: At and for years before decedent's death appellee was a practicing physician at Mace, in Montgomery county, duly licensed under the laws of the state. He held himself out to the public as a general practitioner of medicine. He had been decedent's family physician. Decedent became dangerously ill, and sent for appellee. The messenger informed appellee of decedent's violent sickness, tendered him his fee for his services, and stated to him that no other physician was procurable in time, and that decedent relied on him for attention. No other physician was procurable in time to be of any use, and decedent did rely on appellee for medical assistance. Without any reasons whatever, appellee refused to render aid to decedent. No other patients were requiring appellee's immediate service, and he could have gone to the relief of decedent if he had been willing to do so. Death ensued, without decedent's fault, and wholly from appellee's wrongful act. The alleged wrongful act was appellee's refusal to enter into a contract of employment. Counsel do not contend that, before the enactment of the law regulating the practice of medicine, physicians were bound to render professional service to every one who applied. The act regulating the practice of medicine provides for a board of examiners, standards of qualification, examinations, licenses to those found qualified, and penalties for practicing without license. The act is a preventive, not a compulsive, measure. In obtaining the state's license (permission) to practice medicine, the state does not require, and the licensee does not engage, that he will practice at all or on other terms than he may choose to accept. Counsel's analogies, drawn from the obligations to the public on the part of innkeepers, common carriers, and the like, are beside the mark. Judgment affirmed.

■ WILMINGTON GENERAL HOSPITAL v. MANLOVE
174 A.2d 135 (Del. 1961)

SOUTHERLAND, Chief Justice.

This case concerns the liability of a private hospital for the death of an infant who was refused treatment at the emergency ward of the hospital. The facts are these:

On January 4, 1959, Darien E. Manlove, the deceased infant, then four months old, developed diarrhea. The next morning his parents consulted Dr. Hershon. They asked whether the medicine they had for him was all right and the doctor said that it was. In the evening of the same day Mrs. Manlove took the baby's temperature. It was higher than normal. They called Dr. Hershon, and he prescribed additional medication (streptomycin), which he ordered delivered by a pharmacy.

Mrs. Manlove stayed up with the child that night. He did not sleep. On the morning of January 6th the parents took the infant to Dr. Hershon's office. Dr. Thomas examined the child and treated him for sore throat and diarrhea. He prescribed a liquid diet and some medicine. . . .

On the morning of January 7th (a Wednesday) [the infant's] temperature was still above normal—102. Mr. and Mrs. Manlove determined to seek additional medical assistance. They knew that Dr. Hershon and Dr. Thomas were not in their offices on Wednesdays, and they took their infant to the emergency ward of the Wilmington General Hospital.

There is no real conflict of fact as to what occurred at the hospital. The parents took the infant into the reception room of the Emergency Ward. A nurse was on duty. They explained to the nurse what was wrong with the child, that is, that he had not slept for two nights, had a continuously high temperature, and that he had diarrhea. Mr. Manlove told the nurse that the child was under the care of Dr. Hershon and Dr. Thomas, and showed the nurse the medicines prescribed. The nurse explained to the parents that the hospital could not give treatment because the child was under the care of a physician and there would be danger that the medication of the hospital might conflict with that of the attending physician. The nurse did not examine the child, take his temperature, feel his forehead, or look down his throat. The child was not in convulsions, and was not coughing or crying. There was no particular area of body tenderness.

The nurse tried to get in touch with Dr. Hershon or Dr. Thomas in the hospital and at their offices, but was unable to do so. She suggested that the parents bring the baby Thursday morning to the pediatric clinic.

Mr. and Mrs. Manlove returned home. Mrs. Manlove made an appointment by telephone to see Dr. Hershon or Dr. Thomas that night at eight o'clock. At eight minutes past three o'clock in the afternoon the baby died of bronchial pneumonia. . . .

It was assumed by both parties below that the hospital was a private hospital and not a public one—that is, an institution founded and controlled by private persons and not by public authority. The trial court disagreed, finding a quasi-public status in the receipt of grants of public money and tax exemptions. . . . Hence, the court concluded, liability may be imposed on the defendant in an emergency case.

We are compelled to disagree with the view that the defendant has become a public (or quasi-public) hospital. It is admitted (although the record does not show it) that it is privately owned and operated. We find no dissent from the rule that such a hospital is a private hospital, and may, at least in the absence of control by the legislature, conduct its business largely as it sees fit. . . .

Moreover, the holding that the receipt of grants of public money requires the hospital to care for emergency cases, as distinguished from others, is not logical. Why emergency cases? If the holding is sound it must apply to all the hospital services, and that conclusion, as we shall see, is clearly unsound. . . .

We are of opinion that the defendant is a private and not a public hospital, in so far as concerns the right of a member of the public to demand admission or treatment. What, then, is the liability of a private hospital in this respect?

Since such an institution as the defendant is privately owned and operated, it would follow logically that its trustees or governing board alone have the right to determine who shall be admitted to it as patients. No other rule would be sensible or workable. Such authority as we have found supports this rule. "A private hospital owes the public no duty to accept any patient not desired by it, and it is not necessary to assign any reason for its refusal to accept a patient for hospital service." 41 C. J. S. Hospitals §8, p.345. . . .

. . . Does that rule apply to the fullest extent to patients applying for treatment at an emergency ward? . . .

It may be conceded that a private hospital is under no legal obligation to the public to maintain an emergency ward, or, for that matter, a public clinic. But the maintenance of such a ward to render first-aid to injured persons has become a well-established adjunct to the main business of a hospital. If a person, seriously hurt, applies for such aid at an emergency ward, relying on the established custom to render it, is it still the right of the hospital to turn him away without any reason? In such a case, it seems to us, such a refusal might well result in worsening the condition of the injured person, because of the time lost in a useless attempt to obtain medical aid. Such a set of circumstances is analogous to the case of the negligent termination of gratuitous services, which creates a tort liability. Restatement, Law of Torts, "Negligence," §323. . . .

As above indicated, we are of opinion that liability on the part of a hospital may be predicated on the refusal of service to a patient in case of an unmistakable emergency, if the patient has relied upon a well-established custom of the hospital to render aid in such a case. . . .

Applying this rule here, we inquire, was there an unmistakable emergency? Certainly the record does not support the view that the infant's condition was so desperate that a layman could reasonably say that he was in immediate danger. The learned judge indicated that the fact that death followed in a few hours showed an emergency; but with this we cannot agree. It is hindsight. And it is to be noted that the attending physician, after prescribing for the child one morning before, did not think another examination that night or the next morning was required. If this case had gone to the jury on the record here made, we would have been required to hold that it was insufficient to establish liability. We cannot agree that the mere recitation of the infant's symptoms was, in itself, evidence of an emergency sufficient to present a question for the jury. Before such an issue could arise there would have to be evidence that an experienced nurse should have known that such symptoms constituted unmistakable evidence of an emergency. . . .

The possibility that the case might turn on additional evidence respecting the matters we have touched upon was not considered either by the court or counsel. In the circumstances we think the case should go back for further proceedings. We should add, however, that if plaintiff cannot adduce evidence showing some incompetency of the nurse, or some breach of duty or some negligence, his case must fail. Like the learned judge below, we sympathize with the parents in their loss of a child; but this natural feeling does not permit us to find liability in the absence of satisfactory evidence.

For the reasons above set forth the order denying summary judgment is affirmed, without approving the reasons therefor set forth in the court's opinion.

■ WIDEMAN v. SHALLOWFORD COMMUNITY HOSPITAL
826 F.2d 1030 (11th Cir. 1987)

HILL, Circuit Judge.

This case presents the novel question of whether a county government's alleged practice of using its emergency medical vehicles only to transport patients to certain county hospitals which guarantee the payment of the county's medical bills violates a right protected by the federal constitution. We hold that such a practice, even if proved, would not violate any established constitutional right. . . .

I. BACKGROUND

The facts underlying this case are undeniably tragic. On April 12, 1984, Toni Wideman, who at the time was four months pregnant, began experiencing abdominal pain. She called her obstetrician, Dr. John Ramsey, who instructed her to come immediately to Piedmont Hospital. Ms. Wideman called the 911 emergency telephone number in DeKalb County and requested an ambulance to take her to Piedmont. Three employees of the DeKalb County Emergency Medical Service (EMS) responded to this call. Ms. Wideman claims that she again informed the EMS employees to take her to Piedmont where her doctor was waiting, but they refused and, instead, took her against her wishes to Shallowford Community Hospital. After a substantial delay, during which the attending physician at Shallowford spoke by phone with Dr. Ramsey, Ms. Wideman was transferred to Piedmont. At that point, however, Dr. Ramsey was unable to stop her labor, and Ms. Wideman gave birth to a premature baby, named Ebony Laslun Wideman, who survived for only four hours. . . .

. . . It seems that both parties, as well as the district court, have assumed that the alleged policy violates a cognizable constitutional right, which the plaintiffs characterize as their right to the provision of essential medical treatment and services by the county.[1] However, . . . the proper resolution of this case requires us first to determine whether the Constitution grants a right to medical care and treatment in these circumstances. . . .

III. A. EXISTENCE OF A CONSTITUTIONAL RIGHT TO ESSENTIAL MEDICAL CARE

Beginning from the broadest prospective, we can discern no general right, based upon either the Constitution or federal statutes, to the provision of medical treatment and services by a state or municipality. If such a right exists at all, it must derive from the Fourteenth Amendment's due process clause, which forbids a state to deprive anyone of life, liberty or property without due process of law. The due process clause, however, has traditionally been interpreted as protecting certain "negative liberties," i.e., an individual's right to be free from arbitrary or discriminatory action taken by a state or municipality. This circuit has recognized the "well established notion that the Constitution limits the actions the states can take rather than mandating specific obligations." Bradberry v. Pinellas County, 789 F.2d 1513, 1517 (11th Cir. 1986). . . .

Two Supreme Court decisions dealing with access to abortions also support our conclusion that there is no general right to medical care or treatment provided by the state. In Maher v. Roe, 432 U.S. 464 (1977), two indigent women brought suit challenging a Connecticut regulation prohibiting the funding of abortions that were not medically necessary. The plaintiffs argued under the Fourteenth Amendment

1. The constitutional right alleged by the plaintiffs arguably may be characterized as the much more specific right to the medical care and services of their choice. Ms. Wideman was provided with medical care in this case; indeed, she was rushed to a hospital in an ambulance provided by the county. Her claim appears to be that she should have been able to direct the ambulance wherever she wanted to go. For purposes of our analysis, however, we shall consider the plaintiffs' alleged constitutional right as they have characterized it.

that the state regulation impinged on their constitutional right to an abortion, as recognized in Roe v. Wade, 410 U.S. 113 (1973). The Court upheld the state regulation, concluding that *Roe* did not declare an unqualified constitutional right to an abortion; rather, that case declared a woman's right to be protected from unduly burdensome interference with her freedom to decide whether to terminate her pregnancy. Significantly, in reaching this result, the Court noted that "the Constitution imposes no obligation on the states to pay the pregnancy-related medical expenses of indigent women, or indeed to pay any of the medical expenses of indigents." *Maher*, 432 U.S. at 469 (footnote omitted).

The Court's subsequent decision in Harris v. McRae, 448 U.S. 297 (1980), reinforced the constitutional distinction between requiring the state to provide medical services and prohibiting the state from impeding access to such services. The plaintiffs in *Harris* challenged the constitutionality of the Hyde amendment, which denied public funding for certain medically necessary abortions, as violating their due process liberty interest in deciding whether to terminate a pregnancy. The Supreme Court held that although the liberty protected by the due process clause prohibits unwarranted government interference with freedom of choice in the context of certain personal decisions, "it does not confer an entitlement to such funds as may be necessary to realize all the advantages of that freedom." . . . More recently, the Court has interpreted *Maher* and *Harris* as standing for the proposition that, "as a general matter, the state is under no constitutional duty to provide substantive services for those within its border." Youngberg v. Romeo, 457 U.S. 307, 317 (1982).

Several court of appeals decisions have addressed the issue of whether a state or municipality has a duty under the Fourteenth Amendment to provide various protective services to its citizens. Almost without exception, these courts have concluded that governments are under no constitutional duty to provide police, fire, or other public safety services. . . .

B

That there exists no such general right to the provision of medical care and services by the state, however, does not end our inquiry. Both the Supreme Court and various circuit courts have indicated that the existence of a "special custodial or other relationship" between an individual and the state may trigger a constitutional duty on the part of the state to provide certain medical or other services. In these special circumstances, the state's failure to provide such services might implicate constitutionally protected rights.

For example, the Supreme Court has held that the Eighth Amendment prohibition against cruel and unusual punishments, applicable to the states via the Fourteenth Amendment, requires states to provide medical care for those whom it is punishing by incarceration. . . . Similarly, the Court has held that an involuntarily committed mental patient retains . . . a clear Fourteenth Amendment right "to adequate food, shelter, clothing, and medical care." *Youngberg*, 457 U.S. at 315. . . .

Following this rationale, a constitutional duty can arise only when a state or municipality, by exercising a significant degree of custody or control over an individual, places that person in a worse situation than he would have been had the government not acted at all. Such a situation could arise by virtue of the state affirmatively placing an individual in a position of danger, effectively stripping a person of her ability to defend herself, or cutting off potential sources of private aid. The key concept is the exercise of coercion, dominion, or restraint by the state. . . .

In the present case, we conclude that DeKalb County did not exercise a degree of coercion, dominion, or restraint over Ms. Wideman sufficient to create a "special relationship." . . . The county did not force or otherwise coerce her into its ambulance; it merely made the ambulance available to her, and she entered it voluntarily. Ms. Wideman's physical condition at the time might have required her to seek immediate medical help, and that need might have induced her to make use of the service provided by the county, hoping that she could convince the EMS employees to take her where she wanted to go. Her physical condition, however, cannot be attributed to the county. . . . Therefore, the county was under no affirmative constitutional duty to provide any particular type of emergency medical service for her. . . .

. . . Because the Constitution does not require municipalities to provide any emergency medical services at all, it would be anomalous indeed to hold them liable for providing limited services which happen to be less extensive than a particular citizen may desire. . . .

Notes: The Differing Obligations of Physicians and Hospitals; Hospitals as Quasi-Public Facilities

1. *The "No Duty" Rule.* The complaint and brief in Hurley v. Eddingfield reveal that the deceased patient was in distress during childbirth, yet, as the *Hurley* court suggests, physicians are not obligated to provide care to a particular patient unless they have agreed to do so. A standard characterization of this principle appears in Oliver v. Brock, 342 So. 2d 1, 3 (Ala. 1976):

A physician is under no obligation to engage in practice or to accept professional employment, but when the professional services of a physician are accepted by another person for the purposes of medical or surgical treatment, the relation of physician and patient is created. The relation is a consensual one wherein the patient knowingly seeks the assistance of a physician and the physician knowingly accepts him as patient. The relationship between a physician and patient may result from an express or implied contract, either general or special, and the rights and liabilities of the parties thereto are governed by the general law of contract. . . . 61 Am. Jur. 2d, Physicians, Surgeons, and Other Healers, §96.

This "no duty" rule is consistent with tort law's normal "Good Samaritan" doctrine, which does not require individuals, even professionals, to come to the aid of strangers in distress. A physician's *ethical*, as opposed to legal, duty is somewhat more demanding, however. The American Medical Association's Principles of Medical Ethics state that a "physician shall, in the provision of appropriate patient care, except in emergencies, be free to choose whom to serve. . . ." (Principle VI). Why couldn't this ethical pledge to provide emergency care be converted into an implied promise that physicians make to the public at large? See William E. May, Medical Ethics: Code and Covenant or Philanthropy and Contract?, 5(6) Hastings Ctr. Rep. 29 (1975). Doesn't the public rely on physicians as much as they do on hospital emergency departments? Consider especially Dr. Eddingfield's status as the plaintiff's family physician. Despite these qualms, *Hurley* is still thought to state the prevailing law for physicians.

2. *Triggering a Treatment Relationship.* A physician's complete freedom to refuse treatment exists only if a treatment relationship has not been initiated. Here, the fact that Dr. Eddingfield may have treated the *Hurley* patient in the past did not suffice, because the law considers treatment relationships to coincide with "spells of illness." Thus, once a patient recovers from an illness or stops seeking treatment, a new treatment relationship must be formed in order to invoke a duty of continuing treatment. See, e.g., Castillo v. Emergency Medicine Associates, 372 F.3d 643, 648-652 (4th Cir. 2004).

Consider how this issue might come out differently when the patient receives medical care from a health maintenance organization (HMO). In this regard, see Hand v. Tavera, 864 S.W.2d 678 (Tex. Ct. App. 1993) (holding that "when the health-care plan's insured shows up at a participating hospital emergency department, and the plan's doctor on call is consulted about treatment or admission, there is a physician-patient relationship between the doctor and the insured").

3. *The Hospital's Duty.* Despite the reluctance of the *Manlove* court to find a duty to treat, it is considered a groundbreaking case in that it paved the way for other courts to make more definitive findings of hospital liability for the refusal of emergency care. See, e.g., Stanturf v. Sipes, 447 S.W.2d 558 (Mo. 1969) (hospital may be liable for refusing to treat frostbite victim who could not post $25 deposit); Mercy Medical Center v. Winnebago County, 206 N.W.2d 198 (Wis. 1973) ("It would shock the public conscience if a person in need of medical emergency aid would be turned down at the door of a hospital."); but see Campbell v. Mincey, 413 F. Supp. 16 (N.D. Miss. 1975) (no obligation of hospital emergency department to care for pregnant woman in labor). Many states impose a requirement of open emergency departments by statute or regulation. George D. Pozgar, Legal Aspects of Health Care Administration 235 (10th ed. 2007). See generally Karen Rothenberg, Who Cares? The Evolution of the Legal Duty to Provide Emergency Care, 26 Hous. L. Rev. 21 (1989).

How do you explain the fact that hospitals have a duty to provide emergency care to all who seek it while physicians are under no such obligation? Arguably, it does not make sense to expect physicians to be available at all times, while hospitals can reasonably be expected to always have someone staffing their emergency departments. But what about just expecting physicians to be available during their regular office hours for emergencies? Can't doctors factor into their scheduling the possibility of emergencies? Don't they in fact already do that? Is part of the issue that physicians may not necessarily have the expertise for any emergency patient that comes though the door? Suppose the physician is a dermatologist and is confronted with a cardiac emergency. Is there anything the doctor reasonably could do besides call 911?

Hospitals, too, may be able to limit their obligation according to their capacity or expertise. Suppose a hospital has no emergency department because it specializes in elective surgeries. Or suppose the emergency department is full. When this happens, hospital emergency departments often place themselves on "drive-by" status, which means they alert ambulances not to stop there. One court held this was permissible in the case of a child who consequently suffered brain damage, even though the hospital had treated the child many times in the past and had encouraged his parents to pass up other closer hospitals and come there if he had serious problems. Davis v. Johns Hopkins Hospital, 622 A.2d 128 (Md. 1993). Regulations under the Emergency Medical Treatment and Active Labor Act come to the same conclusion. 42 C.F.R. §489.24(b)(4).

4. *The Meaning of Reliance.* Why is the *Manlove* reliance theory limited to just emergency care? Observe the court's reasoning that "such a refusal [of treatment] might well result in worsening the condition of the injured person, because of the time lost in a useless attempt to obtain medical aid." Presumably, this is true only in a very serious or "unmistakable" emergency. It might be possible, however, to argue for other types of reliance. Suppose, for instance, that a prospective patient chose to live in the community because of the presence of a hospital, and it would thereby frustrate his or her reliance if the hospital could deny care in nonemergencies as well as emergencies. On the other hand, while such patients may have a psychological reliance, they would not suffer a *detrimental* reliance in the sense of a material change in one's position for the worse.

Where reliance is detrimental, should the patient have to demonstrate actual reliance in the particular case, rather than reliance being assumed? The *Manlove* court appeared to treat only the detriment part as requiring proof, not the psychological expectation. Should we presume that patients always legitimately expect emergency departments to be open to them? Consider, for instance, Guerrero v. Copper Queen Hospital, 537 P.2d 1329 (Ariz. 1975), which found that a hospital in a border town owned by a local mining company had a duty to render emergency aid to two severely burned Mexican children who were injured in their home across the border.

5. *Physicians "On Call."* *Hurley* and *Manlove* appear consistent because one is about doctors and the other is about hospitals. But does it make sense for hospitals to have a duty to accept emergency patients if the doctors who work there are free to refuse treatment? Courts generally have resolved this problem by holding that a doctor who is "on call" for a hospital emergency department voluntarily undertakes the hospital's greater duty of care. The leading decision is Hiser v. Randolph, 617 P.2d 774 (Ariz. 1980). At 11:45 P.M. one night, Bonita Hiser came to the emergency department at Mojave County General Hospital in a semi-comatose condition arising out of an exacerbation of her juvenile onset diabetes. Along with the seven other doctors in the area, Dr. Randolph took turns as the on-call physician for the emergency department, a duty for which he was paid $100 per 12-hour shift, and he was on call when Mrs. Hiser came to the hospital. When the emergency department nurse called Dr. Randolph, he refused to come in. He claimed this was because he lacked the expertise to treat diabetes, but there was also evidence that his refusal was based on personal animosity toward Mrs. Hiser or the fact that Mrs. Hiser's husband was a lawyer. Mrs. Hiser died because of the delay in treatment. The court found that Dr. Randolph breached his duty of care arising from his status as an on-call physician. According to the court,

the obviously intended effect of the [hospital's] bylaws and rules and regulations was to obligate the emergency room doctor "on call" to provide emergency treatment to the best of the doctor's ability to any emergency patient of the hospital. Under these circumstances, the lack of a consensual physician-patient relationship before a duty to treat can arise has been waived by the signatory doctors.

But see Childs v. Weis, 440 S.W.2d 104 (Tex. Ct. App. 1969) (physicians on emergency call were under no specific duty to see all patients who presented themselves to the emergency department).

A similar analysis is possible for HMO physicians. See St. Charles v. Kender, 646 N.E.2d 411 (Mass. Ct. App. 1995) (HMO subscriber is a third-party beneficiary of an HMO's contracts with its physicians; contract was breached when physician failed to return patient's calls for an appointment). In Hand v. Tavera, 864 S.W.2d 678 (Tex. Ct. App. 1993), Lewis Hand went to the Humana Hospital (Village Oaks) emergency department because of a three-day headache. He also had high blood pressure, and his medical history revealed that his father had died of an aneurysm. The emergency department physician was able to control Mr. Hand's blood pressure and headache temporarily with medication but ultimately concluded that Mr. Hand should be admitted to the hospital. Hospital admissions required the approval of another physician under the Humana Health Care Plan, so the emergency department physician called Dr. Robert Tavera, the physician responsible that evening for authorizing admissions of Humana patients. Dr. Tavera decided that Mr. Hand should be treated as an outpatient. A few hours after returning home, Mr. Hand suffered a stroke. The trial court granted Dr. Tavera summary judgment on the ground that no patient-physician relationship had been formed, but the appellate court held that a patient-physician relationship existed by virtue of Mr. Hand's membership in the Humana Health Care Plan and Dr. Tavera's designation "as the doctor acting for the Humana plan that night." As the court observed, "Hand paid premiums to Humana to purchase medical care in advance of need . . . and Tavera's medical group agreed to treat Humana enrollees in exchange for the fees received from Humana. In effect, Hand had paid in advance for the services of the Humana plan doctor on duty that night, who happened to be Tavera, and the physician-patient relationship existed."

6. *The Quasi-Public Status of Hospitals.* Another basis for imposing a duty to treat, distinct from the reliance theory, is the assertion that physicians or hospitals owe duties to the public at large simply by virtue of their having chosen to become licensed health care providers. It is a version of this argument that the *Hurley* court rejects with the cryptic comment that "analogies, drawn from the obligations to the public on the part of innkeepers, common carriers, and the like, are beside the mark." In ancient common law, certain occupations and businesses were considered to be "common callings," meaning that they could not turn away customers without a good reason. Innkeepers and public transport ("common carriers") were the classic examples. The reasons for these heightened public service duties were the importance of the service, the monopoly status of the business, and the support it received from the government. See Charles Burdick, The Origin of the Peculiar Duties of Public Service Companies, 11 Colum. L. Rev. 514, 616, 742 (1911); O. W. Holmes, Jr., Common Carriers and the Common Law, 13 Am. L. Rev. 40 (1879). In modern times, these "businesses affected with a public interest" are the public

utilities (electric, phone, trains, etc.), and common law duties of public service have been supplanted by overt government regulation. This body of common law has therefore become somewhat archaic, but it is still sometimes invoked against trade associations or labor unions that refuse membership. See generally Comment, Judicial Intervention in Admission Decisions of Private Professional Associations, 49 U. Chi. L. Rev. 840 (1982); Developments, Judicial Control of Actions of Private Associations, 76 Harv. L. Rev. 983 (1963).

This body of law has been used to characterize hospitals as "quasi-public" facilities for purposes of giving *physicians* rights of access to their medical staffs. Considering that patients are the ultimate customers for whom public benefit is intended, shouldn't this analogy have even more application to them? It would be ironic indeed to insist on physician access but deny patient access. Nevertheless, the *Manlove* court rejected this view. In other states, later decisions have been more receptive to the quasi-public characterization. For instance, in Thompson v. Sun City Community Hospital, 688 P.2d 605 (Ariz. 1984), the court found that a cause of action exists against a hospital that stabilized a patient with a severed artery and then transferred him for financial reasons. The court based the duty to treat on the general public policy embodied in hospital licensing regulations and private accreditation standards. Also, in Payton v. Weaver, the court suggested in dictum that this public service theory could be used to impose a community-wide obligation on kidney dialysis centers to share the burden of treating an unwanted disruptive patient. Cf. A. J. G. Priest, Possible Adaptation of Public Utility Concepts in the Health Care Field, 35 Law & Contemp. Probs. 839 (1970).

7. *The Private Status of Physicians.* Reconsider the situation of physicians. Why shouldn't medical practice by physicians be considered a "common calling" or a quasi-public service? Indeed, it turns out that, in fifteenth-century English law, physicians were included on the list of common callings along with blacksmiths and other important professions. Perhaps today the missing ingredient is that a physician rarely has a local monopoly; usually there are several in town. But not always. One court found a common law duty to treat where the sole physician practice group in town refused to accept a patient who had filed a complaint against one of the doctors in the group. Leach v. Drummond Medical Group, 192 Cal. Rptr. 650 (Cal. Ct. App. 1983).

In a few state statutes, regulatory law imposes some limited duties on physicians to provide care for patients. In Massachusetts, for instance, physicians, as a condition of being licensed, must agree to charge Medicare patients no more than Medicare's "reasonable charge." This has been held not to violate the constitutional rights of physicians. Dukakis v. Massachusetts Medical Society, 815 F.2d 790 (1st Cir. 1987).

8. *Paying vs. Indigent Patients.* Perhaps this body of law is not more developed because doctors and hospitals rarely turn away patients who can pay. For patients who cannot pay, the public service theory is usually no help, since the common law never required common callings to serve people for free. Only the reliance theory reaches this result, but it is restricted to severe emergencies, those in which the patient is worse off for having made a futile attempt to secure service. Only in Arizona have courts used a public service theory to impose a duty to treat patients who cannot pay, and there too the duty is limited to emergency care. (Should it be?)

9. *Enforcement of Public Rights.* For patients who cannot pay, regulatory law may place hospitals under somewhat greater duties than the common law to treat both emergency and nonemergency patients, but these public law duties have been limited and are not enforceable by individual patients.

Consider, for example, tax law. Nonprofit hospitals are considered to be "charities" that are exempt from property and income tax. Part of this charitable status includes an obligation to treat some patients for free. Federal law restricts this free-care obligation to emergency patients, as do most states, but a few states are beginning to require hospitals to devote a certain percentage of their overall services to patients who cannot pay. Once again, however, this is a community service obligation owed to the public at large, not to individual patients, and so it cannot be enforced very easily by private action. Finally, the Joint Commission on Accreditation of Healthcare Organizations (JCAHO) private accreditation standards require hospitals to accept patients without regard to "source of payment," but this is interpreted to mean accepting all patients with some source of payment (e.g., not turning away Medicaid patients) rather than a duty to accept patients who cannot pay.

This leaves us with the following patchwork of laws: for physicians, no common law duty to treat, even in emergencies. For hospitals: (1) a common law duty to treat emergency patients regardless of payment, but only in severe emergencies; (2) common law and regulatory duties to treat all patients who can pay; but (3) no enforceable duty to treat nonemergency or mild emergency patients who cannot pay. This set the stage for enactment of a new federal statute, the Emergency Medical Treatment and Active Labor Act (EMTALA), discussed in the *Burditt* case at page 110.

Notes: Moral and Constitutional Rights to Health Care

1. *Moral Rights to Treatment.* The discussion of legal rights to treatment surely must be informed by how our society views moral rights to health care. What message does society send when the law limits the right to treatment so narrowly as to encompass only serious emergencies? Does the emergency care limitation suggest that we are trying to limit care to the most compelling needs and to avoid people demanding too much care (emergencies being thought of as unpredictable). This might be seen as a partial embodiment of the "rescue principle," which declares that the strongest ethical demand in medicine is to help those in greatest need. In this regard, the moral dimension of medicine is stronger than in any other commercial arena, because there is no equivalent requirement that grocers, restaurants, or hotels provide their services for free to people in dire straits. What justifies this distinction? Is it that if food and housing were available on demand, it would be too easy to abuse the privilege? But what kinds of incentives for patients does a right only to emergency care generate? Is the reluctance of the courts to find even broader rights to health care a reflection of the difficulty in deciding who to hold responsible for vindicating these rights? Or perhaps it reflects the difficulty in defining what a right to health care would include. Consider in this regard the difference between defining a right to housing and a right to health care.

The moral issue can also be debated from a broader, social perspective. So far, we have thought only about whether patients have a right to demand treatment from particular doctors and hospitals. Even where they do not have these private rights, perhaps they have a claim to a more public right, one that society as a whole owes to provide minimally decent health care to all. For some time, we have recognized this claim to basic social support for education and to a more limited extent for food and housing. But for health care, there was no national safety net until the enactment of the Patient Protection and Affordable Care Act in 2010. Importantly, the Act expands Medicaid coverage to all persons whose family income is no more than 138 percent of the federal poverty level. Still, even after the Act goes fully into effect, more than 20 million Americans (many of them undocumented immigrants) will lack health insurance of any kind. Perhaps it was politically and morally sustainable to deny coverage to so many people before enactment of the Affordable Care Act—and to continue denying coverage to millions of Americans—only because private hospital emergency departments exist as a last resort for those without insurance. Could it be, then, that the heightened private law duties of hospitals weakened our nation's public law commitment to health care access? See Mark A. Hall, The Unlikely Case in Favor of Patient Dumping, 28 Jurimetrics 389 (1988). For an argument that private law duties tend to undermine voluntary charity, see Richard Epstein, Mortal Peril: Our Inalienable Right to Health Care? (1997). For responses to Epstein, see Symposium: Is America's Health Care System in Mortal Peril?, 1998 U. Ill. L. Rev. 683.

2. *Positive vs. Negative Liberty.* If there is a moral right to health care generally, it is clearly not vindicated as a substantive due process right by the U.S. Constitution. *Wideman* is a classic statement of the principle that the Bill of Rights embodies primarily negative, not positive, liberties, that is, it is concerned mainly with freedoms from government imposition, not rights to government assistance. Thus, the Constitution becomes relevant to health care when the government bans treatment choices or forces treatment, but not when it simply declines to assist in obtaining treatment. In this regard, the U.S. Constitution differs markedly from constitutional models in Europe. B. Jessie Hill, What Is the Meaning of Health? Constitutional Implications of Defining "Medical Necessity" and "Essential Health Benefits" Under the Affordable Care Act, 38 Am. J.L. & Med. 445 (2012); John A. Robertson, Controversial Medical Treatment and the Right to Health Care, 36(6) Hastings Center Rep. 15 (2006).

Wideman was followed by an important Supreme Court opinion confirming its general analysis in this regard. In DeShaney v. Winnebago County Department of Social Services, 489 U.S. 189 (1989), the Court held that no constitutional violation occurred in a case where a child was left with permanent brain damage when a state social services agency failed to intervene aggressively enough to prevent child abuse. The state had received several reports of severe beatings by the father. The Court reaffirmed "that the due process clauses generally confer no affirmative right to governmental aid," and it reasoned that the state agency had not assumed a "special relationship" with the child by virtue of having made some ineffectual efforts to protect him since the agency did nothing to make him more vulnerable to the danger. See also Archie v. Racine, 847 F.2d 1211 (7th Cir. 1988) (en banc) (§1983 action not maintainable for city rescue service's negligent failure to dispatch ambulance; no constitutional right to treatment exists).

As *Wideman* indicates, government will assume duties to provide health care when it confines individuals in psychiatric hospitals, prisons, or other facilities.

Occasionally, the press report cases of uninsured people committing crimes so they'll have access to health care while incarcerated. Katie Moisse & James Verone, The Medical Motive for His $1 Bank Robbery, ABC News, June 23, 2011, at http://abcnews.go.com/Health/Wellness/james-verone-medical-motive-bank-robbery/story?id=13895584.

3. *Equal Protection.* In Maher v. Roe, 432 U.S. 464, 469-470 (1977), discussed in *Wideman*, the Court identified another possible source of a constitutional duty to treat: "The Constitution imposes no obligation on the states to pay . . . any of the medical expenses of indigents. But when a state decides to alleviate some of the hardships of poverty by providing medical care, the manner in which it dispenses benefits is subject to constitutional limitations." For example, in Memorial Hospital v. Maricopa County, 415 U.S. 250 (1974), the Court struck down Arizona's requirement of a year's residence in a county as a condition of receiving nonemergency medical care at county expense as infringing on the right to travel. Might a state be subject to an equal protection attack for funding some procedures but not others? See Doe v. Colautti, 592 F.2d 704 (3d Cir. 1978) (finding no violation of the equal protection clause when Pennsylvania's medical assistance program provided less generous benefits for psychiatric care than for general medical care). See section A.3 for discussion of statutory protections against discrimination in access to health care.

4. *Legislative Mandates.* In Harris v. McRae, 448 U.S. 297 (1980), another abortion funding case discussed in *Wideman*, the Court addressed a nonconstitutional theory for compelling government funding of health care. States that participate in Medicaid are, generally speaking, required to fund most medically necessary forms of treatment. Beal v. Doe, 432 U.S. 438, 444 (1977). Although *McRae* found this statutory requirement to be inapplicable to abortions, in other cases the medical necessity mandate has proved to be an effective tool for obtaining Medicaid coverage. Ellis v. Patterson, 859 F.2d 52 (8th Cir. 1988) (requiring reasonable funding once a state decides to provide coverage for liver transplants); Rush v. Parham, 625 F.2d 1150 (5th Cir. 1980) (requiring funding for sex change operations in certain circumstances). However, there is no statutory requirement that Medicaid be funded at a level sufficient to cover all people who need it.

▮ BURDITT v. U.S. DEPARTMENT OF HEALTH AND HUMAN SERVICES
934 F.2d 1362 (5th Cir. 1991)

REAVLEY, Circuit Judge.

Hospitals that execute Medicare provider agreements with the federal government pursuant to 42 U.S.C. §1395cc must treat all human beings who enter their emergency departments in accordance with the Emergency Medical Treatment and Active Labor Act (EMTALA), 42 U.S.C. §1395dd. Hospitals and responsible physicians found to have violated EMTALA's requirements are subject to civil money penalties. [This case is an appeal by Dr. Burditt of a $20,000 fine assessed against him by the Department of Health and Human Services. EMTALA also provides for a private cause of action, with prevailing plaintiffs entitled to monetary damages from the offending hospital and appropriate equitable relief. Damages may not be recovered from physicians in a private cause of action, however.]

I.A. FACTS

Mrs. Rosa Rivera arrived in the emergency room of DeTar Hospital in Victoria, Texas at approximately 4:00 P.M. on December 5, 1986. At or near term with her sixth child, she was experiencing one-minute, moderate contractions every three minutes and her membranes had ruptured. Two obstetrical nurses, Tammy Kotsur and Donna Keining, examined her and found indicia of labor and dangerously high blood pressure. Because Rivera had received no prenatal care, and had neither a regular doctor nor means of payment, Kotsur telephoned Burditt, who was next on DeTar's rotating call-list of physicians responsible for such "unaligned" obstetrics patients. Upon hearing Rivera's history and condition, Burditt told Kotsur that he "didn't want to take care of this lady" and asked her to prepare Rivera for transfer to John Sealy Hospital in Galveston, Texas, 170 miles away. Burditt agreed to call back in five to ten minutes.

Kotsur and Keining told the nursing supervisor, Jean Herman, and DeTar's administrator, Charles Sexton, of their belief that it would be unsafe to transfer Rivera. When Burditt called back, Keining told him that, according to Sexton's understanding of hospital regulations and federal law, Burditt would have to examine Rivera and personally arrange for John Sealy to receive her before he could legally transfer her. Keining asked Burditt for permission to start an intravenous push of magnesium sulfate as a precaution against convulsive seizures. Burditt told Keining to begin administering this medication only if Rivera could be transported by ambulance. . . .

Burditt arrived at approximately 4:50 to examine Rivera. He confirmed her blood pressure to be the highest he had ever seen, 210/130, and he assumed that she had been hypertensive throughout her pregnancy. As the experienced head of DeTar's obstetrics and gynecology department, Burditt knew that there was a strong possibility that Rivera's hypertension would precipitate complications which might kill both Rivera and her baby. He also knew that the infants of hypertensive mothers are at higher-than-normal risk of intrauterine growth retardation. He estimated that Rivera's baby was six pounds—less than normal weight—and arranged her transfer to John Sealy, a perinatal facility better equipped than DeTar to care for underweight infants. . . .

At approximately 5:00, Herman showed Burditt DeTar's guidelines regarding EMTALA, but he refused to read them. Burditt told Herman that Rivera represented more risk than he was willing to accept from a malpractice standpoint. Herman explained that Rivera could not be transferred unless Burditt signed a DeTar form entitled "Physician's Certificate Authorizing Transfer." Burditt asked for "that dang piece of paper" and signed his name under the following:

> I have examined the patient, _____, and have determined that, based upon the information available to me at this time, the medical benefits reasonably expected from the provision of appropriate medical treatment at another medical facility outweigh the increased risks to the patient's medical condition from effecting [the] transfer. The basis for my conclusion is as follows: _____

Burditt listed no basis for his conclusion and remarked to Herman that "until DeTar Hospital pays my malpractice insurance, I will pick and choose those patients that I want to treat."

Burditt then went to care for another unaligned patient, Sylvia Ramirez, while the nurses arranged Rivera's transfer. They found another obstetrical nurse, Anita Nichols, to accompany Rivera to John Sealy. Burditt returned to the nurses' station and stayed there from 5:30 to 6:18. He never again examined Rivera or asked about her medical condition, though he inquired several times about the status of her transfer. Burditt delivered the Ramirez baby at 6:22. Afterward, Nichols told him the results of her examination of Rivera and informed him that the ambulance had arrived. Based exclusively on Nichols' statements, Burditt concluded that Rivera's condition had not changed since his examination two hours before. Burditt did not reexamine Rivera though he saw her being wheeled to the ambulance. He did not order any medication or life support equipment for Rivera during her transfer.

Nichols delivered Rivera's healthy baby in the ambulance approximately 40 miles into the 170-mile trip to John Sealy. She directed the driver to nearby Ganado Hospital to get a drug called pitocin to staunch Rivera's bleeding. While there, Nichols telephoned Burditt, who ordered her to continue to John Sealy despite the birth. Instead, per Rivera's wishes, Nichols returned Rivera to DeTar, where Burditt refused to see her because she failed to proceed to John Sealy in accordance with his instructions. Burditt directed that Rivera be discharged if she was stable and not bleeding excessively. A DeTar official pressed Burditt to allow Dr. Shirley Pigott to examine Rivera. Rivera stayed at DeTar under Pigott's care for three days and left in good health. . . .

II.A.1. SCREENING

Because Rivera presented herself to DeTar's emergency department and a request was made on her behalf for care, EMTALA required DeTar to

provide for an *appropriate* medical screening examination *within the capability of the hospital's emergency department* to determine whether or not an emergency medical condition . . . exists or to determine if the individual is in active labor. . . .

42 U.S.C. §1395dd(a) (emphasis added). The parties agree that DeTar appropriately screened Rivera and discovered that she had an "emergency medical condition"—severe hypertension—within the meaning of 42 U.S.C. §1395dd(e)(1).[2]

2. EMTALA defines "emergency medical condition" as
a medical condition manifesting itself by acute symptoms of sufficient severity (including severe pain) such that the absence of immediate medical attention could reasonably be expected to result in—
    (A) placing the patient's health in serious jeopardy,
    (B) serious impairment to bodily functions, or
    (C) serious dysfunction of any bodily organ or part.

42 U.S.C. §1395dd(e)(1) (Supp. IV 1987).

II.A.2. EMERGENCY MEDICAL CONDITION AND ACTIVE LABOR

Patients diagnosed with an "emergency medical condition" or "active labor" must either be treated or be transferred in accordance with EMTALA. Burditt claims that Rivera received all of the care that she was due under EMTALA because he stabilized her hypertension sufficiently for transfer and she was not in active labor when she left DeTar for John Sealy.

II.A.2.a. Unstable Emergency Medical Condition

Rivera's blood pressure was 210/130 at 4:00 and 5:00. This was the last reading known to Burditt before he facilitated her transfer. Nurses also measured her blood pressure as 173/105 at 5:30, 178/103 at 5:45, 186/107 at 6:00, and 190/110 at 6:50. Experts testified that Rivera's hypertension put her at high risk of suffering serious complications, including seizures, heart failure, kidney dysfunction, tubular necrosis, stroke, intracranial bleeding, placental abruption, and fetal hypoxia. This is substantial, if not conclusive evidence that Rivera entered and exited DeTar with an emergency medical condition.

Burditt argues that he fulfilled EMTALA's requirements with respect to Rivera's hypertension by "stabilizing" it, or

provid[ing] such medical treatment of the condition as may be necessary to assure, within reasonable medical probability, that no material deterioration of the condition is likely to result from [a] transfer. . . .

42 U.S.C. §1395dd(e)(4)(A). He claims that the magnesium sulfate that he ordered for Rivera has an antihypertensive effect that complements its primary anticonvulsive purpose.

Development of any of the possible complications could have killed or seriously injured Rivera, her baby, or both, and thus would constitute a "material deterioration" under 42 U.S.C. §1395dd(e)(4)(A). Any deterioration would "result" from transfer in that Rivera would have received better care for any complication at DeTar than in the ambulance. Thus, Burditt could not have stabilized Rivera unless he provided treatment that medical experts agree would prevent the threatening and severe consequences of Rivera's hypertension while she was in transit. [The HHS appeals board] could properly disregard Burditt's testimony and accept that of all other testifying experts in holding that Burditt provided no such treatment, and thus did not stabilize Rivera's emergency medical condition. . . .

II.A.2.b. Active Labor

EMTALA defines "active labor" as labor at a time when

(B) there is inadequate time to effect safe transfer to another hospital prior to delivery, or

(C) a transfer may pose a threat [to] the health and safety of the patient or the unborn child.

42 U.S.C. §1395dd(e)(2)(B)-(C). This statutory definition renders irrelevant any medical definition of active labor. . . .

Burditt challenges the ALJ's finding that, at approximately 5:00, there was inadequate time to safely transfer Rivera to John Sealy before she delivered her baby. Dr. Warren Crosby testified that, based on Burditt's own examination results, Rivera would, more likely than not, deliver within three hours after Burditt [made the decision to transfer her to] John Sealy. . . . Burditt does not challenge [the] conclusion that the ambulance trip from DeTar to John Sealy takes approximately three hours. We therefore hold that [the HHS appeals board] properly concluded that Rivera was in active labor under 42 U.S.C. §1395dd(e)(2)(B).

The ALJ also found that Rivera was in active labor under clause C at the time Burditt examined her. There is always some risk of a vehicular accident in transit, so transfer always "may" pose a threat to the health and safety of the patient or fetus. . . . We believe that Congress intended clause C to extend EMTALA's . . . protection to women in labor who have any complication with their pregnancies regardless of delivery imminency. Because better medical care is available in a hospital than in an ambulance, whether a transfer "may pose a threat" under 42 U.S.C. §1395dd(e)(2) (C) depends on whether the woman in labor has any medical condition that could interfere with the normal, natural delivery of her healthy child. Under the statutory language, a woman in labor is entitled to EMTALA's . . . protections upon a showing of possible threat; it does not require proof of a reasonable medical probability that any threat will come to fruition. . . .

The record overwhelmingly confirms that Rivera's hypertension could have interfered with a normal delivery, and she was thus in active labor under 42 U.S.C. §1395dd(e)(2)(C). . . .

II.A.3. TREAT OR TRANSFER

Upon discovery of active labor or an emergency medical condition, EMTALA usually requires hospitals to treat the discovered condition. Under certain circumstances, however, EMTALA allows hospitals to transfer patients instead of treating them. 42 U.S.C. §1395dd(b)(1)(B). . . . [The court went on to find that Burditt had not satisfied the requirements under EMTALA for a transfer before stabilization. Under EMTALA, transfer is permitted if the patient requests transfer *or* the physician has certified in writing that the medical benefits of transfer outweigh the increased risks to the patient. In addition, the receiving hospital must be capable of providing the needed treatment and must have agreed to accept the transfer. Finally, the transfer must occur with appropriate personnel and transportation, including appropriate life support measures. While Burditt had obtained consent from John Sealy before the transfer, he had not reasonably concluded that the benefits of transfer outweighed the risks nor had he arranged for the transfer with appropriate personnel and transportation.]

II.C. EMTALA's CONSTITUTIONALITY

As his final attempt to escape [liability], Burditt claims that EMTALA effects a public taking of his services without just compensation in contravention of the Constitution's Fifth Amendment.

Assuming *arguendo* that professional services constitute property protected by the takings clause, Burditt has not shown that EMTALA effects a taking. EMTALA imposes no responsibilities directly on physicians; it unambiguously requires hospitals to examine and stabilize, treat, or appropriately transfer all who arrive requesting treatment. Its provision for sanctions against physicians who knowingly violate its requirements is merely an enforcement mechanism that does not alter its explicit assignment of duties.

Governmental regulation that affects a group's property interests "does not constitute a taking of property where the regulated group is not required to participate in the regulated industry." Whitney v. Heckler, 780 F.2d 963, 972 (11th Cir.), *cert. denied*, 479 U.S. 813 (1986).

Two levels of voluntariness undermine Burditt's taking assertion. Only hospitals that voluntarily participate in the federal government's Medicare program must comply with EMTALA. Hospitals must consider the cost of complying with EMTALA's requirements in deciding whether to continue to participate in the Medicare program.

Second, Burditt is free to negotiate with DeTar or another hospital regarding his responsibility to facilitate a hospital's compliance with EMTALA. Thus, physicians only voluntarily accept responsibilities under EMTALA if they consider it in their best interest to do so. Accordingly, Burditt's claim under the takings clause is without merit. . . .

Notes: The Federal Patient Dumping Statute

1. *Historical Background.* Congress passed the Emergency Medical Treatment and Active Labor Act (EMTALA) as part of the Consolidated Omnibus Reconciliation Act of 1986 (COBRA), in response to the perception that state law was too weak to prevent widespread patient dumping. While EMTALA, or COBRA, has worked better than previous legal efforts, in part because of the private right of action, there are still concerns that patient dumping persists at unacceptable levels. One scholar argues, however, that

> EMTALA is a virtual catalogue of how to get a statute wrong. First, generalize from unrepresentative anecdotal evidence in identifying the problem. Draft the statute sloppily, and leave the most important words undefined or defined too broadly. Finance the resulting open-ended entitlement with an unfunded mandate imposed on private parties. . . . [Design the enforcement system] to reward the wrong people. Finally, apply the statute even after the world on which it depended has vanished. Any one of these problems would be bad enough in isolation, but their combined effect is devastating to the interests EMTALA was intended to protect.

David A. Hyman, Dumping EMTALA: When Bad Laws Happen to Good People (1998) (unpublished). As you read the following notes, see if you can determine why someone might reach such a conclusion. Nevertheless, Prof. Hyman acknowledges that

> the statute is wildly popular across the entirety of the political spectrum and among such disparate interest groups as physicians, advocates for the poor, [academics,] and consumer groups. Unlike many reforms, EMTALA does not create a new administrative bureaucracy; it does not favor the interests of the well-connected against the less fortunate; its on-budget costs are modest; and it seems to be no more intrusive than is absolutely necessary to accomplish its objectives.

David A. Hyman, Patient Dumping and EMTALA: Past Imperfect/Future Shock, 8 Health Matrix 29, 29 (1998).

For further discussion of these and other aspects of EMTALA, see Russell Korobkin, Determining Health Care Rights from Behind a Veil of Ignorance, 1998 U. Ill. L. Rev. 801; Sara Rosenbaum et al., EMTALA and Hospital "Community Engagement": The Search for a Rational Policy, 53 Buff. L. Rev. 499 (2005); Karen Rothenberg, Who Cares? The Evolution of the Legal Duty to Provide Emergency Care, 26 Hous. L. Rev. 21 (1989); Dana E. Schaffner, Note, EMTALA: All Bark and No Bite, 2005 U. Ill. L. Rev. 1021; Lawrence E. Singer, Look What They've Done to My Law, Ma: COBRA's Implosion, 33 Hous. L. Rev. 113 (1996); Annot., 104 A.L.R. Fed. 166.

Dr. Michael Burditt was the first physician fined for an EMTALA violation, and his actions were vigorously defended by the Texas Medical Association. For a critical view of the Fifth Circuit's decision in the Burditt case, see David Hyman, Lies, Damned Lies, and Narrative, 73 Ind. L.J. 797, 824-832 (1998).

2. *Screening and Stabilizing.* EMTALA creates two distinct duties. First, the duty to screen patients is triggered by their arrival at the hospital, and it ceases if it is determined they are not in what the statute defines as an "emergency" condition. Second, if patients are in an emergency condition, then the hospital must stabilize them. (The statutory requirements are similar for patients in active labor.) Most litigation has arisen at the first stage, in cases where patients claim the hospital failed entirely to evaluate or recognize their emergency condition. But that is not our main concern here. Our concern is, if there clearly is an emergency, how far does the duty to treat extend? Do hospitals have to perform bypass surgery after they halt a heart attack? Although *Burditt* found that "stabilizing" care was not rendered in that case, what about other typical situations? Consider whether the outcome would be any different under EMTALA than it was under this state law decision: Joyner v. Alton Ochsner Medical Foundation, 230 So. 2d 913 (La. Ct. App. 1970) (auto accident victim did not "require immediate admission" after stabilizing care was rendered, despite "multiple deep facial lacerations, a possible head injury, traumatic damage to the teeth and multiple bruises and contusions of the body, resulting in considerable loss of blood"). Consider whether the duty to treat under EMTALA is as strong as it is under this state law decision: Thompson v. Sun City Community Hospital, 688 P.2d 605 (Ariz. 1984) (a cause of action exists against a hospital that stabilized a patient with a severed artery and then transferred him for financial reasons). Is the federal statute any more demanding than the *Manlove* reliance theory? See generally Mark A. Hall, The Unlikely Case in Favor of Patient Dumping, 28 Jurimetrics J. 389 (1990) ("In the great majority of cases, the federal standard will do nothing to prevent patient dumping. . . . Even for those patients who do require stabilization prior to transfer, the federal law will result only in a delay in the transfer."); Kenneth R. Wing & John R. Campbell, The Emergency Room Admission: How Far Does the "Open Door" Go?, 63 U. Det. L. Rev. 119 (1985).

With an obligation only to stabilize, hospitals may send undocumented immigrants back to their home countries, and many of these patients die because of their inability to access follow-up care upon their return. For discussions of the ethical and financial bind for the hospitals, see Jennifer M. Smith, Screen, Stabilize, and Ship: EMTALA, U.S. Hospitals, and Undocumented Immigrants (International Patient Dumping), 10 Hous. J. Health L. & Pol'y 309 (2010); Maya Babu & Joseph

Wolpin, Undocumented Immigrants, Healthcare Access and Medical Repatriation Following Serious Medical Illness, 3 J. Health & Life Sci. L. 83 (2009); Svetlana Lebedinski, EMTALA: Treatment of Undocumented Aliens and the Financial Burden It Places on Hospitals, 7 J.L. Soc'y 146 (2005-2006). Courts have applied the stabilization requirement of EMTALA only when a hospital discharges a patient or transfers the patient to another hospital, and not when the hospital provides care. Harry v. Marchant, 291 F.3d 767, 770-772 (11th Cir. 2002) (en banc) (observing that the stabilization requirement of EMTALA is defined in terms of transfer or discharge). See also Alvarez-Torres v. Ryder Memorial Hospital, Inc., 582 F.3d 47, 51-52 (1st Cir. 2009); Bryan v. Rectors and Visitors of the University of Virginia, 95 F.3d 349, 352 (4th Cir. 1996).

In its requirement to stabilize emergency patients, EMTALA does not require the impossible. If a hospital does not have the facilities or personnel necessary to fully stabilize a patient, and the patient must be transferred to a more sophisticated hospital to receive needed care, the first hospital can transfer the patient to the more sophisticated hospital without violating EMTALA. The transferring hospital must do all it can to stabilize the patient's condition, but it need not do what it cannot do. Cherukuri v. Shalala, 175 F.3d 446 (6th Cir. 1999) (absolving physician at small rural hospital after the physician transferred two patients who needed surgery to stop internal bleeding from an automobile accident).

3. *The Patient's Indigency.* While the passage of EMTALA was motivated by concerns about private hospitals "dumping" indigent or uninsured patients on public hospitals, the statutory language imposes no requirement that patients show that they were denied emergency services because of indigency or lack of insurance. See 42 U.S.C. §1395dd(a) ("if any individual . . . comes to the emergency department . . . , the hospital must provide for an appropriate medical screening examination within the capability of the hospital's emergency department"). Accordingly, courts have generally held that it is irrelevant why a person did not receive an appropriate screening exam or, if an emergency was identified, why a person did not receive stabilizing care before discharge or transfer. As one court observed, "[EMTALA] applies to any and all patients, not just to patients with insufficient resources." Brooker v. Desert Hospital Corp., 947 F.2d 412, 415 (9th Cir. 1991). Accord Summers v. Baptist Medical Center, 91 F.3d 1132 (8th Cir. 1996); Gatewood v. Washington Healthcare Corp., 933 F.2d 1037, 1040 (D.C. Cir. 1991).

The Supreme Court addressed the motive question in the context of EMTALA's stabilization requirement and rejected any need to show an improper motive. Roberts v. Galen of Virginia, Inc., 525 U.S. 249 (1999). The Court "express[ed] no opinion" on the need to show an improper motive for a claim of inappropriate medical screening.

Perhaps the most controversial extension of EMTALA beyond economic discrimination occurred in the *Baby K* case. In In re Baby K, 16 F.3d 590 (4th Cir. 1994), parents of an anencephalic child sought ventilatory treatment of their child during periodic bouts of respiratory distress. After the second of three such episodes, the hospital sought judicial permission to withhold the ventilator when the child next came to the emergency department. In the view of the hospital, it was medically and ethically inappropriate to ventilate the child given her limited life expectancy, her total absence of consciousness, and the futility of treatment at improving her condition. According to the hospital, the only appropriate treatment for the child was the treatment "it would provide other anencephalic infants—supportive care in the form of warmth, nutrition, and hydration." The court rejected the hospital's argument. It observed that EMTALA requires stabilizing treatment in the event of a medical emergency, and the child's respiratory distress met EMTALA's definition of a medical emergency. If there was to be an exception for "futile" care under EMTALA, Congress would have to write that exception into the statute. The court's opinion in *Baby K* is presented in Chapter 3 with additional discussion.

The *Baby K* decision raises serious questions about the ability of society to contain health care costs. If the hospital in the case could not deny a ventilator to an anencephalic child, how could any emergency medical care be withheld on the ground that its high costs were not justified by its minimal benefit? Is there a distinction between the economic or other discrimination prohibited by EMTALA and the denial of care that results when a hospital is concerned about the limits of society's resources?

Perhaps in recognition of these concerns, the Fourth Circuit limited the impact of *Baby K* two years later. In Bryan v. Rectors and Visitors of the University of Virginia, 95 F.3d 349 (4th Cir. 1996), an EMTALA claim was brought on behalf of a patient who died of a heart attack after her physicians decided that "no further efforts to prevent her death should be made." Twenty days before the heart attack, the patient had been admitted to the hospital in respiratory distress. Eight days before the heart attack, apparently because of the hopelessness of the patient's condition, her physicians decided to withhold further life-sustaining treatment, including cardiopulmonary resuscitation, in the event of a cardiac arrest. When she suffered her heart attack, no efforts were made to prevent her death. According to the court, there was no EMTALA violation because EMTALA "was intended to regulate the hospital's care of the patient only in the immediate aftermath of the act of admitting her for emergency treatment and while it considered whether it would undertake longer-term full treatment or instead transfer the patient to a hospital that could and would undertake that treatment." Id. at 352.

4. *Preventive Dumping.* There has been concern that hospitals would try to evade their EMTALA obligations by dumping patients before they reach the emergency department. For example, when called by a paramedic or emergency medical technician who is transporting a patient by ambulance, the emergency department staff might direct the ambulance to another hospital. Early cases suggested that hospitals would have considerable freedom to prevent patients from reaching the emergency department. See Miller v. Medical Center of Southwest Louisiana, 22 F.3d 626 (5th Cir. 1994) (hospital not liable under EMTALA for refusing to accept the transfer of a patient who needed specialized emergency care beyond the capabilities of the transferring hospital); Johnson v. University of Chicago Hospitals, 982 F.2d 230 (7th Cir. 1992) (hospital not liable for diverting an ambulance to another hospital).

Subsequent amendment of the EMTALA regulations and case law interpreting the amendment have limited the ability of hospitals to engage in preventive dumping. Under one regulation, patients have come to the hospital's emergency department for purposes of EMTALA once they have reached any part of the hospital's property, including a hospital-owned ambulance service. 42 C.F.R. §489.24(b) (2011) (applied in Hernandez v. Starr County Hospital District, 30 F. Supp. 2d 970 (S.D. Tex. 1999); Preston v. Meriter Hospital, Inc., 700 N.W.2d 158 (Wis. 2005)). The same regulation permits hospitals to divert non-hospital-owned ambulance services if the emergency department "does not have the staff or facilities to accept any additional emergency patients." 42 C.F.R. §489.24(b)(4). The Ninth Circuit has interpreted this provision to mean that a hospital violates EMTALA when it diverts a non-hospital-owned ambulance in the absence of an inability to provide treatment for the patient. Arrington v. Wong, 237 F.3d 1066 (9th Cir. 2001); see also Morales v. Sociedad Espanola de Auxilo Mutuo y Beneficencia, 524 F.3d 54 (1st Cir. 2008). See Caroline J. Stalker, Comment, How Far Is Too Far?: EMTALA Moves from the Emergency Room to Off-Campus Entities, 36 Wake Forest L. Rev. 823 (2001).

Note that there is some ambiguity to §489.24(b). Although the regulation seems to limit the ability of hospitals to divert non-hospital-owned ambulances, it also states that "[a]n individual in a non-hospital-owned ambulance off hospital property is not considered to have come to the hospital's emergency department even if a member of the ambulance staff contacts the hospital by telephone or telemetry communications and informs the hospital that they want to transport the individual to the hospital for examination and treatment."

As indicated, under 42 C.F.R. §489.24(b), EMTALA is triggered when an individual comes to areas of the hospital other than the emergency department. Thus, a First Circuit decision emphasizes the point that a hospital's duty to stabilize before transfer applies to any patient in the hospital, "regardless of how that person enters the institution or where within the walls he may be when the hospital identifies the problem." Lopez-Soto v. Hawayek, 175 F.3d 170, 173 (1st Cir. 1999) (observing that the stabilization requirement of EMTALA applies to an individual who "comes to a hospital" and holding that EMTALA applies when a pregnant woman is admitted to the maternity ward and taken to the operating room for a cesarean section, and her infant is born with respiratory distress and needs emergency care).

5. *Dumping After Admission to the Hospital.* Courts disagree as to whether EMTA-LA's stabilization requirement continues to apply once the patient has been admitted to the hospital. Cases have arisen in which patients were admitted to the hospital for treatment and, after a few or more days of treatment, been transferred to another hospital or discharged before their illness was fully treated. Some courts have concluded that the obligation to stabilize exists throughout the patient's visit to the hospital. In addition to *Lopez-Soto*, a First Circuit decision emphasized the point that a hospital's duty to stabilize before transfer applies to any patient in the hospital, "regardless of how that person enters the institution or where within the walls he may be when the hospital identifies the problem." Lopez-Soto v. Hawayek, 175 F.3d 170, 173 (1st Cir. 1999) (observing that the stabilization requirement of EMTALA applies to an individual who "comes to a hospital" and holding that EMTALA applies when a pregnant woman is admitted to the maternity ward and taken to the operating room for a cesarean section, and her infant is born with respiratory distress and needs emergency care). Other courts have concluded that the stabilization requirement ceases upon the patient's admission to the regular hospital. Bryan v. Rectors and Visitors of the University of Virginia, 95 F.3d 349, 352 (4th Cir. 1996); James v. Sunrise Hospital, 86 F.3d 885 (9th Cir. 1996); Bryant v. Adventist Health Systems/West, 289 F.3d 1162 (9th Cir. 2002). Note that in *Bryan* and *Bryant*, the courts were deciding about the stabilization requirement for care rendered during the patient's hospital stay and not in the context of a transfer or discharge. Hence, it is not surprising that the courts were especially concerned about converting state malpractice claims into federal EMTALA claims. See note 6,

infra. In *Bryant*, the Court observed that the stabilization requirement would not cease upon the patient's admission to the hospital "if a patient demonstrates in a particular case that inpatient admission was a ruse to avoid EMTALA's requirements." 289 F.3d at 1169. A federal district court invoked that point in a case in which a patient was sent home after admission but before his injuries had been stabilized. Morgan v. North Mississippi Medical Center, Inc., 403 F. Supp. 2d 1115, 1130 (S.D. Ala. 2005). Although the court denied the hospital's motion to dismiss the EMTALA claim, it ultimately concluded on summary judgment that the hospital had not engaged in a ruse to avoid EMTALA's requirements when it admitted the patient. Morgan v. North Mississippi Medical Center, Inc., 458 F. Supp. 2d 1341 (S.D. Ala. 2006).

In a final rule that took effect in 2003, the Centers for Medicare & Medicaid Services took the position that EMTALA does not apply to individuals who are inpatients or outpatients at a hospital. 42 C.F.R. §489.24(b), (d)(2). The Sixth Circuit, which concluded in the *Thornton* case, supra, that the obligation to stabilize persists through the patient's hospitalization, has rejected the regulation. Moses v. Providence Hospital & Medical Centers, Inc., 561 F.3d 573, 583 (6th Cir. 2009). The Third Circuit, on the other hand, has upheld the regulation. Torretti v. Main Line Hospitals, Inc., 580 F.3d 168, 174-176 (3d Cir. 2009) (interpreting 42 C.F.R. §489.24(b) when an EMTALA claim was brought by an outpatient).

6. *Appropriate Medical Screening.* In interpreting EMTALA's requirement of an "appropriate medical screening examination," courts have recognized an important tension between ensuring access to emergency care for all persons and creating a federal cause of action for charges of malpractice in the emergency department. If a person is sent home from the emergency department after a physician wrongly concludes that there is no serious health problem, the mistaken diagnosis may reflect either the negligent provision of care or the purposeful denial of care. A hospital trying to evade its EMTALA obligations might do so by giving undesired patients short shrift when screening them. At the same time, patients who have been injured by malpractice may try to bring their claim under both state tort law and federal EMTALA law, thereby increasing their potential recovery, gaining access to a federal forum and its quicker judgments, and increasing their bargaining power with the hospitals by virtue of the latter's possible loss of its participation in Medicare. EMTALA claims are often appended to state tort claims when people sue for injuries allegedly caused by inadequate emergency care. Singer, supra note 1, 33 Hous. L. Rev. at 118 & n.22.

Courts have consistently stated that EMTALA cannot be used to bring claims for medical malpractice, and they have tried to distinguish between a denial of care and the negligent provision of care by looking at whether the hospital screened the patient in the same way it screens similarly situated patients. As the D.C. Circuit explained, the issue is whether the hospital "conform[ed] its treatment of a particular patient to its standard screening procedures. . . . [A]ny departure from standard screening procedures constitutes inappropriate screening." Gatewood v. Washington Healthcare Corp., 933 F.2d 1037, 1041 (D.C. Cir. 1991). Similarly, the Fourth Circuit has stated that EMTALA's screening requirement is designed to prevent "disparate treatment." Vickers v. Nash General Hospital, Inc., 78 F.3d 139, 143 (4th Cir. 1996). Hospitals are obligated only to "apply uniform screening procedures to all individuals coming to the emergency room." In re Baby K, 16 F.3d 590, 595 (4th

Cir. 1994). Accord Correa v. Hospital San Francisco, 69 F.3d 1184 (1st Cir. 1995); Summers v. Baptist Medical Center, 91 F.3d 1132, 1138 (8th Cir. 1996); Repp v. Anadarko Municipal Hospital, 43 F.3d 519, 522 (10th Cir. 1994); Holcomb v. Monahan, 30 F.3d 116, 117 (11th Cir. 1994).

The Sixth Circuit has adopted a similar standard, although it has indicated that the departure from the hospital's standard screening procedures must have resulted from some invidious motive like bias against the patient on the basis of "race, sex, politics, occupation, education, personal prejudice, drunkenness, spite . . . distaste for the patient's condition (e.g., AIDS patients). . . ." Cleland v. Bronson Health Care Group, Inc., 917 F.2d 266, 271-272 (6th Cir. 1990); Roberts v. Galen of Virginia, 111 F.3d 405, 408-409 (6th Cir. 1997), rev'd in part, 525 U.S. 249 (1999). Even if the Sixth Circuit requires some invidious motive, would it ever be difficult to find a bias lurking that would be unacceptable under the *Cleland* standard? Perhaps not often, but see Garrett v. Detroit Medical Center, 2007 U.S. Dist. LEXIS 17584 (E.D. Mich. Mar. 14, 2007) (dismissing patient's EMTALA claim on grounds that the defendant hospital transferred the patient to a hospital so he could be treated at a hospital that was "in-network" for his insurance).

Despite the courts' admonition that EMTALA does not create a federal malpractice cause of action, there inevitably will be some overlap between EMTALA claims and malpractice claims. Do you see how a requirement that hospitals provide all patients with their standard screening procedures amounts to requiring that the hospitals provide nonnegligent care? See Demetrios G. Metropoulos, Note, Son of COBRA: The Evolution of a Federal Malpractice Law, 45 Stan. L. Rev. 263 (1992).

As the preceding discussion indicates, courts have interpreted the requirement of an appropriate screening examination as an equal treatment right rather than an entitlement right. But isn't EMTALA a statute that grants an entitlement rather than a right of equal treatment? Is there a way to define appropriate screening examination as an entitlement without turning it even more clearly into the equivalent of nonnegligent care?

2. *Wrongful Reasons to Reject Patients*

While physicians or hospitals may, for most patients, refuse to treat for "good" reasons (such as inability to pay), or even for no particular reason, they may not deny care for the wrong reasons. For example, the federal civil rights acts make it unlawful for physicians and hospitals that receive federal money (such as Medicare and Medicaid) to discriminate on the basis of a patient's race, sex, religion, disability, or other enumerated characteristics. On the other hand, without a statute that specifically prohibits the particular reason for discrimination, morally problematic denials of care are generally permissible, as the *Walker* case at page 131 demonstrates. When a patient is protected from discrimination by a civil rights statute, may a physician nevertheless refuse to treat on grounds of religious belief? The California Supreme Court answered that question for a patient denied fertility services, allegedly on the basis of her sexual orientation. The Court held that a physician may not refuse treatment if it is on a basis protected from discrimination by statute. However, the Court left open the possibility for denying treatment based on a nonprotected status (e.g., unmarried status of parents). North Coast Women's Care Medical Group, Inc.

v. Superior Court, 189 P.3d 959 (Cal. 2008). For further discussion, see Symposium: The Future of Rights of Conscience in Health Care: Legal and Ethical Perspectives, 9(1) Ave Maria Law Rev. (2010).

The following materials focus on disability discrimination as the most recent and controversial form of statutory prohibition. In so doing, we do not mean to neglect the obvious importance of race and gender discrimination laws. At one time in our country's history, it was commonplace, especially in the South, for hospitals to refuse admission to blacks. These and other forms of overt discrimination have now largely disappeared as the result of various prohibitions contained in federal and state regulatory law, as well as in the hospital industry's own private accreditation code. See generally Sara Rosenbaum et al., U.S. Civil Rights Policy and Access to Health Care by Minority Americans, 57 Med. Care Res. & Rev. 226 (2000).

Serious concerns remain, however, over more subtle forms of racial and gender bias in the delivery of health care services. One form occurs in the location of health care facilities, which in inner cities are sometimes older, less accessible, or not as well equipped. See Daniel K. Hampton, Note, Title VI Challenges by Private Parties to the Location of Health Care Facilities: Toward a Just and Effective Action, 37 B.C. L. Rev. 517 (1996). Discrimination can also arise in individual treatment decisions. Numerous studies have documented that physicians treat blacks, and sometimes women, differently for the same medical conditions. For instance, blacks are less likely than whites to receive a kidney transplant, coronary artery bypass surgery, or other major surgical procedures. See page 84. Others respond that these studies are not as conclusive as they may appear because of real or possible differences in income, medical considerations, biological factors, and patient preferences. For more discussion, see page 84.

No cases have yet arisen that attack differential treatment patterns as forms of racial or gender discrimination, but when they do, they will confront the problems of which medical justifications are permissible and the extent to which courts will inquire into the complexities of medical judgment. The outcome of these questions undoubtedly will be influenced by how the courts have resolved similar disputes over disability discrimination.

The analysis of discrimination under disability statutes is inherently complicated. Often a person's disability is relevant in deciding whether the person is a candidate for treatment. For example, it would not make much sense to transplant a kidney or liver into a patient dying of cancer. As we will see, unlawful denials of care can occur both from a refusal to treat at all or a refusal to provide certain kinds of care after the patient-physician relationship is formed.

■ UNITED STATES v. UNIVERSITY HOSPITAL
729 F.2d 144 (2d Cir. 1984)

PRATT, Circuit Judge.

. . . Baby Jane Doe was born on October 11, 1983 at St. Charles Hospital in Port Jefferson, New York. She was suffering from multiple birth defects, the most serious of which were myelomeningocele, commonly known as spina bifida, a condition in which the spinal cord and membranes that envelop it are exposed; microcephaly, an abnormally small head; and hydrocephalus, a condition characterized by an accumulation of fluid in the cranial vault. In addition, she exhibited a "weak face," which prevents the infant from closing her eyes or making a full suck with her tongue; a malformed brain stem; upper extremity spasticity; and a thumb entirely within her fist.

As a result of the spina bifida, the baby's rectal, bladder, leg, and sensory functions were impaired. Due to the combination of microcephaly and hydrocephalus, there was an extremely high risk that the child would be so severely retarded that she could never interact with her environment or with other people.

At the direction of the first pediatric neurosurgeon to examine her, the baby was immediately transferred to University Hospital for dual surgery to correct her spina bifida and hydrocephalus. Essentially, this would entail excising a sac of fluid and nerve endings on the spine and closing the opening, and implanting a shunt to relieve pressure caused by fluid build-up in the cranial cavity. The record indicates that these dual, corrective surgical procedures were likely to prolong the infant's life, but would not improve many of her handicapping conditions, including her anticipated mental retardation.

After consulting with several physicians, nurses, religious advisors, a social worker, and members of their family, the parents of the baby decided to forego the corrective surgery. Instead, they opted for a "conservative" medical treatment consisting of good nutrition, the administration of antibiotics, and the dressing of the baby's exposed spinal sac.

Litigation surrounding Baby Jane Doe began on October 16, when A. Lawrence Washburn, Jr., a Vermont attorney unrelated to the child and her family, commenced a proceeding in New York State Supreme Court seeking appointment of a guardian ad litem for the child and an order directing University Hospital to perform the corrective surgery, [contending that failure to do so would violate Section 504 of the Rehabilitation Act of 1973, 29 U.S.C. §794.] . . .

. . . The Appellate Division found that the "concededly concerned and loving parents have made an informed, intelligent, and reasonable determination based upon and supported by responsible medical authority." As the court elaborated:

> The record confirms that the failure to perform the surgery will not place the infant in imminent danger of death, although surgery might significantly reduce the risk of infection. On the other hand, successful results could also be achieved with antibiotic therapy. Further, while the mortality rate is higher where conservative medical treatment is used, in this particular case the surgical procedures also involved a great risk of depriving the infant of what little function remains in her legs, and would also result in recurring urinary tract and possibly kidney infections, skin infections and edemas of the limbs.

Thus, the Appellate Division determined that the parents' decision was in the best interest of the infant and that there was, therefore, no basis for judicial intervention. . . . [The Appellate Division's decision was affirmed by the New York Court of Appeals, but on the ground that the trial court had abused its discretion in permitting the case to go forward. The Court of Appeals observed that (a) Mr. Washburn (the petitioner) had no direct interest in the case, (b) Mr. Washburn had not contacted the State Department of Social Services, which had primary responsibility under state law for initiating child abuse proceedings, and (c) the trial court had failed to seek the Department of Social Service's assistance.

Meanwhile, as the state court proceedings were unfolding, HHS received a complaint that Baby Jane Doe was being denied medical treatment because of her handicap. In response to the complaint, HHS obtained the record of the state court proceedings and, after personal review by the Surgeon General, requested the infant's medical records from the hospital. When the hospital refused to provide the records, HHS brought its case in federal court, alleging that the hospital was violating Section 504 of the Rehabilitation Act. The federal district court granted summary judgment for the hospital on two grounds: first, the hospital refused to operate on Baby Jane Doe, not because of her handicap, but because her parents did not consent to the procedures; and second, the parents' refusal of treatment was reasonable given the medical options. The federal government appealed, resulting in this opinion.]

To focus more sharply on this central issue, it is first necessary to examine the theory upon which the government predicates its [claim]. The theory rests on two premises. First, the government draws a distinction between decisionmaking based on a "bona fide medical judgment," which without definition it concedes to be beyond the reach of §504, and decisionmaking based solely on an individual's handicap, which it argues is covered by §504. Second, the government identifies Baby Jane Doe's microcephaly, which the record indicates will result in severe mental retardation, as the handicapping condition. From these premises, the government reasons that if a newborn infant suffering from spina bifida and hydrocephalus, but not microcephaly, would receive treatment or services that differ from those provided to an infant suffering from all three defects, or alternatively, if the hospital would seek a state court order compelling surgery in the former case, but not in the latter, then a violation of §504 would have been established. . . .

With this unsettled regulatory background in mind, we turn to the statutory language, which is fundamental to any issue of statutory construction. Section 504 provides in pertinent part as follows:

> No otherwise qualified handicapped individual in the United States, as defined in section 706(7) of this title, shall, solely by reason of his handicap, be excluded from the participation in, be denied the benefits of, or be subjected to discrimination under any program or activity receiving federal financial assistance.

Under 29 U.S.C. §706(7)(B), "the term 'handicapped individual' means . . . any person who (i) has a physical or mental impairment which substantially limits one or more of such person's major life activities, (ii) has a record of such an impairment, or (iii) is regarded as having such an impairment." . . .

[We] next consider whether [Baby Jane Doe] possibly can be considered an "otherwise qualified" handicapped individual or to have been "subjected to discrimination" under §504. These two issues are intertwined.

The leading cases construing the "otherwise qualified" criterion of §504 have involved allegedly discriminatory denials of admission to certain educational programs. Southeastern Community College v. Davis, 442 U.S. 397 (1979); Doe v. New York University, 666 F.2d 761 (2d Cir. 1981). In that context, this court in Doe v. New York University recognized that it is now clear that [the phrase "otherwise qualified handicapped individual"] refers to a person who is qualified *in spite of* her handicap and that an institution is not required to disregard the disabilities of a handicapped applicant, provided the handicap is relevant to reasonable qualifications for acceptance, or to make substantial modifications in its reasonable standards or program to accommodate handicapped individuals but may take an applicant's handicap into consideration, along with all other relevant factors, in determining whether she is qualified for admission. [Id. at 775 (emphasis in original).]

Doe establishes that §504 prohibits discrimination against a handicapped individual only where the individual's handicap is unrelated to, and thus improper to consideration of, the services in question. As defendants here point out, however, where medical treatment is at issue, it is typically the handicap itself that gives rise to, or at least contributes to, the need for services. Defendants thus argue, and with some force, that the "otherwise qualified" criterion of §504 cannot be meaningfully applied to a medical treatment decision. Similarly, defendants argue that it would be pointless to inquire whether a patient who was affected by a medical treatment decision was, "solely by reason of his handicap, . . . subjected to discrimination."

The government's answer to both these arguments is that Baby Jane Doe can be viewed as suffering from not one, but multiple handicaps. Indeed, the crux of the government's case is that her microcephaly is the operative handicap, and that the requested records are necessary to determine whether she has been discriminated against solely for that reason.

Despite its superficial logic, the government's theory is flawed in at least two respects. First, the government's view of "otherwise qualified" is divorced from the statutory language. As the mainstream of cases under §504 exemplifies, the phrase "otherwise qualified" is geared toward relatively static programs or activities such as education, employment, and transportation systems. As a result, the phrase cannot be applied in the comparatively fluid context of medical treatment decisions without distorting its plain meaning. In common parlance, one would not ordinarily think of a newborn infant suffering from multiple birth defects as being "otherwise qualified" to have corrective surgery performed or to have a hospital initiate litigation seeking to override a decision against surgery by the infant's parents. If Congress intended §504 to apply in this manner, it chose strange language indeed.

Second, in arguing that Baby Jane may have been "subjected to discrimination" the government has taken an oversimplified view of the medical decisionmaking process. Where the handicapping condition is related to the (conditions) to be treated, it will rarely, if ever, be possible to say with certainty that a particular decision was "discriminatory." It is at this point that the analogy to race, relied on so heavily by the dissent, breaks down. Beyond the fact that no two cases are likely to be the same, it would invariably require lengthy litigation primarily involving conflicting expert testimony to determine whether a decision to treat, or not to treat, or to litigate or not to litigate, was based on a "bona fide medical judgment," however that phrase might be defined. Before ruling that congress intended to spawn this type of litigation under §504, we would want more proof than is apparent from the face of the statute.

The legislative history, moreover, indicates that congress never contemplated that §504 would apply to treatment decisions of this nature. . . . [According to t]he Senate Report accompanying the 1974 amendments:

> . . . Section 504 was enacted to prevent discrimination against all handicapped individuals . . . in relation to federal assistance in employment, housing, transportation, education, health services, or any other federally-aided programs. Examples of handicapped individuals who may suffer discrimination in receipt of federally-assisted services . . . are as follows: physically or mentally handicapped children who may be denied admission to federally-supported school systems on the basis of their handicap; handicapped persons who may be denied admission to federally-assisted nursing homes on the basis of their handicap; those persons whose handicap is so severe that employment is not feasible but who may be denied the benefits of a wide range of federal programs. . . .

S. Rep. No. 1297, supra at 6388-6389.

This passage provides the best clue to congressional intent regarding §504's coverage of "health services." As Judge Gesell noted in American Academy of Pediatrics v. Heckler, 561 F. Supp. at 401:

> The legislative history . . . [on this subject] focuses on discrimination against adults and older children and denial of access to federal programs. As far as can be determined, no congressional committee or member of the House or Senate ever even suggested that section 504 would be used to monitor medical treatment of defective newborn infants or establish standards for preserving a particular quality of life. No medical group appeared alert to the intrusion into medical practice which some doctors apprehend from such an undertaking, nor were representatives of parents or spokesmen for religious beliefs that would be affected heard. . . .

We are aware, of course, that "where the words and purpose of a statute plainly apply to a particular situation, . . . the fact that the specific application of the statute never occurred to Congress does not bar us from holding that the situation falls within the statute's coverage." United States v. Jones, 607 F.2d 269, 273 (9th Cir. 1979), *cert. denied*, 444 U.S. 1085 (1980). Here, however, the government's theory not only strains the statutory language but also goes well beyond congress's overriding concern with guaranteeing handicapped individuals access to programs or activities receiving federal financial assistance. Further, the situation in question is dramatically different in kind, not just in degree, from the applications of §504 discussed in the legislative history. . . .

This void in the legislative history is conspicuous for another reason. Prior to the enactment of the Rehabilitation Act, congress had passed a number of measures limiting federal involvement in medical treatment decisions. For example, the very first section of the medicare law, . . . codified at 42 U.S.C. §1395, . . . provides that "nothing in this subchapter shall be construed to authorize any federal officer or employee to exercise any supervision or control over the practice of medicine or the manner in which medical services are provided." . . .

In view of this consistent congressional policy against the involvement of federal personnel in medical treatment decisions, we cannot presume that congress intended to repeal its earlier announcements in the absence of clear evidence of congressional intent to do so. . . .

In the present case, Baby Jane Doe has been treated in an evenhanded manner at least to the extent that the hospital has always been and remains willing to perform the dual, corrective surgeries if her parents would consent. Requiring the hospital either to undertake surgery notwithstanding the parents' decision or alternatively, to petition the state court to override the parents' decision, would impose a particularly onerous affirmative action burden upon the hospital. . . .

WINTER, Circuit Judge, dissenting.

Since I believe that §504 applies to the provision of medical services to handicapped infants, I respectfully dissent. . . . Section 504 . . . states with as much clarity as is reasonably possible that in some circumstances recipients of federal financial assistance may not differentiate between individuals on grounds that one or more is handicapped. . . . Although modern courts frequently rely upon legislative history to reach results at odds with the seemingly plain language of a statute, only the most compelling reasons should induce a court to override statutory language because the legislative history is silent on a particular point. Such compelling circumstances might exist in the present case if Congress had no reason to address the questions at hand when it enacted §504. It hardly needs stating that the underlying issues brim with political and moral controversy and portend to extend the hand of the federal government into matters traditionally governed by an interaction of parental judgment and state authority. Were I able to conclude that Congress had no reason to address these issues in its consideration of §504, I would concur with the majority on the grounds that specific consideration by the Congress of this political and moral minefield would be appropriate before applying the statute as written.

However, such a conclusion is untenable since §504 is no first step into a hitherto uncharted legal wilderness. As the Senate Report stated:

> Section 504 was patterned after, and is almost identical to, the antidiscrimination language of section 601 of the Civil Rights Act of 1964, 42 U.S.C. 2000d-1 (relating to race, color, or national origin), and section 901 of the Education Amendments of 1972, 42 U.S.C. 1683 (relating to sex). The section therefore constitutes the establishment of a broad government policy that programs receiving federal financial assistance shall be operated without discrimination on the basis of handicap.

S. Rep. No. 1297, 93d Cong., 2d Sess., *reprinted* in 1974 U.S. Code Cong. & Ad. News 6373, 6390. Section 504 was thus enacted against a background of well understood law which was explicitly designated as a guide to interpretation. Congress was persuaded that a handicapped condition is analogous to race and that, so far as the administration of federal financial assistance is concerned, discrimination on the basis of a handicap should be on statutory par with discrimination on the basis of race.

Once §504's legislative heritage is acknowledged, the "void" in the legislative history is eliminated and the many issues raised by defendants with regard to medical decisions, parental judgments and state authority simply evaporate. The government has never taken the position that it is entitled to override a medical judgment. Its position rather is that it is entitled under §504 to inquire whether a judgment in question is a bona fide medical judgment. While the majority professes uncertainty as to what that means, application of the analogy to race eliminates all doubt. A judgment not to perform certain surgery because a person is black is not a bona fide medical judgment. So too, a decision not to correct a life threatening digestive problem because an infant has Down's Syndrome is not a bona fide medical judgment. The issue of parental authority is also quickly disposed of. A denial of medical treatment to an infant because the infant is black is not legitimated by parental consent. Finally, once the legislative analogy to race is acknowledged, the intrusion on state authority becomes insignificant. . . .

Bragdon v. Abbott, 524 U.S. 624 (1998). Invoking the Americans with Disabilities Act's (ADA's) protection from discrimination based on disability, a woman with HIV infection challenged her dentist's refusal to fill her cavity unless he performed the procedure in a hospital. (The woman, Sidney Abbott, would have been responsible for the cost of using the hospital's facilities.) Important issues in the case were whether HIV infection constitutes a disability for purposes of the ADA and whether the dentist could nevertheless justify denying treatment in his office to protect himself from becoming infected with HIV during the procedure. (The ADA generally tracks the framework of the Rehabilitation Act's protection against discrimination based on disability but expands to more people the protection of the Rehabilitation Act.)

The Court concluded that Ms. Abbott's HIV infection constituted a disability under the ADA on the ground that HIV infection is a "physical . . . impairment that substantially limits one or more . . . major life activities." 42 U.S.C. §12102(2)(A). According to the Court, HIV infection is a physical impairment from the moment of infection because the virus immediately begins to damage an infected person's white blood cells and because of the severity of the disease. As to whether HIV infection substantially limits a major life activity, the Court observed that it might have identified many major life activities substantially limited by HIV infection. Since Ms. Abbott claimed that HIV infection substantially limited her ability to have children, the Court restricted its inquiry to that life activity. As an activity "central to the life process itself," reproduction constitutes a major life activity, wrote the Court. Moreover, HIV infection substantially limits reproduction in two ways: "First, a woman infected with HIV who tries to conceive a child imposes on the man a significant risk of becoming infected. . . . Second, an infected woman risks infecting her child during gestation and childbirth. . . ." The Court also noted that, even though the risk of transmission of HIV from mother to infant could be reduced by treatment to 8 percent, such a risk of transmitting a fatal disease rose to the level of a substantial limitation.

As to whether the dentist could defend his insistence on treatment at a hospital, he would have to show that Ms. Abbott "pose[d] a direct threat to [his] health or safety. . . ." 42 U.S.C. §12182(b)(3), with direct threat defined as "a significant risk to the health or safety of others that cannot be eliminated by a modification of policies, practices, or procedures or by the provision of auxiliary aids or services." Id. In assessing whether the dentist's fear of HIV transmission was objectively reasonable, "the views of public health authorities, such as the U.S. Public Health Service, CDC, and the National Institutes of Health, are of special weight and authority. The views of these organizations are not conclusive, however. A health care professional who disagrees with the prevailing medical consensus may refute it by citing a credible scientific basis for deviating from the accepted norm." The Court remanded the case for consideration of the dentist's defense of a direct threat to his health if he were to fill Ms. Abbott's cavity in his office instead of a hospital.

On remand, the First Circuit found in favor of Ms. Abbott. The court concluded that, because of the availability of universal precautions to prevent transmission of HIV infection from patient to dentist, the dentist could not justify his denial of treatment in terms of the need to protect himself from becoming infected with HIV. Abbott v. Bragdon, 163 F.3d 87 (1st Cir. 1998), *cert. denied*, 526 U.S. 1131 (1999). (Universal precautions are measures that health care providers are supposed to take with every patient to prevent the spread of infectious diseases like HIV and hepatitis. Examples of universal precautions are the wearing of gloves and other protective attire by health care providers, the use of special wastebaskets to dispose of used needles, and sterilization of medical instruments after each use.) The First Circuit decided that once physicians take universal precautions, no significant risk of HIV transmission remains.

▉ GLANZ v. VERNICK
756 F. Supp. 632 (D. Mass. 1991)

MAZZONE, Judge.

In April, 1989, plaintiff's decedent, Raymond Vadnais, brought this suit alleging discrimination in violation of §504 of the Rehabilitation Act of 1973 (the "Act"), 29 U.S.C. §794. . . . The allegations in the complaint can be briefly summarized as follows. In December, 1986, defendant Dr. Vernick saw Mr. Vadnais at the Ear, Nose, and Throat Clinic (the "ENT Clinic") at Beth Israel Hospital and treated him for severe pain in the right ear, at first by prescribing antibiotics and ear drops. In January, 1987, Dr. Vernick diagnosed a perforation in Mr. Vadnais's right ear and, at Mr. Vadnais's third visit, recommended surgery to repair the perforation. After Mr. Vadnais agreed to undergo surgery, Dr. Vernick learned that Mr. Vadnais was infected with HIV and in March, 1987, informed Mr. Vadnais that he would not perform the operation. The ear condition persisted, causing severe pain and discomfort, while Mr. Vadnais continued the ineffective use of antibiotics and ear drops.

In August, 1988, Dr. Yale Berry, unaware of Mr. Vadnais's HIV status, performed the surgery, curing Mr. Vadnais's ear problem. Subsequently, Mr. Vadnais brought this lawsuit seeking . . . compensatory damages for the pain and suffering and emotional distress caused by the delay in receiving corrective surgery, along with punitive damages and attorney's fees. . . .

Count I of the complaint charges that Dr. Vernick, . . . by refusing to perform surgery, unlawfully discriminated against Mr. Vadnais because of his handicap, HIV seropositivity, in violation of §504 of the Rehabilitation Act. . . .

Section 504 states in pertinent part that "no otherwise qualified handicapped individual in the United States . . . shall, solely by reason of his handicap, be excluded from the participation in, be denied the benefits of, or be subjected to discrimination under any program or activity receiving federal financial assistance. . . ." 29 U.S.C. §794.

The defendants argue that summary judgment is appropriate for several . . . reasons . . . [including] the ground that Mr. Vadnais was not "otherwise qualified" for elective ear surgery. They argue that it is proper for a doctor to consider a patient's handicap in determining whether a patient is qualified for surgery. On the basis of this argument, they conclude that Mr. Vadnais was not "otherwise qualified" for surgery because his HIV disease increased his risk of infection, and, furthermore, that the court should defer to the doctor's determination that it was in his patient's best interest to postpone surgery.

The defendants cannot be faulted for considering Mr. Vadnais's handicap in determining whether he was "otherwise qualified" for surgery. In School Bd. v. Arline, 480 U.S. 273, 287-289 (1987) [reprinted in Chapter 6], the Supreme Court held that the defendant school board could consider the risks posed by the plaintiff's contagious disease (tuberculosis) in determining whether she was otherwise qualified to teach school. It follows that, in the present case, the defendants can take into account the risks imposed—both on the patient and on themselves—by the prospect of surgery on an HIV-positive patient. Of course, if they properly conclude that there are risks, they must also consider whether it is possible to make reasonable accommodations to enable the patient to undergo surgery despite those risks.

As the Court made clear in *Arline*, the "otherwise qualified" determination requires an individualized inquiry and appropriate findings of fact. With respect to the defendants' assertions about the risks of surgery, the facts are in dispute. The defendants contend that surgery was postponed because Dr. Vernick thought that Mr. Vadnais was "AIDS positive," because the proposed ear surgery was elective, and because it would pose significant risks to the patient. In addition, they offer Dr. Berry's statement in his deposition that he would not have performed the surgery had he known that Mr. Vadnais had AIDS. The plaintiff offers the contradicting evidence that Mr. Vadnais was HIV-positive and had not yet been diagnosed as having AIDS when surgery was refused. Moreover, Dr. Vernick in answers to interrogatories and Dr. Berry in his deposition stated that they do not consider HIV seropositivity alone as a disqualifying factor for surgery. Based on the evidence that the plaintiff has produced, facts are certainly available to warrant the conclusion that Mr. Vadnais was "otherwise qualified" for surgery. Moreover, the defendants have not produced any evidence that reasonable accommodations could not have been made.

There is some merit to the argument that the court should defer to a doctor's medical judgment. Cf. *Arline*, 480 U.S. at 288 ("courts normally should defer to the reasonable medical judgments of public health officials" when conducting "otherwise qualified" inquiry). Accepting this argument at face value, however, would completely eviscerate §504's function of preventing discrimination against the disabled in the healthcare context. A strict rule of deference would enable doctors to offer merely pretextual medical opinions to cover up discriminatory decisions. The evidentiary approach to §504 cases discussed in Pushkin v. Regents of the Univ. of Colo., 658 F.2d 1372 (10th Cir. 1981), properly balances deference to sound medical opinions with the need to detect discriminatory motives. The plaintiff must first make out a prima facie case that he was otherwise qualified for surgery, and only then does the burden shift to the defendant to show that the plaintiff's handicap made him unqualified. The plaintiff, however, must still be given an opportunity "to prove either that the reason given by defendants is a pretext or that the reason . . . 'encompasses *unjustified* consideration of the handicap itself.'" *Leckelt*, 714 F. Supp. at 1385 (citing *Pushkin*, 658 F.2d at 1387) (emphasis added). . . .

■ WALKER v. PIERCE
560 F.2d 609 (4th Cir. 1977)

BRYAN, Senior Circuit Judge.

Violation of their civil rights was laid in this action for damages and declaratory and injunctive relief by Virgil Walker and Shirley Brown, black females, to Clovis H. Pierce, the attending obstetrician at the Aiken County Hospital in South Carolina for sterilizing them, or threatening to do so, solely on account of their race and number of their children, while they were receiving medical assistance under the Medicaid program. . . .

Centering the controversy is the policy previously announced and constantly pursued in practice by the doctor, testified to by him as follows:

> My policy was with people who were unable to financially support themselves, whether they be on Medicaid or just unable to pay their own bills, if they were having a third child, to request they voluntarily submit to sterilization following the delivery of the third child. If they did not wish this as a condition for my care, then I requested that they seek another physician other than myself.

There is no question of his professional qualifications or experience.

As drawn by the plaintiffs, he is the arch-offender. The accusation is incursion upon their constitutional rights of privacy, due process of law and equal protection of the law as well as of their statutory privileges against discrimination on account of their race and color, all by subjecting or threatening the plaintiffs as citizens of the United States with involuntary sterilization. . . .

Virgil Walker had completed the seventh grade, was separated from her husband and was receiving Aid to Families with Dependent Children and Medicaid benefits. Expecting her fourth child, she first went to Pierce on January 7, 1972. During this consultation, he discussed family planning and his sterilization policy. Walker refused to consent. The issue again came up at the second visit and she again declined. Walker testified that Pierce threatened to have her state assistance terminated unless she cooperated. She called another doctor, but he was not taking new patients.

On February 4, 1972, Spears, a Department of Social Services caseworker assigned to Walker, received a note from Pierce's office asking that he talk with Walker about sterilization. Thereupon, Spears, according to his testimony, spoke with her on February 17th, offering to get her a second doctor. On the other hand, Walker stated that Spears had said there was nothing he could do. Then she returned to Pierce and subsequently signed a consent form for sterilization.

Her fourth child was delivered at the Aiken County Hospital April 16, 1972 by Dr. Billy Burke, an obstetrician who substituted for Pierce on occasion. Burke discussed tubal ligation with Walker. Her response was that she did not want additional children and understood that it would be a permanent sterilization. Two more consent forms were then signed. Pierce performed the operation April 17, 1972. She protested no further because, she said, it would have been futile.

Walker's hospital bills and doctor's fees were paid by Medicaid. Under the South Carolina plan operated by the Department of Social Services, the patient-physician relationship is one of free choice for both parties. The physician, under no contract with the state, simply submits his bill when treatment is concluded to the Medicaid insurance carrier instead of the patient. . . .

We perceive no reason why Dr. Pierce could not establish and pursue the policy he has publicly and freely announced. Nor are we cited to judicial precedent or statute inhibiting this personal economic philosophy. Particularly is this so when all persons coming to him as patients are seasonably made fully aware of his professional attitude toward the increase in offspring and his determination to see it prevail. At no time is he shown to have forced his view upon any mother. Indeed, quite the opposite appears. In the single occasion in this case of a sterilization by this doctor, not just one but three formal written consents were obtained — the first before delivery of the fourth child and two afterwards. . . .

[The court also held that Dr. Pierce was not a state actor and therefore could not be found to have violated his patients' constitutional rights.]

Notes: Discriminatory Denials of Care

1. *Subsequent Developments.* In the end, the parents in *University Hospital* agreed to have a shunt implanted to drain the fluid in their daughter's brain, although the surgery was delayed because of an infection that was likely related to the opening in her spine. The child, Keri-Lynn, has done much better than predicted. Although she is confined to a wheelchair, she can talk, and she attends a school for developmentally disabled children. At age 20, she had attained a first- or second-grade level of scholastic achievement. Experts continued to disagree as to whether surgery to close Keri-Lynn's spine would have improved her outcome. Jamie Talan, A Fighter's Spirit; 20-year-old Keri-Lynn — Baby Jane Doe — Beat Steep Odds, Newsday, Oct. 13, 2003, at A3; B. D. Colen, What Ever Happened to Baby Jane Doe?, 24(3) Hastings Center Rep. 2, 2 (1994).

2. *The Americans with Disabilities Act. University Hospital* and *Glanz* were decided under the Rehabilitation Act, which applies only to federally funded programs or services and federal executive agencies. Since those cases, the Americans with Disabilities Act (ADA) has gone into effect, and its provisions apply to all nonfederal providers of health care services, public or private. The statutory language of the ADA was designed to track the Rehabilitation Act and court decisions interpreting that Act.

For further discussion of the ADA and denials of health care, see Carl H. Coleman, Conceiving Harm: Disability Discrimination in Assisted Reproductive Technologies, 50 UCLA L. Rev. 17 (2002); Mary A. Crossley, Of Diagnoses and Discrimination: Discriminatory Nontreatment of Infants with HIV Infection, 93 Colum. L. Rev. 1581 (1993); E. Haavi Morreim, Futilitarianism, Exoticare, and Coerced Altruism: The ADA Meets Its Limits, 25 Seton Hall L. Rev. 883 (1995); David Orentlicher, Destructuring Disability: Rationing of Health Care and Unfair Discrimination Against the Sick, 31 Harv. C.R.-C.L. L. Rev. 49 (1996); Philip G. Peters, Jr., When Physicians Balk at Futile Care: Implications of the Disability Rights Laws, 91 Nw. U. L. Rev. 798 (1997); and Philip G. Peters, Jr., Health Care Rationing and Disability Rights, 70 Ind. L.J. 491 (1995), which is excerpted below.

3. *Definition of Disability.* As indicated by the Supreme Court in *Bragdon,* one has to determine whether a person is in fact disabled under the ADA or Rehabilitation Act before deciding whether there has been unlawful discrimination on account of disability. Until 1999, it did not seem to be very difficult for plaintiffs to prove that they

were disabled under the ADA. Disability can be shown not only by the presence of a disabling condition but also by a history of a disabling condition or by showing that one is regarded by others as having a disabling condition. 42 U.S.C. §12102(2). Moreover, the legislative history indicated that the judgment whether a patient is disabled should be made assuming that no treatment is provided. Thus, even if a patient's disabling symptoms could be alleviated with medication, the patient would still be considered disabled under the ADA. H.R. Rep. No. 485(II), 101st Cong., 2d Sess., at 52 (1990).

In 1999, the Supreme Court raised the bar on the definition of disability by holding that a person is not actually disabled if medications or medical devices can alleviate the disabling symptoms. Moreover, the Court established a relatively high threshold for showing that one is disabled because of being "regarded as having" a disabling condition. Sutton v. United Air Lines, 527 U.S. 471 (1999). The ADA Amendments Act of 2008 overrode *Sutton* and other narrowing decisions by the Supreme Court. As a result, the definition of disability is consistent again with the legislative history of the ADA. For a discussion of the 2008 Act, see Jeannette Cox, Crossroads and Signposts: The ADA Amendments Act of 2008, 85 Ind. L.J. 187 (2010). For a very helpful discussion about defining disability, see Mary Crossley, The Disability Kaleidoscope, 74 Notre Dame L. Rev. 621 (1999).

4. *When Denial of Treatment Is Discriminatory.* What standard does the *Glanz* court suggest for deciding whether a denial of care constitutes unlawful discrimination on the basis of disability? What theories does the *University Hospital* court use to find no unlawful discrimination when medical care is withheld from a severely disabled newborn? Which of the different approaches do you think makes the most sense?

Note that, while the court's decision in *University Hospital* rested in part on the fact that Baby Jane Doe's parents agreed to the withholding of care, there is much more to the opinion. In addition, another court reached the same result as *University Hospital* in a case in which the parents charged that the physicians' treatment recommendations were biased by the presence of the child's severe disability and that the physicians failed to disclose their bias when obtaining the parents' consent to withhold care. Johnson v. Thompson, 971 F.2d 1487, 1493-1494 (10th Cir. 1992) (citing *University Hospital* for the proposition that, "[w]here the handicapping condition is related to the condition(s) to be treated, it will rarely, if ever, be possible to say . . . that a particular decision was 'discriminatory'"). There are other reasons to discount parental agreement. As Judge Winter observed in his *University Hospital* dissent, parental agreement does not necessarily vitiate a discrimination claim. The parents may not be adequately representing the child's interests.

Both *Glanz* and *University Hospital* take the view that a person's disability can be a relevant consideration in the person's access to health care. If a disability affects the benefit that the patient can receive from health care, then the disability can be a factor in deciding how to treat the patient. But that leaves most disabled persons subject to denials of health care. The immune system compromise of an HIV-infected person, for example, will have wide-ranging effects on that person's response to medical or surgical therapy. Crossley, supra note 3, at 160. Indeed, the argument in *Glanz* that Mr. Glanz's HIV infection would predispose him to infection would apply to any HIV-infected patient undergoing surgery. How do we consider the effects of a person's disability without discriminating unfairly against that person? What if it is true that a disabled person would not gain as much benefit from treatment as a nondisabled person? Is an appropriate analogy the educational services that states are required to provide in the primary public schools for children with disabilities? See New Mexico Association for Retarded Citizens v. New Mexico, 678 F.2d 847, 854-855 (10th Cir. 1982) (requiring special education to ensure that children with disabilities receive an education appropriate to their needs).

To what extent are the costs of care relevant to the analysis? If Baby Jane Doe's care cost thousands instead of hundreds of thousands of dollars, should that make a difference in deciding whether disability discrimination occurred? If you think social costs are relevant, then why does the denial of care by Dr. Pierce seem more troubling than the withholding of care from Baby Jane Doe? Wasn't he also concerned primarily about social costs? Is his decision worse because it was directed toward only the poor, or because welfare status is correlated with race? Or is it that sterilization is reminiscent of discredited eugenic social policies of the past?

Rather than avoiding the care of certain patients by claiming that the patient is not a candidate for care (as in *University Hospital* or *Glanz*), physicians might claim that the patient needs to be referred for more specialized care. In Lesley v. Chie, 250 F.3d 47 (1st Cir. 2001), the U.S. Court of Appeals for the First Circuit addressed a disability discrimination claim in the context of a physician's referral of the patient to a more specialized colleague. In *Leslie,* the court considered "the extent to which a court should defer to a physician's claim that he lacks the experience, knowledge, or other prerequisites necessary to address the medical conditions that allegedly prompted his referral of a patient to another physician." The case arose after an obstetrician referred an HIV-infected, pregnant woman to another hospital for drug therapy designed to prevent transmission of HIV to the woman's child. The other hospital had a special Women and Infants HIV Program. The court found no Rehabilitation Act violation, writing,

> Under the Rehabilitation Act, a patient may challenge her doctor's decision to refer her elsewhere by showing the decision to be devoid of any reasonable medical support. This is not to say, however, that the Rehabilitation Act prohibits unreasonable medical decisions as such. Rather, the point of considering a medical decision's reasonableness in this context is to determine whether the decision was unreasonable in a way that reveals it to be discriminatory. In other words, a plaintiff's showing of medical unreasonableness must be framed within some larger theory of disability discrimination. For example, a plaintiff may argue that her physician's decision was so unreasonable — in the sense of being arbitrary and capricious — as to imply that it was pretext for some discriminatory motive, such as animus, fear, or "apathetic attitudes." See, e.g., Howe v. Hull, 874 F. Supp. 779, 788-89 (N.D. Ohio 1994) (under ADA, jury could find doctor's diagnosis that plaintiff had extremely rare disorder requiring transfer was pretextual, where patient only had an allergic drug reaction, and doctor did not mention the rare disorder in requesting the transfer but only mentioned plaintiff's HIV-status). Or, instead of arguing pretext, a plaintiff may argue that her physician's decision was discriminatory on its face, because it rested on stereotypes of the disabled rather than an individualized inquiry into the patient's condition — and hence was "unreasonable" in that sense. [Id. at 55.]

5. *Infectious Patients.* As *Bragdon* indicates, an outright denial of care on account of the person's HIV status is unlawful disability discrimination. However, *Bragdon* and *Glanz* also indicate that the freedom of a physician to deny care on the basis of a patient's infected status depends not only on whether the infection affects the

patient's ability to benefit from treatment but also on the risk to the physician of becoming infected from the patient. How should the risk be taken into account? What if an orthopedic surgeon refuses to operate on an HIV-infected (or hepatitis-infected) patient on the grounds that orthopedic surgery is "bloody" and involves exposure to sharp edges of bone as well as to sharp surgical instruments? What if the surgeon already provides care to a significant number of HIV-infected patients and the surgeon is trying to have a child? Should it matter whether the denial of care is for elective rather than essential surgical procedures? Consider a dermatologist who refuses to perform a hair transplant on an HIV-infected person on the ground that the procedure invariably causes significant bleeding from the patient's scalp. It is important to note that the circuit courts disagree on exactly when a risk is serious enough to be "significant." For a discussion of the different standards, see Onishea v. Hopper, 171 F.3d 1289, 1296-1299 (11th Cir. 1999) (interpreting "significant risk" in the context of a Rehabilitation Act case).

Concerns about discrimination against HIV-infected physicians are discussed at pages 234-235.

3. Rationing and Discrimination

This section examines whether it is desirable or permissible for insurance providers to exclude some medical conditions or treatments by assessing which medical needs are most demanding and what treatments work the best. The public policy focus here is on how health care resources might be better allocated, and the legal focus is on disability discrimination. As you read this section, realize that, in a world of limited resources, insurance cannot pay for all beneficial medical care that anyone might need. The problem, then, is which approach to limiting insurance benefits makes the most sense, and whether discrimination law allows sensible health care public policy to emerge from either market or political forces.

■ ALEXANDER v. CHOATE
469 U.S. 287 (1985)

Justice MARSHALL delivered the opinion of the Court.

. . . Faced in 1980-1981 with projected state Medicaid costs of $42 million more than the state's Medicaid budget of $388 million, the directors of the Tennessee Medicaid program decided to institute a variety of cost-saving measures. Among these changes was a reduction from 20 to 14 in the number of inpatient hospital days per fiscal year that Tennessee Medicaid would pay hospitals on behalf of a Medicaid recipient. Before the new measures took effect, respondents, Tennessee Medicaid recipients, brought a class action for declaratory and injunctive relief in which they alleged, inter alia, that the proposed 14-day limitation on inpatient coverage would have a discriminatory effect on the handicapped. Statistical evidence, which petitioners do not dispute, indicated that in the 1979-1980 fiscal year, 27.4 percent of all handicapped users of hospital services who received Medicaid required more than 14 days of care, while only 7.8 percent of nonhandicapped users required more than 14 days of inpatient care.

Based on this evidence, respondents asserted that the reduction would violate §504 of the Rehabilitation Act of 1973 . . . [which] provides: "No otherwise qualified handicapped individual . . . shall, solely by reason of his handicap, be excluded from the participation in, be denied the benefits of, or be subjected to discrimination under any program or activity receiving Federal financial assistance." 29 U.S.C. §794. . . .

[The] major thrust of respondents' attack was directed at the use of any annual limitation on the number of inpatient days covered, for respondents acknowledged that, given the special needs of the handicapped for medical care, any such limitation was likely to disadvantage the handicapped disproportionately. . . . [T]he Medicaid programs of only ten states impose such restrictions.[4] Respondents therefore suggested that Tennessee follow these other states and do away with any limitation on the number of annual inpatient days covered. Instead, argued respondents, the state could limit the number of days of hospital coverage on a per-stay basis, with the number of covered days to vary depending on the recipient's illness (for example, fixing the number of days covered for an appendectomy); the period to be covered for each illness could then be set at a level that would keep Tennessee's Medicaid program as a whole within its budget. . . .

The first question the parties urge on the Court is whether proof of discriminatory animus is always required to establish a violation of §504 and its implementing regulations, or whether federal law also reaches action by a recipient of federal funding that discriminates against the handicapped by effect rather than by design. . . . Discrimination against the handicapped was perceived by Congress to be most often the product, not of invidious animus, but rather of thoughtlessness and indifference—of benign neglect. . . . For example, elimination of architectural barriers was one of the central aims of the Act, yet such barriers were clearly not erected with the aim or intent of excluding the handicapped. . . .

At the same time, the position urged by respondents—that we interpret §504 to reach all action disparately affecting the handicapped—is also troubling. Because the handicapped typically are not similarly situated to the nonhandicapped, respondents' position would in essence require each recipient of federal funds first to evaluate the effect on the handicapped of every proposed action that might touch the interests of the handicapped, and then to consider alternatives for achieving the same objectives with less severe disadvantage to the handicapped. The formalization and policing of this process could lead to a wholly unwieldy administrative and adjudicative burden. . . .

To determine which disparate impacts §504 might make actionable, . . . [we must strike] a balance between the statutory rights of the handicapped to be integrated into society and the legitimate interests of federal grantees in preserving the integrity of their programs: While a grantee need not be required to make "fundamental" or "substantial" modifications to accommodate the handicapped, it may be required to make "reasonable" ones. . . .

[A]n otherwise qualified handicapped individual must be provided with meaningful access to the benefit that the grantee offers. The benefit itself, of course, cannot be defined in a way that effectively denies otherwise qualified handicapped

4. As of 1980 the average ceiling in those states was 37.6 days. Six states also limit the number of reimbursable days per admission, per spell of illness, or per benefit period.

individuals the meaningful access to which they are entitled; to assure meaningful access, reasonable accommodations in the grantee's program or benefit may have to be made. In this case, the 14-day limitation will not deny respondents meaningful access to Tennessee Medicaid services or exclude them from those services.

The new limitation does not invoke criteria that have a particular exclusionary effect on the handicapped; the reduction, neutral on its face, does not distinguish between those whose coverage will be reduced and those whose coverage will not on the basis of any test, judgment, or trait that the handicapped as a class are less capable of meeting or less likely of having. Moreover, it cannot be argued that "meaningful access" to state Medicaid services will be denied by the 14-day limitation on inpatient coverage; nothing in the record suggests that the handicapped in Tennessee will be unable to benefit meaningfully from the coverage they will receive under the 14-day rule.[22] The reduction in inpatient coverage will leave both handicapped and nonhandicapped Medicaid users with identical and effective hospital services fully available for their use, with both classes of users subject to the same durational limitation. . . .

To the extent respondents further suggest that their greater need for prolonged inpatient care means that, to provide meaningful access to Medicaid services, Tennessee must single out the handicapped for more than 14 days of coverage, the suggestion is simply unsound. At base, such a suggestion must rest on the notion that the benefit provided through state Medicaid programs is the amorphous objective of "adequate health care." But Medicaid programs do not guarantee that each recipient will receive that level of health care precisely tailored to his or her particular needs. Instead, the benefit provided through Medicaid is a particular package of health care services, such as 14 days of inpatient coverage. That package of services has the general aim of assuring that individuals will receive necessary medical care, but the benefit provided remains the individual services offered—not "adequate health care."[23] . . .

Section 504 does not require the state to alter this definition of the benefit being offered simply to meet the reality that the handicapped have greater medical needs. To conclude otherwise would be to find that the Rehabilitation Act requires states to view certain illnesses, i.e., those particularly affecting the handicapped, as more important than others and more worthy of cure through government subsidization. Nothing in the legislative history of the Act supports such a conclusion. Cf. Doe v. Colautti, 592 F.2d 704 (3d Cir. 1979) (state may limit covered-private-inpatient-psychiatric care to 60 days even though state sets no limit on duration of coverage for physical illnesses). Section 504 seeks to assure evenhanded treatment and the opportunity for handicapped individuals to participate in and benefit from programs receiving federal assistance. The Act does not, however, guarantee

22. The record does not contain any suggestion that the illnesses uniquely associated with the handicapped or occurring with greater frequency among them cannot be effectively treated, at least in part, with fewer than 14 days' coverage. In addition, the durational limitation does not apply to only particular handicapped conditions and takes effect regardless of the particular cause of hospitalization.

23. . . . [W]e express no opinion on whether annual limits on hospital care are in fact consistent with the Medicaid Act. . . .

the handicapped equal results from the provision of state Medicaid, even assuming some measure of equality of health could be constructed. . . .

   We turn next to respondents' alternative contention . . . that all annual durational limitations discriminate against the handicapped because (1) the effect of such limitations falls most heavily on the handicapped and because (2) this harm could be avoided by the choice of other Medicaid plans that would meet the state's budgetary constraints without disproportionately disadvantaging the handicapped. Viewed in this light, Tennessee's current plan is said to inflict a gratuitous harm on the handicapped that denies them meaningful access to Medicaid services. . . .

   On the contrary, to require that the sort of broad-based distributive decision at issue in this case always be made in the way most favorable, or least disadvantageous, to the handicapped, even when the same benefit is meaningfully and equally offered to them, would be to impose a virtually unworkable requirement on state Medicaid administrators. Before taking any across-the-board action affecting Medicaid recipients, an analysis of the effect of the proposed change on the handicapped would have to be prepared. Presumably, that analysis would have to be further broken down by class of handicap—the change at issue here, for example, might be significantly less harmful to the blind, who use inpatient services only minimally, than to other subclasses of handicapped Medicaid recipients; the state would then have to balance the harms and benefits to various groups to determine, on balance, the extent to which the action disparately impacts the handicapped. In addition, respondents offer no reason that similar treatment would not have to be accorded other groups protected by statute or regulation from disparate-impact discrimination.

   It should be obvious that administrative costs of implementing such a regime would be well beyond the accommodations that are required. . . . As a result, Tennessee need not redefine its Medicaid program to eliminate durational limitations on inpatient coverage, even if in doing so the State could achieve its immediate fiscal objectives in a way less harmful to the handicapped. . . .

■ WILL CLINTON'S PLAN BE FAIR?
Ronald Dworkin*
New York Review of Books, Jan. 13, 1994

   Some critics deny that health-care rationing is really necessary: They argue that if the waste and greed in the American health-care system were eliminated, we could save enough money to give men and women all the medical treatment that could benefit them. But . . . the greatest contribution to the rise in medical costs in recent decades has been the availability of new, high-tech means of diagnosis, like magnetic resonance imaging and new and very expensive techniques like organ transplants and, on the horizon, monoclonal-antibody treatment for cancer. . . . Many politicians and some doctors say that much of the new technology is "unnecessary" or "wasteful." They do not mean that it provides no benefit at all. They mean that its benefit is too limited to justify its cost, and this is an argument for rationing, not an argument that rationing is unnecessary. . . . So we cannot . . . avoid the

*Professor of Law and Philosophy, New York University.

question of justice: What is "appropriate" medical care depends on what it would be unfair to withhold on the grounds that it costs too much. That question has been missing from the public debate. . . .

For millennia doctors have paid lip service, at least, to an ideal of justice in medicine which I shall call the rescue principle. It has two connected parts. The first holds that life and health are, as René Descartes put it, chief among all goods: Everything else is of lesser importance and must be sacrificed for them. The second insists that health care must be distributed on grounds of equality: that even in a society in which wealth is very unequal and equality is otherwise scorned, no one must be denied the medical care he needs just because he is too poor to afford it. These are understandable, even noble, ideals. They are grounded in a shared human understanding of the horror of pain, and, beyond that, of the indispensability of life and health to everything else we do. The rescue principle is so ancient, so intuitively attractive, and so widely supported in political rhetoric, that it might easily be thought to supply the right standard for answering questions about rationing. . . .

In past centuries, however, there was not so huge a gap between the rhetoric of the rescue principle and what it was medically possible for a community to do. But now that science has created so many vastly expensive forms of medical care, it is preposterous that a community should treat longer life as a good that it must provide at any cost—even one that would make the lives of its people barely worth living. . . .

The rescue principle does have something helpful, though negative, to say about the other question of justice, which is how health care should be distributed. It says that if rationing is necessary, it should not be done, as it now largely is in the United States, on the basis of money. But we need more positive advice: What should the basis of rationing be? The egalitarian impulse of the principle suggests that medical care should be distributed according to need. But what does that mean—how is need to be measured? Does someone "need" an operation that might save his life but is highly unlikely to do so? Is someone's need for life-saving treatment affected by the quality his life would have if the treatment were successful? Does the age of patient matter—does someone need or deserve treatment less at 70 than a younger age? Why? How should we balance the need of many people for relief from pain or incapacity against the need of fewer people for life-saving care? At one point the procedures of an Oregon commission appointed to establish medical priorities ranked tooth-capping ahead of appendectomy, because so many teeth can be capped for the price of one operation. Why was that so clearly a mistake? . . .

■ HEALTH CARE RATIONING AND DISABILITY RIGHTS
Philip G. Peters, Jr.*
70 Ind. L.J. 491 (1995)

. . . Any criterion suggested for rationing health care will be controversial. The stakes are high and no popular or ethical consensus has emerged. But allocation

*Professor of Law, University of Missouri-Columbia.

decisions are omnipresent and their continuation is inevitable. . . . Americans have never been willing to pay for all the health care that is of any conceivable benefit, nor are they likely to do so in the future. Unfortunately, the existing mechanisms for deciding who receives what care are blunt and often irrational or unfair, reflecting the influence of wealth, employment, habit, cost, and power. . . . Common sense tells us to give priority to services that do the most good. As a result, an approach which would eliminate only the least beneficial or least cost-effective treatments has considerable potential appeal. It offers both the promise of maximizing health care outcomes from limited resources and the surface allure of scientific objectivity and nonpartisan neutrality. . . .

But rationing the least effective care has a dark side beneath its veneer of objectivity. Any health care allocation scheme which attempts to maximize health care outcomes by giving priority to the most effective treatments has the potential to disfavor disabled patients and others, such as the elderly and the frail, whose quality of life is most impaired or whose conditions are most resistant to cure. As a result, the use of effectiveness criteria to allocate health resources may be challenged as violating society's commitment to equality in general, and to protection of those with the greatest need in particular.

The resolution of this conflict between efficiency and equality has dramatic implications for health policy. . . . It arises whenever effectiveness or cost-effectiveness is used by health care providers or insurers to determine which treatments to provide or insure. Those instances range from bedside decisions by clinicians to macroallocation decisions by benefit plans about coverage of conditions such as AIDS, infertility, or mental illness. In each setting, allocations based on medical utility have the potential to disfavor some patients on the basis of their disability. . . .

I. [EFFECTIVENESS MEASURES AND THE OREGON EXPERIMENT]

Health economists have worked for decades on methodologies for calculating both the effectiveness and the cost-effectiveness of health care expenditures.[11] Originally utilized to compare the value of different treatments for the same disease, these methods were later used to compare the cost-effectiveness of treatments for different diseases. Cost-effectiveness calculations have the appeal of incorporating outcomes research, patient preferences, and expected costs into a rational and potentially sophisticated scheme for maximizing health care outcomes from the available resources. . . .

Theoretically, at least, calculating the effectiveness of a medical service is relatively straightforward. This calculation involves both an estimate of the likely outcomes and an assignment of value to those outcomes. The value assigned to an outcome is determined by the impact which the treatment is expected to have on a patient's quality of life. That value is then adjusted to reflect the probability and duration of the expected benefit. The product of this calculus is a single unit which

---

11. . . . American researchers initially derived the methodology from operations research in engineering and mathematics, using it in the health care setting to measure the tradeoff between survival and quality of life that is implicated by some treatment choices such as conservative care versus aggressive care. The British, most notably Alan Williams, then borrowed the concept as a way of suggesting priorities in their national health care system. . . .

expresses the number and quality of additional years that the treatment is likely to confer. These outcome units have been called both Quality-Adjusted Life Years ("QALYs") and Well Years. . . . .

The theoretical value of these calculations cannot be overstated. They provide a common unit of measurement which permits treatments for different diseases to be compared on the basis of their expected benefit or their cost-effectiveness.[16] Using QALYs or their equivalents, comparisons can be made between such disparate treatments as AZT [for AIDS], autologous bone marrow transplants, infertility treatments, mammography screening, early CT scans for head pain, and heroic care for patients in persistent vegetative states. . . .

As the health economist David Hadorn has emphasized, reliable cost-effectiveness data will help health care providers minimize human suffering to the maximum extent possible with the resources society allocates to health care.[17] . . . Current insurance and clinical practices often make the same kinds of calculations regarding treatment value and cost, albeit in a more intuitive manner. . . . QALYs can help improve the process, making it more rational and, therefore, more just. . . . .

QALYs may also help health decisionmakers to avoid what David Eddy has called "rationing by meat ax." By excluding the least effective treatments for conditions that ordinarily are covered by insurance, savings could be generated to fund more comprehensive coverage of treatments for conditions such as mental health that are typically excluded or restricted. Blanket restrictions on treatments for infertility or mental health, for example, could be replaced by narrower exclusions of only those treatments which are least effective.

In addition, the exclusion of whole groups of uninsured persons from programs such as Medicaid could be replaced by the exclusion of marginally effective care. Oregon, for example, replaced a Medicaid system in which a six-year-old child was eligible when a seven-year-old was not, in which pregnant women had coverage but other women did not, and in which single adults with children were covered but those without children or with a spouse were excluded. In its place, the state has instituted a system [described below] that provides protection for [all people below

16. . . . John Rawls includes several helpful illustrations of comparisons based on cost-effectiveness:

> For example, a patient with severe arthritis of the hip who is unable to work and is in severe distress scores a quality of life of 0.7. . . . His expectation of life of ten years is reduced to seven quality adjusted life years. Successful hip replacement, by eliminating disability and distress, restores 3 QALYs to his total, at an average cost of pounds sterling 750 per QALY.
> Another example is a patient with renal failure undergoing renal dialysis twice a week in hospital for a year. He is unable to work and suffers moderate distress with a quality of life of 0.9. However, hemodialysis is life-saving, so every year adds 0.9 to the number of QALYs he would otherwise enjoy, at a cost of pounds sterling 14000 per QALY.

John Rawls, Castigating QALYs, 15 J. Med. Ethics 143, 144-145 (1989).

17. David C. Hadorn, Setting Health Care Priorities in Oregon: Cost-Effectiveness Meets the Rule of Rescue, 265 JAMA 2218, at 2225 (1991) (describing the original Oregon methodology and the modifications undertaken before submission to the federal government for approval). . . .

the poverty line] by prioritizing the treatments covered.[24] . . . This explicit attention to the difficult choices is in marked contrast to current practices, such as those of physicians who use neutral terms such as "futility" to mask intuitive judgments about the value of treatment to the patient. . . .

But measurement of medical effectiveness also presents serious methodological and ethical problems which must be surmounted before its use expands. The methodological problems arise both from the difficulty of obtaining adequate data about outcomes, benefits, and costs and also from predictable issues of study design. Problems of this kind contributed to the failure of Oregon's initial attempt to prioritize medical treatments entirely on the basis of net benefit. . . .

In order to calculate a treatment's medical effectiveness, analysts must estimate its probable outcome and then place a value on that outcome. Both steps could disfavor disabled patients. When outcomes are taken into account, patients with preexisting disabilities, such as diabetes, cancer, or pulmonary disease, could be disfavored because they often have more difficulty fighting unrelated illnesses (comorbidity) than patients who are otherwise healthy.[36] For example, diabetes reduces the probable effectiveness of some treatments for serious heart ailments. Unchecked alcoholism, another disability, could interfere with the success of organ transplantation. . . .

In addition, seriously disabled patients could be disfavored when values are placed on treatment outcomes. For example, QALY use disfavors lifesaving care for patients who are expected to be disabled after treatment, because saving the life of a disabled person with an impaired quality of life will theoretically generate fewer quality-adjusted life years than saving the life of a person whose quality of life after treatment would be better. . . .

The chance that disabled patients will fare unfavorably in QALY calculations is further accentuated by the risk that the scales used to measure quality of life will unfairly underestimate the quality of life of disabled persons. This was precisely the federal government's criticism of the Oregon quality of life measurements. Yet, until the Oregon plan was submitted for federal government approval, no public attention had been called to the discriminatory potential of prioritization on the basis of medical effectiveness. Although the Oregon plan was vilified on other grounds (principally that only poor people would be asked to make sacrifices to

24. Compare the approach of Missouri, which spent nearly $1 million keeping Nancy Cruzan alive in a persistent vegetative state, while providing Medicaid for only 40 percent of its citizens below the poverty level. Leonard M. Fleck, Just Health Care Rationing: A Democratic Decisionmaking Approach, 140 U. Pa. L. Rev. 1597, 1611 (1992).

36. See, e.g., David Orentlicher, Rationing and the Americans with Disabilities Act, 271 JAMA 308, 310 (1994) (recognizing that patients with pulmonary disease are poor candidates for coronary bypass surgery). In another example, an HMO denied payment for a $170,000 liver transplant requested by an e-antigen positive hepatitis-B patient due to the high rate of reinfection of e-antigen positive patients and the liver shortage. Barnett v. Kaiser Found. Health Plan, Inc., Health Care Facility Mgmt. (CCH) ¶22,594 (N.D. Cal. 1993). The HMO's eight-member advisory board had concluded that transplantation was not an appropriate medical treatment for the patient's condition. The federal district court ruled that the HMO had not abused its discretion in considering this factor, even though transplantation might be the patient's only chance of survival. The disability rights laws were apparently not addressed.

help fund an expansion of health care coverage for other poor people), virtually no public debate on disability rights had occurred. As a result, the [first] Bush administration's rejection of the plan because of discrimination against patients with disabilities surprised most observers and caused some speculation that the administration had simply used the disability rights issue to derail a proposal which it found objectionable for other reasons. . . .

Oregon's initial ranking of treatments . . . was based on a pure cost-effectiveness analysis, but problems with that list[44] induced the Oregon Health Services Commission to abandon that list and produce another one . . . using a more intuitive, multifactorial methodology. Nonetheless, considerations of effectiveness continued to play a crucial role . . . at three junctures. First, the Commission divided all treatments into one of seventeen different categories and then ranked these categories. A sampling of the categories illustrates the methodology: "acute fatal, treatment prevents death with full recovery" (ranked #1); "maternity care" (#2); "acute fatal, treatment prevents death without full recovery" (#3); "comfort care" (#7); "acute nonfatal, treatment causes return to previous health state" (#10); and "infertility services" (#15). These rankings gave priority to treatments which produced complete cures over those which ordinarily produce only partial recovery. In this way, the Commission retained a blunt measure of effectiveness in its ranking process. The Commission also considered cost-effectiveness as one of many factors used to create and rank these categories.

Second, the Commission used QALYs to rank treatments within the 17 categories.[51] Third and finally, the Commissioners reviewed the resulting list and adjusted

44. . . . In David Eddy's view, Oregon's inability to estimate accurately either costs or benefits precluded reliance on its initial list. Categories of services and outcomes were defined too broadly. For example, "trouble speaking" could range from mild lisp to mutism. Duration of treatment benefits was poorly differentiated. Cost data were incomplete or inaccurate. And the list generated serious doubts whether the values assigned to treatment outcomes, especially lifesaving treatments, had been accurately measured. David M. Eddy, Oregon's Methods: Did Cost-Effectiveness Analysis Fail?, 266 JAMA 2135 (1991); David M. Eddy, Oregon's Plan: Should It Be Approved?, 266 JAMA 2439 (1991).

Counter-intuitive rankings resulted from these problems. Reportedly, "burn over large areas of the body" scored the same as an "upset stomach." Michael Astrue, then-general counsel of the Department of Health and Human Services, was startled that treatments for ectopic pregnancies and appendicitis were ranked below some dental caps and splints for temporomandibular joint disorder. . . . Unwillingness to accept the implications of cost-effectiveness analysis, especially for the prioritization of noncritical care over life-extending care, may also partially explain the adverse reaction to this list. . . .

51. Benefits were measured using Dr. Robert M. Kaplan's Quality of Well-Being ("QWB") scale. Using the results of a random telephone poll of 1,001 Oregon households in which respondents were asked to rank 23 symptoms and 6 levels of functional impairment, the Commission assigned a value to various states of health, such as requiring a wheelchair or having severe burns. The benefits associated with each treatment were then calculated by using the values for the various outcomes provided by the telephone survey and weighting those values to reflect the probability of their occurrence. Expected outcomes were ascertained by polling practitioners. Outcomes (such as death or return to former health) were estimated five years after treatment. Net benefit (QWB) scores were derived by comparing the QWB score without treatment to the QWB score with treatment. The Commission multiplied the expected QWB by the duration of the benefit (thereby obtaining a measure of quality-adjusted life years or QALYs). In most cases, duration was the patient's life expectancy.

some of the rankings using their "professional judgments and their interpretation of the community values." The Commissioners imposed a "reasonableness" test upon themselves, taking into account effectiveness and cost along with other factors such as public health impact, incidence of condition, and social costs. The result was a ranking of 709 treatments of which 587 were to be funded in the first year. . . .

[T]he Department of Health and Human Services ("HHS") announced that Oregon had been denied a waiver [of the usual Medicaid coverage requirements] because its plan violated the Americans with Disabilities Act ("ADA"). . . . HHS specifically identified two instances in which disabilities had been impermissibly taken into account: (1) the ranking of alcoholic cirrhosis of the liver (#690) below other cirrhoses (#366) and (2) the ranking of extremely low birth weight babies (#708) below heavier babies (#22).

Oregon denied that it had violated the ADA, but nevertheless complied with HHS's demands. Approval was not granted until Oregon had eliminated quality of life data from its formal methodology and had abandoned the separate classification of alcoholic cirrhosis and low birth weight babies. In addition, the newly elected Clinton administration insisted that Oregon no longer disfavor infertility treatments. In March, 1993, the Oregon Commission approved a new list which was based first on mortality and then, as a tie-breaker, on cost considerations. It was then adjusted by the Commission to reflect community values, such as a preference for preventive services and a dislike for medically ineffective care. . . .

This exchange between Oregon and the federal government has dramatic implications for health policy. Oregon's capitulation has cast a shadow over similar endeavors by other states. In its wake, considerable confusion exists about the permissible role of effectiveness in allocating health resources. . . . Alexander Morgan Capron, an . . . advocate of rationing, was . . . dire in his assessment. "As some form of rationing is an inevitable part of all health insurance," he concluded, "the ADA roadblock to rational prioritization of services by their expected benefit should be of grave concern to us all."[70]

Was the federal government correct? Exactly what limits do the disability rights laws place on the use of effectiveness criteria? Answering these questions requires a basic understanding of the disability rights laws.

II. FEDERAL DISABILITY RIGHTS LAW

A. THE BASIC PARADIGM

Two federal statutes protect disabled individuals from improper discrimination in health care decisionmaking: The Rehabilitation Act of 1973 and the more recent Americans with Disabilities Act of 1990 ("ADA"). . . . Although the ADA is much more detailed than the Rehabilitation Act and the wording of the various titles of the ADA are slightly different, the basic paradigm of the two federal laws protecting disability rights can be briefly summarized. Section 504 of the Rehabilitation Act bars discrimination by any program receiving federal financial assistance or any executive agency against an "otherwise qualified" individual with a disability "by

70. Alexander M. Capron, Oregon's Disability: Principles or Politics?, Hastings Ctr. Rep., Nov.-Dec. 1992, at 18, 20.

reason of her or his disability." The ADA extends this prohibition against discrimination "on the basis of" disability to state programs and private entities that do not receive federal funding.

Federal law defines disabled persons as individuals who have a "physical or mental impairment which substantially limits a major life activity," "who have a record of such an impairment," or who are "regarded as having such an impairment." The regulations list examples such as blindness, mental retardation, emotional illness, cancer, heart disease, and HIV infection. . . .

Because functional impairment may affect a person's qualifications for some benefits, the laws governing disability rights permit consideration of a person's disability if the condition legitimately affects that person's ability to meet the essential eligibility requirements. This basic structure is quite different from civil rights legislation governing race because race is presumed to be irrelevant.

While acknowledging that disabilities are sometimes relevant, Congress also recognized that their consideration would often result in the exclusion of disabled persons who could become qualified with modest modifications of policies or practices. To prevent this, Congress required that a reasonable effort be made to accommodate the needs of disabled persons before concluding that they are ineligible. By conferring on people with disabilities this right to affirmative assistance, Congress endorsed, at least in a limited way, an egalitarian approach to distributive justice which allocates extra resources for those persons with the greatest need. . . . To summarize this basic paradigm, a disabled person is qualified to receive health benefits or services if, with reasonable accommodation, she is able to meet the "essential" or "necessary" eligibility criteria. . . .

When the issue is joined, as it was in Oregon, the statutory terms *essential* and *necessary* seem sufficiently elastic to permit courts to consider whether medical utility is a permissible basis for disfavoring disabled patients. In effect, courts would be deciding whether the objective of maximizing health outcomes is an "essential" program objective within the meaning of the equal opportunity laws. . . . HHS did exactly this in responding to the Oregon waiver request. . . .

While the legal status of rationing based on effectiveness is still uncertain, underwriting exclusions based on anticipated cost have express congressional sanction. In the ADA, Congress authorized benefits plans to engage in "the legitimate classification of risk." As a result, plans remain free to consider how various disabilities influence a person's risk of death or illness. This exclusion permits risk-bearing health plans (but not necessarily practicing physicians) to consider the anticipated cost of treating various disabilities. However, the statutory exemption for underwriting practices does not appear to sanction the use of QALYs or other measures of a given treatment's effectiveness. Unlike restrictions based on underwriting risks, eligibility restrictions based on effectiveness are not based on the risk of subscriber illness and its predicted cost. They are based, instead, on predicted outcomes. Patients whose care is relatively ineffective are not necessarily any more costly or financially risky than other patients. . . . As a result, only the cost portion of cost-effectiveness analysis has clear statutory blessing, and even then only when it is part of an underwriting process. . . .

Until the courts rule on this issue, it is possible . . . that employers will be flatly prohibited from adopting health benefits plans that discriminate on the basis of disability for nonunderwriting reasons. . . . [To overcome this objection, employers and insurers will need to establish that] the use of effectiveness criteria is vital to the goal of maximizing health outcomes from fixed resources. . . .

■ RATIONING HEALTH CARE IN BRITAIN AND THE UNITED STATES
Leonard J. Nelson, III*
7 J. Health & Biomed. L. 175 (2011)

Rationing is a "dirty word," "a code word for immoral, inappropriate, or greedy,"[4] and "a four letter word."[5] And not surprisingly, rationing was at the forefront of the recent debate in the United States over health care reform. Former Governor Sarah Palin's Facebook page allegation that the Democrat's health care reform legislation included "death panels," which would ration care for the sick and elderly, was later named "lie of the year" by the fact checkers at Politifacts.com, but it did garner significant attention. . . .

Although [Sarah Palin's] claims are "sensationalistic," they draw attention to a central truth, i.e., . . . that rationing will have to be a part of any publicly subsidized program for the provision of health care to maintain fiscal sustainability. . . . Dr. [Ezekiel Emanuel, former director of bioethics at the NIH,] identified three levels of health care allocation decisions with respect to government health care decisions. First, macro-allocation decisions determine how much of the gross national product ("GNP") to spend on health care services as opposed to national defense, transportation, etc. Second, there is an intermediate level where a determination will be made as to the basic package of health care services that all citizens are entitled to receive. Third, micro-allocation decisions about which patients are eligible to receive particular services. At the intermediate level, he suggested the need for transparency in the form of "public forums to deliberate about which health services should be considered basic and should be socially guaranteed."[6] . . .

Medicare is already engaged in stealth rationing through the Centers for Medicare and Medicaid Services' the use of National Coverage Determinations ("NCDs"), in which CMS refuses to cover expensive new technologies; CMS nevertheless denies taking cost into account in making decisions relating to coverage.[7] . . . [I]t is unlikely that Congress will give CMS the [express] power to ration health care using a cost-effectiveness analysis. . . . As long as Medicare is a service benefit program, it will be very difficult, politically, to control costs. . . .

*Professor, Cumberland School of Law, Samford University, and Senior Scholar, Lister Hill Center for Health Policy, University of Alabama at Birmingham School of Public Health.

4. Peter A. Ubel, Pricing Life: Why It's Time for Health Care Rationing xvii (MIT Press 2001).

5. Henry J. Aaron & William B. Schwartz with Melissa A. Cox, Can We Say No? The Challenge of Rationing Health Care 131 (2005).

6. Ezekiel Emanuel, Where Civic Republicanism Meets Deliberative Democracy, Hastings Center Rep. 12 (Nov.-Dec. 1996).

7. Jacqueline Fox, The Hidden Role of Cost: Medicare Decisions, Transparency and Public Trust, 79 U. Cin. L. Rev. 1 (2010).

[D]uring the debate over health care reform, President Obama spoke of the need for a "very difficult democratic conversation" about health care at the end of life, even expressing doubt about whether his own grandmother should have been given a hip replacement when she was terminally ill. But he also acknowledged that, "It is very difficult to imagine the country making those decisions just through the normal political channels. And that's part of why you have to have some independent group that can give you guidance." . . .

The ongoing debate about the possible role of comparative effectiveness research in health care reform illustrates the political difficulty of rationing health care. . . . The 2009 federal stimulus legislation created [an agency to conduct comparative effectiveness research, which PPACA renamed] the Patient Centered Outcomes Research Institute ("PCORI"). . . . Perhaps in response to concerns about rationing, PPACA expressly precludes the Secretary of the Health and Human Services ("HHS") from relying solely on comparative effectiveness research to deny coverage or from using PCORI sponsored comparative effectiveness research "in a manner that treats extending the life of an elderly, disabled, or terminally ill individual as of lower value than extending the life of an individual who is younger, nondisabled, or not terminally ill." . . . The Secretary is also precluded from using comparative effectiveness "with the intent to discourage an individual from choosing a health care treatment based on how the individual values the tradeoff between extending the length of their life and the risk of disability." . . . [T]hese provisions have been interpreted to prohibit the PCORI "from developing or using cost-per-QALY thresholds," and these provisions have been decried as reflecting "a certain xenophobia toward the kinds of approaches used in Britain, where the National Institute of Health and Clinical Excellence ["NICE"] makes recommendations about technologies and services on the basis of cost-per-QALY thresholds."[8] . . .

[PPACA's] continued reliance on employment-based insurance may make it more difficult to impose rationing in the Medicare program because the standard of care for all is influenced by the care provided through relatively generous employment-based plans. . . . With the exception of "grandfathered" plans, all small group and individual plans offered both within and outside of the exchanges will have to offer at least the "essential health benefits" package. This package is supposed to include the elements of a typical employer plan. [Also, the statute forbids designing "benefits in ways that discriminate against individuals because of their age, disability, or expected length of life" or that are "subject to denial . . . on the basis of the individuals' age or expected length of life or of the individuals' present or predicted disability, degree of medical dependency, or quality of life."] . . .

As noted in the Washington Post, defining the "essential health benefits" is an important and difficult task; "Draw up a package that is too bare-bones and millions of Americans could be deprived of meaningful health coverage when they need it most—undercutting a central goal of the health care law. Add in too many expensive benefits and premiums could spike to unaffordable levels." . . .

PPACA [also] establishes the Independent Payment Advisory Board ("IPAB") for the purpose of reducing the per capita rate of growth in Medicare spending.

---

8. Peter J. Neumann & Milton C. Weinstein, Legislating Against Use of Cost-Effectiveness Information, 363 New Eng. J. Med. 1495, 1495 (2010).

The board is to be composed of fifteen full-time members who are health care experts drawn from various fields. Beginning in 2014, IPAB is required to make annual recommendations to Congress to reduce per capita growth rates when these costs exceed a targeted per capita growth rate that the Chief Actuary of CMS sets. These recommendations will be implemented unless subsequent congressional action blocks them. Notably, a 3/5 vote in the Senate is required to change the IPAB recommendations. But there are some significant limitations on the nature of these recommendations. PPACA provides that these recommendations, "shall not include any recommendation to ration health care, . . . increase Medicare beneficiary cost-sharing[,] . . . or otherwise restrict benefits or modify eligibility criteria." Prior to 2020, the recommendation also cannot include cuts in payment rates for hospitals and suppliers, which PPACA already targets.

. . . Michael Tanner, a health policy expert at the Cato Institute, [notes] that in light of the restrictions on IPAB, it . . . "will end up as neutered as previous attempts to impose fiscal discipline on government health care programs."[9] With all the constraints on its actions, and the possibilities for Congress to void any cuts proposed, it is unlikely IPAB will be successful in reducing costs in the Medicare program. . . .

Health policy experts customarily refer to the health care "Iron Triangle." . . . The three angles of the triangle or triad are cost, access, and quality. It has been observed that, "increasing the performance of the health care system along any one of these dimensions can compromise one or both of the other dimensions, regardless of the amount that is spent on health care."[10] . . . The debate over the impact of PPACA on Medicare costs illustrates the constraints of the iron triangle. . . . While in theory it may be possible to increase health care access, reduce costs, and improve quality, in practice it is virtually impossible. The reduction of costs in public programs without endangering aggregate quality would have to be based on across the board rigorous application of cost-effectiveness analysis that would result in the denial of beneficial treatments to individuals. It is unlikely that Congress has the political will to impose such a regime. . . . Rationing is certainly the third rail of American politics, and the cost controls in PPACA may not be sufficient to save us from ourselves.

Notes: Rationing Insurance Benefits; Disability Discrimination; Cost-Effectiveness Studies

1. *Medical Effectiveness Measures.* It is important to distinguish among ordinary medical effectiveness, comparative effectiveness, cost-effectiveness, and cost-benefit analysis. Ordinary effectiveness determines simply whether a medical procedure works at all. Comparative effectiveness asks whether it works better than another method for the same condition. Cost-effectiveness analysis also asks how much it

9. Michael D. Tanner, Bad Medicine: A Guide to the Real Costs and Consequences of the New Health Care Law 23 (The Cato Institute, 2011) [excerpted at page 57].
10. Fed. Trade Commission & the Department of Justice, Improving Health Care: A Dose of Competition 6 (2004).

costs to achieve an increment in health improvement. And finally, cost-benefit analysis asks whether an effectiveness improvement is actually worth what it costs.

QALYs were devised so that effectiveness can be judged based on quality of life rather than simply number of lives or years of life saved. A generic unit of health improvement also allows comparisons between totally different treatments and disease conditions, such as determining whether prenatal care yields more medical benefit than liver transplants. That kind of comparative cost analysis can help to determine the best use of limited funds, but it cannot tell us what total health expenditures should be, that is, whether to do *both* prenatal care and liver transplants, or *neither* and instead spend the money on education or housing. If that decision is to be made quantitatively, it requires a cost-benefit analysis, which compares the cost of medical procedures with their benefit in terms of dollars. This is obviously much more controversial since it requires that a value be placed on human life and suffering.

It is important to stress that none of the techniques surveyed by Philip Peters goes this far. They only ask, comparatively, whether one benefit is greater than another, not whether the expenditure is worth it at all. But, in adopting the rubric of "comparative effectiveness" rather than "cost effectiveness" in the Affordable Care Act, did Congress mean to say that costs may not be considered at all? For example, it has been estimated that the cost of administering Pap smears, which detect cervical cancer, is roughly $5,000 per additional year of life expectancy for testing every three years but $200,000-400,000 per year of life saved for annual testing. Should insurers, either public or private, be required to fund annual testing? Which would you choose as a patient paying out of pocket? See Sarah Feldman, How Often Should We Screen for Cervical Cancer?, 349 New Eng. J. Med. 1495 (2003) (recommending testing every three years after a series of negative one-year exams).

During the heat of national debate over the Affordable Care Act, political opponents raised yet another storm of controversy over a government blue ribbon panel that happened to issue a recommendation about limiting routine mammography screening to every two years for women over 50, rather than every year and starting at age 40, for women with no prior symptoms or family history of breast cancer. The panel's rationale was to reduce the medical harms from "false positive" results that lead to needless biopsies and surgeries. But, it was also influenced by studies indicating that it would cost $340,000 or more per QALY gained to screen more frequently or at younger ages. See John Schousboe et al., Personalizing Mammography by Breast Density and Other Risk Factors for Breast Cancer, 144 Ann. Intern. Med. 10 (2011).

Discussing comparative medical effectiveness generally, see Eleanor Kinney, Comparative Effectiveness Research Under the Patient Protection and Affordable Care Act, 37 Am. J.L. & Med. 522 (2011); Richard Saver, Health Care Reform's Wild Care: The Uncertain Effectiveness of Comparative Effectiveness Research, 159 U. Pa. L. Rev. 2147 (2011); Sean Tunis, Reflections on Science, Judgment, and Value in Evidence-Based Decision Making, 26 Health Aff. w500 (2007); Note, 21 Ann. Health L. 329 (2012); Symposium, 31 Health Aff. 2225 (2012); Symposium, 29 Health Aff. 1756 (2010). Addressing Medicare's refusal to explicitly consider costs in making its coverage decisions, see Peter J. Neumann et al., Medicare and Cost-Effectiveness Analysis, 353 New Eng. J. Med. 1516 (2006); S. Dhruva et al., CMS's Landmark Decision on CT Colonography, 361 New Eng. J. Med. 1316 (2009); Peter

Neumann, Medicare's National Coverage Decisions for Technologies, 27 Health Aff. 1620 (2008). For broader discussions of the use of cost-benefit analyses in legal and regulatory settings generally, see Matthew Adler & Eric Posner, Cost-Benefit Analysis: Legal, Economic, and Philosophical Perspectives (2001); Symposium, 29 J. Leg. Stud. 837 (2000).

2. *The Scope of Disability Discrimination Laws.* The potential impact of disability discrimination law on many aspects of medical decisionmaking has come to light only gradually. This is because many medical conditions qualify under the broad definition of "disability," explained at page 132, not just stereotypical "handicaps." That being the case, how far might courts and agencies actually go in micromanaging medically informed decisions by covered institutions? Observe how hard the *Choate* Court struggles simply to rule that a facially neutral restriction on coverage is not discriminatory.

The *Choate* precedent has nothing to say, however, about coverage and treatment restrictions that target specific diseases and treatments. It is these restrictions whose legality is still very much in doubt. For instance, most commentators believe that it would clearly violate the ADA and §504 for an employer to exclude or limit coverage for AIDS, and this is the interpretation that the EEOC has taken in a number of enforcement actions. But what about other more common, less objectionable restrictions? In *Choate* the Supreme Court cited approvingly a Second Circuit opinion holding that the limitation of mental health coverage does not violate §504. See also Modderno v. King, 82 F.3d 1059 (D.C. Cir. 1996) (disparity in coverage of mental health treatment is not disability discrimination; to rule otherwise would be "to invite challenges to virtually every exercise of the [insurer's or employer's] discretion with respect to the allocation of benefits amongst an encyclopedia of illnesses"). What is the difference between AIDS restrictions and mental health restrictions? Could it be the fact that many mental health patients are not disabled, whereas all AIDS patients are? Then what about the exclusion of experimental cancer treatment? See Henderson v. Bodine Aluminum, 70 F.3d 958 (8th Cir. 1995) (denying expensive new therapy for breast cancer is potentially discrimination where the plan covers this treatment for other cancers and there is evidence it works for breast cancer). But see Lenox v. Healthwise of Kentucky, 149 F.3d 453 (6th Cir. 1998) (no ADA violation in excluding coverage for heart transplants). See Jane Korn, Cancer and the ADA: Rethinking Disability, 74 S. Cal. L. Rev. 339 (2001).

It is also important to realize how many activities and programs the discrimination laws cover. Section 504 covers federal government jobs, programs, and contractors. The ADA covers state and private entities. It is divided into several titles, each of which covers different realms of activity (employment, transportation, public accommodations). The most obvious application to private health insurance is through the employment title, since insurance is an employment benefit. It is also possible, however, to construe insurance as a public accommodation. The public accommodations title is usually thought of as requiring only physical access to places of business, but some courts initially interpreted this title to require businesses to design their products and services to accommodate disabilities. Regarding insurance, this might mean that not only the refusal to sell insurance but also the terms of coverage would be subject to ADA scrutiny. Several circuit courts, however, have rejected this interpretation, holding instead that the public accommodations title was not intended to "require a seller to alter his product to make it equally valuable to the disabled." Doe v. Mutual of Omaha Insurance Co., 179 F.3d 557 (7th Cir. 1999). See also Parker v. Metropolitan Health, 121 F.3d 1006 (6th Cir. 1997) (en banc). As a consequence, courts have upheld caps of $10,000 on payment for AIDS treatment, when they are in insurance plans not purchased by employers (and therefore not subject to the employment discrimination portion of the ADA). See generally Sharona Hoffman, AIDS Caps, Contraceptive Coverage, and the Law, 23 Cardozo L. Rev. 1313 (2002); Jeffrey S. Manning, Are Insurance Companies Liable Under the Americans with Disabilities Act?, 88 Cal. L. Rev. 607 (2000); Luke Sobota, Does Title III of the ADA Regulate Insurance?, 66 U. Chi. L. Rev. 243 (1999); Comment, 28 Am. J.L. & Med. 107 (2002).

3. *Meaningful Access Without Fundamental Alteration.* Does the Supreme Court's "meaningful access to benefits" test provide a good guide for what's permissible? Meaningful access to *which* benefits? To the particular item of treatment being sought or to insurance coverage generally? See Doe v. Chandler, 83 F.3d 1150 (9th Cir. 1996) (limiting welfare for disabled recipients but not for dependent children does not discriminate against the disabled because states may craft different benefits for different programs).

The *Choate* decision also spoke in terms of avoiding requirements that would fundamentally alter the nature of the product or program. This is the defense on which Philip Peters rests most of his justification for effectiveness analysis in the remainder of his article. (Additional excerpts can be found on the Web site for this book, www.health-law.org.) But this issue is also largely untested in the courts. In contrast with *Choate*, see Olmstead v. L.C., 527 U.S. 581 (1999), which found a potential ADA violation where a state Medicaid plan covered long-term hospitalization for mental illness but not less restrictive community placement options, and the Court suggested that it would not be a "fundamental alteration" to require the state to expand its coverage if doing so can be "reasonably accommodated" without straining the budget for other mental health services. Compare Lovell v. Chandler, 303 F.3d 1039 (9th Cir. 2002) (finding an ADA violation where the state expanded eligibility for Medicaid up to three times the poverty level but excluded disabled participants from the increased eligibility parameters, even though the state said this was all it could afford). See Sara Rosenbaum, *Olmstead v. L.C.*: Implications for Medicaid and Other Publicly Funded Health Services, 12 Health Matrix 93 (2002).

For an argument that these distinctions fail to adequately protect against disability discrimination through disparate impact, see D. Orentlicher, Destructuring Disability: Rationing of Health Care and Unfair Discrimination Against the Sick, 31 Harv. C.R.-C.L. L. Rev. 51 (1996). According to another law professor, "the ADA is an inadequate and even inept tool for resolving whether we should tolerate cost-conscious [insurance] policies" because its concepts are so poorly suited for articulating and understanding the underlying social policy debate. Mary A. Crossley, Medical Futility and Disability Discrimination, 81 Iowa L. Rev. 179 (1995). For additional discussion of ADA issues generally and in insurance coverage and medical care, see Leslie Francis & Anita Silvers, Debilitating *Alexander v. Choate*: "Meaningful Access" to Health Care for People with Disabilities, 35 Fordham Urb. L.J. 447 (2008); Alexander Abbe, "Meaningful Access" to Health Care and the Remedies Available to Medicaid Managed Care Recipients Under the ADA and the Rehabilitation Act, 147 U. Pa. L. Rev. 1161 (1999); Mary Crossley, Becoming Visible: The ADA's Impact on Health Care for Persons with Disabilities, 52 Ala. L. Rev. 51 (2000);

Mary Crossley, The Disability Kaleidoscope, 74 Notre Dame L. Rev. 521 (1999); Maxwell J. Mehlman et al., When Do Health Care Decisions Discriminate Against People with Disabilities?, 22 J. Health Pol. Pol'y & L. 1385 (Dec. 1997).

4. *PPACA: Tossing Around the Hot Potato.* Against this backdrop of uncertainty, is there clarity in PPACA's legislative language that forbids designing "benefits in ways that discriminate against individuals because of their age, disability, or expected length of life" or that are "subject to denial . . . on the basis of the individuals' . . . present or predicted disability, degree of medical dependency, or quality of life"? As Professor Nelson notes, this appears aimed at prohibiting the government's use of QALYs to define the standard set of "essential health benefits" that private insurers must cover (in the individual and small group markets). However, another statutory provision says that "nothing . . . shall be construed to prohibit . . . [health insurers] from carrying out utilization management techniques that are commonly used as of the date of enactment of this Act." Does that mean that rationing, or cost-effectiveness analysis, is fine as long as the government does not do it?

Perhaps due to the controversy over rationing, the Obama administration ruled that each state gets to decide how to define "essential health benefits" for its own jurisdiction. Also, as of early 2013, the federal government so far has avoided even establishing IPAB, Medicare's Independent Payment Advisory Board. The administration may also be awaiting the outcome of a case challenging whether its special legislative rules are constitutional.

For further discussion of the inevitable difficulties in balancing the ACA's competing goals in light of its various restrictions on rationing, see Sara Rosenbaum et al., The Essential Health Benefits Provisions of the Affordable Care Act: Implications for People with Disabilities (Commonwealth Fund, 2011); Alan Cohen, The Debate over Health Care Rationing: Déjà Vu All Over Again?, 49 Inquiry 90 (2012); Emily Stopa, Harnessing Comparative Effectiveness Research to Bend the Cost Curve and Achieve Successful Health Reform, 13 U. Pa. J. Const. L. 815 (2011); Amy B. Monahan, Initial Thoughts on Essential Health Benefits, NYU Review of Employee Benefits and Executive Compensation (2010); Jessica Mantel, Setting National Coverage Standards for Health Plans Under Health Care Reform, 58 UCLA L. Rev. 221 (2010); Timothy S. Jost, The Independent Payment Advisory Board, 363 New Eng. J. Med. 103 (2010); Michael Cook, IPAB: Part of the Solution for Bending the Cost Curve, 4 J. Health & Life Sci. L. 102 (Oct. 2010); James Miller, The Patient-Centered Outcomes Research Institute, 4 J. Health & Life Sci. L. 4 (Oct. 2010); Troy Oechsner & Magda Schaler-Haynes, Keeping It Simple: Health Plan Benefit Standardization and Regulatory Choice Under the Affordable Care Act, 74 Alb. L. Rev. 241 (2011); Ann Marie Marciarille & J. Bradford DeLong, Bending the Health Cost Curve: The Promise and Peril of the Independent Payment Advisory Board, 22 Health Matrix 75 (2012); Institute of Medicine, Essential Health Benefits: Balancing Coverage and Cost (2011); Jesse Hill, What Is the Meaning of Health? Constitutional Implications of Defining "Medical Necessity" and "Essential Health Benefits" Under the Affordable Care Act, 38 Am. J.L. & Med. 445 (2012).

5. *Rationing Criteria and Social Values.* QALYs are objectionable on other moral grounds besides disability discrimination. As discussed most forcefully by David Hadorn and John Harris, cited by Peters, the mathematics of QALYs mean that it is equally as valuable to save ten years from one person's life as it is to save one year of life for ten people. This utilitarian logic does not fit most people's intuitions. See

John Taurek, Should the Numbers Count?, 6 Phil. & Pub. Aff. 293 (1977). On the other hand, if we are to avoid use of rationing criteria that contain any controversial value judgments, we would have to adopt completely arbitrary rationing criteria such as a simple lottery, or treating whoever asks first. Most people would view these "neutral" criteria as even more irrational and objectionable. Einer Elhauge, Allocating Health Care Morally, 82 Cal. L. Rev. 1449 (1994).

The "rescue principle" mentioned by Prof. Dworkin exists in other social arenas such as natural disasters and high-risk recreational activity, where we spend seemingly unlimited amounts responding to crisis situations when people are visibly threatened with death or disability at the same time that we neglect less expensive preventive measures that might avoid situation in the first place. This is also known as the paradox of "statistical versus identifiable lives." If the thrust of this argument is to spend more on prevention, few would disagree, but if the thrust is to spend less on heroic measures, the argument is met with the following response:

> I will risk my life on the roads to do nothing more than secure a bag of potato chips, not to mention take the risk of eating them simply for fleeting gustatory sensations. But should I come up short in the potato chips v. life lottery, and suffer either a car or a cardiovascular accident, I do not expect society to respond by saying, "Well, tough luck, but you made an open-eyed trade-off here." No, I expect EMTs to rush to the scene and pound on my chest and speed me to the hospital in reckless disregard of the laws set down to reduce the risk faced by other travelers in search of potato chips and other goods. This social response, I am suggesting, can be seen as a way of marking the fact that our lives are shot through with incommensurable values, and that we have to wind our way through them in a way that does its best to acknowledge their separate significance.

J. L. Nelson, Publicity and Pricelessness: Grassroots Decisionmaking and Justice in Rationing, 19 J. Med. & Phil. 333 (1994). In a similar vein, Calabresi and Bobbitt explain that rationing is more socially acceptable when the tragic choices are hidden from view, as they are when the harms are merely statistical, than when identifiable victims of rationing can clearly be seen. G. Calabresi & P. Bobbitt, Tragic Choices (1978). Does this mean that effective rationing can be done only out of public view? If so, is that a legitimate reason to promote or tolerate less explicit or "democratic" forms of rationing? Prof. Gregg Bloche argues that health care law and policy is in a "confused, even chaotic state" because it assumes that medical resources can be allocated in a "systematically rational manner," which is not feasible or even desirable considering differing values, limitations on human rationality, and inconsistent understandings about what rationality means or requires. Instead, he urges an "inelegant" approach that "defines our aims more modestly, consistent with a picture of rationality as limited by context, discontinuous across different settings, and changeable with time." Gregg Bloche, The Invention of Health Law, 91 Cal. L. Rev. 247 (2003). Does that make things less confused?

6. *Readings on Rationing.* It is impossible to overemphasize the importance of health care rationing as an aspect of health law and policy. Other aspects of this issue, perhaps the most perplexing of the health care policy issues of our time, are explored in Chapters 1.C.4 and 4.C. For further elaboration of moral and public policy objections to and defenses of QALYs and other criteria for rationing, see

Larry Churchill, Rationing Health Care in America (1987); Frances Kamm, Morality and Mortality (1993); John Kilner, Who Lives? Who Dies? (1990); Paul Menzel, Strong Medicine: The Ethical Rationing of Health Care (1990); Eric Rakowski, Taking and Saving Lives, 93 Colum. L. Rev. 1063 (1993); Matthew D. Adler, QALYs and Policy Evaluation: A New Perspective, 6 Yale J. Health Pol'y L. & Ethics 1 (2006); Sharona Hoffman, Unmanaged Care: Towards Moral Fairness in Health Care Coverage, 78 Ind. L.J. 659 (2003); Norman Daniels & James E. Sabin, Setting Limits Fairly: Can We Learn to Share Medical Resources? (2000); Jennifer Prah Ruger, Health, Capability and Justice: Toward a New Paradigm of Health Ethics, Policy and Law, 15 Cornell J.L. Pub. Pol'y 403 (2006); Amy B. Monahan, Value-Based Mandated Health Benefits, 80 U. Colo. L. Rev. 127-200 (2009); Ani B. Satz, The Limits of Health Care Reform, 59 Ala. L. Rev. 1451 (2008); Symposium, 12 Value in Health S1 (2009).

7. *Oregon's Rationing List.* It is fascinating to observe how Oregon's bold approach actually functioned when implemented in real-world settings. Subsequent evaluation reveals that the list has not generated substantial savings. Many of the items eliminated from funding are fairly "small ticket," are requested only rarely, or were not covered in the first place. In other instances, physicians have been able to obtain coverage by recharacterizing the patient's condition as being more serious. Also, many Oregon Medicaid patients are covered by HMOs in which physicians are paid a capitation payment rather than fee-for-service, so physicians often provide the service even when they are not required to if it is relatively inexpensive. Accordingly, Oregon's expansion of Medicaid eligibility has been financed mostly by increased taxation and legislative appropriations, not by savings from the list. The main impact of the list, according to the following reviews, was its use as a political tool to secure more funds from the legislature. Symposium, 24 J. Health Pol. Pol'y & L. 151 (1999). Once that started to fail, however, Oregon turned to another form of rationing: the lottery. In response to budget cuts during the Great Recession, rather than eliminate its Medicaid expansion, it began to randomly enroll only a fraction of those who were eligible to join. H. Allen et al., What the Oregon Health Study Can Tell Us About Expanding Medicaid, 29 Health Aff. 1498 (2010). For further discussion of the Oregon scheme and the legality of QALYs under the ADA, see Kevin P. Quinn, Viewing Health Care as a Common Good: Looking Beyond Political Liberalism, 73 S. Cal. L. Rev. 277 (2000); Note, 93 Colum. L. Rev. 1985 (1993); Note, 106 Harv. L. Rev. 1296 (1993).

8. *Medicaid Coverage.* Many of the decisions that require Medicaid to fund controversial procedures such as sex-change operations and liver transplants for former alcoholics are reasoned in terms of disability discrimination, even though they are based on the Medicaid statute. They reason that the basic standard of rationality and nonarbitrariness required by the Medicaid statute prevents covering a medically beneficial treatment for some conditions but not for others. Therefore, Medicaid must either exclude the treatment altogether or selectively exclude it under generic criteria such as medically necessary or experimental. See, e.g., Salgado v. Kirschner, 878 P.2d 659 (Ariz. 1994) (unreasonable to cover liver transplant only for children; medically relevant factors, not age alone, should determine coverage).

Imagine that you are in charge of allocating limited government health care funds. Where, if anywhere, would you want to set limits? Would you fund a liver transplant for a patient whose recovery is only 50 percent certain? For a patient with only partial liver dysfunction whose life is not at stake? For an alcoholic? Would you support lung transplants for cigarette smokers? Heart transplants for overeaters? If the legislature appropriated an additional $5 million to use at your discretion, would you choose (1) a large expansion in low-cost prenatal care, which would help decrease the high costs of caring for premature births, or (2) a few expensive organ transplants, or (3) some of both? Which of these decisions would handicap discrimination principles allow? On transplant funding issues generally, see Lisa Deutsch, Medicaid Payment for Organ Transplants: The Extent of Mandated Coverage, 30 Colum. J.L. & Soc. Probs. 185 (1997); Clark Havighurst & Nancy King, Liver Transplantation in Massachusetts: Public Policymaking as Morality Play, 19 Ind. L. Rev. 955 (1986); Note, 79 Minn. L. Rev. 1232 (1995); Note, 89 Nw. U. L. Rev. 268 (1994).

9. *Kidney Dialysis.* Health care rationing issues first came to the public's attention when kidney dialysis was developed in the late 1960s. Moved by the plight of patients dying from kidney failure who could not afford this expensive treatment, Congress in 1973 expanded Medicare to cover virtually all costs for dialysis (and later for kidney transplants), for anyone afflicted with "end stage renal disease" (ESRD), i.e., kidney failure—regardless of whether they were elderly or disabled. This is the only time Congress has enacted a disease-specific insurance program, and may well be the last time. Congress drastically underestimated the costs of this program, which now runs tens of billions of dollars a year and has spawned a huge industry in dialysis clinics. In contrast, British doctors, because of severe overall funding limits, generally do not order dialysis for older patients and those with other serious illnesses. See generally Note, 26 Harv. J. Leg. 225 (1989).

Because undocumented immigrants are not eligible for Medicare, those with kidney failure are served only by safety net hospitals that are willing and able to treat them for free. One such hospital, in Atlanta, faced severe financial shortfalls in 2009 and so made the tough decision to terminate its dialysis program, leaving its existing 50 immigrant patients with no other options in the United States. The hospital offered to transport them to their home countries, but most also could not afford treatment at home, so they remained. Faced with likely deaths, the hospital has balked at several announced deadlines for terminating its dialysis support, and so the situation remains unresolved as of this writing. Lori A. Nessel, The Practice of Medical Repatriation, 55 Wayne L. Rev. 1725 (2009).

10. *Race or Gender Discrimination.* Insurance restrictions can be challenged under other discrimination statutes besides disability. Suppose, for instance, that an excluded disease category has a disproportionate impact on blacks. Most commentators conclude that this alone is not illegal without some indication of racial animus or subterfuge. More compelling, however, is the argument that a treatment exclusion has a categorical effect on only one gender. In Newport News Shipbuilding v. EEOC, 462 U.S. 669 (1993), the Court held that an employer violates Title VII's prohibition of sex discrimination by providing more generous pregnancy benefits to female employees than to the wives of male employees. Similarly, would the exclusion of fertility treatment such as in vitro fertilization constitute either gender or disability discrimination? Saks v. Franklin Covey Co., 316 F.3d 337 (2d Cir. 2003) (no, because infertility is not always a disability, and plan excluded fertility treatment for both men and women). See generally Lisa Kerr, Can Money Buy Happiness? An Examination of the Coverage of Infertility

Services Under HMO Contracts, 49 Case W. Res. L. Rev. 559 (1999); Carl Coleman, Conceiving Harm: Disability Discrimination in Assisted Reproductive Technologies, 50 UCLA L. Rev. 17 (2002). For a related issue, see L. Dechery, Do Employer-Provided Insurance Plans Violate Title VII When They Exclude Treatment for Breast Cancer?, 80 Minn. L. Rev. 945 (1996); Christine Nardi, When Health Insurers Deny Coverage for Breast Reconstructive Surgery: Gender Meets Disability, 1997 Wis. L. Rev. 778.

Civil rights discrimination statutes apply to government programs as well, under Title VI. These statutes have had less effect. A series of public interest lawsuits have attempted to block cities from closing public hospitals in low-income communities, finding that the disparate impact on minorities does not constitute prohibited discrimination. See, e.g., Bryan v. Koch, 627 F.2d 612 (2d Cir. 1980); NAACP v. Wilmington Medical Center, 657 F.2d 1322 (3d Cir. 1981). See generally Jessica Roberts, Health Law as Disability Rights Law, 97 Minn. L. Rev. __ (2013); Marianne Lado, Breaking the Barriers of Access to Health Care: A Discussion of the Role of Civil Rights Litigation, 60 Brook. L. Rev. 239 (1994); Sidney Watson, Reinvigorating Title VI: Defending Health Care Discrimination—It Shouldn't Be So Easy, 58 Fordham L. Rev. 939 (1990).

11. *Impotence and Contraception.* Among the various controversies concerning what health insurance should cover, debates about contraception and sexual health have been especially lively. Following the introduction of Viagra, impotence pills for men were covered by traditional health insurance because it addresses a physical dysfunction often caused by health problems such as heart disease or side effects from medication. However, Viagra is also prescribed in more discretionary situations to enhance sexual performance, especially among elderly men, for whom a decline in sexual vitality is an expected consequence of aging. Rather than drawing age-based lines or crafting sexual performance indicators that would be hard to defend or administer, insurers simply capped the number of Viagra pills permitted per month. (One wonders how they arrived at the cutoff.) See Alison Keith, The Economics of Viagra, 19(2) Health Aff. 147 (Mar. 2000).

The coverage of Viagra highlights the inequities of not covering contraceptives for women, which are similarly important to sexual health. Because fertility is a normal condition, blocking fertility does not fit within the traditional insurance concepts of treatment for illness or disease. Nevertheless, many insurers have agreed to include contraceptive coverage, and the federal government now mandates the same (as part of the Affordable Care Act). Although this contraception mandate exempts churches, it has generated vocal protests and several lawsuits by institutions with religious affiliations, and by private employers and individuals, claiming infringement of religious freedom. See Hobby Lobby Stores v. Sebelius, 133 S. Ct. 641 (2012) (denying injunction); Grote v. Sebelius, 2013 WL 362725 (7th Cir. 2013) (granting preliminary injunction).

For a good overview of this debate, see Hazel Glenn Beh, Sex, Sexual Pleasure, and Reproduction: Health Insurers Don't Want You to Do Those Nasty Things, 13 Wis. Women's L.J. 119 (1998); David Chavking, Medicaid and Viagra: Restoring Potency to an Old Program?, 11 Health Matrix 189 (2000); Sharona Hoffman, AIDS Caps, Contraceptive Coverage, and the Law, 23 Cardozo L. Rev. 1315 (2002). Comment, 35 Tulsa L.J. 399 (2000). For an analysis from the perspective of sex discrimination law, see Sylvia Law, Sex Discrimination and Insurance for Contraception, 73 Wash. L. Rev. 363 (1998). For a constitutional analysis, see Note, 54 Vand. L. Rev. 451 (2001).

12. *Who Decides Medical Effectiveness?* Assuming fair and nondiscriminatory measures of medical effectiveness can be devised, who should apply them? Philip Peters's discussion of QALYs is purposefully somewhat abstract in this regard, because QALYs can be used by any number of decisionmakers to tailor medical decisions. Doctors can use them to trim costs incrementally at the bedside; employers, insurers, and the government can use them to limit the benefit packages they are willing to pay for; and courts can use them to resolve disputes over what those benefit packages actually promise. These notes are focused on the second set of decisionmakers. The two cases in the next section focus on the courts. Physicians as decisionmakers are considered throughout these materials, including under informed consent, malpractice, and financial incentive payments. But what about patients? Could they (or *should* they) have more of a role in deciding what level of cost-effectiveness they are willing to pay for, either when ordering care or selecting insurance? See Russell Korobkin, Bounded Rationality, Moral Hazard and the Case for Relative Value Health Insurance, SSRN 1984937 (2012).

Problem: Allocation Choices in a Public Program

You are CEO of a municipal hospital, funded by the county, looking at next year's budget. This forces you to make tough allocation decisions. Due to your brilliant administrative leadership, the hospital managed to treat all patients who requested service last year, and it still has a $5 million surplus left over. After receiving recommendations from a task force, you have to choose among these three options:

(1) Return the money to the county to help them avoid an anticipated property tax increase.

(2) Buy one Very Big Fancy Machine (VBFM), which, over the course of its five-year useful life, will treat 100 patients a year, with a 1 percent better chance of saving their life compared with existing technologies. In other words, the machine is expected to save five lives at a cost of $1 million/life. On average, each person saved will live for ten more years. (Imagine a machine that helps resuscitate patients in the emergency room.)

(3) Buy 5,000 Really Simple Little Things (RSLTs), which have a 1 percent chance to extend life one year for each person who uses one. In other words, this will provide one additional year for 50 people, at a cost of $100,000 per person. (Imagine an expensive drug that does a better job of delaying but not avoiding death from cancer.)

Now, suppose you learn that patients treated with the VBFM will be left bedridden and debilitated but fully conscious, whereas RSLT patients will be left ambulatory but in pain and with diminished mental capacities. Assuming you were unfettered by the ADA, what do you do? Realizing, however, that the ADA might apply, does it potentially force you to change your mind? What factors determine what effect the ADA might have?

B. THE FIDUCIARY NATURE OF THE TREATMENT RELATIONSHIP

The interactions between healers and those hoping to be healed are complex. Science, sociology, and psychology all provide important perspectives on the rich character of these important relationships. As noted in Chapter 1.A.2 and the Buckman & Sabbagh excerpt at page 15, the experience of illness may include anxiety and physical distress that, combined with the patient's relative lack of knowledge, create a substantial power imbalance between the patient and her caregiver. Moreover, many aspects of the treatment relationship involve sensitive personal matters, ranging from one's weight to one's sexual history and mental health needs. The topics explored in this chapter are united by their focus on the implications of these special vulnerabilities: confidentiality of medical information, informed consent, and conflicts of interest. The final section of the chapter explores research on human subjects, which exposes patients to additional risks along with hope for more effective treatments.

Traditional contract and tort norms have been radically altered in many of these areas through the interventions of courts, legislatures, and administrative agencies. Courts have found protections for patients in the implied or expressed belief that the treatment relationship is a fiduciary one, in which physicians in particular, but some other providers as well, owe heightened duties to protect the vulnerable patient's interests. This chapter explores the extent to which physicians have fiduciary obligations to their patients as well as the implications of those obligations. The chapter also examines when and how special protections for patients have been extended—often by legislation or regulation—beyond the physician-patient relationship to other health care providers and institutional actors.

Fiduciary law is not usually a topic of thorough study in the law school curriculum and it is worth considering its key elements before turning to legislative, regulatory, and judicial approaches to protecting patients' interests. As a common law doctrine, fiduciary law can be thought of as a separate source of distinct legal duties or as a legal status that heightens or alters ordinary contract and tort law duties. Fiduciary principles impose a special measure of loyalty and devotion on several classes of professionals (lawyers, trustees, and general agents) by virtue of their control over an important subject matter, the vulnerability of their clients and the resulting potential for abuse. The materials in Chapter 1.A.2 explain why some courts have found that "the relationship of patients and physicians is a fiduciary one of the highest degree. It involves every element of trust, confidence and good faith."[1] Doctors have a complex body of knowledge and skills that are critical to preserving the life and restoring the health of their patients. Doctors control their patients' welfare in the most vital aspects imaginable. Sick patients, by virtue of their debilitated and vulnerable state, are dependent on their physicians' judgments and actions. Accurate diagnosis requires patients to reveal the most personal details of their lives, and effective treatment often entails invasion of the most essential aspects of bodily intimacy, invading the very blood and guts of our integrated sense of self. Thus many legal decisions and commentators have recognized

---

1. Lockett v. Goodill, 430 P.2d 589, 591 (Wash. 1967).

doctors' fiduciary status.[2] For a sampling of the literature, see Robert Gatter, Faith, Confidence, and Health Care: Fostering Trust in Medicine Through Law, 39 Wake Forest L. Rev. 395, 396 (2004); Thomas L. Hafemeister & Sarah P. Bryan, Beware Those Bearing Gifts: Physicians' Fiduciary Duty to Avoid Pharmaceutical Marketing, 57 U. Kan. L. Rev. 491 (2009); Mark A. Hall, Law, Medicine, and Trust, 55 Stan. L. Rev. 463 (2002); Dayna Bowen Matthew, Implementing American Health Care Reform: The Fiduciary Imperative, 59 Buff. L. Rev. 715 (2011); Maxwell J. Mehlman, Fiduciary Contracting: Limitations on Bargaining Between Patients and Health Care Providers, 51 U. Pitt. L. Rev. 365, 388-416 (1990); and Marc A. Rodwin, Medicine, Money & Morals: Physicians' Conflicts of Interest (1993).

Classifying physicians as fiduciaries might appear to be a simple matter; it is much more difficult, however, to say precisely what obligations result. Fiduciary law is far from a seamless web. There is no integrated body of principles or precise doctrine that applies uniformly to all forms of fiduciary relationships.[3] Nonetheless, there are basic principles of fiduciary obligation that share a broad, familial resemblance across many categories of relationships. One of the common themes is a modification of the ordinary rules of contract. In a classic contractual relationship, neither party has a duty to maintain the secrecy of information provided by the other party, nor a duty to disclose information to the other about the qualities of the product or service sold or the particular needs of the purchaser. *Caveat emptor*, let the buyer beware, is the most common rule associated with classic contract law. Parties to the contract can impose additional obligations on each other only by bargaining for specific contract terms.

Courts have modified the ordinary contract regime by limiting the ability to alter or waive the basic standard of care or by limiting the ability to terminate the relationship. This chapter explains that courts have modified these pure contract principles to provide additional special protections for patients. Courts have used ordinary tort law as well as fiduciary law to achieve these protections, holding, for example, that physicians can be sued for damages if they fail to maintain patient

---

2. Some authorities, however, distinguish confidential relations from fiduciary relations and declare that physicians are subject only to the former. See, e.g., Restatement (Third) of Trusts §2 *cmt b(1)* (2003); 1 Austin W. Scott & William F. Fratcher, The Law of Trusts §2.5, at 43 (4th ed. 1987). The primary thrust of the distinction, however, is one of burden of proof, not scope of obligation. The law does not assume that a position of trust exists in a confidential relation as quickly as it does in a fiduciary one, but where such trust exists, the duties are essentially the same.

3. See L. S. Sealy, Fiduciary Relationships, 1962 Cambridge L.J. 69, 73 (observing that labelling a relationship fiduciary "does not warrant the inference that any particular fiduciary principle or remedy can be applied"). For other works that address fiduciary principles at this more general level, see Deborah A. DeMott, Breach of Fiduciary Duty: On Justifiable Expectations of Loyalty and Their Consequences, 48 Ariz. L. Rev. 25 (2006); Paul D. Finn, Fiduciary Obligations 15-76 (1977); Tamar Frankel, Fiduciary Law, 71 Cal. L. Rev. 795, 808-816 (1983); Tamar Frankel, Fiduciary Duties as Default Rules, 74 Or. L. Rev. 1209 (1995); Marc Rodwin, Medicine, Money & Morals 179-211 (1993); Austin W. Scott, The Fiduciary Principle, 37 Cal. L. Rev. 539, 541 (1949); J. C. Shephard, The Law of Fiduciaries 21-42 (1981); Symposium, The Role of Fiduciary Law and Trust in the Twenty-First Century: A Conference Inspired by the Work of Tamar Frankel, 91 Boston U. L. Rev. 833-1299 (2011).

confidences or to disclose important information about any proposed treatment. State and federal regulators also have responded to the special characteristics of the treatment relationship and the concomitant special duties of health care providers by enacting a wide range of statutes and regulations designed to protect patient confidentiality and to control conflicts of interest.

As you read the following materials, consider how well courts and legislatures have responded to the unique attributes and requirements of the doctor-patient relationship. Are the protections sufficient? Are they excessive or dysfunctional? Should federal or state law be used to address these concerns? When and how should similar obligations be imposed on other types of health care providers? Should similar rules be applied to facilities and institutions such as hospitals and HMOs?

C. CONFIDENTIALITY OF MEDICAL INFORMATION

Both patients and health care providers have long believed that the health care relationship creates a special duty on the part of the provider to protect the patient's interests. One example is the duty to protect the confidentiality of patient information. The common belief that there was such a duty obscured a significant number of important legal questions. What is the source of the obligation? On whom is the duty imposed? What are the limits of the duty? What remedies are available for breaches of confidentiality? Does the system of legal protections effectively balance patient rights, provider duties, and social interests? Historically state courts and legislatures attempted to protect patients' interests in medical privacy by imposing duties to maintain confidentiality on individual health care providers, primarily physicians. There has been a sea change in the last 15 years, as the federal government has flooded the health care system with detailed regulations designed to protect patients' interests in controlling disclosure and use of their medical information. Yet federal regulations—even of the intense sort that will begin this chapter—have not totally displaced the importance of state laws, which in many cases still provide the best avenue for aggrieved patients to challenge breaches of confidentiality.

1. The Federal Duty to Maintain Medical Privacy: Federal Privacy Regulations (HIPAA)

The confidentiality of health information was protected in varying ways by a patchwork of state common law and regulatory approaches for many decades. Critics and patients' rights advocates contended that the framework was seriously deficient because protections varied from place to place and because the narrow focus on physician obligations left vast swaths of the health care system without effective constraints on the disclosure of medical information. At the same time as the complexity and range of participants in the health care system were expanding, technological advances were moving health care records from often illegible paper notes and files found in a single physician's office to comprehensive electronic health records (EHRs) stored in databases that could be accessed by many individuals and institutional participants in health care.

The Health Insurance Portability and Accountability Act of 1996 (HIPAA) was concerned mainly with improving how health insurance is designed and sold, but it also included a set of provisions facilitating the electronic processing of insurance claims and other types of medical information. In order to ensure that greater use of electronic health information would not compromise privacy, the HIPAA statute also required the Secretary of Health and Human Services to issue rules improving privacy protections. The key privacy regulations, which were first issued in 2006 and substantially revised in 2013, are found at 45 C.F.R. §160 et seq.

In general, the federal privacy regulations (the "Privacy Rule") require certain "covered entities" to maintain the confidentiality of defined types of "protected health information" (PHI). Covered entities include health insurers, claims-processing clearinghouses, and health care providers. 45 C.F.R. §160.102(a). These entities must (1) adopt internal procedures to protect the privacy of protected health information; (2) train employees regarding privacy procedures; (3) designate a privacy officer; (4) secure patient records that contain protected information; and (5) establish and enforce agreements with certain third parties (called "business associates") that ensure that they maintain privacy protection for information they have access to. The HITECH Act of 2009 expanded the reach of the Act by imposing many of the Privacy Rule's requirements to business associates. 45 C.F.R. §160.102(b). A "business associate" is "a person [defined to include various organizations and businesses] who" is not an employee of a covered entity but "creates, receives, maintains, or transmits protected health information for a function or activity . . . including claims processing or administration . . . or . . . provides" services such as legal, accounting, or management services. 45 C.F.R. §160.103.

The definition of "health information" is comprehensive. The term means:

> any information, including genetic information, whether oral or recorded in any form or medium, that
>> (1) Is created or received by a health care provider . . . [or a broad range of other entities]; and
>> (2) Relates to the past, present, or future physical or mental health or condition of an individual; the provision of health care to an individual; or the past, present, or future payment for the provision of health care to an individual.

45 C.F.R. §160.103. The Privacy Rule focuses on the protection of a particular subset of health information, called "protected health information," defined as "individually identifiable health information" held or transmitted in electronic media or "transmitted or maintained in any other form or medium." Id. (noting specific exceptions).

The central requirements for using or disclosing PHI are found in a single section, 45 C.F.R. §164.502, but this provision links to and incorporates definitions, standards, and exceptions found in more than 25 other sections or subsections in the Privacy Rule. The Rule thus has gained a reputation for complexity; handbooks, seminars, and training sessions have sprung up to help those working with health care information to master the technical details. A broad summary of the disclosure aspects of the Rule is nonetheless possible.

The standard for the use and disclosure of PHI by covered entities establishes a strict baseline rule of confidentiality, essentially prohibiting *any* use or disclosure of patient medical information, unless a specific regulatory exception applies. The standard provides seven general avenues for disclosure:

1. PHI can be disclosed to the individual or the individual's personal representative (with special rules if there are concerns about abuse or neglect).

2. The information can be used for "treatment, payment, or health care operations" with the patient's general consent (called "TPO" in the increasingly common HIPAA lingo of health lawyers and consultants).

3. The information can be disclosed where the entity receives a more specific "valid authorization," typically via a written and signed document, the nature of which may vary depending on whether the general authorization rule or special rules governing psychotherapy notes, marketing, or sale of PHI apply.

4. A specified subset of PHI can be disclosed without written authorization in certain defined situations after giving the patient an opportunity to object. For example, basic information about an individual's identity and condition can be added to the hospital directory and made available to callers based on an oral agreement after the individual has been given an opportunity to object and can even be provided in emergency circumstances when the individual is unable to communicate approval or disapproval if this would be consistent with any known patient preferences and in the best interests of the patient.

5. An individual's PHI can be disclosed without his or her authorization or agreement in roughly a dozen categories of special circumstances, e.g., where the disclosure is required by law.

6. A "limited data set" that excludes most identifying information can be disclosed for use in public health, research, and operations. Limited types of PHI may also be disclosed in carefully circumscribed circumstances for institutional fundraising and by health plans involved in underwriting decisions.

7. Covered entities are also permitted to disclose PHI "incident to use[s] or disclosures otherwise permitted or required" so long as the covered entity has followed the standards governing the minimum necessary disclosure of information and has put in place proper administrative, physical, and technical safeguards.

45 C.F.R. §164.502. The complex regulatory framework addresses a host of other issues, ranging from the rules governing the creation of de-identified health information that can be used without consent, to the use of health information in research, to the responsibility of the covered entities to ensure that business associates comply with privacy requirements.

Any use or transfer of medical information that does not comply with these detailed rules violates the law, even if completely inadvertent and resulting in no actual harm to the patient, but many such technical violations went unpunished. Thus, enforcement of the Privacy Rule initially appeared lax to some critics, until passage of the HITECH Act in 2009 required the imposition of penalties for all violations. The new regulations issued under the HITECH Act provide that DHHS "will impose a civil money penalty upon a covered entity or business associate" for violations. 45 C.F.R. §160.402(a). The civil penalties begin at a minimum of $100 for inadvertent breaches but rise to a minimum of $50,000 for offenses committed with a higher level of culpability. 45 C.F.R. §160.404. The Rule establishes factors for the Secretary to consider in setting the penalty between the established minimums and maximums. These civil penalty provisions create significant financial exposure for covered entities, even at the lowest dollar level. For example, continuing violations generate a separate violation each day, 45 C.F.R. 160.406. The risk is lessened somewhat by a cap of $1,500,000 placed on the total penalty for identical violations in a calendar year.

Knowing violations of the privacy rules that involve using unique health identifiers or obtaining or disclosing identifiable health information can result in fines and imprisonment. 42 U.S.C. §1320d-6. Notably, the most severe penalties (fines up to $250,000 and ten years imprisonment) are reserved for persons who commit the offense with the "intent to sell, transfer or use individually identifiable health information for commercial advantage, personal gain, or malicious harm."

The Privacy Rule does not explicitly create a private cause of action or remedy and courts have been unwilling to find an implied right of action for individuals harmed by disclosures. Acara v. Banks, 470 F.3d 569 (5th Cir. 2006); Bonney v. Stephens Memorial Hospital, 17 A.3d 123 (Me. 2011); Espinoza v. Gold Cross Services, 234 P.3d 156 (Utah 2010).

The Privacy Rule includes important preemption rules that ultimately reinforce the role of states in establishing and enforcing strict privacy protections. First, HIPAA preemption applies only to state laws that provide weaker protections of privacy; states remain free to adopt and to enforce more protective regimes. 45 C.F.R. §160.201-.205. Second, the Privacy Rule provides that in cases involving civil penalties, the federal penalty "is in addition to any other penalty prescribed by law," 45 C.F.R. §160.418. Plaintiffs are therefore free to pursue whatever damage claims might otherwise be available under state law. This is particularly important given that the federal Privacy Rule does not provide a direct cause of action for individuals injured by improper disclosures. Courts have begun to wrestle with the potential impact of the Privacy Rule on a wide range of state provisions and practices.

■ IN THE MATTER OF MIGUEL M. v. BARRON
950 N.E.2d 107 (N.Y. 2011)

SMITH, J.

We hold that the Privacy Rule adopted by the federal government pursuant to the Health Insurance Portability and Accountability Act (HIPAA) prohibits the disclosure of a patient's medical records to a state agency that requests them for use in a proceeding to compel the patient to accept mental health treatment, where the patient has neither authorized the disclosure nor received notice of the agency's request for the records. . . .

Dr. Charles Barron, as designee of the New York City Department of Health and Mental Hygiene, applied for an order under Mental Hygiene Law §9.60 requiring "assisted outpatient treatment" (AOT) for Miguel M. The petition alleged that Miguel was suffering from a mental illness; that he was unlikely to survive safely in the community without supervision; that he had a history of failing to comply with treatment; that he was unlikely to participate in necessary treatment voluntarily; and that he needed, and would benefit from, AOT to prevent a relapse or deterioration of his mental status, which would be likely to result in serious harm to Miguel or to others.

At the hearing on the petition, Barron offered in evidence records from two hospitals relating to three occasions on which Miguel was hospitalized. A witness called by Barron testified that the hospitals had furnished the records in response to a request—a request made, it is clear from the record, without notice to Miguel. The witness acknowledged that Miguel had not authorized the release of the records, and that no court order for their disclosure had been sought or obtained.

The records were received in evidence over Miguel's objection and Barron's witness described their contents. After the hearing, Supreme Court directed that Miguel "receive and accept assisted outpatient treatment" for a period of six months. The Appellate Division affirmed. We granted leave to appeal, and now reverse. . . .

Mental Hygiene Law §9.60, known as "Kendra's Law," was enacted in 1999. It is named for Kendra Webdale, who was killed by a mentally ill man who pushed her off a subway platform. It says that, on a proper showing, a mentally ill person whose lack of compliance with treatment has, twice within the last 36 months, caused him or her to be hospitalized may be the subject of AOT pursuant to a plan stated in a court order. Public officials identified as "directors of community services" are given the duty of enforcing Kendra's Law, and a petition to require AOT may be filed by a director of community services or his or her designee. [The] Mental Hygiene Law permits disclosure of medical records to a director of community services who requests it in the exercise of his or her duties. Thus, the disclosure of a patient's medical records for purposes of an AOT proceeding is permitted by state law, unless the applicable state law is preempted. Miguel argues that it is.

Miguel says that preemption is found in HIPAA and the Privacy Rule. The Privacy Rule prohibits disclosure of an identifiable patient's health information without the patient's authorization, subject to certain exceptions (45 CFR 164.508[a][1]). HIPAA . . . . and the Privacy Rule say that contrary state laws are preempted unless they offer privacy protections that are "more stringent" than those of the federal law; New York does not offer any more stringent protection that is relevant here. The preemption issue thus comes down to whether the disclosure of Miguel's medical records was permitted by one of the exceptions to the Privacy Rule.

Barron relies on two exceptions, those permitting disclosure for purposes of "public health" and "treatment." It is possible to read the language of both exceptions as covering the disclosure now at issue, but in both cases the reading is strained. Considering the apparent purposes of these two exceptions, we conclude that neither fits these facts.

The public health exception permits disclosure of protected information to:

> [a] public health authority that is authorized by law to collect or receive such information for the purpose of preventing or controlling disease, injury, or disability, including, but not limited to, the reporting of disease, injury, vital events such as birth or death, and the conduct of public health surveillance, public health investigations, and public health interventions.

Barron reasons that disclosure of a mentally ill person's hospital records for purposes of requiring that person to accept AOT protects the public health, because mentally ill people might kill or injure other people—like Kendra Webdale—who, of course, are members of the public. Thus Barron, a person designated to enforce Kendra's Law, would be a "public health authority," collecting information for the "purpose of preventing . . . injury," and his action to require AOT in Miguel's case could be called a public health intervention. We are not convinced, however, that the authors of the Privacy Rule meant "public health" in this literal, but counterintuitive, sense.

The apparent purpose of the public health exception is to facilitate government activities that protect large numbers of people from epidemics, environmental hazards, and the like, or that advance public health by accumulating valuable statistical information. To disclose private information about particular people, for the purpose of preventing those people from harming themselves or others, effects a very substantial invasion of privacy without the sort of generalized public benefit that would come from, for example, tracing the course of an infectious disease. The disclosure to Barron of Miguel's hospital records was not within the scope of the public health exception.

The treatment exception permits disclosure of protected health information "for treatment activities of a health care provider." "Treatment" is defined as:

> the provision, coordination, or management of health care and related services by one or more health care providers, including the coordination or management of health care by a health care provider with a third party; consultation between health care providers relating to a patient; or the referral of a patient for health care from one health care provider to another.

Again, Barron's argument is literalistic: AOT—assisted outpatient treatment—is literally "treatment"—"the provision . . . of health care . . . by one or more health care providers." But the thrust of the treatment exception is to facilitate the sharing of information among health care providers working together. We see no indication that the authors of the regulation meant to facilitate "treatment" administered by a volunteer "provider" over the patient's objection. Disclosure for that purpose is a more serious invasion of privacy than, for example, the transmission of medical records from a patient's primary care physician to a specialist—the sort of activity for which the treatment exception seems primarily designed. The treatment exception is inapplicable here.

We find support for our conclusion that the two exceptions Barron relies on are inapposite in the existence of other exceptions that Barron might have invoked but did not. The Privacy Rule authorizes disclosure of health information, subject to certain conditions, "in the course of any judicial or administrative proceeding," in response to either "an order of a court or administrative tribunal" or "a subpoena, discovery request, or other lawful process" (45 CFR 164.512[e]). Thus, Barron could have pursued Miguel's records either by seeking a court order or by serving a subpoena. To do so in compliance with the Privacy Rule, however, Barron would have had to give notice to Miguel of his request for the records. He could not, absent extraordinary circumstances, have obtained a court order requiring disclosure without giving such notice. And the Privacy Rule's exception for subpoenas and the like is conditioned on "satisfactory assurance" from the person seeking the information to the entity providing it either "that reasonable efforts have been made . . . to ensure that the individual who is the subject of the protected health information . . . has been given notice of the request," or that an order protecting the confidentiality of the information has been sought. In a case, like this one, to which the patient is a party, a request for a protective order would require notice to the patient.

We can see no reason, and Barron has suggested none, why notice should not have been given here. It may well be, in this case as in many others, that no valid ground for withholding the records exists; courts ruling on disclosure issues will surely be conscious, as we are, of the strong public interest in seeing that mentally ill people who might otherwise be dangerous receive necessary treatment. But it seems only fair, and no great burden on the public agencies charged with enforcing Kendra's Law, to give patients a chance to object before the records are delivered.

We emphasize that it is far from our purpose to make the enforcement of Kendra's Law difficult. It may often be possible to avoid all disclosure problems by getting the patient to authorize the disclosure in advance; surely many mentally ill people will, while they are under proper care, recognize that disclosure is very much in their own interest. When there is no advance authorization, patients who are given notice that their records are being sought often may not object; when they do object, their objections may often be overruled. We hold only that unauthorized disclosure without notice is, under circumstances like those present here, inconsistent with the Privacy Rule. . . .

Barron argues in the alternative that, even if the disclosure of the records to him was unlawful—as we have held it was—the Supreme Court did not err by admitting the records into evidence at the AOT hearing. HIPAA, as Barron points out, contains its own remedies for violations: civil penalties and, for the knowing and wrongful disclosure of individually identifiable health information, fines and imprisonment. Neither exclusion of the records from evidence nor suppression of evidence obtained by use of the records is among the remedies listed. Barron cites decisions from other states holding that evidence obtained as a result of a HIPAA violation need not be suppressed in a criminal case. . . .

We assume it is correct that, in a criminal case, a HIPAA or Privacy Rule violation does not always require the suppression of evidence. . . . But this case is different. It is one thing to allow the use of evidence resulting from an improper disclosure of information in medical records to prove that a patient has committed a crime; it is another to use the records themselves, or their contents, in a proceeding to subject to unwanted medical treatment a patient who is not accused of any wrongdoing. Using the records in that way directly impairs, without adequate justification, the interest protected by HIPAA and the Privacy Rule: the interest in keeping one's own medical condition private. We therefore hold that medical records obtained in violation of HIPAA or the Privacy Rule, and the information contained in those records, are not admissible in a proceeding to compel AOT.

Accordingly, the order of the Appellate Division should be reversed, with costs, and the case remitted to Supreme Court for further proceedings in accordance with this opinion.

Notes: HIPAA Privacy Protections

1. *Challenges to HIPAA*. Efforts to challenge HIPAA on constitutional or statutory grounds have failed. In South Carolina Med. Assn. v. Thompson, 327 F.3d 346 (4th Cir. 2003), the court rejected the plaintiffs' claims that the HIPAA regulations constituted an unconstitutionally vague and improper, standardless delegation of

legislative authority. See also Citizens for Health v. Leavitt, Secretary U.S. Department Health and Human Services, 428 F.3d 167 (3d Cir. 2005). For a summary of litigation under HIPAA, see Annot., 194 A.L.R. Fed. 133 (2004).

2. *The Special Nature of Medical Information and EHRs.* The HIPAA privacy standard and related provisions regulating the security of electronic health records (EHRs) represent a very significant investment of public and private resources into the privacy of health care information. The Privacy Rule protects a broad range of information created and held by individual health care providers, practice groups, hospitals, HMOs, and other entities. HIPAA compliance efforts undoubtedly impose hundreds of millions of dollars in costs across the health care system. In theory, our willingness to bear these costs is based on the special character of medical information as distinct from other types of personal information and the nature of the health care provider-patient relationship through which information about health status and treatment are generated. See, e.g., Mark A. Rothstein, The Hippocratic Bargain and Health Information Technology, 38 J.L. Med. & Ethics 7 (2010). Do the costs of the HIPAA privacy regime seem commensurate with the benefits privacy generates for individuals? Are broader social goals served by the Privacy Rule? Are the notice and authorization provisions of HIPAA effective mechanisms for protecting privacy and autonomy or do they merely result in a meaningless flurry of additional paperwork? For a critique, see Fred H. Cate, Protecting Privacy in Health Research: The Limits of Individual Choice, 98 Cal. L. Rev. 1766 (2010).

There are serious concerns about the risks of disclosure associated with creation of EHRs, which can be collected in vast databases of personal health information. The Privacy Rule thus includes specific provisions designed to protect the security of electronic health records. 45 C.F.R. §§164.302-.318. Fears of improper use are legitimate given the frequency of breaches, whether intentional, see Doe v. Walgreens, 2010 WL 4823212 (Tenn. Ct. App.) (Walgreens employee wrongfully accessed Walgreens database and shared co-worker's HIV status with others), or merely negligent, see Milt Freudenheim, Breaches Lead to Push to Protect Medical Data, N.Y. Times, May 30, 2011. HIPAA and the HITECH Act were designed to increase the use of EHRs as a method of reducing costs and improving efficiency and quality of health care. See, e.g., David Blumenthal & Marilyn Tavenner, The "Meaningful Use" Regulation for Electronic Health Records, 363 New Eng. J. Med. 501 (2010) (describing incentives for increased use of EHRs); Symposium, Health IT: The Road to "Meaningful Use," 29 Health Aff. 582-682 (2010). But see Spencer S. Jones et al., Unraveling the IT Productivity Paradox—Lessons for Health Care, 366 New Eng. J. Med. 2243 (2012) (noting debate about actual impact of IT in health care). The privacy components of the legislation were seen as necessary to ensure broader adoption of EHRs. Symposium, The Effects of Health Information Technology on the Physician-Patient Relationship, 38 J.L. Med. & Ethics 6-84 (2010).

The Privacy Rule is focused on "covered entities" and "business associates." Some non-health care providers have attempted to establish Web-based medical records databases, arguing that HIPAA rules do not apply to the arrangements. Perhaps to address consumer concerns about privacy, Microsoft named its product "Microsoft Vault." Should these databases be covered by the Privacy Rule? Eric S. Pasternack, HIPAA in the Age of Electronic Health Records, 41 Rutgers L.J. 817 (2010) (suggesting amendment of HIPAA to address electronic medical records companies).

3. *Genetic Information.* Advances in genetics may create additional privacy concerns. Scientists are increasingly able to link human genes with the risk of developing various human maladies. Individuals have a definite interest in maintaining the confidentiality of their genetic predisposition for a variety of ills. At the same time, other affected family members, insurers, and others have an interest in gaining access to this information. Lawrence O. Gostin & James G. Hodge, Jr., Genetic Privacy and the Law: An End to Genetics Exceptionalism, 40 Jurimetrics J. 21 (1999); Mark A. Hall, Legal Rules and Industry Norms: The Impact of Laws Restricting Health Insurers' Use of Genetic Information, 40 Jurimetrics J. 93 (1999). The federal Genetic Information Nondiscrimination Act of 2008, Pub. L. 110-233, 122 Stat. 881, established special rules protecting the confidentiality of genetic information and restricting the use of this information by insurers and employers. See Jessica L. Roberts, Preempting Discrimination: Lessons from the Genetic Information Nondiscrimination Act, 63 Vand. L. Rev. 439 (2010). The HIPAA Privacy Rule includes certain types of genetic information, including information about family members, in the definition of health information subject to the Rule's protections. 45 C.F.R. §160.103.

4. *The (Limited) Right of Individuals to Control Medical Records.* HIPAA establishes a large reservoir of PHI presumptively under the control of an individual but also establishes significant escape valves through which the flow of PHI is controlled by others. The rule permitting use of PHI for treatment purposes is a major example: Under this provision no separate patient consent is required. The presumption of confidentiality is reduced in some circumstances where common practices and likely preferences of patients would create a default rule of disclosure. 45 C.F.R. §§164.502(a)(1)(v); 164.510. As noted above, this provision eases disclosure of PHI in hospital directories; it also facilitates disclosure to family members and friends involved in the patient's care and to disaster relief organizations. The Rule also establishes that disclosures can be made without any authorization or opportunity to agree or object in any one of a dozen important categories of circumstances. As noted above, this provision establishes that PHI can be disclosed where required by law. Other permitted disclosures include: disclosures for public health activities (a broad category including specific examples such as disease surveillance, notification of exposure to contagious diseases, or FDA-related reports of adverse events); disclosures about victims of abuse, neglect, or domestic violence; disclosures for judicial and administrative proceedings; and disclosures for research or law enforcement purposes, among others. See 45 C.F.R. §164.512. See also U.S. v. Wilk, 572 F.3d 1229 (11th Cir. 2009) (law enforcement and judicial proceedings exception).

Given HIPAA's protective purposes, the court in *Miguel* took a narrow approach to interpreting the scope of HIPPA's exceptions. Does the court's analysis seem persuasive? What will be the impact of the court's ruling on New York's ability to carry out the purposes of Kendra's Law? The court suggests that patients could be asked to pre-authorize release of their medical records. Would this approach cure the harm to an individual's right to control disclosure, given that the records were going to be used to mandate treatment over the patient's current objections? The Privacy Rule allows covered entities to rely on an authorization unless it is known to have been revoked; revocations must be written. 45 C.F.R. §164.508.

5. *Patients' Rights and Medical Records.* Medical records have traditionally been deemed the property of the health care provider who creates them, though patients and others may have access to the information within them. EHRs and the col-

lection and transmission of electronic databases of information have created new challenges and opportunities, including questions about who owns the information contained in a record, as distinct from the physical medium in which the information is stored. See, e.g., Mark A. Hall, Property, Privacy, and the Pursuit of Interconnected Electronic Medical Records, 95 Iowa L. Rev. 631 (2010) (arguing that patients should be given right to monetize access and control rights over medical records); Marc A. Rodwin, Patient Data: Property, Privacy & the Public Interest, 36 Am. J.L. & Med. 586 (2010); Frank Pasquale, Grand Bargains for Big Data: The Emerging Law of Health Information, 72 Md. L. Rev. __ (2013). Cf. Sorrell v. IMS Health, 564 U.S. __ (2011) (discussing economic value of data on physicians' prescription practices; striking down on First Amendment grounds a state ban on sale of information). The HITECH Act gives patients the right to restrict sale of their PHI. 42 U.S.C. §17935(d); 45 C.F.R. §164.508(a)(4) (authorization required).

The Privacy Rule establishes that patients must be given access to most types of their own PHI, with some exceptions, including psychotherapy notes. 45 C.F.R. §164.524. The Rule establishes timelines and procedures for access, including whether or not the denial of access will be considered to be reviewable and the procedures for review. For example, a correctional facility's denial of access on safety grounds would be unreviewable. Also unreviewable would be a denial of an individual's access to "protected health information created or obtained . . . in the course of research that includes treatment" during the research, "provided that the individual . . . agreed to the denial of access" during the consent process for the research. Id. Among other things, this rule protects the integrity of double-blind clinical trials, see section E. Reviewable grounds for denial of access include concerns that "access . . . is reasonably likely to endanger the life or physical safety of the individual or another person." Id. Reviews generally are conducted by licensed health professionals who were not part of the original access decision.

The Privacy Rule also gives individuals a right to amend PHI held within a particular record set. 45 C.F.R. §164.526. Covered entities can deny a request to amend where, for example, the entity believes the PHI "[i]s accurate and complete." The individual retains the right to submit a written statement disagreeing with the denial; the individual's statement must thereafter be transmitted with the disputed PHI along with any rebuttal from the entity. Where the entity accepts the amendment, the Rule creates a process for communicating the correction to persons or entities identified by the individual.

The Privacy Rule gives patients information about different types of disclosures of their PHI. The concept of disclosing disclosures is called "accounting." 45 C.F.R. §164.528. There are numerous exclusions from the accounting duty. One major exclusion involves disclosures made for treatment, payment, and health care operations. Id. Section 13405(c) of the HITECH Act expanded accounting to include treatment-related disclosures through an EHR. Covered entities argued that the expanded accounting provisions might be unduly onerous. Revisions to the Privacy Rule in this area were not yet finalized as of early 2013. See 76 Fed. Reg. 31426 (May 31, 2011). The HITECH Act strengthened protections for patients by requiring notification of data breaches. 42 U.S.C. §17932. "Breach" means the "acquisition, access, use or disclosure of" PHI not otherwise permitted under the Privacy Rule "which compromises the security or privacy of" the PHI. 45 C.F.R. §164.402. Certain inadvertent disclosures within the health care environment are excluded.

Id. Outside of these exclusions, covered entities or business associates must disclose breaches unless they can "demonstrate[] that there is a low probability that the protected health information has been compromised based on a risk assessment." Id. The risk assessment must consider: "[t]he nature and extent of the . . . [PHI] involved including the types of identifiers and the likelihood of re-identification"; "[t]he unauthorized person who used the . . . [PHI] or to whom the disclosure was made"; "[w]hether the . . . [PHI] was actually acquired or viewed"; and "[t]he extent to which the risk to the . . . [PHI] has been mitigated." Id. Covered entities must notify the individuals and the Secretary of HHS about breaches; "prominent media outlets" must be notified about breaches "involving more than 500 residents." 45 C.F.R. §§164.404-.408; see also §164.410 (notification by business associates).

6. *The Standards for Business Associates.* Covered entities are permitted to disclose PHI to "business associates" after "obtain[ing] satisfactory assurance that the business associate will appropriately safeguard the information." 45 C.F.R. §164.502(e) (1). Business associates perform a range of functions from claims management to quality assurance. 45 C.F.R. §160.103 ("business associate"). Critics argued that permitting disclosure of PHI to business associates created a significant risk, as those entities were not directly subject to regulation under HIPAA. The HITECH Act tightened the rules governing business associates by, among other things, directly imposing both security and privacy standards and civil and criminal penalties for violations. 42 U.S.C. §17934; 45 C.F.R. §164.502(a)(3), (4). Disclosures by business associates remain a significant issue. See Kevin Sack, Medical Data of Thousands Posted Online, N.Y. Times, Sept. 9, 2011.

7. *The Intersection of HIPAA with Other Laws Governing Disclosure.* HIPAA interacts with a wide range of federal and state legislation, such as rules governing financial records, public records laws, and state discovery rules. See, e.g., Holman v. Rasak, 785 N.W.2d 98 (Mich. 2010) (HIPAA does not preempt state discovery rules permitting ex parte discovery from plaintiff's treating physician where "reasonable efforts have been made . . . to secure a protective order that meets" HIPAA requirements), cert. denied, 131 S. Ct. 913 (2011); State ex rel. Proctor v. Messina, 320 S.W.3d 145 (Mo. 2010) (en banc) (trial court lacked authority to issue order authorizing ex parte communications under HIPAA); Abbott v. Texas Department of Mental Health and Mental Retardation, 212 S.W.3d 648 (Tex. App. 2006) (HIPAA does not preempt state Public Information Act); State ex rel. Cincinnati Enquirer v. Daniels, 844 N.E.2d 1181 (Ohio 2006) (interaction of HIPAA and Public Records Law); see also Brown v. Mortensen, 253 P.3d 522 (Cal. 2011) (analyzing interaction between HIPAA, the federal Fair Credit Act, and state law in claim involving alleged unlawful disclosure of medical records by debt collector).

8. *The Enforcement Record.* The Privacy Rule is enforced by DHHS's Office of Civil Rights (OCR). The incentives created by the HITECH Act appear to have spurred enforcement, with thousands of complaints investigated and resolved each year. In its first use of the civil monetary damages provisions of the HITECH Act, the OCR imposed a $4.3 million civil penalty against Cignet Health in Maryland based on Cignet's refusal to provide 41 patients with access to their medical records and Cignet's failure to cooperate with the OCR investigation. The OCR secured a $1 million settlement from the Massachusetts General Hospital, one of the nation's most prestigious institutions, based on the breach of privacy arising from an employee leaving records of 192 infectious-disease clinic patients on a subway train. In another noteworthy action, the UCLA Medical Center agreed to pay $865,000

to settle claims of HIPAA violations arising from complaints that UCLA personnel repeatedly and unlawfully accessed information about celebrity patients.

9. *HIPAA Resources.* Information about the current version of the federal rules can be found at www.hhs.gov/ocr/privacy/. See also Patricia I. Carter, The HIPAA Compliance Handbook, 2012; Stephen K. Philips, A Legal Research Guide to HIPAA, 3 J. Health & Life Sci. L. 134 (2010).

Notes: Beyond HIPAA—Constitutional, Common Law, and Statutory Duties to Maintain Confidentiality

1. *Overview.* Long before HIPAA, state courts and legislatures grappled with whether and how information arising from the treatment relationship would be protected from disclosure. The Privacy Rule does not displace other laws that are more protective of privacy. Moreover, the absence of a private cause of action in HIPAA means that patients injured by disclosures must look primarily to other sources of law to secure compensation. It is therefore important to (1) understand the scope and implications of the federal privacy rule; (2) determine whether other federal and state privacy protections are available; and (3) carefully consider the scope of the privacy protections, the persons or entities subject to duties, the limits of the duties, and the available remedies. There are three major sources of duties to maintain the confidentiality of medical information outside the Privacy Rule: federal and state constitutions, statutes, and the common law.

2. *A Constitutional Right of Confidentiality.* The issue of patient confidentiality is of special importance to state and federal health care providers or agencies. Several courts have found that individuals have a constitutionally protected interest in maintaining the privacy of their medical information. See, e.g., Alfred v. Corrections Corp. of America, 2011 WL 2201188 (5th Cir.) (overturning dismissal of prisoner's claim of potential constitutional violation arising from disclosure of his HIV status to another prisoner); Doe v. City of New York, 15 F.3d 264 (2d Cir. 1994) (individuals have a constitutional right of privacy in their medical information; court employs a balancing test to determine whether the government entity's interest in disclosure is "substantial" enough to outweigh the individual's privacy interest). This "informational privacy" interest has its roots in the Supreme Court's decision in Whalen v. Roe, 429 U.S. 589 (1977). In that case, the Court upheld a state program that created a centralized data bank with the names of all persons in the state who had been prescribed certain controlled substances. In dicta, however, the Court noted that the state might have some constitutional obligation to maintain the confidentiality of the information it collected. Constitutional aspects of the obligation to maintain confidentiality will be addressed in more detail in Chapter 6, at pages 680-685.

3. *The Doctrinal Basis for a Common Law Duty to Maintain Confidentiality.* Most states provide a private cause of action against licensed health care providers who impermissibly disclose confidential information obtained in the course of the treatment relationship to third parties. See Annot., 48 A.L.R.4th 668 (1986). Generally, a physician-patient relationship must be formed before the duty to maintain confidences arises. See Howes v. United States, 887 F.2d 729 (6th Cir. 1989) (psychologist and psychiatrist not liable for disclosing information about husband's drug and alcohol use that had been provided by nonpatient wife). Depending on the jurisdiction, the claim may be phrased as a breach of contract, as an act of malpractice, as a breach of fiduciary duty, as an act of fraud/misrepresentation, or as

a breach of a specific civil statute permitting the award of damages. See Biddle v. Warren General Hospital, 715 N.E.2d 518 (Ohio 1999) (finding breach of confidentiality to be an independent tort); Givens v. Mullikin ex rel. Estate of McElwaney, 75 S.W.3d 383 (Tenn. 2002) (implied covenant of confidentiality found in contract for treatment). The duty to maintain confidentiality generally includes the obligation to have in place policies and procedures designed to reduce the risk of accidental or intentional disclosures. Compare Behringer v. The Medical Center at Princeton, 592 A.2d 1251 (N.J. Super. Ct. Law Div. 1991) (hospital liable for failing to have in place policies to protect the confidentiality of the HIV status of a patient-surgeon), with Rosen v. Montgomery Surgical Center, 825 So. 2d 735 (Ala. 2001) (court rejects invasion of privacy claim based on actions of non-physician employee of hospital).

In addition, licensed health care providers who breach the confidentiality of their patients run the risk of professional disciplinary action. See, e.g., Salerian v. Maryland State Board of Physicians, 932 A.2d 1225 (Md. App. 2007) (finding unprofessional conduct where forensic psychiatrist engaged by defense in espionage case disclosed information to subject's wife and media). State privacy rules may also be applied outside the treatment relationship. See Washburn v. Rite Aid Corp., 695 A.2d 495 (R.I. 1997).

The doctrinal basis of the common law claim can be important to prospective plaintiffs. If the claim arises in contract, plaintiffs will have the benefit of the (generally longer) contract statute of limitations. Plaintiffs alleging breaches of contract will also avoid some of the procedural barriers to malpractice suits established as part of tort reform efforts in many states. See, e.g., Pierce v. Caday, 422 S.E.2d 371 (Va. 1992) (breach of confidentiality claim is subject to notice requirements imposed by malpractice reform statutes). A few courts have considered whether breach of confidentiality claims should be subject to the ordinary negligence statute of limitations or the special statute of limitations imposed for malpractice claims. See, e.g., Tighe v. Ginsberg, 540 N.Y.S.2d 99 (App. Div. 1989) (disclosure of medical records is a breach of fiduciary duty subject to the longer negligence statute of limitations). Finally, plaintiffs in contract suits need prove only that the physician failed to honor the degree of confidentiality that was promised. They need not find and present expert medical testimony on the question of whether the health care provider defendant violated the applicable standard of care. Cf. Berger v. Sonneland, 26 P.3d 257 (Wash. 2001) (expert medical testimony required in malpractice claim). Plaintiffs have begun to use the HIPAA Privacy Rule as the source of the standard of care in common law claims for damages. See, e.g., Acosta v. Bynum, 638 S.E.2d 246 (N.C. App. 2006). See also Sharona Hoffman & Andy Podgurski, E-Health Hazards: Provider Liability and Electronic Health Record Systems, 24 Berkeley Tech. L.J. 1523, 1558-1560 (2009).

4. *Statutory Protection.* HIPAA is not the only federal statute protecting the confidentiality of information. The federal Privacy Act of 1974 governs the use of information by federal agencies. See, e.g., FAA v. Cooper, 132 S. Ct. 1441 (2012) (interagency exchange of information relating to an individual's HIV status may have violated Act but sovereign immunity applied to bar claims for emotional or mental distress damages). Many states have passed statutes governing the confidentiality of information provided in the health care provider-patient relationship. Some of these state statutes were enacted to build upon the federal Privacy Rule. See Symposium, 2 Yale J. Health Pol'y L. & Ethics 325 (2002); Center on Medical

Rights and Privacy, Georgetown University, at http://hpi.georgetown.edu/privacy
/records.html (collecting information on state medical records privacy provisions).
Other state provisions protect certain types of health information. See, e.g., Annot.,
12 A.L.R.5th 149 (1993). Do state rules providing additional protection for certain
types of health care information, such as information regarding HIV status, represent good public policy?

5. *Confidentiality as a Rule of Evidence.* The confidentiality of patient-physician
communications is often also protected under rules of evidence. This evidentiary
"privilege" prohibits the discovery of protected information. State rules of evidence
almost always provide for a physician-patient privilege. The rule may be invoked by
the physician or by the patient, but only the patient generally has the power to waive
the privilege. See 81 Am. Jur. 2d Witnesses §§436, 490. The privilege may be limited
to communications with physicians. In Buchanan v. Mayfield, 925 S.W.2d 135 (Tex.
App. 1996), for example, the court held that the statutory privilege accorded to
"confidential communications between a physician and a patient" did not apply to
the communications between a dentist and a patient.

The Federal Rules of Evidence do not include a physician-patient privilege,
see Charles Alan Wright & Kenneth W. Graham, Jr., 25 Fed. Prac. & Proc. Evid.
§5521 (RR 504) (discussing the rejection of a physician-patient privilege under
the federal rules of evidence); Ralph Ruebner & Leslie Ann Reis, Hippocrates to
HIPAA: a Foundation for a Federal Physician-Patient Privilege, 77 Temp. L. Rev. 505
(2004). The Supreme Court recognized a "psychotherapist-patient" privilege under
Rule 501 of the Federal Rules of Evidence in Jaffee v. Redmond, 116 S. Ct. 1923
(1996). Justice Stevens, writing for the majority, found that the privilege was "rooted
in the imperative need for confidence and trust" and that it served important public
and private interests. The majority applied the privilege to shield communications
between a police officer and her social worker therapist, who provided counseling
after the police officer shot an allegedly innocent person. Justice Scalia's dissent
focused on the injustice created by the application of the privilege, including the
loss of evidence of possible wrongdoing. There is no dangerous-patient exception
to the federal psychotherapist-patient testimonial privilege even though the psychotherapist may have the statutory discretion to disclose confidential information
about the patient to prevent harm to a third party or to the patient. U.S. v. Chase,
340 F.3d 978 (9th Cir. 2003).

Is the privilege necessary? Will people seek care from physicians or therapists without its protection? Empirical evidence suggests that perhaps they will. See
Daniel W. Shuman, The Origins of the Physician-Patient Privilege and Professional
Secret, 39 Sw. L.J. 661, 664-665 (1985) (noting the empirical evidence does not fully
support utilitarian proponents of a privilege).

6. *Waiver and Other Exceptions.* The duty to maintain confidentiality is not ordinarily absolute under either common law or statute. Where the duty is derived from
medical ethics and practice, for example, it will be limited by policies that permit
disclosure for the protection of third parties. Statutes protecting the confidentiality
of patient information often contain a general rule of confidentiality and then list
situations under which that confidentiality can be breached. The "exceptions" to the
duty to maintain confidentiality can be quite broad. Generally, patient information
may be revealed when the patient consents, or when disclosure is necessary to protect
the health and safety of either the patient or third parties. In some circumstances,

health care providers may even have a *duty* to breach confidentiality imposed by common law or statute. This issue is discussed in more detail at pages 175-186.

Whether or not a patient has waived his or her right to confidentiality is a significant issue in litigation. See Annot., 21 A.L.R.3d 912 (1968); Reda v. Advocate Health Care, 765 N.E.2d 1002 (Ill. 2002) (plaintiff in neurological injury action had not placed mental condition at issue and had not waived privilege with respect to his mental health records). Should asserting one's fitness to be a parent in a child custody dispute constitute a waiver of the psychiatrist-patient privilege? See Laznovsky v. Laznovsky, 745 A.2d 1054 (Md. 2000) (no). See also Annot., 50 A.L.R.4th 714 (1986).

Should a patient be able to gain access to the identity of other patients? Rogers v. New York University Hospitals Cntr., 795 N.Y.S.2d 438 (N.Y. Sup. 2005) (identity of fellow patient can be released without violating HIPAA privacy); Baptist Memorial Hospital-Union County v. Johnson, 754 So. 2d 1165 (Miss. 2000) (hospital must disclose identity of patient who mistakenly breast-fed another patient's baby); Falco v. Institute of Living, 757 A.2d 571 (Conn. 2000) (psychiatrist-patient privilege prevented disclosure of identity of patient who attacked plaintiff in psychiatric hospital). See also Annot., 66 A.L.R.5th 591 (1999).

7. *Adherence to Confidentiality.* Despite the legal rules, studies regularly demonstrate that patient confidentiality is often breached. See, e.g., Elizabeth A. Kitsis, Shining a Light on Shadowing, 305 JAMA 1029 (2011) (shadowing of physicians by university students and patient privacy); Rebecca Shore et al., Report of the AMA Council on Ethical and Judicial Affairs: Professionalism in the Use of Social Media, 22 J. Clin. Ethics 165 (2011) (noting breaches of patient confidentiality); John C. Moskop, From Hippocrates to HIPAA: Privacy and Confidentiality in Emergency Medicine, 45 Ann. Emerg. Med. 60 (2005); P. A. Ubel et al., Elevator Talk: Observational Study of Inappropriate Comments in a Public Space, 99 Am. J. Med. 190 (1995). What explains the gulf between legal standards and medical practice in this area?

8. *Disclosure of Information About Health Care Providers.* Patients might wish to have access to information about the health status of their health care providers. Should physicians be able to maintain the confidentiality of their own medical information? See infra at page 233 note 8.

2. The Duty to Breach Confidentiality

The duty to maintain confidentiality exists in an uneasy equilibrium with a potentially conflicting duty to breach confidentiality in some circumstances. Recall that the federal Privacy Rule permits some disclosures without patient authorization or opportunity to agree or object. Covered entities:

1. "[M]ay use or disclose protected health information to the extent that such use of disclosure is required by law";
2. "[M]ay disclose . . . [PHI] for . . . public health activities and purposes . . . to" public health authorities for, e.g., disease surveillance activities, prevention of child abuse or neglect, or drug safety monitoring;
3. May disclose PHI to "[a] person who may have been exposed to a communicable disease or may otherwise be at risk of contracting or spreading a disease or condition, if the covered entity or public health authority is authorized by law to

notify such person as necessary in the conduct of a public health intervention or investigation"; and

4. [M]ay, consistent with applicable law and standards of ethical conduct, use or disclose protected health information, if the covered entity, in good faith, believes that the use or disclosure: [] [i]s necessary to prevent or lessen a serious and imminent threat to the health or safety of a person or the public; and [] [is] to a person or persons reasonably able to prevent or lessen the threat, including the target of the threat. . . .

45 C.F.R. §164.512 (a),(b), (c), (j).

Health care providers sometimes have not only a common law or statutory *authority* to breach confidentiality; they also have the *duty* to do so. Failure to meet this obligation can lead to criminal or civil liability. As you read the following materials, consider the perspective of health care providers. Are the rules governing confidentiality and disclosure in hopeless conflict, subjecting health care providers to "Catch-22" liability? Consider also the perspective of patients. Are the limits of confidentiality clear for patients? Is the protection afforded patient-provider communication sufficient to encourage necessary medical treatment? Finally, consider the costs to society created by duties to maintain confidentiality and duties to disclose. When should the interests of third parties be sufficient to outweigh the interests of patients in the confidentiality of medical information?

Florida provides a typical example of laws regarding the mandatory reporting of abuse, neglect, or exploitation of vulnerable adults:

(1) Mandatory reporting.—
(a) Any person, including, but not limited to, any:
1. Physician, osteopathic physician, medical examiner, chiropractic physician, nurse, paramedic, emergency medical technician, or hospital personnel engaged in the admission, examination, care, or treatment of vulnerable adults;
2. Health professional or mental health professional other than one listed in subparagraph 1;
3. Practitioner who relies solely on spiritual means for healing;
4. Nursing home staff; assisted living facility staff; adult day care center staff; adult family-care home staff; social worker; or other professional adult care, residential, or institutional staff; . . .
who knows, or has reasonable cause to suspect, that a vulnerable adult has been or is being abused, neglected, or exploited shall immediately report such knowledge or suspicion to the central abuse hotline.

Fla. Stat. Ann. §415.1034. Section 415.1034(b) describes specific types of information about the alleged victim, perpetrator, and types of injuries. Persons who knowingly and willfully fail to make reports or who prevent others from doing so are subject to misdemeanor criminal liability. Id. §415.111. Persons who report matters in good faith are immune from statutory liability.

Notes: Statutory Disclosure Obligations

1. *Structure of Statutory Obligations.* Each state imposes disclosure obligations on health care professionals by statute. The statute typically will establish (1) who has the duty to disclose information; (2) the events or information that must be

disclosed; (3) to whom the information must be disclosed; and (4) the immunities or liabilities associated with the disclosure obligation. State disclosure obligations generally apply to a wide range of licensed health professions, such as physicians, nurses, nursing home staff members, social workers, and others. The HIPAA privacy rules permit providers to make these disclosures. 45 C.F.R. §164.512.

2. *Types of Disclosure Duties.* Most disclosure obligations are associated with the risk of harm to others through criminal activity or the transmission of disease. The Florida statute focuses on the danger of elder abuse, a matter of particular concern in retirement communities. The disclosure duty stems from concerns that members of this group may not be able to communicate their abuse to others. Like other states, Florida imposes a similar disclosure obligation for instances of suspected child abuse. Fla. Stat. Ann. §39.201 (2012).

States also require physicians and others to report gunshot or knife wounds to police authorities. See, e.g., N.Y. Penal Law §265.25. See generally Mark A. Hall, Hospital and Physician Disclosure of Information Concerning a Patient's Crime, 63 U. Det. L. Rev. 145 (1985). The disclosure will alert appropriate authorities to the probability that a crime has occurred, but it is not especially helpful in preventing imminent harm. Citizens do not have a general obligation to disclose possible criminal activity; what justifies the existence of a disclosure obligation here? Arguably, the health care provider who gives medical treatment to a gunshot victim is more than a passive bystander, insofar as he or she may help perpetrators to elude law enforcement officers. In addition, the ordinary rules favoring confidentiality may not apply; individuals who have been shot or knifed may be highly motivated to seek health care whether or not their treatment will be confidential.

What about wounds not serious enough to fall within the scope of a reporting statute but which might nonetheless reveal evidence of criminal activity? Suppose that a district attorney serves grand jury subpoenas duces tecum on nearly two dozen hospitals, seeking "[a]ny and all records pertaining to any male Caucasian patient between the ages of 30 to 45 years, . . . [treated during a two-day period] for a laceration, puncture wound or slash, or other injury caused by or possibly caused by a cutting instrument and/or sharp object, said injury being plainly observable to a lay person without expert or professional knowledge. . . ." The subpoenas expressly exclude from discovery information obtained by licensed health care professionals obtained while attending the patient and necessary to provide care for the patient. Should the hospitals comply? See In re Grand Jury Investigation in New York County, 779 N.E.2d 173 (N.Y. 2002) (upholding appellate decision quashing the subpoenas); In re Grand Jury Subpoena for Medical Records of Payne, 839 A.2d 837 (N.H. 2004) (statute requiring physicians to report bodily injuries arising from criminal acts insufficient to provide unilateral authority for government subpoena of medical records). Finally, states also require health care providers to report information about individuals who have been diagnosed with certain contagious or transmissible diseases. See pages 687-689.

3. *Disclose to Whom?* States require disclosures to different types of state authorities. Some disclosures are made directly to law enforcement personnel. See, e.g., N.Y. Penal Law §265.25 (McKinney 2012) (gunshot wounds disclosed to police). States have also established special "hotlines" for certain types of disclosures, such as those regarding child or elder abuse. See, e.g., Fla. Stat. Ann. §39.201 (2012). Contagious or transmissible disease reports are most often directed to state public

health authorities. See, e.g., Fla. Stat. Ann. §384.25 (2012) (sexually transmissible diseases reported to health department). The statutes generally provide that the confidentiality of some types of reported information will be protected from further disclosure. See, e.g., id. These confidentiality protections may be constitutionally required. See pages 680-685.

4. *Immunities and Liabilities.* Providers who file mandatory reports about diseases or abuse are usually immune from damages for any mistake and resulting harm. See Zamstein v. Marvasti, 692 A.2d 781 (Conn. 1997). But see Runyon v. Smith, 749 A.2d 852 (N.J. 2000). Less clear is the legal exposure for a professional who is in a position to file a report, but who fails to do so. Under some statutes, a failure to comply with statutory reporting requirements can lead to criminal or civil liability. New York's child abuse reporting statute provides one example of a typical statutory scheme:

1. Any person, official or institution required by this title to report a case of suspected child abuse or maltreatment who willfully fails to do so shall be guilty of a class A misdemeanor.

2. Any person, official or institution required by this title to report a case of suspected child abuse or maltreatment who knowingly and willfully fails to do so shall be civilly liable for the damages proximately caused by such failure.

N.Y. Social Services Law §420.

Should children injured by a provider's failure to report child abuse be permitted to bring suit in jurisdictions where the reporting statute does not include a specific civil remedy? Courts are divided. See Annot., 73 A.L.R.4th 782 (1989). Should a subsequent child abuse victim be permitted to sue the provider on the theory that if the provider had reported the first victim the second victim would not have been at risk? Marcelletti v. Bathani, 500 N.W.2d 124 (Mich. Ct. App. 1993) (no). A provider's failure to follow reporting rules can also spark professional disciplinary action. In the Matter of Schroeder, 415 N.W.2d 436 (Minn. Ct. App. 1988). Should a health care provider have a duty to disclose the limits of confidentiality before providing services to her patients? See Marks v. Tenbrunsel, 910 So. 2d 1255 (Alabama 2005) (patient not permitted to pursue claim against psychologist who reported alleged child abuse even though patient claims he was assured of confidentiality); Hayes v. State, 667 N.E.2d 222 (Ind. Ct. App. 1996) (holding that therapist had no duty to warn client that disclosures of child sexual abuse would be reported to state authorities).

5. *Common Law Disclosure Requirements.* As the next case reveals, disclosure obligations also arise under common law.

■ BRADSHAW v. DANIEL
854 S.W.2d 865 (Tenn. 1993)

ANDERSON, Justice.

We granted this appeal to determine whether a physician has a legal duty to warn a nonpatient of the risk of exposure to the source of his patient's noncontagious disease — Rocky Mountain Spotted Fever. . . .

On July 19, 1986, Elmer Johns went to the emergency room at Methodist Hospital South in Memphis, Tennessee, complaining of headaches, muscle aches, fever, and chills. He was admitted to the hospital under the care and treatment of the defendant, Dr. Chalmers B. Daniel, Jr. Dr. Daniel first saw Johns on July 22, 1986, at which time he ordered the drug Chloramphenicol, which is the drug of choice for a person in the latter stages of Rocky Mountain Spotted Fever. Johns' condition rapidly deteriorated, and he died the next day, July 23, 1986. An autopsy was performed, and the Centers for Disease Control in Atlanta conclusively confirmed, in late September 1986, that the cause of death was Rocky Mountain Spotted Fever. Although Dr. Daniel communicated with Elmer Johns' wife, Genevieve, during Johns' treatment, he never advised her of the risks of exposure to Rocky Mountain Spotted Fever, or that the disease could have been the cause of Johns' death.

A week after her husband's death, on August 1, 1986, Genevieve Johns came to the emergency room of Baptist Memorial Hospital in Memphis, Tennessee, with similar symptoms of chills, fever, mental disorientation, nausea, lung congestion, myalgia, and swelling of the hands. She was admitted to the hospital and treated for Rocky Mountain Spotted Fever, but she died three days later, on August 4, 1986, of that disease. It is undisputed that no patient-physician relationship existed between Genevieve Johns and Dr. Daniel.

The plaintiff, William Jerome Bradshaw, is Genevieve Johns' son. He filed this suit alleging that the defendant's negligence in failing to advise Genevieve Johns that her husband died of Rocky Mountain Spotted Fever, and in failing to warn her of the risk of exposure, proximately caused her death. . . . Dr. Gelfand [an expert witness for the defense] testified that the medical standard of care did not require a physician treating a patient infected with, or suspected of being infected with, Rocky Mountain Spotted Fever to treat the family of the patient in contact with him, or to warn them of the risk of exposure to the disease or the risk of exposure to ticks or tick bites. The plaintiff responded with the affidavit of Dr. Burt Prater. Dr. Prater testified that because of the clustering effect of the disease, the medical standard of care required that a physician treating a patient with symptoms of Rocky Mountain Spotted Fever advise the family of the patient as to the incubation period, the symptoms of the disease, and the need for immediate medical attention upon manifestation of the symptoms. Dr. Prater further testified that the defendant, Dr. Daniel, negligently failed to diagnose Elmer Johns' fatal disease of Rocky Mountain Spotted Fever and failed to warn his wife, Genevieve Johns, of the incubation period of the disease, the symptoms, and the need to seek medical treatment upon manifestation of the symptoms. He also testified that the disease, if untreated, has a 40 percent mortality rate, but if treated promptly, has a 4 percent mortality rate. Based on the affidavits, the defendant's motion for summary judgment was denied. The case was . . . tried before a jury, which returned a verdict of $50,000 against the defendant. . . .

LEGAL DUTY

The defendant physician argues that he owed his patient's wife no legal duty because first, there was no physician-patient relationship, and second, Rocky Mountain Spotted Fever is not a contagious disease and, therefore, there is no duty to warn of the risk of exposure.

We begin our analysis by examining how we determine when a legal duty may be imposed upon one for the benefit of another. While duty was not part of the early English common law jurisprudence of tort liability, it has since become an essential element in negligence cases. . . . [T]he imposition of a legal duty reflects society's contemporary policies and social requirements concerning the right of individuals and the general public to be protected from another's act or conduct. Indeed, it has been stated that "'duty' is not sacrosanct in itself, but is only an expression of the sum total of those considerations of policy which lead the law to say that the plaintiff is entitled to protection." W. Keeton, Prosser and Keeton on the Law of Torts §53 at 358. . . .

The defendant contends that the absence of a physician-patient relationship negates the existence of a duty in this case. While it is true that a physician-patient relationship is necessary to the maintenance of a medical malpractice action, it is not necessary for the maintenance of an action based on negligence, and this Court has specifically recognized that a physician may owe a duty to a nonpatient third party for injuries caused by the physician's negligence, if the injuries suffered and the manner in which they occurred were reasonably foreseeable. Wharton Transport Corp. v. Bridges, 606 S.W.2d 521, 526 (Tenn. 1980) (physician owed duty to third party injured by disabled truck driver's negligence, where the physician was negligent both in his physical examination and certification of the truck driver for the employer).

Here, we are asked to determine whether a physician has an affirmative duty to warn a patient's family member about the symptoms and risks of exposure to Rocky Mountain Spotted Fever, a noncontagious disease. Insofar as we are able to determine, there is no reported decision from this or any other jurisdiction involving circumstances exactly similar to those presented in this case.

We begin by observing that all persons have a duty to use reasonable care to refrain from conduct that will foreseeably cause injury to others. In determining the existence of a duty, courts have distinguished between action and inaction. Professor Prosser has commented that "the reason for the distinction may be said to lie in the fact that by 'misfeasance' the defendant has created a new risk of harm to the plaintiff, while by 'nonfeasance' he has at least made his situation no worse, and has merely failed to benefit him by interfering in his affairs." Prosser, §56 at 373.

Because of this reluctance to countenance nonfeasance as a basis of liability, as a general rule, under the common law, one person owed no affirmative duty to warn those endangered by the conduct of another. Prosser, §56 at 374; Tarasoff v. Regents of University of California, 17 Cal. 3d 425 (1976). To mitigate the harshness of this rule, courts have carved out exceptions for cases in which the defendant stands in some special relationship to either the person who is the source of the danger, or to the person who is foreseeably at risk from the danger. Accordingly,

> while an actor is always bound to prevent his acts from creating an unreasonable risk to others, he is under the affirmative duty to act to prevent another from sustaining harm only when certain socially recognized relations exist which constitute the basis for such legal duty.

Harper & Kime, The Duty to Control the Conduct of Another, 43 Yale L.J. 886, 887 (1934).

One of the most widely known cases applying that principle is *Tarasoff*, supra, in which the California Supreme Court held that when a psychotherapist determines or, pursuant to the standards of his profession, should determine that his patient presents a serious danger of violence to another, the therapist has an affirmative duty to use reasonable care to protect the intended victim against such danger, and the duty may require the physician to warn the intended victim of the danger. The special relationship of the patient to his psychotherapist supported imposition of the affirmative duty to act for the benefit of third persons. . . .

Decisions of other jurisdictions have employed the same analysis and held that the relationship of a physician to his patient is sufficient to support the duty to exercise reasonable care to protect third persons against foreseeable risks emanating from a patient's physical illness. Specifically, other courts have recognized that physicians may be liable to persons infected by a patient, if the physician negligently fails to diagnose a contagious disease, or having diagnosed the illness, fails to warn family members or others who are foreseeably at risk of exposure to the disease. . . . [S]ee generally Annot., 3 A.L.R.5th 370 (1992). . . .

Returning to the facts of this case, first, it is undisputed that there was a physician-patient relationship between Dr. Daniel and Elmer Johns. Second, here, as in the contagious disease context, it is also undisputed that Elmer Johns' wife, who was residing with him, was at risk of contracting the disease. This is so even though the disease is not contagious in the narrow sense that it can be transmitted from one person to another. Both Dr. Daniel and Dr. Prater, the plaintiff's expert, testified that family members of patients suffering from Rocky Mountain Spotted Fever are at risk of contracting the disease due to a phenomenon called clustering, which is related to the activity of infected ticks who transmit the disease to humans. Dr. Prater also testified that Dr. Daniel negligently failed to diagnose the disease and negligently failed to warn his patient's wife, Genevieve Johns, of her risk of exposure to the source of disease. Dr. Daniel's expert disputed these conclusions, but Dr. Daniel conceded there is a medical duty to inform the family when there is a diagnosis of the disease. Thus, this case is analogous to the *Tarasoff* line of cases adopting a duty to warn of danger and the contagious disease cases adopting a comparable duty to warn. Here, as in those cases, there was a foreseeable risk of harm to an identifiable third party, and the reasons supporting the recognition of the duty to warn are equally compelling here.

We, therefore, conclude that the existence of the physician-patient relationship is sufficient to impose upon a physician an affirmative duty to warn identifiable third persons in the patient's immediate family against foreseeable risks emanating from a patient's illness. Accordingly, we hold that under the factual circumstances of this case, viewing the evidence in a light most favorable to the plaintiff, the defendant physician had a duty to warn his patient's wife of the risk to her of contracting Rocky Mountain Spotted Fever, when he knew, or in the exercise of reasonable care, should have known, that his patient was suffering from the disease. Our holding here is necessarily limited to the conclusion that the defendant physician owed Genevieve Johns a legal duty. We express no opinion on the other elements which would be required to establish a cause of action for common-law negligence in this case.

Accordingly . . . this cause is remanded to the trial court for proceedings consistent with this opinion. . . .

Notes: Common Law Duty to Warn

1. *Overview.* Was Dr. Daniel negligent in his treatment of his patient, Elmer Johns? Daniel appropriately identified the cause of Johns' illness and provided treatment. On what basis can he be held liable for injuries to someone who was not his patient? The court notes that the existence of a physician-patient relationship generally is a prerequisite to the maintenance of a malpractice action. It finds, however, that the absence of a relationship is no barrier to an ordinary negligence action. However, the court still must confront whether there is a "special relationship," due to the oft-described distinction between "misfeasance" and "nonfeasance" (creating a risk of harm vs. failing to protect others from a risk of harm created by another). As a general rule, nonfeasance does not constitute actionable negligence. The "special relationship" rule is an exception to this principle. See, e.g., Restatement (Second) Torts §§314, 314A; W. Jonathan Cardi, A Pluralistic Analysis of the Therapist/Physician Duty to Warn Third Parties, 44 Wake Forest L. Rev. 877 (2009); Aaron D. Twerski, The Cleaver, the Violin, and the Scalpel: Duty and the Restatement (Third) of Torts, 60 Hastings L.J. 1 (2008). The key in many third-party liability cases therefore is whether there is a "special relationship" that justifies the imposition of liability for nonfeasance. Note that some jurisdictions are hostile toward the expansion of physicians' duties to third parties. See, e.g., Thapar v. Zezulka, 994 S.W.2d 635 (Tex. 1999).

Once the existence of a duty is established, the court must determine its scope. The scope of the duty is determined in large part by the nature of the risk and the physician's ability to reduce the risk reasonably. Note that in duty to warn situations, some risks can be reduced simply by warning the patient. As an example, suppose that a physician treats a patient for epilepsy and fails to tell the patient to refrain from driving. The patient has a seizure and runs into an oncoming car. Although the physician may have a duty to the driver of the other car, the accident and injury could easily have been avoided by warning the patient not to drive. If the patient had been warned, and had refrained from driving, no breach of confidentiality would have been required and there would have been no conflict between the duty to maintain confidentiality and the duty to protect others from harm. The discussion in this section focuses on the more difficult cases where physicians might have to breach patient confidentiality in order to protect third parties. Note that the federal privacy rules permit covered entities to disclose personally identifiable health information in some circumstances to prevent or reduce the risk of a "serious and imminent threat to health and safety" 45 C.F.R. §164.512(j), supra page 175.

2. *Categorizing Cases: A General Theory of Liability or a Laundry List?* The first problem in these common law liability cases lies in determining the existence of a "special relationship." The *Bradshaw* court notes that the physician-patient relationship has been used to support the imposition of liability in cases involving dangerous psychiatric patients and patients with contagious illnesses. Courts have also noted the importance of the physician-patient relationship in some automobile and child abuse cases. Does this indicate that physicians will always be held liable for injuries caused by or to their patients? Or are courts developing a list of situations in which physicians may be held liable? If so, what principles or factors determine whether the physician owes a duty to the third party? Are disclosure obligations

limited to physicians, or do other types of health care professionals face the same threat of liability?

a. *Contagious Diseases.* One well-developed line of cases holds physicians liable for injuries to nonpatients caused by communicable diseases. Physicians have been held liable for failing to diagnose the contagious condition. See, e.g., Jones v. Stanko, 160 N.E. 456 (Ohio 1928) (physician fails to diagnose smallpox and puts neighbors at risk for infection). But see Ellis v. Peter, 627 N.Y.S.2d 707 (App. Div. 1995) (failure to diagnose TB; no duty to warn). Liability has also been imposed for failure to warn others about the risk of transmission. See, e.g., Skillings v. Allen, 173 N.W. 663 (Minn. 1919) (negligent failure to disclose risk of transmission of scarlet fever); Gammill v. United States, 727 F.2d 950, 954 (10th Cir. 1984) (physician may be found liable for failing to warn persons at risk for exposure of the danger). By contrast, see McNulty v. City of New York, 792 N.E.2d 162 (N.Y. 2003) (defendant physicians did not owe friend of person infected with meningitis a duty to warn her of the risk of infection); Santa Rosa Health Care Corp. v. Garcia, 964 S.W.2d 940 (Tex. 1998) (no duty to warn wife of hemophiliac of risk of HIV). See generally Annot., 3 A.L.R.5th 370 (1992). Note that *Bradshaw* is an extension of this principle — Rocky Mountain Spotted Fever is not contagious but it is likely that others in the patient's household may have come into contact with infected ticks.

Courts also have drawn an analogy between contagious conditions and genetic conditions. What are a physician's obligations when she discovers that a patient has serious hereditable genetic condition? Compare Safer v. Estate of Pack, 677 A.2d 1188 (N.J. Super. 1996) (physicians have a duty to warn those known to be at risk of avoidable harm from genetically transmissible conditions; duty extends to the physician's patient and to members of the immediate family of the patient who may be adversely affected by a failure to warn; physician may have a duty to warn family members), with Pate v. Threlkel, 661 So. 2d 278 (Fla. 1995) (applying contagious disease concepts in context of a genetically transmittable condition but holding that duty met by notifying patient of character of condition). See also Molloy v. Meier, 679 N.W.2d 711 (Minn. 2004) ("physician's duty regarding genetic testing and diagnosis extends beyond the patient to biological parents who foreseeably may be harmed by a breach of that duty"). See generally Mary L. Kovalesky, To Disclose or Not to Disclose: Determining the Scope and Exercise of a Physician's Duty to Warn Third Parties of Genetically Transmissible Conditions, 76 U. Cin. L. Rev. 1019 (2007-2008); Gillian Nycum et al., Intra-Familial Obligations to Communicate Genetic Risk Information: What Foundations? What Forms?, 3 McGill J.L. & Health 21 (2009) (providing international comparisons); Kenneth Offit et al., The "Duty to Warn" a Patient's Family Members About Hereditary Disease Risks, 292 JAMA 1469 (2004); K. Wolff et al., Confidentiality Versus Duty to Inform — An Empirical Study on Attitudes Toward the Handling of Genetic Information, 143 Am. J. Med. Genet. A. 142 (2007) (most respondents wished to be informed about a hereditary disease in their family; study included consideration of conditions under which breach of confidentiality would be deemed acceptable).

The duty to protect third parties from harm in contagious disease cases has become highly controversial because of the risk of HIV transmission. Do physicians have an obligation to warn third parties when their patients continue to engage in activities that present the risk of HIV transmission? The answer is complicated somewhat by the existence of special statutes protecting the confidentiality of HIV-related information, which may restrict the ability to disclose information even when others may be at risk, and by variations in the risk of transmission related to use of condoms and anti-retroviral therapies. See generally Guion L. Johnstone, A Social Worker's Dilemma When a Client Has a Sexually Transmitted Disease, 49 U. Louisville L. Rev. 111 (2010) (reviewing physician obligations); Bernard Friedland, HIV Confidentiality and the Right to Warn—The Health Care Provider's Dilemma, 80 Mass. L. Rev. 3 (1995).

b. *Mental Illness.* Another set of cases concern a mental health professional's duty to protect third parties from his or her patient. The leading case is Tarasoff v. Regents of University of California, 551 P.2d 334 (Cal. 1976), discussed briefly in *Bradshaw.* In *Tarasoff,* a therapist knew that a patient had made threats of violence toward a young woman. The therapist unsuccessfully attempted to commit the patient for treatment. The patient murdered the young woman, whose parents then sued the patient's mental health care providers. The California Supreme Court, relying in part on Restatement (Second) of Torts §315, supra, held that psychotherapists could be held liable for failing to exercise reasonable care to protect a third party where the therapists know or should know that their patient presents a serious danger of violence to another. The court held that therapists might have an obligation to warn those at risk and specifically rejected the defendants' contention that such a warning would impermissibly breach client confidentiality. *Tarasoff* was much discussed by commentators through the late 1970s and 1980s. For a review of *Tarasoff* and its progeny, see Symposium, *Tarasoff* at Thirty, 75 U. Cin. L. Rev. 497-661 (2006). See also W. Jonathon Cardi, A Pluralistic Analysis of the Therapist/Physician Duty to Warn Third Parties, 44 Wake Forest L. Rev. 877 (2009); Annot., 83 A.L.R.3d 1201 (1978).

Tarasoff is an important opinion, almost always cited by courts and legislative bodies whether it is followed or rejected. See, e.g., Munstermann v. Alegent Health-Immanuel Medical Center, 716 N.W.2d 73 (Neb. 2006) (establishing scope of psychiatrist's liability to third parties); Powell v. Catholic Medical Center, 749 A.2d 301 (N.H. 2000) (discussing implications of state codification of *Tarasoff*-type rule); Estates of Morgan v. Fairfield Family Counseling Center, 673 N.E.2d 1311 (Ohio 1997) (psychiatrist-outpatient relationship is a "special relationship" justifying imposition of duty to protect third parties).

Many jurisdictions have adopted only a narrow reading of *Tarasoff* or have rejected it completely. See, e.g., Dawe v. Dr. Reuven Bar-Levav & Associates, 780 N.W.2d 272 (Mich. 2010) (statute codifying narrow mental health professional's duties to warn did not completely abrogate common law duty of care to other patients). In Nasser v. Parker, 455 S.E.2d 502 (Va. 1995), for example, the court considered whether the defendant physician and hospital had a duty to warn a victim about the impending release of a former boyfriend who had threatened to kill her. The court noted the special relationship rule found in §315, but held that no special relationship existed without an additional showing of an ability to control the patient's conduct:

> Accordingly, we disagree with the holding of *Tarasoff* that a doctor-patient relationship or a hospital-patient relationship alone is sufficient, as a matter of law, to establish a "special relation" under Restatement §315(a). Within the context of the Restatement, there is nothing special about the ordinary doctor-patient relationship or hospital-patient relationship. We think there must be added to those ordinary

relationships the factor, required by [Restatement] §319, of taking charge of the patient, meaning that the doctor or hospital must be vested with a higher degree of control over the patient than exists in the ordinary doctor-patient or hospital-patient relationship before a duty arises concerning the patient's conduct.

Id. at 506. See also Boulanger v. Pol, 900 P.2d 823 (Kan. 1995) (no special relationship between psychiatrist and voluntary mental patient); Thapar v. Zezulka, 994 S.W.2d 635 (Tex. 1999) (no duty to warn). See also Cal. Civ. Code §43.92 (limiting *Tarasoff*-type liability).

c. *Driving Impairments.* Most driving impairment cases involve the physician's obligation to warn the patient about the risks of driving. See, e.g., Coombes v. Florio, 877 N.E.2d 567 (Mass. 2007) (divided court holds physician owes a duty of care to third parties to inform his patient of the possible adverse impact of medications on driving ability); Weigold v. Patel, 840 A.2d 19 (Conn. App. 2004) (no liability where patient aware of tendency to fall asleep while driving). See generally Annot., 43 A.L.R.4th 153 (1986). Where a state statute requires physicians to report certain driving impairments, physicians can be held liable for injuries to third parties. See, e.g., Harden by Harden v. Allstate Insurance Co., 883 F. Supp. 963 (D. Del. 1995). But see Praesel v. Johnson, 967 S.W.2d 391 (Tex. 1998) (no negligence per se or common law duty).

3. *A Risk of Harm.* The risk of harm is clear in some cases, particularly those involving serious contagious diseases. The issue is more problematic in the case of psychiatric patients. See, e.g., Douglas Mossman, The Imperfection of Protection Through Detection and Intervention, 30 J. Leg. Med. 109 (2009). Can mental health professionals accurately predict which patients will present a risk of harm to others? The *Tarasoff* court used a professional standard of care to measure the scope of the physicians' obligation to third parties: If the defendant knew or should have known of the risk, using professional judgment, then liability may follow. Tarasoff v. Regents of University of California, 551 P.2d 334 (Cal. 1976). See also Estates of Morgan v. Fairfield Family Counseling Center, 673 N.E.2d 1311, 1325 (Ohio 1997) (psychotherapists need not have perfect predictive power).

4. *Foreseeable and Identifiable Third Parties.* Many contagious disease and psychiatric dangerousness cases suggest that a health care provider's duty to disclose is established by a specific risk to foreseeable and identifiable third parties. See, e.g., *Bradshaw* and *Tarasoff*, supra. This requirement serves at least two purposes: It bolsters the sense that the risk of harm is imminent, and it suggests that a disclosure requirement is reasonable. Where a health care provider knows the identity of the person at risk of harm, it seems reasonable to require that that person be warned about the risk. A few courts have also been willing to impose a duty to breach confidentiality even where the risk is more generalized, however. In Schuster v. Altenberg, 424 N.W.2d 159 (Wis. 1988), the court held that a duty to breach confidentiality existed even in cases where there was no "readily identifiable target" of the patient's violent tendencies. Id. at 172-174. In such cases, the therapist has the duty to inform police so that emergency commitment proceedings can be initiated.

In cases where the claim is based on the physician's failure to disclose information to the *patient* rather than to the injured third parties, courts have not limited liability to situations in which the third party is known or identifiable. See, e.g., Reisner v. Regents of the University of California, 37 Cal. Rptr. 2d 518 (Cal. Ct. App.

1995) (physicians owed a duty to HIV-infected boyfriend to disclose to patient or her parents her HIV status; failure to disclose occurred long before sexual relationship between young people began).

5. *Disclose to Whom?* As noted above, in most cases a physician's duty to third parties is discharged by disclosing the risk to his or her patient. See, e.g., Emerich v. Philadelphia Center for Human Development, Inc., 720 A.2d 1032 (Pa. 1999) (duty satisfied by statement to victim that she should not go to patient's apartment); Pate v. Threlkel, 661 So. 2d 278 (Fla. 1995). Where the patient presents a risk of harm to an identifiable third party, many jurisdictions also will impose a duty to disclose the risk to that person. See, e.g., *Tarasoff*, supra. Sometimes the provider's disclosure obligation can be met through an institutional disclosure mechanism. In Casarez v. NME Hospital, 883 S.W.2d 360 (Tex. App. 1994), for example, a nurse who allegedly contracted HIV from a patient sued the patient's physician for failing to warn him of the patient's condition. The court held that the physician complied with his obligations by notifying the hospital's infection control and quality assurance committees of his patient's condition.

In the absence of a statute, should a court require a physician, who knows that a patient presents a risk of harm through driving, to disclose this information to state authorities? What if the patient is informed of the risk and states that she will continue to drive despite the danger?

6. *Zone of Reasonable Judgment.* Given the conflicting nature of the duties to disclose and to protect confidentiality, and the ambiguities associated with each duty, do physicians have enough guidance to allow them to avoid liability? Even if the duties were precisely defined, it would be tricky at best to walk the narrow line between them. But where the extent of each duty is uncertain, it may be impossible to avoid liability. Disclosing may give rise to damages or ethical sanctions for breach of confidentiality, whereas keeping quiet may result in damages for injuries caused to others. What's a doctor to do? Should the law provide for a neutral zone between these two duties, in which disclosure is discretionary, but not mandatory? In other words, doctors would have a qualified privilege to disclose if they do so in the good faith belief that disclosure is necessary to prevent harm, but could not be sued for failing to disclose unless _____. The issue then becomes: How would you fill in the blank? See Mark A. Hall, Hospital and Physician Disclosure of Information Concerning a Patient's Crime, 63 U. Det. L. Rev. 145 (1985) (advocating a qualified privilege with respect to the duty to report serious crimes committed by patients).

Discussion Problems

Consider how you would analyze the following problems. What law(s) or regulations would apply in your state? Will the health care provider have a duty to maintain confidentiality, the authority to breach confidentiality, or a duty to disclose the information?

- A 30-year-old woman meets with a physician who had also treated her mother. The woman asks the physician for specific information about her mother's medical history. The woman argues that she needs the information to determine whether she is at a significantly higher risk for (a) cancer, (b) high blood pressure, or (c) glaucoma. Should it matter whether the woman's mother is deceased? On this last point, see 45 C.F.R. §164.502(f) ("A covered entity must comply with the [privacy] requirements . . . with respect to the [PHI] of a deceased individual for a period of 50 years following the death of the individual."); and Jessica Berg, Grave Secrets: Legal and Ethical Analysis of Post-mortem Confidentiality, 34 Conn. L. Rev. 81 (2001).

- A drug treatment center's admission form includes the following notice:

> We understand that persons who have problems with drugs and alcohol may fear that treatment information will be disclosed to others, including family members or employers. Rest assured that your medical treatment information will be protected from disclosure as provided by law.

A patient undergoes voluntary HIV testing and receives a positive test result. May or must the treatment center disclose the patient's HIV status to other patients? What if it appears that the HIV-infected patient has begun a sexual relationship with another patient? What if the patient is taking anti-retroviral therapies, which reduce the risk of transmission, and claims that she or he is using safer sexual practices?

- Law enforcement officials are concerned about another possible anthrax bio-terrorism event. Local authorities approach pharmacies in a particular town, seeking information about recent prescriptions for antibiotics. May the pharmacies release the information to law enforcement officials? Suppose that a physician in the town recently received a call from a patient, inquiring about a prescription for an antibiotic thought to be effective against anthrax. May or must the physician disclose this information to anyone?

D. INFORMED CONSENT

1. Goals, Aspirations, Policies

In Chapter 1.A.2 and in the introduction to this chapter we observed that the physician-patient relationship is characterized by a huge imbalance of power, owing to the vulnerability of illness and treatment and physicians' vastly superior knowledge and skills. This power imbalance may be further accentuated by economic and cultural factors. See Chapter 1.C.3. What should the medical and legal response be to these inequalities in the physician-patient relationship? Historically, or perhaps apocryphally, a patient's reverence for her physician was a source of comfort and an important underpinning to the psychology of a cure. A wide range of factors—perhaps among them the anti-establishment views of the 1960s, the consumer movement of the 1970s, the patient advocacy movements of the 1980s and 1990s, the ready availability of health-related information on the Internet, the startling advances and lingering failures of medical progress, and the expansion of specialties such as "bioethics" and "health law"—have combined to challenge the authority and supremacy of the physician. The most prominent legal tool used by those seeking to reform the physician-patient relationship is the doctrine of informed consent. It is believed that requiring physicians to provide more information to their patients will help to redress the power imbalance problems created by the inequality of knowledge. As you read the materials on informed consent, consider how effective the law has been, or conceivably could be, in accomplishing this reformist mission. Consider also what model the reformists envision for the ideal patient-physician interaction, and whether all (or many) patients actually subscribe to that model.

■ PATIENT-CENTERED MEDICINE: A PROFESSIONAL EVOLUTION
Christine Laine & Frank Davidoff*
275 JAMA 152, 152-153 (1996)

In the past, physicians commonly withheld diagnostic information from patients with patients' tacit consent. Hippocrates advocated "concealing most things from the patient while you are attending to him . . . revealing nothing of the patient's future or present condition." . . . The attitude[] of Hippocrates . . . would undoubtedly get [him] into trouble today. Patients increasingly expect to know not only their diagnoses, but also details of pathophysiology, treatment options, and prognosis. . . . Patients expect and often demand information that used to be only within physicians' reach, and physicians increasingly expect to share such information with patients.

The transformation in attitudes surrounding disclosure of diagnoses is particularly striking when one considers cancer. . . . A 1961 study . . . revealed that . . . 90 percent of physicians surveyed preferred not to tell cancer patients their diagnoses. . . . [B]y 1979 . . . 97 percent of physicians surveyed preferred to disclose a diagnosis of cancer. . . .

Beyond "honesty is the best policy," the argument for informing patients is that information enables patients to participate in medical decisions. In more physician-centered days, physicians would decide what was best for their patients, and patient participation was limited to compliance with physicians' orders. As medicine becomes more patient centered, participation begins with the patient helping to decide what the physician will order, and the emphasis shifts from compliance to participation.

■ RETHINKING INFORMED CONSENT
Peter H. Schuck**
103 Yale L.J. 899, 900-905 (1994)

The doctrine requiring physicians to obtain a patient's informed consent before undertaking treatment is relatively young, having first appeared in a recognizable, relatively robust form only in 1957.[1] Yet the values that underlie the doctrine have an ancient pedigree. The consent norm had occupied a prominent and

*Dr. Laine is Editor in Chief, and Dr. Davidoff is an Editor Emeritus, at the Annals of Internal Medicine, published by the American College of Physicians. Dr. Laine is also affiliated with the Division of Internal Medicine at Jefferson Medical College, Thomas Jefferson University.

**Reprinted by permission of The Yale Law Journal Company and Fred B. Rothman & Company. The author is the Simeon E. Baldwin Professor Emeritus of Law and Professor (Adjunct) of Law at Yale Law School.

1. See Jay Katz, The Silent World of Doctor and Patient 48-84 (1984); see also Ruth R. Faden & Tom L. Beauchamp, A History and Theory of Informed Consent 235-273 (1986).

honored place in our legal thought for many centuries before the courts began to develop a jurisprudence of informed consent in health care.[2] Also well established was the cognate notion that consent must be informed or knowledgeable in some meaningful sense if we are to accord it legal or moral significance. . . .

The doctrine of informed consent in health care shared in the more general expansion of American tort liability that proceeded well into the 1980s and that now appears to have stabilized. Everyone, it seems, favors the principle of informed consent; it is "only" the specific details and applications of the doctrine that arouse serious debate. In order to map and enlarge this debate, it is useful to distinguish three different versions of informed consent doctrine. The first is the letter and spirit of the doctrine as developed primarily by courts—the law "in books." The second is the doctrine as imagined, feared, and often caricatured by some physicians—the law "in the mind." The third version, a consequence both of the gap between the first two and of other situational constraints, is the doctrine as actually practiced by clinicians—the law "in action." (Of course, there are almost as many laws-in-action as there are distinct physician-patient relationships.)

Most commentators on informed consent deploy one or more of these versions of the law. Generally (and crudely) speaking, these commentators fall into two camps: idealists and realists. Informed consent idealists—primarily some judges and medical ethicists—advocate a relatively expansive conception of the physician's obligation to disclose and elicit information about risks and alternatives.[18] More specifically, the idealists tend to define informed consent law's pivotal concepts—materiality of risk, disclosure, alternatives, and causation—broadly and subjectively from the perspective of the individual patient rather than that of the professional, while defining the law's exceptions to the duty narrowly. Perhaps most important, idealists emphasize the qualitative dimension of physician-patient interactions concerning treatment decisions. They insist that these interactions be dialogic rather than authoritative, tailored to the individual patient's emotional needs and cognitive capacities rather than formulaic, aimed at maximizing patient autonomy and comprehension rather than mere information flow, and sensitive to the distortions that can be created by power differentials between physician and patient.

The idealists employ a distinctive rhetorical strategy. Capitalizing on the universal support for the principles and goals of informed consent, they point to the often striking difference between the law in books and the law in action—a difference that I call the "informed consent gap." The existence of this gap, they argue, shows that the law in action falls far short of the law in books. Since the law that they think should be in the books is often even more demanding, the true gap is wider still. The problem, then, is not so much the law in books, which tends to demand

2. See, e.g., Ford v. Ford, 10 N.E. 474, 475 (Mass. 1887) [assault defined in part by absence of consent].

18. See, e.g., Canterbury v. Spence, 464 F.2d 772, 787 (D.C. Cir. 1972) (principle of informed consent requires that physician disclose information that reasonable patient would wish to know in making treatment decisions); Truman v. Thomas, 611 P.2d 902, 906-907 (Cal. 1980) (patient must be apprised of risks of not undergoing treatment, even if she has refused treatment); see also Katz, supra note 1, at 48-84.

too little of physicians; rather, it is the laws in action and in the mind. For the idealist, therefore, the goal of reform must be to close the informed consent gap by conforming the law in action, at the very least, to the law now in books.

The realists—primarily practicing physicians—harbor a different vision of informed consent.[20] Although they emphatically do not contest the principle and goals of informed consent, they do question whether most patients really desire the kind of dialogue that the idealists propose. They also question whether, whatever patients desire, the gains in patient autonomy and improved outcomes produced by the dialogue are worth the additional time, money, and needless patient anxiety and confusion that informed consent may entail. Like the idealists, many realists employ a characteristic rhetoric. Rather than master the doctrinal details of the informed consent law in books, they point instead to the law in their minds, which they can easily caricature in order to demonstrate the law's folly. Although some realists do not concede that the law in action actually deviates from the law in their minds, many others readily admit that a gap does in fact exist. To them, however, this gap simply demonstrates how impractical the idealists' vision is and why it cannot be implemented in the demanding world of contemporary clinical practice.

In a real sense, then, informed consent idealists and realists argue past one another, producing a debate that is oblique and inconclusive rather than pointed and fruitful. For several related reasons, it is time to revisit this debate. These reasons include the intense public concern about rising health care costs, the bureaucratization of the physician-patient relationship, and the organization of health care delivery into units with some degree of market power over providers. Is the informed consent gap to be deplored or tolerated? Should physicians' legal obligations to disclose be further expanded, retained in their present form, or reduced? . . .

Notes: The Theory and Practice of Informed Consent

1. *Using Legal Rules to Foster Autonomy.* Peter Schuck suggests that informed consent idealists seek to promote individual autonomy while informed consent realists argue that the goals of complete individual autonomy cannot be met, at least not without great cost. As you read the following materials, identify the interests protected by the informed consent doctrine. A number of commentators have concluded that the doctrine fails to protect individual interests or to promote individual autonomy. See, e.g., Jay Katz, Informed Consent—Must It Remain a Fairy Tale?, 10 J. Contemp. Health L. & Pol'y 69 (1993).

Should we blame the law for this shortcoming, or is it inherently incapable of regulating the subtle and minute interactions between doctors and patients? Dr. Jay Katz, one of the law's most visionary and respected advocates of heightened informed consent, believed that "the radically different climate of physician-patient

---

20. Perhaps the most articulate of the realists is Dr. Thomas P. Duffy. See Thomas P. Duffy, Agamemnon's Fate and the Medical Profession, 9 W. New Eng. L. Rev. 21 (1987) (reviewing and criticizing Jay Katz's approach). Dr. Sherwin Nuland advances a more moderate realist position in his . . . book. See Sherwin B. Nuland, How We Die: Reflections on Life's Final Chapter 258-261, 265-267 (1994) (distinguishing inter alia, between family physicians, who can and should engage in meaningful informed consent dialogue with patients, and specialists, who cannot realistically be expected to do so).

decisionmaking . . . cannot be implemented by judicial, legislative, or administrative orders." Jay Katz, The Silent World of Doctor and Patient 228 (1984). Similarly, a prestigious blue-ribbon ethics commission recognized that

> further evolution of legal standards toward a firmer protection of individual self-determination in medical decisions must be tempered by a recognition of the law's limits as an instrument of social control. . . . [T]he Commission is concerned that efforts to draw the law further into regulating the subtler aspects of relations between patients and health care professionals may prove ineffective, burdensome and ultimately counterproductive.

President's Commission for the Study of Ethical Problems in Medicine and Biomedical and Behavioral Research, Making Health Care Decisions: A Report on the Ethical and Legal Implications of Informed Consent in the Patient-Practitioner Relationship 30, 204, 252 (1982).

For a critique of the current system of patient autonomy and the physician-patient fiduciary relationship see: Omri Ben-Shahar & Carl E. Schneider, The Failure of Mandated Disclosure, 159 U. Pa. L. Rev. 647 (2011); M. Greg Bloche, The Invention of Health Law, 91 Cal. L. Rev. 247 (2003); Roger B. Dworkin, Getting What We Should from Doctors: Rethinking Patient Autonomy and the Doctor-Patient Relationship, 13 Health Matrix 235 (2003); Joan H. Krause, Can Health Law Truly Become Patient-Centered?, 45 Wake Forest L. Rev. 1489 (2010). See also Lisa I. Iezzoni, Survey Shows That at Least Some Physicians Are Not Always Open or Honest with Patients, 31 Health Aff. 383 (2012) (more than 10 percent of surveyed physicians reported telling "patients something untrue in the previous year").

2. *Informed Consent in Practice.* Also consider the problems raised by the implementation of the doctrine. The process of health care decisionmaking described in narratives by physicians often suggests the irrelevance of the legal framework. See, e.g., Atul Gawande, Complications: A Surgeon's Notes on an Imperfect Science (2002). Has the process of providing informed consent through signed consent forms become as ritualized and meaningless as the exchange of a peppercorn in land transactions? Empirical studies often cast doubt on the efficacy of the practice of informed consent. In one pathbreaking article, Alan Meisel and Loren H. Roth reviewed the empirical data on informed consent. Alan Meisel & Loren H. Roth, Toward an Informed Discussion of Informed Consent: A Review of the Empirical Studies, 25 Ariz. L. Rev. 265 (1983). They found that few patients understood or remembered what they had been told about their medical condition and treatment options. Other research confirms these findings. In one typical study, patients facing either anterior cervical fusion or lumbar laminectomy were given a training session on the procedures by a neurosurgeon and a clinical nurse specialist with a master's degree in neurosurgery. D. A. Herz et al., Informed Consent: Is It a Myth?, 30 Neurosurgery 453 (1992). Patients were given a "simple" written test immediately after the training session; the mean patient score was only 43.5 percent. Six weeks later, the mean test score dropped to 38.4 percent. The authors concluded that health care providers "cannot necessarily expect accurate patient or family recall or comprehension. Fulfillment of the doctrine of informed consent by neurosurgeons may very well be mythical." See also A. M. Adams & A. F. Smith, Risk Perception and Communication: Recent Developments and Implications for Anaesthesia, 56 Anaesthesia 745 (2001).

There are a number of explanations for the gap between disclosure and comprehension/retention. Patients are often sick or emotionally vulnerable at the time of the disclosure; information may be presented in a highly technical and incomprehensible fashion; patients may not have the intelligence or educational background necessary to understand medical information; and patients may not feel able to ask important follow-up questions. See, e.g., Yael Schenker et al., Interventions to Improve Patient Comprehension in Informed Consent for Medical and Surgical Procedures: A Systematic Review, 31 Med. Decis. Making 151 (2011). Despite these problems, patients often report that they are satisfied with the informed consent process. See, e.g., F. W. Verheggen et al., Patients' Perceptions on Informed Consent and the Quality of Information Disclosure in Clinical Trials, 29 Patient Educ. Couns. 137 (1996).

Finally, the capacity of patients to understand and to make decisions may be greater than their capacity to participate in carrying out those decisions. A. D. Naik et al. note that the "clinical application of the concept of patient autonomy has centered on the ability to deliberate and make treatment decisions (decisional autonomy) to the virtual exclusion of the capacity to execute the treatment plan (executive autonomy)." A. D. Naik et al., Patient Autonomy for the Management of Chronic Conditions: A Two-Component Re-Conceptualization, 9(2) Am. J. Bioethics 23-30 (2009). For responses, see Symposium, 9(2) Am. J. Bioethics 31-35 (2009).

3. *Information That Is Harmful.* Information is not always welcome. Some types of information may increase anxiety and decrease enjoyment of life without appreciably adding to decisionmaking ability. Imagine a genetic condition associated with the early onset of severe dementia and death for which there is no effective preventive treatment. How many people would want to know how and when they are going to die? The empirical evidence is mixed:

> What studies have been done are not at all clear on the psychological effects of predictive genetic testing. Some commentators have suggested that genetic testing can cause depression and suicide. Studies have demonstrated at least some negative impact on family functioning from predictive testing for Huntington's Disease—a test that can confirm with near-certainty whether one will develop this disabling disease. The data are inconclusive, but likely suffer from substantial selection bias. It may well be that living with the knowledge that one will develop an incurable disease turns out to be better than living with uncertainty. At least it may only be different, rather than "worse." When asked what it was like finally to know that she had Huntington's, one young woman replied that "'[i]t's hard to think the other way anymore of not knowing,' . . . 'It's become a part of my life.'"

Christian Turner, The Burden of Knowledge, 43 Ga. L. Rev. 297, 315 (2009).

Assuming that individuals will have different values and preferences in this area, how do you ask whether someone wants to know without tipping them off to the truth? One solution to this dilemma is to have a more elaborate informed consent process before giving the test, in which patients are told that the information obtained might be upsetting or might affect their personal relationships, etc. Then patients could choose not to be tested at all. See Mark E. Robson et al., American Society of Clinical Oncology Policy Statement Update: Genetic and Genomic Testing for Cancer Susceptibility, 28 J. Clin. Oncol. 893 (2010); Consensus Statement, Genetic Testing for Susceptibility to Adult-Onset Cancer: The Process and Content of Informed Consent, 277 JAMA 1467 (1997). This expansive approach to pretest counseling obviously would put a crimp in the approach that many clinicians take toward routine testing, in which screening tests are done with hardly any notice at all, much less with elaborate informed consent.

Advances in genetics raise an additional dilemma, noted by Roger Dworkin in his article excerpted at page 72. If one patient wants the information and consents to testing, does this invade the privacy of family members who may not want to know the information or even to have the information created? Again, they might suffer either psychological effects or adverse financial effects from insurance or employment. Dworkin argues that genetic medicine requires us to adapt our individual autonomy model of informed consent so that it becomes more family centered. How would one obtain consent from an extended family? Is agreement by every competent adult required, or only a critical mass, or only a single family matriarch or patriarch? See also Gina Kolata, How Do You Live Knowing You Might Have an Alzheimer's Gene?, N.Y. Times, June 7, 2012; Stewart Justman, Uninformed Consent: Mass Screening for Prostate Cancer, 26 Bioethics 143 (2012) (noting that widespread PSA screening creates risk of overdiagnosis and overtreatment for sons of men tested, without demonstrable improvements in health care outcomes).

4. *Do Patients Want Decisional Autonomy?* Several commentators have argued that patients want to be informed but do not actually want to make their own health care decisions. Carl Schneider, a law professor at the University of Michigan, after reviewing empirical studies of patient interest in medical decisionmaking, concluded:

> Taken as a whole, these studies surveyed a considerable variety of populations—from the perfectly well to the dangerously sick. They asked patients about their own conditions and about hypothetical illnesses. They framed their respondent's choices in a variety of ways. And their virtually universal conclusion was that, while patients commonly wish to be informed about their medical circumstances, at least a quite substantial number of them did not want to make their own medical decisions, or perhaps even to participate in those decisions in any very significant way. . . .
>
> One might suppose that if patients were ever to assert their decisional authority it would be after hearing the alarming recitation of risks that characterizes the process of informed consent. Yet a number of studies of that process "strongly suggest that refusals attributable to disclosures are rarely, if ever, seen." Similarly, a study of why patients refuse treatment found an average of 4.6 refusals per 100 patient days. The reasons for refusal were complex, and generally there was more than one "cause" per patient. But two kinds of reasons stood out: first, a failure to tell the patient about the purpose of what was proposed; second, psychological factors, prominently including "characterological factors" (for example, using a refusal to accept treatment as a way of expressing a wish to be cared for) and "other psychoses." While the first of these causes reconfirms the wish for information we have so frequently encountered, neither of them is inconsistent with a reluctance to take control of medical decisions. And the dog that did not bark in the night is the absence of any significant number of patients who heard a doctor's recommendation and reached a different conclusion on the merits.

Carl E. Schneider, Bioethics with a Human Face, 69 Ind. L.J. 1075, 1097, 1099 (1994). Professor Schneider also noted significant evidence that "the more severe a patient's illness, the less likely the patient is to want to make medical decisions." Id.

at 1101. See also Carl E. Schneider, The Practice of Autonomy: Patients, Doctors, and Medical Decisions (1998), which is excerpted at page 69.

5. *Individual Autonomy as a Cultural Norm.* Some have argued that the law in this area represents an obsession with Western values and norms that seem less relevant to those from other cultures. For cultural and comparative perspectives on the doctrine, see Leslie J. Blackhall et al., Ethnicity and Attitudes Toward Patient Autonomy, 274 JAMA 820 (1995); Joseph A. Carrese & Lorna A. Rhodes, Western Bioethics on the Navajo Reservation: Benefit or Harm?, 274 JAMA 826 (1995); Lawrence O. Gostin, Informed Consent, Cultural Sensitivity, and Respect for Persons, 274 JAMA 844 (1995); Frances H. Miller, Denial of Health Care and Informed Consent in English and American Law, 18 Am. J.L. & Med. 37 (1992); Kristina Orfali & Elisa J. Gordon, Autonomy Gone Awry: A Cross-Cultural Study of Parents' Experiences in Neonatal Intensive Care Units, 25 Theoretical Med. & Bioethics 329 (2004). For a critique of informed consent law's application to racial, religious, and ethnic minority patients, see Dayna Bowen Matthew, Race, Religion, and Informed Consent—Lessons from Social Science, 36 J.L. Med. & Ethics 150 (2008).

6. *Individual Autonomy and Medical Research.* Commentators have been particularly concerned with the role of informed consent in medical research. See, e.g., George J. Annas, Questing for Grails: Duplicity, Betrayal and Self-Deception in Postmodern Medical Research, 12 J. Contemp. Health L. & Pol'y 297 (1996); Ruth R. Faden & Tom L. Beauchamp, A History and Theory of Informed Consent 151-232 (1986). The issue is explored in greater depth in section E.

7. *Informed Consent vs. Traditional Malpractice.* Despite academic interest, informed consent theories play a role in a relatively small percentage of claims against physicians, at least as measured by opinions published in computerized databases such as Westlaw. As you read these materials, consider the role that informed consent theories appear to play in traditional malpractice litigation. Of what relevance is it that informed consent claims are rarely brought alone but are most often seen in cases where plaintiffs also are asserting traditional negligence claims?

8. *The Spectrum of Informed Consent Standards.* Both courts and legislatures have participated in the redefinition of the roles in the physician-patient relationship. They have responded to the inequality of knowledge between providers and patients in at least four distinct ways. Some jurisdictions, about half in fact, use some version of a "professional malpractice" standard, under which physicians are required to disclose to patients that information which would have been disclosed by the reasonable, minimally competent physician. A substantial number of states use the "material risk" or "reasonable patient" standard, which requires disclosure of risks that a reasonable patient would consider to be material in making a medical treatment decision. A small number of jurisdictions take an even more protective approach, requiring disclosure of information that a particular patient (as contrasted with a "rational" patient) would have wanted to make his or her decision. Finally, courts seeking tools to regulate the nature of the physician-patient relationship have recently turned to fiduciary law as a source of additional disclosure obligations for physicians.

9. *Additional Commentaries.* The literature in this area is voluminous. Some particularly useful law review commentaries (in addition to those cited in Schuck's article) include Janet L. Dolgin, The Legal Development of Informed Consent

Doctrine: Past and Present, 19 Cambridge Q. Healthcare Ethics 97 (2010); Grant H. Morris, Dissing Disclosure: Just What the Doctor Ordered, 44 Ariz. L. Rev. 313 (2002); William M. Sage, Regulating Through Information: Disclosure Laws and American Health Care, 99 Colum. L. Rev. 1701 (1999); Marjorie Maguire Schultz, From Informed Consent to Patient Choice: A New Protected Interest, 95 Yale L.J. 219 (1985). For a classic attack on the fundamental theory of informed consent liability, see Richard Epstein, Medical Malpractice: The Case for Contract, 1976 Am. B. Found. Res. J. 87 (1976). The major treatise is Fay A. Rozovsky, Consent to Treatment: A Practical Guide (2007). There are several important books on the subject, including Carl E. Schneider, The Practice of Autonomy: Patients, Doctors, and Medical Decisions (1998); Ruth R. Faden & Tom L. Beauchamp, A History and Theory of Informed Consent (1986); Jessica W. Berg et al., Informed Consent: Legal Theory and Practice (2001). For general discussions of informed consent, see Annot., 88 A.L.R.3d 1008 (1978).

2. The Competing Disclosure Standards

■ CANTERBURY v. SPENCE
464 F.2d 772 (D.C. Cir.), cert. denied, 409 U.S. 1064 (1972)

[Appellant Canterbury, a 19-year-old clerk-typist who had experienced persistent back pain, sought care from Dr. Spence. Dr. Spence conducted a number of tests to determine the cause of the back pain and eventually recommended that Canterbury undergo a laminectomy. According to the court, Canterbury "did not raise any objection to the proposed operation nor did he probe into its exact nature." Dr. Spence spoke with Canterbury's mother by telephone. She asked "if the recommended operation was serious and Dr. Spence replied 'not any more than any other operation.'" It is unclear whether Mrs. Canterbury consented to the operation before it took place; she did sign a consent form afterward. The laminectomy was performed without any apparent difficulties. During the recovery period, however, hospital personnel failed to assist Canterbury during the process of voiding, and Canterbury fell out of his bed while attempting to void. Canterbury developed signs of partial paralysis a few hours after the fall, which were only partially improved by another operation.]

At the time of the trial . . . [he] required crutches to walk, still suffered from urinal incontinence and paralysis of the bowels, and wore a penile clamp. . . . [H]e [had] held a number of jobs, but had constant trouble finding work because he needed to remain seated and close to a bathroom. The damages appellant claims include extensive pain and suffering, medical expenses, and loss of earnings.

Appellant filed suit in the district court on March 7, 1963, four years after the laminectomy and approximately two years after he attained his majority. The complaint stated several causes of action against each defendant. Against Dr. Spence it alleged, among other things, negligence in the performance of the laminectomy and failure to inform him beforehand of the risk involved. Against the hospital the complaint charged negligent postoperative care in permitting appellant to remain unattended after the laminectomy, in failing to provide a nurse or orderly to assist him at the time of his fall, and in failing to maintain a side rail on his bed. . . .

At the close of appellant's case in chief, each defendant moved for a directed verdict and the trial judge granted both motions. . . . The judge did not allude specifically to the alleged breach of duty by Dr. Spence to divulge the possible consequences of the laminectomy.

We reverse. The testimony of appellant and his mother that Dr. Spence did not reveal the risk of paralysis from the laminectomy made out a prima facie case of violation of the physician's duty to disclose which Dr. Spence's explanation did not negate as a matter of law. . . .

Suits charging failure by a physician[6] adequately to disclose the risks and alternatives of proposed treatment are not innovations in American law. They date back a good half-century, and in the last decade they have multiplied rapidly. There is, nonetheless, disagreement among the courts and the commentators on many major questions, and there is no precedent of our own directly in point. For the tools enabling resolution of the issues on this appeal, we are forced to begin at first principles.

The root premise is the concept, fundamental in American jurisprudence, that "[e]very human being of adult years and sound mind has a right to determine what shall be done with his own body. . . ."[12] True consent to what happens to one's self is the informed exercise of a choice, and that entails an opportunity to evaluate knowledgeably the options available and the risks attendant upon each. The average patient has little or no understanding of the medical arts, and ordinarily has only his physician to whom he can look for enlightenment with which to reach an intelligent decision. From these almost axiomatic considerations springs the need, and in turn the requirement, of a reasonable divulgence by physician to patient to make such a decision possible.[15]

A physician is under a duty to treat his patient skillfully but proficiency in diagnosis and therapy is not the full measure of his responsibility. The cases demonstrate that the physician is under an obligation to communicate specific information to the patient when the exigencies of reasonable care call for it. . . .

A reasonable revelation in these respects is not only a necessity but, as we see it, is as much a matter of the physician's duty. It is a duty to warn of the dangers lurking in the proposed treatment, and that is surely a facet of due care. It is, too, a duty to impart information which the patient has every right to expect. The patient's

6. Since there was neither allegation nor proof that the appellee hospital failed in any duty to disclose, we have no occasion to inquire as to whether or under what circumstances such a duty might arise.

12. Schloendorff v. Society of New York Hospital, 211 N.Y. 125, 105 N.E. 92, 93 (1914). . . .

15. In duty-to-disclose cases, the focus of attention is more properly upon the nature and content of the physician's divulgence than the patient's understanding or consent. Adequate disclosure and informed consent are, of course, two sides of the same coin—the former a sine qua non of the latter. But the vital inquiry on duty to disclose relates to the physician's performance of an obligation, while one of the difficulties with analysis in terms of "informed consent" is its tendency to imply that what is decisive is the degree of the patient's comprehension. As we later emphasize, physician discharges the duty when he makes a reasonable effort to convey sufficient information although the patient, without fault of the physician, may not fully grasp it. . . .

reliance upon the physician is a trust of the kind which traditionally has exacted obligations beyond those associated with arms length transactions. His dependence upon the physician for information affecting his well-being, in terms of contemplated treatment, is well-nigh abject. As earlier noted, long before the instant litigation arose, courts had recognized that the physician had the responsibility of satisfying the vital informational needs of the patient. More recently, we ourselves have found "in the fiducial qualities of [the physician-patient] relationship the physician's duty to reveal to the patient that which in his best interests it is important that he should know." We now find, as a part of the physician's overall obligation to the patient, a similar duty of reasonable disclosure of the choices with respect to proposed therapy and the dangers inherently and potentially involved.

This disclosure requirement, on analysis, reflects much more of a change in doctrinal emphasis than a substantive addition to malpractice law. It is well established that the physician must seek and secure his patient's consent before commencing an operation or other course of treatment. It is also clear that the consent, to be efficacious, must be free from imposition upon the patient. It is the settled rule that therapy not authorized by the patient may amount to a tort—a common law battery—by the physician. And it is evident that it is normally impossible to obtain a consent worthy of the name unless the physician first elucidates the options and the perils for the patient's edification. Thus the physician has long borne a duty, on pain of liability for unauthorized treatment, to make adequate disclosure to the patient.[36] . . .

Duty to disclose has gained recognition in a large number of American jurisdictions, but more largely on a different rationale. The majority of courts dealing with the problem have made the duty depend on whether it was the custom of physicians practicing in the community to make the particular disclosure to the patient. . . . We agree that the physician's noncompliance with a professional custom to reveal, like any other departure from prevailing medical practice, may give rise to liability to the patient. We do not agree that the patient's cause of action is dependent upon the existence and nonperformance of a relevant professional tradition.

There are, in our view, formidable obstacles to acceptance of the notion that the physician's obligation to disclose is either germinated or limited by medical practice. To begin with, the reality of any discernible custom reflecting a professional consensus on communication of option and risk information to patients is open to serious doubt. We sense the danger that what in fact is no custom at all may be taken as an affirmative custom to maintain silence, and that physician-witnesses to the so-called custom may state merely their personal opinions as to what they or others would do under given conditions. . . . Respect for the patient's right of

36. We discard the thought that the patient should ask for information before the physician is required to disclose. Caveat emptor is not the norm for the consumer of medical services. Duty to disclose is more than a call to speak merely on the patient's request, or merely to answer the patient's questions; it is a duty to volunteer, if necessary, the information the patient needs for intelligent decision. The patient may be ignorant, confused, over-awed by the physician or frightened by the hospital, or even ashamed to inquire. See generally Note, Restructuring Informed Consent: Legal Therapy for the Doctor-Patient Relationship, 79 Yale L.J. 1533, 1545-1551 (1970). . . .

self-determination on particular therapy demands a standard set by law for physicians rather than one which physicians may or may not impose upon themselves.

More fundamentally, the majority rule overlooks the graduation of reasonable-care demands in Anglo-American jurisprudence and the position of professional custom in the hierarchy. . . .

There is . . . no basis for operation of the special medical standard where the physician's activity does not bring his medical knowledge and skills peculiarly into play. . . .

[T]he physician's duty to disclose is governed by the same legal principles applicable to others in comparable situations, with modifications only to the extent that medical judgment enters the picture. We hold that the standard measuring performance of that duty by physicians, as by others, is conduct which is reasonable under the circumstances.

Once the circumstances give rise to a duty on the physician's part to inform his patient, the next inquiry is the scope of the disclosure the physician is legally obliged to make. The courts have frequently confronted this problem but no uniform standard defining the adequacy of the divulgence emerges from the decisions. . . .

The larger number of courts, as might be expected, have applied tests framed with reference to prevailing fashion within the medical profession. . . .

In our view, the patient's right of self-decision shapes the boundaries of the duty to reveal. That right can be effectively exercised only if the patient possesses enough information to enable an intelligent choice. The scope of the physician's communications to the patient, then, must be measured by the patient's need, and that need is the information material to the decision. Thus the test for determining whether a particular peril must be divulged is its materiality to the patient's decision: All risks potentially affecting the decision must be unmasked. And to safeguard the patient's interest in achieving his own determination on treatment, the law must itself set the standard for adequate disclosure.

Optimally for the patient, exposure of a risk would be mandatory whenever the patient would deem it significant to his decision, either singly or in combination with other risks. Such a requirement, however, would summon the physician to second-guess the patient, whose ideas on materiality could hardly be known to the physician. That would make an undue demand upon medical practitioners, whose conduct, like that of others, is to be measured in terms of reasonableness. Consonantly with orthodox negligence doctrine, the physician's liability for nondisclosure is to be determined on the basis of foresight, not hindsight; no less than any other aspect of negligence, the issue on nondisclosure must be approached from the viewpoint of the reasonableness of the physician's divulgence in terms of what he knows or should know to be the patient's informational needs. . . .

From these considerations we derive the breadth of the disclosure of risks legally to be required. The scope of the standard is not subjective as to either the physician or the patient; it remains objective with due regard for the patient's informational needs and with suitable leeway for the physician's situation. In broad outline, we agree that "[a] risk is thus material when a reasonable person, in what the physician knows or should know to be the patient's position, would be likely to attach significance to the risk or cluster of risks in deciding whether or not to forego the proposed therapy."

The topics importantly demanding a communication of information are the inherent and potential hazards of the proposed treatment, the alternatives to that treatment, if any, and the results likely if the patient remains untreated. The factors contributing significance to the dangerousness of a medical technique are, of course, the incidence of injury and the degree of the harm threatened. A very small chance of death or serious disablement may well be significant; a potential disability which dramatically outweighs the potential benefit of the therapy or the detriments of the existing malady may summon discussion with the patient.

There is no bright line separating the significant from the insignificant; the answer in any case must abide a rule of reason. Some dangers—infection, for example—are inherent in any operation; there is no obligation to communicate those of which persons of average sophistication are aware. Even more clearly, the physician bears no responsibility for discussion of hazards the patient has already discovered, or those having no apparent materiality to patients' decision on therapy. . . .

No more than breach of any other legal duty does nonfulfillment of the physician's obligation to disclose alone establish liability to the patient. An unrevealed risk that should have been made known must materialize, for otherwise the omission, however unpardonable, is legally without consequence. Occurrence of the risk must be harmful to the patient, for negligence unrelated to injury is nonactionable. And, as in malpractice actions generally, there must be a causal relationship between the physician's failure to adequately divulge and damage to the patient.

A causal connection exists when, but only when, disclosure of significant risks incidental to treatment would have resulted in a decision against it. The patient obviously has no complaint if he would have submitted to the therapy notwithstanding awareness that the risk was one of its perils. On the other hand, the very purpose of the disclosure rule is to protect the patient against consequences which, if known, he would have avoided by foregoing the treatment. The more difficult question is whether the factual issue on causality calls for an objective or a subjective determination. . . .

It has been assumed that the issue is to be resolved according to whether the factfinder believes the patient's testimony that he would not have agreed to the treatment if he had known of the danger which later ripened into injury. . . .

In our view, this method of dealing with the issue on causation comes in second-best. It places the physician in jeopardy of the patient's hindsight and bitterness. It places the factfinder in the position of deciding whether a speculative answer to a hypothetical question is to be credited. It calls for a subjective determination solely on testimony of a patient-witness shadowed by the occurrence of the undisclosed risk.

Better it is, we believe, to resolve the causality issue on an objective basis: in terms of what a prudent person in the patient's position would have decided if suitably informed of all perils bearing significance. If adequate disclosure could reasonably be expected to have caused that person to decline the treatment because of the revelation of the kind of risk or danger that resulted in harm, causation is shown, but otherwise not. The patient's testimony is relevant on that score of course but it would not threaten to dominate the findings. . . .

In the context of trial of a suit claiming inadequate disclosure of risk information by a physician, the patient has the burden of going forward with evidence tending to establish prima facie the essential elements of the cause of action, and ultimately the burden of proof—the risk of nonpersuasion—on those elements. . . . The burden of going forward with evidence pertaining to a privilege not to disclose, however, rests properly upon the physician. . . .

We now delineate our view on the need for expert testimony in nondisclosure cases. . . .

The guiding consideration our decisions distill, however, is that medical facts are for medical experts and other facts are for any witnesses—expert or not—having sufficient knowledge and capacity to testify to them. It is evident that many of the issues typically involved in nondisclosure cases do not reside peculiarly within the medical domain. Lay witness testimony can competently establish a physician's failure to disclose particular risk information, the patient's lack of knowledge of the risk, and the adverse consequences following the treatment. Experts are unnecessary to a showing of the materiality of a risk to a patient's decision on treatment, or to the reasonably, expectable effect of risk disclosure on the decision. These conspicuous examples of permissible uses of nonexpert testimony illustrate the relative freedom of broad areas of the legal problem of risk nondisclosure from the demands for expert testimony that shackle plaintiffs' other types of medical malpractice litigation. . . .

This brings us to the remaining question . . . whether appellant's evidence was of such caliber as to require a submission to the jury. [T]he evidence was clearly sufficient to raise an issue as to whether Dr. Spence's obligation to disclose information on risks was reasonably met or was excused by the surrounding circumstances. Appellant testified that Dr. Spence revealed to him nothing suggesting a hazard associated with the laminectomy. His mother testified that, in response to her specific inquiry, Dr. Spence informed her that the laminectomy was no more serious than any other operation. When, at trial, it developed from Dr. Spence's testimony that paralysis can be expected in 1 percent of laminectomies, it became the jury's responsibility to decide whether that peril was of sufficient magnitude to bring the disclosure duty into play. There was no emergency to frustrate an opportunity to disclose, and Dr. Spence's expressed opinion that disclosure would have been unwise did not foreclose a contrary conclusion by the jury. There was no evidence that appellant's emotional makeup was such that concealment of the risk of paralysis was medically sound. Even if disclosure to appellant himself might have bred ill consequences, no reason appears for the omission to communicate the information to his mother, particularly in view of his minority. The jury, not Dr. Spence, was the final arbiter of whether nondisclosure was reasonable under the circumstances. . . .

Reversed and remanded for new trial.

■ **CULBERTSON v. MERNITZ**
  602 N.E.2d 98 (Ind. 1992)

KRAHULIK, Justice.

Roland B. Mernitz, M.D., (Appellee-Defendant) seeks transfer from the Court of Appeals' reversal of a summary judgment entered in his favor. Culbertson v. Mernitz (1992), Ind. App., 591 N.E.2d 1040. The issue squarely presented in this petition is whether expert medical testimony is required to establish the standard of care of health care providers on the issue of informed consent. . . .

The facts of the case are as follows. Dr. Mernitz first saw Patty Jo Culbertson on March 28, 1988. Her chief complaint was that of uncontrollable leakage of urine and discharge from the vagina. After performing a physical examination, Dr. Mernitz . . . recommend[ed] . . . that she . . . undergo a surgical procedure known as a MMK [Marshall Marchetti Krantz] procedure in order to suspend the bladder and either a hysterectomy or cryosurgery to freeze the infected tip of the cervix. Dr. Mernitz contends that he advised her of the general risks of any surgery, viz. infection, bleeding, and death, and that, with respect to the bladder suspension, he explained to her the risk that the procedure could fail and the possibility that she would be unable to void. . . . Both parties . . . agree that Dr. Mernitz did not advise her of a risk that the cervix could become adhered to the wall of the vagina.

Following this office visit, Mrs. Culbertson decided to proceed with the bladder suspension and cryosurgery. She was admitted to the hospital and underwent these procedures. Post-surgically, Mrs. Culbertson's cervix adhered to the wall of her vagina. Dr. Mernitz prescribed medication for this condition, but Mrs. Culbertson became dissatisfied with his care and saw another surgeon who eventually performed a total abdominal hysterectomy, bilateral salpingo-oophorectomy which involves the removal of both ovaries, and another bladder suspension.

Following this surgery, Mr. and Mrs. Culbertson filed a proposed complaint against Dr. Mernitz with the Indiana Department of Insurance in four counts. . . . Count II alleged that Dr. Mernitz failed to inform Mrs. Culbertson of the alternatives to surgery and the inherent risks and complications of surgery. . . .

A medical review panel was convened and, after submission of evidence to it, issued its written opinion. . . . With respect to the informed consent issue alleged in Count II, the panel ruled:

> The Panel determines that [Dr. Mernitz] did not advise [Mrs. Culbertson] of the complication of cervical adhesion to the vagina; the Panel further determines that such non-disclosure does not constitute a failure to comply with the appropriate standard of care, as such complication is not considered a risk of such surgery requiring disclosure to the patient.

The Culbertsons filed their civil action in a complaint that mirrored the allegations of the proposed complaint. After answering this complaint, Dr. Mernitz moved for summary judgment relying on the expert opinion issued by the medical review panel. The Culbertsons did not file an affidavit or other evidence in opposition to the motion for summary judgment, but argued to the trial court that the "prudent patient" standard should be utilized in evaluating informed consent claims. The trial court entered summary judgment [for the defendants]. . . . [W]e must determine the role, if any, played by expert medical opinion in resolving claims of medical malpractice premised upon a failure to obtain an informed consent.

The courts, historically, have established the standard of care required of physicians when treating patients. The law requires that a physician treating a patient possess and exercise that degree of skill and care ordinarily possessed and exercised by a physician treating such maladies.

. . . In order for a lay jury to know whether a physician complied with the legally prescribed standard of care, expert testimony has generally been held to be required. This requirement was premised on the logical belief that a non-physician could not know what a reasonably prudent physician would or would not have done under the circumstances of any given case. Therefore, an expert familiar with the practice of medicine needed to establish what a reasonably prudent physician would or would not have done in treating a patient in order to set before the jury a depiction of the reasonably prudent physician against which to judge the actions of the defendant physician. An exception was created in cases of res ipsa loquitur on the premise that in such cases a lay jury did not need guidance from a physician familiar with medical practice as to what was required of a reasonably prudent physician because the deficiency of practice "spoke for itself." Kranda v. Houser-Norborg Med. Corp., 419 N.E.2d 1024, 1042 (Ind. App. 1981). This was the settled law of most American jurisdictions, including Indiana, prior to the early 1970s when two cases on the opposite coasts carved out an additional exception to the requirement of expert medical testimony in the area of "informed consent." [The court summarized Cobbs v. Grant, 8 Cal. 3d 229 (1972), and Canterbury v. Spence, 464 F.2d 772 (D.C. Cir.), cert. denied, 409 U.S. 1064 (1972).]

INFORMED CONSENT IN INDIANA JURISPRUDENCE

[The court reviewed Indiana case law and concluded that Indiana followed the medical malpractice standard in informed consent cases. Under this standard, physicians are required to disclose that which the reasonably careful, skillful, and prudent physician would disclose under the same or similar circumstances. In general, medical expert testimony will be required to determine whether a physician has violated her duty, "unless the situation is clearly within the realm of laymen's comprehension."]

Resolution of the issue of the necessity of expert medical testimony in informed consent cases depends on whether the issue is viewed through the eyes of the physician or the patient. When viewed through the eyes of the physician, it is easy to see that a physician should not be required to guess or speculate as to what a hypothetical "reasonably prudent patient" would "need to know" in order to make a determination. A physician should only be required to do that which he is trained to do, namely, conduct himself as a reasonably prudent physician in taking a history, performing a physical examination, ordering appropriate tests, reaching a diagnosis, prescribing a course of treatment, and in discussing with the patient the medical facts of the proposed procedure, including the risks inherent in either accepting or rejecting the proposed course of treatment. From a physician's viewpoint, he should not be called upon to be a "mind reader" with the ability to peer into the brain of a prudent patient to determine what such patient "needs to know," but should simply be called upon to discuss medical facts and recommendations with the patient as a reasonably prudent physician would.

On the other hand, from the patient's viewpoint, the physician should be required to give the patient sufficient information to enable the patient to reasonably exercise the patient's right of self-decision in a knowledgeable manner. Viewed from this vantage point, the patient does not want the medical profession to determine in a paternalistic manner what the patient should or should not be told concerning the course of treatment. Thus, such a patient would view the reasonably prudent physician standard as destroying the patient's right of self-decision and, impliedly, placing such decision under the exclusive domain of the medical profession. While this viewpoint may or may not have been justified in 1972 when *Canterbury* and *Cobbs* were decided, a review of medical ethics standards of care in 1992 should assuage this fear.

The 1992 Code of Medical Ethics, as prepared by the Council on Ethical and Judicial Affairs of the American Medical Association, sets forth the medical profession's standard on informed consent. It reads as follows:

> The patient's right of self-decision can be effectively exercised only if the patient possesses enough information to enable an intelligent choice. The patient should make his own determination on treatment. The physician's obligation is to present the medical facts accurately to the patient or to the individual responsible for his care and to make recommendations for management in accordance with good medical practice. The physician has an ethical obligation to help the patient make choices from among the therapeutic alternatives consistent with good medical practice. Informed consent is a basic social policy for which exceptions are permitted (1) where the patient is unconscious or otherwise incapable of consenting and harm from failure to treat is imminent; or (2) when risk-disclosure poses such a serious psychological threat of detriment to the patient as to be medically contraindicated. Social policy does not accept the paternalistic view that the physician may remain silent because divulgence might prompt the patient to forego needed therapy. Rational, informed patients should not be expected to act uniformly, even under similar circumstances, in agreeing to or refusing treatment.

We recognize this statement as a reasonable statement on the issue of informed consent. There is no need to change Indiana law on this issue. We therefore hold that, except in those cases where deviation from the standard of care is a matter commonly known by lay persons, expert medical testimony is necessary to establish whether a physician has or has not complied with the standard of a reasonably prudent physician.

In the present case we cannot say that the risk of the adherence of the cervix to the vaginal wall is a matter commonly known to lay persons. Therefore, the Culbertsons needed to provide expert medical testimony to refute the unanimous opinion issued by the medical review panel in order to present a material issue of fact as to what a reasonably prudent physician would have discussed concerning this proposed surgery. Without the presentation of such expert medical opinion, the trial court could only conclude that there was no genuine issue of material fact and that summary judgment should be entered for Dr. Mernitz.

[Justice Dickson's dissenting opinion is omitted.]

Notes: Competing Disclosure Standards

1. *The Objective Patient-Centered Standard vs. the Professional Standard.* Why did the *Canterbury* court reject the professional standard of disclosure? One criticism of the malpractice standard is that it measures the scope of required disclosures by customary practice rather than by the patient's need to know. The *Culbertson* court considered and rejected this argument, noting that the 1992 Code of Medical Ethics promulgated by the American Medical Association recognizes a physician's duty to provide information to patients. See also AMA Code of Medical Ethics,

Opinion 10.01, Fundamental Elements of the Physician-Patient Relationship. Does *Canterbury*'s material risk standard provide any significant additional protections given current norms of medical practice? An empirical study suggests that informed consent claims are more likely to succeed in jurisdictions that have adopted the "patient-centered" standard of disclosure. David M. Studdert et al., Geographic Variation in Informed Consent Law: Two Standards for Disclosure of Treatment Risks, 4 J. Empirical Legal Stud. 103 (2007).

2. *The Implications of* Canterbury*'s Patient-Centered or Material Risk Standard.* How are providers to know whether a risk should be deemed material? Is there any way for a physician to make this determination before providing care for the patient or before litigating the issue? What factors does the court suggest are relevant to the determination of materiality? How would you advise a physician who is considering whether to inform patients about the following risks associated with a particular type of cosmetic surgery: (1) a .01 percent risk of death from anesthesia; (2) a 1 percent risk of severe bleeding that would require a blood transfusion (which carries additional risks, ranging from fever to heart failure to transmission of blood-borne pathogens); (3) a 3 percent risk of postoperative infection (which would require treatment by antibiotics, which carry a small risk of adverse reactions); (4) a 5 percent risk of nerve damage that could lead to localized paralysis and/or loss of sensation; and (5) a 10 percent risk that the cosmetic flaw will not be significantly improved.

Some legislatures have provided "safe harbors" for physicians. In Texas, for example, a Medical Disclosure Panel determines what disclosures should be made for certain types of procedures. Physicians disclosing risks pursuant to the Panel's guidelines enjoy a rebuttable presumption that their informed consent obligations have been met. Failure to follow the guidelines creates a rebuttable presumption of negligence. Tex. Civ. Prac. & Rem. Code §74.106 (2012).

3. *The Professional Disclosure Standard: The Dominant Rule.* About half of the states still follow the "professional" malpractice standard of disclosure rule in informed consent cases. In some states, the standard has been adopted by the courts; in others it has been imposed by the legislature. Jamie Staples King & Benjamin W. Moulton, Rethinking Informed Consent: The Case for Shared Decision-Making, 32 Am. J.L. & Med. 429, 493-501 (2006) (state-by-state summary). In these jurisdictions, medical practice determines whether a particular type of information will be disclosed to patients. The standard protects physicians from liability so long as they disclose that which would be disclosed by the reasonably prudent physician under like or similar circumstances. In *Culbertson,* the court suggests that the professional malpractice standard will protect individual autonomy because it incorporates the view that individuals must be given enough information to make intelligent decisions. Was Mrs. Culbertson given enough information in this case?

4. *The Subjective Patient-Centered Disclosure Standard.* Note that the material risk standard requires the disclosure of information that a reasonable person would consider material in making a determination about treatment. In most circumstances, physicians are not required to provide information about risks that might be considered significant by an individual patient. The *Canterbury* court recognizes this potential defect but finds that the imposition of a subjective disclosure standard would pose an "undue burden" on a physician—unless the physician knows of the patient's idiosyncratic views. See, e.g., Stowell v. Huddleston, 643 F.3d 631

(8th Cir. 2011) (applying state informed consent standard requiring disclosure of risks of particular significance to patient); Lugenbuhl v. Dowling, 676 So. 2d 602 (La. Ct. App. 1996); Robert Gatter, Informed Consent and the Forgotten Duty of Physician Inquiry, 31 Loy. U. Chi. L.J. 557 (2000). The overwhelming majority of those jurisdictions that use the "material risk" standard have followed the *Canterbury* approach by measuring the scope of disclosure by the objective patient. But cf. Macy v. Blatchford, 8 P.3d 204 (Or. 2000) (evidence of sexual relationship between physician and patient relevant to determine whether physician had met his statutory duty to "explain" proposed treatment because of the possible impact of the relationship on the patient's ability to understand).

5. *Expert Testimony Under the Material Risk and Professional Disclosure Standards.* In jurisdictions following the professional disclosure standard, testimony by medical experts obviously will be required to determine whether the defendant met the standard of care. University of Maryland Medical System Corp. v. Waldt, 983 A.2d 112 (Md. 2009) (proposed expert not qualified to testify regarding informed consent claim); Foster v. Oral Surgery Ass'n, 940 A.2d 1102 (Maine 2008) (medical ethicist not qualified as expert). Will a plaintiff in a "material risk" jurisdiction be able to avoid this requirement? Testimony by medical experts will still be required to provide the fact finder with information about the nature and degree of risk associated with particular treatments. See Dunn v. Yager, 58 So. 3d 1171 (Miss. 2011); but see Shortell v. Cavanagh, 15 A.3d 1042 (Conn. 2011) (expert testimony not always required). Experts may also be needed to help the fact finder determine whether the harm suffered by the plaintiff was caused by the procedure or by the plaintiff's underlying injury. See, e.g., Suhadolnik v. Pressman, 254 P.3d 11 (Idaho 2011) (expert testimony and local standard of care); Griffin v. Moseley, 234 P.3d 869 (Mont. 2010) (physician qualified to testify about neurosurgeon's duty to disclose alternative treatments). See generally Annot., 52 A.L.R.3d 1084 (1973).

6. *Whose Duty? Disclosure as a "Professional" Rather Than "Institutional" Obligation.* Another important consequence of the doctrinal origins of the informed consent claim is that its application has been restricted to a limited range of health care professionals. See, e.g., Blotner v. Doreika, 678 S.E.2d 80 (Ga. 2009) (no common law informed consent duty applicable to chiropractors); Foster v. Traul, 120 P.3d 278 (Idaho 2005) (physician has duty to obtain informed consent; hospital merely assists in documentation). Should health care institutions have a duty to disclose some types of risks? Should there be an institutional duty to ensure that patients have given their informed consent to care? If so, what should be the doctrinal source of this obligation?

7. *Informed Consent and Battery.* Why couldn't claims of this type be resolved using principles from battery cases? Plaintiffs pleading informed consent violations as battery actions have two key advantages: They do not have to prove a deviation from the standard of care and they have greater access to punitive damages awards. There are drawbacks, of course; a battery theory is difficult to apply where the medical treatment is noninvasive, and a defendant's insurance policy may exclude coverage for intentional torts. Maryland initially created a narrow form of informed consent claim arising from battery, which required an invasion of the patient's physical integrity, but abandoned the physical invasion requirement in 2009. McQuitty v. Spangler, 976 A.2d 1020 (Md. 2009).

In the typical informed consent claim, the patient has given technical consent to being "touched" by the defendant but argues that consent would not have been given if appropriate disclosures had been made. Courts generally reject battery claims because the patient has "consented" to the touching. In most jurisdictions, battery claims are reserved for those situations in which (1) the patient has not consented to any treatment at all, (2) the health care provider performs a completely different procedure than that for which consent was given, (3) the health care provider performs a procedure on the wrong area of the body, or (4) a different, unconsented-to provider performs the procedure. See, e.g., Gragg v. Calandra, 696 N.E.2d 1282 (Ill. App. Ct. 1998) (allegation that hospital conducted open heart surgery and then maintained patient on life support without patient's or family's consent addressed as medical battery); Coulter v. Thomas, 33 S.W.3d 522 (Ky. 2000) (physician's failure to remove blood pressure cuff as requested by patient addressed in battery claim, not under state informed consent statute); but see Linog v. Yampolosky, 656 S.E.2d 355 (S.C. 2008) (no cause of action for medical battery). See generally Annot., 39 A.L.R.4th 1034 (1985). For a discussion from a medical perspective, see David C. Ring et al., Case 34-2010: A 65-Year-Old Woman with an Incorrect Operation on the Left Hand, 363 New Eng. J. Med. 1950 (2010).

8. *Fraud and Misrepresentation.* Health care providers who misrepresent the risks associated with treatments could be held liable for fraud or misrepresentation. See, e.g., Annot., 42 A.L.R.4th 543 (1985).

9. *Free Speech and Informed Consent.* The First Amendment to the U.S. Constitution protects "freedom of speech." Do governmental efforts to regulate the content of physician-patient communication violate the First Amendment? See, e.g., Lindsey Murtagh & Matthew Miller, Censorship of the Patient-Physician Relationship: A New Florida Law, 306 JAMA 1131 (2011) (state law prohibiting physicians from asking patients about gun ownership). The Supreme Court has upheld the constitutional validity of state laws that impose specific informed consent obligations on physicians performing abortions. Planned Parenthood of Southeastern Pennsylvania v. Casey, 505 U.S. 833, 884 (1992). The issue is considered further in Chapter 5 at pages 494, 511-513.

Notes: The Other Elements of a Nondisclosure Claim

1. *Elements of a Cause of Action.* Plaintiffs in informed consent claims generally will be required to prove (1) that the medical procedure carried a specific risk that was not disclosed, (2) that the physician violated the applicable standard of disclosure, (3) that the undisclosed risk materialized, and (4) that the failure to disclose the information caused the patient's injury.

2. *The Materialization of the Undisclosed Risk.* The plaintiff must show that the undisclosed risk actually materialized into harm. As a result, many failures to disclose information are never litigated. Does this make sense? Can you draw a parallel to the concept of proximate cause in traditional negligence actions? If the purpose of the informed consent doctrine is to protect individual autonomy and to encourage the transfer of information, doesn't a violation of the disclosure obligation cause a cognizable injury even without a physical harm? See Parris v. Limes, 277 P.3d 1259 (Okla. 2012) (patient who underwent post-surgical treatments alleges physician erred in failing to disclose that surgically removed prostate was cancer

free; court finds that the emergence of an undisclosed risk is not required where the patient would not have undergone treatment if he or she had been properly "informed of all the material facts").

Several commentators have argued that individual autonomy would be better protected through the adoption of a "dignitary tort" doctrine, in which the failure to disclose information would be actionable even in the absence of any physical injury. See, e.g., Alan Meisel, A "Dignitary Tort" as a Bridge Between the Idea of Informed Consent and the Law of Informed Consent, 16 L. Med. & Health Care 210, 211-214 (1988); Aaron D. Twerski & Neil B. Cohen, Informed Decision-Making and the Law of Torts: The Myth of Justiciable Causation, 1988 U. Ill. L. Rev. 607, 655; Alan J. Weisbard, Informed Consent: The Law's Uneasy Compromise with Ethical Theory, 65 Neb. L. Rev. 749, 763-764 (1986).

How should damages be measured? "The damages analysis . . . involves a comparison between the condition a plaintiff would have been in had he or she been properly informed and not consented to the risk, with the plaintiff's impaired condition as a result of the risk's occurrence." Howard v. University of Medicine & Dentistry of N.J., 800 A.2d 73 (N.J. 2002). The damages calculations can be more difficult when the patient's initial condition is serious and there are no other alternative treatments.

3. *Objective Causation.* The causation issues associated with informed consent actions are somewhat complex. Most jurisdictions—including those applying the material risk standard—will require proof of objective causation. That is, a plaintiff will be required to show that a reasonable patient would not have undergone the treatment had the risk been disclosed. Does this version of the informed consent doctrine adequately protect the patient's right to the information necessary to participate in medical decisionmaking? Consider the range of circumstances in which the defendant will be found liable for failing to disclose information. The defendant will be held liable only where he or she suggests that a patient undergo a procedure that, had the true risks been disclosed, a reasonable patient would have refused to undergo. Why wouldn't this simply constitute ordinary malpractice? Should plaintiffs be required to show that they would not have undergone the procedure or is it enough to show that a reasonable patient might have sought another opinion or considered a different provider? Compare Spencer v. Goodill, 17 A.3d 552 (Del. 2011) (jury entitled to consider all options that reasonable person might have considered, including seeking second opinion, a different doctor, or a better equipped hospital, even though same operation might ultimately have been pursued) with Orphan v. Pilnik, 940 N.E.2d 555 (N.Y. 2010) (evidence insufficient where "plaintiff . . . alleged only that, if fully informed, she would have sought second opinion").

How much of the "plaintiff's position" is the jury to consider within the limits of objective causation? See Bernard v. Char, 903 P.2d 667, 675-676 (Haw. 1995) (jury permitted to consider whether a reasonable person who was in great pain and who had no health insurance would have opted for tooth extraction or a more expensive root canal procedure); Ashe v. Radiation Oncology Associates, 9 S.W.3d 119, 123-124 (Tenn. 1999) (fact finder applying objective causation rules may take into account characteristics of plaintiff, including "idiosyncrasies, fears, age, medical condition, and religious beliefs"). At what point does the objective causation standard dissolve into a subjective standard?

4. *The Critique of Objective Causation.* Critics of the objective causation standard argue that it undercuts the goal of protecting individual autonomy. The standard is only a rough approximation or a surrogate device for the protection of individual autonomy because it works only so long as the individual is "reasonable." The Oklahoma Supreme Court has agreed:

> The *Canterbury* view certainly severely limits the protection granted an injured patient. To the extent the plaintiff, given an adequate disclosure, would have declined the proposed treatment, and a reasonable person in similar circumstances would have consented, a patient's right of self-determination is irrevocably lost. This basic right to know and decide is the reason for the full-disclosure rule. Accordingly, we decline to jeopardize this right by the imposition of the "reasonable man" standard. . . .
>
> If a plaintiff testifies he would have continued with the proposed treatment had he been adequately informed, the trial is over under either the subjective or objective approach. If he testifies he would not, then the causation problem must be resolved by examining the credibility of plaintiff's testimony. The jury must be instructed that it must find the plaintiff would have refused the treatment if he is to prevail.
>
> Although it might be said this approach places a physician at the mercy of a patient's hindsight, a careful practitioner can always protect himself by insuring that he has adequately informed each patient he treats. If he does not breach this duty, a causation problem will not arise.

Scott v. Bradford, 606 P.2d 554, 559 (Okla. 1979); see also Parris v. Lime, 277 P.3d 1259 (Okla. 2012). Oklahoma's "subjective causation" approach has not gained many adherents. But see Zalazar v. Vercimak, 633 N.E.2d 1223, 1227 (Ill. App. Ct. 1993) (severely limiting the use of objective causation and expert opinion in informed consent cases arising from cosmetic surgery). For a scholarly analysis of the causation issues in informed cases, see Aaron D. Twerski & Neil B. Cohen, Informed Decision-Making and the Law of Torts: The Myth of Justiciable Causation, 1988 U. Ill. L. Rev. 607.

3. Limiting Liability for Failure to Disclose

∎ RIZZO v. SCHILLER
445 S.E.2d 153 (Va. 1994)

HASSELL, Justice.

In this appeal, we consider whether the plaintiffs presented sufficient evidence to establish a prima facie case of medical malpractice against a physician who allegedly failed to obtain the mother's informed consent to use obstetrical forceps to deliver her baby.

Michael Sean Rizzo, Jr., by Pamela Rizzo, his mother and next friend, Pamela Rizzo, individually, and Michael Sean Rizzo, Sr., filed this action against Maurice Schiller, M.D. The plaintiffs alleged that Dr. Schiller, an obstetrician and gynecologist, breached the standard of care owed to them when he assisted Ms. Rizzo with the delivery of Michael. Specifically, the plaintiffs alleged that Dr. Schiller was negligent in the use of obstetrical forceps during the delivery and that he failed to obtain Ms. Rizzo's informed consent to use the forceps.

The case was tried before a jury. The trial court granted Dr. Schiller's motion to strike the plaintiffs' informed consent claim. The case proceeded to the jury on the theory that Dr. Schiller was negligent in the use of the obstetrical forceps. The jury returned a verdict in favor of Dr. Schiller, and we awarded the plaintiffs an appeal on issues related to their informed consent claim.

Pamela Rizzo was admitted to Fairfax Hospital on November 7, 1989, about 9:00 A.M. She was in active labor, and Dr. Schiller was notified of her admission. Upon admission to the hospital, Ms. Rizzo signed the following form:

Authorization for Medical and Surgical Procedures

Patient History No. /P/9456
I hereby authorize Dr. Schiller, and/or other members of the Medical Staff of The Fairfax Hospital of his choice, to perform diagnostic or therapeutic medical and surgical procedures on and to administer anesthetics to Pamela Rizzo. I further authorize The Fairfax Hospital to dispose of any removed tissue or amputated parts.

11/07/89	[Signed] *Pamela S. Rizzo*
(Date)	(Signature)

[Signed] *Vera Thomas*	
(Witness)	(Relationship)

About 12 hours later, Ms. Rizzo's fetal membranes were artificially ruptured at 8:50 P.M., and about 10:00 P.M., she was "pushing with contractions." At 10:15 P.M., Dr. Schiller ordered that Ms. Rizzo be taken to the delivery room. While in the delivery room, Ms. Rizzo made a few, but unsuccessful, attempts to "push" the baby through the birth canal with her abdominal muscles. When Ms. Rizzo's attempts to "push" were unsuccessful, Dr. Schiller told her that he was going to use forceps to deliver the baby. Ms. Rizzo testified that "before I could even get my composure together, ask what they were for, why, [the forceps] were inside me. And my son's head was out, just the head."

[Michael Rizzo developed a subdural hematoma after his birth. Experts testified that the forceps injured his head, causing the hematoma and Michael's subsequently diagnosed cerebral palsy.]

Dr. Arner qualified as an expert witness on the subjects of obstetrics and gynecology and gave the following testimony. Even though Ms. Rizzo had been given certain medication, she was capable of making medical decisions. Ms. Rizzo would have been able to deliver Michael spontaneously, without the use of forceps, had Dr. Schiller simply waited. If forceps are used in "non-emergent situations," the patient should be informed about the use of the forceps and should be given the opportunity to participate in the decision regarding whether the forceps will be used. Dr. Arner opined that Dr. Schiller breached the standard of care owed to Ms. Rizzo because he failed to allow her to participate in the decision to use forceps.

The plaintiffs contend that the trial court erred by striking their evidence because they established a prima facie case that Dr. Schiller failed to obtain Ms. Rizzo's informed consent for the use of obstetrical forceps during Michael's delivery. Dr. Schiller, however, argues that the plaintiffs' evidence fails to establish a prima facie case and that the plaintiffs failed to present evidence of proximate causation. Furthermore, Dr. Schiller asserts that Ms. Rizzo was allowed to participate in the decision to use forceps because she signed the authorization form. We disagree with Dr. Schiller.

In Hunter v. Burroughs, 96 S.E. 360, 366-367 (1918), we held that "it is the duty of a physician in the exercise of ordinary care to warn a patient of the danger of possible bad consequences of using a remedy," but that the physician's failure to warn "is not per se an act of negligence." Rather, the physician owes a duty to make a reasonable disclosure to the patient of all significant facts under the circumstances. This duty is limited to those disclosures that a reasonable medical practitioner would provide under the same or similar circumstances. Bly v. Rhoads, 222 S.E.2d 783, 785-787 (1976). In most cases, expert testimony is necessary to establish those instances where the duty to disclose arises and what disclosures a reasonable medical practitioner would have made under the same or similar circumstances. Id.

We are of opinion that the plaintiffs presented sufficient evidence to establish a prima facie case that Dr. Schiller failed to obtain Ms. Rizzo's informed consent to use the obstetrical forceps. As we have already mentioned, Dr. Arner testified that the appropriate standard of care required that Dr. Schiller inform Ms. Rizzo about the use of the forceps and that she be given an opportunity to participate in the decision whether to use forceps. Ms. Rizzo testified that Dr. Schiller did not disclose any information to her about the use of the forceps and that he used the forceps without her consent.

It is true that Ms. Rizzo signed a document that purportedly is a consent form. However, this form did not inform her of any specific procedures that Dr. Schiller intended to perform; nor did it inform her of foreseeable risks associated with any procedures or risks in failing to perform any procedures. As Dr. Arner observed, the form is so general in nature that "you could also justify amputating her foot." We hold that the duty imposed upon a physician to obtain a patient's informed consent requires more than simply securing the patient's signature on a generalized consent form, similar to the form present here. The law requires informed consent, not mere consent, and the failure to obtain informed consent is tantamount to no consent.

We are also of opinion that the plaintiffs presented sufficient evidence of proximate causation as an element of their prima facie case. Here, the plaintiffs presented evidence from which the jury might have inferred that had Ms. Rizzo been informed of the possible consequences associated with the use of obstetrical forceps, she would have continued to assist in the birth process by "pushing" and that Michael would have been born spontaneously. The plaintiffs also presented evidence from which the jury could have found that but for the use of the forceps, Michael would not have suffered the brain injury.

Accordingly, we will remand this case for a trial of the plaintiffs' claims of lack of informed consent.

Notes: Limiting Liability for Failure to Disclose

1. *Informed Consent and Competence.* The patient's capacity is an important factor in informed consent cases. Physicians must secure consent from someone who

has the legal capacity to give it. See Chapter 3.A.1. See generally Laura B. Dunn et al., Assessing Decisional Capacity for Clinical Research or Treatment: A Review of Instruments, 163 Am. J. Psychiatry 1323 (2006); Marsha Garrison, The Empire of Illness: Competence and Coercion in Health-Care Decision Making, 49 Wm. & Mary L. Rev. 781 (2007); Bruce J. Winick, Competency to Consent to Treatment: The Distinction Between Assent and Objection, 28 Hous. L. Rev. 15 (1991); Annot., 25 A.L.R.3d 1439 (1969). Consent issues are particularly acute in the treatment of minors. See generally Jennifer L. Rosato, Let's Get Real: Quilting a Principled Approach to Adolescent Empowerment in Health Care Decision-Making, 51 DePaul L. Rev. 769 (2002); David Vukadinovich, Minors' Consent Rights to Treatment: Navigating the Complexity of State Laws, 37 J. Health L. 6667 (2004).

Where the patient is incapable of giving consent him- or herself, alternative decisionmaking methods have been adopted by courts and legislatures. These are discussed in Chapter 3.A.3. Did Pamela Rizzo have the capacity to make intelligent health care decisions? Her medical expert testified affirmatively.

2. *The Limits of the Duty to Inform.* Courts and commentators have discussed five general limitations to the duty to disclose:

- *Common Knowledge.* There is no duty to disclose risks "of which persons of average sophistication are aware."
- *Patient Knowledge.* The patient cannot recover for the physician's failure to disclose a risk already known by the patient.
- *Emergencies.* There is no duty to disclose information in an emergency situation where the patient is not competent, immediate treatment is required to prevent more serious harm, and no substitute decisionmaker is available. The issue of decisionmaking for incompetent persons is considered in more detail at pages 303-346.
- *Therapeutic Privilege.* There is no duty to disclose information where the disclosure process would "foreclose rational decision" or "pose psychological damage" to the patient. The *Canterbury* court was particularly concerned about the need to circumscribe this exception lest it swallow the general rule. For academic commentary on the therapeutic exception, see, e.g., Kathleen M. Boozang, The Therapeutic Placebo: The Case for Patient Deception, 54 Fla. L. Rev. 687 (2002); Developments in the Law—Medical Technology and the Law, VI. The Right to Refuse Medical Treatment, 103 Harv. L. Rev. 1643, 1676 (1990). There are few reported applications of the rule. See, e.g., Barrai v. Betwee, 50 P.3d 946 (Haw. 2002) (psychiatrist fails to establish therapeutic privilege exception); and Marsingill v. O'Malley, 58 P.3d 495 (Alaska 2002) (plaintiffs essentially claim that physician should have applied the therapeutic privilege by withholding information about the likelihood that emergency room treatment would be painful or uncomfortable; patient allegedly suffered injuries from her decision to delay seeking emergency medical assistance after hearing about the nature of the likely treatment).
- *Waiver.* Although there are few court decisions on the issue, the disclosure doctrine's grounding in autonomy suggests that patients should be able to refuse information offered by the physician. See Stover v. Association of Thoracic & Cardiovascular Surgeons, 635 A.2d 1047, 1055-1056 (Pa. Super. Ct. 1993); and

Mark A. Hall, A Theory of Economic Informed Consent, 31 Ga. L. Rev. 511 (1997).

These limitations on the duty to disclose may be announced by courts or, in professional disclosure standard jurisdictions, may be established by the testimony of medical experts. The defendant generally has the burden of proving that an exception to the duty to inform is present. For a general discussion of exceptions to the duty to disclose, see Alan Meisel, The "Exceptions" to the Informed Consent Doctrine: Striking a Balance Between Competing Values in Medical Decisionmaking, 1979 Wis. L. Rev. 413.

3. *The "Consent" Process, or the Use of Forms.* Critics of the informed consent process argue that the ideal of a meaningful exchange of information between patient and physician has been replaced with the ritual of the informed consent form. How does the *Rizzo* court analyze the validity of the informed consent document signed by the plaintiff? Why shouldn't a physician be entitled to rely upon informed consent forms as a shield to liability? How was the document defective? Who should draft informed consent documents—health care providers or attorneys? Would a physician relying on the validity of an informed consent form have a malpractice claim against the drafter? Should a physician's failure to obtain a signed consent form give rise to liability? Holley v. Huang, 284 P.3d 81 (Colo. App.) ("because documentation is not required, a failure to document does not constitute a failure to meet the standard of care").

Physician defendants hope that a signed consent form will foreclose any informed consent claim. It is true that a properly completed form can establish at least a presumption that a patient has consented to treatment. Sometimes the presumption is established by statute. See, e.g., Ohio Rev. Code Ann. §2317.54. A form indicating only that a patient has received information and consents is probably not sufficient to benefit from the presumption. See, e.g., Havens v. Hoffman, 902 P.2d 219, 223 (Wyo. 1995) (overturning physician's summary judgment; hospital form is an acknowledgment of the receipt of information but does not indicate the nature of the information disclosed). Should a signed consent form bar recovery where the patient did not read the disclosure before signing and where the physician failed to determine whether the form had been read? Roberts v. Cox, 669 So. 2d 633, 640 (La. Ct. App. 1996) (jury determination that informed consent doctrine satisfied not "manifestly erroneous").

4. *Informed Consent Forms in Hospitals.* Hospital employees, such as nurses, often procure patients' signatures on informed consent forms prior to surgery. Does this mean that hospitals have a duty to obtain the informed consent of patients? Courts routinely find that the answer is "no." The duty to obtain informed consent is the physician's; the hospital's involvement in the process normally is considered to be merely facilitative. Annot., 88 A.L.R.3d 1008 (1978). For a cogent critique, see Robert Gatter, The Mysterious Survival of the Policy Against Informed Consent Liability for Hospitals, 81 Notre Dame L. Rev. 1203 (2006).

5. *Comparative Negligence and Assumption of Risk.* Should patients have an obligation to truthfully disclose information to their physicians? Should the obligation arise only in response to a physician's inquiries, or should patients have a duty to affirmatively disclose matters that a reasonable patient would think might be

relevant to his or her medical treatment? In Brown v. Dibbell, 595 N.W.2d 358 (Wis. 1999), the court held that

> for patients to exercise ordinary care, they must tell the truth and give complete and accurate information about personal, family, and medical histories to a doctor to the extent possible in response to the doctor's requests for information when the requested information is material to a doctor's duty as prescribed by . . . [the informed consent statute] and that a patient's breach of that duty might, under certain circumstances, constitute contributory negligence.

Id. at 368-369. The court did not consider whether patients had a duty to disclose information sua sponte.

Should a defendant physician be able to argue for contributory or comparative negligence where the plaintiff signs a blank consent form, or signs a consent form without reading it? What if a patient fails to ask for clarifications where the consent documents contain inconsistencies or gaps? See Oghia v. Hollan, 363 S.W.3d 30 (Ky. Ct. App. 2012) (comparative negligence applies to informed consent only in extraordinary circumstances not present in case).

An informed consent form is essentially a written documentation of the patient's assumption of the disclosed risks, assumed in order to achieve a procedure's potential benefits. See Karp v. Cooley, 493 F.2d 408 (5th Cir. 1974) (directed verdict for the defendant affirmed; patient undergoing first attempted implantation of a mechanical heart had been given extensive information and counseling about the experimental nature of the treatment and its risks). Patients ordinarily are not permitted, however, to assume the risk that a procedure will be negligently recommended or performed; they assume only the risks that are non-negligently produced. In the typical case, then, a signed informed consent form signifies that the patient was informed of the required risks and agreed to accept those risks; a form is powerful evidence of a physician's compliance with the duty to disclose but is irrelevant to an ordinary malpractice action brought against a physician for delivering substandard care. See Spar v. Cha, 907 N.E.2d 974 (Ind. 2009) ("a waiver of informed consent does not assume risks associated with negligent performance of the underlying procedure or treatment").

As is often true in legal matters, things are not quite this simple, however. Informed consent and ordinary malpractice overlap and interact in several important respects. Where there are alternative standards of care or courses of treatment, obtaining informed consent may be important to the physician's malpractice defense that the physician complied with a "respectable minority" point of view. For instance, informed consent can justify departing from customary practice in order to participate in medical research or to try out an untested procedure. Similarly, informed consent might be used to bolster an affirmative defense that the patient assumed the risk or was contributorily negligent. See, e.g., Smith v. Hull, 659 N.E.2d 185 (Ind. Ct. App. 1995) (in a case involving injuries from treatment for baldness, a contributory negligence finding "was supported by evidence that patient sought out physician and hair injection procedure, received extensive literature and discussed risks with physician, and signed consent forms prior to undergoing procedures, . . . leav[ing] us with little doubt that Smith's desire to sport a full head of hair motivated him to pursue remedies that he knowingly undertook at his own peril").

6. *Injury and Causation.* Note that Ms. Rizzo's claim would have failed if the undisclosed risk had not materialized, that is, if the use of forceps had not resulted in her son's injuries. How did Dr. Schiller's failure to disclose the risks associated with using forceps cause Michael Rizzo's injuries? The court holds that the plaintiffs presented sufficient evidence of proximate causation for a jury to decide in their favor. A jury could have decided that Ms. Rizzo, had she been appropriately informed, might have rejected the use of forceps and continued to "push" and that Michael's brain injuries would not have occurred. Assume that you represent the defendant. What types of counter-evidence might you want to present on this issue?

7. *Alternative Treatments.* Under the professional malpractice standard, a physician must disclose treatment alternatives if the reasonable, competent physician would have done so. The existence of alternative treatments would also be considered "material" under the patient-centered standard of disclosure. See, e.g., Bubb v. Brusky, 768 N.W.2d 903 (Wis. 2009); Annot., 38 A.L.R.4th 900 (1985). But see Cline v. Kresa-Reahl, 728 S.E.2d 87 (W. Va. 2012) (traditional medical malpractice rather than informed consent applies where physician does not disclose information about non-recommended treatment). What should be the physician's disclosure obligation where a treatment alternative is not readily available, perhaps because of cost considerations or geographic location? See, e.g., Mark Hall, A Theory of Economic Informed Consent, 31 Ga. L. Rev. 511 (1997). Should the physician be required to disclose the option of "doing nothing"? See, e.g., Wecker v. Amend, 918 P.2d 658 (Kan. Ct. App. 1996) (yes).

8. *Informed Consent and the Therapeutic Placebo.* Physicians and medical researchers have long believed in the "placebo effect," under which some patients appear to improve after the administration of spurious "treatment," although some recent research results suggest that the effect may be overstated. See Damien G. Finniss et al., Placebo Effects: Biological, Clinical, and Ethical Advances, 375 Lancet 686 (2010). Does the informed consent doctrine implicitly prohibit the use of placebos? Can you design a method of using placebos that would allow physicians (and patients) to gain the benefits of the placebo effect without violating the disclosure doctrine? See Kathleen M. Boozang, The Therapeutic Placebo: The Case for Patient Deception, 54 U. Fla. L. Rev. 687 (2002); Adam J. Kolber, A Limited Defense of Clinical Placebo Deception, 26 Yale L & Pol'y Rev. 75 (2007); Anup Malani, Regulation with Placebo Effects, 58 Duke L.J. 411 (2008); Franklin Miller & Luana Colloca, The Legitimacy of Placebo Treatments in Clinical Practice: Evidence and Ethics, 9 Am. J. Bioethics 39 (2009).

9. *Diagnostic Tests vs. Treatments.* Should the duty to disclose alternatives depend on whether a treatment or a diagnostic test is at issue? See Jandre v. Wisconsin Injured Patients and Families Compensation Fund, 813 N.W.2d 627 (2012). The patient in *Jandre* was brought to the emergency room after he had trouble swallowing his coffee and began drooling; he also experienced slurred speech, facial drooping on the left side, dizziness, and leg weakness. The emergency room physician considered many possible causes, including Bell's Palsy and some form of stroke. She performed a number of diagnostic tests, including using a stethoscope on Jandre's carotid arteries to listen for a blocked artery, but did not order the more reliable carotid ultrasound diagnostic test. She also did not inform Jandre about the availability of the test. The physician incorrectly, but non-negligently, found that Jandre had Bell's palsy. About 11 days after leaving the ER, Jandre suffered a

full-blown stroke that caused physical and cognitive injuries. In a fractured decision, the Wisconsin Supreme Court found that the ER physician had a duty disclose the availability of the carotid ultrasound under the reasonable patient standard. Id. A concurring justice agreed with the result but expressed strong concerns about the policy implications of the decision. Id. at 666. A vigorous dissent warned that the decision would result in strict liability for physicians.

Should physicians be shielded from liability for failure to discuss diagnostic tests for alternative conditions that they have non-negligently eliminated from consideration? Physicians frequently engage in a differential diagnosis analysis, moving from a range of possible conditions of greater or lesser probability to a final diagnosis by analyzing the patient's symptoms, family history, and the results of various diagnostic tests. What are the implications of this decision for physicians engaged in this process? Is the type of fully informed consent the majority imagines a practical possibility in already-overburdened hospital emergency rooms? Will health care costs increase as patients are informed about and demand more diagnostic tests?

10. *Law in Books, Law in Action, and the "New" Model of Shared Decisionmaking.* Does the informed consent duty established under malpractice principles provide adequate protection for patient autonomy? Does it protect physicians from unwarranted intrusions into professional autonomy?

There have been flurries of reformist proposals over the past ten years exploiting the many weaknesses of the current legal approach to informed consent and advocating some form of "shared medical decisionmaking." New models of "shared decisionmaking" in health care promote a dialogue with physicians providing information about risks and probabilities while patients contribute information about values and preferences with the goal of jointly developing a treatment plan. Although the model has many variations, a recent description is typical:

> Shared medical decision-making is a process in which the physician shares with the patient all relevant risk and benefit information on all treatment alternatives and the patient shares with the physician all relevant personal information that might make one treatment or side effect more or less tolerable than others. Then, both parties use this information to come to a mutual medical decision.

Jamie Staples King & Benjamin W. Moulton, Rethinking Informed Consent: The Case for Shared Medical Decision-Making, 32 Am. J.L. & Med. 429, 431 (2006) (citations omitted). The process is often assisted by the use of computer-based or audiovisual "decision aids." This approach may be particularly appropriate for elective procedures or areas in which there are multiple treatment options with varying risks and benefits. Courts typically find, however, that physicians are not required to use any particular means of communicating risk information. Holley v. Huang, 284 P.3d 81 (Colo. App.) ("A doctor may employ any means of communication—such as conversation, writings, video and audio recordings, or some combination of these—that will yield a properly informed consent."). See also Nadia N. Sawicki, Informed Consent Beyond the Physician-Patient Encounter: Tort Implications of Extra-Clinical Decision Support Tools, 21 Ann. Health L. 1 (2012).

Does this recalibration of the role of physicians and patients address the critique of traditional informed consent's focus on information transfer and patient autonomy? Could implementation of shared decisionmaking expand physician liability for failure to disclose low risks that could become relevant in light of a patient's shared values and preferences? See generally Dominick L. Frosch et al., Authoritarian Physicians and Patients' Fear of Being Labeled "Difficult" Among Key Obstacles to Shared Decision Making, 31 Health Aff. 1030 (2012); Jaime S. King et al., The Potential of Shared Decision Making to Reduce Health Disparities, 39 J.L. Med. & Ethics 30 (2011); Dayna Bowen Matthew, Implementing American Health Care Reform: The Fiduciary Imperative, 59 Buff. L. Rev. 715 (2011); Benjamin Moulton & Jaime S. King, Aligning Ethics with Medical Decision-Making: The Quest for Informed Patient Choice, 38 J.L. Med. & Ethics 85 (2010); Carl E. Schneider, Void for Vagueness, Hastings Center Rep. 10 (Jan.-Feb. 2007); Symposium, 70 Med. Care Res. & Rev. 35 (2013). For an article from clinicians' perspective, see Robert A. Olson et al., Oncologists' View of Informed Consent and Shared Decision Making in Paediatric Radiation Oncology, 102 Radiother. Oncol. 210 (2012). States have adopted, or considered implementing, shared decisionmaking pilot projects. Bridget M. Kuehn, States Explore Shared Decision Making, 301 JAMA 2539 (2009).

Discussion Problem: Informed Refusals?

Dr. Claude R. Thomas was Mrs. Rena Truman's personal physician from 1963 to 1969. In 1969, another physician discovered that Mrs. Truman had advanced cervical cancer. Mrs. Truman died in 1970, at the age of 30. Rena Truman's children sued Dr. Thomas for failing to perform a Pap test on Mrs. Truman between 1964 and 1969. Trial testimony indicated that (1) if the Pap smear had been performed during this time period, Mrs. Truman's condition would have been discovered at an earlier stage and she probably would have lived; (2) medical practice required physicians to inform women of the purpose of a Pap test; and (3) Dr. Thomas repeatedly advised Mrs. Truman to undergo the test but did not specifically explain the possible consequences of her refusal. Consider this case under the professional and material risk standards of disclosure. What arguments can you make on behalf of Mrs. Truman's children? What arguments or defenses might you raise on behalf of Dr. Thomas? See Truman v. Thomas, 611 P.2d 902 (Cal. 1980). See also Providence Health Center v. Dowell, 262 S.W.3d 324, 334-335 (Tex. 2008) (O'Neill, dissenting).

4. Fiduciary Obligations, Conflicts of Interest, and Novel Disclosure Obligations

Depending on the jurisdiction, the informed consent doctrine has grown out of the rich soil of cases involving battery, malpractice, and fiduciary law. The doctrine has the potential for continued expansive growth, particularly in those jurisdictions emphasizing a physician's fiduciary obligations over the professional standard of care. In these states, the scope of informed consent is not limited by the current standard of professional conduct. As you read the following cases, consider whether the courts have gone too far or not far enough in regulating the scope of physician disclosure. Does the imposition of liability in these cases seem "just"? Do the courts' decisions seem consistent with the informed consent doctrine they purport to apply? What is the likely impact of these decisions on the nature of physician-patient communications? Are patients more likely to receive important information? What will physicians do to minimize liability?

■ AUTONOMY AND PRIVACY: PROTECTING PATIENTS
FROM THEIR PHYSICIANS
Mary Anne Bobinski
55 U. Pitt. L. Rev. 291, 347-356 (1994)

. . . Jurisdictions with more generous disclosure requirements typically rely, at least in part, on fiduciary principles as a basis for the disclosure obligation. Fiduciary law thus presents a possible avenue for future growth of a more vibrant disclosure duty. Tort law and the law governing fiduciary relationships are similar in that they impose extra-contractual duties on individuals. The two regulatory schemes, however, differ in conception of those duties. Tort law most often imposes general duties irrespective of the status of the parties. The law of fiduciaries, in contrast, is based on the special character of the relationship between two parties. Courts struggling to define the scope of tort-based disclosure duties have often noted the fiducial characteristics of the doctor-patient relationship as a justification for disclosure. This linkage between ordinary tort and fiduciary principles creates the opportunity for both growth and confusion. Ordinary tort duties may be expanded or amplified because of the perceived relevance of fiduciary principles. To date, few courts have explicitly considered the implications of wholesale acceptance of the doctor-patient relationship as one subject to fiduciary law. There has been little judicial analysis of the appropriateness of applying fiduciary-based disclosure obligations to the physician-patient relationship, and virtually no judicial analysis of the special problems presented by provider-associated risk.

The first question is whether the relationship between physicians and patients is a fiduciary one. Fiduciary relationships are generally described as those in which some aspect of the relationship between the parties [such as an imbalance of power or knowledge] justifies the imposition of special obligations on one of them. Several treatises on fiduciary law name the physician-patient relationship as a fiduciary one and the courts have tended to concur. [See page 159.]

Next, the fiduciary duties that physicians owe to patients must be determined. Generally, a fiduciary must act for the benefit of another, but the specific duties imposed on a fiduciary will vary with the scope of the relationship between the parties. The fiduciary owes a duty of loyalty, "good faith, trust, special confidence and candor" to the other party. Obviously, it is not a breach of the fiduciary relationship for the fiduciary to receive compensation for her services. However, the fiduciary can breach her duty by engaging in self-dealing, by receiving bribes or kickbacks, or by misappropriating that knowledge or property which belongs to the entrustor. The role of disclosure in fiduciary law is somewhat complicated. The fiduciary's failure to disclose information to the entrustor can constitute an independent breach of fiduciary duty when the information was gathered in the course of the fiduciary's duties. Disclosure may also help determine whether an apparent breach of fiduciary duties has been "cured" by the consent of the entrustor. The validity of the entrustor's consent will be the important question because the fiduciary's influence over the entrustor may make any consent presumptively invalid. Disclosure in these cases is of evidentiary significance; it may bolster the fiduciary's claim that the entrustor's consent to the transaction was valid. As a substantive matter, disclosure may not be sufficient where the fiduciary's influence over the entrustor makes any—even informed—consent illusory....

This analysis of fiduciary principles assumes that a breach will provide some effective remedy for patients. A fiduciary is liable to the entrustor for a breach of fiduciary duties. A breach of a fiduciary obligation can be remedied by voiding a transaction, by payment by the fiduciary to the trusting party of any impermissible benefits or profits, or by payment by the fiduciary to compensate the other party for actual damages, which may include compensation for personal injury. Courts are divided on whether the entrustor is required to show some specific injury flowed from the fiduciary's breach of her duties.

The significant number of courts that have applied fiduciary principles to the physician-patient relationship can be deceiving. Most courts have failed to consider the broader policy implications of classifying the physician-patient relationship as a fiduciary one; most have also failed to analyze the range of physicians' required fiduciary duties. Some courts have responded to these problems by hedging, noting that the relationship has fiducial "qualities" or "characteristics" or finding that it is a "confidential" relationship....

The . . . [most important] judicial consideration of common law economic disclosure obligations occurred in Moore v. Regents of the University of California....

■ MOORE v. THE REGENTS OF THE UNIVERSITY OF CALIFORNIA
793 P.2d 479 (Cal. 1990), cert. denied, 499 U.S. 936 (1991)

PANELLI, Justice.

We granted review in this case to determine whether plaintiff has stated a cause of action against his physician and other defendants for using his cells in potentially lucrative medical research without his permission. Plaintiff alleges that his physician failed to disclose preexisting research and economic interests in the cells before obtaining consent to the medical procedures by which they were extracted. . . . We hold that the complaint states a cause of action for breach of the physician's disclosure obligations, but not for conversion.

FACTS

. . . The plaintiff is John Moore (Moore), who underwent treatment for hairy-cell leukemia at the Medical Center of the University of California at Los Angeles (UCLA Medical Center). The five defendants are: (1) Dr. David W. Golde (Golde), a physician who attended Moore at UCLA Medical Center; (2) the Regents of the University of California (Regents), who own and operate the university; (3) Shirley G. Quan, a researcher employed by the Regents; (4) Genetics Institute, Inc. (Genetics Institute); and (5) Sandoz Pharmaceuticals Corporation and related entities (collectively Sandoz).

Moore first visited UCLA Medical Center on October 5, 1976, shortly after he learned that he had hairy-cell leukemia. After hospitalizing Moore and "withdrawing extensive amounts of blood, bone marrow aspirate, and other bodily substances,"

Golde confirmed that diagnosis. At this time all defendants, including Golde, were aware that "certain blood products and blood components were of great value in a number of commercial and scientific efforts" and that access to a patient whose blood contained these substances would provide "competitive, commercial, and scientific advantages."

On October 8, 1976, Golde recommended that Moore's spleen be removed. Golde informed Moore "that he had reason to fear for his life, and that the proposed splenectomy operation . . . was necessary to slow down the progress of his disease." Based upon Golde's representations, Moore signed a written consent form authorizing the splenectomy.

Before the operation, Golde and Quan "formed the intent and made arrangements to obtain portions of [Moore's] spleen following its removal" and to take them to a separate research unit. Golde gave written instructions to this effect on October 18 and 19, 1976. These research activities "were not intended to have . . . any relation to [Moore's] medical . . . care." However, neither Golde nor Quan informed Moore of their plans to conduct this research or requested his permission. Surgeons at UCLA Medical Center, whom the complaint does not name as defendants, removed Moore's spleen on October 20, 1976.

Moore returned to the UCLA Medical Center several times between November 1976 and September 1983. He did so at Golde's direction and based upon representations "that such visits were necessary and required for his health and well-being, and based upon the trust inherent in and by virtue of the physician-patient relationship. . . ." On each of these visits Golde withdrew additional samples of "blood, blood serum, skin, bone marrow aspirate, and sperm." On each occasion Moore travelled to the UCLA Medical Center from his home in Seattle because he had been told that the procedures were to be performed only there and only under Golde's direction.

"In fact, [however,] throughout the period of time that [Moore] was under [Golde's] care and treatment, . . . the defendants were actively involved in a number of activities which they concealed from [Moore]. . . ." Specifically, defendants were conducting research on Moore's cells and planned to "benefit financially and competitively . . . [by exploiting the cells] and [their] exclusive access to [the cells] by virtue of [Golde's] on-going physician-patient relationship. . . ."

Sometime before August 1979, Golde established a cell line from Moore's T-lymphocytes.[2] On January 30, 1981, the Regents applied for a patent on the cell line, listing Golde and Quan as inventors. "[B]y virtue of an established policy . . . , [the] Regents, Golde, and Quan would share in any royalties or profits . . . arising out of [the] patent." The patent issued on March 20, 1984, naming Golde and Quan as the inventors of the cell line and the Regents as the assignee of the patent. The Regent's patent also covers various methods for using the cell line to produce lymphokines. Moore admits in his complaint that "the true clinical potential of each

2. A T-lymphocyte is a type of white blood cell. T-lymphocytes produce lymphokines, or proteins that regulate the immune system. Some lymphokines have potential therapeutic value. If the genetic material responsible for producing a particular lymphokine can be identified, it can sometimes be used to manufacture large quantities of the lymphokine through the techniques of recombinant DNA. . . . Moore's T-lymphocytes were interesting to the defendants because they overproduced certain lymphokines, thus making the corresponding genetic material easier to identify. . . .

of the lymphokines . . . [is] difficult to predict, [but] . . . competing commercial firms in these relevant fields have published reports in biotechnology industry periodicals predicting a potential market of approximately $3.01 Billion Dollars by the year 1990 for a whole range of [such lymphokines]. . . ." [Golde and his associates received several hundred thousand dollars over the next three years plus shares of stock, under agreements with Genetics Institute to develop the cell line products.]

Based upon these allegations, Moore attempted to state 13 causes of action.[4] . . . [T]he superior court sustained a general demurrer to the entire complaint. . . .

DISCUSSION

A. BREACH OF FIDUCIARY DUTY AND LACK OF INFORMED CONSENT

Moore repeatedly alleges that Golde failed to disclose the extent of his research and economic interests in Moore's cells[6] before obtaining consent to the medical procedures by which the cells were extracted. These allegations, in our view, state a cause of action against Golde for invading a legally protected interest of his patient. This cause of action can properly be characterized either as the breach of a fiduciary duty to disclose facts material to the patient's consent or, alternatively, as the performance of medical procedures without first having obtained the patient's informed consent.

Our analysis begins with three well-established principles. First, "a person of adult years and in sound mind has the right, in the exercise of control over his own body, to determine whether or not to submit to lawful medical treatment." Cobbs v. Grant, 8 Cal. 3d 229, 242 (1972). Second, "the patient's consent to treatment, to be effective, must be an informed consent." *Cobbs*, 8 Cal. 3d at 242. Third, in soliciting the patient's consent, a physician has a fiduciary duty to disclose all information material to the patient's decision.

These principles lead to the following conclusions: (1) A physician must disclose personal interests unrelated to the patient's health, whether research or economic, that may affect the physician's professional judgment; and (2) a physician's failure to disclose such interests may give rise to a cause of action for performing medical procedures without informed consent or breach of fiduciary duty. . . .

Indeed, the law already recognizes that a reasonable patient would want to know whether a physician has an economic interest that might affect the physician's professional judgment. As the Court of Appeal has said, "[c]ertainly a sick patient deserves to be free of any reasonable suspicion that his doctor's judgment is influenced by a profit motive." Magan Medical Clinic v. Cal. State Bd. of Medical Examiners, 249 Cal. App. 2d 124, 132 (1967). The desire to protect patients from possible conflicts of interest has also motivated legislative enactments. Among these is Business and Professions Code §654.2. Under that section, a physician may not

---

4. (1) "Conversion"; (2) "lack of informed consent"; (3) "breach of fiduciary duty"; (4) "fraud and deceit"; (5) "unjust enrichment"; (6) "quasi-contract"; (7) "bad faith breach of the implied covenant of good faith and fair dealing"; (8) "intentional infliction of emotional distress"; (9) "negligent misrepresentation"; (10) "intentional interference with prospective advantageous economic relationships"; (11) "slander of title"; (12) "accounting"; and (13) "declaratory relief."

6. In this opinion we use the inclusive term cells to describe all of the cells taken from Moore's body, including blood cells, bone marrow, spleen, etc.

charge a patient on behalf of, or refer a patient to, any organization in which the physician has a "significant beneficial interest, unless [the physician] first discloses in writing to the patient, that there is such an interest and advises the patient that the patient may choose any organization for the purposes of obtaining the services ordered or requested by [the physician]." Similarly, under Health and Safety Code §24173, a physician who plans to conduct a medical experiment on a patient must, among other things, inform the patient of "[t]he name of the sponsor or funding source, if any, . . . and the organization, if any, under whose general aegis the experiment is being conducted."

It is important to note that no law prohibits a physician from conducting research in the same area in which he practices. Progress in medicine often depends upon physicians, such as those practicing at the university hospital where Moore received treatment, who conduct research while caring for their patients.

Yet a physician who treats a patient in whom he also has a research interest has potentially conflicting loyalties. This is because medical treatment decisions are made on the basis of proportionality—weighing the benefits to the patient against the risks to the patient. As another court has said, "the determination as to whether the burdens of treatment are worth enduring for any individual patient depends upon the facts unique in each case," and "the patient's interests and desires are the key ingredients of the decision-making process." A physician who adds his own research interests to this balance may be tempted to order a scientifically useful procedure or test that offers marginal, or no, benefits to the patient.[8] The possibility that an interest extraneous to the patient's health has affected the physician's judgment is something that a reasonable patient would want to know in deciding whether to consent to a proposed course of treatment. It is material to the patient's decision and, thus, a prerequisite to informed consent. . . .

We acknowledge that there is a competing consideration. To require disclosure of research and economic interests may corrupt the patient's own judgment by distracting him from the requirements of his health.[9] But California law does not grant physicians unlimited discretion to decide what to disclose. . . .

Accordingly, we hold that a physician who is seeking a patient's consent for a medical procedure must, in order to satisfy his fiduciary duty[10] and to obtain the

---

8. This is, in fact, precisely what Moore has alleged with respect to the postoperative withdrawals of blood and other substances.

9. . . . [A] physician who orders a procedure partly to further a research interest unrelated to the patient's health should not be able to avoid disclosure with the argument that the patient might object to participation in research. In some cases, however, a physician's research interest might play such an insignificant role in the decision to recommend a medically indicated procedure that disclosure should not be required because the interest is not material. By analogy, we have not required disclosure of "remote" risks that "are not central to the decision to administer or reject [a] procedure." Truman v. Thomas, 27 Cal. 3d 285, 293 (1980).

10. In some respects the term fiduciary is too broad. In this context the term fiduciary signifies only that a physician must disclose all facts material to the patient's decision. A physician is not the patient's financial adviser. As we have already discussed, the reason why a physician must disclose possible conflicts is not because he has a duty to protect his patient's financial interests, but because certain personal interests may affect professional judgment.

patient's informed consent, disclose personal interests unrelated to the patient's health, whether research or economic, that may affect his medical judgment.

1. Dr. Golde

We turn now to the allegations of Moore's third amended complaint to determine whether he has stated such a cause of action. . . . Moore alleges that Golde actively concealed his economic interest in Moore's cells during this time period.

> [D]uring each of these visits . . . , and even when [Moore] inquired as to whether there was any possible or potential commercial or financial value or significance of his Blood and Bodily Substances, or whether the defendants had discovered anything . . . which was or might be . . . related to any scientific activity resulting in commercial or financial benefits . . . , the defendants repeatedly and affirmatively represented to [Moore] that there was no commercial or financial value to his Blood and Bodily Substances . . . and in fact actively discouraged such inquiries.

. . . In these allegations, Moore plainly asserts that Golde concealed an economic interest in the postoperative procedures. Therefore, applying the principles already discussed, the allegations state a cause of action for breach of fiduciary duty or lack of informed consent.

We thus disagree with the superior court's ruling that Moore had not stated a cause of action . . . [because he] failed to allege that the operation lacked a therapeutic purpose or that the procedure was totally unrelated to therapeutic purposes. In our view, neither allegation is essential. Even if the splenectomy had a therapeutic purpose, it does not follow that Golde had no duty to disclose his additional research and economic interests. As we have already discussed, the existence of a motivation for a medical procedure unrelated to the patient's health is a potential conflict of interest and a fact material to the patient's decision.

2. The Remaining Defendants

The Regents, Quan, Genetics Institute, and Sandoz are not physicians. In contrast to Golde, none of these defendants stood in a fiduciary relationship with Moore or had the duty to obtain Moore's informed consent to medical procedures. If any of these defendants is to be liable for breach of fiduciary duty or performing medical procedures without informed consent, it can only be on account of Golde's acts and on the basis of a recognized theory of secondary liability, such as respondeat superior. The procedural posture of this case, however, makes it unnecessary for us to address the sufficiency of Moore's secondary-liability allegations. . . .

B. CONVERSION

[The portion of the opinion rejecting Moore's attempt to characterize the invasion of his rights as a conversion is excerpted at page 432. The court reasoned that such an unprecedented extension of property law concepts is not warranted because strict liability would be too threatening to legitimate and socially useful scientific research.] For these reasons, we hold that the allegations of Moore's third amended complaint state a cause of action for breach of fiduciary duty or lack of informed consent, but not conversion.

Mosk, Justice, dissenting.

. . . I disagree with the majority's . . . conclusion that in the present context a nondisclosure cause of action is an adequate—in fact, a superior—substitute for a conversion cause of action. In my view the nondisclosure cause of action falls short on at least three grounds. First, . . . the majority's theory apparently is that the threat of [a damages action based on nondisclosure] . . . will have a prophylactic effect: It will give physician-researchers incentive to disclose any conflicts of interest before treatment, and will thereby protect their patients' right to make an informed decision about what may be done with their body parts.

The remedy is largely illusory. . . . There are two barriers to recovery. First, the patient must show that if he or she had been informed of all pertinent information, he or she would have declined to consent to the procedure in question. . . . The second barrier to recovery is still higher, and is erected on the first: It is not even enough for the plaintiff to prove that he personally would have refused consent to the proposed treatment if he had been fully informed; he must also prove that in the same circumstances no reasonably prudent person would have given such consent. . . . Few if any judges or juries are likely to believe that disclosure of . . . a possibility of research or development would dissuade a reasonably prudent person from consenting to the treatment. For example, in the case at bar no trier of fact is likely to believe that if defendants had disclosed their plans for using Moore's cells, no reasonably prudent person in Moore's position—i.e., a leukemia patient suffering from a grossly enlarged spleen—would have consented to the routine operation that saved or at least prolonged his life. Here . . . a motion for nonsuit for failure to prove proximate cause will end the matter. In this context, accordingly, the threat of suit on a nondisclosure cause of action is largely a paper tiger.

The second reason why the nondisclosure cause of action is inadequate for the task that the majority assign to it is that it fails to solve half the problem before us: It gives the patient only the right to refuse consent, i.e., the right to prohibit the commercialization of his tissue; it does not give him the right to grant consent to that commercialization on the condition that he share in its proceeds. . . . Third, the nondisclosure cause of action fails to reach a major class of potential defendants: all those who are outside the strict physician-patient relationship with the plaintiff. . . .

In sum, the nondisclosure cause of action (1) is unlikely to be successful in most cases, (2) fails to protect patients' rights to share in the proceeds of the commercial exploitation of their tissue, and (3) may allow the true exploiters to escape liability. It is thus not an adequate substitute, in my view, for the conversion cause of action. . . .

Broussard, Justice, concurring and dissenting.

. . . I disagree with the suggestion in [Justice Mosk's] dissenting opinion that defendants will be able to avoid all liability under the breach-of-fiduciary-duty theory simply by showing that plaintiff would have proceeded with the surgical removal of his diseased spleen even if defendants had disclosed their research and commercial interest in his cells. . . . [I]n this context [of a breach of fiduciary duty]—unlike in the traditional "informed consent" context of Cobbs—a plaintiff should not be required to establish that he would not have proceeded with the medical treatment in question if his physician had made full disclosure, but only that the doctor's wrongful failure to disclose information proximately caused the plaintiff some type of compensable damage. . . . [I]n appropriate circumstances, punitive as well as compensatory damages would clearly be recoverable in such an action. Accordingly, [Justice Mosk] underestimates the potential efficacy of the breach-of-fiduciary-duty cause of action in dismissing the action as a "paper tiger."

HOWARD v. UNIVERSITY OF MEDICINE & DENTISTRY OF NEW JERSEY
800 A.2d 73 (N.J. 2002)

LaVecchia, J.

In this appeal we consider what causes of action will lie when a plaintiff contends that a physician misrepresented his credentials and experience at the time he obtained the plaintiff's consent to surgery. . . .

[The plaintiff suffered serious and progressive back injuries in an automobile accident but decided to forgo recommended surgery. The plaintiff was referred to Dr. Heary, a professor at the defendant University, after the plaintiff sustained additional back injuries in a second car accident.] Dr. Heary had two pre-operative consultations with plaintiff. In the first consultation, Dr. Heary determined that plaintiff needed surgery to correct a cervical myelopathy secondary to cervical stenosis and a significantly large C3 C4 disc herniation. Because of the serious nature of the surgery, Dr. Heary recommended that plaintiff's wife attend a second consultation. The doctor wanted to explain again the risks, benefits, and alternatives to surgery, and to answer any questions concerning the procedure.

Plaintiff returned with his wife for a second consultation, but what transpired is disputed. An "Office Note" written by Dr. Heary detailing the contents of the consultation states that "[a]ll alternatives have been discussed and patient elects at this time to undergo the surgical procedure, which has been scheduled for March 5, 1997." Dr. Heary asserts that he informed plaintiff and his wife that the surgery entailed significant risks, including the possibility of paralysis. Plaintiffs dispute that they were informed of such risks. Further, they contend that during the consultation plaintiff's wife asked Dr. Heary whether he was Board Certified and that he said he was. Plaintiffs also claim that Dr. Heary told them that he had performed approximately sixty corpectomies in each of the eleven years he had been performing such surgical procedures. According to Mrs. Howard, she was opposed to the surgery and it was only after Dr. Heary's specific claims of skill and experience that she and her husband decided to go ahead with the procedure.

Dr. Heary denies that he represented that he was Board Certified in Neurosurgery.[1] He also denies that he ever claimed to have performed sixty corpectomies per year for the eleven years he had practiced neurosurgery.

Dr. Heary performed the surgical procedure on March 5, 1997, but it was unsuccessful. A malpractice action was filed alleging that Mr. Howard was rendered quadriplegic as a result of Dr. Heary's negligence. [The plaintiffs sought leave to add a fraud claim to their complaint. The trial court rejected the motion, the appellate division reversed, and the matter was appealed to the state supreme court.]

---

1. Although he was Board Eligible at the time of Mr. Howard's surgery, Dr. Heary did not become Board Certified in Neurosurgery until November 1999. . . .

Presently, a patient has several avenues of relief against a doctor: (1) deviation from the standard of care (medical malpractice); (2) lack of informed consent; and (3) battery. . . . Plaintiffs' motion to amend the complaint to add a fraud claim raises the question whether a patient's consent to surgery obtained through alleged misrepresentations about the physician's professional experience and credentials is properly addressed in a claim of lack of informed consent, or battery, or whether it should constitute a separate and distinct claim based on fraud.

We focus first on the distinction between lack of informed consent and battery as they are recognized in New Jersey. The doctrine of informed consent was tied initially to the tort of battery, but its evolution has firmly established it as a negligence concept. . . . By the mid-twentieth century, as courts began to use a negligence theory to analyze consent causes of action, the case law evolved from the notion of consent to *informed* consent, balancing the patient's need for sufficient information with the doctor's perception of the appropriate amount of information to impart for an informed decision. . . . The doctrine of informed consent continued to be refined. See Natanson v. Kline, 350 P.2d 1093, 1106, modified on other grounds, 354 P.2d 670 (1960) (holding that doctor's required disclosure was "limited to those disclosures which a reasonable medical practitioner would make under the same or similar circumstances," known as the "professional standard"). Eventually, the "prudent patient," or "materiality of risk" standard was introduced. Canterbury v. Spence, 464 F.2d 772, 786-88 (D.C. Cir. 1972), cert. denied, 409 U.S. 1064 (1972). That patient-centered view of informed consent stresses the patient's right to self-determination, and the fiduciary relationship between a doctor and his or her patients. . . . [New Jersey originally followed the professional standard of disclosure but later adopted the patient-centered material risk standard discussed in *Canterbury*.]

Our common law also authorizes a medical battery cause of action where a doctor performs a surgery without consent, rendering the surgery an unauthorized touching. . . . In circumstances where the surgery that was performed was authorized with arguably inadequate information, however, an action for negligence is more appropriate. . . . Thus, although a claim for battery will lie where there has been "ghost surgery"* or where no consent has been given for the procedure undertaken, if consent has been given for the procedure only a claim based on lack of informed consent will lie. A claim based on lack of informed consent properly will focus then on the adequacy of the disclosure, its impact on the reasonable patient's assessment of the risks, alternatives, and consequences of the surgery, and the damages caused by the occurrence of the undisclosed risk. . . .

Few jurisdictions have confronted the question of what cause of action should lie when a doctor allegedly misrepresents his credentials or experience. Research has revealed only one jurisdiction that has allowed a claim based on lack of informed consent under similar circumstances. See Johnson v. Kokemoor, 545 N.W.2d 495 (Wis. 1996) (analyzing doctor's affirmative misrepresentation as claim for lack of informed consent and finding that reasonable person would have considered information regarding doctor's relative lack of experience in performing surgery to have been material in making intelligent and informed decision). Although some suggest

---

*["Ghost surgery" occurs if the patient consents to a surgical procedure to be performed by Physician A but the surgery actually is performed by Physician B. —EDS.]

that a claim based in fraud may be appropriate if a doctor actively misrepresents his or her background or credentials, we are aware of no court that has so held. . . .

The thoughtful decision of the Appellate Division notwithstanding, we are not convinced that our common law should be extended to allow a novel fraud or deceit-based cause of action in this doctor-patient context that regularly would admit of the possibility of punitive damages, and that would circumvent the requirements for proof of both causation and damages imposed in a traditional informed consent setting. We are especially reluctant to do so when plaintiff's damages from this alleged "fraud" arise exclusively from the doctor-patient relationship involving plaintiff's corpectomy procedure. . . . Accordingly, we hold that a fraud or deceit-based claim is unavailable to address the wrong alleged by plaintiff. We next consider whether a claim based on lack of informed consent is the more appropriate analytical basis for the amendment to the complaint permitted by the Appellate Division. . . .

Our case law never has held that a doctor has a duty to detail his background and experience as part of the required informed consent disclosure; nor are we called on to decide that question here. . . . Courts generally have held that claims of lack of informed consent based on a failure to disclose professional-background information are without merit. . . . Although personal credentials and experience may not be a required part of an informed consent disclosure under the current standard of care required of doctors, the question raised in this appeal is whether significant misrepresentations concerning a physician's qualifications can affect the validity of consent obtained. The answer obviously is that they can.

In certain circumstances, a serious misrepresentation concerning the quality or extent of a physician's professional experience, viewed from the perspective of the reasonably prudent patient assessing the risks attendant to a medical procedure, can be material to the grant of intelligent and informed consent to the procedure. See 1 Dan B. Dobbs, *The Law of Torts,* §251 at 660-61 (2001) (citing *Kokemoor, supra,* and discussing that some authority has begun to suggest that patient is entitled to information concerning doctor's experience in performing specific surgery). In *Kokemoor, supra,* the Supreme Court of Wisconsin reviewed a case in which the plaintiff alleged that her surgeon did not obtain her informed consent to perform a surgical procedure because he had misrepresented his experience in response to a direct question during a pre-operative consultation. 545 N.W.2d at 505. At trial, evidence was introduced suggesting that the type of surgery performed—basilar bifurcation aneurysm—was "among the most difficult in all of neurosurgery." Ibid. The court found that evidence of the defendant's lack of experience was relevant to an informed consent claim because "[a] reasonable person in the plaintiff's position would have considered such information material in making an intelligent and informed decision about the surgery." Ibid.

The allegation here is that defendant's misrepresentations concerning his credentials and experience were instrumental in overcoming plaintiff's reluctance to proceed with the surgery. The theory of the claim is not that the misrepresentation induced plaintiff to proceed with unnecessary surgery. . . . Rather, plaintiff essentially contends that he was misled about material information that he required in order to grant an intelligent and informed consent to the performance of the procedure because he did not receive accurate responses to questions concerning defendant's experience in performing corpectomies and whether he was "Board Certified." Plaintiff allegedly was warned of the risk of paralysis from the corpectomy procedure; however, he asserts that if he had known the truth about defendant's qualifications and experience, it would have affected his assessment of the risks of the procedure. Stated differently, defendant's misrepresentations induced plaintiff to consent to a surgical procedure, and its risk of paralysis, that he would not have undergone had he known the truth about defendant's qualifications. Stripped to its essentials, plaintiff's claim is founded on lack of informed consent.

As noted earlier, a patient-specific standard of what is material to a full disclosure does not apply in a claim based on lack of informed consent. Thus, plaintiff's subjective preference for a Board Certified physician, or one who had performed more corpectomies than defendant had performed, is not the actionable standard. Nonetheless, assuming the misrepresentations are proved, if an objectively reasonable person could find that physician experience was material in determining the medical risk of the corpectomy procedure to which plaintiff consented, and if a reasonably prudent person in plaintiff's position informed of the defendant's misrepresentations about his experience would not have consented, then a claim based on lack of informed consent may be maintained.

Modern advances in medicine coupled with the increased sophistication of medical consumers require an evolving notion of the reasonably prudent patient when assessing a claim based on lack of informed consent. . . . That said, most informed consent issues are unlikely to implicate a setting in which a physician's experience or credentials have been demonstrated to be a material element affecting the risk of undertaking a specific procedure. The standard requires proof on which an objectively reasonable person would base a finding that physician experience could have a causal connection to a substantial risk of the procedure. . . .

The alleged misrepresentations in this case about "physician experience" (credentials and surgical experience) provide a useful context for demonstrating the difficulty inherent in meeting the materiality standard required in order for physician experience to have a role in an informed consent case. We recognize that a misrepresentation about a physician's experience is not a perfect fit with the familiar construct of a claim based on lack of informed consent. The difficulty arises because physician experience is not information that directly relates to the procedure itself or one of the other areas of required medical disclosure concerning the procedure, its substantial risks, and alternatives that must be disclosed to avoid a claim based on lack of informed consent. But the possibility of materiality is present. If defendant's true level of experience had the capacity to enhance substantially the risk of paralysis from undergoing a corpectomy, a jury could find that a reasonably prudent patient would not have consented to that procedure had the misrepresentation been revealed. That presumes that plaintiff can prove that the actual level of experience possessed by defendant had a direct and demonstrable relationship to the harm of paralysis, a substantial risk of the procedure that was disclosed to plaintiff. Put differently, plaintiff must prove that the additional undisclosed risk posed by defendant's true level of qualifications and experience increased plaintiff's risk of paralysis from the corpectomy procedure.

The standard for causation that we envision in such an action will impose a significant gatekeeper function on the trial court to prevent insubstantial claims concerning alleged misrepresentations about a physician's experience from proceeding to a jury. We contemplate that misrepresented or exaggerated physician experience would have to significantly increase a risk of a procedure in order for it to affect the judgment of a reasonably prudent patient in an informed consent case. As this case demonstrates, the proximate cause analysis will involve a two-step inquiry.

The first inquiry should be, assuming a misrepresentation about experience, whether the more limited experience or credentials possessed by defendant could have substantially increased plaintiff's risk of paralysis from undergoing the corpectomy procedure. We envision that expert testimony would be required for such a showing. The second inquiry would be whether that substantially increased risk would cause a reasonably prudent person not to consent to undergo the procedure. If the true extent of defendant's experience could not affect materially the risk of paralysis from a corpectomy procedure, then the alleged misrepresentation could not cause a reasonably prudent patient in plaintiff's position to decline consent to the procedure. The court's gatekeeper function in respect of the first question will require a determination that a genuine issue of material fact exists requiring resolution by the factfinder in order to proceed to the second question involving an assessment by the reasonably prudent patient. Further, the trial court must conclude that there is a genuine issue of material fact concerning both questions in order to allow the claim to proceed to trial.

Finally, to satisfy the damages element in a claim based on lack of informed consent, a plaintiff typically has to show a causal connection between the inadequately disclosed risk of the procedure and the injury sustained. . . . If that risk materialized and harmed plaintiff, damages for those injuries are awarded. . . . Here, if successful in his claim based on lack of informed consent, plaintiff may receive damages for injuries caused by an inadequately disclosed risk of the corpectomy procedure. However, as noted, to be successful plaintiff must prove that defendant's allegedly misrepresented qualifications and experience can satisfy the stringent test for proximate causation that is required for physician experience to be material to the substantial risk of the procedure that occurred (paralysis) and injured plaintiff. If he can, then plaintiff may be compensated for that injury caused by the corpectomy irrespective of whether defendant deviated from the standard of care in performing the surgical procedure.

In conclusion, plaintiff's medical malpractice action will address any negligence in defendant's performance of the corpectomy procedure. We hold that in addition plaintiff may attempt to prove that defendant's alleged misrepresentation about his credentials and experience presents a claim based on lack of informed consent to the surgical procedure, consistent with the requirements and limitations that we have imposed on such a claim. . . .

Notes: Fiduciary Principles and the Disclosure of Provider-Associated Risks

1. *Do Fiduciary Principles Add Anything?* Why couldn't the *Moore* court analyze the facts solely using traditional informed consent analysis? Read the opinion to determine (1) the theory underlying the imposition of fiduciary obligations; (2) the scope of the fiduciary duty; (3) the actions that might constitute a breach of the duty; (4) the injury requirements, if any; and (5) the remedies for a breach of fiduciary duty. Do fiduciary duties expand or merely parallel the duties already created under the material risk standard in informed consent cases? What should Golde

have done to avoid liability? Why doesn't the court impose disclosure duties on the other defendants? Would a conversion claim have been an easier basis of recovering damages from all of the defendants? Moore's conversion claim is discussed in more detail in Chapter 4, at pages 439-440. Fiduciary claims might be limited or eliminated where specific legislation governs informed consent actions. Daniels v. Gamma West Brachytherapy, 221 P.3d 256 (Utah 2009).

2. *Causation Problems in* Moore. Who has the better of the causation and damages arguments between Justice Mosk and Justice Broussard? On remand, Moore's claim was settled before going to trial, so the court never had to resolve these issues. The *Howard* court directly confronts the knotty causation questions created by provider-associated risk disclosure claims. Will Mr. Howard be able to recover on his informed consent claim without expert proof that the surgeon violated the standard of care in the conduct of the surgery? Why or why not? See Starozytnyk v. Reich, 871 A.2d 733 (N.J. Super. 2005) (affirming dismissal of plaintiff's informed consent and fiduciary duty claims due to absence of proximate cause); Christine Grady et al., The Limits of Disclosure: What Research Subjects Want to Know About Investigator Financial Interests, 34 J.L. Med. & Ethics 592 (2006) (majority of respondents wanted to know about investigators' interest but "only a minority thought such financial information would influence their decisions about research participation in any way"). Would the fiduciary character of the physician-patient relationship be better protected through the adoption of a new statutory claim that would focus on dignitary harm rather than the types of damages ordinarily recognized in malpractice or fiduciary claims? For a proposal see Caroline Forell & Anna Sortun, The Tort of Betrayal of Trust, 42 U. Mich. J.L. Reform 557 (2008-2009).

3. *Financial Conflicts in Fee-for-Service and Managed Care Arrangements.* The issue of conflicts of interest in medical research identified in *Moore* has continued to attract scrutiny and is discussed further infra at pages 432-436. But aside from research studies, what does *Moore* mean for ordinary medical treatment settings? Does it establish a common law duty for physicians to disclose to patients financial conflicts of interest that could reasonably affect routine treatment recommendations? No one supposes that doctors must disclose the distorting effects of fee-for-service reimbursement, which might result in harms from unnecessary treatment. Cf. Wright v. Jeckle, 144 P.3d 301 (Wash. 2006) (rejecting claim that physician's direct sale of anti-obesity drug constituted a violation of fiduciary duty under state anti-kickback legislation merely because physician profited from sales); and Ambach v. French, 216 P.3d 405 (Wash. 2009) (rejecting Consumer Protection Act claim by patient against physician based in part on extra expense of shoulder surgery compared with alternative treatment). What types of financial arrangements can create a real or perceived conflict of interest? See Association of American Medical Colleges, In the Interest of Patients: Recommendations for Physician Financial Relationships and Clinical Decision Making (2010). See also Symposium, Conflicts of Interest in the Practice of Medicine, 40 J.L. Med. & Ethics 436-522 (2012).

Should there be a duty to disclose incentives related to managed care? Could you argue that incentives to reduce health care expenses in managed care are "common knowledge"? If there is a financial disclosure obligation on the part of physicians participating in managed care arrangements, how great should the financial incentive be before it is considered "material"? Should the plaintiff be required to prove that the incentive was sufficient to affect physician decisionmaking in individual cases? Or can we presume that managed care companies would not use financial incentives unless they worked, by affecting physician decisions at least to some extent? Managed care physicians might argue that incentives are designed only to reduce unnecessary medical care and are not large enough to induce physicians to refrain from making necessary medical referrals. Even if incentives potentially affect necessary care, isn't the threat of a malpractice claim enough to ensure that physicians will still make appropriate referrals, or a sufficient remedy when they fail to do so? Should any duty to disclose managed care incentives be satisfied by a global disclosure when the patient first enrolls (and perhaps once a year thereafter), or must the incentives be repeated each time the patient seeks treatment? For an argument that disclosure at enrollment satisfies the fiduciary obligation, or perhaps acts as a waiver of subsequent disclosures, see Mark A. Hall, A Theory of Economic Informed Consent, 31 Ga. L. Rev. 511 (1997).

4. *Discussing the Costs of Care.* Curiously, there is virtually no legal or ethical guidance on whether physicians should tell patients how much treatment options cost. In the distant past, this may have been because physicians followed an ethic of treat first and bill later, letting patients pay what they were able. In the more recent past, this may be because insurance usually pays for the majority of costs. In the future, however, these cost-insulating features may soon recede, under the influence of "consumer-driven" health insurance plans that expose patients to much greater cost-sharing obligations. See pages 55-56. This will likely generate disputes by patients who feel they were not adequately informed about the costs of the treatments they agreed to. Under the informed consent and fiduciary principles you have learned, should physicians have to volunteer information about costs, or only wait for patients to ask first? Does the answer differ for the costs of the physicians' own services vs. costs charged by other providers, goods, or services the physician may recommend (such as lab tests, drugs, or specialist referrals)? For preliminary discussion, see Haavi Morreim, High-Deductible Health Plans: New Twists on Old Challenges from Tort and Contract, 59 Vand. L. Rev. 1207 (2006); G. Caleb Alexander et al., Rethinking Professional Ethics in the Cost-Sharing Era, 6(4) Am. J. Bioethics W17-W22 (2006); Marshall Kapp, Patient Autonomy in the Age of Consumer-Driven Health Care: Informed Consent and Informed Choice, 28 J. Leg. Med. 91 (2007).

5. *Third-Party Payments and Investment Interests.* As *Moore* briefly indicates, statutory law sometimes requires disclosure of certain kinds of financial conflicts of interest. A prime example is when physicians have investment or ownership interests in the facilities to which they refer their patients. State and federal laws prohibit or regulate these investment interests in many circumstances. Which approach strikes you as more appropriate: disclosure or prohibition/regulation?

Consider as well the many tactics that drug and medical device companies have used to encourage physicians to prescribe their products. Kickbacks and direct financial incentives are illegal; other types of arrangements have elicited increasing attention. See Thomas L. Hafemeister & Sarah P. Bryan, Beware Those Bearing Gifts: Physicians' Fiduciary Duty to Avoid Pharmaceutical Marketing, 57 U. Kan. L. Rev. 491 (2009); Margaret Z. Johns, Informed Consent: Requiring Doctors to Disclose Off-Label Prescriptions and Conflicts of Interest, 58 Hastings L.J. 967 (2007). The Affordable Care Act includes "sunshine" provisions that require drug, device, and medical supply companies to report their payments to physicians. 42 U.S.C.A. §1320a-7h. See Robert Steinbrook & Joseph Ross, 307 JAMA 1029 (2012) (discussing legislation and proposed rules, 76 Fed. Reg. 78742, 78767 (2011)). The federal provisions preempt most state statutes or regulations requiring manufacturers to disclose payments but do not preempt disclosure obligations placed on physicians.

Different types of financial and nonfinancial conflicts of interest permeate medical relationships, as they do most human affairs. (For example, the authors of this book receive modest royalties when their own students purchase it.) How assiduous should physicians be in avoiding or disclosing them? As one specific example among many possible financial and nonfinancial conflicts, should a physician be required to disclose medical errors to patients? Manufacturers can also attempt to influence sales by promoting their products with consumers, who then might exert pressure on their physicians to authorize specific treatments. See Thomas L. Hafemeister & Richard M. Gulbrandsen, The Fiduciary Obligation of Physicians to "Just Say No" If an "Informed" Patient Demands Services That Are Not Medically Indicated, 39 Seton Hall L. Rev. 335 (2009).

6. *Financial Disclosure Claims in the Courts. Moore* appeared to open the door to using informed consent and/or fiduciary theories to protect patients from the risks created by a provider's financial arrangements with third parties, such as managed care organizations. Subsequent courts have tried to push the door shut, at least on some types of claims. In Neade v. Portes, 739 N.E.2d 496 (Ill. 2000), for example, the Illinois Supreme Court rejected the use of fiduciary theories in a case involving managed care incentives. Mr. Neade was only 37 but had a number of significant risk factors for heart disease. Mr. Neade began to experience radiating chest pain and shortness of breath. Mr. Neade's primary physician, Dr. Portes, authorized Mr. Neade's hospitalization. While hospitalized, Mr. Neade underwent a battery of tests that appeared to rule out heart disease. Thereafter, Dr. Portes failed to refer Mr. Neade for more specific tests for heart disease, despite recurring symptoms. Mr. Neade had a heart attack and died. Mr. Neade's estate brought claims for breach of fiduciary duty and medical negligence against Dr. Portes and others. Dr. Portes participated in a risk-sharing agreement with the patient's HMO that arguably gave the physician an incentive to deny referrals to his patients.

Relying in part on some of the language found in the United States Supreme Court's opinion in Pegram v. Herdrich, 530 U.S. 211 (2000) (exploring fiduciary duty under federal ERISA statute), the Illinois Supreme Court rejected the breach of fiduciary duty claim. The Illinois Supreme Court held that a cause of action for breach of fiduciary duty based on a physician's failure to reveal a financial interest in a medical incentive fund essentially duplicated the underlying medical negligence claim:

> [I]t is operative facts together with the injury that we look to in order to determine whether a cause of action is duplicative. In the case at bar, the operative fact in both [the malpractice and fiduciary duty] counts is Dr. Portes' failure to order an angiogram for Mr. Neade. Plaintiff alleges in both counts that Mr. Neade's failure to receive an angiogram is the ultimate reason for his subsequent death. Plaintiff also alleges the same injury in both her medical negligence claim and her breach of fiduciary duty claim, namely, Mr. Neade's death and its effect on plaintiff and her family. We determine that plaintiff's breach of fiduciary duty claim is a re-presentment of her medical negligence claim.
>
> An examination of the elements of a medical negligence claim and breach of fiduciary duty claim illustrates the way in which a breach of fiduciary duty claim

would "boil down to a malpractice claim." *Herdrich*, 530 U.S. at —, 120 S. Ct. at 2157. To sustain an action for medical negligence, plaintiff must show: (1) the standard of care in the medical community by which the physician's treatment was measured; (2) that the physician deviated from the standard of care; and (3) that a resulting injury was proximately caused by the deviation from the standard of care. . . . Thus, the standard of care is the relevant inquiry by which we judge a physician's actions in a medical negligence case. . . .

In contrast to an action for medical negligence, in order to state a claim for breach of fiduciary duty, it must be alleged that a fiduciary duty exists, that the fiduciary duty was breached, and that such breach proximately caused the injury of which the plaintiff complains. . . .

In order to sustain a breach of fiduciary duty claim against Dr. Portes, plaintiff would have to allege, inter alia, that: (1) had she known of the Medical Incentive Fund she would have sought an opinion from another physician; (2) that the other physician would have ordered an angiogram for Mr. Neade; (3) that the angiogram would have detected Mr. Neade's heart condition; and (4) that treatment could have prevented his eventual myocardial infarction and subsequent death. In order to prove the second element, plaintiff would have been required to present expert testimony that the expert, after examining Mr. Neade and considering his history, would have ordered an angiogram. This requirement relates to the standard of care consideration—the first prong in a traditional medical negligence claim—under which a physician is held to "the reasonable skill which a physician in good standing in the community would use." That is precisely what plaintiff must prove to support her breach of fiduciary duty claim. As the Supreme Court stated in *Herdrich*, the breach of fiduciary duty claim "would boil down to a malpractice claim, and the fiduciary standard would be nothing but the malpractice standard traditionally applied in actions against physicians." *Herdrich*, 530 U.S. at —, 120 S. Ct. at 2157. Thus, we need not recognize a new cause of action for breach of fiduciary duty when a traditional medical negligence claim sufficiently addresses the same alleged misconduct. The breach of fiduciary duty claim in the case at bar would be duplicative of the medical negligence claim.

Our decision to refrain from permitting the creation of this new cause of action finds additional support in statutory law. The Illinois legislature has placed the burden of disclosing HMO incentive schemes on HMOs themselves. . . .

Moreover, the outcome that would result if we were to allow the creation of a new cause of action for breach of fiduciary duty against a physician in these circumstances may be impractical. For example, physicians often provide services for numerous patients, many of whom may be covered by different HMOs. In order to effectively disclose HMO incentives, physicians would have to remain cognizant at all times of every patient's particular HMO and that HMO's policies and procedures. See, e.g., Mark Hall, A Theory of Economic Informed Consent, 31 Ga. L. Rev. 511, 525-26 (1997). . . . If we were to recognize a breach of fiduciary duty claim in the context of the case at bar, we fear the effects of such a holding may be unworkable.

Neade v. Portes, 739 N.E.2d. at 502-506. The court also held that evidence of the physician's financial incentives could be relevant on issues relating to interest and bias, in the event that physician testified in the medical negligence trial. Id. at 506.

Chief Justice Harrison dissented:

A complaint against a lawyer for professional malpractice may be couched in either contract or tort. . . . The same rule should apply here. Although this case involves medical rather than legal malpractice, that distinction is insignificant. . . . The right to assert claims for breach of fiduciary duty and negligence in the same professional malpractice action is not unfettered. When the same operative facts support a negligence count and a count for breach of fiduciary duty based on the same injury to the client, the counts are identical and the fiduciary duty count should be dismissed as duplicative. . . . In this case, however, the negligence and breach of fiduciary duty counts asserted by plaintiff are not identical. . . . As the appellate court correctly recognized,

> [i]t is conceivable that a trier of fact could find both that Dr. Portes was within the standard of care and therefore not negligent in relying on the thallium stress test and the EKG in deciding that an angiogram was not necessary and also that Dr. Portes did breach his fiduciary duty in not disclosing his financial incentive arrangement and, as a proximate result thereof, Neade did not obtain a second opinion, suffered a massive coronary infarction, and died.

710 N.E.2d 418. . . .

Id. at 506. For an unsuccessful effort to use fiduciary theories in the context of obesity drug litigation, see Wright v. Jeckle, 90 P.3d 65 (Wash. App. 2004).

7. *Institutional Disclosure Obligations Under Fiduciary Law.* Under common law principles, as *Moore* holds, institutions are generally free from the disclosure duties imposed on physicians. A federal statute, the Employee Retirement Income Security Act of 1974 (ERISA), regulates health plans provided as a benefit of employment. This statute has a number of important implications for the organization and delivery of health care in the United States. For present purposes, it is enough to note that the Supreme Court's decision in *Pegram* left the door open to efforts to use ERISA's fiduciary principles as a tool for imposing disclosure obligations on managed care employee benefit plans.

8. *Nonfinancial Provider-Associated Risks.* Should physicians have a duty to disclose risks to patients that arise from the identity of the provider rather than the type of procedure? *Howard* is part of a small new line of cases considering whether physicians have any duty to disclose provider risks, as distinguished from procedural risks.

a. *Experience and Success Rates.* Health care organizations and purchasers are developing and collecting information about health care outcomes for individual practitioners. Should health care providers have a duty to disclose their own "scorecards" to patients? How does the *Howard* court distinguish between informed consent and misrepresentation claims in this area? Courts generally have considered cases involving misrepresentation of experience under informed consent rather than misrepresentation law. See, e.g., Roderer v. Dash, 233 P.3d 1101 (Alaska 2010); Ray v. Kapiolani Medical Specialists, 259 P.3d 569 (Haw. 2011); Kelly v. Vinzant, 197 P.3d 803 (Kan. 2008); Willis v. Bender, 596 F.3d 1244 (10th Cir. 2010). At least one court has rejected an intentional misrepresentation claim in which the plaintiff did not present expert testimony establishing that his injuries were caused by inexperience. Wooding v. U.S., 2010 WL 781303 (3d Cir. 2010).

For other cases involving physician experience, see Duffy v. Flagg, 905 A.2d 15 (Conn. 2006) (informed consent does not require physician to give detailed account of her past experience with a procedure when answers would not have been relevant to key informed consent issues); DeGennaro v. Tandon, 873 A.2d

191 (Conn. App. 2005) (reasonable patient would consider lack of experience in using equipment, and lack of assistance, to be material information about provider-specific risk); Goldberg v. Boone, 912 A.2d 698 (Md. 2006) (jury should determine whether physician experience is material); Wlosinski v. Cohn, 713 N.W.2d 16 (Mich. App. 2005) ("raw success rates" need not be disclosed; interesting concurring and dissenting opinions); Duttry v. Patterson, 771 A.2d 1255 (Pa. 2001) (physician's personal characteristics and experience irrelevant in informed consent claim; misrepresentation claim possible); Johnson v. Kokemoor, 545 N.W.2d 495 (Wis. 1996) (applying informed consent principles to a case involving a physician's relative lack of experience).

For commentaries on the subject, see Marc D. Ginsberg, Informed Consent: No Longer Just What the Doctor Ordered?, 15 Mich. St. U. J. Med. & L. 17 (2010); Aaron D. Twerski, The Second Revolution in Informed Consent: Comparing Physicians to Each Other, 94 Nw. U. L. Rev. 1 (1999); Aaron D. Twerski & Neil B. Cohen, Comparing Medical Providers: A First Look at the New Era of Medical Statistics, 58 Brook. L. Rev. 5 (1992); Robert Weinstein et al., Infection-Control Report Cards—Ensuring Patient Safety, 353 New Eng. J. Med. 225 (2005); J. Wilks et al., Surgeon with Worst Performance Figures Might Be the Best Option, 323 Brit. Med. J. 1071 (2001).

b. *Abuse of Drug or Alcohol.* Would the reasonable patient consider a physician's cocaine addiction to be a material fact in deciding whether or not to undergo surgery? Would the professional standard of care require such a disclosure? Compare Albany Urology Clinic, P.C. v. Cleveland, 528 S.E.2d 777 (Ga. 2000) (no duty to disclose drug use under common law or state informed consent statute), with Hidding v. Williams, 578 So. 2d 1192 (La. Ct. App. 1991) (physician has duty to reveal his alcoholism; concurring opinion raises interesting causation problem).

c. *Infection with HIV.* There has been a vigorous debate about whether a physician has or should have a duty to disclose his or her HIV status. See, e.g., Mary Anne Bobinski, Autonomy and Privacy: Protecting Patients from Their Physicians, 55 U. Pitt. L. Rev. 291 (1994). The application of the informed consent doctrine to the problem of HIV disclosure in health care is complicated by the fact that many patients are more fearful about the very low risk of HIV transmission from health care worker to patient than they are about other, larger risks. In addition, persons with HIV infection are protected from discrimination under a variety of statutes, including the Americans with Disabilities Act, unless they pose a "significant risk" to the health or safety of others. 42 U.S.C. §§12111-12113. From the perspective of the infected physician, disclosure ought not be required unless there is a significant risk of transmission. From the perspective of the patient, even a "less than significant" risk could be avoided by selecting an (apparently) uninfected health care provider. One court has resolved the conflict in favor of the patient's right to know:

> [Dr. Behringer, a surgeon] argues: (1) the risk of transmission of HIV from surgeon to patient is too remote to require informed consent, and (2) the law of informed consent does not require disclosure of the condition of the surgeon.... [Dr. Behringer] argues that the use of the informed consent form is tantamount to a de facto termination of surgical privileges. [Dr. Behringer] further urges that patient reaction is likely to be based more on public hysteria than on a studied assessment of the actual risk involved.

The answer to these arguments is two-fold. First, it is the duty of the surgeon utilizing the informed consent procedure to explain to the patient the real risk involved. If the patient's fear is without basis, it is likewise the duty of the surgeon to allay that fear. This court recognizes that the burden imposed on the surgeon may not be surmountable absent further education of both the public and the medical community about the realities of HIV and AIDS. Second, the difficulties created by the public reaction to AIDS cannot deprive the patient of making the ultimate decision where the ultimate risk is so significant. The last word has not been spoken on the issue of transmission of HIV and AIDS. Facts accepted at one point in time are no longer accurate as more is learned about this disease and its transmission. . . .

[Dr. Behringer] further argues that there is no requirement under the doctrine of informed consent that a surgeon's physical condition be revealed as a risk of the surgery itself. The informed consent cases are not so narrow as to support that argument. In [a prior New Jersey Supreme Court case] . . . the court spoke of not only an evaluation of the nature of the treatment, but of "any attendant substantial risks." . . .

[Dr. Behringer] urges that these issues should be dealt with on a case-by-case basis, wherein the hospital or medical staff monitors an HIV-positive surgeon and makes a determination as to the surgeon's ability to perform a particular invasive procedure. . . . The position [Dr. Behringer] seeks to implement is replete with the "anachronistic paternalism" rejected in both Canterbury v. Spence, supra, and by the [New Jersey] Supreme Court. . . .

[The court summarized the views of several commentators, one of whom had noted the fiduciary character of the physician-patient relationship.] . . . The obligation of a surgeon performing invasive procedures, such as [Dr. Behringer], to reveal his AIDS condition, is one which requires a weighing of [Dr. Behringer's] rights against the patient's rights. New Jersey's strong policy supporting patient rights, weighed against [Dr. Behringer's] individual right to perform an invasive procedure as a part of the practice of his profession, requires the conclusion that the patient's rights must prevail. At a minimum, the physician must withdraw from performing any invasive procedure which would pose a risk to the patient. Where the ultimate harm is death, even the presence of a low risk of transmission justifies the adoption of a policy which precludes invasive procedures when there is "any" risk of transmission. In the present case, the debate raged as to whether there was "any" risk of transmission, and the informed-consent procedure was left in place. If there is to be an ultimate arbiter of whether the patient is to be treated invasively by an AIDS-positive surgeon, the arbiter will be the fully-informed patient. The ultimate risk to the patient is so absolute—so devastating—that it is untenable to argue against informed consent combined with a restriction on procedures which present "any risk" to the patient.

Estate of Behringer v. Medical Center at Princeton, 592 A.2d 1251, 1279-1283 (N.J. Super. Ct. Div. 1991). Courts have not yet addressed the impact of newer anti-retroviral therapies, which can reduce a patient's viral load and ability to transmit the infection to others.

Problem: *Moore* Liability?

Consider the informed consent doctrine applicable in your state. What types of disclosures would be required in the following situations?

1. A physician recommending a surgical procedure necessary to save the patient's life will earn about $15,000 from the surgery and follow-up care. What if the surgery is for cosmetic purposes?

2. A physician recommends that a patient see a specialist for her condition. The physician is married to the specialist.

3. A physician providing care for an HMO patient earns a flat fee per month per patient. The physician is treating a patient's digestive complaints and suggests that the patient wait two months to see if the condition resolves on its own.

4. A physician providing care for an HMO patient with back pain suggests that the patient take a conservative approach to treatment, delaying expensive diagnostic tests and surgery for as long as possible. The physician's financial arrangements with the HMO include provisions that decrease the physician's income if the physician spends more than an allocated amount on diagnostic tests or hospitalization.

5. A physician describes herself as a social drinker. She only drinks during the evenings and on weekends. On average, she consumes about 21 mixed drinks per week.

6. A general internist learns that he has HIV infection.

7. A physician fails to inform a patient suffering from pancreatic cancer of the patient's low statistical life expectancy. The patient does not make the proper financial arrangements, causing substantial real estate and tax losses. See Arato v. Avedon, 858 P.2d 598 (Cal. 1993).

E. HUMAN EXPERIMENTATION AND RESEARCH

The *Moore* litigation arose because of the alleged conflicts of interest created by the research interests of the defendants. Nightly news stories regularly focus on the results of medical research, touting the next great cures for long-feared diseases (as well as informing us about cures for diseases that we never knew existed). Society clearly has a strong interest in ensuring that medical research is not stymied by excessive regulation. Researchers and biotechnology companies may have significant economic interests in the research enterprise. Statistics are difficult to obtain because medical research is conducted in a range of public and private settings, funded by public and private sources, and regulated either by different federal regulatory entities or by much more diffuse common law rules. Medical research is a significant enterprise involving "an estimated 20 million Americans tak[ing] part in more than 41,000 clinical trials and uncounted more federally funded experiments." Tom Abate, Experiments on Humans: Business of Clinical Trials Soars, but Risk Unknown, S.F. Chron., Aug. 4, 2002, at A1. In 2008, private and public funding for biomedical research totaled $88.8 billion. E. Ray Dorsey et al., Funding of US Biomedical Research, 2003-2008, 303 JAMA 137 (2010).

There are two central concerns in the research context. The first is that experimental treatment is often not done for the patient's immediate benefit. Some patients may approach medical research thinking they will receive better care because it is "state of the art," but this is usually a false impression. Instead, the treatment that is being studied may be riskier; almost certainly its risks are less well known than standard treatment. Also, patients are often "randomized" "blindly" between an "experimental arm" and a "control arm." This means that, by luck of the draw, a significant percentage will receive ordinary treatment or even, in some cases, a placebo; participants generally will not know which type of care they will receive. Moreover, the innovation in treatment may have nothing at all to offer their condition, but may be intended solely to provide an improvement for other patients. The relevant distinction is between "therapeutic" and "nontherapeutic research." Only in the former is there something that a patient might benefit from immediately, but even then, patients are often asked to undergo risks that are greater than the potential rewards in order to further the aims of science.

Fully informed patients may be more than willing to accept these arrangements out of a sense of altruism and a desire to be a part of progress. But there is a second difficulty: How well informed are they, and how freely do they make their decision? Some patients may feel pressured in subtle ways without the knowledge of their physicians. Imagine a physician who eagerly pitches her pet research project, and a patient who fears (irrationally or not?) that disappointing his doctor will jeopardize his treatment. For other patients, coercion could be more overt. The reluctance of well-informed patients to participate in risky experiments might lead researchers either to conceal the experiment or to use patients from vulnerable or socially disadvantaged groups.

These concerns are not merely speculative. The history of medical research reveals both astounding advances and disquieting practices. Scientists have sought to expand the knowledge of human biology, illness, and treatment, often at the expense of the least fortunate in society: slaves, the poor, criminals, and other institutionalized persons. Several twentieth-century examples have left a legacy of fear and mistrust. Nazi scientists conducted a vigorous program of medical research on prisoners and internees during World War II. Their appalling lack of respect for human life and humane principles resulted in the Nuremberg Code. The Code's central tenet is a requirement that human research subjects give consent to participation in any research project. See Evelyn Shuster, Fifty Years Later: The Significance of the Nuremberg Code, 337 New Eng. J. Med. 1436 (1997).

Violations of human rights by researchers are not limited, however, to some distant time and far-off place. Two examples of research abuses in the United States have had a profound impact. In the Tuskegee Study, which ran from the 1950s until the early 1970s, researchers studied the effects of untreated syphilis in a group of African-American men. The researchers purported to treat the men for their ailments but never disclosed to their subjects that they continued to suffer from a highly treatable, yet debilitating illness. The researchers' apparently cavalier disregard for their subjects has resulted in a legacy of distrust among minority and poor communities.

Recent revelations have been no more comforting. In the mid-1990s, the federal government revealed that hundreds of persons had been involuntarily, and in some cases unknowingly, subjected to research in which they were exposed to radiation and other harmful substances. President Clinton was forced to announce the adoption of newly strengthened protections for human subjects participating in classified research projects. Strengthened Protections for Human Subjects of Classified Research, 62 Fed. Reg. 26,367 (1997). See generally U.S. Advisory Comm. on Human Radiation Experiments, Final Report of the Advisory Committee on Human Radiation Experiments (Ruth Faden ed., 1996).

A special set of rules governs the disclosure and consent process in medical research. Federal regulations require an elaborate consent process in order for research to receive federal funding. U.S. Dep't Health & Human Servs., Protection of Human Subjects, 45 C.F.R. §§46.101-.505; U.S. Food & Drug Admin., Protection of Human Subjects, 21 C.F.R. §§50.1 et seq. Entities that accept federally funded research projects also assure that they will protect human subjects in research projects funded by non-federal sources. 45 C.F.R. §46.103(b). Private foundations that fund research usually follow suit. The end result is that the federal regulations effectively govern most planned medical research in the United States. These federal rules, while influential, do not preempt state laws providing greater protection of human subjects. State regulation of research through the common law may become increasingly important.

■WHY INFORMED CONSENT? HUMAN EXPERIMENTATION AND THE ETHICS OF AUTONOMY
Richard W. Garnett*
36 Cath. Law. 455 (1996)

. . . Why does consent have such moral power? Accept for now that our deference to consent is—perhaps mistakenly—rooted in a commitment to human dignity, expressed through respect for autonomy. Is consent's justifying role necessarily required by this commitment to human dignity? Why have we come to think that it is? Does our dignity as persons follow from, or does it instead create and condition, our autonomy? Do we respect consent because one feature of our dignity is that we always know what is best for us? Clearly we do not. . . .

III. Regulating Human Experimentation Through Consent

A. The Nuremberg Code and "Informed Consent"

The Nuremberg Code and the memory of the Nazi doctors' trial animate and permeate modern thinking about regulation of human experimentation. The Code was our most morally rigorous attempt to limit human experimentation. Its most memorable command was that, in medical research, "[t]he voluntary consent of the human subject is absolutely essential."[70] But while the Code has come to stand for "informed consent," it required more. It focused as much on the experiment itself, on the welfare of the subject, and on the conduct of the researcher as it did on the need for the subject's consent. Sadly, this broad focus has received relatively short shrift, and the consent principle has eclipsed the others.

The Code stands tall in memory but its influence has never lived up to its aims. Seen by many as a product of and reaction to Nazi terror, the Code is often dismissed as a context-bound relic, no longer useful for today's researchers. Pragmatists argue that the Code is simply too demanding, that its standards are too high for necessary research to meet, and that its absolutism cannot compete with the utilitarian and impersonal ethics of modern medicine. . . .

---

*Law professor at Notre Dame Law School.

70. The Nazi Doctors and the Nuremberg Code: Human Rights in Human Experimentation 2 (George J. Annas & Michael A. Grodin eds., 1992).

B. REGULATING EXPERIMENTATION AFTER NUREMBERG: THE STANDARD MODEL OF INFORMED CONSENT

. . . Today, human experimentation is regulated by a crazy-quilt of hortatory codes and maxims, scattered federal laws and regulations, and most importantly, by Institutional Review Boards,[85] which provide peer review of proposed experiments. "Informed consent" is still the touchstone, but modern regulations and procedures tolerate and expect deviations from this ideal. Thus, when addressing human experimentation—and they rarely do—courts occasionally mention the [Nuremberg] Code, but generally apply and enforce the more flexible informed consent requirements of later regulations.

The legal doctrine of informed consent as it has developed is quite different from the dignity-based commitment to self-determination animating the Nuremberg Code. The most important feature of today's regulatory regime is that it focuses on the subject's state of mind more than on the experiment itself. What is referred to here as the "Standard Model" of informed consent is this subjectively oriented informed consent in the context of peer review. In practice, research peers have proven insufficiently critical when evaluating proposed experiments. In addition, the informed consent "requirement" is viewed as a chore and a ritual, an impersonal incantation, a hurried signing of papers. We know this is true, yet we cherish the myth of informed consent, skating over its lack of real content or impact. But because the Standard Model is a subterfuge aimed more at easing our consciences than at protecting research subjects, it fails both as a necessary condition for proposed experiments and as a justification for them.

IV. THE STANDARD MODEL IN ACTION: INFORMED CONSENT IN HARD CASES

. . . The Standard Model regulates experiments by requiring the subjects' informed consent. Comparatively little attention is given to the nature of the experiment itself—apart from its riskiness—or to the researcher's goals and intentions. Under the Standard Model, concern may be triggered by some characteristic of the subject (age, health, mental capabilities) or by the experiment's location (prison, hospital, university). These characteristics and locations, however, relate less to whether the researcher's plan is itself ethical, than whether the subject's consent was really given, or was truly informed. When experiments are prohibited, it is due to the quality, or lack thereof, of the consent given, not the propriety of the experiment itself. In these situations, whatever it is that gives the subject's consent its justificatory power—the mysterious indicia of autonomy worth respecting—is deemed lacking. To illustrate this dynamic at work, I review below the operation of the Standard Model in three paradigmatically hard cases.

---

85. For a complete review of the structure and function of Institutional Review Boards, see, e.g., 45 C.F.R. §§46.107-111 (1994); 21 C.F.R. §§56.101-114 (1994). "IRB approval means the determination of the IRB that the research has been reviewed and may be conducted at an institution within the constraints set forth by the IRB and by other institutional and federal requirements." 45 C.F.R. §46.102(h).

A. PRISONERS

Prisoners have long been conveniently immobile, docile, and hence ideal subjects for research and experimentation. . . . Accordingly, experimentation on prisoners is carefully scrutinized under the Standard Model. The Department of Health and Human Services warns that "prisoners may be under constraints because of their incarceration which could affect their ability to make a truly voluntary and uncoerced decision whether or not to participate as subjects in research." . . .

B. THE TERMINALLY ILL

. . . As with prisoners, experimentation with terminally or grieviously ill patients distorts the Standard Model. Like children or the mentally handicapped, dying persons are often thought of as incapable of making informed decisions; and like prisoners, they are viewed as not "really" free, but instead, captive to the course of their disease and therefore under duress. Even when these patients are lucid, we fear their assessment of an experiment's benefits and risks may be skewed; we worry they might submit to quackery in a hopeless and desperate attempt to beat the inevitable. We also worry that the dying may, having abandoned all hope, submit to immoral experiments out of misplaced or entirely genuine altruism. Finally, we fear that we may be tempted to exploit these subjects' despair, incapacity, or altruism, and to railroad through experiments which might not otherwise pass ethical muster. . . .

C. CHILDREN

The use of children poses even thornier problems for research. We need to experiment on children; their problems and illnesses are often sui generis and can only be solved through experiments on them. However, the Standard Model assumes children cannot give adequate consent, and so it gives in to necessity, though the Nuremberg Code insisted that the subject's consent was essential. Because children cannot, by definition, give consent, we settle for less. In addition, because children are a necessary and unique research class, we are forced to face the steely utilitarian calculus that hides beneath the Standard Model's veneer of respect for persons.

The Standard Model requires someone's consent, and parents are the most obvious candidates. However, even parents might not be able to isolate and protect an individual child's safety and dignity, especially when another child is thrown into the equation. The same considerations that call into question whether a prisoner's consent was voluntary or informed might undermine a desperate parent's consent as well. . . .

■ GRIMES v. KENNEDY KRIEGER INSTITUTE, INC.
782 A.2d 807 (Md. 2001)

Opinion by CATHELL, J.

PROLOGUE

We initially note that these are cases of first impression for this Court. For that matter, precious few courts in the United States have addressed the issues presented in the cases at bar. . . .

In these present cases, a prestigious research institute, associated with Johns Hopkins University, based on this record, created a nontherapeutic research program whereby it required certain classes of homes to have only partial lead paint abatement modifications performed, and in at least some instances, including at least one of the cases at bar, arranged for the landlords to receive public funding by way of grants or loans to aid in the modifications. The research institute then encouraged, and in at least one of the cases at bar, required, the landlords to rent the premises to families with young children. In the event young children already resided in one of the study houses, it was contemplated that a child would remain in the premises, and the child was encouraged to remain, in order for his or her blood to be periodically analyzed. In other words, the continuing presence of the children that were the subjects of the study was required in order for the study to be complete. Apparently, the children and their parents involved in the[se] cases . . . were from a lower economic strata and were, at least in one case, minorities.

The purpose of the research was to determine how effective varying degrees of lead paint abatement procedures were. Success was to be determined by periodically, over a two-year period of time, measuring the extent to which lead dust remained in, or returned to, the premises after the varying levels of abatement modifications, and, as most important to our decision, by measuring the extent to which the theretofore healthy children's blood became contaminated with lead, and comparing that contamination with levels of lead dust in the houses over the same periods of time. [Some evidence suggests that families with young children were given priority in renting abated apartments.] . . .

The same researchers had completed a prior study on abatement and partial abatement methods that indicated that lead dust remained and/or returned to abated houses over a period of time. . . . [The researchers also acknowledged that exposure to lead was "particularly hazardous for children."] . . . After publishing this report, the researchers began the present research project in which children were encouraged to reside in households where the possibility of lead dust was known to the researcher to be likely, so that the lead dust content of their blood could be compared with the level of lead dust in the houses at periodic intervals over a two-year period.

Apparently, it was anticipated that the children, who were the human subjects in the program, would, or at least might, accumulate lead in their blood from the dust, thus helping the researchers to determine the extent to which the various partial abatement methods worked. There was no complete and clear explanation in the consent agreements signed by the parents of the children that the research to be conducted was designed, at least in significant part, to measure the success of the abatement procedures by measuring the extent to which the children's blood was being contaminated. It can be argued that the researchers intended that the children be the canaries in the mines but never clearly told the parents. . . .

The researchers and their Institutional Review Board apparently saw nothing wrong with the research protocols that anticipated the possible accumulation of lead in the blood of otherwise healthy children as a result of the experiment, or they believed that the consents of the parents of the children made the research appropriate. Institutional Review Boards (IRB) are oversight entities [that are within the organizational structure of the institution conducting the research]. In research experiments, an IRB can be required in some instances by either federal or state regulation, or sometimes by the conditions attached to governmental grants that are used to fund research projects. Generally, their primary functions are to assess the protocols of the project to determine whether the project itself is appropriate, whether the consent procedures are adequate, whether the methods to be employed meet proper standards, whether reporting requirements are sufficient, and the assessment of various other aspects of a research project. One of the most important objectives of such review is the review of the potential safety and the health hazard impact of a research project on the human subjects of the experiment, especially on vulnerable subjects such as children. Their function is not to help researchers seek funding for research projects.

In the instant case, as is suggested by some commentators as being endemic to the research community as a whole, infra, the IRB involved here, the Johns Hopkins University Joint Committee on Clinical Investigation, in part, abdicated that responsibility, instead suggesting to the researchers a way to miscast the characteristics of the study in order to avoid the responsibility inherent in nontherapeutic research involving children. . . .

While the suggestion of the IRB would not make this experiment any less nontherapeutic or, thus, less regulated, . . . [its action] shows two things: (1) that the IRB had a partial misperception of the difference between therapeutic and nontherapeutic research and the IRB's role in the process and (2) that the IRB was willing to aid researchers in getting around federal regulations designed to protect children used as subjects in nontherapeutic research. An IRB's primary role is to assure the safety of human research subjects—not help researchers avoid safety or health-related requirements. The IRB, in this case, misconceived, at least partially, its own role.

The provisions or conditions imposed by the federal funding entities, pursuant to federal regulations, are conditions attached to funding. As far as we are aware, or have been informed, there are no federal or state (Maryland) statutes that mandate that all research be subject to certain conditions. Certain international "codes" or "declarations" exist (one of which is supposedly binding but has never been so held) that, at least in theory, establish standards. We shall describe them, infra. Accordingly, we write on a clean slate in this case. We are guided, as we determine what is appropriate, by those international "codes" or "declarations," as well as by studies conducted by various governmental entities, by the treatises and other writings on the ethics of using children as research subjects, and by the duties, if any, arising out of the use of children as subjects of research.

Otherwise healthy children, in our view, should not be enticed into living in, or remaining in, potentially lead-tainted housing and intentionally subjected to a research program, which contemplates the probability, or even the possibility, of lead poisoning or even the accumulation of lower levels of lead in blood, in order for the extent of the contamination of the children's blood to be used by scientific researchers to assess the success of lead paint or lead dust abatement measures. Moreover, in our view, parents, whether improperly enticed by trinkets, food stamps, money or other items, have no more right to intentionally and unnecessarily place children in potentially hazardous nontherapeutic research surroundings, than do researchers. In such cases, parental consent, no matter how informed, is insufficient.

While the validity of the consent agreement and its nature as a contract, the existence or nonexistence of a special relationship, and whether the researchers performed their functions under that agreement pursuant to any special relationships are important issues in these cases that we will address, the very inappropriateness of the research itself cannot be overlooked. It is apparent that the protocols of research are even more important than the method of obtaining parental consent and the extent to which the parents were, or were not, informed. If the research methods, the protocols, are inappropriate then, especially when the IRB is willing to help researchers avoid compliance with applicable safety requirements for using children in nontherapeutic research, the consent of the parents, or of any consent surrogates, in our view, cannot make the research appropriate or the actions of the researchers and the Institutional Review Board proper.

The research relationship proffered to the parents of the children the researchers wanted to use as measuring tools, should never have been presented in a nontherapeutic context in the first instance. Nothing about the research was designed for treatment of the subject children. They were presumed to be healthy at the commencement of the project. As to them, the research was clearly nontherapeutic in nature. The experiment was simply a "for the greater good" project.[6] The specific children's health was put at risk, in order to develop low-cost abatement measures that would help all children, the landlords, and the general public as well. . . .

The research project at issue here, and its apparent protocols, differs in large degree from, but presents similar problems as those in the Tuskegee Syphilis Study conducted from 1932 until 1972 . . . the intentional exposure of soldiers to radiation in the 1940s and 50s . . . the tests involving the exposure of Navajo miners to radiation . . . and the secret administration of LSD to soldiers by the CIA and the Army in the 1950s and 60s. . . . [In] the Tuskegee Syphilis Study . . . patients infected with syphilis were not subsequently informed of the availability of penicillin for treatment of the illness, in order for the scientists and researchers to be able to continue research on the effects of the illness. . . . [P]erhaps [the] most notorious . . . [nontherapeutic research project was] the deliberate use of infection . . . in order to study the degree of infection and the rapidity of the course of the disease in the . . . typhus experiments at Buchenwald concentration camp during World War II. These programs were somewhat alike in the vulnerability of the subjects; uneducated African American men, debilitated patients in a charity hospital, prisoners of war, inmates of concentration camps and others falling within the custody and control of the agencies conducting or approving the experiments. In the present case,

6. The ultimate goal was to find the cost of the minimal level of effective lead paint or lead dust abatement costs so as to help landlords assess, hopefully positively, the commercial feasibility of attempting to abate lead dust in marginally profitable, lower-rent urban housing, in order to help preserve such housing in the Baltimore housing market. . . . The tenants involved, presumably, would be from a lower-rent urban class. . . . The children of middle class or rich parents apparently were not involved.

Indeed, the literature on the law and ethics of human experimentation is replete with warnings that all subjects, but especially vulnerable subjects, are at risk of abuse by inclusion [as research subjects]. Those vulnerable subjects included prisoners, who are subject to coercion, . . . children and the elderly . . . and racial minorities, ethnic minorities, and women . . . whom history shows to be the most frequent victims of abuses in human experimentations.

R. Alta Charo, Protecting Us to Death: Women, Pregnancy and Clinical Research Trials, 38 St. Louis U. L.J. 135, 135 (Fall, 1993). . . .

children, especially young children, living in lower economic circumstances, albeit not as vulnerable as the other examples, are nonetheless, vulnerable as well.

It is clear to this Court that the scientific and medical communities cannot be permitted to assume sole authority to determine ultimately what is right and appropriate in respect to research projects involving young children free of the limitations and consequences of the application of Maryland law. The Institutional Review Boards, IRBs, are, primarily, in-house organs. In our view, they are not designed, generally, to be sufficiently objective in the sense that they are as sufficiently concerned with the ethicality of the experiments they review as they are with the success of the experiments. . . . Here, the IRB, whose primary function was to insure safety and compliance with applicable regulations, encouraged the researchers to misrepresent the purpose of the research in order to bring the study under the label of "therapeutic" and thus under a lower safety standard of regulation. The IRB's purpose was ethically wrong, and its understanding of the experiment's benefit incorrect.

The conflicts are inherent. This would be especially so when science and private industry collaborate in search of material gains. Moreover, the special relationship between research entities and human subjects used in the research will almost always impose duties.

In respect to examining that special relationship, we are obliged to further examine its nature and its ethical constraints. In that regard, when contested cases arise, the assessment of the legal effect of research on human subjects must always be subject to judicial evaluation. One method of making such evaluations is the initiation of appropriate actions bringing such matters to the attention of the courts, as has been done in the cases at bar. It may well be that in the end, the trial courts will determine that no damages have been incurred in the instant cases and thus the actions will fail for that reason. In that regard, we note that there are substantial factual differences in the . . . [separate cases under review]. But the actions, themselves, are not defective on the ground that no legal duty can, according to the trial courts, possibly exist. For the reasons discussed at length in the main body of the opinion, a legal duty normally exists between researcher and subject and in all probability exists in the cases at bar. Moreover, as we shall discuss, the consents of the parents in these cases under Maryland law constituted contracts creating duties. Additionally, under Maryland law, to the extent parental consent can ever be effective in research projects of this nature, the parents may not have been sufficiently informed and, therefore, the consents ineffective and, based on the information contained in the sparse records before this court, the research project . . . may have invaded the legal rights of the children subjected to it. . . .

II. FACTS & PROCEDURAL BACKGROUND . . .

The research study [giving rise to these cases] was sponsored jointly by the EPA and the Maryland Department of Housing and Community Development (DHCD). It was thus a joint federal and state project. The Baltimore City Health Department and Maryland Department of the Environment also collaborated in the study. It appears that, because the study was funded and sponsored in part by a federal entity, certain federal conditions were attached to the funding grants and approvals. There are certain uniform standards required in respect to federally funded or approved projects. We, however, are unaware of, and have not been directed to, any federal or state statute or regulation that imposes limits on this Court's powers to conduct its review of the issues presented. None of the parties have questioned this Court's jurisdiction in these cases. Moreover, 45 Code Federal Regulations (C.F.R.) 46.116(e) specifically provides: "The informed consent requirements in this policy are not intended to preempt any applicable federal, state, or local laws which require additional information to be disclosed in order for informed consent to be legally effective." Those various federal or state conditions, recommendations, etc., may well be relevant at a trial on the merits as to whether any breach of a contractual or other duty occurred, or whether negligence did, in fact, occur; but have no limiting effect on the issue of whether, at law, legal duties, via contract or "special relationships" are created in Maryland in experimental nontherapeutic research involving Maryland children. . . .

In summary, KKI conducted a study of five test groups of twenty-five houses each. The first three groups consisted of houses known to have lead present. The amount of repair and maintenance conducted increased from Group 1 to Group 2 to Group 3. The fourth group consisted of houses, which had at one time lead present but had since allegedly received a complete abatement of lead dust. The fifth group consisted of modern houses, which had never had the presence of lead dust. The twenty-five homes in each of the first three testing levels were then to be compared to the two control groups: the twenty-five homes in Group 4 that had previously been abated and the 25 modern homes in Group 5. The research study was specifically designed to do less than full lead dust abatement in some of the categories of houses in order to study the potential effectiveness, if any, of lesser levels of repair and maintenance.

If the children were to leave the houses upon the first manifestation of lead dust, it would be difficult, if not impossible, to test, over time, the rate of the level of lead accumulation in the blood of the children attributable to the manifestation. In other words, if the children were removed from the houses before the lead dust levels in their blood became elevated, the tests would probably fail, or at least the data that would establish the success of the test—or of the abatement results, would be of questionable use. Thus, it would benefit the accuracy of the test, and thus KKI, the compensated researcher, if children remained in the houses over the period of the study even after the presence of lead dust in the houses became evident. . . .

[The consent form for the study provided:]

PURPOSE OF STUDY

As you may know, lead poisoning in children is a problem in Baltimore City and other communities across the country. Lead in paint, house dust and outside soil are major sources of lead exposure for children. Children can also be exposed to lead in drinking water and other sources. We understand that your house is going to have special repairs done in order to reduce exposure to lead in paint and dust. On a random basis, homes will receive one of two levels of repair. We are interested in finding out how well the two levels of repair work. The repairs are not intended, or expected, to completely remove exposure to lead.

We are now doing a study to learn about how well different practices work for reducing exposure to lead in paint and dust. We are asking you and over one hundred other families to allow us to test for lead in and around your homes up to 8 to 9 times over the next two years provided that your house qualifies for the full two years of study. Final eligibility will be determined after the initial testing of your home. We are also doing free blood lead testing of children aged 6 months to 7 years, up to 8 to 9 times over the next two years. We would also like you to respond to a short questionnaire every 6 months. This study is intended to monitor the effects of the repairs and is not intended to replace the regular medical care your family obtains. . . .

BENEFITS

To compensate you for your time answering questions and allowing us to sketch your home we will mail you a check in the amount of $5.00. In the future we would mail you a check in the amount of $15 each time the full questionnaire is completed. The dust, soil, water, and blood samples would be tested for lead at the Kennedy Krieger Institute at no charge to you. We would provide you with specific blood-lead results. We would contact you to discuss a summary of house test results and steps that you could take to reduce any risks of exposure. . . .

On appeal, appellant[s] seek[] review of the Circuit Court's decision granting KKI summary judgment. . . . [They] contend[] that KKI owed a duty of care . . . based on the nature of its relationship with [the children and parents participating in the study] . . . arising out of: (1) a contract between the parties; (2) a voluntary assumption by KKI; (3) a "special relationship" between the parties; and (4) a Federal regulation. . . . [The appellants argued that KKI was negligent in, for example, failing to notify a parent about elevated lead levels in a rental property for nine months, by which time her child had elevated blood levels of lead.]

III. DISCUSSION

A. STANDARD OF REVIEW

We resolve these disputes in the context of the trial court's granting of the appellee's motions for summary judgment in the two distinct cases. The threshold issues before this Court are whether, in the two cases presented, appellee, KKI, was entitled to summary judgment as a matter of law on the basis that no contract existed and that there is inherently no duty owed to a research subject by a researcher. Perhaps even more important is the ancillary issue of whether a parent in Maryland, under the law of this State, can legally consent to placing a child in a nontherapeutic research study that carries with it any risk of harm to the health of the child. We shall resolve all of these primary issues. . . .

B. GENERAL DISCUSSION

Initially, we note that we know of no law, nor have we been directed to any applicable in Maryland courts, that provides that the parties to a scientific study, because it is a scientific, health-related study, cannot be held to have entered into special relationships with the subjects of the study that can create duties, including duties, the breach of which may give rise to negligence claims. We also are not aware of any general legal precept that immunizes nongovernmental "institutional volunteers" or scientific researchers from the responsibility for the breaches of duties arising in "special relationships." Moreover, we, at the very least, hold that, under the particular circumstances testified to by the parties, there are genuine disputes of material fact concerning whether a special relationship existed between KKI and . . . [the appellants]. Concerning this issue, the granting of the summary judgment motions was clearly inappropriate. When a "special relationship" can exist as a matter of law, the issue of whether, given certain facts, a special relationship does exist, when there is a dispute of material fact in that respect, is a decision for the finder of fact, not the trial judge. We shall hold initially that the very nature of nontherapeutic scientific research on human subjects can, and normally will, create special relationships out of which duties arise. Since World War II the specialness or nature of such relationships has been frequently of concern in and outside of the research community.

As a result of the atrocities performed in the name of science during the Holocaust, and other happenings in the World War II era, what is now known as the Nuremberg Code evolved. Of special interest to this Court, the Nuremberg Code, at least in significant part, was the result of legal thought and legal principles, as opposed to medical or scientific principles, and thus should be the preferred standard for assessing the legality of scientific research on human subjects. Under it, duties to research subjects arise. . . . [The court cited a work by distinguished Boston University Professor George Annas detailing the history of the Nuremberg Code and explaining the lack of U.S. case law regarding the regulation of research under the Nuremberg Code or any other source of regulation.] . . .

In arguing that a fuller disclosure should be made when consent is sought for nontherapeutic research, as opposed to therapeutic research, [ethicist Karine] Morin notes:

> Furthermore, as long as courts continue to interpret the doctrine of informed consent in experimentation as it applies in the context of treatment, the uniqueness of the protection needed for human research subjects will be overlooked. Failing to recognize that subjects who volunteer for the sake of the advancement of science are differently situated from patients who stand to benefit from treatment results in an analysis that misconceives the purpose of disclosure. Beyond informing the patient as to means available to treat him or her, a subject must become a voluntary and willing participant in an endeavor that may yield no direct benefit to him or her, or worse, that may cause harm.

Karine Morin, The Standard of Disclosure in Human Subject Experimentation, 19 J. Legal Med. 157, 220 (1998). . . .

[T]here is no[t] [a] complete record of the specific compensation of the researchers involved. Although the project was funded by the EPA, at the request of KKI the EPA has declined to furnish such information to the attorney for one of the parties, who requested it under the federal Freedom of Information Act. Whether the research's character as a co-sponsored state project opens the records under the Maryland Public Information Act has apparently not been considered. Neither is there in the record any development of what pressures, if any, were exerted in respect to the researchers obtaining the consents of the parents and conducting the experiment. Nor, for the same reason, is there a sufficient indication as to the extent to which the Institute has joined with commercial interests, if it has, for the purposes of profit, that might potentially impact upon the researcher's motivations and potential conflicts of interest—motivations that generally are assumed, in the cases of prestigious entities such as Johns Hopkins University, to be for the public good rather . . . [than] a search for profit.

We do note that the institution involved, the respondent here . . . is a highly respected entity, considered to be a leader in the development of treatments, and treatment itself, for children infected with lead poisoning. With reasonable assurance, we can note that its reputation alone might normally suggest that there was no realization or understanding on the Institute's part that the protocols of the experiment were questionable, except for the letter from the IRB requesting that the researchers mischaracterize the study.

We shall further address both the factual and legal bases for the findings of the trial courts, holding, ultimately, that the respective courts erred in both respects.

C. NEGLIGENCE

It is important for us to remember that appellants allege that KKI was negligent. Specifically, they allege that KKI, as a medical researcher, owed a duty of care to them, as subjects in the research study, based on the nature of the agreements between them and also based on the nature of the relationship between the parties. They contend specifically that KKI was negligent because KKI breached its duty to: (1) design a study that did not involve placing children at unnecessary risk; (2) inform participants in the study of results in a timely manner; and (3) to completely and accurately inform participants in the research study of all the hazards and risks involved in the study. . . .

Because this is a review of the granting of the two summary judgments based solely on the grounds that there was no legal duty to protect the children, we are primarily concerned with . . . whether KKI was under a duty to protect appellants from injury.[33] . . .

The relationship that existed between KKI and both sets of appellants in the case at bar was that of medical researcher and research study subject. Though not expressly recognized in the Maryland Code or in our prior cases as a type of relationship which creates a duty of care, evidence in the record suggests that such a relationship involving a duty or duties would ordinarily exist, and certainly could exist, based on the facts and circumstances of each of these individual cases. . . .

IV. THE SPECIAL RELATIONSHIPS

A. THE CONSENT AGREEMENT CONTRACT

Both sets of appellants signed a similar Consent Form prepared by KKI in which KKI expressly promised to: (1) financially compensate (however minimally) appellants for their participation in the study; . . . (2) collect lead dust samples from appellants' homes, analyze the samples, discuss the results with appellants, and discuss steps that could be taken, which could reduce exposure to lead; and (3) collect blood samples from children in the household and provide appellants with the results of the blood tests. In return, appellants agreed to participate in the study,

33. We note that there was little suggestion of actual permanent injury to the children involved with these two cases. Our opinion is not directed to the matter of whether damages can be proven in the present cases.

by: (1) allowing KKI into appellants' homes to collect dust samples; (2) periodically filling out questionnaires; and (3) allowing the children's blood to be drawn, tested, and utilized in the study. If consent agreements contain such provisions, and the trial court did not find otherwise, and we hold from our own examination of the record that such provisions were so contained, mutual assent, offer, acceptance, and consideration existed, all of which created contractual relationships imposing duties by reason of the consent agreement . . . (as well, as we discuss elsewhere, by the very nature of such relationships).

By having appellants sign this Consent Form, both KKI and appellants expressly made representations, which, in our view, created a bilateral contract between the parties. At the very least, it suggests that appellants were agreeing with KKI to participate in the research study with the expectation that they would be compensated, albeit, more or less, minimally, be informed of all the information necessary for the subject to freely choose whether to participate, and continue to participate, and receive promptly any information that might bear on their willingness to continue to participate in the study. This includes full, detailed, prompt, and continuing warnings as to all the potential risks and hazards inherent in the research or that arise during the research. KKI, in return, was getting the children to move into the houses and/or to remain there over time, and was given the right to test the children's blood for lead. As consideration to KKI, it got access to the houses and to the blood of the children that had been encouraged to live in a "risk" environment. In other words, KKI received a measuring tool—the children's blood. Considerations existed, mainly money, food coupons, trinkets, bilateral promises, blood to be tested in order to measure success. "Informed consent" of the type used here, which imposes obligation and confers consideration on both researcher and subject (in these cases, the parents of the subjects) may differ from the more one-sided "informed consent" normally used in actual medical practice. Researcher/subject consent in nontherapeutic research can, and in this case did, create a contract.[35]

B. THE SUFFICIENCY OF THE CONSENT FORM

The consent form did not directly inform the parents of the fact that it was contemplated that some of the children might ingest lead dust particles, and that one of the reasons the blood of the children was to be tested was to evaluate how effective the various abatement measures were.

A reasonable parent would expect to be clearly informed that it was at least contemplated that her child would ingest lead dust particles, and that the degree to which lead dust contaminated the child's blood would be used as one of the ways in which the success of the experiment would be measured. The fact that if such information was furnished, it might be difficult to obtain human subjects for the research, does not affect the need to supply the information, or alter the ethics of failing to provide such information. A human subject is entitled to all material information. The respective parent should also have been clearly informed that in order for the measurements to be most helpful, the child needed to stay in the house

---

35. We make no determination as to whether informed consent in a therapeutic medical context can generate contractual obligations.

until the conclusion of the study. Whether assessed by a subjective or an objective standard, the children, or their surrogates, should have been additionally informed that the researchers anticipated that, as a result of the experiment, it was possible that there might be some accumulation of lead in the blood of the children. The "informed" consent was not valid because full material information was not furnished to the subjects or their parents.

C. SPECIAL RELATIONSHIP

In Case Number 128, Ms. Hughes signed a Consent Form in which KKI agreed to provide her with "specific blood-lead results" and discuss with her "a summary of house test results and steps that [she] could take to reduce any risks of exposure." She contends that this agreement between the parties gave rise to a duty owed by KKI to provide her with that information in a timely manner. She signed the Consent Form on March 10, 1993. The project began almost simultaneously. KKI collected dust samples in the Monroe Street property on March 9, 1993, August 23, 1993, March 9, 1994, September 19, 1994, April 18, 1995, and November 13, 1995. The March 9, 1993 dust testing revealed what the researchers referred to as "hot spots," where the level of lead was "higher than might be found in a completely renovated house." . . . [T]his information was not furnished to Ms. Hughes until December 16, 1993, more than nine months after the samples had been collected and not until after Ericka Grimes's blood was found to contain elevated levels of lead. She contends that not only did KKI have a duty to report such information in a timely manner but that it breached this duty by delaying to such a time that her daughter was allowed to contract lead poisoning. Looking at the relevant facts of Case Number 128, they are susceptible to inferences supporting the position of appellant, Ericka Grimes, and, moreover, that, if true, would create a "special relationship" out of which duties would be created. Therefore, for this reason alone, the grant of summary judgment was improper. . . .

[T]he trial courts appear to have held that special relationships out of which duties arise cannot be created by the relationship between researchers and the subjects of the research. While in some rare cases that may be correct, it is not correct when researchers recruit people, especially children whose consent is furnished indirectly, to participate in nontherapeutic procedures that are potentially hazardous, dangerous, or deleterious to their health. As opposed to compilation of already extant statistics for purposes of studying human health matters, the creation of study conditions or protocols or participation in the recruitment of otherwise healthy subjects to interact with already existing, or potentially existing, hazardous conditions, or both, for the purpose of creating statistics from which scientific hypotheses can be supported, would normally warrant or create such special relationships as a matter of law.

It is of little moment that an entity is an institutional volunteer in a community. If otherwise, the legitimacy of the claim to noble purpose would always depend upon the particular institution and the particular community it is serving in a given case. As we have indicated, history is replete with claims of noble purpose for institutions and institutional volunteers in a wide variety of communities.

Institutional volunteers may intend to do good or, as history has proven, even to do evil and may do evil or good depending on the institution and the community they serve. Whether an institutional volunteer[36] in a particular community should be granted exceptions from the application of law is a matter that should be scrutinized closely by an appropriate public policy maker. Generally, but not always, the legislative branch is appropriately the best first forum to consider exceptions to the tort laws of this State—even then it should consider all ramifications of the policy—especially considering the general vulnerability of subjects of such studies—in this case, small children. In the absence of the exercise of legislative policymaking, we hold that special relationships, out of which duties arise, the breach of which can constitute negligence, can result from the relationships between researcher and research subjects.

D. THE FEDERAL REGULATIONS

A duty may be prescribed by a statute, or a special relationship creating duties may arise from the requirement for compliance with statutory provisions. Although there is no duty of which we are aware prescribed by the Maryland Code in respect to scientific research . . . , federal regulations have been enacted that impose standards of care that attach to federally funded or sponsored research projects that use human subjects. See 45 C.F.R. Part 46 (2000). 45 C.F.R. Part 46, Subpart A, is entitled "Basic HHS Policy for Protection of Human Research Subjects" and Subpart D of the regulation is entitled "Additional Protections for Children Involved as Subjects in Research." . . . [T]his study was funded, and co-sponsored, by the EPA and presumably was therefore subject to these federal conditions. These conditions, if appropriate administrative action has been taken, require fully informed consent in any research using human subjects conducted, supported, or otherwise subject to any level of control or funding by any federal department or agency. . . . .

These federal regulations, especially the requirement for adherence to sound ethical principles, strike right at the heart of KKI's defense of the granting of the Motions for Summary Judgment. Fully informed consent is lacking in these cases. The research did not comply with the regulations. There clearly was more than a minimal risk involved. Under the regulations, children should not have been used for the purpose of measuring how much lead they would accumulate in their blood while living in partially abated houses to which they were recruited initially or encouraged to remain, because of the study. . . .

Clearly, KKI, as a research institution, is required to obtain a human participant's fully informed consent, using sound ethical principles. It is clear from the wording of the applicable federal regulations that this requirement of informed consent continues during the duration of the research study and applies to new or changing risks. In this case, a special relationship out of which duties might arise might be created by reason of the federally imposed regulations. The question becomes whether this duty of informed consent created by federal regulation, as a matter of state law, translates into a duty of care arising out of the unique

36. Moreover, it is not clear that KKI was a mere volunteer in any event. It received funding for developing and conducting the research. Whether it recognized a profit is unknown from the record. The "for profit" nature of some research may well increase the duties of researchers to insure the safety of research subjects, and may well increase researchers' or an institution's susceptibility for damages in respect to any injuries incurred by research subjects.

relationship that is researcher-subject, as opposed to doctor-patient. We answer that question in the affirmative. In this State, it may, depending on the facts, create such a duty.

Additionally, the Nuremberg Code, intended to be applied internationally, and never expressly rejected in this country, inherently and implicitly, speaks strongly to the existence of special relationships imposing ethical duties on researchers who conduct nontherapeutic experiments on human subjects. The Nuremberg Code specifically requires researchers to make known to human subjects of research "all inconveniences and hazards reasonably to be expected; and the effects upon his health or person which may possibly come from his participation in the experiment." The breach of obligations imposed on researchers by the Nuremberg Code, might well support actions sounding in negligence in cases such as those at issue here. We reiterate as well that, given the facts and circumstances of both of these cases, there were, at the very least, genuine disputes of material facts concerning the relationship and duties of the parties, and compliance with the regulations.

V. THE ETHICAL APPROPRIATENESS OF THE RESEARCH

The World Medical Association in its Declaration of Helsinki . . . included a code of ethics for investigative researchers and was an attempt by the medical community to establish its own set of rules for conducting research on human subjects. . . .[39]

The determination of whether a duty exists under Maryland law is the ultimate function of various policy considerations as adopted by either the Legislature, or, if it has not spoken, as it has not in respect to this situation, by Maryland courts. In our view, otherwise healthy children should not be the subjects of nontherapeutic experimentation or research that has the potential to be harmful to the child. It is, first and foremost, the responsibility of the researcher and the research entity to see to the harmlessness of such nontherapeutic research. Consent of parents can never relieve the researcher of this duty. We do not feel that it serves proper public policy concerns to permit children to be placed in situations of potential harm, during nontherapeutic procedures, even if parents, or other surrogates, consent. Under these types of circumstances, even where consent is given, albeit inappropriately, policy considerations suggest that there remains a special relationship between researchers and participants to the research study, which imposes a duty of care. This is entirely consistent with the principles found in the Nuremberg Code.

Researchers cannot ever be permitted to completely immunize themselves by reliance on consents, especially when the information furnished to the subject, or the party consenting, is incomplete in a material respect. A researcher's duty is not created by, or extinguished by, the consent of a research subject or by IRB approval. The duty to a vulnerable research subject is independent of consent, although the obtaining of consent is one of the duties a researcher must perform. All of this is especially so when the subjects of research are children. Such legal duties, and legal protections, might additionally be warranted because of the likely conflict of

39. . . . Declaration of Helsinki, World Medical Assembly (WMA) 18th Assembly (June 1964), amended by 29th WMA Tokyo, Japan (October 1975), 35th WMA Venice, Italy (October 1983) and the 41st WMA Hong Kong (September 1989).

interest between the goal of the research experimenter and the health of the human subject, especially, but not exclusively, when such research is commercialized. There is always a potential substantial conflict of interest on the part of researchers as between them and the human subjects used in their research. If participants in the study withdraw from the research study prior to its completion, then the results of the study could be rendered meaningless. There is thus an inherent reason for not conveying information to subjects as it arises, that might cause the subjects to leave the research project. That conflict dictates a stronger reason for full and continuous disclosure. . . .

A special relationship giving rise to duties, the breach of which might constitute negligence, might also arise because, generally, the investigators are in a better position to anticipate, discover, and understand the potential risks to the health of their subjects. . . .

This duty requires the protection of the research subjects from unreasonable harm and requires the researcher to completely and promptly inform the subjects of potential hazards existing from time to time because of the profound trust that participants place in investigators, institutions, and the research enterprise as a whole to protect them from harm. . . .

While we acknowledge that foreseeability does not necessarily create a duty, we recognize that potential harm to the children participants of this study was both foreseeable and potentially extreme. A "special relationship" also exists in circumstances where such experiments are conducted.

VI. PARENTAL CONSENT FOR CHILDREN TO BE SUBJECTS OF POTENTIALLY HAZARDOUS NONTHERAPEUTIC RESEARCH

The issue of whether a parent can consent to the participation of her or his child in a nontherapeutic health-related study that is known to be potentially hazardous to the health of the child raises serious questions with profound moral and ethical implications. What right does a parent have to knowingly expose a child not in need of therapy to health risks or otherwise knowingly place a child in danger, even if it can be argued it is for the greater good? The issue in these specific contested cases does not relate primarily to the authority of the parent, but to the procedures of KKI and similar entities that may be involved in such health-related studies. The issue of the parents' right to consent on behalf of the children has not been fully presented in either of these cases, but should be of concern not only to lawyers and judges, but to moralists, ethicists, and others. The consenting parents in the contested cases at bar were not the subjects of the experiment; the children were. Additionally, this practice presents the potential problems of children initiating actions in their own names upon reaching majority, if indeed, they have been damaged as a result of being used as guinea pigs in nontherapeutic scientific research. Children, it should be noted, are not in our society the equivalent of rats, hamsters, monkeys, and the like. Because of the overriding importance of this matter and this Court's interest in the welfare of children—we shall address the issue.

Most of the relatively few cases in the area of the ethics of protocols of various research projects involving children have merely assumed that a parent can give informed consent for the participation of their children in nontherapeutic research. . . .

It is not in the best interest of a specific child, in a nontherapeutic research project, to be placed in a research environment, which might possibly be, or which proves to be, hazardous to the health of the child . . . in order to test methods that may ultimately benefit all children. . . .

One simply does not expose otherwise healthy children, incapable of personal assent (consent), to a nontherapeutic research environment that is known at the inception of the research, might cause the children to ingest lead dust. It is especially troublesome, when a measurement of the success of the research experiment is, in significant respect, to be determined by the extent to which the blood of the children absorbs, and is contaminated by, a substance that the researcher knows can, in sufficient amounts, whether solely from the research environment or cumulative from all sources, cause serious and long term adverse health effects. Such a practice is not legally acceptable. . . .

In the[se] case[s], no impartial judicial review or oversight was sought by the researchers or by the parents. . . . Science cannot be permitted to be the sole judge of the appropriateness of such research methods on human subjects, especially in respect to children. We hold that in these contested cases, the research study protocols [presented to the court] . . . were not appropriate. . . .

VII. CONCLUSION

We hold that in Maryland a parent, appropriate relative, or other applicable surrogate, cannot consent to the participation of a child or other person under legal disability in nontherapeutic research or studies in which there is any risk of injury or damage to the health of the subject.

We hold that informed consent agreements in nontherapeutic research projects, under certain circumstances can constitute contracts; and that, under certain circumstances, such research agreements can, as a matter of law, constitute "special relationships" giving rise to duties, out of the breach of which negligence actions may arise. We also hold that, normally, such special relationships are created between researchers and the human subjects used by the researchers. Additionally, we hold that governmental regulations can create duties on the part of researchers towards human subjects out of which "special relationships" can arise. Likewise, such duties and relationships are consistent with the provisions of the Nuremberg Code.

The determination as to whether a "special relationship" actually exists is to be done on a case by case basis. . . . The determination as to whether a special relationship exists, if properly pled, lies with the trier of fact. We hold that there was ample evidence in the cases at bar to support a fact finder's determination of the existence of duties arising out of contract, or out of a special relationship, or out of regulations and codes, or out of all of them, in each of the cases.

We hold that on the present record, the Circuit Courts erred in their assessment of the law and of the facts as pled in granting KKI's motions for summary judgment in both cases before this Court. Accordingly, we vacate the rulings of the Circuit Court for Baltimore City and remand these cases to that court for further proceedings consistent with this opinion. . . .

RAKER, J., concurring in result only:

These appeals present the narrow question of whether the Circuit Courts erred in granting summary judgments to appellee, the Kennedy Krieger Institute, a research entity, on the ground that, as a matter of law, it owed no duty to warn appellants, Ericka Grimes and Myron Higgins, et al., human subjects participating in its research study. I concur in the judgment of the Court only and join in the Court's judgment that the Circuit Courts erred in granting summary judgments to appellee. These cases should be remanded for further proceedings.

I concur in the Court's judgment because I find that appellants have alleged sufficient facts to establish that there existed a special relationship between the parties in these cases, which created a duty of care that, if breached, gives rise to an action in negligence. . . . I would hold that a special relationship giving rise to a duty of care, the breach of which would be the basis for an action in negligence, existed in these cases and would remand the cases at bar to the Circuit Courts for further proceedings. I agree with the majority that this duty includes the protection of research subjects from unreasonable harm and requires the researcher to inform research subjects completely and promptly of potential hazards resulting from participation in the study. . . . As a result of the existence of this tort duty, I find it unnecessary to reach the thorny question, not even raised by any of the parties, of whether the informed consent agreements in these cases constitute legally binding contracts. . . .

As I have indicated, this case presents a narrow question of whether a duty in tort exists between the plaintiffs and the defendants. . . . Nonetheless, the majority appears to have decided the issue of whether such duty of care was, in fact, breached as a matter of law, without a hearing or a trial on the merits.

I cannot join in the majority's sweeping factual determinations. . . .

ON MOTION FOR RECONSIDERATION

PER CURIAM.

The Court has considered the motion for reconsideration and the submissions by the various amici curiae. The motion is denied, with this explanation.

Some of the issues raised in this case, in the briefs and at oral argument, were important ones of first impression in this State, and the Court therefore attempted to address those issues in a full and exhaustive manner. The case reached us in the context of summary judgments entered by the Circuit Court, which entailed rulings that the evidence presented by the plaintiffs, for purposes of the motions, even when taken in a light most favorable to them, was insufficient as a matter of law to establish the prospect of liability. We disagreed with that determination. Although we discussed the various issues and arguments in considerable detail, the only conclusion that we reached as a matter of law was that, on the record currently before us, summary judgment was improperly granted—that sufficient evidence was presented in both cases which, if taken in a light most favorable to the plaintiffs and believed by a jury, would suffice to justify verdicts in favor of the plaintiffs. Thus, the cases were remanded for further proceedings in the Circuit Court. Every issue bearing on liability or damages remains open for further factual development, and any relevant evidence not otherwise precluded under our rules of evidence is admissible.

Much of the argument in support of and in opposition to the motion for reconsideration centered on the question of what limitations should govern a parent's authority to provide informed consent for the participation of his or her minor child in a medical study. In the Opinion, we said at one point that a parent "cannot consent to the participation of a child . . . in nontherapeutic research or studies in which there is any risk of injury or damage to the health of the subject." As we think is clear from Section VI of the Opinion, by "any risk," we meant any articulable risk beyond the minimal kind of risk that is inherent in any endeavor. The context of the statement was a non-therapeutic study that promises no medical benefit to the child whatever, so that any balance between risk and benefit is necessarily negative. As we indicated, the determination of whether the study in question offered some benefit, and therefore could be regarded as therapeutic in nature, or involved more than that minimal risk is open for further factual development on remand.

RAKER, Judge, dissenting.

I respectfully dissent from the order denying the motions for reconsideration. I adhere to the views previously expressed in my concurring opinion filed herein. . . . The majority's discussion of the ability of a parent or guardian to consent to the participation of a minor child in a nontherapeutic research study and the discussion regarding the ethics of the research conducted in these cases involve serious public policy considerations. The statements are a declaration of public policy that, in the posture of this case, are best left to the General Assembly. . . .

Notes: Human Subjects Research

1. *Federal Regulation.* Most of the field of clinical investigation is now very closely regulated by the federal Food and Drug Administration and by the DHHS's Office for Human Research Protections. 45 C.F.R. §§46.101-46.505; 21 C.F.R. §§50.1-50.56; 54.1-54.6; 56.101-56.124. The federal regulatory structure differs from informed consent law in that the penalty for violation is disqualification from federal funding rather than a claim for damages. The regulatory focus, however, mirrors the informed consent themes already introduced in our discussion of fiduciary liability.

The regulations are designed to safeguard individual autonomy from over-reaching by researchers. The mechanism used to provide protection is a combination of mandatory disclosure and individual assent. The researcher is charged with a special obligation to care for his or her research subject and to protect the subject from harm. The federal regulations require prior approval of informed consent process that typically includes written disclosures and consents. These documents are reviewed by interdisciplinary ethical review committees (called "institutional review boards" or "IRBs") located in hospitals, in other medical research centers, and in universities where research is conducted using human subjects. The federal regulations governing research involving human subjects explicitly preserve from preemption foreign, state, or local laws providing additional protections. 45 C.F.R. §46.101(f), (g). The relevant federal agency may also permit federal agencies to apply equivalent or more protective internationally recognized protections for human research subjects in research conducted in foreign countries. Id. §46.101(h).

2. *Basic Definitions: What Is Research?* The federal regulations establish a broad definition of *research* as "a systemic investigation, including research development, testing, and evaluation, designed to develop or contribute to generalizable knowledge." 45 C.F.R. §46.102(d). A "[h]uman subject" is "a living individual about whom the investigator (whether professional or student) conducting research obtains (1) data through intervention or interaction with the individual, or (2) identifiable private information." Id. 46.102(f). Is the line between medical treatment and medical

research always clear? See Lars Noah, Informed Consent and the Elusive Dichotomy Between Standard and Experimental Therapy, 28 Am. J.L. & Med. 361 (2002).

3. *Requirements for Funded Research.* The federal regulations establish several criteria for approval of research:

> (a) In order to approve research covered by this policy the IRB shall determine that all of the following requirements are satisfied:
>
> (1) Risks to subjects are minimized: (i) By using procedures which are consistent with sound research design and which do not unnecessarily expose subjects to risk, and (ii) whenever appropriate, by using procedures already being performed on the subjects for diagnostic or treatment purposes.
>
> (2) Risks to subjects are reasonable in relation to anticipated benefits, if any, to subjects, and the importance of the knowledge that may reasonably be expected to result. In evaluating risks and benefits, the IRB should consider only those risks and benefits that may result from the research (as distinguished from risks and benefits of therapies subjects would receive even if not participating in the research). The IRB should not consider possible long-range effects of applying knowledge gained in the research (for example, the possible effects of the research on public policy) as among those research risks that fall within the purview of its responsibility.
>
> (3) Selection of subjects is equitable. In making this assessment the IRB should take into account the purposes of the research and the setting in which the research will be conducted and should be particularly cognizant of the special problems of research involving vulnerable populations, such as children, prisoners, pregnant women, mentally disabled persons, or economically or educationally disadvantaged persons.
>
> (4) Informed consent will be sought from each prospective subject or the subject's legally authorized representative, in accordance with, and to the extent required by §46.116.
>
> (5) Informed consent will be appropriately documented, in accordance with, and to the extent required by §46.117.
>
> (6) When appropriate, the research plan makes adequate provision for monitoring the data collected to ensure the safety of subjects.
>
> (7) When appropriate, there are adequate provisions to protect the privacy of subjects and to maintain the confidentiality of data.
>
> (b) When some or all of the subjects are likely to be vulnerable to coercion or undue influence, such as children, prisoners, pregnant women, mentally disabled persons, or economically or educationally disadvantaged persons, additional safeguards have been included in the study to protect the rights and welfare of these subjects.

45 C.F.R. §46.111.

Therapeutic research provides the possibility of benefit to the research subject; some risk to the subject might therefore be tolerated so long as it is outweighed by the anticipated benefit and other criteria are met. Nontherapeutic research does not offer a benefit to the subject; the research therefore cannot proceed unless the risks are minimal. The *Grimes* court characterized the lead abatement research as involving more than minimal risk and suggested that parents might not be permitted to consent to nontherapeutic research involving children that poses more than a minimal risk. What is a minimal risk? Federal regulations provide that "minimal risk means that the probability and magnitude of harm or discomfort anticipated in the research are not greater in and of themselves than those ordinarily encountered in daily life. . . ." 45 C.F.R. §46.102(i). Is this the definition used by the *Grimes* court? Why didn't the *Grimes* court consider the risk to be minimal, given that children who live in older housing frequently are exposed to the risk of lead paint? Who should bear the risks of research injuries: research subjects, researchers, or society more broadly? Elizabeth R. Pike, Recovering from Research: A No-Fault Proposal to Compensate Injured Research Participants, 38 Am. J.L. & Med. 7 (2012).

4. *Institutional Review Boards (IRBs).* Under federal law, the membership of an IRB is supposed to be diverse and professionally knowledgeable about research proposals and research ethics. 45 C.F.R. §46.107. The IRB must include at least one member who is unaffiliated with the institution. IRB members may not participate in the review of a research project in which they have a conflict of interest. Id.

The *Grimes* court was skeptical about the independence of IRBs. Commentators have raised many questions about the ability of potentially overworked and conflicted IRBs to safeguard research subjects. These criticisms and various reform proposals are well summarized in Carl Coleman, Rationalizing Risk Assessment in Human Subject Research, 46 Ariz. L. Rev. 1 (2004); Ruth Macklin, How Independent are IRBs? 30 IRB: Ethics & Human Research 15 (2008); Robert Steinbrook, Improving Protection for Research Subjects, 346 New Eng. J. Med. 1425 (2002). The federal government implemented expanded oversight of IRBs in 2009. 45 C.F.R. §46.501-.505. Other mechanisms designed to protect the safety of research subjects include reporting requirements for adverse events and the use of data and safety monitoring committees. See, e.g., Rachel Berhman Sherman et al., New FDA Regulation to Improve Safety Reporting in Clinical Trials, 365 New Eng. J. Med. 3 (2011); and Charles J. Kowalski & Jan L. Hewett, Data and Safety Monitoring Boards: Some Enduring Questions, 37 J.L. Med. & Ethics 496 (2009).

5. *Informed Consent in Research.* The federal regulations focus on the informed consent process as the major tool for protecting human subjects. The informed consent rules are much more detailed in some areas than common law rules but do not preempt those laws. 45 C.F.R. §46.116. Note that federal law prohibits research sponsors from requiring waivers of liability for negligence. Id. Examine the informed consent form excerpted in the *Grimes* decision: In what way(s) was it deficient? For an overview of the current informed consent process globally and the continuing development of the informed consent doctrine, see Jennifer Couture, The Changes in Informed Consent in Experimental Procedures: The Evolution of a Concept, 1 J. Health & Biomed. L. 125 (2004); Lars Noah, Coerced Participation in Clinical Trials: Conscripting Human Research Subjects, 62 Admin L. Rev. 329 (2010); Richard S. Saver, Medical Research and Intangible Harm, U. Cin. L. Rev. 941 (2006).

6. *The Role of Randomized Clinical Trials (RCTs) and Placebos.* The randomized clinical trial is a core feature of biomedical research. In an RCT, research subjects are randomly assigned to receive the treatment under study or to receive another form of treatment or, in some cases, no treatment or a placebo. From an ethical standpoint, an RCT is justified when there is "clinical equipoise," that is, when the differential benefits of the various forms of treatment or non-treatment are not known or are roughly the same. The legitimacy of equipoise has been challenged, in part because of concerns that it is difficult to know when equipoise truly exists. See, e.g., Franklin G. Miller & Stephen Joffe, Equipoise and the Dilemma of Randomized Clinical Trials, 364 New Eng. J. Med. 476 (2011).

Concerns about RCTs are particularly acute in medical research involving placebos, where some level of patient deception about treatment is inherent in the research design. Elana A. Bertam, How Current Informed Consent Protocols Flunk the Sham Surgery Test: A New Frontier in Medicine and Ethics, 14 Quinnipiac Health L.J. 131 (2010). For examples of the ongoing debate about the legitimacy of research trials involving placebos, compare Clifford J. Rosen & Sundeep Khosia, Placebo-Controlled Trials in Osteoporosis—Proceeding with Caution, 363 New Eng. J. Med. 1365 (2010), with C. Michael Stein & Wayne A. Ray, The Ethics of Placebo in Studies with Fracture End Points in Osteoporosis, 363 New Eng. J. Med. 1367 (2010). See also Michael E. Wechsler et al., Active Albuterol or Placebo, Sham Acupuncture, or No Intervention in Asthma, 365 New Eng. J. Med. 119 (2011); Tanguy Leroy et al., Factual Understanding of Randomized Clinical Trials: A Multicenter Case-Control Study in Cancer Patients, 29 Invest. New Drugs 700 (2011).

7. *The Aftermath of* Grimes. There have been few lawsuits involving experimental medicine using either negligence or informed consent theories, despite the huge volume of activity involving research subjects. A few courts have considered whether clinical trial sponsors owe a fiduciary duty to participants. See, e.g., Suthers v. Amgen Inc., 441 F. Supp. 2d 478 (S.D.N.Y. 2006) (plaintiffs' complaint dismissed in case challenging drug company's decision to terminate clinical trial and deny access to experimental drug; no fiduciary duty owed); and Abney v. Amgen Inc., 443 F.3d 540 (6th Cir. 2006) (no fiduciary duty as the clinical trial sponsors were not acting primarily for the benefit of the participants). See also Paul B. Miller & Charles Weijer, Fiduciary Obligation in Clinical Research, 34 J.L. Med. & Ethics 424 (2006); E. Haavi Morreim, The Clinical Investigator as Fiduciary: Discarding a Misguided Idea, 33 J.L. Med. & Ethics 586 (2005); E. Haavi Morreim, Litigation in Clinical Research: Malpractice Doctrines Versus Research Realities, 32 J.L. Med. & Ethics 474 (2004).

Should researchers have any obligation to inform patients about health issues discovered unexpectedly during the course of research, e.g., tumors discovered during scans for other purposes, or genetic anomalies discovered during testing for something else? How should this process be handled in research that might involve biobanks and other forms of archived data sets that may have been collected long ago? Should there be a duty to inform patients that is enforceable under state law? Should different rules apply to international research? See Symposium, Return of Research Results: How Should Research Results Be Handled?, 39 J.L. Med. & Ethics 574 (2011); Symposium, Incidental Findings in Human Subjects Research: From Imaging to Genomics, 36 J.L. Med. & Ethics 216-383 (2008); Matthew P. Gordon, A Legal Duty to Disclose Individual Research Findings to Research Subjects, 64 Food & Drug L.J. 225 (2009); Susan Wolf et al., Managing Incidental Findings and Research Results in Genomic Research Involving Biobanks and Archived Data Sets, 14 Genet. Med. 361 (2012). Should there be an obligation to inform research subjects if later research reveals that a particular genetic finding is associated with heightened risks to health? Cf. Reed E. Pyeritz, The Coming Explosion in Genetic Testing—Is There a Duty to Recontact?, 365 New Eng. J. Med. 1367 (2011).

The *Grimes* decision was understandably controversial. Imagine how medical researchers might feel about a decision that appears to compare a research study sponsored by the federal government and conducted by a leading research institution with Nazi war crimes. The *Grimes* decision sparked a number of commentaries, including Lainie Friedman Ross, In Defense of the Hopkins Lead Abatement Studies, 30 J.L. Med. & Ethics 50 (2002). See also L. Song Richardson, When Human Experimentation Is Criminal, 99 J. Crim. L. & Criminology 89 (2009) (arguing that medical researchers who "conduct experiments on individuals without their knowledge" or who "deliberately fail to disclose to individuals the known and obvious risks of participation in an experiment" should face criminal punishment).

What did the court actually hold in *Grimes*? The lengthy opinion (more than 70 pages, heavily edited here) explores the broad terrain of human subjects research and appears to hold that (1) parents/surrogates cannot consent to the participation of their children/incompetents in nontherapeutic research where there is any risk of injury or damage to the health of the subject; (2) informed consent agreements in nontherapeutic research trials may create "special relationships," and violation of the agreements may be addressed in breach of contract and negligence; and (3) other sources of the "special relationship" include the researcher-subject relationship itself and governmental research regulations. How much does the court majority take back in the per curiam opinion rejecting reconsideration? The court suggests that the parties are free to present evidence on any of these issues. What evidence would you present for either side?

8. *Conflicts of Interest.* The *Grimes* court repeatedly expressed concerns about the conflicts of interest between human subjects and researchers. Researchers may have a financial interest in the subject matter of their research that puts their research subjects at risk or affects the reliability of research results. See *Moore*, supra and note 3 at page 229. News stories regularly reveal shocking conflicts of interest that can jeopardize patient safety and the integrity of research results. See, e.g., Barry Meier & Duff Wilson, Spine Experts Repudiate Medtronic Studies, N.Y. Times, June 29, 2011; Special Issue, The Evolving Safety Profile of rhBMP-2 Use in the Spine, 11 Spine J. A1-A14, 463-539 (2011). See also Robin Fretwell Wilson, The Death of Jesse Gelsinger: New Evidence of the Influence of Money and Prestige in Human Research, 36 Am. J.L. & Med. 295-325 (2010); Symposium, Dangerous Liaisons? Industry Relations with Health Professionals, 37 J.L. Med. & Ethics 398-460 (2009).

A number of influential organizations and scholars have focused on methods of identifying and limiting conflicts of interest between researchers and research subjects. See, e.g., Bernard Lo & Marilyn J. Field eds., Conflict of Interest in Medical Research, Education, and Practice (Institute of Medicine, 2009); Robert Steinbrook, Controlling Conflict of Interest—Proposals from the Institute of Medicine, 360 New Eng. J. Med. 2160 (2009); Kevin P. Weinfurt, Disclosure of Financial Relationships to Participants in Clinical Research, 361 New Eng. J. Med. 916 (2009).

Federal regulations require covered institutions to put in place a conflicts of interest policy that includes a requirement that researchers report, and make publicly accessible, significant financial interests (generally $5,000 or more) "that could directly and significantly affect the design, conduct, or reporting of PHS [Public Health Service]-funded research." 42 C.F.R. §50.601-50.607. The Affordable Care Act includes provisions requiring manufacturers of drugs, biologics, and medical devices to report payments to physicians. 42 U.S.C.A. §1320a-7h; 76 Fed. Reg. 78742, 78767 (2011). The legislation and proposed regulations permit delays in disclosing the payments provided to support research. What justifies the delay in disclosing these payments?

9. *The Economic Interests of Clinical Research Subjects.* Should clinical research subjects share in the economic value of discoveries? The ownership issue, famously

raised in Moore v. Regents of the University of California, 793 P.2d 479 (Cal. 1990), supra, at page 217, has resurfaced. In Washington University v. Catalona, a federal district court found that fully informed tissue donors retained no ownership rights to their biological materials. 437 F. Supp. 2d 985 (2006). Universities were keenly interested in this outcome due to fears that research biobanks would be severely restricted if donor-patients could control the use of their donated tissues. See Leonard Glantz et al., Rules for Donations to Tissue Banks—What Next?, 358 New Eng. J. Med. 298 (2008); Jocelyn Kaiser, Court Decides Tissue Samples Belong to University, Not Patients, 312 Science 345 (2006); Rebecca Skloot, Taking the Least of You, N.Y. Times Magazine, April 16, 2006, at 38.

The economic interests of research subjects have also been debated in the domain of intellectual property law. See, e.g., Greenberg v. Miami Children's Hospital Research Institute, Inc., 264 F. Supp. 2d 1064 (S.D. Fla. 2003), excerpted at page 437 (dismissing all but unjust enrichment claims brought by families whose samples had been used to develop a genetic test for Canavan's Disease). See also Eliot Marshall, Genetic Testing: Families Sue Hospital, Scientist for Control of Canavan Gene, 290 Science 1062 (2000); Charlotte H. Harrison, Neither *Moore* nor the Market: Alternative Models for Compensating Contributors of Human Tissue, 28 Am. J.L. & Med. 77 (2002).

10. *Research on Vulnerable Populations.* As Professor Richard Garnett notes, much of the controversy in human research has surrounded projects involving groups viewed as particularly vulnerable to coercion or abuse. See also Symposium, Vulnerability in Biomedical Research, 37 J.L. Med. & Ethics 6-82 (2009). Should it matter who or what the subject matter of the research is? Is it possible that some of the rules meant to prevent potential research subjects from feeling pressure to participate have gone too far? See David Orentlicher, Making Research a Requirement of Treatment: Why We Should Sometimes Let Doctors Pressure Patients to Participate in Research, 35 Hastings Center Rep. 20 (2005).

a. *Children.* The use of children in research presents special problems because the only "consent" available is parental consent, and parents do not always protect their children from harm. Federal regulations provide special protections for children serving as research subjects. See 45 C.F.R. §§46.401-.409 (DHHS regulations); 21 C.F.R. §§50.50-.56 (FDA regulations). See also NIH Policy Guidance on the Inclusion of Children in Research (1998). Research can be particularly controversial if it involves pregnant women, fetuses, and neonates. 45 C.F.R. §§46.201-.207. See also Chapter 5, at pages 516-571, 601-606; Kristien Hens et al., Children and Biobanks: A Review of the Ethical and Legal Discussion, 130 Hum. Genet. 403 (2011); Valarie Blake et al., Harmonization of Ethics Policies in Pediatric Research, 39 J.L. Med. & Ethics 70 (2011). Most of the commentaries on research involving children assume the existence of an underlying disease or condition that the research seeks to address. Should research on human enhancement, such as through the use of drugs to improve memory or intelligence, be governed by similar rules? See Maxwell J. Mehlman & Jessica W. Berg, Human Subjects Protections in Biomedical Enhancement Research: Assessing Risk and Benefit and Obtaining Informed Consent, 36 J.L. Med. & Ethics 546 (2008).

There are conflicting objectives of scientific research involving children: (1) ensuring that children benefit from the progress in medical care made possible by such research and (2) minimizing the risks to children from their participation in scientific research. See, e.g., Doriane Lambelet Coleman, The Legal Ethics of Pediatric Research, 57 Duke L.J. 517 (2007); Marilyn Field & Richard Behrman, Ethical Conduct of Clinical Research Involving Children (2004); Carrie Fisher & Thomas Keens, Participation of Children in Research, 26 Whittier L. Rev. 823 (2005); and Lainie Friedman Ross, Children in Medical Research: Access Versus Protection (2006).

Despite the controversy, public policymakers sometimes actually seek to encourage research involving children. One example involves pediatric drug testing. Many drugs have been tested only in adults, leaving physicians to choose between denying children access to potentially useful medications and guessing about the correct dosage for pediatric use. Congress has become very involved in the issue. See, e.g., Food and Drug Administration Amendments Act of 2007, Public Law 110-85, Title IV (Pediatric Research Equity Act of 2007), Title V (Best Pharmaceuticals Act for Children of 2007). The FDA Web site includes a collection of material on pediatric issues, www.fda.gov/cder/pediatric/. See also Holly Fernandez Lynch, Give Them What They Want? The Permissibility of Pediatric Placebo-Controlled Trials Under the Best Pharmaceuticals for Children Act, 16 Ann. Health L. 79 (2007).

b. *Patients with Life-Threatening Illnesses.* Research is an important issue for persons with terminal conditions. Where the current, tested treatments are ineffective, people are often tempted to view "research" as providing the best treatment. They may be particularly vulnerable to coercion and the implicit promises and hopes offered by researchers. On the other hand, of course, research in these areas is extremely important for current and future patients. See, e.g., Jerry Menikoff, The Vulnerability of the Very Sick, 37 J.L. Med. & Ethics 51 (2009). The issue is addressed again in Chapter 6's discussion of the power of the state to protect terminally ill persons from potentially harmful drugs.

c. *Mentally Ill/Incompetent Patients.* Similar concerns exist about whether surrogates can give consent for research on mentally ill and other incompetent patients, with the additional concern about who is an appropriate surrogate. See generally Carl H. Coleman, Research with Decisionally Incapacitated Human Subjects: An Argument for a Systemic Approach to Risk-Benefit Assessment, 83 Ind. L.J. 743 (2008); Rebecca Dresser, Dementia Research: Ethics and Policy for the Twenty-First Century, 35 Ga. L. Rev. 661 (2001).

d. *Prisoners.* Should prisoners be permitted to participate in research, even when they "consent"? DHHS regulations provide special protections for prisoners. See 45 C.F.R. §§46.301-.306; OHRP Guidance on the Involvement of Prisoners in Research (2003). The special rules require, for example, that a majority of the IRB members have no other association with the prison and that one member be a prisoner or prisoner representative. Another provision requires assurance that parole boards will not take the prisoner's participation into account; prisoners must also be informed of this policy. See also John F. Edens et al., Voluntary Consent in Correctional Settings: Do Offenders Feel Coerced to Participate in Research?, 29 Behav. Sci. Law 771 (2011) (no); Lawrence O. Gostin, Biomedical Research Involving Prisoners: Ethical Values and Legal Regulation, 297 JAMA 737 (2007) (proposals to modify rules governing research on prisoners); Barron H. Lerner, Subject or Objects? Prisoners and Human Experimentation, 356 New Eng. J. Med. 1806 (2007).

11. *Emergency Research.* Federal regulators recently carved out an exception to the norm of disclosure and consent. FDA regulations now permit research experimentation on patients who have not consented, personally or through surrogates, in certain circumstances. Under the rule, an independent physician and an IRB must agree that the clinical trial concerns a life-threatening condition and that there is no proven, available treatment; that obtaining consent is not feasible; that the research cannot be carried out in another manner; and that the risks and benefits of the experimental procedure are reasonable under the circumstances. 21 C.F.R. §50.24.

The new regulations have been somewhat controversial because they explicitly abandon the Nuremberg Code's requirement of informed consent. See Nuremberg Code, available at http://ohsr.od.nih.gov/guidelines/nuremberg.html. Some commentators also maintain that these regulations allow research that has no therapeutic benefit for the immediate patient since they include patients who are near death with no hope of recovery. For commentaries on the new guidelines, see Gail H. Javitt, Old Legacies and New Paradigms: Confusing "Research" and "Treatment" and Its Consequences in Responding to Emergent Health Threats, 8 J. Health Care L. & Pol'y 38 (2005); Richard S. Saver, Critical Care Research and Informed Consent, 75 N.C. L. Rev. 205 (1996); Jeremy Sugarman, Examining Provisions for Research Without Consent in the Emergency Setting, 37(1) Hastings Center Rep. 12 (Jan.-Feb. 2007); Symposium, In Case of Emergency: No Need for Consent, 27(1) Hastings Center Rep. 7-12 (1997). See also Ian Roberts et al., Effect of Consent Rituals on Mortality in Emergency Care Research, 377 Lancet 1071 (2011) (arguing that UK rules can be unethical if "consent rituals delay the start of a trial treatment such that the treatment effect could be reduced or obscured").

12. *Inclusion of Women and Minorities.* The *Grimes* court focuses on the potential exploitation of the poor and members of minority groups. Commentators have also criticized the failure of medical research to include women and members of minority groups. The federal government responded in the NIH Revitalization Act of 1993, Pub. L. No. 103-43, 107 Stat. 122 (1993). See also NIH Office of Women's Health Research. Significant gaps in research remain. See, e.g., Sara F. Goldkind et al., Enrolling Pregnant Women in Research—Lessons from the H1N1 Influenza Epidemic, 362 New Eng. J. Med. 2241 (2010); P. Kanakamedala & S. Haga, Characterization of Clinical Study Populations by Race and Ethnicity in Biomedical Literature, 22 Ethn. Dis. 96 (2012) (though increasingly common, "reporting of race/ethnicity of study populations is relatively low, ambiguous, and inconsistent").

13. *The FDA's Sentinel System.* The Food and Drug Administration Amendments Act of 2007 (FDAAA), Pub. L. 110-85, included creation of a system designed to promote post-marketing surveillance of the safety of drugs, biologics, and medical devices. A "Mini" Sentinel System database has already been implemented; it includes health data for more than 100 million persons, information about 2.9 billion distributions of prescription drugs, and data from 3 billion health care treatments. The system operates on a "distributed" model in which the data is maintained by the other entities (providers, insurers, or others) rather than being collected into a centralized database; no personally identifiable health information will be transmitted outside the reporting entity. FDA's Sentinel Initiative, www.fda.gov/Safety/FDAsSentinelInitiative/default.htm. See also Asher Mullard, Unleashing the Mini-Sentinel, 11 Nature Rev. 255 (2012); Richard Platt et al., The U.S. Food and Drug

Administration's Mini-Sentinel Program: Status and Direction, 21 Pharmacoepide-
miol. Drug Safety 1 (2012) (Supp. 1). For a discussion of the FDA's authority to
require participation in the project, see Barbara J. Evans, Authority of the Food and
Drug Administration to Require Data Access and Control Use Rights in the Sentinel
Data Network, 65 Food & Drug L.J. 67 (2010). Does the system represent a powerful
tool for medical research unconstrained by consent requirements?

14. *Research in Developing Countries.* It has become increasingly difficult to test
drugs in Western countries because of strict regulations governing safety, difficulties
with compensation, and difficulty in recruiting a statistically meaningful number of
study subjects. Many research-based companies are now outsourcing some of their
trials to developing countries such as India. For a discussion involving testing in
India, see Samiran Nundy & Chandra Gulhati, A New Colonialism? Conducting
Clinical Trials in India, 352 New Eng. J. Med. 1633 (2005). What rules should apply
to human subjects research conducted outside the United States by companies affiliated with U.S. companies, or where the study results will be used to seek approval to
market a drug in the United States? Informed consent issues are particularly salient
in developing countries. See Carol M. Ashton et al., A Taxonomy of Multinational
Ethical and Methodological Standards for Clinical Trials of Therapeutic Interventions, 37 J. Med. Ethics 368 (2011); Dennis M. Coyne, International Pharmaceutical
Mistrials: Existing Law for the Protection of Human Subjects and a Proposal for
Reform, 29 B.U. Int'l L.J. 427 (2011); Roberto Rivera, Informed Consent: An International Researchers' Perspective, 97 Am. J. Public Health 25 (2007) (recommenda-
tions regarding content and process for informed consent); Michael T. Krosin et al.,
Problems in Comprehension of Informed Consent in Rural and Peri-Urban Mali,
West Africa, 3 Clin. Trials 306 (2006).

The issues gained additional public attention in 2011 with the release of a
report by the Presidential Commission for the Study of Bioethical Issues, Research
Across Borders, that considered the protections offered to participants in research
supported by the federal government and carried out in countries around the
world. For an effort to address alleged abuses through U.S. courts, see Abdullahi
v. Pfizer, 562 F.3d 163 (2d Cir. 2009) (permitting claims under Alien Tort Statute,
which alleged violation of customary international law norms regarding consent to
medical experimentation). See also Dennis M. Coyne, International Pharmaceutical Mistrials: Existing Law for the Protection of Foreign Human Subjects and a Proposal for Reform, 29 B.U. Int'l L.J. 427 (2011); Steven W. Postal & Robyn Whipple
Diaz, After Guatemala and Nigeria: The Future of International Clinical Research
Regulation, 24(1) The Health Lawyer 1 (Oct. 2011).

15. *Resources and Commentaries.* The DHHS's Office for Human Research Protections maintains a Web site with links to key federal regulations and documents.
www.hhs.gov/ohrp/. For influential criticisms of human subjects research, see the
articles cited in *Grimes* and George J. Annas, Questing for Grails: Duplicity, Betrayal
and Self-Deception in Research, 12 J. Contemp. Health L. & Pol'y 297 (1996); Jay
Katz, Human Experimentation and Human Rights, 38 St. Louis U. L.J. 7 (1993).
Important books on human subjects research include Baruch A. Brody, The Ethics of Biomedical Research: An International Perspective (1998); Claire Foster,
The Ethics of Medical Research on Humans (2001); Jerry Menikoff & Edward P.
Richards, What the Doctor Didn't Say: The Hidden Truth About Medical Research
(2006).

Postscript: Proposed Revisions to the "Common Rule"

The DHHS issued an Advance Notice of Proposed Rulemaking in July 2011 suggesting the possibility of a substantial overhaul of the federal regulatory structure. 76 Fed. Reg. 44512 (July 26, 2011). The Notice summarized the regulatory structure, long-standing recommendations for revisions made by expert bodies and scholars, and significant changes in the nature of research since the adoption of the Common Rule.

> Since the Common Rule was developed, the landscape of research activities has changed dramatically, accompanied by a marked increase in the volume of research. It is estimated that total spending on health-related research and development by the drug industry and the Federal government has tripled since 1990. While traditional biomedical research conducted in academic medical centers continues to flourish, many studies are now also conducted at community hospitals, outpatient clinics, or physician-based practices. Clinical research is regularly conducted at multiple institutions across the U.S. and other countries. Recruitment firms, bioinformatics specialists, clinical trial coordinating centers, protocol developers, data analysts, contract research organizations (CROs), data and safety monitoring committees, community-based organizations, and other entities have joined investigators and sponsors as part of the clinical research enterprise.
>
> Research has also increased, evolved, and diversified in other areas, such as national security, crime and crime prevention, economics, education, and the environment, using a wide array of methodologies in the social sciences and multidisciplinary studies. The application of technologies such as functional magnetic resonance imaging in neuroscience has led to substantial advances in the understanding of human physiology, cognition, and behavior. The advent of sophisticated computer software programs, the Internet, and mobile technology have created new areas of research activity, particularly within the social and behavioral sciences, exponentially increasing the amount of information available to researchers, while providing the means to access and analyze that information. In many areas of society, researchers are being called upon to provide evidence to more effectively guide social policy and practices.
>
> The rapid growth and expansion of human subjects research has led to many questions about whether the current regulatory framework is adequate and appropriate for the protection of human subjects in the 21st century. Furthermore, decades of experience have revealed a great deal about the functioning—and limitations—of existing regulations, and prompted critical evaluations by the Institute of Medicine (IOM), the U.S. Government Accountability Office, and many scholars. Federal consideration of such revisions to the regulatory schema, in addition to the issues that suggest a need for revision, is not without precedent. In its 2001 concluding report, the National Bioethics Advisory Commission (NBAC) made 30 recommendations that addressed areas including the scope and structure of the oversight system, the level of review applied to research, emphasizing the informed consent process, documentation and waiver of informed consent, protecting privacy and confidentiality, adverse event reporting, and review of cooperative or multi-site research studies. NBAC's recommendations are one source for the revisions in the Common Rule currently being considered. . . .

Id. at 44513 (citations omitted).

The Notice then focused attention on seven key areas of possible reform:

First, the system has been criticized as not adequately calibrating the review process to the risk of research. Critics have raised concerns that some IRBs spend considerable time reviewing minimal risk research, and that some IRBs have a tendency to overestimate the magnitude and probability of reasonably foreseeable risks. Because significantly more research studies require convened IRB review, this greater IRB workload diverts time and resources from review of research that poses greater risks, theoretically resulting in inadequate attention to research that could seriously harm subjects.

Questions have been raised about the appropriateness of the review process for social and behavioral research. . . . While physical risks generally are the greatest concern in biomedical research, social and behavioral studies rarely pose physical risk but may pose psychological or informational risks. . . . Over-regulating social and behavioral research in general may serve to distract attention from attempts to identify those social and behavioral research studies that do pose threats to the welfare of subjects and thus do merit significant oversight.

Second, critics have commented about the inefficiencies of review by multiple IRBs for multi-site studies, which add bureaucratic complexity to the review process and delay initiation of research projects without evidence that multiple reviews provide additional protections to subjects. . . .

Third, questions have been raised about the extent and quality of the protections afforded by current informed consent requirements and practices. A variety of critics have highlighted problems with consent forms. In some research studies, consent forms have become lengthy and are often written in highly technical terms. Many also claim that consent forms have evolved to protect institutions rather than to actually provide salient information to potential human subjects. This is especially problematic if the forms fail to include information that is crucial for making a decision about participation, including appropriate information about financial relationships between researchers and study sponsors, or are written in a way that potential subjects are likely to fail to notice such information. At the same time, others raise concerns about the rigid application of written consent to all forms of research, especially research involving surveys, interviews, focus groups, or other similar methodologies. In these types of research, it has been argued that written documentation of consent is unnecessary and that answering questions should be sufficient to indicate individual consent to participate.

Fourth, increasing use of genetic information, existing (i.e., stored) biospecimens, medical records, and administrative claims data in research has changed the nature of the risks and benefits of research participation. Risks related to these types of research are not physical but informational (e.g., resulting from the unauthorized release of information about subjects). The Privacy Rule promulgated under the Health Insurance Portability and Accountability Act of 1996 (HIPAA) addresses some of these informational risks. . . .

Fifth, the monitoring and evaluation of the current system for protecting human subjects has been criticized. There is concern that current regulations do not provide an ideal mechanism for the collection of information that would allow evaluation of the effectiveness of the research oversight system in protecting human subjects.

Sixth, concerns have been expressed that the current regulatory system does not adequately protect all research subjects. For instance, only some research studies funded by certain Federal agencies or those that involve the development of products subject to regulation by the FDA, are subject to the Common Rule or similar protections. As a result, there are many studies that are not subject to any such Federal oversight, even though they may involve substantial risks to the subjects.

Seventh, the multiple, differing regulatory requirements that can apply to a single research study have been criticized as complex, inconsistent, and lacking in clarity, which results in unwarranted variability across institutions and their IRBs in how the requirements are interpreted and implemented. . . . [For example,] the overlapping, and sometimes, arguably, inconsistent requirements of the Common Rule and the HIPAA Privacy Rule have been criticized as being overly complex, causing confusion and frustration among investigators, IRBs, and others trying to comply with both sets of requirements.

Id. at 44513-44514. The 2013 revisions to the Privacy Rule included provisions designed to reduce the complexity of securing consent to the use of PHI in research. See 45 C.F.R. §164.508(b)(3) (permitting use of compound authorizations involving research in some circumstances).

The Notice included proposed changes to the Common Rule in each of these areas. One key proposed reform would recognize that the only significant risk for many types of studies is the disclosure of information; for these studies an alignment of the Common Rule with the HIPAA privacy provisions could reduce risks enough to avoid the need for IRB review. A second major change would create new streamlined consent procedures for the subsequent use of biospecimens collected outside the research context. See Ezekiel J. Emanuel & Jerry Menikoff, Reforming Regulations Governing Research with Human Subjects, 365 New Eng. J. Med. 1145, 1147 (2011).

The Notice concluded with a list of 74 queries for consideration and feedback. The Notice is just the first stage of a potentially long process for revising the Common Rule. Id. See also Robert Klitzman & Paul Appelbaum, To Protect Human Subjects, Review What Was Done, Not Proposed, 335 Science 1576 (2012). What challenges do you anticipate for the reform process? Are the issues and the proposed reforms raised in the Notice generally appropriate? How would you evaluate whether the reforms are appropriate—based on the opinions of researchers (who might be expected to favor streamlining the system)? The proposed reforms include enhanced efforts to collect data on the problematic research, which could allow resources to be focused on areas (or institutions) presenting the greatest risks.

Problem: Medical Research, Biobanks, and the Privacy Rule

This chapter began with an exploration of the special character of medical information and the complex web of privacy regulations designed to give individuals the right to control use of their protected health information. Privacy concerns pervade medical research. How will medical researchers be able to identify potentially appropriate medical research subjects without having access to medical records? How confidential are the records of medical research projects? These issues are growing increasingly complex, in part due to large-scale research involving medical records, biological samples, and genetic testing. The availability of large sets of patient data and biological samples creates the opportunity to carry out new research strategies that hold great promise for identifying causes and cures for human conditions.

Does the Privacy Rule, discussed supra at pages 161-170, create inordinate barriers to research, particularly research involving large collections of patient data or biobanking? A study by the Institute of Medicine found that the answer was "yes"; the resulting report made a series of recommendations to address the problem. Institute of Medicine, Beyond the HIPAA Privacy Rule: Enhancing Privacy, Improving Health Through Research (2009). The report recommended that HIPAA's Privacy Rule not be applied to research; that PHI related to direct, interventional research with human subjects be regulated under the Common Rule for research; and that "information-based" research (including biobanks) be regulated under a new scheme that would emphasize administrative safeguards rather than requiring patient consent. As one commentator on the report has noted:

> Autonomy and informed consent are vital ethical and legal principles undergirding . . . experimentation on human subjects. But these principles are implicated less strongly, if at all, by data-based health research—research that is becoming more common and more important as more patient data is captured and stored electronically. . . . [T]here is no ethical principle that requires choice as the basis for research involving patient data, especially if identifying information is masked and the use of the data is subject to strong, substantive security and privacy requirements. Regulatory insistence on choice is quite literally allowing people to die and suffer unnecessarily without even providing the benefit of aiding privacy.

Fred Cate, Protecting Privacy in Health Research: The Limits of Individual Choice, 98 Cal. L. Rev. 1765, 1802 (2010). For a pointed critique of the IOM Report, see Mark A. Rothstein, Improve Privacy in Research by Eliminating Informed Consent? IOM Report Misses the Mark, 37 J.L. Med. & Ethics 507 (2009) (The IOM Report "underestimates the risk to individuals, . . . fail[s] to justify abandonment of informed consent . . . overvalues researchers' interests . . . [and] overlook[s] the betrayal of [patient] trust"). Would you support the IOM Report's approach? Do you think that the Privacy Rule's authorization process is realistic and viable for large-scale medical records research projects? Do you think that medical records research conducted without specific patient authorization would injure patient autonomy and the trust necessary to the treatment relationship? What types of evidence would you need to answer these questions? Professors Cate and Rothstein cite to a range of evidence to support their positions, from the meaninglessness of many patient consumer choices, as evidenced by the ubiquitous clicking of "I agree" to software licensing notices (noted by Professor Cates) to surveys demonstrating that most people want to decide whether their PHI is used for research (noted by Professor Rothstein).

The DHHS has modified the Privacy Rule provisions relating to research, though not to the extent advocated by the IOM Report. As of 2013, the Privacy Rule provides three avenues for the use of PHI for research:

1. *De-identification.* The PHI can be "de-identified" by removing more than 18 types of information, ranging from name to any biometric identifiers. De-identified information is not considered to be PHI subject to the protections of the Rule. 45 C.F.R. §164.502(d).

2. *Authorization.* Individuals can provide specific authorization for the use of their PHI in research. 45 C.F.R. §164.508. The authorization for research now is slightly less demanding than the usual authorization provisions under the Privacy Rule. For example, the authorization can be combined with

the informed consent form for the research study. The provider may require completion of the authorization before providing research-related treatment. The authorization need not have a specific expiration date, but instead can state " 'end of the research study,' 'none,' or similar language . . . if the authorization is for . . . research, including the creation and maintenance of a research database or research repository." Id. at §164.508(c)(1)(v). The 2013 revisions to the federal Privacy Rule moved closer to the Common Rule by, for example, permitting 45 C.F.R. §164.508(b)(3) (permitting use of compound authorization for the use of protected health information for research studies with a consent to participate in the research or authorization to create a research database). See also Mark A. Rothstein, HIPAA Privacy Rule 2.0, __ J.L. Med. & Ethics __ (2013).

3. *Substituted Consent by IRB or Privacy Board.* The Privacy Rule permits use of PHI for research where either an IRB or Privacy Board (as defined in the regulations) approves a waiver of the authorization requirement; where the review is necessary to prepare a research protocol and no PHI will leave the entity; or where the research involves decedent's PHI. 45 C.F.R. §164.512(i). An IRB or Privacy Board may waive authorization where (1) "the use or disclosure . . . involves no more than minimal risk to the privacy of individuals"; (2) "The research could not practicably be conducted without the waiver or alteration"; (3) "The research could not practicably be conducted without access to and use of the protected health information; and (4) certain other procedural requirements have been met." Id.

Do the current rules achieve the correct balance between individual control of PHI and the promotion of research, which may improve health care for all? See also Symposium, Biobanking, 130 Hum. Genet. 329-432 (2011); Katherine Drabiak-Syed, State Codification of Federal Regulatory Ambiguities in Biobanking and Genetic Research, 30 J. Leg. Med. 299 (2009).

Problem: DNA Research and Indigenous Communities

The Havasupai people, who live in the Grand Canyon, have been embroiled in a conflict with Arizona State University over the use of the tribe's DNA samples. University researchers took DNA samples from the Havasupai with the hope of finding genetic clues to the tribe's high rate of diabetes. The Havasupai believed that the blood samples were collected solely for diabetes research. However, tribe members discovered that their blood samples were used to study many other issues, including mental illnesses and the tribe's historical migration pattern, which threatened to create conflicts with the tribe's traditional beliefs about its origin.

What types of legal claims might be available to the Havasupai? Who would have standing to bring the claims? How would damages be measured? See Amy Harmon, Indian Tribe Wins Fight to Limit Research of Its DNA, N.Y. Times, April 21, 2010; Michelle M. Mello & Leslie Wolf, The Havasupai Indian Tribe Case—Lessons for Research Involving Stored Biologic Samples, 363 New Eng. J. Med. 204 (2010). See also Debra Harry, Indigenous Peoples and Gene Disputes, 84 Chi.-Kent L. Rev. 147 (2009); Bette Jacobs et al., Bridging the Divide Between Genomic Science and Indigenous Peoples, 38 J.L. Med. & Ethics 684 (2010).

3

The Right and "Duty" to Die

A. REFUSAL OF LIFE-SUSTAINING TREATMENT

In Chapter 2 we saw that patients enjoy a right of informed consent: Physicians may not deliver care to a patient without first informing the patient about the care and its alternatives and obtaining the patient's voluntary and competent consent to the treatment. If the patient must consent to treatment, it follows that the patient also enjoys a right to withhold consent and refuse the treatment.

Ordinarily, this corollary right to refuse treatment is not controversial. Patients with lower back pain from a slipped disk are free to choose between surgery to remove the disk and alternatives like anti-inflammatory drugs, exercise, and chiropractic manipulation. Patients with coronary artery disease may choose among coronary artery bypass surgery, coronary angioplasty, and medical therapies like antianginal drugs.

In many cases, however, a refusal of treatment will result in the patient's death. In such cases, the state (or the health care provider) may want to invoke its interest in preserving life to ensure that the patient receives the treatment necessary to sustain life. The issue, then, is how we balance the individual's right to refuse treatment with the state's or other persons' interest in preserving the patient's life.

It is useful to begin the analysis with the right to accept or refuse life-sustaining treatment when only the patient's interests are directly at stake. For example, an adult patient dying of cancer might reject additional rounds of chemotherapy on the grounds that the treatment is unlikely to provide much benefit but will likely cause significant discomfort. In such a case, the health of another person is not jeopardized by the refusal of treatment.

In later sections and chapters, we will consider whether the patient's right to make treatment decisions becomes circumscribed as we move beyond the core right. Does it matter that a pregnant woman's refusal of treatment will jeopardize the health of her fetus? Does it matter that a patient's refusal of treatment for tuberculosis would place other persons at risk? What if the patient is not refusing offered treatment but is requesting treatment that has not been offered? Does it matter, for example, that the patient is trying to take a lethal drug to end life? Similarly, does it matter that the patient is requesting treatment to sustain life that the patient's physician is unwilling to provide on the ground that the treatment provides little benefit?

Social recognition of the right to refuse life-sustaining treatment reflected the confluence of several factors. In recent decades, advances in medical technology have permitted physicians to save many lives that once were lost to disease or accident. In some cases, however, the person survives with a very poor quality of life and no hope of recovery. While medical care can maintain the person's life for weeks, months, or even years, the greatly diminished quality of life and the burdensomeness of the treatment mean to some individuals that the treatment is not desired. In addition, these life-saving advances in technology have become very costly. If the life that can be saved has a very poor quality and society's limited resources could be used for other patients who would have a better quality of life and who want treatment, then it is not clear that the state has an interest in always preserving the patient's life. Finally, the law not only had recognized a right of informed consent, it also had recognized a right of pregnant women to choose an abortion. In 1973, the U.S. Supreme Court handed down its decision in Roe v. Wade. If the state's interest in preserving the life of a fetus does not overcome the woman's interest in personal autonomy, then it becomes more difficult to justify a state interest in preserving the life of a dying person against the person's will.

There is an extensive literature on the refusal of life-sustaining treatment, including Allen E. Buchanan & Dan W. Brock, Deciding for Others (1989); Robert Burt, Taking Care of Strangers (1979); Margaret L. Campbell & J. Randall Curtis eds., End-of-Life Care (2004); Norman Cantor, Legal Frontiers of Death & Dying (1987); Hastings Center, Guidelines on the Termination of Life-Sustaining Treatment (1987); Alan Meisel & Kathy L. Cerminara, The Right to Die (3d ed. 2004); National Center for State Courts, Guidelines for State Court Decision Making in Life-Sustaining Medical Treatment Cases (rev. 2d ed. 1993); President's Commission for the Study of Ethical Problems in Medicine, Deciding to Forego Life-Sustaining Treatment (1983); Paul Ramsey, Ethics at the Edges of Life (1978).

1. *The Competent Patient*

The right to refuse life-sustaining treatment is most straightforward when the patient possesses decisionmaking capacity and therefore is able to make informed and voluntary decisions about medical care. If the patient is incompetent, we confront an additional issue of how to decide whether the patient's right to refuse treatment is being exercised properly. While we directly consider that issue in the next section, we nevertheless begin our analysis here with cases involving incompetent patients, since it was in those cases that the courts developed the law governing treatment refusals by competent patients.

IN THE MATTER OF KAREN QUINLAN
355 A.2d 647 (N.J. 1976)

HUGHES, Chief Justice.

On the night of April 15, 1975, for reasons still unclear, Karen Quinlan ceased breathing for at least two 15 minute periods. She received some ineffectual mouth-to-mouth resuscitation from friends. She was taken by ambulance to Newton Memorial Hospital. There she had a temperature of 100 degrees, her pupils were unreactive and she was unresponsive even to deep pain. The history at the time of her admission to that hospital was essentially incomplete and uninformative. . . . Dr. Morse and other expert physicians who examined her characterized Karen as being in a "chronic persistent vegetative state." Dr. Fred Plum, one of such expert witnesses, defined this as a "subject who remains with the capacity to maintain the vegetative parts of neurological function but who . . . no longer has any cognitive function." . . . In this respect it was indicated by Dr. Plum that the brain works in essentially two ways, the vegetative and the sapient. He testified:

> We have an internal vegetative regulation which controls body temperature, which controls breathing, which controls to a considerable degree blood pressure, which controls to some degree heart rate, which controls chewing, swallowing and which controls sleeping and waking. We have a more highly developed brain which is uniquely human which controls our relation to the outside world, our capacity to talk, to see, to feel, to sing, to think. Brain death necessarily must mean the death of both of these functions of the brain, vegetative and the sapient. Therefore, the presence of any function which is regulated or governed or controlled by the deeper parts of the brain which in laymen's terms might be considered purely vegetative would mean that the brain is not biologically dead.

. . . The experts believe that Karen [who is 22 years old] cannot now survive without the assistance of the respirator; that exactly how long she would live without it is unknown; that the strong likelihood is that death would follow soon after its removal, and that removal would also risk further brain damage and would curtail the assistance the respirator presently provides in warding off infection. . . .

The further medical consensus was that Karen in addition to being comatose is in a chronic and persistent "vegetative" state, having no awareness of anything or anyone around her and existing at a primitive reflex level. Although she does have some brain stem function (ineffective for respiration) and has other reactions one normally associates with being alive, such as moving, reacting to light, sound and noxious stimuli, blinking her eyes, and the like, the quality of her feeling impulses is unknown. She grimaces, makes stereotyped cries and sounds and has chewing motions. Her blood pressure is normal. . . .

Karen is described as emaciated, having suffered a weight loss of at least 40 pounds, and undergoing a continuing deteriorative process. Her posture is described as fetal-like and grotesque; there is extreme flexion-rigidity of the arms, legs and related muscles and her joints are severely rigid and deformed.

. . . No form of treatment which can cure or improve that condition is known or available. As nearly as may be determined, considering the guarded area of remote uncertainties characteristic of most medical science predictions, she can *never* be restored to cognitive or sapient life. . . .

She is debilitated and moribund and although fairly stable at the time of argument before us (no new information having been filed in the meanwhile in expansion of the record), no physician risked the opinion that she could live more than a year and indeed she may die much earlier. Excellent medical and nursing care so far has been able to ward off the constant threat of infection, to which she is peculiarly susceptible because of the respirator, the tracheal tube and other incidents of care in her vulnerable condition. Her life accordingly is sustained by the respirator and tubal feeding, and removal from the respirator would cause her death soon, although the time cannot be stated with more precision. . . .

[Ms. Quinlan's father asked the superior court to appoint him the guardian of his daughter and to be given the express power to "authorize the discontinuance of all extraordinary medical procedures" sustaining his daughter's life. Ms. Quinlan's father also asked that the treating physicians and hospitals and the local prosecutor be enjoined from interfering with the discontinuation and that the local prosecutor also be enjoined from bringing a criminal prosecution after a discontinuation of treatment. The father's requests were opposed by the doctors, the hospital, the county prosecutor, the State of New Jersey, and Ms. Quinlan's guardian ad litem. The superior court denied the father's request for power to stop treatment.]

III. THE RIGHT OF PRIVACY

It is the issue of the constitutional right of privacy that has given us most concern, in the exceptional circumstances of this case. Here a loving parent, . . . seeks authorization to abandon specialized technological procedures which can only maintain for a time a body having no potential for resumption or continuance of other than a "vegetative" existence.

We have no doubt, in these unhappy circumstances, that if Karen were herself miraculously lucid for an interval (not altering the existing prognosis of the condition to which she would soon return) and perceptive of her irreversible condition, she could effectively decide upon discontinuance of the life-support apparatus, even if it meant the prospect of natural death. To this extent we may distinguish [John F. Kennedy Memorial Hospital v. Heston, 279 A.2d 670 (N.J. 1971)], which concerned a severely injured young woman (Delores Heston), whose life depended on surgery and blood transfusion; and who was in such extreme shock that she was unable to express an informed choice (although the court apparently considered the case as if the patient's own religious decision to resist transfusion were at stake), but most importantly a patient apparently salvable to long life and vibrant health;—a situation not at all like the present case.

We have no hesitancy in deciding, in the instant diametrically opposite case, that no external compelling interest of the state could compel Karen to endure the unendurable, only to vegetate a few measurable months with no realistic possibility of returning to any semblance of cognitive or sapient life. We perceive no thread of logic distinguishing between such a choice on Karen's part and a similar choice which, under the evidence in this case, could be made by a competent patient terminally ill, riddled by cancer and suffering great pain; such a patient would not be resuscitated or put on a respirator . . . , and a fortiori would not be kept *against his will* on a respirator.

Although the Constitution does not explicitly mention a right of privacy, Supreme Court decisions have recognized that a right of personal privacy exists and that certain areas of privacy are guaranteed under the Constitution. . . .

Presumably this right is broad enough to encompass a patient's decision to decline medical treatment under certain circumstances, in much the same way as it is broad enough to encompass a woman's decision to terminate pregnancy under certain conditions.

Nor is such right of privacy forgotten in the New Jersey Constitution. N.J. Const. (1947), Art. I, par. 1.

The claimed interests of the state in this case are essentially the preservation and sanctity of human life and defense of the right of the physician to administer medical treatment according to his best judgment. In this case the doctors say that removing Karen from the respirator will conflict with their professional judgment. The plaintiff answers that Karen's present treatment serves only a maintenance function; that the respirator cannot cure or improve her condition but at best can only prolong her inevitable slow deterioration and death; and that the interests of the patient, as seen by her surrogate, the guardian, must be evaluated by the court as predominant, even in the face of an opinion *contra* by the present attending physicians. Plaintiff's distinction is significant. The nature of Karen's care and the realistic chances of her recovery are quite unlike those of the patients discussed in many of the cases where treatments were ordered. In many of those cases the medical procedure required (usually a transfusion) constituted a minimal bodily invasion and the chances of recovery and return to functioning life were very good. We think that the state's interest *contra* weakens and the individual's right to privacy grows as the degree of bodily invasion increases and the prognosis dims. Ultimately there comes a point at which the individual's rights overcome the state interest. It is for that reason that we believe Karen's choice, if she were competent to make it, would be vindicated by the law. Her prognosis is extremely poor,—she will never resume cognitive life. And the bodily invasion is very great,—she requires 24 hour intensive nursing care, antibiotics, the assistance of a respirator, a catheter and feeding tube. . . .

IV. THE MEDICAL FACTOR

Having declared the substantive legal basis upon which plaintiff's rights as representative of Karen must be deemed predicated, we face and respond to the assertion on behalf of defendants that our premise unwarrantably offends prevailing medical standards. . . .

We glean from the record here that physicians distinguish between curing the ill and comforting and easing the dying; that they refuse to treat the curable as if they were dying or ought to die, and that they have sometimes refused to treat the hopeless and dying as if they were curable. . . . [M]any [physicians] have refused to inflict an undesired prolongation of the process of dying on a patient in irreversible condition when it is clear that such "therapy" offers neither human nor humane benefit. We think these attitudes represent a balanced implementation of a profoundly realistic perspective on the meaning of life and death and that they respect the whole Judeo-Christian tradition of regard for human life. No less would they seem consistent with the moral matrix of medicine, "to heal." . . .

Yet this balance, we feel, is particularly difficult to perceive and apply in the context of the development by advanced technology of sophisticated and artificial life-sustaining devices. For those possibly curable, such devices are of great value, and, as ordinary medical procedures, are essential. Consequently, as pointed out by Dr. Diamond, they are necessary because of the ethic of medical practice. But in light of the situation in the present case (while the record here is somewhat hazy in distinguishing between "ordinary" and "extraordinary" measures), one would have to think that the use of the same respirator or like support could be considered "ordinary" in the context of the possibly curable patient but "extraordinary" in the context of the forced sustaining by cardio-respiratory processes of an irreversibly doomed patient. . . .

The evidence in this case convinces us that the focal point of decision should be the prognosis as to the reasonable possibility of return to cognitive and sapient life, as distinguished from the forced continuance of that biological vegetative existence to which Karen seems to be doomed. [The court granted Mr. Quinlan's request, authorizing him to discontinue his daughter's life support. Surprisingly, Karen ended up living for another ten years without ventilator support.]

■ IN RE CONROY
486 A.2d 1209 (N.J. 1985)

SCHREIBER, Justice.

In 1979 Claire Conroy, who was suffering from an organic brain syndrome that manifested itself in her exhibiting periodic confusion, was adjudicated an incompetent, and plaintiff, her nephew, was appointed her guardian. . . .

During [a July 21-November 17, 1982] hospitalization, Dr. Kazemi observed that Ms. Conroy was not eating adequately, and therefore, on July 23, he inserted a nasogastric tube that extended from her nose through her esophagus to her stomach. Medicines and food were then given to her through this tube. On October 18, the tube was removed, and Ms. Conroy was fed by hand through her mouth for two weeks. However, she was unable to eat a sufficient amount in this manner, and the tube was reinserted on November 3. . . .

At the time of trial, Ms. Conroy [age 84] was no longer ambulatory and was confined to bed, unable to move from a semi-fetal position. She suffered from arteriosclerotic heart disease, hypertension, and diabetes mellitus; her left leg was gangrenous to her knee; she had several necrotic decubitus ulcers (bed sores) on her left foot, leg, and hip; an eye problem required irrigation; she had a urinary catheter in place and could not control her bowels; she could not speak; and her ability to swallow was very limited. On the other hand, she interacted with her environment in some limited ways: she could move her head, neck, hands, and arms to a minor extent; she was able to scratch herself, and had pulled at her bandages, tube, and catheter; she moaned occasionally when moved or fed through the tube, or when her bandages were changed; her eyes sometimes followed individuals in the room; her facial expressions were different when she was awake from when she was asleep; and she smiled on occasion when her hair was combed, or when she received a comforting rub. . . .

[This case arose when Ms. Conroy's guardian, who was also her nephew, petitioned the trial court for permission to discontinue Ms. Conroy's feeding tube. The guardian ad litem opposed the petition, and the trial court granted permission.

The guardian ad litem appealed, and the intermediate court of appeals reversed. At issue in the case was whether Ms. Conroy's feeding tube could be withdrawn. While this case was before the intermediate court of appeals, Ms. Conroy died with her feeding tube in place. The N.J. Supreme Court nevertheless heard the case, as one involving a matter "of substantial importance and . . . capable of repetition but evad[ing] review."]

III

The starting point in analyzing whether life-sustaining treatment may be withheld or withdrawn from an incompetent patient is to determine what rights a competent patient has to accept or reject medical care. It is therefore necessary at the outset of this discussion to identify the nature and extent of a patient's rights that are implicated by such decisions.

The right of a person to control his own body is a basic societal concept, long recognized in the common law. . . .

The doctrine of informed consent is a primary means developed in the law to protect this personal interest in the integrity of one's body. "Under this doctrine, no medical procedure may be performed without a patient's consent, obtained after explanation of the nature of the treatment, substantial risks, and alternative therapies." Cantor, A Patient's Decision to Decline Life-Saving Medical Treatment: Bodily Integrity Versus the Preservation of Life, 26 Rutgers L. Rev. 228, 237 (1973). . . .

The patient's ability to control his bodily integrity through informed consent is significant only when one recognizes that this right also encompasses a right to informed refusal. Thus, a competent adult person generally has the right to decline to have any medical treatment initiated or continued.

The right to make certain decisions concerning one's body is also protected by the federal constitutional right of privacy. . . . While this right of privacy might apply in a case such as this, we need not decide that issue since the right to decline medical treatment is, in any event, embraced within the common-law right to self-determination.

Whether based on common-law doctrines or on constitutional theory, the right to decline life-sustaining medical treatment is not absolute. In some cases, it may yield to countervailing societal interests in sustaining the person's life. Courts and commentators have commonly identified four state interests that may limit a person's right to refuse medical treatment: preserving life, preventing suicide, safeguarding the integrity of the medical profession, and protecting innocent third parties.

The state's interest in preserving life is commonly considered the most significant of the four state interests. It may be seen as embracing two separate but related concerns: an interest in preserving the life of the particular patient, and an interest in preserving the sanctity of all life.

While both of these state interests in life are certainly strong, in themselves they will usually not foreclose a competent person from declining life-sustaining medical treatment for himself. This is because the life that the state is seeking to protect in such a situation is the life of the same person who has competently decided to forego the medical intervention; it is not some other actual or potential life that cannot adequately protect itself.

In cases that do not involve the protection of the actual or potential life of someone other than the decisionmaker, the state's indirect and abstract interest in preserving the life of the competent patient generally gives way to the patient's much stronger personal interest in directing the course of his own life. . . .

[As to the state interest in preventing suicide], declining life-sustaining medical treatment may not properly be viewed as an attempt to commit suicide. Refusing medical intervention merely allows the disease to take its natural course; if death were eventually to occur, it would be the result, primarily, of the underlying disease, and not the result of a self-inflicted injury. In addition, people who refuse life-sustaining medical treatment may not harbor a specific intent to die; rather, they may fervently wish to live, but to do so free of unwanted medical technology, surgery, or drugs, and without protracted suffering. . . . The difference is between self-infliction or self-destruction and self-determination. . . .

The third state interest that is frequently asserted as a limitation on a competent patient's right to refuse medical treatment is the interest in safeguarding the integrity of the medical profession. . . . Medical ethics do not require medical intervention in disease at all costs. . . . Indeed, recent surveys have suggested that a majority of practicing doctors now approve of passive euthanasia and believe that it is being practiced by members of the profession.

Moreover, even if doctors were exhorted to attempt to cure or sustain their patients under all circumstances, that moral and professional imperative, at least in cases of patients who were clearly competent, presumably would not require doctors to go beyond advising the patient of the risks of foregoing treatment and urging the patient to accept the medical intervention. If the patient rejected the doctor's advice, the onus of that decision would rest on the patient, not the doctor. . . .

The fourth asserted state interest in overriding a patient's decision about his medical treatment is the interest in protecting innocent third parties who may be harmed by the patient's treatment decision. [The court cites cases involving minor children who would be abandoned by a parent's death or involving threats to public health or prison security.] . . .

On balance, the right to self-determination ordinarily outweighs any countervailing state interests, and competent persons generally are permitted to refuse medical treatment, even at the risk of death. Most of the cases that have held otherwise, unless they involved the interest in protecting innocent third parties, have concerned the patient's competency to make a rational and considered choice of treatment. . . .

In view of the case law, we have no doubt that Ms. Conroy, if competent to make the decision and if resolute in her determination, could have chosen to have her nasogastric tube withdrawn. Her interest in freedom from nonconsensual invasion of her bodily integrity would outweigh any state interest in preserving life or in safeguarding the integrity of the medical profession. In addition, rejecting her artificial means of feeding would not constitute attempted suicide, as the decision would probably be based on a wish to be free of medical intervention rather than a specific intent to die, and her death would result, if at all, from her underlying medical condition, which included her inability to swallow. Finally, removal of her feeding tube would not create a public health or safety hazard, nor would her death leave any minor dependents without care or support.

It should be noted that if she were competent, Ms. Conroy's right to self-determination would not be affected by her medical condition or prognosis. . . . Of course, a patient's decision to accept or reject medical treatment may be influenced by his medical condition, treatment, and prognosis; nevertheless, a competent person's common-law and constitutional rights do not depend on the quality or value of his life.

[In the section on the incompetent patient, at page 304, we consider the second half of the court's opinion, which discusses how decisions about life-sustaining treatment should be made for patients like Ms. Conroy.]

■ CRUZAN v. DIRECTOR, MISSOURI DEPARTMENT OF HEALTH
497 U.S. 261 (1990)

REHNQUIST, Chief Justice.

. . . On the night of January 11, 1983, Nancy Cruzan lost control of her car as she traveled down Elm Road in Jasper County, Missouri. The vehicle overturned, and Cruzan was discovered lying face down in a ditch without detectable respiratory or cardiac function. Paramedics were able to restore her breathing and heartbeat at the accident site, and she was transported to a hospital in an unconscious state. An attending neurosurgeon diagnosed her as having sustained probable cerebral contusions compounded by significant anoxia (lack of oxygen). The Missouri trial court in this case found that permanent brain damage generally results after six minutes in an anoxic state; it was estimated that Cruzan was deprived of oxygen from 12 to 14 minutes. She remained in a coma for approximately three weeks and then progressed to an unconscious state in which she was able to orally ingest some nutrition. In order to ease feeding and further the recovery, surgeons implanted a gastrostomy feeding and hydration tube in Cruzan with the consent of her then husband. Subsequent rehabilitative efforts proved unavailing. [Now age 31, she] lies in a Missouri state hospital in what is commonly referred to as a persistent vegetative state: generally, a condition in which a person exhibits motor reflexes but evinces no indications of significant cognitive function. The state of Missouri is bearing the cost of her care.

After it had become apparent that Nancy Cruzan had virtually no chance of regaining her mental faculties, her parents asked hospital employees to terminate the artificial nutrition and hydration procedures. . . . The employees refused to honor the request without court approval. [Ms. Cruzan's parents then sought judicial authorization from a state trial court. The trial court granted approval, but the Missouri Supreme Court reversed that decision.] . . .

We granted certiorari to consider the question whether Cruzan has a right under the United States Constitution which would require the hospital to withdraw life-sustaining treatment from her under these circumstances.

At common law, even the touching of one person by another without consent and without legal justification was a battery. Before the turn of the century, this Court observed that "[n]o right is held more sacred, or is more carefully guarded, by the common law, than the right of every individual to the possession and control of his own person, free from all restraint or interference of others, unless by clear and unquestionable authority of law." Union Pacific R. Co. v. Botsford, 141 U.S. 250,

251 (1891). This notion of bodily integrity has been embodied in the requirement that informed consent is generally required for medical treatment. Justice Cardozo, while on the Court of Appeals of New York, aptly described this doctrine: "Every human being of adult years and sound mind has a right to determine what shall be done with his own body; and a surgeon who performs an operation without his patient's consent commits an assault, for which he is liable in damages." Schloendorff v. Society of New York Hospital, 105 N.E. 92, 93 (N.Y. 1914). The informed consent doctrine has become firmly entrenched in American tort law.

The logical corollary of the doctrine of informed consent is that the patient generally possesses the right not to consent, that is, to refuse treatment. Until about 15 years ago and the seminal decision in In re Quinlan, the number of right-to-refuse-treatment decisions was relatively few. Most of the earlier cases involved patients who refused medical treatment forbidden by their religious beliefs, thus implicating First Amendment rights as well as common law rights of self-determination. More recently, however, with the advance of medical technology capable of sustaining life well past the point where natural forces would have brought certain death in earlier times, cases involving the right to refuse life-sustaining treatment have burgeoned. . . .

As these cases demonstrate, the common law doctrine of informed consent is viewed as generally encompassing the right of a competent individual to refuse medical treatment. Beyond that, these cases demonstrate both similarity and diversity in their approaches to decision of what all agree is a perplexing question with unusually strong moral and ethical overtones. . . . This is the first case in which we have been squarely presented with the issue whether the United States Constitution grants what is in common parlance referred to as a "right to die." . . . .

The Fourteenth Amendment provides that no state shall "deprive any person of life, liberty, or property, without due process of law." The principle that a competent person has a constitutionally protected liberty interest in refusing unwanted medical treatment may be inferred from our prior decisions. In Jacobson v. Massachusetts, 197 U.S. 11, 24-30 (1905), for instance, the Court balanced an individual's liberty interest in declining an unwanted smallpox vaccine against the state's interest in preventing disease. Decisions prior to the incorporation of the Fourth Amendment into the Fourteenth Amendment analyzed searches and seizures involving the body under the due process clause and were thought to implicate substantial liberty interests.

Just this Term, in the course of holding that a state's procedures for administering antipsychotic medication to prisoners were sufficient to satisfy due process concerns, we recognized that prisoners possess "a significant liberty interest in avoiding the unwanted administration of antipsychotic drugs under the due process clause of the Fourteenth Amendment." Washington v. Harper, 494 U.S. 210, 221-222 (1990). Still other cases support the recognition of a general liberty interest in refusing medical treatment. Vitek v. Jones, 445 U.S. 480, 494 (1980) (transfer to mental hospital coupled with mandatory behavior modification treatment implicated liberty interests); Parham v. J.R., 442 U.S. 584, 600 (1979) ("[A] child, in common with adults, has a substantial liberty interest in not being confined unnecessarily for medical treatment").

But determining that a person has a "liberty interest" under the due process clause does not end the inquiry; "whether respondent's constitutional rights have been violated must be determined by balancing his liberty interests against the relevant state interests." Youngberg v. Romeo, 457 U.S. 307, 321 (1982).

Petitioners insist that under the general holdings of our cases, the forced administration of life-sustaining medical treatment, and even of artificially delivered food and water essential to life, would implicate a competent person's liberty interest. Although we think the logic of the cases discussed above would embrace such a liberty interest, the dramatic consequences involved in refusal of such treatment would inform the inquiry as to whether the deprivation of that interest is constitutionally permissible. But for purposes of this case, we assume that the United States Constitution would grant a competent person a constitutionally protected right to refuse lifesaving hydration and nutrition. . . .

[While the Court assumed for purposes of the case that Nancy Cruzan had a right to refuse her treatment, it also upheld Missouri's imposition of treatment on the ground that the Missouri Supreme Court had adopted a reasonable procedural standard for deciding when an incompetent person's right to refuse treatment should be invoked. That part of the decision is considered at page 313, in the section on the incompetent patient.]

SCALIA, Justice, concurring.

. . . While I agree with the Court's analysis today, and therefore join in its opinion, I would have preferred that we announce, clearly and promptly, that the federal courts have no business in this field; that American law has always accorded the state the power to prevent, by force if necessary, suicide — including suicide by refusing to take appropriate measures necessary to preserve one's life; that the point at which life becomes "worthless," and the point at which the means necessary to preserve it become "extraordinary" or "inappropriate," are neither set forth in the Constitution nor known to the nine Justices of this Court any better than they are known to nine people picked at random from the Kansas City telephone directory; and hence that . . . [when] a patient no longer wishes certain measures to be taken to preserve his or her life, it is up to the citizens of Missouri to decide, through their elected representatives, whether that wish will be honored. It is quite impossible (because the Constitution says nothing about the matter) that those citizens will decide upon a line less lawful than the one we would choose; and it is unlikely (because we know no more about "life and death" than they do) that they will decide upon a line less reasonable. . . .

Petitioners rely on three distinctions to separate Nancy Cruzan's case from ordinary suicide: (1) that she is permanently incapacitated and in pain; (2) that she would bring on her death not by any affirmative act but by merely declining treatment that provides nourishment; and (3) that preventing her from effectuating her presumed wish to die requires violation of her bodily integrity. None of these suffices. Suicide was not excused even when committed "to avoid those ills which [persons] had not the fortitude to endure." 4 Blackstone, supra, at 189. "The life of those to whom life has become a burden — of those who are hopelessly diseased or fatally wounded — nay, even the lives of criminals condemned to death, are under the protection of the law, equally as the lives of those who are in the full tide of life's enjoyment, and anxious to continue to live." Blackburn v. State, 23 Ohio St. 146, 163 (1873). . . . [Assisted suicide] is declared by the law to be murder, irrespective of the wishes or the condition of the party to whom the poison is administered. . . ." Blackburn, supra, at 163.

The second asserted distinction—suggested by the recent cases canvassed by the Court concerning the right to refuse treatment—relies on the dichotomy between action and inaction. Suicide, it is said, consists of an affirmative act to end one's life; refusing treatment is not an affirmative act "causing" death, but merely a passive acceptance of the natural process of dying. I readily acknowledge that the distinction between action and inaction has some bearing upon the legislative judgment of what ought to be prevented as suicide—though even there it would seem to me unreasonable to draw the line precisely between action and inaction, rather than between various forms of inaction. It would not make much sense to say that one may not kill oneself by walking into the sea, but may sit on the beach until submerged by the incoming tide; or that one may not intentionally lock oneself into a cold storage locker, but may refrain from coming indoors when the temperature drops below freezing. Even as a legislative matter, in other words, the intelligent line does not fall between action and inaction but between those forms of inaction that consist of abstaining from "ordinary" care and those that consist of abstaining from "excessive" or "heroic" measures. Unlike action versus inaction, that is not a line to be discerned by logic or legal analysis, and we should not pretend that it is.

. . . Of course the common law rejected the action-inaction distinction in other contexts involving the taking of human life as well. In the prosecution of a parent for the starvation death of her infant, it was no defense that the infant's death was "caused" by no action of the parent but by the natural process of starvation, or by the infant's natural inability to provide for itself. A physician, moreover, could be criminally liable for failure to provide care that could have extended the patient's life, even if death was immediately caused by the underlying disease that the physician failed to treat.

It is not surprising, therefore, that the early cases considering the claimed right to refuse medical treatment dismissed as specious the nice distinction between "passively submitting to death and actively seeking it. The distinction may be merely verbal, as it would be if an adult sought death by starvation instead of a drug. If the state may interrupt one mode of self-destruction, it may with equal authority interfere with the other." John F. Kennedy Memorial Hosp. v. Heston, 279 A.2d 670, 672-673 (N.J. 1971).

The third asserted basis of distinction—that frustrating Nancy Cruzan's wish to die in the present case requires interference with her bodily integrity—is likewise inadequate, because such interference is impermissible only if one begs the question whether her refusal to undergo the treatment on her own is suicide. It has always been lawful not only for the state, but even for private citizens, to interfere with bodily integrity to prevent a felony. That general rule has of course been applied to suicide. . . . The state-run hospital, I am certain, is not liable under 42 U.S.C. §1983 for violation of constitutional rights, nor the private hospital liable under general tort law, if, in a state where suicide is unlawful, it pumps out the stomach of a person who has intentionally taken an overdose of barbiturates, despite that person's wishes to the contrary. . . .

What I have said above is not meant to suggest that I would think it desirable, if we were sure that Nancy Cruzan wanted to die, to keep her alive by the means at issue here. I assert only that the Constitution has nothing to say about the subject. To raise up a constitutional right here we would have to create out of nothing (for it exists neither in text nor tradition) some constitutional principle whereby, although the state may insist that an individual come in out of the cold and eat food, it may not insist that he take medicine; and although it may pump his stomach empty of poison he has ingested, it may not fill his stomach with food he has failed to ingest. Are there, then, no reasonable and humane limits that ought not to be exceeded in requiring an individual to preserve his own life? There obviously are, but they are not set forth in the due process clause. What assures us that those limits will not be exceeded is the same constitutional guarantee that is the source of most of our protection—what protects us, for example, from being assessed a tax of 100% of our income above the subsistence level, from being forbidden to drive cars, or from being required to send our children to school for 10 hours a day, none of which horribles is categorically prohibited by the Constitution. Our salvation is the equal protection clause, which requires the democratic majority to accept for themselves and their loved ones what they impose on you and me. This Court need not, and has no authority to, inject itself into every field of human activity where irrationality and oppression may theoretically occur, and if it tries to do so it will destroy itself.

Notes: The Individual Interest in Refusing Treatment

1. *Karen Quinlan.* Even though Karen Quinlan's family won the right to have her ventilator discontinued, her physician and the hospital administration refused to comply with the decision of the New Jersey Supreme Court. Rather than turning off the ventilator immediately, Ms. Quinlan's physician, Dr. Morse, spent the next five months "weaning" her from the ventilator so she could breathe on her own. Ms. Quinlan eventually lived for another ten years. Gregory E. Pence, Medical Ethics: Accounts of Ground-Breaking Cases 27 (6th ed. 2011). See also Annette E. Clark, The Right to Die: The Broken Road from *Quinlan* to *Schiavo*, 37 Loy. U. Chi. L.J. 383 (2006).

As the *Quinlan* case illustrates, physicians may incorrectly believe that a patient will be permanently dependent on a ventilator or other medical treatment. Similarly, physicians may incorrectly believe that a patient is terminally ill. People may therefore decline life-sustaining treatment on the basis of mistaken assumptions about their prognoses. How would you respond to the argument that this kind of uncertainty should preclude a patient from refusing life-sustaining treatment?

2. *Persistent Vegetative State, Coma, and Brain Death.* The persistent vegetative state of Karen Quinlan and Nancy Cruzan is often confused with coma and brain death. There is some similarity among the three conditions. With all three, the person suffers a total and sustained loss of consciousness. That is, the cerebral hemispheres, which are responsible for conscious behavior, do not function. Accordingly, the person has no thoughts, feelings, sensations, desires, or emotions. There is no purposeful action, social interaction, memory, pain, or suffering. The person has lost all awareness of self and environment.

Brain death, coma, and the persistent vegetative state differ in the extent to which there is function of the brain stem, the part of the brain that controls unconscious activity. In brain death, there is a nearly complete and an irreversible loss of brain stem function (as well as a complete and irreversible loss of cerebral hemisphere function). As a result, the brain is no longer able to regulate what are known as the body's "vegetative" functions, which include the functions of the heart, lungs, kidneys, intestinal tract, and certain reflex actions. Brain-dead persons appear to be in a deep coma in which they generally do not engage in any spontaneous movement. Moreover, they do not respond to stimuli such as pain, touch, sound, or light. Mechanical measures and other artificial support can maintain a brain-dead person's heartbeat, breathing, and other vegetative functions temporarily, but usually only for a few days or weeks after brain death occurs. As discussed at the end of this chapter, a patient who is brain dead is legally, not just figuratively, dead. As a consequence, patients and families have no choice over "life support"; treatment *must* be withdrawn, not as a matter of the patient's rights, but simply as a matter of medical routine and out of proper respect for the deceased. The one important qualification is when the patient and family have authorized organ donation, in which case "life support" may be continued for a brief time even though the patient is dead in order to keep the organs from deteriorating before "harvesting." See pages 388-394 and 407-414 for further discussion of brain death and its role in organ transplantation.

In contrast to brain-dead persons, patients in a persistent vegetative state are still alive. Because they maintain relatively normal brain stem function, they can usually breathe air, digest food, and produce urine without any assistance. They experience cycles of sleeping, in which their eyes are closed, and waking, in which their eyes are open. They may smile, utter unintelligible sounds, or move their eyes, arms, and legs sporadically. Vegetative state patients also manifest a range of reflex reactions to different stimuli; they will grimace, cough, gag, and move their arms and legs. While all of this activity gives the appearance of consciousness, there is none.

Coma may be viewed as a condition intermediate between brain death and the vegetative state. The brain stem retains some function, but not the range of activity seen in the vegetative state. For example, coma is a sleep-like state in which the eyes remain closed. The patient's breathing is impaired, and many reflexes are absent. Coma and the vegetative state also differ in their duration. Comas rarely last more than two to four weeks, by which time the patient either dies, enters a vegetative state, or regains some degree of consciousness. The duration of the vegetative state, on the other hand, frequently lasts for more than a few weeks. Once it has existed for several months, it is characterized as a persistent vegetative state. Patients can survive for years, even decades, in a persistent vegetative state. In rare cases, patients have regained consciousness from a persistent vegetative state, but these patients usually remain severely disabled neurologically. The Multi-Society Task Force on PVS, Medical Aspects of the Persistent Vegetative State (Second of Two Parts), 330 New Eng. J. Med. 1572 (1994). See also Bryan Jennett, The Vegetative State: Medical Facts, Ethical and Legal Dilemmas (2002).

3. *Sources of a Right to Refuse Life-Sustaining Treatment.* In the early cases that recognized a right to refuse treatment, courts rested the right on two individual interests: the common law right to be free of nonconsensual bodily invasion (i.e., the right to informed consent) and the substantive due process right to make decisions of critical importance to one's destiny (i.e., the right to privacy). As the U.S. Supreme Court began to narrow the reach of the right to privacy, state courts relied more heavily on common law principles of informed consent to find a right to refuse life-sustaining treatment. This trend is reflected in the excerpts printed

above from the *Quinlan* and *Conroy* decisions of the New Jersey Supreme Court. After the *Cruzan* decision, however, courts are again relying on the substantive due process right, although now framed as a liberty interest rather than a privacy right. It is true that the *Cruzan* majority only assumed for purposes of the case that individuals enjoy a constitutional right to refuse life-sustaining treatment. Nevertheless, the decision has been read by courts and commentators as establishing such a right. See, e.g., State v. Pelham, 824 A.2d 1082, 1087 (N.J. 2003) (observing that "[s]ince the 1976 decision in *Quinlan*, numerous other courts, including the United States Supreme Court, have recognized the so-called 'right to die.'"); Browning v. Herbert, 568 So. 2d 4, 10 (Fla. 1990) ("A competent individual has the constitutional right to refuse medical treatment regardless of his or her medical condition," citing *Cruzan*); John A. Robertson, *Cruzan* and the Constitutional Status of Nontreatment Decisions for Incompetent Patients, 25 Ga. L. Rev. 1139 (1991); Mara Silver, Note, Testing Cruzan: Prisoners and the Constitutional Question of Self-Starvation, 58 Stan. L. Rev. 631 (2005).

Although we can easily view the informed consent right and the substantive due process right as independent rights—the first, a right to be free of unwanted bodily invasion; the second, a right to make important personal decisions—the *Cruzan* Court collapsed the two. There, as we saw, the Court turned to common law principles of informed consent as the basis for finding a constitutional liberty interest in refusing life-sustaining treatment. Yet, in terms of underlying principles, it arguably makes more sense to collapse the rights in the other direction. Do you see how the right to informed consent ultimately comes down to a notion of privacy or liberty in making important personal decisions? See, e.g., Schloendorff v. Society of New York Hospital, 105 N.E. 92, 93 (N.Y. 1914) (Cardozo, J.) (holding that surgery without consent is an unlawful assault because "[e]very human being of adult years and sound mind has a right to determine what shall be done with his own body"). In terms of future implications, why do you think the *Cruzan* Court preferred to rest its constitutional right on principles of informed consent rather than on the kind of privacy analysis employed in its abortion cases, Roe v. Wade or Planned Parenthood of Southeastern Pennsylvania v. Casey?

4. *State Action.* In *Cruzan*, the patient was being treated in a state rehabilitation facility, so the Supreme Court did not need to worry whether the state action requirement of the Fourteenth Amendment was satisfied (i.e., the Fourteenth Amendment protects against government, not private, action). Yet, in many cases, it is a private physician or hospital refusing to discontinue life-sustaining treatment. In those cases, it is not clear how the patients could invoke their federal constitutional right to refuse treatment. See Blum v. Yaretsky, 457 U.S. 991, 1004 (1982) (no state action implicated by a private nursing home's decision to transfer a patient despite a reduction in the patient's Medicaid benefits by the state in response to the transfer; "a state normally can be held responsible for a private decision only when it has exercised [such] coercive power . . . that the choice must in law be deemed to be that of the state"). Most likely, state action has not been viewed as an issue in treatment withdrawal cases both because state common law grounds are available to justify withdrawal and because the courts recognize that the state is doing more than refusing to intervene but is also using the threat of criminal liability to effectively force the physician or hospital to treat. See, e.g., In re Colyer, 660 P.2d 738, 742 (Wash. 1983) (finding state action in part because of the state's "capability of

imposing criminal sanctions on the hospital and its staff"). In some cases, a court's finding of state action is difficult to reconcile with the U.S. Supreme Court's state action decisions. See, e.g., Rasmussen v. Fleming, 741 P.2d 674, 682 n.9 (Ariz. 1987) (finding state action on the basis of the state's regulation and licensing of hospitals and physicians and the state's supervisory authority over the guardianship of incapacitated persons).

5. *Withdrawing vs. Withholding.* The *Quinlan* opinion suggests that if the issue had been whether to put Karen Quinlan on a ventilator, she clearly would have enjoyed a right to have the ventilator withheld. At one time, some commentators argued that it was permissible to withhold life-sustaining treatment but not to withdraw such treatment, just as there is no obligation to come to someone's rescue, but there is an obligation not to abandon a rescue. Over time, however, in both ethics and the law, the distinction between withdrawing and withholding was rejected. Indeed, as many commentators have observed, it is arguably worse to withhold than to withdraw. If treatment is withheld, then an opportunity is lost to see if the treatment would provide unexpected benefit. Withdrawal presumably occurs only after it becomes clear that the treatment provides insufficient benefit. Moreover, as suggested by Justice Brennan in his dissent in *Cruzan*, 497 U.S. at 314, if we did not recognize a right to have treatment withdrawn, many people might not seek care in the first place because they would be afraid of not being able to stop treatment once it was started. If the treatment ended up not working and causing greater suffering, the person would be stuck. Do you agree with this latter argument? Is it likely that people would hesitate to seek potentially life-saving care because they might not be able to stop the care at some later time?

Despite years of ethicists and courts rejecting the distinction between withholding and withdrawing, health care providers feel very differently about the two acts. Many physicians believe it is ethically and legally less acceptable to withdraw care than to withhold it. See, e.g., Neil J. Farber et al., Physicians' Decisions to Withhold and Withdraw Life-Sustaining Treatment, 166 Arch. Intern. Med. 560 (2006); Terri R. Fried et al., Limits of Patient Autonomy: Physician Attitudes and Practices Regarding Life-Sustaining Treatments and Euthanasia, 153 Arch. Intern. Med. 722, 723-724 (1993); Philip G. Peters, Jr. et al., Physician Willingness to Withhold Tube Feeding After *Cruzan:* An Empirical Study, 57 Mo. L. Rev. 831, 838-839 (1992).

These feelings are not surprising. It is hard not to feel responsible for a patient's death when you turn off a ventilator and the patient dies within minutes. Two ethics consultants wrote about their experience in discontinuing a ventilator from a competent, 67-year-old patient, Mr. Larson, who was irreversibly dependent on the ventilator because of "post-polio syndrome."

> Although we received grateful hugs from the family and thanks from the health care team, we were struck by the gravity of what we had done. Doubts kept creeping into our minds. We each experienced a wave of disquieting emotion, feelings that we had killed this patient who would have otherwise continued to live connected to the ventilator. We knew intellectually that he had the legal and ethical right to refuse this medical treatment, but the gravity of the decision and our participation haunted us. We returned to our immediate commitments of caring for other patients, one of us responding next to the need of a patient who wanted medical help for a pulmonary problem to prolong his life. Both of us remained preoccupied

throughout the afternoon thinking about Mr. Larson and what we had done. Our respective medical careers have generally been devoted to responding to patient wishes to postpone death and to prolong life. We've seen our patients die of their various diseases, but now our acquiescence in allowing his death caused us much anguish. This anguish continued in both of us for several days. One of us sought counsel from a psychiatrist who reinforced our belief that we did the right thing, counteracting those deep feelings that somehow we had killed this patient. Gradually we came to terms with what had happened. . . . Our consciences were clear, but we were left feeling very impressed with how difficult it had been to honor this man's request.

Miles J. Edwards & Susan W. Tolle, Disconnecting a Ventilator at the Request of a Patient Who Knows He Will Then Die: The Doctor's Anguish, 117 Ann. Intern. Med. 254, 256 (1992).

How should the law take account of these feelings?

6. *Type of Treatment at Stake.* As the *Quinlan* and *Cruzan* cases suggest, it was once unclear legally whether artificial ventilation or artificial nutrition and hydration could be discontinued, and there were many commentators opposed to withdrawal of feeding tubes. See, e.g., Daniel Callahan, On Feeding the Dying, 13(5) Hastings Center Rep. 22 (1983); Mark Siegler & Alan J. Weisbard, Against the Emerging Stream: Should Fluids and Nutritional Support Be Discontinued?, 145 Arch. Intern. Med. 129 (1985). The *Cruzan* case essentially resolved the debate in terms of the law, and now it is widely accepted that patients can refuse any medical treatment. Nevertheless, many physicians are still slow to withdraw feeding tubes because of their personal moral concerns. Cf. Heikki Hinkka et al., Factors Affecting Physicians' Decisions to Forgo Life-Sustaining Treatments in Terminal Care, 28 J. Med. Ethics 109 (2002) (finding that physicians in Finland were much more willing to withhold a ventilator than a feeding tube); Jeffrey S. Rubenstein, Pediatric Resident Attitudes About Technologic Support of Vegetative Patients and the Effects of Parental Input—A Longitudinal Study, 94 Pediatrics 8 (1994) (finding that pediatric residents expressed a much greater willingness to withdraw a ventilator than artificial nutrition and hydration from a child in a persistent vegetative state).

Not all treatment decisions have been so controversial. In particular, do-not-resuscitate (DNR) orders have been accepted medical practice for decades. Such orders, often called DNAR (do-not-attempt-resuscitation) orders, were developed because dying patients do not always want physicians to try to restart their heartbeat when their illness results in the terminal event of cardiac arrest. A DNR order means that cardiopulmonary resuscitation (CPR) will be withheld from the patient. The acceptance of DNR orders is reflected in the hospital accreditation standards of the Joint Commission for the Accreditation of Healthcare Organizations, which *require* hospitals to maintain a specific policy for DNR orders. What is controversial about DNR orders is whether physicians may write them over the objection of the patient or the patient's family, on the ground that CPR serves no useful purpose. This issue will be discussed in greater depth in the section on futility, pages 377-394.

7. *Costs of Care.* While the right to refuse treatment coincides with a trend toward greater recognition of patients' rights, it also coincides, as mentioned in the introduction to this section, with concerns about the high cost of medical care. When the *Cruzan* case was working its way through the courts, it was common to

hear people justify withdrawal of care on the ground that it was costing more than $100,000 a year to keep her alive and that money could be better spent on other kinds of medical care. Does the right to refuse treatment simply reflect the economic cost to society of enforcing a duty to receive life-sustaining treatment?

Much has been made about the high percentage of health care costs that are consumed in the last 6 or 12 months of people's lives. However, there is a good deal of misunderstanding about those costs. First, while one-fourth of Medicare expenditures are consumed in the last 12 months of life, Gerald F. Riley & James D. Lubitz, Long-Term Trends in Medicare Payments in the Last Year of Life, 45 Health Serv. Res. 565 (2010), only 10 to 12 percent of all health care costs go for such care, Ezekiel J. Emanuel & Linda L. Emanuel, The Economics of Dying: The Illusion of Cost Savings at the End of Life, 330 New Eng. J. Med. 540 (1994). Second, physicians tend to treat people aggressively during the last 6 or 12 months of life when it appears that the patient has a reasonable chance of a good recovery. For patients with dismal prognoses, most of the costs of care go to cover nursing home and home health care; in other words, basic supportive care. Anne A. Scitovsky, Medical Care in the Last Twelve Months of Life: The Relation Between Age, Functional Status, and Medical Care Expenditures, 66 Milbank Q. 640 (1988). See also Samuel S. Richardson et al., Use of Aggressive Medical Treatments near the End of Life: Differences Between Patients with and Without Dementia, 42 Health Serv. Res. 183 (2007) (concluding that "during the final 30 days of life, acute care patients with dementia are treated substantially less aggressively than patients without dementia"). For further discussion, see Berhanu Alemayehu & Kenneth E. Warner, The Lifetime Distribution of Health Care Costs, 39 Health Serv. Res. 627 (2004) (finding that nearly half of the lifetime spending for health care occurs after age 65 for the average person, and for those who live at least 85 years, more than a third of their spending occurs after age 85).

Notes: The State's Interest in Preserving Life

1. *The State's Interest.* In *Conroy*, the New Jersey Supreme Court essentially argued that the state's interest in preserving patients' lives is sufficient to justify the imposition of medical treatment only when patients want their lives preserved. The state's primary interest is to protect patients from having their lives taken involuntarily. Similarly, in his dissent in *Cruzan*, Justice Brennan wrote:

> The only state interest asserted here is a general interest in the preservation of life. But the state has no legitimate general interest in someone's life, completely abstracted from the interest of the person living that life, that could outweigh the person's choice to avoid medical treatment. . . . [T]he state's general interest in life must accede to Nancy Cruzan's particularized and intense interest in self-determination in her choice of medical treatment. There is simply nothing legitimately within the state's purview to be gained by superseding her decision.

Cruzan, 497 U.S. at 313-314 (Brennan, J., with Marshall, J., and Blackmun, J., dissenting).

David Blake argues that such a view conflates the value of life with the ability to exercise individual autonomy. Self-determination surely is a critical value, he observes, but there is intrinsic value to a person's life above and beyond the value recognized by that person. David Blake, State Interests in Terminating Medical Treatment, 19(3) Hastings Center Rep. 5 (1989). Why might the state have interests in preserving life even when a competent adult rejects continued life? Consider concerns about preserving the moral worth of society (if patients are allowed to die when they consent, people may have less respect for life and be less troubled when death comes about involuntarily); about preserving freedom of choice in areas of profound consequence to happiness (we do not permit people to become slaves or renounce their right to a divorce); and about avoiding the domination of one group by another (here, preventing the victimization of severely disabled persons). David Orentlicher, Physician-Assisted Dying: The Conflict with Fundamental Principles of American Law, *in* Medicine Unbound: The Human Body and the Limits of Medical Intervention 256 (Blank & Bonnicksen eds., 1994).

2. *Balancing the Individual and State Interests.* If the state's interest in preserving a patient's life exists only insofar as the patient wishes to continue living, then there is no need to balance the state's interest against the individual interest. If the state's interest has some content that is independent of the individual's interest, then that raises the question of how we should balance the state's interest in preserving life with the individual's interest in being able to refuse treatment. Should the right to refuse life-sustaining treatment be unlimited or should it be restricted according to the type of treatment at issue (e.g., a ventilator vs. antibiotics) or the patient's medical condition (e.g., end-stage AIDS vs. pneumonia in an otherwise healthy person). Do you agree with the *Quinlan* court's view that the right to refuse life-sustaining treatment should grow as the degree of bodily invasion increases and the prognosis dims? Should it matter whether the patient is terminally ill or might be able to live for many years?

As the case law has developed, courts have seemingly abandoned any effort to balance the individual's right to refuse treatment with the state's interest in preserving life, almost without exception permitting competent patients to refuse life-sustaining treatment. In the early cases, including *Quinlan*, the courts had suggested that the right to refuse life-sustaining treatment was a right that existed when life could be prolonged for only a short time, with a poor quality of life and at considerable cost to the patient (with cost being measured in terms of pain, other suffering, and economic burden). However, recent cases have not so limited the right.

As we saw, the New Jersey Supreme Court in *Conroy* concluded that:

the right to self-determination ordinarily outweighs any countervailing state interests, and competent persons generally are permitted to refuse medical treatment, even at the risk of death. . . . Ms. Conroy's right to self-determination would not be affected by her medical condition or prognosis. . . . [A] competent person's common-law and constitutional rights do not depend on the quality or value of his life.

486 A.2d at 1225-1226. Two years later, in In re Peter, 529 A.2d 419 (N.J. 1987), involving the removal of a feeding tube from a patient in a persistent vegetative state, the same court wrote:

Medical choices . . . are not to be decided by societal standards of reasonableness or normalcy. Rather, it is the patient's preferences—formed by his or her unique personal experiences—that should control.

The privacy that we accord medical decisions does not vary with the patient's condition or prognosis. The patient's medical condition is generally relevant only to determine whether the patient is or is not competent. . . . [529 A.2d at 423.]

Other courts have taken the same view of the state's interest in preserving life. In the case of Elizabeth Bouvia, an intermediate appeals court permitted a 28-year-old college graduate who retained her full intellectual capacity to refuse a feeding tube. Because of severe cerebral palsy, Ms. Bouvia was quadriplegic, confined to bed, and dependent on others for all of her needs. She also was in continual pain from severe arthritis. She had suffered a series of emotional setbacks when her husband left her and her physical deterioration forced her to drop out of school and become dependent on others. Despondent, she admitted herself to a public hospital as a psychiatric patient, with the apparent intent of starving herself to death using the assistance of pain relief and other comfort care provided by the hospital. After a trial court denied her judicial assistance, she abandoned that effort and lived at several different facilities before seeking permission from a trial court to have her feeding tube withdrawn. In addressing the fact that Ms. Bouvia was not terminally ill, the appellate court wrote,

> All decisions permitting cessation of medical treatment or life-support procedures to some degree hastened the arrival of death. In part, at least, this was permitted because the quality of life during the time remaining in those cases had been terribly diminished. In Elizabeth Bouvia's view, the quality of her life has been diminished to the point of hopelessness, uselessness, unenjoyability and frustration. She, as the patient, lying helplessly in bed, unable to care for herself, may consider her existence meaningless. She cannot be faulted for so concluding. If her right to choose may not be exercised because there remains to her, in the opinion of the court, a physician or some committee, a certain arbitrary number of years, months, or days, her right will have lost its value and meaning. Who shall say what the minimum amount of available life must be? Does it matter if it be 15 to 20 years, 15 to 20 months, or 15 to 20 days, if such life has been physically destroyed and its quality, dignity and purpose be gone? As in all matters lines must be drawn at some point, somewhere, but that decision must ultimately belong to the one whose life is in issue. Here Elizabeth Bouvia's decision to forego medical treatment or life-support through a mechanical means belongs to her. It is not a medical decision for her physicians to make. Neither is it a legal question whose soundness is to be resolved by lawyers or judges. It is not a conditional right subject to approval by ethics committees or courts of law. It is a moral and philosophical decision that, being a competent adult, is hers alone.

Bouvia v. Superior Court, 225 Cal. Rptr. 297, 304-305 (Ct. App. 1986).

According to the *Bouvia* court, a competent adult "has the right to refuse *any* medical treatment, even that which may save or prolong her life." 225 Cal. Rptr. at 300 (emphasis in original). Despite winning her case, Ms. Bouvia did not exercise her right to refuse life-sustaining treatment and is still alive.

The Nevada Supreme Court also has given little weight to the state's interest in preserving life. In McKay v. Bergstedt, 801 P.2d 617 (Nev. 1990), a 31-year-old man, Kenneth Bergstedt, sought permission to discontinue a ventilator. Mr. Bergstedt had been quadriplegic, and therefore ventilator-dependent, since a swimming accident at age ten. He was able to read, watch television, write poetry by orally operating a computer, and move around in a wheelchair. His quadriplegia was irreversible, but he was not terminally ill. When the death of his father appeared imminent, Mr. Bergstedt wanted to end his life because "he despaired over the prospect of life without the attentive care, companionship and love of his devoted father." Id. at 620. His mother had died several years earlier. The court observed that Mr. Bergstedt's desire to end his life was driven primarily by "[f]ear of the unknown," that he was preoccupied with concern "over the quality of his life after the death of his father." Id. at 624. In concluding that Mr. Bergstedt's right to refuse treatment overrode the state's interest in preserving life, the court "attach[ed] great significance to the quality of Kenneth's life as he perceived it under the particular circumstances that were afflicting him." Id. at 625.[1] Like many of the decisions in this area, the Nevada Supreme Court's opinion came down after Mr. Bergstedt died. About a month before the decision, and a week before his father died, Mr. Bergstedt's father disconnected his son's ventilator. Father Succumbs to Cancer After Fulfilling Son's Death Wish, San Diego Union-Tribune, October 12, 1990, at A15.

Although there are some early cases to the contrary,[2] courts have approved refusals of treatments necessary to sustain life even when the treatment is simple and minimally invasive, and the person could readily be restored to good health. In Fosmire v. Nicoleau, 551 N.E.2d 77 (N.Y. 1990), the court recognized the right of a 36-year-old adult to refuse blood transfusions that could restore her to good health following blood loss during a cesarean section. The patient refused the transfusions both because she was a Jehovah's Witness and because she feared that a transfusion would transmit HIV or other infectious organisms. In Stamford Hospital v. Vega, 674 A.2d 821, 824-825 (Conn. 1996), the court also recognized a patient's right to refuse blood transfusions after she had lost a good deal of blood during the vaginal delivery of her child. The patient refused the transfusions because she was a Jehovah's Witness.[3] It is important to recognize that, while a blood transfusion does not have the intrusiveness of a ventilator, Jehovah's Witnesses are expressing a central tenet of their religion when they refuse transfusions. See Dena S. Davis, Does "No" Mean "Yes"? The Continuing Problem of Jehovah's Witnesses and Refusal of Blood Products, 19(3) Second Opinion 34 (1994); Richard Singelenberg, The Blood Transfusion Taboo of Jehovah's Witnesses: Origin, Development and Function of a Controversial Doctrine, 31 Soc. Sci. Med. 515 (1990).

1. The *Bergstedt* court also recognized a fifth state interest beyond the four generally relied on by courts. According to the court, there is an interest "in encouraging the charitable and humane care of afflicted persons." 801 P.2d at 628. Patients contemplating refusal of life-sustaining treatment therefore must be fully informed of the care alternatives that would be available to them if they remained alive. Id.

2. See, e.g., Application of President & Directors of Georgetown College, Inc., 331 F.2d 1000 (D.C. Cir.), *cert. denied*, 377 U.S. 968 (1964) (25-year-old required to accept a blood transfusion to treat severe blood loss from a perforated ulcer); John F. Kennedy Memorial Hospital v. Heston, 279 A.2d 670 (N.J. 1971) (22-year-old required to accept a blood transfusion during surgery that was performed because her spleen was ruptured in an automobile accident).

3. In both *Fasmire* and *Stamford Hospital*, the patient had received transfusions by virtue of a lower court's order before winning on appeal.

Prisoner cases are an area in which courts will require continuation of treatment.[4] In In re Caulk, 480 A.2d 93 (N.H. 1984), a 36-year-old prisoner in good health stopped eating with the intent to end his life because he was serving a 15- to 30-year sentence and was facing additional charges that could ultimately add up to a sentence of life without parole. The court permitted the state to forcibly feed Mr. Caulk, citing concerns about institutional order and the fact that Mr. Caulk was not suffering from any illness. The court also observed that Mr. Caulk's attempt at starvation was frustrating the criminal justice system. Because of his condition, two states that had pending indictments against Mr. Caulk were forced to postpone his trials. As a result, the two states could not meet their duty "to bring to finality pending investigations in such a way that the public knows that the criminal justice system has successfully responded to accusations of criminal behavior." 480 A.2d at 96. See also Polk County Sheriff v. Iowa District Court, 594 N.W.2d 421 (Iowa 1999) (rejecting a pretrial detainee's request to discontinue chronic dialysis); Laurie v. Senecal, 666 A.2d 806 (R.I. 1995) (rejecting healthy prisoner's request to die by refusing food and water); McNabb v. Department of Corrections, 180 P.3d 1257 (Wash. 2008) (rejecting a healthy prisoner's refusal of nutrition and hydration). Note that courts have upheld the right of prisoners to refuse life-sustaining treatment when they are doing so for reasons similar to nonincarcerated persons. Thor v. Superior Court, 855 P.2d 375 (Cal. 1993) (permitting prisoner who was quadriplegic from a neck fracture to refuse a feeding tube); Stouffer v. Reid, 993 A.2d 104 (Md. 2010) (permitting inmate with end-stage renal disease to refuse kidney dialysis); Commonwealth Department of Corrections v. Lindsey, 984 A.2d 573 (Pa. Commw. Ct. 2009) (permitting inmate with "severe kidney ailment" and "gastrointestinal bleeding problem" to refuse blood transfusions).

3. *Burdensome Treatment vs. Burdensome Life.* The nearly unlimited recognition of a right to refuse life-sustaining treatment means that courts have not distinguished between patients who refuse treatment because the treatment itself is not desired and patients who refuse treatment because their life with treatment has become undesirable. The former category includes Jehovah's Witnesses who reject a blood transfusion or a patient with end-stage cancer who rejects an experimental drug with severe side effects. The latter category includes patients like Elizabeth Bouvia and Kenneth Bergstedt. Does it make sense to distinguish between patients who reject treatment and patients who reject life? When a person with kidney failure who is dependent on dialysis becomes tired of the dependency and decides to stop receiving dialysis treatments, is the person rejecting the treatment or life? Even if we could distinguish between rejecting treatment and rejecting life, why does that distinction matter if the right to refuse treatment is based on principles of self-determination and concerns about avoiding suffering?

4. *Practice vs. the Law.* Despite the fairly clear message from appellate courts that competent patients have the right to refuse life-sustaining treatment, irrespective of the prognosis or the type of treatment, actual practices by physicians and lower court judges retain some of the *Quinlan* kind of balancing. For example, as

---

4. As discussed in Chapters 5 and 6, courts have also been much more willing to impose treatment when a third party's interest is at stake, for example, when a woman is pregnant or there is a threat to public health.

discussed in more detail in the note on innocent third parties, pages 295-296, some trial court judges will order blood transfusions for Jehovah's Witnesses despite the religiously based refusal of the patient, only to have the decision reversed on appeal after it is impossible to undo the transfusion. See, e.g., In re Duran, 769 A.2d 497 (Pa. Super. Ct. 2001) (patient received blood transfusion following liver transplant surgery despite written statement before surgery refusing any transfusions). Similarly, in a leading medical ethics guide for practicing physicians, the authors present the following case and analysis:

> Mr. Cure, a 24-year-old graduate student, has been brought to the emergency room (ER) by a friend. Previously in good health, he is complaining of a severe headache and a stiff neck. . . . [Based on physical examination and laboratory tests, a] diagnosis of bacterial meningitis is made. . . .
>
> [Mr. Cure] is informed that he needs immediate hospitalization and administration of antibiotics. Although drowsy, he appears to understand the physician's explanation. He refuses treatment and says he wants to go home. The physician explains the extreme dangers of going untreated and the minimal risks of treatment. [Without treatment, there is a likelihood of death of 60 to 80 percent, with survivors generally having major and permanent neurologic damage. With treatment, there is a greater than 90 percent chance of full recovery.] The young man persists in his refusal. . . .
>
> This patient should be treated despite his refusal. His refusal is enigmatic, insofar as he offers no reason for refusing. Certainly, the physician should suspect an altered mental status due to high fever and brain infection, but this patient . . . communicates articulately, and appears to understand the consequences of his refusal. There is no time for a thorough psychiatric examination. Given the enigmatic nature of his refusal and the urgent, serious need for treatment, the patient should be treated with antibiotics, even against his will. Should there be time, legal authorization should be sought. . . .
>
> . . . It is difficult to believe that this young man wishes to die or become permanently damaged neurologically.

Albert R. Jonsen et al., Clinical Ethics: A Practical Approach to Ethical Decisions in Clinical Medicine 15, 69, 70 (7th ed. 2010).

How should we view the willingness of physicians and courts to override treatment refusals by persons who easily could be restored to good health? Is this a reasonable safeguard against taking too far the important ethical and legal principle of patient autonomy? Or should we worry about physicians and courts going too far the other way in frustrating patient autonomy? In explaining their willingness to override Mr. Cure's refusal of treatment, Jonsen et al. give a reason that is perfectly consistent with respect for patient autonomy. How do they justify their action in terms of individual self-determination? For a similar argument, see Richard A. Epstein, Moral Peril: Our Inalienable Right to Health Care? 300-305 (1997).

Notes: The State's Interest in Preventing Suicide

While we will save most of our analysis of the relationship between withdrawal of life-sustaining treatment and suicide for the section on physician aid in dying, at pages 348-377, it is worth thinking about the distinction now:

1. *The State's Interest in Preventing Suicide.* In discussing the state's interest in preventing suicide, the courts almost summarily dismiss this objection to the withdrawal of life-sustaining treatment. In the *Saikewicz* case, the Massachusetts Supreme Court relegated the concern about suicide to a footnote, began its analysis by stating that "[t]he interest in protecting against suicide seems to require little if any discussion," and completed its analysis by stating that "[t]here is no connection between the conduct here in issue and any state concern to prevent suicide." Superintendent of Belchertown State School v. Saikewicz, 370 N.E.2d 417, 426 n.11 (Mass. 1977). Yet, under a dictionary definition of suicide, would it not be suicide if a patient on a ventilator flipped a switch that turned off the ventilator? (According to Merriam-Webster's Collegiate Dictionary 1177 (11th ed. 2003), suicide is "the act or an instance of taking one's own life voluntarily and intentionally esp. by a person of years of discretion and of sound mind.")

The *Saikewicz* court and the *Conroy* court emphasized that, with withdrawal, the cause of death is natural and the patient has no intent to die. In addition, the *Saikewicz* court observed that "the underlying state interest in this area lies in the prevention of irrational self-destruction." Note that this "irrational self-destruction" argument is a different kind of argument than the "natural cause" and "intent" arguments. Which of these three arguments do you find persuasive? Do you see how the three arguments might play out differently on the question of permitting physician aid in dying? (As discussed in the section on physician aid in dying, this text prefers that term to physician-assisted suicide.)

2. *Distinguishing Treatment Withdrawal from Aid in Dying.* In contrast to the usual judicial analysis, Justice Scalia in his dissent in *Cruzan* saw no distinction between the refusal of life-sustaining treatment and suicide. Indeed, in his view, refusing life-sustaining treatment is a form of suicide. As his analysis suggests, the categories of treatment refusal and suicide are not self-defining but are labels we apply once we have decided whether a particular life-ending act should be permitted. If we do not approve of a life-ending act, we characterize it as suicide or euthanasia; if we approve of a life-ending act, we find some other term to describe it, for example, the withdrawal of life-sustaining treatment. Indeed, at one time, when its propriety was still in question, the withdrawal of life-sustaining treatment was commonly characterized as "passive euthanasia." John A. Robertson, Involuntary Euthanasia of Defective Newborns, 27 Stan. L. Rev. 213, 214-215 & n.16 (1975). Can we find any content to the concept of suicide, or is it simply a way to express a moral conclusion that we have reached on other grounds? One way to answer this question would be to consider two other questions: Do you think that Kenneth Bergstedt was suicidal when he sought discontinuation of his ventilator? Why wouldn't a physician who discontinued Mr. Bergstedt's ventilator be guilty of active euthanasia?

Notes: The Ethical Integrity of the Medical Profession

1. *Professional Objection to Withdrawal.* The state's interest in preserving the ethical integrity of the medical profession has rarely been invoked to prevent the withdrawal of life-sustaining treatment. Courts either conclude that withdrawing treatment is consistent with the ethics of the medical profession (as in *Quinlan* and

Conroy) and/or indicate that the weight of the interest in professional integrity is not sufficient to override the individual interest in refusing life-sustaining treatment (as in *Conroy*).

Still, there may be cases in which the physician has a personal, moral objection to discontinuing life-sustaining treatment. If the patient's right to refuse treatment rests on a principle of individual autonomy, how do we resolve the conflict when the physician invokes the same principle of individual autonomy to resist participation in the patient's death? We might say that the physician's rights are not violated since the physician need only refrain from acting, but is that an answer to the physician who is morally opposed to helping cause a patient's death? There also may be situations in which the hospital or nursing home has an institutional policy against withdrawing life-sustaining treatment. How should these cases be handled?

Courts have responded to this problem in different ways. In Brophy v. New England Sinai Hospital, 497 N.E.2d 626, 639 (Mass. 1986), the court wrote:

> There is nothing in *Saikewicz* and its progeny which would justify compelling medical professionals, in a case such as this, to take active measures which are contrary to their view of their ethical duty toward their patients. There is substantial disagreement in the medical community over the appropriate medical action. It would be particularly inappropriate to force the hospital, which is willing to assist in a transfer of the patient, to take affirmative steps to end the provision of nutrition and hydration to him. A patient's right to refuse medical treatment does not warrant such an unnecessary intrusion upon the hospital's ethical integrity in this case.

Similarly, in Gray v. Romeo, 697 F. Supp. 580 (D.R.I. 1988), the court allowed the hospital to arrange for a transfer of the patient but held that the hospital must accede to the patient's refusal of artificial nutrition and hydration if the patient could not be "promptly transferred to a health care facility that will respect her wishes." Id. at 591.

Two New Jersey courts have refused to permit a transfer of the patient even though a transfer might have been feasible. In both cases, there was no warning of the hospital's policy when the patient was admitted for care; the policy was not formalized until the request was made to stop treatment and the patient had been hospitalized for some time. According to the court in In re Jobes, 529 A.2d 434, 450 (N.J. 1987):

> Mrs. Jobes' family had no reason to believe they were surrendering the right to choose among medical alternatives when they placed her in the nursing home [in 1980]. The nursing home apparently did not inform Mrs. Jobes' family about its policy toward artificial feeding until May of 1985 when they requested that [her feeding tube] be withdrawn. In fact there is no indication that this policy has ever been formalized. Under these circumstances Mrs. Jobes and her family were entitled to rely on the nursing home's willingness to defer to their choice among courses of medical treatment.
>
> We do not decide the case in which a nursing home gave notice of its policy not to participate in the withdrawal or withholding of artificial feeding at the time of a patient's admission. Thus, we do not hold that such a policy is never enforceable. But we are confident in this case that it would be wrong to allow the nursing home to discharge Mrs. Jobes. . . . [Id. at 450.]

Accord In re Requena, 517 A.2d 886 (N.J. Super. Ct. Ch. Div.), aff'd, 517 A.2d 869 (N.J. Super. Ct. App. Div. 1986) (patient had been in the hospital for 17 months and was admitted before the hospital merged with a Catholic hospital).

This issue is also addressed in advance directive statutes. Typically, the statutes direct the physician to arrange for transfer of the patient's care to another physician, without speaking to situations in which a transfer cannot be arranged. Those statutes that do address that situation generally require the physician to comply with the patient's request or bring the case before a court. But see Ind. Code Ann. §16-36-4-13(f) ("If the attending physician, after reasonable investigation, finds no other physician willing to honor the patient's declaration, the attending physician may refuse to withhold or withdraw life prolonging procedures.").

For further discussion of this issue, see George Annas, When Suicide Prevention Becomes Brutality: The Case of Elizabeth Bouvia, 14(2) Hastings Center Rep. 20 (1984); John K. Davis, Conscientious Refusal and a Doctor's Right to Quit, 29 J. Med. Philos. 75 (2004); Anne M. Dellinger & Ann Morgan Vickery, When Staff Object to Participating in Care, 28 J. Health Hosp. Law 269 (1995); Brian C. Kalt, Death, Ethics, and the State, 23 Harv. J.L. & Pub. Pol'y 487 (2000); Note, Life-Sustaining Treatment Law, 47 B.C. L. Rev. 815 (2006); Nadia Sawicki, The Hollow Promise of Freedom of Conscience, 33 Cardozo L. Rev. 1389 (2012); Elizabeth Sepper, Taking Conscience Seriously, 98 Va. L. Rev. 1501 (2012).

2. *Legal Liability.* In addition to moral considerations, provider objection to treatment withdrawal may reflect legal concerns. Although the right to refuse life-sustaining treatment is now well established, in 1983, prosecutors brought criminal charges against two physicians for withdrawing life-sustaining treatment at the behest of the patient's family. Barber v. Superior Court, 195 Cal. Rptr. 478 (Ct. App. 1983). The patient, Clarence Herbert, had suffered a cardiac arrest after intestinal surgery, causing "severe brain damage" and leaving him "in a vegetative state, which was likely to be permanent." Three days later, the family requested that all life-sustaining "machines" be discontinued. The physicians immediately withdrew Mr. Herbert's ventilator, and, two days later, after further consultation with the family, they withdrew Mr. Herbert's feeding tube. After Mr. Herbert died, prosecutors brought murder charges against Mr. Herbert's surgeon and internist. The court recognized the authority of Mr. Herbert's family to refuse life-sustaining treatment on his behalf and therefore concluded that "the [physicians'] omission to continue treatment under the circumstances, though intentional and with knowledge that the patient would die, was not an unlawful failure to perform a legal duty." Id. at 493.

Although no physician has suffered civil or criminal liability for withdrawing life-sustaining treatment at the request of a patient or the patient's family, physicians may express concerns about the risks of legal liability when faced with a request to withdraw treatment. Mildred Z. Solomon et al., Decisions near the End of Life: Professional Views on Life-Sustaining Treatments, 83 Am. J. Public Health 14, 19 (1993). Part of this concern may reflect the fact that, in *Barber*, Mr. Herbert's physicians were in fact prosecuted, but consider whether physicians may rebuff a request to discontinue treatment by pointing to legal concerns as a camouflage, conscious or not, of their moral disagreement with the request. In other words, physicians who think it is morally wrong to discontinue treatment may find it easier—and more persuasive — to say that they cannot stop treatment rather than to acknowledge that they can, but do not want to do so.

Notes: The Protection of Innocent Third Parties

1. *Protecting the Interests of Third Parties.* Courts regularly cite the state's interest in protecting the interests of innocent third parties when a patient wants to refuse life-sustaining medical treatment, particularly when the patient has minor children who would arguably suffer from the loss of a parent. At one time, courts would invoke the interest in innocent third parties to impose treatment. For example, in Application of the President and Directors of Georgetown College, 331 F.2d 1000 (D.C. Cir. 1964), the court ordered blood transfusions for Mrs. Jesse E. Jones, a 25-year-old married woman who was the mother of a seven-month-old child. Mrs. Jones had "lost two thirds of her body's blood supply from a ruptured ulcer" and was refusing transfusion because of her religious beliefs as a Jehovah's Witness. Id. at 1006. The court justified its order on several grounds, including the fact that "Mrs. Jones was *in extremis* and hardly *compos mentis* at the time in question," the state had an interest in preventing the abandonment of her child, Mrs. Jones did not want to die even if she did not want a blood transfusion, and "a life hung in the balance." Id. at 1008-1009.

In more recent cases, courts have generally recognized a parent's right to refuse life-sustaining treatment even though the parent has young children. In In re Debreuil, 629 So. 2d 819 (Fla. 1993), Patricia Debreuil, an otherwise healthy woman, suffered life-threatening bleeding after delivering her fourth child by cesarean section. The trial court ordered transfusions, which were administered, but, on appeal, the Florida Supreme Court held that the trial court erred. According to the court, concerns about the children, who were newborn, 4, 6, and 12 years of age, did not justify the transfusions since the children could be cared for by their father. However, the court "decline[d] at this time to rule out the possibility that some case not yet before us may present a compelling interest to prevent abandonment." Id. at 827. In a similar case, Fosmire v. Nicoleau, 551 N.E.2d 77 (N.Y. 1990), the New York court of appeals also held that the parent had the right to refuse life-sustaining treatment. In that case, Denise Nicoleau had lost a substantial amount of blood after delivering a baby boy via cesarean section. Ms. Nicoleau was married and otherwise in good health. She refused transfusions because of both her religious beliefs as a Jehovah's Witness and her fear of contracting AIDS or other communicable diseases. After the hospital obtained a court order, Ms. Nicoleau received two blood transfusions. The court of appeals held that the trial court erred in ordering the transfusions. Moreover, the court suggested in its dicta that its holding would have been the same even if she had been the only parent available to care for her child: "The state does not prohibit parents from engaging in dangerous activities because there is a risk that their children will be left orphans." Id. at 84. See also Stamford Hospital v. Vega, 674 A.2d 821 (Conn. 1996) (Jehovah's Witness had the right to refuse a blood transfusion needed after she delivered a child although, again, she won on appeal after receiving blood transfusions ordered by the trial court). Still, courts have not yet faced the issue whether a parent would have to receive life-sustaining treatment if the parent's death would leave a minor child as an orphan.

How should courts respond to a single parent's refusal of life-sustaining treatment when the parent has young children? Would it depend on whether the treatment would restore the parent to good health or would only maintain the parent in a severely disabled condition? What if the parent has arranged for a grandparent, aunt, and/or uncle to take care of the children? Is the refusal of life-sustaining treatment by a single parent any different from single parents who engage in risky vocations or avocations? Should we prohibit single parents from being soldiers, police, firefighters, or coal miners? Should exercising your right to procreate require you to forfeit your right to refuse life-sustaining treatment?

2. *Law on the Books vs. Law in Practice.* While appellate courts in recent years have consistently upheld the right of healthy people to refuse blood transfusions, the courts typically do so only after the person has received the transfusion because of an order by a lower court. See Fosmire v. Nicoleau, 551 N.E.2d at 79; Stamford Hospital v. Vega, 674 A.2d at 826; In re Dubreuil, 629 So. 2d at 821. The *Dubreuil* case is particularly striking because the Florida Supreme Court had previously held that a young woman could refuse blood transfusions even though she had minor children. Wons v. Public Health Trust, 541 So. 2d 96 (Fla. 1989). The only apparent difference between the *Dubreuil* and *Wons* cases was that Ms. Dubreuil was estranged from her husband while Ms. Wons was apparently living amicably with her husband. *Dubreuil*, 629 So. 2d at 826. On the other hand, the Florida Supreme Court stated in *Wons* that "these cases demand individual attention. No blanket rule is feasible which could sufficiently cover all occasions in which this situation will arise." 541 So. 2d at 98.

What should we make of the fact that the appellate courts consistently recognize a right of healthy persons to refuse blood transfusions while some trial courts order the blood transfusions? If you were a hospital lawyer, and a physician in your hospital wanted to obtain a court order to transfuse a parent of young children against the parent's wishes, what action would you pursue?

2. The Patient Whose Competence Is Uncertain

In the vast majority of cases, it is clear whether the patient is competent. Most patients either clearly possess decisionmaking capacity or they clearly do not. In some cases, however, whether the patient can competently consent to or refuse treatment is not so easily decided. While patient competence has been a long-standing issue, physicians, lawyers, and other professionals have not yet developed a readily applied standard for assessing competence, perhaps because of its elusive nature. Several different tests have been used for competency: (1) whether the patient expresses a preference for or against treatment; (2) whether the patient's decision is a "reasonable" one; (3) whether the patient's decision is based on "rational" reasons; and (4) whether the patient has the ability to understand or has demonstrated actual understanding. Loren H. Roth et al., Tests of Competency to Consent to Treatment, 134 Am. J. Psychiatry 279 (1977). The latter two of the four tests have emerged as the predominant ones. For example, the New Jersey Supreme Court has written that "[a] competent patient has a clear understanding of the nature of his or her illness and prognosis, and of the risks and benefits of the proposed treatment, and has the capacity to reason and make judgments about that information." In re Farrell, 529

A.2d 404, 413 n.7 (N.J. 1987). Even so, it is not a simple matter to assess a person's capacity for reasoning and understanding nor is it clear what level of understanding a person must be able to exercise to be considered competent. Note also that the tests are not necessarily exclusive. Whether a person exhibits understanding will be judged in part on the rationality of the person's reasoning. For further discussion, see Jessica Wilen Berg et al., Constructing Competence: Formulating Standards of Legal Competence to Make Medical Decisions, 48 Rutgers L. Rev. 345 (1996); Marsha Garrison, The Empire of Illness: Competence and Coercion in Health-Care Decision Making, 49 Wm. & Mary L. Rev. 781 (2007); Daniel Marson & Kellie Ingram, Competency to Consent to Treatment: A Growing Field of Research, 2 J. Ethics Law Aging 59 (1996).

LANE v. CANDURA

376 N.E.2d 1232 (Mass. App. Ct. 1978)

PER CURIAM.

[Ms. Rosaria Candura was a 77-year-old woman with gangrene in her right foot and lower leg. Her physicians recommended amputation without delay, but Ms. Candura refused after originally agreeing to the surgery. She already had undergone two amputative operations on her right foot, losing a toe in one and part of her foot in the other. In explaining her reasons for refusing a third amputative surgery, she said] that she has been unhappy since the death of her husband [two years earlier]; that she does not wish to be a burden to her children; that she does not believe that the operation will cure her; that she does not wish to live as an invalid or in a nursing home; and that she does not fear death but welcomes it....

[The court further found that Ms. Candura] is discouraged by the failure of the earlier operations to arrest the advance of the gangrene. She tends to be stubborn and somewhat irrascible [sic].... [S]he expressed a desire to get well but indicated that she was resigned to death and was adamantly against the operation.... [S]he is lucid on some matters and confused on others. Her train of thought sometimes wanders. Her conception of time is distorted. She is hostile to certain doctors. She is on occasion defensive and sometimes combative in her responses to questioning. But she has exhibited a high degree of awareness and acuity.... [One psychiatrist testified that Ms. Candura lacked decisionmaking capacity, in part because she would not discuss her reasons for refusal with him and because he thought her gangrene might be compromising her thinking. Another psychiatrist, who was able to elicit Ms. Candura's reasons for refusing treatment, testified that she possessed decisionmaking capacity.]

[The court held that Ms. Candura was competent to refuse treatment, noting that her competence had not been questioned until she withdrew her original consent to the surgery; that she had a right to make her own decisions about medical treatment, even if the decisions seemed unwise; that, while she might have symptoms of senility, there was no evidence that her confusion or forgetfulness was interfering with her ability to decide about the surgery; and that her case did not involve] the uninformed decision of a person incapable of appreciating the nature and consequences of her act....

■ DEPARTMENT OF HUMAN SERVICES v. NORTHERN
563 S.W.2d 197 (Tenn. Ct. App. 1978)

TODD, Judge.

[Ms. Mary Northern was a 72-year-old woman with gangrene of both feet who refused her physicians' recommendation of amputative surgery of the feet to prevent her death. A physician reported that] he found the patient to be generally lucid and sane, . . . [but that] she is functioning on a psychotic level with respect to her gangrenous feet. She tends to believe that her feet are black because of soot or dirt. . . . There is an adamant belief that her feet will heal without surgery. . . . There is no desire to die, yet her judgment concerning recovery is markedly impaired. If she appreciated the seriousness of her condition, heard her physicians' opinions, and concluded against an operation, then I would believe she understood and could decide for herself. But my impression is that she does not appreciate the dangers to her life. . . .

[The court found Ms. Northern incompetent to decide about the surgery, basing its decision on her failure to appreciate the nature of her medical condition and her refusal to make a choice between living and keeping her feet. In the view of the court, Ms. Northern was resorting to the "device of denying" her medical condition to avoid having to choose between losing her life and losing her feet.] If, as repeatedly stated, this patient could and would give evidence of a comprehension of the facts of her condition and could and would express her unequivocal desire in the face of such comprehended facts, then her decision, however unreasonable to others, would be accepted and honored by the courts and her doctors. The difficulty is that she cannot or will not comprehend the facts. . . .

[Because of "complications rendering surgery more dangerous," the amputations were not performed. Approximately three months after the court's decision, Ms. Northern died from her gangrene.]

Notes: Assessing Competence

1. *Applying the Tests for Competence.* It makes good sense to consider a patient's degree of understanding and rationality of reasoning, but how should we respond to patients who do not want to explain their decision? What if the patient says, "I don't want the surgery, and it's none of your business why"? The court in *Northern* makes much of Ms. Northern's misunderstanding of what was going on with her feet, but what if she appreciated that her feet were gangrenous but misunderstood other issues? What if she had said that she understood that her feet were gangrenous but that they became that way because she had sinned and that the good Lord would heal them for her now that she was repenting? Would that constitute an incompetent refusal of surgery? For an interesting discussion of religious beliefs and decisionmaking capacity, see Adrienne M. Martin, Tales Publicly Allowed: Competence, Capacity, and Religious Beliefs, 37(1) Hastings Center Rep. 33 (2007) (arguing that religious beliefs that interfere with understanding may make the patient incapacitated but that respect for the patient's religious values may lead us to accept the patient's decision).

In a case similar to *Northern*, a woman refused further dialysis, and cited the burden of the treatment, as well as her belief that Jesus would heal her. Two psychiatrists testified that the woman was depressed and not making a competent decision; a third psychiatrist believed that the woman was making a competent and voluntary refusal of dialysis. The court ordered dialysis, observing that the woman "demonstrated a lack of understanding of the high risk of death without dialysis. She refused to acknowledge the risk inherent in her refusal of treatment and through her other medical choices had demonstrated an unequivocal desire to live." In re J.M., 3 A.3d 651 (N.J. Super. Ct. Ch. Div. 2010).

How accurate are physicians at detecting a patient's incapacity? In a review-of-the-literature study, researchers found that physicians "missed the diagnosis in 58% of patients who were judged incapable" in a formal, independent assessment. On the other hand, physicians generally were correct when they make a diagnosis of incapacity. The researchers also found that the best formal assessment tool for measuring capacity to decide is the Aid to Capacity Evaluation. Laura L. Sessums, Does This Patient Have Medical Decision-Making Capacity?, 306 JAMA 420 (2011).

2. *Adolescents*. Issues of competence also arise for adolescents. There are two separate questions that must be answered: (1) Do minors have capacity to decide for themselves? (2) If not, is the decision one that parents can make for them? In general, the answer to (1) is "no" and to (2) is "yes": Minors usually are held to lack decisionmaking capacity, and parents usually have authority to make decisions on their behalf. Both rules have important exceptions, however. The exceptions to the second rule are discussed below at pages 340-343, where we learn that courts often deny parents authority to refuse life-sustaining treatment for their children. These notes discuss exceptions to the first rule, that is, situations where minors may make important medical decisions for themselves.

While minors generally lack decisionmaking capacity, "mature minors" may be accorded decisionmaking authority if they can show decisionmaking capacity despite their age. For example, in a medical malpractice case, Caldwell v. Bechtol, 724 S.W.2d 739 (Tenn. 1987), the Tennessee Supreme Court considered whether a woman five months shy of her eighteenth birthday could give consent to treatment by an osteopathic physician for her lower back pain. The court stated:

> Several relevant principles from these cases may be stated for this case. Whether a minor has the capacity to consent to medical treatment depends upon the age, ability, experience, education, training, and degree of maturity or judgment obtained by the minor, as well as upon the conduct and demeanor of the minor at the time of the incident involved. Moreover, the totality of the circumstances, the nature of the treatment and its risks or probable consequences, and the minor's ability to appreciate the risks and consequences are to be considered. Guided by the presumptions in the Rule of Sevens, these are questions of fact for the jury to decide. [Id. at 748.]

The Rule of Sevens holds that "under the age of seven, no capacity; between seven and fourteen, a rebuttable presumption of no capacity; between fourteen and twenty-one, a rebuttable presumption of capacity." Id. at 745.

The Supreme Court of Appeals of West Virginia adopted a test very similar to that of the *Caldwell* court in the context of a life-sustaining treatment decision.

In Belcher v. Charleston Area Medical Center, 422 S.E.2d 827 (W. Va. 1992), Larry Belcher, a minor of 17 years and 8 months, suffered from muscular dystrophy, and it appeared that he would become ventilator dependent imminently. His physician and parents decided that Mr. Belcher would not be ventilated or resuscitated in the event of a respiratory arrest, and Mr. Belcher died the following day from a respiratory arrest. An issue before the court was whether his physician should have consulted Mr. Belcher before a decision was made about ventilation and resuscitation. The court wrote:

> Whether the child has the capacity to consent depends upon the age, ability, experience, education, training, and degree of maturity or judgment obtained by the child, as well as upon the conduct and demeanor of the child at the time of the procedure or treatment. The factual determination would also involve whether the minor has the capacity to appreciate the nature, risks, and consequences of the medical procedure to be performed, or the treatment to be administered or withheld. Where there is a conflict between the intentions of one or both parents and the minor, the physician's good faith assessment of the minor's maturity level would immunize him or her from liability for the failure to obtain parental consent. [Id. At 838.]

In In re Swan, 569 A.2d 1202 (Me. 1990), the Maine Supreme Court relied on the statements of a minor, Chad Swan, to permit the withholding of a feeding tube. Mr. Swan was 18 years old at the time of the decision but had become permanently unconscious from an automobile accident at age 17. In permitting the withholding, the court relied on statements that Mr. Swan had made about his wishes regarding life-sustaining treatment. At age 16 he had spoken to his mother about a highly publicized local case in which the patient had also become permanently unconscious from a motor vehicle accident and said, "If I can't be myself . . . no way . . . let me go to sleep." In addition, eight days before his accident, after visiting a comatose friend in the hospital, Mr. Swan told his brother, "I don't ever want to get like that. . . . I would want somebody to let me leave—to go in peace." Id. at 1205. According to the court,

> The fact that Chad made these declarations as to medical treatment before he reached the age of eighteen is at most a factor to be considered by the fact finder in assessing the seriousness and deliberativeness with which his declarations were made. . . . Capacity exists when the minor has the ability of the average person to understand and weigh the risks and benefits. [Id.]

Another leading case discussing the mature minor doctrine in the context of life-sustaining treatment is In re E.G., 549 N.E.2d 322 (Ill. 1989). In that case, a 17-year-old woman with an acute leukemia consented to treatment for her leukemia except for blood transfusions. Her refusal was based on her religious beliefs as a Jehovah's Witness. Her physician testified that, without blood transfusions, E.G. would likely die within a month. With blood transfusions, her chemotherapy had an 80 percent chance of achieving a remission of her leukemia but only a 20 to 25 percent chance of giving E.G. a long-term survival. After the trial court appointed one of the hospital's counsel as E.G.'s temporary guardian, blood transfusions were administered. On appeal, the Illinois Supreme Court held that mature minors enjoy a right to refuse life-sustaining medical treatment. In deciding when that right can be exercised, the court first concluded that, "[w]hen a minor's health and life are at stake," proof of a minor's maturity must be made "by clear and convincing evidence." Id. at 327. In addition, the state's interest in protecting the minor's health "will vary depending upon the nature of the medical treatment involved. Where the health care issues are potentially life threatening, the state's *parens patriae* interest is greater than if the health care matter is less consequential." Id. Minors should be considered mature enough to make their own life-sustaining treatment decisions "[i]f the evidence is clear and convincing that the minor is mature enough to appreciate the consequences of her actions, and . . . the minor is mature enough to exercise the judgment of an adult." Invoking the state's interest in protecting the interests of third parties, the court also wrote that "[i]f a parent or guardian opposes an unemancipated mature minor's refusal to consent to treatment for a life-threatening health problem, this opposition would weigh heavily against the minor's right to refuse." Id. at 328. Since E.G.'s mother agreed with her decision, the court did not indicate how the balance between the minor's right to decide and the state's interest in third parties would play out. In addition, since E.G. had become an adult by the time the decision was issued, the court did not remand the case for determination of her maturity.

Do you agree with the *E.G.* court that the minor's right should depend on whether the "health care issues are potentially life-threatening"? Note that this standard would result in mature minors being governed by something akin to the *Quinlan* substantive standard ("the state's interest *contra* weakens and the individual's right to privacy grows as the degree of bodily invasion increases and the prognosis dims," *Quinlan*, 355 A.2d at 664) and adults by the *Conroy* substantive standard (a competent patient's right to refuse life-sustaining treatment "would not be affected by her medical condition or prognosis," *Conroy*, 486 A.2d at 1226).

Which court do you think has the better approach on the issue of parental disagreement with the child, *E.G.* or *Belcher*?

Not all states recognize a mature minor doctrine. For example, a federal district court in Georgia concluded that Georgia state law grants decisionmaking capacity only in certain statutorily specified situations (e.g., minors who are married, pregnant, or have children) but does not include a mature minor doctrine. Novak v. Cobb County-Kennestone Hospital Authority, 849 F. Supp. 1559, 1575-1576 (N.D. Ga. 1994). Other states have not decided one way or another whether maturity serves as the basis for decisionmaking capacity for a minor. In re Conner, 140 P.3d 1167 (Or. Ct. App. 2006).

For further discussion of these issues, see Rhonda Gay Hartman, Adolescent Decisional Autonomy for Medical Care: Physician Perceptions and Practices, 8 U. Chi. L. Sch. Roundtable 87 (2001); Kimberly M. Mutcherson, Whose Body Is It Anyway? An Updated Model of Healthcare Decision-Making Rights for Adolescents, 14 Cornell J.L. & Pub. Pol'y 251 (2005); Michelle Oberman, Minor Rights and Wrongs, 24 J.L. Med. & Ethics 127 (1996); Jessica A. Penkower, Comment, The Potential Right of Chronically Ill Adolescents to Refuse Life-Saving Medical Treatment—Fatal Misuse of the Mature Minor Doctrine, 45 DePaul L. Rev. 1165 (1996); Jennifer L. Rosato, Let's Get Real: Quilting a Principled Approach to Adolescent Empowerment in Health Care Decision-Making, 51 DePaul L. Rev. 769 (2002); Elizabeth S. Scott, Judgment and Reasoning in Adolescent Decisionmaking, 37 Vill. L. Rev. 1607

(1992); Symposium, Roundtable on Adolescent Decision Making, 15 J. Health Care L. & Pol'y 1-172 (2012); 93 A.L.R.3d 67 (1979).

   3. *Reliability of Patient Decisions.* While a patient may be competent to decide, there still is the question whether the patient has in fact reached a firm and settled decision. We might expect patients to express a good deal of ambivalence when making life-sustaining treatment decisions. When faced with a patient who has come to a decision with some difficulty and gone back and forth on the matter, should we require some kind of waiting period to ensure that the decision really is a reliable one? As discussed in the section on physician aid in dying at page 360, when Oregon adopted its physician aid in dying law, it included a requirement that patients wait at least 15 days from the time they request physician assistance until they can obtain a prescription for a lethal dose of a drug. Should there be a similar waiting period for refusals of life-sustaining treatment? Recall that Kenneth Bergstedt sought and received permission to disconnect his ventilator because he feared what his life would be like after his father died. In that case, Mr. Bergstedt died one week before his father died and one month before the court issued its ruling, apparently because his father disconnected the ventilator. If Mr. Bergstedt had been alive when the court decided the case, should the court have required that Mr. Bergstedt see what his life was like after his father died before deciding whether to refuse the ventilator? How long a trial of living without his father would be sufficient?

   There are studies that have considered whether patients' treatment preferences are stable over time. In these studies, researchers questioned individuals in three categories: people who were healthy; people who had mild health problems; and people who had serious illnesses. The individuals gave their treatment preferences at the outset of the studies, six months later, and one year later. The studies show some differences, but for most people, treatment preferences were stable over the course of a year. Linda L. Emanuel et al., Advance Directives: Stability of Patients' Treatment Choices, 154 Arch. Intern. Med. 209 (1994); Terri R. Fried et al., Inconsistency over Time in the Preferences of Older Persons with Advanced Illness for Life-Sustaining Treatment, 55 J. Am. Geriatrics Soc'y 1014 (2007); Lawrence J. Schneiderman et al., Relationship of General Advance Directive Instructions to Specific Life-Sustaining Treatment Preferences in Patients with Serious Illness, 152 Arch. Intern. Med. 2114 (1992). See also Peter H. Ditto et al., Stability of Older Adults' Preferences for Life-Sustaining Medical Treatment, 22 Health Psychol. 605 (2003) (finding moderate stability in treatment preferences over two-year time period). Changes in health status increase the likelihood that treatment preferences will change, and it appears that patients become more accepting of treatments that provide lower levels of benefit or impose greater levels of discomfort as health status worsens. Fried, supra, at 1010-1011; Terri R. Fried et al., Prospective Study of Health Status Preferences and Changes in Preferences over Time in Older Adults, 166 Arch. Intern. Med. 890 (2006). There also is stability over time in terms of how much patients want their treatment preferences to control once they become unable to decide for themselves and how much they want their medical decisions to be based on what their loved ones or physicians think is in their best interests. Daniel P. Sulmasy et al., How Would Terminally Ill Patients Have Others Make Decisions for Them in the Event of Decisional Incapacity? A Longitudinal Study, 55 J. Am. Geriatrics Soc'y 1981 (2007).

3. *The Incompetent Patient*

When a patient is incompetent, as is common when decisions about life-sustaining treatment are made, a few questions arise: Does the right to refuse life-sustaining treatment survive incompetence? If it does, is the right the same? How is the right invoked on behalf of the patient? You should pay particular attention to the procedural safeguards that the courts have adopted to govern life-sustaining treatment decisions for incompetent patients.

We will begin with two cases from the New Jersey Supreme Court. By way of background, the New Jersey Supreme Court has also adopted procedural safeguards for withdrawal decisions involving competent patients. It is useful to consider how these safeguards change when we move from the competent to the incompetent patient. New Jersey's safeguards for competent patients were developed in In re Farrell, 529 A.2d 404 (N.J. 1987). That case involved a woman, Kathleen Farrell, who became ventilator dependent from amyotrophic lateral sclerosis (ALS, or Lou Gehrig's disease). ALS is a disorder of the nervous system that results in degeneration of the nerves controlling voluntary muscle movements. The disease, whose cause is unknown, gradually leaves people unable to move their muscles. Ultimately, this means that they cannot move their arms or legs, swallow, speak intelligibly, or breathe. At the time of Ms. Farrell's diagnosis, a victim's life expectancy even with life-sustaining treatment was usually one to three years. For "competent patients who are living at home" and "who request the discontinuance of life-sustaining medical treatment," the *Farrell* court adopted the following procedural safeguards:

> First, it must be determined that the patient is competent and properly informed about his or her prognosis, the alternative treatments available, and the risk involved in the withdrawal of the life-sustaining treatment. Then it must be determined that the patient made his or her choice voluntarily and without coercion. . . . These issues are more easily resolved when the patient is in a hospital, nursing home, or other institution, because in those settings the patient is observed by more people. To protect the patient who is at home, we require that two non-attending physicians examine the patient to confirm that he or she is competent and is fully informed about his or her prognosis, the medical alternatives available, the risks involved, and the likely outcome if medical treatment is disconnected.[8] . . . The two independent confirmations of competency that we require should satisfy any questions that might later arise about the propriety of the withholding or withdrawal of treatment. Additionally, this procedural requirement should serve to forestall hasty medical decisions made while a patient is in an emotionally disturbed state because of a sudden illness or major catastrophe. [529 A.2d at 413-415.]

The *Farrell* court also held that there is no need to seek court approval before treatment is withdrawn.

---

8. The procedure we hereby establish for determining the competency of a patient at home who has decided to forgo life-sustaining treatment is likewise applicable to patients in hospitals and nursing homes.

■ **IN RE CONROY**
486 A.2d 1209 (N.J. 1985)

SCHREIBER, Justice.

Plaintiff, Thomas C. Whittemore, nephew and guardian of Claire Conroy, an incompetent, sought permission to remove a nasogastric feeding tube, the primary conduit for nutrients, from his ward, an eighty-four-year-old bedridden woman with serious and irreversible physical and mental impairments who resided in a nursing home. [Additional medical facts for this case are presented in the case excerpt at pages 275-276 in the section on the competent patient. As mentioned there, Ms. Conroy died while her case was before the intermediate court of appeals, but the New Jersey Supreme Court still heard the case as one involving a matter "of substantial importance and . . . capable of repetition but evad[ing] review."]

. . . Ms. Conroy had lived a rather cloistered life. She had been employed by a cosmetics company from her teens until her retirement at age 62 or 63. She had lived in the same home from her childhood until she was placed in the nursing home, had never married, and had very few friends. She had been very close to her three sisters, all of whom had died. . . .

Mr. Whittemore testified that Ms. Conroy feared and avoided doctors and that, to the best of his knowledge, she had never visited a doctor until she became incompetent in 1979. He said that on the couple of occasions that Ms. Conroy had pneumonia, "[y]ou couldn't bring a doctor in," and his wife, a registered nurse, would "try to get her through whatever she had." He added that once, when his wife took Ms. Conroy to the hospital emergency room, "as foggy as she was she snapped out of it, she would not sign herself in and she would have signed herself out immediately." According to the nephew, "[a]ll [Ms. Conroy and her sisters] wanted was to . . . have their bills paid and die in their own house." He also stated that he had refused to consent to the amputation of her gangrenous leg in 1982 and that he now sought removal of the nasogastric tube because, in his opinion, she would have refused the amputation and "would not have allowed [the nasogastric tube] to be inserted in the first place."

Ms. Conroy was a Roman Catholic. The Rev. Joseph Kukura, a Roman Catholic priest and an associate professor of Christian Ethics at the Immaculate Conception Seminary in Mahwah, New Jersey, testified that acceptable church teaching could be found in a document entitled "Declaration of Euthanasia" published by the Vatican Congregation for the Doctrine of the Faith, dated June 26, 1980. The test that this document espoused required a weighing of the burdens and the benefits to the patient of remaining alive with the aid of extraordinary life-sustaining medical treatment. Father Kukura said that life-sustaining procedures could be withdrawn if they were extraordinary, which he defined to embrace "all procedures, operations or other interventions which are excessively expensive, burdensome or inconvenient or which offer no hope of benefit to a patient." Here, he said, the hope of recovery and of returning to cognitive life, even with the nasogastric feeding, was not a reasonable possibility. The means of care were not adding to the value of her life, which was outweighed by the burdens of that life. He therefore considered the use of the nasogastric tube extraordinary. It was his judgment that removal of the tube would be ethical and moral, even though the ensuing period until her death would be painful. . . .

II

This case requires us to determine the circumstances under which life-sustaining treatment may be withheld or withdrawn from an elderly nursing-home resident who is suffering from serious and permanent mental and physical impairments, who will probably die within approximately one year even with the treatment, and who, though formerly competent, is now incompetent to make decisions about her life-sustaining treatment and is unlikely to regain such competence. Subsumed within this question are two corollary issues: what substantive guidelines are appropriate for making these treatment decisions for incompetent patients, and what procedures should be followed in making them. . . .

The *Quinlan* decision dealt with a special category of patients: those in a chronic, persistent vegetative or comatose state. In a footnote, the opinion left open the question whether the principles it enunciated might be applicable to incompetent patients in "other types of terminal medical situations . . . , not necessarily involving the hopeless loss of cognitive or sapient life." 355 A.2d at 671 n.10. We now are faced with one such situation: that of elderly, formerly competent nursing-home residents who, unlike Karen Quinlan, are awake and conscious and can interact with their environment to a limited extent, but whose mental and physical functioning is severely and permanently impaired and whose life expectancy, even with the treatment, is relatively short. The capacities of such people, while significantly diminished, are not as limited as those of irreversibly comatose persons, and their deaths, while no longer distant, may not be imminent. Large numbers of aged, chronically ill, institutionalized persons fall within this general category.

Such people . . . are unable to speak for themselves on life-and-death issues concerning their medical care. This does not mean, however, that they lack a right to self-determination. The right of an adult who, like Claire Conroy, was once competent, to determine the course of her medical treatment remains intact even when she is no longer able to assert that right or to appreciate its effectuation. As one commentator has noted:

> Even if the patient becomes too insensate to appreciate the honoring of his or her choice, self-determination is important. After all, law respects testamentary dispositions even if the testator never views his gift being bestowed. [Cantor, supra, 30 Rutgers L. Rev. at 259.]
> Any other view would permit obliteration of an incompetent's panoply of rights merely because the patient could no longer sense the violation of those rights. [Id. at 252.]

Since the condition of an incompetent patient makes it impossible to ascertain definitively his present desires, a third party acting on the patient's behalf often cannot say with confidence that his treatment decision for the patient will further rather than frustrate the patient's right to control his own body. Nevertheless, the goal of decisionmaking for incompetent patients should be to determine and effectuate, insofar as possible, the decision that the patient would have made if competent. Ideally, both aspects of the patient's right to bodily integrity—the right to consent to medical intervention and the right to refuse it—should be respected.

In light of these rights and concerns, we hold that life-sustaining treatment may be withheld or withdrawn from an incompetent patient when it is clear that the particular patient would have refused the treatment under the circumstances involved. The standard we are enunciating is a subjective one, consistent with the notion that the right that we are seeking to effectuate is a very personal right to control one's own life. The question is not what a reasonable or average person would have chosen to do under the circumstances but what the particular patient would have done if able to choose for himself.

The patient may have expressed, in one or more ways, an intent not to have life-sustaining medical intervention. Such an intent might be embodied in a written document, or "living will," stating the person's desire not to have certain types of life-sustaining treatment administered under certain circumstances. It might also be evidenced in an oral directive that the patient gave to a family member, friend, or health care provider. It might consist of a durable power of attorney or appointment of a proxy authorizing a particular person to make the decisions on the patient's behalf if he is no longer capable of making them for himself. It might take the form of reactions that the patient voiced regarding medical treatment administered to others. It might also be deduced from a person's religious beliefs and the tenets of that religion, or from the patient's consistent pattern of conduct with respect to prior decisions about his own medical care. Of course, dealing with the matter in advance in some sort of thoughtful and explicit way is best for all concerned.

Any of the above types of evidence, and any other information bearing on the person's intent, may be appropriate aids in determining what course of treatment the patient would have wished to pursue. . . .

Although all evidence tending to demonstrate a person's intent with respect to medical treatment should properly be considered by surrogate decisionmakers, . . . the probative value of such evidence may vary depending on the remoteness, consistency, and thoughtfulness of the prior statements or actions and the maturity of the person at the time of the statements or acts. Thus, for example, an offhand remark about not wanting to live under certain circumstances made by a person when young and in the peak of health would not in itself constitute clear proof 20 years later that he would want life-sustaining treatment withheld under those circumstances. In contrast, a carefully considered position, especially if written, that a person had maintained over a number of years or that he had acted upon in comparable circumstances might be clear evidence of his intent.

Another factor that would affect the probative value of a person's prior statements of intent would be their specificity. Of course, no one can predict with accuracy the precise circumstances with which he ultimately might be faced. Nevertheless, any details about the level of impaired functioning and the forms of medical treatment that one would find tolerable should be incorporated into advance directives to enhance their later usefulness as evidence.

Medical evidence bearing on the patient's condition, treatment, and prognosis, like evidence of the patient's wishes, is an essential prerequisite to decisionmaking under the subjective test. . . . [S]ince the goal is to effectuate the patient's right of informed consent, the surrogate decisionmaker must have at least as much medical information upon which to base his decision about what the patient would have chosen as one would expect a competent patient to have before consenting to or rejecting treatment. . . . Particular care should be taken not to base a decision on a premature diagnosis or prognosis.

We recognize that for some incompetent patients it might be impossible to be clearly satisfied as to the patient's intent either to accept or reject the life-sustaining treatment. Many people may have spoken of their desires in general or casual terms, or, indeed, never considered or resolved the issue at all. In such cases, a surrogate decisionmaker cannot presume that treatment decisions made by a third party on the patient's behalf will further the patient's right to self-determination, since effectuating another person's right to self-determination presupposes that the substitute decisionmaker knows what the person would have wanted. Thus, in the absence of adequate proof of the patient's wishes, it is naive to pretend that the right to self-determination serves as the basis for substituted decisionmaking.

We hesitate, however, to foreclose the possibility of humane actions, which may involve termination of life-sustaining treatment, for persons who never clearly expressed their desires about life-sustaining treatment but who are now suffering a prolonged and painful death. An incompetent, like a minor child, is a ward of the state, and the state's *parens patriae* power supports the authority of its courts to allow decisions to be made for an incompetent that serve the incompetent's best interests, even if the person's wishes cannot be clearly established. . . . We therefore hold that life-sustaining treatment may also be withheld or withdrawn from a patient in Claire Conroy's situation if either of two "best interests" tests—a limited-objective or a pure-objective test—is satisfied.

Under the limited-objective test, life-sustaining treatment may be withheld or withdrawn from a patient in Claire Conroy's situation when there is some trustworthy evidence that the patient would have refused the treatment, and the decisionmaker is satisfied that it is clear that the burdens of the patient's continued life with the treatment outweigh the benefits of that life for him. By this we mean that the patient is suffering, and will continue to suffer throughout the expected duration of his life, unavoidable pain, and that the net burdens of his prolonged life (the pain and suffering of his life with the treatment less the amount and duration of pain that the patient would likely experience if the treatment were withdrawn) markedly outweigh any physical pleasure, emotional enjoyment, or intellectual satisfaction that the patient may still be able to derive from life. . . .

In the absence of trustworthy evidence, or indeed any evidence at all, that the patient would have declined the treatment, life-sustaining treatment may still be withheld or withdrawn from a formerly competent person like Claire Conroy if a third, pure-objective test is satisfied. Under that test, as under the limited-objective test, the net burdens of the patient's life with the treatment should clearly and markedly outweigh the benefits that the patient derives from life. Further, the recurring, unavoidable and severe pain of the patient's life with the treatment should be such that the effect of administering life-sustaining treatment would be inhumane. Subjective evidence that the patient would not have wanted the treatment is not necessary under this pure-objective standard. Nevertheless, even in the context of severe pain, life-sustaining treatment should not be withdrawn from an incompetent patient who had previously expressed a wish to be kept alive in spite of any pain that he might experience. . . .

We are aware that it will frequently be difficult to conclude that the evidence is sufficient to justify termination of treatment under either of the "best interests" tests that we have described. Often, it is unclear whether and to what extent a patient such as Claire Conroy is capable of, or is in fact, experiencing pain. Similarly, medical experts are often unable to determine with any degree of certainty the extent of a nonverbal person's intellectual functioning or the depth of his emotional life. When the evidence is insufficient to satisfy either the limited-objective or pure-objective standard, however, we cannot justify the termination of life-sustaining treatment as clearly furthering the best interests of a patient like Ms. Conroy. . . .

The decisionmaking procedure for comatose, vegetative patients suggested in *Quinlan,* namely, the concurrence of the guardian, family, attending physician, and hospital prognosis committee, is not entirely appropriate for patients such as Claire Conroy, who are confined to nursing homes. There are significant differences in the patients, the health-care providers, and the institutional structures of nursing homes and hospitals. . . .

[The court went on to discuss special concerns with treatment withdrawal in nursing homes, including the vulnerability of nursing home residents, the fact that residents are often without any surviving family, the limited role that physicians play in nursing home care, and the occurrence of neglectful and abusive care in nursing homes. Because of these concerns, the court required the involvement of New Jersey's Office of the Ombudsman before the discontinuation of life-sustaining treatment from a patient like Claire Conroy. In addition, two physicians, unaffiliated with the nursing home or with the attending physician, would have to have confirmed the patient's medical condition and prognosis.]

Provided that the two physicians supply the necessary medical foundation, the guardian, with the concurrence of the attending physician, may withhold or withdraw life-sustaining treatment if he believes in good faith, based on the medical evidence and any evidence of the patient's wishes, that it is clear that the subjective, limited-objective or pure-objective test is satisfied. In addition, the ombudsman must concur in that decision. . . . Finally, if the limited-objective or pure-objective test is being used, the family—that is, the patient's spouse, parents, and children, or in their absence, the patient's next of kin, if any—must also concur in the decision to withhold or withdraw life-sustaining treatment. . . .

[The court then concluded that the evidence about Ms. Conroy's condition was insufficient to find that any of these three tests was met in this case. The court did not believe that it was sufficiently clear what decision she personally would have made, nor was it satisfied by the available information about the extent of pleasure or pain she was experiencing before she died. Therefore, were she still alive, the court would have instructed her guardian to find out more about her prior preferences and the benefits and burdens of her life before deciding whether any of the three standards for withdrawing treatment were satisfied.]

■ IN RE JOBES
529 A.2d 434 (N.J. 1987)

GARIBALDI, Justice.

. . . This appeal requires us to develop the guidelines and procedures under which life-sustaining medical treatment may be withdrawn from a non-elderly nursing home patient in a persistent vegetative state who, prior to her incompetency, failed to express adequately her attitude toward such treatment. . . .

[The case arose when the husband and parents of Nancy Jobes asked the nursing home to withdraw Ms. Jobes's feeding tube. The nursing home refused on moral grounds, and the husband sought judicial authorization of the withdrawal. After a seven-day trial, the court approved the removal of the feeding tube but held that the nursing home could refuse to participate in the removal and could require transfer of Ms. Jobes to another facility for discontinuation of the feeding. When the court entered its judgment, it stayed relief pending final determination on appeal, which went directly to this court.]

II

Nancy Ellen Jobes is thirty-one years old. . . . Prior to March of 1980, Mrs. Jobes had no significant mental or physical handicap. She was employed as a certified laboratory technologist, and was four and one-half months pregnant with her first child.

On March 11, 1980, Mrs. Jobes was admitted to Riverside Hospital for treatment of injuries sustained in an automobile accident. Doctors soon determined that her fetus had been killed. During the course of an operation to remove the dead fetus, she sustained a severe loss of oxygen and blood flow to her brain. She suffered massive and irreversible damage to the part of her brain that controls thought and movement. She has never regained consciousness. . . .

She cannot swallow. Originally she was fed and hydrated intravenously, then through a nasogastric tube, then a gastrotomy tube. In June 1985, complications with the gastrotomy tube necessitated an even more direct approach. Since then, Mrs. Jobes has been fed through a j-tube inserted—through a hole cut into her abdominal cavity—into the jejunum of her small intestine. Water and a synthetic, pre-digested formula of various amino acids are pumped through the j-tube continuously. . . .

IV

Mrs. Jobes' closest friends, her cousin, her clergyman, and her husband offered testimony that was intended to prove that if she were competent, Mrs. Jobes would refuse to be sustained by the j-tube. Deborah Holdsworth, a registered nurse and life-long friend of Mrs. Jobes, recalled a conversation in 1971 in which Mrs. Jobes stated that if she were ever crippled like the children with multiple sclerosis and muscular dystrophy that Ms. Holdsworth cared for, she would not want to live. Ms. Holdsworth also recalled telling Mrs. Jobes on numerous occasions that she, Holdsworth, would not want to live like Karen Quinlan did after the removal of her respirator. She recalled that Mrs. Jobes had not disagreed with her, but could not recall Mrs. Jobes' position any more clearly than that. Finally Holdsworth recalled that in late 1979 Mrs. Jobes specifically stated that she would not want to be kept alive on a respirator like a patient suffering from amyotrophic lateral sclerosis whom Ms. Holdsworth had described to her.

Another friend of Mrs. Jobes' since childhood, Donna DeChristofaro, testified that in Autumn 1979 Mrs. Jobes had told her that "it was a shame that [Karen Quinlan] hadn't died when they removed the respirator; that that wasn't living, it was existing; that she had wished that God had taken her then. . . ."

Mrs. Jobes' first cousin, Dr. Cleve Laird, recalled a discussion he had with her in the summer of 1975 about a victim of an automobile accident who was being kept alive by a cardiac stimulator:

> She said that she wouldn't want those measures taken in her case and that she certainly wouldn't want to live that way. I said, well, they wouldn't do that to me because I carried and still carry a form of identification that says that I do not wish to have any heroic measures taken in case of massive injury.
>
> Subsequent to that she became interested in where I had gotten that and I told her that it was pretty common both at Baylor where I had taught prior to going up to Massachusetts and also at Harvard. I said that I would send her a card. My wife was there and I turned around to her and told her why didn't she send one. Then we moved on into discussion of other technical things.

Dr. Laird testified that his wife had sent the card to Mrs. Jobes, and that Mrs. Jobes thanked them for it in a note she sent them at Christmas. The card has not been found.

John Jobes testified that if his wife were competent, she would "definitely" choose to terminate the artificial feeding that sustains her in her present condition. He generally recalled her having stated that she would not want to be kept alive under Karen Quinlan's circumstances. She did this frequently when the *Quinlan* case was in the news, mostly during 1976-1977.

The Reverend George A. Vorsheim, minister of the Morris Plains Presbyterian Church, testified that he had married the Jobes, and that he was familiar with them and with Mrs. Jobes' parents. They are all members of the Presbyterian Church (U.S.A.). The Reverend Mr. Vorsheim testified that Mrs. Jobes was raised in the Presbyterian Faith, and that in the Presbyterian Faith there is no religious requirement to perpetuate life by artificial means nor is there any doctrine prohibiting life-sustaining medical treatment. The Presbyterian Church leaves decisions like the one at issue here to the individual conscience. . . .

V

In *Conroy* and *Peter* we have described the type of evidence that can establish a person's medical preferences under the "subjective test." We have explained that the probative value of prior statements offered to prove a patient's inclination for or against medical treatment depends on their specificity, their "remoteness, consistency and thoughtfulness . . . [,] and the maturity of the person at the time of the statements. . . ." *Conroy*, 486 A.2d at 1230. All of the statements about life-support that were attributed to Mrs. Jobes were remote, general, spontaneous, and made in casual circumstances. Indeed, they closely track the examples of evidence that we have explicitly characterized as unreliable.

Other than her prior statements, the only evidence of Mrs. Jobes' intent that the trial court relied on was her membership in the Presbyterian Church. There is no specific evidence of her personal belief in the tenets of that Church; nevertheless, we have consistently recognized that "a person's religious affiliation and the tenets of that religion may furnish evidence of his or her intent with regard to medical decisions." *Conroy*, supra, 98 N.J. at 362. In this case, however, Mrs. Jobes' minister testified that her religion neither requires nor forbids medical treatment like that at issue here. Therefore, Mrs. Jobes' religious affiliation does not offer much guidance in determining what her preference would be in this situation.

Thus, we conclude that although there is some "trustworthy" evidence that Mrs. Jobes, if competent, would want the j-tube withdrawn, it is not sufficiently "clear and convincing" to satisfy the subjective test. Therefore, we must determine the guidelines and procedures under which life-sustaining medical treatment may be withdrawn from a patient like Mrs. Jobes when there is no clear and convincing proof of her attitude toward such treatment.

VI

Because of the unique problems involved in decisionmaking for any patient in the persistent vegetative state, we necessarily distinguish their cases from cases involving other patients. Accordingly, in *Peter* we held that neither the life-expectancy test nor the balancing tests set forth in *Conroy* are appropriate in the case of a persistently vegetative patient. Those holdings are equally relevant in this case. In any case involving a patient in the persistent vegetative state, "we look instead primarily to *Quinlan* for guidance." *Peter*, 529 A.2d at 425 [observing that "[w]hile a benefits-burdens analysis is difficult with marginally cognitive patients like Claire Conroy, it is essentially impossible with patients in a persistent vegetative state. By definition such patients, like Ms. Peter, do not experience any of the benefits or burdens that the *Conroy* balancing tests are intended or able to appraise"]. . . .

In light of Karen Quinlan's inability to assert her right to decline continued artificial respiration, we determined that "[t]he only practical way to prevent destruction of the right [was] to permit the guardian and family of Karen to render their best judgment, subject to the qualifications [t]hereinafter stated, as to whether she would exercise it in [her] circumstances." 355 A.2d at 664. The term *substituted judgment* is commonly used to describe our approach in *Quinlan*. This approach is intended to ensure that the surrogate decisionmaker effectuates as much as possible the decision that the incompetent patient would make if he or she were competent. Under the substituted judgment doctrine, where an incompetent's wishes are not clearly expressed, a surrogate decisionmaker considers the patient's personal value system for guidance. The surrogate considers the patient's prior statements about and reactions to medical issues, and all the facets of the patient's personality that the surrogate is familiar with—with, of course, particular reference to his or her relevant philosophical, theological, and ethical values—in order to extrapolate what course of medical treatment the patient would choose.

In *Quinlan* we held that the patient's family members were the proper parties to make a substituted medical judgment on her behalf. We make the same determination today. Almost invariably the patient's family has an intimate understanding of the patient's medical attitudes and general world view and therefore is in the best position to know the motives and considerations that would control the patient's medical decisions. . . .

Family members are best qualified to make substituted judgments for incompetent patients not only because of their peculiar grasp of the patient's approach to life, but also because of their special bonds with him or her. Our common human experience informs us that family members are generally most concerned with the welfare of a patient. It is they who provide for the patient's comfort, care, and best interests, and they who treat the patient as a person, rather than a symbol of a cause. Where strong and emotional opinions and proponents exist on an issue involving the treatment of an incompetent, extreme care must be exercised in determining who will act as his or her surrogate decisionmaker. We believe that a family member is generally the best choice.

As we stated in *Farrell*:

> Our common human experience teaches us that family and close friends care most and best for a patient. They offer love and support and concern, and have the best interest of the patient at heart. The importance of the family in medical treatment decisions is axiomatic.

> [F]amilies commonly exhibit the greatest degree of concern about the welfare of ailing family members. It is they who come to the hospital and involve themselves in the sick person's care and comfort. Competent patients usually actively solicit the advice and counsel of family members in decisionmaking. Family members routinely ask questions of the medical staff about the patient's condition and prognosis; one study found they frequently asked more questions than patients themselves did. Family members, in fact, commonly act as advocates for patients in the hospital, looking out for their comfort, care, and best interests. . . . [Newman, Treatment Refusals for the Critically Ill: Proposed Rules for Family, the Physician and the State, III N.Y. L. Sch. Human Rights Annual 35 (1985).]

> The law has traditionally respected the private realm of family life which the state cannot enter. . . . We believe that this tradition of respect for and confidence in the family should ground our approach to the treatment of the sick. [Farrell, 529 A.2d at 414. . . .]

Normally those family members close enough to make a substituted judgment would be a spouse, parents, adult children, or siblings. Generally in the absence of such a close degree of kinship, we would not countenance health care professionals deferring to the relatives of a patient, and a guardian would have to be appointed. However, if the attending health care professionals determine that another relative, e.g., a cousin, aunt, uncle, niece, or nephew, functions in the role of the patient's nuclear family, then that relative can and should be treated as a close and caring family member.

There will, of course, be some unfortunate situations in which family members will not act to protect a patient. We anticipate that such cases will be exceptional. Whenever a health-care professional becomes uncertain about whether family members are properly protecting a patient's interests, termination of life-sustaining treatment should not occur without the appointment of a guardian. . . .

Mrs. Jobes is blessed with warm, close, and loving family members. It is entirely proper to assume that they are best qualified to determine the medical decisions she would make. Moreover, there is some trustworthy evidence that supports their judgment of Mrs. Jobes' personal inclinations. Therefore, we will not presume to disturb their decision.

Thus, we hold that the right of a patient in an irreversibly vegetative state to determine whether to refuse life-sustaining medical treatment may be exercised by the patient's family or close friend. If there are close and caring family members who are willing to make this decision there is no need to have a guardian appointed. We require merely that the responsible relatives comply with the medical confirmation procedures that we henceforth establish. . . .

VII

. . . For non-elderly non-hospitalized patients in a persistent vegetative state who, like Mrs. Jobes, have a caring family or close friend, or a court-appointed guardian in attendance, we hold that the surrogate decisionmaker who declines life-sustaining medical treatment must secure statements from at least two independent physicians knowledgeable in neurology that the patient is in a persistent vegetative state and that there is no reasonable possibility that the patient will ever recover to a cognitive, sapient state. If the patient has an attending physician, then that physician likewise must submit such a statement. These independent neurological confirmations will substitute for the concurrence of the prognosis committee for patients who are not in a hospital setting and thereby prevent inappropriate withdrawal of treatment. In a proper case, however, they should not be difficult to obtain, and this requirement should not subject the patient to undesired treatment.

As long as the guidelines we hereby establish are followed in good faith, no criminal or civil liability will attach to anyone involved in the implementation of a surrogate decision to decline medical treatment. Accordingly, judicial review of such decisions is not necessary or appropriate. . . .

IX

. . . If a disagreement arises among the patient, family, guardian, or doctors, or if there is evidence of improper motives or malpractice, judicial intervention will be required. We expect, however, that disagreements will be rare and that intervention seldom will be necessary. We emphasize that even in those few cases in which the courts may have to intervene, they will not be making the ultimate decision whether to terminate medical treatment. Rather, they will be acting to insure that all the guidelines and procedures that we have set forth are properly followed. . . .

■ CRUZAN v. DIRECTOR, MISSOURI DEPARTMENT OF HEALTH
497 U.S. 261 (1990)

REHNQUIST, Chief Justice.

[The facts of this case and the Court's discussion of the existence of a right to refuse treatment are excerpted at pages 277-281 in the section on the competent patient. Ms. Cruzan suffered severe brain damage from an automobile accident that left her in a persistent vegetative state. A few years later, when her parents sought to have Ms. Cruzan's feeding tube discontinued, the Missouri Supreme Court found there to be insufficient evidence that Ms. Cruzan would want the treatment withdrawn. The primary evidence of her wishes were thoughts expressed about a year before the accident "in somewhat serious conversation with a housemate friend that if sick or injured she would not wish to continue her life unless she could live at least halfway normally."]

. . . Petitioners go on to assert that an incompetent person should possess the same right in this respect as is possessed by a competent person. . . .

The difficulty with petitioners' claim is that in a sense it begs the question: An incompetent person is not able to make an informed and voluntary choice to exercise a hypothetical right to refuse treatment or any other right. Such a "right" must be exercised for her, if at all, by some sort of surrogate. Here, Missouri has in effect recognized that under certain circumstances a surrogate may act for the patient in electing to have hydration and nutrition withdrawn in such a way as to cause death, but it has established a procedural safeguard to assure that the action of the surrogate conforms as best it may to the wishes expressed by the patient while competent. Missouri requires that evidence of the incompetent's wishes as to the withdrawal of treatment be proved by clear and convincing evidence. The question, then, is whether the United States Constitution forbids the establishment of this procedural requirement by the state. We hold that it does not.

Whether or not Missouri's clear and convincing evidence requirement comports with the United States Constitution depends in part on what interests the state may properly seek to protect in this situation. Missouri relies on its interest in the protection and preservation of human life, and there can be no gainsaying this interest. As a general matter, the states—indeed, all civilized nations—demonstrate their commitment to life by treating homicide as a serious crime. Moreover, the majority of states in this country have laws imposing criminal penalties on one who assists another to commit suicide. We do not think a state is required to remain neutral in the face of an informed and voluntary decision by a physically able adult to starve to death.

But in the context presented here, a state has more particular interests at stake. The choice between life and death is a deeply personal decision of obvious and overwhelming finality. We believe Missouri may legitimately seek to safeguard the personal element of this choice through the imposition of heightened evidentiary requirements. It cannot be disputed that the due process clause protects an interest in life as well as an interest in refusing life-sustaining medical treatment. Not all incompetent patients will have loved ones available to serve as surrogate decisionmakers. And even where family members are present, "[t]here will, of course, be some unfortunate situations in which family members will not act to protect a patient." In re Jobes, 529 A.2d 434, 447 (N.J. 1987). A state is entitled to guard against potential abuses in such situations. . . . Finally, we think a state may properly decline to make judgments about the "quality" of life that a particular individual may enjoy, and simply assert an unqualified interest in the preservation of human life to be weighed against the constitutionally protected interests of the individual.

In our view, Missouri has permissibly sought to advance these interests through the adoption of a "clear and convincing" standard of proof to govern such proceedings. . . . "This Court has mandated an intermediate standard of proof—'clear and convincing evidence'—when the individual interests at stake in a state proceeding are both 'particularly important' and 'more substantial than mere loss of money.'" Santosky v. Kramer, 455 U.S. 745, 756 (1982) (quoting Addington, supra, [441 U.S.] at 424). Thus, such a standard has been required in deportation proceedings, in denaturalization proceedings, in civil commitment proceedings, and in proceedings for the termination of parental rights. . . .

We think it self-evident that the interests at stake in the instant proceedings are more substantial, both on an individual and societal level, than those involved in a run-of-the-mine civil dispute. But not only does the standard of proof reflect the importance of a particular adjudication, it also serves as "a societal judgment about how the risk of error should be distributed between the litigants." *Santosky*, 455 U.S., at 755. The more stringent the burden of proof a party must bear, the more that party bears the risk of an erroneous decision. We believe that Missouri may permissibly place an increased risk of an erroneous decision on those seeking to terminate an incompetent individual's life-sustaining treatment. An erroneous decision not to terminate results in a maintenance of the status quo; the possibility of subsequent developments such as advancements in medical science, the discovery of new evidence regarding the patient's intent, changes in the law, or simply the unexpected death of the patient despite the administration of life-sustaining treatment at least create the potential that a wrong decision will eventually be corrected or its impact mitigated. An erroneous decision to withdraw life-sustaining treatment, however, is not susceptible of correction.

It is also worth noting that most, if not all, states simply forbid oral testimony entirely in determining the wishes of parties in transactions which, while important, simply do not have the consequences that a decision to terminate a person's life does. . . . There is no doubt that statutes requiring wills to be in writing, and statutes of frauds which require that a contract to make a will be in writing, on occasion frustrate the effectuation of the intent of a particular decedent, just as Missouri's requirement of proof in this case may have frustrated the effectuation of the not fully-expressed desires of Nancy Cruzan. But the Constitution does not require general rules to work faultlessly; no general rule can.

In sum, we conclude that a state may apply a clear and convincing evidence standard in proceedings where a guardian seeks to discontinue nutrition and hydration of a person diagnosed to be in a persistent vegetative state.

Petitioners alternatively contend that Missouri must accept the "substituted judgment" of close family members even in the absence of substantial proof that their views reflect the views of the patient. . . .

No doubt is engendered by anything in this record but that Nancy Cruzan's mother and father are loving and caring parents. If the state were required by the United States Constitution to repose a right of "substituted judgment" with anyone, the Cruzans would surely qualify. But we do not think the due process clause requires the state to repose judgment on these matters with anyone but the patient herself. Close family members may have a strong feeling—a feeling not at all ignoble or unworthy, but not entirely disinterested, either—that they do not wish to witness the continuation of the life of a loved one which they regard as hopeless, meaningless, and even degrading. But there is no automatic assurance that the view of close family members will necessarily be the same as the patient's would have been had she been confronted with the prospect of her situation while competent. All of the reasons previously discussed for allowing Missouri to require clear and convincing evidence of the patient's wishes lead us to conclude that the State may choose to defer only to those wishes, rather than confide the decision to close family members.

O'CONNOR, Justice, concurring.

[In her concurrence, Justice O'Connor suggested that the Constitution gives individuals the right to have their life-sustaining treatment decisions made by a formally appointed surrogate decisionmaker (e.g., through a durable power of attorney).]

BRENNAN, Justice, with whom MARSHALL, Justice, and BLACKMUN, Justice, join, dissenting.

. . . As the majority recognizes, Missouri has a *parens patriae* interest in providing Nancy Cruzan, now incompetent, with as accurate as possible a determination of how she would exercise her rights under these circumstances. Second, if and when it is determined that Nancy Cruzan would want to continue treatment, the state may legitimately assert an interest in providing that treatment. But until Nancy's wishes have been determined, the only state interest that may be asserted is an interest in safeguarding the accuracy of that determination.

Accuracy, therefore, must be our touchstone. Missouri may constitutionally impose only those procedural requirements that serve to enhance the accuracy of a determination of Nancy Cruzan's wishes or are at least consistent with an accurate determination. The Missouri "safeguard" that the Court upholds today does not meet that standard. The determination needed in this context is whether the incompetent person would choose to live in a persistent vegetative state on life support or to avoid this medical treatment. Missouri's rule of decision imposes a markedly asymmetrical evidentiary burden. Only evidence of specific statements of treatment choice made by the patient when competent is admissible to support a finding that the patient, now in a persistent vegetative state, would wish to avoid further medical treatment. Moreover, this evidence must be clear and convincing. No proof is required to support a finding that the incompetent person would wish to continue treatment.

A

The majority offers several justifications for Missouri's heightened evidentiary standard. First, the majority explains that the state may constitutionally adopt this rule to govern determinations of an incompetent's wishes in order to advance the state's substantive interests, including its unqualified interest in the preservation of human life. Missouri's evidentiary standard, however, cannot rest on the state's own interest in a particular substantive result. To be sure, courts have long erected clear and convincing evidence standards to place the greater risk of erroneous decisions on those bringing disfavored claims. In such cases, however, the choice to discourage certain claims was a legitimate, constitutional policy choice. In contrast, Missouri has no such power to disfavor a choice by Nancy Cruzan to avoid medical treatment, because Missouri has no legitimate interest in providing Nancy with treatment until it is established that this represents her choice. Just as a state may not override Nancy's choice directly, it may not do so indirectly through the imposition of a procedural rule. . . .

The majority claims that the allocation of the risk of error is justified because it is more important not to terminate life support for someone who would wish it continued than to honor the wishes of someone who would not. An erroneous decision to terminate life support is irrevocable, says the majority, while an erroneous decision not to terminate "results in a maintenance of the status quo." But, from the point of view of the patient, an erroneous decision in either direction is irrevocable. An erroneous decision to terminate artificial nutrition and hydration, to be sure, will lead to failure of that last remnant of physiological life, the brain stem, and result in complete brain death. An erroneous decision not to terminate life support, however, robs a patient of the very qualities protected by the right to avoid unwanted medical treatment. His own degraded existence is perpetuated; his family's suffering is protracted; the memory he leaves behind becomes more and more distorted.

Even a later decision to grant him his wish cannot undo the intervening harm. But a later decision is unlikely in any event. "[T]he discovery of new evidence," to which the majority refers, is more hypothetical than plausible. The majority also misconceives the relevance of the possibility of "advancements in medical science," by treating it as a reason to force someone to continue medical treatment against his will. The possibility of a medical miracle is indeed part of the calculus, but it is a part of the patient's calculus. If current research suggests that some hope for cure or even moderate improvement is possible within the lifespan projected, this is a factor that should be and would be accorded significant weight in assessing what the patient himself would choose.[18]

B

Even more than its heightened evidentiary standard, the Missouri court's categorical exclusion of relevant evidence dispenses with any semblance of accurate factfinding. The court adverted to no evidence supporting its decision, but held that no clear and convincing, inherently reliable evidence had been presented to show that Nancy would want to avoid further treatment. In doing so, the court failed to consider statements Nancy had made to family members and a close friend. The court also failed to consider testimony from Nancy's mother and sister that they were certain that Nancy would want to discontinue artificial nutrition and hydration, even after the court found that Nancy's family was loving and without malignant motive. The court also failed to consider the conclusions of the guardian ad litem, appointed by the trial court, that there was clear and convincing evidence that Nancy would want to discontinue medical treatment and that this was in her best interests. The court did not specifically define what kind of evidence it would consider clear and convincing, but its general discussion suggests that only a living will or equivalently formal directive from the patient when competent would meet this standard.

Too few people execute living wills or equivalently formal directives for such an evidentiary rule to ensure adequately that the wishes of incompetent persons will be honored. While it might be a wise social policy to encourage people to furnish such instructions, no general conclusion about a patient's choice can be drawn from the absence of formalities. The probability of becoming irreversibly vegetative is so low that many people may not feel an urgency to marshal formal evidence of their preferences. Some may not wish to dwell on their own physical deterioration and mortality. Even someone with a resolute determination to avoid life support under circumstances such as Nancy's would still need to know that such things as living

---

18. For Nancy Cruzan, no such cure or improvement is in view. So much of her brain has deteriorated and been replaced by fluid, see App. to Pet. for Cert. A94, that apparently the only medical advance that could restore consciousness to her body would be a brain transplant.

wills exist and how to execute one. Often legal help would be necessary, especially given the majority's apparent willingness to permit states to insist that a person's wishes are not truly known unless the particular medical treatment is specified.

. . . When Missouri enacted a living will statute, it specifically provided that the absence of a living will does not warrant a presumption that a patient wishes continued medical treatment. Thus, apparently not even Missouri's own legislature believes that a person who does not execute a living will fails to do so because he wishes continuous medical treatment under all circumstances.

The testimony of close friends and family members, on the other hand, may often be the best evidence available of what the patient's choice would be. It is they with whom the patient most likely will have discussed such questions and they who know the patient best. . . .

. . . The rules by which an incompetent person's wishes are determined must represent every effort to determine those wishes. The rule that the Missouri court adopted and that this Court upholds, however, skews the result away from a determination that as accurately as possible reflects the individual's own preferences and beliefs. It is a rule that transforms human beings into passive subjects of medical technology. . . .

D

Finally, I cannot agree with the majority that where it is not possible to determine what choice an incompetent patient would make, a state's role as *parens patriae* permits the state automatically to make that choice itself. Under fair rules of evidence, it is improbable that a court could not determine what the patient's choice would be. Under the rule of decision adopted by Missouri and upheld today by this Court, such occasions might be numerous. But in neither case does it follow that it is constitutionally acceptable for the state invariably to assume the role of deciding for the patient. A state's legitimate interest in safeguarding a patient's choice cannot be furthered by simply appropriating it.

The majority justifies its position by arguing that, while close family members may have a strong feeling about the question, "there is no automatic assurance that the view of close family members will necessarily be the same as the patient's would have been had she been confronted with the prospect of her situation while competent." I cannot quarrel with this observation. But it leads only to another question: Is there any reason to suppose that a state is more likely to make the choice that the patient would have made than someone who knew the patient intimately? To ask this is to answer it. . . .

. . . A state may ensure that the person who makes the decision on the patient's behalf is the one whom the patient himself would have selected to make that choice for him. And a state may exclude from consideration anyone having improper motives. But a state generally must either repose the choice with the person whom the patient himself would most likely have chosen as proxy or leave the decision to the patient's family.

Notes: Deciding for the Incompetent Patient

1. *Nancy Cruzan.* After the U.S. Supreme Court upheld the Missouri Supreme Court's holding that there was not sufficient evidence to show that Nancy Cruzan

would want her feeding tube withdrawn, Ms. Cruzan's family returned to a state trial court with new evidence of her wishes. Because of wide publicity about her case, friends who had discussed end-of-life decisionmaking with Ms. Cruzan came forward with additional testimony about her wishes. These friends had not come forward sooner because they knew Ms. Cruzan under her married name, Nancy Davis, and she had taken her maiden name back when she divorced her husband shortly before her accident. The state did not oppose withdrawal of the feeding tube, and the court ruled in favor of the family. The feeding tube was withdrawn, and Ms. Cruzan died shortly thereafter, five months after the U.S. Supreme Court's decision. Gregory E. Pence, Medical Ethics: Accounts of Ground-Breaking Cases 30 (6th ed. 2011). For additional discussion of the *Cruzan* case, see Yale Kamisar, When Is There a Constitutional "Right to Die"? When Is There No Constitutional "Right to Live"?, 25 Ga. L. Rev. 1203 (1991); Thomas W. Mayo, Constitutionalizing the "Right to Die," 49 Md. L. Rev. 103 (1990).

2. *The Right of Incompetent Patients.* In *Conroy,* the court held that a competent adult's right to refuse life-sustaining medical treatment remains intact when the person loses competence. Similarly, the *Saikewicz* court wrote that "[t]he recognition of that right must extend to the case of an incompetent, as well as a competent, patient because the value of human dignity extends to both." Superintendent of Belchertown State School v. Saikewicz, 370 N.E.2d 417, 427 (Mass. 1977). Is it so clear that the right to refuse life-sustaining treatment should survive incompetence? If the right is justified by principles of self-determination, why should the right exist for individuals who can no longer express their preferences?

Consider the following explanations for a right to refuse life-sustaining treatment for incompetent persons:

a. We can justify the extension of the right to refuse treatment by analogy to a person's right to dispose of property at death through a will. By letting people pass their wealth on to their family or other chosen beneficiaries, we do not discourage people from engaging in socially desirable activities while they are alive (e.g., wealth-generating activities.) In addition, we want people to be able to ensure the financial security of their loved ones. Both justifications arguably apply to treatment withdrawals. Do you see how this is so?

b. To properly understand the right to refuse treatment, we need to consider not only who gets to make the treatment decision but also who does not get to make the decision. When individuals enjoy a right to refuse treatment, they gain personal control over an important aspect of their lives, and they also are freed from government control over that important aspect. This anti-totalitarian justification for the right to refuse treatment is still very much present for incompetent persons. Giles Scofield, The Calculus of Consent, 20(1) Hastings Center Rep. 44 (1990); Jed Rubenfeld, The Right of Privacy, 102 Harv. L. Rev. 737 (1989).

c. Incompetent persons may not have any interests in self-determination, but they do have interests in being spared from suffering and in being treated with dignity. A right to refuse treatment is essential to ensure that incompetent persons do not undergo unjustified suffering from the imposition of medical treatment. It is also essential to ensure that incompetent persons are not robbed of their dignity.

Which of these statements do you think explain(s) or should explain the right to refuse treatment for incompetent persons? Would the nature of the right vary depending on which of the explanations actually is at work? That is, do any of the explanations justify a broader right than the other explanations? Would explanation c. justify withdrawal of Nancy Jobes's or Nancy Cruzan's feeding tube?

In thinking about why we permit the right to refuse treatment to survive incompetence, does your explanation account for why we do not permit the right to vote to survive incompetence? Suppose a person had voted consistently as a Democrat and explained such voting on the basis that Democrats were more likely to provide adequate funding for nursing homes and other long-term care. Should that person's ballot be cast for Democratic candidates even after the person becomes incompetent?

3. *Variation in Procedural Rules.* The recognition of a right to refuse treatment for incompetent persons still leaves the question as to how the right should be implemented. In *Cruzan*, the U.S. Supreme Court gave states broad leeway to adopt procedural rules for deciding when life-sustaining treatment can be withdrawn from incompetent persons.

In general, states will permit withdrawal of treatment if there is clear and convincing evidence of the patient's treatment preferences from written or oral statements made by the patient before losing competence. Evidence of the patient's wishes is clear and convincing when it is "sufficient to persuade the trier of fact that the patient had a firm and settled commitment" to decline treatment. In re Westchester County (O'Connor), 531 N.E.2d 607, 613 (N.Y. 1988). If clear and convincing evidence does not exist, there is considerable variation from state to state as to whether treatment may be discontinued.

As we have seen, New Jersey has adopted different standards for patients in different conditions. For patients who are permanently unconscious and who did not leave clear and convincing evidence of their wishes, family members may decide on the patient's behalf under a "substituted judgment" standard in which the family members draw on their knowledge of the patient to reach "as much as possible the decision that the incompetent patient would make if he or she were competent." *Jobes*, 529 A.2d at 444. For patients who have some degree of consciousness and have a short life expectancy (but are not expected to die imminently), treatment withdrawals must be justified either by clear and convincing evidence that this is what the patient would have wanted (*Conroy*'s "subjective" standard) or by a demonstration that the pain and suffering of continued treatment markedly outweigh the benefits of continued treatment (*Conroy*'s two "objective" or "best interests" standards).

Other states have not varied their standard in terms of the patient's condition. Some courts, for example, have adopted a simple best interests standard for cases in which the patient's preferences cannot be established. See, e.g., Rasmussen v. Fleming, 741 P.2d 674, 689 (Ariz. 1987) (observing that "[w]here no reliable evidence of a patient's intent exists, as here, the substituted judgment standard provides little, if any, guidance to the surrogate decisionmaker and should be abandoned in favor of the 'best interests' standard"); In re Torres, 357 N.W.2d 332, 338-339 (Minn. 1984).

A good illustration of the best interests standard is the court's discussion in *Saikewicz*. Although the court stated that it was employing a substituted judgment approach, it actually was employing a best interests approach. Indeed, inasmuch as Mr. Saikewicz had never been competent, it made no sense to employ a substituted judgment, or, as one expert testified in a case involving a profoundly retarded patient, it "would be similar to asking whether 'if it snowed all summer would it then be winter?'" In re Storar, 420 N.E.2d 64, 72-73 (N.Y. 1981). The analysis of the *Saikewicz* court follows:

> . . . In short, the decision in cases such as this should be that which would be made by the incompetent person, if that person were competent, but taking into account the present and future incompetency of the individual as one of the factors which would necessarily enter into the decisionmaking process of the competent person. . . .

> The two factors considered by the probate judge to weigh in favor of administering chemotherapy were: (1) the fact that most people elect chemotherapy and (2) the chance of a longer life. Both are appropriate indicators of what Saikewicz himself would have wanted, provided that due allowance is taken for this individual's present and future incompetency. . . . With regard to the second factor, the chance of a longer life carries the same weight for Saikewicz as for any other person, the value of life under the law having no relation to intelligence or social position. Intertwined with this consideration is the hope that a cure, temporary or permanent, will be discovered during the period of extra weeks or months potentially made available by chemotherapy. The guardian ad litem investigated this possibility and found no reason to hope for a dramatic breakthrough in the time frame relevant to the decision.

> The probate judge identified six factors weighing against administration of chemotherapy. Four of these—Saikewicz's age,[17] the probable side effects of treatment, the low chance of producing remission, and the certainty that treatment will cause immediate suffering—were clearly established by the medical testimony to be considerations that any individual would weigh carefully. A fifth factor—Saikewicz's inability to cooperate with the treatment—introduces those considerations that are unique to this individual and which therefore are essential to the proper exercise of substituted judgment. The judge heard testimony that Saikewicz would have no comprehension of the reasons for the severe disruption of his formerly secure and stable environment occasioned by the chemotherapy. He therefore would experience fear without the understanding from which other patients draw strength. The inability to anticipate and prepare for the severe side effects of the drugs leaves room only for confusion and disorientation. The possibility that such a naturally uncooperative patient would have to be physically restrained to allow the slow intravenous administration of drugs could only compound his pain and fear, as well as possibly jeopardize the ability of his body to withstand the toxic effects of the drugs.

> The sixth factor identified by the judge as weighing against chemotherapy was "the quality of life possible for him even if the treatment does bring about remission." To the extent that this formulation equates the value of life with any measure of the quality of life, we firmly reject it. A reading of the entire record clearly reveals, however, the judge's concern that special care be taken to respect the dignity and worth of Saikewicz's life precisely because of his vulnerable position. The judge, as well as all the parties, was keenly aware that the supposed inability of Saikewicz, by virtue of his mental retardation, to appreciate or experience life had no place in the decision before them. Rather than reading the judge's formulation in a manner

---

17. This factor is relevant because of the medical evidence in the record that people of Saikewicz's age do not tolerate the chemotherapy as well as younger people and that the chance of remission is decreased. Age is irrelevant, of course, to the question of the value or quality of life.

that demeans the value of the life of one who is mentally retarded, the vague, and perhaps ill-chosen, term "quality of life" should be understood as a reference to the continuing state of pain and disorientation precipitated by the chemotherapy treatment. Viewing the term in this manner, together with the other factors properly considered by the judge, we are satisfied that the decision to withhold treatment from Saikewicz was based on a regard for his actual interests and preferences and that the facts supported this decision. Superintendent of Belchertown State School v. Saikewicz, 370 N.E.2d 417, 431-432 (Mass. 1977).

Other states permit family members or guardians to employ a *Jobes*-like substituted judgment standard for all incompetent patients. Brophy v. New England Sinai Hospital, Inc., 497 N.E.2d 626, 634-635 (Mass. 1986); In re Tavel, 661 A.2d 1061, 1068-1069 (Del. 1995). As the Indiana Supreme Court wrote:

> Respect for patient autonomy does not end when the patient becomes incompetent. In our society, health care decisionmaking for patients typically transfers upon incompetence to the patient's family. . . . Even when they have not left formal advance directives or expressed particular opinions about life-sustaining medical treatment, most Americans want the decisions about their care, upon their incapacity, to be made for them by family and physician, rather than by strangers or by government. [In re Lawrence, 579 N.E.2d 32, 39 (Ind. 1991).]

Illinois also relies on family decisionmaking, although not for all patients. The Illinois Supreme Court struggled with the question of treatment withdrawal in In re Estate of Longeway, 549 N.E.2d 292 (Ill. 1989), and In re Greenspan, 558 N.E.2d 1194 (Ill. 1990), and Rudy Linares highlighted the need for better legal guidance when he discontinued a ventilator from his 15-month-old child while holding medical staff at bay with a gun. John D. Lantos et al., The Linares Affair, 17 L. Med. & Health Care 308 (1989). In response, the Illinois legislature passed its Health Care Surrogate Act. 755 Ill. Comp. Stat. 40. The Act applies to incompetent patients who have not executed a living will or durable power of attorney for health care and who either are terminally ill, are permanently unconscious, or have some other incurable or irreversible condition "that imposes severe pain or otherwise imposes an inhumane burden on the patient," and for which life-sustaining medical treatment "provides only minimal medical benefit." 755 Ill. Comp. Stat. 40/10. For persons covered by the Act, life-sustaining treatment decisions are to be made by family members or close friends. The Act instructs surrogate decisionmakers to decide first on the basis of how they believe the patient would have decided. Essentially, then, surrogates are governed first by New Jersey's "subjective" and "substituted judgment" standards. If surrogates are unable to figure out what the patient would have wanted, decisions for the patient "shall be made on the basis of the patient's best interests *as determined by the surrogate decision maker.*" 755 Ill. Comp. Stat. 40/20(b)(1) (emphasis added). The best interests judgment is to be made by weighing the benefits to and burdens on the patient from treatment against the burdens and benefits of the treatment itself.

At one time New York employed essentially the same standard for all patients that Missouri adopted for cases like the *Cruzan* case—a strict version of *Conroy's* subjective standard. The New York Court of Appeals not only required clear and convincing evidence of the patient's wishes, as in *Conroy*, but also adopted a strict view of clear and convincing evidence, requiring proof sufficient to persuade the trier of fact that the patient held a firm and settled commitment to the termination of life supports *under the circumstances like those presented.* As a threshold matter, the trier of fact must be convinced, as far as is humanly possible, that the strength of the individual's beliefs and the durability of the individual's commitment to those beliefs makes a recent change of heart unlikely. The persistence of the individual's statements, the seriousness with which those statements were made and the inferences, if any, that may be drawn from the surrounding circumstances are among the factors which should be considered.

O'Connor, 531 N.E.2d at 613 (emphasis added).

In 2010, the New York legislature replaced the *O'Connor* standard with an approach much like that of New Jersey. Under the Family Health Care Decisions Act, family members or close friends may refuse life-sustaining treatment for patients who are terminally ill or permanently unconscious. In addition, for patients who have an incurable condition, family members or close friends may refuse life-sustaining treatment that is inhumane or extraordinarily burdensome. N.Y. Pub. Health Law §2994-d. The legislative language comes largely from the recommendations of the New York State Task Force on Life and the Law's report, When Others Must Choose: Deciding for Patients Without Capacity (1992 and 1993 Supplement).

Most states now have statutes authorizing surrogate decisionmaking in the event that the patient did not execute an advance directive. Like Illinois and New York, they tend to restrict the surrogate's authority in terms of the patient's condition. For example, in Maryland, the patient must be terminally ill or permanently unconscious, or must have an "end-stage condition," defined as an "advanced, progressive, irreversible condition . . . [t]hat has caused severe and permanent deterioration indicated by incompetency and complete physical dependency." Md. Code Ann., Health Gen. §5-601(i). Still, the Uniform Health Care Decisions Act and surrogate statutes in some states recognize the authority of surrogates to make life-sustaining treatment decisions without qualification in terms of the patient's condition. See, e.g., Uniform Health Care Decisions Act §5(a) (1993); D.C. Code Ann. §21-2210; Va. Code Ann. §54.1-2986. For further discussion, see Diane E. Hoffmann, The Maryland Health Care Decisions Act: Achieving the Right Balance?, 53 Md. L. Rev. 1064 (1994); Aaron N. Krupp, Health Care Surrogate Statutes: Ethics Pitfalls Threaten the Interests of Incompetent Patients, 101 W. Va. L. Rev. 99 (1998); Jerry A. Menikoff et al., Beyond Advance Directives—Health Care Surrogate Laws, 327 New Eng. J. Med. 1165 (1992); Charles P. Sabatino, The New Uniform Health Care Decisions Act: Paving a Health Care Decisions Superhighway?, 53 Md. L. Rev. 1238 (1994); Marah Stith, The Semblance of Autonomy: Treatment of Persons with Disabilities Under the Uniform Health-Care Decisions Act, 22 Issues L. & Med. 39 (2006).

Which of the different approaches for deciding about end-of-life care for incompetent persons make the most sense to you? Or, is it better, in a pluralistic society, to have different approaches in different states?

4. *General Trends in Procedural Rules.* Despite the state-to-state variation, some patterns do emerge. In particular, states tend to adopt stricter procedural rules when the incompetent patient is neither terminally ill nor permanently unconscious. In such cases, the patient has some degree of consciousness and may live for a year or more. The *Conroy* case falls into this category, and the New

Jersey Supreme Court adopted a stricter standard than it did in the *Jobes* case for patients who are permanently unconscious. The California Supreme Court also has adopted strict standards for patients who are neither terminally ill nor permanently unconscious. In *Wendland*, the court required clear and convincing evidence that patients would have refused treatment under the circumstances in which they now find themselves, or clear and convincing evidence that withdrawal of treatment would be in the patient's best interests. Conservatorship of Wendland, 28 P.3d 151 (Cal. 2001). (The court did not "attempt to define the extreme factual predicates that, if proved by clear and convincing evidence, might support a [surrogate's] decisions that withdrawing life support would be in the best interest of a conscious [patient]." Id. at 174. The court did observe that a surrogate's "own subjective judgment that the [patient] d[oes] not enjoy a satisfactory quality of life" is insufficient. Id.)

Other courts have adopted the strict subjective standard of *Conroy* and *Wendland* but have not included an alternative objective standard. For example, in the *Martin* case, the Michigan Supreme Court adopted a purely subjective standard for patients who are neither terminally ill nor permanently unconscious, a standard similar to New York's old *O'Connor* standard. For such patients in Michigan, in the absence of a written directive expressing the patient's preferences, prior oral statements will be sufficient to justify withdrawal of treatment "[o]nly when the patient's prior statements clearly illustrate a serious, well thought out, consistent decision to refuse treatment under these exact circumstances or circumstances highly similar to the current situation." In re Martin, 538 N.W.2d 399, 411 (Mich. 1995).

In Michael Martin's case, this test was not satisfied despite considerable testimony suggesting he would not want treatment provided. Mr. Martin had suffered serious injuries, including a head injury, from an automobile accident that left him "unable to walk or talk, and rendered him dependent on a colostomy for defecation and a gastrostomy tube for nutrition." He was able to understand "only very short and very simple questions." He could not "accurately comprehend questions that are lengthy, verbose, or that require the retention of multiple thoughts." In particular, he could not understand "his physical capabilities and medical condition." Id. at 402-404. Mr. Martin's wife testified to eight years of discussions regarding his wishes in the event of a serious accident or disabling illness, the most recent discussion occurring one month before his accident. These discussions took place after the Martins watched movies about people who could no longer take care of themselves because of an accident or illness.

> Mike stated to me on several occasions: "That's bullshit. I would never want to live like that." He also said to me, "Please don't ever let me exist that way because those people don't even have their dignity." . . . [Regarding a movie about a football player with a terminal illness,] Mike said to me after we saw it together: "If I ever get sick don't put me on any machines to keep me going if there is no hope of getting better." He also said that if I ever put him on machines to keep him alive: "I'll always haunt you, Mary." Then he would say, "Do you understand?" I always said "Yes." We watched this movie at least two or three times and had virtually the same discussion each time. . . . Mike was an avid hunter and frequently expressed concerned [sic] about a hunting accident. Mike frequently told me that if he ever had an accident from which he would "not recover" and "could not be the same person," he did "not want to live that way." He would say, "Mary, promise me you wouldn't let me live like

> that if I can't be the person I am right now, because if you do, believe me I'll haunt you every day of your life." [Id. at 412.]

The Michigan court found that this testimony did not represent clear and convincing evidence of Mr. Martin's wishes. Two of his co-workers stated that, while Mr. Martin had indicated his desire not to be kept alive if in a vegetative state, Mr. Martin's present condition was not "the type referred to in conversations with them before his injury." In addition, several witnesses testified that, after his accident, Mr. Martin would shake his head no "when asked if he ever felt that he did not want to continue living." Id. at 412-413. For discussion of the *Martin* case, see the articles by Andrew J. Broder and Ronald E. Cranford, and by Thomas J. Marzen and Daniel Avila in Symposium Issue: Assisted Suicide, Health Care and Medical Treatment Choices, 72 U. Det. Mercy L. Rev. 719 (1995). For another case requiring clear evidence of the patient's wishes before removing a life-sustaining treatment from a patient who is neither terminally ill nor permanently unconscious, see Spahn v. Eisenberg, 563 N.W.2d 485 (Wis. 1997). Cf. In re D.L.H., 2 A.3d 505 (Pa. 2010) (interpreting Pennsylvania's health care representative statute to require the provision of life-preserving treatment for incompetent patients who are neither terminally ill nor permanently unconscious and who have not appointed a health care agent).

Does it make sense to vary the procedural rules depending on the patient's medical condition? If we have a different procedural standard for patients like Mr. Martin or Ms. Conroy than we do for patients like Ms. Jobes, have we maintained the principle that the substantive right to refuse life-sustaining treatment is not altered by incompetence? Should we be concerned about the fact that stricter procedural standards are likely to affect people differently depending on their socioeconomic status?

Although it is controversial whether clear and convincing evidence of the patient's wishes should be required before discontinuing life-sustaining treatment, it is less controversial when courts impose strict standards for establishing the patient's prognosis. If life-sustaining treatment is withdrawn because the patient is terminally ill or permanently unconscious, for example, we would want to be reasonably sure that the patient really is terminally ill or permanently unconscious. The Alabama Supreme Court came to that conclusion when it adopted a clear and convincing evidence standard for deciding that a patient is permanently unconscious for purposes of carrying out the patient's advance directive in the event of permanent unconsciousness. Knight v. Beverly Health Care Bay Manor Health Care Center, 820 So. 2d 92, 102 (Ala. 2001).

5. *The Patient's Best Interests.* While most courts and commentators believe that decisions for incompetent patients should reflect a judgment of what the patient would have wanted based on the patient's statements and values while competent, others disagree. Rebecca Dresser and John Robertson contend that medical decisions for incompetent persons should be based on an assessment of the patient's current best interests, that the incompetent person is very different from the person's previously competent self:

> It is wrong to assume that the incompetent patient's prior competent preferences are the best indicator of the patient's current interests. If we could determine the choice that these patients would make if suddenly able to speak—if they could tell

us what their interests in their compromised states are—such choices would reflect their current and future interests as incompetent individuals, not their past preferences. . . . When people become incompetent and seriously ill, . . . their interests may radically change. With their reduced mental and physical capacities, what was once of extreme importance to them no longer matters, while things that were previously of little moment assume much greater significance. An existence that seems demeaning and unacceptable to the competent person may still be of value to the incompetent patient, whose abilities, desires and interests have greatly narrowed.

Rebecca S. Dresser & John A. Robertson, Quality of Life and Non-Treatment Decisions for Incompetent Patients: A Critique of the Orthodox Approach, 17 L. Med. & Health Care 234 (1989).

Some support for this view comes from the empirical literature. Studies consistently indicate that healthy persons underestimate the quality of life of disabled persons. That is, when healthy persons are asked to estimate the quality of life of disabled persons, they give a lower quality of life than that given by the disabled persons about their own quality of life. David Orentlicher, Destructuring Disability: Rationing of Health Care and Unfair Discrimination Against the Sick, 31 Harv. C.R.-C.L. L. Rev. 49, 69 (1996). In addition, people who become disabled find that they have a higher quality of life than they thought they would. Norman F. Boyd et al., Whose Utilities for Decision Analysis?, 10 Med. Decis. Making 58 (1990). See also Terri R. Fried et al., Prospective Study of Health Status Preferences and Changes in Preferences over Time in Older Adults, 166 Arch. Intern. Med. 890 (2006) (finding that patients more accepting of diminished health status as their own health declines); Peter A. Ubel et al., Mismanaging the Unimaginable: The Disability Paradox and Health Care Decision Making, 24(4) Health Psychol. S57 (2005).

Which approach do you prefer, a "subjective" and/or "substituted judgment" approach based on the patient's statements and values while competent, or an "objective" approach based on the patient's current best interests?

In a study of patients on dialysis because of kidney failure, the patients were asked to consider whether they would want dialysis continued if they developed advanced Alzheimer's disease. They were then asked how much leeway they would want their family and physician to have in terms of overriding their wishes if overriding would be in their best interests. The researchers found that 39 percent of the patients would want their family and physicians to have "no leeway" in overriding their wishes, 31 percent of the patients would want their family and physicians to have "complete leeway" in overriding their wishes, and the remaining 30 percent of patients would want their family and physician to have some leeway (19 percent a "little leeway" and 11 percent a "lot of leeway"). Ashwini Sehgal et al., How Strictly Do Dialysis Patients Want Their Advance Directives Followed?, 267 JAMA 59 (1992). In another study of patients who were either seriously ill or at least 80 years old, researchers asked the patients about their wishes for CPR in the event of cardiac arrest. They then asked the patients whether their wishes about CPR should be followed if they lost decisionmaking capacity, or whether the CPR decision should be made by their family and physician. More than 70 percent of the patients preferred that their family and physician decide about CPR. Christina M. Puchalski, Patients Who Want Their Family and Physician to Make Resuscitation Decisions for Them: Observations from SUPPORT and HELP, 48(5) J. Am. Geriatrics Soc'y S84 (2000).

See also Daniel P. Sulmasy et al., How Would Terminally Ill Patients Have Others Make Decisions for Them in the Event of Decisional Incapacity? A Longitudinal Study, 55 J. Am. Geriatrics Soc'y 1981 (2007) (finding that most patients wanted their decisions to be based on a mix of their expressed preferences and what their loved ones and physicians thought was in their best interests). How do these studies affect your feelings about a subjective vs. objective standard?

For further discussion, see Norman L. Cantor, Discarding Substituted Judgment and Best Interests: Toward a Constructive Preference Standard for Dying, Previously Competent Patients Without Advance Directives, 48 Rutgers L. Rev. 1193 (1996); Rebecca Dresser, Missing Persons: Legal Perceptions of Incompetent Persons, 46 Rutgers L. Rev. 609 (1994).

6. *Family Decisionmaking.* For an argument in favor of family decisionmaking in all cases of incompetent persons, see Nancy K. Rhoden, Litigating Life and Death, 102 Harv. L. Rev. 375, 437-439 (1988) (emphasis in original):

> Families have historically exercised and continue to exercise a great deal of autonomy over decisions about procreation, education, and the upbringing of children. Family members have likewise attended to other members during their illnesses and have helped make their treatment choices for them. Not surprisingly, polls repeatedly show that patients, and members of society in general, believe that family members should function as surrogate decisionmakers. In short, there is a deep-rooted and almost instinctual sense that a close family member should make decisions. Most readers will understand this if they consider whom they would want to make treatment decisions for themselves — their families or physicians and hospital administrators.
>
> Moreover, because of the nature of the family as an association, its members are in the best position to reproduce preferences of an incompetent patient. . . . Not only are family members most likely to be privy to any relevant statements that patients have made on the topics of treatment or its termination, but they also have longstanding knowledge of the patient's character traits. Although evidence of character traits may seem inconclusive to third parties, closely related persons may, quite legitimately, "just know" what the patient would want in a way that transcends purely logical evidence. . . . Family members also *care* most: . . . humans naturally care most for those closest to them.
>
> Moreover, no patient is an island. The family is the context within which a person first develops her powers of autonomous choice, and the values she brings to these choices spring from, and are intertwined with, the family's values. A parent may understand a child's values because she helped to form them, a child may grasp a parent's values because the parent imparted them to her, and a couple may have developed and refined their views in tandem.

Rhoden recommends a presumption in favor of the family's choice, except that when "the patient recognizes caretakers and can interact with her environment in some way — even if she is completely nonverbal — then the patient has an interest in living, and foregoing treatment, unless it is excessively burdensome, is not a reasonable choice." Id. at 442.

Interestingly, Rhoden's approach and the best interests approach of Dresser and Robertson may not be that different in the end in terms of the kinds of decisions that would be made for incompetent persons. Dresser and Robertson generally would respect families' judgments as to whether treatment is in the patient's best interests except that it would not be acceptable for a family to decline treatment when the patient is a conscious, incompetent person "who can experience enjoyment and pleasure, and whose conditions and necessary treatment interventions impose on them small or moderate burdens." Dresser & Robertson, 17 L. Med. & Health Care at 242. In other words, Dresser and Robertson defer to the family as a general matter, as does Rhoden, and they limit the family's authority in essentially the same situations.

In thinking about family decisionmaking as an approach, consider the following results from the empirical literature:

> Several studies have examined the accuracy of surrogate decisionmakers by presenting individuals with hypothetical scenarios and asking them to indicate their treatment preferences for each scenario. Potential surrogates are simultaneously asked to predict the preferences of the individuals. These studies consistently demonstrate that the potential surrogates' predictions do not reach a statistically significant degree of agreement with the choices of the individuals. This holds true even when individuals chose people that they would feel most comfortable with as surrogate decisionmakers.

David Orentlicher, The Limitations of Legislation, 53 Md. L. Rev. 1255, 1278 (1994). Do these results affect your view as to the appropriate role of family decisionmaking? How do you respond to the concern of the *Cruzan* majority that family members are not disinterested parties to the decision? How might a patient's children react to the prospects of several more months or years of hospital or nursing home costs for the patient?

Note that family decisionmaking and substituted judgment approaches overlap substantially. In *Jobes*, for example, the court approved substituted judgments by families, and other courts or statutes also authorize family members to make substituted judgments for incompetent patients.

For further discussion, see Kathleen M. Boozang, An Intimate Passing: Restoring the Role of Family and Religion in Dying, 58 U. Pitt. L. Rev. 549 (1997); Allen E. Buchanan, The Limits of Proxy Decisionmaking for Incompetents, 29 UCLA L. Rev. 386 (1981); Jacqueline J. Glover, Should Families Make Health Care Decisions?, 53 Md. L. Rev. 1158 (1994); John Hardwig, What About the Family?, 20(2) Hastings Center Rep. 5 (1990); Nancy S. Jecker, The Role of Intimate Others in Medical Decision Making, 30 Gerontologist 65 (1990); James L. Nelson, Taking Families Seriously, 22(4) Hastings Center Rep. 6 (1992); David I. Shalowitz et al., The Accuracy of Surrogate Decision Makers, 166 Arch. Intern. Med. 493 (2006).

7. *Disagreements Among Family Members.* An important concern with family decisionmaking is how to resolve disagreements among family members. To some extent, this issue is addressed by state statutes governing surrogate decisionmaking. Typically, these statutes establish a hierarchy of family members according to their authority to make decisions on behalf of the patient. See, e.g., Md. Code Ann., Health-Gen. §5-605(a)(2) (establishing a hierarchy of legal guardian (if one has been appointed), spouse, adult child, parent, adult brother or sister, other close relative or friend). However, not all states have such statutes, and even when they exist, physicians may be reluctant to implement a request by some family members to discontinue treatment over the objections of other family members.

Courts also are reluctant to permit withdrawal of treatment in the presence of a disagreement among family members. Indeed, the reluctance to order withdrawal of treatment in the midst of a family dispute may explain many of the court decisions that seem most at odds with the ethical and legal principles underlying the law in this area. For example, in the *Martin* case, supra pages 324-325, in which Mr. Martin's wife seemed to be acting on repeatedly expressed wishes of her husband when she asked that treatment be discontinued, the court's decision to require treatment may have reflected the opposition of Mr. Martin's parents to withdrawal as much it reflected a desire for stricter standards for patients who are neither terminally ill nor permanently unconscious. Similarly in *Spahn*, supra page 325, there was a disagreement between the patient's sister and niece. Even more problematic is the court's decision in Couture v. Couture, 549 N.E.2d 571, 576 (Ohio Ct. App. 1989). In that case, a patient's divorced parents disagreed as to whether his artificial nutrition and hydration should be discontinued. The patient was in a persistent vegetative state, and the appellate court upheld the lower court's finding of clear and convincing evidence that Mr. Couture would want the treatment discontinued. Nevertheless, the court ordered that the treatment be continued.

Perhaps the most extreme family dispute occurred in the case of Terri Schiavo in Florida. A dispute between Ms. Schiavo's husband and parents resulted in nearly seven years of litigation with more than a dozen state and federal court decisions, statutes by the Florida Legislature and Congress, and intervention by Governor Jeb Bush and President George W. Bush. Ms Schiavo's husband requested the withdrawal of her feeding tube after she had been in a persistent vegetative state for several years. After reviewing the testimony, the trial court judge concluded that there was clear and convincing evidence that Terri would not want a feeding tube, based on her prior oral statements to family members. In re Schiavo, 780 So. 2d 176, 179-180 (Fla. Ct. App. 2001). Ms. Schiavo's parents petitioned successfully for reinsertion of the feeding tube, and after a second removal and reinsertion in 2003, Ms. Schiavo's feeding tube was finally removed in March 2005. Her death ensued 13 days later. For further discussion, see symposia at 22 Const. Commentary 383 (2005) and 35 Stetson L. Rev. 1 (2005); Barbara A. Noah, Politicizing the End of Life: Lessons from the Schiavo Controversy, 59 U. Miami L. Rev. 107 (2004); Lois Shepherd, Shattering the Neutral Surrogate Myth in End-of-Life Decisionmaking: Terri Schiavo and Her Family, 35 Cumb. L. Rev. 575 (2004/2005). For a timeline of the case and links to key documents and other resources, see the University of Miami Bioethics Program's Web site.

For discussions of the role of mediation and alternative dispute resolution more generally in resolving disagreements, see I. Glenn Cohen, Negotiating Death: ADR and End of Life Decision-Making, 9 Harv. Negotiation L. Rev. 253 (2004); Nancy Neveloff Dubler & Carol B. Liebman, Bioethics Mediation: A Guide to Shaping Shared Solutions (2004); Robert Gatter, Unnecessary Adversaries at the End of Life: Mediating End-of-Life Treatment Disputes to Prevent Erosion of Physician-Patient Relationships, 79 B.U. L. Rev. 1091 (1999); Diane E. Hoffmann, Mediating Life and Death Decisions, 36 Ariz. L. Rev. 821 (1994).

8. *Ethics Committees and Consultants.* Many commentators and courts have encouraged resort to ethics committees and/or ethics consultants to help resolve disagreements among patients, family members, and health care providers. Indeed, the *Quinlan* court suggested that physicians might routinely turn to a hospital ethics

committee for guidance when faced with requests by a patient or family to discontinue life-sustaining treatment. *Quinlan*, 355 A.2d at 668-669 (citing Karen Teel, The Physician's Dilemma: A Doctor's View: What the Law Should Be, 27 Baylor L. Rev. 6 (1975)). There are two basic types of committees, with many variations. "Prognosis committees" are composed primarily of medical personnel and their principal role is to help clinicians resolve questions about the patient's medical condition and likely outcomes of treatment. Full-fledged "ethics committees" include physicians, nurses, social workers, ethicists, lawyers, clergy, and others, including community representatives, and they serve as an interface between clinicians and families. Whereas ethics committees tend to be ongoing, standing committees, prognosis committees may be ad hoc committees constituted as particular cases arise. In re Colyer, 660 P.2d 738, 749 & n.7 (Wash. 1983). Note too that courts in some cases require or recommend confirmation of prognosis by independent consulting physicians rather than a committee. In re Conroy, 486 A.2d 1209, 1242 (N.J. 1985).

Prodded partly by accreditation requirements, hospitals are increasingly likely to have the full-fledged ethics committees that are available to consider ethical questions that arise in the hospital, and to serve in an advisory role to the patients and physicians involved. In their advisory role, they make no formal decisions and issue nothing of binding force. Ethics committees may, however, develop binding hospital policies and protocols for dealing with specific recurring ethical issues. They also provide ethics education to clinicians. Committee on Bioethics, Institutional Ethics Committees, 107 Pediatrics 205 (2001) (reaffirmed October 2008, 123 Pediatrics 1421 (2009)). It is also becoming more common for hospitals to have ethics consultants, who are physician or nonphysician ethicists whom treating physicians can call on for advice, much as they call on medical specialists for consultation.

An important question is what the goals of the ethics committee or consultant should be. Is it to reach the ethically "correct" result, or is it to guide the involved parties to a result that all can accept? While these two goals may be compatible, they may also be in conflict, and there is often a tendency to view compromise as a desirable goal. The issue whether to aim for the right result or an amicable outcome raises the further question as to whether ethics can lead us to a correct answer or only provide analytic tools to better understand the issues at stake. There are also important legal issues, including whether committee proceedings are confidential and whether committee members are subject to tort liability for their decisions.

For further discussion, see Alan Meisel & Kathy L. Cerminara, The Right to Die §3.25 (3d ed. 2004); Judith Wilson Ross et al., Health Care Ethics Committees: The Next Generation (1993); David C. Blake, The Hospital Ethics Committee: Health Care's Moral Conscience or White Elephant?, 22(1) Hastings Center Rep. 5 (1992); John C. Fletcher & Mark Siegler, What Are the Goals of Ethics Consultation? A Consensus Statement, 7 J. Clin. Ethics 122 (1996); Diane Hoffmann, Evaluating Ethics Committees: A View from the Outside, 71 Milbank Q. 667 (1993); Diane Hoffmann & Anita Terzian, The Role and Legal Status of Health Care Ethics Committees in the U.S., *in* Legal Perspectives in Bioethics (Ana Ilitis et al. eds., 2008); Thaddeus Pope, Multi-Institutional Healthcare Ethics Committees: The Procedurally Fair Internal Dispute Resolution Mechanism, 31 Campbell L. Rev. 257 (2009); Bethany Spielman, Has Faith in Health Care Ethics Consultants Gone Too Far? Risks of an Unregulated Practice and a Model Act to Contain Them, 85 Marq. L. Rev. 161 (2001); Robin Wilson, Hospital Ethics Committees as the Forum of Last Resort: An

Idea Whose Time Has Not Come, 76 N.C. L. Rev. 353 (1998); Symposium: Hospital Ethics Committees and the Law, 50 Md. L. Rev. 742 (1991).

For an interesting historical perspective on hospital ethics committees, including discussion of their use to approve abortions, allocate limited kidney dialysis slots, and review decisions to withdraw life-sustaining treatment from seriously disabled newborns, see George J. Annas, Ethics Committees: From Ethical Comfort to Ethical Cover, 21(3) Hastings Center Rep. 18 (1991).

9. *Resort to the Courts.* Courts routinely discourage judicial intervention into end-of-life cases, on the basis either that these are matters for legislatures to work out or that these are matters that are best resolved by patients, families, and physicians. Two typical statements follow:

> . . . Because the issue with all its ramifications is fraught with complexity and encompasses the interests of the law, both civil and criminal, medical ethics and social morality, it is not one which is well-suited for resolution in an adversary judicial proceeding. It is the type [of] issue which is more suitably addressed in the legislative forum, where fact finding can be less confined and the viewpoints of all interested institutions and disciplines can be presented and synthesized. In this manner only can the subject be dealt with comprehensively and the interests of all institutions and individuals be properly accommodated. [Satz v. Perlmutter, 379 So. 2d 359, 260 (Fla. 1980).]

> . . . [J]udicial review of a competent patient's refusal of life-sustaining medical treatment is generally not appropriate. Only unusual circumstances, such as a conflict among the physicians, or among the family members, or between the physicians and the family or other health care professionals, would necessitate judicial intervention. . . .
>
> No matter how expedited, judicial intervention in this complex and sensitive area may take too long. Thus, it could infringe the very rights that we want to protect. The mere prospect of a cumbersome, intrusive, and expensive court proceeding during such an emotional and upsetting period in the lives of a patient and his or her loved ones would undoubtedly deter many persons from deciding to discontinue treatment. And even if the patient or the family were willing to submit to such a proceeding, it is likely that the patient's rights would nevertheless be frustrated by judicial deliberation. Too many patients have died before their right to reject treatment was vindicated in court. Even in this case—where the judicial system acted in an extremely prompt and efficient manner (only 14 days elapsed between the filing of the complaint and the grant of the petition for certification)—we were unable to act in time. Mrs. Farrell died shackled to the respirator. [In re Farrell, 529 A.2d 404, 415 (N.J. 1987).]

Other concerns with judicial involvement include the consequences of forcing the family and physicians into an adversarial posture and the requirement that the court issue its decision based on the state of affairs that existed at the time the record was made despite the possibility of rapidly changing facts. See In re L.H.R., 321 S.E.2d 716, 720-721 (Ga. 1984); William J. Curran, The *Saikewicz* Decision, 298 New Eng. J. Med. 499 (1978).

Nevertheless, some courts have required judicial review of treatment withdrawal cases, requirements that have proven to be short-lived. The Massachusetts Supreme Court, in the *Saikewicz* case, required probate court approval before life-sustaining treatment could be withdrawn from incompetent persons. *Saikewicz*, 370 N.E.2d at

433-434. Not surprisingly, medical reaction to the *Saikewicz* court's requirement of judicial involvement was immediate and overwhelmingly disapproving. Hospital attorneys were also generally opposed to the decision. Civil rights groups and many academic lawyers, on the other hand, supported the court's holding. Impassioned debate took up many pages of volumes 4 and 5 of the *American Journal of Law & Medicine* (1978-1979). Ultimately, the issue was dissipated two years later by a subsequent Massachusetts Supreme Court decision in which the court wrote that "our opinions should not be taken to establish any requirement of prior judicial approval that would not otherwise exist." In re Spring, 405 N.E.2d 115, 120 (Mass. 1980).

In 1989, the Illinois Supreme Court also imposed a requirement of a court order for cases in which family members or other surrogate decisionmakers seek to discontinue artificial nutrition and hydration from an incompetent person. In re Longeway, 549 N.E.2d 292, 300-301 (Ill. 1989). Despite the court's holding, there was no surge in petitions for court orders to withdraw feeding tubes. Some hospitals and nursing homes continued to stop artificial nutrition and hydration without seeking judicial approval; others may have simply continued to provide artificial nutrition and hydration. In 1991, the Illinois legislature eliminated the need for judicial approval when it passed the state's Health Care Surrogate Act. 755 Ill. Comp. Stat. 40.

Notes: Advance Planning

As the court opinions regularly observe, people can avoid many of the problems with end-of-life decisionmaking by executing a living will, durable power of attorney for health care, or other advance directive while competent. All states have either a living will or power of attorney statute and almost all states have both. Alan Meisel & Kathy L. Cerminara, The Right to Die §§7.01, 7.13 (3d ed. 2009 Supp.). The statutes typically state that the rights granted therein are cumulative with other rights individuals might have with respect to end-of-life medical decisions.

1. *Living Wills.* The first living will statute was enacted in California in 1976; the document is called a "living" will because it takes effect while the testator is still alive. With a living will, also called a treatment directive, a person describes the circumstances under which treatment would not be desired. A person also might use a living will to indicate a desire that treatment *not* be withheld as long as life can be prolonged. Indeed, Indiana's living will statute includes two forms, one a typical "living will declaration" to express a desire that treatment be withheld, the other a "life prolonging procedures declaration" to express a desire that treatment be provided. Ind. Stat. Ann. §§16-36-4-10, 16-36-4-11. The Indiana statute also states that a life prolonging procedures declaration has conclusive weight while a living will declaration has "great weight." Ind. Stat. Ann. §16-36-4-8 (f)-(g).

Living wills have several drawbacks. If a person gives specific instructions, the document will not provide guidance in unanticipated situations. If a person instead tries to give general guidance that can be applied to any particular situation, then there will likely be a good deal of ambiguity in the living will, ambiguity that may lead different people to different interpretations of the person's wishes. Some statutes apply only to patients with terminal illnesses and persistent vegetative states, and some statutes restrict the circumstances under which artificial nutrition and hydration may be withdrawn. People can avoid such limitations by attaching addenda or using one of the model forms available from national organizations, although most people are likely to use the statutory form out of either convenience or unawareness of the alternatives. David Orentlicher, Advance Medical Directives, 263 JAMA 2365 (1990). See also Leslie Francis, The Evanescence of Living Wills, 14 J. Contemp. L. 27 (1988); Symposium, Advance Directive Instruments for End-of-Life and Health Care Decision Making, 4 Psychol. Pub. Pol'y & L. 579 (1998); Katherine Taylor, Compelling Pregnancy at Death's Door, 7 Colum. J. Gender & L. 85 (1997).

For a case illustrating the problems that patients can experience with having their living wills followed, see Wright v. Johns Hopkins Health Systems Corp., 728 A.2d 166 (Md. 1999) (discussed, infra, page 337).

2. *Proxy Appointments.* Rather than giving treatment instructions, a person might choose to appoint a proxy or surrogate decisionmaker by executing a durable power of attorney for health care. By doing so, the individual can transfer authority to make medical decisions to someone else. Durable powers of attorney were created because under the common law, all agency power ceases when the principal becomes incompetent. With a "durable" power of attorney, the proxy's agency authority survives the incompetence of the patient. Technically, durable powers of attorney for health care are actually "springing" powers of attorney. In other words, strictly speaking, a durable power of attorney takes effect while the principal is still competent and continues to have effect if the principal becomes incompetent. A springing power of attorney, on the other hand, does not take effect until the principal becomes incompetent. Despite the inaccuracy of the term, powers of attorney for health care are universally characterized as durable powers of attorney.

With a power of attorney, a person can avoid many of the problems with living wills. Power of attorney statutes generally apply to patients in any condition and with regard to any treatment. It is unusual for them to qualify the surrogate's authority to situations in which the patient is terminally ill or to restrict the surrogate's authority to decline artificial nutrition and hydration. Accordingly, people can provide for the exercise of their right to refuse treatment in all circumstances. Since proxies have broad authority, they are able to make decisions even when patients have not expressed their wishes or expressed them in too vague a way to be sure what the patient intended. Of course, some people may not have anyone whom they trust enough to appoint as a proxy. For a decision recognizing broad surrogate authority, see Stein v. County of Nassau, 642 F. Supp. 2d 135 (E.D.N.Y. 2009), in which the court held that under New York's health care proxy statute, surrogates have authority to make medical decisions in any setting, including the patient's home, not just in hospitals. The court of appeals vacated the trial court's holding on the ground that the New York statute required the attending physician to certify in writing that the patient lacked decisionmaking capacity, and no such certification had been made. Stein v. Barthelson, 419 Fed. Appx. 617 (2d Cir. 2011).

Some people choose to combine a treatment directive with a power of attorney, giving some instructions and leaving authority to the surrogate for situations not covered by their instructions. What do you see as the problem with this approach?

3. *Statutory Forms.* Advance directive laws typically include a statutory form but generally state that individuals need not use the statutory form. However, in a few states, the statutes require compliance with the statutory form. See, e.g., Texas

Medical Power of Attorney, Tex. Health & Safety Code §§166.163, 166.164. What would be the legal significance of a handwritten living will that does not follow the statutory format?

4. *Limitations of Advance Directives.* For all of their usefulness, advance directives have been disappointing in practice. Most people do not fill them out, even when encouraged to do so by physicians. Moreover, as indicated, when living wills are executed, they are often too vague to give sufficient guidance. Most troubling is the fact that, even when living wills give sufficient guidance, they are often overridden by physicians.

Although courts have clearly and emphatically recognized that end-of-life-decisions should be based on patient preferences and values, empirical studies indicate that it is the physician's preferences and values that seem to drive decisions regarding the withdrawal of life-sustaining medical treatment. David Orentlicher, The Limitations of Legislation, 53 Md. L. Rev. 1255, 1280-1288 (1994). In one study, after nursing home residents completed living wills, researchers followed the residents to determine whether subsequent medical decisions were consistent with them. The researchers found that physicians overrode the living wills 25 percent of the time. Marion Danis et al., A Prospective Study of Advance Directives for Life-Sustaining Care, 324 New Eng. J. Med. 882 (1991). While a 75 percent agreement may seem good, the study suggests that physicians overrode the patient's preferences the majority of the time when there was a disagreement between the patient's choice and the physician's preferences:

> [I]n most end-of-life situations, physicians and patients probably agree on whether treatment should be provided, and much of the 75 percent consistency between the living wills and the physicians' decisions can be explained by a sharing of values between patients and physicians. When there is disagreement between physicians and patients, however, it follows that the physicians' preferences generally prevail. Assuming that there is a 60 percent agreement rate and a 40 percent disagreement rate between patients and physicians, then a 25 percent override rate means that physicians prevail in 62.5 percent of the disagreements (25 percent/40 percent).

Orentlicher, The Limitations of Legislation, at 1282. This predominance of physicians' values also can be found in situations involving competent patients or in which family members have decisionmaking authority. David Orentlicher, The Illusion of Patient Choice in End-of-Life Decisions, 267 JAMA 2101, 2101-2102 (1992). See also Susan Adler Channick, The Myth of Autonomy at the End-of-Life: Questioning the Paradigm of Rights, 44 Vill. L. Rev. 577 (1999); Kenneth E. Covinsky et al., Communication and Decision-Making in Seriously Ill Patients: Findings of the SUPPORT Project, 48(5) J. Am. Geriatrics Soc'y S187 (2000) (reporting that physicians wrote DNR orders for only 52 percent of patients who said they did not want CPR and that physicians frequently misjudged patient willingness to live in a nursing home). In a recent study, researchers found close agreement between patient preferences and the care that they received when patients requested limited care but not when patients requested all care possible. Maria J. Silveira, Advance Directives and Outcomes of Surrogate Decision Making Before Death, 362 New Eng. J. Med. 1211 (2010). (Note that this study was based on interviews with patient proxies after the patient's death.)

Moreover, physicians' personal values often diverge from the principles that have become widely recognized in ethics and the law. Even though patients are as free to have treatment withdrawn as to have it withheld, many physicians believe it is ethically and legally less acceptable to withdraw care than to withhold it, as discussed at pages 284-285 in the section on the competent patient. Similarly, even though the patient's right to refuse treatment applies to all medical treatments, whether the decision to withhold or withdraw involves a ventilator, CPR, or a feeding tube, physicians often express a greater reluctance to withdraw some treatments than others, particularly feeding tubes. See, e.g., Heikki Hinkka et al., Factors Affecting Physicians' Decisions to Forgo Life-Sustaining Treatments in Terminal Care, 28 J. Med. Ethics 109 (2002); William R. Mower & Larry J. Baraff, Advance Directives: Effect of Type of Directive on Physicians' Therapeutic Decisions, 153 Arch. Intern. Med. 375, 380 Table 3 (1993); Mildred Z. Solomon et al., Decisions near the End of Life: Professional Views on Life-Sustaining Treatments, 83 Am. J. Public Health 14, 18 Table 4 (1993). See also David A. Asch et al., The Sequence of Withdrawing Life-Sustaining Treatment from Patients, 107 Am. J. Med. 153 (1999) (finding that when life-sustaining treatment is withdrawn from patients, intravenous fluids and tube feedings are the last treatments to be withdrawn); David A. Asch & Nicholas A. Christakis, Why Do Physicians Prefer to Withdraw Some Forms of Life Support over Others?, 34 Med. Care 103 (1996) (finding that physicians prefer to withdraw treatments that are scarce, expensive, emotionally taxing, high technology, and rapidly fatal when withdrawn).

It is not only physicians who view feeding tubes differently than dialysis, ventilators, or other treatments. Statutory treatment of end-of-life decisions indicates that this view is shared more widely. In one study, researchers found that 20 states set more stringent standards for withdrawal of artificial nutrition and hydration than for withdrawal of other treatments. Carol E. Sieger et al., Refusing Artificial Nutrition and Hydration: Does Statutory Law Send the Wrong Message?, 50 J. Am. Geriatrics Soc'y 544 (2002). Not all of those standards have been constitutionally valid. According to an opinion by the Oklahoma Attorney General, Oklahoma's advance directive statute was unconstitutional when it limited the withholding of artificial nutrition and hydration from patients who were terminally ill or persistently unconscious. Okla. Att'y Gen. Op., No. 06-7 (Apr. 6, 2006). In response, the Oklahoma legislature amended its statute to create a presumption that patients wish to have artificial nutrition and hydration provided unless they give contrary directions in an advance directive or leave other clear and convincing evidence of their wishes, their physician knows that the patient would not want these treatments, or it would be futile or inhumane to provide artificial nutrition and hydration. 63 Okla. Stat. tit. 63, §§3080.3-3080.4.

Knowing that physicians may not follow instructions in an advance directive and that they may also impose their views on surrogate decisionmakers, what advice might you give to clients who want to ensure that their wishes are carried out?

For an interesting study of efforts to ensure that patients have advance directives or surrogates, see Daniel P. Kessler & Mark B. McClellan, Advance Directives and Medical Treatment at the End of Life, 23 J. Health Econ. 111 (2004) (finding that state laws with incentives for physicians or hospitals to comply with advance directives reduce the probability of patients dying in an acute care hospital, that laws requiring the appointment of a surrogate in the absence of an advance directive increase the probability of receiving acute care in the last month of life, but decrease the probability of receiving nonacute care, and that neither type of law leads to any savings in medical expenditures).

5. *Patient Self-Determination Act.* The federal government has tried to facilitate advance planning with the enactment of the Patient Self-Determination Act. The Act applies to health care institutions that receive Medicare or Medicaid funds. Under the Act, people must be informed of their rights regarding medical decision-making, including the right to refuse life-sustaining treatment, when they are admitted to a hospital or nursing home, come under the care of a home health agency or hospice, or enroll in a health maintenance organization (HMO). These institutions must also inquire as to whether patients have an advance directive and document any directive in the patient's medical record. The institutions must ensure that they are in compliance with state law regarding advance directives and must not condition their provision of care on whether a patient has an advance directive. John La Puma, David Orentlicher & Robert J. Moss, Advance Directives on Admission: Clinical Implications and Analysis of the Patient Self-Determination Act of 1990, 266 JAMA 402 (1991); Susan M. Wolf et al., Sources of Concern About the Patient Self-Determination Act, 325 New Eng. J. Med. 1666 (1991).

A government study of the implementation of the Act found that facilities failed to document whether the patient had completed an advance directive in 20 percent of cases. In addition, for 40 percent of the individuals with advance directives, there was no copy of the directive in the person's medical record. Office of Inspector General, Department of Health and Human Services, Patient Advance Directives: Facility and Patient Responses (August 1993).

Other studies have found little evidence that the Act has affected the use of advance directives or do-not-resuscitate orders. David W. Baker et al., Changes in the Use of Do-Not-Resuscitate Orders After Implementation of the Patient Self-Determination Act, 18 J. Gen. Internal Med. 353 (2003) (but finding a small shift toward addressing resuscitation status earlier in a patient's hospital stay); Eric D. Morrell et al., The Do-Not-Resuscitate Order: Associations with Advance Directives, Physician Specialty, and Documentation of Discussion 15 Years After the Patient Self-Determination Act, 34 J. Med. Ethics 642 (2008); Joan Teno et al., Advance Directives for Seriously Ill Hospitalized Patients: Effectiveness with the Patient Self-Determination Act and the SUPPORT Intervention, 45 J. Am. Geriatrics Soc'y 500 (1997) (but finding greater likelihood of documentation of existing advance directives). See also Edward J. Larson & Thomas A. Eaton, The Limits of Advance Directives: A History and Assessment of the Patient Self-Determination Act, 32 Wake Forest L. Rev. 249 (1997). But see Nicholas G. Castle & Victor Mor, Advance Care Planning in Nursing Homes: Pre- and Post-Patient Self-Determination Act, 33 Health Serv. Res. 101 (1998) (finding evidence that the PSDA has promoted advance planning).

6. *Physician Orders for Life-Sustaining Treatment.* If treatment can be withdrawn based on clear and convincing evidence of the patient's wishes, does it matter whether the wishes are documented by the patient or by someone else?

Physicians can create advance directives for their patients by documenting patient preferences in their medical records. While this option followed from principles of end-of-life law, states also have passed statutes recognizing "physician orders for life-sustaining treatment" or POLST. POLST translate the general guidance that patients might provide in a living will into specific physician orders regarding treatment. Because POLST take the form of physician orders, they have the potential for being more effective than patient-written advance directives in carrying out the patient's wishes. In particular, POLST address the problem of physicians overriding patient advance directives (discussed, supra, note 4). For further discussion, see Judy Citko et al., The National POLST Paradigm Initiative, 2nd Edition #178, 14 J. Palliative Med. 241 (2011); Diane Meier & Larry Beresford, POLST Offers Next State in Honoring Patient Preferences, 12 J. Palliative Med. 291 (2009). (While POLST is the original name, states have chosen a variety of names, including Medical Order for Life-Sustaining Treatment (MOLST) and Physician Order Regarding Treatment (PORT). Alan Meisel & Kathy L. Cerminara, The Right to Die §1A.07[D] (3d ed. 2009 Supp.)).

7. *Enforcement of the Legal Standards.* As discussed at pages 294 and 334-335, end-of-life decisions may be driven more by the physician's views or the hospital's legal defensiveness than by the patient's preferences. One way to address the failure to follow patients' wishes is to hold physicians and institutions liable in tort suits when they ignore the patient's preferences. Individuals or their families have sued providers for administering unwanted life-sustaining treatment, but courts have generally refused to impose liability.

In an Ohio case, for example, the patient, a Mr. Winter, had stated his desire not to be resuscitated in the event of cardiac arrest. He wanted to avoid the fate of his wife, whose health seriously deteriorated after she received cardiopulmonary resuscitation (CPR). Mr. Winter's physician wrote a do-not-resuscitate (DNR) order in the medical chart, but Mr. Winter was resuscitated nevertheless. Two days later, Mr. Winter suffered a stroke, and he required nursing home care until his death two years later. The court permitted nominal damages only for the battery of receiving unwanted CPR, holding that the stroke was not a direct result of the CPR. Anderson v. St. Francis-St. George Hospital, 671 N.E.2d 225 (Ohio 1996).

Maryland's supreme court also rejected a claim based on wrongful administration of life-sustaining care. In Wright v. Johns Hopkins Health Systems Corp., 728 A.2d 166 (Md. 1999), a man with HIV disease, Robert Lee Wright, Jr., had executed a living will declining life-sustaining care, and he had also requested a DNR order on the hospital's HIV Case Management Plan of Care. More than a year later, when he was terminally ill with AIDS, Mr. Wright received a blood transfusion on what was supposed to be the final day of a three-day hospitalization for treatment of his AIDS. Immediately following the transfusion, Wright suffered a cardiac arrest and was resuscitated despite his advance planning. The cardiac arrest left him with severe brain damage, and he died ten days later, still in the hospital. The court upheld summary judgment in favor of the hospital on two grounds. First, by its language, the living will took effect when Wright had been "certified [to have] a terminal condition by two (2) physicians," and that certification had not occurred. Id. at 175. Second, although Wright had requested a DNR order, hospital policy set forth the physician's responsibility to discuss the withholding of CPR when patients had an irreversible disease and death was imminent or there was a high probability of cardiac arrest during the current hospitalization. Although Wright's life expectancy was less than six months, his death was not imminent. Id. at 177.

Other cases rejecting damages include Duarte v. Chino Community Hospital, 85 Cal. Rptr. 2d 521 (Ct. App. 1999); Taylor v. Muncie Medical Investors, 727 N.E.2d 466, 471 (Ind. Ct. App. 2000). For a case rejecting a lawsuit by parents for the undesired resuscitation of a premature infant, see Miller v. HCA, Inc., 118 S.W.3d 758 (Tex. 2003).

For a decision recognizing a cause of action and remanding for trial, see Gragg v. Calandra, 696 N.E.2d 1282 (Ill. Ct. App. 1998). In addition, there have been some jury verdicts and settlements in which damages were recovered. Scheible v. Joseph L. Morse Geriatric Center, Inc., 988 So. 2d 1130 (Fla. Ct. App. 2008); Rose Gasner, Financial Penalties for Failing to Honor Patient Wishes to Refuse Treatment, 11 St. Louis U. Pub. L. Rev. 499 (1992). In one case, a jury awarded $16.5 million after a hospital continued life-sustaining treatment over the apparent objections of the patient's family members. Andrew J. Broder, "She Don't Want No Life Support," 75 U. Det. Mercy L. Rev. 595 (1998). In that case, the hospital claimed at trial that family members agreed to the provision of treatment. The trial judge reduced the verdict to $1.43 million, and a settlement was reached while the appeal was pending.

Courts have not only been reluctant to authorize damages for the imposition of unwanted life-sustaining treatment, they have sometimes required families to pay hospital bills that accrued during the time between the family's request that treatment be stopped and the issuance of a court order upholding the family's request. Grace Plaza of Great Neck, Inc. v. Elbaum, 623 N.E.2d 513 (N.Y. 1993); First Healthcare Corp. v. Rettinger, 467 S.E.2d 243 (N.C. 1996).

Since some of the courts' reluctance to award damages reflects a sense that the law regarding withdrawal of treatment was not well established when the cases arose, courts in the future may be more willing to assess damages for the unwanted imposition of treatment. But even then tort law principles may yield low levels of damages. Alan Meisel & Kathy L. Cerminara, The Right to Die §11.01[A] (3d ed. 2009 and 2010 Supps.).

Why do you suppose that courts are so reluctant to impose damages in these cases?

Courts' reluctance to award damages for unwanted life-sustaining treatment may explain in part why some hospitals will not honor a patient's request to discontinue treatment in the absence of a court order. Court cases arise even when the patient's wishes and the law clearly support withdrawal. See, e.g., Bartling v. Superior Court, 209 Cal. Rptr. 220 (Ct. App. 1984) (hospital refused to remove ventilator upon request of competent adult patient). To some extent, the hospitals are likely acting on the basis of religious or other moral scruples. It may also be the case that the hospital's attorneys view the legal risks, however minimal, as existing primarily on the side of withdrawing treatment. As discussed at page 294, regarding the ethical integrity of the medical profession, even though no physician or hospital has been held civilly or criminally liable for withdrawing life-sustaining treatment at the behest of the patient or family, criminal charges were lodged against two physicians in Barber v. Superior Court, 195 Cal. Rptr. 478 (Ct. App. 1983). Moreover, most lawyers would probably prefer to explain to a jury why they kept someone alive too long than why they let someone die prematurely.

For further discussion, see Holly Fernandez Lynch et al., Compliance with Advance Directives, 29 J. Leg. Med. 133 (2008); Adam A. Milani, Better Off Dead Than Disabled?: Should Courts Recognize a "Wrongful Living" Cause of Action When Doctors Fail to Honor Patients' Advance Directives?, 54 Wash. & Lee L. Rev. 149 (1997); A. Samuel Oddi, The Tort of Interference with the Right to Die: The Wrongful Living Cause of Action, 75 Geo. L.J. 625 (1986); Philip G. Peters, Jr., The

Illusion of Autonomy at the End of Life: Unconsented Life Support and the Wrong-ful Life Analogy, 45 UCLA L. Rev. 673 (1998); Annot., Tortious Maintenance or Removal of Life Supports, 58 A.L.R.4th 222 (1987). For a related issue, consider "wrongful life" and "wrongful birth" causes of action when a child is born with a dis-ability that could have been detected with prenatal screening.

8. *Further Reading.* Good discussions of advance directives and/or the Patient-Self Determination Act can be found in Norman L. Cantor, Advance Directives and the Pursuit of Death with Dignity (1993); Rebecca Dresser, Precommitment: A Misguided Strategy for Securing Death with Dignity, 81 Tex. L. Rev. 1823 (2003); Angela Fagerlin & Carl E. Schneider, Enough: The Failure of the Liv-ing Will, 34(2) Hastings Center Rep. 30 (2004); Lesley S. Castillo et al., Lost in Translation: The Unintended Consequences of Advance Directive Law on Clini-cal Care, 154 Ann. Intern. Med. 121 (2011); Bernard Lo & Robert Steinbrook, Resuscitating Advance Directives, 164 Arch. Intern. Med. 1501 (2004); Practicing the PSDA: A Hastings Center Report Special Supplement, 21(5) Hastings Center Rep. S1-S16 (1991); Joan M. Teno et al., Association Between Advance Directives and Quality of End-of-Life Care: A National Study, 55 J. Am. Geriatrics Soc'y 189 (2007).

Problems: Interpreting and Drafting Advance Directives

1. Karen Thomas was a 65-year-old woman with a severe narrowing of her left carotid artery (one of the two main arteries that carries blood to the brain). Because of the high risk of a disabling stroke, her physician recommended surgery to correct the narrowing. When he explained that there was a small risk that the surgery itself would precipitate a stroke or heart attack, Ms. Thomas told her physician about her living will. Four years earlier, after her husband had died of a prolonged illness, Ms. Thomas had executed the will, and she told her surgeon that she wished her will to be carried out in the event that she became incapacitated as a result of the surgery. She also told the surgeon that she considered life to be worth living only if she could live independently. Her living will included the following passage:

> If a situation should arise in which there is no reasonable expectation of my recov-ery from physical or mental disability, I request that I be allowed to die and not be kept alive by artificial means or heroic measures. I do not fear death itself as much as the indignities of deterioration, dependence, and hopeless pain. I therefore ask that medications be mercifully administered to me to alleviate suffering, even though this may hasten the moment of death. This request is made after careful consideration. I hope that you who care for me will feel morally bound to follow its mandate.

Ms. Thomas's surgery went well, and she awoke with full neurological func-tion. However, shortly thereafter, she began to experience progressively worsening weakness on her right side and other abnormalities consistent with a serious stroke on the left side of her brain. She was taken back to the operating room, and her surgeons removed a large clot in a main artery that delivers blood to the left side of the brain. Nevertheless, Ms. Thomas continued to manifest signs of a severe stroke, with paralysis of her right side and loss of consciousness with responsiveness only to painful stimuli. Over the next week, Ms. Thomas showed no improvement in her condition, and, because of a pneumonia, needed a ventilator to ensure adequate oxygenation. Ms. Thomas' brother reminded the hospital of her living will and requested that the ventilator be discontinued. Her physician asked for a neurology consult, and the neurologists indicated that it could take several months before her ultimate prognosis became clear. They felt there was a 10 percent chance that she could recover most of her mental and physical capacity, although she might always need a wheelchair, a 30 percent chance that she would die without recovering consciousness, and a 60 percent chance that she would be seriously and permanently disabled. If you were the hospital's attorney, and Ms. Thomas's physician asked for your guidance, what would you say and/or do? (This case is a modified version of a case presented in Stuart J. Eisendrath & Albert R. Jonsen, The Living Will: Help or Hindrance?, 249 JAMA 2054 (1983).)

2. As an exercise to promote understanding of advance directives, you will serve as the "attorney" of a layperson you know and assist your "client" in filling out an advance directive. The exercise also requires you to write a one-page, single-spaced report about the reasoning behind the choices made and your impressions of the process. Your responsibility is to help your client understand the advance directive process and reach some resolution of the necessary decisions (e.g., whom to appoint as an agent, in what circumstances treatment may be withdrawn). If the person you approach is willing to discuss these decisions with you but unwilling to commit to any definitive answers, that is all right. Just leave the form blank and explain the client's reasoning in your report. It is your responsibility to select an advance directive form to be used. You may want to use the statutory form for your state, which you can find in your state's statutory code, or you may want to use a generic form. You can find several generic forms at the Web site for the University of Buffalo Center for Clinical Ethics, http://wings.buffalo.edu/faculty/research/bioethics/adv-dir.html. You may also use an advance directive form that you find elsewhere. The Web site for this book (www.health-law.org) also has a list of discussion questions you may want to use with your client. After your completed advance directive and one-page report are due, you will be given a patient scenario. You should then write down what would be the effect of your client's advance directive and ask your client whether that effect is consistent with what the client would want done if the client were ever in the condition described in the scenario. If it is unclear what outcome would result from the advance directive, or if the result would depend on information not available, then you should indicate that such is the case.

Notes: Young Children and Adolescents (Not Competent)

1. *Presumption of Parental Authority.* As mentioned at page 299, parents generally have authority to make medical decisions, including decisions about life-sustaining medical treatment on behalf of their children. The usual standard for parental decisionmaking is a best interests standard. Alan Meisel & Kathy L. Cerminara, The Right to Die §9.05[A] (3d ed. 2009 Supp.). The child's lack of decisionmaking capacity precludes the adoption of a standard based solely on the child's wishes. Still, one can consider the child's desires even if they are not determinative. Over time, courts have refined the best interests standard for children, as illustrated by the following standard from California:

We conclude that a court making the decision of whether to withhold or withdraw life-sustaining medical treatment from a dependent child should consider the following factors: (1) the child's present levels of physical, sensory, emotional and cognitive functioning; (2) the quality of life, life expectancy and prognosis for recovery with and without treatment, including the futility of continued treatment; (3) the various treatment options, and the risks, side effects, and benefits of each; (4) the nature and degree of physical pain or suffering resulting from the medical condition; (5) whether the medical treatment being provided is causing or may cause pain, suffering, or serious complications; (6) the pain or suffering to the child if the medical treatment is withdrawn; (7) whether any particular treatment would be proportionate or disproportionate in terms of the benefits to be gained by the child versus the burdens caused to the child; (8) the likelihood that pain or suffering resulting from withholding or withdrawal of treatment could be avoided or minimized; (9) the degree of humiliation, dependence and loss of dignity resulting from the condition and treatment; (10) the opinions of the family, the reasons behind those opinions, and the reasons why the family either has no opinion or cannot agree on a course of treatment; (11) the motivations of the family in advocating a particular course of treatment; and (12) the child's preference, if it can be ascertained, for treatment. [In re Christopher I, 106 Cal. App. 4th 533, 551 (Ct. App. 2003) (followed by J. N. v. Superior Court, 156 Cal. App. 4th 523, 534 (Ct. App. 2007).]

As the best interests standard suggests, parents will be denied authority to refuse life-sustaining treatment in some situations. The classic cases are those involving families of Jehovah's Witnesses where the children need blood transfusions and their parents decline the transfusions on religious grounds. In those cases, the courts have held that the children must be given the transfusions. See, e.g., In re McCauley, 565 N.E.2d 411 (Mass. 1991) (eight-year-old child needed blood transfusion as part of treatment for an acute leukemia); In re Cabrera, 552 A.2d 1114 (Pa. Super. Ct. 1989) (six-year-old child with sickle cell anemia who had already suffered two strokes needed weekly blood transfusions over at least a year's time to reduce the risk of a recurrence of her strokes from 70 percent to 10 percent). In ordering treatment, the courts typically cite Prince v. Massachusetts, 321 U.S. 158, 170 (1944), where the Court wrote:

> Parents may be free to become martyrs themselves. But it does not follow they are free, in identical circumstances, to make martyrs of their children before they have reached the age of full and legal discretion when they can make that choice for themselves.

As the *Prince* excerpt indicates, the theory of these cases is that the children must be given an opportunity to reach adulthood to decide for themselves which religious tenets they will follow. What is the problem with this theory?

2. *Applying the Best Interests Standard to Children.* The hard question in this area is where the limits of parental authority end, and when a refusal of treatment becomes child neglect or abuse. At either end of the spectrum, the law is fairly clear. Courts have had no trouble holding that, when a child can readily be restored to good health or when treatment poses little risk, parents may *not* refuse a life-sustaining treatment, such as a blood transfusion (*McCauley* and *Cabrera*, supra, In re L.S., 87 P.3d 521 (Nev. 2004)), antibiotics (Walker v. Superior Court, 763 P.2d 852 (Cal. 1988) (upholding conviction of Christian Science parents of involuntary

manslaughter for withholding treatment for meningitis from nine-month-old child)), or abdominal surgery (Commonwealth v. Twitchell, 617 N.E.2d 609 (Mass. 1993) (finding that Christian Science parents were not entitled to withhold intestinal surgery from their two-year-old child, but overturning their conviction for involuntary manslaughter on grounds that they were prevented from presenting the affirmative defense that they were misled as to their risk of prosecution by an opinion of the state's Attorney General)). Similarly, courts have had no trouble holding that parents *may* refuse life-sustaining ventilators or feeding tubes when the child is irreversibly unconscious. See, e.g., In re L.H.R., 321 S.E.2d 716 (Ga. 1984) (permitting the removal of a ventilator from a several-month-old child in an irreversible coma); In re P.V.W., 424 So. 2d 1015 (La. 1982) (permitting the removal of artificial life supports from an infant who had been irreversibly comatose since birth); In re Guardianship of Crum, 580 N.E.2d 876 (Ohio Prob. Ct. 1991) (permitting the removal of a feeding tube from a 17-year-old who was irreversibly unconscious); In re Guardianship of Myers, 610 N.E.2d 663 (Ohio Prob. Ct. 1993) (permitting the removal of a feeding tube from a minor, apparently an adolescent, who was irreversibly unconscious).

Other decisions, however, are not so clear. Some treatments will have a low likelihood of success and may carry substantial risks. As the following cases indicate, the courts have not come to a consensus on the extent of parental discretion:

Newmark v. Williams, 588 A.2d 1108 (Del. 1991). A three-year-old boy was diagnosed as having an aggressive malignancy of the immune system, Burkitt's lymphoma. By the time a diagnosis was made during surgery for an intestinal obstruction, the cancer had spread elsewhere in the boy's body. His physician recommended that he be treated with a heavy regimen of chemotherapy. According to the medical testimony, there was a 40 percent chance of a "cure." Without treatment, he would likely die within six to eight months. Medical testimony also indicated that the treatment itself was quite toxic and might prove fatal. The boy's parents declined the chemotherapy in favor of care from a Christian Science practitioner. Given the substantial risks of treatment and the less than 50 percent chance of success, the court upheld the parental refusal of treatment.

In re Hamilton, 657 S.W.2d 425 (Tenn. Ct. App. 1983). A 12-year-old girl was diagnosed with Ewing's sarcoma, a bone cancer for which the girl had a 25 to 50 percent chance of long-term remission with treatment. Without treatment, she would likely die within six to nine months. Her father, a lay minister of the Church of God of the Union Assembly, refused treatment on religious grounds. Given the apparent certainty of death without treatment, and the reasonable possibility of long-term success with treatment, the court overrode the parental refusal of treatment. The court seemed to consider the fact that the family's religious sect did not refuse all kinds of medical treatment.

In re Hofbauer, 393 N.E.2d 1009 (N.Y. 1979). A seven-year-old boy developed Hodgkin's lymphoma, and his parents rejected conventional radiation and chemotherapy in favor of metabolic therapy, which included injections of laetrile. The parents explained that they were concerned about the side effects of conventional treatment and that they would agree to conventional therapy if the boy's physician, who was a proponent of metabolic therapy, so advised. The physician testified that the boy was responding well to the metabolic therapy and indicated that he would use conventional treatment if there was a significant deterioration in the boy's condition. The court found that, given these considerations, the family was acting reasonably.

Custody of a Minor, 393 N.E.2d 836 (Mass. 1979). A three-year-old boy was being treated with conventional medical therapy for an acute leukemia, and the leukemia was in remission with a chance of cure as high as 80 percent. However, the boy's parents decided to discontinue his chemotherapy and substitute metabolic therapy, involving the daily taking of enzymes, laetrile, and megadoses of vitamins. The child's leukemia reappeared, and the trial court ordered resumption of conventional chemotherapy, whereupon the leukemia went back into remission, albeit with the chance of cure now at 50 percent. The parents agreed to continue with conventional chemotherapy but also wanted to continue with the metabolic therapy. The trial court ordered the parents to stop the metabolic therapy. The state supreme court affirmed the trial court's order, observing that the metabolic therapy was not only ineffective in treating the leukemia but also posed significant risks of toxicity from the megadoses of vitamins and from the laetrile. In particular, noted the court, laetrile can be broken down in the body to cyanide, leading to chronic cyanide poisoning and eventually to blindness, deafness, and an inability to walk.

In re Phillip B., 156 Cal. Rptr. 48 (Ct. App. 1979). A 12-year-old boy with Down syndrome suffered from a congenital heart defect that, without surgical correction, would result in gradually worsening incapacity and, ultimately, an early death. The parents opposed surgery. Because of the child's Down syndrome and the fact that his heart defect had caused changes in his lung's blood vessels over time, his risk of death from the surgery—5 to 10 percent—was higher than usual, and he had a higher than usual risk of postoperative complications. Because of the child's elevated risks from surgery, the court upheld the parents' decision to refuse surgery. (Subsequently, volunteers at a facility where Phillip B. resided successfully petitioned to become his guardians and for authorization for medical testing, Guardianship of Phillip B., 188 Cal. Rptr. 781 (Ct. App. 1983).)

Which of these court decisions do you think are correctly decided?

For other interesting cases, see In re Nicholas E., 720 A.2d 562 (Me. 1998) (permitting mother to refuse aggressive antiviral drug therapy to treat HIV infection in her four-year-old son); In re Gianelli, 834 N.Y.S.2d 623 (NY. Sup. Ct. 2007) (denying parents' request to withdraw ventilator from a 14-year-old child who had a lethal genetic disease and a life expectancy of no more than two years but who was still "aware and enjoy[ed] TV and videos"); In re Martin F. v. D.L., 820 N.Y.S.2d 759 (N.Y. Sup. Ct. 2006) (deferring to parent's refusal of antipsychotic drug for three-year-old child).

3. *Bibliography.* Good discussions of this topic include Joseph Goldstein, Medical Care for the Child at Risk: On State Supervention of Parental Autonomy, 86 Yale L.J. 645 (1977); Martin T. Harvey, Adolescent Competency and the Refusal of Medical Treatment, 13 Health Matrix 297 (2003); Jennifer L. Rosato, Using Bioethics Discourse to Determine When Parents Should Make Health Care Decisions for Their Children: Is Deference Justified?, 73 Temp. L. Rev. 1 (2000); Lainie Ross, Children, Families, and Health Care Decision Making (1998); Walter Wadlington, Medical Decision Making for and by Children: Tensions Between Parent, State, and Child, 1994 U. Ill. L. Rev. 311; Annot., Physician's Treatment of Child Without Parental Consent, 67 A.L.R.4th (1989).

Notes: Severely Disabled Newborns

1. *Historical Background and Congressional Action.* Treatment of severely disabled newborns generated considerable debate in the 1980s in conjunction with several celebrated cases in which parents sought to withhold life-sustaining treatment from children born with Down syndrome or other, more serious conditions. One case involved the death in 1982 of a Bloomington, Indiana, infant with Down syndrome. The child suffered from several congenital abnormalities associated with Down syndrome, including an esophageal obstruction that prevented oral feeding but that could have been corrected by surgery. The parents declined surgery, and the child died after a trial court and the local Child Protection Committee upheld the parents' decision. In response to the case, the U.S. Department of Health and Human Services adopted rules under the Rehabilitation Act of 1973 to regulate treatment decisions for severely disabled newborns, but the Supreme Court invalidated the rules as not justified by any evidence that such persons were being discriminated against in the provision of health care. Bowen v. American Hospital Association, 476 U.S. 610 (1986).

Also in response to the controversy generated by the Bloomington case, Congress enacted provisions of the Child Abuse Amendments of 1984 to address concerns about the "withholding of medically indicated treatment from disabled infants with life-threatening conditions." 42 U.S.C.A. §5106a(b)(10) (West 1995) (now §5106a(b)(2)(B). Regulations adopted under this legislation are in effect; the regulations condition federal grants for child abuse prevention on whether states establish programs or procedures to respond to cases of alleged "medical neglect." 45 C.F.R. §1340.15). As to the definition of medical neglect,

The term "medical neglect" includes, but is not limited to, the withholding of medically indicated treatment from a disabled infant with a life-threatening condition.

The term "withholding of medically indicated treatment" means the failure to respond to the infant's life-threatening conditions by providing treatment . . . which, in the treating physician's . . . reasonable medical judgment, will be most likely to be effective in ameliorating or correcting all such conditions, except that the term does not include the failure to provide treatment (other than appropriate nutrition, hydration, or medication) to an infant when, in the treating physician's . . . reasonable medical judgment any of the following circumstances apply:

(i) The infant is chronically and irreversibly comatose;

(ii) The provision of such treatment would merely prolong dying, not be effective in ameliorating or correcting all of the infant's life-threatening conditions, or otherwise be futile in terms of the survival of the infant; or

(iii) The provision of such treatment would be virtually futile in terms of the survival of the infant and the treatment itself under such circumstances would be inhumane. [45 C.F.R. §1340.15(b).]

In the interpretive guidelines to these regulations, the Department of Health and Human Services observed that the "third key feature" of the definition of "withholding of medically indicated treatment" is "that even when one of [the] three circumstances is present, and thus failure to provide treatment is not a 'withholding of medically indicated treatment,' the infant must nonetheless be provided with appropriate nutrition, hydration, and medication." 45 C.F.R. pt. 1340, app. While the interpretive guidelines suggest that nutrition and hydration may never be with-held from a newborn, some commentators have argued that there is ambiguity in the qualifying use of "appropriate" before "nutrition, hydration, and medication." One could interpret the term as meaning that nutrition and hydration must be provided and that the way in which it is provided must be appropriate for the child (e.g., the composition of the feedings must meet the dietary needs of the child or the method of feeding, by oral feeding or a feeding tube, must be tailored to the child's condition). Alternatively, one could interpret "appropriate" as meaning that nutrition and hydration must be provided only when it is appropriate given the child's overall medical condition and that, for some newborns, parents may reason-ably conclude that artificial nutrition and hydration should be withdrawn. Lawrence J. Nelson et al., Forgoing Medically Provided Nutrition and Hydration in Pediatric Patients, 23 J.L. Med. & Ethics 33, 40-41 (1995).

The reach of the federal regulations is limited because it is a condition for grants, not a substantive standard directly applicable to parents, physicians, or hos-pitals. Indeed, as indicated in the previous notes section, courts do permit parents to decline artificial nutrition and hydration for their irreversibly unconscious children. Moreover, while there have been cases in which the regulations were at issue, the courts generally have concluded that the parents could proceed with their decision to decline treatment. In re AMB, 640 N.W.2d 262 (Mich. Ct. App. 2001) (finding the Child Abuse Amendments inapplicable for a newborn with heart defects incom-patible with long-term survival); Mary A. Crossley, Of Diagnoses and Discrimination: Discriminatory Nontreatment of Infants with HIV Infection, 93 Colum. L. Rev. 1581, 1613-1614 n.134 (1993) (describing a case in which parents could decline CPR for a child who was irreversibly unconscious and a case in which parents could decline ventilation for a terminally ill child with severe mental and physical disabilities); Carol R. Leicher & Francis J. DiMario, Termination of Nutrition and Hydration in a Child with Vegetative State, 148 Arch. Pediatr. Adolesc. Med. 87 (1994) (describing a case in which parents could decline artificial nutrition and hydration for a perma-nently unconscious child). However, a decision by a Wisconsin court of appeals took a strict view of the Child Abuse Amendments. In a case involving a child born after 23 weeks of gestation who was given maximal life-prolonging treatment, the parents sued, claiming that they were not sufficiently informed of their child's prognosis when they agreed to some of the life-saving measures. The court rejected the par-ents' claim, concluding that under both the Amendments and Wisconsin end-of-life law, the parents did not have the right to refuse life-sustaining treatment for their infant. Montalvo v. Borkovec, 647 N.W.2d 413 (Wis. Ct. App. 2002).

Even if courts defer to parental decisions, parental wishes may be frustrated by the unwillingness of physicians to withdraw or withhold care, either out of personal conviction or because of a belief that the federal regulations mandate care. Early data suggested that the regulations were having a significant impact on physician practices. In a survey of pediatric neurologists, researchers found that 75 percent of the responders stated that "they 'never' recommend the withholding of fluids and nutrition." Stephen Ashwal et al., The Persistent Vegetative State in Children: Report of the Child Neurology Society Ethics Committee, 32 Ann. Neurol. 570, 573 (1992). In a survey in which neonatologists were asked to consider cases of infants with a short life expectancy and severe neurologic disabilities, many responders reported that the federal regulations required the provision of treatment that was not in the best interests of the child. Many also reported that the regulations had led them to change their practices. Loretta M. Kopelman et al., Neonatologists Judge the "Baby Doe" Regulations, 318 New Eng. J. Med. 677 (1988). More recent reports suggest that there may not have been a substantial impact overall from the Child Abuse Amendments on clinical practice. Charity Scott, Baby Doe at Twenty-Five, 25 Ga. St. U. L. Rev. 801, 807-811 (2009).

For further discussion of the Child Abuse Amendments, see the articles in the "Baby Doe at Twenty-Five" symposium of the Georgia State Law Review (vol. 25, no. 4); Loretta Kopelman, The Best Interests Standard for Incompetent or Incapacitated Patients of All Ages, 35 J.L. Med. & Ethics 187 (2007); Dianne Koller Fine, Government as God: An Update on Federal Intervention in the Treatment of Critically Ill Newborns, 34 New Eng. L. Rev. 343 (2000).

For a discussion of the potential use of EMTALA (the federal law providing a right to emergency medical care, see Chapter 2.A.1) to override parental decision-making, see Sadath A. Sayeed, The Marginally Viable Newborn: Legal Challenges, Conceptual Inadequacies, and Reasonableness, 34 J.L. Med. & Ethics 600 (2006) (discussing the interaction of EMTALA with the Born Alive Infant Protection Act of 2002).

2. *Rehabilitation Act and Americans with Disabilities Act.* While there has not been much litigation over the regulations implementing the Child Abuse Amendments of 1984, there has been some important litigation of treatment decisions for severely disabled newborns under §504 of the Rehabilitation Act of 1973. Section 504 prohibits recipients of federal funds from discriminating against "otherwise qualified" disabled persons solely on the basis of their disability. 29 U.S.C. §794. The Americans with Disabilities Act of 1990 extends the protections of §504 to virtually all health care settings. In the §504 cases, the claim is that denying treatment to the newborn is an unlawful act of discrimination. In these cases, the courts have permitted the withholding of treatment. For example, in United States v. University Hospital, 729 F.2d 144 (2d Cir. 1984), the issue was whether surgery could be withheld from an infant with spina bifida, a condition of variable severity in which there is incomplete closure of the tissues surrounding the spinal cord. In this case, the infant had serious physical problems like impaired bowel and bladder function and was thought to have such compromised mental function that she would "never interact with her environment or other people." Id. at 146. The surgery, which would have closed the opening in her spine and implanted a shunt to drain excessive fluid buildup in her brain, was likely to prolong the infant's life but not do anything to treat her disabilities. A state appellate court had refused to intervene, noting that, while the surgery would enhance the infant's chances of living, it also might aggravate her disabilities. In also refusing to intervene, the Second Circuit wrote:

Doe [v. New York University, 666 F.2d 761 (2d Cir. 1981),] establishes that §504 prohibits discrimination against a handicapped individual only where the individual's handicap is unrelated to, and thus improper to consideration of, the services in question. As defendants here point out, however, where medical treatment is at issue, it is typically the handicap itself that give rise to, or at least contributes to, the need for services. Defendants thus argue, and with some force, that the "otherwise qualified" criterion of §504 cannot be meaningfully applied to a medical treatment decision. Similarly, defendants argue that it would be pointless to inquire whether a patient who was affected by a medical treatment decision, was "solely by reason of his handicap . . . subjected to discrimination."

. . . Where the handicapping condition is related to the condition(s) to be treated, it will rarely, if ever, be possible to say with certainty that a particular decision was "discriminatory."

729 F.2d at 156-157. See also Johnson v. Thompson, 971 F.2d 1487 (10th Cir. 1992) (finding no violation of §504 when surgery was withheld from children with spina bifida).

In the end, the parents in *University Hospital* agreed to have a shunt implanted to drain the fluid in their daughter's brain, although the surgery was delayed because of an infection that was likely related to the opening in her spine. The child, Keri-Lynn, has done much better than predicted. She is confined to a wheelchair, but she not only can talk, she also attends a school for developmentally disabled children. At age 20, she had attained a first- or second-grade level of scholastic achievement. Experts continued to disagree as to whether surgery to close Keri-Lynn's spine would have improved her outcome. Jamie Talan, A Fighter's Spirit; 20-Year-Old Keri-Lynn—Baby Jane Doe—Beat Steep Odds, Newsday, October 13, 2003, at A3; B. D. Colen, What Ever Happened to Baby Jane Doe?, 24(3) Hastings Center Rep. 2, 2 (1994); Kathleen Kerr, Proving Their Prognosis Wrong; Baby Jane Doe Busy Learning, Laughing, Newsday, Sept. 2, 1990, at 7. The *University Hospital* decision is excerpted on pages 122-128 and discussed on pages 132-135. The ADA is discussed further in Chapter 2.A.3.

3. *The Role of Physicians.* There have been important changes with respect to parental discretion over the past two decades because of changes in physicians' views as to what constitutes appropriate care for seriously disabled newborns. Partly because advances in medical care are resulting in better outcomes and partly because of changing social attitudes about disabled infants, physicians are becoming more aggressive in recommending treatment. For example, while many physicians once believed it reasonable to withhold surgery to correct an intestinal obstruction in a child with Down syndrome and allow the child to die, it would probably be very difficult today to find a physician taking that position. Sarah Glazer, Born Too Soon, Too Small, Too Sick; Whatever Happened to Baby Doe?, Washington Post, Apr. 2, 1991, at Z8; Betty Wolder Levin et al., Treatment Choice for Infants in the Neonatal Intensive Care Unit at Risk for AIDS, 265 JAMA 2976, 2978 Table 3 (1991). Since courts are likely to defer to physicians as to whether treatment is necessary, the range of parental discretion has been narrowing. Indeed, it is not clear that the *Phillip B.* case discussed at page 343 would come out the same way if it were decided today.

4. *Additional Readings.* For further discussion of this topic, see Robert F. Weir, Selective Nontreatment of Handicapped Newborns: Moral Dilemmas in Neonatal Medicine (1984); Legislative Workshop, Baby Doe: Problems and Legislative Proposals, 1984 Ariz. St. L.J. 601; Benjamin H. Levi, Withdrawing Nutrition and Hydration from Children: Legal, Ethical, and Professional Issues, 42 Clin. Pediatr. 139 (2003); Martha Minow, Beyond State Intervention in the Family: For Baby Jane Doe, 18 U. Mich. J.L. Reform 933 (1985); Nancy K. Rhoden, Treatment Dilemmas for Imperiled Newborns: Why Quality of Life Counts, 58 S. Cal. L. Rev. 1283 (1985); Carl E. Schneider, Rights Discourse and Neonatal Euthanasia, 76 Cal. L. Rev. 151

(1988); George P. Smith, II, Murder, She Wrote or Was It Merely Selective Nontreatment?, 8 J. Contemp. Health L. & Pol'y 49 (1992).

B. PHYSICIAN AID IN DYING

We have seen that the competent patient has an almost unlimited right to refuse medical treatment even though death might result. An important question is whether this strong right should be extended to permit a patient to hasten death by taking a lethal dose of a drug.

As a preliminary matter, it is worth considering the different descriptive terms used for this topic. Although courts commonly talk about "physician-assisted suicide," others prefer "physician aid in dying," "death with dignity," or similar terms. Choice of terms depends a good deal on whether one views decisions by dying persons to manage their deaths with self-administered medications as "suicides" or more like decisions to refuse life-sustaining medical treatment. Following the recommendation of the American Public Health Association, this text will use the term "physician aid in dying."

■ WASHINGTON v. GLUCKSBERG
521 U.S. 702 (1997)

REHNQUIST, Chief Justice.

The question presented in this case is whether Washington's prohibition against "causing" or "aiding" a suicide offends the Fourteenth Amendment to the United States Constitution. We hold that it does not.

It has always been a crime to assist a suicide in the state of Washington. In 1854, Washington's first Territorial Legislature outlawed "assisting another in the commission of self-murder." Today, Washington law provides: "A person is guilty of promoting a suicide attempt when he knowingly causes or aids another person to attempt suicide." Wash. Rev. Code §9A.36.060(1) (1994). "Promoting a suicide attempt" is a felony, punishable by up to five years' imprisonment and up to a $10,000 fine. . . .

Petitioners in this case are the state of Washington and its Attorney General. Respondents Harold Glucksberg, M.D., Abigail Halperin, M.D., Thomas A. Preston, M.D., and Peter Shalit, M.D., are physicians who practice in Washington. These doctors occasionally treat terminally ill, suffering patients, and declare that they would assist these patients in ending their lives if not for Washington's assisted-suicide ban. In January 1994, respondents, along with three gravely ill, pseudonymous plaintiffs who have since died and Compassion in Dying, a nonprofit organization that counsels people considering physician-assisted suicide, sued in the United States district court, seeking a declaration that Wash. Rev. Code §9A.36.060(1) (1994) is, on its face, unconstitutional.

The plaintiffs asserted "the existence of a liberty interest protected by the Fourteenth Amendment which extends to a personal choice by a mentally competent, terminally ill adult to commit physician-assisted suicide." . . . [T]he district court agreed and concluded that Washington's assisted-suicide ban is unconstitutional because it "places an undue burden on the exercise of [that] constitutionally protected liberty interest." . . .

A panel of the court of appeals for the Ninth Circuit reversed. . . . Compassion in Dying v. Washington, 49 F.3d 586, 591 (1995). The Ninth Circuit reheard the case en banc, reversed the panel's decision, and affirmed the district court. Compassion in Dying v. Washington, 79 F.3d 790, 798 (1996). . . . The court . . . concluded that "the Constitution encompasses a due process liberty interest in controlling the time and manner of one's death . . ." [and] that the state's assisted-suicide ban was unconstitutional "as applied to terminally ill competent adults who wish to hasten their deaths with medication prescribed by their physicians." . . . We granted certiorari and now reverse.

I

We begin, as we do in all due-process cases, by examining our nation's history, legal traditions, and practices. In almost every state — indeed, in almost every Western democracy — it is a crime to assist a suicide. The states' assisted-suicide bans are not innovations. Rather, they are longstanding expressions of the states' commitment to the protection and preservation of all human life. . . .

More specifically, for over 700 years, the Anglo-American common-law tradition has punished or otherwise disapproved of both suicide and assisting suicide. [The court continues by noting that English law initially treated suicide as a form of murder, with the person's real and personal property being forfeited to the king. Only the personal property was forfeited, however, if the suicide was motivated by serious illness. Beginning in 1701, the colonies, and later the states, rescinded their laws criminalizing suicide because of the unfairness to the decedent's family, rather than out of any acceptance of suicide.]

That suicide remained a grievous, though nonfelonious, wrong is confirmed by the fact that colonial and early state legislatures and courts did not retreat from prohibiting assisting suicide. . . . And the prohibitions against assisting suicide never contained exceptions for those who were near death. . . . By the time the Fourteenth Amendment was ratified, it was a crime in most states to assist a suicide. . . . In this century, the Model Penal Code also prohibited "aiding" suicide, prompting many states to enact or revise their assisted-suicide bans. . . .

The Washington statute at issue in this case, Wash. Rev. Code §9A.36.060 (1994), was enacted in 1975 as part of a revision of that state's criminal code. . . . In 1991, Washington voters rejected a ballot initiative which, had it passed, would have permitted a form of physician-assisted suicide. . . .

California voters rejected an assisted-suicide initiative similar to Washington's in 1993. On the other hand, in 1994, voters in Oregon enacted, also through ballot initiative, that state's "Death with Dignity Act," which legalized physician-assisted suicide for competent, terminally ill adults. Since the Oregon vote, many proposals to legalize assisted-suicide have been and continue to be introduced in the states' legislatures, but none has been enacted. And just last year, Iowa and Rhode Island joined the overwhelming majority of states explicitly prohibiting assisted suicide. . . .

Attitudes toward suicide itself have changed since [the thirteenth century], but our laws have consistently condemned, and continue to prohibit, assisting suicide. . . . Against this backdrop of history, tradition, and practice, we now turn to respondents' constitutional claim.

II

The due process clause guarantees more than fair process, and the "liberty" it protects includes more than the absence of physical restraint. The clause also provides heightened protection against government interference with certain fundamental rights and liberty interests. In a long line of cases, we have held that, in addition to the specific freedoms protected by the Bill of Rights, the "liberty" specially protected by the due process clause includes the rights to marry, to have children, to direct the education and upbringing of one's children, to marital privacy, to use contraception, to bodily integrity, and to abortion. We have also assumed, and strongly suggested, that the due process clause protects the traditional right to refuse unwanted lifesaving medical treatment. *Cruzan*, 497 U.S., at 278-279.

But we "have always been reluctant to expand the concept of substantive due process because guideposts for responsible decisionmaking in this unchartered area are scarce and open-ended." *Collins*, 503 U.S., at 125. By extending constitutional protection to an asserted right or liberty interest, we, to a great extent, place the matter outside the arena of public debate and legislative action. We must therefore "exercise the utmost care whenever we are asked to break new ground in this field," ibid., lest the liberty protected by the due process clause be subtly transformed into the policy preferences of the members of this Court.

Our established method of substantive-due-process analysis has two primary features: First, we have regularly observed that the due process clause specially protects those fundamental rights and liberties which are, objectively, "deeply rooted in this nation's history and tradition," *Moore*, 431 U.S. at 503 (plurality opinion), and "implicit in the concept of ordered liberty," such that "neither liberty nor justice would exist if they were sacrificed," Palko v. Connecticut, 302 U.S. 319, 325, 326 (1937). Second, we have required in substantive-due-process cases a "careful description" of the asserted fundamental liberty interest. *Flores*, 507 U.S. at 302. . . .

Turning to the claim at issue here, the court of appeals stated that "properly analyzed, the first issue to be resolved is whether there is a liberty interest in determining the time and manner of one's death," or, in other words, "is there a right to die?" Similarly, respondents assert a "liberty to choose how to die" and a right to "control of one's final days," and describe the asserted liberty as "the right to choose a humane, dignified death," and "the liberty to shape death." . . .

Respondents contend that in *Cruzan* we "acknowledged that competent, dying persons have the right to direct the removal of life-sustaining medical treatment and thus hasten death" and that "the constitutional principle behind recognizing the patient's liberty to direct the withdrawal of artificial life support applies at least as strongly to the choice to hasten impending death by consuming lethal medication." . . .

The right assumed in *Cruzan*, however, was not simply deduced from abstract concepts of personal autonomy. Given the common-law rule that forced medication was a battery, and the long legal tradition protecting the decision to refuse unwanted medical treatment, our assumption was entirely consistent with this nation's history and constitutional traditions. The decision to commit suicide with the assistance of another may be just as personal and profound as the decision to refuse unwanted medical treatment, but it has never enjoyed similar legal protection. Indeed, the two acts are widely and reasonably regarded as quite distinct. In *Cruzan* itself, we recognized that most states outlawed assisted suicide—and even more do today—and we certainly gave no intimation that the right to refuse unwanted medical treatment could be somehow transmuted into a right to assistance in committing suicide.

Respondents also rely on *Casey*. There, the Court's opinion concluded that "the essential holding of Roe v. Wade should be retained and once again reaffirmed." *Casey*, 505 U.S., at 846. . . . In reaching this conclusion, the opinion discussed in some detail this Court's substantive-due-process tradition of interpreting the due process clause to protect certain fundamental rights and "personal decisions relating to marriage, procreation, contraception, family relationships, child rearing, and education," and noted that many of those rights and liberties "involve the most intimate and personal choices a person may make in a lifetime."

The court of appeals, like the district court, found *Casey* "highly instructive" and "almost prescriptive" for determining "what liberty interest may inhere in a terminally ill person's choice to commit suicide":

> Like the decision of whether or not to have an abortion, the decision how and when to die is one of "the most intimate and personal choices a person may make in a lifetime," a choice "central to personal dignity and autonomy." [79 F.3d, at 813-814.]

Similarly, respondents emphasize the statement in *Casey* that:

> At the heart of liberty is the right to define one's own concept of existence, of meaning, of the universe, and of the mystery of human life. Beliefs about these matters could not define the attributes of personhood were they formed under compulsion of the State. [*Casey*, 505 U.S., at 851.]

By choosing this language, the Court's opinion in *Casey* described, in a general way and in light of our prior cases, those personal activities and decisions that this Court has identified as so deeply rooted in our history and traditions, or so fundamental to our concept of constitutionally ordered liberty, that they are protected by the Fourteenth Amendment. The opinion moved from the recognition that liberty necessarily includes freedom of conscience and belief about ultimate considerations to the observation that "though the abortion decision may originate within the zone of conscience and belief, it is more than a philosophic exercise." *Casey*, 505 U.S., at 852. That many of the rights and liberties protected by the due process clause sound in personal autonomy does not warrant the sweeping conclusion that any and all important, intimate, and personal decisions are so protected, and *Casey* did not suggest otherwise.

The history of the law's treatment of assisted suicide in this country has been and continues to be one of the rejection of nearly all efforts to permit it. That being the case, our decisions lead us to conclude that the asserted "right" to assistance in committing suicide is not a fundamental liberty interest protected by the due process clause. The Constitution also requires, however, that Washington's assisted-suicide ban be rationally related to legitimate government interests. This requirement is unquestionably met here. As the court below recognized, Washington's assisted-suicide ban implicates a number of state interests.

First, Washington has an "unqualified interest in the preservation of human life." The state's prohibition on assisted suicide, like all homicide laws, both reflects and advances its commitment to this interest. . . .

. . . The court of appeals also recognized Washington's interest in protecting life, but held that the "weight" of this interest depends on the "medical condition and the wishes of the person whose life is at stake." Washington, however, has rejected this sliding-scale approach and, through its assisted-suicide ban, insists that all persons' lives, from beginning to end, regardless of physical or mental condition, are under the full protection of the law. As we have previously affirmed, the states "may properly decline to make judgments about the 'quality' of life that a particular individual may enjoy," *Cruzan*, 497 U.S., at 282. This remains true, as *Cruzan* makes clear, even for those who are near death.

Relatedly, all admit that suicide is a serious public-health problem, especially among persons in otherwise vulnerable groups. . . . The state has an interest in preventing suicide, and in studying, identifying, and treating its causes.

Those who attempt suicide—terminally ill or not—often suffer from depression or other mental disorders. Research indicates, however, that many people who request physician-assisted suicide withdraw that request if their depression and pain are treated. The New York Task Force, however, expressed its concern that, because depression is difficult to diagnose, physicians and medical professionals often fail to respond adequately to seriously ill patients' needs. Thus, legal physician-assisted suicide could make it more difficult for the state to protect depressed or mentally ill persons, or those who are suffering from untreated pain, from suicidal impulses.

The state also has an interest in protecting the integrity and ethics of the medical profession. In contrast to the court of appeals' conclusion that "the integrity of the medical profession would [not] be threatened in any way by [physician-assisted suicide]," the American Medical Association, like many other medical and physicians' groups, has concluded that "physician-assisted suicide is fundamentally incompatible with the physician's role as healer." American Medical Association, Code of Ethics §2.211 (1994). And physician-assisted suicide could, it is argued, undermine the trust that is essential to the doctor-patient relationship by blurring the time-honored line between healing and harming.

Next, the state has an interest in protecting vulnerable groups—including the poor, the elderly, and disabled persons—from abuse, neglect, and mistakes. . . . We have recognized [in *Cruzan*] . . . the real risk of subtle coercion and undue influence in end-of-life situations. . . . If physician-assisted suicide were permitted, many might resort to it to spare their families the substantial financial burden of end-of-life health-care costs.

The state's interest here goes beyond protecting the vulnerable from coercion; it extends to protecting disabled and terminally ill people from prejudice, negative and inaccurate stereotypes, and "societal indifference." The state's assisted-suicide ban reflects and reinforces its policy that the lives of terminally ill, disabled, and elderly people must be no less valued than the lives of the young and healthy, and that a seriously disabled person's suicidal impulses should be interpreted and treated the same way as anyone else's.

Finally, the state may fear that permitting assisted suicide will start it down the path to voluntary and perhaps even involuntary euthanasia. The court of appeals struck down Washington's assisted-suicide ban only "as applied to competent, terminally ill adults who wish to hasten their deaths by obtaining medication prescribed by their doctors." Washington insists, however, that the impact of the court's decision will not and cannot be so limited. . . . The court of appeals' decision, and its expansive reasoning, provide ample support for the state's concerns. The court noted, for example, that the "decision of a duly appointed surrogate decision maker is for all legal purposes the decision of the patient himself," that "in some instances, the patient may be unable to self-administer the drugs and . . . administration by the physician . . . may be the only way the patient may be able to receive them,'" and that not only physicians, but also family members and loved ones, will inevitably participate in assisting suicide. Thus, it turns out that what is couched as a limited right to "physician-assisted suicide" is likely, in effect, a much broader license, which could prove extremely difficult to police and contain.

This concern is further supported by evidence about the practice of euthanasia in the Netherlands. The Dutch government's own study revealed that in 1990, there were 2,300 cases of voluntary euthanasia (defined as "the deliberate termination of another's life at his request"), 400 cases of assisted suicide, and more than 1,000 cases of euthanasia without an explicit request. In addition to these latter 1,000 cases, the study found an additional 4,941 cases where physicians administered lethal morphine overdoses without the patients' explicit consent. This study suggests that, despite the existence of various reporting procedures, euthanasia in the Netherlands has not been limited to competent, terminally ill adults who are enduring physical suffering, and that regulation of the practice may not have prevented abuses in cases involving vulnerable persons, including severely disabled neonates and elderly persons suffering from dementia. . . . Washington, like most other states, reasonably ensures against this risk by banning, rather than regulating, assisting suicide.

We need not weigh exactly the relative strengths of these various interests. They are unquestionably important and legitimate, and Washington's ban on assisted suicide is at least reasonably related to their promotion and protection. We therefore hold that Wash. Rev. Code §9A.36.060(1) (1994) does not violate the Fourteenth Amendment, either on its face or "as applied to competent, terminally ill adults who wish to hasten their deaths by obtaining medication prescribed by their doctors." 79 F.3d, at 838.[24]

. . . Throughout the nation, Americans are engaged in an earnest and profound debate about the morality, legality, and practicality of physician-assisted suicide. Our holding permits this debate to continue, as it should in a democratic society. The decision of the en banc court of appeals is reversed, and the case is remanded for further proceedings consistent with this opinion. . . .

24. . . . We emphasize that we today reject the court of appeals' specific holding that the statute is unconstitutional "as applied" to a particular class. Justice Stevens agrees with this holding, but would not "foreclose the possibility that an individual plaintiff seeking to hasten her death, or a doctor whose assistance was sought, could prevail in a more particularized challenge." Our opinion does not absolutely foreclose such a claim. However, given our holding that the due process clause of the Fourteenth Amendment does not provide heightened protection to the asserted liberty interest in ending one's life with a physician's assistance, such a claim would have to be quite different from the ones advanced by respondents here.

■VACCO v. QUILL
521 U.S. 793 (1997)

REHNQUIST, Chief Justice.

In New York, as in most states, it is a crime to aid another to commit or attempt suicide, but patients may refuse even lifesaving medical treatment. The question presented by this case is whether New York's prohibition on assisting suicide therefore violates the equal protection clause of the Fourteenth Amendment. We hold that it does not.

Petitioners are various New York public officials. Respondents Timothy E. Quill, Samuel C. Klagsbrun, and Howard A. Grossman are physicians who practice in New York. They assert that although it would be "consistent with the standards of [their] medical practices" to prescribe lethal medication for "mentally competent, terminally ill patients" who are suffering great pain and desire a doctor's help in taking their own lives, they are deterred from doing so by New York's ban on assisting suicide. Respondents, and three gravely ill patients who have since died, sued the state's Attorney General in the United States district court. They urged that because New York permits a competent person to refuse life-sustaining medical treatment, and because the refusal of such treatment is "essentially the same thing" as physician-assisted suicide, New York's assisted-suicide ban violates the equal protection clause.

The district court disagreed: "It is hardly unreasonable or irrational for the state to recognize a difference between allowing nature to take its course, even in the most severe situations, and intentionally using an artificial death-producing device." . . .

The court of appeals for the Second Circuit reversed. The court determined that, despite the assisted-suicide ban's apparent general applicability, "New York law does not treat equally all competent persons who are in the final stages of fatal illness and wish to hasten their deaths," because "those in the final stages of terminal illness who are on life-support systems are allowed to hasten their deaths by directing the removal of such systems; but those who are similarly situated, except for the previous attachment of life-sustaining equipment, are not allowed to hasten death by self-administering prescribed drugs." . . . We granted certiorari and now reverse.

The equal protection clause commands that no state shall "deny to any person within its jurisdiction the equal protection of the laws." This provision creates no substantive rights. Instead, it embodies a general rule that states must treat like cases alike but may treat unlike cases accordingly. If a legislative classification or distinction "neither burdens a fundamental right nor targets a suspect class, we will uphold [it] so long as it bears a rational relation to some legitimate end." Romer v. Evans, 517 U.S. (slip op., at 10) (1996).

New York's statutes outlawing assisting suicide affect and address matters of profound significance to all New Yorkers alike. They neither infringe fundamental rights nor involve suspect classifications. These laws are therefore entitled to a "strong presumption of validity." Heller v. Doe, 509 U.S. 312, 319 (1993).

On their faces, neither New York's ban on assisting suicide nor its statutes permitting patients to refuse medical treatment treat anyone differently than anyone else or draw any distinctions between persons. Everyone, regardless of physical condition, is entitled, if competent, to refuse unwanted lifesaving medical treatment;

no one is permitted to assist a suicide. Generally speaking, laws that apply evenhandedly to all "unquestionably comply" with the equal protection clause. New York City Transit Authority v. Beazer, 440 U.S. 568, 587 (1979).

The court of appeals, however, concluded that some terminally ill people—those who are on life-support systems—are treated differently than those who are not, in that the former may "hasten death" by ending treatment, but the latter may not "hasten death" through physician-assisted suicide. This conclusion depends on the submission that ending or refusing lifesaving medical treatment "is nothing more nor less than assisted suicide." Unlike the court of appeals, we think the distinction between assisting suicide and withdrawing life-sustaining treatment, a distinction widely recognized and endorsed in the medical profession and in our legal traditions, is both important and logical; it is certainly rational.

The distinction comports with fundamental legal principles of causation and intent. First, when a patient refuses life-sustaining medical treatment, he dies from an underlying fatal disease or pathology; but if a patient ingests lethal medication prescribed by a physician, he is killed by that medication.

Furthermore, a physician who withdraws, or honors a patient's refusal to begin, life-sustaining medical treatment purposefully intends, or may so intend, only to respect his patient's wishes and "to cease doing useless and futile or degrading things to the patient when [the patient] no longer stands to benefit from them." Assisted Suicide in the United States, Hearing before the Subcommittee on the Constitution of the House Committee on the Judiciary, 104th Cong., 2d Sess., 368 (1996) (testimony of Dr. Leon R. Kass). The same is true when a doctor provides aggressive palliative care; in some cases, painkilling drugs may hasten a patient's death, but the physician's purpose and intent is, or may be, only to ease his patient's pain. A doctor who assists a suicide, however, "must, necessarily and indubitably, intend primarily that the patient be made dead." Id. at 367. Similarly, a patient who commits suicide with a doctor's aid necessarily has the specific intent to end his or her own life, while a patient who refuses or discontinues treatment might not.

The law has long used actors' intent or purpose to distinguish between two acts that may have the same result. Put differently, the law distinguishes actions taken "because of" a given end from actions taken "in spite of" their unintended but foreseen consequences. . . .

Given these general principles, it is not surprising that many courts, including New York courts, have carefully distinguished refusing life-sustaining treatment from suicide. . . . Similarly, the overwhelming majority of state legislatures have drawn a clear line between assisting suicide and withdrawing or permitting the refusal of unwanted lifesaving medical treatment by prohibiting the former and permitting the latter. . . .

For all these reasons, we disagree with respondents' claim that the distinction between refusing lifesaving medical treatment and assisted suicide is "arbitrary" and "irrational." Granted, in some cases, the line between the two may not be clear, but certainty is not required, even were it possible. Logic and contemporary practice support New York's judgment that the two acts are different, and New York may therefore, consistent with the Constitution, treat them differently. By permitting everyone to refuse unwanted medical treatment while prohibiting anyone from assisting a suicide, New York law follows a longstanding and rational distinction.

New York's reasons for recognizing and acting on this distinction—including prohibiting intentional killing and preserving life; preventing suicide; maintaining physicians' role as their patients' healers; protecting vulnerable people from indifference, prejudice, and psychological and financial pressure to end their lives; and avoiding a possible slide towards euthanasia—are discussed in greater detail in our opinion in *Glucksberg*. These valid and important public interests easily satisfy the constitutional requirement that a legislative classification bear a rational relation to some legitimate end.

The judgment of the court of appeals is reversed. . . .

O'CONNOR, Justice, concurring [joined by Justices Ginsburg and Breyer in substantial part.]

Death will be different for each of us. For many, the last days will be spent in physical pain and perhaps the despair that accompanies physical deterioration and a loss of control of basic bodily and mental functions. Some will seek medication to alleviate that pain and other symptoms.

The Court frames the issue in this case as whether the due process clause of the Constitution protects a "right to commit suicide which itself includes a right to assistance in doing so," and concludes that our nation's history, legal traditions, and practices do not support the existence of such a right. I join the Court's opinions because I agree that there is no generalized right to "commit suicide." But respondents urge us to address the narrower question whether a mentally competent person who is experiencing great suffering has a constitutionally cognizable interest in controlling the circumstances of his or her imminent death. I see no need to reach that question in the context of the facial challenges to the New York and Washington laws at issue here. The parties and amici agree that in these states a patient who is suffering from a terminal illness and who is experiencing great pain has no legal barriers to obtaining medication, from qualified physicians, to alleviate that suffering, even to the point of causing unconsciousness and hastening death. In this light, even assuming that we would recognize such an interest, I agree that the state's interests in protecting those who are not truly competent or facing imminent death, or those whose decisions to hasten death would not truly be voluntary, are sufficiently weighty to justify a prohibition against physician-assisted suicide.

Every one of us at some point may be affected by our own or a family member's terminal illness. There is no reason to think the democratic process will not strike the proper balance between the interests of terminally ill, mentally competent individuals who would seek to end their suffering and the state's interests in protecting those who might seek to end life mistakenly or under pressure. As the Court recognizes, states are presently undertaking extensive and serious evaluation of physician-assisted suicide and other related issues. In such circumstances, "the . . . challenging task of crafting appropriate procedures for safeguarding . . . liberty interests is entrusted to the 'laboratory' of the states . . . in the first instance." Cruzan v. Director, Missouri Department of Health, 497 U.S. 261, 292 (1990) (O'Connor, J., concurring) (citing New State Ice Co. v. Liebmann, 285 U.S. 262, 311 (1932)). . . .

STEVENS, Justice, concurring in the judgments.

The Court ends its opinion with the important observation that our holding today is fully consistent with a continuation of the vigorous debate about the "morality, legality, and practicality of physician-assisted suicide" in a democratic society. I write separately to make it clear that there is also room for further debate about the limits that the Constitution places on the power of the states to punish the practice.

I

The morality, legality, and practicality of capital punishment have been the subject of debate for many years. In 1976, this Court upheld the constitutionality of the practice in cases coming to us from Georgia, Florida, and Texas. In those cases we concluded that a state does have the power to place a lesser value on some lives than on others; there is no absolute requirement that a state treat all human life as having an equal right to preservation. Because the state legislatures had sufficiently narrowed the category of lives that the state could terminate, and had enacted special procedures to ensure that the defendant belonged in that limited category, we concluded that the statutes were not unconstitutional on their face. In later cases coming to us from each of those states, however, we found that some applications of the statutes were unconstitutional.

Today, the Court decides that Washington's statute prohibiting assisted suicide is not invalid "on its face," that is to say, in all or most cases in which it might be applied. That holding, however, does not foreclose the possibility that some applications of the statute might well be invalid. . . .

History and tradition provide ample support for refusing to recognize an open-ended constitutional right to commit suicide. Much more than the state's paternalistic interest in protecting the individual from the irrevocable consequences of an ill-advised decision motivated by temporary concerns is at stake. There is truth in John Donne's observation that "No man is an island." The state has an interest in preserving and fostering the benefits that every human being may provide to the community—a community that thrives on the exchange of ideas, expressions of affection, shared memories and humorous incidents as well as on the material contributions that its members create and support. . . .

But just as our conclusion that capital punishment is not always unconstitutional did not preclude later decisions holding that it is sometimes impermissibly cruel, so is it equally clear that a decision upholding a general statutory prohibition of assisted suicide does not mean that every possible application of the statute would be valid. . . .

III

. . . Although as a general matter the state's interest in the contributions each person may make to society outweighs the person's interest in ending her life, this interest does not have the same force for a terminally ill patient faced not with the choice of whether to live, only of how to die. Allowing the individual, rather than the state, to make judgments "about the 'quality' of life that a particular individual may enjoy," does not mean that the lives of terminally-ill, disabled people have less value than the lives of those who are healthy. Rather, it gives proper recognition to the individual's interest in choosing a final chapter that accords with her life story, rather than one that demeans her values and poisons memories of her.

Similarly, the state's legitimate interests in preventing suicide, protecting the vulnerable from coercion and abuse, and preventing euthanasia are less significant in this context. I agree that the state has a compelling interest in preventing persons from committing suicide because of depression, or coercion by third parties. But the state's legitimate interest in preventing abuse does not apply to an individual who is not victimized by abuse, who is not suffering from depression, and who makes a rational and voluntary decision to seek assistance in dying. . . .

Relatedly, the state and amici express the concern that patients whose physical pain is inadequately treated will be more likely to request assisted suicide. Encouraging the development and ensuring the availability of adequate pain treatment is of utmost importance; palliative care, however, cannot alleviate all pain and suffering. See Orentlicher, Legalization of Physician Assisted Suicide: A Very Modest Revolution, 38 Boston College L. Rev. 443, 454 (1997) ("Greater use of palliative care would reduce the demand for assisted suicide, but it will not eliminate [it]"). An individual adequately informed of the care alternatives thus might make a rational choice for assisted suicide. For such an individual, the state's interest in preventing potential abuse and mistake is only minimally implicated.

The final major interest asserted by the state is its interest in preserving the traditional integrity of the medical profession. The fear is that a rule permitting physicians to assist in suicide is inconsistent with the perception that they serve their patients solely as healers. But for some patients, it would be a physician's refusal to dispense medication to ease their suffering and make their death tolerable and dignified that would be inconsistent with the healing role. For doctors who have long-standing relationships with their patients, who have given their patients advice on alternative treatments, who are attentive to their patient's individualized needs, and who are knowledgeable about pain symptom management and palliative care options, heeding a patient's desire to assist in her suicide would not serve to harm the physician-patient relationship. Furthermore, because physicians are already involved in making decisions that hasten the death of terminally ill patients—through termination of life support, withholding of medical treatment, and terminal sedation—there is in fact significant tension between the traditional view of the physician's role and the actual practice in a growing number of cases.

As the New York State Task Force on Life and the Law recognized, a state's prohibition of assisted suicide is justified by the fact that the "ideal" case in which "patients would be screened for depression and offered treatment, effective pain medication would be available, and all patients would have a supportive committed family and doctor" is not the usual case. New York State Task Force on Life and the Law, When Death Is Sought: Assisted Suicide and Euthanasia in the Medical Context 120 (May 1994). Although, as the Court concludes today, these potential harms are sufficient to support the state's general public policy against assisted suicide, they will not always outweigh the individual liberty interest of a particular patient. Unlike the court of appeals, I would not say as a categorical matter that these state interests are invalid as to the entire class of terminally ill, mentally competent patients. I do not, however, foreclose the possibility that an individual plaintiff seeking to hasten her death, or a doctor whose assistance was sought, could prevail in a more particularized challenge. Future cases will determine whether such a challenge may succeed. . . .

Notes: Physician Aid in Dying

1. *Factual Background.* The debate over physician aid in dying was sparked anew in March 1989, when a distinguished group of physicians argued in favor of physician aid in dying as a last resort for relieving patient suffering. Sidney H. Wanzer et al., The Physician's Responsibility Toward Hopelessly Ill Patients: A Second Look, 320 New Eng. J. Med. 844 (1989), and in June 1990 when Dr. Jack Kevorkian, a retired pathologist living in Michigan, assisted the dying of Janet Adkins. Ms. Adkins was a 54-year-old woman in the early stages of Alzheimer's disease who decided to end her life before she became even more affected. Lisa Belkin, Doctor Tells of First Death Using His Suicide Device, N.Y. Times, June 6, 1990, at A1.

While Kevorkian's license to practice medicine was revoked, he continued to aid patient dying. By December 1997, he had disclosed his assistance in more than 50 deaths, and his attorney indicated that he had assisted in the range of 100 deaths.

Kevorkian lost his constitutional challenge to Michigan's prohibition of physician aid in dying, People v. Kevorkian, 527 N.W.2d 714 (Mich. 1994), and was prosecuted four different times, but juries acquitted him in three trials and a mistrial was declared in the fourth prosecution. When he crossed the line from aid in dying to euthanasia, however, Kevorkian was convicted. On March 26, 1999, a jury found him guilty of second-degree murder for administering a fatal injection to Thomas Youk, a 52-year-old man suffering from amyotrophic lateral sclerosis (ALS or Lou Gehrig's disease). Pam Belluck, Dr. Kevorkian Is a Murderer, the Jury Finds, N.Y. Times, Mar. 27, 1999, at A1. This was the case in which Kevorkian taped the patient's death, and the tape was televised by *60 Minutes* in November 1998. On April 13, 1999, the trial court judge sentenced Kevorkian to 10 to 25 years in prison. Dirk Johnson, Kevorkian Sentenced to 10 to 25 Years in Prison, N.Y. Times, Apr. 14, 1999, at A1. Eight years later, Kevorkian was released from prison on parole. Monica Davey, Kevorkian Freed After Years in Prison for Aiding Suicide, N.Y. Times, June 2, 2007, at A3. On June 3, 2011, Kevorkian died of natural causes at the age of 83. Keith Schneider, Doctor Who Helped End Lives, N.Y. Times, June 4, 2011, at A1.

The fact that Kevorkian was convicted despite his earlier escapes from punishment can be attributed to a few factors: (1) this was a case of euthanasia rather than aid in dying; (2) during his interview on *60 Minutes*, Kevorkian indicated that he chose euthanasia rather than aid in dying to advance his agenda rather than to serve the patient's needs (and Youk could have chosen aid in dying); (3) Kevorkian was aggressively flouting the law with the televising of Youk's death; and (4) Kevorkian defended himself rather than relying on a lawyer to make his case.

Dr. Timothy Quill also focused discussion on physician aid in dying by disclosing in 1991 that he prescribed a lethal dose of barbiturates for a cancer patient who was terminally ill. Timothy E. Quill, Death and Dignity: A Case of Individualized Decision Making, 324 New Eng. J. Med. 691 (1991). In Quill's case, prosecutors were unable to persuade a grand jury to bring an indictment. Lawrence K. Altman, Jury Declines to Indict a Doctor Who Said He Aided in a Suicide, N.Y. Times, July 27, 1991, at A1.

The absence of a conviction for either Kevorkian or Quill for aid in dying did not reflect a gap in the law. In both Michigan and New York, the law prohibited aid in dying. However, juries are generally unwilling to convict physicians who help dying patients self-administer a lethal dose of drugs. Prosecutions of a physician for either aid in dying or euthanasia are rare. Convictions are almost unheard of, with only one case reported in the literature before Kevorkian's, a case in which a physician injected his mother-in-law with a fatal dose of Demerol. The mother-in-law suffered from advanced Alzheimer's disease, and the physician pled guilty to a charge of manslaughter and was sentenced to two years' probation after a plea-bargain. Maria T. CeloCruz, Aid-in-Dying: Should We Decriminalize Physician-Assisted Suicide and Physician-Committed Euthanasia?, 18 Am. J.L. & Med. 369, 377-383 (1992); Leonard Glantz, Withholding and Withdrawing Treatment: The Role of the Criminal Law, 15 L. Med. & Health Care 231, 232 (1987). For a case in which a physician was acquitted of charges of performing euthanasia, on grounds that his treatment fell within the standard of care for palliative care, see State v. Naramore, 965 P.2d 211 (Kan. 1998).

The legal system is also sympathetic to cases of aid in dying and euthanasia involving family members or close friends of the patient, but to a lesser extent than with physicians. Family members have been convicted of criminal charges, but they are likely to be sentenced leniently.

2. *Legalized Aid in Dying in Oregon.* In November 1994, Oregon voters approved by referendum the Oregon Death with Dignity Act, a law that permits mentally competent, terminally ill persons to obtain a prescription from their physicians for a lethal dose of a drug. The statute requires patients to make their request for aid in dying orally and in writing and to reiterate their request orally at least 15 days after the initial request. The physician is required to inform the patient of the medical diagnosis, prognosis, and alternatives to aid in dying, and must refer the patient to a consulting physician to confirm both the diagnosis and that the patient is competent and making a voluntary and informed decision. If either physician believes that the patient suffers from a psychiatric disorder or from a depression that impairs judgment, the patient must be referred for counseling. Or. Rev. Stat. §§127.800-.897.

A constitutional challenge to the statute was brought, and the district court judge enjoined the law. According to the court, terminally ill persons were denied equal protection by the statute because the state did not employ the same safeguards to protect terminally ill persons from impaired judgment or abuse as used to protect nonterminally ill persons. Lee v. Oregon, 891 F. Supp. 1429 (D. Or. 1995). On appeal, the Ninth Circuit held that the plaintiffs did not have standing to challenge the Oregon statute and so vacated the district court judgment and remanded with instructions to dismiss for lack of jurisdiction. Lee v. Oregon, 107 F.3d 1382, 1392 (9th Cir. 1997). After the Ninth Circuit's decision, the Oregon legislature voted to send the Death with Dignity Act back to the electorate for a second vote by referendum in November 1997. Oregon's voters reaffirmed their earlier approval, this time by a larger margin, 60 to 40 percent versus 51 to 49 percent in 1994.

The first public report of a death under Oregon's aid in dying law came on March 25, 1998. Timothy Egan, First Death Under an Assisted-Suicide Law, N.Y. Times, Mar. 26, 1998, at A14. After the report, it was disclosed that the law had been invoked earlier by another patient. On August 18, 1998, the Oregon Department of Human Resources (now Human Services) released data on the first ten patients who exercised their rights under the Death with Dignity Act, and since then the Department has issued annual reports describing Oregon's experience with aid in dying. The full reports are available at the Web site of the Department (http://public.health.oregon.gov/ProviderPartnerResources/Evaluationresearch /deathwithdignityact/Pages/index.aspx); summaries have been published for the earlier years in the *New England Journal of Medicine.*

Through December 31, 2011, physicians had written 935 prescriptions under the Death with Dignity Act, and 596 patients had taken the lethal medication (64 percent), a small number were still alive, and the rest died of their illnesses). Oregon Public Health Division, Oregon's Death with Dignity Act (2011). Between one-fifth and one-fourth of 1 percent of deaths in Oregon are by aid in dying. The most common diagnosis has been cancer (81 percent), and the patients have been similar to other dying patients with regard to sex, race, urban or rural residence, health insurance coverage, and hospice enrollment. The level of education has been higher for patients who choose aid in dying. The most common concerns of patients choosing aid in dying have been loss of autonomy, decreased ability to participate in enjoyable activities, and loss of dignity.

Researchers studying patients' reasons for aid in dying have found similar results to those of the Department of Human Services. According to one study, loss of independence, a desire to control the circumstances of death, and concerns about future pain and quality of life are leading reasons for patients to invoke the Death with Dignity Act. Linda Ganzini et al., Oregonians' Reasons for Requesting Physician Aid in Dying, 169 Arch. Intern. Med. 489 (2009). Similarly, another study found that reasons for pursuing aid in dying included loss of function and other physical consequences of illness, loss of sense of self and a desire for control, and fears about the future. Depression was not a significant factor. Robert A. Pearlman et al., Motivations for Physician-Assisted Suicide, 20 J. Gen. Intern. Med. 234 (2005). See also Linda Ganzini et al., Experiences of Oregon Nurses and Social Workers with Hospice Patients Who Requested Assistance with Suicide, 347 New Eng. J. Med. 582 (2002) (finding loss of autonomy and a desire to control the circumstances of death as leading reasons).

Researchers also have looked at physicians' responses to requests under the Oregon Act. A study found that physicians in Oregon grant roughly one in six requests for a lethal prescription and that one in ten requests actually result in aid in dying. Physicians did not provide a prescription in 82 percent of cases because the physician was not willing to aid in dying ever (29 percent), the physician was not willing to assist in the particular case (24 percent), the patient died before meeting Oregon's legal requirements or before receiving a prescription (22 percent), the patient had a change of mind before meeting Oregon's legal requirements or before receiving a prescription (17 percent), or the patient did not meet Oregon's legal requirements (15 percent). While 20 percent of requests came from patients with depression, none of their requests were granted. Linda Ganzini et al., Physicians' Experiences with the Oregon Death with Dignity Act, 342 New Eng. J. Med. 557 (2000). Data from the Netherlands suggest that physicians there are more likely to grant a patient's request for physician aid in dying or euthanasia. Jansen-van der Weide et al., Granted, Undecided, Withdrawn, and Refused Requests for Euthanasia and Physician-Assisted Suicide, 165 Arch. Intern. Med. 1698 (2005) (finding in a physician survey that 44 percent of explicit requests for physician aid in dying or euthanasia were granted).

For more discussion of the Oregon experience, see Herbert Hendin & Kathleen Foley, Physician-Assisted Suicide in Oregon: A Medical Perspective, 106 Mich. L. Rev. 1613 (2008); Susan Okie, Physician-Assisted Suicide—Oregon and Beyond, 352 New Eng. J. Med. 1627 (2005); Jackson Pickett, Can Legalization Improve End-of-Life Care? An Empirical Analysis of the Results of the Legalization of Euthanasia and Physician-Assisted Suicide in the Netherlands and Oregon, 16 Elder L.J. 333 (2009); Robert Steinbrook, Physician-Assisted Suicide in Oregon—An Uncertain Future, 346 New Eng. J. Med. 460 (2002); Kathryn Tucker, In the Laboratory of the States: The Progress of *Glucksberg*'s Invitation to States to Address End-of-Life Choice, 106 Mich. L. Rev. 1593 (2008).

The Task Force to Improve the Care of Terminally Ill Oregonians has published a 91-page guidebook on the Oregon law, Oregon's Death with Dignity Act: A Guidebook for Health Care Providers. The Task Force represents 25 health care professional organizations, state agencies, and health care systems. You can find the Guidebook at the Web site of the Center for Ethics in Health Care at Oregon Health Sciences University. For an article observing that efforts to address patients' concerns can diminish the desire for physician aid in dying, see Paul B. Bascom & Susan W. Tolle, Responding to Requests for Physician-Assisted Suicide: "These Are Uncharted Waters for Both of Us . . . ," 288 JAMA 91 (2002).

3. *States' Rights and the Right to Die.* As controversial end-of-life decisions have worked their way through state courts and legislatures, federal government officials have sometimes tried to intervene. Earlier, on page 329 the *Schiavo* discussion referenced congressional and presidential involvement. Federal intervention has been even more active with respect to Oregon's Death with Dignity Act.

In November 2001, Attorney General John Ashcroft tried to reverse the federal government's policy on physician aid in dying in Oregon. Under a June 1998 declaration by Ashcroft's predecessor, Janet Reno, the Drug Enforcement Administration (DEA) did not intervene when physicians used federally controlled prescription drugs to assist a patient's death under Oregon law. Ashcroft's directive to the DEA specifically allowed for the revocation of drug prescription licenses of doctors who participated in aid in dying using federally controlled substances. His directive did not speak to criminal prosecution of the doctors, but they would have been subjected to severe prison sentences under the Controlled Substances Act.

The U.S. Court of Appeals for the Ninth Circuit rejected Attorney General Ashcroft's effort to override Oregon's law, holding that he lacked authority under the Controlled Substances Act to intervene. Oregon v. Ashcroft, 368 F.3d 1118 (9th Cir. 2004). In January 2006, the Supreme Court affirmed the Ninth Circuit, concluding that the Controlled Substances Act does not give the Attorney General authority to declare "illegitimate a medical standard for care and treatment of patients that is specifically authorized under state law." Gonzales v. Oregon, 546 U.S. 243 (2006).

Previously, members of Congress were unsuccessful in their efforts to override Oregon's law. Companion bills were introduced in the U.S. House and Senate that would have permitted the DEA to revoke a physician's registration to prescribe federally controlled substances if the physician prescribed a lethal dose of drugs under Oregon's law. Neither bill was passed, and Congress considered a new bill, the Pain Relief Promotion Act, during 1999 and 2000, that would have overridden Oregon's law by stating that no drugs regulated as controlled substances by the federal government could be used to aid in dying. For a discussion of the Act, see David

Orentlicher & Arthur Caplan, The Pain Relief Promotion Act of 1999: A Serious Threat to Palliative Care, 283 JAMA 255 (2000).

Many commentators have criticized federal involvement in end-of-life decisions as being politically motivated; others see value in the federal oversight. For further discussion, see Brian Bix, Physician-Assisted Suicide and Federalism, 17 Notre Dame J.L. Ethics & Pub Pol'y 53 (2003); Steven G. Calabresi, The Terri Schiavo Case: In Defense of the Special Law Enacted by Congress and President Bush, 100 Nw. U. L. Rev. 151 (2006); Lars Noah, Ambivalent Commitments to Federalism in Controlling the Practice of Medicine, 53 U. Kan. L. Rev. 149 (2004); Adam M. Samaha, Undue Process: Congressional Referral and Judicial Resistance in the Schiavo Controversy, 22 Const. Commentary 505 (2005); Marc Spindelman, A Dissent from the Many Dissents from Attorney General Ashcroft's Interpretation of the Controlled Substances Act, 19 Issues L. & Med. 3 (2003). Similar issues arise with federal intrusion into state decisions to allow marijuana use for medical purposes. See Chapter 6.

4. *Aid in Dying in Other States.* Even before Oregon legalized aid in dying, studies suggested that physician aid in dying and physician-caused euthanasia occur on a regular, albeit infrequent, basis in the United States. Anthony L. Back et al., Physician-Assisted Suicide and Euthanasia in Washington State: Patient Requests and Physician Responses, 275 JAMA 919 (1996); Ezekiel J. Emanuel et al., The Practice of Euthanasia and Physician-Assisted Suicide in the United States, 280 JAMA 506 (1998); Diane E. Meier et al., A National Survey of Physician-Assisted Suicide and Euthanasia in the United States, 338 New Eng. J. Med. 1193 (1998).

In a national survey regarding requests for physician aid in dying or euthanasia, physicians reported that patients receiving aid in dying had a "substantial burden of physical pain and distress," and were "expected to die of their illness within a short time." For euthanasia, physicians reported that the patients were "imminently dying, bedridden, and severely uncomfortable." About 20 to 30 patients who died by aid in dying or euthanasia were reported to be depressed, but patients with depression were significantly less likely to have their requests granted. Diane E. Meier et al., Characteristics of Patients Requesting and Receiving Physician-Assisted Death, 163 Arch. Intern. Med. 1537 (2003).

5. *The Patient-Plaintiffs in* Glucksberg. The Supreme Court provided little information about the patients who claimed a constitutional right to aid in dying in the *Glucksberg* case. In contrast, when the Ninth Circuit found such a right, it provided the following descriptions:

> Jane Roe is a 69-year-old retired pediatrician who has suffered since 1988 from cancer which has now metastasized throughout her skeleton. Although she tried and benefitted temporarily from various treatments including chemotherapy and radiation, she is now in the terminal phase of her disease. In November 1993, her doctor referred her to hospice care. Only patients with a life expectancy of less than six months are eligible for such care.
>
> Jane Roe has been almost completely bedridden since June of 1993 and experiences constant pain, which becomes especially sharp and severe when she moves. The only medical treatment available to her at this time is medication, which cannot fully alleviate her pain. In addition, she suffers from swollen legs, bed sores, poor appetite, nausea and vomiting, impaired vision, incontinence of bowel, and general weakness. . . .

John Doe is a 44-year-old artist dying of AIDS. Since his diagnosis in 1991, he has experienced two bouts of pneumonia, chronic, severe skin and sinus infections, grand mal seizures and extreme fatigue. He has already lost 70 percent of his vision to cytomegalovirus retinitis, a degenerative disease which will result in blindness and rob him of his ability to paint. His doctor has indicated that he is in the terminal phase of his illness.

John Doe is especially cognizant of the suffering imposed by a lingering terminal illness because he was the primary caregiver for his long-term companion who died of AIDS in June of 1991. He also observed his grandfather's death from diabetes preceded by multiple amputations as well as loss of vision and hearing. Mr. Doe is mentally competent, understands there is no cure for AIDS and wants his physician to prescribe drugs which he can use to hasten his death.

James Poe is a 69-year-old retired sales representative who suffers from emphysema, which causes him a constant sensation of suffocating. He is connected to an oxygen tank at all times, and takes morphine regularly to calm the panic reaction associated with his feeling of suffocation. Mr. Poe also suffers from heart failure related to his pulmonary disease which obstructs the flow of blood to his extremities and causes severe leg pain. There are no cures for his pulmonary and cardiac conditions, and he is in the terminal phase of his illness. Mr. Poe is mentally competent and wishes to commit suicide by taking physician-prescribed drugs.

Compassion in Dying v. Washington, 79 F.3d 790, 794-795 (9th Cir. 1996).

6. *Substantive Due Process.* As discussed in the Court's opinions, a right to aid in dying can be analogized to the right to refuse unwanted medical treatment and the right to abortion.

The right to refuse treatment: The Supreme Court had no trouble upholding the traditional distinction between the withdrawal of life-sustaining treatment and physician aid in dying. The Ninth and Second Circuits in *Glucksberg* and *Quill*, however, found the distinction to be unconstitutional, at least for persons who are terminally ill. Consider the following arguments for the distinction. Do they really explain why treatment withdrawal and aid in dying should be treated differently?

a. "[D]eclining life-sustaining medical treatment may not properly be viewed as an attempt to commit suicide. Refusing medical intervention merely allows the disease to take its natural course; if death were eventually to occur, it would be the result, primarily, of the underlying disease, and not the result of a self-inflicted injury." In re Conroy, 486 A.2d 1209, 1224 (N.J. 1985).

b. "[P]eople who refuse life-sustaining medical treatment may not harbor a specific intent to die; rather, they may fervently wish to live, but to do so free of unwanted medical technology, surgery, or drugs, and without protracted suffering." In re Conroy, 486 A.2d 1209, 1224 (N.J. 1985).

c. The right to die is only a right to refuse unwanted bodily invasion. As the Massachusetts Supreme Court wrote in the *Saikewicz* case, "[A] person has a strong interest in being free from nonconsensual invasion of his bodily integrity." Superintendant of Belchertown v. Saikewicz, 370 N.E.2d 417, 424 (Mass. 1977). Similarly, the right to abortion is essentially the right to avoid an unwanted invasion of the body by a fetus. Aid in dying in contrast is a right to demand a bodily invasion, and there is no tradition in the law of such a right.

d. If physicians began to dispense death-causing agents, patients would develop a profound distrust of the medical profession. "[I]f physicians become killers or are even merely licensed to kill, the profession—and, therewith, each physician—will never again be worthy of trust and respect as healer and comforter and protector of life in all its frailty." Willard Gaylin et al., Doctors Must Not Kill, 259 JAMA 2140, 2141 (1988).

e. "How easily will [physicians] be able to care wholeheartedly for patients when it is always possible to think of killing them as a 'therapeutic option'? Shall it be penicillin and a respirator one more time, or perhaps just an overdose of morphine this time? Physicians get tired of treating patients who are hard to cure, who resist their best efforts, who are on their way down—'gorks,' 'gomers,' and 'vegetables' are only some of the less than affectionate names they receive from the house officers. Won't it be tempting to think that death is the best treatment for the little old lady 'dumped' again on the emergency room by the nearby nursing home?" Leon Kass, Neither for Love nor Money: Why Doctors Must Not Kill, 94 Pub. Int. 25, 35 (Winter 1989).

f. Many physicians are poorly trained in the relief of pain and other symptoms of suffering, and studies indicate that half of terminally ill patients receive inadequate pain control during their hospitalizations. Joanne Lynn et al., Perceptions by Family Members of the Dying Experience of Older and Seriously Ill Patients, 126 Ann. Intern. Med. 97 (1997). It would be dangerous to legalize aid in dying before we ensure that physicians are providing appropriate palliative care to their patients.

g. "Two strong movements have each begun to enlist many enthusiastic adherents throughout the nation: a movement toward managed care as a means of cost control and a movement toward managed death through euthanasia and assisted suicide. . . . In managed care, . . . [physicians] are usually given financial incentives to control costs while maintaining quality. . . . As providers of managed care, many physicians will be motivated by concern for quality, but concerns about cost will also be significant. Their concern for quality will probably be made explicit, but their concern for cost will generally be left unspoken. As providers of managed death, many physicians will be sincerely motivated by respect for patient autonomy, but the cost factor will always lurk silently in the background. This will be especially true if they are providing managed death in a setting of managed care." Daniel P. Sulmasy, Managed Care and Managed Death, 155 Arch. Intern. Med. 133, 133, 134 (1995).

h. "Is this the kind of choice, assuming that it can be made in a fixed and rational manner, that we want to offer a gravely ill person? Will we not sweep up, in the process, some who are not really tired of life, but think others are tired of them; some who do not really want to die, but who feel they should not live on, . . . Will not some feel an obligation to have themselves 'eliminated' in order that funds allocated for their terminal care might be better used by their families or, financial worries aside, in order to relieve their families of the emotional strain involved?" Yale Kamisar, Some Non-Religious Views Against Proposed "Mercy-Killing" Legislation, 42 Minn. L. Rev. 669, 690 (1958).

i. "Studies of suicide have found that 90 to 100 percent of the victims die while they have a diagnosable psychiatric illness, an observation that is equally true in suicides among the elderly. The elderly appear to be more prone than younger victims to take their lives during the type of acute depressive episode that responds most effectively to available, modern treatments. . . . One study showed that of 44 patients in the later stages of cancer, only 3 had considered suicide, and each of them had a severe clinical depression. . . . [T]he medical literature is replete with studies demonstrating that primary care physicians often fail to recognize treatable depression in their patients, particularly the elderly. . . . Our data on suicides among the elderly show that 75 percent of those who took their lives had seen a primary care physician during the month before death, yet their psychiatric disturbances usually went undetected or were inadequately treated." Yeates Conwell & Eric D. Caine, Rational Suicide and the Right to Die: Reality and Myth, 325 New Eng. J. Med. 1100, 1101-1102 (1991).

j. "Slavery was long ago outlawed on the ground that one person should not have the right to own another, even with the other's permission. Why? Because it is a fundamental moral wrong for one person to give over his life and fate to another, whatever the good consequences, and no less a wrong for another person to have that kind of total, final power. Like slavery, dueling was long ago banned on similar grounds: even free, competent individuals should not have the power to kill each other, whatever their motives, whatever the circumstances. Consenting adult killing, like consenting adult slavery or degradation, is a strange route to human dignity." Daniel Callahan, When Self-Determination Runs Amok, 22(2) Hastings Center Rep. 52, 52 (1992).

k. "It is not medicine's place to determine when lives are not worth living or when the burden of life is too great to be borne. Doctors have no conceivable way of evaluating such claims on the part of patients, and they should have no right to act in response to them. Medicine should try to relieve human suffering, but only that suffering which is brought on by illness and dying as biological phenomena, not that suffering which comes from anguish or despair at the human condition." Callahan, supra, at 52, 55.

The right to abortion: In some ways, a right to aid in dying seems more defensible than a right to abortion. The life being ended is the life of the person making the decision rather than the life of a third party. Moreover, what is being taken away is a short period of great suffering rather than a potential for a full span of a healthy and productive life. In other ways, the right to aid in dying is the harder case. In particular, the life of a person rather than a pre-viable fetus is being taken.

How well the analogy works depends on which theory you accept for the right to abortion. Consider the following arguments for a right to abortion. How well do they support a right to aid in dying?

a. "Our law affords constitutional protection to personal decisions relating to marriage, procreation, contraception, family relationships, child rearing and education. [These] matters, involving the most intimate and personal choices a person may make in a lifetime, choices central to personal dignity and autonomy, are central to the liberty protected by the Fourteenth Amendment. At the heart of liberty is the right to define one's own concept of existence, of meaning, of the universe, and of the mystery of human life. Beliefs about these matters could not define the attributes of personhood were they formed under compulsion of the state." Planned Parenthood of Southeastern Pennsylvania v. Casey, 505 U.S. 833, 851 (1992).

b. "It is a deeply rooted principle of American law that an individual is ordinarily not required to volunteer aid to another individual who is in danger or in need of assistance. In brief, our law does not require people to be Good Samaritans. . . . [I]f we require a pregnant woman to carry the fetus to term and deliver it—if we forbid abortion, in other words—we are compelling her to be a Good Samaritan. . . . [I]f we consider the generally very limited scope of obligations of samaritanism under our law, and if we consider the special nature of the burdens imposed on pregnant women by laws forbidding abortion, we must eventually conclude that the equal protection clause forbids imposition of these burdens on pregnant women." Donald H. Regan, Rewriting Roe v. Wade, 77 Mich. L. Rev. 1569, 1569 (1979).

c. "The distinctive and singular characteristic of the laws against which the right to privacy has been applied lies in their *productive or affirmative* consequences. There are perhaps no legal proscriptions with more profound, more extensive, or more persistent affirmative effects on individual lives than the laws struck down as violations of the right to privacy. Anti-abortion laws . . . involve the forcing of lives into well-defined and highly confined institutional layers. . . . They affirmatively and very substantially shape a person's life; they direct a life's development along a particular avenue. These laws do not simply proscribe one act or remove one liberty; they inform the totality of a person's life. . . . Anti-abortion laws produce motherhood: They take diverse women with every variety of career, life-plan, and so on, and make mothers of them all. . . . For a period of months and quite possibly years, forced motherhood shapes women's occupations and preoccupations in the minutest detail; it creates a perceived identity for women and confines them to it. . . ." Jed Rubenfeld, The Right of Privacy, 102 Harv. L. Rev. 737, 784, 788 (1989).

7. *The Patient's Condition.* An important question in determining due process rights in end-of-life care is whether the critical issue is the physician's action or the patient's condition. We have seen that the courts permit withdrawal of treatment regardless of the patient's condition but are generally unwilling to recognize a right to aid in dying (or euthanasia), also regardless of the patient's condition. In contrast, when the Ninth and Second Circuits in *Glucksberg* and *Quill* recognized a right to aid in dying, the courts suggested that the critical question is not the nature of the physician's action but the condition of the patient. That is, the critical issue is whether the patient has an irreversible and fatal medical problem, not whether there is a withdrawal of treatment or aid in dying. Consider the following perspectives:

Suppose the doctor agrees to withhold treatment [from a dying patient], as the conventional doctrine says he may. The justification for his doing so is that the patient is in terrible agony, and since he is going to die anyway, it would be wrong to prolong his suffering needlessly. But now notice this. If one simply withholds treatment, it may take the patient longer to die, and so he may suffer more than he would if more direct action were taken and a lethal injection given. This fact provides strong reason for thinking that, once the initial decision not to prolong his agony has been made, active euthanasia is actually preferable to passive euthanasia, rather than the reverse. To say otherwise is to endorse the option that leads to more suffering rather than less, and is contrary to the humanitarian impulse that prompts the decision not to prolong his life in the first place. [James Rachels, Active and Passive Euthanasia, 292 New Eng. J. Med. 78, 78 (1975).]

There are two individuals, one of whom is twenty-eight years old, is despondent from a recent romantic breakup and, because of an acute asthma attack, is temporarily ventilator dependent. Other than the asthma, this person is in good health. The other individual is eighty-two years old, is wracked with pain from widely metastatic cancer and has no more than a few weeks to live. Assume that both of these individuals wish to end their lives, the twenty-eight-year-old by refusing the ventilator and the eighty-two-year-old by suicide. Under current law, the twenty-eight-year-old may have the ventilator discontinued while the eighty-two-year-old generally lacks a right to suicide assistance.

Yet, in terms of the reasons why we recognize a right to refuse life-sustaining treatment, it would be more justifiable for a physician to assist the eighty-two-year-old's suicide than to accede to the twenty-eight-year-old's refusal of the ventilator. . . .

[T]he right to refuse life-sustaining treatment arose out of a sense that hopelessly ill patients should be able to refuse treatment that provides little, if any, benefit and merely prolongs the dying process. Society's interest in preserving a patient's life becomes attenuated when there is little life left to save, and treatment becomes burdensome rather than beneficial. In the same way, society's interest in preserving the life of the eighty-two-year-old becomes attenuated—the patient's remaining life is very short and overcome by severe suffering. Conversely, imposing a ventilator on the twenty-eight-year-old would not result in the brief prolongation of a dying process but the long extension of a life that likely would become very much valued by the patient. If we were to decide these cases strictly on their own merits, we would probably permit physicians to assist the suicide of the eighty-two-year-old but not permit them to withdraw the ventilator from the twenty-eight-year-old. [David Orentlicher, The Legalization of Physician-Assisted Suicide: A Very Modest Revolution, 38 B.C. L. Rev. 443, 462-463 (1997).]

If the patient's condition is more critical than the nature of the physician's act, does this imply that the appropriate standard for both the right to refuse life-sustaining treatment and a right to aid in dying is the standard of the *Quinlan* court, that the individual's right should "grow [] as the degree of bodily invasion increases and the prognosis dims. Ultimately there comes a point at which the individual's rights overcome the state interest. . . ." *Quinlan*, 355 A.2d at 664.

8. *Equal Protection.* The *Quill* court addressed the question whether a right to refuse life-sustaining treatment implies a right to physician aid in dying under the equal protection clause. In the lawsuit over Oregon's statute legalizing physician aid in dying, on the other hand, the federal district court in *Lee* used the equal protection clause to limit the ability of states to permit aid in dying. See supra, at page 360.

If the Second Circuit in *Quill* used the equal protection clause to strike down a prohibition on aid in dying, and the district court in *Lee* used the equal protection clause to strike down a statute permitting aid in dying, do the two opinions simply demonstrate that the equal protection clause is hopelessly indeterminate, or is there a way to reconcile the two rulings?

If we accept the logic of the *Lee* court, must we require the same safeguards for withdrawal of life-sustaining treatment that we require for aid in dying? Aren't patients on life-sustaining treatment given less protection from abuse or impaired judgment than persons who are not being sustained by medical treatment but who want to die? Isn't it easier for a patient like Kenneth Bergstedt, at pages 288-289, to end his life involuntarily than a person who isn't dependent on a ventilator?

9. *Limiting a Right to Aid in Dying.* In *Glucksberg* and *Quill*, the Supreme Court echoed concerns from many commentators that a right to aid in dying cannot be easily cabined. As one scholar has observed,

[i]f personal autonomy and the termination of suffering are supposed to be the touchstones for physician-assisted suicide, why exclude those with nonterminal illnesses or disabilities who might have to endure greater pain and suffering *for much longer periods of time* than those who are expected to die in the next few weeks or months? If the terminally ill do have a right to assisted suicide, doesn't someone who must continue to live what *she considers* an intolerable or unacceptable existence *for many years*

have an equal—or even greater—right to assisted suicide? . . . [I]f, as proponents of assisted suicide maintain, there is no significant difference between the right to assisted suicide and the right to reject unwanted life-saving treatment, it is fairly clear that, once established, the right to assisted suicide would not be limited to the terminally ill. For the right of a person to reject life-sustaining medical treatment *has not been so limited.*

Yale Kamisar, Against Assisted Suicide—Even a Very Limited Form, 72 U. Det. Mercy L. Rev. 735, 740-741 (1995) (emphasis in original).

Is the Court's observation in *Glucksberg* correct that, if we permit physician aid in dying for terminally ill persons, we must also permit euthanasia for terminally ill persons who lack the physical ability to self-administer a lethal dose of medication? Is the Court also correct that we must honor the living will of a patient who requested euthanasia in the event of terminal illness? Must we permit aid in dying for patients who are not terminally ill but who have an incurable and irreversible illness and are suffering greatly?

For an argument that a right to aid in dying is not readily susceptible to expansion, see David Orentlicher & Christopher M. Callahan, Feeding Tubes, Slippery Slopes, and Physician-Assisted Suicide, 25 J. Leg. Med. 389 (2004).

10. *Palliative Sedation.* In her concurring opinion, Justice O'Connor suggested that dying patients have a constitutional right to alleviate their suffering, but that such a right would not imply a right to aid in dying since patients are able to obtain medications to relieve their suffering "even to the point of causing unconsciousness and hastening death."

It is well accepted in ethics and law that physicians can administer medications to relieve pain or other suffering even if doing so poses some increased risk of death for the patient. Under this principle of "double effect," the risk of death is acceptable as long as the medication is used in a reasonable effort to treat the patient's suffering. By way of analogy, we permit physicians to perform open heart surgery, despite the risk of patient death, because the primary purpose of the surgery is to treat the patient's heart disease, and the benefits of the surgery are reasonable when compared with the risks.

In some cases, as Justice O'Connor noted, the patient must be sedated into unconsciousness to relieve the suffering. In these cases, the patient is sedated into a coma from which the patient usually dies in a few days, either because the patient is at the end stage of the underlying illness or because food and water are withheld.

Is there a good reason to permit palliative sedation (once, and at the time of *Glucksberg* and *Quill,* called "terminal sedation") but not to permit aid in dying? From the patient's perspective, which is the more desirable approach? Do you see how palliative sedation could be viewed as a form of euthanasia? See David Orentlicher, The Supreme Court and Physician-Assisted Suicide: Rejecting Assisted Suicide but Embracing Euthanasia, 337 New Eng. J. Med. 1236 (1997) (and a fuller version of the argument in 24 Hastings Const. L.Q. 947 (1997)). In the Netherlands, where both practices are permitted, one study found that palliative sedation is "typically used to address severe physical and psychological suffering in dying patients, whereas perceived loss of dignity during the last phase of life is a major problem for patients requesting euthanasia." Judith A. C. Rietjens et al., Terminal Sedation and Euthanasia, 166 Arch. Intern. Med. 749 (2006). But see Jean-Jacques Georges et al.,

Differences Between Terminally Ill Cancer Patients Who Died After Euthanasia Had Been Performed and Terminally Ill Cancer Patients Who Did Not Request Euthanasia, 19 Palliative Med. 578 (2005) (finding that patients choosing euthanasia had much higher levels of severe pain, vomiting, and nausea than patients who did not choose euthanasia).

States have begun to recognize a right to palliative care in their legislatures and courts. California in 2008 and New York in 2010 passed statutes requiring physicians to advise terminally ill patients of their options for end-of-life care, including hospice care, and treatment to relieve pain and other symptoms. Cal. Health & Safety Code §442.5; N.Y. Pub. Health Law §2997-c. In one important difference between the two statutes, the duty to provide information is not triggered in California until the patient requests information. In addition to these statutory rights, patients have received damages awards from doctors and other health care providers for the failure to provide adequate pain relief. Tolliver v. Visiting Nurse Ass'n of Midlands, 771 N.W. 2d 908 (Neb. 2009); Ben Rich, Physicians' Legal Duty to Relieve Suffering, 175 West. J. Med. 151 (2001). But see McGregor v. Hospice Care of Louisiana in Baton Rouge, 2009 WL 838621 (La. Ct. App. 2009) (rejecting breach of contract claim for failure to provide a pain-free death).

If there is a right to receive medications to alleviate the symptoms of disease, is there also a right to receive medications to treat the disease itself? In a surprising decision in favor of patients' rights based on *Cruzan* and *Glucksberg*, a panel of the D.C. Circuit initially found a limited constitutional right of terminally ill persons to receive experimental cancer chemotherapy or other potentially therapeutic drugs without Food and Drug Administration (FDA) approval when there are no other therapeutic options left. Abigail Alliance v. Eschenbach, 445 F.3d 470 (D.C. Cir. 2006). This decision was reversed by the en banc court, however, 495 F.3d 695 (D.C. Cir. 2007), which reasoned that such a right is not deeply rooted in the nation's history and tradition, considering the long history of the regulation of pharmacists and pharmaceuticals. During the litigation, the FDA proposed a new rule to give terminally ill patients greater access to experimental drugs. 71 Fed. Reg. 75147 (2006). For further discussion of *Abigail Alliance*, see Chapter 6.D.1; Rebecca Dresser, Investigational Drugs and the Constitution, 36(6) Hastings Center Rep. 9 (2006); Peter Jacobson & Wendy Parmet, A New Era of Unapproved Drugs: The Case of *Abigail Alliance v. Von Eschenbach*, 297 JAMA 205 (2007); John Robertson, Controversial Medical Treatment and the Right to Health Care, 36(6) Hastings Center Rep. 15 (2006).

For discussion of the medical and ethical aspects of palliative sedation, see Nathan I. Cherny & Russell K. Portenoy, Sedation in the Management of Refractory Symptoms: Guidelines for Evaluation and Treatment, 10(2) J. Palliative Care 31 (1994); National Ethics Committee, Veterans Health Administration, The Ethics of Palliative Sedation as a Therapy of Last Resort, 23 Am. J. Hosp. Palliat. Care 483 (2007); Bernard Lo & Gordon Rubenfeld, Palliative Sedation in Dying Patients, 294 JAMA 1810 (2005); Timothy E. Quill et al., Last-Resort Options for Palliative Sedation, 154 Ann. Intern. Med. 421 (2009); Robert D. Truog et al., Barbiturates in the Care of the Terminally Ill, 327 New Eng. J. Med. 1678 (1992). See also George P. Smith, II, Refractory Pain, Existential Suffering, and Palliative Care: Releasing an Unbearable Lightness of Being, 20 Cornell J.L. & Pub. Pol'y 469 (2011).

11. *Predicting Patient Outcome.* An important concern about a right of terminally ill persons to aid in dying is the reliability of a physician's prediction that a

patient will die soon (e.g., within six months). For many patients, it is difficult to predict when they will die. Certainty varies not only from patient to patient but also from disease to disease—while predictions are fairly reliable for patients with cancers, they are rather unreliable for patients with emphysema or congestive heart failure. Ellen Fox et al., Evaluation of Prognostic Criteria for Determining Hospice Eligibility in Patients with Advanced Lung, Heart, or Liver Disease, 282 JAMA 1638 (1999); Joanne Lynn et al., Defining the "Terminally Ill": Insights from SUPPORT, 35 Duq. L. Rev. 311 (1996). Still, among all patients certified as likely to die within six months for purposes of hospice benefits under Medicare, 81 percent die within six months. Medicare Payment Advisory Commission, Healthcare Spending and the Medicare Program: A Data Book 2010 (June 2010). (And physicians might be quicker to diagnose a patient as terminally ill to establish eligibility for Medicare benefits than to establish eligibility for physician aid in dying.)

If we reject a right to aid in dying for the terminally ill because of uncertainties as to when a patient is terminally ill, does it follow that we should reject a right to refuse life-sustaining treatment because patients might refuse treatment on the mistaken assumption either that they are terminally ill or that, while not terminally ill, they will be permanently dependent on a ventilator or other treatment?

12. *Refusing Food and Water.* Some commentators have argued that patients who are not dependent upon life-sustaining treatment but who desire aid in dying can always end their lives by refraining from eating and drinking. James L. Bernat et al., Patient Refusal of Hydration and Nutrition: An Alternative to Physician-Assisted Suicide or Voluntary Active Euthanasia, 153 Arch. Intern. Med. 2723 (1993). While some courts and commentators have suggested that death by starvation is painful, Brophy v. New England Sinai Hospital, 497 N.E.2d 626, 641 n.2 (Mass. 1986) (Lynch, J., dissenting), there actually seems to be little discomfort from dying by withdrawal of nutrition and hydration, and the discomfort can easily be relieved with appropriate care. Robert J. Sullivan, Accepting Death Without Artificial Nutrition or Hydration, 8 J. Gen. Intern. Med. 220, 221 (1993). In most cases, death will occur within a few days. If people can end their lives by starvation, or, for that matter, by a number of ways described in Derek Humphrey, Final Exit: The Practicalities of Self-Deliverance and Assisted Suicide for the Dying (1991), why do patients request aid in dying? Note that, even with cessation of eating and drinking, it still may take several weeks in rare cases for the patient to die. Sullivan, supra, at 221-222.

13. *Conscientious Objection.* Living will statutes routinely recognize a conscientious objection on the part of physicians who are unwilling to participate in a withdrawal of life-sustaining treatment. Cal. Prob. Code §4734; Ohio Rev. Code Ann. §2133.10(A); Pa. Cons. Stat. tit. 20, §5424(a). If the physician believes that it is morally wrong to discontinue life-sustaining treatment, then the physician may withdraw from the case and arrange for another physician to carry out the patient's request. To the physician with a conscientious objection of this sort, withdrawal of treatment is understood to cause the patient's death; it does not matter that the physician is doing so by omission or "inaction." To the conscientious objector, withdrawing treatment is just as much an action as aiding in dying. If the physician who opposes withdrawal of treatment may equate it to aid in dying, does it follow that the physician who supports aid in dying may equate it to withdrawal of treatment?

14. *Euthanasia.* While most of the legal activity surrounding this issue in the United States has focused on aid in dying, some statutory proposals and cases seek a

right to euthanasia. As mentioned, the California and Washington legislative initiatives that were defeated would have granted a right to both aid in dying and euthanasia. Also, a California man sought a declaratory judgment permitting him to have his body preserved cryogenically before he died in the hope that physicians could reanimate his body once a cure was found for his brain cancer. Since the "freezing" process would result in the man's death, his claim rested on the existence of a constitutional right to euthanasia, but the court held that no such right exists. Donaldson v. Van de Kamp, 4 Cal. Rptr. 2d 59 (Ct. App. 1992). (Normally, cryopreservation takes place after the person dies.)

15. *Other Countries.* Australia's Northern Territory became the first jurisdiction to legalize euthanasia when it enacted the Rights of the Terminally Ill Act in May 1996. The legislation took effect on July 1, 1996, and the first reported death under the Act occurred on September 22, 1996. The law permitted euthanasia and aid in dying for terminally ill persons after evaluation by two physicians, including a psychiatrist, and after a nine-day waiting period. Robert L. Schwartz, Rights of the Terminally Ill Act of the Australian Northern Territory, 5 Cambridge Q. Healthcare Ethics 157 (1996). In March 1997, after four persons had invoked the law, the Australian Parliament repealed the legislation. Reuters, Euthanasia Law Struck Down in Australia, N.Y. Times, March 27, 1997, at A15.

In the Netherlands, euthanasia and aid in dying were treated as criminal acts, but they were not prosecuted if performed under guidelines that were developed between 1973 and 1984 by the legal system and the medical profession. In 2001, legislation formally legalized aid in dying and euthanasia in accordance with existing practices, with some extension of those practices. The legislation took effect in April 2002.

In the Netherlands, the patient must be competent and have made a consistent, persistent, and voluntary request for euthanasia or aid in dying. The patient need not be terminally ill but must be incurably ill and experiencing unbearable suffering that cannot be relieved. The patient's physician must consult with an experienced colleague before acceding to the patient's request. Maurice A. M. Wachter, Active Euthanasia in the Netherlands, 262 JAMA 3316 (1989).

As discussed in *Glucksberg*, there is evidence that the guidelines for euthanasia and aid in dying were not rigorously followed in a substantial number of cases before 2002. Empirical data indicate that in about one-fourth of cases of euthanasia or aid in dying, physicians did not observe the strict criteria for those procedures. In these cases, the patient "had in a previous phase of his or her illness expressed a wish for euthanasia should suffering become unbearable," the patient was "near to death and clearly suffering grievously, yet verbal contact had become impossible," or the decision had been discussed with the patient but the patient's wishes had not been expressed explicitly and persistently. Paul J. van der Maas et al., Euthanasia and Other Medical Decisions Concerning the End of Life, 338 Lancet 669, 672 (1991); Paul J. van der Maas et al., Euthanasia, Physician-Assisted Suicide, and Other Medical Practices Involving the End of Life in the Netherlands, 1990-1995, 335 New Eng. J. Med. 1699, 1701 (1996). In response to this evidence, the Royal Dutch Medical Association issued new guidelines in August 1995 that emphasized that existing rules needed to be followed and that stated that euthanasia should not be performed unless aid in dying is not an option (e.g., because the patient is too sick to swallow the lethal drug) and that the consulting physician may not have a professional or family relationship with the patient or physician. Marlise Simons, Dutch Doctors to Tighten Rules on Mercy Killings, N.Y. Times, Sept. 11, 1995, at A3. A subsequent study found that rates of aid in dying and euthanasia had stabilized between 1995 and 2001, with physicians becoming somewhat more reluctant to engage in the two practices. Bregje D. Onwuteaka-Philipsen, Euthanasia and Other End-of-Life Decisions in the Netherlands in 1990, 1995, and 2001, 362 Lancet 395 (2003).

After the 2002 legalization of euthanasia and aid in dying, it appears that physicians have become more reluctant to employ those practices. A survey of Dutch physicians in 2005 found a significant decrease in the use of aid in dying and euthanasia, accompanied by greater use of palliative sedation. For example, the euthanasia rate in 2005 was 1.7 percent of all deaths, down from 2.6 percent in 2001 and equal to the rate in 1990. In addition, the rate of life-ending acts without a current explicit request from the patient dropped from 0.7 percent in 2001 to 0.4 percent in 2005. The researchers observed that the reduction in aid in dying and euthanasia may have reflected a substitution of palliative sedation for the two practices and/or a decline in the likelihood that physicians would attribute patient death to the effects of opioid administration. As to the latter, it is possible that physicians were less likely in 2005 than in previous years to mitakenly believe that their use of opioids to treat patient suffering had hastened patient deaths. Agnes van der Heide et al., End-of-Life Practices in the Netherlands Under the Euthanasia Act, 356 New Eng. J. Med. 1957 (2007). Dutch patients who request aid in dying or euthanasia are more likely to be depressed than comparable patients who do not make such a request. However, doctors refuse the requests most of the time for depressed patients, and the prevalence of depression among those who receive aid in dying or euthanasia is no higher than among similar patients who do not request aid in dying or euthanasia. Ilana Levene & Michael Parker, Prevalence of Depression in Granted and Refused Requests for Euthanasia and Assisted Suicide: A Systematic Review, 37 J. Med. Ethics 205 (2011).

In addition to legalizing existing rules for non-prosecuted euthanasia and aid in dying for competent persons, the 2002 law also permits euthanasia by advance directive. In a survey of physicians asking about euthanasia by advance directive in 2000-2001, before its recognition under the law, researchers found that 29 percent of the physicians had treated demented patients with a euthanasia advance directive, but only 3 percent of the physicians complied with such a directive, and 54 percent reported that they never would comply with such a directive. Mette L. Rurup et al., Physicians' Experiences with Demented Patients with Advance Euthanasia Directives in the Netherlands, 53 J. Am. Geriatrics Soc'y 1138 (2005).

For a comprehensive discussion of euthanasia and aid in dying in the Netherlands before legalization, see John Griffiths et al., Euthanasia & Law in the Netherlands (1998).

In Belgium, final approval was given in 2002 to legislation permitting euthanasia under rules like those in the Netherlands. In 2007, euthanasia in Belgium accounted for 0.5 percent of all deaths, with most of the patients terminally ill from cancer and experiencing unbearable physical suffering. Tinne Smets et al., Legal Euthanasia in Belgium: Characteristics of All Reported Euthanasia Cases, 48 Med. Care 187 (2010). In Germany, euthanasia is prohibited by law, but aid in dying is not. However, physicians are legally obligated to try to resuscitate persons who have attempted suicide. Consequently, while aid in dying is practiced in Germany, the assistance is usually provided by family members or friends rather than physicians. The German Society for Humane Dying is a large, private, nonmedical organization that provides advice to members about aid in dying after they have been members for at least a year. Margaret P. Battin, Assisted Suicide: Can We Learn from Germany?, 22(2) Hastings Center Rep. 44 (1992). Switzerland permits aid in dying without the involvement of a physician; there, too, lay assistance is common. Samia A. Hurst & Alex Mauron, Assisted Suicide and Euthanasia in Switzerland: Allowing a Role for Non-Physicians, 326 BMJ 271 (2003). Concerns have been raised by the practice of "suicide tourism," in which individuals from other countries where physician aid in dying is illegal travel to Switzerland to end their lives. For further discussion, see Alan Meisel & Kathy L. Cerminara, The Right to Die §12.07[B] (3d ed. 2011 Supp.).

16. *Additional Arguments.* Consider the following additional arguments regarding aid in dying (or euthanasia):

The common concern that assisted suicide will shorten life may be mistaken. Seriously ill patients often face an option of treatment that has a small but still significant chance of prolonging life. At the same time, there may be a substantial risk that the treatment will fail and only cause painful and debilitating side effects. The prospect of the treatment failure and the side effects will discourage many patients from accepting the treatment. A small chance of success may not be enough to overcome a high risk of great suffering. If a right to assisted suicide existed, however, those same patients would be more likely to accept the treatment. The patients would know that, if the treatment did not work, they would always have the option of ending their suffering through physician assisted suicide. The patients would not have to fear the consequences of treatment failure. They also would know that, with their physician's guidance, their suicide attempt would be more dignified, less painful and less likely to fail and leave the patient in a condition of even greater suffering. [David Orentlicher, The Legalization of Physician-Assisted Suicide: A Very Modest Revolution, 38 B.C. L. Rev. 443, 452-453 (1997).]

[P]hysician assisted suicide has been prohibited not because it is meaningfully different from withdrawal of life-sustaining treatment, but because the distinction between suicide assistance and treatment withdrawal served as a useful proxy for distinguishing between morally acceptable and morally unacceptable decisions by patients to end their lives. Society commonly implements its principles through generally valid rules rather than through case-by-case determinations, recognizing that the rules will not fit every case perfectly but also recognizing the infeasibility of case-by-case determinations. The distinction between suicide assistance and treatment withdrawal is an example of rule-based lawmaking that, in the view of the public and the courts, was an effective way to ensure that patients could end their lives only when they were morally justified in doing so.

    Now, however, the distinction between physician assisted suicide and withdrawal of life-sustaining treatment has lost its utility as a moral proxy. . . . [T]here are many patients desiring assisted suicide whose wishes to end their lives are morally justified—in society's view. The distinction between assisted suicide and withdrawal of treatment no longer does a good job of sorting morally valid from morally invalid requests by patients to end their lives. Accordingly, the distinction is being replaced—and may continue to be replaced—by new proxy distinctions that allow for physician assisted suicide in limited situations. [Id. at 445.]

See also David Orentlicher, Matters of Life and Death: Making Moral Theory Work in Medical Ethics and the Law 16-23 (2001).

17. *State Law Activity Outside of Oregon.* The Supreme Court's rejection of a federal constitutional right has shifted the aid in dying debate back to the state courts and legislatures. . Voters in Maine rejected aid in dying by referendum in 2000 on a 51.5 percent to 48.5 percent vote, and an aid in dying referendum lost by 71 percent to 29 percent in Michigan in 1998.

Washington became the second state to permit physician aid in dying, in November 2008. A voter initiative—the Washington Death with Dignity Act—that was patterned on the Oregon Death with Dignity Act passed with 58 percent support. Rev. Code Wash. §70.245. Through mid-2012, 265 had patients received a prescription for life-ending medication, and as in Oregon, a substantial number of patients died without using their prescriptions. In 2011, for example, 103 prescriptions were reported, with 70 deaths by ingestion of the prescribed medication, 19 deaths without ingestion of the medication, and 5 deaths of persons whose ingestion status was not known. Among the patients who died, whether by taking the prescribed medication or not, nearly 80 percent had cancer, and the main concerns of the patients were loss of autonomy, diminished ability to engage in activities that made life enjoyable, and a loss of dignity. Reports are available at the Web site of the Washington State Department of Health's Center for Health Statistics. For commentary, see Robert Steinbrook, Physician-Assisted Death—From Oregon to Washington State, 359 New Eng. J. Med. 2513 (2008).

Bills to legalize aid in dying have been introduced in other state legislatures, and several states have enacted or reaffirmed their prohibitions of aid in dying in recent years. For updates on legislative activity, see the Death with Dignity National Center Web site, at www.deathwithdignity.org/news/statenews.asp.

Seriously ill persons also have gone to state court for relief, arguing for a right to aid in dying under state constitutional law. In December 2009, the Montana Supreme Court held that physician aid in dying is permissible under state law. Baxter v. State, 224 P.3d 1211 (Mont. 2009). The trial court had recognized a right to physician aid in dying under the Montana constitution, but the Supreme Court vacated the constitutional ruling and rested its holding on Montana statutory law. According to the Supreme Court, "a terminally ill patient's consent to physician aid in dying constitutes a statutory defense to a charge of homicide against the aiding physician." Litigation in other states has been unsuccessful so far. See Sampson v. Alaska, 31 P.3d 88 (Alaska 2001); Krischer v. McIver, 697 So. 2d 97 (Fla. 1997).

For an interesting argument that physician aid in dying should not be legalized but that there should be an affirmative defense to charges of aid in dying when the patient is competent, terminally ill, and suffering, see James A. Tulsky et al., A Middle Ground on Physician-Assisted Suicide, 5 Cambridge Q. Healthcare Ethics 33 (1996).

18. *Further Readings.* For additional discussions of physician aid in dying, see Margaret P. Battin, Physician-Assisted Dying and the Slippery Slope: The Challenge of Empirical Evidence, 45 Willamette L. Rev. 91 (2008); Daniel Callahan & Margot White, The Legalization of Physician-Assisted Suicide: Creating a Regulatory Potemkin Village, 30 U. Rich. L. Rev. 1 (1996); Ronald Dworkin, Life's Dominion: An Argument About Abortion, Euthanasia, and Individual Freedom (1993); Leonard M. Fleck, Just Caring: Assisted Suicide and Health Care Rationing, 72 U. Det. Mercy L. Rev. 873 (1995); Sylvia A. Law, Physician-Assisted Death: An Essay on Constitutional Rights and Remedies, 55 Md. L. Rev. 292 (1996); Thomas Marzen,

"Out, Out Brief Candle": Constitutionally Prescribed Suicide for the Terminally Ill, 21 Hastings Const. L.Q. 799 (1994); Physician-Assisted Suicide: Expanding the Debate (Margaret P. Battin et al. eds., 1998); Robert A. Sedler, Constitutional Challenges to Bans on "Assisted Suicide": The View from Without and Within, 21 Hastings Const. L.Q. 777 (1994); Symposium, 106 Mich. L. Rev. 1453 (2008); Symposium: Physician-Assisted Suicide, 82 Minn. L. Rev. 885 (1998); Symposium: Visions of Death and Dying, 24 Hastings Const. L.Q. 833 (1997); Symposium, Physician-Assisted Suicide, 35 Duq. L. Rev. 1 (1996).

Problem: Is It Aid in Dying or Is It Withdrawal of Treatment?*

Laura is a chronically depressed woman in her late 60s who has very symptomatic arthritis and is seriously overweight. The arthritis causes her chronic pain, which in turn has led her to become addicted to pain medications. Her arthritis and obesity have also caused her to be nonambulatory. Four days ago, Robert, Laura's husband, came into the room at home where Laura appeared injured. Robert called the paramedics, and Laura was brought to the hospital. Robert says that, at the time he called the paramedics, he had not realized that Laura had shot herself with a pistol to the head (actually under her chin with an exit wound in the forehead). He says if he had known, he would not have called them. What happened next was that Laura was taken to surgery and found to have sustained considerable damage to her head but not much damage to the brain except some to the frontal lobes. The surgeons indicate that although the patient is intubated and ventilator-dependent, it is because of the mechanical damage and edema in her neck, and they feel they will be able to take her off the ventilator shortly. Because her brain damage is minimal and involving only the frontal lobes, without the development of meningitis, she is not expected to have any loss of movement or sensation. [Injuries to the frontal lobes can cause a number of personality changes. People with such injuries may become indifferent to the problems of others, give little thought to the effects of their conduct on others, exhibit socially inappropriate behavior like telling silly or tasteless jokes, and become distractible and given to euphoria and emotional outbursts. There also is often a reduction in worry, anxiety, depression, and sensitivity to stressful stimuli, and patients who suffer from chronic pain often complain less of the pain after a frontal lobe injury. There may be compromise of memory or intellectual skills, including problem solving ability, or there may be very little effect on memory and intellect.]

Shortly after Laura's arrival to the hospital, Robert brought a copy of the state's standard Durable Power of Attorney for Health Care (DPAHC) form, which was signed by Laura, duly witnessed, and dated three months before the date of her gunshot wound. Laura had designated Robert as her DPAHC agent. Robert told the hospital doctors and staff that he and his family were aware of the emotional and physical pain and suffering that Laura had experienced over the years and understood that she was depressed (indeed, she had attempted suicide in the 1970s with pills), but she really did not want to live and suffer from her infirmities any longer and she wanted to end the suffering, and, as her agent, he wanted them to stop the emergency treatment and let her die.

*This problem was adapted from a case originally presented by Maurice Bernstein, M.D., University of Southern California School of Medicine, and Scott Rae, Ph.D., Talbot School of Theology, Biola University (California).

Emergency treatment was continued despite the protestations of Robert and the family, who wanted to let Laura die. Currently, Laura is under morphine pain management in the intensive care unit, still ventilator-dependent and unable to communicate, is not deteriorating and indeed her doctors are optimistic about a possible recovery. "A recovery . . . , but to what?" Robert and family say. "A return to the misery of her life before she shot herself and possibly with some additional impairments?" What Robert and the family want the medical staff to do is take Laura off the ventilator and let her die.

You work in the office of the hospital's legal counsel who receives a call from the physicians taking care of Laura asking for legal advice. They want to know whether the law permits, requires, or forbids them to comply with the family's request to discontinue the ventilator. The legal counsel asks you for a memo analyzing the legal issues raised by this case. What would you write in the memo? In considering whether discontinuation of the ventilator would constitute withdrawal of life-sustaining treatment or aid in dying, do you see how the answer depends on your theory as to why aid in dying is different from withdrawal of treatment?

C. FUTILITY

While cases about life-sustaining medical treatment have generally involved situations in which the patient or patient's proxy wanted to stop treatment over the objection of physicians or the hospital, cases are also arising in which the positions are reversed: the patient or proxy wants to continue with treatment, but the physicians or hospital want to stop providing care. In such cases, the patient or family asserts the patient's right to make medical decisions; the physicians or hospital argue that the treatment is medically "futile," that it does not provide sufficient—or any—medical benefit and therefore ought not to be offered to the patient.

■ IN RE BABY K
16 F.3d 590 (4th Cir. 1994)

WILKINS, Circuit Judge.

The Hospital instituted this action against Ms. H, Mr. K, and Baby K, seeking a declaratory judgment that it is not required under the Emergency Medical Treatment and Active Labor Act (EMTALA), 42 U.S.C.A. §1395dd (West 1992),[2] to

2. The Hospital also sought declaratory relief under §504 of the Rehabilitation Act of 1973 (Rehabilitation Act), 29 U.S.C.A. §794 (West Supp. 1993); the Americans with Disabilities Act of 1990 (ADA), 42 U.S.C.A. §§12101 et seq. (West 1993); the Child Abuse Prevention and Treatment Act (Child Abuse Act), 42 U.S.C.A. §§5101-5106h (West Supp. 1993); and the statutes and common law of Virginia. In addressing these provisions, the district court concluded that a failure to provide respiratory support to Baby K because of her condition of anencephaly would constitute discrimination in violation of the ADA and the Rehabilitation Act but declined to rule on the application of the Child Abuse Act or Virginia law. Because we conclude that the Hospital has a duty to render stabilizing treatment under EMTALA, we need not address its obligations under the remaining federal statutes or the laws of Virginia.

provide treatment other than warmth, nutrition, and hydration to Baby K, an anencephalic infant. Because we agree with the district court that EMTALA gives rise to a duty on the part of the Hospital to provide respiratory support to Baby K when she is presented at the Hospital in respiratory distress and treatment is requested for her, we affirm.

I

Baby K was born at the Hospital in October of 1992 with anencephaly, a congenital malformation in which a major portion of the brain, skull, and scalp are missing. While the presence of a brain stem does support her autonomic functions and reflex actions, because Baby K lacks a cerebrum, she is permanently unconscious. Thus, she has no cognitive abilities or awareness. She cannot see, hear, or otherwise interact with her environment.

When Baby K had difficulty breathing on her own at birth, Hospital physicians placed her on a mechanical ventilator. This respiratory support allowed the doctors to confirm the diagnosis and gave Ms. H, the mother, an opportunity to fully understand the diagnosis and prognosis of Baby K's condition. The physicians explained to Ms. H that most anencephalic infants die within a few days of birth due to breathing difficulties and other complications. Because aggressive treatment would serve no therapeutic or palliative purpose, they recommended that Baby K only be provided with supportive care in the form of nutrition, hydration, and warmth. Physicians at the Hospital also discussed with Ms. H the possibility of a "Do Not Resuscitate Order" that would provide for the withholding of lifesaving measures in the future.

The treating physicians and Ms. H failed to reach an agreement as to the appropriate care. Ms. H insisted that Baby K be provided with mechanical breathing assistance whenever the infant developed difficulty breathing on her own, while the physicians maintained that such care was inappropriate. As a result of this impasse, the Hospital sought to transfer Baby K to another hospital. This attempt failed when all of the hospitals in the area with pediatric intensive care units declined to accept the infant. In November of 1992, when Baby K no longer needed the services of an acute-care hospital, she was transferred to a nearby nursing home.

Since being transferred to the nursing home, Baby K has been readmitted to the Hospital three times due to breathing difficulties. Each time she has been provided with breathing assistance and, after stabilization, has been discharged to the nursing home. Following Baby K's second admission, the Hospital filed this action to resolve the issue of whether it is obligated to provide emergency medical treatment to Baby K that it deems medically and ethically inappropriate. Baby K's guardian ad litem and her father, Mr. K, joined in the Hospital's request for a declaration that the Hospital is not required to provide respiratory support or other aggressive treatments. . . .

II

Congress enacted EMTALA in response to its "concern that hospitals were 'dumping' patients [who were] unable to pay, by either refusing to provide emergency medical treatment or transferring patients before their emergency conditions were stabilized." Brooks v. Maryland General Hospital Inc., 996 F.2d 708, 710 (4th Cir. 1993). Through EMTALA, Congress sought "to provide an 'adequate first response to a medical crisis' for all patients," Baber v. Hospital Corp. of America, 977 F.2d 872, 880 (4th Cir. 1992), by imposing two duties on hospitals that have entered into Medicare provider agreements.

First, those hospitals with an emergency medical department must provide an appropriate medical screening to determine whether an emergency medical condition exists for any individual who comes to the emergency medical department requesting treatment. A hospital fulfills this duty if it utilizes identical screening procedures for all patients complaining of the same condition or exhibiting the same symptoms.

An additional duty arises if an emergency medical condition is discovered during the screening process. EMTALA defines an "emergency medical condition" as including:

> a medical condition manifesting itself by acute symptoms of sufficient severity (including severe pain) such that the absence of immediate medical attention could reasonably be expected to result in—
>
> (i) placing the health of the individual . . . in serious jeopardy,
> (ii) serious impairment to bodily functions, or
> (iii) serious dysfunction of any bodily organ or part. [42 U.S.C.A. §1395dd(e)(1)(A).]

When an individual is diagnosed as presenting an emergency medical condition:

> the hospital must provide either—
>
> (A) within the staff and facilities available at the hospital, for such further medical examination and such treatment as may be required to stabilize the medical condition, or
>
> (B) for the transfer of the individual to another medical facility in accordance with subsection (c) of this section. [42 U.S.C.A. §1395dd(b)(1).]

The treatment required "to stabilize" an individual is that treatment "necessary to assure, within reasonable medical probability, that no material deterioration of the condition is likely to result from or occur during the transfer of the individual from a facility." 42 U.S.C.A. §1395dd(e)(3)(A). Therefore, once an individual has been diagnosed as presenting an emergency medical condition, the hospital must provide that treatment necessary to prevent the material deterioration of the individual's condition or provide for an appropriate transfer to another facility.

In the application of these provisions to Baby K, the Hospital concedes that when Baby K is presented in respiratory distress a failure to provide "immediate medical attention" would reasonably be expected to cause serious impairment of her bodily functions. Thus, her breathing difficulty qualifies as an emergency medical condition, and the diagnosis of this emergency medical condition triggers the duty of the hospital to provide Baby K with stabilizing treatment or to transfer her in accordance with the provisions of EMTALA. Since transfer is not an option available to the Hospital at this juncture,[5] the Hospital must stabilize Baby K's condition. . . .

5. In order for a hospital to transfer a patient prior to stabilization, EMTALA requires: (1) the patient or a person acting on the patient's behalf to request a transfer in writing after

III

. . . As the Hospital acknowledged during oral argument, Baby K resides at the nursing home for months at a time without requiring emergency medical attention. Only when she has experienced episodes of bradypnea or apnea[9] has Baby K required respiratory support to prevent serious impairment of her bodily functions. It is bradypnea or apnea, not anencephaly, that is the emergency medical condition that brings Baby K to the Hospital for treatment. . . . The Hospital does not allege that it would refuse to provide respiratory support to infants experiencing bradypnea or apnea who do not have anencephaly. Indeed, a refusal to provide such treatment would likely be considered as providing no emergency medical treatment. . . .

[The Hospital argues] that, in redressing the problem of disparate emergency medical treatment, Congress did not intend to require physicians to provide medical treatment outside the prevailing standard of medical care. The Hospital asserts that, because of their extremely limited life expectancy and because any treatment of their condition is futile, the prevailing standard of medical care for infants with anencephaly is to provide only warmth, nutrition, and hydration. Thus, it maintains that a requirement to provide respiratory assistance would exceed the prevailing standard of medical care. However, the plain language of EMTALA requires stabilizing treatment for any individual who comes to a participating hospital, is diagnosed as having an emergency medical condition, and cannot be transferred. . . . The Hospital has been unable to identify, nor has our research revealed, any statutory language or legislative history evincing a congressional intent to create an exception to the duty to provide stabilizing treatment when the required treatment would exceed the prevailing standard of medical care. We recognize the dilemma facing physicians who are requested to provide treatment they consider morally and ethically inappropriate, but we cannot ignore the plain language of the statute because "to do so would 'transcend our judicial function.'" *Baber*, 977 F.2d at 884. The appropriate branch to redress the policy concerns of the Hospital is Congress. . . .

---

being informed of the risks involved and the obligations of the hospital under EMTALA; or (2) a proper certification that the medical benefits expected from the transfer outweigh the risks involved. 42 U.S.C.A. §1395dd(c)(1). In addition, the transfer must meet the criteria for an appropriate transfer which include the requirement that a qualified receiving facility agree to accept that the patient and to provide appropriate medical treatment. 42 U.S.C.A. §1395dd(c)(1)(B), (c)(2). Since Ms. H objects to the transfer of Baby K, since the Hospital has not obtained a certificate that the benefits of a transfer would outweigh the medical risks involved, and since no qualified medical facility has agreed to accept Baby K, the requirements for transfer prior to stabilization have not been met. If Ms. H requests a transfer or the Hospital obtains a certification that the benefits of a transfer would outweigh the risks involved, and all of the requirements for an appropriate transfer are met, then the Hospital could, of course, transfer Baby K to another qualified medical facility prior to stabilization.

9. Bradypnea is an "abnormal slowness of breathing." Dorland's Illustrated Medical Dictionary 230 (27th ed. 1988). In an infant who has established and sustained spontaneous breathing, apnea describes the cessation of respiration for more than sixty seconds. Id. at 112.

IV

It is beyond the limits of our judicial function to address the moral or ethical propriety of providing emergency stabilizing medical treatment to anencephalic infants. We are bound to interpret federal statutes in accordance with their plain language and any expressed congressional intent. Congress rejected a case-by-case approach to determining what emergency medical treatment hospitals and physicians must provide and to whom they must provide it; instead, it required hospitals and physicians to provide stabilizing care to any individual presenting an emergency medical condition. EMTALA does not carve out an exception for anencephalic infants in respiratory distress any more than it carves out an exception for comatose patients, those with lung cancer, or those with muscular dystrophy—all of whom may repeatedly seek emergency stabilizing treatment for respiratory distress and also possess an underlying medical condition that severely affects their quality of life and ultimately may result in their death. Because EMTALA does not provide for such an exception, the judgment of the district court is affirmed.

■ CAUSEY v. ST. FRANCIS MEDICAL CENTER
719 So. 2d 1072 (La. Ct. App. 1998)

BROWN, J.

The facts of this end of life drama are not materially disputed. Believing it medically and ethically inappropriate, a physician and hospital withdrew life-sustaining care to a 31-year-old, quadriplegic, end-stage renal failure, comatose patient over the strongly expressed objections of the patient's family. . . .

FACTS

Having suffered cardiorespiratory arrest, Sonya Causey was transferred to St. Francis Medical Center (SFMC) from a nursing home. She was comatose, quadriplegic and in end-stage renal failure. Her treating physician, Dr. Herschel R. Harter, believed that continuing dialysis would have no benefit. Although Dr. Harter agreed that with dialysis and a ventilator Mrs. Causey could live for another two years, he believed that she would have only a slight (1% to 5%) chance of regaining consciousness. Because Mrs. Causey's family demanded aggressive life-sustaining care, Dr. Harter sought unsuccessfully to transfer her to another medical facility willing to provide this care.

Dr. Harter enlisted support from SFMC's Morals and Ethics Board. The Board agreed with Dr. Harter's opinion to discontinue dialysis, life-support procedures, and to enter a "no-code" status (do not resuscitate). Mrs. Causey was taken off a feeding tube and other similar devices. The day the ventilator was removed, Mrs. Causey died of respiratory and cardiac failure.

Plaintiffs, the husband, father and mother of Sonya Causey, brought this petition for damages against SFMC and Dr. Harter. Defendants filed an exception of prematurity asserting that this action was covered under Louisiana's Medical Malpractice Act, which requires that malpractice claims be first submitted to a medical review panel before any action can be filed. . . .

DISCUSSION

Patient participation in medical decision-making is now well-established. Recognizing individual autonomy and the right to self-determination, our state legislature enacted a statute granting a competent, terminally ill person the right to *refuse* medical treatment.

In the *Karen Quinlan* case the court rejected a physician's adamant stand that he had a moral duty to treat to the last gasp. In that case, the father, not the physician, was given the power to decide whether his comatose daughter's life-prolonging care was beneficial. . . .

Now the roles are reversed. Patients or, if incompetent, their surrogate decision-makers, are demanding life-sustaining treatment regardless of its perceived futility, while physicians are objecting to being compelled to prolong life with procedures they consider futile. . . .

The problem is not with care that the physician believes is harmful or literally has no effect. For example, radiation treatment for Mrs. Causey's condition would not have been appropriate. This is arguably based on medical science. Rather, the problem is with care that has an effect on the dying process, but which the physician believes has no benefit. Such life-prolonging care is grounded in beliefs and values about which people disagree. Strictly speaking, if a physician can keep the patient alive, such care is not medically or physiologically "futile;" however, it may be "futile" on philosophical, religious or practical grounds.

Placement of statistical cut-off points for futile treatment involves subjective value judgments. The difference in opinion as to whether a 2% or 9% probability of success is the critical point for determining futility can be explained in terms of personal values, not in terms of medical science. When the medical professional and the patient, through a surrogate, disagree on the worth of pursuing life, this is a conflict over values, i.e., whether extra days obtained through medical intervention are worth the burden and costs.

SFMC had in place a Futile Care Policy which allowed for the discontinuance of medical care over and above that necessary for comfort and support if the probability of improving the patient's condition was slight and would serve only to prolong life in that condition. The inclusion of non-medical persons on the Morals and Ethics Board signals that this is not strictly a physiological or medical futility policy, but a policy asserting values and beliefs on the worth of sustaining life, even in a vegetative condition.

Futility is a subjective and nebulous concept which, except in the strictest physiological sense, incorporates value judgments. Obviously, in this case, subjective personal values of the benefit of prolonging life with only a slight possibility of improvement dictated SFMC's and Dr. Harter's decision.

To focus on a definition of "futility" is confusing and generates polemical discussions. We turn instead to an approach emphasizing the standard of medical care.

Physicians are professionals and occupy a special place in our community. They are licensed by society to perform this special role. No one else is permitted to use life-prolonging technology, which is considered by many as "fundamental" health care. The physician has an obligation to present all medically acceptable treatment options for the patient or her surrogate to consider and either choose or reject; however, this does not compel a physician to provide interventions that in his view would be harmful, without effect or "medically inappropriate." In recognizing a terminal patient's right to refuse care, La. R.S. 40:1299.58.1(a)(4) states that the statute is not to be construed "to require the application of *medically inappropriate* treatment or life-sustaining procedures to any patient or to interfere with *medical judgment* with respect to the application of medical treatment or life-sustaining procedures." (Emphasis added). Unfortunately, "medically inappropriate" and "medical judgment" are not defined. . . .

Standards of medical malpractice require a physician to act with the degree of skill and care ordinarily possessed by those in that same medical specialty acting under the same or similar circumstances. Departure from this prevailing standard of care, coupled with harm, may result in professional malpractice liability. A finding that treatment is "medically inappropriate" by a consensus of physicians practicing in that specialty translates into a standard of care. Thus, in this case, whether Dr. Harter and SFMC met the standard of care concerning the withdrawal of dialysis, life-support procedures and the entering of a "no code" status must be determined. . . . [T]he Medical Malpractice Act is applicable and the matter should first be submitted to a medical review panel.

[Although multiple experts supported the withdrawal of care in their testimony to the medical review panel, the *Causey* case was settled before trial on remand.]

Notes: Medical Futility

1. *What Really Happened in* Baby K? Baby K, whose name was Stephanie Keene, ultimately lived for two-and-a-half years in a pediatric nursing facility. She died in the emergency room of Fairfax Hospital in Fairfax, Virginia—the same hospital that brought the *Baby K* case—after being taken there by ambulance for the sixth time. Her anencephaly had been diagnosed by ultrasound during the sixteenth week of her gestation, and her mother, Contrenia Harrell, decided to carry her to term, believing (according to press accounts) that "'all life is precious'" and that God would guide Stephanie's life. Other local hospitals reportedly refused to accept a transfer of Baby K shortly after her birth.

Baby K's medical bills ultimately reached almost $1 million. They were covered in part by her mother's insurance with an HMO and in part by Medicaid. They often do not pay the full costs of treatment. Nevertheless, hospital officials stated that the costs of Baby K's care were not a factor in the hospital's lawsuit. Even so, the hospital may have been thinking about the implications of the case for future patients, and the cost of caring for patients like Baby K are likely to be an issue for other hospitals as health insurers increasingly employ capitation rates for reimbursement, and as Medicare and Medicaid continue to limit their reimbursement rates.

An important question is who should make the treatment decision for a patient like Baby K? Do you think the insurers should have a stake in the decision? Would it be reasonable to tell Baby K's mother she can insist on treatment but not on payment, thereby remaining liable for the bills? If she still insisted on treatment, but the hospital knew she could never pay, should it still have to treat?

2. *A Medical Miracle?* Some might scoff at Ms. Harrell's reported belief in a medical miracle, but one may in fact have occurred here. As the court noted, anencephalic children generally do not live very long; fewer than 10 percent of such children survive more than a week. Baby K may be the longest-lived child with anencephaly. Rather than a miracle, however, her length of life may indicate that the general lack of aggressive treatment for anencephalic children results in their actual lifespans being considerably shorter than their potential lifespans.

3. An important issue raised by the *Baby K* case is whether a denial of treatment would violate the Americans with Disabilities Act (and the Rehabilitation Act). Although the Fourth Circuit declined to decide this issue, supra page 377 n.2, the court did allude to the issue in its opinion, supra page 380. There, the Court observes that the hospital would provide ventilator support to infants in respiratory distress who were not anencephalic. This argument is analogous to the argument raised in the *University Hospital* case, reprinted at pages 122-128 and discussed at pages 132-135 and 346-347. In *University Hospital*, there were charges of discrimination when potentially life-prolonging treatments were withheld from a seriously disabled infant. The crux of the argument is as follows: Anti-discrimination law requires similarly situated persons to be treated alike. Is *Baby K* similarly situated to other infants needing ventilator treatment because she is also in respiratory distress, or is she not similarly situated because her respiratory distress is related to her anencephaly rather than to a condition that is more responsive to medical treatment? A major concern in these cases is whether scarce resources can be allocated. For a relevant discussion of this concern in the context of allocating organs for transplantation, see pages 454-459. For further discussion of the Americans with Disabilities Act, see Chapter 2.A.3.

The implications of *Baby K* for hospitals trying to limit health care costs is serious. Perhaps in recognition of that fact, the Fourth Circuit cabined the holding of *Baby K* two years later in Bryan v. Rectors and Visitors of the University of Virginia, 95 F.3d 349 (4th Cir. 1996) (discussed at pages 118-119). In *Bryan*, the court rejected the family's claim when physicians withheld resuscitative treatment from a hopelessly ill patient who died of a heart attack 20 days after her hospital admission.

4. *Literature on Futility.* While there are a relatively small number of court cases involving "futility," there is already an extensive literature on the topic of medical futility. Useful readings on the issue include Mary Ann Baily, Cost and End-of-Life-Care: Futility, Autonomy, and Cost in End-of-Life Care, 39 J.L. Med. & Ethics 172 (2011); Leslie Blackhall, Must We Always Use CPR?, 317 New Eng. J. Med. 1281 (1987); Allen S. Brett & Laurence B. McCullough, When Patients Request Specific Interventions: Defining the Limits of the Physician's Obligation, 315 New Eng. J. Med. 1347 (1986); Council on Ethical and Judicial Affairs, Guidelines for the Appropriate Use of Do-Not-Resuscitate Orders, 265 JAMA 1868 (1991); Paul R. Helft et al., The Rise and Fall of the Futility Movement, 343 New Eng. J. Med. 293 (2000); Jerry Menikoff, Demanded Medical Care, 30 Ariz. St. L.J. 1091 (1998); David Orentlicher, Matters of Life and Death, 123-166 (2002); Thaddeus Mason Pope, Surrogate Selection: An Increasingly Viable, but Limited, Solution to Intractable Futility Disputes, 3 St. Louis U. J. Health L. & Pol'y 183 (2010); Tom Tomlinson & Howard Brody, Futility and the Ethics of Resuscitation, 264 JAMA 1276 (1990); Robert Truog, Medical Futility, 25 Ga. St. U.L. Rev. 985 (2009); Robert D. Truog et al., The Problem with

Futility, 326 New Eng. J. Med. 1560 (1992); and a symposium in the June 2011 issue of the *Journal of Bioethical Inquiry*.

Other useful articles include contributions to a Symposium on Medical Futility, 25 Seton Hall L. Rev. 873-1026 (1995); Mary A. Crossley, Medical Futility and Disability Discrimination, 81 Iowa L. Rev. 179 (1995); Philip G. Peters, Jr., When Physicians Balk at Futile Care: Implications of the Disability Rights Laws, 91 Nw. U. L. Rev. 798 (1997); and Lance K. Stell, Stopping Treatment on Grounds of Futility: A Role for Institutional Policy, 11 St. Louis U. Pub. L. Rev. 481 (1992).

5. *Defining Futility.* Futility is generally analyzed under two rubrics: qualitative and quantitative futility. Under qualitative futility, the claim is that medical treatment cannot provide a sufficient benefit to justify its use. Some commentators argue that there is qualitative futility when the patient would not recover enough to go home from the hospital, some find qualitative futility when the patient is permanently unconsciousness, and others believe there is futility only when treatment cannot provide a physiological benefit. In this third view, treatment is not futile as long as it can prolong life or affect the quality of life in any way.

Under quantitative futility, the claim is that there is too low a likelihood that medical treatment will have its desired effect. Here, too, there is disagreement as to when futility exists. Some would find futility when a particular treatment has been consistently unsuccessful for at least 100 tries. Lawrence J. Schneiderman et al., Medical Futility: Its Meaning and Ethical Implications, 112 Ann. Intern. Med. 949 (1990). Others would place it at different likelihoods of success. In one study, researchers discussed with internal medicine residents the reasons why the residents wrote do-not-resuscitate (DNR) orders for their patients. In two-thirds of the cases in which quantitative futility was a contributing factor to the DNR order, the likelihood that the patient would be resuscitated and be able to go home from the hospital was 1 percent or less. In 9 percent of cases, on the other hand, the likelihood of success was 20 percent or more. J. Randall Curtis et al., Use of the Medical Futility Rationale in Do-Not-Attempt-Resuscitation Orders, 273 JAMA 124, 126-127 (1995). Of course, one's view about quantitative futility depends on the qualitative benefit to be gained. The greater the potential qualitative benefit, the lower the likelihood of benefit before a treatment would be considered futile.

6. *Comparison with* Quinlan. In 1991, doctors at Hennepin County Medical Center unsuccessfully invoked futility to discontinue a ventilator from a patient in a persistent vegetative state. In re Wanglie, No. PX-91-283 (Hennepin County Prob. Ct. Minn., July 1, 1991), discussed in Steven H. Miles, Informed Demand for "Nonbeneficial" Medical Treatment, 325 New Eng. J. Med. 512 (1991).

The *Wanglie* case is exactly the reverse of the *Quinlan* case. Both cases involved a patient who was permanently unconscious and thought to be ventilator dependent. In *Quinlan*, the family was in court trying to have the ventilator stopped. In *Wanglie*, the family was in court trying to have the ventilator continued. If ventilator treatment for Mrs. Wanglie was futile, how could it not have been futile for Ms. Quinlan? Why do you suppose the hospital in *Wanglie* asked the court to appoint a conservator for Mrs. Wanglie rather than simply to authorize discontinuation of her ventilator?

7. *Other Futility Cases.* In futility cases, courts so far have split between siding with the patient or the patient's family and siding with the physicians and hospital.

For cases rejecting futility, in addition to *Baby K* and *Wanglie*, there is In re Jane Doe, 418 S.E.2d 3 (Ga. 1992). In that case, an adolescent suffered from a severe and degenerative neurological disease that left her comatose or nearly comatose. Jane Doe's physicians and hospital wanted to de-escalate life support and enter a DNR order, and her parents split on the issue. Although the case was brought at least in part as a futility case, the positions of the parties changed during the judicial proceedings such that the Georgia Supreme Court ended up deciding the case on the issue of resolving parental disagreements over CPR. The court held that a DNR order could not be written without the consent of both parents.

In another unreported case, In re Ryan N. Nguyen, #94206074-5 (Wash. Super. Ct., Spokane County, Nov. 22, 1994), the futility argument also was rejected. Ryan Nguyen was born six weeks early and was diagnosed with severe brain damage, an intestinal blockage, and malfunctioning kidneys. The hospital where he was being treated could not provide the necessary dialysis, and two academic medical centers refused to accept a referral, in at least one case on the ground that the child had such a dismal prognosis. The family obtained a court order for treatment, and the publicity resulted in a hospital offering to provide care. Ultimately, Ryan's intestinal blockage was cleared, his kidney problems resolved, and it turned out that he had not suffered any irreversible brain injury. Alexander Morgan Capron, Baby Ryan and Virtual Futility, 25(2) Hastings Center Rep. 20 (1995).

For a case accepting futility in addition to *Bryan* and *Causey*, consider the *Gilgunn* case. Gilgunn v. Massachusetts General Hospital, No. 92-4820 (Mass. Super. Ct. Suffolk Cty., April 22, 1995). In that case, Catherine Gilgunn became comatose and terminally ill at age 71, and her physicians decided to write a do-not-resuscitate order and discontinue her ventilator over the objections of one of her children. Alexander Morgan Capron, Abandoning a Waning Life, 25(4) Hastings Center Rep. 24 (1995). After Mrs. Gilgunn died, her daughter sued the hospital and physician, and the jury decided in favor of the defendants. This case, however, may not tell us very much about the law on futility since the verdict was not appealed, and the jury may have sided with the hospital and physicians on any of several theories. Capron, supra, at 25-26.

Nearly a decade after the *Gilgunn* case, Massachusetts General Hospital sought judicial permission to discontinue aggressive treatment of a patient severely disabled by ALS (Lou Gehrig's disease), over the objections of the patient's daughter. For the most part in this case, the hospital did not succeed with its futility argument. The trial court upheld the patient's appointment of her daughter as health care proxy and also ordered the writing of a do-not-resuscitate order (which by the time of the decision had been agreed to by the daughter) on the grounds that CPR would be both "inappropriate and harmful." The court also instructed the daughter to make future medical decisions based on the daughter's assessment of the patient's best interests. The court felt that the patient's condition had deteriorated in ways unanticipated by the patient and that the patient's wishes were no longer ascertainable. (In the appointment, the patient directed her daughter to decide on the basis of her wishes unless her wishes were unknown, in which case her daughter was supposed to decide on the basis of an assessment of best interests.) In re Barbara Howe, No. 03 P 1255 (Mass. Prob. & Fam. Ct., Suffolk Div., March 22, 2004). A year later, the daughter and hospital were back in court and settled the dispute with an agreement that the hospital would maintain ventilator support for three more months and then be free to discontinue treatment. Ms. Howe died 26 days before the expiration of the three-month period. John J. Paris et al., *Howe v. MGH* and *Hudson v. Texas Children's Hospital:* Two Approaches to Resolving Family-Physician Disputes in End-of-Life Care, 26 J. Perinatology 726 (2006).

Betancourt v. Trinitas Hospital involved a patient in a persistent vegetative state for whom physicians wanted to write a DNR order and discontinue dialysis. Family members sought an injunction against these steps, and the New Jersey trial court rejected the hospital's futility argument. While the appeal was pending, the patient died, and the court of appeals dismissed the case as moot. The court also called on the legislature, executive branch, and appropriate commissions to develop policy for cases involving claims of futility. 1 A.3d 823 (N.J. Ct. App. 2010). Note that the New Jersey Supreme Court did not dismiss the *Conroy* case as moot even though Ms. Conroy died while the appeal was pending in her case.

8. *Futility Statutes.* As in Louisiana, some states have addressed futility by statute. See Cal. Prob. Code §§4735-4736 (modifying Section 7(f) of the Uniform Health Care Decisions Act (1993); Md. Code Ann., Health—General §5-611; Tex. Health & Safety Code Ann. §166.046; Va. Code Ann. §54.1-2990.

The Texas statute is notable for the procedures it sets out to invoke futility. In Texas, a physician's refusal to honor a request for treatment requires review by an ethics or medical committee, and the patient or surrogate decisionmaker is entitled to attend the committee's meeting and receive a written explanation for the committee's decision. If the patient or family disagrees with a committee's decision affirming the refusal, the physician must make a reasonable effort to transfer the patient to a physician who will provide the desired treatment. Although treatment must be provided pending transfer, there is no obligation to provide treatment beyond the tenth day after a committee decision in favor of refusing treatment.

While some view the Texas approach as a model, Paris et al., *Howe v. MGH,* supra, it has provoked considerable controversy in some cases when doctors and hospitals have invoked it, and family members have been able to delay the withdrawal of treatment through court challenges. The Texas Senate passed legislation in 2007 that would have amended the statute, but the bill died in the House. Michael Grabell, Boy at Center of Ethics Case Dies, Dallas Morning News (Central Edition), May 31, 2007, at 1B.

9. *Futility in Practice.* What do you make of the fact that the physicians in *Baby K* were willing to provide the child with nutrition and hydration but not a ventilator to ensure adequate oxygenation? If a ventilator is futile because the child is anencephalic, then why isn't a feeding tube futile? Conversely, if we say that Mrs. Wanglie is entitled to a ventilator because it could maintain her life, would we also say she is entitled to a heart valve replacement if one were needed to maintain her life?

Is there some difference between *Bryan, Causey,* and *Gilgunn,* on one hand, and many of the other cases presented (e.g., *Baby K, Howe, Jane Doe, Wanglie,* and *Ryan Nguyen*) that might explain why the two groups of cases came out differently?

10. *Additional Views.* Consider the following perspectives on futility:

  a. "In the event that the patient or surrogate requests a treatment that the responsible health care professional regards as clearly futile in achieving its physiological objective and so offering no physiological benefit to the patient, the professional has no obligation to provide it. However, the health care professional's value judgment that although a treatment will produce physiological benefit, the benefit is not sufficient to warrant the treatment, should not be used as a basis for determining a treatment to be futile." Guidelines on the Termination of Life-Sustaining Treatment and the Care of the Dying: A Report of the Hastings Center 32 (1987).

b. "The argument that physician judgments about the futility of CPR are improper simply because they incorporate value judgments relies on a principle that has implausible implications for the rest of medical practice. . . . If the physician cannot refuse because, as a matter of principle, he or she is forbidden to employ 'value judgments,' then no justification can remain for refusal to provide a computed tomographic scan for the anxious patient with a headache, who also may have attached symbolic importance to the procedure, and no justification is available for resisting a family's demand that even 'physiologically futile' resuscitation efforts must continue indefinitely. . . . The real question can no longer be *whether* value judgments can be made concerning the provision of CPR or other medical techniques; rather, the question is *which* value judgments physicians may use in deciding whether to meet patients' demands." Tom Tomlinson & Howard Brody, Futility and the Ethics of Resuscitation, 264 JAMA 1276, 1277-1278 (1990)

c. Claims that a particular treatment is "futile" are really claims that the treatment is too expensive at a time when health care resources are severely strained. Physicians prefer to characterize a treatment as futile rather than as too costly for the same reason that judges prefer to justify a decision on the ground that it is compelled by precedent rather than to acknowledge the indeterminacy in the law and concede that they are deciding on the basis of personal philosophy. By characterizing a treatment as medically futile and therefore of no purpose, physicians can hide the fact that they are rationing care, and thereby avoid patient challenges to their rationing decisions. It is much easier for a patient to challenge a rationing decision than a "medical" decision. Calling a treatment futile serves another purpose. It permits physicians to regain some of the authority they have lost since the mid-1960s when medical ethics and the law began to give greater recognition to patient autonomy. If a treatment decision is viewed as a medical decision rather than a value judgment, then physicians can colorably claim that the decision is exclusively for them to make.

Notes: Brain Death

Although futility has been debated seriously as an issue only since the late 1980s, the development of the concept of brain death in the late 1960s and early 1970s can be seen as an early manifestation of the futility concern.

1. *Medical Background.* Traditionally, death was pronounced based on the cessation of the beating of the heart and the breathing of the lungs. In other words, death was determined on the basis of "cardiopulmonary" criteria. Typically at death, a person's heart stops functioning because of injury or illness. The person's lungs and brain also stop functioning because they are deprived of their blood flow. Since it is a much simpler matter to detect loss of heart and lung function than to detect loss of brain function, cardiopulmonary criteria for death were adopted. In some cases, injury or illness causes loss of brain function first, and without the regulation of the brain, the lungs also stop functioning (i.e., the breathing of the lungs is controlled by the brain stem—the beating of the heart is also regulated by the brain stem, but the heart can pump an adequate amount of blood in the absence of brain stem function). When the lungs stop, the heart is deprived of oxygen, and it then

ceases beating. Historically, loss of lung and heart function followed within minutes of the loss of brain function, and patients who had lost brain function satisfied cardiopulmonary criteria for death.

With advances in medical technology, however, it became possible to support a person's heart and lungs with mechanical ventilation even after cessation of brain function. According to cardiopulmonary criteria, these persons were not dead, but to many observers, they seemed to have lost their vitality. Patients who have lost all brain function appear to be in a very deep coma. (Interestingly, spontaneous movements are more common in brain-dead patients than once thought. In a study, researchers found that 39 percent of their brain-dead patients exhibited spontaneous movements of their fingers, toes, and arms. These movements are believed to reflect spinal cord reflexes, and, in fact, no brain activity was seen on EEGs during the movements. Gustavo Saposnik et al., Spontaneous and Reflex Movements in Brain Death, 54 Neurology 221 (2000).) Mechanical measures and other artificial support can maintain brain-dead patients' heartbeat and breathing temporarily, but usually only for a few weeks or months, after cessation of brain function. But see D. Alan Shewmon, Chronic "Brain Death": Meta-Analysis and Conceptual Consequences, 51 Neurology 1538 (1998) (describing the maintenance of a heartbeat in brain-dead patients for more than a year, including one patient for more than 14 years). Because of the profound loss of functioning, the permanence of the condition, and the inability to prolong the state for very long, many observers questioned whether it made sense to provide treatment to these patients.

Ordinarily, such questioning might lead to a right to have medical treatment withdrawn when a person's brain stops functioning, just as Karen Quinlan's persistent vegetative state led the New Jersey Supreme Court to recognize her right to have her ventilator withdrawn. Instead, "brain" criteria for death were developed. In a report that was highly influential in leading to the acceptance of "brain death," the authors wrote:

> Our primary purpose is to define irreversible coma as a new criterion for death. There are two reasons why there is need for a definition: (1) Improvements in resuscitative and supportive measures have led to increased efforts to save those who are desperately injured. Sometimes these efforts have only partial success so that the result is an individual whose heart continues to beat but whose brain is irreversibly damaged. The burden is great on patients who suffer permanent loss of intellect, on their families, on the hospitals, and on those in need of hospital beds already occupied by these comatose patients. (2) Obsolete criteria for the definition of death can lead to controversy in obtaining organs for transplantation.

Report of the Ad Hoc Committee of the Harvard Medical School to Examine the Definition of Brain Death, A Definition of Irreversible Coma, 205 JAMA 85, 85 (1968).

As this excerpt suggests, the adoption of brain criteria for death may have been motivated primarily by futility-type concerns—the high burdens and low benefits of treatment—as well as by concerns about the shortage of organs for transplantation. Philosophical considerations about the meaning of life seemingly played little role in the change.

In the next chapter, we take up the issues of organ transplantation related to brain death. Here, we consider the implications for patient autonomy of brain criteria for death. By defining patients as dead when they lose brain function, it would seem to follow that one could not choose for oneself or one's family member to have mechanical ventilation continued after cessation of brain function. That implication has been confirmed by the law.

2. *Adoption of Brain Criteria for Death.* Kansas was the first state to adopt a brain death statute, and its constitutionality was upheld in State v. Schaffer, 574 P.2d 205 (1977). It did so in the context of a murder prosecution, where the defendant had argued that the doctors who removed life support, and not himself, caused the death of the victim. A later case adopting the brain death definition as a matter of common law provides a particularly thorough explanation of the relationship between the definition of death and homicide statutes. People v. Eulo, 472 N.E.2d 286 (N.Y. 1984). Death by brain criteria is accepted in every state as well as the District of Columbia. Alan Meisel & Kathy L. Cerminara, The Right to Die §6.04[A] (3d ed. 2011 Supp.). The Uniform Determination of Death Act has been enacted by statute in a majority of states. Several states, like Washington, have adopted brain death by court decision, and the remainder of the states have enacted brain death legislation without relying on the uniform law.

In re Bowman, 617 P.2d 731 (Wash. 1980) (en banc), provides a good discussion of the principles undergirding brain death. According to the court,

> [d]eath is both a legal and medical question. Traditionally, the law has regarded the question of at what moment a person died as a question of fact to be determined by expert medical testimony. However, recognizing that the law has independent interests in defining death which may be lost when deference to medicine is complete, courts have established standards which, although based on medical knowledge, define death as a matter of law. Thus, the law has adopted standards of death but has turned to physicians for the criteria by which a particular standard is met. [Id. at 734.]

3. *The Meaning of Adopting Brain Criteria for Death.* It is not clear what the significance has been of changing the definition of death to include cessation of brain function. We could characterize the change as substituting brain death for cardiopulmonary death. Under this view, the essence of personhood is found in the functioning of the mind rather than the body, so that death occurs when the brain stops functioning. We can identify brain death either directly, by showing the absence of brain function, or indirectly, by showing the absence of cardiac function (i.e., once the heart stops pumping blood to the brain, the brain cells die). According to another view, life requires the presence of both brain and cardiopulmonary function. Once one of the two functions is lost, the person is dead.

A third view, and the one given by most commentators to explain the development of neurological criteria for death, is that death has always meant loss of the body's integrative capacity. Under this view, death occurs when the body loses its ability to function as an integrated whole rather than as a collection of independently functioning cells or tissues. President's Commission for the Study of Ethical Problems in Medicine and Biomedical and Behavioral Research, Defining Death: A Report on the Medical, Legal, and Ethical Issues in the Determination of Death 32-38 (1981); Alexander M. Capron & Leon Kass, A Statutory Definition of the Standards for Determining Human Death: An Appraisal and a Proposal, 121 U. Pa.

L. Rev. 87, 102 (1972). After all, a person's cells can be maintained indefinitely in the laboratory, but we would not therefore say that the person is still alive. The body retains some ability to integrate bodily functions as long as there is some brain function, but once the brain ceases all function, the body has lost its integrative capacity. Again, we can measure loss of integrative function either directly, by establishing loss of brain function, or indirectly, by establishing loss of cardiopulmonary function. According to this view, we always thought of death as the loss of integrative capacity, but, until recently, we were able to determine its existence only when the heart stopped beating. Once we were able to support cardiopulmonary function artificially even after loss of brain function, we were able to have different ways to measure death. Under the integrative capacity view, the definition of death did not change; rather, we have only changed the criteria for ascertaining death.

4. *Loss of Integrative Capacity.* While the President's Commission and others accept integrative capacity as the basis for life, there are serious problems with this theory. First, it turns out that people who are dead according to neurological criteria still maintain some integrative capacity. For example, their brains still regulate water retention by the kidneys to ensure the appropriate balance among water, blood cells, and other components of blood in the body's bloodstream. In addition, many patients who are dead by brain criteria have some electrical activity on their electroencephalograms (EEGs), and they "frequently respond to surgical incision at the time of organ procurement with a significant rise in both heart rate and blood pressure." Robert D. Truog, Is It Time to Abandon Brain Death?, 27(1) Hastings Center Rep. 29, 29-30 (1997). Proponents of the integrative capacity theory respond that death occurs when there is loss of all critical or essential bodily functions. James L. Bernat, Brain Death: Occurs Only with Destruction of the Cerebral Hemispheres and the Brain Stem, 49 Arch. Neurol. 569, 569 (1992), but that begs the question of what bodily functions are critical.

A second problem with the integrative capacity theory is that it does not seem to explain how people think about death. The fact that we still use the term "brain death" and speak of keeping "brain dead" patients on "life support" suggests that people think of death by neurological criteria differently than death by cardiopulmonary criteria. Indeed, in one study, physicians and nurses likely to be involved in organ procurement for transplantation were asked to explain why they thought a person was dead when the brain stopped functioning. While 25 percent of the physicians and nurses gave loss of integrative capacity as their reason, 36 percent spoke in terms of loss of consciousness and 32 percent indicated that they really did not believe the patient was dead, explaining that the patient would die soon no matter what was done or that the patient's quality of life was unacceptable. Stuart J. Youngner, Defining Death: A Superficial and Fragile Consensus, 49 Arch. Neurol. 570, 571 (1992). See also Richard Willing, Brain-Dead Woman Dies After Baby Born, USA Today, Aug. 4, 2005, at 3A (marking woman's death when ventilator was discontinued nearly three months after declaration of death by brain criteria).

5. *Choosing a Definition of Death.* How should we define death? How do we choose among cardiopulmonary death, brain death, and upper brain death (i.e., loss of consciousness)? What is the moral, philosophical, or legal principle that helps us decide what it means to be dead? If the issue is whether the person has the essential characteristics of a human being, why not require only permanent

loss of consciousness before declaring someone dead? Is it because unconscious persons do things that make them appear to be conscious (e.g., random or reflexive movements of the eyes, arms, or legs)? Or is it that we cannot be sure they are really unconscious and therefore those things that look like conscious activity may really reflect conscious activity? For useful readings on these issues, see Alexander Morgan Capron, Brain Death—Well Settled yet Still Unresolved, 344 New Eng. J. Med. 1244 (2001); Michael B. Green & Daniel Wikler, Brain Death and Personal Identity, 9 Phil. & Pub. Aff. 105 (1980); Jeff McMahan, An Alternative to Brain Death, 34 J.L. Med. & Ethics 44 (2006); President's Commission for the Study of Ethical Problems in Medicine and Biomedical and Behavioral Research, Defining Death (1981); Tom Stacy, Death, Privacy, and the Free Exercise of Religion, 77 Cornell L. Rev. 490 (1992); Robert M. Veatch, The Whole-Brain-Oriented Concept of Death: An Outmoded Philosophical Formulation, 3 J. Thanatology 13 (1975); Stuart J. Youngner et al. eds., The Definition of Death: Contemporary Controversies (1999).

6. *Lack of Patient or Family Choice.* When a person has been declared dead, that person's legal representative (in this case the guardian ad litem) cannot insist that the patient be maintained on a ventilator. Indeed, in In re *Bowman,* the court automatically assumed that the declaration of death by brain criteria foreclosed a choice of continued treatment. 617 P.2d at 420-421. Although *Bowman* involved child abuse and a guardian ad litem, the same result has been reached when foul play was not involved and the parents had religious reasons for wanting to continue ventilation of their child. In re Long Island Jewish Medical Center, 641 N.Y.S.2d 989 (Sup. Ct. 1996).

Does it necessarily follow from the fact that a person is dead that we do not respect the person's or the family's wishes for ventilation to be continued until the heart stops beating? We can point to public health concerns to explain why a person must be buried or cremated after cardiopulmonary death, but what is the justification for insisting that a ventilator be discontinued after brain death? Would it matter if the person could pay for the costs of the continued treatment, through either an insurance policy or personal wealth?

7. *Single or Multiple Definitions.* Must we have a standard definition of death to which everyone subscribes? In New Jersey, under the determination of death statute, people are dead when either their heart and lungs or their brain stops functioning. However,

> [t]he death of an individual shall not be declared upon the basis of neurological criteria . . . when the licensed physician authorized to declare death, has reason to believe, on the basis of information in the individual's available medical records, or information provided by a member of the individual's family or any other person knowledgeable about the individual's personal religious beliefs that such a declaration would violate the personal religious beliefs of the individual. In these cases, death shall be declared, and the time of death fixed, solely upon the basis of cardiorespiratory criteria. . . . [N.J. Stat. Ann. 26:6A-5.]

In New York, a New York State Department of Health Regulation provides that hospitals shall establish "a procedure for the reasonable accommodation of the individual's religious or moral objection to the determination" of death by neurological criteria. N.Y. Comp. Codes R. & Regs. tit. 10, §400.16(e)(3). New York physicians and hospitals vary in the extent to which they will continue treatment of a brain-dead person under that provision, but the regulation's requirement of reasonable accommodation does not mandate the continuation of treatment beyond the time necessary for the family to obtain an independent medical opinion and try to arrange for transfer of the patient to another facility. *Long Island Jewish*, 641 N.Y.S.2d at 992. California also has an accommodation provision much like the New York provision. Under California law, families that have "any special religious or cultural practices or concerns" about brain death are entitled to a "reasonably brief period of accommodation." Cal. Health & Safety Code §1254.4.

Could we permit all persons to decide when they are dead, as long as their definition of death falls within a reasonable range, say as long as the definition is permanent unconsciousness, brain death, or cardiac death? Would this be any different from the current status of abortion law, which essentially allows women to decide when their fetus becomes a person, as long as the woman chooses some point between conception and viability? For an argument that the free exercise clause of the First Amendment gives patients and their families a right to determine when death occurs, see Stacy, supra page 392.

We might also want to have different definitions of death depending on the reasons for wanting to know whether the patient is still alive. In this regard, see Roger Dworkin, Death in Context, 48 Ind. L.J. 623 (1975). Dworkin argues that "the effort devoted to defining death is wasted at best, counterproductive at worst," because of the variety of contexts in which the issue is relevant, namely: (1) procedural issues such as when the statutes of limitations begin to run for wrongful death actions and murder prosecutions; (2) numerous property and wealth devolution issues such as who died first for purposes of probating the wills of two people with interests in each other's estates; and (3) status relationships such as when remarriage is valid. Consider, for instance, that one accepted departure from the uniform definition of death is the presumption in many states that a person is dead who is missing for more than seven years.

8. *Criteria for Brain Death.* Guidelines for determining brain death have been published by medical specialty societies. Guidelines and discussion of brain death in adults can be found at Eelco F. M. Wijdicks, The Diagnosis of Brain Death, 344 New Eng. J. Med. 1215 (2001); Report of the Quality Standards Subcommittee of the American Academy of Neurology, Evidence-Based Guideline Update: Determining Brain Death in Adults, 74 Neurology 1911 (2010). Guidelines and discussion of brain death in children can be found at American Academy of Pediatrics, Report of Special Task Force: Guidelines for the Determination of Brain Death in Children, 80 Pediatrics 298 (1987); Joan Lynch & Maher K. Eldadah, Brain-Death Criteria Currently Used by Pediatric Intensivists, 31 Clin. Pediatr. 457 (1992). See also Eelco F. M. Wijdicks ed., Brain Death (2001).

Perhaps in part because of disagreement over the validity of the guidelines for determining brain death in children, one study demonstrated considerable deviation from the guidelines by pediatric intensive care specialists. Rodrigo E. Mejia & Murray M. Pollack, Variability in Brain Death Determination Practices in Children, 274 JAMA 550 (1995). Similarly, the guidelines for determining brain death in adults were issued in part because of variation in practice among neurologists diagnosing death by brain criteria. Eelco Wijdicks, Determining Brain Death in Adults, 45 Neurology 1003 (1995). See also Stuart J. Youngner et al., "Brain Death" and Organ Retrieval: A Cross-Sectional Survey of Knowledge and Concepts Among Health Professionals, 261 JAMA 2205 (1989) (finding in a survey of 39 medical personnel responsible for identifying brain-dead patients that one-third were unable to identify the correct legal and medical criteria for death and apply them to two simple cases).

4

Organ Transplantation: The Control, Use, and Allocation of Body Parts

This chapter explores another dimension of personal control over medical decisions: the supply and distribution of lifesaving organs for transplantation. Because of the serious shortage of transplantable organs, this is a topic that sparks much debate: Can financial payments to organ donors be used to increase the supply of organs? Can organs or other tissues be taken without permission? When organs are in short supply and lives of those who need them are at stake, who gets them first and who decides? These questions range broadly among issues and themes that are addressed elsewhere in this book, but they are more compelling here because the stakes are so clearly life-and-death, and because the use of body parts is so infused with moral and emotional value.

We start by focusing on who controls the decision for organ donation. We have seen that patients may refuse unwanted offers of medical treatment even if doing so results in death. Courts have concluded that the state has a weaker interest than the patient in deciding how to balance concerns about bodily integrity with concerns about the preservation of the patient's own life. What if, on the other hand, there are other lives at stake? Does the state have a greater interest than the patient in making medical decisions when the issue is balancing the individual's concerns with the needs of other persons? That question extends beyond this chapter since an individual's medical decisions can implicate the interests of other persons in a number of ways. In Chapter 3, we considered situations in which a person's death would leave minor children without one of their parents. In Chapters 5 and 6, we consider situations in which a fetus's health is at stake or in which a person's illness poses a public health threat to other persons.

In this chapter, the question is how the balance of affected interests is struck with respect to bodily organs and tissues. The state may perceive an interest in overriding a person's desire to maintain bodily integrity after death by taking kidneys or tissues from cadavers for persons who need a transplant. Or the state may perceive an interest in protecting individuals from unwise decisions to give up their organs while they are still alive. In some cases, then, the question is whether the state can require a transfer of organs (e.g., remove corneas from cadavers for transplantation); in other cases, the question is whether the state can make it harder for people to give up their organs (e.g., prohibit sales of kidneys). Should the balance be struck by individuals since it is their body, or by the state since it has a longer- and broader-range view of both individual and collective interests, or should there be a division of responsibility? As we will see, much of the law in this area has developed in response to the shortage of organs for transplantation, so before we begin, it is helpful to understand more about the need for organ donation and the existing sources of supply.

Good background readings include Michelle Goodwin, Black Markets: The Supply and Demand of Body Parts (2006); Organ Substitution Technology: Ethical, Legal, and Public Policy Issues (Deborah Matheiu ed., 1988); The Ethics of Organ Transplantation (Wayne Shelton & John Balint eds., 2001); Organ Donation: Legal, Ethical, and Policy Issues (Bethany Spielman ed., 1996); Robert M. Veatch, Transplantation Ethics (2000); Organ Transplantation: Meanings and Realities (Stuart J. Youngner et al. eds., 1996).

Note: The Shortage of Organs for Transplantation

The shortage of organs for transplantation is substantial. In December 2012, there were more than 127,000 registrations, and more than 117,000 people on waiting lists for transplantation of a kidney, liver, heart, lung, intestine, or pancreas. (The number of registrations exceeds the number of people waiting since individuals may register on the waiting lists of more than one transplant center. On the other hand, many candidates are temporarily classified as "inactive" by their transplant programs because "they are medically unsuitable for transplantation or need to complete other eligibility requirements.") More than 6,500 people die each year waiting for an organ to become available, and more than 3,000 people are removed from the waiting list because they become too sick to receive a transplant. Even these statistics understate the problem. Given the serious shortage of organs for transplantation, many individuals never make it onto a waiting list since it is clear that they will not have sufficient priority to receive a transplant. (Current and historical data on organ transplantation can be found on the Web site of the Organ Procurement and Transplantation Network (OPTN). Other useful information can be found at the Web site of the United Network for Organ Sharing (UNOS).)

The gap between need and supply reflects a number of considerations. First, in a substantial percentage of cases in which a person dies and the person's organs could be transplanted, there is no transplantation. Physicians may neglect to ask for permission, or family members may refuse to donate the decedent's organs. Physicians are often uncomfortable raising the issue of transplantation, fearing that it will only aggravate the family's grief. Families may deny permission for transplantation because they have religious or other objections to the removal of a body's organs after death. Deborah Matheiu, Introduction, *in* Organ Substitution Technology: Ethical,

Legal, and Public Policy Issues 33, 34-35 (Deborah Matheiu ed., 1988). Efforts have been made to encourage the use of organ donor cards, but most people do not fill them out, sometimes because of fears that their physicians will hasten their death, sometimes because of unwillingness to consider their mortality, sometimes because of religious conviction or a desire for an intact body. But even when people do fill out organ donor cards and physicians know that they have done so, the cards may not ensure organ retrieval unless family consent can be obtained. Many physicians will not remove a deceased person's organs without family consent despite the fact that ethics and the law give priority to the decedent's previously expressed wishes. Indeed, according to the Revised Uniform Anatomical Gift Act, if a person does not revoke a decision to donate before dying, other persons are generally barred from amending or revoking the decedent's consent to donate. Rev. Unif. Anatomical Gift Act §8(a) (2006). This provision is designed to strengthen a similar provision in the previous Uniform Act, according to which a decedent's decision to donate is "irrevocable and does not require the consent or concurrence of any person after the donor's death." Unif. Anatomical Gift Act §2(h) (1987). Even before the 2006 revision a number of states enacted legislation to firmly indicate that the decedent's wishes control. See, e.g., Ind. Code §29-2-16-2.5. For further discussion, see James R. Rodrigue et al., Organ Donation Decision: Comparison of Donor and Nondonor Families, 6 Am. J. Transplantation 190 (2006); Laura A. Siminoff et al., Factors Influencing Families' Consent for Donation of Solid Organs for Transplantation, 286 JAMA 71 (2001); Dave Wendler & Neal Dickert, The Consent Process for Cadaveric Organ Procurement: How Does It Work? How Can It Be Improved?, 285 JAMA 329 (2001).

The gap between need and supply of organs also reflects the fact that, while the number of transplants each year has been increasing, the number of waiting list registrations has been growing twice as fast. The number of waiting list registrations rose from 16,000 to nearly 120,000 between 1988 and 2010, but the number of transplants rose from about 13,000 to nearly 29,000. This continually growing gap between candidates for transplant and available organs reflects several factors. The number of persons who die in a way that leaves their organs suitable for transplantation is being reduced by the enactment of laws requiring seat belts or motorcycle helmets, the use of air bags in automobiles, gun control legislation, and the stricter enforcement of laws that prohibit driving under the influence of alcohol. At the same time, progress in medicine is increasing the number of persons who could benefit from a transplant.

A. ORGAN DONATION

1. Competent Organ Donors

Traditionally, organ donation has been governed by state law. The National Organ Transplant Act of 1984 added a good deal of federal regulation. The Act created the Organ Procurement and Transportation Network as a private, nonprofit entity to determine standards for organ allocation and to establish a system for matching organ donors with recipients. 42 U.S.C. §274(b). The Act also imposed a ban on the sale of organs or other tissues used in transplantation. 42 U.S.C. §274e. However, the ban does not apply to blood, sperm, or ova.

When patients are alive, they are free to donate renewable tissues (e.g., blood and semen) and tissues that are not necessary to maintain health (e.g., ova). They may also sell these tissues (though there is controversy about the selling of ova). On the other hand, people may not donate or sell life-necessary organs (e.g., hearts). In between these two extremes are donations—but not sales—of organs or parts of organs where there may be a significant health risk to the donor. For example, a person might want to donate a kidney to a family member. Since people typically have two kidneys, the donor ordinarily would function reasonably well without the second kidney. As with any major surgery, however, there are some risks from the donation—the chance of dying is about 0.03 percent. Dorry L. Segev et al., Perioperative Mortality and Long-Term Survival Following Live Kidney Donation, 303 JAMA 959 (2010). In addition, if something happened to the remaining kidney, there would be no backup. The long-term consequences for a kidney donor are not definitively known, but they appear to be minimal. To date, studies of kidney donors have not found any long-term medical problems related to the donation. Segev et al., supra; Hassan N. Ibrahim et al., Long-Term Consequences of Kidney Donation, 360 New Eng. J. Med. 459 (2009). Surveys of insurers generally find that kidney donation does not raise premiums for health or life insurance, but some donors have reported problems. Aaron Spital & Tomoko Kokmen, Health Insurance for Kidney Donors: How Easy Is It to Obtain?, 62 Transplantation 1356 (1996); R. C. Yang et al., Life Insurance for Living Kidney Donors: A Canadian Undercover Investigation, 9 Am. J. Transplantation 1585 (2009); Aaron Spital & Cheryl Jacobs, Life Insurance for Kidney Donors: Another Update, 74 Transplantation 972 (2002).

It may be that the absence of problems reflects in part a screening process for donation that selects individuals who are healthier than the average person. Also, even if kidney donation does not raise the risk of hypertension, kidney donors who develop hypertension for other reasons might be more vulnerable to kidney damage from the high blood pressure. Ingela Fehrman-Ekholm & Gilbert T. Thiel, Long-Term Risks After Kidney Donation, in Living Donor Kidney Transplantation 99, 106-107, 110 (Robert S. Gaston & Jonas Wadström eds., 2005).

Because of the risks to the donor—even if small—and concerns about donor motivation, donation of kidneys by living persons still provokes some controversy. When the donation occurs within the family, there are concerns about coercion; when the donation is extrafamilial, there are concerns about hidden payments or psychological stability of the donor. Nevertheless, transplant centers generally welcome donation of kidneys within families. When there is no close relationship between the donor and recipient, however, transplant centers are decidedly less enthusiastic about donations from living persons. Megan Crowley-Matoka & Galen Switzer, Nondirected Living Donation: A Survey of Current Trends and Practices, 79 Transplantation 515 (2005). Still, such donations are becoming more common, and studies suggest that transplant centers can screen potential donors to ensure that their desire to donate does not reflect psychopathology. Martin D. Jendrisak et al., Altruistic Living Donors: Evaluation for Nondirected Kidney or Liver Donation, 6 Am. J. Transplantation 115 (2006); Paul E. Morrissey et al., Good Samaritan Kidney Donation, 27 Transplantation 1369 (2005). See also M. A. Dew et al., Guidelines for the Psychosocial Evaluation of Living Unrelated Kidney Donors in the United States, 7 Am. J. Transplantation 1047 (2007).

Similar issues are raised with regard to donations of a partial liver, lung, or pancreas. In those cases, the concerns are accentuated since the risks to the donor are greater and the procedures are still being developed. Consequently, these transplants are largely limited to circumstances in which the donor has a close relationship to the recipient. For discussion of concerns regarding partial-liver transplants, see David C. Cronin II et al., Transplantation of Liver Grafts from Living Donors into Adults—Too Much, Too Soon, 344 New Eng. J. Med. 1633 (2001); Rafik M. Ghobrial et al., Donor Morbidity After Living Donation for Liver Transplantation, 135 Gastroenterology 468 (2008); John F. Renz & Robert S. Brown, Jr., The Dilemma of Adult-to-Adult Living Donor Liver Transplantation, *in* Liver Transplantation: Challenging Controversies and Topics 65 (Gregory T. Everson & James F. Trotter eds., 2009); James F. Trotter et al., Adult-to-Adult Transplantation of the Right Hepatic Lobe from a Living Donor, 346 New Eng. J. Med. 1074 (2002).

People also may agree while competent to have their organs (and other tissues) taken for transplantation after they die. These donations are governed by the relevant state's version of the Revised Uniform Anatomical Gift Act, 8A U.L.A. 1 (Supp. 2007), or the Uniform Anatomical Gift Act, 8A U.L.A. 3 or 69 (2003). Some version of the 1968 Act was adopted by every state and the District of Columbia within four years of the Act's issuance. By the time the 1987 Act was issued, some states had already adopted at least one of the new provisions, and by 1992, 46 states and the District of Columbia had done so. Fred H. Cate, Human Organ Transplantation: The Role of Law, 20 Iowa J. Corp. L. 69, 71-74 (1994). The 2006 Revised Act quickly elicited interest. By 2012, 45 states had adopted the Act.

Under all versions of the Act, competent adults may make a gift of their organs, with the gift to take effect upon their deaths. The gift may be for education, research, transplantation, or other therapy. For individuals who have not made a gift and who have not expressed opposition to the use of their organs, family members may authorize the taking of their organs. The 1987 Act added a few new provisions: hospitals must ask adult patients whether they want to be organ donors after death (routine inquiry); hospitals must discuss with family members their authority to authorize the taking of organs from deceased patients (routine request); medical examiners may authorize the taking of organs after autopsy if they do not find any objection after reasonable efforts to ascertain the person's or family's wishes; and, as with federal law, sales are prohibited. There is also duplication of federal law with respect to routine requests. That step is required of hospitals as a condition of receiving Medicare and Medicaid reimbursement. 42 U.S.C. §1320b-8. The 2006 Revised Act eliminated the ability of medical examiners to authorize organ retrieval in the absence of consent, in light of case law questioning that authority (discussed in section B.1, infra). Rev. Unif. Anatomical Gift Act §23 (2006). It also expanded the list of persons who may consent to organ donation after a person's death to include adult grandchildren, adults who "exhibited special care and concern for the decedent," and health care agents. Id. at §9(a).

2. Incompetent Organ "Donors"

An important issue is whether the right of a competent person to donate organs survives incompetence. Is the issue analogous to whether the right to refuse life-sustaining treatment survives incompetence? We worry about abuse with organ transplantation—society might be too willing to take organs from incompetent persons to give the organs to competent persons—but we also worry about life-sustaining treatment being withdrawn too quickly from incompetent persons. Are there any important differences between the two concerns about abuse?

■ STRUNK v. STRUNK
445 S.W.2d 145 (Ky. Ct. App. 1969)

OSBORNE, Judge.

The specific question involved upon this appeal is: Does a court of equity have the power to permit a kidney to be removed from an incompetent ward of the state upon petition of his . . . mother, for the purpose of being transplanted into the body of his brother, who is dying of a fatal kidney disease? We are of the opinion it does.

The facts of the case are as follows: Arthur L. Strunk, 54 years of age, and Ava Strunk, 52 years of age, of Williamstown, Kentucky, are the parents of two sons. Tommy Strunk is 28 years of age, married, an employee of the Penn State Railroad and a part-time student at the University of Cincinnati. Tommy is now suffering from chronic glomerulus nephritis, a fatal kidney disease. He is now being kept alive by frequent treatment on an artificial kidney, a procedure which cannot be continued much longer.

Jerry Strunk is 27 years of age, incompetent, and through proper legal proceedings has been committed to the Frankfort State Hospital and School, which is a state institution maintained for the feebleminded. He has an I.Q. of approximately 35, which corresponds with the mental age of approximately six years. He is further handicapped by a speech defect, which makes it difficult for him to communicate with persons who are not well acquainted with him. When it was determined that Tommy, in order to survive, would have to have a kidney the doctors considered the possibility of using a kidney from a cadaver if and when one became available or one from a live donor if this could be made available. The entire family, his mother, father and a number of collateral relatives were tested. Because of incompatibility of blood type or tissue none were medically acceptable as live donors. As a last resort, Jerry was tested and found to be highly acceptable. . . . The mother . . . petitioned the county court for authority to proceed with the operation. The court found that the operation was necessary, that under the peculiar circumstances of this case it would not only be beneficial to Tommy but also beneficial to Jerry because Jerry was greatly dependent upon Tommy, emotionally and psychologically, and that his well-being would be jeopardized more severely by the loss of his brother than by the removal of a kidney. . . .

A psychiatrist, in attendance to Jerry, who testified in the case, stated in his opinion the death of Tommy under these circumstances would have "an extremely traumatic effect upon him" (Jerry).

The Department of Mental Health of this Commonwealth has entered the case as amicus curiae and on the basis of its evaluation of the seriousness of the operation as opposed to the traumatic effect upon Jerry as a result of the loss of Tommy, recommended to the court that Jerry be permitted to undergo the surgery. Its recommendations are as follows:

. . . Jerry Strunk, a mental defective, has emotions and reactions on a scale comparable to that of normal person. He identifies with his brother Tom; Tom is his model, his tie with his family. Tom's life is vital to the continuity of Jerry's improvement at Frankfort State Hospital and School. The testimony of the hospital representative reflected the importance to Jerry of his visits with his family and the constant inquiries Jerry made about Tom's coming to see him. Jerry is aware he plays a role in the relief of this tension. We the Department of Mental Health must take all possible steps to prevent the occurrence of any guilt feelings Jerry would have if Tom were to die.

The necessity of Tom's life to Jerry's treatment and eventual rehabilitation is clearer in view of the fact that Tom is his only living sibling and at the death of their parents, now in their fifties, Jerry will have no concerned, intimate communication so necessary to his stability and optimal functioning.

The evidence shows that at the present level of medical knowledge, it is quite remote that Tom would be able to survive several cadaver transplants. Tom has a much better chance of survival if the kidney transplant from Jerry takes place.

Upon this appeal we are faced with the fact that all members of the immediate family have recommended the transplant. The Department of Mental Health has likewise made its recommendation. The county court has given its approval. The circuit court has found that it would be to the best interest of the ward of the state that the procedure be carried out. Throughout the legal proceedings, Jerry has been represented by a guardian ad litem, who has continually questioned the power of the state to authorize the removal of an organ from the body of any incompetent who is a ward of the state. . . .

The renal transplant is becoming the most common of the organ transplants. This is because the normal body has two functioning kidneys, one of which it can reasonably do without, thereby making it possible for one person to donate a kidney to another. Testimony in this record shows that there have been over 2,500 kidney transplants performed in the United States up to this date. The process can be effected under present techniques with minimal danger to both the donor and the donee. Doctors Hamburger and Crosneir describe the risk to the donor as follows:

> This discussion is limited to renal transplantation, since it is inconceivable that any vital organ other than the kidney might ever be removed from a healthy living donor for transplantation purposes. The immediate operative risk of unilateral nephrectomy in a healthy subject has been calculated as approximately 0.05 percent. The long-term risk is more difficult to estimate, since the various types of renal disease do not appear to be more frequent or more severe in individuals with solitary kidneys than in normal subjects. On the other hand, the development of surgical problems, trauma, or neoplasms, with the possible necessity of nephrectomy, do increase the long-term risks in living donors; the long-term risk, on this basis, has been estimated at 0.07 percent. These data must, however, be considered in the light of statistical life expectancy which, in a healthy 35-year-old adult, goes from 99.3 percent to 99.1 percent during the next five succeeding years; this is an increase in risk equal to that incurred by driving a car for 16 miles every working day. The risks incurred by the donor are therefore very limited, but they are a reality, even if, until now, there have been no reports of complications endangering the life of a donor anywhere in the world. Unfortunately, there is no doubt that, as the number of renal transplants increases, such an incident will inevitably be recorded. Hamburger and Crosneir, Moral and Ethical Problems in Transplantation, *in* Human Transplantation 37 (Rapaport and Dausset ed. 1968). . . .

We are of the opinion that a chancery court does have sufficient inherent power to authorize the operation. The circuit court having found that the operative procedures in this instance are to the best interest of Jerry Strunk and this finding having been based upon substantial evidence, we are of the opinion the judgment should be affirmed. . . .

STEINFELD, Judge, dissenting.

Apparently because of my indelible recollection of a government which, to the everlasting shame of its citizens, embarked on a program of genocide and experimentation with human bodies I have been more troubled in reaching a decision in this case than in any other. My sympathies and emotions are torn between a compassion to aid an ailing young man and a duty to fully protect unfortunate members of society. . . .

The majority opinion is predicated upon the finding of the circuit court that there will be psychological benefits to the ward but points out that the incompetent has the mentality of a six-year-old child. It is common knowledge beyond dispute that the loss of a close relative or a friend to a six-year-old child is not of major impact. Opinions concerning psychological trauma are at best most nebulous. Furthermore, there are no guarantees that the transplant will become a surgical success, it being well known that body rejection of transplanted organs is frequent. The life of the incompetent is not in danger, but the surgical procedure advocated creates some peril. . . .

Unquestionably the attitudes and attempts of the . . . members of the family of the two young men whose critical problems now confront us are commendable, natural and beyond reproach. However, they refer us to nothing indicating that they are privileged to authorize the removal of one of the kidneys of the incompetent for the purpose of donation, and they cite no statutory or other authority vesting such right in the courts. The proof shows that less compatible donors are available and that the kidney of a cadaver could be used, although the odds of operational success are not as great in such case as they would be with the fully compatible donor brother.

I am unwilling to hold that the gates should be open to permit the removal of an organ from an incompetent for transplant, at least until such time as it is conclusively demonstrated that it will be of significant benefit to the incompetent. The evidence here does not rise to that pinnacle. To hold that . . . guardians or courts have such awesome power even in the persuasive case before us, could establish legal precedent, the dire result of which we cannot fathom. Regretfully I must say no.

■ IN RE PESCINSKI
226 N.W.2d 180 (Wis. 1975)

WILKIE, Chief Justice.

Does a county court have the power to order an operation to be performed to remove a kidney of an incompetent ward, under guardianship of the person, and transfer it to a sister where the dire need of the transfer is established but where no consent has been given by the incompetent or his guardian ad litem, nor has any benefit to the ward been shown?

That is the issue presented on appeal here. The trial court held that it did not have that power and we agree. The appellant, Janice Pescinski Lausier, on her own petition, was appointed guardian of the person of her brother, the respondent, Richard Pescinski. In 1958, Richard was declared incompetent and was committed to Winnebago State Hospital. He has been a committed mental patient since that date, classified as a schizophrenic, chronic, catatonic type.

On January 31, 1974, Janice Pescinski Lausier petitioned for permission to Dr. H. M. Kauffman to conduct tests to determine whether Richard Pescinski was a suitable donor for a kidney transplant for the benefit of his sister, Elaine Jeske. Elaine had both kidneys surgically removed in 1970, because she was suffering from kidney failure diagnosed as chronic glomerulonephritis. In order to sustain her life, she was put on a dialysis machine, which functions as an artificial kidney. Because of the deterioration of Elaine, the petition contended that a kidney transplant was needed. Subsequent tests were completed establishing that Richard was a suitable donor, and a hearing was then held on the subject of whether permission should be granted to perform the transplant. The guardian ad litem would not give consent to the transplant and the county court held that it did not have the power to give consent for the operation.

At the time of the hearing Elaine was 38 and her brother Richard was 39. Evidence was produced at the hearing that the other members of the Pescinski family had been ruled out as possible donors on the basis of either age or health. The father, aged 70, and the mother, aged 67, were eliminated as possible donors by Dr. Kauffman because, as a matter of principle, he would not perform the operation on a donor over 60. A similar rationale was applied by Dr. Kauffman as to all of the six minor children of Elaine, the doctor concluding that he "would not personally use their kidneys" as a matter of his "own moral conviction." Mrs. Jeske's sister, Mrs. Lausier, was excluded as a donor because she has diabetes. Another brother, Ralph Pescinski, testified that he was 43 years old, had been married 20 years and had 10 children, 9 of whom remained at home. He is a dairy farmer and did not care to be a donor because there would be nobody to take over his farm and he felt he had a duty to his family to refuse. He further testified that he had a stomach disorder which required a special diet and had a rupture on his left side. He had been to see Dr. Capati at the Neillsville Clinic, who told him he should not get involved and that his family should come first.

The testimony showed that Richard was suffering from schizophrenia—catatonic type, and that while he was in contact with his environment there was marked indifference in his behavior. Dr. Hoffman, the medical director at the Good Samaritan Home, West Bend, Wisconsin, testified that in layman's terms Richard's mental disease was a flight from reality. He estimated Richard's mental capacity to be age 12. No evidence in the record indicates that Richard consented to the transplant. Absent that consent, there is no question that the trial court's conclusion that it had no power to approve the operation must be sustained.

"A guardian of the person has the care of the ward's person and must look to the latter's health, education, and support." 39 Am. Jur. 2d, Guardian and Ward, p.60, §68. The guardian must act, if at all, "loyally in the best interests of his ward." Guardianship of Nelson, 123 N.W.2d 505, 509 (Wis. 1963). There is absolutely no evidence here that any interests of the ward will be served by the transplant.

. . . . We decline to adopt the concept of "substituted judgment" which was specifically approved by the Kentucky Court of Appeals in Strunk v. Strunk. . . . .

As the dissenting opinion in Strunk v. Strunk points out, "substituted judgment" is nothing more than an application of the maxim that equity will speak for one who cannot speak for himself. Historically, the substituted judgment doctrine was used to allow gifts of the property of an incompetent. If applied literally, it would allow a trial court, or this court, to change the designation on a life insurance policy or make an election for an incompetent widow, without the requirement of a statute authorizing these acts and contrary to prior decisions of this court.

We conclude that the doctrine should not be adopted in this state.

We, therefore, must affirm the lower court's decision that it was without power to approve the operation, and we further decide that there is no such power in this court. An incompetent particularly should have his own interests protected. Certainly no advantage should be taken of him. In the absence of real consent on his part, and in a situation where no benefit to him has been established, we fail to find any authority for the county court, or this court, to approve this operation. . . .

DAY, Justice, dissenting. . . .

. . . . The guardian ad litem for the incompetent in this case has interposed strong objection to the transplant from Richard Pescinski to his sister, who . . . has now deteriorated to the point of confinement in a wheelchair. We were advised that without a kidney transplant death for her is quite imminent. The brother, on the other hand, the incompetent, is in good health. The medical testimony is that the removal of one of his kidneys would be of minimal risk to him and that he would function normally on one kidney for the rest of his natural life, as do thousands of others in similar circumstances. . . . To avoid the concerns expressed by the guardian ad litem, there are certain definite standards which could and should be imposed. First of all, a strong showing should be made that without the kidney transplant the proposed donee or recipient stands to suffer death. This is certainly the evidence here. Secondly, that reasonable steps have been taken to try and acquire a kidney from other sources and the record is clear that such attempt was made here. Because of the fact that the donee has had six children, she has built up certain chemical resistance to the receipt of foreign tissue into her body which can be overcome only by a transplant from one close to her by blood such as a brother or sister. The testimony showed the impracticality of acquiring a kidney from either her other brother or her sister. No suitable kidney from a cadaver has been found since her kidneys were removed in 1970. The next showing that should be made is that the incompetent proposed donor is closely related by blood to the proposed donee, such as a brother or sister, which of course is the case here. Showing should be made that the donor, if competent, would most probably consent because of the normal ties of family. Here, the trial court specifically found ". . . the conclusion would appear to be inescapable that the ward [the incompetent proposed donor] would so consent and that such authorization should be granted." Another showing should be that the proposed incompetent donor is in good health and that was shown here. And lastly, that the operation is one of minimal risk to the donor and that the donor could function normally on one kidney following such operation. The medical testimony is all to the effect that the donor would undergo minimal risk and would be able to function normally on one kidney. In fact, the testimony is that a person can function on as little as one tenth of one normal kidney.

With these guidelines the fear expressed that institutions for the mentally ill will merely become storehouses for spare parts for people on the outside is completely unjustified. I agree with the trial court that if the brother here were competent in all probability he would be willing to consent to the transplant to save his sister's life. For him it would be a short period of discomfort which would not affect his ability either to enjoy life or his longevity. . . .

Notes: The Incompetent Organ Donor

1. *The Appropriate Legal Standard.* Which decision do you prefer, *Strunk* or *Pescinski*? Consider the following perspective:

> Despite widespread acceptance in the United States, few other nations allow routine use of minors or mentally incompetent persons as organ donors. Judicial decisions of United States courts seem to be without parallel in any other country. . . . By legislation, Mexico and British Columbia prohibit organ donation by minors and incompetent persons. Restriction on such donations have been enacted by France and Australia. The Council of Europe has recommended that organ donation from wards be forbidden except when the donor, having capacity of understanding, has given consent. . . .

Rodney K. Adams, Live Organ Donors and Informed Consent: A Difficult Minuet, 8 J. Leg. Med. 555, 572 (1987). (The Council of Europe does condone removal of regenerative tissue like bone marrow from persons lacking capacity to consent in limited circumstances (e.g., the recipient must be a sibling of the donor). Council of Europe, Additional Protocol to the Convention on Human Rights and Biomedicine, on Transplantation of Organs and Tissues of Human Origin (January 24, 2002).) For cases in agreement with *Strunk*, see Hart v. Brown, 289 A.2d 386 (Conn. Super. Ct. 1972); In re Doe, 481 N.Y.S.2d 932 (App. Div. 1981); Little v. Little, 576 S.W.2d 493 (Tex. Ct. App. 1979). For a case in agreement with *Pescinski*, see In re Richardson, 284 So. 2d 185 (La. Ct. App. 1973).

Are the two decisions consistent with each other? Is the dissent in *Strunk* correct that we should not base the decision on supposed psychological benefit to Jerry Strunk inasmuch as such benefit is highly speculative? What about having Strunk's brother not visit him for a couple of weeks to see if he is adversely affected by his brother's absence? Were the outcomes different in *Strunk* and *Pescinski* because Strunk could relate to his sibling while Pescinski could not? Or because the recipient in *Strunk* would have been a man, and the recipient in *Pescinski* a woman? What incentives do you think the court in *Pescinski* might have been trying to avoid? After the Wisconsin Supreme Court denied her request for organ transplantation, Elaine Jeske died of kidney failure.

Which of the following factors should a court consider in deciding whether to order a transplantation from an incompetent person, and how should they be weighed: benefit to the recipient of the organ; risk to the donor; the relationship between the donor and recipient; the availability of alternative donors; and the feelings of the donor about the procedure? Do you agree with Justice Day's dissent in

Pescinski on this question? Why do you suppose he believed that Richard Pescinski, if competent, would agree to be a donor when the other brother, Ralph Pescinski, did not agree to be a donor?

2. *Additional Readings.* For further discussion of these issues, see Charles Baron et al., Live Organ and Tissue Transplants from Minor Donors in Massachusetts, 55 B.U. L. Rev. 159 (1975); Cara Cheyette, Note, Organ Harvests from the Legally Incompetent: An Argument Against Compelled Altruism, 41 B.C. L. Rev. 465 (2000); Michelle Goodwin, My Sister's Keeper: Law, Children, and Compelled Donation, 29 W. New Eng. L. Rev. 357 (2007); Michael T. Marley, Note, Proxy Consent to Organ Donation by Incompetents, 111 Yale L.J. 1215 (2002); Sara Lind Nygren, Note, Organ Donation by Incompetent Patients: A Hybrid Approach, 2006 U. Chi. Legal F. 471; John Robertson, Organ Donations by Incompetents and the Substituted Judgment Doctrine, 76 Colum. L. Rev. 48 (1976).

Problem: Conceiving a Child to Make Tissue Available for Transplantation

A couple, John and Joanne, have a 10-year-old daughter with leukemia who will almost certainly die within five years without a stem cell transplant. (Historically, stem cells for transplantation were taken from the donor's bone marrow, but now stem cells can often be retrieved as well from a donor's circulating blood or a newborn's umbilical cord blood.) With a transplant, there is a 70 percent chance of a long-term survival. Family members and friends have been tested to see if their stem cells are compatible, but none are candidates for transplantation. Despite a nationwide search to find a compatible donor, none has been found. John and Joanne decide to conceive another child in the hope that this child's stem cells will be suitable for transplantation in their daughter. There is a 25 percent chance that a new child will have compatible cells, but the odds can be improved to 100 percent with preimplantation genetic screening. With this approach, a couple can create embryos through in vitro fertilization. The embryos can then be tested to see if the new child's stem cells will be compatible with the existing child. Yury Verlinsky et al., Preimplantation HLA Testing, 291 JAMA 2079 (2004). If John and Joanne bear a child, and the child's cells are compatible, then physicians would perform a transplant with stem cells from umbilical cord blood after birth or other stem cells when the new child is older. There is no risk to the child from using its umbilical cord blood; the risk that the child would die from a surgery to remove her marrow is unknown, but probably in the range of 1/25,000 to 1/100,000. The risk of serious complications from using stem cells from circulating blood is also very low. Should John and Joanne be able to conceive the child and consent to the transplantation? [This problem is based on the Ayala case, in which a couple conceived a child to serve as a bone marrow donor for their daughter. Diane M. Gianelli, Bearing a Donor? Ethical Concerns Raised over Having a Baby for Marrow Match, American Medical News, Mar. 2, 1990, at 3. For further discussion, see Katrien Devolder, Preimplantation HLA Typing: Having Children to Save Our Loved Ones, 31 J. Med. Ethics 582 (2005); Susan M. Wolf et al., Using Preimplantation Genetic Diagnosis to Create a Stem Cell Donor: Issues, Guidelines & Limits, 31 J.L. Med. & Ethics 327 (2003).]

3. Redefining Death

According to the law of every state, organs necessary for life (e.g., the heart or an entire liver) cannot be removed from a person for transplantation unless the person is dead (the "dead donor" rule). Moreover, even with kidneys, which can be donated while the person is alive, more than half of organs for transplantation come from cadavers. This is both because two kidneys can be taken from dead persons and only one kidney from a living person, and also because persons are more reluctant to donate a kidney while alive than once dead. Most kidney transplants from a live donor go to a family member.

Most organs taken from dead persons come from patients whose death is diagnosed by cessation of brain function ("brain death") rather than from patients whose death is diagnosed by cessation of cardiopulmonary function (loss of heart and lung function). This is because the blood flow of brain-dead patients can be maintained with the provision of artificial life supports until the organs are removed for transplantation. Without continued blood supply, organs in the body deteriorate and quickly become unavailable for transplantation.

As discussed in Chapter 3, when a person is brain dead, the heart and lungs will ordinarily also stop working unless the person is maintained on a ventilator. Artificial ventilation and other medical support can maintain a brain-dead person's heartbeat and breathing for days to months but not indefinitely. Pregnant women have been maintained in brain death until their fetuses mature enough to be delivered by cesarean section. David R. Field et al., Maternal Brain Death During Pregnancy: Medical and Ethical Issues, 260 JAMA 816 (1988) (describing a case in which a brain-dead, pregnant woman was maintained on a ventilator for nine weeks). There is some question whether cessation of heartbeat and respiration are really inevitable after brain death. While it appears that most brain-dead patients cannot be maintained more than two or three months, some have been maintained for more than a year, including one patient for more than 14 years. D. Alan Shewmon, Chronic "Brain Death": Meta-Analysis and Conceptual Consequences, 51 Neurology 1538 (1998).

Some commentators have proposed that death be redefined so that more persons would be candidates for organ transplantation. In particular, it has been argued that brain death should be defined by whether there is brain function sufficient to achieve consciousness, not by whether there is brain function at all. If brain death were defined by the absence of consciousness, then anencephalic children and permanently unconscious persons would be dead, and their organs could be removed for transplantation. Other commentators have suggested that we no longer use death as the sole criterion for removing life-necessary organs but permit removal of life-necessary organs from living persons in limited situations. See, e.g., Robert D. Truog, Is It Time to Abandon Brain Death?, 29(1) Hastings Center Rep. 29, 34 (1997) (suggesting a focus on the ethical concerns of consent and harm, which would allow a person to give consent to organ retrieval if the person became permanently unconscious in the future).

The question, then, for this section is whether the need for more organs is sufficient reason for the state to either change the definition of death or permit individuals to donate their own organs or the organs of family members before death occurs. Does the individual's right to control bodily integrity and to make decisions about important personal matters include a right to decide when life-necessary organs may be given to others?

■ IN RE T.A.C.P.
609 So. 2d 588 (Fla. 1992)

KOGAN, Justice.

We have for review an order of the trial court certified by the Fourth District Court of Appeal as touching on a matter of great public importance requiring immediate resolution by this court. We frame the issue as follows: Is an anencephalic newborn considered "dead" for purposes of organ donation solely by reason of its congenital deformity? We have jurisdiction.

I. FACTS

At or about the eighth month of pregnancy, the parents of the child T.A.C.P. were informed that she would be born with anencephaly. This is a birth defect invariably fatal, in which the child typically is born with only a "brain stem" but otherwise lacks a human brain. In T.A.C.P.'s case, the back of the skull was entirely missing and the brain stem was exposed to the air, except for medical bandaging. The risk of infection to the brain stem was considered very high. Anencephalic infants sometimes can survive several days after birth because the brain stem has a limited capacity to maintain autonomic bodily functions such as breathing and heartbeat. This ability soon ceases, however, in the absence of regulation from the missing brain.

In this case, T.A.C.P. actually survived only a few days after birth. . . .

On the advice of physicians, the parents continued the pregnancy to term and agreed that the mother would undergo cesarean section during birth. The parents agreed to the cesarean procedure with the express hope that the infant's organs would be less damaged and could be used for transplant in other sick children. Although T.A.C.P. had no hope of life herself, the parents both testified in court that they wanted to use this opportunity to give life to others. However, when the parents requested that T.A.C.P. be declared legally dead for this purpose, her health care providers refused out of concern that they thereby might incur civil or criminal liability.

The parents then filed a petition in the circuit court asking for a judicial determination. After hearing testimony and argument, the trial court denied the request on grounds that §382.009(1), Florida Statutes (1991), would not permit a determination of legal death so long as the child's brain stem continued to function. On appeal, the Fourth District summarily affirmed but then certified the trial court's order to this court for immediate resolution of the issue. We have accepted jurisdiction to resolve this case of first impression.

II. THE MEDICAL NATURE OF ANENCEPHALY

Although appellate courts appear never to have confronted the issues there already is an impressive body of published medical scholarship on anencephaly. From our review of this material, we find that anencephaly is a variable but fairly well defined medical condition. Experts in the field have written that anencephaly is the most common severe birth defect of the central nervous system seen in the United States, although it apparently has existed throughout human history.

A statement by the Medical Task Force on Anencephaly ("Task Force") printed in the New England Journal of Medicine generally described "anencephaly" as "a congenital absence of major portions of the brain, skull, and scalp, with its genesis in the first month of gestation." David A. Stumpf et al., The Infant with Anencephaly, 322 New Eng. J. Med. 669, 669 (1990). The large opening in the skull accompanied by the absence or severe congenital disruption of the cerebral hemispheres is the characteristic feature of the condition.

The Task Force defined anencephaly as diagnosable only when all of the following four criteria are present:

(1) A large portion of the skull is absent. (2) The scalp, which extends to the margin of the bone, is absent over the skull defect. (3) Hemorrhagic, fibrotic tissue is exposed because of defects in the skull and scalp. (4) Recognizable cerebral hemispheres are absent. [Id. at 670.]

Anencephaly is often, though not always, accompanied by defects in various other body organs and systems, some of which may render the child unsuitable for organ transplantation. . . .

The Task Force stated that most reported anencephalic children die within the first few days after birth, with survival any longer being rare. After reviewing all available medical literature, the Task Force found no study in which survival beyond a week exceeded 9 percent of children meeting the four criteria. Two months was the longest confirmed survival of an anencephalic, although there are unconfirmed reports of one surviving three months and another surviving fourteen months. [This decision preceded the *Baby K* case, page 377, involving an anencephalic child who lived for two years.] The Task Force reported, however, that these survival rates are confounded somewhat by the variable degrees of medical care afforded to anencephalics. Some such infants may be given considerable life support while others may be given much less care.

The Task Force reported that the medical consequences of anencephaly can be established with some certainty. All anencephalics by definition are permanently unconscious because they lack the cerebral cortex necessary for conscious thought. Their condition thus is quite similar to that of persons in a persistent vegetative state. Where the brain stem is functioning, as it was here, spontaneous breathing and heartbeat can occur. In addition, such infants may show spontaneous movements of the extremities, "startle" reflexes, and pupils that respond to light. Some may show feeding reflexes, may cough, hiccup, or exhibit eye movements, and may produce facial expressions.

The question of whether such infants actually suffer from pain is somewhat more complex. It involves a distinction between "pain" and "suffering." The Task Force indicated that anencephaly in some ways is analogous to persons with cerebral brain lesions. Such lesions may not actually eliminate the reflexive response to a painful condition, but they can eliminate any capacity to "suffer" as a result of the condition. Likewise, anencephalic infants may reflexively avoid painful stimuli where the brain stem is functioning and thus is able to command an innate, unconscious withdrawal response; but the infants presumably lack the capacity to suffer.

It is clear, however, that this incapacity to suffer has not been established beyond all doubt. . . .

There appears to be general agreement that anencephalics usually have ceased to be suitable organ donors by the time they meet all the criteria for "whole brain death," i.e., the complete absence of brain-stem function. There also is no doubt that a need exists for infant organs for transplantation. Nationally, between 30 and 50 percent of children under two years of age who need transplants die while waiting for organs to become available.

III. Legal Definitions of "Death" & "Life"

[The court discussed the history of the cardiopulmonary definition of death and the development of a definition of death based on cessation of brain function. The court then discusses Florida's approach to defining death.]

Indeed, Florida appears to have struck out on its own. The statute cited as controlling by the trial court does not actually address itself to the problem of anencephalic infants, nor indeed to any situation other than patients actually being sustained by artificial life support. The statute provides:

> For legal and medical purposes, *where respiratory and circulatory functions are maintained by artificial means of support* so as to preclude a determination that these functions have ceased, the occurrence of death *may* be determined where there is the irreversible cessation of the functioning of the entire brain, including the brain stem, determined in accordance with this section.

§382.009(1), Fla. Stat. (1991) (emphasis added). A later subsection goes on to declare:

> Except for a diagnosis of brain death, the standard set forth in this section is not the exclusive standard for determining death or for the withdrawal of life-support systems.

§382.009(4), Fla. Stat. (1991). This language is highly significant for two reasons.

First, the statute does not purport to codify the common law standard applied in some other jurisdictions, as does the uniform act. The use of the permissive word *may* in the statute in tandem with the savings clause of §382.009(4) buttresses the conclusion that the legislature envisioned other ways of defining "death." Second, the statutory framers clearly did not intend to apply the statute's language to the anencephalic infant not being kept alive by life support. To the contrary, the framers expressly limited the statute to that situation in which "respiratory and circulatory functions are maintained by artificial means of support." . . .

The parties have cited to no authorities directly dealing with the question of whether anencephalics are "alive" or "dead." Our own research has disclosed no other federal or Florida law or precedent arguably on point or applicable by analogy. We thus are led to the conclusion that no legal authority binding upon this court has decided whether an anencephalic child is alive for purposes of organ donation. In the absence of applicable legal authority, this court must weigh and consider the public policy considerations at stake here.

IV. COMMON LAW & POLICY

Initially, we must start by recognizing that §382.009, Florida Statutes (1991), provides a method for determining death in those cases in which a person's respiratory and circulatory functions are maintained artificially. §382.009(4), Fla. Stat. (1991). Likewise, we agree that a cardiopulmonary definition of death must be accepted in Florida as a matter of our common law, applicable whenever §382.009 does not govern. Thus, if cardiopulmonary function is not being maintained artificially as stated in §382.009, a person is dead who has sustained irreversible cessation of circulatory and respiratory functions as determined in accordance with accepted medical standards. We have found no credible authority arguing that this definition is inconsistent with the existence of death, and we therefore need not labor the point further.

The question remaining is whether there is good reason in public policy for this court to create an additional common law standard applicable to anencephalics. Alterations of the common law, while rarely entertained or allowed, are within this court's prerogative. However, the rule we follow is that the common law will not be altered or expanded unless demanded by public necessity, or where required to vindicate fundamental rights. We believe, for example, that our adoption of the cardiopulmonary definition of death today is required by public necessity and, in any event, merely formalizes what has been the common practice in this state for well over a century.

Such is not the case with petitioners' request. Our review of the medical, ethical, and legal literature on anencephaly discloses absolutely no consensus that public necessity or fundamental rights will be better served by granting this request.... .

There is an unquestioned need for transplantable infant organs. Yet some medical commentators suggest that the organs of anencephalics are seldom usable, for a variety of reasons, and that so few organ transplants will be possible from anencephalics as to render the enterprise questionable in light of the ethical problems at stake—even if legal restrictions were lifted.

Others note that prenatal screening now is substantially reducing the number of anencephalics born each year in the United States and that, consequently, anencephalics are unlikely to be a significant source of organs as time passes. And still others have frankly acknowledged that there is no consensus and that redefinition of death in this context should await the emergence of a consensus.

A presidential commission in 1981 urged strict adherence to the Uniform Determination of Death Act's definition, which would preclude equating anencephaly with death. President's Commission for the Study of Ethical Problems, Biomedical, and Behavioral Research, Defining Death: Medical, Legal and Ethical Issues in the Determination of Death 2 (1981). Several sections of the American Bar Association have reached much the same conclusion. National Conference on Birth, Death, and Law, Report on Conference, 29 Jurimetrics J. 403, 421 (Lori B. Andrews et al. eds., 1989).

Some legal commentators have urged that treating anencephalics as dead equates them with "nonpersons," presenting a "slippery slope" problem with regard to all other persons who lack cognition for whatever reason. Others have quoted physicians involved in infant-organ transplants as stating, "The slippery slope is real," because some physicians have proposed transplants from infants with defects less severe than anencephaly.

We express no opinion today about who is right and who is wrong on these issues—if any "right" or "wrong" can be found here. The salient point is that no consensus exists as to: (a) the utility of organ transplants of the type at issue here; (b) the ethical issues involved; or (c) the legal and constitutional problems implicated.

V. CONCLUSIONS

Accordingly, we find no basis to expand the common law to equate anencephaly with death. We acknowledge the possibility that some infants' lives might be saved by using organs from anencephalics who do not meet the traditional definition of "death" we reaffirm today. But weighed against this is the utter lack of consensus, and the questions about the overall utility of such organ donations. The scales clearly tip in favor of not extending the common law in this instance. . . .

Notes: Redefining Death

1. *The T.A.C.P. Decision.* At the end of Section III of the opinion, the court observed that there was no binding legal authority on the issue of whether an anencephalic child is alive for purposes of organ donation. Accordingly, said the court, it was an issue for the court to decide after weighing the public policy considerations at stake. What standard did the court employ for deciding whether to expand the common law in this case? Is it so clear that organ retrieval from anencephalic infants did not satisfy the court's standard? Why isn't the desire to avoid needless deaths a sufficiently strong basis for changing the common law? Were the justifications behind the court's adoption of the cardiopulmonary definition of death any more compelling? The court points to the lack of consensus on the issue, but doesn't the lack of consensus cut both ways (i.e., how should the court decide when there is no consensus for either position)? Should the court feel bound by its perception of academic opinion?

2. *The Role of Utilitarian Justifications.* Although it may seem too utilitarian to change the definition of death in order to facilitate organ transplantation, we saw in Chapter 3 that utilitarian concerns essentially were responsible when the definition of death was changed to include the cessation of brain function. In justifying a change in the definition of death, the influential Harvard Medical School report cited the burdens of treating brain-dead persons, including the diversion of resources from other patients, and the difficulty in obtaining organs for transplantation. Report of the Ad Hoc Committee of the Harvard Medical School to Examine the Definition of Brain Death, A Definition of Irreversible Coma, 205 JAMA 85, 85 (1968), excerpted at page 389. In other words, there are two important questions here. First, is there a principled difference between permitting organ retrieval from anencephalic infants now and permitting organ retrieval from brain-dead persons 35 years ago? Or is the real difference the fact that many more organs can be retrieved from brain-dead persons than from anencephalic infants? Second, even if there is no principled difference, might we still want to say that it would be wrong to retrieve organs from anencephalic infants? For further discussion, see Jay A. Friedman, Taking the Camel by the Nose: The Anencephalic as a Source for Pediatric

Organ Transplants, 90 Colum. L. Rev. 917 (1990); Fazal Khan & Brian Lea, Paging King Solomon: Towards Allowing Organ Donation from Anencephalic Infants, 6 Ind. Health L. Rev. 17 (2009); Margaret Lock, Twice Dead: Organ Transplants and the Reinvention of Death (2002); D. Alan Shewmon et al., The Use of Anencephalic Infants as Organ Sources, 261 JAMA 1773 (1989).

3. *Modifying the "Dead Donor" Rule.* Some commentators have proposed that, rather than change the definition of death to facilitate organ donation, we should modify the dead donor rule. Instead of insisting that people be dead before taking their heart, liver, lungs, and kidneys for transplantation, we would permit organ donation before death, in limited circumstances. For example, people could direct in a living will that, in the event of a condition of permanent unconsciousness, they want their organs taken for transplantation. Or, parents of anencephalic children could be given the opportunity to choose among continuing treatment, stopping treatment, or donating their child's organs before the child dies. Robert M. Arnold & Stuart J. Youngner, The Dead Donor Rule: Should We Stretch It, Bend It, or Abandon It?, 2 Kennedy Inst. Ethics J. 263 (1993); Council on Ethical and Judicial Affairs, American Medical Association, The Use of Anencephalic Neonates as Organ Donors, 273 JAMA 1614 (1995) (position reversed in Charles W. Plows, Reconsideration of AMA Opinion on Anencephalic Neonates as Organ Donors, 275 JAMA 443 (1996)); Sheldon F. Kurtz & Michael J. Saks, Living Organ Donor Act, 18 Iowa J. Corp. L. 523, 561 (1993).

Would this approach be more acceptable than changing the definition of death? Do you think that the reasons for having the dead donor rule apply when a person is permanently unconscious? Can we distinguish the removal of organs from permanently unconscious persons from other actions that we already permit? For example, can we really distinguish taking a ventilator away from a permanently unconscious person, because the ventilator could be better used by someone else, from taking the lungs from a permanently unconscious person, because the lungs could be better used by someone else? Indeed, if we had consent to take the lungs from the person's advance directive, would it be less troublesome than taking away a ventilator when doing so would be over the objections of the family and in disregard of the patient's advance directive?

4. *Donation After "Cardiopulmonary Death."* Given the substantial shortage of organs for transplantation, greater efforts are being made to increase the number of organs taken from persons who die from cessation of cardiopulmonary function. One approach is to infuse cold fluids into the cadaver to rapidly cool the organs and prevent their deterioration. Another approach, for patients whose ventilators are being withdrawn, is to perform the withdrawal in an operating room. That way, once the ventilator is withdrawn and the patient dies, action can be taken quickly to maintain the vitality of the organs before they are removed for transplantation.

The ratio of "cardiopulmonary death" donors to "brain death" donors is about 1:8 in the United States but more than 1:4 in some organ procurement organizations. In the UK, the ratio is about 2:3. Data so far indicate that kidney transplants fare as well after cardiopulmonary death as after brain death but that liver transplants are not as successful after cardiopulmonary death. Janet M. Bellingham et al., Donation After Cardiac Death: A 29-Year Experience, 150 Surgery 692 (2011).

While donation after cardiopulmonary death is becoming more common, critics argue the patients may not be truly dead when they are declared dead. When organ donation is planned for someone after cardiopulmonary death, physicians typically declare death after cardiopulmonary function has ceased for five minutes. (Data indicate that hearts do not spontaneously resume circulatory function after two minutes of cessation.) But does it matter that cardiopulmonary resuscitation can restore circulatory function? In addition, it usually takes more than five minutes without blood flow for the brain to die. Jerry Menikoff, The Importance of Being Dead, 18 Issues L. & Med. 3 (2002).

For further discussion, see Institute of Medicine, Organ Donation: Opportunities for Action 127-160 (2006); Procuring Organs for Transplant: The Debate over Non-Heart-Beating Cadaver Protocols (Robert M. Arnold et al. eds., 1995); Ethics Committee, American College of Critical Care Medicine, Society of Critical Care Medicine, Recommendations for Nonheartbeating Organ Donation, 29 Critical Care Med. 1826 (2001) (currently under revision); Markus Weber et al., Kidney Transplantation from Donors Without a Heartbeat, 347 New Eng. J. Med. 248 (2002).

B. OWNERSHIP AND CONTROL OF THE BODY

1. Mandates or Incentives for Organ Donation

At one time, states commonly permitted the removal of corneas and other tissues or organs from persons who died and were undergoing an autopsy by a coroner or medical examiner. In such cases, the legislatures probably reasoned, the body was being cut open and some tissue permanently removed anyway as part of the autopsy. The 1987 Uniform Anatomical Gift Act encouraged the passage of such statutes in its §4. But the 2006 Revised Uniform Anatomical Gift Act eliminated §4, and most states have followed the 2006 Act. Still, some states have retained the coroner/medical examiner authority, particularly for corneas.

If additional tissue can be used to improve the health of a living person, particularly if the tissue is the cornea, whose absence would not be detectable by looking at the corpse, then should we not give preference to the living person over the dead person? Is there any reason to limit mandatory "donation" to cadavers undergoing an autopsy? Why not take organs and tissues from every cadaver? Why not require living persons to give up renewable tissues, like bone marrow, for transplantation? To the extent that takings of organs or tissues raise concerns about people being deprived of their body parts without their consent and without compensation, can we answer those concerns by offering financial incentives for organ donation?

■ STATE v. POWELL
497 So. 2d 1188 (Fla. 1986)

OVERTON, Justice.

This is a petition to review a circuit court order finding unconstitutional §732.9185, Florida Statutes (1983), which authorizes medical examiners to remove corneal tissue from decedents during statutorily required autopsies when such tissue is needed for transplantation. The statute prohibits the removal of the corneal tissue if the next of kin objects, but does not require that the decedent's next of kin be notified of the procedure. The Fifth District Court of Appeal certified that this case presents a question of great public importance requiring immediate resolution by this court. We accept jurisdiction . . . , and, for the reasons expressed below, find that the statute is constitutional.

The challenged statute provides:

Corneal removal by medical examiners.—

(1) In any case in which a patient is in need of corneal tissue for a transplant, a district medical examiner or an appropriately qualified designee with training in ophthalmologic techniques may, upon request of any eye bank authorized under s. 732.918, provide the cornea of a decedent whenever all of the following conditions are met:

(a) A decedent who may provide a suitable cornea for the transplant is under the jurisdiction of the medical examiner and an autopsy is required in accordance with s. 406.11.

(b) No objection by the next of kin of the decedent is known by the medical examiner.

(c) The removal of the cornea will not interfere with the subsequent course of an investigation or autopsy.

(2) Neither the district medical examiner nor his appropriately qualified designee nor any eye bank authorized under s. 732.918 may be held liable in any civil or criminal action for failure to obtain consent of the next of kin.

The trial court decided this case by summary judgment. The facts are not in dispute. On June 15, 1983, James White drowned while swimming at the city beach in Dunellon, Florida. Associate Medical Examiner Dr. Thomas Techman, who is an appellant in this cause, performed an autopsy on James' body at Leesburg Community Hospital. On July 11, 1983, Anthony Powell died in a motor vehicle accident in Marion County. Medical Examiner Dr. William H. Shutze, who is also an appellant in this cause, performed an autopsy on Anthony's body. In each instance, under the authority of §732.9185, the medical examiner removed corneal tissue from the decedent without giving notice to or obtaining consent from the parents of the decedent.

James' and Anthony's parents, who are the appellees in this case, each brought an action claiming damages for the alleged wrongful removal of their sons' corneas and seeking a judgment declaring §732.9185 unconstitutional. . . .

In addressing the issue of the statute's constitutionality, we begin with the premise that a person's constitutional rights terminate at death. If any rights exist, they belong to the decedent's next of kin.

Next, we recognize that a legislative act carries with it the presumption of validity and the party challenging a statute's constitutionality must carry the burden of establishing that the statute bears no reasonable relation to a permissible legislative objective. In determining whether a permissible legislative objective exists, we must review the evidence arising from the record in this case.

The unrebutted evidence in this record establishes that the state of Florida spends approximately $138 million each year to provide its blind with the basic necessities of life. At present, approximately 10 percent of Florida's blind citizens are candidates for cornea transplantation, which has become a highly effective procedure for restoring sight to the functionally blind. As advances are made in the field, the number of surgical candidates will increase, thereby raising the demand for suitable corneal tissue. The increasing number of elderly persons in our population has also created a great demand for corneas because corneal blindness often is age-related. Further, an affidavit in the record states:

> Corneal transplants are particularly important in newborns. The brain does not learn to see if the cornea is not clear. There is a critical period in the first few months of life when the brain "learns to see." If the cornea is not clear, the brain not only does not "learn to see," but the brain loses its ability to "learn to see." Hence, corneal transplant in children must be made as soon as practicable after the problem is discovered. Without the medical examiner legislation, there would be virtually no corneal tissue available for infants and these children would remain forever blind.

The record reflects that the key to successful corneal transplantation is the availability of high-quality corneal tissue and that corneal tissue removed more than ten hours after death is generally unsuitable for transplantation. The implementation of §732.9185 in 1977 has, indisputably, increased both the supply and quality of tissue available for transplantation. Statistics show that, in 1976, only 500 corneas were obtained in Florida for transplantation while, in 1985, more than 3,000 persons in Florida had their sight restored through corneal transplantation surgery.

The record also demonstrates that a qualitative difference exists between corneal tissue obtained through outright donation and tissue obtained pursuant to §732.9185. In contrast to the tissue donated by individuals, which is largely unusable because of the advanced age of the donor at death, approximately 80 to 85 percent of tissue obtained through medical examiners is suitable for transplantation. The evidence establishes that this increase in the quantity and quality of available corneal tissue was brought about by passage of the statute and is, in large part, attributable to the fact that §732.9185 does not place a duty upon medical examiners to seek out the next of kin to obtain consent for cornea removal. An affidavit in the record reveals that, before legislation authorized medical examiners in California to remove corneas without the consent of the next of kin, the majority of the families asked by the Los Angeles medical examiner's office responded positively; however, approximately 80 percent of the families could not be located in sufficient time for medical examiners to remove usable corneal tissue from the decedents.

An autopsy is a surgical dissection of the body; it necessarily results in a massive intrusion into the decedent. This record reflects that cornea removal, by comparison, requires an infinitesimally small intrusion which does not affect the decedent's appearance. With or without cornea removal, the decedent's eyes must be capped to maintain a normal appearance.

Our review of §732.9185 reveals certain safeguards which are apparently designed to limit cornea removal to instances in which the public's interest is greatest and the impact on the next of kin the least: corneas may be removed only if the decedent is under the jurisdiction of the medical examiner; an autopsy is mandated by Florida law; and the removal will not interfere with the autopsy or an investigation of the death. Further, medical examiners may not automatically remove tissue from all decedents subject to autopsy; rather, a request must be made by an eye bank based on a present need for the tissue.

We conclude that this record clearly establishes that this statute reasonably achieves the permissible legislative objective of providing sight to many of Florida's blind citizens.

We next address the trial court's finding that §732.9185 deprives appellees of a fundamental property right. All authorities generally agree that the next of kin have no property right in the remains of a decedent. Although, in Dunahoo v. Bess, 200 So. 541, 542 (1941), this court held that a surviving husband had a "property right" in his wife's body which would sustain a claim for negligent embalming, . . . [m]ore recently, we affirmed the district court's determination that the next of kin's right in a decedent's remains is based upon "the personal right of the decedent's next of kin to bury the body rather than any property right in the body itself." Jackson v. Rupp, 228 So. 2d 916, 918 (Fla. 4th DCA 1969), *affirmed*, 238 So. 2d 86 (Fla. 1970). The view that the next of kin has no property right but merely a limited right to possess the body for burial purposes is universally accepted by courts and commentators. Prosser states:

> A number of decisions have involved the mishandling of dead bodies. . . . In these cases the courts have talked of a somewhat dubious "property right" to the body, usually in the next of kin, which did not exist while the decedent was living, cannot be conveyed, can be used only for the one purpose of burial, and not only has no pecuniary value but is a source of liability for funeral expenses. It seems reasonably obvious that such "property" is something evolved out of thin air to meet the occasion, and that it is in reality the personal feelings of the survivors which are being protected, under a fiction likely to deceive no one but a lawyer.

W. Prosser, The Law of Torts, 43-44 (2d ed. 1955). . . .

Under the facts and circumstances of these cases, we find no taking of private property by state action for a non-public purpose in violation of article X, §6, of the Florida Constitution. We note that the right to bring an action in tort does not necessarily invoke constitutional protections. Decisions of the United States Supreme Court have clearly established that the loss of a common law right by legislative act does not automatically operate as a deprivation of substantive due process. Tort actions may be restricted when necessary to obtain a permissible legislative objective.

Appellees also assert that their right to control the disposition of their decedents' remains is a fundamental right of personal liberty protected against unreasonable governmental intrusion by the due process clause. Appellees argue that, because the statute permits the removal of a decedent's corneas without reference to his family's preferences, it infringes upon a right, characterized as one of religion, family, or privacy, which is fundamental and must be subjected to strict scrutiny. . . .

We reject appellees' argument. The cases cited recognize only freedom of choice concerning personal matters involved in existing, ongoing relationships among living persons as fundamental or essential to the pursuit of happiness by free persons. We find that the right of the next of kin to a tort claim for interference with burial, established by this court in *Dunahoo*, does not rise to the constitutional dimension of a fundamental right traditionally protected under either the United States or Florida Constitution. Neither federal nor state privacy provisions protect an individual from every governmental intrusion into one's private life, especially when a statute addresses public health interests.

The record contains no evidence that the appellees' objections to the removal of corneal tissues for human transplants are based on any "fundamental tenets of their religious beliefs." Wisconsin v. Yoder, 406 U.S. at 218. . . .

In conclusion, we hold that §732.9185 is constitutional because it rationally promotes the permissible state objective of restoring sight to the blind. In so holding, we note that laws regarding the removal of human tissues for transplantation implicate moral, ethical, theological, philosophical, and economic concerns which do not readily lend themselves to analysis within a traditional legal framework. Applying constitutional standards of review to §732.9185 obscures the fact that at the heart of the issue lies a policy question which calls for a delicate balancing of societal needs and individual concerns more appropriately accomplished by the legislature. . . .

■ BROTHERTON v. CLEVELAND
923 F.2d 477 (6th Cir. 1991)

MARTIN, Circuit Judge.

Deborah S. Brotherton, the wife of decedent Steven Brotherton, appeals the dismissal of her §1983 claim for wrongful removal of her deceased husband's corneas. Because we find that Deborah Brotherton has a protected property interest in her husband's corneas and that the removal of those corneas was caused by established state procedures, we reverse.

On February 15, 1988, Steven Brotherton was found "pulseless" in an automobile and was taken to Bethesda North Hospital in Cincinnati, Ohio. He was pronounced dead on arrival. The hospital asked Deborah Brotherton to consider making an anatomical gift; she declined, based on her husband's aversion to such a gift, and her refusal was documented in the hospital's "Report of Death."

Because Steven Brotherton's death was considered a possible suicide, his body was taken to the Hamilton County coroner's office. An autopsy of Steven Brotherton's body was performed on February 16, 1988; after the autopsy, the coroner permitted Steven Brotherton's corneas to be removed and used as anatomical gifts. The coroner's office had called the Cincinnati Eye Bank, which sent the technician who removed the corneas. Deborah Brotherton did not learn that her husband's corneas had been removed until she read the autopsy report.

Bethesda North Hospital made no attempt to inform the coroner's office of Deborah Brotherton's objection to making an anatomical gift, and the coroner's office did not inquire into whether there was an objection. Ohio Rev. Code §2108.60 permits a coroner to remove the corneas of autopsy subjects without consent, provided that the coroner has no knowledge of an objection by the decedent, the decedent's spouse, or, if there is no spouse, the next of kin, the guardian, or the person authorized to dispose of the body. The custom and policy of the Hamilton County coroner's office is not to obtain a next of kin's consent or to inspect the medical records or hospital documents before removing corneas. [Indeed, when personnel at the eye bank started asking about the existence of objections to removals, the coroner instructed his staff to withhold information about next of kin. Brotherton v. Cleveland, 173 F.3d 552, 556 (6th Cir. 1999).]

Deborah Brotherton, on her own behalf and on behalf of her children, as well as a purported class of similarly situated plaintiffs, filed this case under 42 U.S.C. §1983, alleging that her husband's corneas were removed without due process of law and in violation of the equal protection clause. She also asserted pendent state law claims for emotional distress. . . .

A majority of the courts confronted with the issue of whether a property interest can exist in a dead body have found that a property right of some kind does exist and often refer to it as a "quasi-property right." . . . However, two Ohio appellate courts which have been confronted with determining the nature of the right have avoided characterizing it in this manner.

In *Carney*, an appellate court ruled on who has standing to bring a claim for mishandling a dead body. The court stated that calling the right to control the dead body of a relative a "quasi-property right" would create a legal fiction and concluded:

> This court rejects the theory that a surviving custodian has quasi-property rights in the body of the deceased, and acknowledges the cause of action for mishandling of a dead body as a subspecies of the tort of infliction of emotional distress. *Carney*, 33 Ohio App. 3d at 37. . . .

In *Everman*, an appellate court rejected the argument that a husband's right to possession of his deceased wife's body for purposes of preparation, mourning, and burial is protected against unreasonable search or seizure. In so ruling, the court stated:

> There is no issue in this case of the possessory right of a spouse or other appropriate member of the family of a deceased for the purposes of preparation, mourning and burial. This right is recognized by law and by the decisions. This is not the [sic] say that a person has a property right in the body of another, living or dead, or that a corpse may not be temporarily held for investigation as to the true cause of death. *Everman*, 54 Ohio App. 3d at 122.

Evading the question of whether to call the spouse's interest "property," the *Everman* court recognized that Ohio does grant that right which resides at the very core of a property interest: the right to possess.

The concept of "property" in the law is extremely broad and abstract. The legal definition of "property" most often refers not to a particular physical object, but rather to the legal bundle of rights recognized in that object. Thus, "property" is often conceptualized as a "bundle of rights." The "bundle of rights" which have been associated with property include the rights to possess, to use, to exclude, to profit, and to dispose. . . . .

Though some early American cases adopted the English common-law rule that there was no property right in a dead body, other cases held that the rule was unsound in light of the rights of next of kin with regard to burial. The tendency to classify the bundle of rights granted by states as a property interest of some type was a direct function of the increased significance of those underlying rights. The prevailing view of both English and American courts eventually became that next of kin have a "quasi-property" right in the decedent's body for purposes of burial or other lawful disposition.

The importance of establishing rights in a dead body has been, and will continue to be, magnified by scientific advancements. The recent explosion of research and information concerning biotechnology has created a market place in which human tissues are routinely sold to and by scientists, physicians and others. The human body is a valuable resource. As biotechnology continues to develop, so will the capacity to cultivate the resources in a dead body. A future in which hearts, kidneys, and other valuable organs could be maintained for expanded periods outside a live body is far from inconceivable.

Thankfully, we do not need to determine whether the Supreme Court of Ohio would categorize the interest in the dead body granted to the spouse as property, quasi-property or not property. Although the existence of an interest may be a matter of state law, whether that interest rises to the level of a "legitimate claim of entitlement" protected by the due process clause is determined by federal law. This determination does not rest on the label attached to a right granted by the state but rather on the substance of that right.

Ohio Rev. Code §2108.02(B), as part of the Uniform Anatomical Gift Act governing gifts of organs and tissues for research or transplants, expressly grants a right to Deborah Brotherton to control the disposal of Steven Brotherton's body. *Everman* expresses the recognition that Deborah Brotherton has a possessory right to his body. *Carney* allows a claim for disturbance of his body. Although extremely regulated, in sum, these rights form a substantial interest in the dead body, regardless of Ohio's classification of that interest. We hold the aggregate of rights granted by the state of Ohio to Deborah Brotherton rises to the level of a "legitimate claim of entitlement" in Steven Brotherton's body, including his corneas, protected by the due process clause of the Fourteenth Amendment.

We also hold the removal of Steven Brotherton's corneas were caused by established state procedures and that Ohio failed to provide the necessary predeprivation process. The Supreme Court has often reiterated that a property interest may not be destroyed without a hearing. See, e.g., Logan v. Zimmerman Brush Co., 455 U.S. 422, 434 (1982). In *Logan*, the Supreme Court ruled that the timing of a hearing depends upon the accommodation of competing interests involved, which include: the importance of the private interests, the length and finality of deprivation, and the magnitude of governmental interest. The Court added that deprivation of property resulting from an established state procedure can only satisfy due process if there is a predeprivation hearing. . . .

It is the policy and custom of the Hamilton County coroner's office not to review medical records or paperwork pertaining to a corpse prior to the removal of corneas. This intentional ignorance is induced by Ohio Rev. Code §2108.60 which allows the office to take corneas from the bodies of deceased without considering the interest of any other parties, as long as they have no knowledge of any objection to such a removal. After the cornea is removed, it is not returned and the corpse is permanently diminished. The only governmental interest enhanced by the removal of the corneas is the interest in implementing the organ/tissue donation program; this interest is not substantial enough to allow the state to consciously disregard those property rights which it has granted. Moreover, predeprivation process undertaken by the state would be a minimal burden to this interest. This court does not at this time need to establish the type or extent of predeprivation process required by the due process clause; we merely hold that the policy and custom of the Hamilton

County coroner's office is an established state procedure necessitating predeprivation process. . . . [The litigation in *Brotherton* was finally settled ten years after this decision with a change in policy at the coroner's office and the payment of $5.25 million into a settlement fund to compensate the class of people harmed by the coroner's practices. Brotherton v. Cleveland, 141 F. Supp. 2d 894 (S.D. Ohio 2001).]

■ McFALL v. SHIMP
10 Pa. D. & C. 3d 90 (Allegheny County 1978)

FLAHERTY, Judge.

Plaintiff, Robert McFall, suffers from a rare bone marrow disease and the prognosis for his survival is very dim, unless he receives a bone marrow transplant from a compatible donor. Finding a compatible donor is a very difficult task and limited to a selection among close relatives. After a search and certain tests, it has been determined that only defendant [David Shimp] is suitable as a donor. Defendant refuses to submit to the necessary transplant, and before the court is a request for a preliminary injunction which seeks to compel defendant to submit to further tests, and, eventually, the bone marrow transplant. [McFall had aplastic anemia, and Shimp was his first cousin.]

Although a diligent search has produced no authority, plaintiff cites the ancient statute of King Edward I, 811 Westminster 2, 13 Ed. I, c.24, pointing out, as is the case, that this court is a successor to the English courts of Chancery and derives power from this statute, almost 700 years old. The question posed by plaintiff is that, in order to save the life of one of its members by the only means available, may society infringe upon one's absolute right to his "bodily security"?

The common law has consistently held to a rule which provides that one human being is under no legal compulsion to give aid or to take action to save another human being or to rescue. A great deal has been written regarding this rule which, on the surface, appears to be revolting in a moral sense. Introspection, however, will demonstrate that the rule is founded upon the very essence of our free society. It is noteworthy that counsel for plaintiff has cited authority which has developed in other societies in support of plaintiff's request in this instance. Our society, contrary to many others, has as its first principle, the respect for the individual, and that society and government exist to protect the individual from being invaded and hurt by another. Many societies adopt a contrary view which has the individual existing to serve the society as a whole. In preserving such a society as we have, it is bound to happen that great moral conflicts will arise and will appear harsh in a given instance. In this case, the chancellor is being asked to force one member of society to undergo a medical procedure which would provide that part of that individual's body would be removed from him and given to another so that the other could live. Morally, this decision rests with defendant, and, in the view of the court, the refusal of defendant is morally indefensible. For our law to *compel* defendant to submit to an intrusion of his body would change every concept and principle upon which our society is founded. To do so would defeat the sanctity of the individual, and would impose a rule which would know no limits, and one could not imagine where the line would be drawn.

This request is not to be compared with an action at law for damages, but rather is an action in equity before a chancellor, which, in the ultimate, if granted, would require the forceable submission to the medical procedure. For a society which respects the rights of *one* individual, to sink its teeth into the jugular vein or neck of one of its members and suck from it sustenance for *another* member, is revolting to our hard-wrought concepts of jurisprudence. Forceable extraction of living body tissue causes revulsion to the judicial mind. Such would raise the spectre of the swastika and the Inquisition, reminiscent of the horrors this portends.

This court makes no comment on the law regarding plaintiff's rights in an action at law for damages, but has no alternative but to deny the requested equitable relief. An order will be entered denying the request for a preliminary injunction. . . .

[Mr. McFall died two weeks after the court's opinion was issued. For details about the case, see Fordham E. Huffman, Comment, Coerced Donation of Body Tissues: Can We Live with *McFall v. Shimp*?, 40 Ohio St. L.J. 409 (1979); Alan Meisel & Loren H. Roth, Must a Man Be His Cousin's Keeper?, 8(5) Hastings Center Rep. 5 (1978) (observing that newspaper accounts reported strong pressures from Shimp's wife and mother for him not to donate and that Shimp explained his refusal in terms of the risks of anesthesia, concerns that the procedure would aggravate existing aches and pains, and the possibility that his job-related exposure to chemicals might interfere with the regeneration of his bone marrow).]

Notes: Obligations to Give Up Organs and Tissues; Autopsies

1. *The Family's Property Rights.* Which of the two courts, *Powell* or *Brotherton,* has the better analysis on the issue of whether the family has a property right? If the family can choose whether or not to donate the organs of a person who has just died, doesn't that make it clear that the family possesses a property right in the decedent's organs?

The *Powell* court cited the various safeguards in the Florida statute "which are apparently designed to limit cornea removal to instances in which the public's interest is greatest and the impact on the next of kin the least." The opinion suggests that these safeguards played an important role in the court's decision, but are they required under the court's standard that a statute is valid unless it "bears no reasonable relation to a permissible legislative objective"?

2. *Authority for Autopsies.* As the first two cases illustrate, state law gives broad authority for coroners or medical examiners to perform autopsies in cases of unnatural death or for public health reasons, despite any objection by the family. In a full autopsy, internal organs are removed, examined, and placed back in the body, but not necessarily reattached with any care or precision. These statutes are widely regarded as constitutional and are rarely challenged. See, e.g., Rielly v. City of New York, 1992 WL 368082 (E.D.N.Y. 1992) (autopsy statute that permits performance of procedure without consent of relatives when part of a criminal homicide investigation is "plainly" constitutional). The reasoning is both that important public health and law enforcement objectives outweigh any private interests, and also that opening and examining a corpse does not clearly infringe any constitutionally protected interest. An autopsy may not constitute a deprivation of "property" at all since, after the body is examined, it is returned to the family more or less intact.

The constitutionality of autopsy statutes is buttressed by the fact that they frequently allow the family to object for religious reasons.

While there is no constitutional obstacle to performing autopsies in the proper manner, if this authority is abused, courts do recognize that families have protected interests in the nature of a quasi-property right to respectful treatment and to exercise some control over the disposition of the decedent's body. In one case, a court allowed a constitutional tort action against a part-time coroner who also ran an eye bank and was allegedly caught stealing eyeballs from corpses before sewing the eyelids shut. Whaley v. County of Tuscola, 58 F.3d 1111 (6th Cir. 1995). See also Whitehair v. Highland Memory Gardens, 327 S.E.2d 438 (W. Va. 1985) (tort suit allowed for mishandling of corpse during interment process). But see Hinkle v. City of Clarksburg, 81 F.3d 416 (4th Cir. 1996) (medical examiners entitled to qualified immunity on claim that they improperly disposed of decedent's internal organs); Arnaud v. Odom, 870 F.2d 304, 309 (5th Cir. 1989) (no §1983 due process claim against physician for performing unauthorized experiments on decedent during autopsy because state law provided adequate postdeprivation remedy of action for tampering with a corpse); Albrecht v. Treon, 617 F.3d 890 (6th Cir. 2010) (no §1983 due process claim when coroner discarded decedent's brain after an autopsy because no property rights of the family were infringed).

3. *The Process Due the Family.* Powell, *Brotherton,* and other cases have clearly established the state's right to take corneas for transplantation from bodies that are undergoing an autopsy by the state (in the absence of an objection). See Erik S. Jaffee, Note, "She's Got Bette Davis['s] Eyes": Assessing the Nonconsensual Removal of Cadaver Organs Under the Takings and Due Process Clauses, 90 Colum. L. Rev. 528 (1990); Annot., 54 A.L.R.4th 1214 (1987). *Brotherton,* however, requires some kind of process before the corneas can be taken. What kind of process do you think *Brotherton* requires? Would it have been sufficient if the coroner had reviewed Mr. Brotherton's medical records to see if an objection to tissue removal had been registered? Should the coroner have to contact the family to ascertain their wishes before taking any corneas? What if, after reasonable efforts to contact family members, they cannot be reached before the autopsy? (Perhaps family members are out of town or overseas and are not responding to messages left on their telephone answering machine.)

For a case with a result similar to that in *Brotherton,* see Newman v. Sathya-vaglswaran, 287 F.3d 786 (9th Cir. 2002) (expressing great concern with the absence of pre-removal process before retrieval of corneas, but leaving for future proceedings exactly what process is due). Before the *Newman* litigation commenced, and in response to an article in the *Los Angeles Times* about alleged trafficking in corneas by the Los Angeles County Coroner's Office, California amended its cornea removal statute to require consent by the decedent or a surrogate decisionmaker. 1998 Cal. Adv. Legis. Serv. 887. The current statute can be found at Cal. Gov't Code §27491.47. (Mr. Newman had been under the custody of the Los Angeles County Coroner's Office when his corneas were taken.)

In response to *Brotherton* and *Newman,* the Revised Uniform Anatomical Gift Act §23 (2006) removed the authority of coroners to release corneas (or other tissues or organs) in the absence of consent. For more background, see the discussion of Sections 22 and 23 of the Revised Act in the "Summary of the Changes in the Revised Act." The Revised Act has substantially curtailed the use of cornea removal statutes in the United States. By 2012, 45 states had enacted the 2006 Revision, though not all of them repealed their cornea provisions. Thus, *Powell* and *Brotherton* now serve as constitutional baselines in the event that attitudes change, and states reconsider the use of coroner statutes.

4. *Retrieving Visceral Organs in Coroners' Cases.* A number of states had gone even further than Florida and Ohio and enacted statutory provisions allowing coroners or medical examiners to remove hearts, lungs, kidneys, livers, and other visceral organs for transplantation if (a) there had been no objection by the decedent while alive or by family members either before or after the decedent's death, and (b) efforts to contact the family had not been successful. The widespread adoption of the 2006 Act has eliminated most of these provisions. But even when in effect, they did not necessarily result in the retrieval of organs. Coroners and medical examiners were reluctant to remove visceral organs for transplantation without the family's permission. In Texas, in the first year after medical examiners were given authority to remove visceral organs without consent, that authority was used only twice. Coroners and medical examiners are not the only persons reluctant to remove organs without family consent. Even in cases in which a person has completed an organ donor card, transplant surgeons often will not remove the person's organs without the family's permission. David Orentlicher, Organ Donation—The Willing Donor, *in* Ethics in Emergency Medicine 214, 217 (Kenneth V. Iserson et al. eds., 2d ed. 1995).

While the 2006 Act has led states to revoke the authority of coroners or medical examiners to remove hearts, livers, kidneys, and other organs in the absence of consent, some states retained their cornea removal provisions when they adopted the 2006 Act. See, e.g., Ind. Code §29-2-16.1-3 (requiring consent for organs); Ind. Code §36-2-14-19 (allowing cornea removal). Interestingly, in Montana, the legislature followed the provisions of the Revised Uniform Anatomical Gift Act on coroners and medical examiners, but also retained its statutory provision granting authority to retrieve organs and tissues in the absence of consent. Compare Mont. Code Ann. §72-17-215 with §72-17-217.

5. *Presumed Consent More Broadly.* A number of commentators have argued that retrieval of organs should not have been limited to coroners' cases but should become a routine practice for all deceased persons. Under this "presumed consent" approach, the law would shift the presumption that people do not want to donate their organs in the absence of explicit consent to a presumption that people do want to donate their organs in the absence of an explicit refusal. See Paul T. Menzel, Strong Medicine (1990); Jesse Dukeminier & David Sanders, Organ Transplantation: A Proposal for Routine Salvaging of Cadaver Organs, 279 New Eng. J. Med. 413 (1968); Arthur J. Matas et al., A Proposal for Cadaver Organ Procurement: Routine Removal with Right of Informed Refusal, 10 J. Health Pol. Pol'y & L. 231 (1985); Theodore Silver, The Case for a Post-Mortem Organ Draft and a Proposed Model Organ Draft Act, 68 B.U. L. Rev. 681 (1988). For a dissenting view, see Robert M. Veatch & J. B. Pitt, The Myth of Presumed Consent: Ethical Problems in New Organ Procurement Strategies, 27 Transplant. Proc. 1888 (1995).

Presumed consent has been enacted in several European countries, in part as a response to a recommendation of the Council of Europe in 1978, but, even in countries with presumed consent, physicians still typically ask the family for consent to take the organs. Austria, and to some extent Belgium, are apparently the only European countries with a true presumed consent system, and there is some evidence that presumed consent has meaningfully increased the rate of organ retrieval. Hakan Gabel, How Presumed Is Presumed Consent?, 28 Transplant. Proc. 27 (1996); Maxwell J. Mehlman, Presumed Consent to Organ Donation: A Reevaluation, 1 Health Matrix 31 (1991); Paul Michielsen, Presumed Consent to Organ Donation: 10 Years' Experience in Belgium, 89 J. Roy. Soc. Med. 663 (1996). Perhaps because family consent is typically sought in most presumed consent countries, studies generally do not find higher rates for organ donation in those countries. Chris Rudge, Organ Donation and the Law, 82 Transplantation 1140 (2006). However, in a study controlling for other variables that influence organ donation, researchers found organ donation rates 25 to 30 percent higher in presumed consent countries. The authors suggested that the legislative presumption of consent may affect family decisionmaking, such that families are more likely to consent to organ donation when the law authorizes presumed consent. Alberto Abadie & Sebastien Gay, The Impact of Presumed Consent Legislation on Cadaveric Organ Donation: A Cross-Country Study, 25 J. Health Economics 599 (2006). For a review of the law and practice in European countries with presumed consent, see Anke Janssen & Sjef Gevers, Explicit or Presumed Consent and Organ Donation Post-Mortem: Does It Matter?, 24 Med. Law 575 (2005).

If we allow states to conduct autopsies without permission in criminal cases, does it follow that we should allow removal of organs from all dead persons for transplantation? Would a presumed consent law be constitutional assuming an adequate option to register objection? If the relevant issues are the violation of the person's bodily integrity and the benefit to society, how does an autopsy to solve a crime compare with a removal of organs to save a life or to improve someone's health? How does being subject to organ removal after death compare to being subject to a military draft while alive?

Assuming policy and constitutional objections to presumed consent laws could be overcome, it is not clear how great an impact they would have. As mentioned in the previous note, the laws permitting coroners to remove organs did not seem to have been employed very much for visceral organs despite their widespread use for removal of corneas. In this regard, it is instructive that the two countries in which the practical impact of presumed consent laws has been greatest—Austria and Belgium—are countries with a tradition of routine autopsies in the absence of consent. Michielsen, supra, at 663. In addition, it appears that presumed consent laws may succeed in part because they are combined with other measures to increase the organ supply. M. F. X. Gnant et al., The Impact of the Presumed Consent Law and a Decentralized Organ Procurement System on Organ Donation: Quadruplication in the Number of Organ Donors, 23 Transplant. Proc. 2685 (1991); Kieran Healy, Do Presumed-Consent Laws Raise Organ Procurement Rates?, 55 DePaul L. Rev. 1017 (2006).

For an argument that the enactment of the cornea provisions represented a limited experiment with presumed consent in the United States and that the repeal of those provisions after the 2006 Act reflects a societal judgment against presumed consent, see David Orentlicher, Presumed Consent to Organ Donation: Its Rise and Fall in the United States, 61 Rutgers L. Rev. 295 (2009).

6. *Required Request and Mandated Choice.* States have tried to increase organ donation through the adoption of "required request" laws. These laws, which almost

all states have, require hospitals to ensure that families are asked for permission to retrieve organs from patients who die. Required request is also a condition for hospitals to receive Medicare and Medicaid reimbursement. 42 U.S.C. §1320b-8. Required request was designed to overcome the reluctance of physicians to raise the issue of organ donation with families, but the laws have not had much impact. In a study to ascertain why required request was not working, researchers found that families were generally asked about organ donation, but family members frequently refused consent. Laura A. Siminoff et al., Public Policy Governing Organ and Tissue Procurement in the United States: Results from the National Organ and Tissue Procurement Study, 123 Ann. Intern. Med. 10 (1995). See also Ellen Sheehy et al., Estimating the Number of Potential Organ Donors in the United States, 349 New Eng. J. Med. 667 (2003) (finding that "[l]ack of consent to a request for donation was the primary cause of the gap between the number of potential donors and the number of actual donors"). In recent years, organ procurement organizations have raised the consent rate by family members by improving the way they discuss the possibility of donation. Patricia A. Webster & Lori Markham, Pediatric Organ Donation: A National Survey Examining Consent Rates and Characteristics of Donor Hospitals, 10 Pediatr. Crit. Care Med. 500, 503 (2009).

A number of commentators have urged the adoption of "mandated choice" laws, under which all competent adults would have to explicitly state whether or not they wish to be organ donors after they die. The choice might be required at the time of obtaining a driver's license or filing a tax return. Supporters of mandated choice observe that it would place the decision in the hands of the individual rather than in the hands of family members, and they suggest that people might be more willing to agree to a donation while alive than are their family members who are asked when the person has just died. Council on Ethical and Judicial Affairs, American Medical Association, Strategies for Cadaveric Organ Procurement: Mandated Choice and Presumed Consent, 272 JAMA 809 (1994); Sheldon F. Kurtz & Michael J. Saks, Cadaveric Organ Donor Act, 18 Iowa J. Corp. L. 523, 527 (1993); Aaron Spital, Mandated Choice for Organ Donation: Time to Give It a Try, 125 Ann. Intern. Med. 66 (1996).

However, since mandated choice is likely to be implemented without the prospective donor receiving much information, refusals may be common. Data from a Texas routine request program were consistent with this fear. In Texas (as in other states), driver's license applicants were automatically asked whether they want to be organ donors, and the refusal rate was as high as 80 percent. Ultimately, Texas repealed its mandated choice law. Laura A. Siminoff & Mary Beth Mercer, Public Policy, Public Opinion, and Consent for Organ Donation, 10 Cambridge Q. Healthcare Ethics 377, 380 (2001).

7. *Taking Tissue from Living Persons.* The *McFall* case may have come from a local Pennsylvania court, but it nevertheless represents the state of the law. There is no case that has required one person to give up tissue for the benefit of another person over the first person's objection. A subsequent case went even further and denied access to the name of a potential donor, whom the dying person wanted to contact and try to persuade to serve as a donor. In Head v. Colloton, 331 N.W.2d 870 (Iowa 1983), William Head, who was living in Texas, needed a bone marrow transplant to treat his leukemia. He had heard that the University of Iowa maintained a registry of potential bone marrow donors, and, through conversations with a staff member,

discovered that a woman in the registry might have compatible tissue for donation. The woman had been entered into the registry without her knowledge—she had been tested at one time to see if she could be a blood platelet donor to a family member—and the registry's practice was to ask potential donors whether they were willing as a general matter to participate in bone marrow transplants. When this woman was contacted, she indicated that she would consider donation but only for a family member. Mr. Head then filed suit, seeking disclosure of the woman's name to the court or his attorney so the woman could be informed about Mr. Head's situation and asked if she would consider donation in this particular case. The court held that, while the bone marrow registry was a public record under Iowa law, it was a confidential record to which public access must be denied.

If we consider just the case itself, the result in *Head* may seem problematic. However, from a broader perspective, why do you think the court felt it had to preserve the confidentiality of the woman's name? Does your answer explain why the court was not even willing to require the bone marrow registry to send the woman a letter about Mr. Head without disclosing the woman's name to Mr. Head?

8. *The Other Side of the Argument.* Is it so obvious that *McFall* and *Head* are correctly decided? Most persons share the *McFall* court's abhorrence at the idea of an involuntary taking of a person's tissue for use by another person. Yet, our society already condones behavior that is arguably more coercive. If given the choice between paying taxes and donating blood every three months, which would you choose? Of course, there are health risks with bone marrow donation. Most donors experience tiredness, pain at the donation site (i.e., the upper part of the pelvic bone), and low back pain. In one study, donors generally recovered within two weeks, but 10 percent took more than a month to recover fully. David F. Stroncek et al., Experiences of the First 493 Unrelated Marrow Donors in the National Marrow Donor Program, 81 Blood 1940 (1993). Life-threatening problems occur between 0.1 and 0.3 percent of the time, and the risk of death is about 1 in 10,000. Dennis L. Confer et al., Bone Marrow and Peripheral Blood Cell Donors and Donor Registries, *in* Thomas' Hematopoietic Cell Transplantation 544, 549-551 (F. R. Applebaum et al. eds., 4th ed. 2009). Consider also the following argument:

> [I]f you are talking about fairness, I really do not understand why the fact that I have inherited good kidneys, or good bone marrow, . . . or indeed inherited a good environment, gives me more rights than the person who has inherited bad ones. I am not sure that a person deserves inherited desirable body parts any more than he or she deserves inherited wealth. . . . Consider this situation from a Rawlsian point of view. If one did not know whether or not one would have good marrow or kidneys, then what would one say if asked whether one preferred the right to obtain somebody else's bone marrow or kidneys or the right to retain one's own? In the real world, where there are more people who have good kidneys than there are people who need them, it is all too easy to vote against a law which mandates donation. But what about voting behind a Rawlsian veil, where we would not know whether we were the needy or the well-endowed?

Guido Calabresi, Do We Own Our Bodies?, 1 Health Matrix 5, 16 (1991). Calabresi observes that laws requiring organ or tissue donation might only be passed by the majority if the potential donors were relatively weak politically and the potential recipients were relatively powerful politically, and that such laws would therefore "have to be constitutionally suspect." Id. at 11-12. But what if discrimination were not an issue?

> Now consider a communitarian-based law under which . . . *everyone* would have to be donors because we wanted to show that we are *all* willing to take on the burden. . . . Of course, it is unlikely that a legislature would actually do this, which again says something about whether or not we as a society are sufficiently concerned about "life" to be *nondiscriminating* communitarians. If we were, then I would argue the law might well be constitutional. [Id. at 13.]

Advances in medicine have resulted in a procedure that replaces bone marrow transplants in most cases. Rather than harvesting adult blood stem cells from bone marrow for transplantation in cases like *McFall*, doctors can retrieve stem cells from the donor's circulating blood after giving the donor a drug to stimulate stem cell production. Like bone marrow donation, this peripheral blood stem cell donation is generally safe, although rare serious complications can occur, including death. It is not clear whether the risk of death differs between bone marrow and peripheral cell donation. Confer et al., supra, at 552-553. Because it is less invasive to retrieve stem cells from peripheral blood, recovery time is generally shorter. While researchers have not seen long-term side effects from the drugs used to stimulate peripheral stem cell production, there are concerns that the drugs might raise the risk of leukemia. Derwood Pamphilon et al., The Use of Granulocyte-Colony-Stimulating Factor in Volunteer Unrelated Hemopoietic Stem Cell Donors, 48 Transfusion 1495 (2008).

9. *The "Trolley Problem."* Moral theorists have posed the following dilemma: If a trolley conductor is steering a runaway car through a crowded city and must choose between two tracks, it is morally permissible, and perhaps mandatory, to choose the track that will result in harm to fewer people, even if in doing so the conductor will purposefully kill someone. That being the case, why can't a physician take five life-necessary organs from one person in order to save the lives of five other persons, or even take tissue from a person for whom it is not life-necessary to give it to another person for whom it would be life-sustaining? The possible answers turn out to be more complicated than you would first think, and lead to fascinating extrapolations. For discussion, see Michael J. Costa, The Trolley Problem Revisited, 24 S.J. Phil. 437 (1986); Frances M. Kamm, Harming Some to Save Others, 57 Phil. Stud. 227 (1989); Adam Kolber, A Matter of Priority: Transplanting Organs Preferentially to Registered Donors, 55 Rutgers L. Rev. 671 (2003); James A. Montmarquet, On Doing Good: The Right and the Wrong Way, 79 J. Phil. 439 (1982); Eric Rakowski, Taking and Saving Lives, 93 Colum. L. Rev. 1063 (1993); Judith Jarvis Thomson, The Trolley Problem, 94 Yale L.J. 1395 (1985); Judith Jarvis Thomson, The Realm of Rights 176-202 (1990).

Problem: Obligatory Stem Cell Donation

Suppose a legislature, concerned about the shortage of stem cell donors for transplants, passed a law requiring that all persons be included in a national stem cell registry. People would automatically be registered at birth by having a small amount of additional blood taken at the time that blood was taken for routine newborn medical testing. Other persons would have to bring a certificate showing that they had registered before they could obtain or renew a driver's license or begin a new academic year in school. When someone needed a stem cell transplant (either from bone marrow or peripheral blood), the person's physician could check with the registry for a match. If a match was found, the person who matched would have to donate stem cells for a transplant. People could be excused from having to donate if they had religious objections or had a medical reason that disqualified them as a donor (just as the military excuses conscientious objectors and those with health problems from the draft). Should this law be constitutional? If constitutional, is it good policy? Would it matter whether the state paid some compensation to the donors as it does with military or jury duty? Would any constitutional concerns be eliminated if the law simply required automatic registration, leaving with the individual the decision whether to donate stem cells if a match occurred?

Consider the following variation on the facts: A Chernobyl-like disaster occurs in the United States, and, because of the nuclear fallout, tens or hundreds of thousands of persons need stem cell transplants. In response to the disaster, Congress passes a law requiring all healthy adults to register as potential stem cell donors. Do your answers to the previous questions come out any differently?

Notes: Financial Incentives for Organ Donation

1. *Proposals for Financial Incentives.* Another obvious way to increase the supply of transplantable organs is with financial inducement. A number of commentators have criticized the federal law that prohibits payment for organs. 42 U.S.C. §274e. They propose that people should be able either to sell their tissues and body parts that are not essential for life, as they now do with blood products, or to receive payment now for a promise to give up their organs when they die. T. Randolph Beard & David L. Kaserman, On the Ethics of Paying Organ Donors: An Economics Perspective, 55 DePaul L. Rev. 827 (2006); Richard A. Epstein, Mortal Peril: Our Inalienable Right to Health Care? 249-261 (1997); Henry Hansmann, The Economics and Ethics of Markets for Human Organs, 14 J. Health Pol. Pol'y & L. 57 (1989); Debra Satz, Why Some Things Should Not Be for Sale: The Moral Limits of Markets (2010); Richard Schwindt & Aidan R. Vining, Proposal for a Future Delivery Market for Transplant Organs, 11 J. Health Pol. Pol'y & L. 483 (1986); James S. Taylor, Stakes and Kidneys: Why Markets in Human Body Parts Are Morally Imperative (2005); Note, The Sale of Human Body Parts, 72 Mich. L. Rev. 1182 (1974).

In 2000, Pennsylvania enacted a statute authorizing payments of $3,000 to families for medical or funeral expenses of the decedent. 20 Pa. Cons. Stat. Ann. §8622. The federal prohibition against sales of organs has prevented the statute from taking effect. In June 2002, the American Medical Association called for pilot studies of financial incentives for organ donation. Deborah Josefson, AMA Considers Whether to Pay for Donation of Organs, 324 Brit. Med. J. 1541 (2002).

In January 2004, Wisconsin enacted a state tax deduction for live organ donors that passes muster under federal law. Organ donors can deduct up to $10,000 from adjusted gross income for travel expenses, lodging expenses, or lost wages that are not reimbursed (a donor can claim the deduction only once). Wis. Stat. §71.05(10) (i). Under federal law, "valuable consideration" may not be paid for a human organ, but valuable consideration does not include "the expenses of travel, housing, and lost wages incurred by the donor of a human organ in connection with the donation of the organ." 42 U.S.C. §274e(c)(2). Since Wisconsin's enactment, several states have passed similar statutes. With regard to the concern that payments will have a coercive effect on poor people, why is Wisconsin's approach particularly good?

Such incentives would increase the organ supply, it is argued. But see Jeffrey M. Prottas, Buying Human Organs—Evidence That Money Doesn't Buy Everything, 53 Transplantation 1371 (1992). In addition, considerations of justice also can support payments to donors. Noting that transplant surgeons, organ recipients, and others involved in transplantation benefit, commentators argue that donors also ought to benefit. A third argument in favor of some kind of payment is that we may have fewer problems with donors or their families wanting to be involved with recipients or feeling that the recipient owes them something. Thomas Murray has observed that gift-giving, unlike business dealings, can result in open-ended human relationships:

> In short, gifts create moral relationships that are much more open-ended, less speci-
> fiable, and less contained than contracts. Contracts are well suited to the market-
> place where a strictly limited relationship for a narrow purpose—trading goods or
> services—is desired. Gifts are better for initiating and sustaining more rounded
> human relationships, where future expectations are unknown, and where the ex-
> change of goods is secondary in importance to the relationship itself.

Thomas H. Murray, Gifts of the Body and the Needs of Strangers, 17(2) Hastings Center Rep. 30, 31 (1987) (but preferring a system of donation for organs because of the important social values that it promotes).

After studying the relations between organ recipients and the donor or the donor's family, Renée Fox and Judith Swazey concluded that

> [w]hat recipients believe they owe to donors and the sense of obligation they feel
> about repaying "their" donor for what has been given, weigh heavily on them. This
> psychological and moral burden is especially onerous because the gift the recipient
> has received from the donor is so extraordinary that it is inherently unreciprocal.
> It has no physical or symbolic equivalent. As a consequence, the giver, the receiver,
> and their families may find themselves locked in a creditor-debtor vise that binds
> them one to another in a mutually fettering way. We have called these aspects of
> the gift-exchange dimensions of transplantation, "the tyranny of the gift." . . . In the
> case of a live kidney donation, for example, the donor may exhibit a great deal of
> "proprietary interest" in the health, work, and private life of the close relative who
> has received his or her organ. . . . Recipients of cadaveric organ transplants also
> suffer from the magnitude of the gift they have received and from its unrequitable
> nature. . . . [T]he import of what has been given may not only drive close relatives of
> a cadaver donor to seek out the recipient but also, especially with heart transplants,
> to relate to this person as if he or she embodied the living spirit of the donor. How-
> ever painful it may be for the recipients and their families to be united with their
> organ donors' kin, they are likely to feel obligated to yield to them because of their
> ineffable sense of indebtedness. . . .

Renée C. Fox & Judith P. Swazey, Spare Parts: Organ Replacement in American Society 40-41 (1992).

Do we want open-ended relationships between organ donors and recipients?

2. *Concerns with Financial Incentives.* Opponents of organ sales claim that it will undermine altruistic sentiments in society. Proponents counter that we do not lose altruism by using tax deductions to encourage charitable contributions and that, in any event, altruism in society is not based on what kind of organ donation system we have. Opponents also worry that organ sales "commodify" the body (i.e., turn the body into a commodity). Proponents respond that society already permits a great deal of commodification when it permits people to work for a wage. Should we be more worried about commodifying people by buying their organs than commodifying people when we pay them for the fruits of their minds? There is also a concern about desperate persons taking unacceptable risks for pay. In response to this concern, there have been proposals to pay people for their organs, but only if the organs are taken after death, with payment to the person's heirs:

> My proposed solution is a futures market in which healthy individuals would be given the opportunity to contract for the sale of their body tissue for delivery after their death. If the vendor's organs are harvested and transplanted, a payment in the range of $5,000 for each major organ and lesser amounts for minor tissue would be made to his estate or designee. The hospital in which the vendor dies, as any bailee entrusted with valuable property, would have the legal duty to preserve his cadaver in a manner suitable for organ harvesting and to notify the purchasing agency of the decedent's condition so that it may harvest his organs. The proposal speaks only to increasing the supply of organs, not to allocating them. . . . The futures market I propose avoids three potential ethical and political pitfalls. First, because there will be no acquisition of organs from live donors, it does not raise the spectre of exploiting the poor. Second, because the market need not be used to allocate the harvested organs, the rich need have no greater access than the poor. Finally, because people will be selling their own organs, their next of kin will not be required to traffic in the decedents' remains.

Lloyd R. Cohen, Increasing the Supply of Transplant Organs: The Virtues of a Futures Market, 58 Geo. Wash. L. Rev. 1, 2 (1989).

Are there in fact good reasons for denying a person the freedom to sell a kidney? We might be concerned about a system in which the wealthy are able to obtain kidneys more easily than the poor, but suppose we permit sales of organs only if the organ is sold to the United Network for Organ Sharing (UNOS), which in turn would allocate the organ according to its customary criteria? Organ selling seems ghoulish, but is there more than an aesthetic preference that underlies the opposition to sales? Are the reasons for opposing sales sufficient to deny poor persons the means to purchase basic necessities for their families? Might the prohibition on sales exist so that we can, as a society, avoid having to deal with the reality of people being so desperately poor as to want to sell a kidney?

For empirical evidence on organ selling by living persons in a country where the practice is not prohibited by law, see Madhav Goyal et al., Economic and Health Consequences of Selling a Kidney in India, 288 JAMA 1589 (2002) (finding that the sale of a kidney "does not lead to a long-term economic benefit and may be associated with a decline in health"). See also S. A. A. Naqvi, Health Status and Renal Function Evaluation of Kidney Vendors: A Report from Pakistan, 8 Am. J. Transplantation 1444 (2008); Benita S. Padilla, Regulation Compensation for Kidney Donors in the Philippines, 14 Curr. Opin. Organ Transplant. 120 (2009); Adibul Hasan S. Rizvi et al., Regulated Compensated Donation in Pakistan and Iran, 14 Curr. Opin. Organ Transplant. 124 (2009).

For further discussion of the concerns raised by organ selling, see Robert Arnold et al., Financial Incentives for Cadaver Organ Donation: An Ethical Reappraisal, 73 Transplantation 1361 (2002) (representing the ethics committee of the American Society of Transplant Surgeons); Margaret Jane Radin, Market-Inalienability, 100 Harv. L. Rev. 1849 (1987) (arguing that we should prevent commodification when doing so is necessary to foster personhood and human flourishing); Simon Rippon, Imposing Options on People in Poverty: The Harm of a Live Donor Organ Market, J. Med. Ethics online (June 28, 2012) (observing that if individuals had the option to sell their organs, people living in poverty would face strong social pressures to sell their organs to pay off their debts or fund basic necessities).

3. *Costs of Financial Incentives.* In considering the option of financial incentives, you may be concerned about the added cost to organ transplantation from the need to pay donors. But why is that a problem if a life is saved? Is it clear that the cost of transplantation will go up? Finally, consider the fact that educational campaigns to increase organ donation are also costly.

2. Ownership of Human Tissue

Whether organs and other tissues can be taken involuntarily or can be willingly sold depends in part on whether we think people have a property interest in their body. That issue is explored in the following case, but in a somewhat different context: using human tissue for research purposes rather than for transplantation. As you read this case, consider whether the court's answer to the ownership question can be generalized to other contexts, or whether the court creates a special rule just for medical research.

■ MOORE v. THE REGENTS OF THE UNIVERSITY OF CALIFORNIA
793 P.2d 479 (Cal. 1990)

PANELLI, Justice.

[The facts of this case are presented at page 217. After holding that people have a right of informed consent when a researcher profits from studying and using their cells, the court considered whether use of a person's cells without permission violates the person's property rights.]

. . . Moore also attempts to characterize the invasion of his rights as a conversion—a tort that protects against interference with possessory and ownership interests in personal property. He theorizes that he continued to own his cells following their removal from his body, at least for the purpose of directing their use, and that he never consented to their use in potentially lucrative medical research. . . .

No court, however, has ever in a reported decision imposed conversion liability for the use of human cells in medical research. While that fact does not end our inquiry, it raises a flag of caution. In effect, what Moore is asking us to do is to impose a tort duty on scientists . . . [that] would affect medical research of importance to all of society, implicat[ing] policy concerns far removed from the traditional, two-party ownership disputes in which the law of conversion arose. . . .

"To establish a conversion, plaintiff must establish an actual interference with his *ownership or right of possession.* . . . Where plaintiff neither has title to the property alleged to have been converted, nor possession thereof, he cannot maintain an action for conversion." (Del E. Webb Corp. v. Structural Materials Co., 123 Cal. App. 3d 593, 610-611 (1981)) (emphasis added).

Moore . . . argues that "[i]f the courts have found a sufficient proprietary interest in one's persona, how could one not have a right in one's own genetic material, something far more profoundly the essence of one's human uniqueness than a name or a face?" However, . . . the goal and result of defendants' efforts has been to manufacture lymphokines. Lymphokines, unlike a name or a face, have the same molecular structure in every human being and the same important functions in every human being's immune system. Moreover, the particular genetic material which is responsible for the natural production of lymphokines, and which defendants use to manufacture lymphokines in the laboratory, is also the same in every person; it is no more unique to Moore than the number of vertebrae in the spine or the chemical formula of hemoglobin.

. . . [T]he Court of Appeal in this case concluded that "[a] patient must have the ultimate power to control what becomes of his or her tissues. To hold otherwise would open the door to a massive invasion of human privacy and dignity in the name of medical progress." Yet one may earnestly wish to protect privacy and dignity without accepting the extremely problematic conclusion that interference with those interests amounts to a conversion of personal property. Nor is it necessary to force the round pegs of "privacy" and "dignity" into the square hole of "property" in order to protect the patient, since the fiduciary-duty and informed-consent theories protect these interests directly by requiring full disclosure. . . .

Finally, the subject matter of the Regents' patent—the patented cell line and the products derived from it—cannot be Moore's property. This is because the patented cell line is both factually and legally distinct from the cells taken from Moore's body. Federal law permits the patenting of organisms that represent the product of "human ingenuity," but not naturally occurring organisms. Human cell lines are patentable because "[l]ong-term adaptation and growth of human tissues and cells in culture is difficult—often considered an art . . . ," and the probability of success is low. U.S. Congress, Office of Technology Assessment, New Developments in Biotechnology: Ownership of Human Tissues and Cells 33 (1987). It is this *inventive effort* that patent law rewards, not the discovery of naturally occurring raw materials. . . .

Of the relevant policy considerations, two are of overriding importance. The first is protection of a competent patient's right to make autonomous medical decisions. . . . This policy weighs in favor of providing a remedy to patients when physicians act with undisclosed motives that may affect their professional judgment. The second important policy consideration is that we not threaten with disabling civil liability innocent parties who are engaged in socially useful activities, such as researchers who have no reason to believe that their use of a particular cell sample is, or may be, against a donor's wishes. . . .

We need not, however, make an arbitrary choice between liability and nonliability. Instead, an examination of the relevant policy considerations suggests an appropriate balance: Liability based upon existing disclosure obligations, rather than an unprecedented extension of the conversion theory, protects patients' rights of privacy and autonomy without unnecessarily hindering research. . . .

Research on human cells plays a critical role in medical research. This is so because researchers are increasingly able to isolate naturally occurring, medically useful biological substances and to produce useful quantities of such substances through genetic engineering. These efforts are beginning to bear fruit. Products developed through biotechnology that have already been approved for marketing in this country include treatments and tests for leukemia, cancer, diabetes, dwarfism, hepatitis-B, kidney transplant rejection, emphysema, osteoporosis, ulcers, anemia, infertility, and gynecological tumors, to name but a few.

The extension of conversion law into this area will hinder research by restricting access to the necessary raw materials. Thousands of human cell lines already exist in tissue repositories. . . . These repositories respond to tens of thousands of requests for samples annually. Since the patent office requires the holders of patents on cell lines to make samples available to anyone, many patent holders place their cell lines in repositories to avoid the administrative burden of responding to requests. At present, human cell lines are routinely copied and distributed to other researchers for experimental purposes, usually free of charge. This exchange of scientific materials, which still is relatively free and efficient, will surely be compromised if each cell sample becomes the potential subject matter of a lawsuit. . . .

[T]he theory of liability that Moore urges us to endorse threatens to destroy the economic incentive to conduct important medical research. If the use of cells in research is a conversion, then with every cell sample a researcher purchases a ticket in a litigation lottery. Because liability for conversion is predicated on a continuing ownership interest, "companies are unlikely to invest heavily in developing, manufacturing, or marketing a product when uncertainty about clear title exists." (OTA Rep., supra, at p. 27.) . . .

BROUSSARD, Justice, concurring and dissenting.

. . . If this were a typical case in which a patient consented to the use of his removed organ for general research purposes and the patient's doctor had no prior knowledge of the scientific or commercial value of the patient's organ or cells, I would agree that the patient could not maintain a conversion action. In that common scenario, the patient has abandoned any interest in the removed organ and is not entitled to demand compensation if it should later be discovered that the organ or cells have some unanticipated value. I cannot agree, however, with the majority that a patient may never maintain a conversion action for the unauthorized use of his excised organ or cells, even against a party who knew of the value of the organ or cells before they were removed and breached a duty to disclose that value to the patient. . . .

Although the majority opinion, at several points, appears to suggest that a removed body part, by its nature, may never constitute "property" for purposes of a conversion action, there is no reason to think that the majority opinion actually intends to embrace such a broad or dubious proposition. If, for example, another medical center or drug company had stolen all of the cells in question from the UCLA Medical Center laboratory and had used them for its own benefit, there would be no question but that a cause of action for conversion would properly lie against the thief, and the majority opinion does not suggest otherwise. Thus, the majority's analysis cannot rest on the broad proposition that a removed body part is not property, but rather rests on the proposition that a *patient* retains no ownership interest in a body part once the body part has been removed from his or her body. . . .

MOSK, Justice, dissenting.

. . . The majority's third and last reason for their conclusion that Moore has no cause of action for conversion under existing law is that "the subject matter of the Regents' patent — the patented cell line and the products derived from it — cannot be Moore's property." The majority then offer a dual explanation: "This is because the patented cell line is both *factually* and *legally* distinct from the cells taken from Moore's body" (emphasis added). Neither branch of the explanation withstands analysis.

. . . For present purposes no distinction can be drawn between Moore's cells and the Mo cell line. It appears that the principal reason for establishing a cell line is not to "improve" the quality of the parent cells but simply to extend their life indefinitely, in order to permit long-term study and/or exploitation of the qualities already present in such cells. The complaint alleges that Moore's cells naturally produced certain valuable proteins in larger than normal quantities; indeed, that was why defendants were eager to culture them in the first place. Defendants do not claim that the cells of the Mo cell line are in any degree more productive of such proteins than were Moore's own cells. . . .

I do not question that the cell line is primarily the product of defendants' inventive effort. Yet likewise no one can question Moore's crucial contribution to the invention — an invention named, ironically, after him: But for the cells of Moore's body taken by defendants, there would have been no Mo cell line. Thus the complaint alleges that Moore's "Blood and Bodily Substances were absolutely essential to defendants' research and commercial activities . . . and that defendants could not have applied for and had issued to them the Mo cell-line patent and other patents described herein without obtaining and culturing specimens of plaintiff's Blood and Bodily Substances." . . . Defendants admit this allegation by their demurrers, as well they should: For all their expertise, defendants do not claim they could have extracted the Mo cell line out of thin air.

Nevertheless the majority conclude that the patent somehow cut off all Moore's rights — past, present, and future — to share in the proceeds of defendants' commercial exploitation of the cell line derived from his own body tissue. The majority cite no authority for this unfair result, and I cannot believe it is compelled by the general law of patents: A patent is not a license to defraud. Perhaps the answer lies in an analogy to the concept of "joint inventor." . . .

Although a patient who donates cells does not fit squarely within the definition of a "joint inventor," the policy reasons that inform joint inventor patents should also apply to cell donors. Neither John Moore nor any other patient whose cells become the basis for a patentable cell line qualifies as a "joint inventor" because he or she did not further the development of the product in any intellectual or conceptual sense. Nor does the status of patients as sole owners of a component part make them deserving of joint inventorship status. What the patients did do, knowingly or unknowingly, is collaborate with the researchers by donating their body tissue. . . . By providing the researchers with unique raw materials, without which the resulting product could not exist, the donors become necessary contributors to the product. Concededly, the patent is not granted for the cell as it is found in nature, but for the modified biogenetic product. However, the uniqueness of the product that gives rise to its patentability stems from the uniqueness of the original cell. *A patient's claim to share in the profits flowing from a patent would be analogous to that of an inventor whose collaboration was essential to the success of a resulting product. The patient was not a coequal, but was a necessary contributor to the cell line.* (Danforth, Cells, Sales, and Royalties: The Patient's Right to a Portion of the Profits, 6 Yale L. & Pol'y Rev. 179, 197 (1988) (emphasis added).) . . .

The majority begin their analysis by stressing the obvious facts that research on human cells plays an increasingly important role in the progress of medicine, and that the manipulation of those cells by the methods of biotechnology has resulted in numerous beneficial products and treatments. Yet it does not necessarily follow that, as the majority claim, application of the law of conversion to this area "will hinder research by restricting access to the necessary raw materials," i.e., to cells, cell cultures, and cell lines. . . .

To begin with, if the relevant exchange of scientific materials was ever "free and efficient," it is much less so today. Since biological products of genetic engineering became patentable in 1980, human cell lines have been amenable to patent protection and, as the court of appeal observed in its opinion below, "The rush to patent for exclusive use has been rampant." Among those who have taken advantage of this development, of course, are the defendants herein. . . . With such patentability has come a drastic reduction in the formerly free access of researchers to new cell lines and their products: The "novelty" requirement for patentability prohibits public disclosure of the invention at all times up to one year before the filing of the patent application. Thus defendants herein recited in their patent specification, "At no time has the Mo cell line been available to other than the investigators involved with its initial discovery." . . .

Secondly, to the extent that cell cultures and cell lines may still be "freely exchanged," e.g., for purely research purposes, it does not follow that the researcher who obtains such material must necessarily remain ignorant of any limitations on its use: By means of appropriate recordkeeping, the researcher can be assured that the source of the material has consented to his proposed use of it, and hence that such use is not a conversion. . . . "Record keeping would not be overly burdensome because researchers generally keep accurate records of tissue sources for other reasons: to trace anomalies to the medical history of the patient, to maintain title for other researchers and for themselves, and to insure reproducibility of the experiment." Toward the Right of Commerciality, 34 UCLA L. Rev. at 241. As the Court of Appeal correctly observed, any claim to the contrary "is dubious in light of the meticulous care and planning necessary in serious modern medical research." . . .

A second policy consideration adds notions of equity to those of ethics. Our society values fundamental fairness in dealings between its members, and condemns the unjust enrichment of any member at the expense of another. This is particularly true when, as here, the parties are not in equal bargaining positions. We are repeatedly told that the commercial products of the biotechnological revolution "hold the promise of tremendous profit." Toward the Right of Commerciality, 34 UCLA

L. Rev. at 211. In the case at bar, for example, the complaint alleges that the market for the kinds of proteins produced by the Mo cell line was predicted to exceed $3 billion by 1990. . . .

There is, however, a third party to the biotechnology enterprise—the patient who is the source of the blood or tissue from which all these profits are derived. While he may be a silent partner, his contribution to the venture is absolutely crucial. . . . Yet defendants deny that Moore is entitled to any share whatever in the proceeds of this cell line. This is both inequitable and immoral. . . .

The majority's final reason for refusing to recognize a conversion cause of action on these facts is that "there is no pressing need" to do so because the complaint also states another cause of action that is assertedly adequate to the task [—the nondisclosure cause of action]. . . .

I disagree . . . with the majority's . . . conclusion that in the present context a nondisclosure cause of action is an adequate—in fact, a superior—substitute for a conversion cause of action. [Justice Mosk then goes on to point out how difficult it is for patients to win damages in informed consent cases. He also points out that an informed consent claim would be good only against the patient's physician, in this case Dr. Golde, but not against other persons or institutions outside the patient-physician relationship who benefited from the patient's cells.]

GREENBERG v. MIAMI CHILDREN'S HOSPITAL RESEARCH INSTITUTE, INC.
264 F. Supp. 2d 1064 (S.D. Fla. 2003)

MORENO, Judge . . .

I. BACKGROUND . . .

The Complaint alleges a tale of a successful research collaboration gone sour. In 1987, Canavan disease still remained a mystery—there was no way to identify who was a carrier of the disease, nor was there a way to identify a fetus with Canavan disease. Plaintiff Greenberg approached Dr. Matalon, a research physician . . . for assistance. Greenberg requested Matalon's involvement in discovering the genes that were ostensibly responsible for this fatal disease, so that tests could be administered to determine carriers and allow for prenatal testing for the disease. [Canavan disease is a genetic disorder of the neurologic system that usually causes death by age 4 and is more common among Jews from Eastern Europe and among Saudi Arabians. If both parents carry the gene for Canavan disease, their children face a 25 percent chance of developing the disease.]

At the outset of the collaboration, Greenberg and the Chicago Chapter of the National Tay-Sachs and Allied Disease Association, Inc. ("NTSAD") located other Canavan families and convinced them to provide tissue (such as blood, urine, and autopsy samples), financial support, and aid in identifying the location of Canavan families internationally. The other individual Plaintiffs began supplying Matalon with the same types of information and samples beginning in the late 1980s. . . .

The individual Plaintiffs allege that they provided Matalon with these samples and confidential information "with the understanding and expectations that such samples and information would be used for the specific purpose of researching Canavan disease and identifying mutations in the Canavan disease which could lead to carrier detection within their families and benefit the population at large." Plaintiffs further allege that it was their "understanding that any carrier and prenatal testing developed in connection with the research for which they were providing essential support would be provided on an affordable and accessible basis, and that Matalon's research would remain in the public domain to promote the discovery of more effective prevention techniques and treatments and, eventually, to effectuate a cure for Canavan disease." This understanding stemmed from their "experience in community testing for Tay-Sachs disease, another deadly genetic disease that occurs most frequently in families of Ashkenazi Jewish descent."

There was a breakthrough in the research in 1993. Using Plaintiffs' blood and tissue samples, familial pedigree information, contacts, and financial support, Matalon and his research team successfully isolated the gene responsible for Canavan disease. After this key advancement, Plaintiffs allege that they continued to provide Matalon with more tissue and blood in order to learn more about the disease and its precursor gene.

In September 1994, unbeknownst to Plaintiffs, a patent application was submitted for the genetic sequence that Defendants had identified. This application was granted in October 1997, and Dr. Matalon was listed as an inventor on the gene patent and related applications for the Canavan disease, Patent No. 5,679,635 (the "Patent"). Through patenting, Defendants acquired the ability to restrict any activity related to the Canavan disease gene, including without limitation: carrier and prenatal testing, gene therapy and other treatments for Canavan disease and research involving the gene and its mutations.

Although the Patent was issued in October 1997, Plaintiffs allege that they did not learn of it until November 1998, when MCH (Miami Children's Hospital) revealed their intention to limit Canavan disease testing through a campaign of restrictive licensing of the Patent. . . . Defendant MCH also began restricting public accessibility through negotiating exclusive licensing agreements and charging royalty fees. . . .

. . . . Plaintiffs generally seek a permanent injunction restraining Defendants from enforcing their patent rights, damages in the form of all royalties Defendants have received on the Patent as well as all financial contributions Plaintiffs made to benefit Defendants' research. Plaintiffs allege that Defendants have earned significant royalties from Canavan disease testing in excess of $75,000 through enforcement of their gene patent, and that Dr. Matalon has personally profited by receiving a recent substantial federal grant to undertake further research on the gene patent. . . .

III. ANALYSIS . . .

A. LACK OF INFORMED CONSENT

[The court rejected a duty for researchers to disclose their economic interests, distinguishing Moore v. Regents of the University of California on the ground that the researcher in that case also provided care to Mr. Moore, while Dr. Matalon did not provide care to any of the plaintiffs.] . . .

C. UNJUST ENRICHMENT

In Count III of the Complaint, Plaintiffs allege that MCH is being unjustly enriched by collecting license fees under the Patent. Under Florida law, the elements of a claim for unjust enrichment are (1) the plaintiff conferred a benefit on the defendant, who had knowledge of the benefit; (2) the defendant voluntarily accepted and retained the benefit; and (3) under the circumstances it would be inequitable for the defendant to retain the benefit without paying for it. The Court finds that Plaintiffs have sufficiently alleged the elements of a claim for unjust enrichment to survive Defendants' motion to dismiss.

While the parties do not contest that Plaintiffs have conferred a benefit to Defendants, including, among other things, blood and tissue samples and soliciting financial contributions, Defendants contend that Plaintiffs have not suffered any detriment, and note that no Plaintiff has been denied access to Canavan testing. Furthermore, the Plaintiffs received what they sought—the successful isolation of the Canavan gene and the development of a screening test. Plaintiffs argue, however, that when Defendants applied the benefits for unauthorized purposes, they suffered a detriment. Had Plaintiffs known that Defendants intended to commercialize their genetic material through patenting and restrictive licensing, Plaintiffs would not have provided these benefits to Defendants under those terms.

Naturally, Plaintiffs allege that the retention of benefits violates the fundamental principles of justice, equity, and good conscience. While Defendants claim that they have invested significant amounts of time and money in research, with no guarantee of success and are thus entitled to seek reimbursement, the same can be said of Plaintiffs. Moreover, Defendants' attempt to seek refuge in the endorsement of the U.S. Patent system, which gives an inventor rights to prosecute patents and negotiate licenses for their intellectual property fails, as obtaining a patent does not preclude the Defendants from being unjustly enriched. The Complaint has alleged more than just a donor-donee relationship for the purposes of an unjust enrichment claim. Rather, the facts paint a picture of a continuing research collaboration that involved Plaintiffs also investing time and significant resources in the race to isolate the Canavan gene. Therefore, given the facts as alleged, the Court finds that Plaintiffs have sufficiently pled the requisite elements of an unjust enrichment claim and the motion to dismiss for failure to state a claim is DENIED as to this count. . . .

E. CONVERSION

The Plaintiffs allege in Count V of their Complaint that they had a property interest in their body tissue and genetic information. . . . The Court disagrees and declines to find a property interest for the body tissue and genetic information voluntarily given to Defendants. These were donations to research without any contemporaneous expectations of return of the body tissue and genetic samples, and thus conversion does not lie as a cause of action.

In Florida, the tort of "conversion is an unauthorized act which deprives another of his property permanently or for an indefinite time." Using property given for one purpose for another purpose constitutes conversion.

First, Plaintiffs have no cognizable property interest in body tissue and genetic matter donated for research under a theory of conversion. This case is similar to *Moore v. Regents of the University of California,* where the Court declined to extend liability under a theory of conversion to misuse of a person's excised biological materials. The plaintiff in *Moore* alleged that he had retained a property right in excised bodily material used in research, and therefore retained some control over the results of that research. The California Supreme Court, however, disagreed and held that the use of the results of medical research inconsistent with the wishes of the donor was not conversion, because the donor had no property interest at stake after the donation was made. . . .

Second, limits to the property rights that attach to body tissue have been recognized in Florida state courts. For example, *in State v. Powell, 497 So. 2d 1188, 1192 (Fla. 1986),* the Florida Supreme Court refused to recognize a property right in the body of another after death. Similarly, the property right in blood and tissue samples also evaporates once the sample is voluntarily given to a third party.

. . . Plaintiffs cite a litany of cases in other jurisdictions that have recognized that body tissue can be property in some circumstances. *See, e.g., Brotherton v. Cleveland, 923 F.2d 477, 482 (6th Cir. 1991)* (aggregate of rights existing in body tissue is similar to property rights); *York v. Jones, 717 F. Supp. 421, 425 (E.D. Va. 1989)* (couple granted property rights in their frozen embryos). These cases, however, do not involve voluntary donations to medical research. . . .

The Court finds that Florida . . . law do[es] not provide a remedy for Plaintiffs' donations of body tissue and blood samples under a theory of conversion liability. Indeed, the Complaint does not allege that the Defendants used the genetic material for any purpose but medical research. Plaintiffs claim that the *fruits* of the research, namely the patented material, was commercialized. This is an important distinction and another step in the chain of attenuation that renders conversion liability inapplicable to the facts as alleged. If adopted, the expansive theory championed by Plaintiffs would cripple medical research as it would bestow a continuing right for donors to possess the results of any research conducted by the hospital. At the core, these were donations to research without any contemporaneous expectations of return. Consequently, the Plaintiffs have failed to state a claim upon which relief may be granted on this issue. Accordingly, this claim is DISMISSED. . . .

Notes: Human Tissue in Research

1. *Subsequent Developments.* When the *Moore* case went back to the trial court on remand, the parties settled for an undisclosed amount of money. Ultimately, researchers figured out how to produce large amounts of lymphokines without using Mr. Moore's cell line. The *Greenberg* case also was settled, with Miami Children's Hospital permitted to license and collect royalty fees for the laboratory test for the Canavan gene, but obligated to allow license-free use of the Canavan gene in research to cure Canavan disease. Note, 93 Geo. L.J. 365, 376 (2004).

2. Washington University v. Catalona. While *Moore* and *Greenberg* involved disputes between patients and researchers, disputes also may arise between researchers and their institutions. When a highly respected researcher of prostate cancer, Dr. William Catalona, moved from Washington University, St. Louis, to Northwestern

B. **Ownership and Control of the Body**   441

University, he wanted to take a repository of prostate tissue, blood, and DNA samples that he had collected from patients and that he used in his research. On summary judgment, a federal trial court concluded that the patients had donated their tissue samples to Washington University, which enjoyed ownership rights over those samples. The court therefore held that neither the patients nor Dr. Catalona could insist that Washington University transfer the samples to Northwestern University. Wash. Univ. v. Catalona, 437 F. Supp. 2d 985 (E.D. Mo. 2006). For further discussion of this case, see Lori Andrews, Who Owns Your Body? A Patient's Perspective on *Washington University v. Catalona*, 34 J.L. Med. Ethics 398 (2006).

3. *Reconciling* Moore *and* Greenberg *with* McFall. Are the results in *Moore* and *Greenberg* consistent with the result in McFall v. Shimp, supra page 421? If the state cannot force Mr. Shimp to give up his bone marrow for the greater good of society, why can it force Mr. Moore and others to relinquish control over their cells for the same reason? Does Shimp win and the others lose only because the cells were already outside their bodies, and they therefore suffered no invasion of their bodily integrity? But didn't Moore consent to subsequent invasions of his bodily integrity after the surgery only because of Dr. Golde's deception? Does the *Moore* case simply prove Judge Calabresi's point at page 427 that we see ourselves as the Shimps and users of lymphokines of society, but not as the McFalls or Moores of society?

4. *Frozen Embryos.* In Davis v. Davis, 842 S.W.2d 588 (Tenn. 1992), the Tennessee Supreme Court held that frozen embryos could not be used for procreation without the consent of both the woman and man who contributed the egg and sperm, respectively. If Moore and Greenberg lost in their cases because there was no bodily invasion, then how do we reconcile the *Davis* case with the *Moore* and *Greenberg* cases?

5. *Researchers Profiting from Mr. Moore's Cells.* Why should everyone but Moore be able to benefit financially from the use of his cells? We might argue that the difference between paying researchers and paying patients is the fact that we worry about patients assuming undue health risks for pay, but we do not have to worry about researchers putting themselves at risk of personal harm if they benefit financially from their work. What is the counter to this argument?

Does *Greenberg*'s theory of unjust enrichment provide adequate protection for patients?

Just as researchers can earn substantial sums by manipulating a person's cells in research, so can companies realize large profits by processing a cadaver's tissues for transplantation. Although federal law prohibits payments to the decedent's family for skin, tendons, bone, heart valves, and other tissues, 42 U.S.C. §274e, tissue banks can receive reasonable payments for their retrieval and storage costs, and tissue processors can charge what the market will bear for tissues used in transplants. In contrast to the substantial regulation of the organ transplant system, the law provides considerably less oversight of the tissue processing and transplant industry. For more discussion, see Robert A. Katz, The Re-Gift of Life: Can Charity Law Prevent For-Profit Firms from Exploiting Donated Tissue and Nonprofit Tissue Banks?, 55 DePaul L. Rev. 943 (2006); Michelle Oberman, When the Truth Is Not Enough: Tissue Donation, Altruism, and the Market, 55 DePaul L. Rev. 903 (2006).

6. *Additional Readings.* Additional readings on this topic include Lori B. Andrews, My Body, My Property, 16(5) Hastings Center Rep. 28 (1986); George J. Annas, Outrageous Fortune: Selling Other People's Cells, 20(6) Hastings Center

Rep. 36 (1990); R. Alta Charo, Body of Research—Ownership and Use of Human Tissue, 355 New Eng. J. Med. 1517 (2006); Donna M. Gitter, Ownership of Human Tissue: A Proposal for Federal Recognition of Human Research Participants' Property Rights in Their Biological Material, 61 Wash. & Lee L. Rev. 257 (2004); Michele Goodwin, Formalism and the Legal Status of Body Parts, 2006 U. Chi. Legal F. 317; Natalie Ram, Assigning Rights and Protecting Interests: Constructing Ethical and Efficient Legal Rights in Human Tissue, 23 Harv. J.L. & Tech. 119 (2009).

C. ALLOCATION OF ORGANS

So far, we have been discussing issues about organ procurement and proposals to increase the supply of organs. Another critical issue is organ allocation: among those in need of an organ transplant, to whom will an available organ be given? The important law for this issue is the National Transplant Act of 1984. As mentioned above, the Act created the OPTN as a private, nonprofit entity to oversee the retrieval and allocation of organs for transplantation. Since 1986, the Secretary of Health and Human Services has awarded successive contracts to the United Network for Organ Sharing (UNOS) to operate the OPTN. UNOS is a membership organization that includes the 58 organ procurement organizations throughout the country, as well as more than 300 transplant surgery centers, medical laboratories that perform tests for organ matching, volunteer and advocacy groups, and members of the general public. The organ procurement organizations are responsible for securing organs in their geographic area and allocating the organs to patients in need. OPTN/UNOS issues allocation guidelines for the procurement organizations to follow, and while the guidelines differ for hearts, livers, kidneys, and other organs, they generally rely on criteria such as the likelihood of a successful transplant, time spent on the waiting list, and medical urgency (i.e., is the person likely to die or suffer irreparable injury if a transplant is not performed soon). A person's place of residence may also play a critical role. Preference for a transplant is given to people on the local waiting list, and people tend to appear only on the waiting list for their area. Often the different criteria come into conflict. A patient may gain priority because of an urgent need for a liver transplant, but then have the priority offset by a short life expectancy even with a transplant.

While OPTN/UNOS guidelines govern the allocation of organs for persons who are on a waiting list for a transplant, there are no standard rules for deciding when a person is added to a waiting list. Accordingly, while transplant centers exhibit considerable agreement in their policies, they also vary in their approaches. In deciding whom to place on the wait list, transplant centers tend to consider several factors: the likelihood that the transplant surgery will go well, the length of time that the recipient will benefit from the transplant before either the transplant is "rejected" by the patient or the patient dies, and the quality of life that the recipient will experience with the transplant. For indirect measures of these factors, transplant centers look at the severity and cause of organ failure, the presence in the recipient of other illnesses that affect either life expectancy or the ability to tolerate major surgery, the patient's age, and psychosocial criteria (e.g., alcohol or other drug abuse, psychiatric illness, mental retardation, and lack of compliance with treatment regimens in the past).

With liver transplantation, for example, a number of unofficial policies have developed. Patients with liver cancer generally do not do well with a transplant because of recurrence of the cancer, and transplant centers typically limit transplants to liver cancer patients whose cancers are found early and have not yet spread. Maria Varela et al., Hepatoma, *in* Medical Care of the Liver Transplant Patient 119, 120 (Paul G. Killenberg & Pierre-Alain Clavien eds., 3d ed. 2006). Other patients who are denied liver transplants are those who currently engage in drug abuse, have AIDS or other severe infections, have a non-liver, non-skin cancer, or have suffered irreversible brain injury from their liver failure. Don C. Rockey, Selection and Evaluation of the Recipient (Including Retransplantation), *in* Medical Care of the Liver Transplant Patient, supra, at 3, 6-10. Transplantation for patients with liver failure from alcohol abuse is common, but there is variation among centers in deciding which persons with alcoholic liver disease should be considered for transplantation. Factors that are used to select candidates include documented abstinence from alcohol (typically at least six months), evidence of social stability (e.g., employment, permanent residence, and marriage), presence of a good family or social support system, absence of illicit substance use, absence of psychiatric illness, and compliance with recommendations by the patient's treating physicians. See Sheila Jowsey & Terry Schneekloth, Psychosocial Assessment of Adult Liver Transplant Recipients, *in* Transplantation of the Liver 395, 401 (Ronald W. Busuttil & Goran K. Klintmalm eds., 2d ed. 2005); see also Seonaid McCallum & George Masterton, Liver Transplantation for Alcoholic Liver Disease: A Systematic Review of Psychosocial Selection Criteria, 41 Alcohol & Alcoholism 358 (2006) (finding that social stability, past compliance with medical care, and other variables, but not duration of pre-transplant abstinence from alcohol use, are good predictors of post-transplant success). Some transplant centers are now performing transplants for some patients with HIV infection. Michelle E. Roland et al., HIV-Infected Liver and Kidney Transplant Recipients: 1- and 3-Year Outcomes, 8 Am. J. Transplantation 355 (2008).

Ability to pay is also an obstacle for many potential organ transplant recipients. Medicare pays for kidney transplants, but not for all of the associated costs (e.g., coverage is temporary for drugs to prevent rejection of the transplanted organ by the recipient's immune system that have to be taken as long as the organ is still functioning). Medicare also pays for heart, lung, and liver transplants, but restricts the pool of potential recipients by requiring them to meet certain medical criteria and to qualify for Social Security disability benefits. In addition, with these organs, Medicare also does not pay all of the associated medical costs. Some recipients can rely on private insurance or Medicaid, but those patients too may receive only partial reimbursement for the costs of the transplant and its follow-up care. Accordingly, for some people, the costs of a transplant may preclude its availability. Even for people who receive a transplant, financial considerations may compromise the long-term success of the procedure. Data suggest that an important reason for failure of organs a few years after transplantation is the unaffordability of the drugs to suppress the recipient's immune system. Lisa M. Willoughby et al., Health Insurance Considerations for Adolescent Transplant Recipients as They Transition to Adulthood, 11 Pediatric Transplantation 127 (2007).

Finally, cases involving celebrities suggest that social value considerations may affect allocation decisions (e.g., the liver transplant for Mickey Mantle in June 1995).

■ OPTN/UNOS POLICY FOR ORGAN DISTRIBUTION

OPTN/UNOS prescribes policies for allocation of each type of organ. Below you will find an excerpt from the liver allocation policy. The excerpt reflects the OPTN/UNOS policy for ranking adults waiting for liver transplants. There are additional provisions for children waiting for transplants that can be found at the OPTN Web site. As you work through the policy, consider the following questions. If a liver becomes available after a death in Chicago, and there is a person waiting for a liver in Gary, IN, Indianapolis, IN, Fargo, ND, and Los Angeles, CA, how will OPTN/UNOS rank the four people who are waiting (assuming they all have the same MELD score)? What if the person from Indianapolis is Status 1A, and the person from Fargo has a MELD score of 5? For a map of the organ procurement regions, see http://optn.transplant.hrsa.gov/members/regions.asp. You can find a list of organ procurement organizations (OPOs) (the local geographic units in the policy) by searching for OPOs at http://optn.transplant.hrsa.gov/members/search.asp. Note that some OPOs cross state boundaries (e.g., the New England Organ Bank), some follow a state's boundaries (e.g., Alabama Organ Center), and some serve part of a single state (e.g., OneLegacy in the Los Angeles area). For state-by-state and county-by-county information on OPO locations, see http://opotxfind.hrsa.gov/Search_OPO_OTC.aspx.

OPTN/UNOS Policy 3.6 — December 13, 2012

3.6 *ALLOCATION OF LIVERS.* Unless otherwise approved according to [other OPTN/UNOS policies], the allocation of livers according to the following point system is mandatory. For the purpose of enabling physicians to apply their consensus medical judgment for the benefit of liver transplant candidates as a group, each patient will be assigned [either] a status code or [a] probability of candidate death derived from a mortality risk score corresponding to the degree of medical urgency as described in Policy 3.6.4 below. Mortality risk scores shall be determined by the prognostic factors specified in Table[] 1 . . . and calculated in accordance with the Model for End-Stage Liver Disease (MELD) Scoring System . . . described in Policy 3.6.4.1 . . . Candidates will be stratified within MELD . . . score by blood type similarity as described in Policy 3.6.2. No individual or property rights are conferred by this system of liver allocation.

Livers will be offered to candidates with an assigned Status of 1A . . . in descending point sequence with the candidate having the highest number of points receiving the highest priority before being offered for candidates listed in other categories. . . . Following Status 1, livers will be offered to candidates based upon their probability of candidate death derived from assigned MELD . . . scores, as applicable, in descending point sequence with the candidate having the highest probability ranking receiving the highest priority before being offered to candidates having lower probability rankings. . . .

[Priority Ranking for Adults on the Liver Wait List]

Combined Local and Regional

1. Status 1A candidates in descending point order
. . . .

Local and Regional

[2]. Candidates with [MELD] Scores >= 35 in descending order of mortality risk (MELD) scores, with Local candidates ranked above Regional candidates at each level of MELD score

Local

[3]. Candidates with [MELD] Scores 29-34 in descending order of mortality risk scores (probability of candidate death)

National

[4]. Liver-Intestine candidates in descending order of Status and mortality risk scores (probability of candidate death)

Local

[5]. Candidates with [MELD] Scores 15-28 in descending order of mortality risk scores (probability of candidate death)

Regional

[6]. Candidates with [MELD] Scores 15-34 in descending order of mortality risk scores (probability of candidate death)

National

[7]. Status 1A candidates in descending point order
[8]. Candidates with [MELD] Scores >= 15 in descending order of mortality risk scores (probability of candidate death)

Local

[9]. Candidates with [MELD] Scores < 15 in descending order of mortality risk scores (probability of candidate death)

Regional

[10]. Candidates with [MELD] Scores < 15 in descending order of mortality risk scores (probability of candidate death)

National

[11]. Candidates with [MELD] scores < 15 in descending order of mortality risk scores (probability of candidate death)....

The liver must be transplanted into the original designee or be released back to the Host OPO or to the Organ Center for distribution. . . . The final decision whether to use the liver will remain the prerogative of the transplant surgeon and/

or physician responsible for the care of that candidate. This will allow physicians and surgeons to exercise judgment about the suitability of the liver being offered for their specific candidate; to be faithful to their personal and programmatic philosophy about such controversial matters as the importance of cold ischemia and anatomic anomalies; and to give their best assessment of the prospective recipient's medical condition at the moment. If a liver is declined for a candidate, a notation of the reason for the decision not to accept the liver for that candidate must be made on the appropriate form and promptly submitted. . . .

3.6.1 Preliminary Stratification. For every potential liver recipient, the acceptable donor size must be determined by the responsible surgeon. The Match System will consider only potential liver recipients who are an acceptable size for that particular donor liver.

3.6.2 Blood Type Similarity Stratification/Points. For Status 1A . . . transplant candidates, those with the same ABO type as the liver donor shall receive 10 points. Candidates with compatible but not identical ABO types shall receive 5 points, and candidates with incompatible types shall receive 0 points. . . . Within each [MELD] score, donor livers shall be offered to transplant candidates who are ABO-identical with the donor first, then to candidates who are ABO-compatible, followed by candidates who are ABO-incompatible with the donor.

3.6.2.1 Allocation of Blood Type O Donors. With the Exception of Status 1A . . . candidates, blood type O donors may only be allocated to blood type O candidates, or B candidates with a MELD . . . score greater than or equal to 30. . . .

3.6.2.2 Liver Allocation to Candidates Willing to Accept an Incompatible Blood Type. For Status 1A . . . , candidates or candidates with a match MELD . . . score of 30 and greater, centers may specify on the Waiting List those candidates who will accept a liver from a donor of any blood type.

3.6.3 Time Waiting. Transplant candidates on the Waiting List shall accrue waiting time within Status 1A . . . or any assigned MELD . . . score; however, waiting time accrued while listed at a lower [MELD] score will not be counted toward liver allocation if the candidate is upgraded to a higher [MELD] score. . . . For example, if there are 2 persons with a MELD score of 30 who were both of identical blood types with the donor, the candidate with the longest accrued waiting time in MELD score 30 or higher would receive the first offer. Waiting time will not be accrued by candidates awaiting a liver transplant while they are registered on the Waiting List as inactive.

Candidates in Status 1A . . . will receive waiting time points based on their waiting time in that Status. Ten points will be accrued by the candidate waiting for the longest period for a liver transplant and proportionately fewer points will be accrued by those candidates with shorter tenure. For example, if there were 75 persons of O blood type waiting who were of a size compatible with a blood group O donor, the person waiting the longest would accrue 10 points (75/75 x 10). A person whose rank order was 60 would accrue 2 points. ((75-60)/75 x 10 = 2).

3.6.4 Degree of Medical Urgency. Each candidate is assigned a status code or mortality risk score (probability of candidate death) which corresponds to how medically urgent it is that the candidate receive a transplant.

3.6.4.1 Adult Candidate Status. Medical urgency is assigned to an adult liver transplant candidate (greater than or equal to 18 years of age) based on either the criteria defined below for Status 1A, or the candidate's mortality risk score as determined by the prognostic factors specified in Table 1 and calculated in accordance with the MELD Scoring System. A candidate who does not have a MELD score that, in the judgment of the candidate's transplant physician, appropriately reflects the candidate's medical urgency, may nevertheless be assigned a higher MELD score upon application by his/her transplant physician(s) and justification to the applicable Regional Review Board that the candidate is considered, by consensus medical judgment, using accepted medical criteria, to have an urgency and potential for benefit comparable to that of other candidates having the higher MELD score. The justification must include a rationale for incorporating the exceptional case as part of MELD calculation. . . .

Status Definition

7   A candidate listed as Status 7 is temporarily inactive. Candidates who are considered to be temporarily unsuitable transplant candidates are listed as Status 7, temporarily inactive.

1A   A candidate greater than or equal to 18 years of age listed as Status 1A has fulminant liver failure with a life expectancy without a liver transplant of less than 7 days. For the purpose of Policy 3.6, fulminant liver failure shall be defined as described in (i)-(iv). . . .

    (i)   fulminant hepatic failure defined as the onset of hepatic encephalopathy within 8 weeks of the first symptoms of liver disease. The absence of pre-existing liver disease is critical to the diagnosis. . . . or

    (ii) primary non-function of a transplanted liver within 7 days of implantation [primary non-function is to be distinguished from secondary non-function, or loss of function from problems external to the liver, like heart disease]; . . . or

    (iii) hepatic artery thrombosis in a transplanted liver within 7 days of implantation, with evidence of severe liver injury, . . . or

    (iv) acute decompensated Wilson's disease [a rare, inherited disease that results in damage to the liver and the brain]. . . .

Candidates who are listed as a Status 1A automatically revert back to their most recent MELD Score after 7 days unless these candidates are relisted as Status 1A by an attending physician. . . .

All other adult liver transplant candidates on the Waiting List shall be assigned a mortality risk score calculated in accordance with the MELD scoring system. . . .

[For pediatric liver allocation, there is a status 1B as well as 1A.]

[Table 1 describes the MELD scoring system, which is based on three laboratory values, with a maximum score of 40. The three laboratory values are serum bilirubin (a measure of liver function), INR (a measure of blood-clotting ability that reflects liver function), and serum creatinine (a measure of kidney function).]

3.6.4.1.1 Adult Candidate Reassessment and Recertification Schedule. The appropriateness of the MELD score assigned to each candidate listing shall be reassessed and recertified by the listing transplant center to the OPTN Contractor in accordance with the following schedule:

Adult Candidate Reassessment and Recertification Schedule

Status 1A	Status recertification every 7 days.	Laboratory values must be no older than 48 hours.
MELD Score 25 or greater	Status recertification every 7 days.	Laboratory values must be no older than 48 hours.
Score ≤ 24 but > 18	Status recertification every 1 month.	Laboratory values must be no older than 7 days.
Score ≤ 18 but ≥ 11	Status recertification every 3 months.	Laboratory values must be no older than 14 days.
Score ≤ 10 but > 0	Status recertification every 12 months.	Laboratory values must be no older than 30 days.

Notes: Criteria for Rationing Organs

1. *Local vs. National Standards for Listing.* As we have seen, UNOS guidelines kick in only after patients have been selected for the waiting list. Getting on the waiting list can be a much more important step, and transplant centers are free to develop their own policies. Is that appropriate, or should UNOS issue national guidelines for determining when a patient will be added to the waiting list?

In the past, UNOS has suggested it would develop standard criteria for deciding when a person should be placed on the waiting list for either a kidney or liver. Such criteria would help address the problem of some transplant centers being too quick to place a patient on a waiting list (sometimes doing so on the theory that, by the time the patient reaches the top of the list, the patient will be ready for a transplant).

Note that to some extent, the allocation guidelines also give guidance for adding people to the waiting list. For example, if a patient's liver disease is severe enough for the patient to qualify for Status 1A once listed or the patient has a high MELD score, the disease is also severe enough that the patient should be listed.

For an example of professional guidelines for listing candidates for organ transplantation, see Michael R. Lucey et al., Minimal Criteria for Placement of Adults on the Liver Transplant Waiting List: A Report of the National Conference Organized by the American Society of Transplant Physicians and the American Association for the Study of Liver Diseases, 3 Liver Transplantation 628 (1997); Mandeep R. Mehra et al., Listing Criteria for Heart Transplantation: International Society for Heart and Lung Transplantation Guidelines for the Care of Cardiac Transplant Candidates—2006, 25 J. Heart & Lung Transplantation 1024 (2006).

For a discussion of the inequities in listing, see Michele Goodwin, Altruism's Limits: Law, Capacity, and Organ Commodification, 56 Rutgers L. Rev. 305, 330-339 (2004).

2. *Relative Weights of Different Criteria.* Under the UNOS policy for liver transplantation, the greatest weights are given to medical urgency and the length of time that the recipient will benefit from the transplant. Medical urgency comes into play through the criteria for Status 1A and the MELD score ranking. Patients do not qualify for Status 1A unless their life expectancy without a transplant is less than seven days, and sicker patients have higher MELD scores.

The length of time that the recipient will benefit from the transplant is reflected in two ways. First, and more importantly, there is consideration of the patient's life expectancy with a transplant. Adult patients qualify for Status 1A only if they suffer from "fulminant" liver failure. These patients, whose liver failure has usually come on suddenly, typically live longer with a liver transplant than patients with "chronic" or long-standing liver failure. If the liver failure has existed for only a short time, then almost all of its harm to the body can be reversed with a liver transplant. When the liver failure has been long-standing, then much of its damage to the body is permanent and cannot be reversed. As a result, the patient might die even though the new liver is functioning well. (Note that some patients qualify for Status 1A if they've experienced unsuccessful liver transplant surgery. These patients might have developed their initial need for a transplant after chronic liver failure.)

Length of benefit from the transplant is also reflected in consideration of the likelihood that the liver will be rejected by the recipient's immune system. Under Policy 3.6.2, points are given for blood type similarity (maximum of ten points) since rejection of the transplant is less likely when blood types are compatible.

Some consideration in the UNOS liver policy is given to concerns of equity in access; this is done in the awarding of points for time on the waiting list and for blood type similarity. The relationship between equity and points for blood type similarity is somewhat complicated. First, Policy 3.6.2.1 has special rules for blood type O patients. Second, under Policy 3.6.2, if the donor and recipient have *identical* blood types, ten points are given. Five points are given for *compatible* blood types. These rules in Policies 3.6.2.1 and 3.6.2 exist because patients with blood type O would be disadvantaged if livers were allocated only on the basis of blood type compatibility. Livers from type O donors are good transplants for recipients of any blood type (i.e., type O people are "universal" donors), but type O recipients must rely almost exclusively on livers from type O donors. If only compatibility mattered, livers from type O donors would be scattered among recipients of all blood types, thereby decreasing the pool of "good" livers for blood type O patients and increasing the pool of "good" livers for patients of other blood types.

For suggestions to improve the use of MELD scores, see Kiran M. Bambha & Scott W. Biggins, Inequities of the Model for End-Stage Liver Disease, 13 Curr. Opin. Organ Transplant. 227 (2008).

For allocation of kidneys, UNOS assigns different relative weights. The most important difference is the unimportance of medical urgency in kidney allocation. Urgency rarely affects kidney allocation decisions since patients on the waiting list usually can be maintained on dialysis while awaiting a transplant. The greatest weight for kidney transplants is given to the length of time in which the recipient will benefit from the transplant. Most of the points for ranking potential recipients come from measuring the likelihood that the transplanted organ will be rejected, as reflected in the compatibility of tissue matching between the donor and recipient. Tissue compatibility is associated with a greater length of time in which the kidney functions in the recipient. Significant consideration under the UNOS policy is also given to the fact that some potential recipients are highly "sensitized" to foreign tissues (i.e., tissues from other persons) and are therefore much less likely to find a kidney that they would not reject immediately. Common causes of tissue sensitization are blood transfusions, pregnancy, and receipt of an organ transplant previously (i.e., situations in which the patient has been exposed to tissue from another person). Tissue compatibility is given greater weight with kidneys than livers because rejection of the transplanted organ is more frequently a problem with kidney transplants.

Although length of benefit is very important with kidney allocation, it is measured only in terms of the likelihood that the kidney will be rejected, without consideration of the patient's life expectancy with a functioning transplant. That is, there is nothing analogous for kidney allocation to the distinction in liver allocation between fulminant and chronic liver failure. This may simply reflect the fact that the distinction between fulminant and chronic liver failure dates only to November 1996. Why else might life expectancy with a transplant be more important with a liver transplant? (Life expectancy with a kidney transplant may not show up in the UNOS policy, but it undoubtedly is considered by physicians when they decide whether to place a patient with kidney failure on the transplant waiting list.) Life expectancy may become part of the UNOS kidney allocation policy soon. In September 2012, UNOS invited public comment on a proposal to give priority to the 20 percent of individuals on the waiting list with the longest estimated post-transplant survival.

3. *The Controversial Nature of Allocation Criteria.* Since the allocation of organs may have life and death consequences, there often is considerable controversy over the selection criteria, as occurred in November 1996 when UNOS proposed an amendment of the criteria for allocation of livers. The proposed policy gave greater weight to the patient's life expectancy with a transplant and less weight to the patient's medical urgency. Under the pre-proposal policy, urgency was the dominant consideration. Patients were classified as Status 1 if they were expected to die within seven days without a transplant, regardless of whether they suffered from fulminant or chronic liver failure. To give greater weight to expected benefit, the proposed policy limited Status 1 only to patients whose need for a transplant was urgent *and* who were suffering from fulminant liver failure. Patients with chronic liver failure could not qualify for Status 1 even if their need for a liver was urgent. When the 1996 proposal was announced, there were charges of discrimination against alcoholics since alcohol abuse is one of the most common causes of chronic liver failure.

Because of the public outcry, the liver allocation rules underwent multiple modifications between 1996 and 2002. The U.S. Department of Health and Human Services provided guidance through amendment of its regulations governing organ transplantation at 42 C.F.R. 6 §§121.1 et seq. (2002). For discussion of the controversy, see Dulcinea A. Grantham, Transforming Transplantation: The Effect of the Health and Human Services Final Rules on the Organ Allocation System, 35 U.S.F. L. Rev. 751 (2001).

4. *Legal Rights to a Transplant.* Does a potential recipient of an organ ever enjoy a legal right to the organ? Recall from the liver allocation policy that UNOS has tried to foreclose that possibility. According to the policy, "[n]o individual or property rights are conferred by this system of liver allocation." Allocation policies for other organs, however, do not have a similar statement.

The rights of a potential recipient were explored to some extent in Colavito v. New York Organ Donor Network, Inc., 860 N.E.2d 713 (N.Y. 2006) and 486 F.3d 78 (2d Cir. 2007). That case arose after a widow tried to donate a kidney from her deceased husband to the husband's longtime friend. One of the kidneys was sent to the friend's hospital, but anatomical abnormalities (renal artery aneurysms) made the kidney unsuitable for transplantation. When the friend's surgeon asked for the second kidney, he was told that it had already been transplanted into another person. The widow argued that she intended for any donation to be limited to the longtime friend, and there were questions whether the second kidney had in fact been transplanted when the call came from the friend's doctor. As it turned out, immunological testing demonstrated that the kidneys were not compatible with the friend and could not have been transplanted into him. For that reason, the New York Court of Appeals did not decide whether a disappointed transplant recipient might have a cause of action under New York public health law for failure to receive the transplant. The court did conclude that a disappointed transplant recipient is not able to bring a cause of action for conversion.

Whether or not potential recipients enjoy legal rights to a transplant, they may have a valid claim if they lose an opportunity for an organ because of a transplant program's malfeasance. Litigation against the liver transplant program at University of California-Irvine precipitated a shutting down of the program by the federal government. A patient sued the program, claiming that it wrongfully denied her an organ on many occasions over a four-year period. In supporting her claim, the patient cited a UNOS document indicating that the transplant program had declined organs offered by UNOS for the woman approximately 40 times. Irvine v. Regents of the University of California, 57 Cal. Rptr. 3d 500 (Ct. App. 2007) (reinstating claim and remanding for consideration by the trial court). During its investigation of the program, Medicare found that the program lacked adequate staffing, resulting in a very high level of deaths among patients on the waiting list. Charles Ornstein & Alan Zarembo, Hospital Halts Liver Transplant Program, L.A. Times, Nov. 11, 2005, at A1.

5. *Local vs. National Waiting Lists.* Another controversial issue has been the use of local, regional, and national waiting lists rather than a single national list. As the liver allocation policy indicates, people on the local waiting list generally have priority over people on the regional waiting list, who in turn have priority over people on the national waiting list. Some people are listed on multiple local waiting lists, and some health care plans require their members to be listed on the local waiting list for transplant "centers of excellence," but most people are listed only on the local waiting list where they reside. In recent years, the emphasis on geography has been reduced. In December 2010, for example, Status 1A patients on the regional waiting list were given parity with Status 1A patients on the local waiting list.

As a result of the emphasis on local lists, patients in some parts of the country may wait only a few days for a new organ while patients in other parts of the country may wait a few months or longer, or die while waiting. This disparity explained in part why former baseball star Mickey Mantle received a liver two days after going on the waiting list. In the region for his organ procurement agency, there was a waiting list at the time of only 3.3 days for someone with Mantle's severity of illness, while the national average was 78 days. For all liver transplants regardless of severity of illness, the average wait varied across the country from 18 to 443 days.

The use of local waiting lists also means that persons with a relatively low priority for an organ transplant will receive organs before persons with a higher priority who live in other parts of the country. At one time, local waiting lists primarily reflected the inability to transport an organ from one part of the country to another before the organ deteriorated, but currently, kidneys and livers generally can be retrieved from a deceased person in one region and flown to a recipient in another region. (Hearts and lungs can be preserved outside the body for 4-6 hours, livers for 12-24 hours, and kidneys for 48-72 hours.) Why do you suppose, then, that priority is given first to people in the local area or region?

6. *Social Worth.* When kidney dialysis first became available, there were not enough dialysis machines for all those who needed treatment. Hospitals therefore established committees to decide who would receive dialysis. One member of such a committee was quoted as follows:

> The choices were hard. . . . I remember voting against a young woman who was a known prostitute. I found I couldn't vote for her, rather than another candidate, a young wife and mother. I also voted against a young man who, until he learned he had renal failure, had been a ne'er do-well, a real playboy. He promised he would reform his character, go back to school, and so on, if only he were selected for treatment. But I felt I'd lived enough to know that a person like that won't really do what he was promising at the time.

Renée C. Fox & Judith P. Swazey, The Courage to Fail 232 (1974). Discomfort with the selection process led Congress in 1972 to provide Medicare coverage for any person with kidney failure who needed dialysis. Roger W. Evans et al., Implications for Health Care Policy: A Social and Demographic Profile of Hemodialysis Patients in the United States, 245 JAMA 487 (1981).

Most commentators reject social worth as a criterion for organ allocation. Some of the reasons are presented in the following passage:

> A patient's contribution to society—or social worth—should not be a factor in allocation decisions. Such judgments are usually defended as attempts to maximize the return on society's investment in medical resources. One common use is to justify the denial of care to the elderly, who some argue no longer make a positive contribution to the social good. . . .
>
> A social worth criterion can also be used to justify discrimination against the young and virtually any other group not actively involved in the economic productivity of society, on the grounds that those who have put the most into society are entitled to get the most back out of it. Distinctions can be made among economic contributions as well; for instance, white collar workers with higher salaries may be favored over blue collar workers or the working poor. Social worth can also be measured by noneconomic criteria. Artists, writers, musicians, and other cultural elite may be favored over average citizens, and people with dependents may be preferred over those without families.
>
> Because of the pluralistic values of society, any single definition of social contribution or social worth is inherently suspect. Social worth judgments often reflect the preferences and values of individual decision makers rather than any objective criteria. In addition, by assuming that members of a certain group make greater social contributions than others, a social worth criterion ignores diversity and the value of each individual.

Council on Ethical and Judicial Affairs, American Medical Association, Ethical Considerations in the Allocation of Organs and Other Scarce Medical Resources Among Patients, 155 Arch. Intern. Med. 29 (1995).

While social worth criteria may generally be inappropriate, might there be some circumstances when they are relevant? Consider the following perspective:

> Yet Dr. [Mark] Siegler said he would exempt Mickey Mantle from his rule [that people with liver failure from alcoholism should go to the bottom of the transplant waiting list] because the baseball legend is "a real American hero." He said Mr. Mantle, "who captured the imagination of a generation through his skill and ability and personality," should not be lumped in with the rest of the population. . . . "I think we have to give deference to the rare heroes in American life," he added. "We don't have enough of these people in America, and when one comes along, we have got to take them with all their warts and failures and treat them differently."

Gina Kolata, Transplants, Morality and Mickey, N.Y. Times, June 11, 1995, §4, at 5.

Is Dr. Siegler's proposal any different than our country's practice of spending millions of dollars more to protect the President from assassination than to protect the lives of citizens living in high crime areas? Or what if you were a hospital attorney and you received a call from the transplant service because a liver was available for transplantation but the person at the top of the waiting list was someone who had been convicted multiple times for child sex abuse? Would it matter if the person was still in prison? Would it matter if the person was serving a life sentence without parole?

Is it consistent to consider costs when rationing care but not to consider social value? For example, assume we would deny someone care because the costs of the care are very high (e.g., $500,000), and the benefits of care seem very low (e.g., an extra few months of life in a permanently unconscious state). If the costs to society of the person's medical treatment matter, then why doesn't it matter whether the person will recover with treatment, return to work, and benefit society?

As mentioned, commentators generally reject social worth as a legitimate criterion. Nevertheless, it is still an unwritten consideration employed by physicians who refer patients for transplants or by transplant surgeons who accept patients on referral.

7. *Individual Responsibility.* Should we take into account the extent to which people are "responsible" for their need for an organ transplant? For example, should people who need a liver because of alcoholic liver disease be given lower priority than people who need a transplant because of a congenital defect in their liver? Consider the following affirmative response to this question:

> We suggest that patients who develop ESLD [end-stage liver disease] through no fault of their own (e.g., those with congenital biliary atresia or primary biliary cirrhosis) should have a higher priority in receiving a liver transplant than those whose liver disease results from failure to obtain treatment for alcoholism. . . . Although alcoholics cannot be held responsible for their disease, once their condition has been diagnosed they can be held responsible for seeking treatment and preventing the complication of ARESLD [alcohol-related end-stage liver disease]. . . . We are not suggesting that some lives and behaviors have greater value than others. . . . But we are holding people responsible for their personal effort. . . .

Much of the initial success in securing public and political approval for liver transplantation was achieved by focusing media and political attention not on adults but on children dying of ESLD. The public may not support transplantation for patients with ARESLD in the same way that they have endorsed this procedure for babies born with biliary atresia. . . . Just because a majority of the public holds these views does not mean they are right, but the moral intuition of the public . . . reflects community values that must be seriously considered.

Alvin H. Moss & Mark Siegler, Should Alcoholics Compete Equally for Liver Transplantation?, 265 JAMA 1296-1297 (1991).

In response to the argument that persons with alcohol-related liver failure are being singled out when other persons become sick as a result of voluntary behavior, including smokers with chronic lung disease, athletes who sustain injuries, and people who develop coronary artery disease from poor diet and insufficient exercise, Moss and Siegler respond,

[t]he critical distinguishing factor for treatment of ARESLD is the scarcity of the resource needed to treat it. The resources needed to treat most of these other conditions are only moderately or relatively scarce, and patients with these diseases or injuries can receive a share of the resources . . . roughly equivalent to their need. [Id. at 1296.]

In a companion article a different perspective was presented:

We could rightly preclude alcoholics from transplantation only if we assume that qualification for a new organ requires some level of moral virtue or is canceled by some level of moral vice. But there is absolutely no agreement—and there is likely to be none—about what constitutes moral virtue and vice and what rewards and penalties they deserve. The assumption that undergirds the moral argument for precluding alcoholics is thus unacceptable. Moreover, even if we could agree . . . upon the kind of misconduct we would be looking for, the fair weighting of such a consideration would entail highly intrusive investigations into patients' moral habits—investigations universally thought repugnant. . . . We do not seek to determine whether a particular transplant candidate is an abusive parent or a dutiful daughter, whether candidates cheat on their income taxes or their spouses, or whether potential recipients pay their parking tickets or routinely lie when they think it is in their best interests. We refrain from considering such judgments for several good reasons: (1) We have genuine and well-grounded doubts about comparative degrees of voluntariness and, therefore, *cannot pass judgment fairly.* (2) Even if we could assess degrees of voluntariness reliably, we *cannot know what penalties different degrees of misconduct deserve.* (3) *Judgments of this kind could not be made consistently in our medical system*—and a fundamental requirement of a fair system in allocating scarce resources is that it treat all in need of certain goods on the same standard, without unfair discrimination by group.

Carl Cohen et al., Alcoholics and Liver Transplantation, 265 JAMA 1299, 1299-1300 (1991) (emphasis in original).

8. *Quality of Life.* The UNOS guidelines do not include a criterion for quality of life, perhaps because persons with a permanently low quality of life never make it

onto a waiting list. In a survey of pediatric transplant centers, researchers found that more than 40 percent of programs would automatically deny an organ transplant to a child suffering from severe (IQ < 35) or profound (IQ < 20) neurodevelopmental delay. Christopher T. Richards et al., Use of Neurodevelopmental Delay in Solid Organ Transplant Decisions, 13 Pediatric Transplantation 843, 847-848 (2009).

Should quality of life matter?

> . . . If for example some people were given life-saving treatment in preference to others because they had a better quality of life than those others, or more dependents and friends, or because they were considered more useful, this would amount to regarding such people as more valuable than others on that account. Indeed it would be tantamount, literally, to sacrificing the lives of others so that they might continue to live.
>
> Because my own life would be better and even of more value to me if I were healthier, fitter, had more money, more friends, more lovers, more children, more life expectancy, more everything I want, it does not follow that others are entitled to decide that because I lack some or all of these things I am less entitled to health care resources, or less worthy to receive those resources, than others, or that those resources would somehow be wasted on me.

John Harris, QALYfying the Value of Life, 13 J. Med. Ethics 117, 121 (1987).

> The appeal of considering [duration and quality of life] can be brought out by a contrast with an alternative position, namely that what is valuable are lives, not lifeyears or their quality. From this point of view society should aim purely and simply to keep the number of deaths to a minimum. It would follow that one should strive to save a baby who can only live another hour of acute suffering just as much as one who will have a happy and fruitful existence for three score years and ten. The two individuals are both human and subjects of consciousness; and surely at least some of the significance that is attributed to these characteristics is adventitious. An evaluation of life and lives without regard to actual or potential [length and quality of life] seems very incomplete. . . . Surely health is a *sine qua non* for the whole gamut of activities, experiences, aspirations and attainment of goals which make our lives valuable to us.

John Cubbon, The Principle of QALY Maximisation as the Basis for Allocating Health Care Resources, 17 J. Med. Ethics 181, 182 (1991).

9. *The Tension Between Social Utility and Equality.* As the previous notes suggest, in choosing criteria for allocating organs, a critical concern is the tension between maximizing social utility and treating all persons equitably. The local guidelines used by transplant programs to decide whether a patient should be placed on the waiting list tend to emphasize utilitarian criteria, including likelihood that the transplant surgery will go well and expected duration of benefit for the recipient. The UNOS guidelines for ranking persons on the waiting list give more weight to equitable considerations like time spent waiting for an organ. How do you think the balance should be drawn? In that regard, consider the following perspectives:

> . . . The fundamental ethical conflict in the distribution of scarce resources is between doing the most good with a scarce resource and ensuring that it is distributed fairly. How these values should be traded off, particularly when the good in ques-

tion is needed for life itself, is controversial among not only moral philosophers but also the general public. As a result, there is a strong temptation to seek to avoid or obscure the ethical or value judgments in selection of recipients, and the principal means of doing so is by appeals . . . to medical criteria for selecting recipients. . . .

It is important to emphasize that there are *no* value-neutral selection criteria that could permit bypassing the need to make ethical judgments in the recipient selection process. Notions of medical criteria, medical eligibility, or medical need for treatment, so common in medical practice generally, implicitly embody value judgments when used in determining how a scarce resource like organ transplantation will be distributed. . . .

I believe the crux of the fairness issue is whether it requires some form of random selection among all those in need . . . or whether it merely requires that irrelevant grounds such as racial or other prejudices not be allowed to influence the selection process. These two interpretations of what fairness requires—the equal chance or lottery interpretation and the no-irrelevant-distinctions interpretation—have dramatically different implications. If fairness requires that all in need have equal chances of being selected, then that interpretation will be in strong conflict with the various factors [e.g., length of life and quality of life gained from a transplant] . . . that are relevant in doing the most good possible with these scarce resources. . . . A simple lottery selection process among all who want and might receive any benefit from transplantation would require random selection between [a 25-year-old person in otherwise good health and a 70-year-old person for whom the transplant is unlikely to be successful and who is expected even with a transplant to die from an unrelated medical condition within one or two years after transplantation]. Even the hardiest of egalitarians and the strongest proponents of fairness are very unlikely to be willing to support a random selection process between these two patients.

However, it also seems unacceptable to let very small differences in the expected good to be produced determine whether one gives the transplant to one rather than another patient, at least if doing so means ignoring the requirement of fairness that all in need be given an equal chance to be selected. . . .

What is the alternative interpretation of the requirement of equity or fairness in the selection of recipients? I have already indicated one aspect of this interpretation, that no irrelevant bases such as race or gender influence the selection process; fairness will thus exclude some factors from influencing the selection process. With this alternative interpretation, how do we respond to the idea that none morally deserves the benefit more than another and so each should be given an equal chance to be selected? There are at least two possible lines of argument in this case that are not themselves incompatible.

The first holds that what fairness requires is that all members of society must have a roughly equal input into the decision process that will determine what criteria are to be employed for selection of recipients. Moreover, that decision process should be one that imposes some condition of impartiality on those taking part in it, so that participants do not simply tailor their proposals to suit their own known interests. . . .

The second line of argument . . . offers an alternative substantive interpretation. . . . According to this argument, which persons happen to become diseased and in need of an organ for transplant, which properties particular patients happen to have that influence their relative desirability or undesirability for transplant within a system that attempts to do the most good with scarce organs . . . are all essentially random matters. They are all outcomes of a biological and social lottery. In this argument, the randomization that fairness requires is not to be imposed by a deliberate lottery after all the facts are known about how each particular individual will fare under the system. Instead, fairness is achieved by randomization at an earlier stage, in the interplay of forces that determine who will and who will not be favored by a system that distributes organs according to the criterion that benefit is to be maximized. . . .

Dan W. Brock, Ethical Issues in Recipient Selection for Organ Transplantation, *in* Organ Substitution Technology: Ethical, Legal, and Public Policy Issues 86, 87-95 (Deborah Matheiu ed., 1988).

Brock goes on to describe three methods for choosing organ recipients from a waiting list of persons who are candidates for organ transplantation: a simple random lottery, use of medical criteria to rank candidates in terms of the benefit they will likely receive from a transplant, and a weighted lottery in which a candidate's chance of being picked for an organ transplant would depend on the medical benefit expected from an organ transplant. With a weighted lottery, anyone on the waiting list would have a shot at a new organ, but persons with a relatively low expected benefit would have a low likelihood of being chosen to receive the organ. Id. at 96-97. For example, he suggests placing patients into categories of low, medium, and high expected benefit with the medium patients having twice the likelihood of receiving an organ as the low patients, and the high patients having thrice the likelihood of receiving an organ as the low patients.

Brock suggests that there may be no unfairness when medical criteria are used since the winners and losers are ultimately determined by a "biological and social lottery." In that regard, consider the following argument:

. . . [T]he environment is shaped not simply by natural, inevitable forces but also has been shaped to serve the interests of some segments of society at the expense of others. The socio-political environment cannot always be justified by the operation of neutral or objective principles or by principles that are otherwise morally valid.

. . . Social norms develop not because they are pre-ordained, but because they serve the needs of social groups that are dominant either in numbers or power. . . .

Social forces cause disability by commission when environmental pollution leads to lung diseases or cancers, when lead-based paint damages the neurological systems of children, or when unchecked violence results in traumatic injury.

Social organization causes disability by omission when priorities are established for medical research and treatment. Some illnesses, such as heart disease and cancer, are the subject of vast research expenditures, while other illnesses receive disproportionately little federal research funding. Patients with intensively studied diseases are much more likely to be saved from disabling symptoms than patients with neglected diseases. . . . Moreover, when treatments are developed for a particular disease, they are often based on the norm of a patient without any coexisting illnesses. As a result, patients with multiple illnesses are less able to benefit from treatment. For example, persons with chronic lung disease are less likely to be viewed as appropriate candidates for coronary artery surgery. . . .

All of the[se] disadvantaging aspects of social structure . . . may act to limit a disabled person's access to organ transplants. If there had been more aggressive efforts in the past to treat disabling conditions targeted by eligibility criteria for transplantation, they would not now have as much effect as they do on organ transplant success. Unfortunately, much of the neglect of certain diseases reflects the invidious prejudices that people have about those diseases. Psychiatric illnesses have not often been viewed as real illnesses, for example; other diseases, like obesity, have been ignored because they have been viewed as self-inflicted.

David Orentlicher, Destructuring Disability: Rationing of Health Care and Unfair Discrimination Against the Sick, 31 Harv. C.R.-C.L. L. Rev. 49, 66-71 (1996).

While it is useful to frame the debate in terms of the trade-off between social utility and social equality, it is also important to understand how unhelpful this framing can be. It is not clear what content exists in the idea that people need to be treated as equals. Peter Westen, The Empty Idea of Equality, 95 Harv. L. Rev. 537 (1982). We can all agree that equal treatment is a moral imperative, but we can also agree that we do not want to treat everyone in the same way. People are different, and those differences need to be recognized. For example, we require all children to attend school (or be schooled at home), but we do not impose the same requirement on adults. Accordingly, we need to decide when people are the same for purposes of organ transplantation and when they are different. In this regard, it is not clear whether differences in expected length of life or expected quality of life mean that people should be treated differently for purposes of kidney transplantation or whether length and quality of life are irrelevant to organ allocation decisions.

10. *Racial Inequity*. One important area of concern in terms of equity is the evidence that African Americans are disadvantaged when it comes to receiving kidney transplants. Despite the fact that African Americans are more likely than whites to need a kidney transplant, they are less likely to receive a transplant. The disparity in access to kidney transplants remains even after researchers control for confounding variables like cause of the kidney failure, age, and family income. Much of the difference may reflect the fact that white persons waiting for a kidney are more likely to have a good tissue match with an available organ since most organs come from whites. Important questions are whether the effects of poorer tissue matching can be overcome by immunosuppressive drugs and whether achieving more successful transplants is sufficient reason to disadvantage a racial group that is already disadvantaged in the health care system. See Ian Ayres et al., Unequal Racial Access to Kidney Transplantation, 46 Vand. L. Rev. 805 (1993); Council on Ethical and Judicial Affairs, Black-White Disparities in Health Care, 263 JAMA 2344 (1990); Arnold M. Epstein et al., Racial Disparities in Access to Renal Transplantation, 343 New Eng. J. Med. 1537 (2000); Sayeed K. Malek et al., Racial and Ethnic Disparities in Kidney Transplantation, 24 Transplant International 419 (2011).

The inequities in allocation may reflect and/or contribute to a lower trust in the organ retrieval and allocation systems and a lower willingness to donate organs among African Americans. Laura A. Siminoff et al., Racial Disparities in Preferences and Perceptions Regarding Organ Donation, 21 J. Gen. Intern. Med. 995 (2006). These issues are compounded by organ procurement organization staff being less likely to discuss organ donation or to discuss the details of organ donation with African American family members. Laura A. Siminoff et al., Comparison of Black and White Families' Experiences and Perceptions Regarding Organ Donation Requests, 31 Crit. Care Med. 146 (2003).

In response to the concerns about racial disparities in kidney transplantation, OPTN/UNOS amended its allocation policy in November 2002 to increase minority access to kidney transplants. Recent studies had indicated that OPTN/UNOS could reduce its emphasis on tissue matching while still maintaining a high rate of long-term success. Accordingly under the new policy, tissue matching is relevant only in a few areas (i.e., when the donor and recipient match perfectly or when there is matching at the "DR locus"). The change in policy has reduced the magnitude of the disparities. Malek et al., supra, at 421.

Racial disparities also existed in liver transplantation, but adoption of the MELD scores has resulted in elimination of an association between race and the receipt of a liver transplant once patients are added to the wait list. However, disparities based on the sex of the patient remain, with women less likely than men to receive a transplant. Cynthia A. Moylan et al., Disparities in Liver Transplantation Before and After Introduction of the MELD Score, 300 JAMA 2371 (2008). In addition, disparities on the basis of race still exist with respect to being referred to a transplant center for evaluation. A. K. Mathur et al., Race and Ethnicity in Access to and Outcomes of Liver Transplantation, 9 Am. J. Transplantation 2662 (2009).

11. *The Americans with Disabilities Act.* The Americans with Disabilities Act (ADA), 42 U.S.C. §§12101-12213, prohibits discrimination against persons with disabilities in employment, education, housing, health care, and other services on account of their disabilities, unless the disabilities are relevant to the decision being made. Thus, for example, a construction company could refuse to hire someone confined to a wheelchair as a roofer but could not refuse to hire that person as a desk clerk. Similarly, an organ transplant program could not deny a kidney transplant to a blind person simply because the person is blind. Discrimination is also prohibited when it results from more "neutral" criteria that have a disproportionate effect (disparate impact) on persons with disabilities. For example, it might violate the ADA to deny an organ transplant to persons without a driver's license since a requirement to have a driver's license disadvantages blind persons. Which of the criteria for organ allocation discussed above potentially implicate the ADA? So far, no cases have been decided on this question.

Even if the person's disability is relevant to the decision being made, the person may not be denied the benefit if "reasonable accommodations" would overcome the effects of the disability. In some cases, a person's psychiatric condition might interfere with the success of an organ transplant. If psychiatric counseling would keep the condition under control, the organ transplant program might have to provide the counseling as part of its treatment program.

Another important question is whether the ADA limits the ability of transplant programs to take into account unrelated medical considerations that affect a person's likelihood of benefiting from a new organ. For example, would it violate the ADA if a transplant candidate is denied a kidney because the candidate has lung disease in addition to kidney failure, and the lung disease will shorten the person's life expectancy? Most likely, the lung disease would be considered a "relevant" difference under the ADA, but other criteria used by transplant programs (e.g., lack of mental retardation) are suspect under the ADA.

For further discussion, see David Orentlicher, Psychosocial Assessment of Organ Transplant Candidates and the Americans with Disabilities Act, 18 Gen. Hosp. Psychiatry 5S (1996); David Orentlicher, Destructuring Disability: Rationing of Health Care and Unfair Discrimination Against the Sick, 31 Harv. C.R.-C.L. L. Rev. 49 (1996). The role of the ADA in governing other kinds of rationing decisions is also taken up in Chapter 2.A.3.

12. *Absolute vs. Relative Scarcity.* Organ allocation presents a compelling case to consider criteria for rationing limited medical resources because the short supply of organs creates a situation of absolute scarcity: We know that giving an organ to one person rather than others means some people will die. Financial resources are also scarce, and affect organ transplantation as well as other life-saving medical procedures, but they are not scarce in the same absolute sense. Instead, we must decide in more relative terms which medical conditions or procedures deserve more funding than others, and whether medical needs are more demanding than other social needs. Resource allocation issues at this broader level are debated in many of the same moral terms as have been introduced here, but the legal context is framed in terms of the right to payment under public and private insurance, and in terms of disability discrimination.

13. *Additional Reading.* For additional discussion of organ allocation issues, see Douglas J. Besharov & Jessica Dunsay Silver, Rationing Access to Advanced Medical Techniques, 8 J. Leg. Med. 507 (1987); F. Daniel Davis, The Ethics of Organ Allocation (2007) (paper prepared for the President's Council on Bioethics); Richard A. Epstein, Mortal Peril: Our Inalienable Right to Health Care? 263-282 (1997); John F. Kilner, Who Lives? Who Dies? Ethical Criteria in Patient Selection (1990); Robert Veatch, Transplantation Ethics (2000); David L. Weimer, Medical Governance (2010).

5

Reproductive Rights and Genetic Technologies

This chapter examines both the state's right to regulate individual reproductive capacity and the use of genetic technologies. We treat reproduction as a discrete subject area, separate from the state's ability to control other sorts of human behavior, because human reproduction raises especially controversial moral, ethical, and legal issues. Reproduction is not just another bodily function; the creation of human life implicates profound moral and religious issues not encountered in other medical arenas. Therefore, many special constitutional, statutory, and common law rules have been developed to resolve disputes arising from human reproductive capacity. As you study this chapter, consider whether the rules adopted differ significantly from the rules used in other, similar disputes and whether these differences are warranted from a public policy or legal standpoint. Reproduction is at least partly a question of genetics, but advances in genetics have profound implications beyond reproduction. The final section of this chapter will focus on the legal implications of advances in genetics outside of reproduction.

This chapter will focus initially on four broad aspects of reproductive health law. The first two sections of the chapter explore the conflict between state and individual interests in controlling reproductive capacity. Do people have a constitutionally protected interest in either procreating or in refraining from procreation? Do states have the power to control or to influence personal reproductive decisions? The third section explores the legal recognition of fetal interests as distinguishable from and sometimes conflicting with those of parents. Should pregnant women be subjected to criminal or civil sanctions where their behavior presents risks of fetal injury? The fourth section focuses on the moral, ethical, and legal implications of new reproductive technologies. Who should be considered to be the legal parents of a child who is conceived from donor sperm and egg and gestated by a willing surrogate? The fifth and final section of the chapter explores the legal implications of advances in genetics and the regulation of genetic technologies. Should cloning and related procedures be allowed for reproductive, research, or therapeutic purposes? Should scientists be permitted to patent life forms and genes?

Note: Many Streams or One River: Reproductive Rights and Substantive Due Process

We all have an interest in controlling our own reproductive capacity. Through reproduction, we transmit our individual genetic heritage to a new generation, and in the process are likely to experience the rewards and pains of parenting. Biological reproduction is also associated with cultural reproduction: the ability to pass along values, religious beliefs, and one's cultural heritage. The burdens of reproduction are well known. For women, pregnancy and delivery present certain health risks. For both women and men, unwanted parenthood can be emotionally and financially burdensome. Techniques for avoiding reproduction, such as abstinence, condoms, and oral contraceptives, each have their drawbacks.

Government entities can also have an interest in controlling the reproductive capacity of certain individuals or groups. In societies struggling with overpopulation, the government may have an interest in discouraging reproduction. What is more, historically many governments have expressed an interest in preventing reproduction by some individuals, such as persons with disabilities or members of disfavored ethnic or racial minorities. Other societies, on the other hand, may wish to encourage stable or increasing rates of reproduction. This can be accomplished by restricting access to technologies designed to prevent reproduction. Additionally, many societies have sought to protect the new life created through procreation, sometimes at the very earliest stages of its existence within a woman's body. Finally, legislation in these areas often reflects moral and religious perspectives on sexuality, procreation, and fetal interests.

It is therefore not surprising that courts and legislatures have been occupied with the task of balancing these often conflicting individual and social interests. What is the nature of a person's interest in controlling reproduction? Do we have a constitutional right to control procreative capacity that is distinguishable from the right to control medical treatment? Is the right to procreate the mirror image of the right not to procreate? When may the state intrude on personal procreative choice, by either attempting to prevent or to encourage procreation?

Judicial review of state policies under the Constitution's Fourteenth Amendment due process clause raises some troubling constitutional history. You will recall from basic constitutional law that, in the early part of the last century, the Supreme Court took an "activist" approach to reviewing the constitutional validity of state economic regulation under the due process clause. In Lochner v. New York, 198 U.S. 45 (1905), the Court struck down a state's regulation of maximum work hours as a violation of the fundamental right to contract. However, the onslaught of programs in the late 1930s designed to ameliorate the Depression caused the Court to retreat by substituting a more deferential, rational basis, standard of review of state economic regulation. Thereafter, the *Lochner* era of "substantive due process" was thoroughly repudiated as a valid form of judicial review for economic regulation. See Ferguson v. Skrupa, 372 U.S. 726 (1963). It survived only for legislation that affects special categories of "fundamental" interests or liberties, and even then remains under suspicion and sometimes even under attack.

Courts attempting to define the nature of individual interests in procreation and to mark the permissible scope of state regulation have struggled in the shadow of the *Lochner* era. Judges have been forced to confront three important issues. What is the constitutional source of the right to procreate? What are the permissible limits of state regulation? Will the judiciary be able to avoid another *Lochner* debacle in which there is widespread criticism of its fundamental authority to engage in searching substantive due process review?

A. A RIGHT TO PROCREATE?

■ BUCK v. BELL
274 U.S. 200 (1927)

HOLMES, Justice.

This is a writ of error to review a judgment of the Supreme Court of Appeals of the State of Virginia, affirming a judgment of the Circuit Court of Amherst County, by which the defendant in error, the superintendent of the State Colony for Epileptics and Feeble Minded, was ordered to perform the operation of salpingectomy upon Carrie Buck, the plaintiff in error, for the purpose of making her sterile. 130 S.E. 516. The case comes here upon the contention that the statute authorizing the judgment is void under the Fourteenth Amendment as denying to the plaintiff in error due process of law and the equal protection of the laws.

Carrie Buck is a feeble-minded white woman who was committed to the State Colony above mentioned in due form. She is the daughter of a feeble-minded mother in the same institution, and the mother of an illegitimate feeble-minded child. She was 18 years old at the time of the trial of her case in the Circuit Court in the latter part of 1924. An Act of Virginia approved March 20, 1924 recites that the health of the patient and the welfare of society may be promoted in certain cases by the sterilization of mental defectives, under careful safeguard, etc.; that the sterilization may be effected in males by vasectomy and in females by salpingectomy, without serious pain or substantial danger to life; that the Commonwealth is supporting in various institutions many defective persons who if now discharged would become a menace but if incapable of procreating might be discharged with safety and become self-supporting with benefit to themselves and to society; and that experience has shown that heredity plays an important part in the transmission of insanity, imbecility, etc. The statute then enacts that whenever the superintendent of certain institutions including the above named State Colony shall be of opinion that it is for the best interest of the patients and of society that an inmate under his care should be sexually sterilized, he may have the operation performed upon any patient afflicted with hereditary forms of insanity, imbecility, etc., on complying with the very careful provisions by which the act protects the patients from possible abuse.

The superintendent first presents a petition to the special board of directors of his hospital or colony, stating the facts and the grounds for his opinion, verified by affidavit. Notice of the petition and of the time and place of the hearing in the institution is to be served upon the inmate, and also upon his guardian, and if there is no guardian the superintendent is to apply to the Circuit Court of the County to appoint one. If the inmate is a minor notice also is to be given to his parents, if any, with a copy of the petition. The board is to see to it that the inmate may attend the hearings if desired by him or his guardian. The evidence is all to be reduced to writing, and after the board has made its order for or against the operation, the superintendent, or the inmate, or his guardian, may appeal to the Circuit Court of the County. The Circuit Court may consider the record of the board and the evidence before it and such other admissible evidence as may be offered, and may affirm, revise, or reverse the order of the board and enter such order as it deems just. Finally any party may apply to the Supreme Court of Appeals, which, if it grants the appeal, is to hear the case upon the record of the trial in the Circuit Court and may enter such order as it thinks the Circuit Court should have entered. There can be no doubt that so far as procedure is concerned the rights of the patient are most carefully considered, and as every step in this case was taken in scrupulous compliance with the statute and after months of observation, there is no doubt that in that respect the plaintiff in error has had due process at law.

The attack is not upon the procedure but upon the substantive law. It seems to be contended that in no circumstances could such an order be justified. It certainly is contended that the order cannot be justified upon the existing grounds. The judgment finds the facts that have been recited and that Carrie Buck "is the probable potential parent of socially inadequate offspring, likewise afflicted, that she may be sexually sterilized without detriment to her general health and that her welfare and that of society will be promoted by her sterilization," and thereupon makes the order. In view of the general declarations of the Legislature and the specific findings of the Court obviously we cannot say as matter of law that the grounds do not exist, and if they exist they justify the result. We have seen more than once that the public welfare may call upon the best citizens for their lives. It would be strange if it could not call upon those who already sap the strength of the state for these lesser sacrifices, often not felt to be such by those concerned, in order to prevent our being swamped with incompetence. It is better for all the world, if instead of waiting to execute degenerate offspring for crime, or to let them starve for their imbecility, society can prevent those who are manifestly unfit from continuing their kind. The principle that sustains compulsory vaccination is broad enough to cover cutting the Fallopian tubes. Jacobson v. Massachusetts, 197 U.S. 11. Three generations of imbeciles are enough.

But, it is said, however it might be if this reasoning were applied generally, it fails when it is confined to the small number who are in the institutions named and is not applied to the multitudes outside. It is the usual last resort of constitutional arguments to point out shortcomings of this sort. But the answer is that the law does all that is needed when it does all that it can, indicates a policy, applies it to all within the lines, and seeks to bring within the lines all similarly situated so far and so fast as its means allow. Of course so far as the operations enable those who otherwise must be kept confined to be returned to the world, and thus open the asylum to others, the equality aimed at will be more nearly reached.

Judgment affirmed.

SKINNER v. OKLAHOMA
316 U.S. 535 (1942)

DOUGLAS, Justice.

This case touches a sensitive and important area of human rights. Oklahoma deprives certain individuals of a right which is basic to the perpetuation of a race—the right to have offspring. Oklahoma has decreed the enforcement of its law against petitioner, overruling his claim that it violated the Fourteenth Amendment. Because that decision raised grave and substantial constitutional questions, we granted the petition for certiorari.

The statute involved is Oklahoma's Habitual Criminal Sterilization Act. Okla. Stat. Ann. tit. 57, §171, et seq. That Act defines an "habitual criminal" as a person who, having been convicted two or more times for crimes "amounting to felonies involving moral turpitude" either in an Oklahoma court or in a court of any other state, is thereafter convicted of such a felony in Oklahoma and is sentenced to a term of imprisonment in an Oklahoma penal institution. Machinery is provided for the institution by the Attorney General of a proceeding against such a person in the Oklahoma courts for a judgment that such person shall be rendered sexually sterile. Notice, an opportunity to be heard, and the right to a jury trial are provided. The issues triable in such a proceeding are narrow and confined. If the court or jury finds that the defendant is an "habitual criminal" and that he "may be rendered sexually sterile without detriment to his or her general health," then the court "shall render judgment to the effect that said defendant be rendered sexually sterile," by the operation of vasectomy in case of a male and of salpingectomy in case of a female. Only one other provision of the Act is material here and that is [the section] which provides that "offenses arising out of the violation of the prohibitory laws, revenue acts, embezzlement, or political offenses, shall not come or be considered within the terms of this Act."

Petitioner was convicted in 1926 of the crime of stealing chickens and was sentenced to the Oklahoma State Reformatory. In 1929 he was convicted of the crime of robbery with fire arms and was sentenced to the reformatory. In 1934 he was convicted again of robbery with firearms and was sentenced to the penitentiary. He was confined there in 1935 when the Act was passed. In 1936 the Attorney General instituted proceedings against him. Petitioner in his answer challenged the Act as unconstitutional by reason of the Fourteenth Amendment. A jury trial was had. The court instructed the jury that the crimes of which petitioner had been convicted were felonies involving moral turpitude and that the only question for the jury was whether the operation of vasectomy could be performed on petitioner without detriment to his general health. The jury found that it could be. A judgment directing that the operation of vasectomy be performed on petitioner was affirmed by the Supreme Court of Oklahoma by a 5-4 decision. 115 P.2d 123.

Several objections to the constitutionality of the Act have been pressed upon us. It is urged that the Act cannot be sustained as an exercise of the police power in view of the state of scientific authorities respecting inheritability of criminal traits. It is argued that due process is lacking because under this Act, unlike the act upheld in Buck v. Bell, 274 U.S. 200, the defendant is given no opportunity to be heard on the issue as to whether he is the probable potential parent of socially undesirable offspring. It is also suggested that the Act is penal in character and that the sterilization provided for is cruel and unusual punishment and vocative of the Fourteenth Amendment. We pass those points without intimating an opinion on them, for there is a feature of the Act which clearly condemns it. That is its failure to meet the requirements of the equal protection clause of the Fourteenth Amendment.

We do not stop to point out all of the inequalities in this Act. A few examples will suffice. In Oklahoma grand larceny is a felony. Larceny is grand larceny when the property taken exceeds $20 in value. Embezzlement is punishable "in the manner prescribed for feloniously stealing property of the value of that embezzled." Hence he who embezzles property worth more than $20 is guilty of a felony. A clerk who appropriates over $20 from his employer's till and a stranger who steals the same amount are thus both guilty of felonies. If the latter repeats his act and is convicted three times, he may be sterilized. But the clerk is not subject to the pains and penalties of the Act no matter how large his embezzlements nor how frequent his convictions. A person who enters a chicken coop and steals chickens commits a felony; and he may be sterilized if he is thrice convicted. If, however, he is a bailee of the property and fraudulently appropriates it, he is an embezzler. Hence no matter how habitual his proclivities for embezzlement are and no matter how often his conviction, he may not be sterilized. Thus the nature of the two crimes is intrinsically the same and they are punishable in the same manner. Furthermore, the line between them follows close distinctions. . . . Whether a particular act is larceny by fraud or embezzlement turns not on the intrinsic quality of the act but on when the felonious intent arose. . . .

It was stated in Buck v. Bell, supra, that the claim that state legislation violates the equal protection clause of the Fourteenth Amendment is "the usual last resort of constitutional arguments." Under our constitutional system the states in determining the reach and scope of particular legislation need not provide "abstract symmetry." They may mark and set apart the classes and types of problems according to the needs and as dictated or suggested by experience. . . . Thus, if we had here only a question as to a state's classification of crimes, such as embezzlement or larceny, no substantial federal question would be raised. For a state is not constrained in the exercise of its police power to ignore experience which marks a class of offenders or a family of offenses for special treatment. Nor is it prevented by the equal protection clause from confining "its restrictions to those classes of cases where the need is deemed to be clearest." . . .

But the instant legislation runs afoul of the equal protection clause, though we give Oklahoma that large deference which the rule of the foregoing cases requires. We are dealing here with legislation which involves one of the basic civil rights of man. Marriage and procreation are fundamental to the very existence and survival of the race. The power to sterilize, if exercised, may have subtle, far reaching and devastating effects. In evil or reckless hands it can cause races or types which are inimical to the dominant group to wither and disappear. There is no redemption for the individual whom the law touches. Any experiment which the state conducts is to his irreparable injury. He is forever deprived of a basic liberty. We mention these matters not to reexamine the scope of the police power of the states. We advert to them merely in emphasis of our view that strict scrutiny of the classification which a state makes in a sterilization law is essential, lest unwittingly or otherwise invidious discriminations are made against groups or types of individuals in violation of the constitutional guaranty of just and equal laws. The guaranty of "equal protection of the laws is a pledge of the protection of equal laws." Yick Wo v. Hopkins, 118 U.S. 356, 369. When the law lays an unequal hand on those who have committed intrinsically the same quality of offense and sterilizes one and not the other, it has made as an invidious a discrimination as if it had selected a particular race or nationality for oppressive treatment. Sterilization of those who have thrice committed grand larceny with immunity for those who are embezzlers is a clear, pointed, unmistakable discrimination. Oklahoma makes no attempt to say that he who commits larceny by trespass or trick or fraud has biologically inheritable traits which he who commits embezzlement lacks. Oklahoma's line between larceny by fraud and embezzlement is determined, as we have noted, "with reference to the time when the fraudulent intent to convert the property to the taker's own use" arises. We have not the slightest basis for inferring that that line has any significance in eugenics nor that the inheritability of criminal traits follows the neat legal distinctions which the law has marked between those two offenses. In terms of fines and imprisonment the crimes of larceny and embezzlement rate the same under the Oklahoma code. Only when it comes to sterilization are the pains and penalties of the law different. The equal protection clause would indeed be a formula of empty words if such conspicuously artificial lines could be drawn. In Buck v. Bell, supra, the Virginia statute was upheld though it applied only to feebleminded persons in institutions of the state. But it was pointed out that "so far as the operations enable those who otherwise must be kept confined to be returned to the world, and thus open the asylum to others, the equality aimed at will be more nearly reached." Here there is no such saving feature. Embezzlers are forever free. Those who steal or take in other ways are not. If such a classification were permitted, distinctions which are "very largely dependent upon history for explanation" could readily become a rule of human genetics.

Reversed.

STONE, Chief Justice, concurring.

I concur in the result, but I am not persuaded that we are aided in reaching it by recourse to the equal protection clause.

If Oklahoma may resort generally to the sterilization of criminals on the assumption that their propensities are transmissible to future generations by inheritance, I seriously doubt that the equal protection clause requires it to apply the measure to all criminals in the first instance, or to none.

Moreover, if we must presume that the legislature knows—what science has been unable to ascertain—that the criminal tendencies of any class of habitual offenders are transmissible regardless of the varying mental characteristics of its individuals, I should suppose that we must likewise presume that the legislature, in its wisdom, knows that the criminal tendencies of some classes of offenders are more likely to be transmitted than those of others. And so I think the real question we have to consider is not one of equal protection, but whether the wholesale condemnation of a class to such an invasion of personal liberty, without opportunity to any individual to show that his is not the type of case which would justify resort to it, satisfies the demands of due process. . . .

Science has found and the law has recognized that there are certain types of mental deficiency associated with delinquency which are inheritable. But the state does not contend—nor can there be any pretense—that either common knowledge or experience, or scientific investigation, has given assurance that the criminal tendencies of any class of habitual offenders are universally or even generally inheritable. In such circumstances, inquiry whether such is the fact in the case of any particular individual cannot rightly be dispensed with. Whether the procedure by which a statute carries its mandate into execution satisfies due process is a matter of judicial cognizance. A law which condemns, without hearing, all the individuals of a class to so harsh a measure as the present because some or even many merit condemnation, is lacking in the first principles of due process. . . .

[Justice Jackson's concurring opinion is omitted.]

Notes: The Right to Procreate

1. *The Right to Procreate.* Did Justice Holmes suggest that there was a "fundamental" right to procreate? What standard of review did the *Buck* court apply to its review of the Virginia sterilization statute? The Court cites Jacobson v. Massachusetts, 197 U.S. 11 (1904), for the proposition that the state's interest in protecting public health was sufficient to support a program of compulsory vaccination. Are there any significant differences between the intrusions to individual liberty created by vaccination as opposed to sterilization? Note that the historical record suggests that Carrie Buck and her family did not actually suffer from "feeble-mindedness." See University of Virginia, Eugenics Historical Materials, available at www.hsl.virginia .edu/historical/eugenics/. See also Paul A. Lombardo, Three Generations, No Imbeciles: Eugenics, the Supreme Court, and *Buck v. Bell* (2008); Edward J. Larson, Putting Buck v. Bell in Scientific and Historical Context, 39 Pepp. L. Rev. 119 (2011); Victoria Nourse, Buck v. Bell: A Constitutional Tragedy from a Lost World, 39 Pepp. L. Rev. 101 (2011). See also Thomas v. Hickman, 2009 WL 1273190 (E.D. Cal. 2009) (prisoner claims Fourteenth Amendment violation of right to procreate, alleging medical procedure resulted in sterilization without consent).

The *Skinner* decision is often thought to have overruled Buck v. Bell. Is this so? Does Justice Douglas identify the right to procreate as "fundamental"? Of what significance is the fact that *Skinner* was decided as an equal protection case rather than a substantive due process case? What was the flaw in the Oklahoma statute? Does the Court's analysis suggest that mandatory sterilization statutes could be upheld if they were supported by sufficiently rigorous scientific evidence about the heritability of a socially costly trait? There was no evidence of a hereditable condition in Jack Skinner's case. He had lost a foot in an accident and had difficulty finding work to support himself and his wife. See Lombardo, supra. For recent explorations of the right to procreate, see Carter J. Dillard, Rethinking the Procreative Right, 10 Yale Hum. Rts. & Dev. L.J. 1, 3 (2007) (suggesting narrow definition of right); John A. Robertson, Assisting Reproduction, Choosing Genes, and the Scope of Reproductive Freedom, 76 Geo. Wash. L. Rev. 1490 (2009) (right to procreate, assisted reproductive technologies, and gene selection).

2. *Eugenics. Buck* and *Skinner* arose from what might be called the first wave of the genetic revolution. Public interest in genetics and Darwinism was high during the early 1900s. Leading commentators suggested that individuals and society should consider whether patterns of reproductive behavior were likely to "improve" or lead to the "deterioration" of the human stock. These eugenic theories were combined with fears about the "quality" of immigrants and other disfavored members

of society, whose reproductive tendencies were viewed as a potential assault upon society. The sterilization statutes at issue in *Buck* and *Skinner* were the legislative outgrowth of these popular concerns.

During and after World War II, eugenic theories became closely associated with Nazi atrocities, which included forced sterilizations and the extermination of those deemed to sap the strength of the "Aryan race." The scientific and moral flaws of early eugenic theories were exposed and publicized. Public reaction against state-organized eugenic policies became quite strong. Despite this change in public attitudes, some social programs designed to "encourage" sterilization among poor persons or those with mental disabilities continued well into the 1960s. See, e.g., The Oxford Handbook of the History of Eugenics (Alison Bashford & Philippa Levine eds., 2010); Genes and Human Self-Knowledge: Historical and Philosophical Reflections on Modern Genetics (Robert F. Weir et al. eds., 1994); Note, 72 Geo. Wash. L. Rev. 862 (2004).

We are now in the second wave of the genetic revolution. At the turn of the century, scientists in the United States and elsewhere joined together to identify and map the human "genome," the sequence of genes found in human beings. The "working draft" was completed in 2000 but the process of identifying, understanding, and exploiting knowledge about specific human genes is still in the early stages. The federal government's Human Genome Web site offers a number of useful resources. See http://genomics.energy.gov/. Genetic information can be used, for good or for ill, by individuals, employers, insurance companies, health care providers, and government entities. The Genetic Information Nondiscrimination Act of 2008, P.L. 110-233, 122 Stat. 881 (2008), prohibits some forms of genetic discrimination in employment and insurance. See, e.g., Timothy J. Aspinwall, Imperfect Remedies: Legislative Efforts to Prevent Genetic Discrimination, 19 Ann. Health L. 121 (2009-2010); Kathy L. Hudson et al., Keeping Pace with the Times—The Genetic Information Nondiscrimination Act of 2008, 358 New Eng. J. Med. 2661 (2008). Many ethicists argue that people will benefit as advances in genetics produce better information to use in making decisions about whether and how to reproduce. Does it matter, from an ethical or legal standpoint, whether efforts to avoid the reproduction of certain "traits" arise from public or private action? Should it matter whether advances in genetics are used to avoid traits considered to be harmful or to acquire traits considered to be desirable? See, e.g., Bernard G. Prusak, Rethinking "Liberal Eugenics": Reflections and Questions on Habermas on Bioethics, 35(6) Hastings Center Rep. 31 (Nov.-Dec. 2005). We will return to these questions as we consider the connections between genetic information and the use of abortion or assisted reproduction.

3. *Sterilization of Incompetent Persons. Buck* explored the state's ability to impose sterilization upon the mentally incompetent. The issue still arises. See Vaughn v. Ruoff, 253 F.3d 1124 (8th Cir. 2001) (government social worker not entitled to qualified immunity on claim that she violated constitutional rights of mildly retarded woman by threatening loss of children if woman refused to consent to sterilization). The modern debate has centered on the ability of courts to authorize sterilizations when sought by the family or guardian of an incompetent person. In these cases, the "state" is involved only in the sense that the guardians seek judicial authorization of the sterilization procedure. Courts have been confronted with two separate issues: (1) Does this court have jurisdiction over the subject matter of the dispute?

(2) What substantive and procedural rules should be applied to resolve the dispute? The resolution of the second issue is particularly difficult because of the potential conflict between the incompetent's rights to procreate and to refrain from procreation. See, e.g., In re Hayes, 608 P.2d 635 (Wash. 1980).

In *Hayes*, the mother of a girl with severe mental retardation sought a court order specifically authorizing her daughter's sterilization. The trial court held that it did not have the authority to authorize the sterilization. On appeal, the Washington Supreme Court held that the lower court did have jurisdiction over the question and that a petition for sterilization could be granted "in the rare and unusual case that sterilization is in the best interest of the retarded person." 608 P.2d at 637. The court established a framework of procedural and substantive protections designed to ensure that sterilization was necessary to serve the best interests of the individual rather than for the convenience of her caretakers. See also Guardianship of Mary Moe, 960 N.E.2d 350 (Mass. App. 2012) (overturning abortion order under substituted judgment standard and sterilization order where "judge appears to have simply produced the requirement out of thin air"); In re Valerie N., 707 P.2d 760 (Cal. 1985) (en banc) (ban on sterilization of incompetent persons violates their constitutionally protected liberty interests); In re Wirsing, 573 N.W.2d 51 (Mich. 1998) (probate court had jurisdiction to authorize guardian's consent to sterilization; clear and convincing evidence not required). Note that the vast majority of these sterilizations are performed on women. Does this present any ethical or legal concerns? Do statutes prohibiting disability-based discrimination affect the legality of these sterilizations? See Kerry Lynn Macintosh, Brave New Eugenics: Regulating Assisted Reproductive Technologies in the Name of Better Babies, 2010 U. Ill. J.L. Tech. & Pol'y 257 (2010) (drawing connection between constraints on use of assisted reproduction and eugenic sterilizations); Vanessa Volz, A Matter of Choice: Women with Disabilities, Sterilization, and Reproductive Autonomy in the Twenty-First Century, 27 Women's Rts. L. Rep. 203 (2006).

Title II of the Americans with Disabilities Act (ADA) prohibits disability-based discrimination in the provision of public services. 42 U.S.C.A. §§12131-12165. Some rulings by the Supreme Court have raised doubts about whether Title II could be applied to secure monetary damages from states without running afoul of the sovereign immunity provisions of the Eleventh Amendment to the U.S. Constitution. In Tennessee v. Lane, 124 S. Ct. 1978 (2004), the Court held that Title II could be applied in cases involving a valid exercise of congressional power to enforce the Fourteenth Amendment. The Title II claim was upheld in *Lane* because the contested state action affected the fundamental right of access to the courts. The reasoning suggests that claimants might be able to use Title II of the ADA to contest state efforts to bar reproduction by persons with disabilities because these policies might be viewed as impairing the fundamental right to procreate. Cf. *Lane*, 124 S. Ct. at 1989 n.8 (noting that state policies preventing marriage of persons with disabilities provided part of basis for enactment of Title II).

4. *"Temporary Mandatory Sterilization" or Mandatory Birth Control.* Is the state also precluded from mandating birth control? Most cases have arisen when judges have ordered defendants to refrain from reproducing or have ordered defendants to use long-acting contraceptives as a condition of probation. See, e.g., State v. Talty, 814 N.E.2d 1201 (Ohio 2004) (invalidating condition where no provision to lift order when child support payments current); and State v. Oakley, 629 N.W.

2d 200 (Wis. 2001) (upholding probation condition that defendant avoid having another child absent showing his willingness to provide financial support for children). See also A. Felecia Epps, Unacceptable Collateral Damage: The Danger of Probation Conditions Restricting the Right to Have Children, 38 Creighton L. Rev. 611 (2005); Symposium, Long Term Contraception, Hastings Center Rep. S1-S33 (Jan.-Feb. 1995). Women are much more likely to be the targets of reproductive restrictions than men. See Rachel Roth, "No New Babies?" Gender Inequality and Reproductive Control in the Criminal Justice and Prison Systems, 12 Am. U. J. Gender & Soc. Pol'y & L. 391 (2004). But see Smith v. Superior Court, 725 P.2d 1101 (Ariz. 1986).

5. *Governmental Encouragement.* More subtle problems are raised when governmental action is not overtly coercive, but merely seeks to encourage reproductive restraint by structuring government benefit or taxation programs to discriminate against large families. In Dandridge v. Williams, 397 U.S. 471 (1970), the Supreme Court upheld a Maryland regulation limiting payments under the state's Aid for Dependent Children program (AFDC) to no more than $240 or $250 per family. As a result of the regulation, AFDC payments equaling a calculated subsistence standard went only to families with fewer than five or six children. 397 U.S. at 509-510 n.2 (Marshall, J., dissenting). The Court did not answer plaintiffs' contentions that the regulation infringed parents' rights "to freedom of choice concerning procreation and reproduction and to marital privacy." Brief for Appellees at 31. See Yvette Barksdale, And the Poor Have Children: A Harm-Based Analysis of Family Caps and the Hollow Procreative Rights of Welfare Beneficiaries, 14 Law & Ineq. 1 (1995); Rebekah J. Smith, Family Caps in Welfare Reform: Their Coercive Effects and Damaging Consequences, 29 Harv. J.L. & Gender 151 (2006).

6. *"Private" Coercion.* In Walker v. Pierce, 560 F.2d 609 (4th Cir. 1977), cert. denied, 434 U.S. 1075 (1978), two African-American women claimed that the defendant, obstetrician Pierce, had sterilized or threatened to sterilize them because of their race, number of children, and status as recipients of publicly funded Medicaid benefits. Dr. Pierce's policy was to refuse to provide obstetrical services to poor women with more than two children unless the women agreed to undergo sterilization after delivery of their third child. The plaintiffs argued that Dr. Pierce had acted "under the color of state law" and that this policy violated their constitutional rights to privacy, due process, and equal protection. The court rejected the claims, in part because it found that Dr. Pierce's connection to the state Medicaid program and a hospital that had received federal funds was not sufficient to make him a state actor subject to liability for the violation of constitutional rights under 42 U.S.C. §1983. The court noted:

We perceive no reason why Dr. Pierce could not establish and pursue the policy he has publicly and freely announced. Nor are we cited to judicial precedent or statute inhibiting this personal economic philosophy. Particularly is this so when all persons coming to him as patients are seasonably made fully aware of his professional attitude toward the increase in offspring and his determination to see it prevail. At no time is he shown to have forced his view upon any mother. Indeed, quite the opposite appears. In the single occasion in this case of a sterilization by this doctor, not just one but three formal written consents were obtained, the first before delivery of the fourth child and two afterwards.

560 F.2d at 613. Federal regulations now require specific informed consent and other procedures to reduce the risk of coerced sterilizations in programs supported by federal funds. 42 C.F.R. §§50.201-210.

Problem: Sterilization and Advances in Genetics

Scientists completed the map of the human genome sequence—part of the billion-dollar Human Genome Project—in 2000. Researchers are now focused on understanding the operational significance of genes, identifying the structure and function of the thousands of proteins manufactured according to genetic instructions, and exploring the implications for the human condition. Scientific advances are likely to create more uncertainty in the short term. News stories frequently report the discovery of genes "associated with" certain human traits or diseases, but an association may be strong or weak and the mechanism may be simple or complex to understand. Therapies for genetic conditions are extremely rare. The behavioral implications of genetics are particularly controversial. See Behavioral Genetics: The Clash of Culture and Biology (Ronald A. Carson et al. eds., 1999).

Consider the development and use of genetic tests for the following conditions:

1. Gene A is a "dominant" trait. Because we ordinarily carry two copies of each gene, only one of which is passed to our offspring, a child of someone who carries one of these genes has a 50 percent chance of receiving this gene and of experiencing its bad effects. Gene A is a late-onset genetic disorder. Persons with the defective gene will develop Alzheimer's disease in their 50s. See Gina Kolata, How Do You Live Knowing You Might Have an Alzheimer's Gene?, N.Y. Times, June 7, 2012.

2. Gene B is a recessive trait and will be expressed only if a child receives the "defective" gene from each parent. Statistically speaking, for two parents who each carry one of these genes, there is a 25 percent chance of their passing two defective genes to their offspring. Children with two B genes develop a painful disorder that leads to death, usually by the age of five. See Emily Rapp, Notes from a Dragon Mom, N.Y. Times, Oct. 15, 2011.

3. Genetic trait C is caused by a large number of different genetic mutations. Scientists have developed a test that will identify 75 percent of these mutations, but trait C is not always expressed in persons who have these mutations and it is also found in persons who do not have these mutations. Persons with C have shortened life spans; with proper medical care they may live into their 20s or beyond.

4. Hypothetical genetic trait D is associated with higher rates of criminal conduct. Persons who inherit one copy of the gene are 10 percent more likely to be convicted of a violent crime than the general population. Persons with two copies of the gene are 30 percent more likely to be convicted of a violent crime. Although geneticists cannot completely explain the correlation between this gene and criminal conduct, they do believe that the gene is associated with greater risk taking and lower social empathy. Cf. A. Reif et al., Nature and Nurture Predispose to Violent Behavior: Serotonergic Genes and Adverse Childhood Environment, 32 Neuropsychopharmacology 2375

(2007); K. Blum et al., Sex, Drugs, and Rock 'N' Roll: Hypothesizing Common Mesolimbic Activation as a Function of Reward Gene Polymorphisms, 44 J. Psychoactive Drugs 38 (2012).

Is there any basis for restricting the reproduction of any of these persons? Could the risks of reproduction be used to justify premarital screening for one or more of these conditions? See Chapter 6 at page 674. Could a state require individuals who carry one or more of these genes to be counseled about the possible reproductive consequences? The ethical norms governing genetic counselors typically prohibit coercion or directive counseling while encouraging focus on the patient's values and preferences. See Robert Wachbroit & David Wasserman, Patient Autonomy and Value—Neutrality in Nondirective Genetic Counseling, 6 Stan. L. & Pol'y Rev. 103 (1995).

Could a state prohibit reproduction for persons who carry two copies of the hypothetical gene associated with trait D? With one copy? Does *Skinner* stand for the proposition that the state can never prohibit reproduction? Or must the state merely have an adequate scientific basis and apply its standard uniformly? Could the state argue that it has a compelling interest in protecting the child from being born? See Dena Davis, Genetic Dilemmas: Reproductive Technology, Parental Choices, and Children's Futures (2009); Perfecting Pregnancy: Law, Disability and the Future of Reproduction (Isabel Karpin & Kristin Savell eds., 2012); Mary Anne Bobinski, Genetics and Reproductive Decision Making, *in* The Human Genome Project and the Future of Health Care 79-107 (1996); Lois Shepherd, Protecting Parents' Freedom to Have Children with Genetic Differences, 1995 U. Ill. L. Rev. 761. Genetic progress may not provide benefits to all groups in society. See Mary Briody Mahowald, Genes, Women, Equality (1999); Sonia Suter, A Brave New World of Designer Babies, 22 Berkeley Tech. L.J. 897 (2007); Symposium, Communities of Color and Genetic Testing: Purpose, Voice & Values, 27 Seton Hall L. Rev. 887 (1997).

Problem: The Ashley Treatment

Ashley is a profoundly disabled 6-year-old with the mental capacity of a 3-month-old whose parents have asked a Seattle-area hospital for surgery to remove her uterus and to prevent breast growth, along with hormone treatments to restrain her growth. Should the treatment be provided? With what procedural and substantive protections? See Peter Singer, A Convenient Truth, N.Y. Times, Jan. 26, 2007 (discussing the Ashley case and the hospital's agreement with the parents' requests).

Ashley's parents argued that the procedures were in her best interests, as she would avoid the discomfort of menstruation and the expected development of large breasts; moreover, her smaller stature would permit the parents to include her more readily in family outings and activities. A state investigation later concluded that the procedures should not have been done without a court order. Christine Ryan, Revisiting the Legal Standards That Govern Requests to Sterilize Profoundly Incompetent Children: In Light of the "Ashley Treatment," Is a New Standard Appropriate?, 77 Fordham L. Rev. 287 (2008) (noting investigation report available at www.disabilityrightswa.org). See also Alicia Ouellette, Shaping Parental

Authority over Children's Bodies, 85 Ind. L.J. 955 (2010); Ed Pilkington & Karen McVeigh, 'Ashley Treatment' on Rise amid Concerns from Disability Groups, The Guardian, Mar. 15, 2012.

Problem: Chemical or Surgical Castration of Male Sex Offenders

Should the government's purpose matter in sterilization cases? In most of the cases discussed above, the state intended to restrict a person's ability to procreate, either because of eugenic ideology or because of a judgment that the individual would not provide properly for a child. Consider the movement in the 1990s to require male sex offenders to undergo "chemical castration" as a condition of probation. See, e.g., Daniel L. Icenogle, Sentencing Male Sex Offenders to the Use of Biological Treatments, 15 J. Leg. Med. 279 (1994). Courts and legislatures hoped to reduce recidivism rates by reducing the offender's sexual drive; the effect on reproduction, therefore, was merely incidental. Appellate courts struck down early efforts to impose chemical castration in the criminal context. See, e.g., People v. Gauntlett, 352 N.W.2d 310 (Mich. Ct. App.), modified on other grounds, 353 N.W.2d 463 (Mich. 1984) (unlawful condition of probation). Legislatures responded by explicitly authorizing the use of chemical castration as a condition of probation for certain sex offenders. See, e.g., Cal. Penal Code §645 (authorizing chemical castration). Should prisoners be entitled to voluntarily consent to castration? See Tex. Gov't Code Ann. §§501.061-.062 (repeat sex offenders authorized to voluntarily undergo orchiectomy, also known as surgical castration). Could a physician ethically perform an orchiectomy on a physically healthy male? If so, under what circumstances? Compare your views with the provisions of the Texas law. For a discussion on the efficacy of treatments for sexual offenders, see Abby Goodnough & Monica Davey, For Sex Offenders, Dispute on Therapy's Benefits, N.Y. Times, Mar. 6, 2007.

Assume that your client, Greg Aya, has been convicted of child molestation on three different occasions. His female victims were all less than 13 years old. Under the applicable California statute, chemical castration must be imposed as a condition of probation. The procedure will require Greg to receive regular shots of a drug that will reduce his sex drive and which will likely impair his sexual functioning. The treatment is to continue until the state's experts certify that it is "no longer necessary." Can you devise a challenge to the California statute and its application to Greg? Will cases such as *Skinner* be useful? Should it matter whether Greg will have an opportunity to "bank" frozen sperm for possible future procreation? Are there any other sources of relevant law? Will you be successful? See People v. Foster, 124 Cal. Rptr. 2d 22 (Cal. App. 4 Dist. 2002). See also Houston v. State, 852 So. 2d 425 (Fla. App. 2003) (trial court failed to follow requirements of chemical castration statute); Bruno v. State, 837 So. 2d 521 (Fla. App. 2003) (surgical castration not authorized for violation of statute at issue in case; illegal sentence resulting from negotiated plea agreement must be set aside). For more on the legal and ethical issues surrounding chemical castration of male sex offenders, see Lystra Batchoo, Voluntary Surgical Castration of Sex Offenders: Waiving the Eighth Amendment Protection from Cruel and Unusual Punishment, 72 Brook. L. Rev. 689 (2007); Karen Harrison, Legal and Ethical Issues When Using Antiandrogenic Pharmacotherapy with

Sex Offenders, 3 Sexual Offender Treatment (2008); Marnie E. Rice & Grant T. Harris, Is Androgen Deprivation Therapy Effective in the Treatment of Sex Offenders?, 17 Psychol. Pub. Pol'y & L. 315 (2011); Catherine Rylyk, Note: Lest We Regress to the Dark Ages: Holding Voluntary Surgical Castration Cruel and Unusual, Even for Child Molesters, 16 Wm. & Mary Bill Rts. J. 1305 (2008).

B. A RIGHT TO AVOID PROCREATION?

Court decisions identifying a constitutionally protected interest in being able to procreate without impermissible state interference are relatively uncontroversial since state efforts to limit procreation are quite intrusive. The procedure at issue in *Skinner* involved surgery and the permanent alteration of reproductive capacity. In contrast, state restrictions on access to contraception implicate individual interests in a fashion that is arguably less intrusive. Do individuals have a right to *avoid* reproduction that includes the right to use contraceptive technology? Does the right extend to postconception techniques of avoiding reproduction, such as abortion? The next set of cases considers the constitutional validity of state efforts to restrict access to contraception and abortion. As you read these cases, try to identify the source and scope of an individual's right to avoid procreation. What types of state regulation are permissible? Does the validity of state regulation depend on its purpose or effect?

1. Contraception

GRISWOLD v. CONNECTICUT
381 U.S. 479 (1965)

DOUGLAS, Justice.

. . . . The statutes whose constitutionality is involved in this appeal are §§53-32 and 54-196 of the General Statutes of Connecticut (1958 rev.). The former provides: "Any person who uses any drug, medicinal article or instrument for the purpose of preventing conception shall be fined not less than fifty dollars or imprisoned not less than sixty days nor more than one year or be both fined and imprisoned." Section 54-196 provides: "Any person who assists, abets, counsels, causes, hires or commands another to commit any offense may be prosecuted and punished as if he were the principal offender."

The appellants[, physicians who prescribed contraceptives to married persons,] were found guilty as accessories and fined $100 each, against the claim that the accessory statute as so applied violated the Fourteenth Amendment. . . .

[W]e are met with a wide range of questions that implicate the due process clause of the Fourteenth Amendment. Overtones of some arguments suggest that Lochner v. State of New York, 198 U.S. 45, should be our guide. But we decline that invitation. . . . We do not sit as a super-legislature to determine the wisdom, need, and propriety of laws that touch economic problems, business affairs, or social conditions. This law, however, operates directly on an intimate relation of husband and wife and their physician's role in one aspect of that relation.

The association of people is not mentioned in the Constitution nor in the Bill of Rights. The right to educate a child in a school of the parents' choice—whether public or private or parochial—is also not mentioned. Nor is the right to study any particular subject or any foreign language. Yet the First Amendment has been construed to include certain of those rights.

By Pierce v. Society of Sisters, 268 U.S. 510, the right to educate one's children as one chooses is made applicable to the states by the force of the First and Fourteenth Amendments. By Meyer v. State of Nebraska, 262 U.S. 390, the same dignity is given the right to study the German language in a private school. In other words, the state may not, consistently with the spirit of the First Amendment, contract the spectrum of available knowledge. The right of freedom of speech and press includes not only the right to utter or to print, but the right to distribute, the right to receive, the right to read. . . . Without those peripheral rights the specific rights would be less secure. . . .

The foregoing cases suggest that specific guarantees in the Bill of Rights have penumbras, formed by emanations from those guarantees that help give them life and substance. Various guarantees create zones of privacy. The right of association contained in the penumbra of the First Amendment is one, as we have seen. The Third Amendment in its prohibition against the quartering of soldiers "in any house" in time of peace without the consent of the owner is another facet of that privacy. The Fourth Amendment explicitly affirms the "right of the people to be secure in their persons, houses, papers, and effects, against unreasonable searches and seizures." The Fifth Amendment in its self-incrimination clause enables the citizen to create a zone of privacy which government may not force him to surrender to his detriment. The Ninth Amendment provides: "The enumeration in the Constitution, of certain rights, shall not be construed to deny or disparage others retained by the people." The Fourth and Fifth Amendments were described in Boyd v. United States, 116 U.S. 616, 630, as protection against all governmental invasions "of the sanctity of a man's home and the privacies of life." We have had many controversies over these penumbral rights of "privacy and repose." These cases bear witness that the right of privacy which presses for recognition here is a legitimate one.

The present case, then, concerns a relationship lying within the zone of privacy created by several fundamental constitutional guarantees. And it concerns a law which, in forbidding the use of contraceptives rather than regulating their manufacture or sale, seeks to achieve its goals by means having a maximum destructive impact upon that relationship. Such a law cannot stand in light of the familiar principle, so often applied by this Court, that a "governmental purpose to control or prevent activities constitutionally subject to state regulation may not be achieved by means which sweep unnecessarily broadly and thereby invade the area of protected freedoms." NAACP v. Alabama, 377 U.S. 288, 307. Would we allow the police to search the sacred precincts of marital bedrooms for telltale signs of the use of contraceptives? The very idea is repulsive to the notions of privacy surrounding the marriage relationship.

We deal with a right of privacy older than the Bill of Rights—older than our political parties, older than our school system. Marriage is a coming together for better or for worse, hopefully enduring, and intimate to the degree of being sacred. It is an association that promotes a way of life, not causes; a harmony in living, not political faiths; a bilateral loyalty, not commercial or social projects. Yet it is an association for as noble a purpose as any involved in our prior decisions.

Reversed.

GOLDBERG, Justice, whom the Chief Justice and BRENNAN, Justice, join, concurring.

I agree with the Court that Connecticut's birth-control law unconstitutionally intrudes upon the right of marital privacy, and I join in its opinion and judgment. . . . I do agree that the concept of liberty protects those personal rights that are fundamental, and is not confined to the specific terms of the Bill of Rights. My conclusion that the concept of liberty is not so restricted and that it embraces the right of marital privacy though that right is not mentioned explicitly in the Constitution is supported both by numerous decisions of this Court, referred to in the Court's opinion, and by the language and history of the Ninth Amendment. . . .

[I]t should be said of the Court's holding today that it in no way interferes with a state's proper regulation of sexual promiscuity or misconduct [such as "adultery, homosexuality, and the like"]. . . .

HARLAN, Justice, concurring.

. . . In my view, the proper constitutional inquiry in this case is whether this Connecticut statute infringes the due process clause of the Fourteenth Amendment because the enactment violates basic values "implicit in the concept of ordered liberty," Palko v. State of Connecticut, 302 U.S. 319, 325. . . . I believe that it does. While the relevant inquiry may be aided by resort to one or more of the provisions of the Bill of Rights, it is not dependent on them or any of their radiations. The due process clause of the Fourteenth Amendment stands, in my opinion, on its own bottom.

WHITE, Justice, concurring.

In my view this Connecticut law as applied to married couples deprives them of "liberty" without due process of law, as that concept is used in the Fourteenth Amendment. I therefore concur in the judgment of the Court reversing these convictions under Connecticut's aiding and abetting statute. . . .

In these circumstances one is rather hard pressed to explain how the ban on use by married persons in any way prevents use of such devices by persons engaging in illicit sexual relations and thereby contributes to the state's policy against such relationships. . . . I find nothing in this record justifying the sweeping scope of this statute, with its telling effect on the freedoms of married persons, and therefore conclude that it deprives such persons of liberty without due process of law.

STEWART, Justice, whom BLACK, Justice, joins, dissenting.

Since 1879 Connecticut has had on its books a law which forbids the use of contraceptives by anyone. I think this is an uncommonly silly law. As a practical matter, the law is obviously unenforceable, except in the oblique context of the present case. As a philosophical matter, I believe the use of contraceptives in the relationship of marriage should be left to personal and private choice, based upon each individual's moral, ethical, and religious beliefs. As a matter of social policy, I think professional counsel about methods of birth control should be available to all, so that each individual's choice can be meaningfully made. But we are not asked in this case to say whether we think this law is unwise, or even asinine. We are asked to hold that it violates the United States Constitution. And that I cannot do.

In the course of its opinion the Court refers to no less than six Amendments to the Constitution: the First, the Third, the Fourth, the Fifth, the Ninth, and the Fourteenth. But the Court does not say which of these Amendments, if any, it thinks is infringed by this Connecticut law.

We are told that the due process clause of the Fourteenth Amendment is not, as such, the "guide" in this case. With that much I agree. There is no claim that this law, duly enacted by the Connecticut legislature, is unconstitutionally vague. There is no claim that the appellants were denied any of the elements of procedural due process at their trial, so as to make their convictions constitutionally invalid. And, as the Court says, the day has long passed since the due process clause was regarded as a proper instrument for determining "the wisdom, need, and propriety" of state laws. *Compare* Lochner v. State of New York, 198 U.S. 45, *with* Ferguson v. Skrupa, 372 U.S. 726. . . .

As to the First, Third, Fourth, and Fifth Amendments, I can find nothing in any of them to invalidate this Connecticut law. . . . [Moreover] the Ninth Amendment . . . was . . . adopted by the states simply to make clear that the adoption of the Bill of Rights did not alter the plan that the Federal Government was to be a government of express and limited powers, and that all rights and powers not delegated to it were retained by the people and the individual states. . . .

What provision of the Constitution, then, does make this state law invalid? The Court says it is the right of privacy "created by several fundamental constitutional guarantees." With all deference, I can find no such general right of privacy in the Bill of Rights, in any other part of the Constitution, or in any case ever before decided by this Court.

At the oral argument in this case we were told that the Connecticut law does not "conform to current community standards." But it is not the function of this Court to decide cases on the basis of community standards. We are here to decide cases "agreeably to the Constitution and laws of the United States." It is the essence of judicial duty to subordinate our own personal views, our own ideas of what legislation is wise and what is not. If, as I should surely hope, the law before us does not reflect the standards of the people of Connecticut, the people of Connecticut can freely exercise their true Ninth and Tenth Amendment rights to persuade their elected representatives to repeal it. That is the constitutional way to take this law off the books.

Notes: A Right to Avoid Procreation

1. *Another Constitutional Right?* Does the Court settle on the source of a constitutional right to avoid procreation in *Griswold*? Justice Douglas reviews a number of different parts of the Bill of Rights before concluding that their "penumbra" was sufficiently broad to encompass the right of married couples to use contraceptives. Is Douglas's attempt to find textual support for this right persuasive? Note that Justices Goldberg and White were dissatisfied with Douglas's analysis, preferring to rest the decision on the Ninth Amendment and the "liberty" clause of the Fourteenth

Amendment, respectively. Justice Stewart raises the specter of *Lochner* in his dissent, arguing that the majority is substituting its own judgment for the will of the people of Connecticut, as delivered by their elected representatives. See generally I. Glenn Cohen, The Constitution and the Rights Not to Procreate, 60 Stan. L. Rev. 1135 (2008) (exploring unbundling of right not to procreate).

2. *Individuals or Married Couples.* Left unresolved in *Griswold* was the question whether the right to use contraceptives belonged to the individual or was instead some protected aspect of the marital relationship. In Eisenstadt v. Baird, 405 U.S. 438 (1972), Baird was convicted for "exhibiting contraceptive[s] . . . in the course of delivering a lecture on contraception to . . . students at Boston University" and "for giving a young woman a package of [contraceptive] foam at the end of his address." The Massachusetts statute at issue imposed a maximum five-year prison term for distribution of contraceptives unless certain statutory requirements were met. The statute permitted a physician to prescribe contraceptives to married persons to prevent pregnancy. Single persons were denied access to contraceptives to prevent pregnancy; however, any adult could obtain contraceptives to prevent the spread of disease. The Court struck down the statutory scheme under a rational basis, equal protection standard. The Court's holding suggested, without explicitly deciding, that individuals might have a fundamental liberty interest in decisions to avoid procreation:

> [W]hatever the rights of the individual to access to contraceptives may be, the rights must be the same for the unmarried and the married alike.
>
> If under Griswold [v. Connecticut, 381 U.S. 479 (1965),] the distribution of contraceptives to married persons cannot be prohibited, a ban on distribution to unmarried persons would be equally impermissible. It is true that in *Griswold* the right of privacy in question inhered in the marital relationship. Yet the marital couple is not an independent entity with a mind and heart of its own, but an association of two individuals each with a separate intellectual and emotional makeup. If the right of privacy means anything, it is the right of the individual, married or single, to be free from unwarranted governmental intrusion into matters so fundamentally affecting a person as the decision whether to bear or beget a child.
>
> On the other hand, if *Griswold* is no bar to a prohibition on the distribution of contraceptives, the state could not, consistently with the equal protection clause, outlaw distribution to unmarried but not to married persons. In each case the evil, as perceived by the state, would be identical, and the underinclusion would be invidious. . . . We hold that by providing dissimilar treatment for married and unmarried persons who are similarly situated, Massachusetts General Laws Ann., c. 272, §§21 and 21A, violate the equal protection clause.

Id. at 453-455.

3. *Judicial Review of Social Legislation.* According to some, the Supreme Court is essentially an antidemocratic institution in which life-tenured political appointees wield the potential power to reverse the will of the democratically elected representatives of the majority. Are you troubled by the Court's lack of deference to the will of the people as embodied in their statutes? What limits, if any, does the Court place upon itself? Are those limits meaningful? Does the very process of judicial review of social legislation betray our society's ultimate discomfort with democracy?

4. *Minors and Contraception.* The next dispute, inevitably, involved the ability of the state to regulate access to contraceptives for minors. In Carey v. Population Services, 431 U.S. 678 (1977), the Court struck down a New York statute that criminalized distribution of condoms to persons under 16 years of age and provided that condoms could be distributed only by licensed pharmacists to persons over 16. Justice Brennan, writing for the plurality, found that minors had a limited constitutional right of access to contraceptives and that the state had failed to show that its regulation served a "significant state interest." Justices White and Powell would have invalidated the statute as irrational without finding that minors had a protected constitutional interest. Justice Rehnquist authored a spirited dissent. The Court's doctrinal difficulties in this case mirror its fractured decisionmaking in abortion cases involving minors, see page 510.

Do parents have a constitutional right to be consulted (or informed) when professional clinics offer contraceptive advice or services to minor children living with their parents? In Doe v. Irwin, 615 F.2d 1162 (6th Cir. 1980), the court held that there was no such parental right and reversed the district court's finding that a state-funded family planning center's practice of distributing contraceptives to unemancipated minors without parental notice or consultation violated the parents' constitutional right to oversee the care, custody, and nurturing of their children. Do parents have a constitutional right to prevent schools from distributing condoms to their children? See Parents United for Better Schools, Inc. v. Board of Education, 148 F.3d 260 (3d Cir. 1998) (voluntary high school condom distribution program does not violate parents' fundamental rights where parents could refuse to let children participate); Curtis v. School Committee of Falmouth, 652 N.E.2d 580 (Mass. 1995) (upholding voluntary, noncoercive program), cert. denied, 116 S. Ct. 753 (1996). Should schools learning that a minor is pregnant be required to notify the minor's parents? Melissa Prober, Please Don't Tell My Parents: The Validity of School Policies Mandating Parental Notification of a Student's Pregnancy, 71 Brook. L. Rev. 557 (2005).

Family planning counseling for minors may raise special problems of medical ethics for physicians and other health care personnel. Elise D. Berlan & Terrill Bravender, Confidentiality, Consent, and Caring for the Adolescent Patient, 21 Curr. Opin. Pediatr. 450 (2009); David A. Klein & Jeffrey W. Hutchinson, Providing Confidential Care for Adolescents, 85 Am. Fam. Physician 556 (2012); Ryan E. Lawrence et al., Adolescents, Contraception and Confidentiality: A National Survey of Obstetrician-Gynecologists, 84 Contraception 259 (2011). Should a physician who discovers that a minor is engaged in sexual activity have a duty to report the situation as a case of potential child abuse? See Jodi Rudoren, Judge Blocks Law to Report Sex Under 16, N.Y. Times, Apr. 19, 2006, at A16.

The Supreme Court's jurisprudence governing access to abortion for minors has also influenced some legislatures to consider restrictions on minors' access to contraception. Some research suggests that these proposals might cause minors to turn to other, potentially less effective methods of avoiding pregnancy. Rachel K. Jones et al., Adolescents' Reports of Parental Knowledge of Adolescents' Use of Sexual Health Services and Their Reactions to Mandated Parental Notification for Prescription Contraception, 293 JAMA 340 (2005). Currently, "21 states and the District of Columbia explicitly allow all minors to consent to contraceptive services" and "25 states explicitly permit minors to consent to contraceptive services in one or more circumstances," leaving four states with "no explicit policy." Guttmacher

Institute, Minors' Access to Contraceptive Services, Feb. 1, 2013 (most recent briefing available at www.guttmacher.org/sections/contraception.php).

5. *Paying for Contraceptives.* Contraceptives remain controversial, largely due to religious and moral views regarding the procreative purpose of sexual activity. See, e.g., R. Alta Charo, Warning: Contraceptive Drugs May Cause Political Headaches, 366 New Eng. J. Med. 1361 (2012). Should public and private insurers provide coverage for contraceptives? Is this a policy argument or could a failure to provide contraceptive coverage be considered impermissible sex discrimination? See Sylvia A. Law, Sex Discrimination and Insurance for Contraception, 73 Wash. L. Rev. 363 (1998). Courts have also been asked to determine whether the failure to pay for prescription contraceptives under various health plans violates federal or state law. See, e.g., Catholic Charities of Sacramento, Inc. v. Superior Court, 85 P.3d 67 (Cal.), cert. denied, 125 S. Ct. 53 (2004) (upholding state Women's Contraceptive Equity Act in constitutional challenge brought by employer which opposed contraceptives on religious grounds); and Standridge v. Union Pac. R.R. Co. (In re Union Pac. R.R. Employment Practices Litigation), 479 F. 3d 936 (8th Cir. Neb. Mar. 15, 2007) (finding employer did not violate Title VII by failing to cover prescription contraception for women). State and federal legislative initiatives in this area are summarized in the National Conference of State Legislatures, Health Insurance Coverage for Contraceptives (available at NCSL Web site, www.ncsl.org). Following the recommendations of an Institute of Medicine panel, the Obama administration announced in 2012 that contraception coverage without co-pays or deductibles should be provided in the basic package of health care benefits required in the Affordable Care Act. The initial proposal, which exempted churches but not other institutions with religious affiliations, such as universities and hospitals, was modified to insulate certain religiously affiliated organizations from paying for or providing information about the coverage, 45 C.F.R. §147.130(a)(1)(iv), though the Obama administration was suggesting additional revisions to the policy as of February 2013. See also Timothy Stoltzfus Jost, Religious Freedom and Women's Health — The Litigation on Contraception, 368 New Eng. J. Med. 4 (2013).

6. *Emergency Contraception.* Emergency contraception, also known as the "morning-after pill," should be taken as soon as possible after unprotected intercourse to prevent conception or the implantation of a fertilized egg in a woman's uterus. It appears to work in most cases by "delaying or preventing ovulation, but prevention of implantation cannot be ruled out." Alastair J. J. Wood et al., The Politics of Emergency Contraception, 366 New Eng. J. Med. 101 (2012). Those who believe that human life begins at the fertilization of an ovum view the drug as an abortifacient because it in some cases may work by preventing the implantation of a fertilized egg. But see Pam Belluck, Abortion Qualms on Morning-After Pill May Be Unfounded, N.Y. Times, June 5, 2012.

State regulations initially focused on the role of pharmacists in dispensing the prescriptions, including providing "right of conscience" protections for pharmacists who refused to dispense the drug based on their personal moral or religious beliefs. See the National Conference of State Legislatures, Emergency Contraception Laws (available at NCSL Web site); Noesen v. State Department of Regulation and Licensing, Pharmacy Examining Bd., 751 N.W.2d 385 (Wis. App. 2008) (state board permitted to discipline pharmacists who refused to refill a prescription for birth control pills and refused to transfer the prescription to another pharmacy). After some controversy, the FDA approved over-the-counter (OTC) sales of Plan B emergency contraception for women over age 17. Frank Davidoff & James Trussell, Plan B and the Politics of Doubt, 296 JAMA 1775 (2006); Cynthia Harper et al., Over-the-Counter Access to Emergency Contraception for Teens, 77 Contraception 230 (2008) (noting arguments supporting OTC for teens). See also Anspach v. City of Philadelphia, Department of Public Health, 503 F.3d 256 (3d Cir. 2007) (rejecting First and Fourteenth Amendment claims brought by parents and unemancipated minor against clinic that provided emergency contraception to minor at her request). The debate about whether the drug should be available OTC for minors flared up in 2012 when the Secretary of Health and Human Services ordered the FDA commission not to approve OTC sales for minors. See Wood, supra.

Problem: Incompetent Persons and Long-Term Contraception

Grace and Tony Jones have a daughter, Alice, who is 17 years old. Alice has a low IQ. She attends school along with other children in the neighborhood but takes part in special classes designed to meet her intellectual and emotional needs. Alice is a friendly person who takes a great interest in others and in animals. She has an ordinary interest in sexual activity and often talks about looking forward to having her own child. On the other hand, she is not fond of going to her physician and has a low tolerance for pain. She is easily distractible and must be reminded by others to bathe and eat. Alice's parents are concerned about her future, particularly because they are entering their 50s and can foresee a period of declining health. They want to ensure that Alice is not "burdened by the trauma and responsibility of childrearing or the loss of a child by adoption." They have heard that forced sterilization of minors and incompetents is very controversial. (See discussion at page 469.) As an alternative, they have approached Alice's physician to have Alice undergo insertion of an IUD contraceptive, which could prevent against pregnancy for several years. If this is not possible, they want Alice to be given a birth control pill prescription. How would you advise Alice's physician? Are there any potential sources of liability? In what ways is this situation similar to the sterilization cases? In what ways is it different? Are the differences legally significant? What sources of law would you examine to determine the physician's obligations? Could the ADA be relevant? Would you seek a court order, and if so, of what type?

2. Abortion

▮ ROE v. WADE
410 U.S. 113 (1973)

BLACKMUN, Justice.

[Roe challenged the constitutional validity of a Texas statute that made it a crime to procure an abortion, except where necessary to save the life of the pregnant woman. The Court held that the statute violated the Fourteenth Amendment's due process clause. Justice Blackmun recognized that states had two separate interests in regulating abortion: (1) an interest in protecting the health and safety of women; and (2) an interest in protecting fetal life. These interests had to be weighed against the rights of the woman and her fetus. The Court first held that women had a protected "privacy" interest in the abortion decision:]

This right of privacy, whether it be founded in the Fourteenth Amendment's concept of personal liberty and restrictions upon state action, as we feel it is, . . . is broad enough to encompass a woman's decision whether or not to terminate her pregnancy. The detriment that the state would impose upon the pregnant woman by denying this choice altogether is apparent. Specific and direct harm medically diagnosable even in early pregnancy may be involved. Maternity, or additional offspring, may force upon the woman a distressful life and future. Psychological harm may be imminent. Mental and physical health may be taxed by child care. There is also the distress, for all concerned, associated with the unwanted child, and there is the problem of bringing a child into a family already unable, psychologically and otherwise, to care for it. In other cases, as in this one, the additional difficulties and continuing stigma of unwed motherhood may be involved. All these are factors the woman and her responsible physician necessarily will consider in consultation. . . .

[A] state may properly assert important interests in safeguarding health, in maintaining medical standards, and in protecting potential life. At some point in pregnancy, these respective interests become sufficiently compelling to sustain regulation of the factors that govern the abortion decision. The privacy right involved, therefore, cannot be said to be absolute. In fact, it is not clear to us that the claim asserted by some amici that one has an unlimited right to do with one's body as one pleases bears a close relationship to the right of privacy previously articulated in the Court's decisions. The Court has refused to recognize an unlimited right of this kind in the past. Jacobson v. Massachusetts, 197 U.S. 11 (1905) (vaccination); Buck v. Bell, 274 U.S. 200 (1927) (sterilization). [See also the assisted suicide cases in Chapter 3.]

We, therefore, conclude that the right of personal privacy includes the abortion decision, but that this right is not unqualified and must be considered against important state interests in regulation. . . .

Where certain "fundamental rights" are involved, the Court has held that regulation limiting these rights may be justified only by a "compelling state interest," and that legislative enactments must be narrowly drawn to express only the legitimate state interests at stake. . . .

The appellee and certain amici argue that the fetus is a "person" within the language and meaning of the Fourteenth Amendment. . . . If this suggestion of personhood is established, the appellant's case, of course, collapses, for the fetus' right to life would then be guaranteed specifically by the Amendment. . . . [The Court rejects this claim, noting that "person" in the Constitution is never used in a way that suggests it could have any prenatal application.] . . .

The pregnant woman cannot be isolated in her privacy. She carries an embryo and, later, a fetus, if one accepts the medical definitions of the developing young in the human uterus. The situation therefore is inherently different from [prior cases]. . . .

[W]e do not agree that, by adopting one theory of life, Texas may override the rights of the pregnant woman that are at stake. We repeat, however, that the state does have an important and legitimate interest in preserving and protecting the health of the pregnant woman . . . . and that it has still another important and legitimate interest in protecting the potentiality of human life. These interests are separate and distinct. Each grows in substantiality as the woman approaches term and, at a point during pregnancy, each becomes "compelling."

With respect to the state's important and legitimate interest in the health of the mother, the "compelling" point, in the light of present medical knowledge, is at approximately the end of the first trimester. This is so because of the now-established medical fact that until the end of the first trimester mortality in abortion may be less than mortality in normal childbirth. It follows that, from and after this point, a state may regulate the abortion procedure to the extent that the regulation reasonably relates to the preservation and protection of maternal health. . . .

This means, on the other hand, that, for the period of pregnancy prior to this "compelling" point, the attending physician, in consultation with his patient, is free to determine, without regulation by the state, that, in his medical judgment, the patient's pregnancy should be terminated. If that decision is reached, the judgment may be effectuated by an abortion free of interference by the state.

With respect to the state's important and legitimate interest in potential life, the "compelling" point is at viability. This is so because the fetus then presumably has the capability of meaningful life outside the mother's womb. State regulation protective of fetal life after viability thus has both logical and biological justifications. If the state is interested in protecting fetal life after viability, it may go so far as to proscribe abortion during that period, except when it is necessary to preserve the life or health of the mother. . . .

[The Court then applied these standards to invalidate the Texas abortion statute.]

Affirmed in part and reversed in part.

REHNQUIST, Justice, dissenting.

The Court's opinion brings to the decision of this troubling question both extensive historical fact and a wealth of legal scholarship. While the opinion thus commands my respect, I find myself nonetheless in fundamental disagreement with those parts of it that invalidate the Texas statute in question, and therefore dissent. . . .

I would reach a conclusion opposite to that reached by the Court. I have difficulty in concluding, as the Court does, that the right of "privacy" is involved in this case. . . . If the Court means by the term *privacy* no more than that the claim of a person to be free from unwanted state regulation of consensual transactions may be a form of "liberty" protected by the Fourteenth Amendment, there is no doubt that similar claims have been upheld in our earlier decisions on the basis of that liberty. . . . The test traditionally applied in the area of social and economic legislation is whether or not a law such as that challenged has a rational relation to a valid state objective. Williamson v. Lee Optical Co., 348 U.S. 483, 491 (1955). The due process clause of the Fourteenth Amendment undoubtedly does place a limit, albeit a broad one, on legislative power to enact laws such as this. If the Texas statute were to prohibit an abortion even where the mother's life is in jeopardy, I have little doubt that such a statute would lack a rational relation to a valid state objective under the test stated in *Williamson,* supra. But the Court's sweeping invalidation of any restrictions on abortion during the first trimester is impossible to justify under that standard, and the conscious weighing of competing factors that the Court's opinion apparently substitutes for the established test is far more appropriate to a legislative judgment than to a judicial one. . . .

While the Court's opinion quotes from the dissent of Mr. Justice Holmes in Lochner v. New York, 198 U.S. 45, 74 (1905), the result it reaches is more closely attuned to the majority opinion of Mr. Justice Peckham in that case. As in *Lochner* and similar cases applying substantive due process standards to economic and social welfare legislation, the adoption of the compelling state interest standard will inevitably require this Court to examine the legislative policies and pass on the wisdom of these policies in the very process of deciding whether a particular state interest put forward may or may not be "compelling." The decision here to break pregnancy into three distinct terms and to outline the permissible restrictions the state may impose in each one, for example, partakes more of judicial legislation than it does of a determination of the intent of the drafters of the Fourteenth Amendment. . . .

To reach its result, the Court necessarily has had to find within the scope of the Fourteenth Amendment a right that was apparently completely unknown to the drafters of the Amendment. . . .

There apparently was no question concerning the validity of this provision or of any of the other state statutes when the Fourteenth Amendment was adopted. The only conclusion possible from this history is that the drafters did not intend to have the Fourteenth Amendment withdraw from the states the power to legislate with respect to this matter.

For all of the foregoing reasons, I respectfully dissent.

Notes: Roe v. Wade

1. *Abortion Statistics.* Abortion is a relatively common medical procedure in the United States. According to federal government statistics, "825,564 abortions were reported to CDC for 2008" from 47 states, the District of Columbia, and New York City, with about one-fifth of all pregnancies ending in abortion. Karen Pazol et al., Abortion Surveillance—United States, 2008, 60 MMWR 1, 11 (Nov. 25, 2011) (No. SS-15). For an overall review of the topic from a public health perspective, see Cynthia C. Harper et al., Abortion in the United States, 26 Annu. Rev. Public Health 501 (2005).

2. *Fetal Personhood.* The "personhood" of the fetus is an area of significant religious and philosophical debate. It is clear that many major religions treat an unborn child as a person from the moment of conception. Philosophers and bioethicists have also argued for the special, human nature of the fetus. Is it possible to argue that fetuses are "persons" for constitutional purposes? If a fetus is a constitutional person then it would be protected under the due process and equal protection clauses. How does the Court deal with this issue? Did the Texas criminal abortion statute indicate that Texas believed that fetuses were persons? See also Christopher Robert Kaczor, The Ethics of Abortion: Women's Rights, Human Life, and the Question of Justice (2011); Bonnie Steinbeck, Life Before Birth: The Moral and Legal Status of Embryos and Fetuses (2d ed. 2011); Note, What We Talk About When We Talk About Persons: The Language of a Legal Fiction, 114 Harv. L. Rev. 1745 (2001). Would a fetus's status as a person automatically mean that abortion would be prohibited by the constitution? In DeShaney v. Winnebago County Department

of Social Services, 489 U.S. 189 (1989), the Supreme Court held that the state did not owe any affirmative duty to protect a child from private violence inflicted by his father. What are the implications of this in the abortion context? Would *DeShaney* be relevant if a plaintiff argued that the state's failure to criminalize abortion while criminalizing other types of homicide violated the EPC clause? See Lee v. Oregon, 107 F.3d 182 (9th Cir. 1997) (holding plaintiffs did not have standing to bring equal protection challenge to Oregon's assisted suicide statute), cert. denied sub nom. Lee v. Harcleroad, 522 U.S. 927 (1997).

3. *Sources of Authority in Constitutional Interpretation.* In the full opinion, Justice Blackmun engages in a painstaking analysis of historical, legal, medical, and religious attitudes toward abortion. By what theory is this discussion constitutionally relevant? Is this an argument that the framers of the Fourteenth Amendment considered procreative liberty to be fundamental? Even if this doubtful proposition were accurate, should it be determinative? In other contexts, some have argued that the Constitution should evolve over time; could not the controversy over abortion indicate heightened sensitivity to the rights of others that should be incorporated into the Constitution? If the Constitution can grow to recognize a woman's right to choose, can it also grow to recognize fetal rights? In the unedited opinion, Justice Blackmun also details the opinions of various medical organizations. Should the medical profession have special influence on the establishment of constitutional norms where they concern biological processes?

4. *The "Right to Privacy."* What is the nature of the right to privacy? Does Justice Blackmun succeed in adequately describing its source, scope, and limits? Note that the Court adopts the theory that the source of the right is the liberty clause of the Fourteenth Amendment. How would Justice Rehnquist determine whether the right to choose abortion is "fundamental"? Does his charge of "Lochnerism" seem valid?

5. *The State's Interest.* Justice Blackmun contends that the interests of the pregnant woman and the state can be weighed and evaluated through the use of the trimester framework. Does he adequately explain what the state's interest is in the first trimester? What types of state regulation would be supported by this interest? Is Justice Blackmun's discussion of the importance of viability convincing? Or does it constitute *ipse dixit*?

6. *Additional Ethical or Moral Aspects of Abortion.* Abortion implicates our definition of personhood, the value of potential human life, and the obligations of health professionals to "do no harm", and to serve patients' medical needs. The law on abortion does not differentiate among the various possible nontherapeutic reasons underlying a woman's decision to end a pregnancy, but ethicists, philosophers, and religious groups often make these distinctions. Consider the following rationales for abortion:

   a. Should abortion be used explicitly as a means of after-the-fact birth control? See Judith Jarvis Thomson, A Defense of Abortion, 1 Phil. & Pub. Aff. 47 (1971) (mounting a defense of abortion, but suggesting that abortion merely as birth control exceeds ethical bounds). The issue is of increasing importance to those who fear that the increasing availability of pharmaceutical abortions might increase use of abortion as a method of family planning. See, e.g., Karen Pazol et al., Abortion Surveillance—United

States, 2008, 60 MMWR 1, 11 (Nov. 25, 2011) (No. SS-15) ("The use of medical abortion increased 17% from 2007 to 2008.").

b. Should abortion be used to eliminate multiple births? Pregnancies with multiple fetuses carry health risks for the fetuses and for the expectant mother. Obstetricians have the ability to selectively reduce the number of fetuses in multifetal pregnancies. Is there an ethical basis justifying selection reduction from triplets to twins that would not apply to the reduction of twins to a singleton fetus? For a discussion of the clinical and ethical issues, see Judith F. Daar, Selective Reduction of Multiple Pregnancy: Lifeboat Ethics in the Womb, 25 U.C. Davis L. Rev. 773 (1992); Mark Evans et al., Update on Selective Reduction, 25 Prenatal Diag. 807 (2005).

c. Should abortion be used to avoid the birth of a child with birth defects? If so, which defects? Why shouldn't this be considered an impermissible form of disability-based discrimination or eugenics? Genetic screening is already used to identify the sex of the fetus, sometimes to avoid a sex-linked genetic disorder but other times to ensure parental control over gender. Should parents be able to use genetic screening to identify the sex of a child so that they can abort a child of the "wrong" gender? See Ariz. Rev. Stat. §13-3603.02 (prohibiting performing or soliciting abortions based on sex or race of fetus). See also Susannah Baruch et al., Genetic Testing of Embryos: Practices and Perspectives of U.S. IVF Clinics, 89 Fertility & Sterility 1053 (2008); John F. Muller, Disability, Ambivalence, and the Law, 37 Am. J.L. & Med. 469 (2011); Erik Parens & Adrienne Asch, the Disability Rights Critique of Prenatal Genetic Testing, 29 Hastings Center Rep. 40 (Sept.-Oct. 1999) (special supp.); Stanford Symposium on Preimplantation Genetic Diagnosis, 85 Fertility & Sterility 1631-1660 (2006). See also Jennifer Steinhauer, House Rejects Bill to Ban Sex-Selective Abortions, N.Y. Times, May 31, 2012.

d. What about using abortion to "deselect" other characteristics, such as size, hair color, or personality, assuming that genetic science progressed to make this possible? At some point, prospective parents may be able to create even more detailed shopping lists. Is there anything ethically or legally wrong with permitting parents to abort pregnancies until they conceive a fetus with a projected IQ greater than 125? See Greer Conley et al., Prenatal Whole Genome Sequencing: Just Because We Can, Should We?, 42(4) Hastings Center Rep. 28 (July-Aug. 2012); Owen D. Jones, Reproductive Autonomy and Evolutionary Biology: A Regulatory Framework for Trait-Selection Technologies, 19 Am. J.L. & Med. 187 (1993); Maxwell J. Mehlman, The Law of Above Averages: Leveling the New Genetic Enhancement Playing Field, 85 Iowa L. Rev. 517 (2000); John A. Robertson, Genetic Selection of Offspring Characteristics, 76 B.U. L. Rev. 421 (1996); Stanford Symposium on Preimplantation Genetic Diagnosis, supra.

7. *Abortion Politics.* Those who hoped that a Supreme Court decision in this area would resolve the issue have been greatly disappointed. The *Roe* decision helped to fuel another 40 years of debate about abortion, the Constitution, and state regulation. "Pro-life" or "anti-choice" advocates were not vanquished, but in fact seemed invigorated by the Court's rejection of most types of state abortion

regulation. Abortion continued to be a political issue; federal, state, and local political candidates announced their positions even in races where the controversy was largely irrelevant given the nature of the office being elected. "Pro-life" or "anti-choice" activists worked for a constitutional amendment. State legislatures continued to regulate abortion, sending test case after test case to the courts. "Pro-choice" or "pro-abortion" advocates fought in the courts and the legislatures to preserve constitutional protections for women seeking abortions. While it would be naive to imagine that the judicial selection process before *Roe* was apolitical, it is clear that the abortion debate produced a new "litmus test" for potential state and federal judicial nominees. Cf. Linda Greenhouse, Democracy and the Courts: The Case of Abortion, 61 Hastings L.J. 1333 (2010). The cases and notes in the remainder of this section will summarize the judicial response to changes in the political battle lines.

8. *Supreme Court Abortion Jurisprudence Between* Roe *and* Casey. For a summary of some of the important post-*Roe* cases, see Rachael K. Pirner & Laurie B. Williams, *Roe* to *Casey*: A Survey of Abortion Law, 32 Washburn L.J. 166 (1993).

■ PLANNED PARENTHOOD OF SOUTHEASTERN PENNSYLVANIA v. CASEY
505 U.S. 833 (1992)

O'CONNOR, KENNEDY, and SOUTER, Justices.

I

Liberty finds no refuge in a jurisprudence of doubt. Yet 19 years after our holding that the Constitution protects a woman's right to terminate her pregnancy in its early stages, Roe v. Wade, 410 U.S. 113 (1973), that definition of liberty is still questioned. Joining the respondents as amicus curiae, the United States, as it has done in five other cases in the last decade, again asks us to overrule *Roe*.

At issue in these cases are five provisions of the Pennsylvania Abortion Control Act of 1982 as amended in 1988 and 1989. 18 Pa. Cons. Stat. §§3203-3220 (1990). The Act requires that a woman seeking an abortion give her informed consent prior to the abortion procedure, and specifies that she be provided with certain information at least 24 hours before the abortion is performed. For a minor to obtain an abortion, the Act requires the informed consent of one of her parents, but provides for a judicial bypass option if the minor does not wish to or cannot obtain a parent's consent. Another provision of the Act requires that, unless certain exceptions apply, a married woman seeking an abortion must sign a statement indicating that she has notified her husband of her intended abortion. The Act exempts compliance with these three requirements in the event of a "medical emergency." In addition to the above provisions regulating the performance of abortions, the Act imposes certain reporting requirements on facilities that provide abortion services. . . .

After considering the fundamental constitutional questions resolved by *Roe*, principles of institutional integrity, and the rule of stare decisis, we are led to conclude this: The essential holding of Roe v. Wade should be retained and once again reaffirmed. . . .

II

Constitutional protection of the woman's decision to terminate her pregnancy derives from the due process clause of the Fourteenth Amendment. . . .

Our law affords constitutional protection to [certain] personal decisions relating to marriage, procreation, contraception, family relationships, child rearing, and education. . . . These matters, involving the most intimate and personal choices a person may make in a lifetime, choices central to personal dignity and autonomy, are central to the liberty protected by the Fourteenth Amendment. At the heart of liberty is the right to define one's own concept of existence, of meaning, of the universe, and of the mystery of human life. Beliefs about these matters could not define the attributes of personhood were they formed under compulsion of the state.

These considerations begin our analysis of the woman's interest in terminating her pregnancy but cannot end it, for this reason: Though the abortion decision may originate within the zone of conscience and belief, it is more than a philosophic exercise. Abortion is a unique act. It is an act fraught with consequences for others: for the woman who must live with the implications of her decision; for the persons who perform and assist in the procedure; for the spouse, family, and society which must confront the knowledge that these procedures exist, procedures some deem nothing short of an act of violence against innocent human life; and, depending on one's beliefs, for the life or potential life that is aborted. Though abortion is conduct, it does not follow that the state is entitled to proscribe it in all instances. That is because the liberty of the woman is at stake in a sense unique to the human condition and so unique to the law. The mother who carries a child to full term is subject to anxieties, to physical constraints, to pain that only she must bear. That these sacrifices have from the beginning of the human race been endured by woman with a pride that ennobles her in the eyes of others and gives to the infant a bond of love cannot alone be grounds for the state to insist she make the sacrifice. Her suffering is too intimate and personal for the state to insist, without more, upon its own vision of the woman's role, however dominant that vision has been in the course of our history and our culture. The destiny of the woman must be shaped to a large extent on her own conception of her spiritual imperatives and her place in society.

It should be recognized, moreover, that in some critical respects the abortion decision is of the same character as the decision to use contraception, to which Griswold v. Connecticut, Eisenstadt v. Baird, and Carey v. Population Services International, afford constitutional protection. We have no doubt as to the correctness of those decisions. . . .

While we appreciate the weight of the arguments made on behalf of the state in the case before us, arguments which in their ultimate formulation conclude that *Roe* should be overruled, the reservations any of us may have in reaffirming the central holding of *Roe* are outweighed by the explication of individual liberty we have given combined with the force of stare decisis. We turn now to that doctrine.

[In Part III, the Justices reviewed the importance of *stare decisis* in constitutional cases, and concluded that *Roe* should not be overruled.]

IV

From what we have said so far it follows that it is a constitutional liberty of the woman to have some freedom to terminate her pregnancy. We conclude that the basic decision in *Roe* was based on a constitutional analysis which we cannot now repudiate. The woman's liberty is not so unlimited, however, that from the outset the state cannot show its concern for the life of the unborn, and at a later point in fetal development the state's interest in life has sufficient force so that the right of the woman to terminate the pregnancy can be restricted. . . .

We conclude the line should be drawn at *viability*, so that before that time the woman has a right to choose to terminate her pregnancy. We adhere to this principle for two reasons. First, as we have said, is the doctrine of *stare decisis*. Any judicial act of line-drawing may seem somewhat arbitrary, but *Roe* was a reasoned statement, elaborated with great care. We have twice reaffirmed it in the face of great opposition. . . .

The second reason is that the concept of viability, as we noted in *Roe*, is the time at which there is a realistic possibility of maintaining and nourishing a life outside the womb, so that the independent existence of the second life can in reason and all fairness be the object of state protection that now overrides the rights of the woman. See Roe v. Wade, 410 U.S., at 163. . . . [T]here may be some medical developments that affect the precise point of viability, but this is an imprecision within tolerable limits. . . . The viability line also has, as a practical matter, an element of fairness. In some broad sense it might be said that a woman who fails to act before viability has consented to the state's intervention on behalf of the developing child.

The woman's right to terminate her pregnancy before viability is the most central principle of Roe v. Wade. It is a rule of law and a component of liberty we cannot renounce. . . . On the other side of the equation is the interest of the state in the protection of potential life. The *Roe* Court recognized the state's "important and legitimate interest in protecting the potentiality of human life." The weight to be given this state interest, not the strength of the woman's interest, was the difficult question faced in *Roe*. . . . [W]e have concluded that the essential holding of *Roe* should be reaffirmed.

Yet it must be remembered that Roe v. Wade speaks with clarity in establishing not only the woman's liberty but also the state's "important and legitimate interest in potential life." That portion of the decision in *Roe* has been given too little acknowledgment and implementation by the Court in its subsequent cases. Those cases decided that any regulation touching upon the abortion decision must survive strict scrutiny, to be sustained only if drawn in narrow terms to further a compelling state interest. Not all of the cases decided under that formulation can be reconciled with the holding in *Roe* itself that the state has legitimate interests in the health of the woman and in protecting the potential life within her. In resolving this tension, we choose to rely upon *Roe*, as against the later cases. . . . Most of our cases since *Roe* have involved the application of rules derived from the trimester framework. . . .

We reject the trimester framework, which we do not consider to be part of the essential holding of *Roe*. Measures aimed at ensuring that a woman's choice contemplates the consequences for the fetus do not necessarily interfere with the right recognized in *Roe*, although those measures have been found to be inconsistent with the rigid trimester framework announced in that case. A logical reading of the central holding in *Roe* itself, and a necessary reconciliation of the liberty of the woman and the interest of the state in promoting prenatal life, require, in our view, that we abandon the trimester framework as a rigid prohibition on all provability regulation aimed at the protection of fetal life. The trimester framework suffers from these basic flaws: In its formulation it misconceives the nature of the pregnant woman's interest; and in practice it undervalues the state's interest in potential life, as recognized in *Roe*. . . .

The very notion that the state has a substantial interest in potential life leads to the conclusion that not all regulations must be deemed unwarranted. Not all burdens on the right to decide whether to terminate a pregnancy will be undue. In our view, the undue burden standard is the appropriate means of reconciling the state's interest with the woman's constitutionally protected liberty. . . . Because we set forth a standard of general application to which we intend to adhere, it is important to clarify what is meant by an undue burden.

A finding of an undue burden is a shorthand for the conclusion that a state regulation has the purpose or effect of placing a substantial obstacle in the path of a woman seeking an abortion of a nonviable fetus. A statute with this purpose is invalid because the means chosen by the state to further the interest in potential life must be calculated to inform the woman's free choice, not hinder it. And a statute which, while furthering the interest in potential life or some other valid state interest, has the effect of placing a substantial obstacle in the path of a woman's choice cannot be considered a permissible means of serving its legitimate ends. . . . Understood another way, we answer the question, left open in previous opinions discussing the undue burden formulation, whether a law designed to further the state's interest in fetal life which imposes an undue burden on the woman's decision before fetal viability could be constitutional. The answer is no.

Some guiding principles should emerge. What is at stake is the woman's right to make the ultimate decision, not a right to be insulated from all others in doing so. Regulations which do no more than create a structural mechanism by which the state, or the parent or guardian of a minor, may express profound respect for the life of the unborn are permitted, if they are not a substantial obstacle to the woman's exercise of the right to choose. Unless it has that effect on her right of choice, a state measure designed to persuade her to choose childbirth over abortion will be upheld if reasonably related to that goal. Regulations designed to foster the health of a woman seeking an abortion are valid if they do not constitute an undue burden. . . .

We give this summary:

(a) To protect the central right recognized by Roe v. Wade while at the same time accommodating the state's profound interest in potential life, we will employ the undue burden analysis as explained in this opinion. An undue burden exists, and therefore a provision of law is invalid, if its purpose or effect is to place a substantial obstacle in the path of a woman seeking an abortion before the fetus attains viability.

(b) We reject the rigid trimester framework of Roe v. Wade. To promote the state's profound interest in potential life, throughout pregnancy the state may take measures to ensure that the woman's choice is informed, and measures designed to advance this interest will not be invalidated as long as their purpose is to persuade the woman to choose childbirth over abortion. These measures must not be an undue burden on the right.

(c) As with any medical procedure, the state may enact regulations to further the health or safety of a woman seeking an abortion. Unnecessary health regulations that have the purpose or effect of presenting a substantial obstacle to a woman seeking an abortion impose an undue burden on the right.

(d) Our adoption of the undue burden analysis does not disturb the central holding of Roe v. Wade, and we reaffirm that holding. Regardless of whether exceptions are made for particular circumstances, a state may not prohibit any woman from making the ultimate decision to terminate her pregnancy before viability.

(e) We also reaffirm *Roe*'s holding that "subsequent to viability, the state in promoting its interest in the potentiality of human life may, if it chooses, regulate, and even proscribe, abortion except where it is necessary, in appropriate medical judgment, for the preservation of the life or health of the mother." Roe v. Wade, 410 U.S., at 164-165.

These principles control our assessment of the Pennsylvania statute, and we now turn to the issue of the validity of its challenged provisions.

V

A

Because it is central to the operation of various other requirements, we begin with the statute's definition of medical emergency. . . . [T]he court of appeals construed the phrase "serious risk" to include those circumstances. It stated: "we read the medical emergency exception as intended by the Pennsylvania legislature to assure that compliance with its abortion regulations would not in any way pose a significant threat to the life or health of a woman." . . . We adhere to that course today, and conclude that, as construed by the court of appeals, the medical emergency definition imposes no undue burden on a woman's abortion right.

B

We next consider the informed consent requirement. Except in a medical emergency, the statute requires that at least 24 hours before performing an abortion a physician inform the woman of the nature of the procedure, the health risks of the abortion and of childbirth, and the "probable gestational age of the unborn child." The physician or a qualified nonphysician must inform the woman of the availability of printed materials published by the state describing the fetus and providing information about medical assistance for childbirth, information about child support from the father, and a list of agencies which provide adoption and other services as alternatives to abortion. An abortion may not be performed unless the woman certifies in writing that she has been informed of the availability of these printed materials and has been provided them if she chooses to view them.

Our prior decisions establish that as with any medical procedure, the state may require a woman to give her written informed consent to an abortion. In this respect, the statute is unexceptional. Petitioners challenge the statute's definition of informed consent because it includes the provision of specific information by the doctor and the mandatory 24-hour waiting period. The conclusions reached by a majority of the Justices in the separate opinions filed today and the undue burden standard adopted in this opinion require us to overrule in part some of the Court's past decisions, decisions driven by the trimester framework's prohibition of all previability regulations designed to further the state's interest in fetal life. . . .

To the extent [that our prior decisions] find a constitutional violation when the government requires, as it does here, the giving of truthful, nonmisleading information about the nature of the procedure, the attendant health risks and those of childbirth, and the "probable gestational age" of the fetus, those cases go too far, are inconsistent with *Roe*'s acknowledgment of an important interest in potential life, and are overruled. . . .

Whether the mandatory 24-hour waiting period is . . . invalid because in practice it is a substantial obstacle to a woman's choice to terminate her pregnancy is a close question. The findings of fact by the district court indicate that because of the distances many women must travel to reach an abortion provider, the practical effect will often be a delay of much more than a day because the waiting period requires that a woman seeking an abortion make at least two visits to the doctor. The district court also found that in many instances this will increase the exposure of women seeking abortions to "the harassment and hostility of anti-abortion protestors demonstrating outside a clinic." As a result, the district court found that for those women who have the fewest financial resources, those who must travel long distances, and those who have difficulty explaining their whereabouts to husbands, employers, or others, the 24-hour waiting period will be "particularly burdensome."

These findings are troubling in some respects, but they do not demonstrate that the waiting period constitutes an undue burden. We do not doubt that, as the district court held, the waiting period has the effect of "increasing the cost and risk of delay of abortions," but the district court did not conclude that the increased costs and potential delays amount to substantial obstacles. . . .

We also disagree with the district court's conclusion that the "particularly burdensome" effects of the waiting period on some women require its invalidation. A particular burden is not of necessity a substantial obstacle. Whether a burden falls on a particular group is a distinct inquiry from whether it is a substantial obstacle even as to the women in that group. And the district court did not conclude that the waiting period is such an obstacle even for the women who are most burdened by it. Hence, on the record before us, and in the context of this facial challenge, we are not convinced that the 24-hour waiting period constitutes an undue burden. . . .

c

Pennsylvania's abortion law provides, except in cases of medical emergency, that no physician shall perform an abortion on a married woman without receiving a signed statement from the woman that she has notified her spouse that she is about to undergo an abortion. The woman has the option of providing an alternative signed statement certifying that her husband is not the man who impregnated her; that her husband could not be located; that the pregnancy is the result of spousal sexual assault which she has reported; or that the woman believes that notifying her husband will cause him or someone else to inflict bodily injury upon her. A physician who performs an abortion on a married woman without receiving the appropriate signed statement will have his or her license revoked, and is liable to the husband for damages. . . .

The spousal notification requirement is thus likely to prevent a significant number of women from obtaining an abortion. It does not merely make abortions a little more difficult or expensive to obtain; for many women, it will impose a substantial obstacle. We must not blind ourselves to the fact that the significant number of women who fear for their safety and the safety of their children are likely to be deterred from procuring an abortion as surely as if the Commonwealth had outlawed abortion in all cases. . . .

The husband's interest in the life of the child his wife is carrying does not permit the state to empower him with this troubling degree of authority over his wife. The contrary view leads to consequences reminiscent of the common law. A husband has no enforceable right to require a wife to advise him before she exercises her personal choices. If a husband's interest in the potential life of the child outweighs a wife's liberty, the state could require a married woman to notify her husband before she uses a postfertilization contraceptive. Perhaps next in line would be a statute requiring pregnant married women to notify their husbands before engaging in conduct causing risks to the fetus. After all, if the husband's interest in the fetus' safety is a sufficient predicate for state regulation, the state could reasonably conclude that pregnant wives should notify their husbands before drinking alcohol or smoking. Perhaps married women should notify their husbands before using contraceptives or before undergoing any type of surgery that may have complications affecting the husband's interest in his wife's reproductive organs. And if a husband's interest justifies notice in any of these cases, one might reasonably argue that it justifies exactly what the *Danforth* Court held it did not justify—a requirement of the husband's consent as well. A state may not give to a man the kind of dominion over his wife that parents exercise over their children.

[The statute] embodies a view of marriage consonant with the common-law status of married women but repugnant to our present understanding of marriage and of the nature of the rights secured by the Constitution. Women do not lose their constitutionally protected liberty when they marry. The Constitution protects all individuals, male or female, married or unmarried, from the abuse of governmental power, even where that power is employed for the supposed benefit of a member of the individual's family. These considerations confirm our conclusion that [the spousal notification provision] is invalid.

D

We next consider the parental consent provision. Except in a medical emergency, an unemancipated young woman under 18 may not obtain an abortion unless she and one of her parents (or guardian) provides informed consent as defined above. If neither a parent nor a guardian provides consent, a court may authorize the performance of an abortion upon a determination that the young woman is mature and capable of giving informed consent and has in fact given her informed consent, or that an abortion would be in her best interests.

We have been over most of this ground before. Our cases establish, and we reaffirm today, that a state may require a minor seeking an abortion to obtain the consent of a parent or guardian, provided that there is an adequate judicial bypass procedure. Under these precedents, in our view, the one-parent consent requirement and judicial bypass procedure are constitutional. . . .

VI

Our Constitution is a covenant running from the first generation of Americans to us and then to future generations. It is a coherent succession. Each generation must learn anew that the Constitution's written terms embody ideas and aspirations that must survive more ages than one. We accept our responsibility not to retreat from interpreting the full meaning of the covenant in light of all of our precedents. We invoke it once again to define the freedom guaranteed by the Constitution's own promise, the promise of liberty. . . .

BLACKMUN, Justice, concurring in part, concurring in the judgment in part, and dissenting in part.

Three years ago, in Webster v. Reproductive Health Serv., 492 U.S. 490 (1989), four Members of this Court appeared poised to "cas[t] into darkness the hopes and visions of every woman in this country" who had come to believe that the Constitution guaranteed her the right to reproductive choice. All that remained between the promise of *Roe* and the darkness of the plurality was a single, flickering flame. Decisions since Webster gave little reason to hope that this flame would cast much light. . . . But now, just when so many expected the darkness to fall, the flame has grown bright.

I do not underestimate the significance of today's joint opinion. Yet I remain steadfast in my belief that the right to reproductive choice is entitled to the full protection afforded by this Court before *Webster*. And I fear for the darkness as four Justices anxiously await the single vote necessary to extinguish the light. . . .

Make no mistake, the joint opinion of Justices O'Connor, Kennedy, and Souter is an act of personal courage and constitutional principle. . . .

Today, no less than yesterday, the Constitution and decisions of this Court require that a state's abortion restrictions be subjected to the strictest of judicial scrutiny. Our precedents and the joint opinion's principles require us to subject all non-de minimis abortion regulations to strict scrutiny. Under this standard, the Pennsylvania statute's provisions requiring content-based counseling, a 24-hour delay, informed parental consent, and reporting of abortion-related information must be invalidated. . . .

In one sense, the Court's approach is worlds apart from that of The Chief Justice and Justice Scalia. And yet, in another sense, the distance between the two approaches is short—the distance is but a single vote.

I am 83 years old. I cannot remain on this Court forever, and when I do step down, the confirmation process for my successor well may focus on the issue before us today. That, I regret, may be exactly where the choice between the two worlds will be made.

REHNQUIST, Chief Justice, with whom WHITE, SCALIA, and THOMAS, Justices, join, concurring in the judgment in part and dissenting in part.

The joint opinion, following its newly-minted variation on *stare decisis*, retains the outer shell of Roe v. Wade, but beats a wholesale retreat from the substance of that case. We believe that *Roe* was wrongly decided, and that it can and should be overruled consistently with our traditional approach to *stare decisis* in constitutional cases. We would adopt the approach of the plurality in Webster v. Reproductive

Health Services, 492 U.S. 490 (1989), and uphold the challenged provisions of the Pennsylvania statute in their entirety. . . .

In construing the phrase *liberty* incorporated in the due process clause of the Fourteenth Amendment, we have recognized that its meaning extends beyond freedom from physical restraint. In Pierce v. Society of Sisters, 268 U.S. 510 (1925), we held that it included a parent's right to send a child to private school; in Meyer v. Nebraska, 262 U.S. 390 (1923), we held that it included a right to teach a foreign language in a parochial school. Building on these cases, we have held that the term *liberty* includes a right to marry, Loving v. Virginia, 388 U.S. 1 (1967); a right to procreate, Skinner v. Oklahoma ex rel. Williamson, 316 U.S. 535 (1942); and a right to use contraceptives. Griswold v. Connecticut, 381 U.S. 479 (1965); Eisenstadt v. Baird, 405 U.S. 438 (1972). But a reading of these opinions makes clear that they do not endorse any all-encompassing "right of privacy." . . .

Nor do the historical traditions of the American people support the view that the right to terminate one's pregnancy is "fundamental." . . .

We think, therefore, both in view of this history and of our decided cases dealing with substantive liberty under the due process clause, that the Court was mistaken in *Roe* when it classified a woman's decision to terminate her pregnancy as a "fundamental right" that could be abridged only in a manner which withstood "strict scrutiny." . . .

The joint opinion of Justices O'Connor, Kennedy, and Souter cannot bring itself to say that *Roe* was correct as an original matter, but the authors are of the view that "the immediate question is not the soundness of *Roe*'s resolution of the issue, but the precedential force that must be accorded to its holding." Instead of claiming that *Roe* was correct as a matter of original constitutional interpretation, the opinion therefore contains an elaborate discussion of *stare decisis*. This discussion of the principle of *stare decisis* appears to be almost entirely dicta, because the joint opinion does not apply that principle in dealing with *Roe*. *Roe* decided that a woman had a fundamental right to an abortion. The joint opinion rejects that view. *Roe* decided that abortion regulations were to be subjected to "strict scrutiny" and could be justified only in the light of "compelling state interests." The joint opinion rejects that view. *Roe* analyzed abortion regulation under a rigid trimester framework, a framework which has guided this Court's decisionmaking for 19 years. The joint opinion rejects that framework.

The sum of the joint opinion's labors in the name of *stare decisis* and "legitimacy" is this: Roe v. Wade stands as a sort of judicial Potemkin Village, which may be pointed out to passers by as a monument to the importance of adhering to precedent. But behind the facade, an entirely new method of analysis, without any roots in constitutional law, is imported to decide the constitutionality of state laws regulating abortion. Neither *stare decisis* nor "legitimacy" are truly served by such an effort.

We have stated above our belief that the Constitution does not subject state abortion regulations to heightened scrutiny. Accordingly, we think that the correct analysis is that set forth by the plurality opinion in *Webster*. A woman's interest in having an abortion is a form of liberty protected by the due process clause, but states may regulate abortion procedures in ways rationally related to a legitimate state interest. . . .

We therefore would hold that each of the challenged provisions of the Pennsylvania statute is consistent with the Constitution. It bears emphasis that our conclusion in this regard does not carry with it any necessary approval of these regulations. Our task is, as always, to decide only whether the challenged provisions of a law comport with the United States Constitution. If, as we believe, these do, their wisdom as a matter of public policy is for the people of Pennsylvania to decide.

■ GONZALES v. CARHART
550 U.S. 124 (2007)

KENNEDY, J.

These cases require us to consider the validity of the Partial-Birth Abortion Ban Act of 2003 (Act), 18 U.S.C. §1531, a federal statute regulating abortion procedures. In recitations preceding its operative provisions the Act refers to the Court's opinion in Stenberg v. Carhart, 530 U.S. 914 (2000), which [struck down Nebraska's restriction on] abortion procedures used in the later stages of pregnancy. Compared to the state statute at issue in *Stenberg*, the Act is more specific concerning the instances to which it applies and in this respect more precise in its coverage. We conclude the Act should be sustained against the objections lodged by the broad, facial attack brought against it. . . .

I

A

The Act proscribes a particular manner of ending fetal life, so it is necessary here, as it was in *Stenberg*, to discuss abortion procedures in some detail. . . .* Abortion methods vary depending to some extent on the preferences of the physician and, of course, on the term of the pregnancy and the resulting stage of the unborn child's development. Between 85 and 90 percent of the approximately 1.3 million abortions performed each year in the United States take place in the first three months of pregnancy, which is to say in the first trimester. . . . The Act does not regulate these procedures.

Of the remaining abortions that take place each year, most occur in the second trimester. The surgical procedure referred to as "dilation and evacuation" or "D & E" is the usual abortion method in this trimester. . . . Although individual techniques for performing D & E differ, the general steps are the same. . . . A doctor must first dilate the cervix at least to the extent needed to insert surgical instruments into the uterus and to maneuver them to evacuate the fetus. . . .

The abortion procedure that was the impetus for the numerous bans on "partial-birth abortion," including the Act, is a variation of this standard. . . . The medical community has not reached unanimity on the appropriate name for this D & E variation. It has been referred to as "intact D & E," "dilation and extraction" (D & X), and "intact D & X." . . . For discussion purposes this D & E variation will

---

*[Justice Kennedy's opinion includes graphic descriptions of various second-term abortion procedures that have been shortened and summarized in this edited version of the opinion. — EDS.]

be referred to as intact D & E. The main difference between the two procedures is that in intact D & E a doctor extracts the fetus intact or largely intact with only a few passes [through the cervix, instead of extracting it in pieces]. . . . Intact D & E gained public notoriety when, in 1992, Dr. Martin Haskell gave a presentation describing his method of performing the operation. . . .

D & E and intact D & E are not the only second-trimester abortion methods. Doctors also may abort a fetus through medical induction. The doctor medicates the woman to induce labor, and contractions occur to deliver the fetus. Induction, which unlike D & E should occur in a hospital, can last as little as 6 hours but can take longer than 48. It accounts for about five percent of second-trimester abortions before 20 weeks of gestation and 15 percent of those after 20 weeks. Doctors turn to two other methods of second-trimester abortion, hysterotomy [removal of the fetus via an incision in the abdomen and uterine wall] and hysterectomy [removal of the uterus], only in emergency situations because they carry increased risk of complications. . . .

B

After Dr. Haskell's procedure received public attention, with ensuing and increasing public concern, bans on "partial birth abortion" proliferated. By the time of the *Stenberg* decision, about 30 States had enacted bans designed to prohibit the procedure. . . . In 1996, Congress also acted to ban partial-birth abortion. President Clinton vetoed the congressional legislation, and the Senate failed to override the veto. Congress approved another bill banning the procedure in 1997, but President Clinton again vetoed it. In 2003, after this Court's [5-4] decision in *Stenberg* [striking down Nebraska's ban], Congress passed [and President Bush signed] the Act at issue here. . . .

The Act responded to *Stenberg* in two ways. First, Congress made factual findings. Congress determined that this Court in *Stenberg* "was required to accept the very questionable findings issued by the district court judge," . . . but that Congress was "not bound to accept the same factual findings." Congress found, among other things, that "[a] moral, medical, and ethical consensus exists that the practice of performing a partial-birth abortion . . . is a gruesome and inhumane procedure that is never medically necessary and should be prohibited." . . . Second, and more relevant here, the Act's language differs from that of the Nebraska statute struck down in *Stenberg*. . . . [The court then summarized the provisions of the Act.]

II

The principles set forth in the joint opinion in *Planned Parenthood of Southeastern Pa. v. Casey*, [supra at page 488] did not find support from all those who join the instant opinion. . . . Whatever one's views concerning the *Casey* joint opinion, it is evident a premise central to its conclusion — that the government has a legitimate and substantial interest in preserving and promoting fetal life — would be repudiated were the Court now to affirm the judgments of the Courts of Appeals.

[Applying the principles of *Casey*] . . . we must determine whether the Act furthers the legitimate interest of the Government in protecting the life of the fetus that may become a child. . . . We assume the following principles for the purposes of this opinion. Before viability, a State "may not prohibit any woman from making the ultimate decision to terminate her pregnancy" [*Casey*, 505 U.S. at 879 (plurality opinion)]. It also may not impose upon this right an undue burden, which exists if a regulation's "purpose or effect is to place a substantial obstacle in the path of a woman seeking an abortion before the fetus attains viability." . . . On the other hand, "[r]egulations which do no more than create a structural mechanism by which the State, or the parent or guardian of a minor, may express profound respect for the life of the unborn are permitted, if they are not a substantial obstacle to the woman's exercise of the right to choose." . . . *Casey*, in short, struck a balance. The balance was central to its holding. We now apply its standard to the cases at bar. . . .

[The Act] regulates and proscribes, with exceptions or qualifications to be discussed, performing the intact D & E procedure. Respondents agree the Act encompasses intact D & E, but they contend its additional reach is both unclear and excessive. Respondents assert that, at the least, the Act is void for vagueness because its scope is indefinite. In the alternative, respondents argue the Act's text proscribes all D & Es. Because D & E is the most common second-trimester abortion method, respondents suggest the Act imposes an undue burden. In this litigation the Attorney General does not dispute that the Act would impose an undue burden if it covered standard D & E.

We conclude that the Act is not void for vagueness, does not impose an undue burden from any overbreadth, and is not invalid on its face.

The Act punishes "knowingly perform[ing]" a "partial-birth abortion." §1531 (a). It defines the unlawful abortion in explicit terms. . . . "As generally stated, the void-for-vagueness doctrine requires that a penal statute define the criminal offense with sufficient definiteness that ordinary people can understand what conduct is prohibited and in a manner that does not encourage arbitrary and discriminatory enforcement." . . . The Act satisfies both requirements. . . .

Unlike the statutory language in *Stenberg* that prohibited the delivery of a "'substantial portion'" of the fetus—where a doctor might question how much of the fetus is a substantial portion—the Act defines the line between potentially criminal conduct on the one hand and lawful abortion on the other. . . . Doctors performing D & E will know that if they do not deliver a living fetus to an anatomical landmark [referring to the delivery of the fetus to a certain point as specified in the statute] they will not face criminal liability. This conclusion is buttressed by the intent that must be proved to impose liability. The Court has made clear that scienter requirements alleviate vagueness concerns. . . .

We next determine whether the Act imposes an undue burden, as a facial matter, because its restrictions on second-trimester abortions are too broad. A review of the statutory text discloses the limits of its reach. The Act prohibits intact D & E; and, notwithstanding respondents' arguments, it does not prohibit the D & E procedure in which the fetus is removed in parts. . . .

IV

. . . The abortions affected by the Act's regulations take place both previability and postviability. . . . Under the principles accepted as controlling here, . . . the question is whether the Act, measured by its text in this facial attack, imposes a substantial obstacle to late-term, but previability, abortions. The Act does not on its face impose a substantial obstacle, and we reject this further facial challenge to its validity.

A

The Act's purposes are set forth in recitals preceding its operative provisions. A description of the prohibited abortion procedure demonstrates the rationale for the congressional enactment. The Act proscribes a method of abortion in which a fetus is killed just inches before completion of the birth process. Congress stated as follows: "Implicitly approving such a brutal and inhumane procedure by choosing not to prohibit it will further coarsen society to the humanity of not only newborns, but all vulnerable and innocent human life, making it increasingly difficult to protect such life." The Act expresses respect for the dignity of human life.

Congress was concerned, furthermore, with the effects on the medical community and on its reputation caused by the practice of partial-birth abortion. The findings in the Act explain: "Partial-birth abortion . . . confuses the medical, legal, and ethical duties of physicians to preserve and promote life, as the physician acts directly against the physical life of a child, whom he or she had just delivered, all but the head, out of the womb, in order to end that life." There can be no doubt the government "has an interest in protecting the integrity and ethics of the medical profession." Washington v. Glucksberg, 521 U.S. 702 (1997). . . .

Casey reaffirmed these governmental objectives. The government may use its voice and its regulatory authority to show its profound respect for the life within the woman. A central premise of the opinion was that the Court's precedents after *Roe* had "undervalue[d] the State's interest in potential life." 505 U.S. at 873 (plurality opinion). . . . The plurality opinion indicated "[t]he fact that a law which serves a valid purpose, one not designed to strike at the right itself, has the incidental effect of making it more difficult or more expensive to procure an abortion cannot be enough to invalidate it." *Id.* at 874. This was not an idle assertion. The three premises of *Casey* must coexist. . . . The third premise, that the State, from the inception of the pregnancy, maintains its own regulatory interest in protecting the life of the fetus that may become a child, cannot be set at naught by interpreting *Casey*'s requirement of a health exception so it becomes tantamount to allowing a doctor to choose the abortion method he or she might prefer. Where it has a rational basis to act, and it does not impose an undue burden, the State may use its regulatory power to bar certain procedures and substitute others, all in furtherance of its legitimate interests in regulating the medical profession in order to promote respect for life, including life of the unborn.

The Act's ban on abortions that involve partial delivery of a living fetus furthers the Government's objectives. No one would dispute that, for many, D & E is a procedure itself laden with the power to devalue human life. Congress could nonetheless conclude that the type of abortion proscribed by the Act requires specific regulation because it implicates additional ethical and moral concerns that justify a special prohibition. Congress determined that the abortion methods it proscribed had a "disturbing similarity to the killing of a newborn infant," and thus it was concerned with "draw[ing] a bright line that clearly distinguishes abortion and infanticide." . . . The Court has in the past confirmed the validity of drawing boundaries to prevent certain practices that extinguish life and are close to actions that are condemned. *Glucksberg* found reasonable the State's "fear that permitting assisted suicide will start it down the path to voluntary and perhaps even involuntary euthanasia." 521 U.S. at 732-35. . . .

Respect for human life finds an ultimate expression in the bond of love the mother has for her child. The Act recognizes this reality as well. Whether to have an abortion requires a difficult and painful moral decision. . . . While we find no reliable data to measure the phenomenon, it seems unexceptionable to conclude some women come to regret their choice to abort the infant life they once created and sustained. Severe depression and loss of esteem can follow. . . .

In a decision so fraught with emotional consequence some doctors may prefer not to disclose precise details of the means that will be used, confining themselves to the required statement of risks the procedure entails. From one standpoint this ought not to be surprising. Any number of patients facing imminent surgical procedures would prefer not to hear all details, lest the usual anxiety preceding invasive medical procedures become the more intense. This is likely the case with the abortion procedures here in issue. . . .

It is, however, precisely this lack of information concerning the way in which the fetus will be killed that is of legitimate concern to the State. *Casey*, 505 U.S. at 873 (plurality opinion) ("States are free to enact laws to provide a reasonable framework for a woman to make a decision that has such profound and lasting meaning"). The State has an interest in ensuring so grave a choice is well informed. It is self-evident that a mother who comes to regret her choice to abort must struggle with grief more anguished and sorrow more profound when she learns, only after the event, what she once did not know . . . [about how the procedure is performed].

It is a reasonable inference that a necessary effect of the regulation and the knowledge it conveys will be to encourage some women to carry the infant to full term, thus reducing the absolute number of late-term abortions. The medical profession, furthermore, may find different and less shocking methods to abort the fetus in the second trimester, thereby accommodating legislative demand. The State's interest in respect for life is advanced by the dialogue that better informs the political and legal systems, the medical profession, expectant mothers, and society as a whole of the consequences that follow from a decision to elect a late-term abortion. . . . In sum, we reject the contention that the congressional purpose of the Act was "to place a substantial obstacle in the path of a woman seeking an abortion." 505 U.S. at 878 (plurality opinion).

B

The Act's furtherance of legitimate government interests bears upon, but does not resolve, the next question: whether the Act has the effect of imposing an unconstitutional burden on the abortion right because it does not allow use of the barred procedure where "'necessary, in appropriate medical judgment, for [the] preservation of the . . . health of the mother.'" [citing Ayotte v. Planned Parenthood of Northern New Eng., 546 U.S. 320.] . . . The prohibition in the Act would be unconstitutional, under precedents we here assume to be controlling, if it "subject[ed] [women] to significant health risks." [*Id.* at 328.] . . . In *Ayotte* the parties agreed a health exception to the challenged parental-involvement statute was necessary "to avert serious and often irreversible damage to [a pregnant minor's] health." . . . Here, by contrast, whether the Act creates significant health risks for women has been a contested factual question. The evidence presented in the trial courts and before Congress demonstrates both sides have medical support for their position. . . .

The question becomes whether the Act can stand when this medical uncertainty persists. The Court's precedents instruct that the Act can survive this facial attack. The Court has given state and federal legislatures wide discretion to pass legislation in areas where there is medical and scientific uncertainty. [The Court cites, among other cases, Jacobson v. Massachusetts, 197 U.S. 11 (1905), discussed in Chapter 6 at page 654.] . . . Physicians are not entitled to ignore regulations that direct them to use reasonable alternative procedures. The law need not give abortion doctors unfettered choice in the course of their medical practice, nor should it elevate their status above other physicians in the medical community. . . . Medical uncertainty does not foreclose the exercise of legislative power in the abortion context any more than it does in other contexts. . . . The medical uncertainty over whether the Act's prohibition creates significant health risks provides a sufficient basis to conclude in this facial attack that the Act does not impose an undue burden. . . .

In reaching the conclusion the Act does not require a health exception we reject certain arguments made by the parties on both sides of these cases. On the one hand, the Attorney General urges us to uphold the Act on the basis of the congressional findings alone. Although we review congressional factfinding under a deferential standard, we do not in the circumstances here place dispositive weight on Congress' findings. The Court retains an independent constitutional duty to review factual findings where constitutional rights are at stake. . . . As respondents have noted, and the District Courts recognized, some recitations in the Act are factually incorrect. . . .

On the other hand, relying on the Court's opinion in Stenberg, respondents contend that an abortion regulation must contain a health exception "if 'substantial medical authority supports the proposition that banning a particular procedure could endanger women's health.'" . . . As illustrated by respondents' arguments and the decisions of the Courts of Appeals, Stenberg has been interpreted to leave no margin of error for legislatures to act in the face of medical uncertainty. . . . A zero tolerance policy would strike down legitimate abortion regulations, like the present one, if some part of the medical community were disinclined to follow the proscription. This is too exacting a standard to impose on the legislative power, exercised in this instance under the Commerce Clause, to regulate the medical profession. Considerations of marginal safety, including the balance of risks, are within the legislative competence when the regulation is rational and in pursuit of legitimate ends. When standard medical options are available, mere convenience does not suffice to displace them; and if some procedures have different risks than others, it does not follow that the State is altogether barred from imposing reasonable regulations. The Act is not invalid on its face where there is uncertainty over whether the barred procedure is ever necessary to preserve a woman's health, given the availability of other abortion procedures that are considered to be safe alternatives. . . .

In these circumstances the proper means to consider exceptions is by as-applied challenge. . . . This is the proper manner to protect the health of the woman if it can be shown that in discrete and well-defined instances a particular condition has or is likely to occur in which the procedure prohibited by the Act must be used. In an as-applied challenge the nature of the medical risk can be better quantified and balanced than in a facial attack. . . .

Respondents have not demonstrated that the Act, as a facial matter, is void for vagueness, or that it imposes an undue burden on a woman's right to abortion based on its overbreadth or lack of a health exception. For these reasons the judgments of the Courts of Appeals for the Eighth and Ninth Circuits are reversed. . . .

[Justices Roberts, Scalia, Thomas, and Alito joined the majority opinion. Justice Thomas wrote a concurring opinion, joined by Justice Scalia, "reiterat[ing] my view that the Court's abortion jurisprudence . . . has no basis in the Constitution."]

GINSBURG, J., dissenting. . . .

Seven years ago, in *Stenberg*, . . . the Court invalidated a Nebraska statute criminalizing the performance of a medical procedure that, in the political arena, has been dubbed "partial-birth abortion." . . . [T]he Court held the Nebraska statute unconstitutional in part because it lacked the requisite protection for the preservation of a woman's health. . . .

Today's decision is alarming. It refuses to take *Casey* and *Stenberg* seriously. It tolerates, indeed applauds, federal intervention to ban nationwide a procedure found necessary and proper in certain cases by the American College of Obstetricians and Gynecologists (ACOG). It blurs the line, firmly drawn in *Casey* between previability and postviability abortions. And, for the first time since *Roe*, the Court blesses a prohibition with no exception safeguarding a woman's health.

I dissent from the Court's disposition. Retreating from prior rulings that abortion restrictions cannot be imposed absent an exception safeguarding a woman's health, the Court upholds an Act that surely would not survive under the close scrutiny that previously attended state-decreed limitations on a woman's reproductive choices.

I

As *Casey* comprehended, at stake in cases challenging abortion restrictions is a woman's "control over her [own] destiny." . . . Women, it is now acknowledged, have the talent, capacity, and right "to participate equally in the economic and social life of the Nation." . . . Their ability to realize their full potential, the Court recognized, is intimately connected to "their ability to control their reproductive lives." . . . Thus, legal challenges to undue restrictions on abortion procedures do not seek to vindicate some generalized notion of privacy; rather, they center on a woman's autonomy to determine her life's course, and thus to enjoy equal citizenship stature. See, e.g., Siegel, Reasoning from the Body: A Historical Perspective on Abortion Regulation and Questions of Equal Protection, 44 Stan. L. Rev. 261 (1992); Law, Rethinking Sex and the Constitution, 132 U. Pa. L. Rev. 955 (1984).

In keeping with this comprehension of the right to reproductive choice, the Court has consistently required that laws regulating abortion, at any stage of pregnancy and in all cases, safeguard a woman's health. . . . We have thus ruled that a State must avoid subjecting women to health risks not only where the pregnancy itself creates danger, but also where state regulation forces women to resort to less safe methods of abortion. . . .

[The courts below] made findings after full trials at which all parties had the opportunity to present their best evidence. . . . According to the expert testimony plaintiffs introduced, the safety advantages of intact D & E are marked for women with certain medical conditions, for example, uterine scarring, bleeding disorders, heart disease, or compromised immune systems. . . . Further, plaintiffs' experts testified that intact D & E is significantly safer for women with certain pregnancy-related conditions, such as placenta previa and accreta and for women carrying fetuses with certain abnormalities, such as severe hydrocephalus. . . . Based on thoroughgoing review of the trial evidence and the congressional record, each of the District Courts to consider the issue rejected Congress' findings as unreasonable and not supported by the evidence. . . . The District Courts' findings merit this Court's respect. . . .

II

The Court offers flimsy and transparent justifications for upholding a nation-wide ban on intact D & E. . . . The law saves not a single fetus from destruction, for it targets only a *method* of performing abortion. . . . And surely the statute was not designed to protect the lives or health of pregnant women. . . . In short, the Court upholds a law that, while doing nothing to "preserv[e] . . . fetal life," . . . bars a woman from choosing intact D & E although her doctor "reasonably believes [that procedure] will best protect [her]." . . .

Ultimately, the Court admits that "moral concerns" are at work, concerns that could yield prohibitions on any abortion. . . . Notably, the concerns expressed are untethered to any ground genuinely serving the Government's interest in preserving life. By allowing such concerns to carry the day and case, overriding fundamental rights, the Court dishonors our precedent. . . .

Revealing in this regard, the Court invokes an antiabortion shibboleth for which it concededly has no reliable evidence: Women who have abortions come to regret their choices, and consequently suffer from "[s]evere depression and loss of esteem." . . .[7] Because of women's fragile emotional state and because of the "bond of love the mother has for her child," the Court worries, doctors may withhold information about the nature of the intact D & E procedure. . . . The solution the Court approves, then, is *not* to require doctors to inform women, accurately and adequately, of the different procedures and their attendant risks. . . . Instead, the Court deprives women of the right to make an autonomous choice, even at the expense of their safety. . . . This way of thinking reflects ancient notions about women's place in the family and under the Constitution-ideas that have long since been discredited. . . .

One wonders how long a line that saves no fetus from destruction will hold in face of the Court's "moral concerns." . . . The Court's hostility to the right *Roe* and *Casey* secured is not concealed. Throughout, the opinion refers to obstetrician-gynecologists and surgeons who perform abortions not by the titles of their medical specialties, but by the pejorative label "abortion doctor." . . . A fetus is described

---

7. The Court is surely correct that, for most women, abortion is a painfully difficult decision. . . . But "neither the weight of the scientific evidence to date nor the observable reality of 33 years of legal abortion in the United States comports with the idea that having an abortion is any more dangerous to a woman's long-term mental health than delivering and parenting a child that she did not intend to have. . . ." Cohen, Abortion and Mental Health: Myths and Realities, 9 Guttmacher Policy Rev. 8 (2006). . . .

as an "unborn child," and as a "baby," . . . second-trimester, previability abortions are referred to as "late-term," . . . ; and the reasoned medical judgments of highly trained doctors are dismissed as "preferences" motivated by "mere convenience." . . . Instead of the heightened scrutiny we have previously applied, the Court determines that a "rational" ground is enough to uphold the Act. . . . And, most troubling, *Casey*'s principles, confirming the continuing vitality of "the essential holding of *Roe*" are merely "assume[d]" for the moment, . . . rather than "retained" or "reaffirmed" . . . .

Though today's opinion does not go so far as to discard *Roe* or *Casey*, the Court, differently composed than it was when we last considered a restrictive abortion regulation, is hardly faithful to our earlier invocations of "the rule of law" and the "principles of *stare decisis*." . . . In candor, the Act, and the Court's defense of it, cannot be understood as anything other than an effort to chip away at a right declared again and again by this Court. . . .

[This dissent was joined by Justices Stevens, Souter, and Breyer.]

Notes: The Post-*Casey* Landscape and the Implications of *Gonzales*

1. Stare Decisis. Did *Casey* overturn *Roe*? Does the Court's discussion of *stare decisis* in the abortion cases seem persuasive? What does it mean to reaffirm Roe v. Wade while overturning the trimester framework, as the Court did in *Casey*? What types of cases are now likely to have different results?

The *Gonzales* Court clearly was forced to wrestle with the significance of *stare decisis* given the Court's invalidation of a similar statute in *Stenberg*. In *Stenberg*, the majority seemed to constrain the state's ability to prohibit abortion procedures:

> In sum, Nebraska has not convinced us that a health exception is "never necessary to preserve the health of women." . . . Rather, a statute that altogether forbids D & X [referred to as an "intact D & E" in *Gonzales*] creates a significant health risk. The statute consequently must contain a health exception. This is not to say . . . that a State is prohibited from proscribing an abortion procedure whenever a particular physician deems the procedure preferable. . . . But where substantial medical authority supports the proposition that banning a particular abortion procedure could endanger women's health, *Casey* requires the statute to include a health exception when the procedure is " 'necessary, in appropriate medical judgment, for the preservation of the life or health of the mother.' "

530 U.S. 914 at 937-938. Does the *Gonzales* majority overturn *Stenberg*?

The *Gonzales* case gave the newly constituted Supreme Court—with Justices Alito and Roberts and without Justices Rehnquist and O'Connor—an opportunity to revisit its approach to the jurisprudence of abortion. Justice Kennedy held the pivotal swing vote in a classic 5-4 split, a position often previously occupied by Justice Sandra Day O'Connor. Justice Kennedy's dissent in *Stenberg* argued that the Court's invalidation of Nebraska's ban on the abortion procedure was inconsistent with *Casey*'s stated deference to a state's legitimate interest in "promot[ing] the life of the unborn and to ensure respect for all human life and its potential." His majority decision in *Gonzales* emphasizes and relies upon this portion of *Casey*.

What does *Gonzales* suggest about the future of abortion jurisprudence? See Neal Devins, How Planned Parenthood v. Casey (Pretty Much) Settled the Abortion Wars, 118 Yale L.J. 1318 (2009) (arguing that *Casey* stabilized abortion politics); Reva B. Siegel, Dignity and the Politics of Protection: Abortion Restrictions Under *Casey/Carhart,* 117 Yale L.J. 1694 (2008). The decision suggested that governments would be given more latitude to regulate abortion to protect "moral values" and women's interests (as defined by the *Gonzales* majority rather than by Justice Ginsburg). Justice Ginsburg explicitly discusses the impact of the changes in the Court's membership since *Casey* and *Stenberg* in her dissent and expresses concern about the future of the abortion right. See R. Alta Charo, The Partial Death of Abortion Rights, 356 New Eng. J. Med. 2125 (2007). Justices Souter and Stevens have since been replaced by Justices Kagan and Sotomayor, who are presumed to support the continuation of constitutional protections.

2. *A Fundamental Right?* Is a woman's right to choose whether or not to have an abortion still a "fundamental right"? What is a "liberty interest"? The composition of the Court changed between *Casey, Stenberg,* and *Gonzales.* How many Justices actually supported the use of the "undue burden" test? *Gonzales* suggested that there were at least five, as Justice Kennedy seemed not yet willing to abandon *Casey.* The views of Chief Justice Roberts and Justice Alito were not completely clear as they joined Justice Kennedy's majority decision "assuming" that the principles of *Casey* applied. Neither joined in Justice Thomas's dissent repudiating *Roe* and its progeny. What types of proof might be relevant to determining whether a state regulation poses an "undue burden" on a woman's abortion right post-*Casey* and post-*Gonzales?*

3. *A New Court and New Legislative Challenges.* Changes in the political climate and the composition of the Supreme Court have resulted in sharp increases in state legislation relating to abortion, including efforts to preemptively ban abortion should *Roe v. Wade* be overturned. See, e.g., National Conference of State Legislatures, Abortion Laws (available at NCSL Web site); Rachel Benson Gold & Elizabeth Nash, Troubling Trend: More States Hostile to Abortion Rights as Middle Ground Shrinks, 15 Guttmacher Pol'y Rev. 14 (2012) ("States enacted 92 provisions restricting abortion in 2011, nearly triple the previous record of 34 in 2005.").

4. *Abortion and Equal Protection.* Some commentators have argued that restrictions on abortion ought to be challenged under equal protection grounds. Justice Ginsburg's dissent in *Gonzales* begins with a description of the abortion right as necessary to ensure women's liberty and equality. Is there any other support for this view in the Court's recent decisions? See Jennifer S. Hendricks, Body and Soul: Equality, Pregnancy, and the Unitary Right to Abortion, 45 Harv. C.R.-C.L. L. Rev. 329 (2010); Priscilla J. Smith, Give Justice Ginsburg What She Wants: Using Sex Equality Arguments to Demand Examination of the Legitimacy of State Interests in Abortion Regulation, 34 Harv. J.L. & Gender 377 (2011). But see Charles I. Lugosi, Conforming to the Rule of Law: When Person and Human Being Finally Mean the Same Thing in Fourteenth Amendment Jurisprudence, 22 Issues L. & Med. 119 (2006) (arguing that the Supreme Court should reconsider its failure to find fetuses protected under the Equal Protection Clause). For an interesting alternative argument, see Andrew Koppelman, Originalism, Abortion, and the Thirteenth Amendment, 112 Columbia L. Rev. 1917 (2012) (arguing that banning abortion and compelling women to bear children would violate the Thirteenth Amendment).

5. *The Undue Burden Standard Applied.* As might be expected, *Casey* has been cited in more than 1,200 judicial decisions since its publication. It has been used to

uphold some state abortion regulations, see, e.g., Barnes v. Moore, 970 F.2d 12 (5th Cir. 1992), and to strike down others, see, e.g., Stenberg v. Carhart, supra. Litigants have sought to use *Casey* in other socially controversial areas. See, e.g., Washington v. Glucksberg, 521 U.S. 702 (1997) (Court rejects view that *Casey* supports a constitutional right to assisted suicide). Will the Court's decision in *Gonzales* have a ripple effect in other areas? See Abigail Alliance for Better Access to Developmental Drugs v. von Eschenbach, 495 F.3d 695, 714 (D.C. Cir. 2007) (en banc) (citing *Gonzales* in case involving limiting patient access to experimental therapies for the power of legislatures to act even where scientific uncertainty exists).

6. *Later Abortions.* Second-trimester abortions are relatively rare. Karen Pazol et al., Abortion Surveillance—United States, 2008, 60 MMWR 1, 15 (Nov. 25, 2011) (No. SS-15) (7.3% of reported abortions occurred at 14 to 20 weeks of gestation; only 1.3% occurred at 21 weeks or greater). See also Lisa Haddad et al., Changes in Abortion Provider Practices in Response to the Partial-Birth Abortion Ban Act of 2003, 79 Contraception 379 (2009).

What explains the significant legislative activity in this area, given the relative rarity of these procedures? The *Stenberg* decision discussed in *Gonzales* arguably presented a blueprint for states interested in enacting limits on late-term abortions, yet most legislatures did not review or revise their partial-birth abortion bans to conform with *Stenberg*'s criteria. Why did Congress finally enact the "partial-birth" abortion ban after the Court's decision in *Stenberg*? A relatively new type of state legislation focuses on the concept of fetal pain as a basis for banning later abortions, typically after 20 weeks. See Neb. Rev. St. §38-2021 (unprofessional conduct includes performance of abortion in violation of Pain-Capable Unborn Child Protection Act). Suppose that the medical evidence indicated that fetuses could feel pain at a point close to viability. Would the state interest in preventing fetal pain be compelling? Would the interest be compelling if evidence suggested the experience of pain earlier in pregnancy? See I. Glenn Cohen & Sadath Sayeed, Fetal Pain, Abortion, Viability and the Constitution, 39 J.L. Med. & Ethics 235 (2011) (finding legislation unconstitutional but noting close question).

Most states have enacted legislation limiting or prohibiting later abortions or banning "partial-birth" abortion. Guttmacher Institute, State Policies on Later Abortions (Nov. 1, 2012) (listing states and status of court challenges); Guttmacher Institute, An Overview of Abortion Laws (Feb. 1, 2013) (19 states have attempted to ban partial-birth abortions), both available at www.guttmacher.org/. Late-term abortions remain extremely controversial. Joe Stumpe, Jurors Acquit Kansas Doctor in a Late-Term Abortion Case, N.Y. Times, Mar. 28, 2009, at A11; Monica Davey, Abortion Foe Found Guilty in Doctor's Killing, N.Y. Times, Jan. 30, 2010, at A12.

Notes: Forty Years of Abortion Jurisprudence

1. *Regulation of Abortion Providers.* The Supreme Court held in *Roe*, at least by implication, that states could require that first-trimester abortions be performed by physicians. 410 U.S. 113, 163 (1973). The state's interest in the health of a pregnant woman would become compelling at the point where the risks of the abortion outweighed the risks of carrying the pregnancy to term, or at the end of the first trimester. After this point, "a state may regulate the abortion procedure to the extent that the regulation reasonably relates to the preservation and protection of maternal

health." States may establish requirements for providers and facilities. At the point of fetal viability, sometime around the end of the second trimester, a state may assert its compelling interest in protecting fetal life by prohibiting abortion, except where the procedure was necessary to preserve the life or health of the pregnant woman. Id. Is *Gonzales* consistent with this framework? What interests support regulation of the type of abortion procedure used prior to viability? The Supreme Court confirmed that states may require that physicians perform abortions in Mazurek v. Armstrong, 520 U.S. 968 (1997) (rejecting contention that requirement placed an undue burden on access to abortion). See also Guttmacher Institute, An Overview of Abortion Laws (Feb. 1, 2013) (39 states require use of licensed physicians), available at www.guttmacher.org/.

States have increased reporting, facilities, and inspection requirements for abortion providers. These regulations generally reduce the number of abortion providers and increase the costs of providing the procedure. Although many regulations will be upheld given the Supreme Court's explicit authorization of certain forms of state provider regulation, providers and activists have successfully challenged some provisions under the undue burden standard. In 2012, for example, a lower court issued a preliminary injunction against enforcement of a new Mississippi statute requiring abortion providers to have hospital admitting privileges and to be board certified in obstetrics and gynecology; the legislation had threatened to close the state's only abortion clinic. Jackson Women's Health Organization v. Currier, 2012 WL 2886715 (S.D. Miss.) See also Choice Incorporated of Texas v. Greenstein, 691 F.3d 710 (5th Cir. 2012) (dismissing as not ripe an action challenging changes in Louisiana's regulation of abortion clinics); Theodore Joyce, The Supply-Side Economics of Abortion, 365 New Eng. J. Med. 1466 (2011) (discussing Kansas licensing rules that would have eliminated two of three providers in state); Dawn Johnson, "TRAP"ing *Roe* in Indiana and a Common-Ground Alternative, 118 Yale L.J. 1356 (2009) (noting impact of increasing regulation of providers).

Women who face difficulties accessing surgical abortions may turn to mifepristone. In 2000, mifepristone was approved by the FDA for use in terminating pregnancies in accordance with particular dosing requirements. Subsequent research resulted in changes in the clinical practice for the use of the drug, including a reduction in the required dosage and a slight expansion of the gestational period during which the drug could be used. Should states be able to ban this "off-label" use of mifepristone and require adherence to the original FDA approval? Planned Parenthood Southwest Ohio Region, 696 F.3d 490 (6th Cir. 2012) (yes). Can a state criminally prosecute a woman for terminating her pregnancy using a drug purchased over the Internet? McCormack v. Hiedeman, 694 F.3d 1004 (9th Cir. 2012) (finding undue burden where state felony statute used to prosecute woman where pregnancy not terminated by physician under regulatory regime).

2. *Government Funding for Abortion.* Restrictions on government funding for abortions were the first real political and legal successes for abortion opponents. In Maher v. Roe, 432 U.S. 464 (1977), the Supreme Court upheld the constitutional validity of a Connecticut welfare rule that provided Medicaid recipients with coverage for pregnancy services but not for nontherapeutic abortion services. In Harris v. McRae, 448 U.S. 297 (1980), the Court upheld the "Hyde Amendment," which prohibited the use of federal funds contributed to the Medicaid program to reimburse the cost of most abortions even when they were medically necessary. The Court found that state and federal funding restrictions did not violate the due

process or equal protection clause because, while women had a constitutional right to choose abortion, they did not have a constitutional right to make the government pay for it. The government, the Court held, was free to establish programs that provided pregnancy benefits while denying coverage for abortion:

> But, regardless of whether the freedom of a woman to choose to terminate her pregnancy for health reasons lies at the core or the periphery of the due process liberty recognized in [Roe v. Wade], it simply does not follow that a woman's freedom of choice carries with it a constitutional entitlement to the financial resources to avail herself of the full range of protected choices. . . . [A]lthough government may not place obstacles in the path of a woman's exercise of her freedom of choice, it need not remove those not of its own creation. Indigence falls in the latter category. The financial constraints that restrict an indigent woman's ability to enjoy the full range of constitutionally protected freedom of choice are the product not of governmental restrictions on access to abortions, but rather of her indigence. Although Congress has opted to subsidize medically necessary services generally, but not certain medically necessary abortions, the fact remains that the Hyde Amendment leaves an indigent woman with at least the same range of choice in deciding whether to obtain a medically necessary abortion as she would have had if Congress had chosen to subsidize no health care costs at all. We are thus not persuaded that the Hyde Amendment impinges on the constitutionally protected freedom of choice recognized in [Roe].

448 U.S. 297 at 316-317. Federal funding for abortion is the subject of regular congressional debate, and the abortion coverage exclusion occasionally expands and narrows as the result of political campaigns waged by pro-choice and anti-abortion forces.

State courts have sometimes found a state constitutional right to Medicaid funding for abortions, requiring that states fund these services even in the absence of federal assistance. See, e.g., State Department of Health & Human Services v. Planned Parenthood of Alaska, Inc., 28 P.3d 904 (Alaska 2001). Other states have statutory or constitutional provisions that *prohibit* expenditure of state funds on abortions. These jurisdictions have been confronted with somewhat of a dilemma because federal law requires that states provide funding for abortion in some limited circumstances, and federal law of course is supreme even when weighed against a state constitutional provision. See Dalton v. Little Rock Family Planning Services, 516 U.S. 474 (1996). See generally Guttmacher Institute, State Funding of Abortion Under Medicaid (Nov. 1, 2012), available at www.guttmacher.org. Government funding returned as a controversial issue in the late 1980s with the adoption of new regulations implementing federal funding of family planning clinics under Title X of the Public Health Service Act. 42 U.S.C. §§300 to 300a-6. The Act specified that federal funds could not be "used in programs where abortion is a method of family planning." Id. §300a-6. The regulations placed three different conditions on recipients of Title X federal funds. The first, and most controversial, set of provisions came to be known as the "gag clause." Title X providers were prohibited from counseling about abortion or providing abortion referrals as a method of family planning. The Title X project was forbidden from providing an abortion referral even when specifically requested by a patient. Project personnel were permitted to state: "The project does not consider abortion an appropriate method of family planning and therefore does not counsel or refer for abortion." 42 C.F.R. §59.8(b) (5) (1989). The regulations also restricted Title X projects from encouraging, promoting, or advocating abortion as a method of family planning through lobbying, educational programs, or other activities. 42 C.F.R. §59.10(a) (1989). Finally, Title X projects had to be organized so that they were "physically and financially separate" from abortion activities. 42 C.F.R. §59.9 (1989). The Supreme Court rejected claims that the regulations violated the First Amendment in Rust v. Sullivan, 500 U.S. 173 (1991). The Court relied on the Harris v. McRae line of federal funding cases to hold that the regulations merely implemented a permissible governmental objective: ensuring that federal funds were used only for family planning purposes, not the promotion of abortion. Id. at 192-200. The gag rule was rescinded in the Clinton Administration. See Standards of Compliance for Abortion-Related Services in Family Services Projects, 65 Fed. Reg. 41,270 (2000).

There was intense debate over the coverage of abortion services in the federal Patient Protection and Affordable Care Act. The final legislation and regulations impose strict accounting requirements designed to ensure that federal funds are not used for abortion services. States may prohibit coverage of abortion services, but if they do not, the new insurance exchanges are permitted to sell insurance that covers abortion. However, no federal funds may be used to subsidize that portion of the coverage. See Susan A. Cohen, Insurance Coverage of Abortion: The Battle to Date and the Battle to Come, 13 Guttmacher Pol'y Rev. 2 (2010); Guttmacher Institute, Restricting Insurance Coverage of Abortion (2013). See also Lisa C. Ikemoto, Abortion, Contraception and the ACA: The Realignment of Women's Health, 55 How. L.J. 731 (2012); Roy G. Spece, Jr., The Purpose Prong of Casey's Undue Burden Test and Its Impact on the Constitutionality of Abortion Insurance Restrictions in the Affordable Care Act or Its Progeny, 33 Whittier L. Rev. 77 (2011).

The latest round of the funding battle involves state efforts to cut off funding for Planned Parenthood's family planning and other health services because of the organization's involvement in providing abortion services. Compare Planned Parenthood Ass'n of Hidalgo County Texas, Inc. v. Suehs, 692 F.3d 343 (5th Cir. 2012) (regulation barring organization from receiving funds under state health program if it promotes elective abortion or is affiliated with organizations promoting elective abortion does not violate First Amendment) with Planned Parenthood of Indiana, Inc. v. Commissioner of Indiana State Department of Health, 699 F.3d 962 (7th Cir. 2012) (upholding preliminary injunction against state law excluding health care providers who performed abortion from participation in Medicaid because federal law gives patients freedom of choice among qualified providers; state permitted to ban abortion-related providers from receiving funds under separate federal block grant program).

3. *Minors and Abortion.* Does the right established in Roe v. Wade apply to minors as well? Even if one accepts the proposition that women have a right to choose abortion, it does not necessarily follow that minors should be given the right to secure an abortion without parental notification or even consent. The Supreme Court has supported a minor's right of access to contraceptives, but the risks associated with an abortion clearly outweigh those created by the use of condoms. Parents ordinarily must give consent for their children to undergo medical procedures, absent an emergency, and abortion is a morally and religiously sensitive medical procedure. Notifying a parent of a child's pregnancy can, additionally, give parents important

information about a child's participation in sexual activities. On the other hand, children have constitutional rights in many circumstances. A significant percentage of teenagers may have the maturity to make their own abortion determinations. Further, a minor's right to make these decisions free from parental interference may be an important issue in abusive or incestuous homes.

The post-*Roe* Supreme Court struggled to determine whether and when a minor had a right to choose abortion. See, e.g., Ohio v. Akron Center for Reproductive Health, 497 U.S. 502 (1990); Hodgson v. Minnesota, 497 U.S. 417 (1990). These decisions were marked by deep divisions within the Court, with a majority of Justices upholding state parental notification or consent rules so long as they were accompanied by a judicial bypass procedure that permitted a mature minor to obtain judicial approval of her decision. The *Casey* court affirmed the continuing validity of *Hodgson* and *Akron* by upholding Pennsylvania's parental consent or judicial bypass procedure. More recently, the Supreme Court found that New Hampshire's parental notification law, which prohibited physicians from performing abortions on minors without prior written notice to a parent or guardian, could be unconstitutional in a medical emergency. The matter was remanded to the Court of Appeals for a determination of whether the remedy could be narrowed to prevent invalidation of the entire legislation. Ayotte v. Planned Parenthood, 546 U.S. 320 (2006). See Note, 119 Harv. L. Rev. 2552 (2006). See also State v. Planned Parenthood of Alaska, 171 P.3d 577 (Alaska 2007) (statute requiring parental consent struck down under state constitution; consent requirement more intrusive than notification and not the least restrictive way of achieving the state interests).

May states require minors to prove they are mature enough to make a decision about abortion by clear and convincing evidence? See In re B.S., 74 P.3d 285 (Ariz. App. 2003) (applying this standard). Can a trial court judge rely on a minor's failure to consult with her mother about proposed abortion as evidence for finding that she lacks the maturity required to make the decision? In re Doe, 33 A.3d 615 (Pa. 2011) (probably not, but see dissent). See also Zbaraz v. Madigan, 572 F.3d 370 (7th Cir. 2009) (rejecting facial challenge to judicial bypass standards for immature minors); and In re Petition of Anonymous 3, 782 N.W.2d 591 (Neb. 2010) (de novo review of record; no parental notification required as minor was emancipated). For a summary of the law involving minors and abortion, see Guttmacher Institute, Parental Involvement in Minors' Abortions (as of Feb. 1, 2013), available at: www.guttmacher .org; Carol Sanger, Decisional Dignity: Teenage Abortion, Bypass Hearings, and the Misuse of Law, 18 Colum. J. Gender & L. 409 (2009); and National Conference of State Legislatures, Parental Consent or Notification for Abortion (available at NCSL Web site). See also Theodore Joyce et al., Changes in Abortions and Births and the Texas Parental Notification Law, 354 New Eng. J. Med. 1031 (2006) (analysis of data to determine impact of law on abortion rates).

4. *Informed Consent and Waiting Periods.* A number of state legislatures have sought to regulate the informed consent process for abortions in two ways. First, states have sought to require abortion providers to disclose specific types of information about, for example, fetal age and development, or the availability of paternity support actions under state law. Second, states have enacted "waiting periods," under which women are required to wait some statutorily established period of time (one to three days) between being given information about the abortion procedure and undergoing the procedure itself. Guttmacher Institute, Counseling and Waiting

Periods for Abortion (2013). Waiting periods can be particularly problematic for women who must travel significant distances to secure access to abortion services.

Before *Casey*, courts generally invalidated attempts to dictate the specifics of what doctors must disclose to their patients—particularly scripts that were blatant attempts to discourage the procedure. See Akron v. Akron Center for Reproductive Health, 462 U.S. 416 (1983) (striking requirement that woman be informed, inter alia, that "the unborn child is a human life from the moment of conception"). The *Casey* decision reopened this avenue for state regulation, by upholding a Pennsylvania informed consent provision and 24-hour waiting rule because they did not impose an "undue burden" on women seeking an abortion. See, e.g., Cincinnati Women's Services, Inc. v. Taft, 468 F.3d 361 (6th Cir. 2006) (upholding Ohio's requirement of an informed consent process with physician 24 hours before procedure). See also Annot., 119 A.L.R.5th 315 (2004). The *Gonzales* decision supports state efforts to impose significant message-oriented informed consent provisions.

State legislatures have been particularly active in expanding informed consent provisions related to (1) the human status of the fetus under state law; (2) fetal development as assessed by sonogram results or heart auscultation; and (3) abortion and mental health. Opponents have argued that statements about the status of the fetus violate the First Amendment rights of physicians to avoid compelled speech; that the provisions requiring women to view sonograms or to listen to heart auscultation are not medically necessary; and that the required disclosures about fetal pain and mental health are inaccurate and misleading.

The courts have not been sympathetic to claims that the disclosure requirements violate physician's First Amendment rights. Citing Rust v. Sullivan, supra, Planned Parenthood v. Casey, supra, and Gonzales v. Carhart, supra, courts have held that physician speech can be subject to reasonable regulation via informed consent so long as the required information is relevant, truthful, and non-misleading. In Planned Parenthood of Minnesota, North Dakota, South Dakota v. Rounds, 653 F.3d 662 (8th Cir. 2011), the court upheld a South Dakota law requiring physicians to provide oral advisories about the human status of the fetus, the protected nature of the relationship between the woman and the fetus, and the fact that the abortion will terminate that relationship. This case has a complicated procedural history: The judgment was vacated, 662 F.3d 1072 (8th Cir. 2011), but a subsequent en banc decision noted that the panel holding on this issue was still in force, 686 F.3d 889, 893 n.1 (8th Cir. 2012) (en banc).

The U.S. Court of Appeals for the Fifth Circuit reviewed and rejected claims that Texas's sonogram and heartbeat requirements violated physicians' First Amendment rights or constituted an undue burden on the woman's abortion right. Texas Medical Providers Performing Abortion Services v. Lakey, 667 F.3d 570, 580 (5th Cir. 2012) (rejecting physicians' First Amendment claims). The court noted that standard medical practice supported the use of sonograms and measures to hear the fetal heartbeat. The state law simply required that this relevant, truthful, and non-misleading information be shared with pregnant women unless they certified that they fell into one of three excluded groups (involving women whose pregnancy came from certain types of rapes, minors in a judicial bypass procedure, or fetuses with an "irreversible medical condition or abnormality"). Id. at 578-579. See also John A. Robertson, Abortion and Technology: Sonograms, Fetal Pain, Viability, and

Early Prenatal Diagnosis, 14 U. Pa. J. Const. L. 327, 349-357 (2011); Jeannie Suk, The Trajectory of Trauma: Bodies and Minds of Abortion Discourse, 110 Colum. L. Rev. 1193 (2010).

The *Gonzales* majority noted the possibility that women would suffer psychologically from participating in the abortion procedure. But see Trine Munk-Olsen et al., Induced First-Trimester Abortion and Risk of Mental Disorder, 364 New Eng. J. Med. 332 (2011) ("relative risk of psychiatric contact did not differ significantly after abortion as compared with before abortion . . . but did increase after childbirth"). State legislatures have begun to incorporate the idea of mental or emotional sequelae from abortion into their informed consent provisions. The Eighth Circuit reviewed and upheld a requirement that a physician disclose the "[i]ncreased risk of suicide ideation and suicide" to women considering abortion. Planned Parenthood Minnesota, supra, 686 F.3d at 894. The plaintiffs argued that most research demonstrated that there was no causal link between abortion and suicide and that any increased prevalence of suicide in women who had undergone abortion was related to other life factors rather than the abortion itself. The court found that the required disclosure was truthful and non-misleading, noting that physicians were free to explain the absence of scientific evidence that the abortion procedure itself leads to an increased risk of suicide. 686 F.3d 889, at 893-906.

Do physicians have a duty to warn patients about the "abortion trauma syndrome" under the common law? Does it matter whether a jurisdiction follows the "material risk" or "professional" standard of disclosure? See Emily Bazelon, Is There a Post-Abortion Syndrome?, N.Y. Times Magazine, Jan. 21, 2006, at 41. Nada L. Stotland, The Myth of the Abortion Trauma Syndrome, 268 JAMA 2078 (1992).

Physicians have always had a duty to disclose information to women undergoing the abortion procedure. The ordinary rules governing disclosure (see Chapter 2.D) apply unless a state has enacted a specific informed consent procedure for abortion. As you recall, the two major disclosure standards are the "malpractice" standard and the "material risk" standard. There are few reported decisions in which patients have brought informed consent claims against their physicians. See, e.g., Humes v. Clinton, 792 P.2d 1032 (Kan. 1990) (no recovery for emotional distress caused by physician's failure to disclose risks where no physical injury occurs); Boes v. Deschu, 768 S.W.2d 205 (Mo. Ct. App. 1989) (plaintiff subjected to coercive "anti-abortion" counseling states claim for intentional infliction of emotional distress); Acuna v. Turkish, 930 A.2d 416 (N.J. 2007) (rejecting informed consent claim arising from asserted failure to disclose human status of fetus); Rodriguez v. Epstein, 664 N.Y.S.2d 20 (App. Div. 1997) (physicians not required to refer patients in counseling on alternatives to elective abortion); Spencer v. Seikel, 742 P.2d 1126 (Okla. 1987) (physician not liable for failing to inform plaintiff that late-term abortion might be available in other states). See also Bendar v. Rosen, 588 A.2d 1264 (N.J. Super. Ct. App. Div. 1991) (facts are as complex as those found in the typical Torts final; court upholds jury award for psychological trauma following an abortion).

5. *Spousal Notification/Consent.* In Planned Parenthood of Central Missouri v. Danforth, 428 U.S. 52 (1976), the Supreme Court appeared to eliminate any question about whether putative fathers have an interest in blocking an abortion. There, the Court invalidated a requirement that the spouse consent to a woman's abortion unless necessary to save her life. The Court reasoned that

the state cannot delegate to a spouse a veto power which the state itself is absolutely and totally prohibited from exercising. . . . [W]hen the wife and the husband disagree on this decision, the view of only one of the two marriage partners can prevail. Inasmuch as it is the woman who physically bears the child and who is the more directly and immediately affected by the pregnancy, as between the two, the balance weighs in her favor.

Courts generally refuse to give genetic fathers any right to prevent an abortion. Annot., 62 A.L.R.3d 1097 (1975). The *Casey* plurality struck down Pennsylvania's spousal notification requirement using the undue burden standard.

6. *Conscience Provisions.* Generally, private facilities and actors are not required to participate in abortions. See Lisa C. Ikemoto, When a Hospital Becomes Catholic, 47 Mercer L. Rev. 1087 (1996). Under federal law, private hospitals, which are not state actors, are free to decide for themselves not to perform abortions. See 20 U.S.C. §1688 ("Nothing in this chapter shall be construed to require or prohibit any person, or public or private entity, to provide or pay for any benefit or service, including the use of facilities, related to abortion."). But see Doe v. Bridgeton Hospital Ass'n, Inc., 389 A.2d 526 (N.J. Super. Ct. Law Div. 1978) (private hospitals required to provide access to abortions under state constitution).

Consider also the rights of individual health care practitioners (as opposed to facilities) to refuse to participate in abortions. Following *Roe*, Congress and many state legislatures moved quickly to enact so-called conscience clause statutes that protect physicians, nurses, and other medical personnel from retaliatory measures for refusing to participate in abortions. See 42 U.S.C. §300a-7 (known as the "Church Amendment"); Shelton v. University of Medicine & Dentistry of New Jersey, 223 F.3d 220 (3d Cir. 2000) (hospital provided reasonable accommodations to nurse's religious beliefs regarding abortions); Judith F. Daar, A Clash at the Bedside: Patient Autonomy v. A Physician's Professional Conscience, 44 Hastings L.J. 1241, 1274 (1993) (comparing protection for physician conscience in death and dying and abortion cases); Mark L. Rienzi, The Constitutional Right Not to Participate in Abortions: *Roe, Casey,* and the Fourteenth Amendment Rights of Healthcare Providers, 87 Notre Dame L. Rev. 1 (2011) (arguing provider's right to refuse merits constitutional recognition). The FDA's approval of mifepristone and emergency contraception (which some argued served as an abortifacient) generated claims that pharmacists should have a similar right of conscience. See Kansas St. Ann. §65-443 (2012) (conscience provision amended to include coverage of prescriptions); and Robin Fretwell Wilson, The Limits of Conscience: Moral Clashes over Deeply Divisive Healthcare Procedures, 34 Am. J.L. & Med. 41 (2008). Justice Kennedy's opinion in *Gonzales,* supra, notes that states have the power to regulate abortion "to protect[] the integrity and ethics of the medical profession." Some commentators have argued that health care workers should also be deemed to have a right of conscience supporting their interest in providing abortion services. See, e.g., Lisa H. Harris, Recognizing Conscience in Abortion Provision, 367 New Eng. J. Med. 981 (2012); Elizabeth Sepper, Taking Conscience Seriously, 98 Va. L. Rev. 1501 (2012) (noting need to balance institutional and provider claims of conscience); Steph Sterling & Jessica L. Waters, Beyond Religious Refusals: The Case for Protecting Health Care Workers' Provision of Abortion Care, 34 Harv. J.L. & Gender 463 (2011).

7. *Abortion Protesters.* Courts and legislatures have also struggled to resolve the controversies created by abortion protesters. Anti-abortion protesters have sought to block clinic doors and to engage in "sidewalk counseling" of women attempting to gain access to abortion clinics. Theoretically, protesters might be charged with violation of state trespass laws. Compare Joan Teshima, Annot., Trespass: State Prosecution for Unauthorized Entry or Occupation, for Public Demonstration Purposes, of Business, Industrial, or Utility Premises, 41 A.L.R.4th 773 (1985), with James O. Pearson, Jr., Annot., "Choice of Evils," Necessity, Duress, or Similar Defense to State or Local Criminal Charges Based on Acts of Public Protest, 3 A.L.R.5th 521 (1992). Abortion clinics and their supporters have also sought to use the federal Racketeer Influenced and Corrupt Organizations Act (RICO). In Scheidler v. National Organization of Women, 547 U.S. 9 (2006), the Supreme Court rejected efforts to use RICO and the Hobbs Act's extortion provisions in a class action brought by NOW against individuals and organizations involved in anti-abortion protests.

State and local officials sometimes have been overwhelmed by the numbers and commitment of protesters. See Operation Save America v. City of Jackson, 275 P.3d 438 (Wyo. 2012) (TRO entered to restrict abortion protest in and around town square during Boy Scout festival found unconstitutional). Judges have issued injunctions designed to create a "buffer zone" around clinics, attempting to balance the need to protect free speech against the harms protesters inflict on the clinics and their patients. The Supreme Court opinions in this area are complex. See, e.g., Schenck v. Pro-Choice Network of Western New York, 519 U.S. 357 (1997) (upholding "fixed" 15-foot buffer zones but striking down "floating" buffer zone established around people and vehicles; floating buffer zones unnecessarily burdened speech); Madsen v. Women's Health Center, 512 U.S. 753 (1994) ("In evaluating a content-neutral injunction, the governing standard is whether the injunction's challenged provisions burden no more speech than necessary to serve a significant government interest."); McCullen v. Coakley, 571 F.3d 167 (1st Cir. 2009) (rejecting facial challenge to Massachusetts legislation providing 35-foot buffer zone around abortion facilities), cert. denied, 130 S. Ct. 1881 (2010). See also Bray v. Alexandria Women's Health Clinic, 506 U.S. 263 (1993) (42 U.S.C. §1985 does not protect women seeking abortion from the concerted activities of abortion protesters).

Clinic defenders turned to other forums for additional relief. Congress enacted statutory protections in the Freedom of Access to Clinic Entrances Act of 1994. 18 U.S.C. §248. See also Planned Parenthood of Columbia/Williamette, Inc. v. American Coalition of Life Activists, 422 F.3d 949 (9th Cir. 2005), cert. denied, 126 S. Ct. 1912 (2006) (publication of names and addresses of abortion providers through "guilty" posters and Internet Web site are "threat[s] of force" giving rise to liability for punitive damages under FACE; amount reduced). See generally Guttmacher Institute, Protecting Access to Clinics (2013).

Problem: Late-Trimester Abortions

Suppose that Annie Grey is 28 weeks pregnant when she discovers that she is carrying a fetus with anencephaly. She does not want to give birth to a child who will have no higher brain functions and who will have little chance of surviving past the first few weeks of life. She wants to undergo a late-term abortion. Consider the relevant federal and state statutes. Are abortions for women in Annie's situation legal in your state? See Guttmacher Institute, State Policies on Later Abortions (2013). If they are legal, are there any physicians who are willing to perform the procedure? How would you find out? If they are not legal, is there any mechanism to prevent Annie from traveling to another state or country where the procedure would be legal? Susan Frelich Appleton, Gender, Abortion, and Travel After *Roe*'s End, 51 St. Louis U. L.J. 655 (2007); Joseph W. Dellapenna, Abortion Across State Lines, 2008 BYU L. Rev. 1651 (2008). Who would have standing to bring such a claim? Could you argue that medical providers who permit the use of testing to identify and abort fetuses likely to be born with disabilities have violated the ADA? Would public health institutions engaging in the policy violate the equal protection clause? Would you have to show that a fetus was a "person"? Martha A. Field, Killing the "Handicapped"—Before and After Birth, 16 Harv. Women's L.J. 79 (1993); Dov Fox & Christopher Griffin, Jr., Disability-Selective Abortion and the Americans with Disabilities Act, 2009 Utah L. Rev. 845; Janet Malek, Deciding Against Disability: Does the Use of Reproductive Genetic Technologies Express Disvalue for People with Disabilities?, 36 J. Med. Ethics 217 (2010).

C. STATE OR FEDERAL RECOGNITION OF FETAL INTERESTS

1. Introduction

This section considers what steps government can take to protect potential life, apart from restricting abortions. There are a variety of alternative legal mechanisms for protecting fetal interests. Tort law could be used to recover damages for fetal injuries and to deter conduct that puts fetuses at risk of injury. Criminal law could be used to punish those who injure fetuses. Governments also may establish the importance of fetal interests via proclamations and even by the allocation of public funds. See generally Sara Dubow, Ourselves Unborn: A History of the Fetus in Modern America (2011).

The Supreme Court's procreation jurisprudence presents no barrier to the preferential allocation of public funds toward childbearing rather than abortion or to the development of a particularized abortion informed consent statute. See supra at pages 508-510. Yet *Skinner, Roe, Casey,* and *Gonzales* do not resolve the validity of other governmental efforts to value and protect fetal interests. *Skinner* suggested that individuals have a fundamental liberty interest in deciding to procreate. *Roe* held that a fetus was not a "person" entitled to protection under the Fourteenth Amendment and prohibited the state from adopting a definition of fetal personhood that would infringe on a woman's right to choose abortion. However, *Casey* suggests that the Supreme Court will be much more deferential toward a state's asserted desire to protect fetuses, at least so long as the measures taken to protect the fetus do not "unduly" infringe a woman's abortion option. Furthermore, *Casey* reiterates *Roe*'s holding that a state's interest in fetal life becomes compelling at the point of viability. At viability, the state may prohibit abortion completely unless the procedure is necessary for the health or life of the pregnant woman. The Supreme Court's decision in *Gonzales* affirmed the government's ability to promote fetal interests and to define the scope of what might be medically appropriate, even before viability. See Randy Beck, *Gonzales, Casey,* and the Viability Rule, 103 Nw. U. L. Rev. 249 (2009) (criticizing Supreme Court's approach to viability). The abortion cases suggest that the Court would not permit states to value the fetus's potential life more than the life of the pregnant woman.

This brief summary demonstrates that the abortion cases are not very helpful in establishing the scope of governmental power to protect fetal life outside of the abortion context, when the risk to the fetus comes from something other than the pregnant woman's right to choose abortion. Courts have struggled to determine the appropriate constitutional balance between a state's interest in protecting fetal life and a woman's right to engage in activities that might put her fetus at risk. The first part of this section briefly summarizes state and federal recognition of fetal interests. The second part of the section focuses on two of the most difficult areas for courts and commentators: forced medical treatment for pregnant women and criminal prosecution of pregnant women for conduct presenting a risk to their fetus.

a. State Law and Fetal Personhood

State law protections for fetal interests have grown in recent years in areas ranging from tort law, to criminal law, to medical research. State courts generally resolve the question of a fetus's personhood by interpreting and applying the words of statutes or precedents rather than searching for a unitary definition of personhood that could be applied to fetuses in all areas of the law. Does this strike you as the correct approach? What prevents states from adopting a unitary concept of personhood that could be applied across different areas of law? Wouldn't such an approach comport more closely with the centrality of personhood to most ethical, moral, and jurisprudential theories? See, e.g., Note, What We Talk About When We Talk About Persons: The Language of a Legal Fiction, 114 Harv. L. Rev. 1745 (2001). See also In the Matter of the Unborn Child of Starks, 18 P.3d 342 (Okla. 2001). States have taken up the issue through legislation, enacting provisions that define the fetus as a human being under state law. See 720 Ill. Comp. Stat. Ann. §510/1.

States have been particularly quick to recognize fetal interests in tort law. The old black-letter rule was that fetuses could only recover for injuries sustained in utero if they were born alive. Roland F. Chase, Annot., Liability for Prenatal Injuries, 40 A.L.R.3d 1222 (1971). Parents could not recover for the wrongful death of their unborn children. These tort rules have undergone significant revision. A majority of states now permit suits on behalf of injured fetuses, even when stillborn, if the injury was sustained after the point of viability. Annot., Right to Maintain Action or to Recover Damages for Death of Unborn Child, 84 A.L.R.3d 411 (1978). A few states even permit tort claims where the injury was sustained prior to viability. See, e.g., Nealis v. Baird, 996 P.2d 438 (Okla. 1999) (wrongful death statute covers nonviable fetus born alive); Wiersma v. Maple Leaf Farms, 543 N.W.2d 787 (S.D. 1996) (wrongful death statute provides cause of action for loss of nonviable unborn child).

Tort claims involving fetal injury often involve substantial causation issues: the plaintiff must prove that the tortfeasor actually caused legally cognizable harm. This burden of proof may be difficult to meet where the pregnancy is in the earliest stages at the time of the fetal injury because of the significant rate of spontaneous abortion or miscarriage during this period. See also Agota Peterfy, Commentary, Fetal Viability as a Threshold to Personhood: A Legal Analysis, 16 J. Leg. Med. 607 (1995).

Does a fetus have similar rights to be free of injuries caused by its mother? There are several problems with these claims: the parental immunity doctrine will protect the pregnant woman in some jurisdictions; there are difficulties establishing the appropriate standard of care; and there are also public policy concerns with imposing liability for maternal conduct. See Thomas M. Fleming, Annot., Right of Child to Action Against Mother for Infliction of Prenatal Injuries, 78 A.L.R.4th 1082 (1991). Only a handful of courts have even considered the issue; litigation of this sort typically arises only when mothers arrange to have their children sue them in order to draw resources from their homeowners' or automobile insurance policies. Most courts have rejected the claims. See Stallman v. Youngquist, 531 N.E.2d 355 (Ill. 1988) (car accident); Remy v. MacDonald, 801 N.E.2d 260 (Mass. 2004) (car accident; summarizing case law); Chenault v. Huie, 989 S.W.2d 474 (Tex. App. 1999) (grossly negligent use of illicit drugs). The *Stallman* court's criticism of the liability claim was pointed:

> It is clear that the recognition of a legal right to begin life with a sound mind and body on the part of a fetus which is assertable after birth against its mother would have serious ramifications for all women and their families, and for the way in which society views women and women's reproductive abilities. The recognition of such a right by a fetus would necessitate the recognition of a legal duty on the part of the woman who is the mother; a legal duty, as opposed to a moral duty, to effectuate the best prenatal environment possible. . . . Any action which negatively impacted on fetal development would be a breach of the pregnant woman's duty to her developing fetus. Mother and child would be legal adversaries from the moment of conception until birth. . . .
>
> The relationship between a pregnant woman and her fetus is unlike the relationship between any other plaintiff and defendant. No other plaintiff depends exclusively on any other defendant for everything necessary for life itself. No other defendant must go through biological changes of the most profound type, possibly at the risk of her own life, in order to bring forth an adversary into the world. It is, after all, the whole life of the pregnant woman which impacts on the development of the fetus. As opposed to the third-party defendant, it is the mother's every waking and sleeping moment which, for better or worse, shapes the prenatal environment which forms the world for the developing fetus.

531 N.E.2d at 359-360. But see Grodin v. Grodin, 301 N.W.2d 869 (Mich. Ct. App. 1980) (child's mother potentially liable to child for prenatal injuries); Tesar v. Anderson, 789 N.W.2d 351 (Wis. App. 2010) (public policy does not preclude action by father against mother's insurer where mother's negligent driving resulted in stillborn birth). A few courts have considered whether maternal negligence should be imputed to her child in the child's action against third parties for prenatal conduct. See, e.g., Hogle v. Hall, 916 P.2d 814 (Nev. 1996) (no).

States may also use the criminal law to protect fetal interests. Criminal prosecutions against "strangers" have generally fallen into two categories: (1) traditional crimes and (2) special criminal statutes protecting fetuses. Attempts to prosecute third parties for traditional crimes such as murder or manslaughter typically fail. Homicide convictions, for example, require the death of a "person," usually defined as a person born alive. A defendant who violently assaults a pregnant woman might be prosecuted for a homicide if the fetus is born alive but then dies as a result of the criminal conduct. Cf. Mamta K. Shah, Note, Inconsistencies in the Legal Status of an Unborn Child: Recognition of a Fetus as Potential Life, 29 Hofstra L. Rev. 931, 933-949 (2001). See also State v. Courchesne, 998 A.2d 1 (Conn. 2010) (infant born alive who subsequently dies due to injuries sustained in utero is "person" under murder statute); State v. Horne, 319 S.E.2d 703 (S.C. 1984) (death of unborn viable fetus supports manslaughter conviction).

A majority of states have enacted special statutes designed to criminalize conduct related to fetuses. Feticide statutes are a common example. Prosecutions under these provisions are less controversial, in part because legislative intent is clear. The statutes generally include specific exceptions for a woman exercising her right to choose abortion and for abortion providers. Mamta K. Shah, supra; Alan S. Wasserstrom, Annot., Homicide Based on Killing of Unborn Child, 64 A.L.R.5th 671 (1998). See also People v. Davis, 872 P.2d 591 (Cal. 1994). Many states reviewed and revised criminal laws governing fetuses in the aftermath of some highly publicized cases involving the murder of pregnant women. See also National Conference of State Legislatures, Fetal Homicide Laws (available at NCSL Web site) (citing 38 states with legislation as of Feb. 2013). Do feticide statutes demonstrate irreconcilable conflicts in the law given that third parties can be subjected to criminal penalties for conduct permissible when undertaken by the pregnant woman? See Luke M. Milligan, A Theory of Stability: John Rawls, Fetal Homicide, and Substantive Due Process, 87 B.U. L. Rev. 1177 (2007); Carolyn B. Ramsey, Restructuring the Debate over Fetal Homicide Laws, 67 Ohio St. L.J. 721 (2006) (arguing that abortion rights are not inconsistent with feticide prosecutions). Criminal prosecution of women for risky prenatal activity is a controversial area that will be considered in more detail below.

States can also show respect for fetuses, and indirectly disfavor abortion, by restricting the use of fetal tissue produced in spontaneous or planned abortions. A number of state legislatures have prohibited the use of fetal remains in medical research or have otherwise attempted to restrict fetal experimentation. Violators may be criminally prosecuted. See, e.g., Mo. Ann. Stat. §188.036 (purports to ban abortions performed to obtain fetal material for experimentation); N.D. Cent. Code §14-02.2-02 (fetal experimentation restrictions); 18 Pa. Cons. Stat. Ann. §3216 (fetal experimentation restrictions). These statutes may be implicated in stem cell research, discussed below at page 601.

b. Federal Recognition of Fetal Interests

The federal government has had fewer opportunities to show its interest in fetal well-being, but federal activity is prominent in three areas: (1) the allocation of funds designed to protect fetal health; (2) the adoption of legislation designed to criminally or civilly penalize risky conduct; and (3) the dramatic debates about the permissibility of embryonic stem cell research.

The federal government wields enormous power through its capacity to tie the expenditure of federal dollars to particular policy objectives. For many years, the eligibility rules for the federal-state Medicaid program were the most important federal expression of interest in fetal well-being through the provision of Medicaid coverage for pregnant women. Coverage for pregnant women near or below the federal poverty level has expanded over the past two decades. See 42 U.S.C. §§1396a(a)(i) (10)(A)(III), 1396d(n). Health insurance coverage for pregnant women is an indirect indication of the value of fetal life. See also 42 C.F.R. §457.10 (unborn children eligible for health coverage under State Children's Health Insurance Program). Federal funding for stem cell research, which raises the specter of the use and destruction of embryos, will be discussed in the final section of this chapter, at page 603.

Congress has also sought to recognize and to protect fetal interests more directly. The federal Partial-Birth Abortion Ban Act of 2003 discussed supra, at page 497, recognizes a private cause of action to protect fetal interests. The Act gives certain relatives of a fetus subjected to the prohibited procedure a right to recover civil damages. 18 U.S.C.A. §1531. Congress also expanded federal criminal law to recognize the distinct offense of injuring or killing a fetus.

The federal Unborn Victims of Violence Act of 2004, 18 U.S.C.A. §1841, was enacted in the aftermath of a highly publicized murder of a pregnant woman. The Act provides:

(a)(1) Whoever engages in conduct that violates any of [certain enumerated] . . . provisions of law . . . and thereby causes the death of, or bodily injury . . . [to] a child, who is in utero at the time the conduct takes place, is guilty of a separate offense under this section.

(2)(A) Except as otherwise provided in this paragraph, the punishment for that separate offense is the same as the punishment provided under Federal law for that conduct had that injury or death occurred to the unborn child's mother.

(B) An offense under this section does not require proof that

(i) the person engaging in the conduct had knowledge or should have had knowledge that the victim of the underlying offense was pregnant; or

(ii) the defendant intended to cause the death of, or bodily injury to, the unborn child.

(C) If the person engaging in the conduct thereby intentionally kills or attempts to kill the unborn child, that person shall instead of being punished under subparagraph (A), be punished as provided under . . . for intentionally killing or attempting to kill a human being.

(D) Notwithstanding any other provision of law, the death penalty shall not be imposed for an offense under this section. . . .

Constitutionally protected abortion procedures are exempted. Id. See generally Carolyn B. Ramsey, Restructuring the Debate over Fetal Homicide Laws, 67 Ohio St. L.J. 721 (2006).

2. Pregnant Women and Forced Medical Treatment

A pregnant woman presents a unique dilemma for health care providers. The woman's autonomy interests must be fully recognized as a matter of law and medical ethics. Yet the woman's decisions about medical treatment can have an immediate impact on the fetus, whose interests also demand respect. The health care professional's legal and ethical obligations to the fetus, as a being separate and distinct from her mother, are a matter of greater controversy. Should a physician's obligation to the fetus ever override the obligation to a pregnant patient? When and how should courts or legislatures intervene in this potential conflict? Are the rules developed in this area truly sui generis, or should they be applied to situations in which third parties make demands for biological support from other persons? Compare the following material, for instance, with the discussion in Chapter 4 of whether people can be forced to donate life-saving organs or tissue at little risk to themselves.

■ IN RE A.C.
573 A.2d 1235 (D.C. App. 1990) (en banc)

TERRY, Associate Judge.

I

. . . This case came before the trial court when George Washington University Hospital petitioned the emergency judge in chambers for declaratory relief as to how it should treat its patient, A.C., who was close to death from cancer and was twenty-six and one-half weeks pregnant with a viable fetus. After a hearing lasting approximately three hours, which was held at the hospital (though not in A.C.'s room), the court ordered that a cesarean section be performed on A.C. to deliver the fetus. Counsel for A.C. immediately sought a stay in this court, which was unanimously denied by a hastily assembled division of three judges. In re A.C., 533 A.2d 611 (D.C. 1987). The cesarean was performed, and a baby girl, L.M.C., was delivered. Tragically, the child died within two and one-half hours, and the mother died two days later.

Counsel for A.C. now maintain that A.C. was competent and that she made an informed choice not to have the cesarean performed. Given this view of the facts, they argue that it was error for the trial court to weigh the state's interest in preserving the potential life of a viable fetus against A.C.'s interest in having her decision respected. They argue further that, even if the substituted judgment procedure had been followed, the evidence would necessarily show that A.C. would not have wanted the cesarean section. Under either analysis, according to these arguments, the trial court erred in subordinating A.C.'s right to bodily integrity in favor of the state's interest in potential life. . . .

II

[A.C. had suffered from cancer for 14 years. During a period of remission, she married and conceived a child. At 25 weeks in her pregnancy, her doctors found a terminal, inoperable tumor in her lung. She decided to continue her pregnancy and to receive palliative treatment, apparently with the desire to extend her life at least to the twenty-eighth week of pregnancy, when the prognosis for the fetus would be much better if intervention were necessary. However, as her condition worsened during her twenty-sixth week, her stated desire to have the baby became more equivocal. Her mother opposed the operation, but her husband "was too distraught to testify and uttered only a few words at the hearing."]

After hearing this testimony and the arguments of counsel, the trial court made oral findings of fact. It found, first, that A.C. would probably die, according to uncontroverted medical testimony, "within the next twenty-four to forty-eight hours"; second, that A.C. was "pregnant with a twenty-six and a half week viable fetus who, based upon uncontroverted medical testimony, has approximately a 50 to 60 percent chance to survive if a cesarean section is performed as soon as possible"; third, that because the fetus was viable, "the state has [an] important and legitimate interest in protecting the potentiality of human life"; and fourth, that there had been some testimony that the operation "may very well hasten the death of [A.C.]," but that there had also been testimony that delay would greatly increase the risk to the fetus and that "the prognosis is not great for the fetus to be delivered post-mortem. . . ." Most significantly, the court found:

> The court is of the view that it does not clearly know what [A.C.'s] present views are with respect to the issue of whether or not the child should live or die. She's presently unconscious. As late as Friday of last week, she wanted the baby to live. As late as yesterday, she did not know for sure.

Having made these findings of fact and conclusions of law, and expressly relying on In re Madyun, 114 Daily Wash. L. Rptr. 2233 (D.C. Super. Ct. July 26, 1986), the court ordered that a cesarean section be performed to deliver A.C.'s child. . . .

[After the judge's order was communicated to A.C. by her doctors, she at first agreed to the operation, but shortly later she refused. Although she appeared lucid, her doctors differed in their opinions as to whether she had reached a truly competent and informed decision one way or the other.] After hearing this new evidence, the court found that it was "still not clear what her intent is" and again ordered that a cesarean section be performed. . . . The operation took place, but the baby lived for only a few hours, and A.C. succumbed to cancer two days later.

IV

A. INFORMED CONSENT AND BODILY INTEGRITY

A number of learned articles have been written about the propriety or impropriety of court-ordered cesarean sections. E.g., Johnsen, The Creation of Fetal Rights: Conflicts with Women's Constitutional Rights to Liberty, Privacy, and Equal Protection, 95 Yale L.J. 599 (1986); Kolder, Gallagher & Parsons, Court-Ordered Obstetrical Interventions, 316 New Eng. J. Med. 1192 (1987) (hereafter Obstetrical Interventions); Rhoden, The Judge in the Delivery Room: The Emergence of Court-Ordered Caesareans, 74 Cal. L. Rev. 1951 (1986); Robertson, Procreative Liberty and the Control of Conception, Pregnancy, and Childbirth, 69 Va. L. Rev. 405 (1983). Commentators have also considered how medical decisions for incompetent persons which may involve some detriment or harm to them should be made. . . . These and other articles demonstrate the complexity of medical intervention cases, which become more complex with the steady advance of medical technology. From a recent national survey, it appears that over the five years preceding the survey there were 36 attempts to override maternal refusals of proposed medical treatment, and that in 15 instances where court orders were sought to authorize cesarean interventions, 13 such orders were granted. Obstetrical Interventions, supra, 316 New Eng. J. Med. at 1192-1193. . . . Nevertheless, there is only one published decision from an appellate court that deals with the question of when, or even whether, a court may order a cesarean section: Jefferson v. Griffin Spalding County Hospital Authority, 247 Ga. 86, 274 S.E.2d 457 (1981).

Jefferson is of limited relevance, if any at all, to the present case. In *Jefferson* there was a competent refusal by the mother to undergo the proposed surgery, but the evidence showed that performance of the cesarean was in the medical interests of both the mother and the fetus.[7] . . .

[O]ur analysis of this case begins with the tenet common to all medical treatment cases: that any person has the right to make an informed choice, if competent to do so, to accept or forego medical treatment. . . .

[C]ourts do not compel one person to permit a significant intrusion upon his or her bodily integrity for the benefit of another person's health. See, e.g., . . . McFall v. Shimp, 10 Pa. D. & C.3d 90 (Allegheny County Ct. 1978). In *McFall* the court refused to order Shimp to donate bone marrow which was necessary to save the life of his cousin, McFall:

> The common law has consistently held to a rule which provides that one human being is under no legal compulsion to give aid or to take action to save another human being or to rescue. . . . For our law to compel defendant to submit to an intrusion of his body would change every concept and principle upon which our society is founded. To do so would defeat the sanctity of the individual, and would impose a rule which would know no limits, and one could not imagine where the line would be drawn.

Id. at 91. [This case is excerpted and discussed at page 419.] Even though Shimp's refusal would mean death for McFall, the court would not order Shimp to allow his body to be invaded. It has been suggested that fetal cases are different because a woman who "has chosen to lend her body to bring [a] child into the world" has an enhanced duty to assure the welfare of the fetus, sufficient even to require her to undergo cesarean surgery. Robertson, Procreative Liberty, supra, 69 Va. L. Rev. at 456. Surely, however, a fetus cannot have rights in this respect superior to those of a person who has already been born.[8] . . .

7. Because the patient in *Jefferson* had a placenta previa which blocked the birth canal, doctors estimated that without cesarean intervention there was a 99 percent chance that her full-term fetus would perish and a 50 percent chance that the mother would die as well. The mother was unquestionably competent to make her own treatment decisions, but refused a cesarean because of her religious beliefs. A trial court gave custody of the fetus to state human resources officials and ordered a cesarean section; the Georgia Supreme Court denied the parents' motion for a stay. [Nevertheless, the mother went into hiding, and both she and the child survived without the operation.]

8. There are also practical consequences to consider. What if A.C. had refused to comply with a court order that she submit to a cesarean? Under the circumstances she obviously could not have been held in civil contempt and imprisoned or required to pay a daily fine until compliance. . . . Enforcement could be accomplished only through physical force or its equivalent. A.C. would have to be fastened with restraints to the operating table, or perhaps involuntarily rendered unconscious by forcibly injecting her with an anesthetic, and then subjected to unwanted major surgery. Such actions would surely give one pause in a civilized society, especially when A.C. had done no wrong. Cf. Rochin v. California, 342 U.S. 165, 169, 72 S. Ct. 205, 208, 96 L. Ed. 183 (1952).

In those rare cases in which a patient's right to decide her own course of treatment has been judicially overridden, courts have usually acted to vindicate the state's interest in protecting third parties, even if in fetal state. . . .

We hold, however, that without a competent refusal from A.C. to go forward with the surgery, and without a finding through substituted judgment that A.C. would not have consented to the surgery, it was error for the trial court to proceed to a balancing analysis, weighing the rights of A.C. against the interests of the state.

There are two additional arguments against overriding A.C.'s objections to caesarean surgery. First . . . [court orders diminish the patient's trust in her physician and may deter women from seeking care]. . . . Second, and even more compellingly, any judicial proceeding in a case such as this will ordinarily take place—like the one before us here—under time constraints so pressing that it is difficult or impossible for the mother to communicate adequately with counsel, or for counsel to organize an effective factual and legal presentation in defense of her liberty and privacy interests and bodily integrity. . . .

In this case A.C.'s court-appointed attorney was unable even to meet with his client before the hearing. By the time the case was heard, A.C.'s condition did not allow her to be present, nor was it reasonably possible for the judge to hear from her directly. The factual record, moreover, was significantly flawed because A.C.'s medical records were not before the court and because Dr. Jeffrey Moscow, the physician who had been treating A.C. for many years, was not even contacted and hence did not testify.[17] . . .

C. THE TRIAL COURT'S RULING . . .

What a trial court must do in a case such as this is to determine, if possible, whether the patient is capable of making an informed decision about the course of her medical treatment. If she is, and if she makes such a decision, her wishes will control in virtually all cases. If the court finds that the patient is incapable of making an informed consent (and thus is incompetent), then the court must make a substituted judgment. This means that the court must ascertain as best it can what the patient would do if faced with the particular treatment question. Again, in virtually all cases the decision of the patient, albeit discerned through the mechanism of substituted judgment, will control. We do not quite foreclose the possibility that a conflicting state interest may be so compelling that the patient's wishes must yield, but we anticipate that such cases will be extremely rare and truly exceptional. This is not such a case.

Having said that, we go no further. We need not decide whether, or in what circumstances, the state's interests can ever prevail over the interests of a pregnant

17. In an affidavit filed after the hearing, Dr. Moscow said that if he had been notified of the proceedings, he would have come to the hospital immediately and would have testified that a cesarean section was medically inadvisable *both for A.C. and for the fetus.* Dr. Moscow also viewed the hospital's handling of A.C.'s case as deficient in several other significant respects. In these circumstances we think it unfortunate that Dr. Moscow was not called by representatives of the hospital and made available to the court when the hospital decided to seek judicial guidance.

patient. We emphasize, nevertheless, that it would be an extraordinary case indeed in which a court might ever be justified in overriding the patient's wishes and authorizing a major surgical procedure such as a cesarean section.[23]

. . . If the substituted judgment procedure were to be followed, there is evidence going both ways as to what decision A.C. would have made, and we see no point in requiring the court now to make that determination when it can have no practical effect on either A.C. or L.M.C.

Accordingly, we vacate the order of the trial court and remand the case for such further proceedings as may be appropriate.

BELSON, Associate Judge, concurring in part and dissenting in part.

I agree with much of the majority opinion, but I disagree with its ultimate ruling that the trial court's order must be set aside, and with the narrow view it takes of the state's interest in preserving life and the unborn child's interest in life. . . . I would hold that in those instances, fortunately rare, in which the viable unborn child's interest in living and the state's parallel interest in protecting human life come into conflict with the mother's decision to forgo a procedure such as a cesarean section, a balancing should be struck in which the unborn child's and the state's interests are entitled to substantial weight.

It was acknowledged in Roe v. Wade, 410 U.S. 113 (1973), that the state's interest in potential human life becomes compelling at the point of viability. . . . When the unborn child reaches the state of viability, the child becomes a party whose interests must be considered. . . .

The balancing test should be applied in instances in which women become pregnant and carry an unborn child to the point of viability. This is not an unreasonable classification because, I submit, a woman who carries a child to viability is in fact a member of a unique category of persons. Her circumstances differ fundamentally from those of other potential patients for medical procedures that will aid another person, for example, a potential donor of bone marrow for transplant. This is so because she has undertaken to bear another human being, and has carried an unborn child to viability. Another unique feature of the situation we address arises from the singular nature of the dependency of the unborn child upon the mother. A woman carrying a viable unborn child is not in the same category as a relative,

23. In particular, we stress that nothing in this opinion should be read as either approving or disapproving the holding in In re Madyun, supra. There are substantial factual differences between Madyun and the present case. In this case, for instance, the medical interests of the mother and the fetus were in sharp conflict; what was good for one would have been harmful to the other. In *Madyun,* however, there was no real conflict between the interests of mother and fetus; on the contrary, there was strong evidence that the proposed cesarean would be beneficial to both. Moreover, in *Madyun* the pregnancy was at full term, and Mrs. Madyun had been in labor for two and a half days; in this case, however, A.C. was barely two-thirds of the way through her pregnancy, and there were no signs of labor. If another *Madyun*-type case ever comes before this court, its result may well depend on facts that we cannot now foresee. For that reason (among others), we defer until another day any discussion of whether *Madyun* was rightly or wrongly decided. [Elsewhere the court also limited its reasoning to those cases involving "a major bodily invasion," reserving judgment on when "lesser invasions" would be permitted and on "where the line should be drawn between 'major' and 'minor' surgery."]

friend, or stranger called upon to donate bone marrow or an organ for transplant. Rather, the expectant mother has placed herself in a special class of persons who are bringing another person into existence, and upon whom that other person's life is totally dependent. Also, uniquely, the viable unborn child is literally captive within the mother's body. No other potential beneficiary of a surgical procedure on another is in that position.

For all of these reasons, . . . I cannot agree that in cases where a viable unborn child is in the picture, it would be extremely rare, within that universe, to require that the mother accede to the vital needs of the viable unborn child.[8]

For the reasons stated above, I would affirm.

Notes: Forced Medical Treatment

1. *Abortion and Cesareans.* How should the state's interest in protecting viable fetuses, recognized in *Roe, Casey,* and subsequent case law affect a woman's right to control her own medical treatment? Should these decisions be limited to the abortion context in which they arose? Does the underlying reasoning—that the state's compelling interest can override a woman's constitutionally protected right to choose abortion—seem transferable where the constitutional interests at stake are a woman's right to choose her own medical care and to be free from extreme invasions to her bodily integrity? Recall that Cruzan v. Director, Missouri Department of Health, 497 U.S. 261 (1990), suggests that the right to control end-of-life treatment decisions has a constitutional dimension. If a state interest is compelling in one circumstance, wouldn't it be compelling in the other? In which cases would the In re A.C. court permit forced medical interventions to preserve the fetus?

2. *Moral or Legal Obligations to Protect Fetuses?* Generations of law students have considered the hypothetical of the champion swimmer who observes a person drowning offshore. The bystander is said to have a moral, but not a legal, obligation to attempt to save the drowning swimmer. Is the pregnant woman in the same position as the expert swimmer? Which of the following factors should be considered ethically or legally relevant to the resolution of these cases: Whether the woman became pregnant by choice? Whether she intends to carry the fetus to term? The gestational age of the fetus? The probability of harm to the fetus? The degree of harm to the fetus? The probability and degree of harm confronted by the pregnant woman? Whether the proposed medical treatment would benefit the woman as well as the fetus? The nature of the intrusion into the woman's autonomy? The rationale for the woman's refusal of treatment? What other factors might you consider? Do pregnant women have an ethical duty to protect their fetuses from harm? Should

8. To the contrary, it appears that a majority of courts faced with this issue have found that the state's compelling interest in protection of the unborn child should prevail. See Noble-Allgire, Court-Ordered Cesarean Sections, 10 J. Legal Med. 211, 236 (1989). I add that in mapping this uncharted area of the law, we can draw lines, and a line I would draw would be to preclude the use of physical force to perform an operation. The force of the court order itself as well as the use of the contempt power would, I think, be adequate in most cases. See id. at 243.

pregnant women have a legal obligation to protect their fetuses from harm, just as parents have a legal obligation to safeguard their children?

For a detailed analysis of the ethical and legal aspects of these cases, see David Orentlicher, Matters of Life and Death: Making Moral Theory Work in Medical Ethics and the Law 91-120 (2001) (arguing that pregnant women may have both a moral and a legal obligation to protect their fetuses, at least under some circumstances, but noting that the creation of a legal obligation could create a perverse incentive for pregnant women to avoid prenatal care). See also April L. Cherry, The Free Exercise Rights of Pregnant Women Who Refuse Medical Treatment, 69 Tenn. L. Rev. 563 (2002); Daniel R. Levy, The Maternal Conflict: The Right of a Woman to Refuse a Cesarean Section Versus the State's Interest in Saving the Life of the Fetus, 108 W. Va. L. Rev. 97 (2005); Michelle Oberman, Mothers and Doctors' Orders: Unmasking the Doctor's Fiduciary Role in Maternal-Fetal Conflicts, 94 Nw. U. L. Rev. 451 (2000).

3. *Court-Ordered Medical Interventions.* The *A.C.* court implies, in dicta, that the state's interest in fetal life might override a woman's interest in avoiding some minimally intrusive medical interventions. Should the state's interest in preserving the life of a viable fetus outweigh a woman's right to refuse routine prenatal care? Antibiotics? A physician's recommendation of complete bed rest for three months? The use of forceps? A cesarean section delivery?

Most of the reported cases involve cesareans. The Kolder study described by the *A.C.* court also found:

> Among 21 cases in which court orders were sought, the orders were obtained in 86 percent; in 88 percent of those cases, the orders were received within six hours. Eighty-one percent of the women involved were black, Asian, or Hispanic, 44 percent were unmarried, and 24 percent did not speak English as their primary language. All the women were treated in a teaching-hospital clinic or were receiving public assistance. . . .

Veronica E. Kolder et al., Court-Ordered Obstetrical Interventions, 316 New Eng. J. Med. 1192, 1192 (1987). The In re A.C. decision is regarded by most law review commentators as the dominant judicial approach, at least at the appellate level. See also In re Baby Boy Doe, a Fetus, 632 N.E.2d 326, 330 (Ill. App. Ct. 1994) (Illinois courts should not balance the rights of the viable fetus against the woman's right to control her treatment; "a woman's competent choice in refusing medical treatment as invasive as a cesarean section . . . must be honored, even in circumstances where the choice may be harmful to her fetus."). But see Pemberton v. Tallahassee Memorial Regional Center, 66 F. Supp. 2d 1247 (N.D. Fla. 1999).

In *Pemberton,* a woman subjected to a state-court-ordered cesarean section brought §1983 and §1985 claims in federal court against the regional hospital, claiming that its actions had violated her constitutional rights to "bodily integrity . . . to refuse unwanted medical treatment . . . to make important personal and family decisions without undue governmental interference . . . [and] her right to religious freedom." Id. at 1251. The court rejected the claims, noting:

> Ms. Pemberton was at full term and actively in labor. It was clear that one way or the other, a baby would be born (or stillborn) very soon, certainly within hours.

> Whatever the scope of Ms. Pemberton's personal constitutional rights . . . they clearly did not outweigh the interests of the State of Florida in preserving the life of the unborn child. . . . Bearing an unwanted child is surely a greater intrusion on the mother's constitutional interests than undergoing a caesarean section to deliver a child that the mother affirmatively desires to deliver. [Id. at 1251-1252.]

Could a woman's refusal of a cesarean section recommended by her physicians be used as evidence of neglect? New Jersey Division of Youth and Family Services v. V.M. and B.G., 974 A.2d 448 (N.J. Super. 2009) (no); and Jessica L. Waters, In Whose Best Interest?, 34 Harv. J.L. & Gender 81 (2011).

Cases involving less intrusive measures are less common. See, e.g., Burton v. State, 49 So. 3d 263 (Fla. App. 2010) (overturning lower court order requiring pregnant woman "to submit to any medical treatment deemed necessary by the attending obstetrician, including detention in the hospital for enforcement of bed-rest . . ."); Barbara F. v. Bristol Division of the Juvenile Court Department, 735 N.E.2d 357 (Mass. 2000) (discussing case involving protective custody of pregnant woman who had religious objections to prenatal care); Taft v. Taft, 446 N.E.2d 395 (Mass. 1983) (rejecting husband's effort to obtain a court order requiring pregnant wife to undergo "purse string" operation on cervix). See also Julie D. Cantor, Court-Ordered Care—A Complication of Pregnancy to Avoid, 366 New Eng. J. Med. 2237 (2012) (discussing *Burton*, supra, and reviewing cases); April L. Cherry, The Detention, Confinement, and Incarceration of Pregnant Women for the Benefit of Fetal Health, 16 Colum. J. Gender & L. 147 (2007). Clashes between optimal fetal development and basic lifestyle choices such as whether to smoke, what to eat, and how to conduct childbirth are likely to arise with much greater frequency in the future due to rapid advances of medical science on three fronts: (1) understanding the fetal developmental process; (2) refining diagnostic techniques that detect fetal problems; and (3) developing modes of surgical and medical intervention that allow in utero therapy. See, e.g., Bernard M. Dickens & Rebecca J. Cook, Legal and Ethical Issues in Fetal Surgery, 115 Int'l J. Gynecol. Obstet. 80 (2011).

A maternal-fetal conflict may also arise when a woman needs medication that can negatively impact her fetus. See, e.g., Guardianship of J.D.S., 864 So. 2d 534 (Fla. App. 2004) (state law does not permit appointment of guardian for a fetus in case involving incompetent pregnant women whose medications posed risk to fetus). See also Linda C. Fentiman, The New "Fetal Protection": The Wrong Answer to the Crisis of Inadequate Health Care for Women and Children, 84 Denv. U. L. Rev. 537 (2006); April L. Cherry, *Roe*'s Legacy: The Nonconsensual Medical Treatment of Pregnant Women and Implications for Female Citizenship, 6 U. Pa. J. Const. L. 723 (2004).

4. *Medical Predictions and Medical Ethics.* In a surprising number of the reported cases, such as the principal case and *Jefferson*, described in n.7 of the opinion, the doctors' predictions of the need for fetal intervention proved completely wrong. Sometimes the strength of the medical evidence appears to be exaggerated by the court. See *Pemberton*, 66 F. Supp. at 1250 n.2 (noting that the underlying court order exaggerated the degree of certainty of the underlying medical testimony).

The absence of predictive certainty has played at least some role in the development of the ethical guidelines of medical societies. See, e.g., Committee on Ethics

Opinion, American College of Obstetricians and Gynecologists, Maternal Decision Making, Ethics, and the Law, No. 321 (Nov. 2005) (noting limitation of medical knowledge and predictions; concluding that "[e]fforts to use the legal system to protect the fetus by constraining pregnant women's decision making or punishing them erode a woman's basic rights to privacy and bodily integrity and are not justified"), available at www.acog.org/Resources_And_Publications/Committee_Opinions_List. The American Medical Association House of Delegates-approved policy provides:

> Court Ordered Medical Treatments And Legal Penalties For Potentially Harmful Behavior By Pregnant Women: (1) Judicial intervention is inappropriate when a woman has made an informed refusal of a medical treatment designed to benefit her fetus. If an exceptional circumstance could be found in which a medical treatment poses an insignificant or no health risk to the woman, entails a minimal invasion of her bodily integrity, and would clearly prevent substantial and irreversible harm to her fetus, it might be appropriate for a physician to seek judicial intervention. However, the fundamental principle against compelled medical procedures should control in all cases which do not present such exceptional circumstances.

AMA, H-420.969, Legal Interventions During Pregnancy, available through: www.ama-assn.org/ama/pub/about-ama/our-people/house-delegates/policyfinder.page?.

5. *State or Private Interests.* Should it matter whether the action to force a cesarean is brought by private parties or by the state? In re A.C. was initiated by a hospital, which sought a declaratory judgment permitting the surgery. In re Baby Boy Doe, supra note 3, was pursued by the Illinois state attorney's office. Should the hospital be able to assert the state's interest in protecting fetuses? In the employment context, the Supreme Court has held that policies purportedly designed to protect fetuses that discriminate against fertile women constitute impermissible sex discrimination under Title VII of the Civil Rights Act. Int'l Union, United Automobile, Aerospace and Agricultural Implement Workers of America, UAW v. Johnson Controls, 499 U.S. 187 (1991). Johnson Controls argued that its policy of discriminating against fertile woman was justified as a "bona fide occupational qualification [BFOQ] necessary to the normal operation" of its business. The Court rejected the claim, holding that "Johnson Controls' professed moral and ethical concerns about the welfare of the next generation do not suffice to establish a BFOQ of female sterility." The Civil Rights Act provisions apply only to employment, not to a hospital's treatment of its patients, but the Court's reasoning suggests that private third parties might be restricted from discriminating against women in order to protect fetuses. For more information on the *Johnson Controls* decision, see Mary Becker, Reproductive Hazards After *Johnson Controls*, 31 Hous. L. Rev. 43 (1994); Elaine Draper, Reproductive Hazards and Fetal Exclusion Policies After *Johnson Controls*, 12 Stan. L. & Pol'y Rev. 117 (2001).

6. *Testing and Medical Treatment for HIV Transmission.* Many women with HIV infection are pregnant or hope to become pregnant. Pregnant women who take anti-retroviral drugs and deliver through cesarean section can reduce the risk of HIV transmission from 25-30 percent to a little over 2 percent. Is the risk of HIV transmission from woman to child sufficient to support a program of mandatory HIV testing for pregnant women? Does your answer depend on the use to be made

of the test information? What if it is used to "encourage" HIV-infected pregnant women to abort? To get treatment for themselves or their children? Many states have enacted statutes designed to encourage the use of "routine" HIV testing for pregnant women. See Leslie E. Wolf et al., Legal Barriers to Implementing Recommendations for Universal Routine Prenatal HIV Testing, 32 J.L. Med. & Ethics 137 (2004). The federal Centers for Disease Control and Prevention has issued new guidelines encouraging HIV screening for pregnant women. Bernard M. Branson et al., Revised Recommendations for HIV Testing of Adults, Adolescents, and Pregnant Women in Health Care Settings, 55 MMWR Recomm. Rep. 1 (2006) (RR-14) (recommending directive counseling); and Lawrence O. Gostin, HIV Screening in Health Care Settings: Public Health and Civil Liberties in Conflict?, 296 JAMA 2023 (2006). See discussion at page 677.

Should women with HIV infection be forced to take anti-retroviral therapy? Is this the type of "lesser" invasion of liberty that a court might accept? See In re the Termination of Parental Rights to Aaliyah W. v. Abigail W., 2011 WL 446866 (Wis. App. 2011) (noting detention of pregnant woman in hospital to ensure HIV treatment necessary to protect unborn child). See also Michael A. Grizzi, Compelled Antiviral Treatment of HIV Positive Women, 5 UCLA Women's L.J. 473 (1995); Margot Kaplan, "A Special Class of Persons": Pregnant Women's Right to Refuse Medical Treatment After Gonzales v. Carhart, 13 J. Const. L. 145 (2010). You should reconsider these problems after reading Chapter 6's discussion of public health laws under which people can be screened for diseases and forced to undergo treatment to protect the health of third parties. See pages 698-699. Are the rules governing forced medical treatment for pregnant women consistent with other public health policies? Are any differences explained by the lesser weight given to the state's interest in protecting fetuses, even viable ones?

7. *Brain Death and Pregnancy.* Are there any legal or ethical problems associated with maintaining a brain-dead woman on life support to permit her fetus to mature with the hope that it can be delivered alive? See Alexis Gregorian, Post-Mortem Pregnancy: A Proposed Methodology for the Resolution of Conflicts over Whether a Brain Dead Pregnant Woman Should Be Maintained on Life-Sustaining Treatment, 19 Ann. Health L. 401 (2010); Daniel Sperling, Maternal Brain Death, 30 Am. J.L. & Med. 453 (2004). See also Majid Esmaeilzadeh et al., One Life Ends, Another Begins: Management of a Brain-Dead Pregnant Mother, 8 BMC Med. 74 (2010); David R. Field et al., Maternal Brain Death During Pregnancy, 260 JAMA 816 (1988) (patient maintained in a brain-dead state for nine weeks at a cost of $217,784 before delivery of an infant weighing about 3 pounds).

Problem: Pregnancy and Living Wills

Janet Kuan was 24 weeks pregnant when an aneurysm burst in her brain. She was rushed to the hospital and into surgery, but she experienced extensive brain damage. Although her brain stem is still functioning—and she can breathe without a respirator—all of her higher brain functions have irreversibly ceased. Janet's physicians agree that she is in a permanent vegetative state.

Two years ago, Janet filled out a living will form provided to her by her physician. The form indicated that she wished to refuse "life-sustaining treatments" if she were reliably diagnosed as suffering from a "terminal condition," which was defined to include a "permanent vegetative state." The form also included the following language: "Pursuant to state law, this document becomes null and void and will be given no effect if I am pregnant at the time I am diagnosed with the terminal condition." Janet had crossed out this language in the form and written: "I do not wish to be treated if I am terminally ill and pregnant."

Janet's husband, Nick, wants Janet to be kept alive using a feeding tube and whatever other means are necessary. He hopes that the child can be delivered alive. Janet's parents are repelled by the thought of their child being used as an incubator. What should Janet's physicians do? If the courts become involved, how should they rule and for what reasons?

Many states have enacted living will statutes that purport to restrict the ability of pregnant women to refuse life-sustaining treatment. Assess the validity of these statutes under *Cruzan*, supra at pages 277 and 313, and the majority and dissenting opinions in *A.C.* Should it matter whether the fetus is viable? Would the In re A.C. majority approve the application of the statute to void a pregnant woman's decision not to pursue life-sustaining treatment under the theory that the treatment would extend rather than diminish her life expectancy? Should it matter whether the life-sustaining treatment is more or less invasive than a cesarean section? For a discussion of these issues, see Timothy J. Burch, Incubator or Individual?: The Legal and Policy Deficiencies of Pregnancy Clauses in Living Will and Advanced Health Care Directive Statutes, 54 Md. L. Rev. 528 (1995); Note, 84 Minn. L. Rev. 971 (2000); Katherine A. Taylor, Compelling Pregnancy at Death's Door, 7 Colum. J. Gender & L. 85 (1997).

Problem: Cesarean Deliveries

Conflicts over cesarean births are also connected to debates about whether women who have had a cesarean delivery may subsequently deliver vaginally without undue risk to themselves or to their children. See, e.g., Jun Zhang et al., Contemporary Cesarean Delivery Practice in the United States, 203 Am. J. Obstet. Gynecol. 326.e1 (2010) (noting decline in rate of vaginal birth after cesarean delivery (VBAC) despite evidence supporting attempt at vaginal delivery). Concerns about the risks have led physicians and hospitals to refuse to offer vaginal delivery as an option to women who have had a cesarean section delivery in the past. Kimberly D. Gregory et al., Trends and Patterns of Vaginal Birth After Cesarean Availability in the United States, 34 Semin. Perinatol. 237 (2010) (noting physicians' concerns about legal risks). Should a woman who has previously had a cesarean delivery have a right to give birth vaginally despite any increased risk? Is this a matter that can and should be dealt with using the informed consent process? If the informed consent process is legally adequate, would there be any heightened malpractice risk for the health care providers? See AMA, H-420.969, Legal Interventions During Pregnancy, supra. Can the woman waive her child's right to bring a claim for damages? Is the woman's right to choose vaginal birth related in any way to her right to refuse life-sustaining treatment?

Problem: Access to Drugs Associated with Birth Defects

How should the FDA regulate medications that could have a negative impact on fetuses if taken by pregnant women? Accutane® (used to treat acne), thalidomide (used to treat leprosy), and other products are associated with a significant risk of severe birth defects. Should the products be banned for all, prescribed only for those women who are willing to demonstrate that they are not pregnant and will not become pregnant, or prescribed for anyone with suitable warnings? See Ami E. Doshi, The Cost of Clear Skin: Balancing the Social and Safety Costs of IPledge with the Efficacy of Accutane (Isotretinoin), 37 Seton Hall L. Rev. 625 (2007); Richard A. Epstein, Regulatory Paternalism in the Market for Drugs: Lessons from Vioxx and Celebrex, 5 Yale J. Health Pol'y L. & Ethics 741 (2005); Lars Noah, Too High a Price for Some Drugs? The FDA Burdens Reproductive Choice, 44 San Diego L. Rev. 231 (2007); Toby L. Schonfeld et al., iPledge Allegiance to the Pill: Evaluation of Year 1 of a Birth Defect Prevention and Monitoring System, 37 J.L. Med. & Ethics 104 (2009).

3. Pregnant Women and Drug Use

■ WHITNER v. SOUTH CAROLINA
492 S.E.2d 777 (S.C. 1997), cert. denied, 523 U.S. 1145 (1998)

TOAL, Justice.

This case concerns the scope of the child abuse and endangerment statute in the South Carolina Children's Code (the Code), S.C. Code Ann. §20-7-50 (1985) [the "statute"]. We hold the word child as used in that statute includes viable fetuses.

On April 20, 1992, Cornelia Whitner (Whitner) pled guilty to criminal child neglect for causing her baby to be born with cocaine metabolites in its system by reason of Whitner's ingestion of crack cocaine during the third trimester of her pregnancy. The circuit court judge sentenced Whitner to eight years in prison. Whitner did not appeal her conviction.

Thereafter, Whitner filed a petition for Post Conviction Relief (PCR), pleading the circuit court's lack of subject matter jurisdiction to accept her guilty plea. . . .

Under South Carolina law, a circuit court lacks subject matter jurisdiction to accept a guilty plea to a nonexistent offense. For the sentencing court to have had subject matter jurisdiction to accept Whitner's plea, criminal child neglect would have to include an expectant mother's use of crack cocaine after the fetus is viable. . . .

[The statute] provides:

> Any person having the legal custody of any child or helpless person, who shall, without lawful excuse, refuse or neglect to provide . . . the proper care and attention for such child or helpless person, so that the life, health or comfort of such child or helpless person is endangered or is likely to be endangered, shall be guilty of a misdemeanor and shall be punished within the discretion of the circuit court.

The state contends this section encompasses maternal acts endangering or likely to endanger the life, comfort, or health of a viable fetus.

Under the Children's Code, "child" means a "person under the age of 18." The question for this Court, therefore, is whether a viable fetus is a "person" for purposes of the Children's Code.

In interpreting a statute, this court's primary function is to ascertain the intent of the legislature. Of course, where a statute is complete, plain, and unambiguous, legislative intent must be determined from the language of the statute itself. We should consider, however, not merely the language of the particular clause being construed, but the word and its meaning in conjunction with the purpose of the whole statute and the policy of the law. Finally, there is a basic presumption that the legislature has knowledge of previous legislation as well as of judicial decisions construing that legislation when later statutes are enacted concerning related subjects.

South Carolina law has long recognized that viable fetuses are persons holding certain legal rights and privileges. . . . [The court summarized the treatment of fetuses under state tort law, noting that the state wrongful death statute had been interpreted to permit actions brought on behalf of viable fetuses even where they were not born alive.]

More recently, we held the word *person* as used in a criminal statute includes viable fetuses. State v. Horne, 319 S.E.2d 703 (S.C. 1984), concerned South Carolina's murder statute, S.C. Code Ann. §16-3-10 (1976). The defendant in that case stabbed his wife, who was nine months' pregnant, in the neck, arms, and abdomen. Although doctors performed an emergency cesarean section to deliver the child, the child died while still in the womb. The defendant was convicted of voluntary manslaughter and appealed his conviction on the ground South Carolina did not recognize the crime of feticide.

This court disagreed. In a unanimous decision, we held it would be "grossly inconsistent . . . to construe a viable fetus as a 'person' for the purposes of imposing civil liability while refusing to give it a similar classification in the criminal context." 319 S.E.2d at 704. Accordingly, the court recognized the crime of feticide with respect to viable fetuses.

Similarly, we do not see any rational basis for finding a viable fetus is not a "person" in the present context. Indeed, it would be absurd to recognize the viable fetus as a person for purposes of homicide laws and wrongful death statutes but not for purposes of statutes proscribing child abuse. Our holding . . . that a viable fetus is a person rested primarily on the plain meaning of the word *person* in light of existing medical knowledge concerning fetal development. We do not believe that the plain and ordinary meaning of the word *person* has changed in any way that would now deny viable fetuses status as persons.

The policies enunciated in the Children's Code also support our plain meaning reading of "person." . . . The abuse or neglect of a child at any time during childhood can exact a profound toll on the child herself as well as on society as a whole. However, the consequences of abuse or neglect which takes place after birth often pale in comparison to those resulting from abuse suffered by the viable fetus before birth. This policy of prevention supports a reading of the word *person* to include viable fetuses. Furthermore, the scope of the Children's Code is quite broad. It applies "to all children who have need of services." When coupled with the comprehensive remedial purposes of the Code, this language supports the inference that the legislature intended to include viable fetuses within the scope of the Code's protection.

Whitner advances several arguments against an interpretation of "person" as used in the Children's Code to include viable fetuses. We shall address each of Whitner's major arguments in turn.

Whitner's first argument concerns the number of bills introduced in the South Carolina General Assembly in the past five years addressing substance abuse by pregnant women. . . . We disagree with Whitner's conclusion about the significance of the proposed legislation. Generally, the legislature's subsequent acts "cast no light on the intent of the legislature which enacted the statute being construed." . . .

Whitner also argues an interpretation of the statute that includes viable fetuses would lead to absurd results obviously not intended by the legislature. Specifically, she claims if we interpret "child" to include viable fetuses, every action by a pregnant woman that endangers or is likely to endanger a fetus, whether otherwise legal or illegal, would constitute unlawful neglect under the statute. For example, a woman might be prosecuted . . . for smoking or drinking during pregnancy. Whitner asserts these "absurd" results could not have been intended by the legislature and, therefore, the statute should not be construed to include viable fetuses.

We disagree for a number of reasons. First, the same arguments against the statute can be made whether or not the child has been born. After the birth of a child, a parent can be prosecuted . . . for an action that is likely to endanger the child without regard to whether the action is illegal in itself. For example, a parent who drinks excessively could, under certain circumstances, be guilty of child neglect or endangerment even though the underlying act—consuming alcoholic beverages—is itself legal. Obviously, the legislature did not think it "absurd" to allow prosecution of parents for such otherwise legal acts when the acts actually or potentially endanger the "life, health or comfort" of the parents' born children. We see no reason such a result should be rendered absurd by the mere fact the child at issue is a viable fetus.

Moreover, we need not address this potential parade of horribles advanced by Whitner. In this case, which is the only case we are called upon to decide here, certain facts are clear. Whitner admits to having ingested crack cocaine during the third trimester of her pregnancy, which caused her child to be born with cocaine in its system. Although the precise effects of maternal crack use during pregnancy are somewhat unclear, it is well documented and within the realm of public knowledge that such use can cause serious harm to the viable unborn child. . . . There can be no question here Whitner endangered the life, health, and comfort of her child. We need not decide any cases other than the one before us.

We are well aware of the many decisions from other states' courts throughout the country holding maternal conduct before the birth of the child does not give rise to criminal prosecution under state child abuse/endangerment or drug distribution statutes. . . . Many of these cases were prosecuted under statutes forbidding delivery or distribution of illicit substances and depended on statutory construction of the terms "delivery" and "distribution." . . . Obviously, such cases are inapplicable to the present situation. The cases concerning child endangerment statutes or construing the terms *child* and *person* are also distinguishable, because the states in which these cases were decided have entirely different bodies of case law from South Carolina. . . .

[Previous tort and criminal law cases] were decided primarily on the basis of the meaning of "person" as understood in the light of existing medical knowledge, rather than based on any policy of protecting the relationship between mother and child. As a homicide case, *Horne* also rested on the state's — not the mother's — interest in vindicating the life of the viable fetus. Moreover, the United States Supreme Court has repeatedly held that the states have a compelling interest in the life of a viable fetus [citing *Roe* and *Casey*]. . . . If, as Whitner suggests we should, we read *Horne* only as a vindication of the mother's interest in the life of her unborn child, there would be no basis for prosecuting a mother who kills her viable fetus by stabbing it, by shooting it, or by other such means, yet a third party could be prosecuted for the very same acts. We decline to read *Horne* in a way that insulates the mother from all culpability for harm to her viable child. . . .

[T]he dissent implies that we have ignored the rule of lenity requiring us to resolve any ambiguities in a criminal statute in favor of the defendant. The dissent argues that "[a]t most, the majority only suggests that the term *child* . . . is ambiguous," and that the ambiguity "is created not by reference to our decisions under the Children's Code or by reference to the statutory language and applicable rules of statutory construction, but by reliance on decisions in two different fields of the law, civil wrongful death and common law feticide."

Plainly, the dissent misunderstands our opinion. First, we do not believe the statute is ambiguous and, therefore, the rule of lenity does not apply. Furthermore, our interpretation of the statute is based primarily on the plain meaning of the word *person* as contained in the statute. We need not go beyond that language. However, because our prior decisions . . . support our reading of the statute, we have discussed the rationale underlying those holdings. We conclude that both statutory language and case law compel the conclusion we reach. We see no ambiguity. . . .

C. CONSTITUTIONAL ISSUES

[The court quickly disposed of any constitutional impediments to child endangerment prosecutions of drug-using pregnant women. It rejected Whitner's "notice" claim because the statute clearly and unambiguously covered viable fetuses and Whitner therefore had notice of the potential for prosecution. The court also rejected Whitner's claim that prosecution improperly violated her 14th Amendment "privacy" interests. The court found that the statute merely created an additional penalty for conduct that was already illegal — use of crack cocaine — and did not improperly penalize Whitner for choosing to carry her pregnancy to term.]

WALLER and BURNETT, JJ., concur.

FINNEY, Chief Justice:
I respectfully dissent, and would affirm the grant of post-conviction relief to respondent Whitner.

The issue before the court is whether a fetus is a "child" within the meaning of . . . a statute which makes it a misdemeanor for a "person having legal custody of any child or helpless person" to unlawfully neglect that child or helpless person. Since this is a penal statute, it is strictly construed against the state and in favor of respondent.

The term *child* . . . is defined as a "person under the age of 18" unless a different meaning is required by the circumstances. . . . More importantly, it is apparent from a reading of the entire statute that the word *child* . . . means a child in being and not a fetus. A plain reading of the entire child neglect statute demonstrates the intent to criminalize only acts directed at children, and not those which may harm fetuses. First, [the statute] . . . does not impose criminal liability on every person who neglects a child, but only on a person having legal custody of that child. The statutory requirement of legal custody is evidence of intent to extend the statute's reach only to children, because the concept of legal custody is simply inapplicable to a fetus. Second, [the statute refers to other statutory sections] . . . for the definition of neglect. [These sections] . . . define[] a neglected child as one harmed or threatened with harm, and further defines harm. The vast majority of acts which constitute statutory harm under [these provisions] are acts which can only be directed against a child, and not towards a fetus.[2] . . .

At most, the majority only suggests that the term *child* as used in [the child neglect statute at issue] is ambiguous. This suggestion of ambiguity is created not by reference to our decisions under the Children's Code or by reference to the statutory language and applicable rules of statutory construction, but by reliance on decisions in two different fields of the law, civil wrongful death and common law feticide. Even if these wrongful death, common law, and Children's Code decisions are sufficient to render the term *child* in [the statute] . . . ambiguous, it is axiomatic that the ambiguity must be resolved in respondent's favor.

I would affirm.

MOORE, Justice:

I concur with the dissent in this case but write separately to express my concerns with today's decision. In my view, the repeated failure of the legislature to pass proposed bills addressing the problem of drug use during pregnancy is evidence the child abuse and neglect statute is not intended to apply in this instance. This court should not invade what is clearly the sole province of the legislative branch. At the very least, the legislature's failed attempts to enact a statute regulating a pregnant woman's conduct indicate the complexity of this issue. While the majority opinion is perhaps an argument for what the law should be, it is for the General Assembly, and not this court, to make that determination by means of a clearly drawn statute. With today's decision, the majority not only ignores legislative intent but embarks on a course rejected by every other court to address the issue. . . .

■ FERGUSON v. CITY OF CHARLESTON
532 U.S. 67 (2001)

STEVENS, J.

In this case, we must decide whether a state hospital's performance of a diagnostic test to obtain evidence of a patient's criminal conduct for law enforcement

2. Examples include condoning delinquency, using excessive corporal punishment, committing sexual offenses against the child, and depriving her of adequate food, clothing, shelter or education.

purposes is an unreasonable search if the patient has not consented to the procedure. More narrowly, the question is whether the interest in using the threat of criminal sanctions to deter pregnant women from using cocaine can justify a departure from the general rule that an official nonconsensual search is unconstitutional if not authorized by a valid warrant.

I

In the fall of 1988, staff members at the public hospital operated in the city of Charleston by the Medical University of South Carolina (MUSC) became concerned about an apparent increase in the use of cocaine by patients who were receiving prenatal treatment. In response to this perceived increase, as of April 1989, MUSC began to order drug screens to be performed on urine samples from maternity patients who were suspected of using cocaine. If a patient tested positive, she was then referred by MUSC staff to the county substance abuse commission for counseling and treatment. However, despite the referrals, the incidence of cocaine use among the patients at MUSC did not appear to change.

Some four months later, Nurse Shirley Brown, the case manager for the MUSC obstetrics department, heard a news broadcast reporting that the police in Greenville, South Carolina, were arresting pregnant users of cocaine on the theory that such use harmed the fetus and was therefore child abuse.[1] Nurse Brown discussed the story with MUSC's general counsel, Joseph C. Good, Jr., who then contacted Charleston Solicitor Charles Condon in order to offer MUSC's cooperation in prosecuting mothers whose children tested positive for drugs at birth.

After receiving Good's letter, Solicitor Condon took the first steps in developing the policy at issue in this case. . . . [The policy is called] "POLICY M-7," dealing with the subject of "Management of Drug Abuse During Pregnancy." . . .

The first three pages of Policy M-7 set forth the procedure to be followed by the hospital staff to "identify/assist pregnant patients suspected of drug abuse." . . . The first section, entitled the "Identification of Drug Abusers," provided that a patient should be tested for cocaine through a urine drug screen if she met one or more of nine criteria . . . [including no or late prenatal care]. It also stated that a chain of custody should be followed when obtaining and testing urine samples, presumably to make sure that the results could be used in subsequent criminal proceedings. The policy also provided for education and referral to a substance abuse clinic for patients who tested positive. Most important, it added the threat of law enforcement intervention that "provided the necessary 'leverage' to make the [p]olicy effective." . . . That threat was, as respondents candidly acknowledge, essential to the program's success in getting women into treatment and keeping them there.

The threat of law enforcement involvement was set forth in two protocols, the first dealing with the identification of drug use during pregnancy, and the second with identification of drug use after labor. Under the latter protocol, the police were

1. Under South Carolina law, a viable fetus has historically been regarded as a person; in 1995, the South Carolina Supreme Court held that the ingestion of cocaine during the third trimester of pregnancy constitutes criminal child neglect. Whitner v. South Carolina, 492 S.E.2d 777 (S.C. 1995), cert. denied, 523 U.S. 1145 (1998).

to be notified without delay and the patient promptly arrested. Under the former, after the initial positive drug test, the police were to be notified (and the patient arrested) only if the patient tested positive for cocaine a second time or if she missed an appointment with a substance abuse counselor. . . . [although at least one patient was arrested after an initial positive drug screen.] In 1990, however, the policy was modified at the behest of the solicitor's office to give the patient who tested positive during labor, like the patient who tested positive during a prenatal care visit, an opportunity to avoid arrest by consenting to substance abuse treatment.

The last six pages of the policy contained forms for the patients to sign, as well as procedures for the police to follow when a patient was arrested. The policy also prescribed in detail the precise offenses with which a woman could be charged, depending on the stage of her pregnancy[, with the charges as well as their nature and severity changing with each stage]. . . . Other than the provisions describing the substance abuse treatment to be offered to women who tested positive, the policy made no mention of any change in the prenatal care of such patients, nor did it prescribe any special treatment for the newborns.

II

Petitioners are 10 women who received obstetrical care at MUSC and who were arrested after testing positive for cocaine. Four of them were arrested during the initial implementation of the policy; they were not offered the opportunity to receive drug treatment as an alternative to arrest. The others were arrested after the policy was modified in 1990; they either failed to comply with the terms of the drug treatment program or tested positive for a second time. Respondents include the city of Charleston, law enforcement officials who helped develop and enforce the policy, and representatives of MUSC.

Petitioners' complaint challenged the validity of the policy under various theories, including the claim that warrantless and nonconsensual drug tests conducted for criminal investigatory purposes were unconstitutional searches. Respondents advanced two principal defenses to the constitutional claim: (1) that, as a matter of fact, petitioners had consented to the searches; and (2) that, as a matter of law, the searches were reasonable, even absent consent, because they were justified by special non-law-enforcement purposes. . . . The District Court rejected the second defense because the searches in question "were not done by the medical university for independent purposes. [Instead,] the police came in and there was an agreement reached that the positive screens would be shared with the police." . . . Accordingly, the District Court submitted the factual defense to the jury with instructions that required a verdict in favor of petitioners unless the jury found consent. . . . The jury found for respondents.

Petitioners appealed, arguing that the evidence was not sufficient to support the jury's consent finding. The Court of Appeals for the Fourth Circuit affirmed, but without reaching the question of consent. . . .

We granted certiorari, 528 U.S. 1187 (2000), to review the appellate court's holding on the "special needs" issue. Because we do not reach the question of the sufficiency of the evidence with respect to consent, we necessarily assume for purposes of our decision—as did the Court of Appeals—that the searches were conducted without the informed consent of the patients. We conclude that the judgment should be reversed and the case remanded for a decision on the consent issue.

III

Because MUSC is a state hospital, the members of its staff are government actors, subject to the strictures of the Fourth Amendment. . . . Moreover, the urine tests conducted by those staff members were indisputably searches within the meaning of the Fourth Amendment. Skinner v. Railway Labor Executives' Assn., 489 U.S. 602, 617 (1989). . . . Neither the District Court nor the Court of Appeals concluded that any of the nine criteria used to identify the women to be searched provided either probable cause to believe that they were using cocaine, or even the basis for a reasonable suspicion of such use. Rather, the District Court and the Court of Appeals viewed the case as one involving MUSC's right to conduct searches without warrants or probable cause. . . . Furthermore, given the posture in which the case comes to us, we must assume for purposes of our decision that the tests were performed without the informed consent of the patients. . . .

Because the hospital seeks to justify its authority to conduct drug tests and to turn the results over to law enforcement agents without the knowledge or consent of the patients, this case differs from the four previous cases in which we have considered whether comparable drug tests "fit within the closely guarded category of constitutionally permissible suspicionless searches." Chandler v. Miller, 520 U.S. 305, 309 (1997). . . .

In each of . . . [the prior] cases, we employed a balancing test that weighed the intrusion on the individual's interest in privacy against the "special needs" that supported the program. As an initial matter, we note that the invasion of privacy in this case is far more substantial than in those cases. In the previous four cases, there was no misunderstanding about the purpose of the test or the potential use of the test results, and there were protections against the dissemination of the results to third parties. . . . The reasonable expectation of privacy enjoyed by the typical patient undergoing diagnostic tests in a hospital is that the results of those tests will not be shared with nonmedical personnel without her consent. . . .[2] In none of our prior cases was there any intrusion upon that kind of expectation.[3]

The critical difference between those four drug-testing cases and this one, however, lies in the nature of the "special need" asserted as justification for the warrantless searches. In each of those earlier cases, the "special need" that was advanced as a justification for the absence of a warrant or individualized suspicion was one divorced from the State's general interest in law enforcement. . . . In this

---

2. There are some circumstances in which state hospital employees, like other citizens, may have a duty to provide law enforcement officials with evidence of criminal conduct acquired in the course of routine treatment, see, e.g., S. C. Code Ann. §20-7-510 (2000) (physicians and nurses required to report to child welfare agency or law enforcement authority "when in the person's professional capacity the person" receives information that a child has been abused or neglected). While the existence of such laws might lead a patient to expect that members of the hospital staff might turn over evidence acquired in the course of treatment to which the patient had consented, they surely would not lead a patient to anticipate that hospital staff would intentionally set out to obtain incriminating evidence from their patients for law enforcement purposes.

3. In fact, we have previously recognized that an intrusion on that expectation may have adverse consequences because it may deter patients from receiving needed medical care. . . .

case, however, the central and indispensable feature of the policy from its inception was the use of law enforcement to coerce the patients into substance abuse treatment. This fact distinguishes this case from circumstances in which physicians or psychologists, in the course of ordinary medical procedures aimed at helping the patient herself, come across information that under rules of law or ethics is subject to reporting requirements, which no one has challenged here. See, e.g., Council on Ethical and Judicial Affairs, American Medical Association, PolicyFinder, Current Opinions E-5.05 (2000) (requiring reporting where "a patient threatens to inflict serious bodily harm to another person or to him or herself and there is a reasonable probability that the patient may carry out the threat"). . . .

Respondents argue in essence that their ultimate purpose—namely, protecting the health of both mother and child—is a beneficent one. . . . In looking to the programmatic purpose, we consider all the available evidence in order to determine the relevant primary purpose. . . . Tellingly, the document codifying the policy incorporates the police's operational guidelines. It devotes its attention to the chain of custody, the range of possible criminal charges, and the logistics of police notification and arrests. Nowhere, however, does the document discuss different courses of medical treatment for either mother or infant, aside from treatment for the mother's addiction.

Moreover, throughout the development and application of the policy, the Charleston prosecutors and police were extensively involved in the day-to-day administration of the policy. . . .

While the ultimate goal of the program may well have been to get the women in question into substance abuse treatment and off of drugs, the immediate objective of the searches was to generate evidence for law enforcement purposes . . . in order to reach that goal. . . . The threat of law enforcement may ultimately have been intended as a means to an end, but the direct and primary purpose of MUSC's policy was to ensure the use of those means. In our opinion, this distinction is critical. Because law enforcement involvement always serves some broader social purpose or objective, under respondents' view, virtually any nonconsensual suspicionless search could be immunized under the special needs doctrine by defining the search solely in terms of its ultimate, rather than immediate, purpose. . . . Such an approach is inconsistent with the Fourth Amendment. Given the primary purpose of the Charleston program, which was to use the threat of arrest and prosecution in order to force women into treatment, and given the extensive involvement of law enforcement officials at every stage of the policy, this case simply does not fit within the closely guarded category of "special needs."[4]

The fact that positive test results were turned over to the police does not merely provide a basis for distinguishing our prior cases applying the "special needs" balancing approach to the determination of drug use. It also provides an affirmative reason for enforcing the strictures of the Fourth Amendment. While state hospital employees, like other citizens, may have a duty to provide the police with evidence of criminal conduct that they inadvertently acquire in the course of routine treat-

---

4. It is especially difficult to argue that the program here was designed simply to save lives. Amici claim a near consensus in the medical community that programs of the sort at issue, by discouraging women who use drugs from seeking prenatal care, harm, rather than advance, the cause of prenatal health. . . .

ment, when they undertake to obtain such evidence from their patients for the specific purpose of incriminating those patients, they have a special obligation to make sure that the patients are fully informed about their constitutional rights, as standards of knowing waiver require. . . .

As respondents have repeatedly insisted, their motive was benign rather than punitive. Such a motive, however, cannot justify a departure from Fourth Amendment protections, given the pervasive involvement of law enforcement with the development and application of the MUSC policy. The stark and unique fact that characterizes this case is that Policy M-7 was designed to obtain evidence of criminal conduct by the tested patients that would be turned over to the police and that could be admissible in subsequent criminal prosecutions. While respondents are correct that drug abuse both was and is a serious problem, "the gravity of the threat alone cannot be dispositive of questions concerning what means law enforcement officers may employ to pursue a given purpose." . . . The Fourth Amendment's general prohibition against nonconsensual, warrantless, and suspicionless searches necessarily applies to such a policy. . . .

Accordingly, the judgment of the Court of Appeals is reversed, and the case is remanded for further proceedings consistent with this opinion.

It is so ordered.

KENNEDY, J., concurring:

I agree that the search procedure in issue cannot be sustained under the Fourth Amendment. My reasons for this conclusion differ somewhat from those set forth by the Court, however, leading to this separate opinion. . . .

In my view, it is necessary and prudent to be explicit in explaining the limitations of today's decision. The beginning point ought to be to acknowledge the legitimacy of the State's interest in fetal life and of the grave risk to the life and health of the fetus, and later the child, caused by cocaine ingestion. Infants whose mothers abuse cocaine during pregnancy are born with a wide variety of physical and neurological abnormalities. . . . There should be no doubt that South Carolina can impose punishment upon an expectant mother who has so little regard for her own unborn that she risks causing him or her lifelong damage and suffering. The State, by taking special measures to give rehabilitation and training to expectant mothers with this tragic addiction or weakness, acts well within its powers and its civic obligations.

The holding of the Court, furthermore, does not call into question the validity of mandatory reporting laws such as child abuse laws which require teachers to report evidence of child abuse to the proper authorities, even if arrest and prosecution is the likely result. . . . [W]e must accept the premise that the medical profession can adopt acceptable criteria for testing expectant mothers for cocaine use in order to provide prompt and effective counseling to the mother and to take proper medical steps to protect the child. If prosecuting authorities then adopt legitimate procedures to discover this information and prosecution follows, that ought not to invalidate the testing. . . .

SCALIA, J., dissenting:

There is always an unappealing aspect to the use of doctors and nurses, ministers of mercy, to obtain incriminating evidence against the supposed objects of their ministration—although here, it is correctly pointed out, the doctors and nurses were ministering not just to the mothers but also to the children whom their cooperation with the police was meant to protect. But whatever may be the correct social judgment concerning the desirability of what occurred here, that is not the issue in the present case. . . . The question before us is a narrower one: whether, whatever the desirability of this police conduct, it violates the Fourth Amendment's prohibition of unreasonable searches and seizures. In my view, it plainly does not. . . .

It is rudimentary Fourth Amendment law that a search which has been consented to is not unreasonable. There is no contention in the present case that the urine samples were extracted forcibly. The only conceivable bases for saying that they were obtained without consent are the contentions (1) that the consent was coerced by the patients' need for medical treatment, (2) that the consent was uninformed because the patients were not told that the tests would include testing for drugs, and (3) that the consent was uninformed because the patients were not told that the results of the tests would be provided to the police. . . .

Until today, we have never held—or even suggested—that material which a person voluntarily entrusts to someone else cannot be given by that person to the police, and used for whatever evidence it may contain. . . . Today's holding would be remarkable enough if the confidential relationship violated by the police conduct were at least one protected by state law. . . . But today's holding goes even beyond that, since there does not exist any physician-patient privilege in South Carolina. . . .

There remains to be considered the first possible basis for invalidating this search, which is that the patients were coerced to produce their urine samples by their necessitous circumstances, to-wit, their need for medical treatment of their pregnancy. If that was coercion, it was not coercion applied by the government—and if such nongovernmental coercion sufficed, the police would never be permitted to use the ballistic evidence obtained from treatment of a patient with a bullet wound. And the Fourth Amendment would invalidate those many state laws that require physicians to report gunshot wounds, . . . evidence of spousal abuse, . . . and (like the South Carolina law relevant here, see S. C. Code Ann. §20-7-510 (2000)) evidence of child abuse. . . .

I think it clear, therefore, that there is no basis for saying that obtaining of the urine sample was unconstitutional. The special-needs doctrine is thus quite irrelevant, since it operates only to validate searches and seizures that are otherwise unlawful. In the ensuing discussion, however, I shall assume (contrary to legal precedent) that the taking of the urine sample was (either because of the patients' necessitous circumstances, or because of failure to disclose that the urine would be tested for drugs, or because of failure to disclose that the results of the test would be given to the police) coerced. Indeed, I shall even assume (contrary to common sense) that the testing of the urine constituted an unconsented search of the patients' effects. On those assumptions, the special-needs doctrine would become relevant; and, properly applied, would validate what was done here. . . .

The cocaine tests started in April 1989, neither at police suggestion nor with police involvement. Expectant mothers who tested positive were referred by hospital staff for substance-abuse treatment . . . —an obvious health benefit to both mother and child. . . . Thus, in their origin—before the police were in any way involved—the tests had an immediate, not merely an "ultimate," . . . purpose of improving maternal and infant health. Several months after the testing had been initiated . . . [the hospital invited police involvement.] . . . Why would there be any reason to believe that, once this policy of using the drug tests for their "ultimate" health benefits had been adopted, use of them for their original, immediate, benefits somehow disappeared, and testing somehow became in its entirety nothing more than a "pretext" for obtaining grounds for arrest?

In sum, there can be no basis for the Court's purported ability to "distinguish this case from circumstances in which physicians or psychologists, in the course of ordinary medical procedures aimed at helping the patient herself, come across information that . . . is subject to reporting requirements," . . . .

But as far as the Fourth Amendment is concerned: There was no unconsented search in this case. And if there was, it would have been validated by the special-needs doctrine. For these reasons, I respectfully dissent.

Notes: Maternal Substance Abuse

1. *Prevalence and Effect of Maternal Substance Abuse.* Thousands of children are born each year to women who have used tobacco, alcohol, or illegal drugs during pregnancy. In 2009-2010, 4.4 percent of all pregnant women aged 15-44 reported using illicit drugs in the last month. Drug use was more prevalent in young pregnant women (16.2% for young women aged 15-17 compared to 1.9% for women aged 26-44). Just over 16 percent of pregnant women aged 15-44 reported using tobacco products within the past month. More than 10 percent of pregnant women in this age range reported drinking alcohol. Substance Abuse and Mental Health Services Administration, U.S. Department of Health and Human Services, 2010 National Survey on Drug Use and Health. The type of substance used varies by race and socioeconomic status, although there is some evidence that the overall use of potentially injurious substances is consistent across all groups. See S. L. Hans, Demographic and Psychosocial Characteristics of Substance-Abusing Pregnant Women, 26 Clin. Perinatology 55 (1999).

Illicit drugs, alcohol, tobacco, and other substances can injure developing fetuses. Research findings include higher rates of prematurity, lower birth weights, and cognitive/behavioral abnormalities. It is important to recognize, however, that other related factors may contribute to some of these problems, including inadequate diet, poor prenatal care, and a less than optimal developmental environment. See, e.g., Sonia Minnes et al., Prenatal Tobacco, Marijuana, Stimulant, and Opiate Exposure: Outcomes and Practical Implications, 6 Addict. Sci. Clin. Pract. 57 (2011); Linda L. LaGasse et al., Prenatal Methamphetamine Exposure and Childhood Behavior Problems at 3 and 5 Years of Age, 129 Pediatrics 681 (2012); Ashley H. Schempf & Donna M. Strobino, Illicit Drug Use and Adverse Birth Outcomes: Is It Drugs or Context?, 85 J. Urban Health 858 (2008). Should policies developed to deal with the use of illicit drugs by pregnant women be applied to the use of harmful, but legal, substances? The *Whitner* court suggests that such prosecutions are possible but potentially problematic from a constitutional standpoint.

2. *Two Views on Legislative Intent.* Determining whether traditional child endangerment, drug delivery, or other statutes apply to the problem of risky prenatal conduct is initially a problem of statutory interpretation. Does the statute

apply to fetuses explicitly or will a court find that the legislature intended for the provision to apply to fetuses? The vast majority of states that have considered the statutory interpretation questions in the criminal context have found that the legislature did not intend to include fetuses. For an excellent review of the relevant cases, see Linda C. Fentiman, In the Name of Fetal Protection: Why American Prosecutors Pursue Drug Users (and Other Countries Don't), 18 Colum. J. Gender & L. 647 (2009). See also Michele Goodwin, Precarious Moorings: Tying Fetal Drug Law Policy to Social Profiling, 42 Rutgers L.J. 659 (2011); Michelle Goodwin, Prosecuting the Womb, 76 Geo. Wash. L. Rev. 1657 (2008); James G. Hodge, Jr., Prosecution of Mother for Prenatal Substance Abuse Based on Endangerment of or Delivery of Controlled Substances to Child, 70 A.L.R.4th 461 (1999). The Editorial Staff of the Yale Journal of Health Policy, Law, and Ethics, Synopsis of State Case and Statutory Law, 1 Yale J. Health Pol'y L. & Ethics 215 (2001) [hereinafter Synopsis of State Case and Statutory Law]. See also State v. Ikerd, 850 A.2d 516 (N.J. Super. 2004) (holding that "a pregnant, drug-addicted woman who has violated the conditions of her probation cannot be sentenced to prison for the avowed purpose of safeguarding the health of her fetus."). *Whitner*, therefore, represents the minority view. The decision could still be "right" for purposes of South Carolina law. Do you agree that the state legislature intended that the child endangerment statute be applied to a pregnant woman's behavior toward her fetus? Why would the legislature attempt to enact legislation on the subject if the child endangerment statute already provided a remedy? How persuasive is the majority's statutory interpretation? Is the legislature likely to "correct" the court if it is wrong?

South Carolina continues to follow the *Whitner* approach. In State v. McKnight, 576 S.E.2d 168 (S.C. 2003), the South Carolina Supreme Court cited *Whitner* in affirming a defendant's conviction of homicide by child abuse through prenatal use of cocaine. The defendant gave birth to a stillborn child estimated to be at 34-37 weeks of gestation; metabolites of cocaine were found during an autopsy of the fetus. The defendant was sentenced to a 20-year term of imprisonment. The court later determined that McKnight had received ineffective assistance of counsel and reversed her conviction. State v. McKnight, 661 S.E.2d 354 (S.C. 2008).

The defendant in *Whitner* argued that South Carolina's recognition of tort and criminal law actions arising from fetal injuries was an attempt to protect a woman's relationship with her fetus rather than an effort to protect a fetal right to be free from harm. The court rejected the argument, finding that state case law was based on the definition of "person" and noting the state's compelling interest in protecting fetal life. Other courts have accepted the defendant's view and have restricted actions brought against the woman, as opposed to some third party, on the theory that the state's interest is in protecting the woman's interest in the fetus.

State ex rel. Angela M.W. v. Kruzicki, 561 N.W.2d 729 (Wis. 1997), is typical of the majority approach. Angela M.W.'s obstetrician reported her to county authorities because of her persistent drug use during pregnancy. The county filed a motion to take Angela's unborn child (and, by necessity, Angela herself) into custody; the order was granted by the juvenile court. The county then filed a petition asserting that the unborn child was a "child in need of protection or services" under state law because Angela was endangering her fetus's health. The relevant statute defined "child" as a "person who is less than 18 years of age." Angela brought and lost an action in the court of appeals, seeking her release or a stay of the juvenile court proceedings. In the course of these proceedings, Angela gave birth to a baby boy.

The Wisconsin Supreme Court reversed the court of appeals, with three justices dissenting. 561 N.W.2d 729 (Wis. 1997) (The court issued its decision despite the child's birth and Angela's release from confinement under an exception to the mootness doctrine often used in litigation involving pregnancy. See Roe v. Wade, supra.). The court agreed that the definition of "child" was ambiguous under the statutory scheme but held that the legislature had not intended to include unborn fetuses in the definition. The court noted, for example, that the statute used "child" in a number of ways that were inconsistent with the inclusion of viable fetuses. The majority did not reach the constitutional issues because it was able to overturn the custodial order on statutory interpretation grounds alone. See also Ian Vandewalker, Taking the Baby Before It's Born: Termination of the Parental Rights of Women Who Use Illegal Drugs While Pregnant, 32 NYU Rev. L. & Soc. Change 423 (2008).

Note that some states have attempted to prosecute pregnant drug users under statutes that make it a criminal offense to "deliver" drugs to another "person." The prosecutions proceeded on the theory that a pregnant woman who had ingested illegal drugs within a few days of giving birth was capable of transmitting drug metabolites to her newborn during the brief time period between birth and the cutting of the umbilical cord—when the child was a "person." Courts have rejected these prosecutions, holding that the legislatures did not intend this application of the drug delivery statutes. See, e.g., Synopsis of State Case and Statutory Law, supra; Johnson v. State, 602 So. 2d 1288 (Fla. 1992).

3. *The Constitution and the Prosecution of Pregnant Women.* Most attempted prosecutions have failed on the basis of statutory interpretation and legislative intent. Courts, therefore, have rarely reached the constitutional objections to the prosecution of pregnant women. Of course a state legislature could easily surmount the statutory interpretation obstacles to criminal prosecution by enacting legislation that clearly imposes criminal punishments on pregnant women who injure their fetuses. Courts reviewing this type of legislation would be forced to confront potential due process and equal protection challenges. How would you frame the constitutional questions?

The *Whitner* court's constitutional analysis was cursory. The majority defended child endangerment prosecutions from constitutional attack by noting that the underlying drug use was already criminal. Would it be unconstitutional to prosecute pregnant women for conduct that, while potentially injurious, was otherwise legal? How would you analyze the prosecution of a woman for smoking tobacco after fetal viability? The dissenting justices in State ex rel. Angela M.W. seemed to argue that such prosecutions would also be permissible under the due process and equal protection clauses:

> Angela next contends that the custodial effect of the protective order violated her due process liberty interest under the United States Constitution. . . . In regard to the state interest implicated here, the United States Supreme Court has determined [that] . . . the state's interest in protecting the life and health of an unborn child becomes compelling and dominant once the fetus reaches viability. . . . In the present case, there is no dispute that Angela's child was a viable fetus when the petition was filed, that Angela was actively using cocaine, and that the use of cocaine put the child at substantial risk of great bodily harm or possibly death. As such, the state has

a compelling state interest to protect Angela's fetus under *Roe* [and] *Casey*. . . . [If *Roe* stands for the proposition that the state's interest in a viable fetus can override a woman's wish to terminate the pregnancy, why shouldn't the state be able to] protect the viable fetus from maternal conduct which functionally presents the same risk and portends the same result, the death of the viable fetus? . . .

The next issue therefore is whether the infringement on Angela's liberty is narrowly tailored to further the compelling state interest. I conclude that it is. The Children's Code specifies the procedures necessary to further the state's compelling interest in the protection of children. These procedures must be complied with before the state can exercise its right to detain and ultimately protect a child. [The procedures include a post-detention hearing to determine whether there is probable cause to exercise jurisdiction over the child and whether the child will be "subject to injury if . . . not taken into protective custody."] . . . In light of all the statutorily imposed procedures necessary to detain a child, it is clear that the means by which the state's compelling interest is served are narrowly tailored to [meet the state's interest in protecting children]. . . .

Finally, Angela argues that if the state is allowed to intervene when the mother ingests cocaine, this will "open the door" for the state to intervene whenever a mother acts in any manner that is potentially harmful to her viable fetus. Angela cites as examples the possibility of state intervention if a mother smokes or refuses to take her prenatal vitamins. This argument is not a realistic one because [the statute] . . . contains the necessary protections against unreasonable or unjustified intervention by the state. . . . Clearly, the Children's Code enables the state to intervene only when a child faces substantial risk. Thus, [the statute] . . . contains the necessary stopping point to protect against Angela's slippery slope argument. In fact, if this were not true, then the same argument would have validity under the Children's Code even if the child has been born [citing Whitner v. State, supra].

State ex rel. Angela M.W. v. Kruzicki, 561 N.W.2d 729, 747-749 (Wis. 1997) (Crooks, J., dissenting).

Do you agree with the dissent's disposition of the constitutional questions? Do the abortion cases stand for the proposition that the state's compelling interest in fetal life can outweigh more than a woman's right to terminate her pregnancy? How would you characterize the nature of the pregnant woman's interests? Is the use of forced confinement and drug treatment a measure narrowly tailored to achieve the state's objectives? Compare the dissent's analysis with the majority and dissenting opinions in In re A.C. See also Nancy Ehrenreich, The Colonization of the Womb, 43 Duke L.J. 492 (1993).

4. *Medical Care for Pregnant Women and the Fourth Amendment.* The *Ferguson* case might be viewed as the natural outgrowth of the criminalization of drug use by pregnant women. Note that the Court does not find fault with the state law criminalizing prenatal drug abuse. What were the constitutional defects of the hospital policy in *Ferguson?* State law often requires health care providers to report matters such as child abuse and gunshot wounds. See Chapter 2, at page 176. Do reports under these statutes present the same Fourth Amendment problems as the hospital policy in *Ferguson?* For a summary of state testing and reporting rules, see Synopsis of State Case and Statutory Law, supra. See also The American College of Obstetricians and Gynecologists, Committee Opinion, Substance Abuse Reporting and Pregnancy: The Role of the Obstetrician-Gynecologist, 117 Obstet. Gynecol. 200 (2011).

On remand in *Ferguson*, the United States Court of Appeals for the Fourth Circuit issued a lengthy opinion holding that: (1) a mother's Fourth Amendment interests are not implicated by newborn urine testing; (2) the MUSC's policy of testing patients' urine for evidence of cocaine was not designed to further medical care; (3) the hospital's consent forms did not adequately inform patients about the use of urine tests for law enforcement purposes; and (4) patients who presented themselves to the hospital for treatment could not be said to have impliedly consented to the urine search policy. Ferguson v. City of Charleston, South Carolina, 308 F.3d 380 (4th Cir. 2002). The court also held that two patients had sufficient knowledge of the law enforcement purposes of the testing to imply consent. Id. Could a state require welfare recipients to undergo warrantless, suspicionless drug testing as a condition of receiving benefits? Marchwinski v. Howard, 113 F. Supp. 2d 1134 (E.D. Mich. 2000) (no), upheld on rehearing en banc, 60 Fed. Appx. 601 (6th Cir. 2003) (judgment of the district court reinstated by equally divided vote of the appeals court en banc).

5. *The Criminal Model vs. the Treatment Model.* Punitive prenatal substance abuse policies clearly might deter drug-addicted women from seeking prenatal care. Not surprisingly, the AMA's policy favors treatment over criminal liability: "Criminal sanctions or civil liability for harmful behavior by the pregnant woman toward her fetus are inappropriate. . . . Pregnant substance abusers should be provided with rehabilitative treatment appropriate to their specific physiological and psychological needs." AMA, H-420.969 Legal Interventions During Pregnancy. Critics of the criminal model also note that pregnant women have faced difficulties accessing treatment programs. Janet W. Steverson & Traci Rieckmann, Legislating for the Provision of Comprehensive Substance Abuse Programs for Pregnant and Mothering Women, 16 Duke J. Gender L. & Pol'y 315 (2009). See Elaine W. v. Joint Diseases North General Hospital, 613 N.E.2d 523 (N.Y. 1993) (exclusion of pregnant women from treatment program).

Whitner and *Ferguson* were followed by a new wave of legislation focused on the therapeutic solution to risky maternal conduct. See Synopsis of State Case and Statutory Law, supra; Elizabeth E. Coleman & Monica K. Miller, Assessing Legal Responses to Prenatal Drug Use: Can Therapeutic Responses Produce More Positive Outcomes Than Punitive Responses?, 20 J.L. & Health 35 (2007); Lynn M. Paltrow, Governmental Responses to Pregnant Women Who Use Alcohol or Other Drugs, 8 DePaul J. Health Care L. 461 (2005). One possible noncriminal approach to prenatal substance abuse is civil commitment. See Chapter 6, at pages 706-707. Does this approach avoid any of the drawbacks of criminal prosecution? See David F. Chavkin, "For Their Own Good": Civil Commitment of Alcohol and Drug-Dependent Women, 37 S.D. L. Rev. 224 (1991/1992).

D. USING REPRODUCTIVE TECHNOLOGIES TO CREATE NEW FAMILIES

Technological advances in reproduction have cast into question some long-established legal doctrines. Who is the father of a child conceived through artificial insemination (AI)? Who is the mother of a child born through the use of in vitro fertilization (IVF) techniques and surrogacy? Is it possible to have two fathers or two mothers? Is it possible to have more than two parents? These questions are intrinsically important because of the joys, legal rights, and obligations that go along with parenthood. Yet the answers to these questions also can have important consequences for our ideas of what "parenthood," "fatherhood," or "motherhood" means.

Some of the issues considered in this section build upon those discussed in section A of this chapter. Litigants often assert their constitutional right to control procreation, for example, in arguing for particular legal treatment of a reproductive technology. Moreover, the struggle for control between individuals and the state is a consistent theme of the cases in section A and in this section. Nonetheless, there are important differences in the cases in these sections.

In the earlier section, the state's attempt to control most often took the form of regulations or of outright prohibition of the use of the technology itself, such as state attempts to restrict access to abortion. In this section, we are concerned primarily with state attempts to control outcome rather than use. Only with respect to cloning, discussed in the final section of this chapter, have states begun to impose blanket prohibitions on the use of reproductive technologies to facilitate reproduction. Most state regulation focuses on the manner in which the technology is used and seeks to establish the legal status of participants in the process. These efforts have been resisted by individuals who have sought to use contractual agreements or existing statutory mechanisms to establish legal status and relationships. The primary issue therefore has been whether individuals or the state controls the legal status of participants in reproductive ventures.

1. Parenting Possibilities

■ ASSISTED REPRODUCTIVE TECHNOLOGY AND THE FAMILY*
John A. Robertson**
47 Hastings L.J. 911 (1996)

More than one in eight married couples in the United States suffer from infertility (defined as a lack of pregnancy after a year of unprotected intercourse). Although some couples adopt or choose to remain childless, many turn to physicians for help in forming families. The list of assisted reproductive techniques (ARTs) available for treating infertility now includes intrauterine insemination (IUI), ovulation induction, in vitro fertilization (IVF), intracytoplasmic sperm injection, sperm donation, egg donation, embryo donation, and gestational surrogacy.

The growth of the contemporary infertility industry has been largely spurred by the development of IVF. The first American birth resulting from in vitro fertilization occurred in 1981. By 1988, 15,000 stimulated IVF cycles occurred in more than 100 clinics. In 1994, more than 300 clinics performed more than 35,000 cycles, resulting in more than 6,000 births. . . .

The use of assisted reproductive techniques by infertile couples is a family-centered act, reflecting couples' desire to form families with biologically related offspring. Although adoption and foster parenting can provide parenting experiences, only ARTs enable one or both partners to have some biologic tie, either genetic or gestational, to their children. While some critics of ARTs disapprove of the emphasis these technologies place on genetic ties, our culture, our law, and our social and psychological understandings of reproduction and parenting define parental and offspring roles largely though not exclusively in genetic or biologic terms. In this context, the development of safe and effective ARTs appears to be positive: It reduces the suffering of childless couples by making it possible for them to realize their procreative goals.

Yet many people have doubts about ARTs and the industry that has grown up around them. Some of these doubts concern the morality and consequences of interfering with nature or manipulating the earliest stages of life. Others focus on the consequences for offspring, for participants (including the couples directly involved and the collaborating donors and surrogates), and for women and families generally. Some have criticized the industry's emphasis on profits and its lack of regulation—which has recently received considerable attention because of allegations of the theft of eggs and embryos by leading doctors at a California fertility center. . . .

My basic premise is that ARTs support the traditional notion of the family, even though they depart from the conventional method of producing children through coital conception. Despite the differences in the method of conception, the goal of an ART is a child biologically related to one or both rearing parents—a goal similar to that sought through coital conception. The family project in each case should be treated equally. The use of gamete donors and surrogates, however, requires special attention because of the potential problems that the resulting desegregation of the genetic, gestational, and social aspects of procreation pose for participants and offspring. . . .

ARTs, Freedom, and the Family

Before addressing current policy issues, it is useful to consider briefly the connection between the use of ARTs and personal and procreative liberty. Critics of ARTs have often called for prohibition or regulation without realizing the impact such restrictions would have on procreative freedom, a freedom that is highly valued in other contexts. Yet the right of infertile couples to use these techniques is as important as their right to conceive coitally or to avoid reproduction once pregnancy has occurred. The argument in support of the rights of infertile couples to use ARTs to form families can be briefly stated.

Although it is not mentioned explicitly in the Constitution, courts would no doubt recognize as fundamental the right of a married couple to reproduce coitally, because of the traditional association of reproduction and childbearing with marriage, and the independent importance of reproduction in people's lives. Since an infertile couple or individual has the same interest in bearing and rearing offspring as a fertile couples does, their right to use noncoital techniques to treat infertility should have equivalent respect. This is clearest when the couple's own gametes will be involved, such as IUI and IVF, but it should also be recognized when one partner does not contribute genetically or gestationally to reproduction. Thus laws that restrict or prohibit access to ARTs should be judged under the same exacting standard that would apply to direct restrictions on coital reproduction—the need to show a compelling state interest not achievable by less restrictive means. Under this standard, most objections to ARTs are insufficient to justify banning or unduly burdening their use, though there is considerable room for reasonable regulation designed to assure that consumers fully understand and freely choose the particular ART at issue. . . .

■ASSISTED REPRODUCTIVE TECHNOLOGY SURVEILLANCE—UNITED STATES, 2009

Saswati Sunderam et al.
61 Morbidity & Mortality Weekly Rep. 1-3 (2012)

Since the birth of the first U.S. infant conceived with Assisted Reproductive Technology (ART) in 1981, use of advanced technologies to overcome the problem of infertility has increased steadily, as has the number of fertility clinics providing ART services and procedures in the United States.

In 1992, Congress passed the Fertility Clinic Success Rate and Certification Act . . . , which requires that all U.S. fertility clinics performing ART procedures report data to CDC annually on every ART procedure initiated. . . . The ART Success Rates Reports contain national summaries as well as specific details for each fertility clinic.

Despite its increasing use, ART is associated with potential risks to the mother and fetus. Multiple-infant births are associated with greater health problems for mothers and infants, including higher rates of caesarean deliveries, prematurity, low birthweight, infant death, and disability. In addition, concerns exist regarding elevated risks of birth defects, genetic abnormalities, and imprinting disorders (Beckwith-Wiedermann syndrome and Angelman syndrome) associated with infertility and infertility treatments with ART. Because multiple embryos are transferred in the majority of ART procedures, ART has been associated with a substantial risk for multiple-gestation pregnancy and multiple births. Further, even singleton infants conceived with ART have a higher risk of low birthweight. CDC also performs in-depth analyses of infant health outcomes reported by U.S. fertility clinics. . . .

ART [in this Report] includes fertility treatments in which both eggs and sperm are handled in the laboratory (i.e., IVF and related procedures). ART [reporting] does not include treatments in which only sperm are handled (i.e., intrauterine insemination) or procedures in which a woman takes drugs only to stimulate egg production without the intention of having eggs retrieved. . . .

Of 484 fertility clinics in the U.S. states and territories that performed ART procedures in 2009, a total of 441 (91%) provided data to CDC. . . .

The use of ART has grown substantially in the United States since the beginning of ART surveillance. In 1996 (the first full year for which ART data were reported to CDC), 20,597 infants were born from 64,036 ART cycles. Since then, the number of cycles reported to CDC has more than doubled while the number of infants born from ART procedures has nearly tripled. In 2009, a total of 146,244 cycles resulted in 60,190 live-born infants, which is approximately 1.4% of total U.S.

live-births. The impact of ART on multiple births and poor birth outcomes, how-ever, is substantial because almost half of ART infants (47%) were born in multiple births (compared with only 3% of infants among the general birth population). On average, in all states and territories, more than one embryo was transferred among women aged <35 years, thus resulting in high rates of multiple births. National rates of elective single-embryo transfer procedures were low, especially among women aged >35 years. As a result, the rates of low birthweight and preterm births were substantially higher among ART infants (32% and 33% respectively) than in the general population (8% and 12% respectively). Overall, 19% of all twin births and 34% of triplet or higher order birth infants were conceived with ART. . . .

ART use varied widely by state, especially after controlling for the size of the population in reproductive age. Residents of California, New York, Illinois, New Jersey, Massachusetts, and Texas reported 46% of ART births but only 34% of all U.S. births. . . . This divergence might be explained in part by variations in state health insurance coverage. Certain states (Massachusetts, Illinois, and New Jersey) had mandated comprehensive insurance coverage for ART procedures that must cover at least four cycles of IVF. This type of mandated insurance has been associ-ated with greater use of ART. . . .

Although many factors (e.g., a patient's age and diagnostic factors) influence elective single-embryo transfer rates, increasingly, research shows that broad insur-ance mandates for IVF result not only in large increases in access to ART services but also in substantially fewer aggressive treatments, with fewer embryos transferred within a procedure. . . . In the United States, private insurance coverage of ART is rare. Even where mandated, coverage for infertility treatment often varies in scope, with some states requiring that all insurers cover ART whereas others require restricted coverage or merely offer plans that include ART coverage. The high use of eSET [elective Single Embryo Transfer] in Massachusetts and Illinois is consis-tent with the recommendations of the American Society for Reproductive Medicine (ASRM) on eSET. ESET rates also exceeded the national average in a number of states that do not have mandated insurance coverage for ART, especially among women aged <35 years, suggesting greater compliance with ASRM guidelines. . . .

In the United States, on average, more than one embryo was transferred in ART procedures, even among younger women. Because most states do not have mandated insurance coverage, and the majority of insurance plans do not cover IVF treatments, to control costs, patients and providers might be willing to transfer mul-tiple embryos to maximize the chance of live-birth delivery in a single procedure. Evidence also suggests that after years of failure to conceive, infertile couples might prefer multiple births, especially twins, in their desire to achieve parenthood, and might not estimate the risks of such pregnancies accurately. Infertile women might be more receptive to the idea of a multiple birth than fertile women. . . .

The economic costs of multiple births are also much higher compared with singleton births. The mean medical cost of delivering a singleton baby was esti-mated to be $9,329, whereas a set of twins costs $20,318, and triplets have a delivery expense of $153,335. . . .

The rates of low birthweight and very low birthweight infants were dispropor-tionately higher among ART infants than in the general birth population. . . . The contribution of ART to preterm births in the United States, most of which are also low birthweight, is a key concern. . . . Preterm births are a leading cause of infant mortality and morbidity, and preterm infants are at increased risk for death and have more health and developmental problems than full-term infants. The health risks associated with preterm births have contributed to increasing health-care costs. . . .

CONCLUSION

ART-conceived infants now represent a substantial proportion of infants born in the United States, ranging from 0.2% to 4% of all infants born in U.S. states and territories. The majority of these infants were born from multiple-gestation pregnancies and resulted in multiple births. This report is the first to document the contribution of ART to multiple births, low birthweight, and preterm births by each state/territory and allows State Health Departments to monitor the extent of ART-related adverse perinatal outcomes in their individual state and territories.

Comprehensive insurance coverage of ART might increase access to fertility treatments. It also might increase the use of elective single-embryo transfers, where feasible. Further research is needed to ascertain the influence of state insurance mandates on ART use and outcomes, as well as the economic costs of multiple births, including out-of-pocket costs to patients. Addressing the risk of multiple births also requires understanding the perspectives of couples undergoing infertility treatments who might not fully consider the risks of multiple births, especially twins. Clinicians and patients should continue to strengthen and support ongoing efforts to limit the number of embryos transferred and encourage wider implementation of elective single-embryo transfers, when feasible, as one mechanism of promoting singleton infant births among ART-conceived pregnancies. . . .

Further efforts also are needed to monitor the use of non-ART infertility treatments and their role in the rising number of multiple births. Despite its substantial impact on adverse birth outcomes, ART only partially explains the overall prevalence of these adverse outcomes in the United States. Preterm births resulting from controlled ovarian stimulation (superovulation-intrauterine insemination and conventional ovulation induction) might contribute as much as ART to multiple gestations. More research is needed to identify the causes and consequences of preterm births that occur because of infertility treatments and to institute guidelines to reduce the number of multiple gestations. The risk for multiple gestations associated with these treatments is less well documented, as clinics are not mandated to report data on the use of non-ART infertility treatments.

Notes: Parenting Possibilities

1. *Reproductive Alternatives.* How important is it to have a child? How important is it to have a child that is genetically related to you or to your partner? See L. Jill Halman et al., Attitudes about Infertility Interventions Among Fertile and Infertile Couples, 82 Am. J. Public Health 191 (1992); Gina Kolata, The Heart's Desire, N.Y. Times, May 11, 2004, at D1 (discussing costs and methods of treating infertility). Professor Robertson reviews the prevalence of infertility in our society. An estimated 10 percent of the reproductive-age population is infertile. Katie S. Murray et al., The Effect of the New 2010 World Health Organization Criteria for Semen Analyses on Male Infertility, 98 Fertility & Sterility 1428 (2012) (infertility defined as "inability to achieve a pregnancy through national means after a year; about one-half of cases of infertility are related to males"); The Practice Committee of the ASRM, Diagnostic Evaluation of the Infertile Male: A Committee Opinion, 98 Fertility & Sterility 294 (2012) ("Approximately 8% to 15% of couples are unable to conceive after one year of unprotected intercourse."). The data on infertility understate the population of those potentially interested in making use of these techniques. Single people and gay or lesbian couples have also sought to make use of alternative approaches to reproduction.

Current forms of alternative reproduction involve separating the contribution of gametes (eggs and sperm) from gestation. Reproductive projects therefore can involve:

- intended parent(s) (one or more),
- donors or providers of the sperm and oocytes (who may or may not be intended parents), and
- a provider of the womb (who may be a gestational surrogate or an intended parent).

The individuals making use of these new approaches to reproduction may use the same technique in an effort to achieve different results. For example, a physician might use donor eggs and sperm along with IVF to create an embryo that is implanted into a woman. The parties participating in this process might intend in one case that the woman bearing the child be recognized as the legal mother of the child, while a different set of parties using the same techniques might hope that the woman bearing the child will be recognized only as a gestational surrogate who has no legal relationship or claim on the child to whom she gives birth. The CDC report excerpted above does not focus on this aspect of the use of ART but simply reports the total number of procedures and births.

The participants in alternative reproduction can be connected with each other through:

- formal legal ties (e.g., married or participants in domestic partnerships),
- informal agreements between family members or friends (such as when a sister or friend agrees to serve as an oocyte donor or gestational surrogate),
- more formalized agreements or contracts that seek to establish the rights and obligations of relatives, friends, and "strangers."

See, e.g., The Ethics Committee of ASRM, Using Family Members as Gamete Donors of Surrogates, 98 Fertility & Sterility 797 (2012) (analyzing ethical aspects of specific intrafamilial arrangements). The reproductive arrangements can be facilitated or directed by third parties or health care providers who "package" arrangements for intended parents.

2. *Regulation.* Should states or the federal government regulate the use of reproductive technology? Do the risks associated with multiple embryo transfers support direct regulation or indirect regulation through the tort system? How should our legal system determine the legal rights and responsibilities of participants in reproductive activities? Consider some of the possible reproductive alternatives. Who do you think should be considered to be the "legal" parent(s) of the child produced by these arrangements? What factors motivate your judgments? Should states enact legislation regulating the use of alternative reproduction and defining the legal status of the participants? What should be the guiding principles of the legislation? What standards should courts use in the absence of legislation? Should the intent of the parties always govern the use of these techniques and the status of the parties? What should happen where the parties no longer agree on these matters? When, if ever, should states or courts override the intent of the parties? Is there any constitutional limit on state regulation or legislation that overrides the intent of the parties? The situation is made even more complex by the potential for human cloning, discussed below in section E.

ART regulation involves the intersection of matters typically regulated at the state level (family law, medical practice) with issues amenable to federal regulation (interstate commerce, human subjects research, the donation and use of human cells). Not surprisingly, regulation in the United States has been piecemeal, with significant regulatory gaps. Courts therefore have been forced to step in to resolve the implications of new reproductive technologies. See generally Susan Frelich Appleton, Illegitimacy and Sex, Old and New, 20 Am. U. J. Gender Soc. Pol'y & L. 347 (2012) (noting similarities between old legal treatment of illegitimacy and regulation of ARTs); David Adamson, Regulation of Assisted Reproductive Technologies in the United States, 39 Fam. L.Q. 727 (2005).

3. *Standards, Guidelines, and Studies.* Commissions and other advisory groups have issued numerous recommendations. See National Conference of the Commissioners on Uniform State Laws, Uniform Parentage Act (2002); National Conference of the Commissioners on Uniform State Laws, Uniform Probate Code (2008); American Bar Association, Model Act Governing Assisted Reproductive Technology (2008); Charles P. Kindregan, Jr., Clarifying the Law of ART: The New American Bar Association Model Act Governing Assisted Reproductive Technology, 42 Fam. L.Q. 203 (2008); President's Council on Bioethics, Reproduction and Responsibility: The Regulation of New Biotechnologies (2004).

The President's Council recommended that Congress consider a package of legislative initiatives that would prohibit: certain human-nonhuman hybrids, the use of women's uteruses for anything other than human reproduction, the use of certain methods to create children, the use of embryos after a designated stage of development, and the commercialization of embryos. The Council also recommended that professional organizations act to ensure that members follow the organization's guidelines. President's Council on Bioethics, Reproduction and Responsibility: The Regulation of New Biotechnologies 205-224 (2004). Professional societies and organizations have issued guidelines. See, e.g., the various guidelines from the

Society for Assisted Reproduction Technology and the American Society for Reproductive Medicine (ASRM) that are cited throughout this section.

4. *International Developments.* The use of ARTs has also been controversial around the world. For data on the use of ART worldwide, see Karl G. Nygren et al., International Committee for Monitoring Assisted Reproductive Technology (ICMART) World Report: Assisted Reproductive Technology 2003, 95 Fertility & Sterility 2209, 2221 (2011) (estimated 232,380 babies born from ART worldwide in 2003). Several countries have enacted comprehensive legislation designed to cover the use of ARTs and new genetic technologies such as cloning. Canada enacted the Assisted Human Reproduction Act in 2004. One major purpose of the Act is to prevent the commercialization of reproductive technologies. Thus, the Act prohibits payment for sperm or egg donors. Critics argue that the decommercialization will reduce the supplies of sperm and eggs available for use. See Barbara von Tigerstrom, Federal Health Legislation and the Assisted Human Reproduction Act Reference, 74 Sask. L. Rev. 33 (2011) (analyzing impact of Supreme Court of Canada decision striking down portions of Act but upholding restrictions on commercialization and posthumous reproduction). See also the U.K.'s Human Fertilisation & Embryology Authority, at www.hfea.gov.uk. Alicia Ouelette et al., Lessons Across the Pond: Assisted Reproductive Technology in the United Kingdom and the United States, 31 Am. J.L. & Med. 419 (2005); Richard F. Storrow, Religious, Feminism and Abortion: The Regulation of Assisted Reproduction in Two Catholic Countries, 42 Rutgers L. Rev. 725 (2011).

5. *Reproductive Tourism.* As ART has developed and improved, couples have demonstrated willingness to travel, resulting in "reproductive tourism." Karl Nygren et al., Cross-Border Fertility Care—International Committee Monitoring Assisted Reproductive Technologies Global Survey: 2006 Data and Estimates, 94 Fertility & Sterility e4 (2010); and Special Contributions on Cross-Border Fertility Care, 94 Fertility & Sterility e1-26 (2010). The activities involved in the reproductive project can span the boundaries of states and countries, such as when intended parents make use of gestational surrogates located in India. I. Glenn Cohen, Circumvention Tourism, 97 Cornell L. Rev. 1309 (2012); I. Glenn Cohen, Protecting Patients with Passports: Medical Tourism and the Patient Protective Argument, 95 Iowa L. Rev. 1467 (2010); I. Glenn Cohen, Medical Tourism: The View from Ten Thousand Feet, 40(2) Hastings Center Rep. 11 (Mar.-Apr. 2010); Lisa C. Ikemoto, Reproductive Tourism: Equality Concerns in the Global Market for Fertility Services, 27 Law & Ineq. J. 277 (2009); Richard F. Storrow, Travel into the Future of Reproductive Technology, 79 UKMC L. Rev. 295 (2010).

6. *Commentaries.* This is yet another area rich with commentaries. Early, influential articles include: R. Alta Charo, And Baby Makes Three—or Four, or Five, or Six: Redefining the Family After the Reprotech Revolution, 15 Wis. Women's L.J. 231 (2000); Janet L. Dolgin, Choice, Tradition, and the New Genetics: The Fragmentation of the Ideology of Family, 32 Conn. L. Rev. 523 (2000); Thomas H. Murray, What Are Families For? Getting to an Ethics of Reproductive Technology, 32(3) Hastings Center Rep. 41 (May-June 2002) (suggesting that emphasis on procreative liberty risks disregard for the interests of children); Dorothy E. Roberts, Race and the New Reproduction, 47 Hastings L.J. 935 (1996); John A. Robertson, Children of Choice: Freedom and the New Reproductive Technologies (1994); John A. Robertson, Procreative Liberty and the Control of Conception, Pregnancy, and Childbirth, 69 Va. L. Rev. 405 (1983). John A. Robertson, Procreative Liberty and Harm to Offspring in

Assisted Reproduction, 30 Am. J.L. & Med. 7 (2004); John A. Robertson, Procreative Liberty in the Era of Genomics, 29 Am. J.L. & Med. 439 (2003).

Problem: ART and the Constitution

In the article excerpted above, Professor Robertson suggests that constitutional protection of the right to procreate extends to the use of new reproductive technologies, even where the resulting child will not be biologically related to the intended parents. See also John A. Robertson, Assisting Reproduction, Choosing Genes, and the Scope of Reproductive Freedom, 76 Geo. Wash. L. Rev. 1490 (2008). Do you agree?

While the language in *Skinner* (page 465) is broad and general, the Supreme Court has been disinclined in recent years to find constitutional protection for activities not deeply rooted in history and tradition. See Troxel v. Granville, 530 U.S. 57 (2000) (parents have fundamental right to make child-rearing decisions; Constitution limits state's ability to presume interaction with grandparents is in the best interests of a child); Michael H. v. Gerald D., 491 U.S. 110 (1989) (rejecting claim of married woman's male lover that he had constitutional right to establish a parenting relationship with his genetic child, born of his lover during her marriage to another man). Will courts find that procreative liberty is limited to "natural" procreation, via sexual reproduction? What will be the limits of constitutional protection for procreative liberty? Does our right to procreative liberty extend beyond genetic parenting, to include the use of donated gametes? If genetic parenting is constitutionally significant, will cloning be given any constitutional protection?

For an examination on the constitutionality of regulating ART and possible regulatory schemes, see Naomi R. Cahn, The New Kinship, 100 George. L.J. 367 (2012); Radhika Rao, Equal Liberty: Assisted Reproductive Technology and Reproductive Equality, 76 Geo. Wash. L. Rev. 1457 (2008); Marsha Garrison, Regulating Reproduction, 76 Geo. Wash. L. Rev. 1623 (2008); June Carbone, If I Say "Yes" to Regulations Today, Will You Still Respect Me in the Morning?, 76 Geo. Wash. L. Rev. 1747 (2008); Debora Spar & Anna M. Harrington, Building a Better Baby Business, 10 Minn. J.L. Sci. & Tech. 41 (2009); Catherine A. Clements, What About the Children? A Call for Regulation of Assisted Reproductive Technology, 84 Ind. L.J. 331 (2008). Professor I. Glenn Cohen has challenged the theoretical and philosophical bases for the regulation of many forms of ART. He is particularly skeptical of state regulations justified as furthering the "best interests of the child," pointing out that many forms of regulation would prevent the birth of a child and noting the difficulty with state claims that it would be better not to be born alive than to be born using a particular form of ART. I. Glenn Cohen, Regulating Reproduction: The Problem with Best Interests, 96 Minn. L. Rev. 423 (2011); and I. Glenn Cohen, Beyond Best Interests, 96 Minn. L. Rev. 1187 (2012).

Notes: Genetics and Reproduction

1. *Genetic Testing.* Reproductive and genetic technologies can be combined, with interesting policy dilemmas as one major consequence. Genetic testing can

be employed at various stages in reproduction, with ethical and religious concerns generally increasing at each stage. Individuals can be tested before donating their gametes, the preembryo can be tested after conception but before implantation, or the embryo and fetus can be tested after implantation. Genetic testing after implantation clearly raises the possibility of abortion, with all the attendant controversy. Initially, genetic tests during pregnancy involved blood and ultrasound tests followed by a physically invasive amniocentesis test during the second trimester that carried some risk for the fetus. Mark I. Evans & Michael Kilpatrick, Noninvasive Prenatal Diagnosis: 2010, 30 Clin. Lab. Med. 655 (2010). The latest genetic tests use fetal DNA found in blood samples from the pregnant woman and can be performed at ten weeks. Noninvasive prenatal genetic testing (NIPT) permits women to gain access to a wider range of fetal characteristics during a period of pregnancy when abortion is still relatively accessible. See Stephanie A. Devaney, Noninvasive Fetal Sex Determination Using Cell-Free Fetal DNA, 306 JAMA 627 (2011); Henry T. Greely, Get Ready for the Flood of Fetal Gene Screening, 469 Nature 289 (2011). The ability to conduct genetic testing has advanced more quickly than the ability to translate the results into useable knowledge for clinicians or parents. See, e.g., Teri A. Manolio, Genomewide Association Studies and Assessment of the Risk of Disease, 363 New Eng. J. Med. 166 (2010); Andrew Pollack, DNA Blueprint for Fetus Built Using Tests of Parents, N.Y. Times, June 6, 2012.

A number of commentators have written about genetic testing and reproduction. See, e.g., Carolyn Jacobs Chachkin, What Potent Blood: Non-Invasive Prenatal Genetic Diagnosis and the Transformation of Modern Prenatal Care, 33 Am. J.L. & Med. 9 (2007); Amber R. Cooper & Emily S. Jungheim, Preimplantation Genetic Testing: Indications and Controversies, 30 Clin. Lab. Med. 519 (2010); Judith F. Daar, Embryonic Genetics, 2 St. Louis U. J. Health L. & Pol'y 81 (2008); Barbara Katz Rothman, The Tentative Pregnancy: Prenatal Diagnosis and the Future of Motherhood (1986); President's Council on Bioethics, Reproduction and Responsibility: The Regulation of New Biotechnologies (2004); Sonia M. Suter, The Routinization of Prenatal Testing, 28 Am. J.L. & Med. 233 (2002).

2. *"Negative" vs. "Positive" Eugenics and Genetic Enhancement.* Persons who take advantage of prenatal screening may use information about their child's genetic characteristics in deciding whether to continue the pregnancy to term. Preimplantation genetic screening can be combined with IVF so that only genetically desirable embryos are implanted in a woman's uterus. NIPT will now provide information about genetic conditions such as Down Syndrome much earlier in pregnancy. Peter A. Benn & Audrey R. Chapman, Practical and Ethical Considerations of Noninvasive Prenatal Diagnosis, 301 JAMA 2154 (2009) (noting the possibility that rates of abortion could increase in part due to indirect pressure on parents); Darrin P. Dixon, Informed Consent or Institutionalized Eugenics?, 24 Issues L. & Med. 3 (2008) (pressures result in high abortion rates for fetuses diagnosed with Down syndrome). Could a state restrict access to genetic screening tests in order to further its interest in protecting fetal life? The state would not restrict abortion, per se, but merely limit parental access to information. See Rachel Rebouché & Karen H. Rothenberg, Mixed Messages: The Intersection of Prenatal Genetic Testing and Abortion, 55 How. L.J. 983 (2012).

Should it matter whether parents are engaging in "negative" versus "positive" eugenics? In the first, parents seek to avoid some abnormal and seriously disabling genetic condition. In the second, they hope to acquire a child with some particularly socially desirable traits. Do parents have a duty to use preimplantation genetic diagnosis (PGD) to prevent the birth of a child with a seriously disabling condition? See Janet Malek & Judy Daar, The Case for a Parental Duty to Use Preimplantation Genetic Diagnosis for Medical Benefit, 12 Am. J. Bioethics 3 (2012) (ethical duty and potential parental duty under tort law). Would a "negative" eugenics program discriminate against fetuses on the basis of their disability? Note, Regulating Preimplantation Genetic Diagnosis: The Pathologization Problem, 118 Harv. L. Rev. 2770 (2005). What if the parents sought to use these technologies to choose the gender of their child, perhaps by implanting only the embryos of the "correct" gender? Compare the discussion of sex selection and abortion, supra, pages 486-487, and Judith F. Daar, ART and the Search for Perfectionism: On Selecting Gender, Genes, and Gametes, 9 J. Gender Race & Just. 241 (2005); Susannah Baruch et al., Genetic Testing of Embryos: Practices and Perspectives of U.S. IVF Clinics, 89 Fertility & Sterility 5 (2007) (majority of surveyed IVF clinics will participate in sex-selection at parental request); Jaime S. King, Politics and Fetal Diagnostics Collide, 491 Nature 33 (2012) (noting legislative efforts to restrict testing and abortion based on sex or other characteristics); Jaime S. King, Not This Child: Constitutional Questions in Regulating Noninvasive Prenatal Genetic Diagnosis and Selective Abortion, 60 UCLA L. Rev. 2 (2012).

3. *Gene Therapy, Genetic Engineering, and Genetic Enhancement.* At some future point, effective genetic engineering and genetic therapy technologies may be developed. While the terms are not always used consistently, "gene therapy" most often refers to treating a genetic disorder, either through traditional medical or genetic means. Genetic engineering typically refers to altering an individual's genes. Somatic genetic engineering or therapy involves changing the genetic content of a person's non-reproductive cells. Germ-line genetic engineering or therapy involves changing the genetic content of a person's reproductive cells or gametes. Germ-line genetic engineering could be very appealing to those who have serious genetic conditions that limit their ability or desire to reproduce. Yet the scientific risks and ethical concerns related to genetic engineering are greatest when the "treatment," perhaps more realistically called an "experiment," also involves future generations.

Advances in genetics may also empower humans to "enhance" their offspring. Enhancement may occur by taking genes associated with desirable traits from third parties for incorporation into one's gametes or embryos. "Enhancement" might also be achieved through the use of non-human genetic materials or engineered materials. Although all such research would be controversial, incorporation of novel genes into the germ line once again would be the most risky, controversial, and morally problematic. See, e.g., Harry Adams, A Human Germline Modification Scale, 32 J.L. Med. & Ethics 164 (2004); Roberta M. Berry, Genetic Enhancement in the Twenty-First Century: Three Problems in Legal Imagining, 34 Wake Forest L. Rev. 715 (1999); Maxwell J. Mehlman, The Law of Above Averages: Leveling the New Genetic Enhancement Playing Field, 34 Wake Forest L. Rev. 561 (1999); Robert Sparrow, A Not-So-New Eugenics, 41(1) Hastings Center Rep. 32 (Jan.-Feb. 2011); Daniel L. Tobey, What's Really Wrong with Genetic Enhancement: A Second Look at Our Posthuman Future, 6 Yale J.L. & Tech. 54 (2003-2004).

Should the federal government or state governments restrict access to these technologies? Should regulation distinguish between somatic cell therapy and germ-line therapy, assuming that researchers are able to confidently predict whether germ-line cells will be affected by a treatment? How should regulation proceed, perhaps with a permanent, total ban on germ-line research? See, e.g., Jonathan Kimmelman, The Ethics of Human Gene Transfer, 9 Nature Reviews Genetics 239 (2008); Maxwell J. Mehlman, Any DNA to Declare? Regulating Offshore Access to Genetic Enhancement, 28 Am. J.L. & Med. 179 (2002); Michael Sandel, The Case Against Perfection: Ethics in an Age of Genetic Engineering (2007).

Assuming that research goes forward, are you concerned about equality of access to genetic screening tests and/or genetic therapies? What if access to genetic technologies could reify class differences—permitting the wealthy to ensure the future success of their offspring through positive genetic engineering? Is this any different from current practices that permit the wealthy to send their children to expensive private schools? See generally Dov Fox, Silver Spoons and Golden Genes: Genetic Engineering and the Egalitarian Ethos, 33 Am. J.L. & Med. 567 (2007); Ronald M. Green, Babies by Design: The Ethics of Genetic Choice (2007); LeRoy Walters & Julie Palmer, The Ethics of Human Gene Therapy (1996).

2. Gamete Donation

The donation of gametes—sperm and ova—encompasses old and new uses of reproductive technology. Artificial insemination, also known as intrauterine insemination (IUI), is the oldest assisted reproductive technique; in its simplest form, it requires no medical expertise or specialized equipment. The two major types of IUI used today involve (1) using the sperm of the husband or male partner (AIH); or (2) using the sperm of a third-party donor (AID). AIH can compensate for certain types of male infertility. AID provides a substitute source of male gametes in the case of profound male infertility or compensates for the absence of a male partner for single heterosexual women or lesbians. See Harvey L. Fiser & Paula K. Garrett, Life Begins at Ejaculation: Legislating Sperm as the Potential to Create Life and the Effects on Contracts for Artificial Insemination, 21 Am. U. L. Gender Soc. Pol'y & L. 39 (2012); Walter Wadlington, Artificial Insemination: The Dangers of a Poorly Kept Secret, 64 Nw. U. L. Rev. 777 (1970). Most of the legal and policy debates have focused on AID. In the Internet age, it should not be surprising that sperm banks offer information about potential donors online. Couples or single women searching for a suitable donor may select various donor characteristics, may hear an audiotape of the donor's voice, and may even be able to see a donor's baby picture. See Anetta Pietrzak, The Price of Sperm, 14 J.L. & Fam. Stud. 121 (2012).

Donation of an egg (also called an oocyte) is much more medically complex and invasive. Prospective donors must undergo medical treatment to stimulate their ovaries to produce multiple eggs. The donor is monitored through ultrasound exams and blood tests to determine whether there are a sufficient number of eggs to warrant harvesting. The eggs must be retrieved from inside the woman's body using an ultrasound-guided needle or through a laparoscopic procedure. See Kara N. Maxwell, The Incidence of Both Serious and Minor Complications in Young Women Undergoing Oocyte Donation, 90 Fertility & Sterility 2165 (2008) (0.7% rate of serious complications, 8.5% rate of minor complications involving medical attention). Until recently, the technical challenges associated with freezing oocytes meant that "fresh" donated eggs would need to be fertilized using sperm in the laboratory (using IVF), creating a preembryo that could either be frozen or implanted in a woman's uterus. (The legal and ethical aspects of embryo donation and use will be discussed in great detail below, at pages 567-581.) "Egg banks" are now becoming more common on the Internet, with Web sites offering to match infertile women with prospective egg donors having certain characteristics.

Recent advances in cryopreservation may result in greater use of oocyte cryopreservation by women who wish to preserve their reproductive potential. See Society for Assisted Reproductive Technology (SART) and the Practice Committee of the American Society for Reproductive Medicine (ASRM), Mature Oocyte Cryopreservation: A Guideline, 99 Fertility & Sterility 37 (2013) (concluding cryopreservation of oocytes no longer experimental but recommending that cryopreservation use be limited to women with the medical need to preserve capacity and not for women seeking to delay reproduction); Elia A. Rybak & Harry J. Lieman, Egg Freezing, Procreative Liberty, and ICSI: The Double Standards Confronting Elective Self-Donation of Oocytes, 92 Fertility & Sterility 1509 (2009) (arguing that cryopreservation should be available for women seeking to maximize their reproductive potential); The Practice Committee of the ASRM, ASRM Practice Committee Response to Rybak and Lieman, 92 Fertility & Sterility 1513 (2009).

Gamete donation is governed by federal regulations and the voluntary guidelines of professional organizations. 21 C.F.R. §§1271.45-1271.90 (donor eligibility and screening rules); Ethics Committee of the ASRM, Interests, Obligations, and Rights of the Donor in Gamete Donation, 91 Fertility & Sterility 22 (2009); Practice Committees of ASRM and SART, Recommendations for Gamete and Embryo Donation: A Committee Opinion, 99 Fertility & Sterility 47 (2013). The federal regulations require entities that provide ART to register with the government; organizations that participate in gamete donation are subject to inspection and other oversight. The regulations and guidelines generally require quarantine of the donation and evaluation and testing of the gamete donor for certain communicable and genetic conditions. Interestingly, these guidelines apply to sperm but not to oocytes. Recommendations for Gamete and Embryo Donation, supra, at 52-53 (cryopreservation of oocytes necessary for quarantine process "cannot be performed reliably," contrary to Mature Oocyte Cryopreservation: A Guideline, supra).

The Practice Committees' guidelines also require screening and evaluation of potential gamete recipients. Are health care providers who refuse to provide reproductive technology services to persons with hereditary conditions or disabilities engaged in impermissible disability-based discrimination under the ADA? See The Ethics Committee of the ASRM, Human Immunodeficiency Virus and Infertility Treatment, 94 Fertility & Sterility 11 (2010) (clinics should offer services to HIV-infected patients and couples where appropriate); Carl H. Coleman, Conceiving Harm: Disability Discrimination in Assisted Reproductive Technologies, 50 UCLA L. Rev. 17 (2002); and 21 C.F.R. §1271.90 (exceptions from donor screening requirements). Gamete providers have established systems that support parental efforts to use race as a factor in selecting donors. Should this be permissible? See Dov Fox, Note, Racial Classification in Assisted Reproduction, 118 Yale L.J. 1844 (2009) (practices legal but "pernicious").

Who is the father of a child produced through IUI? Should a child produced within a marriage be presumed to be the child of the husband? Should genetic parentage govern over social norms or the parties' expectations? The AI provisions of the 1973 version of the Uniform Parentage Act (UPA), adopted in some form or another in most states, were designed to eliminate ambiguity and to relieve prospective donors of the risk of unwanted paternity. National Conference of Commissioners on Uniform State Laws (NCCUSL), UPA §5 (1973). The 1973 Act provided a legal mechanism for recognizing the infertile husband as the father of a child born through insemination of his wife using donor sperm. The husband was required to give written consent, the procedure had to be performed under the supervision of a physician, and the records were subject to inspection by a court upon a showing of good cause. Under the 1973 UPA, the sperm donor was not considered the father so long as the sperm was provided to a licensed physician for insemination of a "married woman." This restrictive language placed the donor at risk if the sperm was used in the insemination of a woman who was not legally married—and consequently made IUI for single or lesbian women difficult to obtain in some states. Other states adopted a version of the rule that simply omitted the word "married," eliminating the legal barrier to the use of IUI for unmarried women. Many providers nonetheless continued to deny access to these services to unmarried women.

Discriminatory conduct by providers might violate ethical guidelines and state laws prohibiting discrimination by places of public accommodation or businesses. North Coast Women's Care Medical Group, Inc. v. San Diego Superior Court, 189 P.3d 959 (Cal. 2008) (upholding discrimination claim against fertility providers based on sexual orientation or marital status against claimed violation of free exercise of religion rights of defendants). See also The Ethics Committee of the ASRM, Access to Fertility Treatment by Gays, Lesbians, and Unmarried Persons, 92 Fertility & Sterility 1190 (2009) (concluding that "programs should treat all requests for assisted reproduction equally without regard to marital status or sexual orientation"); Holly J. Harlow, Paternalism Without Paternity: Discrimination Against Single Women Seeking Artificial Insemination by Donor, 6 S. Cal. Rev. L. & Women's Stud. 173 (1996); Richard F. Storrow, Marital Status and Sexual Orientation Discrimination in Infertility Care, 3 L.J. for Social Justice 99 (2012).

Until recently, the law presumed that the woman who gave birth to a child was the child's mother. The 1973 UPA did not consider the legal consequences of egg donation, IVF, or gestational surrogacy. Courts were forced to resolve the first disputes without the assistance of special legislation. NCCUSL adopted a Uniform Act on the Status of Children of Assisted Conception in the late 1980s; the Act treated egg and sperm donation roughly equivalently. States began to enact gamete and embryo donation provisions in the early 1990s.

The UPA was revised in 2002 and now provides:

§701. Scope of Article. This [article] does not apply to the birth of a child conceived by means of sexual intercourse[, or as the result of a [lawful] gestational agreement . . .].

§702. Parental Status of Donor. A donor is not a parent of a child conceived by means of assisted reproduction.

§703. Paternity of Child of Assisted Reproduction. A man who provides sperm for, or consents to, assisted reproduction by a woman as provided in Section 704 with the intent to be the parent of her child, is a parent of the resulting child.

§704. Consent to Assisted Reproduction. (a) Consent by a woman, and a man who intends to be a parent of a child born to the woman by assisted reproduction must be in a record signed by the woman and the man. This requirement does not apply to a donor.

(b) Failure [sic] a man to sign a consent required by subsection (a), before or after birth of the child, does not preclude a finding of paternity if the woman and the man, during the first two years of the child's life resided together in the same household with the child and openly held out the child as their own.

The Act also limits the period of time in which the husband can challenge his paternity following the use of assisted conception, with some exceptions. UPA §705 (2002) (available at: http://uniformlaws.org/).

Notes: Gamete Donation

1. *Gamete Donation.* The trend in the law is to treat the donation of sperm and eggs as legally similar. Do you agree? Should the greater degree of medical and physical intrusion involved in egg donation have any legal significance? See generally Anne Reichman Schiff, Solomonic Decisions in Egg Donation: Unscrambling the Conundrum of Legal Maternity, 80 Iowa L. Rev. 265 (1995). Should it be permissible to compensate gamete donors? The 2002 UPA provides that a "donor" is "an individual who produces eggs or sperm used for assisted reproduction, whether or not for consideration." UPA §102(8) (2002). Sperm donors typically are compensated less than $100 per deposit; egg donors might receive $3,500 to $5,000 per cycle, plus expenses. Should the amount of the compensation be regulated? Ethics Committee of the ASRM, Financial Compensation of Oocyte Donors, 88 Fertility & Sterility 305 (2007) (suggesting that payments over $5,000 require justification and that payments over $10,000 are inappropriate). See also Sonia M. Suter, Giving In to Baby Markets: Regulation Without Prohibition, 16 Mich. J. Gender & L. 217 (2009); Jason Keehn et al., Recruiting Egg Donors Online: Analysis of In Vitro Fertilization Clinic and Agency Websites' Adherence to [ASRM] Guidelines, 98 Fertility & Sterility 995 (2012). For a discussion of restrictions on the recruitment of gamete donors in other countries, see the sources cited above at page 555.

Both the 1973 and 2002 versions of the UPA refuse to apply the "donation" rules when the child is conceived through sexual intercourse. See UPA §701 (2002). Why doesn't the UPA permit the parties to execute a document indicating that the sexual activity is for the purpose of donating gametes? In Ferguson v. McKiernan, the court noted the parental responsibilities created in sexual reproduction under state law and the differential treatment of non-coital reproduction:

> In the case of traditional sexual reproduction, there simply is no question that the parties to any resultant conception and birth may not contract between themselves to deny the child the support he or she requires. . . . In the institutional sperm donation case, however, there appears to be a growing consensus that clinical, institutional sperm donation neither imposes obligations nor confers privileges upon the sperm donor. Between these poles lies a spectrum of arrangements that exhibit characteristics of each extreme to varying degrees — informal agreements between friends to conceive a child via sexual intercourse; non-clinical non-sexual insemination; and so on.

940 A.2d 1236, 1246 (Pa. 2007) (upholding informal agreement and protecting sperm donor from parental support because facts most closely mirrored the institutional sperm donation arrangement). Should courts and legislatures extend gamete donation rules to embryo donations? How should courts and legislatures deal with

the possibility of procreation using gametes derived from embryonic stem cells, that is, from parents who were never born? See Heidi Mertes & Guido Pennings, Embryonic Stem Cell-Derived Gametes and Genetic Parenthood: A Problematic Relationship, 17 Cambridge Q. Healthcare Ethics 7 (2008). See also Debra J. H. Mathews et al., Pluripotent Stem Cell-Derived Gametes: Truth and (Potential) Consequences, 5 Cell Stem Cell 11 (2009).

2. *Difficulties in the Application of the 1973 UPA Approach.* The 1973 UPA imposed a variety of requirements, such as physician supervision and written consent by the husband. Where the criteria were not satisfied, the donor might be given—or forced to accept—parental rights and obligations. Cf. Jhordan C. v. Mary K., 224 Cal. Rptr. 530 (Ct. App. 1986); Weaver v. Guinn, 31 P.3d 1119 (Or. Ct. App. 2001). Where there have been technical violations of a state's AI statute, in a manner agreed to by the participants, courts sometimes have reached the statutory results through equitable doctrines such as estoppel or ratification. See, e.g., E.E. v. O.M.G.R., 20 A.3d 1171 (N.J. Super. 2011) (self-administered AI; best interests of child met through sole custody to biological mother without support order from biological father); K.B. v. N.B., 811 S.W.2d 634 (Tex. Ct. App. 1991), cert. denied, 504 U.S. 918 (1992). Adherence to the criteria, on the other hand, did not necessarily shield the participants from the claims of donors seeking parental rights. See Janssen v. Alicea, 30 So. 3d 680 (Fla. Dist. Ct. App. 2010) (reversing summary judgment were genuine issues of fact with respect to whether man was sperm donor or part of "commissioning couple"); McIntyre v. Crouch, 780 P.2d 239 (Or. Ct. App. 1989) (termination of donor's parental rights might be unconstitutional where "donor" argues that sperm was provided with understanding that he would be considered father). See generally Annot., 83 A.L.R.4th 295 (1991).

In recent years, there has been a resurgence of litigation surrounding some of the implications of IUI for nontraditional families. The use of IUI by lesbian couples created a new wave of litigation testing the legal recognition of the nonbiological lesbian parent of the resulting child. See, e.g., Kristine H. v. Lisa R., 117 P.3d 690 (Cal. 2005) (birth mother estopped from contesting maternity of her former partner with whom she had previously obtained a stipulated judgment declaring that both were the parents of a child born through AI); K.M. v. E.G., 117 P.3d 673 (Cal. 2005) (woman who provided ova to her female partner for IVF is a legal parent of the children born through this arrangement along with the birth mother; law terminating parental rights of sperm donor not applied to the partner who donated ova); Elisa B. v. The Superior Court of El Dorado County, 117 P.3d 660 (Cal. 2005) (woman is legally a parent despite lack of biological connection based on conduct holding the children born to her female partner through AI as her own). See E. Gary Spitko, The Constitutional Function of Biological Paternity: Evidence of the Biological Mother's Consent to the Biological Father's Co-Parenting of Her Child, 48 Ariz. L. Rev. 97 (2006); Ann K. Wooster, Adoption of Child by Same-Sex Partners, 61 A.L.R.6th 1 (2011).

3. *Changes in the 2002 UPA.* The 1973 UPA was adopted by 13 states; the 2002 UPA or its amendments had been adopted by eight states as of early 2013. The revised UPA resolves some, but not all, of the gaps in the 1973 model act. The 2002 UPA makes clear that a donor is not the legal parent whether or not the assisted reproduction participants are married. The revised UPA also provides that donors have no parental rights and no right to seek such rights, UPA §702 cmt., yet the

language is unlikely to deter courts from resolving fraud or misrepresentation claims brought by sperm donors who want to maintain a relationship with their biological offspring. See note 2, supra. The new Act also eliminates the requirement that the donor provide his sperm to a physician. UPA §102(8) (2002). The 2002 UPA continues the presumption that a woman who gives birth to a child is the mother of the child, unless the child is conceived as part of a gestational surrogacy contract authorized and approved under state law. UPA §201 (2002). This presumption provides additional protection for egg donors, by emphasizing that the woman who gives birth is the mother rather than the donor. But see T.M.H. v. D.M.T., 79 So. 3d 787 (Dist. Ct. App. Fla. 2011) (statute terminating parental rights of egg donor unconstitutional as applied to woman who gave ova to partner for use in ART). Would you suggest any additional changes to the UPA? Does the right to procreate noted in *Skinner* have any impact on the enforceability of any aspect of the UPA? How does your own state law treat the rights and responsibilities of sperm and egg donors?

4. *Tort and Criminal Liability.* Will a physician be liable for genetically defective gametes? Current guidelines suggest screening donors for family histories of genetic disorders as well as for sexually transmitted diseases such as HIV. See Practice Committees of ASRM and SART, Recommendations for Gamete and Embryo Donation: A Committee Opinion, 99 Fertility & Sterility 47 (2013); Ethics Committee of the ASRM, Disclosure of Medical Errors Involving Gametes and Embryos, 96 Fertility & Sterility 1312 (2011). Tort claims can be difficult to assert if donors can remain anonymous. But see Johnson v. Superior Court, 95 Cal. Rptr. 2d 864 (2000) (tort action claiming failure to disclose sperm donor had family history of autosomal dominant polycystic kidney disease; court compels donor's deposition and record production). There are occasional errors in the donation process. See also Andrews v. Keltz, 838 N.Y.S.2d 363 (N.Y. Super. 2007) (third party's sperm used in IVF instead of husband's; limited emotional distress damages); Harnicher v. University of Utah Medical Center, 962 P.2d 67 (Utah 1998) (defendants allegedly used wrong donor's sperm, resulting in triplets; insufficient proof of negligent infliction of emotional distress); Cynthia R. Mabry, "Who Is My Real Father?" The Delicate Task of Identifying a Father and Parenting Children Created from an In Vitro Mix-Up, 18 Nat'l Black L.J. 1 (2004-2005).

Should sperm banks be held liable for the negligent destruction of donated sperm? Practice Committee of the ASRM, Recommendations for Development of an Emergency Plan for In Vitro Fertilization Programs: A Committee Opinion, 98 Fertility & Sterility e3 (2012). How would you measure the damages? See Kurchner v. State Farm Fire & Casualty Co, 858 So. 2d 1220 (Fla. App. 2003) (destruction of sperm not "bodily injury" and loss not covered under insurance policy). For three bizarre cases, see James v. Jacobson, 6 F.3d 233 (4th Cir. 1993) (noting criminal prosecution of physician who used his own sperm in providing AI services to more than 70 women); Judy Siegel-Itkovich, Doctor's Licence Suspended After He Admitted Removing Ova Without Consent, 334 BMJ 557 (2007) (physician removed hundreds of ova without patient consent for use in ART); Stone v. Regents, University of California, 92 Cal. Rptr. 2d 94 (Ct. App. 1999) (physician allegedly engaged in "egg stealing").

5. *Posthumous Reproduction.* The ability to donate and store gametes (and embryos) means that it is possible to parent a child after one's death. What ethical

and legal issues are raised by this possibility? One key question involves control—who has the right to decide whether to use stored gametes for reproductive purposes? See Hecht v. Superior Court., 59 Cal. Rptr. 2d 222 (Ct. App. 1996), review denied (Cal. 1997) (after a six-year battle, a deceased man's frozen sperm were awarded to his girlfriend as designated in his will, over the objections of the decedent's adult children). Should parents have the authority to direct collection of gametes from their children before or immediately after birth? See Michelle Goodwin & Naomi Duke, Capacity and Autonomy: A Thought Experiment on Minors' Access to Assisted Reproductive Technology, 34 Harv. J.L. & Gender 503 (2011). See generally Sara E. Barton, Population-Based Study of Attitudes Toward Posthumous Reproduction, 98 Fertility & Sterility 735 (2012) ("[a]lmost 50% of the general population support posthumous reproduction in men and women" with a "majority favor[ing] prior consent from the deceased"); Sharona Hoffman & Andrew P. Morriss, Birth After Death: Perpetuities and the New Reproductive Technologies, 38 Ga. L. Rev. 575 (2004); John A. Robertson, Posthumous Reproduction, 69 Ind. L.J. 1027 (1994); Anne Reichman Schiff, Arising from the Dead: Challenges of Posthumous Procreation, 75 N.C. L. Rev. 901 (1997); Carson Strong, Ethical and Legal Aspects of Sperm Retrieval After Death or Persistent Vegetative State, 27 J.L. Med. & Ethics 347 (1999).

The posthumous birth raises another set of issues: Should the child be considered the legal child of the decedent? What is the impact on the child's ability to inherit or to take part in family/survivors benefits programs? The traditional rule is that a man cannot be the father of a child born more than nine to ten months after his death. The 2002 UPA provides:

§707. Parental Status of Deceased Individual. If an individual who consented in a record to be a parent by assisted reproduction dies before placement of eggs, sperm, or embryos, the deceased individual is not a parent of the resulting child unless the deceased spouse consented in a record that if assisted reproduction were to occur after death, the deceased individual would be a parent of the child.

See also National Conference of Commissioners on Uniform State Laws, Uniform Probate Code §§2-120, 2-121 (2008 Amendments) (consent required; time limits established for posthumous reproduction); ABA Model Act Governing Assisted Reproductive Technology (2008) (decedent must have consented in record to become parent by posthumous reproduction); Kristine S. Knaplund, Children of Assisted Reproduction, 45 U. Mich. J.L. Reform 899 (2012) (analyzing posthumous reproduction provisions of the UPC). Posthumous reproduction can also have an impact on benefits provided under private and public plans. The Supreme Court upheld the Social Security Administration's determination that state intestacy law determines whether posthumously conceived children qualify for federal benefits. Astrue v. Capato, 132 S. Ct. 2021 (2012). See also Khabbaz v. Commissioner, Social Security Administration, 930 A.2d 1180 (N.H. 2007) (posthumously conceived child not considered surviving issue under state intestacy law); Woodward v. Commissioner of Social Security, 760 N.E.2d 257 (Mass. 2002) (children can inherit if wife establishes genetic relationship and decedent's consent to posthumous reproduction and support).

6. *Anonymity.* Artificial insemination has a long history, and the early presumption was that anonymity was a necessary part of the arrangement. Anonymity helped

to ensure that the sperm donor would not be held liable for child support in an era of ambiguous obligations. Anonymity also allowed the receiving couple both to claim parentage over the child born as a result of AI and could help to conceal the male partner's infertility in a less sympathetic era. Yet the legal and social climate has changed considerably in the past few decades. Adopted children and those who have given children up for adoption have pushed for the creation of mechanisms that allow adopted children to learn the identity of their birth parents. These efforts have borne fruit in other countries. See, e.g., U.K. Human Fertilization and Embryology Authority, at www.hfea.gov.uk/5526.html. But see Pratten v. British Columbia, 2012 BCCA 480 (rejecting claim that differential treatment of children born from adoption and AI violated Canadian Charter).

Should the open adoption and adoption registry concepts be mirrored in the world of gamete donation? Do children born of AI have a right to information about their genetic parents? Is openness necessary to prevent accidental incest? See Jacqueline Mroz, From One Sperm Donor, 150 Children, N.Y. Times, Sept. 6, 2011. Will greater openness reduce the supply of gametes and, if so, should that influence the development of the law in this area? Gaia Bernstein, Unintended Consequences: Prohibition of Gamete Donor Anonymity and the Fragile Practice of Surrogacy, __ Ind. Health L. Rev. __ (2013); Naomi R. Cahn, The New Kinship, 100 Geo. L.J. 367 (2012) (advocating openness and registry process); I. Glenn Cohen, Response: Rethinking Sperm-Donor Anonymity: Of Changed Selves, Nonidentity, and One-Night Stands, 100 Geo. L.J. 431 (2012) (offering response to Prof. Cahn); Patricia P. Mahlstedt et al., The Views of Adult Offspring of Sperm Donation, 93 Fertility & Sterility 2236 (2010) (offspring favored release of donor information or identity); Ethics Committee of the ASRM, Interests, Obligations, and Rights of the Donor in Gamete Donation, 91 Fertility & Sterility 22 (2009) (donors should be informed of information-sharing practices and cautioned "that policies cannot be guaranteed if laws of individual circumstances change"); Sonia M. Suter, Giving In to Baby Markets: Regulation Without Prohibition, 16 Mich. J. Gender & L. 217 (2009) (suggesting greater openness).

Problem: Ovary Transplantation

Researchers have demonstrated some success in autologous transplantation of ovarian tissue. Alberto Revelli et al., Live Birth After Orthotopic Grafting of Autologous Cryopreserved Ovarian Tissue and Spontaneous Conception in Italy, 99 Fertility & Sterility 227 (2013); Michael Grynberg et al., Ovarian Tissue and Follicle Transplantation as an Option for Fertility Preservation, 97 Fertility & Sterility 1260 (2012). Heterologous transplantation is more complex because of the risk of tissue rejection and the need for the transplant recipient to take immunosuppressing drugs. Would transplantation of an ovary from a donor present any particular legal or ethical challenges? Should live donors be permitted to gift an ovary (women ordinarily have two)? Should an ovary donor be treated like an egg donor or should the person to whom the ovary is donated now be deemed to be the "owner" of the ova generated by the ovary despite the lack of genetic connection? See Roger G. Gosden, Ovary and Uterus Transplantation, 136 Reproduction 671 (2008) (reviewing advances supporting potential for transplantation); Mohamed A. Bedaiwy et al.,

Reproductive Organ Transplantation: Advances and Controversies, 90 Fertility & Sterility 2031 (2008). Should parents have the authority to initiate cryopreservation of a child's ovarian tissue to preserve potential future fertility where the child's fertility might be at risk due to illness or medical treatment? See Gregory Dolin et al., Medical Hope, Legal Pitfalls: Potential Legal Issues in the Emerging Field of Oncofertility, 49 Santa Clara L. Rev. 673 (2009).

3. In Vitro Fertilization and Frozen Embryos

In vitro fertilization (IVF) involves the fertilization of eggs by sperm in a laboratory setting. The first known "test tube" baby was born in the late 1970s. The birth was controversial. A congressional committee held hearings on the topic of federal funding for related research projects. See, e.g., Walter Wadlington, Artificial Conception: The Challenge for Family Law, 69 Va. L. Rev. 465 (1983). Critics argued that IVF was unnatural, that it supplanted God in the creation of new life, that it could lead to embryo farms, and that children born from IVF might have genetic or other health problems. Forty years later, IVF has become an accepted infertility procedure. Success rates approach those of natural reproduction for younger patients but are lower for older women using their own oocytes. Barbara Luke et al., Cumulative Birth Rates with Linked Assisted Reproductive Technology Cycles, 366 New Eng. J. Med. 2483 (2012). Does the broad acceptance of IVF illustrate what philosopher Bertrand Russell once observed (in An Outline of Intellectual Rubbish: A Hilarious Catalogue of Organized and Individual Stupidity 20 (1943)), that "[e]very advance in civilization has been denounced as unnatural while it was recent"?

IVF is physically and emotionally taxing for participants. The woman providing the eggs (who may either be a donor or the intended parent) must undergo the hormone therapy and egg-extraction procedures described supra at page 559. These hormone treatments cause ovarian hyperstimulation syndrome in less than 5 percent of IVF cycles; the syndrome ordinarily resolves within a few weeks but in very rare cases can lead to death. Bradley J. Van Voorhis, In Vitro Fertilization, 356 New Eng. J. Med. 379, 382 (2007) (video of oocyte extraction available online). The man providing the sperm (either the donor or the intended parent) must undergo screening and sample collection. The intended carrier of the embryo—either the gestational surrogate or the intended mother—must undergo treatment to ensure that her uterus is prepared to receive the embryo at the time of implantation (which may occur soon after fertilization or after unfreezing stored embryos). IVF is not associated with an increased risk of birth defects. Michael J. Davies et al., Reproductive Technologies and the Risk of Birth Defects, 366 New Eng. J. Med. 1803 (2012) (IVF birth defect risk "no longer significant after adjusting for parental factors").

"Multiple births are the most frequent complication of IVF, contributing to a virtual epidemic of multiple gestations in the United States." Bradley J. Van Voorhis, supra, at 382; see also Saswati Sunderam et al., Assisted Reproductive Technology Surveillance—United States, 2009, supra page 550. IVF is associated with multiple births because physicians seeking to achieve a pregnancy often transfer multiple embryos in one cycle in hopes that at least one will be retained and the pregnancy brought to term. Multiple gestations are more risky for both the pregnant woman and the resulting children, who may be born with low birth weight and other special medical needs. Yet even singleton pregnancies induced through IVF are associated with higher rates of complications, and "some studies have suggested that assisted reproductive technology is associated with an increased risk of birth defects." Bradley J. Van Voorhis, supra, at 382. See also Louise M. Stewart, In Vitro Fertilization and Breast Cancer: Is There Cause for Concern?, 98 Fertility & Sterility 334 (2012) (increased rate of breast cancer for women beginning IVF at younger ages).

These procedures are fairly expensive. A single cycle of IVF can cost $10,000 or more. Given a 28 percent success rate per cycle, expenses of $40,000 to $50,000 per live birth are common. Van Voorhis, supra; Tarun Jain et al., Insurance Coverage and Outcomes of In Vitro Fertilization, 347 New Eng. J. Med. 661 (2002). Many people would not be able to afford IVF if required to pay out of pocket; health insurance coverage for IVF is therefore an important issue. Historically, insurance companies argued that IVF procedures were excluded as "experimental" or that they were not covered "treatments" because they did not address the underlying medical condition of infertility and required "treatment" of third parties (such as the sperm donor). The more common current technique is to include a specific exclusion for infertility treatment within the health insurance plan or contract. Edward L. Raymond, Jr., Annot., Coverage of Artificial Insemination Procedures or Other Infertility Treatments by Health, Sickness, or Hospitalization Insurance, 80 A.L.R.4th 1059 (1990). A few states require that insurance contracts sold within the state provide coverage for IVF, although this requirement cannot be applied to self-insured employee benefit plans. The Affordable Care Act does not mandate coverage of infertility care. See K. Omurtag & G. D. Adamson, The Affordable Care Act's Impact on Fertility Care, __ Fertility & Sterility __ (Nov. 5, 2012 advance epub); Judith Daar, Federalizing Embryo Transfers, 23 Colum. J. Gender & L. 257 (2012) (linking proposed expansion of insurance coverage to proposed federal regulation of transfers). Do health plans limiting or denying coverage for infertility treatment violate the ADA or the Pregnancy Discrimination Act? See supra at Chapter 2.A.3; and Saks v. Franklin Covey Co., 316 F.3d 337 (2d Cir. 2003) (holding that exclusions of coverage for male and female infertility treatments did not violate the Pregnancy Discrimination Act or Title VII's ban on sex discrimination). For an article on whether infertility treatment costs can be deducted as a medical expense under the Internal Revenue Code, see Katherine T. Pratt, Inconceivable? Deducting the Costs of Fertility Treatment, 89 Cornell L. Rev. 1121 (2004).

Consumers of infertility services may be vulnerable to unscrupulous practitioners. Congressional concern with this problem led to passage of the Fertility Clinic Success Rate and Certification Act of 1992, Pub. L. No. 102-493, codified at 42 U.S.C.A. §§263a-1 to -7 (2006). Clinic success rates are available online. CDC, Assisted Reproductive Technology (ART), at www.cdc.gov/art/ARTReports.htm. Some providers enter into shared risk agreements with patients under which, for example, patients pay a flat fee that is refunded if a pregnancy is not achieved after a set number of cycles of IVF. See, e.g., Jim Hawkins, Financing Fertility, 47 Harv. J. on Legis. 115 (2010) (finding evidence that the providers fail to comply with voluntary self-regulation in shared-risk arrangements; arguing for consumer protection legislation); Eric D. Levens & Michael J. Levy, Ethical Application of Shared Risk Programs in Assisted Reproductive Technology, 95 Fertility & Sterility 2198 (2011).

Problems: Ethical Aspects of IVF

- *The Risk of Failure vs. the Risk of Sextuplets.* How many embryos should be transferred to a woman's uterus at one time? Should the number be set by individual physicians, ethical guidelines, or a standard of care enforceable in a malpractice action? The problem arises in part because of the relatively high expense and low success rate of IVF. Physicians might transfer two to three embryos in hopes of achieving a single live birth, depending in the age of the woman and other factors. But multiple embryo transfers increase the risk of a multiple pregnancy, which brings greater health risks for the woman and fetuses. The "remedy" is selective abortion, discussed supra at page 486. Should the birth of sextuplets become prima facie evidence of unethical or negligent conduct by an infertility center? See Practice Committee of the ASRM, Multiple Gestation Associated with Infertility Therapy: An [ASRM] Practice Committee Opinion, 97 Fertility & Sterility 825 (2012); Practice Committees of SART and ASRM, Criteria for Number of Embryos to Transfer, 99 Fertility & Sterility 44 (2013) (guidelines developed to reduce number of multifetal pregnancies; specific number of embryos transferred should depend on factors including patients' age, with single embryo transfer option offered to women under age 35 with a favorable prognosis). Should states limit the number of transfers by legislation? See Theresa Glennon, Choosing One: Resolving the Epidemic of Multiples in Assisted Reproduction, 55 Vill. L. Rev. 147 (2010) (reviewing risks and options to reduce multiple embryo transfers in the United States); S. Ory, The American Octuplet Experience: A Transformative Event, 93 Fertility & Sterility 337 (2010) (noting potential for state legislation after well-publicized birth of octuplets).

- *Postmenopausal Reproduction.* Should access to IVF be restricted based on the age of the intended mother? Researchers can use hormone therapy to sustain a pregnancy even after menopause. See Shari Roan, Woman Gives Birth at 63, L.A. Times, Apr. 24, 1997, at A1 (USC physicians announce birth of baby girl to 63-year-old woman). The USC pregnancy was produced using a donor egg; the recipient's own ovaries stopped producing new eggs at menopause. Is the ethical analysis the same for men and women seeking to reproduce later in life? See Ethics Committee of the American Society for Reproductive Medicine, Oocyte Donation to Postmenopausal Women, 82 Fertility & Sterility S254 (Supp. 1 2004); Kathryn C. Humm & Denny Sakkas, Role of Increased Male Age in IVF and Egg Donation: Is Sperm DNA Fragmentation Responsible?, 99 Fertility & Sterility 30 (2013); David R. Meldrum, Aging Gonads, Gland, and Gametes: Immutable or Partially Reversible Changes? 99 Fertility & Sterility 1 (2013).

- *Preimplantation Genetic Diagnosis (PGD).* Genetic tests can be used to select which preembryos will be implanted. PGD raises important issues related to informed consent and malpractice. See, e.g., Tochi Amagwula, Preimplantation Genetic Diagnosis: A Systematic Review of Litigation in the Face of New Technology, 98 Fertility & Sterility 1277 (2012); The Practice Committees of the SART & ASRM, Preimplantation Genetic Testing, 90 Fertility & Sterility S136 (2008). Much of the commentary by ethicists has focused on the use of tests to avoid the implantation of embryos with disabling genetic conditions or to select offspring of a certain sex. See page 558. Are there any limits on parental ability to select for traits that might be considered to be disabilities? Should it be permissible for deaf parents to use PGD to ensure that they have deaf offspring? Consider the "rights-based" analysis of reproduction, which focuses on the right of the parent to reproduce and to use technology to achieve a healthy child. Under a rights-based approach, when may the state interfere with parental reproductive choices? Could a parent be held liable for intentionally selecting an injurious genetic characteristic for his or her child? Now consider an ethics-based approach to the problems of reproduction. What ethical norms would you apply to a parent's use of reproductive technologies? How would you capture the interests of the child and society? See Susannah Baruch et al., Genetic Testing of Embryos: Practices and Perspectives of U.S. IVF Clinics, 89 Fertility & Sterility 1053 (2008) (small percentage of surveyed IVF clinics reported receiving such requests); Kirsten Rabe Smolensky, Creating Children with Disabilities, 60 Hastings L.J. 299 (2008) (exploring parental tort liability); I. Glenn Cohen, Intentional Diminishment, the Non-Identity Problem, and Legal Liability, 60 Hastings L.J. 347 (2008) (response to Smolensky); Alicia R. Ouellette, Insult to Injury, 60 Hastings L.J. 397 (2008) (response to Smolensky).

- *Children of the Unborn.* Tissue from the ovaries of aborted female fetuses theoretically could be used to create a new life. Other than the obvious opportunities for impossible brain teasers, is there any moral or policy problem with being the child of someone who was never born? Would *Roe* and *Casey* bar state attempts to restrict the use of fetal reproductive tissue? See Jonathan Hersey, Comment, Enigma of the Unborn Mother: Legal and Ethical Considerations of Aborted Fetal Ovarian Tissue and Ova Transplantations, 43 UCLA L. Rev. 159 (1995); John A. Robertson, Ethical Issues in Ovarian Transplantation and Donation, 73 Fertility & Sterility 443, 445 (2000); see also Dori C. Woods & Jonathan L. Tilly, The Next (Re)Generation of Ovarian Biology and Fertility in Women: Is Current Science Tomorrow's Practice?, 98 Fertility & Sterility 3 (2012) (noting challenges to efforts to obtain oocytes from embryonic or induced pluripotent human stem cells).

- *Embryo "Cloning" or "Twinning."* This type of "cloning" differs from that discussed infra at pages 607-609 because it begins with an egg that has been fertilized by sperm. Early embryos can be stimulated to divide and can be separated to create artificial identical twins. One of the twin's embryos could be frozen, allowing the twin to be born long after its genetically identical sibling. Does this process present any ethical or legal dilemmas? See Andrea L. Bonnicksen, Ethical and Policy Issues in Human Embryo Twinning, 4 Cambridge Q. Healthcare Ethics 268 (1995).

■ J.B. v. M.B. & C.C.
783 A.2d 707 (N.J. 2001)

PORITZ, C.J.

In this case, a divorced couple disagree about the disposition of seven preembryos . . . that remain in storage after the couple, during their marriage, undertook in vitro fertilization procedures. We must first decide whether the husband and wife have entered into an enforceable contract that is now determinative on the disposition issue. If not, we must consider how such conflicts should be resolved by our courts.

Although the reproductive technology to accomplish in vitro fertilization has existed since the 1970s, there is little case law to guide us in our inquiry. . . .

J.B. and M.B. were married in February 1992. After J.B. suffered a miscarriage early in the marriage, the couple encountered difficulty conceiving a child and sought medical advice from the Jefferson Center for Women's Specialties. Although M.B. did not have infertility problems, J.B. learned that she had a condition that prevented her from becoming pregnant. On that diagnosis, the couple decided to attempt in vitro fertilization at the Cooper Center for In Vitro Fertilization, P.C. (the Cooper Center). . . .

The Cooper Center's consent form describes the procedure. . . . The consent form also contains language discussing the control and disposition of the preembryos. . . .

The in vitro fertilization procedure was carried out in May 1995 and resulted in eleven preembryos. Four were transferred to J.B. and seven were cryopreserved. J.B. became pregnant . . . and gave birth to the couple's daughter on March 19, 1996. In September 1996, however, the couple separated, and J.B. informed M.B. that she wished to have the remaining preembryos discarded. M.B. did not agree.

J.B. filed a complaint for divorce on November 25, 1996, in which she sought an order from the court "with regard to the . . . frozen embryos." In a counterclaim filed on November 24, 1997, M.B. demanded judgment compelling his wife "to allow the . . . frozen embryos currently in storage to be implanted or donated to other infertile couples." J.B. filed a motion for summary judgment on the preembryo issue in April 1998 alleging, in a certification filed with the motion, that she had intended to use the preembryos solely within her marriage to M.B. She stated . . . "I endured the in vitro process and agreed to preserve the preembryos for our use in the context of an intact family." . . . M.B., in a cross-motion filed in July 1998, described his understanding very differently. . . . His certification stated: . . . "For me, as a Catholic, the I.V.F. procedure itself posed a dilemma. We discussed this issue extensively and had agreed that no matter what happened the eggs would be either utilized by us or by other infertile couples." . . .

The couple's final judgment of divorce, entered in September 1998, resolved all issues except disposition of the preembryos. Shortly thereafter, the trial court granted J.B.'s motion for summary judgment on that issue. . . . Because the husband was "fully able to father a child," and because he sought control of the preembryos "merely to donate them to another couple," the court concluded that the wife had "the greater interest and should prevail."

The Appellate Division affirmed. . . . We . . . now modify and affirm the judgment of the Appellate Division. . . .

M.B. contends that the judgment of the court below violated his constitutional rights to procreation and the care and companionship of his children. He also contends that his constitutional rights outweigh J.B.'s right not to procreate because her right to bodily integrity is not implicated, as it would be in a case involving abortion. He asserts that religious convictions regarding preservation of the preembryos, and the State's interest in protecting potential life, take precedence over his former wife's more limited interests. Finally, M.B. argues that the Appellate Division should have enforced the clear agreement between the parties to give the preembryos a chance at life. He believes that his procedural due process rights have been violated because he was not given an opportunity to introduce evidence demonstrating the existence of that agreement, and because summary judgment is inappropriate in a case involving novel issues of fact and law.

J.B. argues that the Appellate Division properly held that any alleged agreement between the parties to use or donate the preembryos would be unenforceable as a matter of public policy. She contends that New Jersey has "long recognized that individuals should not be bound by agreements requiring them to enter into family relationships or [that] seek to regulate personal intimate decisions relating to parenthood and family life." J.B. also argues that in the absence of an express agreement establishing the disposition of the preembryos, a court should not imply that an agreement exists. It is J.B.'s position that requiring use or donation of the preembryos would violate her constitutional right not to procreate. Discarding the preembryos, on the other hand, would not significantly affect M.B.'s right to procreate because he is fertile and capable of fathering another child. . . .

M.B. contends that he and J.B. entered into an agreement to use or donate the preembryos, and J.B. disputes the existence of any such agreement. As an initial matter, then, we must decide whether this case involves a contract for the disposition of the cryopreserved preembryos resulting from in vitro fertilization. We begin, therefore, with the consent form provided to J.B. and M.B. by the Cooper Center. . . . That form states, among other things:

> The control and disposition of the embryos belongs to the Patient and her Partner. You will be asked to execute the attached legal statement regarding control and disposition of cryopreserved embryos.

The attachment, executed by J.B. and M.B., provides further detail in respect of the parties' "control and disposition":

> I, J.B. (patient), and M.B. (partner) agree that all control, direction, and ownership of our tissues will be relinquished to the IVF Program under the following circumstances:
>
> 1. A dissolution of our marriage by court order, unless the court specifies who takes control and direction of the tissues, or
> 2. In the event of death of both of the above named individuals, or unless provisions are made in a Will, or
> 3. When the patient is no longer capable of sustaining a normal pregnancy, however, the couple has the right to keep embryos maintained for up to two years before making a decision [regarding a] "host womb" or
> 4. At any time by our/my election which shall be in writing, or
> 5. When a patient fails to pay periodic embryo maintenance payment.

The consent form, and more important, the attachment, do not manifest a clear intent by J.B. and M.B. regarding disposition of the preembryos in the event of "[a] dissolution of [their] marriage." Although the attachment indicates that the preembryos "will be relinquished" to the clinic if the parties divorce, it carves out an exception that permits the parties to obtain a court order directing disposition of the preembryos. . . . Clearly, the thrust of the document signed by J.B. and M.B. is that the Cooper Center obtains control over the preembryos unless the parties choose otherwise in writing, or unless a court specifically directs otherwise in an order of divorce.

The conditional language employed in the attachment stands in sharp contrast to the language in the informed consents provided by the hospital in Kass v. Kass, 696 N.E.2d 174 (N.Y. 1998). . . . In *Kass*, the New York Court of Appeals enforced a couple's memorialized decision to donate their preembryos for scientific research when they could not agree on disposition. . . . The court found that the parties had signed an unambiguous contract to relinquish control of their preembryos to the hospital for research purposes in the event of a dispute. . . . In that case, the parties executed several forms before undergoing in vitro fertilization. . . . Informed Consent No. 2 stated: "In the event of divorce, we understand that legal ownership of any stored . . . [preembryos] must be determined in a property settlement and will be released as directed by order of a court of competent jurisdiction." Addendum No. 2-1 further elaborated:

> In the event that we . . . are unable to make a decision regarding the disposition . . . we now indicate our desire for the disposition of . . . [preembryos] and direct the IVF Program to (choose one):
>
>> Our frozen pre-zygotes may be examined by the IVF Program for biological studies and be disposed of by the IVF Program for approved research investigation as determined by the IVF Program.

Moreover, before the parties divorced, they drafted and signed an " 'uncontested divorce' agreement" indicating that their preembryos "should be disposed of [in] the manner outlined in our consent form and [neither party] will lay claim to custody of these . . . [preembryos]." . . .

The *Kass* court found that the parties had agreed to donate their preembryos for IVF research if they could not together decide on another disposition. . . . That holding is based on language entirely different from the language in the form in this case. Here, the parties have agreed that on the dissolution of their marriage the Cooper Center obtains control of the preembryos unless the court specifically makes another determination. Under that provision, the parties have sought another determination from the court.

M.B. asserts, however, that he and J.B. jointly intended another disposition. Because there are no other writings that express the parties' intentions, M.B. asks the Court either to remand for an evidentiary hearing on that issue or to consider his certified statement. . . .

We find no need for a remand to determine the parties' intentions at the time of the in vitro fertilization process. Assuming that it would be possible to enter into a valid agreement at that time irrevocably deciding the disposition of preembryos in circumstances such as we have here, a formal, unambiguous memorialization of the parties' intentions would be required to confirm their joint determination. The parties do not contest the lack of such a writing. We hold, therefore, that J.B. and M.B. never entered into a separate binding contract providing for the disposition of the cryopreserved preembryos now in the possession of the Cooper Center.

In essence, J.B. and M.B. have agreed only that on their divorce the decision in respect of control, and therefore disposition, of their cryopreserved preembryos will be directed by the court. In this area, however, there are few guideposts for decision-making. Advances in medical technology have far outstripped the development of legal principles to resolve the inevitable disputes arising out of the new reproductive opportunities now available. For infertile couples, those opportunities may present the only way to have a biological family. Yet, at the point when a husband and wife decide to begin the in vitro fertilization process, they are unlikely to anticipate divorce or to be concerned about the disposition of preembryos on divorce. As they are both contributors of the genetic material comprising the preembryos, the decision should be theirs to make. See generally Davis v. Davis, 842 S.W.2d 588, 597 (Tenn. 1992) (stating that donors should retain decision-making authority with respect to their preembryos). . . .

But what if, as here, the parties disagree. Without guidance from the Legislature, we must consider a means by which courts can engage in a principled review of the issues presented in such cases in order to achieve a just result. Because the claims before us derive, in part, from concepts found in the Federal Constitution and the Constitution of this State, we begin with those concepts.

Both parties . . . invoke the right to privacy in support of their respective positions. More specifically, they claim procreational autonomy as a fundamental attribute of the privacy rights guaranteed by both the Federal and New Jersey Constitutions. Their arguments are based on various opinions of the United States Supreme Court that discuss the right to be free from governmental interference with procreational decisions. . . . In Skinner v. Oklahoma [supra at page 465], the Court spoke of that most "basic liberty[]" when rejecting, on equal protection grounds, an Oklahoma statute that required sterilization of certain repeat criminal offenders. 316 U.S. at 541. . . .

This Court also has recognized the fundamental nature of procreational rights [when we] observed . . . that "the rights of personal intimacy, of marriage, of sex, of family, of procreation . . . are fundamental rights protected by both the federal and state Constitutions." . . .

Those decisions provide a framework within which disputes over the disposition of preembryos can be resolved. In *Davis, supra*, for example, a divorced couple could not agree on the disposition of their unused, cryopreserved preembryos . . . [842 S.W.2d 588, 589 (Tenn. 1992)]. The Tennessee Supreme Court balanced the right to procreate of the party seeking to donate the preembryos (the wife), against the right not to procreate of the party seeking destruction of the preembryos (the husband). . . .

We agree with the Tennessee Supreme Court that "ordinarily, the party wishing to avoid procreation should prevail." . . . M.B.'s right to procreate is not lost if he is denied an opportunity to use or donate the preembryos. M.B. is already a father and is able to become a father to additional children, whether through natural procreation or further in vitro fertilization. In contrast, J.B.'s right not to procreate may be lost through attempted use or through donation of the preembryos. Implantation, if successful, would result in the birth of her biological child and could have life-long emotional and psychological repercussions.[7] . . . Her fundamental right not to procreate is irrevocably extinguished if a surrogate mother bears J.B.'s child. We will not force J.B. to become a biological parent against her will.

The court below "concluded that a contract to procreate is contrary to New Jersey public policy and is unenforceable." . . . That determination follows the reasoning of the Massachusetts Supreme Judicial Court in A.Z. v. B.Z., wherein an agreement to compel biological parenthood was deemed unenforceable as a matter of public policy. 725 N.E.2d 1051, 1057-58 (2000). The Massachusetts court likened enforcement of a contract permitting implantation of preembryos to other contracts to enter into familial relationships that were unenforceable under the laws of Massachusetts, i.e., contracts to marry or to give up a child for adoption prior to the fourth day after birth. . . .

[T]he laws of New Jersey also evince a policy against enforcing private contracts to enter into or terminate familial relationships. . . .[8]

Enforcement of a contract that would allow the implantation of preembryos at some future date in a case where one party has reconsidered his or her earlier acquiescence raises similar issues. If implantation is successful, that party will have been forced to become a biological parent against his or her will.

We note disagreement on the issue both among legal commentators and in the limited case law on the subject. *Kass*, supra, held that "agreements between progenitors, or gamete donors, regarding disposition of their . . . [preembryos] should generally be presumed valid and binding, and enforced in a dispute between them. . . ." 696 N.E.2d at 180. The New York court emphasized that such agreements would "avoid costly litigation," "minimize misunderstandings and maximize procreative liberty by reserving to the progenitors the authority to make what is in the first instance a quintessentially personal private decision."[9] . . . Yet, as discussed above,

7. The legal consequences for J.B. also are unclear. See N.J.A.C. 8:2-1.4(a) (stating "the woman giving birth shall be recorded as a parent"). We note without comment that a recent case before the Chancery Division in Bergen County concluded that seventy-two hours must pass before a non-biological surrogate mother may surrender her parental rights and the biological mother's name may be placed on the birth certificate. A.H.W. v. G.H.B., 772 A.2d 948 (2000). In Arizona, an appellate court determined that a statute allowing a biological father but not a biological mother to prove paternity violated the Equal Protection Clause. Soos v. Superior Court, 897 P.2d 1356, 1361 (1995). In California, the legal mother is the person who "intended to bring about the birth of a child that she intended to raise as her own." Johnson v. Calvert, 851 P.2d 776, 782 (Cal. 1993), cert. denied, 510 U.S. 874, and cert. dismissed, Baby Boy J. v. Johnson, 510 U.S. 938 (1993).

8. Currently, a minority of states have passed legislation addressing in vitro fertilization. See, e.g., Cal. Penal Code §367g (West 1999) (permitting use of preembryos only pursuant to written consent form); Fla. Stat. ch. 742.17 (1997) (establishing joint decision-making authority regarding disposition of preembryos); La. Rev. Stat. Ann. §§ 9:121 to 9:133 (West 1991) (establishing fertilized human ovum as a biological human being that cannot be intentionally destroyed); Okla. Stat. Ann. tit. 10, §556 (West 2001) (requiring written consent for embryo transfer); Tex. Family code Ann. §151.103 (West 1996) (establishing parental rights over child resulting from preembryo).

9. The Supreme Court of Tennessee, in dicta, also stated "that an agreement regarding disposition of any untransferred preembryos in the event of contingencies (such as the death of one or more of the parties, divorce, financial reversals, or abandonment of the program) should be presumed valid and should be enforced as between the progenitors." *Davis, supra*, 842 S.W.2d at 597.

the Massachusetts Supreme Judicial Court as well as our Appellate Division have declared that when agreements compel procreation over the subsequent objection of one of the parties, those agreements are violative of public policy. *A.Z., supra,* 725 N.E.2d at 1057-58; *J.B., supra,* 331 N.J. Super. at 234. . . .

We recognize that persuasive reasons exist for enforcing preembryo disposition agreements. Both the *Kass* and *Davis* decisions pointed out the benefits of enforcing agreements between the parties. . . . We also recognize that in vitro fertilization is in widespread use, and that there is a need for agreements between the participants and the clinics that perform the procedure. We believe that the better rule, and the one we adopt, is to enforce agreements entered into at the time in vitro fertilization is begun, subject to the right of either party to change his or her mind about disposition up to the point of use or destruction of any stored preembryos.

The public policy concerns that underlie limitations on contracts involving family relationships are protected by permitting either party to object at a later date to provisions specifying a disposition of preembryos that that party no longer accepts. Moreover, despite the conditional nature of the disposition provisions, in the large majority of cases the agreements will control, permitting fertility clinics and other like facilities to rely on their terms. Only when a party affirmatively notifies a clinic in writing of a change in intention should the disposition issue be reopened. Principles of fairness dictate that agreements provided by a clinic should be written in plain language, and that a qualified clinic representative should review the terms with the parties prior to execution. Agreements should not be signed in blank, as in *A.Z., supra,* 725 N.E.2d at 1057, or in a manner suggesting that the parties have not given due consideration to the disposition question. Those and other reasonable safeguards should serve to limit later disputes.

Finally, if there is disagreement as to disposition because one party has reconsidered his or her earlier decision, the interests of both parties must be evaluated. . . . Because ordinarily the party choosing not to become a biological parent will prevail, we do not anticipate increased litigation as a result of our decision. In this case, after having considered that M.B. is a father and is capable of fathering additional children, we have affirmed J.B.'s right to prevent implantation of the preembryos. We express no opinion in respect of a case in which a party who has become infertile seeks use of stored preembryos against the wishes of his or her partner, noting only that the possibility of adoption also may be a consideration, among others, in the court's assessment.

Under the judgment of the Appellate Division, the seven remaining preembryos are to be destroyed. It was represented to us at oral argument, however, that J.B. does not object to their continued storage if M.B. wishes to pay any fees associated with that storage. M.B. must inform the trial court forthwith whether he will do so; otherwise, the preembryos are to be destroyed.

The judgment of the Appellate Division is affirmed as modified.

VERNIERO, J., concurring.

I join in the disposition of this case and in all but one aspect of the Court's opinion. I do not agree with the Court's suggestion, in dicta, that the right to procreate may depend on adoption as a consideration. . . . I also write to express my view that the same principles that compel the outcome in this case would permit an infertile party to assert his or her right to use a preembryo against the objections of the other party, if such use were the only means of procreation. In that instance, the balance arguably would weigh in favor of the infertile party absent countervailing factors of greater weight. I do not decide that profound question today, and the Court should not decide it or suggest a result, because it is absent from this case.

[Justice Zazzali's concurring opinion is omitted.]

Notes: Frozen Embryo Disputes

1. *Family, Property, or Contract Law?* Should preembryos be treated as the property or as the children of one or both parents? The *Davis* litigation, cited in *J.B.*, has influenced all subsequent decisions. Davis v. Davis, 842 S.W.2d 588 (Tenn. 1992), on rehearing in part, 1992 WL 341632 (Tenn. 1992), cert. denied sub nom. Stowe v. Davis, 507 U.S. 911 (1993). As in most frozen embryo disputes, the litigants were divorcing and could not agree on the disposition of their frozen embryos, which had been produced in more hopeful times. The *Davis* trial court resolved the frozen embryo dispute as though the embryos were children of the marriage. 842 S.W.2d at 589. The wife was awarded "custody" so that she could arrange to have the embryos implanted. The trial court's holding was exceedingly controversial—in part because it implicitly challenged the characterization of embryos and fetuses as nonpersons in abortion law—and the decision was promptly appealed. The Tennessee Supreme Court rejected the notion that the preembryos were "persons," finding instead that the preembryos had a special status:

> To our way of thinking, the most helpful discussion on this point is found . . . in the ethical standards set by The American Fertility Society. . . .
>
> [T]he preembryo deserves respect greater than that accorded to human tissue but not the respect accorded to actual persons. The preembryo is due greater respect than other human tissue because of its potential to become a person and because of its symbolic meaning for many people. Yet, it should not be treated as a person, because it has not yet developed the features of personhood, is not yet established as developmentally individual, and may never realize its biologic potential. . . .
>
> We conclude that preembryos are not, strictly speaking, either "persons" or "property," but occupy an interim category that entitles them to special respect because of their potential for human life. It follows that any interest that [the genetic parents] . . . have in the preembryos in this case is not a true property interest. However, they do have an interest in the nature of ownership, to the extent that they have decisionmaking authority concerning disposition of the preembryos, within the scope of policy set by law. . . .

Davis, 842 S.W.2d at 596. What does it mean to give the embryos "special respect" because of their potential for human life? What are the practical implications of this "respect"? What does it mean to say that the progenitors have decisional authority, particularly since most disputes arise because the genetic parents disagree about the decision to make? Post-*Davis*, the Iowa Supreme Court has "identified three primary approaches to resolving disputes over the disposition of frozen embryos . . . (1) the contractual approach; (2) the contemporaneous mutual consent model; and (3) the [interests] balancing test [used in *J.B.* and in *Davis* where the parties had not executed an agreement]." In re Witten, 672 N.W.2d 768 (Iowa 2003).

2. *Disposing of Frozen Embryos by Contract or Mutual Agreement?* As noted in the *J.B.* decision, supra, there is substantial disagreement about whether the parties can contractually bind themselves to a particular form of embryo disposition even after one or both parties changes his or her preference. Does the *J.B.* court enforce the agreement signed by the parties? The informed consent form/disposition agreement appears to give the Cooper Center control over the embryos upon the divorce of the parties, absent a court order or a written agreement of the parties. Perhaps the court's decision actually fulfills the contract's terms. What about the alleged additional agreement between the parties, the one that M.B. claimed that he should have a right to prove? Why doesn't M.B. have a right to present evidence about his agreement with his wife regarding the disposition of the embryos? The court appears to impose a judicially constructed "statute of frauds," requiring that such agreements be written.

The New Jersey court also holds that "[w]e believe that the better rule, and the one we adopt, is to enforce agreements entered into at the time in vitro fertilization is begun, subject to the right of either party to change his or her mind about disposition up to the point of use or destruction of any stored preembryos." *J.B.*, supra. Does this mean that the court favors the use of binding predisposition contracts? Probably not, given that the court will only enforce agreements so long as the parties don't change their minds. This certainly is not the traditional legal approach to the enforcement of contracts.

It appears that other courts might enforce disposition agreements in some circumstances. The *Davis* court noted in dicta, for example:

> We believe, as a starting point, that an agreement regarding disposition of any untransferred preembryos in the event of contingencies (such as the death of one or more of the parties, divorce, financial reversals, or abandonment of the program) should be presumed valid and should be enforced as between the progenitors. This conclusion is in keeping with the proposition that the progenitors, having provided the gametic material giving rise to the preembryos, retain decisionmaking authority as to their disposition.
>
> At the same time, we recognize that life is not static, and that human emotions run particularly high when a married couple is attempting to overcome infertility problems. It follows that the parties' initial "informed consent" to IVF procedures will often not be truly informed because of the near impossibility of anticipating, emotionally and psychologically, all the turns that events may take as the IVF process unfolds. Providing that the initial agreements may later be modified by agreement will, we think, protect the parties against some of the risks they face in this regard. But, in the absence of such agreed modification, we conclude that their prior agreements should be considered binding.

Davis, 842 S.W.2d at 597. See also Kass v. Kass, 696 N.E.2d 174 (N.Y. 1998) (enforcing dispositional terms of signed consents, which assigned preembryos for research purposes); In re Dahl and Angle, 194 P.3d 834 (Or. App. 2008) ("courts should give effect to a valid agreement evincing the parties' intent"); Roman v. Roman, 193 S.W.3d 40 (Tex. App. 2006) (embryo agreement terms should be enforced).

The contractual approach has been described as "[t]he currently prevailing view." In re Witten, 672 N.W.2d 768, 776 (Iowa 2003). The *Witten* court nonetheless rejected the contractual approach because it provides "'insufficient[] protect[ion] for] the individual and societal interests at stake.'" Id. at 777. The court agreed with critics of the contractual approach who argued that preferences regarding embryo disposition cannot be known in advance. Id. The court noted:

> We have considered and rejected the arguments of some commentators that embryo disposition agreements are analogous to antenuptial agreements and divorce stipulations, which courts generally enforce. . . . Whether embryos are viewed as having life or simply as having the potential for life, this characteristic or potential renders embryos fundamentally distinct from the chattels, real estate, and money that are the subjects of antenuptial agreements. Divorce stipulations are also distinguishable. While such agreements may address custody issues, they are contemporaneous with the implementation of the stipulation, an attribute noticeably lacking in disposition agreements.

In re Witten, 672 N.W.2d at 781-782. The court rejected the balancing of interests approach because it would require the court to make sensitive value judgments about procreation particularly within the dominion of individuals. The court thus adopted the contemporaneous agreement standard: "A better principle to apply . . . is the requirement of contemporaneous mutual consent. Under that model, no transfer, release, disposition, or use of the embryos can occur without the signed authorization of both donors. If a stalemate results, the status quo would be maintained. . . . Thus, any expense [for embryo storage] should logically be borne by the person opposing destruction." Id. at 783. See also A.Z. v. B.Z., 725 N.E.2d 1051 (Mass. 2000) (court expresses doubt about whether informed consent forms offered by clinic and signed by parties reflected their intent); Deborah L. Forman, Embryo Disposition and Divorce: Why Clinic Consent Forms Are Not the Answer, 24 J. Am. Acad. Matrim. L. 57 (2011) (offering critique of reliance on forms).

3. *Frozen Embryos and the Constitution.* Frozen embryos occupy a peculiar position under the law. Who should have power to exercise control over the embryos? Are these questions answered by an analysis of the "right to procreate" or the "right not to procreate"? Women invest more "sweat equity" in in vitro reproduction than men. Women must undergo arduous hormone therapy and ovum retrieval procedures. Men must produce a sperm sample, typically under less harrowing conditions. Should this difference in investments affect the outcome? See Ruth Colker, Pregnant Men Revisited or Sperm Is Cheap, Eggs Are Not, 47 Hastings L.J. 1063 (1996). If procreation had occurred in the ordinary fashion, a man's ability to decline the opportunity of fatherhood would have ended with the procreative act itself. A man cannot require that a woman undergo an abortion, for example; see page 513. Should courts use a similar analogy when considering frozen embryo disputes, denying genetic parents the opportunity to reject parenthood once they have committed their gametes to the enterprise? See Kass v. Kass, 1995 WL 110368 (N.Y. Sup. Ct.) (unpublished opinion), rev'd, 663 N.Y.S.2d 581 (App. Div. 1997).

Most courts following the balancing of interests approach have favored the right not to procreate. In *J.B.*, supra, for example, the court anticipates that the party who does not wish to procreate will "ordinarily . . . prevail." The *Davis* court reached a similar result for cases not governed by a preexisting contractual agreement:

> If no prior agreement exists, then the relative interests of the parties in using or not using the preembryos must be weighed. Ordinarily, the party wishing to avoid procreation should prevail, assuming that the other party has a reasonable possibility of achieving parenthood by means other than use of the preembryos in question.

If no other reasonable alternatives exist, then the argument in favor of using the preembryos to achieve pregnancy should be considered. However, if the party seeking control of the preembryos intends merely to donate them to another couple, the objecting party obviously has the greater interest and should prevail. But the rule does not contemplate the creation of an automatic veto, and in affirming the judgment of the court of appeals, we would not wish to be interpreted as so holding. . . .

842 S.W.2d at 604. See also A.Z. v. B.Z., 725 N.E.2d 1051 (Mass. 2000) (husband's interest in avoiding procreation outweighed defendant's interest in having additional children; husband should not be forced to become a parent). See also I. Glenn Cohen, The Right Not to Be a Genetic Parent, 81 S. Cal. Rev. 1115 (2008); I. Glenn Cohen, The Constitution and the Rights Not to Procreate, 60 Stan. L. Rev. 1135 (2008). When, if ever, would these courts authorize the use of embryos over the objection of one of the parties? What is the significance of the dispute between the majority and concurring opinions in *J.B.* regarding the ability to adopt? A Pennsylvania appellate court using a balancing of interests approach in a case where the parties had no disposition agreement awarded frozen embryos to a woman who had undergone cancer treatment and would not otherwise be able to bear a genetically related child. Reber v. Reiss, 42 A.3d 1131 (Pa. Super. 2012). The court considered but rejected the argument that the woman could achieve parenthood through adoption. Id. at 1138-1139 (adoption is "laudable" but not the same as genetic parenting and adoption option not practically available to woman due to her age and health history).

4. *Genetic Parenthood and Frozen Embryo Disputes.* In In re Litowitz, the Washington Supreme Court confronted a frozen embryo dispute in which one of the parties was not genetically related to the embryos. 48 P.3d 261 (Wash. 2002), opinion amended, 53 P.3d 516 (2002), cert. denied sub nom. Litowitz v. Litowitz, 537 U.S. 1191 (2003). Becky M. Litowitz was unable to produce oocytes or to bear a child. She and her then-husband David J. Litowitz entered into an agreement with an egg donor to obtain eggs that could be fertilized with David's sperm and then implanted in a gestational surrogate. The Litowitz marriage crumbled before the birth of their first child produced according to this arrangement. The parties could not agree to the disposition of the remaining frozen embryos. The trial court gave the embryos to the husband for implantation in another surrogate "based on the best interest of the child." Id. at 264.

The Washington Supreme Court took a different approach. The court held that Becky Litowitz's rights would be determined by contract because she had no biological connection to the preembryos. Id. at 267. Becky argued that she and David had equal rights to the embryos because the egg donor contract provided that the "intended parents" were the owners of the donated eggs. Id. at 267-268. The court rejected this claim, holding that the egg donor contract did not apply once the eggs had been fertilized. Id. at 268. The court then turned to the cryopreservation contract the parties entered into with the fertility clinic. That contract provided that the preembryos should be "thawed out and not allowed to undergo further development" after five years. Id. at 271. Given that the five years had expired, the court suggested that the embryos might already have been destroyed or could be destroyed in accordance with the parties' expressed wishes.

5. *Legislation.* Several states have enacted legislation establishing special consent and dispute resolution rules for the allocation of frozen embryos. See, e.g., N.J. Stat.

Ann. §26:2 Z-2 (enacted 2003; persons providing infertility treatment must provide certain options for the disposal of embryos including for use in research); National Conference of State Legislatures, Gamete and Embryo Disposition Laws (updated through 2007) (available at NCSL Web site). Some jurisdictions focus on regulating the informed consent process. See, e.g., Cal. H & S Code §125315 (patients must be given options for disposition in the event of separation or divorce). Other jurisdictions give the partner wishing to avoid procreation the right to withdraw consent any time before the use of the embryos. See, e.g., Colo. Rev. Stat. §19-4-106. Several states have enacted rules governing embryo adoption. See National Conference of State Legislatures, supra. Legislation may be helpful in some circumstances but is not likely to resolve the need for judicial determinations completely. How should courts resolve embryo disputes when the parties have failed to execute an agreement about the disposition of embryos as required by state law?

6. *Commentators.* Professor Robertson is the leading commentator on frozen embryo disputes; he served as an expert in the *Davis* trial and has written extensively on the subject. See, e.g., John A. Robertson, Precommitment Strategies for Disposition of Frozen Embryos, 50 Emory L.J. 990 (2001). See also Jessica Berg, Owning Persons: The Application of Property Theory to Embryos and Fetuses, 40 Wake Forest L. Rev. 159 (2005); Carl H. Coleman, Procreative Liberty and Contemporaneous Choice: An Inalienable Rights Approach to Frozen Embryo Disputes, 84 Minn. L. Rev. 55 (1999) (cited by the court in In re Witten); Janet L. Dolgin, The "Intent" of Reproduction: Reproductive Technologies and the Parent-Child Bond, 26 Conn. L. Rev. 1261 (1994); Theresa M. Erickson & Megan T. Erickson, What Happens to Embryos When a Marriage Dissolves? Embryo Disposition and Divorce, 35 Wm. Mitchell L. Rev. 469 (2009); Elizabeth E. Swire, The Disposition of Cryopreserved Embryos: Why Embryo Adoption Is an Inapposite Model for Application to Third Party Assisted Reproduction, 35 Wm. Mitchell L. Rev. 489 (2009); Ellen Waldman, The Parent Trap: Uncovering the Myth of "Coerced Parenthood" in Frozen Embryo Disputes, 53 Am. U. L. Rev. 1021 (2004) (discusses and critiques the dominance of the right to not procreate in frozen embryo disputes). See generally Annot., 87 A.L.R.5th 253 (2001).

7. *Lost Embryos; Donated Embryos.* Should couples be permitted to sue infertility centers that lose or destroy frozen embryos? See Jeter v. Mayo Clinic Arizona, 121 P.3d 1256 (Ariz. 2005) (rejecting wrongful death claim but permitting certain other claims to go forward); Miller v. American Infertility Group of Illinois, S.C., 897 N.E.2d 837 (Ill. App. 2008) (no wrongful death claim before embryo is implanted). See also Charles P. Kindregan, Jr., & Maureen McBrien, Embryo Donation: Unresolved Legal Issues in the Transfer of Surplus Cryopreserved Embryos, 49 Vill. L. Rev. 169 (2004).

4. Traditional and Gestational Surrogacy

■R.R. v. M.H.
689 N.E.2d 790 (Mass. 1998)

WILKINS, C.J.

On a report by a judge in the Probate and Family Court, we are concerned with the validity of a surrogacy parenting agreement between the plaintiff (father) and the defendant (mother). Both the mother and the father are married but not to each other. A child was conceived through artificial insemination of the mother with the father's sperm, after the mother and father had executed the surrogate parenting agreement. The agreement provided that the father would have custody of the child. During the sixth month of her pregnancy and after she had received funds from the father pursuant to the surrogacy agreement, the mother changed her mind and decided that she wanted to keep the child.

The father thereupon brought this action. . . . The question of the enforceability of the surrogacy agreement is before us and, although we could defer any ruling until there is a final judgment entered, the issue is one on which we elect to comment because it is fully briefed and is of importance to more than the parties. This court has not previously dealt with the enforceability of a surrogacy agreement. . . .

The baby girl who is the subject of this action was born on August 15, 1997. . . . The defendant mother and the plaintiff father are her biological parents. The father and his wife, who live in Rhode Island, were married in June, 1989. The wife is infertile. Sometime in 1994, she and the father learned of an egg donor program but did not pursue it because the procedure was not covered by insurance and had a relatively low success rate. Because of their ages (they were both in their forties), they concluded that pursuing adoption was not feasible. In April, 1996, responding to a newspaper advertisement for surrogacy services, they consulted a Rhode Island attorney who had drafted surrogacy contracts for both surrogates and couples seeking surrogacy services. On the attorney's advice, the father and his wife consulted the New England Surrogate Parenting Advisors (NESPA), a for-profit corporation that helps infertile couples find women willing to act as surrogate mothers. They entered into a contract with NESPA in September, 1996, and paid a fee of $6,000. Meanwhile, in the spring of 1996, the mother, who was married and had two children, responded to a NESPA advertisement. She reported to NESPA that her family was complete and that she desired to allow others less fortunate than herself to have children. The mother submitted a surrogacy application to NESPA. The judge found that the mother was motivated to apply to NESPA by a desire to be pregnant, in order to earn money, and to help an infertile couple.

In October, Dr. Angela Figueroa of NESPA brought the mother together with the father and his wife. They had a seemingly informative exchange of information and views. The mother was advised to seek an attorney's advice concerning the surrogacy agreement. Shortly thereafter, the mother, the father, and his wife met again to discuss the surrogacy and other matters. The mother also met with a clinical psychologist as part of NESPA's evaluation of her suitability to act as a surrogate. The psychologist, who also evaluated the father and his wife, advised the mother to consult legal counsel, to give her husband a chance to air his concerns, to discuss arrangements for contact with the child, to consider and discuss her expectations concerning termination of the pregnancy, and to arrange a meeting between her husband and the father and his wife. The psychologist concluded that the mother was solid, thoughtful, and well grounded, that she would have no problem giving the child to the father, and that she was happy to act as a surrogate. The mother told the psychologist that she was not motivated by money, although she did plan to use the funds received for her children's education. The mother's husband told the psychologist by telephone that he supported his wife's decision.

The mother signed the surrogate parenting agreement and her signature was notarized on November 1. The father signed on November 18. The agreement stated that the parties intended that the "Surrogate shall be inseminated with the semen of Natural Father" and "that, on the birth of the child or children so conceived, Natural Father, as the Natural Father, will have the full legal parental rights of a father, and surrogate will permit Natural Father to take the child or children home from the hospital to live with he [sic] and his wife." The agreement acknowledged that the mother's parental rights would not terminate if she permitted the father to take the child home and have custody, that the mother could at any time seek to enforce her parental rights by court order, but that, if she attempted to obtain custody or visitation rights, she would forfeit her rights under the agreement and would be obligated to reimburse the father for all fees and expenses paid to her under it. . . . .

The agreement provided for compensation to the mother in the amount of $10,000 "for services rendered in conceiving, carrying and giving birth to the Child." Payment of the $10,000 was to be made as follows: $500 on verification of the pregnancy; $2,500 at the end of the third month; $3,500 at the end of the sixth month; and $3,500 at the time of birth "and when delivery of child occurs." The agreement stated that no payment was made in connection with adoption of the child, the termination of parental rights, or consent to surrender the child for adoption. The father acknowledged the mother's right to determine whether to carry the pregnancy to term, but the mother agreed to refund all payments if, without the father's consent, she had an abortion that was not necessary for her physical health. The father assumed various expenses of the pregnancy, including tests, and had the right to name the child. The mother would be obliged, however, to repay all expenses and fees for services if tests showed that the father was not the biological father of the child, or if the mother refused to permit the father to take the child home from the hospital. The agreement also provided that the mother would maintain some contact with the child after the birth. The judge found that the mother entered into the agreement on her own volition after consulting legal counsel. There was no evidence of undue influence, coercion, or duress. The mother fully understood that she was contracting to give custody of the baby to the father. She sought to inseminate herself on November 30 and December 1, 1996. The attempt at conception was successful.

The lawyer for the father sent the mother a check for $500 in December, 1996, and another for $2,500 in February. In May, the father's lawyer sent the mother a check for $3,500. She told the lawyer that she had changed her mind and wanted to keep the child. She returned the check uncashed in the middle of June. The mother has made no attempt to refund the amounts that the father paid her, including $550 that he paid for pregnancy-related expenses.

Approximately two weeks after the mother changed her mind and returned the check for $3,500, and before the child was born, the father commenced this action against the mother seeking to establish his paternity, alleging breach of contract, and requesting a declaration of his rights under the surrogacy agreement. Subsequently, the wife's husband was added as a defendant. The judge appointed a guardian ad litem to represent the interests of the unborn child. Proceedings were held on . . . . the mother's motion to determine whether surrogacy contracts are enforceable in Massachusetts. . . . .

A significant minority of States have legislation addressing surrogacy agreements. Some simply deny enforcement of all such agreements. . . . . Others expressly deny enforcement only if the surrogate is to be compensated. . . . Some States have simply exempted surrogacy agreements from provisions making it a crime to sell babies. . . . A few States have explicitly made unpaid surrogacy agreements lawful. . . . Florida, New Hampshire, and Virginia require that the intended mother be infertile. . . . New Hampshire and Virginia place restrictions on who may act as a surrogate and require advance judicial approval of the agreement. . . . Last, Arkansas raises a presumption that a child born to a surrogate mother is the child of the intended parents and not the surrogate. . . .

There are few appellate court opinions on the enforceability of traditional surrogacy agreements. . . .

The best known opinion is that of the Supreme Court of New Jersey in the *Matter of Baby M.*, 537 A.2d 1227 (N.J. 1988), where the court invalidated a compensated surrogacy contract because it conflicted with the law and public policy of the State. . . . The Baby M surrogacy agreement involved broader concessions from the mother than the agreement before us because it provided that the mother would surrender her parental rights and would allow the father's wife to adopt the child. . . . The agreement, therefore, directly conflicted with a statute prohibiting the payment of money to obtain an adoption and a statute barring enforcement of an agreement to adoption made prior to the birth of the child. . . . The court acknowledged that an award of custody to the father was in the best interests of the child, but struck down orders terminating the mother's parental rights and authorizing the adoption of the child by the husband's wife. . . . The court added that it found no "legal prohibition against surrogacy when the surrogate mother volunteers, without any payment, to act as a surrogate and is given the right to change her mind and to assert her parental rights." . . .

The case before us concerns traditional surrogacy, in which the fertile member of an infertile couple is one of the child's biological parents. Surrogate fatherhood, the insemination of the fertile wife with sperm of a donor, often an anonymous donor, is a recognized and accepted procedure. . . . If the mother's husband consents to the procedure, the resulting child is considered the legitimate child of the mother and her husband. *G. L. c. 46, §4B*. . . . Section 4B does not comment on the rights and obligations, if any, of the biological father, although inferentially he has none. In the case before us, the infertile spouse is the wife. No statute decrees the consequences of the artificial insemination of a surrogate with the sperm of a fertile husband. This situation presents different considerations from surrogate fatherhood because surrogate motherhood is never anonymous and her commitment and contribution is unavoidably much greater than that of a sperm donor.[10]

We must face the possible application of *G. L. c. 46, §4B*, to this case. Section 4B tells us that a husband who consents to the artificial insemination of his wife with the sperm of another is considered to be the father of any resulting child. In the case before us, the birth mother was married at the time of her artificial

10. A situation which involves considerations different from those in the case before us arises when the birth mother has had transferred to her uterus an embryo formed through in vitro fertilization of the intended parents' sperm and egg. This latter process in which the birth mother is not genetically related to the child (except coincidentally if an intended parent is a relative) has been called gestational surrogacy. . . .

insemination. . . . It is doubtful, however, that the Legislature intended §4B to apply to the child of a married surrogate mother. . . .

Policies underlying our adoption legislation suggest that a surrogate parenting agreement should be given no effect if the mother's agreement was obtained prior to a reasonable time after the child's birth or if her agreement was induced by the payment of money. Adoption legislation is, of course, not applicable to child custody, but it does provide us with some guidance. Although the agreement makes no reference to adoption and does not concern the termination of parental rights or the adoption of the child by the father's wife, the normal expectation in the case of a surrogacy agreement seems to be that the father's wife will adopt the child with the consent of the mother (and the father). Under *G. L. c. 210, §2*, adoption requires the written consent of the father and the mother but, in these circumstances, not the mother's husband. Any such consent, written, witnessed, and notarized, is not to be executed "sooner than the fourth calendar day after the date of birth of the child to be adopted." Id. That statutory standard should be interpreted as providing that no mother may effectively agree to surrender her child for adoption earlier than the fourth day after its birth, by which time she better knows the strength of her bond with her child. Although a consent to surrender custody has less permanency than a consent to adoption, the legislative judgment that a mother should have time after a child's birth to reflect on her wishes concerning the child weighs heavily in our consideration whether to give effect to a prenatal custody agreement. No private agreement concerning adoption or custody can be conclusive in any event because a judge, passing on custody of a child, must decide what is in the best interests of the child.[11]

Adoptive parents may pay expenses of a birth parent but may make no direct payment to her. See *G. L. c. 210, §11A*. . . . Even though the agreement seeks to attribute that payment of $10,000, not to custody or adoption, but solely to the mother's services in carrying the child, the father ostensibly was promised more than those services because, as a practical matter, the mother agreed to surrender custody of the child. She could assert custody rights, according to the agreement, only if she repaid the father all amounts that she had received and also reimbursed him for all expenses he had incurred. The statutory prohibition of payment for receiving a child through adoption suggests that, as a matter of policy, a mother's agreement to surrender custody in exchange for money (beyond pregnancy-related expenses) should be given no effect in deciding the custody of the child.

The mother's purported consent to custody in the agreement is ineffective because no such consent should be recognized unless given on or after the fourth day following the child's birth. In reaching this conclusion, we apply to consent to custody the same principle which underlies the statutory restriction on when a mother's consent to adoption may be effectively given. Moreover, the payment of money to influence the mother's custody decision makes the agreement as to custody void. Eliminating any financial reward to a surrogate mother is the only way to assure that no economic pressure will cause a woman, who may well be a member

11. In the case of a divorce, a judge may approve an agreement between parents concerning child custody unless the judge makes specific findings that the agreement would not be in the best interests of the child. *G. L. c. 208, §31.*

of an economically vulnerable class, to act as a surrogate. It is true that a surrogate enters into the agreement before she becomes pregnant and thus is not presented with the desperation that a poor unwed pregnant woman may confront. However, compensated surrogacy arrangements raise the concern that, under financial pressure, a woman will permit her body to be used and her child to be given away.

There is no doubt that compensation was a factor in inducing the mother to enter into the surrogacy agreement and to cede custody to the father. If the payment of $10,000 was really only compensation for the mother's services in carrying the child and giving birth and was unrelated to custody of the child, the agreement would not have provided that the mother must refund all compensation paid (and expenses paid) if she should challenge the father's right to custody. Nor would the agreement have provided that final payment be made only when the child is delivered to the father. We simply decline, on public policy grounds, to apply to a surrogacy agreement of the type involved here the general principle that an agreement between informed, mature adults should be enforced absent proof of duress, fraud, or undue influence.

We recognize that there is nothing inherently unlawful in an arrangement by which an informed woman agrees to attempt to conceive artificially and give birth to a child whose father would be the husband of an infertile wife. We suspect that many such arrangements are made and carried out without disagreement.

If no compensation is paid beyond pregnancy-related expenses and if the mother is not bound by her consent to the father's custody of the child unless she consents after a suitable period has passed following the child's birth, the objections we have identified in this opinion to the enforceability of a surrogate's consent to custody would be overcome. Other conditions might be important in deciding the enforceability of a surrogacy agreement, such as a requirement that (a) the mother's husband give his informed consent to the agreement in advance; (b) the mother be an adult and have had at least one successful pregnancy; (c) the mother, her husband, and the intended parents have been evaluated for the soundness of their judgment and for their capacity to carry out the agreement; (d) the father's wife be incapable of bearing a child without endangering her health; (e) the intended parents be suitable persons to assume custody of the child; and (f) all parties have the advice of counsel. The mother and father may not, however, make a binding best-interests-of-the-child determination by private agreement. Any custody agreement is subject to a judicial determination of custody based on the best interests of the child.

The conditions that we describe are not likely to be satisfactory to an intended father because, following the birth of the child, the mother can refuse to consent to the father's custody even though the father has incurred substantial pregnancy-related expenses. A surrogacy agreement judicially approved before conception may be a better procedure, as is permitted by statutes in Virginia and New Hampshire. A Massachusetts statute concerning surrogacy agreements, pro or con, would provide guidance to judges, lawyers, infertile couples interested in surrogate parenthood, and prospective surrogate mothers.

We do not reach but comment briefly on the mother's argument that the agreement was unconscionable. She actively sought to become a surrogate and entered into the surrogacy agreement voluntarily, advised by counsel, not under duress, and fully informed. Unconscionability is not apparent on this record.

A declaration shall be entered that the surrogacy agreement is not enforceable. Such further orders as may be appropriate, consistent with this opinion, may be entered in the Probate and Family Court.

■ CULLITON v. BETH ISRAEL DEACONESS MEDICAL CENTER
756 N.E.2d 1133 (Mass. 2001)

GREANEY, J.

We transferred this case here on our own motion to decide whether a judge in the Probate and Family Court had authority to act on the plaintiffs' complaint that sought declaratory and injunctive relief by way of a judgment ordering the defendant Beth Israel Deaconess Medical Center (hospital) "to enter MARLA CULLITON as the mother, and STEVEN CULLITON as the father [,] on the birth certificates of unborn Baby A and unborn Baby B." The children, twins, were born while the case was pending appeal. They are the genetic children of the plaintiffs, who had embryos . . . that had been created from the plaintiff Steven Culliton's sperm . . . and the plaintiff Marla Culliton's ova . . . . implanted into the uterus of the defendant Melissa Carroll, who agreed to act as a gestational carrier for the plaintiffs pursuant to a gestational carrier contract with them. The judge ordered the entry of a judgment dismissing the complaint because of a "lack of clarity and certainty as to this court's authority" to grant the relief sought. We conclude that the judge had authority to decide the merits of the complaint. We also conclude that, on the facts of this case, a judgment should enter declaring that the plaintiffs are the legal parents of the children, and ordering the hospital, through its reporters, to place the plaintiffs' names on all "record[s] of birth" created pursuant to G. L. c. 46, §§1, 3, 3A, listing the plaintiffs as the mother and father, respectively, of the children.

The facts of this case are undisputed. We now summarize those facts and provide an overview of the case's procedural background. The plaintiffs and the defendant Melissa Carroll (gestational carrier), a single woman over the age of twenty-one years who had "at least one previous live birth," entered into a gestational carrier contract. Pursuant to the contract, the gestational carrier agreed to have implanted into her uterus embryos that were created from the sperm of Steven Culliton and the ova of Marla Culliton; to carry and deliver any child resulting from the embryo implantation; and, upon the birth of any child resulting from the embryo implantation, to permit the plaintiffs to have sole physical and legal custody of the child or children. For her role, the gestational carrier was to receive certain financial compensation.[6] The contract appears to have been executed because Marla "is capable of conceiving a child, but incapable of bearing and giving birth to a child without unreasonable risk to her health."

---

6. Under the contract, the plaintiffs agreed to pay the gestational carrier for certain medical expenses, maternity clothing, travel expenses, childcare expenses, legal expenses, telephone expenses, medically necessitated lost wages, psychological counselling expenses, health insurance expenses, and living expenses. According to the contract, payment of these expenses was not conditioned "upon the termination of any parental rights or the placement of the child with [the plaintiffs]."

The gestational carrier underwent the embryo implantation and became pregnant with twins. A few months later, the plaintiffs filed a verified complaint in the Probate and Family Court seeking a declaration of paternity and maternity, as well as a prebirth order directing the hospital at which the gestational carrier was expected to deliver to designate the plaintiffs as the father and mother of the children on their birth certificates. Together with the complaint, the plaintiffs and the gestational carrier filed a stipulation for the entry of judgment in the plaintiffs' favor. . . .

A judge in the Probate and Family Court, concluding that he did not have the authority to issue a prebirth order of parentage, ordered the entry of a judgment of dismissal. . . . The plaintiffs filed a notice of appeal, and the case was entered in the Appeals Court. That court, on motion by the plaintiffs, entered a preliminary injunction enjoining the hospital from issuing birth certificates until resolution of the appeal. The day before we transferred the case here, the twins were born. After transfer, we entered an order continuing the injunction in effect. . . .

The judge acted prudently in seeking to place this case before us as quickly as possible because, as he correctly noted, there is no direct legal "authority for issuing a pre-birth order regarding parentage under the facts of this case." Authority elsewhere is sparse and not altogether consistent [citing cases from Ohio, New Jersey, New York, and California].

The pregnancy in issue is not governed by the statutes referred to by the [trial] judge. General Laws c. 209C, for instance, establish procedures for determining paternity and maternity for children "born out of wedlock." See G. L. c. 209C, §1. . . . While the twins technically were born out of wedlock, because the gestational carrier was not married when she gave birth to them, it is undisputed that the twins were conceived by a married couple. In these circumstances the children should be presumed to be the children of marriage. . . . Conversely, problems would have arisen if the gestational carrier had been married at the time of birth, for, in those circumstances, under G. L. c. 209C, her husband would be presumed to be the father of the children to whom she gave birth. . . . Additionally, under the statute, in contested cases, one method of proving paternity involves soliciting testimony from one parent concerning the occurrence of "sexual intercourse" with the other party during the "probable period of conception." . . . As shown by the facts of this case, reproductive advances have eliminated the necessity of having sexual intercourse in order to procreate. It is apparent, after examining the paternity statute in detail, that the statute is simply an inadequate and inappropriate device to resolve parentage determinations of children born from this type of gestational surrogacy.

Nor does the adoption statute, G. L. c. 210, furnish any better guidance. While this court has previously looked to the adoption statute in deciding whether to enforce a traditional surrogacy agreement, . . . see [citing R.R. v. M.H., supra], the court did so "to assure that no economic pressure will cause a woman . . . to act as a surrogate. . . . Compensated surrogacy arrangements raise the concern that, under financial pressure, a woman will permit her body to be used and her child to be given away." . . . In such an arrangement, the surrogate is both the genetic mother of the child and the mother who carries the child through pregnancy and delivery. The child is thus, undisputedly, "her" child to be surrendered for adoption. Here, where it is undisputed that the plaintiffs were not donating an embryo or embryos to the gestational carrier, and that the twins have no genetic relation to the gestational carrier, the concerns are different. . . . Also, in these circumstances, applying the four-day waiting period of G. L. c. 210, §2, to this gestational carrier arrangement would work unintended, and possibly detrimental, results. The duties and responsibilities of parenthood (for example, support and custody) would lie with the gestational carrier for at least four days; the gestational carrier could be free to surrender the children for adoption; and the genetic parents of the children would be forced to go through the adoption process, possibly having to wait as long as six months, see G. L. c. 210, §5A . . . , before becoming the legal parents of the children. As is evident from its provisions, the adoption statute was not intended to resolve parentage issues arising from gestational surrogacy agreements.

Contrary to the plaintiffs' contention, G. L. c. 46, §4B, does not authorize the relief sought in this case. That statute provides that "any child born to a married woman as a result of artificial insemination with the consent of her husband, shall be considered the legitimate child of the mother and such husband." G. L. c. 46, §4B. As we explained in R.R. v. M.H., supra at 510, §4B "seems to concern the status of a child born to a fertile mother whose husband, presumably infertile, consented to her artificial insemination with the sperm of another man so that the couple could have a child biologically related to the mother." The situation that §4B addresses is not present here. The statute does not apply. . . .

Here, where (a) the plaintiffs are the sole genetic sources of the twins; (b) the gestational carrier agrees with the orders sought; (c) no one, including the hospital, has contested the complaint or petition; and (d) by filing the complaint and stipulation for judgment the plaintiffs agree that they have waived any contradictory provisions in the contract (assuming those provisions could be enforced in the first place), we conclude that pursuant to the Probate and Family Court's general equity jurisdiction under G. L. c. 215, §6, the judge had authority to consider the merits of the relief sought here.[9]

This conclusion acknowledges the importance of establishing the rights and responsibilities of parents as soon as is practically possible. By enacting G. L. c. 46, which contains provisions establishing a process for the issuance of accurate birth certificates on which the "parents" of a newly born child are listed, the Legislature has also recognized and addressed, in some measure, this concern. Delays in establishing parentage may, among other consequences, interfere with a child's medical treatment in the event of medical complications arising during or shortly after birth; may hinder or deprive a child of inheriting from his legal parents should a legal parent die intestate before a postbirth action could determine parentage; may hinder or deprive a child from collecting Social Security benefits under 42 U.S.C. §402(d) (Supp. 1999); and may result in undesirable support obligations as well as

---

9. This conclusion takes into account a fact apparently overlooked by the plaintiffs, namely, that a hospital's reporters do not "issue" birth certificates. Rather, they furnish certain information pursuant to G. L. c. 46, §§1, 3, 3A, including the identity of the "parents" of the child born, which, in turn, is used by city and town clerks to "record" a complete "return of birth," which is commonly known as a person's birth certificate, see G. L. c. 46, §§1, 3, 3A, 4A. City or town clerks, the Commissioner of Public Health, or the State Registrar of Vital Records and Statistics may then furnish or "issue" a certified copy of the birth record to a parent. See G. L. c. 46, §§2A, 19, 19B, 19C.

custody disputes (potentially more likely in situations where the child is born with congenital malformations or anomalies, or medical disorders and diseases). . . . Our holding provides that such consequences, at least in some circumstances, can be minimized or avoided, thus furnishing a measure of stability and protection to children born through such gestational surrogacy arrangements. See E.N.O. v. L.M.M., 711 N.E.2d 886 (Mass. 1999), cert. denied, 528 U.S. 1005 (1999) ("the court's duty as parens patriae necessitates that its equitable powers extend to protecting the best interests of children.").

[W]e suggested [in a previous case] that a protocol for these types of cases be established. Such a protocol becomes increasingly necessary as infertile couples, and others, take advantage of existing and emerging assisted reproductive technologies, and as children are conceived and born through these technologies. . . . While responding to some parentage issues arising through artificial insemination, see G. L. c. 46, §4B, the Legislature has not enacted laws to determine parentage of children born from other methods of reproductive technologies or assisted conception. The Legislature is the most suitable forum to deal with the questions involved in this case, and other questions as yet unlitigated, by providing a comprehensive set of laws that deal with the medical, legal, and ethical aspects of these practices. . . .

The judgment of dismissal is vacated. The preliminary injunction enjoining the hospital from complying with its statutory obligations for the children is dissolved. A judgment is to enter declaring the plaintiffs as the legal parents of the children and ordering the hospital, through its reporters, to place the plaintiffs' names on its "record[s] of birth" created pursuant to G. L. c. 46, §§1, 3, 3A, listing the plaintiffs as the mother and father, respectively, of the children.

So ordered.

Notes: Traditional and Gestational Surrogacy

1. *One Plus One Equals Three?* Do *R.R.* and *Culliton* give consistent treatment to the legal "weight" of genetic parenthood and gestational parenthood? The modern approach is to treat egg donation and sperm donation as equivalent legal acts with equivalent consequences. See supra at page 562. A gamete donor is thus legally permitted to terminate his or her parental rights at the time of the donation. According to *Culliton,* a gestational surrogate may also enter into a binding agreement to forgo whatever parental rights she might have before the birth of the child. What prevents an egg donor who is also a gestational surrogate from entering into a binding agreement to forgo her parental rights? Why does the *R.R.* court turn instead to the laws governing adoption for standards to be applied in traditional surrogacy cases?

Perhaps the distinction is that the parties in *Culliton* sought an agreed court order and there was no dispute that required a court to weigh the gestational surrogate's interests. See Steven H. Snyder & Mary Patricia Byrn, The Use of Prebirth Parentage Orders in Surrogacy Proceedings, 39 Fam. L.Q. 633 (2005). The *Culliton* court notes the gestational carrier's agreement. The New Jersey courts have struggled with the framework for gestational surrogacy, finding in a 2011 case that state law permits a declaration of maternity to a biologically or gestationally related woman and not to the intended nonbiological, nongestational intended mother. In re T.J.S., 16 A.3d 386 (N.J. Super. Ct. 2011) (intended mother not entitled to declaration of maternity; differential treatment of infertile husband and infertile wife under Parentage Act does not violate equal protection), aff'd, 54 A.3d 263 (N.J. 2012) (affirmed by equally divided court with per curiam and dissenting opinions). See also Kate Zernike, Court's Split Decision Provides Little Clarity on Surrogacy, N.Y. Times, Oct. 24, 2012.

Is there a legal or ethical basis for reaching a different result if the gestational carrier does not agree? In Johnson v. Calvert, 851 P.2d 776 (Cal. 1993) (en banc), cert. denied, 510 U.S. 874 (1993), cert. dismissed by Baby Boy J. v. Johnson, 510 U.S. 938 (1993), the California Supreme Court rejected a claim by a gestational surrogate that she should be recognized as the mother of the resulting child and given visitation privileges. The court found that state laws addressing the determination of maternity were ambiguous and held that the original intent of the parties should determine the outcome:

> Because two women each have presented acceptable proof of maternity, we do not believe this case can be decided without enquiring into the parties' intentions as manifested in the surrogacy agreement. . . . Mark and Crispina are a couple who desired to have a child of their own genetic stock but are physically unable to do so without the help of reproductive technology. . . . The parties' aim was to bring Mark's and Crispina's child into the world, not for Mark and Crispina to donate a zygote to Anna. . . . No reason appears why Anna's later change of heart should vitiate the determination that Crispina is the child's natural mother.
>
> We conclude that although the Act recognizes both genetic consanguinity and giving birth as means of establishing a mother and child relationship, when the two means do not coincide in one woman, she who intended to procreate the child — that is, she who intended to bring about the birth of a child that she intended to raise as her own — is the natural mother under California law. . . .

851 P.2d at 782. The court rejected Anna's claim that the surrogacy contract violated public policy, noting that gestational surrogacy is distinguishable from adoption and that public policy favored giving women the same right to enter into contracts as men. See also The Practice Committee of the ASRM, Recommendations for Practices Utilizing Gestation Carriers: An ASRM Practice Committee Guideline, 97 Fertility & Sterility 1301 (2012); Noa Ben-Asher, The Curing Law: On the Evolution of Baby-Making Markets, 30 Cardozo L. Rev. 1885 (2009) (critiquing the distinction between gestational and traditional surrogacy); Todd M. Krim, Beyond Baby M: International Perspectives on Gestational Surrogacy and the Demise of the Unitary Biological Mother, 5 Ann. Health L. 193 (1996). The end result in practice is that infertile couples split the biological and legal transactions into two parts by using an egg donor and a different gestational surrogate. See, e.g., Raftopol v. Ramey, 12 A.3d 783 (Conn. 2011) (gestational carrier does not have parental rights to child; domestic partner who was intended co-parent in valid gestational agreement gains status without separate adoption proceeding); J.F. v. D.B., 879 N.E.2d 740 (Ohio 2007) (gestational surrogacy contract prohibiting gestational surrogate with no genetic connection to child from asserting parental rights does not violate public policy).

Some women who are incapable of producing suitable ova may seek to bear and rear children created with donor ova. In this circumstance, the parties intend that the gestational mother serve as the legal mother, even though she has no genetic relationship with the child. The physical arrangements in these two situations are similar (woman gives birth to a child with whom she has no genetic relationship), but the parties' preliminary intentions differ. How should the courts treat disputes arising out of these arrangements? Note that the 2002 UPA contains the presumption, found in most state laws, that a woman who gives birth to a child is the child's mother. UPA §201(a)(1) (2002). The Act also includes alternate provisions applicable in states that permit gestational surrogacy. Id. §201(a)(1), (4). In addition, the UPA provides that mechanisms for challenging paternity may also be used to challenge maternity. Id. §106; see also Soos v. Superior Court, County of Maricopa, 897 P.2d 1356 (Ariz. Ct. App. 1995) (statute that allowed biological father to prove paternity while denying genetic mother that right violates equal protection clause). Does this provision lessen the maternal security of an intended mother who gives birth to a baby produced from a donor egg? Could the woman argue that she did not "donate" the egg? See supra at page 563 n.2.

The Tennessee Supreme Court considered a case questioning the legal status of a woman who gave birth to triplets who had been conceived using IVF, donor eggs, and her male partner's sperm. In re C.K.G., 173 S.W.3d 714 (Tenn. 2005). The woman sought custody of the children when the couple separated. Her former partner objected, asserting that the woman was not the mother or a legal parent of the children because she was merely a gestational surrogate who has no genetic or legally enforceable tie to the children. The trial court held that the woman was the birth mother and legal mother; the appeals court affirmed using the intent of the parties as the legally relevant test, see Johnson v. Calvert, supra. The Tennessee Supreme Court affirmed that the woman was the legal mother on different grounds. The court rejected the intent test as straying too far from Tennessee's statutory framework and the genetics test because it would reach unintended results in cases involving egg donors. 173 S.W.3d at 724-725. The court instead adopted a "narrow" ruling limited to the specific facts and focusing on several factors: genetics, intent, gestation, and the "absence of controversy between the gestator and the genetic 'mother.'" Based on its analysis of these factors, the court decided that the woman who gave birth to the triplets was the legal mother and entitled to share custody with the genetic father. Id. at 730.

2. *Constitutional Considerations.* How does the right to procreate apply to surrogacy arrangements? Does the Massachusetts court in *R.R.* consider whether infertile couples have a constitutionally protected interest in the enforcement of their surrogacy arrangement? In *Baby M*, the court considered and rejected the genetic father's constitutional claims:

> Both parties argue that the Constitutions—state and federal—mandate approval of their basic claims. The source of their constitutional arguments is essentially the same: the right of privacy, the right to procreate, the right to the companionship of one's child, those rights flowing either directly from the Fourteenth Amendment or by its incorporation of the Bill of Rights, or from the Ninth Amendment, or through the penumbra surrounding all of the Bill of Rights. They are the rights of personal intimacy, of marriage, of sex, of family, of procreation. . . . The right asserted by the Sterns is the right of procreation; that asserted by Mary Beth Whitehead is the right to the companionship of her child. We find that the right of procreation does not extend as far as claimed by the Sterns. . . . The right to procreate very simply is the right to have natural children, whether through sexual intercourse or artificial insemination. It is no more than that. Mr. Stern has not been deprived of that right.

Through artificial insemination of Mrs. Whitehead, Baby M is his child. The custody, care, companionship, and nurturing that follow birth are not parts of the right to procreation; they are rights that may also be constitutionally protected, but that involve many considerations other than the right of procreation. . . .

Mrs. Whitehead, on the other hand, asserts a claim that falls within the scope of a recognized fundamental interest protected by the Constitution. As a mother, she claims the right to the companionship of her child. This is a fundamental interest, constitutionally protected. Furthermore, it was taken away from her by the action of the court below. Whether that action under these circumstances would constitute a constitutional deprivation, however, we need not and do not decide. By virtue of our decision Mrs. Whitehead's constitutional complaint—that her parental rights have been unconstitutionally terminated—is moot. . . .

In re Baby M, 537 A.2d 1227, 1253-1255 (N.J. 1988).

3. *Traditional Surrogacy Contracts.* Why does the *R.R.* court refuse to enforce the surrogacy contract? Is there a way to write an enforceable traditional surrogacy contract in Massachusetts? Are the factors the court suggests ones that a court or legislature should devise? Why does the court reject the surrogate's claim that the contract was unconscionable? What is the legal distinction between refusing to enforce a contract and declaring it unconscionable? See also A.L.S. ex rel. J.P. v. E.A.G., 2010 WL 4181449 (Minn. App. 2011) (traditional surrogate was legal and biological mother of resulting child).

What explains discomfort with surrogacy contracts? The development of private law in the nineteenth century can be viewed, under one theory, as the movement from status to contract. See H. Maine, Ancient Law (1939) (originally published in 1884). Many years before the development of doctrines tested on today's bar exams, an individual was born into a network of social relationships that established his or her legal rights and duties to others and to the state. This status-based idea of legal relationships is reflected in matters ranging in time from feudal law to the old law of master and servant to modern family law. Surrogacy contracts could be viewed as part of a continued assault on status-based law by contractarian principles. See, e.g., Janet L. Dolgin, Status and Contract in Surrogate Motherhood: An Illumination of the Surrogacy Debate, 38 Buff. L. Rev. 515 (1990).

Discomfort with traditional surrogacy arrangements is intertwined with concerns about economic exploitation. The *Baby M* court issued the classic statement regarding the need for courts to protect surrogates:

Intimated, but disputed, is the assertion that surrogacy will be used for the benefit of the rich at the expense of the poor. See, e.g., Radin, Market Inalienability, 100 Harv. L. Rev. 1849, 1930 (1987). In response it is noted that the Sterns are not rich and the Whiteheads not poor. Nevertheless, it is clear to us that it is unlikely that surrogate mothers will be as proportionately numerous among those women in the top 20 percent income bracket as among those in the bottom 20 percent. Ibid. Put differently, we doubt that infertile couples in the low-income bracket will find upper income surrogates. . . .

The point is made that Mrs. Whitehead agreed to the surrogacy arrangement, supposedly fully understanding the consequences. Putting aside the issue of how compelling her need for money may have been, and how significant her understanding of the consequences, we suggest that her consent is irrelevant. There are, in a civilized society, some things that money cannot buy. In America, we decided long ago that merely because conduct purchased by money was "voluntary" did not mean that it was good or beyond regulation and prohibition. West Coast Hotel Co. v. Parrish, 300 U.S. 379 (1937). Employers can no longer buy labor at the lowest price they can bargain for, even though that labor is "voluntary," 29 U.S.C. §206 (1982), or buy women's labor for less money than paid to men for the same job, 29 U.S.C. §206(d), or purchase the agreement of children to perform oppressive labor, 29 U.S.C. §212, or purchase the agreement of workers to subject themselves to unsafe or unhealthful working conditions, 29 U.S.C. §§651 to 678 (Occupational Safety and Health Act of 1970). There are, in short, values that society deems more important than granting to wealth whatever it can buy, be it labor, love, or life. . . .

The surrogacy contract is based on principles that are directly contrary to the objectives of our laws. It guarantees the separation of a child from its mother; it looks to adoption regardless of suitability; it totally ignores the child; it takes the child from the mother regardless of her wishes and her maternal fitness; and it does all of this, it accomplishes all of its goals, through the use of money.

Beyond that is the potential degradation of some women that may result from this arrangement. In many cases, of course, surrogacy may bring satisfaction, not only to the infertile couple, but to the surrogate mother herself. The fact, however, that many women may not perceive surrogacy negatively but rather see it as an opportunity does not diminish its potential for devastation to other women.

In sum, the harmful consequences of this surrogacy arrangement appear to us all too palpable. In New Jersey the surrogate mother's agreement to sell her child is void. Its irrevocability infects the entire contract, as does the money that purports to buy it. . . .

In re Baby M, 537 A.2d 1227, 1249-1250 (N.J. 1988). How would you describe the court's attitude toward women who wish to become surrogates? Empowering? Respectful? Paternalistic? Baby M's analysis of the evils of surrogacy can be compared with the pro-contract views of the proponents of law and economics and the views of some feminists. See, e.g., Lori Andrews, Beyond Doctrinal Boundaries: A Legal Framework for Surrogate Motherhood, 81 Virginia L. Rev. 2343 (1995); Richard Epstein, Surrogacy: The Case for Full Contractual Enforcement, 81 Va. L. Rev. 2305 (1995); Richard A. Posner, The Ethics and Economics of Enforcing Contracts of Surrogate Motherhood, 5 J. Contemp. Health L. & Pol'y 21, 31 (1989). See also Susan Frelich Appleton, Reproduction and Regret, 23 Yale J.L. & Feminism 257 (2011) (drawing together cases from abortion, surrogacy, and gamete donation).

4. *The 2002 UPA and Gestational Surrogacy.* Most states do not have legislation on surrogacy or have banned the practice. Are you surprised by this legislative response? Why have so many states prohibited surrogacy agreements? Note that a ban on surrogacy agreements is not technically a ban on surrogacy itself; the ban merely impedes the creation of enforceable agreements in which money is paid to the surrogate. While this undoubtedly has the effect of diminishing the business of surrogacy, surrogate arrangements are still possible between family members, for example, who are motivated by nonmonetary factors. Thirteen states specifically permit surrogacy under some circumstances. Darra L. Hofman, "Mama's Baby, Daddy's Maybe": A State-by-State Survey of Surrogacy Laws and Their Disparate Gender Impact, 35 Wm. Mitchell L. Rev. 449 (2009) (Arkansas, California, Florida, Illinois, Nevada, New Hampshire, New Jersey, North Dakota, Tennessee, Texas, Utah, Virginia, and Washington).

States that permit contractual arrangements typically limit their use to gestational surrogacy, where the surrogate has no genetic relationship with the resulting child. Are contractual models the appropriate mechanism for dealing with gestational disputes? What if major contractual terms were never decided by the parties—such as payment, visitation rights, and so forth? Should a court fill in these terms?

The revised UPA offers the choice of recognizing gestational surrogacy agreements as an alternative rather than as the uniform consensus approach:

§801. Gestational Agreement Authorized.

(a) A prospective gestational mother, her husband if she is married, a donor or the donors, and the intended parents may enter into a written agreement providing that:

(1) the prospective gestational mother agrees to pregnancy by means of assisted reproduction;

(2) the prospective gestational mother, her husband if she is married, and the donors relinquish all rights and duties as the parents of a child conceived through assisted reproduction; and

(3) the intended parents become the parents of the child.

(b) The man and the woman who are the intended parents must both be parties to the gestational agreement.

(c) A gestational agreement is enforceable only if validated as provided in Section 803.

(d) A gestational agreement does not apply to the birth of a child conceived by means of sexual intercourse.

(e) A gestational agreement may provide for payment of consideration.

(f) A gestational agreement may not limit the right of the gestational mother to make decisions to safeguard her health or that of the embryos or fetus. . . .

§803. Hearing to Validate Gestational Agreement.

(a) If the requirements of subsection (b) are satisfied, a court may issue an order validating the gestational agreement and declaring that the intended parents will be the parents of a child born during the term of the agreement.

(b) The court may issue an order under subsection (a) only on finding that:

(1) the residence requirements of Section 802 have been satisfied and the parties have submitted to the jurisdiction of the court under the jurisdictional standards of this [Act];

(2) unless waived by the court, the [relevant child-welfare agency] has made a home study of the intended parents and the intended parents meet the standards of fitness applicable to adoptive parents;

(3) all parties have voluntarily entered into the agreement and understand its terms;

(4) adequate provision has been made for all reasonable health-care expense associated with the gestational agreement until the birth of the child, including responsibility for those expenses if the agreement is terminated; and

(5) the consideration, if any, paid to the prospective gestational mother is reasonable.

§806. Termination of Gestational Agreement.

(a) After issuance of an order under this [article], but before the prospective gestational mother becomes pregnant by means of assisted reproduction, the prospective gestational mother, her husband, or either of the intended parents may terminate the gestational agreement by giving written notice of termination to all other parties.

(b) The court for good cause shown may terminate the gestational agreement.

(c) An individual who terminates a gestational agreement shall file notice of the termination with the court. On receipt of the notice, the court shall vacate the order issued under this [article]. An individual who does not notify the court of the termination of the agreement is subject to appropriate sanctions.

(d) Neither a prospective gestational mother nor her husband, if any, is liable to the intended parents for terminating a gestational agreement pursuant to this section.

§807. Parentage Under Validated Gestational Agreement.

(a) Upon birth of a child to a gestational mother, the intended parents shall file notice with the court that a child has been born to the gestational mother within 300 days after assisted reproduction. Thereupon, the court shall issue an order:

(1) confirming that the intended parents are the parents of the child;

(2) if necessary, ordering that the child be surrendered to the intended parents; and

(3) directing the [agency maintaining birth records] to issue a birth certificate naming the intended parents as parents of the child. . . .

(c) If the intended parents fail to file notice required under subsection (a), the gestational mother or the appropriate State agency may file notice with the court that a child has been born to the gestational mother within 300 days after assisted reproduction. Upon proof of a court order issued pursuant to Section 803 validating the gestational agreement, the court shall order the intended parents are the parents of the child and are financially responsible for the child.

§809. Effect of Nonvalidated Gestational Agreement.

(a) A gestational agreement, whether in a record or not, that is not judicially validated is not enforceable.

(b) If a birth results under a gestational agreement that is not judicially validated as provided in this [article], the parent-child relationship is determined as provided in [Article] 2.

(c) Individuals who are parties to a nonvalidated gestational agreement as intended parents may be held liable for support of the resulting child, even if the agreement is otherwise unenforceable. The liability under this subsection includes assessing all expenses and fees. . . .

The UPA offers a strong judicial review model for gestational surrogacy arrangements. Note the many terms and conditions placed on the gestational surrogacy contract. Are any of the requirements ethically or legally dubious? Should a gestational surrogate have the same right to freely make an abortion decision as other pregnant women? See Kevin Yamamoto & Shelby A. D. Moore, A Trust Analysis of a Gestational Carrier's Right to Abortion, 70 Fordham L. Rev. 93 (2001). What is the practical effect of §809?

The UPA is but one of several model approaches. The ABA Model Act (2008) also offers two options for gestational surrogacy: judicial preauthorization or "administrative" guidelines for determining the enforceability of the agreement. See, e.g., Christine Metteer Lorillard, Informed Choices and Uniform Decisions: Adopting the ABA's Self-Enforcing Administrative Model to Ensure Successful Surrogacy Arrangements, 16 Cardozo J.L. & Gender 237 (2010); Kristine S. Knaplund, Children of Assisted Reproduction, 45 U. Mich. J.L. Reform 899 (2012) (comparing UPA and UPC surrogacy provisions).

Challenges to state surrogacy legislation are relatively rare. In J.R. v. Utah, 261 F. Supp. 2d 1268 (2003), the court found that the plaintiffs had standing to challenge a portion of the then-applicable state law that prevented them from establishing that they were the legal parents of twins born as a result of a gestational surrogacy agreement. Utah's UPA now authorizes certain gestational agreements. Utah Code Ann. §78B-15-801.

5. *Surrogacy and Intentional Parenting.* In In re Buzzanca, a California court considered the impact of assisted reproduction involving a donated embryo and a gestational surrogate. 72 Cal. Rptr. 2d 280 (Ct. App. 1998). Luanne and John Buzzanca agreed to create a child by using a donor embryo implanted into a gestational surrogate. John filed for divorce shortly before the birth of Jaycee. John alleged that the couple did not have children; Luanne contended that they were expecting their first child from the surrogate. Id. at 282. The surrogate did not want to parent the child. The trial court found that Jaycee did not have any parents. Id. at 283. The appellate court rejected this conclusion, finding that the AI statute applied to both intended parents and that John became Jaycee's father by causing the child's conception. Id. at 284-288, 292. The intent of the parties was only relevant to a point, however, as John was barred from asserting that Luanne had promised to assume responsibility for Jaycee's care. Id. at 292. See also Doe v. Doe, 710 A.2d 1297 (Conn. 1998) (nonbiological mother given custody of child conceived as a result of a surrogacy arrangement in which her husband's sperm had been used to impregnate a third party) (modified by CGS §7-48a "each birth certificate shall be filed with the name of the birth mother recorded. If the birth is subject to a gestational agreement, the Department of Public Health shall create a replacement certificate in accordance with an order from a court of competent jurisdiction not later than forty-five days after receipt of such order or forty-five days after the birth of the child, whichever is later.").

6. *Tort Law Implications of Surrogacy Arrangements.* What tort claims might arise from these arrangements? Could the parents in *R.R.* sue the fertility clinic or psychologist for failure to appropriately screen surrogates for latent traditionally maternal instincts? What would be the damages? Could the fertility clinic be liable if a child from a surrogacy arrangement is born with a genetic defect? See Summer James et al., Avoiding Legal Pitfalls in Surrogacy Arrangements, 21 Reproductive BioMedicine 862 (2010) (reviewing legal issues for endocrinologists).

7. *Womb Transplants.* Uterus transplants may provide an alternative to gestational surrogacy for some women. Arthur L. Caplan et al., Moving the Womb, 37(3)

Hastings Center Rep. 18 (May-June 2007). What are the advantages and disadvantages of this approach? The uterus can be obtained from deceased donors much like other organs. Should a live donor be permitted to gift a uterus, perhaps after a vigorous informed consent process that includes explicit recognition that the donor will no longer be able to gestate a child? Womb transplants impose significant surgical risks on the recipient, including the need to take immunosuppressive drugs and the risk of rejection. Fetuses carried in the transplanted uterus would also be exposed to additional risk. Should these risks be considered "unnecessary" because of the available alternative of surrogacy? Id. Mats Brännström et al., Uterus Transplantation: Animal Research and Human Possibilities, 97 Fertility & Sterility 1269 (2012); Ivo Brosens et al., Uterus Transplantation in the Human: A Complex Surgical, Medical and Ethical Challenge, 28 Human Reproduction 292 (2013); Roger G. Gosden, Ovary and Uterus Transplantation, 136 Reproduction 671 (2008) (reviewing advances supporting potential for transplantation); Giuseppe Del Priore et al., Uterine Transplantation—A Real Possibility? The Indianapolis Consensus, 28 Human Reproduction 288 (2013); David Orentlicher, Toward Acceptance of Uterus Transplants, 42 Hastings Center Rep. 12 (2012); Roni Rabin, Prospect of Womb Transplant Raises Hopes and Red Flags, N.Y. Times, Jan. 1, 2007, at F5. For a discussion of the role of artificial wombs in debates about abortion and surrogacy, see Jennifer S. Hendricks, Not of Woman Born: A Scientific Fantasy, 623 Case W. Res. L. Rev. 399 (2011).

8. *Commentaries.* The surrogate motherhood controversy has generated profuse commentary in legal, medical, philosophical, and popular journals. In addition to the books and articles cited above, see Margaret Friedlander Brinig, A Maternalistic Approach to Surrogacy, 81 Va. L. Rev. 2377 (1995); R. Alta Charo, And Baby Makes Three—or Four, or Five, or Six: Redefining the Family After the Reprotech Revolution, 15 Wis. Women's L.J. 231 (2000); Rachel Cook et al. eds., Surrogate Motherhood: International Perspectives (2003); Janet L. Dolgin, An Emerging Consensus: Reproductive Technology and the Law, 23 Vt. L. Rev. 225 (1998); Janet L. Dolgin, Choice, Tradition, and the New Genetics: The Fragmentation of the Ideology of Family, 32 Conn. L. Rev. 523 (2000); Helene S. Shapo, Assisted Reproduction and the Law: Disharmony on a Socially Divisive Issue, 100 Nw. U. L. Rev. 465 (2006); Molly J. Walker Wilson, Precommitment in Free-Market Procreation: Surrogacy, Commissioned Adoption, and Limits on Human Decision Making Capacity, 31 J. Legis. 329 (2005); see also Danny R. Veilleux, Annot., Validity and Construction of Surrogate Parenting Agreement, 77 A.L.R.4th 70 (1989).

Problems: Determining Parentage

The explosive growth of reproductive technologies creates an almost bewildering array of parenting possibilities. The statutes and cases in this section demonstrate that the rules governing the determination of parentage are still in flux. The most established technology—AI or IUI—is regulated by statutes that attempt to allocate parenting rights and responsibilities. Consumers of donated sperm nonetheless confront some legal uncertainties. Technologies designed to provide the female components of the reproductive process—eggs and a uterus—are less well regulated, and significant areas of legal uncertainty still remain. States appear to be moving toward treating egg donation as the equivalent of sperm donation. See 2002 UPA. Conflicts over the disposition of frozen embryos also can be difficult to resolve, with courts suggesting that they will enforce the prior agreements of progenitors but balking at the imposition of parenthood on a presently unwilling individual. Gestational surrogates appear to have fewer legally protected interests than traditional surrogates (in which both egg and uterus are provided by one donor). The state of legal confusion, however, does not prevent these transactions from going forward. Consumers and sellers of reproductive services, and their lawyers, attempt to meet the objectives of the parties within whatever legal framework is available. A poor use of reproductive technology can result in substantial emotional and financial costs for the participants, as well as in professional disciplinary or malpractice liability for the health care providers and attorneys. See generally Linda S. Anderson, Adding Players to the Game: Parentage Determinations When Assisted Reproductive Technology Is Used to Create Families, 62 Ark. L. Rev. 29 (2009).

1. *Sperm Donation and IUI.* Assume you are in a jurisdiction that has adopted the 2002 version of UPA's provisions governing gamete donation (see pages 561, 563). Melissa and Julie wish to have and raise a child together. Their friend, David, volunteers to provide sperm that will be used to artificially inseminate Julie. How should the transaction be structured to ensure that David will not have any parental rights and obligations? How could the parties use IUI and ensure that David will be considered to be the resulting child's legal father? Will Melissa have any legally recognized relationship with the child? Could such a relationship be created?

2. *Egg Donation and Surrogacy.* Latisha and Michael Bates have been married for eight years. Pregnancy and/or the hormonal treatments necessary for egg harvesting would injure Latisha's health. The couple still wants very much to have a child, preferably one that is genetically related to Michael. They have heard about surrogacy arrangements and would like to hire a surrogate to bear their child. Assume you are in a jurisdiction with laws like those in Massachusetts. Could the Bateses enter into a surrogacy agreement with their neighbor, Paula? What should be the terms? Will the agreement be enforceable? What type of compensation, if any, will the Bateses be able to give Paula? Who will be the parents of the resulting child? Can the parties do anything to ensure that Latisha and Michael will be considered to be the parents?

Now assume that the Bateses make a separate arrangement with an egg donor, Ala Truistic, whose egg would be fertilized with Michael's sperm and implanted in Paula's uterus for gestation. Could Ala be paid any compensation for undergoing the procedures necessary for egg donation? Could Paula be compensated for enduring the pregnancy? Who would be the mother? Consider this question first based under the Massachusetts cases, supra at pages 581-590. Then consider the 2002 UPA approach. Who would be considered to be the legal parents of any resulting child?

Suppose that Ala donates several eggs that are fertilized with Michael's sperm. The eggs are donated pursuant to a written agreement that provides that Ala is donating the eggs "for use by Michael and Latisha Bates, a married couple, for use in raising the resulting child in a loving home." Latisha files for divorce from Michael after the eggs are fertilized and the resulting embryos are frozen but before implantation into Paula. Suppose that Ala now wants to control the disposition of the frozen embryos on the theory that the donation contract has been breached.

Could you make any arguments on her behalf? Suppose that Michael wants to control the disposition of the embryos on the theory that Ala's ability to exercise reproductive choices ended with her donation?

3. *Reproductive Tourism.* Kerry and Chris are married and would like to obtain donor eggs and sperm and the services of a surrogate to bear a child for them. Suppose your clients live in a state that has prohibited surrogacy. Kerry and Chris have heard that low-cost surrogacy services are available in India and have asked your advice about any legal, ethical, or social concerns with pursuing their family objectives in India. How would you advise your clients? Would your advice be the same if your clients lived in California, which permits gestational surrogacy agreements that meet certain criteria, including separate legal representation for each party? See Ann. Cal. Fam. Code §7962 (2013). See generally sources cited supra at page 555 n.5 on reproductive tourism; Erica Davis, The Rise of Gestational Surrogacy and the Pressing Need for International Regulation, 21 Minn. J. Int'l L. 120 (2012) (discussing cross-border regulatory issues and risk of stateless, parentless children); Leora I. Gabry, Procreating Without Pregnancy: Surrogacy and the Need for a Comprehensive Regulatory Scheme, 45 Colum. J.L. & Soc. Probs. 415, 439-442 (2012) (summarizing economic and legal aspects of Indian surrogacy market); Molly McDonough, Prominent Lawyer Pleads Guilty in Baby-Selling Ring, ABA Journal, Aug. 10, 2011; J. Brad Reich & Dawn Swink, Outsourcing Human Reproduction: Embryos and Surrogacy Services in the Cyberprocreative Era, 14 J. Health Care L. & Pol'y 241 (2011); France: Surrogacy Ban Affirmed, N.Y. Times, Apr. 7, 2011 (French court rejects French citizenship for girls born to U.S. surrogate mother on behalf of French couple).

E. ETHICAL AND LEGAL IMPLICATIONS OF ADVANCES IN GENETICS

1. Introduction

The fifth and final section of the chapter explores the legal implications of advances in genetics and the regulation of genetic technologies. In some senses these advances have already played a significant role in the chapter's coverage of reproduction: advances in understanding heredity and genetics undercut the scientific foundation for the eugenics theories underlying the laws challenged in Buck v. Bell, supra at page 463, and Skinner v. Oklahoma, supra at page 465. Genetic testing provides the technical capacity for parents to identify the sex of a fetus and to learn whether the fetus has certain genetic anomalies; the woman carrying the fetus may decide to abort based on the results of these tests. See page 487. The process greatly increases the possibility of using genetic information to shape offspring. This can be seen in Internet Web sites for sperm and egg donors, which appear to offer recipients the ability to select donors based on characteristics commonly understood to have a genetic component such as height, hair and eye color, and intelligence. IVF provides an even more direct opportunity to perform genetic testing on the preembryos and to use the results to determine which embryos will be selected for transplantation. Genetic testing can be used to screen for disabling genetic conditions as well as to select for some characteristics, see pages 182-183.

The final section of this chapter will focus more directly on the implications of scientific discoveries in this area. Should cloning and related procedures be allowed for reproductive, research, or therapeutic purposes? Should scientists be permitted to patent life forms and genes? How should society balance the positive incentives created from intellectual property ownership rules with the need to ensure equitable access to important new developments?

2. Human Stem Cell Research

As noted supra at page 519, federal and state governments have struggled with the ethical and legal implications of research involving certain types of stem cells that are derived from human embryos. Understanding the debate requires familiarity with some basic biology. The human body contains hundreds of different types of specialized cells capable of performing different functions. Heart muscle cells, nerve cells (neurons), and liver cells all perform different functions. Certain types of stem cells are "undifferentiated" (they have not yet become specialized cells), "pluripotent" (they have the capacity to become any type of specialized cell), and "self-replicating" (they can replicate in a proper laboratory setting). Stem cells can be found in all stages of human development from embryos (up to about seven weeks of development), fetuses (from the eighth week of development to birth), children, and adults.

There are several uses for stem cells. At a basic level, researchers hope to use stem cells to understand more about the process by which stem cells are able to differentiate into one of hundreds of specialized cells in the human body. Once more is understood about this process, it is possible that researchers will be able to develop clinical uses for stem cells by, for example, using stem cells to generate differentiated cells that could be used to replace heart muscle injured in a heart attack, nerve cells for those who have suffered spinal cord injuries, or insulin-producing cells for persons with diabetes. Stem cell research thus offers the tantalizing possibility of enormous tangible benefits to persons suffering from cardiovascular disease, diabetes, or spinal cord injuries, along with other conditions. Researchers hope that mastery of the process of cellular differentiation, combined with a ready supply of human stem cells, could halt or reverse the progress of these diseases. See U.S. Department of Health and Human Services, Regenerative Medicine, at http://stemcells.nih.gov/info/Regenerative_Medicine/. However, there are significant questions about the clinical use of pluripotent stem cells, including concerns about increased cancer risks. Riikka J. Lund et al., Genetic and Epigenetic Stability of Human Pluripotent Stem Cells, 13 Nature Reviews Genetics 732 (2012).

One specific type of stem cell research is tied to the ongoing debates about cloning and to the destruction of embryos. The use of ordinary stem cells for treatment could give rise to an immune reaction in the recipient of the stem cells, as the body will treat the cells as foreign matter. One way to avoid this reaction involves using somatic cell nuclear transplantation (often referred to as SCNT in the scientific literature). This technique involves taking the genetic materials from a somatic cell[2] from the intended recipient and transplanting this material into an oocyte

---

2. Somatic cells are ordinary cells from the body containing a full complement of genes as opposed to germ-line cells (sperm and egg cells), which contain only half of a person's genes.

(a human egg cell) that has had its original genetic material removed. The oocyte is then manipulated into beginning the process of cell division and the creation of an embryo. The embryo will contain stem cells that could be extracted and used to create specialized cells that would no longer be viewed as foreign by the recipient and thus would not create the risk of tissue rejection and the need for the recipient to take immune-suppressing drugs. This procedure is known as "therapeutic" cloning because, as in reproductive cloning, an embryo is created with virtually the same genetic identity as another human being.[3] Therapeutic cloning is different from reproductive cloning because the resulting embryo is never implanted in a uterus with the hope of producing a human being; instead the goal is to provide a therapeutic treatment using embryonic stem cells. The following diagram compares natural reproduction, therapeutic cloning, and reproductive cloning:

Diagram 1: Normal Reproduction, Reproductive Cloning, and Therapeutic Cloning[4]

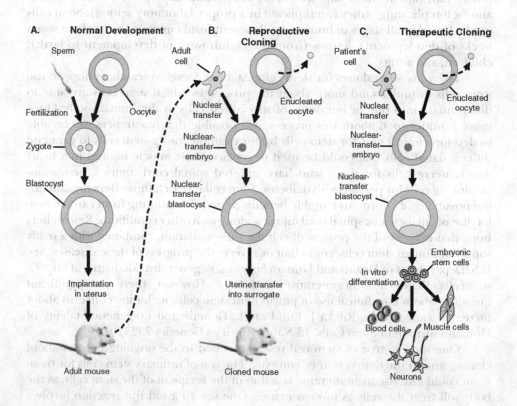

3. The cloned embryo will not be completely identical because the genetic material found in the oocyte's mitochondria is not removed; mitochondrial DNA from the donor oocyte therefore will be reproduced in the embryo.

4. Adapted from Konrad Hochedlinger & Rudolf Jaenisch, Nuclear Transplantation, Embryonic Stem Cells, and the Potential for Cell Therapy, 349 New Eng. J. Med. 275 (2003).

Stem cell research involving human embryonic stem cells provokes debates about fetal interests. To those who believe that personhood begins at the union of a sperm and egg, research using embryonic stem cells involves the sacrifice of human life for scientific progress. Furthermore, the successful development of treatments using embryonic stem cells might require the commercialized production and exploitation of human embryos. The use of embryonic stem cells implicates strongly held views regarding the status of embryos and fetuses and the degree to which they command special respect and concern. Many ethicists and others object to the creation of potential human life solely for the purpose of producing stem cells. Many also object to the extraction of stem cells from embryos or fetuses originally created for other purposes, such as through ordinary pregnancy or the use of in vitro fertilization, even if the potential for human life will never be realized because of a woman's right to choose to terminate her pregnancy or because embryos created for assisted human reproduction are no longer needed for this purpose.

Embryonic stem cells have been easier to harvest and considered more likely to be pluripotent than adult stem cells. See generally National Institutes of Health, Stem Cell Information, available at http://stemcells.nih.gov. Embryonic stem cell research has expanded worldwide over the past decade and the first clinical trials of related therapies are now under way. Uri Ben-David et al., Expanding the Boundaries of Embryonic Stem Cells, 10 Cell Stem Cell 666 (2012) (summarizing breadth of research projects around the world).

Researchers have developed a third approach to generating human stem cells that might be used for clinical therapies without the risk of generating an immune response. Researchers begin with cells from adults, resetting differentiated cells to create induced pluripotent stem cells that have properties similar to embryonic stem cells. Praschant Mali & Linzhao Cheng, Concise Review: Human Cell Engineering: Cellular Reprogramming and Genome Editing, 30 Stem Cells 75 (2012). It is not yet clear whether induced pluripotent stem cells can produce the same potential benefits as embryonic stem cells. See Josipa Bilic & Juan Carlos Izpisua Belmonte, Concise Review: Induced Pluripotent Stem Cells Versus Embryonic Stem Cells: Close Enough or Yet Too Far Apart?, 30 Stem Cells 33 (2012); Mira C. Puri & Andras Nagy, Concise Review: Embryonic Stem Cells Versus Induced Pluripotent Stems Cells: The Game Is On, 30 Stem Cells 10 (2012).

The federal debate about human stem cell research has focused on funding for research involving embryonic stem cells. Federal law "prohibits NIH from funding '(1) the creation of a human embryo or embryos for research purposes; or (2) research in which a human embryo or embryos are destroyed, discarded, or knowingly subjected to risk of injury or death greater than that allowed for research on fetuses in utero under 45 C.F.R. 46.204(b) and [42 U.S.C. §289g(b)].'" Sherley v. Sebelius, 689 F.3d 776, 779 (D.C. Cir. 2012) (quoting the Dickey-Wicker Amendment inserted by Congress into appropriations bills since 2006). This language leaves open the question of whether federal funding could be used for research involving embryonic stem cells so long as the specific research project does not involve the destruction of human embryos. Id.

In 2001, President Bush authorized federal funding for research involving embryonic stem cells so long as the cell lines were already in existence at the time of the announcement and were derived from embryos originally created for use in assisted reproduction but were no longer going to be used for this purpose. Exec. Order No.

13,435, 72 Fed. Reg. 34,591 (2007) (formalizing 2001 policy announcement). Stem cell research remained a sensitive political issue through the decade, driven in part by public pleas for expansions in governmental funding from prominent individuals such as Christopher Reeve, an actor paralyzed in a riding accident; Michael J. Fox, an actor with Parkinson's disease; and former First Lady Nancy Reagan, whose husband, former President Ronald Reagan, eventually died from Alzheimer's disease.

The federal funding debate during the 2000s sparked a parallel debate in the states. The gap in federal funding sparked concerns that important stem cell research projects and leading researchers might leave the United States for other, more hospitable jurisdictions around the world. Some argued that the United States might lose access to important and potentially lucrative scientific developments. Stem cell activists began to promote state funding of stem cell research as a method of ensuring that U.S. researchers could remain at the forefront of the field. Several states provided funding and support for stem cell research—including embryonic stem cell research—through successful voter or legislative initiatives. See, e.g., the Web site for the California Institute for Regenerative Medicine, established as the result of a voter initiative, at www.cirm.ca.gov; Institute of Medicine, The California Institute for Regenerative Medicine: Science, Governance, and the Pursuit of Cures (2012) (reviewing successes and challenges).

Given limited federal involvement in human stem cell-related research during much of the 2000s, other groups generated ethical guidelines and procedures governing the derivation and use of stem cells. See National Academies, Stem Cells at the Academies, (2010); and International Society for Stem Cell Research (ISSCR), Guidelines for the Conduct of Human Embryonic Stem Cell Research.

President Obama issued an executive order in 2009 permitting federal funding for research using stem cells from embryos where appropriate procedures and consents had been employed to develop the stem cells. Exec. Order 13,505, 74 Fed. Reg. 10,667 (2009). See also Joel B. Finkelstein, Change in Federal Stem Cell Funding Policy Spurs Interest in Field, 101 J. Natl. Cancer Inst. 626 (2009). The approach was reflected in new federal regulations. Guidelines for Human Stem Cell Research, 74 Fed. Reg. 32,170-02 (2009). See also Sherley v. Sebelius, 689 F.3d 776, 781 (D.C. Cir. 2012) (affirming "that NIH had reasonably interpreted Dickey-Wicker's ban on funding 'research in which . . . embryos are destroyed' to allow federal funding of ESC research").

The 2009 NIH regulations focus on defining the circumstances in which federal funding will be available for stem cell research. Federal funding still cannot be used to create new lines of embryonic stem cells under the Dickey-Wicker ban. Federal funding is available only for research involving embryonic stem cells derived from IVF embryos originally created for reproductive purposes. The NIH guidelines provide paths to possible federal funding for research using embryonic stem cells created before or after the development of the federal guidelines, within or outside the United States. Ethical guidelines developed by other groups, such as the National Academies, retain their importance in the wide range of areas outside the ambit of federal funding and oversight, including the creation of the embryonic stem cells lines themselves, the use of embryonic stem cells from embryos created for research purposes (rather than for IVF), the creation of induced pluripotent human stem cells, and the use of human stem cells in various forms of non-federally funded research.

Notes: Human Stem Cell Research

1. *Resources on Stem Cell Research.* Stem cell research has attracted an enormous amount of commentary from individuals and specialized, expert committees or groups. For more information about stem cell research and the implications for law and ethics see, e.g., Symposium, 38 J.L., Med. & Ethics 175-351 (2010); Stem Cell Symposium, 9 Yale J. Health Pol'y L. & Ethics 483-622 (2009); Russell Korobkin, Stem Cell Century: Law and Policy for a Breakthrough Technology (2009) (with contributions from Stephen R. Munzer); and the National Academies and ISSCR Web sites noted above.

2. *The Destruction of Pre-Existing Embryos Originally Created for Reproductive Purposes.* Many existing stem cell lines were derived from very early embryos, more scientifically known as morulae or blastocysts, originally created as a part of assisted human reproduction but no longer needed for that purpose. The NIH guidelines squarely cover using human embryonic stem cells derived in this fashion for research. The guidelines developed by the National Academies provide overlapping guidance that is more prescriptive in some areas.

Should the "intended parents" of an embryo be required to consent to the use of the embryo even if it was created solely through the use of donor gametes? The answer is "yes" under both the NIH and National Academies guidelines. Should gamete donors be required to consent to the use of the resulting embryo in research? Consent from gamete donors is not specifically required under the NIH guidelines but is required under the National Academies approach. NIH Guidelines for Human Stem Cell Research, 74 Fed. Reg. 32170-02, 32173; National Academies, Guidelines for Human Embryonic Stem Cell Research (2010), supra, at 5 & Appendix C, §3.2, 3.3 (consent requirement met by simple written agreement that embryo research is one possible use of material). See also Ethics Committee of the ASRM, Donating Spare Embryos for Stem Cell Research, 91 Fertility & Sterility 667 (2009).

3. *The Creation of Embryos for Stem Cell Research.* The NIH guidelines do not apply to the creation of embryos for research purposes, and research involving embryonic stem cells derived from embryos created for research purposes is not eligible for federal funding. The NIH guidelines attempt to ensure that individuals who have created embryos for IVF are not paid or otherwise pressured to release the embryos for research. 74 Fed. Reg. 32170-02, 32174. What rules should apply outside the context of federally funded research? See, e.g., Sandra A. Caron et al., Proposed Oocyte Donation Guidelines for Stem Cell Research, 94 Fertility & Sterility 2503 (2010).

Compensation for human cells, blood, and tissues is controversial and sometimes prohibited entirely. See Chapter 4.B and Flynn v. Holder, 684 F.3d 852 (9th Cir. 2012) (holding that federal ban on compensation for bone marrow donations did not apply to blood stem cells obtained through peripheral blood stem cell apheresis). But, as noted, supra, at 562, gamete donors may be compensated. Oocyte donation is an invasive and potentially risky procedure. Is it unethical to ask women who will receive no direct medical or financial benefit to bear the risks of oocyte donation? See Russell Korobkin, Buying and Selling Human Tissues for Stem Cell Research, 49 Ariz. L. Rev. 45 (2007); Debora Spar, The Egg Trade—Making Sense of the Market for Human Oocytes, 356 New Eng. J. Med. 1289 (2007) (noting inconsistency in permitting payment to oocyte donors for reproduction but not for research). In 2009, the board charged with administering state funds for stem cell research in New York authorized payments to women donating oocytes for research that were comparable to the sums available to oocyte donors in assisted reproduction. Pamela Foohey, Paying Women for Their Eggs for Use in Stem Cell Research, 30 Pace L. Rev. 900 (2010). The National Academies' 2010 guidelines continued to prohibit direct payment to oocyte donors, while noting that "states and other entities may choose to set their own policies." National Academies, Guidelines for Human Embryonic Stem Cell Research (2010), supra, at 5.

4. *Regulating the Creation and Use of Induced Pluripotent Human Stem Cells.* The NIH Human Stem Cell Guidelines note that the ordinary rules governing research on human subjects, including informed consent, privacy protection, and Institutional Review Board oversight, might apply to research involving human adult stem cells or induced pluripotent stem cells. 74 Fed. Reg. 32174, see also Chapter 2.E. The NIH Human Stem Cell Guidelines do not focus on the specific informed consent provisions that should be used for donors of somatic cells that might be used to create human pluripotent stem cells. The National Academies' Guidelines suggest that the informed consent requirements should be the same as those used for donors in embryonic stem cell research. National Academies, Guidelines for Human Embryonic Stem Cell Research (2010), supra, at Appendix C, §3.6. For a sample consent, see Stanford University, Stem Cell Research Oversight, http://scro .stanford.edu/resources/forms_templates/index.html.

5. *Oversight vs. Regulation and the Creation of Chimeras.* Stem cell research could involve mixing human and animal cells, tissues, or genetic materials in new ways. This type of research often is described as the creation of human-animal hybrids or modern-day "chimeras," drawing on ancient Greek myths about monsters with attributes of humans and other animals. Federal regulation of stem cell research has been indirect rather than direct, using the incentive of federal funding to induce researchers toward some types of research and away from others and relying on the existing framework of human subjects research protection as a general safety net. Thus the federal regulations tie funding to certain informed consent requirements and prohibit federal funding of certain types of research, such as the introduction of human embryonic stem cells or induced pluripotent human stem cells into non-human primate blastocysts or "[r]esearch involving the breeding of animals . . . where the human stem cells might contribute" genetic material to the animal's offspring. 74 Fed. Reg. 32170-02, 32174. The National Academies' Guidelines include both procedural protections, such as the creation of institutional Embryonic Stem Cell Research Oversight Committees to review certain types of research, and outright prohibitions of certain forms of research, such as research that could introduce human neural tissue into animals or that could transmit human genes through breeding. National Academies, Guidelines for Human Embryonic Stem Cell Research (2010), supra, at Appendix C, §§1.3(b), 1.3(c), 6. These guidelines are voluntary. Should federal or state governments simply prohibit these types of research? See Ariz. Rev. Stat. Ann. §36-2311-2312.

6. *Therapeutic Cloning.* Part of the controversy surrounding therapeutic cloning arises from the fact that it involves the creation of embryos that are then destroyed to extract embryonic stem cells. Should the fact that the embryos are cloned create any additional ethical concerns? Is the line between therapeutic and reproductive

cloning as clear as Diagram 1 would suggest? The next section will explore the cloning debate in more detail.

3. Human Reproductive Cloning

Scientists reported the first successful reproductive cloning of a mammal early in 1997. Wilmut et al., Viable Offspring Derived from Fetal and Adult Mammalian Cells, 385 Nature 810 (1997). Reproductive cloning essentially involves the creation of a sort of time-delayed nearly identical twin. An ovum's nucleus is replaced by the nucleus of a mature adult cell that contains the core genetic identity of an individual being. The ovum is induced to divide and to produce living offspring that have virtually the same genetic identity as the donor of the original genetic material ("virtually," because cloning does not now involve the transfer of genetic material found outside the nucleus in the mitochondria. Cf. Anthony H. Shapira, Mitochondrial Diseases, 379 Lancet 1825 (2012); R. Sanders Williams, Another Surprise from the Mitochondrial Genome, 347 New Eng. J. Med. 609 (2002) (brief summary of knowledge regarding mitochondrial DNA)).

This is not the "cloning" of late-night science fiction films—a single cell does not grow in a laboratory and give rise to an adult being with the same memories and abilities as the original being. See Nancy L. Segal, Human Cloning: Insights from Twins and Twin Research, 53 Hastings L.J. 1073 (2002). Neither Hitler nor Gandhi could be absolutely replicated. But the development of mammalian cloning nonetheless raised the significant possibility that people might now be able to pass on their genetic heritage to future generations without engaging in the shuffling and mixing of genes that occurs in sexual reproduction. This could be an important tool for persons who do not have gametes or who cannot reproduce sexually within their relationships. David Orentlicher, Beyond Cloning: Expanding Reproductive Options for Same-Sex Couples, 66 Brook. L. Rev. 651 (2000-2001).

The immediate response to the birth of Dolly, the cloned sheep, was largely negative. President Bill Clinton announced that federal funds would not be used for human reproductive cloning research. The FDA reacted swiftly, asserting jurisdiction over clinical research using cloning technology for human reproduction in 1998. Researchers were warned not to pursue human reproductive cloning without following the FDA's investigational new drug (IND) regulations.

Commentators argued that research into human reproductive cloning should be banned for a number of reasons. Would cloning stifle the normal evolutionary process, which depends on new combinations of genes created through sexual reproduction? Would cloning encourage unduly egocentric reproduction—perhaps the creation of 50 genetic copies of a wealthy real estate developer or writer of health law casebooks? Would cloning encourage reproduction for profit—50 genetic copies of LeBron James or Bill Gates? Perhaps cloning would be used to create genetically identical persons who could provide "spare parts," such as organs or tissue for their creator. See, e.g., Human Cloning Requires a Moratorium, Not a Ban, 386 Nature 1 (1997); Elizabeth Pennisi & Nigel Williams, Will Dolly Send in the Clones?, 275 Science 1415 (1997). If nothing else, negative responses to the possibility of human reproductive cloning have revealed our fears about genetic determinism and our belief that "normal" reproduction represents something different—and better—than selfish egotism.

Scientific and ethical advisory boards weighed in on reproductive cloning in the early 2000s. See, e.g., President's Council on Bioethics, Human Cloning and Human Dignity: An Ethical Inquiry (2002); National Research Council, Scientific and Medical Aspects of Human Reproductive Cloning (2002) (focusing on medical risks that make the procedure unsafe for participants and offspring). These advisory groups uniformly recommended at least a moratorium if not a permanent ban on human cloning for reproduction. The virtual uniformity of views regarding the inadvisability of human cloning reflected the fact that mammalian cloning appeared to be extraordinarily difficult to achieve and to entail significant risks of genetic and other abnormalities. This raises the possibility that the debate may become less one sided if human cloning should ever become less medically risky. When and how would researchers determine the safety of human cloning if the practice is banned? See also The Ethics Committee of the ASRM, Human Somatic Cell Nuclear Transfer and Cloning, 98 Fertility & Sterility 804 (2012) (human reproductive cloning currently unethical due to medical risk and availability of alternative reproduction; noting difficulty of ethical analysis if safety concerns reduced in the future).

Congress considered banning reproductive cloning in the early 2000s but the proposed legislation stalled due to a clash between lawmakers who favored permitting therapeutic cloning and those who believed that therapeutic and reproductive cloning were indistinguishable misuses of human embryos. See, e.g., George J. Annas, Cloning and the U.S. Congress, 346 New Eng. J. Med. 1599 (2002). More than a dozen states have banned human reproductive cloning. National Conference of State Legislatures, Human Cloning Laws (updated to 2008) (available at NCSL Web site). The U.N. General Assembly adopted a nonbinding declaration urging nations to ban reproductive and therapeutic human cloning. United Nations Declaration on Human Cloning.

Notes: Human Reproductive Cloning

1. *Cloning as Procreation?* Reproductive cloning would produce a child who, from a genetic standpoint, would be similar to an identical twin of the genetic progenitor. From one genetic perspective, the child would not be the "child" of anyone, because reproduction involves the mixing of parental genes, not the duplication of those genes. Could you even develop an argument that the U.S. Constitution's protection of procreative liberty includes a right to cloning? See generally Robert A. Burt, Constitutional Constraints on the Regulation of Cloning, 9 Yale J. Health Pol'y L. & Ethics 495 (2009); John A. Robertson, Liberty, Identity, and Human Cloning, 76 Tex. L. Rev. 1371 (1998); Cass R. Sunstein, Is There a Constitutional Right to Clone?, 53 Hastings L.J. 987 (2002). What about the treatment of a cloned child under state law—to whom would the UPA assign parental rights?

2. *The Ethics of Cloning.* The President's Bioethics Advisory Council unanimously found that human reproductive cloning is unethical. President's Council Human Cloning Report ch. 5 (2002). The Council viewed human cloning as a particularly risky type of human experimentation in which it is impossible to obtain the consent of the party at the most risk, the cloned child. Unlike other groups,

the Council found that "safety is not a temporary ethical concern. It is rather an enduring moral concern that might not be surmountable and should thus preclude work toward the development of cloning techniques to produce children." Id. at 14. The President's Council identified several "specific ethical issues and objections to cloning human children: (1) problems of identity and individuality; (2) concerns regarding manufacture; (3) the prospects of a new eugenics; (4) troubled family relations; and (5) effects on society [through, e.g., permitting dehumanizing practices]." Id. at 18. How would you weigh these ethical objections? How many of them do you think apply to other uses of reproductive technology?

3. *Comparing Regulatory Regimes.* Several countries have enacted comprehensive legislation designed to address assisted reproductive technologies, embryo research, and cloning. Are there any lessons in this legislation for the United States? Canada's Assisted Human Reproduction Act, http://laws.justice.gc.ca/en/A-13.4/, prohibits germ-line engineering, the creation of chimeras, human reproductive cloning, sex selection unless it is being used to treat or prevent a sex-linked disease, and creation of human embryos solely for research, as well as payment of surrogates or payment for gametes. See also Barbara von Tigerstrom, Federal Health Legislation and the Assisted Human Reproduction Act Reference, 74 Sask. L. Rev. 33 (2011) (summarizing impact of Supreme Court of Canada decision on validity of legislation). The United Kingdom has had legislation in place since 1990. The Human Fertilization and Embryology Act creates the Human Fertilization and Embryology Authority, whose responsibilities include licensing ART clinics, gamete and embryo storage facilities, and licensing and monitoring human embryo research. Human reproductive cloning is prohibited but therapeutic cloning research is permitted. See www.hfea.gov.uk.

4. *Commentaries.* In addition to the sources noted above, see Ronald Chester, Cloning Embryos from Adult Human Beings: The Relative Merits of Reproductive, Research and Therapeutic Uses, 39 New Eng. L. Rev. 583 (2005); Rudolf Jaenisch, Human Cloning—The Science and Ethics of Nuclear Transplantation, 351 New Eng. J. Med. 2787 (2004); Leon R. Kass & James Q. Wilson, The Ethics of Human Cloning (1998); Symposium on Human Cloning: Legal, Social, and Moral Perspectives for the Twenty-First Century, 27 Hofstra L. Rev. 473-668 (1999).

Problem: Human Cloning

Your client, Chris Jacobs, wants to create a child through cloning. Chris is preparing to go to an unnamed foreign country where experts believe they have perfected the process. The nucleus from some of Chris's cells will be inserted into a donor's eggs, whose nuclei have been removed. The eggs will be stimulated into developing into embryos, which will then be implanted into a gestational surrogate. The surrogate will then relinquish the child to Chris. Chris hopes to be a parent within a year. How would you counsel Chris? Do you have any ethical, professional disciplinary, or malpractice concerns? Assume that Chris brings a child back to this country. How would you go about attempting to establish that Chris is the child's parent? Examine the relevant statutes in your state. Who is the child's parent? See also I. Glenn Cohen, Medical Tourism: The View from 10,000 Feet, 40(2) Hastings Center Rep. 11 (Mar.-Apr. 2010).

4. Intellectual Property and the Ownership of Genetic Discoveries

■ DIAMOND v. CHAKRABARTY
447 U.S. 303 (1980)

BURGER, C.J.

We granted certiorari to determine whether a live, human-made micro-organism is patentable subject matter under 35 U.S.C. §101.

In 1972, respondent Chakrabarty, a microbiologist, filed a patent application, assigned to the General Electric Co. The application asserted 36 claims related to Chakrabarty's invention of "a bacterium from the genus Pseudomonas containing therein at least two stable energy-generating plasmids, each of said plasmids providing a separate hydrocarbon degradative pathway."[5] This human-made, genetically engineered bacterium is capable of breaking down multiple components of crude oil. Because of this property, which is possessed by no naturally occurring bacteria, Chakrabarty's invention is believed to have significant value for the treatment of oil spills.

Chakrabarty's patent claims were of three types: first, process claims for the method of producing the bacteria; second, claims for an inoculum comprised of a carrier material floating on water, such as straw, and the new bacteria; and third, claims to the bacteria themselves. The patent examiner allowed the claims falling into the first two categories, but rejected claims for the bacteria. His decision rested on two grounds: (1) that micro-organisms are "products of nature," and (2) that as living things they are not patentable subject matter. . . . [T]he Patent Office Board of Appeals . . . affirmed the Examiner on the second ground. Relying on the legislative history of the 1930 Plant Patent Act, in which Congress extended patent protection to certain asexually reproduced plants, the Board concluded that §101 was not intended to cover living things such as these laboratory created micro-organisms. . . .

[The case went through a circuitous appeal process finally resulting in a decision by Court of Customs and Patent Appeals reversing the patent examiner and Board of Appeals.] The Commissioner of Patents and Trademarks . . . sought certiorari, and we granted the writ. . . .

II

The Constitution grants Congress broad power to legislate to "promote the Progress of Science and useful Arts, by securing for limited Times to Authors and Inventors the exclusive Right to their respective Writings and Discoveries." Art. I, §8, cl. 8. The patent laws promote this progress by offering inventors exclusive rights

---

5. Plasmids are hereditary units physically separate from the chromosomes of the cell. In prior research, Chakrabarty and an associate discovered that plasmids control the oil degradation abilities of certain bacteria. In particular, the two researchers discovered plasmids capable of degrading camphor and octane, two components of crude oil. In the work represented by the patent application at issue here, Chakrabarty discovered a process by which four different plasmids, capable of degrading four different oil components, could be transferred to and maintained stably in a single *Pseudomonas* bacterium, which itself has no capacity for degrading oil.

for a limited period as an incentive for their inventiveness and research efforts. . . . The authority of Congress is exercised in the hope that "[t]he productive effort thereby fostered will have a positive effect on society through the introduction of new products and processes of manufacture into the economy, and the emanations by way of increased employment and better lives for our citizens." [Kewanee Oil Co. v. Bicron Corp., 416 U.S. 470, 480 (1974)].

The question before us in this case is a narrow one of statutory interpretation requiring us to construe 35 U.S.C. §101, which provides: "Whoever invents or discovers any new and useful process, machine, manufacture, or composition of matter, or any new and useful improvement thereof, may obtain a patent therefore, subject to the conditions and requirements of this title." [] Specifically, we must determine whether respondent's micro-organism constitutes a "manufacture" or "composition of matter" within the meaning of the statute.[6] . . .

III

. . . Guided by [] canons of construction, this Court has read the term "manufacture" in §101 in accordance with its dictionary definition to mean "the production of articles for use from raw or prepared materials by giving to these materials new forms, qualities, properties, or combinations, whether by hand-labor or by machinery." American Fruit Growers, Inc. v. Brogdex Co., 283 U.S. 1 (1931). . . . In choosing such expansive terms as "manufacture" and "composition of matter," modified by the comprehensive "any," Congress plainly contemplated that the patent laws would be given wide scope.

The relevant legislative history also supports a broad construction. The Patent Act of 1793, authored by Thomas Jefferson, defined statutory subject matter as "any new and useful art, machine, manufacture, or composition of matter, or any new or useful improvement [thereof]." The Act embodied Jefferson's philosophy that "ingenuity should receive a liberal encouragement." . . . In 1952, when the patent laws were recodified, Congress replaced the word "art" with "process," but otherwise left Jefferson's language intact. The Committee Reports accompanying the 1952 Act inform us that Congress intended statutory subject matter to "include anything under the sun that is made by man."

This is not to suggest that §101 has no limits or that it embraces every discovery. The laws of nature, physical phenomena, and abstract ideas have been held not patentable. . . . Thus, a new mineral discovered in the earth or a new plant found in the wild is not patentable subject matter. Likewise, Einstein could not patent his celebrated law that $E = mc^2$; nor could Newton have patented the law of gravity. Such discoveries are "manifestations of . . . nature, free to all men and reserved exclusively to none."

Judged in this light, respondent's micro-organism plainly qualifies as patentable subject matter. His claim is not to a hitherto unknown natural phenomenon, but to a nonnaturally occurring manufacture or composition of matter—a product of human ingenuity "having a distinctive name, character [and] use." The point is underscored dramatically by comparison of the invention here with that in [Funk

---

6. This case does not involve the other "conditions and requirements" of the patent laws, such as novelty and nonobviousness. 35 U.S.C. §101, 103.

Brothers Seed Co. v. Kalo Inoculant Co, 333 U.S. 127, 130 (1948)]. There, the patentee had discovered that there existed in nature certain species of root-nodule bacteria which did not exert a mutually inhibitive effect on each other. He used that discovery to produce a mixed culture capable of inoculating the seeds of leguminous plants. Concluding that the patentee had discovered "only some of the handiwork of nature," the Court ruled the product nonpatentable:

> Each of the species of root-nodule bacteria contained in the package infects the same group of leguminous plants which it always infected. No species acquires a different use. The combination of species produces no new bacteria, no change in the six species of bacteria, and no enlargement of the range of their utility. Each species has the same effect it always had. The bacteria perform in their natural way. Their use in combination does not improve in any way their natural functioning. They serve the ends nature originally provided and act quite independently of any effort of the patentee.

Here, by contrast, the patentee has produced a new bacterium with markedly different characteristics from any found in nature and one having the potential for significant utility. His discovery is not nature's handiwork, but his own; accordingly it is patentable subject matter under §101.

IV

Two contrary arguments are advanced, neither of which we find persuasive. [The Court discussed arguments that Congressional enactment of the] . . . 1930 Plant Patent Act, which afforded patent protection to certain asexually reproduced plants, and the 1970 Plant Variety Protection Act, which authorized protection for certain sexually reproduced plants but excluded bacteria from its protection . . . [indicated] congressional understanding that the terms "manufacture" or "composition of matter" do not include living things; if they did, the petitioner argues, neither Act would have been necessary. . . . [The Court rejected these claims, noting that] Congress . . . explained at length its belief that the work of the plant breeder "in aid of nature" was patentable invention. . . .

Congress thus recognized that the relevant distinction was not between living and inanimate things, but between products of nature, whether living or not, and human-made inventions. Here, respondent's micro-organism is the result of human ingenuity and research. Hence, the passage of the Plant Patent Act affords the Government no support. . . .

In particular, we find nothing in the exclusion of bacteria from plant variety protection to support the petitioner's position. . . . The legislative history gives no reason for this exclusion. As the Court of Customs and Patent Appeals suggested, it may simply reflect congressional agreement with [that court's previous holding that "bacteria were not plants for the purposes of the 1930 Act"]. . . . Or it may reflect the fact that prior to 1970 the Patent Office had issued patents for bacteria under §101.[9]. . . .

9. In 1873, the Patent Office granted Louis Pasteur a patent on "yeast, free from organic germs of disease, as an article of manufacture." And in 1967 and 1968, immediately prior to the passage of the Plant Variety Protection Act, that Office granted two patents which, as the petitioner concedes, state claims for living micro-organisms.

The petitioner's second argument is that . . . genetic technology was unforeseen when Congress enacted §101. From this it is argued that resolution of the patentability of inventions such as respondent's should be left to Congress. The legislative process, the petitioner argues, is best equipped to weigh the competing economic, social, and scientific considerations involved, and to determine whether living organisms produced by genetic engineering should receive patent protection. . . . The subject-matter provisions of the patent law have been cast in broad terms to fulfill the constitutional and statutory goal of promoting "the Progress of Science and the useful Arts" with all that means for the social and economic benefits envisioned by Jefferson. Broad general language is not necessarily ambiguous when congressional objectives require broad terms. . . . Congress employed broad general language in drafting §101 precisely because such inventions are often unforeseeable.[10]

To buttress his argument, the petitioner, with the support of amicus, points to grave risks that may be generated by research endeavors such as respondent's. The briefs present a gruesome parade of horribles. Scientists, among them Nobel laureates, are quoted suggesting that genetic research may pose a serious threat to the human race, or, at the very least, that the dangers are far too substantial to permit such research to proceed apace at this time. We are told that genetic research and related technological developments may spread pollution and disease, that it may result in a loss of genetic diversity, and that its practice may tend to depreciate the value of human life. These arguments are forcefully, even passionately, presented; they remind us that, at times, human ingenuity seems unable to control fully the forces it creates—that with Hamlet, it is sometimes better "to bear those ills we have than fly to others that we know not of."

It is argued that this Court should weigh these potential hazards in considering whether respondent's invention is patentable subject matter under §101. We disagree. The grant or denial of patents on micro-organisms is not likely to put an end to genetic research or to its attendant risks. The large amount of research that has already occurred when no researcher had sure knowledge that patent protection would be available suggests that legislative or judicial fiat as to patentability will not deter the scientific mind from probing into the unknown any more than Canute could command the tides. Whether respondent's claims are patentable may determine whether research efforts are accelerated by the hope of reward or slowed by want of incentives, but that is all.

What is more important is that we are without competence to entertain these arguments—either to brush them aside as fantasies generated by fear of the unknown, or to act on them. The choice we are urged to make is a matter of high policy for resolution within the legislative process after the kind of investigation, examination, and study that legislative bodies can provide and courts cannot. That

---

10. Even an abbreviated list of patented inventions underscores the point: telegraph (Morse, No. 1,647); telephone (Bell, No. 174,465); electric lamp (Edison, No. 223,898); airplane (the Wrights, No. 821,393); transistor (Bardeen & Brattain, No. 2,524,035); neutronic reactor (Fermi & Szilard, No. 2,708,656); laser (Schawlow & Townes, No. 2,929,922). See generally Revolutionary Ideas, Patents & Progress in America, United States Patent and Trademark Office (1976).

process involves the balancing of competing values and interests, which in our democratic system is the business of elected representatives. . . .

Congress is free to amend §101 so as to exclude from patent protection organisms produced by genetic engineering. . . . Or it may choose to craft a statute specifically designed for such living things. But, until Congress takes such action, this Court must construe the language of §101 as it is. The language of that section fairly embraces respondent's invention. Accordingly, the judgment of the Court of Customs and Patent Appeals is *affirmed.*

BRENNAN, J., dissenting [joined by Justices White, Marshall, and Powell].

I agree with the Court that the question before us is a narrow one. Neither the future of scientific research, nor even, the ability of respondent Chakrabarty to reap some monopoly profits from his pioneering work, is at stake. Patents on the processes by which he has produced and employed the new living organism are not contested. The only question we need decide is whether Congress, exercising its authority under Art. I, §8, of the Constitution, intended that he be able to secure a monopoly on the living organism itself, no matter how produced or how used. Because I believe the Court has misread the applicable legislation, I dissent.

The patent laws attempt to reconcile this Nation's deep seated antipathy to monopolies with the need to encourage progress. . . . Given the complexity and legislative nature of this delicate task, we must be careful to extend patent protection no further than Congress has provided. . . . [W]e are not dealing—as the Court would have it—with the routine problem of "unanticipated inventions." . . . In [the two Plant Acts] . . . Congress has addressed the general problem of patenting animate inventions and has chosen carefully limited language granting protection to some kinds of discoveries, but specifically excluding others. . . .

Because Congress thought it had to legislate in order to make agricultural "human-made inventions" patentable and because the legislation Congress enacted is limited, it follows that Congress never meant to make items outside the scope of the legislation patentable.

Second, the 1970 Act clearly indicates that Congress has included bacteria within the focus of its legislative concern, but not within the scope of patent protection. Congress specifically excluded bacteria from the coverage of the 1970 Act. The Court's attempts to supply explanations for this explicit exclusion ring hollow. . . . It is the role of Congress, not this Court, to broaden or narrow the reach of the patent laws. This is especially true where, as here, the composition sought to be patented uniquely implicates matters of public concern.

■ MAYO COLLABORATIVE SERVICES v. PROMETHEUS LABORATORIES, INC.
132 S. Ct. 1289 (2012)

BREYER, J.

Section 101 of the Patent Act [35 U.S.C. §101] defines patentable subject matter. It says:

Whoever invents or discovers any new and useful process, machine, manufacture, or composition of matter, or any new and useful improvement thereof, may obtain a patent therefor, subject to the conditions and requirements of this title.

The Court has long held that this provision contains an important implicit exception. "[L]aws of nature, natural phenomena, and abstract ideas" are not patentable. Thus, the Court has written that "a new mineral discovered in the earth or a new plant found in the wild is not patentable subject matter. Likewise, Einstein could not patent his celebrated law that $E = mc^2$; nor could Newton have patented the law of gravity. Such discoveries are 'manifestations of . . . nature, free to all men and reserved exclusively to none.'" Chakrabarty, 447 U.S. 303, 309 (quoting Funk Brothers Seed Co. v. Kalo Inoculant Co., 333 U.S. 127, 130 (1948)).

"Phenomena of nature, though just discovered, mental processes, and abstract intellectual concepts are not patentable, as they are the basic tools of scientific and technological work." Gottschalk v. Benson, 409 U.S. 63, 67(1972). And monopolization of those tools through the grant of a patent might tend to impede innovation more than it would tend to promote it.

The Court has recognized, however, that too broad an interpretation of this exclusionary principle could eviscerate patent law. For all inventions at some level embody, use, reflect, rest upon, or apply laws of nature, natural phenomena, or abstract ideas. Thus, in [Diamond v. Diehr] the Court pointed out that "'a process is not unpatentable simply because it contains a law of nature or a mathematical algorithm.'" 450 U.S. 175, 187. It added that "an application of a law of nature or mathematical formula to a known structure or process may well be deserving of patent protection." Diehr, supra, at 187. And it emphasized . . . "'While a scientific truth, or the mathematical expression of it, is not a patentable invention, a novel and useful structure created with the aid of knowledge of scientific truth may be.'" 450 U.S. at 188 (quoting [Mackay Radio & Telegraph Co. v. Radio Corp. of America], 450 U.S. 86, 188 (1939)). See also Funk Brothers, supra, at 130 ("If there is to be invention from [a discovery of a law of nature], it must come from the application of the law of nature to a new and useful end").

Still, as the Court has also made clear, to transform an unpatentable law of nature into a patent-eligible application of such a law, one must do more than simply state the law of nature while adding the words "apply it."

The case before us lies at the intersection of these basic principles. It concerns patent claims covering processes that help doctors who use thiopurine drugs to treat patients with autoimmune diseases determine whether a given dosage level is too low or too high. The claims purport to apply natural laws describing the relationships between the concentration in the blood of certain thiopurine metabolites and the likelihood that the drug dosage will be ineffective or induce harmful side-effects. We must determine whether the claimed processes have transformed these unpatentable natural laws into patent-eligible applications of those laws. We conclude that they have not done so and that therefore the processes are not patentable.

Our conclusion rests upon an examination of the particular claims before us in light of the Court's precedents. Those cases warn us against interpreting patent statutes in ways that make patent eligibility "depend simply on the draftsman's art" without reference to the "principles underlying the prohibition against patents for [natural laws].″ [Parker v. Flook, 437 U.S. 584, 593 (1978)]. They warn us against upholding patents that claim processes that too broadly preempt the use of a natural law. And they insist that a process that focuses upon the use of a natural law also contain other elements or a combination of elements, sometimes referred to as an "inventive concept," sufficient to ensure that the patent in practice amounts to significantly more than a patent upon the natural law itself.

We find that the process claims at issue here do not satisfy these conditions. In particular, the steps in the claimed processes (apart from the natural laws themselves) involve well-understood, routine, conventional activity previously engaged in by researchers in the field. At the same time, upholding the patents would risk disproportionately tying up the use of the underlying natural laws, inhibiting their use in the making of further discoveries.

I

A

The patents before us concern the use of thiopurine drugs in the treatment of autoimmune diseases, such as Crohn's disease and ulcerative colitis. When a patient ingests a thiopurine compound, his body metabolizes the drug, causing metabolites to form in his bloodstream. Because the way in which people metabolize thiopurine compounds varies, the same dose of a thiopurine drug affects different people differently, and it has been difficult for doctors to determine whether for a particular patient a given dose is too high, risking harmful side effects, or too low, and so likely ineffective.

At the time the discoveries embodied in the patents were made, scientists already understood that the levels in a patient's blood of certain metabolites, including, in particular, 6-thioguanine and its nucleotides (6-TG) and 6-methyl-mercaptopurine (6-MMP), were correlated with the likelihood that a particular dosage of a thiopurine drug could cause harm or prove ineffective. But those in the field did not know the precise correlations between metabolite levels and likely harm or ineffectiveness. The patent claims at issue here set forth processes embodying researchers' findings that identified these correlations with some precision.

More specifically, the patents—U.S. Patent No. 6,355,623 ('623 patent) and U.S. Patent No. 6,680,302 ('302 patent)—embody findings that concentrations in a patient's blood of 6-TG or of 6-MMP metabolite beyond a certain level (400 and 7000 picomoles per 8×10^8 red blood cells, respectively) indicate that the dosage is likely too high for the patient, while concentrations in the blood of 6-TG metabolite lower than a certain level (about 230 picomoles per 8×10^8 red blood cells) indicate that the dosage is likely too low to be effective.

The patent claims seek to embody this research in a set of processes. Like the Federal Circuit we take as typical claim 1 of the '623 Patent, which describes one of the claimed processes as follows:

A method of optimizing therapeutic efficacy for treatment of an immune-mediated gastrointestinal disorder, comprising:

(a) administering a drug providing 6-thioguanine to a subject having said immune-mediated gastrointestinal disorder; and

(b) determining the level of 6-thioguanine in said subject having said immune-mediated gastrointestinal disorder,

wherein the level of 6-thioguanine less than about 230 pmol per 8 x 10⁸ red
blood cells indicates a need to increase the amount of said drug subsequently administered to said subject and

wherein the level of 6-thioguanine greater than about 400 pmol per 8 x 10⁸
red blood cells indicates a need to decrease the amount of said drug subsequently
administered to said subject. '623 patent, col.20, ll.10-20, 2 App. 16.

For present purposes we may assume that the other claims in the patents do
not differ significantly from claim 1.

B

Respondent, Prometheus Laboratories, Inc. (Prometheus), is the sole and
exclusive licensee of the '623 and '302 patents. It sells diagnostic tests that embody
the processes the patents describe. For some time petitioners, Mayo Clinic Rochester and Mayo Collaborative Services (collectively Mayo), bought and used those
tests. But in 2004 Mayo announced that it intended to begin using and selling its
own test—a test using somewhat higher metabolite levels to determine toxicity (450
pmol per 8 x 10⁸ for 6-TG and 5700 pmol per 8 x 10⁸ for 6-MMP). Prometheus then
brought this action claiming patent infringement.

The District Court found that Mayo's test infringed [various aspects of the
claimed patent]. . . . Nonetheless the District Court ultimately granted summary
judgment in Mayo's favor. The court reasoned that the patents effectively claim
natural laws or natural phenomena—namely the correlations between thiopurine
metabolite levels and the toxicity and efficacy of thiopurine drug dosages—and so
are not patentable.

On appeal, the Federal Circuit reversed. It pointed out that in addition to these
natural correlations, the claimed processes specify the steps of (1) "administering
a [thiopurine] drug" to a patient and (2) "determining the [resulting metabolite]
level." These steps, it explained, involve the transformation of the human body or
of blood taken from the body. Thus, the patents satisfied the Circuit's "machine
or transformation test," which the court thought sufficient to "confine the patent
monopoly within rather definite bounds," thereby bringing the claims into compliance with §101. 581 F.3d 1336, 1345, 1346-1347 (2009) (internal quotation marks
omitted).

Mayo filed a petition for certiorari. We granted the petition, vacated the judgment, and remanded the case for reconsideration in light of Bilski, 130 S. Ct. 3218,
which clarified that the "machine or transformation test" is not a definitive test of
patent eligibility, but only an important and useful clue. 130 S. Ct., at 3234-3235.
On remand the Federal Circuit reaffirmed its earlier conclusion. It thought that the
"machine-or-transformation test," understood merely as an important and useful
clue, nonetheless led to the "clear and compelling conclusion . . . that the . . . claims
. . . do not encompass laws of nature or preempt natural correlations." 628 F.3d
1347, 1355 (2010). Mayo again filed a petition for certiorari, which we granted.

II

Prometheus' patents set forth laws of nature—namely, relationships between
concentrations of certain metabolites in the blood and the likelihood that a dosage
of a thiopurine drug will prove ineffective or cause harm. Claim 1, for example,

states that if the levels of 6-TG in the blood (of a patient who has taken a dose of a thiopurine drug) exceed about 400 pmol per 8×10^8 red blood cells, then the administered dose is likely to produce toxic side effects. While it takes a human action (the administration of a thiopurine drug) to trigger a manifestation of this relation in a particular person, the relation itself exists in principle apart from any human action. The relation is a consequence of the ways in which thiopurine compounds are metabolized by the body—entirely natural processes. And so a patent that simply describes that relation sets forth a natural law.

The question before us is whether the claims do significantly more than simply describe these natural relations. To put the matter more precisely, do the patent claims add enough to their statements of the correlations to allow the processes they describe to qualify as patent-eligible processes that apply natural laws? We believe that the answer to this question is no.

A

If a law of nature is not patentable, then neither is a process reciting a law of nature, unless that process has additional features that provide practical assurance that the process is more than a drafting effort designed to monopolize the law of nature itself. A patent, for example, could not simply recite a law of nature and then add the instruction "apply the law." Einstein, we assume, could not have patented his famous law by claiming a process consisting of simply telling linear accelerator operators to refer to the law to determine how much energy an amount of mass has produced (or vice versa). Nor could Archimedes have secured a patent for his famous principle of flotation by claiming a process consisting of simply telling boat builders to refer to that principle in order to determine whether an object will float.

What else is there in the claims before us? The process that each claim recites tells doctors interested in the subject about the correlations that the researchers discovered. In doing so, it recites an "administering" step, a "determining" step, and a "wherein" step. These additional steps are not themselves natural laws but neither are they sufficient to transform the nature of the claim.

First, the "administering" step simply refers to the relevant audience, namely doctors who treat patients with certain diseases with thiopurine drugs. That audience is a pre-existing audience; doctors used thiopurine drugs to treat patients suffering from autoimmune disorders long before anyone asserted these claims. In any event, the "prohibition against patenting abstract ideas 'cannot be circumvented by attempting to limit the use of the formula to a particular technological environment.'" Bilski, supra, 130 S. Ct., at 3230 (quoting Diehr, 450 U.S., at 191-192).

Second, the "wherein" clauses simply tell a doctor about the relevant natural laws, at most adding a suggestion that he should take those laws into account when treating his patient. That is to say, these clauses tell the relevant audience about the laws while trusting them to use those laws appropriately where they are relevant to their decisionmaking (rather like Einstein telling linear accelerator operators about his basic law and then trusting them to use it where relevant).

Third, the "determining" step tells the doctor to determine the level of the relevant metabolites in the blood, through whatever process the doctor or the laboratory wishes to use. As the patents state, methods for determining metabolite levels were well known in the art. Indeed, scientists routinely measured metabolites as part of their investigations into the relationships between metabolite levels and efficacy and toxicity of thiopurine compounds. Thus, this step tells doctors to engage in well-understood, routine, conventional activity previously engaged in by scientists who work in the field. Purely "conventional or obvious" "[pre]-solution activity" is normally not sufficient to transform an unpatentable law of nature into a patent-eligible application of such a law. Flook, 437 U.S., at 590.

Fourth, to consider the three steps as an ordered combination adds nothing to the laws of nature that is not already present when the steps are considered separately. . . . Anyone who wants to make use of these laws must first administer a thiopurine drug and measure the resulting metabolite concentrations, and so the combination amounts to nothing significantly more than an instruction to doctors to apply the applicable laws when treating their patients.

The upshot is that the three steps simply tell doctors to gather data from which they may draw an inference in light of the correlations. To put the matter more succinctly, the claims inform a relevant audience about certain laws of nature; any additional steps consist of well-understood, routine, conventional activity already engaged in by the scientific community; and those steps, when viewed as a whole, add nothing significant beyond the sum of their parts taken separately. For these reasons we believe that the steps are not sufficient to transform unpatentable natural correlations into patentable applications of those regularities. . . .

3

The Court has repeatedly emphasized . . . a concern that patent law not inhibit further discovery by improperly tying up the future use of laws of nature. Thus, in *Morse* the Court set aside as unpatentable Samuel Morse's general claim for "'the use of the motive power of the electric or galvanic current . . . however developed, for making or printing intelligible characters, letters, or signs, at any distances,'" [O'Reilly v. Morse, 15 How. 62, 86 (1854)]. The Court explained:

> For aught that we now know some future inventor, in the onward march of science, may discover a mode of writing or printing at a distance by means of the electric or galvanic current, without using any part of the process or combination set forth in the plaintiff's specification. His invention may be less complicated—less liable to get out of order—less expensive in construction, and in its operation. But yet if it is covered by this patent the inventor could not use it, nor the public have the benefit of it without the permission of this patentee.

These statements reflect the fact that, even though rewarding with patents those who discover new laws of nature and the like might well encourage their discovery, those laws and principles, considered generally, are "the basic tools of scientific and technological work." Benson, supra, at 67. And so there is a danger that the grant of patents that tie up their use will inhibit future innovation premised upon them, a danger that becomes acute when a patented process amounts to no more than an instruction to "apply the natural law," or otherwise forecloses more future invention than the underlying discovery could reasonably justify. See generally W. Landes & R. Posner, The Economic Structure of Intellectual Property Law 305-306 (2003) (The exclusion from patent law of basic truths reflects "both . . . the enormous potential for rent seeking that would be created if property rights could be obtained in them and . . . the enormous transaction costs that would be imposed on would-be users [of those truths]").

The laws of nature at issue here are narrow laws that may have limited applications, but the patent claims that embody them nonetheless implicate this concern. They tell a treating doctor to measure metabolite levels and to consider the resulting measurements in light of the statistical relationships they describe. In doing so, they tie up the doctor's subsequent treatment decision whether that treatment does, or does not, change in light of the inference he has drawn using the correlations. And they threaten to inhibit the development of more refined treatment recommendations (like that embodied in Mayo's test), that combine Prometheus' correlations with later discovered features of metabolites, human physiology or individual patient characteristics. The "determining" step too is set forth in highly general language covering all processes that make use of the correlations after measuring metabolites, including later discovered processes that measure metabolite levels in new ways.

We need not, and do not, now decide whether were the steps at issue here less conventional, these features of the claims would prove sufficient to invalidate them. For here, as we have said, the steps add nothing of significance to the natural laws themselves. Unlike, say, a typical patent on a new drug or a new way of using an existing drug, the patent claims do not confine their reach to particular applications of those laws. The presence here of the basic underlying concern that these patents tie up too much future use of laws of nature simply reinforces our conclusion that the processes described in the patents are not patent eligible, while eliminating any temptation to depart from case law precedent.

III

We have considered several further arguments in support of Prometheus' position. But they do not lead us to adopt a different conclusion. First, the Federal Circuit, in upholding the patent eligibility of the claims before us, relied on this Court's determination that "[t]ransformation and reduction of an article 'to a different state or thing' is the clue to the patentability of a process claim that does not include particular machines." Benson, supra, 93 S. Ct. 253. It reasoned that the claimed processes are therefore patent eligible, since they involve transforming the human body by administering a thiopurine drug and transforming the blood by analyzing it to determine metabolite levels. 628 F.3d, at 1356-1357.

The first of these transformations, however, is irrelevant. As we have pointed out, the "administering" step simply helps to pick out the group of individuals who are likely interested in applying the law of nature. And the second step could be satisfied without transforming the blood, should science develop a totally different system for determining metabolite levels that did not involve such a transformation. Regardless, in stating that the "machine-or-transformation" test is an "important and useful clue " to patentability, we have neither said nor implied that the test trumps the "law of nature" exclusion. Bilski, supra, 130 S. Ct., at 3225-3227 (emphasis added). That being so, the test fails here.

Second, Prometheus argues that, because the particular laws of nature that its patent claims embody are narrow and specific, the patents should be upheld. Thus, it encourages us to draw distinctions among laws of nature based on whether or not they will interfere significantly with innovation in other fields now or in the future.

But the underlying functional concern here is a relative one: how much future innovation is foreclosed relative to the contribution of the inventor. A patent upon a narrow law of nature may not inhibit future research as seriously as would a patent upon Einstein's law of relativity, but the creative value of the discovery is also considerably smaller. And, as we have previously pointed out, even a narrow law of nature (such as the one before us) can inhibit future research.

In any event, our cases have not distinguished among different laws of nature according to whether or not the principles they embody are sufficiently narrow. And this is understandable. Courts and judges are not institutionally well suited to making the kinds of judgments needed to distinguish among different laws of nature. And so the cases have endorsed a bright-line prohibition against patenting laws of nature, mathematical formulas and the like, which serves as a somewhat more easily administered proxy for the underlying "building-block" concern.

Third, the Government argues that . . . other statutory provisions—those that insist that a claimed process be novel, 35 U.S.C. §102, that it not be "obvious in light of prior art," §103, and that it be "full[y], clear[ly], concise[ly], and exact[ly]" described, §112—can [address any concerns]. . . . In particular, it argues that these claims likely fail for lack of novelty under §102. . . . [The government's] approach, however, would make the "law of nature" exception to §101 patentability a dead letter. . . .

Fourth, Prometheus, supported by several amici, argues that a principle of law denying patent coverage here will interfere significantly with the ability of medical researchers to make valuable discoveries, particularly in the area of diagnostic research. That research, which includes research leading to the discovery of laws of nature, is expensive; it "ha[s] made the United States the world leader in this field"; and it requires protection. Brief for Respondent 52.

Other medical experts, however, argue strongly against a legal rule that would make the present claims patent eligible, invoking policy considerations that point in the opposite direction. The American Medical Association, the American College of Medical Genetics, the American Hospital Association, the American Society of Human Genetics, the Association of American Medical Colleges, the Association for Molecular Pathology, and other medical organizations tell us that if "claims to exclusive rights over the body's natural responses to illness and medical treatment are permitted to stand, the result will be a vast thicket of exclusive rights over the use of critical scientific data that must remain widely available if physicians are to provide sound medical care." Brief for American College of Medical Genetics et al. as Amici Curiae 7; see also App. to Brief for Association Internationale pour la Protection de la Propriete Intellectuelle et al. as Amici Curiae A6, A16 (methods of medical treatment are not patentable in most of Western Europe).

We do not find this kind of difference of opinion surprising. Patent protection is, after all, a two-edged sword. On the one hand, the promise of exclusive rights provides monetary incentives that lead to creation, invention, and discovery. On the other hand, that very exclusivity can impede the flow of information that might permit, indeed spur, invention, by, for example, raising the price of using the patented ideas once created, requiring potential users to conduct costly and time-consuming searches of existing patents and pending patent applications, and requiring the negotiation of complex licensing arrangements. At the same time, patent law's general rules must govern inventive activity in many different fields of human endeavor, with the result that the practical effects of rules that reflect a general effort to balance these considerations may differ from one field to another.

In consequence, we must hesitate before departing from established general legal rules lest a new protective rule that seems to suit the needs of one field produce unforeseen results in another. And we must recognize the role of Congress in crafting more finely tailored rules where necessary. Cf. 35 U.S.C. §§161-164 (special rules for plant patents). We need not determine here whether, from a policy perspective, increased protection for discoveries of diagnostic laws of nature is desirable. . . .

For these reasons, we conclude that the patent claims at issue here effectively claim the underlying laws of nature themselves. The claims are consequently invalid. And the Federal Circuit's judgment is reversed.

■ HARVARD COLLEGE v. CANADA (COMMISSIONER OF PATENTS)
2002 SCC 76, 219 D.L.R. (4th) 577 (Supreme Court of Canada 2002)

BASTARACHE J. . . .

This appeal raises the issue of the patentability of higher life forms within the context of the Patent Act, R.S.C. 1985, C. P-4. The respondent, the President and Fellows of Harvard College, seeks to patent a mouse that has been genetically altered to increase its susceptibility to cancer, which makes it useful for cancer research. The patent claims also extend to all non-human mammals which have been similarly altered. . . .

The Commissioner of Patents upheld the Patent Examiner's refusal to grant the patent. This decision was in turn upheld by the Federal Court Trial Division, but was overturned by a majority of the Federal Court of Appeal. . . . To refuse a patent, the Commissioner must be satisfied that the applicant is not "by law" entitled to the patent, wording which indicates that the Commissioner has no discretion independent of the Patent Act to consider the public interest when granting or denying a patent. . . . [Therefore], the sole question is whether Parliament intended the definition of invention, and more particularly the words "manufacture" or "composition of matter", within the context of the Patent Act,[7] to encompass higher life forms such as the oncomouse [so-called in reference to "oncology" or cancer].

II. FACTUAL BACKGROUND. . . .

On June 21, 1985, the respondent, the President and Fellows of Harvard College ("Harvard"), applied for a patent on an invention entitled "transgenic animals". The invention aims to produce animals with a susceptibility to cancer for purposes of animal carcinogenic studies. The animals can be used to test a material

---

7. [According to the] *Patent Act*, R.S.C. 1985, c. P-4: . . . "invention" means any new and useful art, process, machine, manufacture or composition of matter, or any new and useful improvement in any art, process, machine, manufacture or composition of matter. . . .

suspected of being a carcinogen by exposing them to the material and seeing if tumours develop. Because the animals are already susceptible to tumour develop-ment, ... the animals will be expected to develop tumours in a shorter time period. The animals can also be used to test materials thought to confer protection against the development of cancer. ...

The technology by which a cancer-prone mouse ("oncomouse") is produced is described in the patent application disclosure. The oncogene (the cancer-promoting gene) is obtained from the genetic code of a non-mammal source, such as a virus. A vehicle for transporting the oncogene into the mouse's chromosomes is constructed using a small piece of bacterial DNA referred to as a plasmid. The plas-mid, into which the oncogene has been "spliced", is injected into fertilized mouse eggs, preferably while they are at the one-cell stage. The eggs are then implanted into a female host mouse, or "foster mother", and permitted to develop to term. .... those [offspring] that contain the oncogene are called "founder" mice. ...

In its patent application, the respondent seeks to protect both the process by which the oncomice are produced and the end product of the process, i.e. the founder mice and the offspring whose cells are affected by the oncogene. The pro-cess and product claims also extend to all non-human mammals. ...

V. ANALYSIS ...

The sole question in this appeal is whether the words "manufacture" and "composition of matter", in the context of the Patent Act [see note 7 above], are sufficiently broad to include higher life forms. If these words are not sufficiently broad to include higher life forms, it is irrelevant whether this Court believes that higher life forms such as the oncomouse ought to be patentable. ...

Having considered the relevant factors, I conclude that Parliament did not intend to include higher life forms within the definition of invention found in the Patent Act. .... I do not believe that a higher life form such as the oncomouse is easily understood as either a "manufacture" or a "composition of matter". For this reason, I am not satisfied that the definition of "invention" in the Patent Act is suf-ficiently broad to include higher life forms. This conclusion is supported by the fact that the patenting of higher life forms raises unique concerns which do not arise in respect of non-living inventions and which are not addressed by the scheme of the Act. Even if a higher life form could, scientifically, be regarded as a "composi-tion of matter," ... the patenting of higher life forms is a highly contentious and complex matter that raises serious practical, ethical and environmental concerns. [Therefore,] [a]bsent explicit legislative direction, the Court should not order the Commissioner to grant a patent on a higher life form. ...

In *Chakrabarty*, the majority [of the U.S. Supreme Court] attributed the widest meaning possible to the phrases "composition of matter" and "manufacture" for the reason that inventions are, necessarily, unanticipated and unforeseeable. .... I agree that the definition of invention in the Patent Act is broad. Because the Act was designed in part to promote innovation, it is only reasonable to expect the definition of invention to be broad enough to encompass unforeseen and unanticipated tech-nology. I cannot however agree with the suggestion that the definition is unlimited in the sense that it includes "anything under the sun that is made by man". In draft-ing the Patent Act, Parliament chose to adopt an exhaustive definition that limits invention to any "art, process, machine, manufacture or composition of matter". Parliament did not define "invention" as "anything new and useful made by man". By choosing to define invention in this way, Parliament signalled a clear intention to include certain subject matter as patentable and to exclude other subject matter as being outside the confines of the Act. . . .

[T]he word ["manufacture"] would commonly be understood to denote a non-living mechanistic product or process. . . . In *Chakrabarty*, . . . "manufacture" was defined as "the production of articles for use from raw or prepared materials by giving to these materials new forms, qualities, properties, or combinations, whether by hand-labor or by machinery." . . . Is a mouse an "article" [or] "material" . . . ? In my view, while a mouse may be analogized to a "manufacture" when it is produced in an industrial setting, the word in its vernacular sense does not include a higher life form. . . .

As regards the meaning of the words "composition of matter", I believe that they must be defined more narrowly than was the case in *Chakrabarty*. . . . It [] is significant that the word "matter" captures but one aspect of a higher life form. As defined by the Oxford English Dictionary . . . "matter" is a "[p]hysical or corporeal substance in general, . . . contradistinguished from immaterial or incorporeal substance (spirit, soul, mind), and from qualities, actions, or conditions". . . . Higher life forms are generally regarded as possessing qualities and characteristics that transcend the particular genetic material of which they are composed. A person whose genetic make-up is modified by radiation does not cease to be him or herself. Likewise, the same mouse would exist absent the injection of the oncogene into the fertilized egg cell; it simply would not be predisposed to cancer. The fact that it has this predisposition to cancer that makes it valuable to humans does not mean that the mouse, along with other animal life forms, can be defined solely with reference to the genetic matter of which it is composed. The fact that animal life forms have numerous unique qualities that transcend the particular matter of which they are composed makes it difficult to conceptualize higher life forms as mere "composition[s] of matter". It is a phrase that seems inadequate as a description of a higher life form. . . . It simply does not follow from the objective of promoting ingenuity that all inventions must be patentable. . . .

The respondent . . . submits that there is . . . no evidentiary or legal basis for the distinction the Patent Office has made between lower life forms such as bacteria, yeast and moulds, and higher life forms such as plants and animals. . . .

[I]t is up to Parliament and not the courts to assess the validity of the distinction drawn by the Patent Office between higher life forms and lower life forms. Yet, even if this Court were to alter the status quo and find higher life forms patentable, it would be unable to avoid engaging in line-drawing. The majority of the Federal Court of Appeal, which found that the Patent Act did apply to higher life forms, was nonetheless compelled to draw a distinction between higher life forms and human beings. In doing so, it merely substituted one line, that between humans and animals, for the line preferred by the Patent Office, that between higher and lower life forms. In my opinion, the decision to move the line in this manner was ill-advised. As I stated earlier when considering the definition of invention, the patenting of all plants and animals, and not just human beings, raises several concerns that are not appropriately dealt with in the Patent Act. In addition, a judicially crafted exception from patentability for human beings does not adequately address issues such as what defines a human being and whether parts of the human body as opposed to the entire person would be patentable....

Appeal allowed.

[Justice Binnie's dissenting opinion omitted. The Justices were split 5-4.]

Notes on Ownership

1. *Intellectual Property Doctrine.* As noted in *Chakrabarty,* the Patent Act establishes a broad right to patent "any new and useful [invention], . . . subject to the conditions and requirements of this title." 35 U.S.C.A. §101. Although not emphasized in *Chakrabarty,* these conditions require that the invention be "novel," "non-obvious," and "adequately enabled and described." A patent gives an inventor a monopoly over the use of the discovery for a 20-year period. The owner can profit from the discovery directly or through "licensing" the use of the discovery to third parties who pay the inventor a "royalty." The Patent Act gives patent holders the right to bring a civil action against infringers for injunctive relief and damages (usually at least what would have been the reasonable royalty payments but treble damages are possible in cases of intentional infringement). 35 U.S.C.A. §§281-287.

As emphasized by the Court in *Mayo v. Prometheus,* ownership of intellectual property creates incentives for innovation but this also can result in barriers to accessing the invention itself and to innovation in related areas. The patent owner has the right to exclude others from using the invention. If the patent holder does not make use of the patent or offer other users licenses at a reasonable fee, then the innovation may not be available to the public, defeating the overriding purpose of offering patent protection in the first place. Patent law attempts to balance these competing policy considerations by, for example, ensuring that laws of nature and abstract ideas cannot be patented.

The field of intellectual property is vast, and there are numerous books, articles, and treatises. Some basic reference works are Donald S. Chisum, Chisum on Patents (this 28-volume loose-leaf publication demonstrates the breadth of the field); Janice M. Mueller, Introduction to Patent Law (2009); Craig Allen Nord et al., The Law of Intellectual Property (2011). For an international perspective, see Oliver Mills, Biotechnological Innovation, Moral Rights and Patent Law (2005). For some especially relevant publications, see Dan Burk & Mark Lemley, Policy Levers in Patent Law, 89 Va. L. Rev. 1575 (2003); Rebecca S. Eisenberg, Wisdom of the Ages or Dead-Hand Control? Patentable Subject Matter for Diagnostic Methods After In re Bilski, 3 Case W. Res. J.L. Tech. & Internet 1 (2012); Rebecca S. Eisenberg, Patents and the Progress of Science, 56 U. Chi. L. Rev. 1017 (1989); Sapna Kumar & Arti Rai, Synthetic Biology: The Intellectual Property Puzzle, 85 Tex. L. Rev. 1745 (2007); Arti K. Rai, Patent Validity Across the Executive Branch: Ex Ante Foundations for Policy Development, 61 Duke L.J. 1237 (2012) (exploring role of executive branch agencies, such as the NIH, in the development of patent policy, including DNA-patenting debates); Arti Rai ed., Intellectual Property and Biotechnology (2011); Note, Recent Legislation, Patent Law, 125 Harv. L. Rev. 1290 (2012) (analyzing Leahy-Smith America Invents Act reforms, including major change from "first to invent" to "first inventor to file" priority standard and new administrative processes for patent challenges).

2. *Patenting Life Forms. Chakrabarty* was a 5-4 decision involving a closely contested question of federal statutory interpretation. Congress did not accept the Court's implicit invitation to override its decision. See Anna Lumelsky, Diamond v. Chakrabarty: Gauging Congress's Response to Dynamic Statutory Interpretation by the Supreme Court, 39 U.S.F. L. Rev. 641 (2005). The Supreme Court of Canada's 5-4 decision in the Harvard Mouse case was equally controversial. As Justice Binnie noted in his dissent, "the oncomouse has been held patentable, and is now patented" in 16 jurisdictions including the United States. Two additional countries have issued patents for similar inventions. "Indeed, we were not told of any country with a patent system comparable to Canada's (or otherwise) in which a patent on the oncomouse had been applied for and been refused." 2002 SCC 76 at ¶2. The Supreme Court of Canada revisited the patentability of life forms in another 5-4 decision upholding patents for plants genetically modified to resist application of an herbicide used to control weeds. Schmeiser v. Monsanto, 2004 SCC 34 (2004). Animal patents are relatively common in the United States. See Tracie Letterman et al., Patently Cruel, 40 Brief 39 (Summer 2011) (noting 800 PTO-approved patents on live animals since approval of Harvard Mouse; summarizing current efforts to challenge animal patents).

3. *IP and the Access Debate.* Intellectual property ownership rules give patent holders monopoly power to extract significant profits from their inventions, or to block others from using, or even experimenting with, their inventions. The concept of ownership itself can be controversial. Activists in some countries and cultures have argued that intellectual property regimes have failed to protect local communities from corporations that have allegedly exploited local knowledge of traditional medicines. See, e.g., Jim Chen, There's No Such Thing as Biopiracy . . . and It's a Good Thing Too, 37 McGeorge L. Rev. 1 (2006); Jonathan Curci, The Protection of Biodiversity and Traditional Knowledge in International Law of Intellectual Property (2010); George Frisvold & Kelly Day-Rubenstein, Bioprospecting and Biodiversity Conservation: What Happens When Discoveries Are Made?, 50 Ariz. L. Rev. 545 (2008); Cynthia M. Ho, Access to Medicine in the Global Economy (2011); Daniel Robinson, Confronting Biopiracy: Challenges, Cases and International Debates (2011).

When medical technologies are involved, intellectual property rights generate considerable controversy if they threaten to retard biomedical research or block access to essential life-saving innovations. An example of this problem can be found in Chapter 4.B.2.'s discussion of Greenberg v. Miami Children's Hospital Research Institute, Inc., 264 F. Supp. 2d 1064 (S.D. Fla. 2003), at page 437, which involves a patent on the gene that causes Canavan's disease—a fatal brain disorder that is most prevalent in children of eastern and central European Jewish descent. Families affected with the disease who had provided biological samples to the researchers who discovered the gene sued (unsuccessfully) to block enforcement of patent rights because they felt the owners were obstructing access to the gene test in order to increase their profits. Patent law addresses concerns such as these in several ways.

a. *"March-In" Rights and Compulsory Licensing.* First, patents can be overridden for pressing public policy considerations. Without going into details here, various sources of law allow (1) the U.S. government to "march in" and reclaim pharmaceutical patents from private entities whose research the government funded, if the private patent holder fails to develop or market the product; (2) courts to refuse to enjoin patent infringement where the infringement serves an important public purpose; and (3) in some countries, compulsory licensing to protect public health, meaning that the government can force companies to sell essential patented medical products at reasonable prices. Exercises of these special powers are rare and controversial, however. See generally National Research Council of the Nat'l Academies, Reaping the Benefits of Genomic and Proteomic Research: Intellectual Property Rights, Innovation, and Public Health 146-147 (2006). For more on the Bayh-Dole Act and "march-in" rights, see 35 U.S.C. §203; Board of Trustees of the Leland Stanford Junior University v. Roche Molecular Systems, Inc., 131 S. Ct. 2188 (2011) (analyzing impact of Bayh-Dole Act on inventor's assignment of rights to federally funded inventions). For a discussion of the judicial power to deny an injunction where infringement serves the public interest, see eBay, Inc. v. MercExchange, L.L.C., 547 U.S. 388 (2006). For more on compulsory licensing, see Richard A. Epstein, Questioning the Frequency and Wisdom of Compulsory Licensing for Pharmaceutical Patents, 78 U. Chi. L. Rev. 71 (2011); Donald Harris, TRIPS After Fifteen Years: Success or Failure, as Measured by Compulsory Licensing, 18 J. Intell. Prop. L. 367 (2011); Rudolf V. Van Puymbroeck, Basic Survival Needs and Access to Medicines—Coming to Grips with TRIPS: Conversion + Calculation, 38 J.L. Med. & Ethics 520 (2010); Simone A. Rose, On Purple Pills, Stem Cells, and Other Market Failures: A Case for a Limited Compulsory Licensing Scheme for Patent Property, 48 How. L.J. 579 (2005).

b. *Access to Research Materials.* There have been numerous reports of IP-fueled restrictions on access to biomedical research materials such as cell lines, cancer drugs, and gene-altered mice. U.S. law only dimly recognizes a vague research exemption to patent rights, similar to, but much narrower than, the "fair use" exception under copyright law. Madey v. Duke University, 307 F.3d 1351 (Fed. Cir. 2002); Katherine J. Standburg, What Does the Public Get? Experimental Use and the Patent Bargain, 2004 Wis. L. Rev. 81 (2004); Comment, 113 Yale L.J. 261 (2003). These concerns have resulted in various studies and recommendations, either for a more explicit research exemption in the law, or for biomedical patent holders to adopt "best practices" in their licensing and patent enforcement practices for researchers. See, e.g., David H. Ledbetter, Gene Patenting and Licensing: The Role of Academic Researchers and Advocacy Groups, 10 Genet. Med. 314 (2008); Aaron D. Levine, Access to Human Embryonic Stem Cell Lines, 29 Nature Biotechnology 1079 (2011) (study finds significant delays for human embryonic stem cell researchers); Principles and Guidelines for Recipients of NIH Research Grants and Contracts on Obtaining and Disseminating Biomedical Research Resources, 62 Fed. Reg. 72090 (1999); NIH, Best Practices for the Licensing of Genomic Inventions, 70 Fed. Reg. 18413 (2005); National Research Council of the Nat'l Academies, Reaping the Benefits of Genomic and Proteomic Research: Intellectual Property Rights, Innovation, and Public Health 140-144 (2006).

c. *Medical Process Patents.* Many countries bar patents for medical processes, such as innovations in surgical procedures or medical protocols, for public policy reasons. This is not the law in the United States. Instead, medical processes are inherently patentable, if other requirements are met (such as novelty, nonobviousness, etc.). However, medical ethics disfavor seeking patent protection, and a special statutory amendment (35 U.S.C. §287(c)) prevents patent holders from enforcing their rights against health care practitioners, making such patents generally not worth the effort. See Aaron Kesselheim & Michelle Mello, Medical-Process Patents: Monopolizing the Delivery of Health Care, 355 New Eng. J. Med. 2036 (2006); Note, 13 Colum. Sci. & Tech. L. Rev. 206 (2012); Note, 91 Minn. L. Rev. 1088 (2007). See also John C. Newman & Robin Feldman, Copyright and Open Access at the Bedside, 365 New Eng. J. Med. 2447 (2011) (exploring intersection of copyright with medical practice in context of commonly used mental state examination).

In addition, *Prometheus,* supra, emphasizes that to be patentable, medical processes must do more than simply restate and apply natural laws. Commentators have noted that the reasoning in *Prometheus* could be used to challenge a broad range of patents relating to medical procedures and diagnostic tests. See, e.g., Bernard Chao, Moderating *Mayo,* 107 Nw. U. L. Rev. 423 (2012); Tamsen Valoir, Mayo v. Prometheus: Natural Law or Mental Step?, 24 Intell. Prop. & Tech. L.J. 3 (2012); Note, 126 Harv. L. Rev. 347 (2012). Commentators focused in particular on the implications of *Prometheus* for litigation involving diagnostic tests for genes and gene mutations that are the focus of the next section of this chapter. See Jeffrey L. Fox, Industry Reels as Prometheus Falls and Myriad Faces Further Reviews, 30 Nature Biotechnology 373 (2012).

5. Intellectual Property, Human Genes, and Human Stem Cells

One consequence of the Human Genome Project was the race by researchers, universities, and companies to patent human genes, diagnostic tests, and other procedures or products related to human genes. See Michael J. Malinowski & Radhika Rao, Legal Limits on Genetic Research and the Commercialization of Its Results, 54 Am. J. Comp. L. 45, 47-49 (2006) ("[c]ompanies and universities have obtained patents on more than 4,000 human genes, almost 20 percent of the roughly 24,000 human genes"). Human gene patents raise two different types of issues: Are these genetic discoveries patentable under the specific requirements of U.S. law? Do moral or other policy considerations justify restricting patent rights relating to genetic aspects of life forms generally or humans in particular? These are separate issues because U.S. patent law does not explicitly provide the U.S. Patent and Trademark Office (PTO) with the right to refuse patent applications based on general moral or policy grounds not otherwise found within the terms of the patent legislation. See Cynthia M. Ho, Splicing Morality and Patent Law: Issues Arising from Mixing Mice and Men, 2 Wash. U. J.L. & Pol'y 247 (2000).

As Malinowski and Rao note, determining the validity of a gene-related patent required the PTO to ensure that the patent application demonstrated an invention rather than simply the discovery of a natural phenomenon:

> [Some] object that DNA sequences should not be patentable because they are discoveries of nature that are the common heritage of all rather than man-made inventions. Nevertheless, current U.S. policy . . . permits patents on human genes [as "composition[s] of matter."] . . . While newly-discovered plants, minerals, and other natural phenomena cannot be patented because they exist without human intervention, isolated and purified versions of naturally occurring substances are patentable. Gene patents lie at the intersection of these two lines of precedent because they involve isolated and purified DNA sequences from living organisms.

Malinowski & Rao, supra, 54 Am. J. Comp. L. at 48-49.

Relying in part on researchers' claims that they had isolated and purified genetic DNA, the PTO initially took a relatively lenient approach to human gene patents. This led to widespread criticism that premature gene patents were preventing even more productive research efforts. Although the PTO's gene patenting policies had not been formally rejected in court, these concerns caused the PTO to toughen its standards on the secondary considerations required for patentability (such as utility, nonobviousness, and adequate description), even as it continued to view human genes as inherently patentable subject matter. The PTO's 2001 guidelines required applicants to precisely identify the gene, what useful functions it controlled, and perhaps also the molecular details of the proteins coded for by the gene and how they related to these functions. U.S. Patent and Trademark Office, Utility Examination Guidelines, 66 Fed. Reg. 1092 (2001) (revised guidelines governing gene patents). For a major report, see National Research Council of the Nat'l Academies, Reaping the Benefits of Genomic and Proteomic Research: Intellectual Property Rights, Innovation, and Public Health 140-144 (2006). There are numerous articles and journal symposia addressing gene patenting and related issues. For a sampling, see Helen M. Berman & Rochelle Dreyfuss, Reflections on the Science and Law of Structural Biology, Genomics, and Drug Development, 53 U.C.L.A. L. Rev. 871 (2006); Christopher M. Holman, Trends in Human Gene Patent Litigation, 322 Science 198 (2008); Symposium, Who Owns Your Body?, 84 Chi.-Kent L. Rev. 3-224 (2010).

As of early 2013, the stage was set for a clash in the Supreme Court between the traditional view that gene patents are valid and the Mayo v. Prometheus-fueled view that at least some gene patents may be an invalid effort to patent laws of nature. The litigation involves the validity of patent claims held by Myriad Genetics on two genes (BRCA1 and BRCA2) associated with susceptibility to breast and ovarian cancer. The plaintiffs in the case included various scientific and medical groups concerned with ensuring broad access to gene-related research along with women's groups and patients. The federal district court held that all of the challenged claims were invalid under §101, in part because the claims reflected products of nature and abstract mental processes rather than patentable inventions. Ass'n for Molecular Pathology v. U.S. Patent and Trademark Office, 702 F. Supp. 2d 181, 229-232, 236-237 (S.D.N.Y. 2010) (lengthy subsequent history includes rejection of the district court approach by the Federal Circuit). See also Aaron S. Kesselheim & Michelle M. Mello, Gene Patenting—Is the Pendulum Swinging Back?, 362 New Eng. J. Med. 1855 (2010).

On appeal, the Federal Circuit affirmed in part and reversed in part. The Federal Circuit initially invalidated Myriad's patent claims relating to "comparing" or "analyzing" DNA sequences as reflecting laws of nature and abstract mental steps but upheld the validity of the patent claims on isolated gene molecules or sequences. Ass'n for Molecular Pathology v. U.S. Patent and Trademark Office, 653 F.3d 1329 (Fed. Cir. 2011); and Note, 125 Harv. L. Rev. 658 (2011). The Supreme Court granted certiorari and remanded the case to the Federal Circuit to consider in light of Mayo Collaborative Services v. Prometheus Laboratories, Inc., supra at page 614, 132 S. Ct. 1794 (2012).

Commentators predicted that *Mayo* would not significantly impact the Federal Circuit's decision, in part because of the court's reputation for patent-friendly decisions and in part because the *Mayo* decision involved process patents rather than the product patents at the heart of Myriad's most significant patent claims. On remand, as predicted, the Federal Circuit once again found the methods of analyzing sequences patent ineligible and reaffirmed Myriad's patent on the "isolated" genes:

> [W]e reverse the district court's decision that Myriad's composition claims to "isolated" DNA molecules cover patent-ineligible products of nature under § 101 because each of the claimed molecules represents a nonnaturally occurring composition of matter. We also reverse the district court's decision that Myriad's method claim to screening potential cancer therapeutics via changes in cell growth rates of transformed cells is directed to a patent-ineligible scientific principle. We affirm the court's decision, however, that Myriad's method claims directed to "comparing" or "analyzing" DNA sequences are patent ineligible; such claims include no transformative steps and cover only patent-ineligible abstract, mental steps.

Ass'n for Molecular Pathology v. U.S. Patent and Trademark Office, 689 F.3d 1303, 1309 (Fed. Cir. 2012).

Judge Bryson dissented in part, relying on *Mayo* to argue that Myriad should not be permitted to patent isolated DNA and mRNA, molecules that occur in nature:

> Just as a patent involving a law of nature must have an "inventive concept" that does "significantly more than simply describe . . . natural relations," *Mayo*, 132 S. Ct. at 1294, 1297, a patent involving a product of nature should have an inventive concept that involves more than merely incidental changes to the naturally occurring product. In cases such as this one, in which the applicant claims a composition of matter that is nearly identical to a product of nature, it is appropriate to ask whether the applicant has done "enough" to distinguish his alleged invention from the similar product of nature. Has the applicant made an "inventive" contribution to the product of nature? Does the claimed composition involve more than "well-understood, routine, conventional" elements? Here, the answer to those questions is no.
>
> Neither isolation of the naturally occurring material nor the resulting breaking of covalent bonds makes the claimed molecules patentable. We have previously stated that "isolation of interesting compounds is a mainstay of the chemist's art," and that "[i]f it is known how to perform such an isolation doing so 'is likely the product not of innovation but of ordinary skill and common sense.'" Aventis Pharma Deutschland GmbH v. Lupin, Ltd., 499 F.3d 1293, 1302 (Fed. Cir. 2007), quoting KSR Int'l Co. v. Teleflex, Inc., 550 U.S. 398, 421, 127 S. Ct. 1727, 167 L. Ed. 2d 705 (2007). Similarly, the structural changes ancillary to the isolation of the gene do not render these claims patentable. The cleaving of covalent bonds incident to isolation is itself not inventive, and the fact that the cleaved molecules have terminal groups that differ from the naturally occurring nucleotide sequences does nothing to add any inventive character to the claimed molecules. The functional portion of the composition—the nucleotide sequence—remains identical to that of the naturally occurring gene.
>
> The majority suggests that I have "focus[ed] not on the differences between isolated and native DNAs, but on one similarity: their informational content." In light of *Mayo*, that approach seems appropriate. The informational content of the nucleotide sequences is the critical aspect of these molecules; the terminal groups added to the molecules when the covalent bonds are broken—to which the majority

and concurring opinions attribute such significance—are not even mentioned in the claims. The nucleotide sequences of the claimed molecules are the same as the nucleotide sequences found in naturally occurring human genes. In my view, that structural similarity dwarfs the significance of the structural differences between isolated DNA and naturally occurring DNA, especially where the structural differences are merely ancillary to the breaking of covalent bonds, a process that is itself not inventive.

689 F.3d at 1355 (Bryson, J., dissenting).

The Supreme Court granted certiorari again, and a decision is expected by June 2013. (An edited version will be provided on the Web site to this casebook, www.health-law.org.)

The *Myriad* litigation has attracted considerable commentary. See, e.g., Allison W. Dobson & James P. Evans, Gene Patents in the US—Focusing on What Really Matters, 13 Genome Biology 161 (2012); Robin Feldman, Whose Body Is It Anyway?, supra; Samantak Ghosh, Gene Patents: Balancing the Myriad Issues Concerning the Patenting of Natural Products, 27 Berkeley Tech. L.J. 241 (2012); Isabelle Huys et al., The Fate and Future of Patents on Human Genes and Genetic Diagnostic Methods, 13 Nature Reviews Genetics 441 (2012); Simone A. Rose, Semiconductor Chips, supra; Symposium, Who Owns Your Body?, 84 Chi.-Kent L. Rev. 224 (2009).

The controversy over human gene patents is only part of the picture. Human stem cells have also been patented in the United States. Karl Bergman & Gregory D. Graff, The Global Stem Cell Patent Landscape, 25 Nature Biotechnology 419 (2007); Jeanne F. Loring & Cathryn Campbell, Intellectual Property and Human Embryonic Stem Cell Research, 311 Science 1716 (2006); Mark L. Rohrbaugh, Intellectual Property of Human Pluripotent Stem Cells *in* National Institutes of Health, Regenerative Medicine 53-54 (2006); Symposium, 39 New Eng. L. Rev. 501 (2005). This too is controversial, not only because the patents involve human cells and sometimes the destruction of human embryos, but also because patent holders have been accused of limiting the ability of researchers to pursue potentially important research of great public benefit. The holders of patents covering two of the most useful lines of human stem cells (WARF and Geron) claimed that their patents covered all similar human stem cells, even if they were derived from other sources. The patent owners imposed significant licensing costs on researchers, including the right to receive royalties if research using the stem cells resulted in additional products with commercial value.

Again, the U.S. Patent and Trademark Office, rather than relenting on whether human stem cells are fundamentally patentable subject matter, began to question stem cell patents on more technical grounds. For example, in 2007, it revoked three such patents previously issued to the University of Wisconsin because the cells "appeared to be the same as, or obvious variations of, cells described in earlier scientific papers or in patents issued to others." Andrew Pollack, 3 Patents on Stem Cells Are Revoked in Initial Review, N.Y. Times, Apr. 3, 2007, at C2. See also John M. Golden, WARF's Stem Cell Patents and Tensions Between Public and Private Sector Approaches to Research, 38 J.L., Med. & Ethics 314 (2010); Fiona Murray, The Stem-Cell Market—Patents and the Pursuit of Scientific Progress, 356 New Eng. J. Med. 2341 (2007); Simon Rose, Semiconductor Chips, Genes, and Stem

Cells: New Wine for New Bottles?, 38 Am. J.L. & Med. 113 (2012) (noting WARF's request to reopen prosecution of amended stem cell claims).

Some authors have suggested that stem cells be provided sui generis treatment. See, e.g., Stephen Munzer, How to Integrate Administrative Law and Tort Law: The Regulation of Stem Cell Products, 64 Admin. L. Rev. 743 (2012) (suggesting revisions to FDA and tort approaches); Simon A. Rose, Semiconductor Chips, Genes, and Stem Cells: New Wine for New Bottles?, 38 Am. J.L. & Med. 113 (2012) (arguing for sui generis IP approach for "isolated genes, stem cells, and related bioproducts"); David E. Winickoff et al., Opening Stem Cell Research and Development: A Policy Proposal for the Management of Data, Intellectual Property, and Ethics, 9 Yale J. Health Pol'y L. & Ethics 52, 59 (2009). European courts have rejected patents on embryonic stem cell lines created from the destruction of embryos. See, e.g., Nuala Moran, European Court Bans Embryonic Stem Cell Patents, 29 Nature Biotechnology 1057 (2011); Ned Stafford, Patents Cannot Be Given for Research Methods That Destroy Healthy Human Embryos to Obtain Stem Cells, German Court Rules, 345 BMJ e8248 (2012).

If human genes, cells, and tissues have been patented, should courts also allow the patenting of human beings? The 2011 Leahy-Smith America Invents Act included a provision relating to 35 U.S.C.A. §101 that mirrored previous PTO announcements and guidelines in providing that "[n]otwithstanding any other provision of law, no patent may issue on a claim directed to or encompassing a human organism." P.L. 112-29, 125 Stat. 284, 340 (2011). See also Seán M. Coughlin, The Newman Application and the USPTO's Unnecessary Response: Patentability of Humans and Human Embryos, 5 Chi.-Kent J. Intell. Prop. 90 (2006); Note, Designer Human Embryos: A Challenge for Patent Law and Regulation, 30 Quinnipiac L. Rev. 767 (2012).

Problem: Patenting Human Genes

The "Genomic Research and Accessibility Act" was introduced in the U.S. House of Representatives by a Republican and a Democrat sponsor early in 2007. The Act provides:

> Notwithstanding any other provision of law, no patent may be obtained for a nucleotide sequence, or its functions or correlations, or the naturally occurring products it specifies.

H.R. 977, 110th Cong., 1st Sess. (2007). Would you support the bill? Are you concerned about promoting innovation, ensuring access, the moral or ethical aspects of humanity, or other factors? See Michael Crichton, Patenting Life, N.Y. Times, Feb. 13, 2007, at A19 (op-ed supporting the bill).

Problem: Patenting Chimeras

"Chimeras" in mythology were a combination of three different animals. Modern-day researchers are combining two or more different species in a variety of ways. Hybrids can be created through genetic manipulation (inserting the gene of one species into the genes of another species) or through manipulating the combination of nuclear material from different species to create a new organism. Each cell of the new organism will have the newly inserted gene or new genetic combination. Chimeras can be created through combining the stem cells of one organism with the embryo of another; the resulting organism will have cells of different genetic heritage within it. There has been considerable attention to whether and how to limit the creation of chimeras or hybrids using human genes and/or stem cells. See section E.2, supra. Animal-human combinations are becoming commonplace in research. One example is the development of mice with human immune systems created by the addition of human genes; another is the mixing of mouse and human stem cells to create mice with human brain cells. See, e.g., Andrew Pollack, Seeking Cures, Patients Enlist Mice Stand-Ins, N.Y. Times, Sept. 25, 2012.

Should researchers be able to patent human-animal chimeras or hybrids? The PTO rejected a patent application for a human-animal chimera in 2005, citing among other things, the Thirteenth Amendment prohibition against slavery. See U.S. Patent Application 20030079240; Mary Ann Liebert, No Patent on Embryonic Human-Animal Chimera, 24 Biotechnology L. Rep. 290 (2005); Sander Rabin, The Human Use of Humanoid Beings: Chimeras and Patent Law, 24 Nature Biotechnology 517 (2006). At what point should use of human genes or tissues result in an inability to patent? What is the definition of "human" under the Leahy-Smith Innovation Act, supra? For more recent developments, see Ryan Hagglund, Patentability of Human-Animal Chimeras, 25 Santa Clara Computer & High Tech. L.J. 51 (2008); Gregory R. Hagen & Sébastien A. Gittens, Patenting Part-Human Chimeras, Transgenics and Stem Cells for Transplantation in the United States, Canada, and Europe, 14 Rich. J.L. & Tech. 11, 16 (2008); Laura A. Keay, Morality's Move Within U.S. Patent Law: From Moral Utility to Subject Matter, 40 AIPLA Q.J. 409 (2012); Note, Presumed Sapient: A Proposed Test for the Constitutional Personhood and Patentability of Human-Animal Chimeras and Hybrids, 46 U.S.F. L. Rev. 1075 (2012).

Problem: Synthetic Biology

The cases and commentaries to date have focused on issues connected with human genes. One of the consequences of genetic research more generally is the slowly developing ability of scientists to create and use DNA segments that can be selected to create new forms of life. This research raises significant intellectual property issues. As noted by Sapna Kumar and Arti Rai, intellectual property rules have the potential to stifle development of the field. For example, "foundational patents" on basic approaches and mechanisms could block development. Or, separate, smaller "building blocks" could be held by multiple inventors in ways that create "patent thickets" or "anticommons" hindering development. Sapna Kumar & Arti Rai, Synthetic Biology: The Intellectual Property Puzzle, 85 Tex. L. Rev. 1745 (2007) (analyzing issues and potential solutions).

Beyond intellectual property rules, synthetic biology also challenges our society's general strategy of using funding carrots and voluntary guidelines to direct research toward or away from certain areas. The synthesis of new forms of life could present substantial risks and benefits. See, e.g., Carl Zimmer, Amateurs Are

New Fear in Creating Mutant Virus, N.Y. Times, Mar. 5, 2012 (noting debate over publication of research reporting modification of H5N1 bird flu virus heightening transmissibility between mammals). What form of regulation seems appropriate and feasible? The National Science Advisory Board for Biosecurity (NSABB) initially recommended against publication of the H5N1 research. See Declan Butler, Post-Mortem on Mutant Flu, 484 Nature 150 (2012); Editorial, Publishing Risky Research, 485 Nature 5 (2012). Challenges to public health will provide a focus to the issues considered in Chapter 6.

Note: Concluding Thoughts

This chapter has examined the state's right to regulate individual reproductive capacity and the implications of advances in genetic technology. You are now in a position to assess whether the legal treatment of reproductive issues is united by any common constitutional theme or policy, or whether this chapter's topics are united only by their biological underpinnings. For interesting commentary that takes this perspective, see Note, Guiding Regulatory Reform in Reproduction and Genetics, 120 Harv. L. Rev. 574 (2006) (comparing and contrasting regulatory approaches to reproduction and genetics). You might also have developed some views on whether the Supreme Court has arrived at a firmer constitutional basis for judicial review of state legislation than in the *Lochner* debacle. You can appreciate the role that advances in genetics have played in reproduction along with some of the larger issues raised by the intersection of those advances with intellectual property law. You can consider the implications of advances in genetics for insurance coverage. You can look forward to being able to place the reproductive case law in context with material in other chapters. What is the nature of a person's interest in controlling reproduction? Do we have a constitutional right to control procreative capacity that is distinguishable from the right to control medical treatment? See Chapters 2-4. How is state regulation to protect the health of pregnant women or to safeguard fetal life similar to or different from other types of state regulation? See Chapter 6.

6

Public Health Law

Our lives are a tenuous gift, subject to revocation by injury, illness, and death. What is the proper role of government in safeguarding people from illness or injury? Should this responsibility be exercised by federal, state, or local government? To what extent should the need to protect public health outweigh the interests of persons subjected to coercive regulation? This chapter will consider these important questions.

Section A introduces some traditional public health strategies designed to reduce the transmission of disease and to protect individuals from injury. It is important to understand the potential scope of these measures before considering their legal implications. Medical and legal approaches to solving public health threats often seem to conflict, or at least to operate with different assumptions. Even the "simple" process of identifying and assessing the severity of public health threats can raise a number of important legal and policy questions.

Section B provides a sketch of legal underpinnings for state or federal attempts to protect public health. Traditionally, states have had the primary authority and responsibility for public health under their "police power," whether exercised directly or delegated to local governmental authorities. The federal government does not have any constitutional authority to regulate to protect the public health. Instead, its power comes from the authority to regulate the relationship between the United States and foreign countries, to regulate interstate commerce, and to spend to promote the public welfare. U.S. Const. art. 1, §8. This basic constitutional division of authority has blurred over time. These constitutional rules are supplemented by some important statutory developments, particularly the widespread effect of statutes that prohibit discrimination against persons with disabilities. International aspects of public health law are increasingly important given the need to identify and coordinate the response to global public health threats. The United States is also an active participant in developing and funding global public health initiatives targeting issues ranging from HIV to malaria.

What distinguishes "public health" law from other categories of legal regulation? It can be difficult to discern a unifying theme. Consider licensing requirements for restaurants, funding for waste treatment plants, food and drug regulations, federal support of the Centers for Disease Control and Prevention and the National Institutes of Health or for global health initiatives, rules governing quarantines and civil commitments, licensure of health care providers, and environmental regulation. It is hard to imagine a more diverse set of policies. Yet each is founded upon governmental interests in protecting health. Seen in this light, many of the topics discussed in other chapters could be considered specific examples of "public health law." State or federal attempts to control the physician-patient relationship, to control the dying process, or to regulate organ transplantation, abortion, and reproductive technologies can be justified by the need to protect the health of members of our society. The major distinction between these topics and those traditionally considered the domain of "public health law" is the identification of the "public" protected. Government regulations considered elsewhere in this book are concerned mainly with protecting the individual patient. In contrast, public health policies traditionally have protected society "at large" from threats to public health. Public health focuses on the health of populations.

The range of potential public health topics is so large that only a small subset of public health policies has been selected for consideration here. In section C, we focus on traditional public health interventions. This section explores the legal authority for disease testing and reporting statutes, quarantine, commitment, and mandatory treatment. Section D focuses on restrictions on consumer choices to protect public health. The federal government's regulation of pharmaceuticals is a particularly important example of this type of regulatory structure. The medical marijuana movement provides an opportunity to consider federal-state conflicts in public health policy. The chapter concludes with an exploration of public health approaches to the "epidemic" of obesity.

The main theme that connects these different topics is the attempt to balance the state's interest in protecting the public at large with an individual's right to freedom from coercion or constraint. As you read these materials, consider whether the balance struck between public needs and individual rights is appropriate. Will the state's interest in public health always outweigh the assertion of individual interests? What role will the courts take in ensuring that the threat to health is real and that the public health measures employed are likely to reduce the risk? Consider also the wide range of threats to public health that public health entities must address. Can the same government agencies and statutory/regulatory framework be used to address the public health risks presented by avian influenza, bioterrorism, and obesity?

A. PUBLIC HEALTH STRATEGIES

1. Medical and Legal Views of Public Health

What does it mean to protect the public's health? Health professionals tend to give a four-step answer to this question. First, potential threats to public health must be understood. Scientists work to identify "injuries" to public health and to connect those harms with their causes. Suppose that your fellow law students suddenly began to experience high fevers, swelling of their extremities, lung congestion, unconsciousness, and then rapid death. Part of the medical response would be to identify the cause of this problem—perhaps exposure to a contagious disease or an environmental toxin. Similarly, suppose that scientists observed increasing rates of morbidity and mortality from lung cancer or heart disease in society. They might then attempt to identify the causes of these conditions, such as use of tobacco products or ingestion of trans fats.

The second task is to identify a mechanism for eliminating or reducing the threat. Identifying a "cure" for the malady afflicting your classmates might be a part of this task. But researchers might also try to reduce exposure to the causal agent. If the disease is spread by exposure to rodent feces, for example, public health officials would probably develop recommendations to minimize exposure to this source and to safely clean your law school's food service area. Similarly, medical authorities might develop educational or regulatory campaigns designed to discourage smoking or consumption of trans fats.

The third step is implementation. The protective mechanisms developed in step two must be implemented. Governments must be convinced to spend scarce resources and/or to create appropriate laws or regulations to address the problem. In this stage, scientists must work with other groups in society, such as political interest groups, trade associations, lobbyists, public health officials, and legislators.

The fourth step, at least ideally, involves evaluation of the policy's outcomes. Have the new rules regarding food service sanitation actually reduced the premature death rate? Do people actually have a better diet and smoke less? If not, how can these policies be improved? Empirical research into the impact of public health law is an important example of this evaluation process.

■ HISTORY OF CDC
Centers for Disease Control
45 MMWR 526 (1996)

. . . When CDC's name changed in 1970, from the Communicable Disease Center to the Centers for Disease Control, CDC scientists were poised to accept new challenges. The most notable of the agency's many achievements in the following ten years was its role in global smallpox eradication, a program that finally succeeded because of the application of scientific principles of surveillance to a complex problem. In the realm of infectious diseases, CDC maintained its preeminence, identifying the Ebola virus and the sexual transmission of hepatitis B, and isolating the hepatitis C virus and the bacterium causing Legionnaires disease. The Study of the Effectiveness of Nosocomial Infection Control (SENIC) was the most expensive study the agency had ever undertaken and proved for the first time the effectiveness of recommended infection-control practices. Other studies included identification of the association of Reye's syndrome with aspirin use, the relation between liver cancer and occupational exposure to vinyl chloride, and the harmful effects of the popular liquid protein diet.

The 1980s institutionalized what is considered to be a critically important scientific activity at CDC—the collaboration of laboratorians and epidemiologists. The decade began with the national epidemic of toxic-shock syndrome, documentation of the association with a particular brand of tampons, and the subsequent withdrawal of that brand from the market. CDC collaboration with the National Center for Health Statistics (NCHS) resulted in the removal of lead from gasoline, which in turn has markedly decreased this exposure in all segments of the population. The major public health event of the 1980s was the emergence of AIDS. CDC helped lead the response to this epidemic, including characterization of the syndrome and defining risk factors for disease. . . .

The 1990s have been characterized by continuing applications of CDC's classic field-oriented epidemiology, as well as by the development of new methodologies. For example, the disciplines of health economics and decision sciences were merged to create a new area of emphasis—prevention effectiveness—as an approach for making more rational choices for public health interventions. In 1993, the investigation of hantavirus pulmonary syndrome required a melding between field epidemiology and the need for sensitivity to and involvement of American Indians and their culture. Similarly, the response to global problems with Ebola virus and plague underscore the importance of adapting these new methodologies. Other major CDC contributions to the world's health include global polio eradication efforts and efforts to prevent neural tube defects. Finally, in October 1992, Congress changed CDC's official name to the Centers for Disease Control and Prevention, to recognize CDC's leadership role in prevention. Today, CDC is both the nation's prevention agency and a global leader in public health. As the world enters the new millennium, CDC will remain the agency ready to address the challenges to its vision of healthy people in a healthy world through prevention.

■ SUMMARY OF NOTIFIABLE DISEASES— UNITED STATES, 2010

Deborah A. Adams et al.

59(53) MMWR 1, 2, 6-7 (June 1, 2012)

BACKGROUND

. . . A notifiable disease is one for which regular, frequent, and timely information regarding individual cases is considered necessary for the prevention and control of the disease. A brief history of the reporting of nationally notifiable infectious diseases in the United States is available at http://wwwn.cdc.gov/nndss/script/history.aspx. In 1961, CDC assumed responsibility for the collection and publication of data on nationally notifiable diseases. . . .

Notifiable disease reporting at the local level protects the public's health by ensuring the proper identification and follow-up of cases. Public health workers ensure that persons who are already ill receive appropriate treatment; trace contacts who need vaccines, treatment, quarantine, or education; investigate and halt outbreaks; eliminate environmental hazards; and close premises where spread has occurred. Surveillance of notifiable conditions helps public health authorities to monitor the effect of notifiable conditions, measure disease trends, assess the effectiveness of control and prevention measures, identify populations or geographic areas at high risk, allocate resources appropriately, formulate prevention strategies, and develop public health policies. Monitoring surveillance data enables public health authorities to detect sudden changes in disease occurrence and distribution, identify changes in agents and host factors, and detect changes in health-care practices.

The list of nationally notifiable infectious diseases is revised periodically. A disease might be added to the list as a new pathogen emerges, or a disease might be deleted as its incidence declines. Public health officials at state health departments and CDC collaborate in determining which diseases should be nationally notifiable. CSTE [Council of State and Territorial Epidemiologists], with input from CDC, makes recommendations annually for additions and deletions. Although disease reporting is mandated by legislation or regulation at the state and local levels, state reporting to CDC is voluntary. Reporting completeness of notifiable diseases is highly variable and related to the condition or disease being reported. . . . The list of diseases considered notifiable varies by state and year. Current and historic national public health surveillance case definitions used for classifying and enumerating cases consistently across reporting jurisdictions are available at www.cdc.gov/nndss. . . .

REVISED INTERNATIONAL HEALTH REGULATIONS

In May 2005, the World Health Assembly adopted revised International Health regulations (IHR) . . . that went into effect in the United States on July 18, 2007. This international legal instrument governs the role of the World Health Organization (WHO) and its member countries, including the United States, in identifying, responding to, and sharing information about Public Health Emergencies of International Concern (PHEIC). A PHEIC is an extraordinary event that 1) constitutes a public health risk to other countries through international spread of disease, and 2) potentially requires a coordinated international response.

The IHR are designed to prevent and protect against the international spread of diseases while minimizing the effect on world travel and trade. Countries that have adopted these rules have a much broader responsibility to detect, respond to, and report public health emergencies that potentially require a coordinated international response in addition to taking preventive measures. The IHR will help countries work together to identify, respond to, and share information about PEHIC.

The revised IHR is a conceptual shift from a predefined disease list to a framework of reporting and responding to events on the basis of an assessment of public health criteria, including seriousness, unexpectedness, and international travel and trade implications. PHEIC are events that fall within those criteria (further defined in a decision algorithm in Annex 2 of the revised IHR). Four conditions always constitute a PHEIC and do not require the use of the IHR decision instrument in Annex 2: Severe Acute Respiratory Syndrome (SARS), smallpox, poliomyelitis caused by wild-type poliovirus, and human influenza caused by a new subtype. Any other event requires the use of the decision algorithm in Annex 2 of the IHR to determine if it is a potential PHEIC. Examples of events that require the use of the decision instrument include, but are not limited to, cholera, pneumonic plague, yellow fever, West Nile fever, viral hemorrhagic fevers, and meningococcal disease. Other biologic, chemical, or radiologic events might fit the decision algorithm and also must be reportable to WHO. All WHO member states are required to notify WHO of a potential PHEIC. WHO makes the final determination about the existence of a PHEIC.

Health-care providers in the United States are required to report diseases, conditions, or outbreaks as determined by local, state, or territorial law and regulation, and as outlined in each state's list of reportable conditions. All health-care providers should work with their local, state, and territorial health agencies to identify and report events that might constitute a potential PHEIC occurring in their location. U.S. State and Territorial Departments of Health have agreed to report information about a potential PHEIC to the most relevant federal agency responsible for the event. In the case of human disease, the U.S. State or Territorial Departments of Health will notify CDC rapidly through existing formal and informal reporting mechanisms. . . . CDC will further analyze the event based on the decision algorithm in Annex 2 of the IHR and notify the U.S. Department of Health and Human Services (DHHS) Secretary's Operations Center (SOC), as appropriate.

DHHS has the lead role in carrying out the IHR, in cooperation with multiple federal departments and agencies. The DHHS SOC is the central body for the United States responsible for reporting potential events to WHO. The United States has 48 hours to assess the risk of the reported event. If authorities determine that a potential PHEIC exists, the WHO member country has 24 hours to report the event to WHO.

An IHR decision algorithm . . . has been developed to help countries determine whether an event should be reported. If any two of the following four questions can be answered in the affirmative, then a determination should be made that a potential PHEIC exists and WHO should be notified:

- Is the public health impact of the event serious?
- Is the event unusual or unexpected?
- Is there a significant risk of international spread?
- Is there a significant risk of international travel or trade restrictions? . . . .

▮ THE LAW AND THE PUBLIC'S HEALTH: A STUDY
OF INFECTIOUS DISEASE LAW IN THE
UNITED STATES*
Lawrence O. Gostin, Scott Burris & Zita Lazzarini
99 Colum. L. Rev. 59 (1999)

Public health is typically regarded as a scientific pursuit, and, undoubtedly, our understanding of the etiology and response to disease is heavily influenced by

*Reprinted with permission. Lawrence O. Gostin is a law professor at Georgetown University. Scott Burris is a law professor at Temple University's Beasley School of Law. Zita Lazzarini is a professor and Director of the Division of Medical Humanities, Health Law & Ethics at the University of Connecticut School of Medicine.

scientific inquiry. Less well understood is the role of law in public health. Law is an essential part of public health practice. Law defines the jurisdiction of public health officials and specifies the manner in which they may exercise their authority. The law is a tool in public health work, which is used to establish norms for healthy behavior and to help create the social conditions in which people can be healthy. The most important social debates about public health take place in legal fora—legislatures, courts, and administrative agencies—and in the law's language of rights, duties, and justice. . . .

The Institute of Medicine (IOM), in its foundational 1988 report, "The Future of Public Health" (the IOM Report), agreed that law was essential to public health, but cast serious doubt on the soundness of public health's legal basis in the United States. . . .[2]

Communicable disease control has occupied American governments from the earliest years of European settlement, and it was in response to epidemics that formal health agencies were first created. Throughout the history of the United States, each state, through the exercise of its police powers, has enacted a web of legislation to control infectious disease. These laws range from generic statutes establishing powers relating to communicable and sexually transmitted disease, to disease-specific laws relating, for example, to tuberculosis or HIV/AIDS. Although the threat of communicable diseases in America has declined throughout the last century, new diseases such as AIDS, hepatitis C, and hantavirus have emerged as major threats, and old diseases such as tuberculosis and E. coli have returned with new virulence.

Communicable disease law has deep historical roots, yet remains centrally important to legal institutions and to the public's health. Our approach to reform, however, is based on a broader notion of the determinants of health and the role of the state in promoting it, a view in which the distinction between communicable and noncommunicable health threats is, in many ways, unimportant. Thus, many of our points about communicable disease law apply to public health regulation as a whole.

Our frankly utilitarian premise is that public health law ought to be as effective as possible in helping public health agencies create the conditions necessary for health. To do this, the law must reflect our best understanding of how public health agencies work to promote health, as well as the political conditions in which these agencies operate. . . .

The essential job of public health agencies is to identify what makes us healthy and what makes us sick, and then to take the steps necessary to make sure we encounter a maximum of the former and a minimum of the latter. At first glance, this would seem to be a rather uncontroversial goal, but we will show that the pursuit of public health creates fundamental social disputes virtually by definition. Public health is rooted in the biomedical and social sciences, but from the moment of asserting some collective responsibility for the population's health, through the process of defining the determinants of health and disease, to the implementation of programs, the practice of public health entails judgments that challenge deeply ingrained social attitudes and practices.

2. Committee for the Study of the Future of Public Health, IOM, Nat'l Acad. of Sci., The Future of Public Health 1-6 (1988). . . .

Three distinct accounts of disease and health are widely used in public health practice today. . . . The microbial model focuses on the pathogens that are the immediate causes of many illnesses. The microbial model produces interventions designed to kill the pathogen or isolate it from human beings; it also tends to produce political disputes about the proper scope and exercise of the state's power to attack the pathogen by controlling the human being who carries it. The behavioral model looks primarily at the behavior that exposes us to pathogens or that otherwise tends to produce illness and premature death. The idea that behavior is an important factor in health and disease is widely accepted, but health efforts on the behavioral model are nonetheless often controversial. When the government gives advice about how to have safer sex or how to reduce the risk of drug injection, many people see an official endorsement of what they regard as deviant behavior. When the state uses its power to discourage smoking, to require a motorcycle helmet, or even to prevent dental caries through water fluoridation, many people see unacceptable paternalism. The ecological model takes the broadest view of what makes people ill or well, seeking the causes of disease in the way society organizes itself, produces and distributes wealth, and interacts with the natural environment. Such an approach operates unavoidably as a critique of the status quo, pointing to such fundamental social causes of disease as poverty, racism, and severe income inequality. The ecological model also implicates our collective responsibility for unhealthy behavior, suggesting the importance of social factors in producing, for example, the levels of drug abuse and unsafe sex that fuel the HIV and hepatitis epidemics. Each of these models of disease and health is rooted in the sciences of medicine and epidemiology and provides complementary ways of understanding and fighting disease, but each also entails judgments about who is responsible for illness and who must change to produce health. . . .

We name five perennially significant political problems inherent in modern public health practice. The first is the problem of popular apathy about public health programs. Much of what public health agencies do is to prevent injury and disease, often by getting people at low risk to refrain from behaviors they enjoy or profit from. . . .

Second, public health agencies have a jurisdiction problem. Many societal and environmental factors that influence public health are beyond the reach of health agencies. Occupational safety, environmental protection, food safety, and the prevention of violence and accidents are normally the province of other agencies, and much of the behavior that public health tries to change—eating a diet high in fat, for example—is not subject to direct legal regulation at all.

Third, public health agencies must confront the problem of stigma and social hostility. Communicable disease control has traditionally had to deal with barriers thrown up by the social reaction to disease. In their time, diseases like cholera, yellow fever, tuberculosis, and syphilis were all attributed to sin or vice, and the shame and social risk of having such conditions often led the sick to conceal their illness and to avoid medical and public health services. The problem of stigma and social hostility has been an important factor in HIV prevention since the earliest days of the epidemic.

The fourth problem involves the legitimacy of government action in certain realms of human behavior. The problem of legitimacy arises whenever public health measures are perceived to exceed the bounds of proper government action.

Whether framed in terms of paternalism, endorsement, neutrality, or simple libertarianism, the legitimacy issue turns on the belief that there are certain things government simply ought not do, no matter how laudable its objectives.

Finally, health agencies face a problem of trust. Because so much of what public health does depends upon voluntary cooperation by those at risk and the support of the population at large, health officials must appear credible in the advice they render and trustworthy in their practices. If the public perceives health officials as simply the tool of an overreaching government or suspects that they have been captured by "special interests," their ability to win compliance and support is compromised.

As if these built-in challenges were not enough, communicable disease control faces economic and structural barriers: the decline in the public health infrastructure for monitoring and controlling disease; the transformation of the health care system, including expansion of managed care and integrated delivery systems; and the emergence and resurgence of infectious disease threats. . . .

"Public health" refers both to a goal for the health of a population and to professional practices aimed at its attainment. . . . At a minimum, the goal of public health is to attain the highest level and widest distribution of physical and mental health that a society reasonably can achieve within the limits of the resources it chooses to devote to the task. . . .

Even this carefully narrowed definition places the goal of public health at the intersection of deep social fault lines. First, it posits that public health is a function of the health of populations, not individuals. Geoffrey Rose has brilliantly described the practical implications of this difference for disease prevention, including most notably the "prevention paradox." This is the apparently iron law holding that those measures that have the greatest potential for improving public health (like seatbelt use) offer little absolute benefit to any individual, while measures that heroically save individual lives (like heart transplants) make no significant contribution to the population's health. Public health, in other words, has as its chief duty the unenviable tasks of providing common goods and controlling negative externalities, both difficult at best. . . .

The ability of public health work to attract support is, however, essential to its success, for, as the definition of public health also reminds us, public health operates in a world of choices in the allocation of limited resources. The great sanitarian Herman Biggs famously remarked that "public health is purchasable," but because there will always be limits on how much we are willing to buy, public health will always turn on allocational decisions. Thus, public health, as both a goal and a practice, is as inherently political (i.e., concerned with the allocation of resources in society) as it is technological (i.e., concerned with the deployment of professional knowledge of illness).

Finally, public health's desire for optimally healthy populations builds into the definition a concern for distributive justice that must, on occasion, challenge the current distribution of wealth. A society in which the more prosperous segment of the population enjoys health conditions that are as good as any in the world, but where many are living substantially below the norm, is not a nation with good public health. . . .

Nineteenth-century sanitarians focused on providing clean water, adequate sewers, pure food, safe workplaces, and hygienic dwellings to the urban poor who were at greatest risk for the most common communicable diseases. Toward this end, boards of health were created and given increasingly broad powers to investigate and abate nuisances endangering health, and an administrative and legal infrastructure was built of food safety laws, building codes, social welfare programs, and water bureaus. But as early as the turn of this century, the escalating success of biomedical science was changing public health, moving its center away from a broad social, environmental focus to a more individualized, medical one based on germ theory. Health leaders . . . pushed for the legal authority to deploy modern "epidemiological methods" of disease control, in which pathogens were to be identified through individual testing or population screening and reporting, and then eliminated through vaccination, treatment, isolation, or quarantine. With good diagnostic tools and surveillance, disease outbreaks could be spotted early. With quick and effective treatments, patients could be rendered noninfectious with little disruption to their lives or society's business. The pathogen, not social conditions, was thought to be the problem, and through modern methods like these, the pathogen could be defeated. Health authorities sought the power to test suspected carriers, screen populations (such as marriage license applicants and newborns), trace partners, and require treatment. The social vision and reform agenda that had focused sanitary reformers on slums and sewer lines was replaced with a concern for biomedical research, vaccination, and timely medical treatment. It was in the early- to mid-twentieth century, the heyday of the microbial model of disease, that communicable disease law assumed the form in which it largely exists to this day.

Health departments are influenced by this history, even as they try to adapt to changes in social conditions and threats to health. Health departments today are generally organized to serve four "core functions": health promotion and disease prevention; assessment, data collection, and data analysis; medical services; and leadership and policy development. . . .

The main job of health agencies is to directly promote good health and prevent illness. To this end, modern public health practice deploys measures based on all three of the major models of disease causation. Health departments continue to employ traditional measures aimed at finding and controlling pathogens (e.g., testing, screening, reporting, contact tracing, vaccination, compulsory treatment, and isolation). Health departments also oversee the purity of water supplies and the hygienic conditions of food service establishments. Law provides both jurisdiction over the problem and the authority to require compliance. Law, in the form of privacy rules and due process requirements, also helps assure that measures involving the control of individuals are, and are perceived to be, rational, fair, and as harmless to the individual as possible.

Health departments also devote significant resources to changing behavior in the population. As chronic, nonmicrobial diseases such as cancer and heart disease came to dominate the mortality tables, public health focused its attention on risk-enhancing behavior such as smoking, high-fat diets, and inactivity. Significant behavioral sources of traumatic injury and death, such as teen violence and drunken driving, have also been treated as public health problems. Changing behavior has, of course, become crucial in controlling communicable diseases like HIV, as well. Risk-factor screening (for cholesterol or high blood pressure, for example), individualized counseling, and health education are standard tools of behavior change, but so is the law. Law is used to reduce unsafe behavior by both direct (e.g., helmet laws for motorcyclists and drunk driving laws) and indirect (e.g., taxes and subsidies) means, the goals of which are to make healthier behavior less costly and unhealthy behavior more expensive.

Influenced by ecological thinking about disease, public health workers have recognized the importance of addressing the social causes of unhealthy individual behavior. Individual choices depend in substantial part on the options provided by society and on the behavioral cues with which individual decisionmakers are bombarded in any social setting. They also depend upon material conditions, like the distribution of wealth and government policies. Health workers now routinely design interventions that attempt to address social factors such as stigma, discrimination, and sexism. Public health officials have become advocates of policies, such as the elimination of legal barriers to sterile hypodermic syringes and needles, that make it possible for individuals to make healthier choices. Using tools of economics and marketing, public health authorities have begun to develop programs to influence individual behavior choices by changing the prevailing social norms.

Ecological strategies address environmental problems, land use, patterns of commerce, and medical and commercial use of antimicrobials, as well as social, political, and economic conditions that influence population movement and changes in standards of living. With such broad targets, health measures aimed at ecological causes of disease quickly bring health agencies to the outer bounds of their statutory jurisdiction. . . .

Notes: Traditional Public Health Strategies

1. *Sources of Information.* There are a broad range of measures designed to improve public health, ranging from improved sanitation to vaccination, screening programs, and education about health threats such as tobacco. There are different sources of information on all of these public health topics. The Centers for Disease Control and Prevention (CDC) is a world leader in identifying threats to public health and in developing recommendations to reduce health risks. Its publication, the aptly named Morbidity and Mortality Weekly Report (MMWR), is a major source of data on a variety of threats to public health, but particularly for data on contagious diseases. The publication is not for the fainthearted or for those with any tendencies toward hypochondria. The MMWR's pages are regularly filled with detailed case descriptions of everything from infectious diseases to the disastrous effects of ingesting commercially prepared, improperly refrigerated potato soup. The CDC maintains extensive online resources. See, e.g., CDC homepage, www.cdc .gov/; MMWR homepage, www.cdc.gov/mmwr/.

2. *Conflicts Between Medical and Legal Norms.* Where should public health policies be developed—in legislative bodies, in administrative agencies, or somewhere else? Should physicians or lawyers have primary control over the development and implementation of public health strategies? What role should the courts take in overseeing public health measures? Medical or scientific authorities and lawyers tend to have somewhat different perspectives on public health strategies. Historically, public health officials focused on the medical or scientific aspects of public health policies and paid little attention to their impact on individual liberty. The article by Professors Gostin, Burris, and Lazzarini was one of the early publications

in a significant effort to study and to reform public health law that is still under way. The CDC established a public health law program, see www.cdc.gov/phlp/ and assisted in the creation of academic centers of study, see www.publichealthlaw.net/. Professor Gostin is a leader in the reform of public health law. See Lawrence O. Gostin, Public Health Law: Power, Duty, Restraint (2d ed. 2008) [hereinafter Public Health Law].

3. *Jurisdictional Issues.* Public health threats often span jurisdictional boundaries. The federal government plays an important role in addressing threats that cross international or state boundaries. 42 U.S.C. §§264-272; CDC, Specific Laws and Regulations Governing the Control of Communicable Disease. The CDC periodically issues guidelines regarding monitoring airplane passengers for infections. See Centers for Disease Control, Interim Guidance for Airlines Regarding Flight Crews Arriving from Domestic and International Areas Affected by Swine Influenza.

The CDC plays an important role in collecting data from states about the incidence of disease, and the federal government is responsible for making determinations under WHO's International Health Regulations (www.who.int/ihr/en/). Yet, mandatory disease reporting is established by state law, reporting to the CDC is voluntary, and there are gaps and difficulties in comparing the voluntarily reported state data. Is the constitutional balance between state and federal authority in protecting public health appropriate? Has the federal government achieved virtual authority over public health matters by tying state receipt of federal funding to compliance with federal requirements? See Rebecca Katz & Sara Rosenbaum, Challenging Custom: Rethinking National Population Surveillance Policy in a Global Public Health Age, 35 J. Health Pol. Pol'y & L. 1027 (2010) (suggesting possible expansion of federal involvement in disease surveillance); Kumanan Wilson et al., Strategies for Implementing the New International Health Regulations in Federal Countries, 86(3) Bull. World Health Organ. 215 (2008). Given the nature of the threats to public health, should the United States work with other countries toward more powerful international institutions and standards? Lawrence O. Gostin & Emily A. Mok eds., Symposium, Global Health Governance, 38 J.L. Med. & Ethics 451-646 (2010).

A different form of jurisdictional conflict arises as public health policies move beyond traditional responses to infectious diseases into addressing chronic diseases caused by behavioral choices, disparities in health related to social determinants of the health of populations, and complex threats such as climate change. Public Health Law at 38-41; CDC Health Disparities and Inequalities Report—United States, 60 MMWR 1 (Supp. 2011).

As one example, public health organizations are beginning to address climate change as a new threat to public health. See CDC, Climate Change and Human Health (www.cdc.gov/climateandhealth). What are the advantages and disadvantages of addressing global warming as a public health issue? What effect does framing the issue in this way have on federal and state governments' ability to regulate human activities that contribute to global warming? Greenhouse gas emissions are typically seen as matters for environmental regulation rather than as public health threats remedied through, e.g., nuisance actions. See, e.g., American Electric Power Co. Inc. v. Connecticut, 564 U.S., 131 S. Ct. 2527 (2011) (federal legislation and proposed EPA action on greenhouse gases displaces availability of nuisance claim under federal law; availability of state law nuisance claims to be determined on remand); Massachusetts et al. v. Environmental Protection Agency et al., 549 U.S. 497 (2007) (EPA has jurisdiction over greenhouse gas emissions under the Clean Air Act). The CDC and WHO focus on planning for the health care outcomes of global warming rather than on reduction or elimination of the underlying problem.

4. *The International Health Regulations (IHR) and the 2009 H1N1 Pandemic.* The H1N1 epidemic in 2009 provided an opportunity to test the international health law framework. H1N1 was a novel influenza virus; the impact on public health thus could have ranged from minimal to severe. The WHO attempted to use its powers under the IHR to guide the global response; ultimately the morbidity and mortality associated with the virus proved to be within normal ranges. Critics charged that public health authorities overreacted to the threat and noted challenges in producing the H1N1 vaccine. An expert review panel concluded:

> The IHR helped make the world better prepared to cope with public-health emergencies. The core national and local capacities called for in the IHR are not yet fully operational and are not now on a path to timely implementation worldwide. . . .
>
> The world is ill-prepared to respond to a severe influenza pandemic or to any similarly global, sustained and threatening public-health emergency. Beyond implementation of core public-health capacities called for in the IHR, global preparedness can be advanced through research, reliance on a multisectoral approach, strengthened health-care delivery systems, economic development in low and middle-income countries and improved health status.

Report of the Review Committee on the Functioning of the International Health Regulations in Relation to Pandemic (H1N1) 2009, 11-12 (2011).

China confined many North American travelers to hotels and hospitals during the H1N1 outbreak. See Andrew Jacobs, Mexico Objects to Quarantine in China, N.Y. Times, May 4, 2009. The Review Committee noted that a number of countries failed to comply with WHO guidance regarding the lack of justification for restrictions and travel and trade. The Committee concluded: "The most important structural shortcoming of the IHR is the lack of enforceable sanctions. For example, if a country fails to explain why it has adopted more restrictive traffic and trade measures than those recommended by WHO, no legal consequences follow." Id. at 12.

5. *Fear.* What would be your response to an apparently serious, contagious illness spreading among your classmates? Dangerous contagious diseases can create a state euphemistically called "anxiety," better known as fear or panic. Fear can motivate a wide range of responses, some helpful from a public health standpoint, but some not. What should be the role of public health officials in addressing public concerns? Should courts worry more about too weak or too vigilant public health responses? See also Cass R. Sunstein, Laws of Fear: Beyond the Precautionary Principle (2005); Luc Bonneux & Wim Van Damme, An Iatrogenic Pandemic of Panic, 332 BMJ 786 (2006). For more on this topic, see Albert Camus, The Plague (1947) or the portions of the Bible (especially Exodus, Deuteronomy, and Amos) dealing with plagues and public reactions to contagious diseases.

6. *Other Resources.* There are a number of excellent books and articles on public health measures from medical and legal perspectives. In addition to the sources noted above, see Dan Beauchamp, The Health of the Republic: Epidemics, Medicine, and Moralism as Challenges to Democracy (1990); Allan M. Brandt, No Magic Bullet: A Social History of Venereal Disease in the United States Since 1880 (1985); Scott Burris et al., Making the Case for Laws That Improve Health: A Framework for Public Health Law Research, 88 Milbank Q. 169 (2010); Committee on Public Health Strategies to Improve Health, Institute of Medicine, For the Public's Health: Revitalizing Law and Policy to Meet New Challenges (2011); David P. Fidler & Lawrence O. Gostin, Biosecurity in the Global Age: Biological Weapons, Public Health, and the Rule of Law (2007); David P. Fidler, SARS: Governance and the Globalization of Disease (2004); Frank P. Grad, Public Health Law Manual (2004); Kenneth R. Wing & Benjamin Gilbert, The Law and the Public's Health (7th ed. 2006); Wendy E. Parmet, Populations, Public Health, and the Law (2009); Alexandra Minna Stern & Howard Markel, International Efforts to Control Infectious Diseases, 1851 to the Present, 292 JAMA 1474 (2004); Symposium, Public Health in Law, 10 J. Health Care L. & Pol'y 1 (2007). For an effort to provide guidance for lawyers and judges in a health emergency, see Michael Colodner ed., New York State Public Health Legal Manual (2011).

7. *Assessing Public Health Threats.* What are the greatest threats to public health? Infectious conditions? Bioterrorism? Environmental hazards such as climate change? Dietary and lifestyle choices? How would you identify the "greatest" threat? By number of persons affected? By the severity of the harm? Now consider the appropriate role of government in responding to the risks you have identified. Should the government develop a response to one or more of these risks? What type of response seems justified: public education or using regulations to reduce risks? Where should governments apply their scarce resources and why? The next case addresses some of these issues, in the context of OSHA regulation. Although the Occupational Safety and Health Administration is not considered one of the classic public health agencies, the following case focuses on a workplace health risk peculiar to hospitals—contagious disease—that is at the core of classic public health regulation. Moreover, this case explains the fundamentals of risk assessment that are the basis for all public health measures.

2. Risk Assessment and Regulatory Competence

■ AMERICAN DENTAL ASSOCIATION v. MARTIN
984 F.2d 823 (7th Cir. 1993)

POSNER, Circuit Judge.

In 1991 the Occupational Safety and Health Administration promulgated a rule on occupational exposure to bloodborne pathogens. 29 C.F.R. §1910.1030. The rule is designed to protect health care workers from viruses, particularly those causing Hepatitis B and AIDS, that can be transmitted in the blood of patients. Promulgated after a protracted notice-and-comment rulemaking proceeding, the rule and its supporting reasons occupy 178 densely packed pages in the Federal Register. Most employers in the health care industry have accepted the rule, which in essence requires compliance with procedures for health care workers recommended by the Centers for Disease Control (since renamed the Centers for Disease Control and Prevention), the federal agency responsible for the control of contagious diseases. Many of these employers, indeed, had adopted the procedures as soon as the CDC recommended them. Three employer groups, however, challenge the rule—dentists, represented by the American Dental Association, and medical-personnel and home-health employers, both represented by the Home Health Services and Staffing Association. Medical-personnel firms supply health care workers on a temporary basis to hospitals and nursing homes, while home-health firms supply such workers to patients at home.

As of 1991, there had been only 24 confirmed cases of U.S. health care workers infected with the AIDS virus by patients since AIDS was first diagnosed in 1981. Hepatitis B is a far more common disease than AIDS, though less scary, publicized, or stigmatized. . . . Although most infected persons recover uneventfully, about 1 percent die and about 6 to 10 percent of adult (and a much higher percentage of child) victims of Hepatitis B become carriers. . . . Nonetheless, because of the greater virulence of the Hepatitis B virus (HBV) and the fact that many health care workers are not vaccinated, patient-communicated Hepatitis B kills about 200 health workers in the United States per year—roughly 100 times the number of such workers infected by patient-communicated HIV [human immunodeficiency virus]. The precautions against infection of health care workers by the two viruses is similar, except that the vaccine against HBV offers a protection that has no counterpart with regard to HIV, and contaminated laundry poses a danger of spreading HBV that also has no counterpart with regard to HIV.

OSHA's rule reflects the public-health philosophy of "universal precautions," which means precautions against the blood of every patient, not just the blood of patients known or believed likely to be carriers of HBV or HIV. The precautions are various. They include engineering controls (such as requirements for the location of sinks), work practice controls (such as standards of care in handling contaminated sharp instruments, such as needles), requirements for personal protective equipment such as gloves, masks, goggles, and gowns, requirements for housekeeping (covering such things as the cleaning of contaminated surfaces and laundry and the disposal of contaminated waste), reporting requirements, and provisions for medical care. The rule requires the employer to offer employees who are at risk of exposure to the blood of patients the Hepatitis B vaccine at the employer's own expense, though it allows the employees to decline to be vaccinated. An employee who is involved in an "exposure incident," such as being stuck with a contaminated needle, must be offered at the employer's expense a confidential blood test for HBV and HIV; that is, only the employee is entitled to the result of the test.

In deciding to impose this extensive array of restrictions on the practice of medicine, nursing, and dentistry, OSHA did not (indeed is not authorized to) compare the benefits with the costs and impose the restrictions on finding that the former exceeded the latter. Instead it asked whether the restrictions would materially reduce a significant workplace risk to human health without imperiling the existence of, or threatening massive dislocation to, the health care industry. For this is the applicable legal standard. 29 U.S.C. §655(b) (5); Industrial Union Dept., AFL-CIO v. American Petroleum Institute, 448 U.S. 607, 642-645, 655-656 (1980) (the "benzene" case) (plurality opinion); American Textile Mfrs. Institute, Inc. v. Donovan, 452 U.S. 490, 509-512, 530-536 (1981) (the "cotton dust" case). The agency focused on HBV rather than on HIV because of the minute number of health care workers who have been infected by the latter virus. It estimated that the rule would eliminate between 113 and 129 annual deaths of health care workers from Hepatitis B, and a somewhat higher figure (187 to 197) if deaths of nonworkers infected by health-care workers who (but for the rule) would be carriers are factored in as well. (In making this additional calculation, OSHA expressed an uncharacteristic, but as it seems to us commendable, concern with the indirect effects of its rule. On the other hand it did not consider the reduction in medical care that might result from the rule's effect in making the practice of medicine more costly—more on this shortly.) Most of these deaths would be avoided by the vaccine, but by no means all, because the vaccine is not a hundred percent effective and, more important, because many health care workers refuse to be vaccinated. Hence the other parts of the rule would have a positive effect even on Hepatitis B; and there is no vaccine (or cure) for AIDS.

OSHA's evaluation of the effects of the rule, relying as it does on the undoubted expertise of the Centers for Disease Control, cannot seriously be faulted, at least by judges. Hence we cannot say that the rule, viewed as a whole, flunks the test of material reduction of a significant risk to workplace health. As for the impact on the health care industry, OSHA estimated the total cost of compliance with the rule at $813 million a year, clearly not enough to break the multi-hundred-billion-dollar healthcare industry. The rule's implicit valuation of a life is high—about $4 million—but not so astronomical, certainly by regulatory standards, . . . as to call the rationality of the rule seriously into question, especially when we consider that neither Hepatitis B nor AIDS is a disease of old people. . . . Nor is death the only consequence of these diseases. AIDS causes protracted pain and disability before death, and Hepatitis B causes pain and disability and often permanent liver damage, even when the patient "recovers."

No doubt the agency's $813 million estimate is an underestimate. It ignores . . . many or most time costs. . . . But the petitioners made no effort in the rulemaking proceeding to quantify these costs or to provide any basis for supposing them to be huge.

OSHA also exaggerated the number of lives likely to be saved by the rule by ignoring lives likely to be sacrificed by it, since the increased cost of medical care, to the extent passed on to consumers, will reduce the demand for medical care, and some people may lose their lives as a result. The agency's consideration of the indirect costs of the rule is thus incomplete. How many lives the rule is likely to sacrifice, however, we do not know; and again the petitioners make no effort to come up with a number. So while $4 million doubtless underestimates the agency's implicit valuation of each life actually likely to be saved by the rule, we do not know how great the underestimate is and we cannot resolve our doubts against the agency. We add that the $4 million ignores the benefits to workers who will be spared illness—remember that 99 times as many people get Hepatitis B as die from it.

As an original matter we might have been inclined to think that the regulation of the safety of the medical and dental workplace could be left largely to the market, that doctors, dentists, and other health care workers have a stronger incentive than the government to protect themselves from health hazards at reasonable cost, that their employees are compensated in their wages for what is after all a modest risk, and that health care workers who refuse to be vaccinated against Hepatitis B are knowingly assuming the risk and should be left to bear the consequences without government interference. But the occupational safety and health law is constructed on different premises that we are not free to question, and perhaps the infectious character of HIV and HBV warrants even on narrowly economic grounds more regulation than would be necessary in the case of a noncommunicable disease. . . .

So in the main the [bloodborne pathogen] rule must be upheld. Which is not to say that it is a good rule. It may be unnecessary; it may go too far; its costs may exceed its benefits. . . . But our duty as a reviewing court of generalist judges is merely to patrol the boundary of reasonableness, and . . . OSHA's bloodborne-pathogens rule—accepted as it has been by most health care industries and based as it is on the recommendations of the nation's, perhaps the world's, leading repository of knowledge about the control of infectious diseases—does not cross it. . . .

COFFEY, Circuit Judge, concurring in part, dissenting in part.

Section 3(8) of the Occupational Safety and Health Act defines "occupational safety and health standard" as a standard which requires the adoption of practices "reasonably necessary or appropriate to provide safe or healthful employment and places of employment." 29 U.S.C. §652(8). . . .

The rule adopted can best be classified as an attempt to try to kill a fly with a sledgehammer. The rule was drafted partially in response to the public hysteria surrounding AIDS. . . . The rule was not drafted in response to an established significant risk of harm to employees. The dangers of transmitting the blood-borne pathogen hepatitis B have been well-established for years yet for reasons unexplained OSHA did not concern itself with that risk in the workplace prior to November 1987. . . . The rule unduly burdens health care employers, including but not limited to dentists, doctors and hospitals, while offering but minimal benefit to their employees, and furthermore it is estimated that it will increase health care costs some $817 million annually. Additionally, the rule duplicates the scientifically based and well-reasoned guidelines of the Centers for Disease Control and Prevention (CDC) a governmental agency medically and scientifically qualified to determine and evaluate if there is in fact a significant risk in the health care area and, if so, propose reasonable, efficient guidelines. . . .

I suggest that the United States Congress must address the question of whether there is a need to duplicate the education, investigation and prevention efforts of the CDC and state health agencies, thus increasing health care costs, and whether OSHA is the proper agency to regulate health care given their lack of experience, knowledge and expertise in comparison to the CDC and state health agencies. In the alternative, the entire rule should be remanded to OSHA. . . .

I am cognizant of the need for dental and medical regulations and safeguards to insure and prevent the spread of infection, but fail to understand why OSHA must assert authority over the health care field when it lacks the required medical knowledge, training, and experience, much less expertise. . . . There is no need for four separate entities (OSHA, CDC, state agencies, and professional organizations) to regulate the health care industry. . . . One qualified entity can most effectively and efficiently regulate the health care profession. I see no reason why the respective states are unable to continue to regulate the medical and dental profession as the states have traditionally done in the past and presently do in many other professional fields including but not limited to law, engineering and architecture. . . .

Finally, there is little doubt that lobbyists and the media in all probability have greatly impacted OSHA's rulemaking.

Notes: Risk Assessment by Legislatures, Agencies, and Courts

1. *Is Any Action Required?* Identify the risk the bloodborne pathogen rule was designed to reduce. Was this a risk in need of reduction? How would you answer that question? Posner contends, in dictum, that the whole concept of an occupational safety and health statute is unnecessary because it is in workers' own interests to practice safe work habits and because workers in unsafe workplaces may be choosing to risk injury in exchange for higher wages. Judge Coffey criticizes the bloodborne pathogen standard from a different standpoint; he argues that it provides little marginal benefit over guidelines already issued by the CDC that were already being implemented in most workplaces. In your view, is the bloodborne pathogen standard necessary and appropriate? Should the answer be influenced by the fact that the rule was precipitated by a fear of HIV even though the long-standing risk of hepatitis was much more serious? Is this a case of overreaction to irrational hysteria, or was HIV simply the impetus to take action that was long overdue? To what extent is risk assessment an essentially political determination rather than a mathematical calculation? Consumer activists and industry groups regularly lobby government to promote action (or inaction). See, e.g., Jock McCulloch & Geoffrey Tweedale, Defending the Indefensible (2008) (asbestos industry).

2. *Administrative Competence.* Assuming some action was necessary, is OSHA the correct agency to act? OSHA's bloodborne pathogen rule was a departure from OSHA's historical focus on traditional sources of risk in the workplace such as machinery and chemicals. What do you think of Judge Coffey's contention that the states or the CDC are better able to regulate the health care professions? OSHA tried but failed to regulate workplace exposure to tuberculosis in the late 1990s. See Institute of Medicine, Tuberculosis in the Workplace (2001). OSHA regulations continue to generate controversy. See generally Cass R. Sunstein, Is OSHA Unconstitutional?, 94 Va. L. Rev. 1407 (2008).

3. *Risk Assessment Literature.* The vast academic literature on risk assessment explores how and why societies and individuals choose to respond to some risks but not others, and at what costs. For a small sampling, see Stephen Breyer, Breaking the Vicious Cycle: Toward Effective Risk Regulation (1993); Elizabeth Fisher, Risk Regulation and Administrative Constitutionalism (2010); Public Health Law at 54-62; Kip Viscusi, Fatal Tradeoffs: Public and Private Responsibilities for Risk (1992); Cass R. Sunstein, Laws of Fear: Beyond the Precautionary Principle (2005); Richard H. Thaler & Cass R. Sunstein, Nudge (2009); Matthew D. Adler, Against "Individual Risk": A Sympathetic Critique of Risk Assessment, 153 U. Pa. L. Rev. 1121 (2005); R. Keeney, Decisions About Life-Threatening Risks, 331 New Eng. J. Med. 193 (1994).

Problem: State Law, Disaster-Planning, and Bioterrorism Preparedness

The United States has been fortunate not to have experienced many large-scale public health disasters since the influenza epidemic in the early part of the 1900s. But concerns about bioterrorism spurred public health officials and researchers in the early 2000s to review the ability of state and local governments to respond to public health emergencies. Medical journals increased their coverage of illnesses and injuries associated with potential terrorist attacks after 9/11. See, e.g., Luciana Borio et al., Consensus Statement, Hemorrhagic Fever Viruses and Biological Weapons: Medical and Public Health Management, 287 JAMA 2391 (2002); Julie Louise Gerberding et al., Bioterrorism Preparedness and Response: Clinicians and Public Health Agencies as Essential Partners, 287 JAMA 898 (2002).

Attention shifted from bioterrorism to natural disasters in the aftermath of events such as the Indian Ocean tsunami (2004), Hurricane Katrina (2005), and earthquakes with serious health implications in Haiti (2010) and Japan (2011). See Symposium, 4 Harv. L. & Pol'y Rev. 263 (2010); Symposium, 25 Health Aff. 898 (2006); Symposium, 2 J. Health & Biomed. L. 157 (2006); Symposium, 58 Admin. L. Rev. 551 (2006). Public health officials also began to devote considerable attention to planning responses to a possible new influenza pandemic. See, e.g., Symposium, St. Louis U. J. Health L. & Pol'y 1 (2010); Leslie E. Gerwin, Planning for Pandemic: A New Model for Governing Public Health Emergencies, 37 Am. J.L. & Med. 129 (2011); Lawrence O. Gostin, Public Health Strategies for Pandemic Influenza, 295 JAMA 1700 (2006); and CDC, www.flu.gov/. According to some estimates, a new pandemic influenza could cause global mortality of 62 million people, with many of the deaths occurring in the developing world. C. J. Lopez, Estimation of Potential Global Pandemic Influenza Mortality on the Basis of Vital Registry Data from the 1918-1920 Pandemic: A Quantitative Analysis, 368 Lancet 2211 (2006).

Professor Lawrence Gostin and the Center for Law and the Public's Health at Georgetown and Johns Hopkins Universities prepared the Model State Emergency Health Powers Act to facilitate discussion of the legal aspects of disaster preparedness, available at www.publichealthlaw.net (Dec. 21, 2001 version) (hereinafter MSEHPA). The Center's Web site includes information about state legislation related to the model act. Center for Law and the Public's Health, Model Laws. See also Lawrence O. Gostin et al., The Model State Emergency Health Powers Act: Planning for and Response to Bioterrorism and Naturally Occurring Infectious Diseases, 288 JAMA 622 (2002); William Martin, Legal and Public Policy Responses of States to Bioterrorism, 94 Am. J. Public Health 1093 (2004). Has your state adopted any of the MSEHPA provisions or reviewed and revised its public health emergency powers in the past decade?

The Model Act includes rules and procedures designed to improve detection of a public health emergency and then establishes rules and procedures that take effect only in a public health emergency. The definition of "public health emergency" is therefore critical to the Act's operation:

A "public health emergency" is an occurrence or imminent threat of an illness or health condition that:
    (1) is believed to be caused by any of the following:
        (i) bioterrorism;
        (ii) the appearance of a novel or previously controlled or eradicated infectious agent or biological toxin;
        (iii) [a natural disaster]
        (iv) [a chemical attack or accidental release; or]
        (v) [a nuclear attack or accident] . . . and
    (2) poses a high probability of any of the following harms;
        (i) a large number of deaths in the affected population;

(ii) a large number of serious or long-term disabilities in the affected population; or

(iii) widespread exposure to an infectious or toxic agent that poses a significant risk of substantial future harm to a large number of people in the affected population.

MSEHPA §104(m) (emphasis omitted; items in brackets are optional provisions). Note that the Act attempts to give states the option of creating a single legal framework for the public health response to a wide range of crises. As you review the Act's provisions through the remainder of this chapter, consider whether you would advise a state to adopt a single framework. Should the same rules apply in a bioterrorism incident as in a natural disaster? Does that Act—created in the shadow of 9/11—give adequate and appropriate guidance for other types of health emergencies?

B. THE SOURCE AND LIMIT OF AUTHORITY TO PROTECT PUBLIC HEALTH

This section explores the fundamental source and scope of the government's authority to pursue various public health measures. The first case is an historical one that establishes the constitutional basis for constraining individual liberties. The second case looks at the limits imposed by the more contemporary concern about disability discrimination. Although each case focuses on a specific public health measure, the general principles these cases establish permeate all of the public health topics that we encounter in the remainder of the chapter.

1. Constitutional Principles

■ JACOBSON v. COMMONWEALTH OF MASSACHUSETTS

197 U.S. 11 (1905)

HARLAN, J.

This case involves the validity, under the Constitution of the United States, of certain provisions in the statutes of Massachusetts relating to vaccination.

[A Massachusetts statute permitted cities to require vaccination and revaccination of all inhabitants of a city; noncompliant citizens over the age of 21 could be charged a fine of $5.00. The city of Cambridge adopted a smallpox vaccination regulation under this statute. Jacobson refused to be vaccinated for smallpox and these proceedings were instituted against him. He was found guilty and jailed until he paid the $5.00 fine.] . . .

The authority of the state to enact this statute is to be referred to what is commonly called the police power,—a power which the state did not surrender when becoming a member of the Union under the Constitution. Although this court has refrained from any attempt to define the limits of that power, yet it has distinctly recognized the authority of a state to enact quarantine laws and "health laws of every description"; indeed, all laws that relate to matters completely within its territory and which do not by their necessary operation affect the people of other states. According to settled principles, the police power of a state must be held to embrace, at least, such reasonable regulations established directly by legislative enactment as will protect the public health and the public safety. It is equally true that the state may invest local bodies called into existence for purposes of local administration with authority in some appropriate way to safeguard the public health and the public safety. The mode or manner in which those results are to be accomplished is within the discretion of the state, subject, of course, so far as federal power is concerned, only to the condition that no rule prescribed by a state, nor any regulation adopted by a local governmental agency acting under the sanction of state legislation, shall contravene the Constitution of the United States, nor infringe any right granted or secured by that instrument. A local enactment or regulation, even if based on the acknowledged police powers of a state, must always yield in case of conflict with the exercise by the general government of any power it possesses under the Constitution, or with any right which that instrument gives or secures.

We come, then, to inquire whether any right given or secured by the Constitution is invaded by the statute as interpreted by the state court. The defendant insists that his liberty is invaded when the state subjects him to fine or imprisonment for neglecting or refusing to submit to vaccination; that a compulsory vaccination law is unreasonable, arbitrary, and oppressive, and, therefore, hostile to the inherent right of every freeman to care for his own body and health in such way as to him seems best; and that the execution of such a law against one who objects to vaccination, no matter for what reason, is nothing short of an assault upon his person. But the liberty secured by the Constitution of the United States to every person within its jurisdiction does not import an absolute right in each person to be, at all times and in all circumstances, wholly freed from restraint. There are manifold restraints to which every person is necessarily subject for the common good. . . .

Applying these principles to the present case, it is to be observed that the legislature of Massachusetts required the inhabitants of a city or town to be vaccinated only when, in the opinion of the board of health, that was necessary for the public health or the public safety. The authority to determine for all what ought to be done in such an emergency must have been lodged somewhere or in some body; and surely it was appropriate for the legislature to refer that question, in the first instance, to a board of health composed of persons residing in the locality affected, and appointed, presumably, because of their fitness to determine such questions. To invest such a body with authority over such matters was not an unusual, nor an unreasonable or arbitrary, requirement. Upon the principle of self-defense, of paramount necessity, a community has the right to protect itself against an epidemic of disease which threatens the safety of its members. It is to be observed that when the regulation in question was adopted smallpox, according to the recitals in the regulation adopted by the board of health, was prevalent to some extent in the city of Cambridge, and the disease was increasing. If such was the situation,—and nothing is asserted or appears in the record to the contrary,—if we are to attach any value whatever to the knowledge which, it is safe to affirm, in common to all civilized peoples touching smallpox and the methods most usually employed to eradicate that disease, it cannot be adjudged that the present regulation of the board of health was not necessary in order to protect the public health and secure the public safety.

Smallpox being prevalent and increasing at Cambridge, the court would usurp the functions of another branch of government if it adjudged, as matter of law, that the mode adopted under the sanction of the state, to protect the people at large was arbitrary, and not justified by the necessities of the case. We say necessities of the case, because it might be that an acknowledged power of a local community to protect itself against an epidemic threatening the safety of all might be exercised in particular circumstances and in reference to particular persons in such an arbitrary, unreasonable manner, or might go so far beyond what was reasonably required for the safety of the public, as to authorize or compel the courts to interfere for the protection of such persons. . . .

There is, of course, a sphere within which the individual may assert the supremacy of his own will, and rightfully dispute the authority of any human government, — especially of any free government existing under a written constitution, to interfere with the exercise of that will. But it is equally true that in every well-ordered society charged with the duty of conserving the safety of its members the rights of the individual in respect of his liberty may at times, under the pressure of great dangers, be subjected to such restraint, to be enforced by reasonable regulations, as the safety of the general public may demand. . . . [Citing rules governing the quarantine of persons exposed to contagious diseases and mandatory military service.] It is not, therefore, true that the power of the public to guard itself against imminent danger depends in every case involving the control of one's body upon his willingness to submit to reasonable regulations established by the constituted authorities, under the sanction of the state, for the purpose of protecting the public collectively against such danger. . . .

Looking at the propositions embodied in the defendant's rejected offers of proof, it is clear that they are more formidable by their number than by their inherent value. . . . We must assume that, when the statute in question was passed, the legislature of Massachusetts was not unaware of these opposing theories [about the safety and efficacy of vaccination], and was compelled, of necessity, to choose between them. . . . Upon what sound principles as to the relations existing between the different departments of government can the court review this action of the legislature? If there is any such power in the judiciary to review legislative action in respect of a matter affecting the general welfare, it can only be when that which the legislature has done comes within the rule that, if a statute purporting to have been enacted to protect the public health, the public morals, or the public safety, has no real or substantial relation to those objects, or is, beyond all question, a plain, palpable invasion of rights secured by the fundamental law, it is the duty of the courts to so adjudge, and thereby give effect to the Constitution. Mugler v. Kansas, 123 U.S. 623, 661.

Whatever may be thought of the expediency of this statute, it cannot be affirmed to be, beyond question, in palpable conflict with the Constitution. Nor, in view of the methods employed to stamp out the disease of smallpox, can anyone confidently assert that the means prescribed by the state to that end has no real or substantial relation to the protection of the public health and the public safety. Such an assertion would not be consistent with the experience of this and other countries whose authorities have dealt with the disease of smallpox. . . .

[T]he police power of a state, whether exercised directly by the legislature, or by a local body acting under its authority, may be exerted in such circumstances, or

by regulations so arbitrary and oppressive in particular cases, as to justify the interference of the courts to prevent wrong and oppression. Extreme cases can be readily suggested. Ordinarily such cases are not safe guides in the administration of the
law. It is easy, for instance, to suppose the case of an adult who is embraced by the
mere words of the act, but yet to subject whom to vaccination in a particular condition of his health or body would be cruel and inhuman in the last degree. We are
not to be understood as holding that the statute was intended to be applied to such
a case, or, if it was so intended, that the judiciary would not be competent to interfere and protect the health and life of the individual concerned. . . . Until otherwise
informed by the highest court of Massachusetts, we are not inclined to hold that the
statute establishes the absolute rule that an adult must be vaccinated if it be apparent or can be shown with reasonable certainty that he is not at the time a fit subject
of vaccination, or that vaccination, by reason of his then condition, would seriously
impair his health, or probably cause his death. No such case is here presented. It is
the cause of an adult who, for aught that appears, was himself in perfect health and
a fit subject of vaccination, and yet, while remaining in the community, refused to
obey the statute and the regulation adopted in execution of its provisions for the
protection of the public health and the public safety, confessedly endangered by the
presence of a dangerous disease.

We now decide only that the statute covers the present case, and that nothing
clearly appears that would justify this court in holding it to be unconstitutional and
inoperative in its application to the plaintiff in error. The judgment of the court
below must be affirmed. It is so ordered. Mr. Justice BREWER and Mr. Justice PECKHAM
dissent.

Notes: The State Police Power and Federalism

1. *Interpreting* Jacobson. The *Jacobson* case, while ancient in constitutional law
terms, is often cited as the authoritative statement of the scope of the state's police
power, Lawrence O. Gostin, *Jacobson v. Massachusetts* at 100 Years: Police Power and
Civil Liberties in Tension, 95 Am. J. Public Health 576 (2005), and has guided the
development of the law in areas ranging from abortion to end-of-life decisionmaking, see, e.g., Gonzales v. Carhart, 550 U.S. 124 (2007); Cruzan v. Director, Missouri
Department of Health, 497 U.S. 261 (1990). Professor Gostin argues that:

> *Jacobson* established a floor of constitutional protection. Public health powers are
> constitutionally permissible only if they are exercised in conformity with five stan-
> dards . . . [:]
> *Public Health Necessity.* Public health powers are exercised under the theory that
> they are necessary to prevent an avoidable harm. . . . The standard of public health
> necessity requires, at a minimum, that the subject of the compulsory intervention
> actually pose a threat to the community. . . .
> *Reasonable Means.* . . . The methods used . . . must be designed to prevent or ame-
> liorate th[e] threat. The *Jacobson* Court adopted a means/ends test that required
> a reasonable relationship between the public health intervention and the achieve-
> ment of a legitimate public health objective. . . . [T]he methods adopted must have
> a "real and substantial relation" to protection of the public health, and cannot be "a
> plain, palpable invasion of rights."

Proportionality. . . . [A] public health regulation is unconstitutional if the human burden imposed is wholly disproportionate to the expected benefit. . . .

Harm Avoidance. . . . The control measure itself . . . should not pose a health risk to its subject.

Fairness. [Although] [t]he facts in *Jacobson* did not require the Supreme Court to enunciate a standard of fairness under the Equal Protection Clause of the Four-teenth Amendment [the standard had already been established under federal law].

Public Health Law at 126-128. Do you agree with this analysis of *Jacobson*? Is the end result consistent with the current approach to judicial review under the strict scru-tiny or rational basis standards? Gostin notes the possibility of a "sliding scale" for review that would "subject[] public health policies to increasingly demanding levels of constitutional review . . . [a]s the intrusiveness and unfairness of the public health policy grows." Id. at 143-144. Commentators agree that public health measures will elicit even greater judicial scrutiny if they infringe on fundamental rights or operate based on suspect or quasi-suspect classifications.

Do individuals have a liberty interest in avoiding vaccination? Do individuals have a protected liberty interest in engaging in behaviors that could help spread disease? Or do individuals have a fundamental right to bodily integrity that is out-weighed by the state's compelling interest in protecting public health? *Jacobson's* discussion of these issues seems a little murky to the modern eye. The Court sug-gests at times that there simply is no liberty interest in conduct that puts others at risk. Yet, the Court's analysis ultimately is consistent with the more modern balanc-ing approach: Whatever liberty interest individuals have can be outweighed where the state has a compelling interest in protecting public health, assuming the public health measure is appropriately tailored to meet that objective. Under what facts could Jacobson have avoided vaccination without penalty? For more on *Jacobson's* relevance today, see Jessica Berg, All for One and One for All: Informed Consent and Public Health, 50 Hous. L. Rev. 1 (2012); Mary Holland, Compulsory Vaccina-tion, the Constitution, and the Hepatitis B Mandate for Infants and Young Children, 12 Yale J. Health Pol'y L. & Ethics 39 (2012); Wendy Parmet et al., Individual Rights Versus the Public's Health—100 Years After *Jacobson v. Massachusetts*, 352 New Eng. J. Med. 652 (2005); and Michael H. Shapiro, Updating Constitutional Doctrine: An Extended Response to the Critique of Compulsory Vaccination, 12 Yale J. Health Pol'y L. & Ethics 87 (2012). See also Workman v. Mingo County Board of Education, 2011 WL 1042330 (4th Cir. 2011) (rejecting parent's challenge to state laws requir-ing vaccination as condition of admission to school); Coshow v. City of Escondido, 34 Cal. Rptr. 3d 19 (2005) (rejecting substantive due process challenge to fluorida-tion of drinking water).

2. *Delegation.* The police power is the power of the "state" to protect its citizens. The power is most often initially invested in the state legislature by the state constitu-tion. The legislature therefore may pass statutes designed to protect the public. The state legislature also can delegate the power in at least two different directions. It may establish some administrative agency in the executive branch, such as a state health department, which will be given statutory authority to oversee some aspects of public health. The legislature may also delegate some portion of its authority to other politi-cal entities within the state, such as to counties, cities, or local health entities.

As an initial matter, it is important to determine whether the entity exercis-ing the police power has the constitutional authority to do so. See Wong Wai v.

Williamson, 103 F. 1 (C.C. N.D. Cal. 1900) (court notes that San Francisco Board of Supervisors, rather than the Board of Health, was the entity with authority to issue ordinances to protect public health). Other, related questions include examining the delegation of authority from the legislature to the entity to ensure that the entity has not exceeded or improperly exercised its authority under the terms of the grant. In *Jacobson*, for example, the Court noted that the state may give some public health authority to local bodies, and that, in this case, the Massachusetts legislature had delegated to the local Board of Health the determination of when vaccinations were necessary. The delegation itself can also be challenged as "standardless" or as not providing sufficient guidance to the entity given the authority to exercise the police power.

3. *Due Process and Equal Protection.* Courts in the early 1900s were extremely deferential to a state's power to protect public health. Thus, courts would uphold a state's public health action so long as it was not "arbitrary" or "unreasonable" or "unnecessary" to protect public health. See *Jacobson,* supra. Under current constitutional law doctrines, individuals have a protected liberty interest in maintaining their own bodily integrity and in exercising at least some decisionmaking power with respect to their medical treatment. See Chapters 3-5, especially the discussions of *Cruzan* (pages 277 and 313) and *Casey* (page 488). Persons subjected to coercive state policies may also assert their First Amendment right to the free exercise of religion and their Fourth Amendment right to be free from unreasonable searches and seizures. Under the modern approach, a state may infringe a fundamental right to serve a compelling state interest only so long as the infringement is narrowly tailored to meet that interest. Consider whether and how this standard has been incorporated into modern public health decisions as you read the remaining cases in this chapter. See also Public Health Law at 113-146.

Under the equal protection clause, class-based legislation will be reviewed under one of three standards: (1) suspect classifications (those based on race, for example, or those that intrude on other fundamental rights) will be subjected to strict scrutiny; (2) quasi-suspect classifications (such as gender) will receive intermediate scrutiny; and (3) all other legislative classifications will be reviewed under the rational basis standard. There is some suggestion that the Supreme Court will apply a heightened rational basis review standard (sometimes called "rational basis with bite") to some classifications, see, e.g., Romer v. Evans, 517 U.S. 620 (1996) (Court uses "rational basis" standard to strike down state measure that specifically prejudiced persons seeking legislative bans on discrimination against homosexuals); City of Cleburne v. Cleburne Living Center, 473 U.S. 432 (1985) (invalidating application of zoning ordinance to group home for persons with mental disabilities under "rational basis" standard).

4. *Statutory Construction.* Courts generally follow the rule of statutory construction that exhorts that ambiguous statutes should be construed to avoid constitutional defects. In *Jacobson,* for example, the Court grafts an exception onto the vaccination rule. What constitutional defect is remedied by this procedure?

5. *Compulsory Vaccination and Religious or Philosophical Objections.* Compulsory smallpox vaccination opened the door to broader immunization campaigns. Later programs were targeted at early vaccination of children prior to attending public school. In another classic decision, the U.S. Supreme Court held that parental religious objections to vaccination would not justify avoiding vaccination

of children despite the First Amendment's protection of religious freedom. See Prince v. Massachusetts, 321 U.S. 158 at 166-167 (1944); and Workman v. Mingo County Board of Education, 2011 WL 1042330 (4th Cir. 2011) (state not required to include religious exemption in mandatory vaccination law). On religious objection to health measures generally, see Annot., 94 A.L.R.5th 613 (2001). Many states have implemented vaccination regimes that permit parents with religious or philosophical objections to avoid vaccinating their children. Low immunization rates have been tied to outbreaks of preventable disease. Point-Counterpoint, Personal Belief Exemptions, 37 J. Health Pol. Pol'y & L. 129-147 (2011); Alison Buttenheim et al., Exposure of California Kindergartners to Students with Personal Belief Exemptions from Mandated School Entry Vaccinations, 102 Am. J. Public Health e59 (2012).

6. *Vaccine Safety*. Childhood vaccinations continue to be controversial, despite the unified efforts of public health authorities to reassure the public about the safety and efficacy of the vaccinations. See, e.g., the CDC's Vaccine and Immunization Web site, at www.cdc.gov/vaccines/; WHO, Immunization Safety, at www.who.int/immunization_safety/en/. Use your favorite Internet search engine to find information by combining "vaccine" with "risks" or "danger." Do the "official" Web sites provide sufficient information to counteract the "scary" vaccine Web sites? See also Katherine M. Harris et al., Influenza Vaccine—Safe, Effective, and Mistrusted, 363 New Eng. J. Med. 2183 (2010); Allison Kennedy et al., Confidence About Vaccines in the United States: Understanding Parents' Perceptions, 30 Health Aff. 1151 (2011); Gregory A. Poland & Robert M. Jacobson, The Age-Old Struggle Against the Antivaccinationalists, 364 New Eng. J. Med. 97 (2011).

7. *Vaccine Production and Distribution*. Vaccines must be developed, manufactured, and distributed if they are to be used to protect public health. Much of this activity occurs in the private sector as pharmaceutical companies work to discover and develop vaccines, to secure governmental approval for their use, and to establish economically beneficial manufacturing and distribution arrangements. There are substantial concerns about whether this system is capable of meeting the public health needs of the United States and other countries. See David P. Fidler & Lawrence O. Gostin, The WHO Pandemic Influenza Preparedness Framework: A Milestone in Global Governance for Health, 306 JAMA 200 (2011) (discussing new, nonbinding WHO framework for Pandemic Influenza Preparedness (PIP)).

These concerns were reinforced when vaccine production lagged in response to the H1N1 pandemic in 2009. New approaches to vaccines are being developed and implemented. See Rino Rappuoli et al., Vaccine Discovery and Translation of New Vaccine Technology, 378 Lancet 360 (2011). The CDC Web site provides information on current vaccine shortages, at: www.cdc.gov/vaccines/vac-gen/shortages/. How should access to vaccines be rationed during times of shortage? Should this be seen as a medical or legal issue? Nimalan Arinaminpathy et al., Effective Use of a Limited Antiviral Stockpile for Pandemic Influenza, 6 J. Bioethical Inq. 171 (2009); and Michelle M. Mello & Troyen A. Brennan, Legal Concerns and the Influenza Vaccine Shortage, 294 JAMA 1817 (2005).

Health care providers are often given priority in vaccination schemes, at least in part because they may be at increased risk of acquiring and then passing on infection to others. Should priority access to vaccines be translated into a mandate that health care providers undergo vaccination? See Arthur Caplan, Time to Mandate Influenza Vaccination in Health-Care Workers, 378 Lancet 310 (2011); Wendy E. Parmet, Pandemics, Populism and the Role of Law in the H1N1 Vaccine Campaign, 4 St. Louis U. J. Health L. & Pol'y 113 (2010); Wendy E. Parmet, Pandemic Vaccines—The Legal Landscape, 362 New Eng. J. Med. 1949 (2010). See also Mark A. Rothstein, Should Health Care Providers Get Treatment Priority in an Influenza Epidemic?, 38 J.L. Med. & Ethics 412 (2010). Should the existence of vaccine or treatment priorities be related to legal obligations compelling the health care providers to work during a health emergency? See Carl H. Coleman, Beyond the Call of Duty: Compelling Health Care Professionals to Work During an Influenza Pandemic, 94 Iowa L. Rev. 1 (2008).

8. *Federal Authority over Public Health.* These days we are most likely to see the federal government as a pervasive force in our lives, with its influence—for good or for bad—exerted over everything from the national defense, to the organization of our health care system, to the problem of educational standards in our local schools. Constitutionally speaking, the national government has limited powers and may exercise authority only in those areas ceded by the states to the federal government within that document. Somewhat surprisingly, given the undeniable breadth and scope of federal health and safety regulation, the federal government does not have any direct constitutional authority to protect the public health. Congress and the executive branch have not been deterred by this gap in authority. Instead, Congress has achieved many of the same objectives through the exercise of its powers to regulate the relationship between the United States and foreign countries, to regulate interstate commerce, and to spend to promote the public welfare. U.S. Const. art. 1, §8. For a sampling of federal public health initiatives, see Public Health Law at 156-157 (Box 8). James Hodge et al., The Pandemic and All-Hazards Preparedness Act: Improving Public Health Emergency Response, 297 JAMA 1708 (2007) (evaluating federal legislation).

9. *State vs. Federal Authority.* A state's power to regulate in order to protect the public health can also be limited by conflicts with federal authority over interstate or international matters. States often attempt to establish standards that can have a negative impact on interstate commerce. Should a state or local government be permitted to legislate to improve roadway safety within its borders? City of Columbus v. Ours Garage & Wrecker Service, Inc., 536 U.S. 424 (2002) (preserving local tow truck rule from federal preemption despite generally broad federal preemptive authority). In general, state power in areas of federal jurisdiction, including interstate commerce, is severely restricted by federal supremacy and preemption. Compare Pliva v. Mensing, 131 S. Ct. 2567 (2011) (state warning claim preempted by federal law governing generic drugs when impossible for manufacturer to comply with both state and federal warning requirements), with Wyeth v. Levine, 555 U.S. 555 (2009) (state failure to warn claim not preempted by FDA labeling rule for non-generic drug as possible for manufacturer to comply with both federal and state rules). See also National Meat Association v. Harris, 132 S. Ct. 965 (2012) (Federal Meat Inspection Act preempts application of California Penal Code provision banning sale of meat from "nonambulatory" animals to humans).

Problem: Bioterrorism and Smallpox Vaccination

Routine vaccination for smallpox ended in the early 1970s, when it appeared that the only smallpox virus on earth was safely contained in scientific laboratories in the United States and Russia. The federal government began to reconsider its vaccination policies in 2001, amidst growing concern about the threat that smallpox would be used as a weapon of bioterrorism. The initial problem was the production of new smallpox vaccine. The federal government arranged to purchase several hundred million doses of vaccine. The second issue involved the appropriate distribution strategy. The smallpox vaccine carries a significant risk of disease or death for persons with compromised immune systems (e.g., persons with HIV, or transplant recipients) as well as for people with a history of eczema or atopic dermatitis. A massive vaccination program could put millions at risk, whether or not they underwent vaccination directly, because of the live viral particles that would be shed from the vaccination site of those who did receive the vaccine. Yet, delaying vaccination programs until after the first case of smallpox could result in thousands of preventable deaths.

What smallpox vaccine distribution policy do you favor? Use Web-based public health resources to find the federal government's current smallpox vaccination strategy. What ethical and/or legal constraints should govern the development and implementation of mandatory or voluntary vaccination policies?

See generally CDC Smallpox, available at www.bt.cdc.gov/agent/smallpox /vaccination/ for the most current federal plans for the distribution of smallpox vaccine in the event of a confirmed case. For a discussion of the failure of the federal government's initial smallpox vaccination campaign, see Jay Gold Rathbun, The Smallpox Vaccination Campaign of 2003: Why Did It Fail and What Are the Lessons for Bioterrorism Preparedness?, 64 La. L. Rev. 851 (2004).

Problem: HPV Vaccination

There are two FDA-approved vaccines designed to protect against infection by particular strains of the Human Papillomavirus (HPV): one for girls and one for boys and girls. Vaccination is recommended for girls but merely approved for boys. 59(20) MMWR 630 (May 28, 2010); 59(20) MMWR 626 (May 28, 2010). HPV is the most common sexually transmitted disease, with infection rates of 40-50 percent among sexually active young people. While apparently harmless in many cases, HPV can cause cervical cancer in women, other cancers in men and women, and genital warts. See CDC, Vaccines and Preventable Diseases: HPV Vaccination. The vaccines require three separate doses costing several hundred dollars. The vaccine should be administered before the recipient has been exposed to the disease via sexual activity.

Should HPV vaccine be added to the list of mandatory childhood vaccinations for girls? For boys? What factors do you think should be relevant to this decision? Is there any problem with mandating a vaccine for girls (who face the risk of cervical cancer) but not boys (who can transmit the disease and face the risk of other medical conditions from HPV)? For more information on the controversy, see Lawrence O. Gostin, Mandatory HPV Vaccination and Political Debate, 306 JAMA 1699

(2011); Jane J. Kim, Weighing the Benefits and Costs of HPV Vaccination of Young Men, 364 New Eng. J. Med. 393 (2011) (analyzing factors weighing against recommending routine HPV vaccination of young men, including cost-benefit analyses); James Colgrove et al., HPV Vaccination Mandates—Lawmaking amid Political and Scientific Controversy, 363 New Eng. J. Med. 785 (2011) (analyzing data on reasons for rejection of mandates in most jurisdictions).

2. Disability Discrimination

Despite its age, *Jacobson* still sets the basic framework for debating the constitutional legitimacy of various public health interventions. That debate has expanded in recent years, however, to incorporate a new concern, one that has a statutory origin: disability discrimination. The following case explains how concepts of disability discrimination relate to contagious diseases. As with *Jacobson*, the case's relevance extends far beyond the particular dispute since it establishes broad principles that apply throughout the public health arena.

■ SCHOOL BOARD OF NASSAU COUNTY v. ARLINE
480 U.S. 273 (1987)

BRENNAN, Justice.

Section 504 of the Rehabilitation Act of 1973, 29 U.S.C. §794 (Act), prohibits a federally funded state program from discriminating against a handicapped individual solely by reason of his or her handicap. This case presents the questions whether a person afflicted with tuberculosis, a contagious disease, may be considered a "handicapped individual" within the meaning of §504 of the Act, and, if so, whether such an individual is "otherwise qualified" to teach elementary school.

I

From 1966 until 1979, respondent Gene Arline taught elementary school in Nassau County, Florida. She was discharged in 1979 after suffering a third relapse of tuberculosis within two years. After she was denied relief in state administrative proceedings, she brought suit in federal court, alleging that the school board's decision to dismiss her because of her tuberculosis violated §504 of the Act . . . [which] reads in pertinent part:

> No otherwise qualified handicapped individual . . . shall, solely by reason of his handicap, be excluded from participation in, be denied the benefits of, or be subjected to discrimination under any program or activity receiving Federal financial assistance. . . .

29 U.S.C. §794. In 1974 Congress expanded the definition of "handicapped individual" for use in §504 to read as follows:

> [A]ny person who (i) has a physical or mental impairment which substantially limits one or more of such person's major life activities, (ii) has a record of such an impairment, or (iii) is regarded as having such an impairment.

The amended definition reflected Congress' concern with protecting the handicapped against discrimination stemming not only from simple prejudice, but also from "archaic attitudes and laws" and from "the fact that the American people are simply unfamiliar with and insensitive to the difficulties confront[ing] individuals with handicaps." S. Rep. No. 93-1297, p.50 (1974), U.S. Code Cong. & Admin. News 1974, p.6400. To combat the effects of erroneous but nevertheless prevalent perceptions about the handicapped, Congress expanded the definition of "handicapped individual" so as to preclude discrimination against "[a] person who has a record of, or is regarded as having, an impairment [but who] may at present have no actual incapacity at all." Southeastern Community College v. Davis, 442 U.S. 397, 405-406, n.6 (1979).

Petitioners concede that a contagious disease may constitute a handicapping condition to the extent that it leaves a person with "diminished physical or mental capabilities," and concede that Arline's hospitalization for tuberculosis in 1957 demonstrates that she has a record of a physical impairment. Petitioners maintain, however, that Arline's record of impairment is irrelevant in this case, since the school board dismissed Arline not because of her diminished physical capabilities, but because of the threat that her relapses of tuberculosis posed to the health of others.

We do not agree with petitioners that, in defining a handicapped individual under §504, the contagious effects of a disease can be meaningfully distinguished from the disease's physical effects on a claimant in a case such as this. Arline's contagiousness and her physical impairment each resulted from the same underlying condition, tuberculosis. It would be unfair to allow an employer to seize upon the distinction between the effects of a disease on others and the effects of a disease on a patient and use that distinction to justify discriminatory treatment.

Allowing discrimination based on the contagious effects of a physical impairment would be inconsistent with the basic purpose of §504, which is to ensure that handicapped individuals are not denied jobs or other benefits because of the prejudiced attitudes or the ignorance of others. By amending the definition of "handicapped individual" to include not only those who are actually physically impaired, but also those who are regarded as impaired and who, as a result, are substantially limited in a major life activity, Congress acknowledged that society's accumulated myths and fears about disability and disease are as handicapping as are the physical limitations that flow from actual impairment. Few aspects of a handicap give rise to the same level of public fear and misapprehension as contagiousness. Even those who suffer or have recovered from such noninfectious diseases as epilepsy or cancer have faced discrimination based on the irrational fear that they might be contagious. . . . We conclude that the fact that a person with a record of a physical impairment is also contagious does not suffice to remove that person from coverage under §504.

IV

The remaining question is whether Arline is otherwise qualified for the job of elementary schoolteacher. To answer this question in most cases, the district court will need to conduct an individualized inquiry and make appropriate findings of fact. Such an inquiry is essential if §504 is to achieve its goal of protecting handicapped individuals from deprivations based on prejudice, stereotypes, or unfounded fear, while giving appropriate weight to such legitimate concerns of grantees as avoiding exposing others to significant health and safety risks. The basic factors to be considered in conducting this inquiry are well established. In the context of the employment of a person handicapped with a contagious disease, we agree with amicus American Medical Association that this inquiry should include:

> [findings of] facts, based on reasonable medical judgments given the state of medical knowledge, about (a) the nature of the risk (how the disease is transmitted), (b) the duration of the risk (how long is the carrier infectious), (c) the severity of the risk (what is the potential harm to third parties) and (d) the probabilities the disease will be transmitted and will cause varying degrees of harm.

In making these findings, courts normally should defer to the reasonable medical judgments of public health officials. The next step in the "otherwise-qualified" inquiry is for the court to evaluate, in light of these medical findings, whether the employer could reasonably accommodate the employee. . . .

Because of the paucity of factual findings by the district court, we, like the court of appeals, are unable at this stage of the proceedings to resolve whether Arline is "otherwise qualified" for her job. . . .

We remand the case to the district court to determine whether Arline is otherwise qualified for her position. The judgment of the court of appeals is Affirmed.

[The dissenting opinion of Chief Justice Rehnquist and Justice Scalia is omitted.]

Notes: Balancing Risk Reduction with Other Values

1. *Disability Discrimination Law.* The *Arline* case was decided under the federal Rehabilitation Act of 1973, which prohibits disability-based discrimination by the federal government, federal contractors, and recipients of federal funds. 29 U.S.C. §§701-796. Congress later enacted the Americans with Disabilities Act (ADA), 42 U.S.C. §§12101-12213, to expand protection against discrimination by private employers, public entities, and public accommodations. Thus, these disability discrimination principles apply to virtually all of the different public health measures encountered in this chapter.

The two Acts have similar definitions of disability: A person is disabled under the statutes if she (1) has a physical or mental impairment that substantially limits her ability to engage in one or more major life activities; (2) has a record of such an impairment; or (3) is regarded as being impaired. 42 U.S.C. §12102(2). A person who meets one of these three tests will be protected from discrimination so long as she meets the essential qualifications and does not present a "direct threat" or a "significant risk" to the health or safety of others, with or without reasonable accommodation. See, e.g., id. at §12111(3) (defining direct threat) and §12113(b) (direct threat defense). Thus, as in *Arline*, persons with contagious diseases are protected from discrimination unless they present a significant risk to others.

How should employers and the courts assess the degree and probability of risk? In *Arline*, the Supreme Court suggested that "courts normally should defer to the reasonable medical judgments of public health officials," supra at page 663. In Bragdon v. Abbott, the Court described a more nuanced approach:

> In assessing the reasonableness of [a defendant's] actions, the views of public health authorities such as the U.S. Public Health Service, CDC, and the National Institutes of Health, are of special weight and authority. *Arline*, [480 U.S.] at 288; 28 C.F.R. pt. 36, App. B, p. 626 (1997). The views of these organizations are not conclusive, however. A health care professional who disagrees with the prevailing medical consensus may refute it by citing a credible scientific basis for deviating from the accepted norm.

524 U.S. 624, 650 (1998). See also Samuel R. Bagenstos, The Americans with Disabilities Act as Risk Regulation, 101 Colum. L. Rev. 1479 (2001).

2. *TB, HIV, and "Disability."* On remand, the district court found that Arline did not present a significant risk to the health and safety of others. Arline v. School Board of Nassau County, 692 F. Supp. 1286 (M.D. Fla. 1988). Although Arline was infected with TB, the decision was clearly potentially relevant to discrimination against persons with HIV infection or AIDS. The next question, however, was whether a person with HIV infection had a "disability" as defined in the statutes. The Supreme Court finally addressed this question in Bragdon v. Abbott, 524 U.S. 624 (1998). Sidney Abbott was infected with HIV but appeared otherwise healthy. Bragdon refused to fill Abbott's cavity in his dental office, offering to do so in a local hospital if Abbott would pay the hospital charges. Abbott brought a disability-based discrimination claim. The Court held that Abbott was a person with a disability because she had a physical impairment that substantially limited her ability to engage in the major life activity of reproduction. The "substantial limitation" was not physical inability to reproduce but the fact that HIV could be transmitted to her sexual partner or to her offspring in the process.

3. *Direct Threat.* Employers, public entities, and places of public accommodation are permitted to discriminate against a person with a disability where that person poses a significant risk to the health or safety of others. Employers have successfully relied upon the "direct threat" exclusion in a number of cases. See, e.g., Jakubowski v. Christ Hospital, 627 F.3d 195 (6th Cir. 2010) (medical resident with Asperger's Disorder); Turco v. Hoechst Celanese Corp., 101 F.3d 1090 (5th Cir. 1996) (diabetic presents direct threat in workplace with heavy machinery and dangerous chemicals). In most cases involving HIV infection, courts have rejected "direct threat" claims asserted by employers or others. See, e.g., Doe v. Deer Mountain Day Camp, 682 F. Supp. 2d 324 (S.D.N.Y. 2010) (HIV-infected applicant to basketball camp); Chalk v. United States District Court Central District of California, 840 F.2d 701 (9th Cir. 1988) (HIV-infected teacher).

The risk of HIV transmission within health care settings has provoked the greatest policy debate. Should HIV-infected health care providers be permitted to continue to practice? See Waddell v. Valley Force Dental Associates, 276 F.3d 1275 (11th Cir.) (HIV-infected dental hygienist posed a direct threat to patients that could not be eliminated with reasonable accommodations). Should health care providers be permitted to discriminate against HIV-infected patients? Bragdon v. Abbott, 524 U.S. 624 (1998) (HIV-infected patient did not pose significant risk to health and safety of dentist through filling of cavity).

Where should the burden of proof lie in "direct threat" litigation? Compare McKenzie v. Benton, 388 F.3d 1342 (10th Cir. 2004) (plaintiff has burden of proving she did not pose a direct threat), cert. denied, 544 U.S. 1048 (2005) with Branham v. Snow, 392 F.3d 896 (7th Cir. 2004) (defendant has burden of proof for the defense of direct threat). See also S. R. Christie, AIDS, Employment, and the Direct Threat Defense: The Burden of Proof and the Circuit Court Split, 76 Fordham L. Rev. 235 (2007).

4. *Other State and Local Laws.* Virtually every state has its own disability discrimination statutes. The great majority have already declared AIDS and HIV infection covered under these state laws. There are also more general antidiscrimination laws in most states related to public accommodations and private housing. About half the states have enacted HIV-specific statutes, either as independent new provisions or as amendments to existing legislation. How will other contagious diseases be treated under these statutes?

5. *Disability Discrimination and State Public Health Regulation. Jacobson* seemed to stand for the proposition that the state had broad powers to regulate to protect the public health, even when those regulations intruded on personal liberty. You might predict that courts would use a very loose standard of review when considering the constitutional validity of state public health regulation. Do the ADA and the Rehabilitation Act fundamentally change this understanding of the relative power of the state and the judiciary in public health matters? These laws prevent government from discriminating against persons with disabilities in public services and in federally funded programs. How might these principles limit the actions of public health authorities? See Wendy F. Hensel & Leslie E. Wolf, Playing God: The Legality of Plans Denying Scarce Resources to People with Disabilities in Public Health Emergencies, 63 Fla. L. Rev. 725 (2011); Scott Burris, Rationality Review and the Politics of Public Health, 34 Vill. L. Rev. 933 (1989).

The Supreme Court's decision in Board of Trustees of the University of Alabama v. Garrett, 531 U.S. 356 (2001), cast doubt on whether and how the ADA might be applied to the states. In *Garrett,* the Court held that Congress had exceeded its Fourteenth Amendment authority in attempting to abrogate states' Eleventh Amendment immunity under Title I of the ADA. State employees were denied the ability to bring actions for money damages under the ADA in federal court. Id. Injunctive and declaratory relief remain available.

Similar concerns are raised by Title II of the ADA's prohibition against disability-based discrimination in public services. In Tennessee v. Lane, 541 U.S. 509 (2004), the Court held that Title II could be used to recover money damages in cases involving a valid exercise of congressional power to enforce the Fourteenth Amendment. See City of Boerne v. Flores, 521 U.S. 507 (1997) (setting forth test used to determine whether a congressional enactment is a valid effort to enforce the Fourteenth Amendment). Abrogation of state immunity was upheld in *Lane* because the action contested under Title II involved a fundamental right—access to the courts. In United States v. Georgia et al., the Court held that Title II of the ADA validly abrogates state sovereign immunity "for conduct that actually violates the Fourteenth Amendment." 546 U.S. 151 (2006) (emphasis omitted). See also Phiffer v. Columbia River Correctional Institute, 384 F.3d 791 (9th Cir. 2004), cert. denied, 546 U.S. 1137 (2006) (inmate suffering from osteoarthritis and osteoporosis denied accommodation for his disabilities; state not entitled to Eleventh Amendment immunity from the inmate's suit under Title II of the ADA). Case law must be monitored to determine whether and how Title II might be applied in other public health cases. The Rehabilitation Act's provisions prohibiting disability-based discrimination by recipients of federal funds might grow in importance if *Lane* signals sharp restrictions in the application of Title II of the ADA to cases involving state public services. See, e.g., Constantine v. Rectors and Visitors of George Mason University, 411 F.3d 474 (4th Cir. 2005).

6. *Summary.* Persons seeking to challenge the validity of public health measures may look to the federal constitution, federal statutes such as the ADA and Rehabilitation Act, state constitutions, state statutes, and state regulations. You may wish to consider each of these potential limitations on public health initiatives throughout the remainder of this chapter.

C. REGULATING MEDICAL TREATMENT TO PROTECT PUBLIC HEALTH

There are many types of governmental intervention into the treatment relationship. Much of the discussion in previous chapters might be characterized, one way or another, as governmental regulation of this important relationship. The policies examined in sections C.1-C.4 below are distinguished from those studied in earlier chapters, however, by their explicit and unique grounding in a governmental interest in protecting the community's health beyond the health of the individual. The analytical focus in these sections is the sacrifice of individual autonomy to serve the public health. Traditional public health measures often involve significant intrusions into bodily integrity, privacy, and freedom of movement. How much of a sacrifice can be exacted? In what circumstances? With what level of judicial oversight?

1. Testing and Public Health

Section A, above, discusses primary public health techniques, including the identification of threats to public health and the development of strategies to address those threats. Traditionally, public health authorities have used five strategies to respond to certain types of contagious diseases. *Testing* is used to identify persons who are infected with the disease. The individual might then be *treated,* if any treatment is available, or might be *confined* to protect others from the disease. *Reporting* allows state and federal public health officials to gather specific information about people who have been infected and also permits general epidemiological research into the rate and distribution of infection within a population of people. *Contact tracing* is used to alert people who have had contact with an infected person of the possibility of exposure to the disease. If such an individual tests positive for the relevant condition, a new round of testing, reporting, and tracing can begin.

Each of these public health strategies entails some risk to individual liberty. Mandatory testing can be physically intrusive; it also violates the concept of individual autonomy and control over one's medical care. Reporting violates the norms of confidentiality and can expose an individual to the risk of additional, more intrusive public health interventions. Contact tracing might threaten the confidentiality of the "source" individual, and can lead to additional harms. Should courts weigh the protection of public health against individual liberties in determining the validity of public health programs? These traditional public health strategies have never been employed for all contagious illnesses; instead they have been reserved for particularly serious and particularly transmissible conditions. How should public health authorities determine whether and when to employ these techniques? Mandatory reporting will be explored in section C.2. Treatment and confinement will be considered in section C.4.

■ STATE v. HANDY
44 A.3d 776 (Vt. 2012)

JOHNSON, J.

Following defendant's conviction for a sex offense, the superior court, criminal division, granted the State's motion to compel defendant to submit to testing for sexually transmitted diseases under the authority of 13 V.S.A. §3256, which does not require probable cause or a warrant for testing. On appeal, defendant argues that the statute is unconstitutional because it does not serve any special need beyond law enforcement justifying abandonment of the normal probable-cause and warrant requirements and because, even if such a special need were present, the governmental goals advanced by the statute do not outweigh his constitutionally protected privacy interests. We affirm the trial court's order compelling the testing, but we remand the matter for the court to issue an order restricting the victim's disclosure of the test results.

In November 2009, defendant was convicted of lewd or lascivious conduct as the result of his having had nonconsensual sexual intercourse with the victim in a public place on October 28, 2007. In March 2010, at the behest of the victim, the State moved for the trial court to order defendant to submit to testing for sexually transmitted diseases based on his conviction for a crime involving a sexual act that created a risk of exposing the victim to the etiologic agent for acquired immune deficiency syndrome (AIDS). Upon completion of a brief nonevidentiary hearing, the trial court issued an order concluding that it was compelled to grant the State's motion under §3256, even though it had been nearly three years since the assault occurred, and that the statute was constitutional. . . .

On appeal, defendant argues that the trial court erred by concluding that the purposes underlying §3256 represented special needs sufficient to abandon the warrant and probable-cause requirements under Article Eleven of the Vermont Constitution, and further that, even if the statute represented such special needs, those special needs did not overcome his constitutionally protected privacy rights.

Article Eleven is implicated in this case because the taking of a blood sample or cheek swab is unquestionably a search that triggers constitutional protections. Article Eleven, like the Fourth Amendment, "does not contemplate an absolute prohibition on warrantless searches or seizures, but circumstances under which warrantless searches or seizures are permitted must be jealously and carefully drawn." State v. Welch, 624 A.2d 1105, 1110 (1992). Toward that end, this Court has adopted as part of its Article Eleven jurisprudence, in the context of administrative searches, the "special needs" standard of review set forth by Justice Blackman in his dissent in O'Connor v. Ortega, 480 U.S. 709 (1987).* Similarly, other jurisdictions have applied a special-needs analysis in reviewing constitutional challenges to statutes compelling sex offenders to submit to testing, at the request of the victim, for sexually transmitted diseases. See, e.g., State v. Houey, 651 S.E.2d 314, 316-317 (2007) (applying special-needs test in rejecting constitutional challenge to federal statute allowing victims to obtain HIV testing of sexual assault perpetrators).

Under the standard adopted in [previous cases], we will abandon the probable-cause and warrant requirements only under exceptional circumstances when the State demonstrates that special needs beyond normal law enforcement make those requirements impracticable and those special needs outweigh countervailing privacy interests. It is the State's burden, then, to show both that there are special needs outside law enforcement making warrants impracticable and that those needs outweigh any countervailing privacy rights upon which the warrantless search intrudes. . . .

Section 3256 addresses both the testing of the perpetrator and the testing and support of the victim of unlawful sexual conduct. . . . Upon the request of the victim "at any time after the commission of a crime involving a sexual act," the state "shall" provide to the victim various services, including "counseling regarding human immunodeficiency virus (HIV)," confidential testing "for HIV and other sexually-transmitted diseases," counseling regarding "the accuracy of the testing, and the risk of transmitting HIV and other sexually-transmitted diseases to the victim as the result of the crime involving a sexual act," and "prophylaxis treatment, crisis counseling, and support services." . . .

At issue in this appeal are the . . . subsections of the statute that concern the testing of convicted sex offenders. The victim of a sexual act "which creates a risk of transmission of the etiologic agent for AIDS" may obtain an order requiring the perpetrator "convicted" of an offense based on that act to be tested for AIDS and other sexually transmitted diseases. If the court determines that the offender has been convicted of a crime involving a sexual act with the victim, as defined in the statute, "the court shall order the test to be administered," id. §3256(c). "The results of the offender's test shall be disclosed only to the offender and the victim," and the test results and record of the court proceedings "shall be sealed," id. §3256(j).

. . . As courts in other jurisdictions have uniformly held in examining similar statutes, statutes such as these are directed at public health matters, not law enforcement, and therefore satisfy the first part of the special-needs standard. . . . Moreover, the courts have also recognized that imposing probable-cause and warrant requirements would be entirely impracticable in this context because many sexually transmitted diseases, and most particularly the AIDS virus, have no outward manifestations that would permit a probable-cause determination for obtaining a warrant. Hence, requiring probable cause and a warrant for such searches would effectively preclude the testing of sex offenders and thus negate the statute. . . .

*[The special needs exception to the warrant and probable cause requirements of the Fourth Amendment is also discussed in Ferguson v. City of Charleston, 532 U.S. 67 (2001), excerpted at page 536. — Eds.]

[Next], we must balance the governmental interests forwarded by §3256 against the privacy interests invaded by the statute. We first examine the privacy interests at stake here because they are more straightforward. At the outset, we recognize that the statute's targeted class — convicted sex offenders — has greatly diminished privacy interests, particularly with respect to precluding the testing of bodily fluids forced upon their victims in criminal sexual acts. See In re Juveniles, 847 P.2d at 460 ("For sexual offenders in particular, their expectation in privacy in bodily fluids is greatly diminished because they have engaged in a class of criminal behavior which presents the potential of exposing others to the AIDS virus."). Moreover, the taking of a blood sample or a cheek swab is a relatively minimal intrusion on privacy.

On the other hand, courts have recognized "that the information obtained as the result of a positive HIV test may have a devastating impact on individuals who would prefer not to know their true status" and that "persons with AIDS are often stigmatized and subject to social disapproval." People v. Adams, 597 N.E.2d 574, 582-83 (Ill. 1992). "Mandatory testing and disclosure of HIV status thus threaten privacy interests beyond the taking of the blood sample, particularly because of the social stigma, harassment, and discrimination often suffered by individuals who have AIDS or who are HIV-positive." In re J.G., 701 A.2d 1260, 1267 (N.J. 1997).

The degree to which convicted sex offenders may be subject to this more significant invasion of privacy associated with mandatory HIV testing "is a function of how widely the results are disseminated." Gov't of Virgin Islands v. Roberts, 756 F. Supp. 898, 902 (D. V.I. 1991). "The risk of stigmatic harm therefore speaks not to whether the search should transpire in the first instance, but rather to the extent to which the private medical facts learned from the procedure should be disclosed." Id. In short, the only privacy interest of any significance in this context is the risk of public dissemination of positive test results.

We now examine the other side of the equation — the governmental interest in testing sex offenders. On its face, the statute begs several questions. How does the testing of sex offenders following conviction contribute to the state's interest in public health and, more specifically, the well-being of the victims of sex crimes? What is the nexus between testing offenders following conviction and providing relevant information to victims about their risk of contracting sexually transmitted infectious diseases? Given that testing offenders after conviction apparently would not provide any information as to when a sexually transmitted disease was contracted relative to the timing of the sex offense for which they were convicted, how does the testing further the state's public health interest?

None of these questions was addressed at the nonevidentiary hearing before the trial court. . . . [An analysis of the legislative history of the mandatory testing provision reveals that it] was a controversial proposition that had been introduced in various bills and debated and negotiated in legislative committees over several legislative sessions. . . . The medical expert testified [during the legislative process] that . . . [t]he latency period between exposure to the virus and the accumulation of sufficient antibodies to result in a positive test is normally between six weeks and six months. For a victim potentially exposed to the AIDS virus to benefit from prophylaxis treatment aimed at reducing the chances of incurring the virus, the treatment must commence within a seventy-two-hour period. Therefore, testing the offender following conviction cannot inform a decision as to whether to begin the rigorous prophylaxis treatment. Nor would such testing normally precede the six-week-to-six-month latency period during which the victim's own testing might not yet reveal the presence of the virus. Hence, neither a negative nor a positive result from the offender's testing would appear to have any value for the victim. Moreover, any positive test result from the offender would have limited value for the additional reasons that the tests do not indicate when the virus was incurred and that the chances of passing the virus on to a sexual assault victim are very small. Indeed, even those who testified in support of testing offenders acknowledged that such testing provided little or no medically useful information for victims of sexual crimes.

Faced with this testimony, the chairs of both the House and Judiciary Committees acknowledged the apparent lack of medical usefulness in testing offenders, but explained that the State of Vermont would not be eligible to receive roughly $175,000 per year in federal grants to fund testing and counseling for sexual assault victims . . . unless the statute required testing the perpetrators. This appears to be the principal driving force behind incorporating in §3256 the sections compelling the testing of sex offenders upon the request of the victim.

If retaining federal funding were the sole governmental interest supporting the challenged portion of the statute, then the constitutionality of the law would be suspect because there would be no nexus between the law's intrusion on even the diminished privacy interest here and the information obtained from that intrusion. That is not the case, however. There was additional testimony before the legislative committees in support of testing offenders unrelated to preserving federal grant money. . . . Courts have . . . recognized the psychological benefit for victims of having the perpetrator tested even if such testing, as a practical matter, provides little or no useful medical information to the victim. . . .

We concur. One hardly need document the obvious trauma and suffering endured by victims of sexual assault. . . . When that trauma is further exacerbated by a legitimate fear of contracting a life-threatening sexually transmitted disease, the desire of victims to have the perpetrator tested to allay their fears is entirely understandable and real. Therefore, although the consensus among medical experts is that testing offenders—particularly following conviction after months or even years have passed—has little or no direct medical benefit to victims, testing offenders can provide to victims some psychological benefit that outweighs the offenders' significantly diminished interest in preventing the testing of bodily fluids forced upon their unwilling victims.

Accordingly, as long as the trial court imposes restrictions that comport with the statute's obvious intent to prevent public dissemination of the perpetrator's test results, we find no constitutional infirmity to the statute. . . . To safeguard defendant's privacy interests in not having any potential positive test results disseminated publicly, we remand the matter for the court to order the victim not to disclose defendant's test results to anyone except for the victim's medical provider or counselor, who, in turn, would have an obligation to keep confidential information revealed by their patients. . . .

Notes: Testing Programs

1. *Voluntary Screening.* Voluntary screening programs present the fewest constitutional objections. A voluntary program is consistent with the norms of patient consent for medical treatment. In practice, a voluntary program can operate along a spectrum of voluntariness and consent: A patient may have an opportunity to give specific, sometimes written consent after a discussion of the test's risks and benefits. A patient can be told that testing is "routine" and will be performed unless the patient "opts out" or objects. Finally, a patient's consent to medical treatment can be deemed to cover a particular test without any specific discussion or explicit opportunity to object.

A voluntary screening program can be established through the development of professional norms of practice or through governmental intervention. When the link between maternal age and Down syndrome was recognized, for example, prenatal screening for the condition became widespread. In part because of the risk of malpractice liability, physicians began to routinely advise women of the risk of Down syndrome and to offer prenatal screening.

Governmental bodies have also required that certain screening tests be offered to selected populations. For example, newborn screening programs for genetic and other conditions are often established under state law. See Ellen Wright Clayton, State Run Newborn Screening in the Genomic Era, or How to Avoid Drowning When Drinking from a Firehose, 38 J.L. Med. & Ethics 697 (2010); Paul A. Levy, An Overview of Newborn Screening, 31 J. Dev. Behav. Pediatr. 622 (2010); Proceedings: Newborn Screening for Nontreatable Disorders, 19 Health Matrix 137-204 (2009). Do ethnically focused testing programs create any special concerns? Cynthia F. Hinton et al., Ethical Implications and Practical Considerations of Ethnically Targeted Screening for Genetic Disorders: The Case of Hemoglobinopathy Screening, 16 Ethnicity & Health 377 (2011). Some of these programs, while officially voluntary, can as a practical matter result in coercive testing. This is particularly so where individuals either do not understand that testing is being performed or do not understand their right to refuse the procedure. For an interesting case dealing with the liability implications of state newborn screening programs, see Creason v. State Department of Health Services, 957 P.2d 1323 (Cal. 1998).

2. *"Conditional" Screening.* Conditional screening programs occupy an uneasy middle ground between voluntary and mandatory testing programs. Conditional screening occurs where testing is required as a condition of participation in some activity or for the receipt of some benefit. Conditional screening seems most like voluntary screening where the activity or benefit are of little consequence to the individual to be tested. A rule that requires HIV screening of blood donors, for example, seems more like a voluntary testing program because no one is compelled to donate blood and the benefits of donation are largely emotional. See Cal. Health & Safety Code §§1603.3, 1644.5 (HIV screening of blood and tissue donors).

Conditional screening seems much more like mandatory screening where the activity or benefit are of great importance. Rules that require testing applicants for marriage licenses for sexually transmitted diseases or that impose HIV testing on hospital patients or in employment seem closer to mandatory testing. Certainly, a person can avoid testing, but only by refraining from participating in a valued activity. For that reason, the legal analysis of these programs is likely to be similar to that employed for traditional mandatory screening programs.

3. *Premarital Screening.* Various states in the United States and some countries have conditioned issuance of a marriage license on submission of evidence that the participants had undergone a premarital examination and testing for certain diseases. Some states have repealed their premarital testing provisions, often because they were considered to be inefficient: Not many cases of infection were identified, and transmission would often already have been accomplished via premarital sexual activity. See, e.g., N.Y. Dom. Rel. §13-a. Repealed. L. 1985, 674, §1, eff. Aug. 1, 1985. Should states consider expanding their premarital testing statutes to include mandatory HIV screening or, as science advances, genetic screening? Compare Edmund C. Tamon & Shant S. Boyajian, Learning from History: What the Public Health Response to Syphilis Teaches Us About HIV/AIDS, 26 J. Contemp. Health L. & Pol'y 253 (2010) (arguing for expansion of HIV screening akin to response to syphilis before 1945), with Michael Closen et al., Mandatory Premarital HIV Testing: Political Exploitation of the AIDS Epidemic, 69 Tul. L. Rev. 71 (1994). See also Ill. Rev. Stat. ch. 40, §204 (1987) (repealed). How would you analyze the constitutionality of a statute requiring premarital testing for some sexually transmitted disease or for genetic conditions that might be inherited by offspring?

4. *Medical Testing in Private and Public Employment.* Should private entities be entitled to screen individuals for unwanted medical conditions? The ADA regulates employer use of medical examinations. The Act sets up three different rules. Employers may not impose medical exams or ask questions designed to ferret out applicants' disabilities during the pre-offer stage. Employers may ask whether an applicant will be able to perform the essential functions of a job, with or without reasonable accommodations. After extending a conditional offer of employment, the employer may require that all prospective employees undergo a medical screening exam. The exam does not need to be job related, but the employer must offer a nondiscriminatory rationale for retracting a job offer after an employment physical. Once employed, an individual may only be subjected to mandatory medical exams that are job related and consistent with business necessity. See, e.g., Deborah F. Buckman, Construction and Application of §102(d) of Americans with Disabilities Act (42 U.S.C.A. §12112(d)) Pertaining to Medical Examinations and Inquiries, 159 A.L.R. Fed. 89 (2000).

The government-as-employer often must comply with certain constitutional rules, including those protecting individual rights as well as the ADA. See Local 1812, American Federation of Government Employees v. Department of State, 662 F. Supp. 50 (D.D.C. 1987). But see Norman-Bloodsaw v. Lawrence Berkeley Laboratory, 135 F.3d 1260 (9th Cir. 1998) (noting that employees had a protected privacy interest in intimate personal matters such as syphilis, sickle-cell trait, and pregnancy; case remanded for further fact finding regarding employee authorization and government's need for information); and Elizabeth Pendo, Race, Sex, and Genes at Work: Uncovering the Lessons of Norman-Bloodsaw, 10 Hous. J. Health L. & Pol'y 227 (2010) (providing historical background on the case along with implications for Genetic Information Nondiscrimination Act of 2008). Should the federal government require HIV screening for state department employees or military personnel? The U.S. State Department eliminated its HIV testing requirement in 2008, shortly before a scheduled trial on the issue. See Taylor v. Rice, 451 F.3d 898 (D.C. Cir. 2006).

5. *Mandatory Screening.* Mandatory screening programs impose testing on all persons who fit within some defined group. Examples of current mandatory screening programs include: premarital testing for sexually transmitted diseases; mandatory drug testing of certain employees; mandatory HIV or other testing for those convicted of sexual offenses; and mandatory TB screening for prisoners. In each of these cases, states have sought to enhance safety or health by identifying those who might present a risk to others. Does the rationale applied in *Handy* suggest that each of these programs will be found to be constitutional under the Fourth Amendment? Can you think of any other constitutional objections? Should HIV screening be mandated in some sports, like boxing? See Corona v. State, 100 Cal. Rptr. 3d 591 (App. 2009). HIV testing was eliminated as a mandatory component of medical screening for immigration in 2009. Julia Preston, Obama Lifts a Ban on Entry into U.S. by H.I.V.-Positive People, N.Y. Times, Oct. 30, 2009.

6. *STD Testing for Persons Convicted of Sexual Crimes.* What public health objectives are served by testing persons convicted of sexual crimes for sexually transmitted diseases (STDs)? Will the testing program necessarily prevent future transmission of disease? Does the disclosure of the test result to the survivor of a sexual assault provide useful information? Unfortunately, as noted in *Handy*, HIV testing performed years after a sexual assault will be too late to provide useful medical information for the survivor. Were you persuaded by the *Handy* court's finding that the psychological benefits to survivors are sufficient to justify HIV testing for the perpetrators of sexual crimes? Testing convicted defendants for HIV and other STDs is very popular among legislators, in part because of the incentives created by a federal link between state HIV testing rules and eligibility for federal funds. See, e.g., N.Y. Crim. Proc. Law §390.15 (legislative history including link to federal law). See also Michael P. Bruyere, Damage Control for Victims of Physical Assault—Testing the Innocent for AIDS, 21 Fla. St. U. L. Rev. 945 (1994); Steven Eisenstat, An Analysis of the Rationality of Mandatory Testing for the HIV Antibody: Balancing the Governmental Public Health Interests with the Individual's Privacy Interest, 52 U. Pitt. L. Rev. 327 (1991).

As noted in *Handy*, mandatory testing programs generally are held to implicate the Fourth Amendment's right to be free from unreasonable searches and seizures. The Fourth Amendment requires that searches be reasonable, balancing the government's interest in the search against the individual's liberty interests. Not all searches require a warrant or individualized suspicion. Courts have developed the "special governmental needs" exception to the warrant requirement. Under this approach, applied in *Handy*, a warrantless search may be upheld where it serves some special governmental purpose important enough to outweigh an individual's reasonable expectation of privacy. As the *Handy* court noted, concerns about public health and safety easily fall within the category of "special needs." What public health objectives were supported by coercive testing of persons convicted of sexual offenses? Why does the court hold that the intrusion into individual liberty is "minimal" when balanced against the governmental need? What types of personal interests are at stake? Which is most important, the physical intrusion created by the blood test? The use of an HIV antibody test? The disclosure of the test result to others? Do you agree with the court's balancing analysis? See also Ferguson v. City of Charleston at page 536.

7. *Equal Protection.* In People v. Adams, 597 N.E.2d 574 (Ill. 1992), cited in *Handy,* the court upheld a mandatory HIV testing law applicable to persons convicted of prostitution. The court found that the testing program could be upheld under the special needs exception to the warrant requirement. In addition, the court considered and rejected an equal protection claim:

> [The defendants argue that the HIV testing statute violates the equal protection clause because] . . . the measure is both overinclusive and underinclusive in scope. The defendants believe that the statute is overinclusive in scope because it includes within its scope offenses [such as solicitation] having no risk of AIDS transmission. . . . The defendants maintain that the statute is underinclusive in scope because it fails to require HIV testing for certain criminal and noncriminal conduct [such as adultery, fornication, and bigamy] that is as likely to result in the transmission of AIDS as prostitution, the offense charged here. . . . The defendants contend that the extent to which the challenged statute is alternately overinclusive and underinclusive demonstrates the absence of any legitimate governmental purpose that would sustain it. . . .
>
> The present statute does not impinge upon the exercise of a fundamental right or operate against a suspect class. Thus, under the standard of review appropriate here, the statute need not establish a perfect fit between the desired end and the means chosen to achieve that end. . . . [The testing] requirement bears a rational relationship to the state interest in combating the spread of AIDS. In sum, we conclude that the testing provision, as applied to the present defendants, does not deny them equal protection of the laws, under either the federal or state Constitutions. . . .

Id. at 585-586.

8. *TB and HIV Testing in Prisons.* Contagious diseases also present complex constitutional issues within prisons. Prisoners do not lose all of their constitutional rights by virtue of their confinement. Prisoners may thus assert their right to be free from unreasonable searches, to make medical decisions, to pursue their religious beliefs, and to be free from cruel and unusual punishment. U.S. Const. amends. I, V, VIII, XIV. Prisoners may also be able to assert statutory claims, such as prohibitions against disability-based discrimination. 29 U.S.C. §794 (Rehabilitation Act provisions prohibiting disability-based discrimination by federal entities or recipients of federal funds); 42 U.S.C. §12132 (ADA prohibition of disability-based discrimination by public entities). But see pages 667-668. Prison officials are nonetheless given considerable latitude in devising prison rules that, while impinging on individual liberties, are considered reasonable in light of the prison's legitimate penological goals. See Turner v. Safely, 482 U.S. 78, 89 (1987); and Johnson v. California, 543 U.S. 499 (2005) (*Turner* applies to restriction of rights that are inconsistent with incarceration but not to policies contravening racial equality). See also Thompson v. City of Los Angeles, 885 F.2d 1439, 1447 (9th Cir. 1989) (prison officials have compelling interest in disease prevention).

Should correctional facilities be permitted to test inmates for the presence of contagious conditions? Most courts have answered affirmatively. See, e.g., Moore v. Mabus, 976 F.2d 268 (5th Cir. 1992) ("identification and segregation of HIV-positive prisoners obviously serves a legitimate penological purpose"); Hasenmeier-McCarthy v. Rose, 986 F. Supp. 464 (S.D. Ohio 1998) (forcible administration of TB test performed pursuant to legitimate penological interest in detecting and controlling communicable disease). A number of commentators have written on the problems of HIV and TB in correctional facilities. See John V. Jacobi, Prison Health, Public Health: Obligations and Opportunities, 31 Am. J.L. & Med. 447 (2005); John D. Kraemer, Screening of Prisoners for HIV: Public Health, Legal, and Ethical Implications, 13 Mich. St. U. J. Med. & L. 187 (2009); James Less Pope, HIV Testing in State Correctional Systems, 22 J.L. & Health 17 (2009).

Persons who knowingly put others at risk for HIV transmission, through sexual or other activity, can be prosecuted for assault, attempted murder, or for violation of HIV-specific criminal statutes. Adeline Delavande et al., Criminal Prosecution and Human Immunodeficiency Virus-Related Risky Behavior, 53 J.L. & Econ. 741 (2010); Zita Lazzarini et al., Evaluating the Impact of Criminal Laws on HIV Risk Behavior, 30 J.L. Med. & Ethics 239 (2002). Prosecution is difficult unless it can be shown that the defendant knew that he or she was HIV infected. Should test results obtained from convicted defendants or prisoners be used in subsequent prosecutions to prove that the defendant must have known of his or her HIV status at the time of the risky act? See State ex rel. J.G., 701 A.2d 1260 (N.J. 1997) (no).

9. *HIV Screening for Pregnant Women and Newborns.* The risk of HIV transmission from woman to child during pregnancy is less than 30 percent without treatment. In the 1990s, proponents of mandatory or routine HIV testing for pregnant women noted that the risk of HIV transmission through pregnancy could be reduced significantly. Transmission rates drop to less than 2 percent if pregnant women are aware of their infection, take antiretroviral therapies, and use special procedures during birth and during the newborn's first days and months of life. Edward M. Connor et al., Reduction of Maternal-Infant Transmission of Human Immunodeficiency Virus Type 1 with Zidovudine Treatment, 331 New Eng. J. Med. 1173 (1994).

Given this sharp reduction in the risk of transmission, a number of states considered whether to adopt mandatory or routine maternal screening for HIV. See Comment, 45 Am. U. L. Rev. 1185 (1996); Tex. Health & Safety Code §81.090 (routine screening with "opt-out"). In the mid-2000s, public health officials recommended routine screening coupled with directive counseling. Bernard M. Branson et al., Revised Recommendations for HIV Testing of Adults, Adolescents, and Pregnant Women in Health Care Settings, 55 MMWR 1 (2006) (RR-14) (recommending directive counseling). See also Lawrence O. Gostin, HIV Screening in Health Care Settings: Public Health and Civil Liberties in Conflict?, 296 JAMA 2023 (2006).

Problem: Routine HIV Screening for All

Should mandatory or routine HIV testing be imposed for all adults and adolescents? What would be the benefits and risks of such testing program? See Howard Libman, Screening for HIV Infection: A Healthy, "Low-Risk" 42-Year-Old Man, 306 JAMA 637 (2011); A. David Paltiel et al., Expanded Screening for HIV in the United States — An Analysis of Cost-Effectiveness, 352 New Eng. J. Med. 586 (2005); see also Samuel Bossette, Routine Screening for HIV Infection — Timely and Cost-Effective, 352 New Eng. J. Med. 620 (2005). Should the law protect the right of individuals not to know their HIV status? Cf. Christian Turner, The Burden of Knowledge, 43 Ga. L. Rev. 297 (2009).

The CDC now recommends routine HIV testing for most adolescents and adults in health care settings. The recommendations specify that patients should be told about the testing and be given an opportunity to decline. Do you agree with this approach? Bernard M. Branson et al., Revised Recommendations for HIV Testing of Adults, Adolescents, and Pregnant Women in Health Care Settings, 55 MMWR Recomm. Rep. 1 (2006) (RR-14); Matthew W. Pierce et al., Testing Public Health Ethics: Why the CDC's HIV Screening Recommendations May Violate the Least Infringement Principle, 39 J.L. Med. & Ethics 263 (2011). The CDC estimated in 2009 that 45 percent of adults between the ages of 18 and 65 had ever been tested for HIV, only a 5 percent increase over the level of testing that existed before the expansion in the CDC's guidelines in 2006. Libman, supra, at 641. What would explain the apparent resistance to the implementation of the CDC's recommendations? Would you expect that continuing stigma associated with HIV would be more or less important than legal barriers? Should insurance plans cover the costs of routine HIV screening? Ronald Bayer & Gerald Oppenheimer, Routine HIV-Screening—What Counts as Evidence-Based Policy?, 365 New Eng. J. Med. 1265 (2011) (discussing possibility that U.S. Preventive Services Task Force might join CDC in recommending routine screening, which would result in broader insurance coverage for screening).

Examine your jurisdiction's rules regarding HIV testing. Could the CDC's recommendations be adopted without legislative changes? Has your state's legislation changed in response to the recommendations? See Libman, supra, at 641 (as of 2006, 16 states had laws or regulations creating impediments to implementation of the CDC guidelines); A. P. Mahajan et al., Consistency of State Statutes with the Centers for Disease Control and Prevention HIV Testing Recommendations for Health Care Settings, 150 Ann. Intern. Med. 263 (2009); Lauren E. Palmer, Solving the HIV Testing Problem: An Analysis of New York's New Legislation, 4 Alb. Gov't L. Rev. 758 (2011); Colleen Snyder, Chapter 550: Relaxing Consent Requirements for HIV Testing, 39 McGeorge L. Rev. 567 (2008). For the international debate on "opt-in" or "opt-out" testing, see Ronald Bayer & Claire Edington, HIV Testing, Human Rights, and Global AIDS Policy: Exceptionalism and Its Discontents, 34 J. Health Pol. Pol'y & L. 301 (2009). Could the CDC's recommendations be used to establish a new standard of care in medical practice with respect to HIV screening? Should physician's failure to implement HIV screening lead to liability for failure to diagnose HIV infection through proof, for example, that earlier testing would have permitted early use of antiretroviral therapies or prevented HIV transmission to others? Interestingly, although the CDC guidelines are advisory, in 2011 public health authorities implemented a new campaign to increase rates of HIV testing, called: "HIV Screening. Standard Care." See www.actagainstaids.org/; CDC, HIV Testing in Healthcare Settings.

Problem: State Law, Disaster-Planning, and
Bioterrorism Preparedness

The Model State Emergency Health Powers Act (MSEHPA) described above at pages 653-654, includes rules and procedures designed to improve detection of a public health emergency and then establishes rules and procedures that take effect only in a public health emergency. As noted above, a public health emergency is one that is caused by bioterrorism, novel infectious agents, natural disasters, or certain other enumerated events.

The Model Act includes provisions authorizing mandatory medical examinations and tests:

> Medical examination and testing. During a state of public health emergency the public health authority may perform physical examinations and/or tests as necessary for the diagnosis or treatment of individuals.
>
> (a) Medical examinations or tests may be performed by any qualified person authorized to do so by the public health authority.
>
> (b) Medical examinations or tests must not be such as are reasonably likely to lead to serious harm to the affected individual.
>
> (c) The public health authority may isolate or quarantine, pursuant to Section 604 [discussed supra at pages 410-412], any person whose refusal of medical examination or testing results in uncertainty regarding whether he or she has been exposed to or is infected with a contagious or possibly contagious disease or otherwise poses a danger to public health.

MSEHPA §602.

Evaluate the constitutionality of the Model Act's testing provisions. Should it matter how a public health emergency is declared and whether there can be judicial review of the decision? Should it matter whether public health authorities have any reason to suspect that an individual has been exposed to a contagious disease or transmissible condition? Compare the Model Act's provisions to the relevant public health statute in your own state. Do the public health authorities in your state have explicit authority to mandate medical tests or examinations? If so, do you see any similarities or differences between your state law and the Model Act? Which seems better from a legal or policy standpoint? Should the same testing rules apply in bioterrorism incidents as during natural disasters or a natural epidemic such as avian influenza? Would you recommend the adoption of the Model Act's testing provision?

2. Confidentiality, Reporting, and Contact Tracing

Testing programs, whether public or private, create opportunities for additional public health interventions. What use should be made of a test result? One possibility is that the individual tested could be counseled about the significance of the test result and given information about how to safeguard her own health or the health of others with whom she may have contact. Testing can thus be an opportunity to improve public health through targeted education. See Public Health Law at 395-410.

Other public health interventions might proceed along a different path. State reporting statutes require specified entities to report information to state health authorities. The federal CDC collects and disseminates information about some types of health threats at the national level. See CDC's Vision for Public Health Surveillance in the 21st Century, 61 MMWR 1-40 (2012) (July 27 Supp.). Common examples of reporting statutes include those that govern gunshot wounds, suspected child abuse, and certain diseases, such as plague or HIV. See page 176. In some cases, reporting statutes are an "early warning" system that can alert public health officials to serious epidemics. More prosaically, the information could promote better health budgeting as states reallocate funds and personnel to emerging health threats. Public health officials could follow up case reports with notices about treatment or other options. Finally, the information could be used to protect those exposed to disease. Contact tracing programs attempt to identify and notify persons who have been exposed to a person with a contagious condition.

Each of these public health strategies begins with the disclosure of an individual's health status to others. Do individuals have a right to confidentiality that protects them from disclosures about their health status? The answer may depend on the nature of the information and the public interest asserted in its disclosure.

■ WHALEN v. ROE
429 U.S. 589 (1977)

Stevens, J.

The constitutional question presented is whether the state of New York may record, in a centralized computer file, the names and addresses of all persons who have obtained, pursuant to a doctor's prescription, certain drugs for which there is both a lawful and an unlawful market.

The district court enjoined enforcement of the portions of the New York State Controlled Substances Act of 1972 which require such recording on the ground that they violate appellees' constitutionally protected rights of privacy. We noted probable jurisdiction of the appeal by the Commissioner of Health, 424 U.S. 907, and now reverse.

Many drugs have both legitimate and illegitimate uses. In response to a concern that such drugs were being diverted into unlawful channels, in 1970 the New York legislature created a special commission to evaluate the state's drug-control laws. The commission found the existing laws deficient in several respects. There was no effective way to prevent the use of stolen or revised prescriptions, to prevent unscrupulous pharmacists from repeatedly refilling prescriptions, to prevent users from obtaining prescriptions from more than one doctor, or to prevent doctors from over-prescribing, either by authorizing an excessive amount in one prescription or by giving one patient multiple prescriptions. In drafting new legislation to correct such defects, the commission consulted with enforcement officials in California and Illinois where central reporting systems were being used effectively.

The new New York statute classified potentially harmful drugs in five schedules.[7] Drugs, such as heroin, which are highly abused and have no recognized medical use, are in Schedule I; they cannot be prescribed. Schedules II through V include drugs which have a progressively lower potential for abuse but also have a

7. These five schedules conform in all material aspects with the drug schedules in the Federal Comprehensive Drug Abuse Prevention and Control Act of 1970. 21 U.S.C. §801 et seq.

recognized medical use. Our concern is limited to Schedule II which includes the most dangerous of the legitimate drugs.[8]

With an exception for emergencies, the Act requires that all prescriptions for Schedule II drugs be prepared by the physician in triplicate on an official form. The completed form identifies the prescribing physician; the dispensing pharmacy; the drug and dosage; and the name, address, and age of the patient. One copy of the form is retained by the physician, the second by the pharmacist, and the third is forwarded to the New York State Department of Health in Albany. A prescription made on an official form may not exceed a 30-day supply, and may not be refilled.

The district court found that about 100,000 Schedule II prescription forms are delivered to a receiving room at the Department of Health in Albany each month. They are sorted, coded, and logged and then taken to another room where the data on the forms is recorded on magnetic tapes for processing by a computer. Thereafter, the forms are returned to the receiving room to be retained in a vault for a five-year period and then destroyed as required by the statute. . . .

A few days before the Act became effective, this litigation was commenced by a group of patients regularly receiving prescriptions for Schedule II drugs, by doctors who prescribe such drugs, and by two associations of physicians. After various preliminary proceedings, a three-judge district court conducted a one-day trial. Appellees offered evidence tending to prove that persons in need of treatment with Schedule II drugs will from time to time decline such treatment because of their fear that the misuse of the computerized data will cause them to be stigmatized as "drug addicts."

I

The district court found that the state had been unable to demonstrate the necessity for the patient-identification requirement on the basis of its experience during the first 20 months of administration of the new statute. . . .

State legislation which has some effect on individual liberty or privacy may not be held unconstitutional simply because a court finds it unnecessary, in whole or in part. For we have frequently recognized that individual states have broad latitude in experimenting with possible solutions to problems of vital local concern.

The New York statute challenged in this case represents a considered attempt to deal with such a problem. It is manifestly the product of an orderly and rational legislative decision. It was recommended by a specially appointed commission which held extensive hearings on the proposed legislation, and drew on experience with similar programs in other states. There surely was nothing unreasonable in the assumption that the patient-identification requirement might aid in the enforcement of laws designed to minimize the misuse of dangerous drugs. For the requirement could reasonably be expected to have a deterrent effect on potential violators as well as to aid in the detection or investigation of specific instances of apparent abuse. At the very least, it would seem clear that the state's vital interest in controlling the distribution of dangerous drugs would support a decision to experiment

8. These include opium and opium derivatives, cocaine, methadone, amphetamines, and methaqualone. Pub. Health Law §3306. These drugs have accepted uses in the amelioration of pain and in the treatment of epilepsy, narcolepsy, hyperkinesia, schizo-affective disorders, and migraine headaches.

with new techniques for control. For if an experiment fails—if in this case experience teaches that the patient-identification requirement results in the foolish expenditure of funds to acquire a mountain of useless information—the legislative process remains available to terminate the unwise experiment. It follows that the legislature's enactment of the patient-identification requirement was a reasonable exercise of New York's broad police powers. The district court's finding that the necessity for the requirement had not been proved is not, therefore, a sufficient reason for holding the statutory requirement unconstitutional.

II

Appellees contend that the statute invades a constitutionally protected "zone of privacy." The cases sometimes characterized as protecting "privacy" have in fact involved at least two different kinds of interests. One is the individual interest in avoiding disclosure of personal matters, and another is the interest in independence in making certain kinds of important decisions. Appellees argue that both of these interests are impaired by this statute. The mere existence in readily available form of the information about patients' use of Schedule II drugs creates a genuine concern that the information will become publicly known and that it will adversely affect their reputations. This concern makes some patients reluctant to use, and some doctors reluctant to prescribe, such drugs even when their use is medically indicated. It follows, they argue, that the making of decisions about matters vital to the care of their health is inevitably affected by the statute. Thus, the statute threatens to impair both their interest in the nondisclosure of private information and also their interest in making important decisions independently.

We are persuaded, however, that the New York program does not, on its face, pose a sufficiently grievous threat to either interest to establish a constitutional violation.

Public disclosure of patient information can come about in three ways. Health Department employees may violate the statute by failing, either deliberately or negligently, to maintain proper security. A patient or a doctor may be accused of a violation and the stored data may be offered in evidence in a judicial proceeding. Or, thirdly, a doctor, a pharmacist, or the patient may voluntarily reveal information on a prescription form.

The third possibility existed under the prior law and is entirely unrelated to the existence of the computerized data bank. Neither of the other two possibilities provides a proper ground for attacking the statute as invalid on its face. There is no support in the record, or in the experience of the two states that New York has emulated, for an assumption that the security provisions of the statute will be administered improperly. And the remote possibility that judicial supervision of the evidentiary use of particular items of stored information will provide inadequate protection against unwarranted disclosures is surely not a sufficient reason for invalidating the entire patient-identification program.

Even without public disclosure, it is, of course, true that private information must be disclosed to the authorized employees of the New York Department of Health. Such disclosures, however, are not significantly different from those that were required under the prior law. Nor are they meaningfully distinguishable from a host of other unpleasant invasions of privacy that are associated with many facets of health care. Unquestionably, some individuals' concern for their own privacy may lead them to avoid or to postpone needed medical attention. Nevertheless, disclosures of private medical information to doctors, to hospital personnel, to insurance companies, and to public health agencies are often an essential part of modern medical practice even when the disclosure may reflect unfavorably on the character of the patient. Requiring such disclosures to representatives of the state having responsibility for the health of the community, does not automatically amount to an impermissible invasion of privacy.

Appellees also argue, however, that even if unwarranted disclosures do not actually occur, the knowledge that the information is readily available in a computerized file creates a genuine concern that causes some persons to decline needed medication. The record supports the conclusion that some use of Schedule II drugs has been discouraged by that concern; it also is clear, however, that about 100,000 prescriptions for such drugs were being filled each month prior to the entry of the district court's injunction. Clearly, therefore, the statute did not deprive the public of access to the drugs.

Nor can it be said that any individual has been deprived of the right to decide independently, with the advice of his physician, to acquire and to use needed medication. Although the state no doubt could prohibit entirely the use of particular Schedule II drugs, it has not done so. This case is therefore unlike those in which the Court held that a total prohibition of certain conduct was an impermissible deprivation of liberty. Nor does the state require access to these drugs to be conditioned on the consent of any state official or other third party. Within dosage limits which appellees do not challenge, the decision to prescribe, or to use, is left entirely to the physician and the patient.

We hold that neither the immediate nor the threatened impact of the patient-identification requirements in the New York State Controlled Substances Act of 1972 on either the reputation or the independence of patients for whom Schedule II drugs are medically indicated is sufficient to constitute an invasion of any right or liberty protected by the Fourteenth Amendment. . . .

Reversed.

Notes: Informational Privacy

1. *Informational vs. Decisional Privacy.* Does *Whalen* clearly establish that we have a fundamental constitutional right to maintain the privacy of our medical information? To the contrary, the Court upholds the validity of a state public health statute that required physicians to report sensitive information about individual prescription drug use. The constitutional protection of confidentiality is at best found in the margins of the decision, in the Court's suggestion that a constitutional right to privacy might have been implicated if the state's reporting mechanism had failed to protect patient information from improper disclosure. Justice Brennan concurred in the Court's opinion with the understanding that constitutional norms were implicated and that widespread dissemination of private information could only be justified by a compelling governmental objective. Justice Stewart's concurrence rested on his understanding that the opinion did not establish a constitutional right to privacy.

The technological capacity to collect and store information has increased dramatically since *Whalen*. Data that once could only be stored on mainframe computers can now be kept on laptops and moved via USB drives or email attachments. Hackers and unauthorized employees may access supposedly secure computerized information. Does this affect your view of whether constitutional protection for privacy is desirable and realistic? See Amy L. Fairchild, The Democratization of Privacy: Public-Health Surveillance and Changing Conceptions of Privacy in Twentieth-Century America in History and Health Policy in the United States (Rosemary A. Stevens et al. eds., 2006); Milt Freudenheim, Breaches Lead to Push to Protect Medical Data, N.Y. Times, May 30, 2011 (including example of stolen government laptop with unencrypted medical data). The HIPAA electronic records and confidentiality provisions discussed in Chapter 2.C create clear standards for confidentiality but offer no private right of action for breaches.

2. *Nomenclature. Whalen* suggests that the "right to privacy" encompasses both decisional and informational privacy. In recent years, the Supreme Court has retreated from the use of "privacy" as a basis for protecting individual decisionmaking from governmental intrusion. Most Justices now tend to refer to a "protected liberty interest" in making certain types of decisions free from unwarranted governmental interference. The Court has not taken the opportunity to revisit and more clearly delineate an individual's protected liberty interest in the privacy of information. The current status of the right remains, at best, unclear. See NASA v. Nelson, 131 S. Ct. 746 (2011) (assuming without deciding the existence of the right but finding no violation). See also Mark A. Rothstein, Constitutional Right to Informational Health Privacy in Critical Condition, 39 J.L. Med. & Ethics 280 (2011); and Ferguson v. City of Charleston at page 536.

3. *Confidentiality in the Courts of Appeal. Whalen's* unstable foundation, some courts have at least tentatively erected a constitutional confidentiality doctrine. The debate has centered on the standard of review to be applied to state measures that intrude on individual privacy. The Tenth Circuit requires a compelling state interest for privacy intrusions. Stidham v. Peace Officer Standards & Training, 265 F.3d 1144 (10th Cir. 2001). A few federal courts of appeal have adopted an intermediate standard of review, employing a balancing test to weigh an individual's interest in privacy against the governmental objective. See Overstreet v. Lexington-Fayette Urban County Government, 305 F.3d 566 (6th Cir. 2002) (balancing test applies only when disclosure implicates fundamental rights); Denius v. Dunlap, 209 F.3d 944 (7th Cir. 2000) (noting relevance of type of information); C.N. v. Ridgewood Board of Education, 430 F.3d 159 (3d Cir. 2005) (balancing test includes consideration of seven factors); Matson v. Board of Education, 631 F.3d 57 (2d. Cir. 2011) (level of privacy related to character of medical information and associated risk to individual). Some courts of appeal apply only a rational basis standard of review. See also National Federation of Federal Employees v. Greenberg, 983 F.2d 286, 293-294 (D.C. Cir. 1993) (critique of *Whalen's* "uncharted terrain").

Which of the following measures would likely withstand constitutional attack in which jurisdictions?

1. A statute requiring physicians to report the names and addresses of persons diagnosed with AIDS.
2. A statute requiring disclosure of a surgeon's HIV status to her patients.
3. A statute requiring persons with TB to post the information on their doors in at least 12-point type.

Commentators have argued that individual privacy is increasingly at risk because of a number of trends, including expanded governmental involvement in health care and the resurgence of dangerous contagious diseases such as HIV and TB. Some interesting sources include: Jessica Berg, All for One and One for All: Informed Consent and Public Health, 50 Hous. L. Rev. 1 (2012); Amy L. Fairchild et al., Searching Eyes: Privacy, the State, and Disease Surveillance in America (2007); Public Health Law at 321-322; Seth F. Kreimer, Sunlight, Secrets, and Scarlet Letters: The Tension Between Privacy and Disclosure in Constitutional Law, 140 U. Pa. L. Rev. 1 (1991); Neil M. Richards, Essay, The Information Privacy Law Project, 94 Geo. L.J. 1087 (2006); Daniel J. Solove, A Taxonomy of Privacy, 154 U. Pa. L. Rev. 477 (2006).

4. *Statutory and Common Law Protections.* The confidentiality of health-related information is protected by statute and common law as well. See Chapter 2.C; and Soumitra Sengupta et al., A Model for Expanded Public Health Reporting in the Context of HIPAA, 15 J. Am. Med. Inform. Assoc. 569 (2008). Yet none of these sources of protection is absolute. Each has an extensive list of express or implied exceptions. Typically, for example, physicians are permitted to disclose confidential medical information if "*required or authorized by law*," such as under HIPAA or state reporting statutes. See, e.g., 45 C.F.R. §164.512 (a), (b) (HIPAA authorization for use and disclosure without authorization or opportunity to agree or object where otherwise required by law or for certain public health activities); Tex. Occ. Code Ann. §159.004. See also FAA v. Cooper, 132 S. Ct. 1441 (2012) (exchange of information about individual's HIV status between federal agencies may have violated Privacy Act but sovereign immunity barred damage claims for emotional or mental distress).

MIDDLEBROOKS v. STATE BOARD OF HEALTH
710 So. 2d 891 (Ala. 1998)

MADDOX, Justice.

This case presents the issue whether §22-11A-2, Ala.Code 1975, which requires physicians, dentists, and certain other persons to report cases or suspected cases of "notifiable diseases" and health conditions, such as HIV infections and AIDS cases, to the Alabama State Board of Health, is discriminatory and therefore violates the Equal Protection Clause of the Fourteenth Amendment to the Constitution of the United States.

Dr. Mark Middlebrooks, a physician practicing in Jefferson County, specializes in infectious diseases. Through his practice, Dr. Middlebrooks diagnoses and treats patients who are infected with HIV and AIDS. Under the provisions of §22-11A-2, Dr. Middlebrooks is within the class of persons required to report all cases of HIV infection and AIDS to the State Board of Health. The required reports are to include the names and addresses of persons infected.[1]

1. Section 22-11A-2 provides, in part:

Each physician, dentist, nurse, medical examiner, hospital administrator, nursing home administrator, laboratory director, school principal, and day care center director shall be responsible to report cases or suspected cases of notifiable diseases and health conditions. The report shall contain such information, and be delivered in such

In July 1993, Dr. Middlebrooks was contacted by officials of the Jefferson County Health Department, who requested that he comply with the reporting mandate of the statute and with the rules of the State Board of Health. . . . Dr. Middlebrooks provided certain statistical data, as the statute and regulatory rules required, but he refused to provide the names and addresses of his patients.

On September 8, 1994, the State Board of Health filed this action against Dr. Middlebrooks, seeking to compel him to disclose the names and addresses of his HIV and AIDS patients, as required by statute and rule. On March 13, 1996, the trial court entered an order compelling disclosure; Dr. Middlebrooks appealed.

Dr. Middlebrooks primarily contends that the statutory and regulatory scheme violates the Equal Protection Clause of the Fourteenth Amendment because persons or entities not listed in the statute are authorized by regulations adopted by the Federal Food and Drug Administration to sell confidential HIV-testing kits and the sellers of those kits are not required to report the names and addresses of the purchasers. Dr. Middlebrooks argues that he is subjected to discriminatory treatment because he is required to report the names and addresses of his HIV and AIDS patients while those who sell the testing kits and out-of-state testing laboratories that evaluate the test results are not required to report the names and addresses of those persons who test positive.

In order to address Dr. Middlebrooks's arguments, we believe it essential to discuss briefly the right of privacy in regard to disclosure of medical information relating to diseases such as HIV and AIDS.

The United States Supreme Court has stated:

> [D]isclosures of private medical information to doctors, to hospital personnel, to insurance companies, and to public health agencies are often an essential part of modern medical practice even when the disclosure may reflect unfavorably on the character of the patient. Requiring such disclosures to representatives of the State having responsibility for the health of the community, does not automatically amount to an impermissible invasion of privacy.

Whalen v. Roe, 429 U.S. 589, 602 (1977). In United States v. Westinghouse Electric Corp., 638 F.2d 570, 578 (3d Cir. 1980), the United States Court of Appeals for the

---

a manner, as may be provided for from time to time by the rules of the state board of health. All medical and statistical information and reports required by this chapter shall be confidential and shall not be subject to the inspection, subpoena, or admission into evidence in any court, except proceedings brought under this chapter to compel the examination, testing, commitment or quarantine of any person or upon the written consent of the patient, or if the patient is a minor, his parent or legal guardian. Any physician or other person making any report required by this chapter or participating in any judicial proceeding resulting therefrom shall, in doing so, be immune from any civil or criminal liability, that might otherwise be incurred or imposed.

The rules of the State Board of Health define HIV and AIDS as "notifiable diseases" and require the reporting person to give the patient's name and address and certain laboratory data. Alabama *Administrative Code*, Chapter 420-4-1 et seq.

Third Circuit established factors for a court to consider when determining "whether an invasion into an individual's records is justified." Those factors are:

the type of record requested, the information it does or might contain, the potential for harm in any subsequent nonconsensual disclosure, the injury from disclosure to the relationship in which the record was generated, the adequacy of safeguards to prevent unauthorized disclosure, the degree of need for access, and whether there is an express statutory mandate, articulated public policy, or other recognizable public interest militating toward access. [Id.]

After weighing the *Westinghouse* factors, we hold that the prevention of the spread of HIV and AIDS is a legitimate governmental interest, and that, even in regard to HIV and AIDS, where, in some situations, the disclosure may reflect unfavorably on the character of the patient, . . . the State can require disclosure to representatives of the State having responsibility for the health of the community, and that the disclosure required by §22-11A-2 does not amount to an impermissible invasion of privacy. The statute and the regulatory rules adopted pursuant thereto have adequate safeguards to protect the medical records from unauthorized disclosure.

Now that we have determined that §22-11A-2 does not violate the right to privacy, we must decide whether Dr. Middlebrooks's constitutional right to equal protection is violated by the fact that §22-11A-2 does not apply to the stores that market and sell at-home HIV testing kits and out-of-state testing labs that analyze the results of the tests.

The purpose of the Equal Protection Clause is to prevent states from enacting legislation that treats persons "similarly situated" differently. City of Cleburne v. Cleburne Living Center, Inc., 473 U.S. 432, 439 (1985). "It does not, however, require that a statute necessarily apply equally to all persons or require that things different in fact be treated in law as though they were the same." McClendon v. Shelby County, 484 So. 2d 459, 464 (Ala. Civ. App. 1985).

We conclude that the State has made a reasonable classification in this instance. It appears to us that the out-of-state testing labs that analyze the results of the testing kits are not, as to those required to report HIV and AIDS cases under §22-11A-2, similarly situated.[3]

We conclude that the trial judge properly ordered Dr. Middlebrooks to disclose to the State Board of Health the names of his patients infected with HIV and AIDS. The judgment is, therefore, affirmed.

Notes: Reporting and Contact Tracing

1. Middlebrooks *Analysis*. What standard of review does the court apply to Dr. Middlebrooks's constitutional claims? Given the standard of review, could

3. We note, from the Board's brief, that Alabama, like other states, is attempting to get a waiver of the federal rule that permits the sale of testing kits within the state. In any event, it appears to us that the out-of-state testing labs do not know the identity of the persons that are being tested. The vendors of the testing kits are not similarly situated, because they merely sell the kits and have no information on whether a particular purchaser is HIV- or AIDS-positive.

Dr. Middlebrooks have relied on public health experts who question whether states should require name-specific HIV reporting? Most public health officials strongly support names-based reporting. See, e.g., CDC, Guidelines for National Human Immunodeficiency Virus Case Surveillance, Including Monitoring for Human Immunodeficiency Infection and Acquired Immunodeficiency Syndrome, 48 MMWR 1 (1999) (RR-13). Most states now require physicians and others to report the names of persons tested for HIV. See CDC, Diagnoses of HIV Infection and AIDS in the United States and Dependent Areas, 2009, 21 HIV Surveillance Report 5-6 (2011). Why isn't the state reporting scheme irrational under the equal protection clause? Does it help or hurt the equal protection clause analysis if state residents can obtain anonymous HIV antibody testing at clinics in the state or if individuals are permitted to use false names when registering for testing?

2. *Reporting Requirements.* States currently require physicians to report a wide range of health conditions to public health authorities. New reporting requirements are typically added piecemeal and spread throughout the state's code of laws. See, e.g., Cal. Health & Safety Code §120250 (duty to report infectious, contagious, or communicable diseases); Cal. Penal Code §11166 (duty to report child abuse); Cal. Welf. & Inst. Code §15630 (duty to report elder or dependent adult abuse). See also page 176.

3. *Contact Tracing and Partner Notification.* Contact tracing programs provide a mechanism for the notification of persons who may have been exposed to a contagious or transmissible condition. These programs have a long history, particularly for sexually transmitted diseases such as syphilis or gonorrhea and are now being applied to HIV infection. See, e.g., CDC, Recommendations for Partner Service Programs for HIV Infection, Syphilis, Gonorrhea, and Chlamydial Infection, 57 MMWR 1 (2008) (RR-9); Mary R. Reichler et al., Evaluation of Investigations Conducted to Detect and Prevent Transmission of Tuberculosis, 287 JAMA 991 (2002) (reviewing data and concluding that improvements are needed in TB contact investigation techniques); Janet S. St. Lawrence et al., STD Screening, Testing, Case Reporting, and Clinical Partner Notification Practices: A National Survey of US Physicians, 92 Am. J. Public Health 1784 (2002); James M. Tesoriero et al., The Effect of Names-Based Reporting and Partner Notification on HIV Testing in New York State, 98 Am. J. Public Health 728 (2008) (HIV reporting not associated in decreased willingness to be tested); Theresa Yuricic, An Examination of Partner Notification Laws: What Does Partner Notification Mean for HIV/AIDS in the African-American Community?, 3 S. Regional Black L. Students Ass'n L.J. 121 (2009).

Contact tracing programs typically are required to protect the confidentiality of the source individual. The programs nonetheless increase the risk that an individual's identity will be disclosed to third parties. Suppose, for example, that an individual notified about possible exposure to a sexually transmitted disease has had only one sexual partner. See Jane K. Stoever, Stories Absent from the Courtroom: Responding to Domestic Violence in the Context of HIV and AIDS, 87 N.C. L. Rev. 1157 (2009).

Consider Iowa's approach to the issues:

§141A.5. Partner Notification Program—HIV.

1. The department shall maintain a partner notification program for persons known to have tested positive for HIV infection.

2. In administering the program, the department shall provide for the following:

a. A person who tests positive for HIV infection shall receive post-test counseling, during which time the person shall be encouraged to refer for counseling and HIV testing any person with whom the person has had sexual relations or has shared drug injecting equipment.

b. The physician or other health care provider attending the person may provide to the department any relevant information provided by the person regarding any person with whom the tested person has had sexual relations or has shared drug injecting equipment.

c. (1) Devise a procedure, as a part of the partner notification program, to provide for the notification of an identifiable third party who is a sexual partner of or who shares drug injecting equipment with a person who has tested positive for HIV, by the department or a physician, when all of the following situations exist:

(a) A physician for the infected person is of the good faith opinion that the nature of the continuing contact poses an imminent danger of HIV transmission to the third party.

(b) When the physician believes in good faith that the infected person, despite strong encouragement, has not and will not warn the third party and will not participate in the voluntary partner notification program.

(2) Notwithstanding subsection 3, the department or a physician may reveal the identity of a person who has tested positive for HIV infection pursuant to this subsection only to the extent necessary to protect a third party from the direct threat of transmission. This subsection shall not be interpreted to create a duty to warn third parties of the danger of exposure to HIV through contact with a person who tests positive for HIV infection.

(3) The department shall adopt rules . . . to implement this paragraph "c". The rules shall provide a detailed procedure by which the department or a physician may directly notify an endangered third party.

3. In making contact the department shall not disclose the identity of the person who provided the names of the persons to be contacted and shall protect the confidentiality of persons contacted.

4. The department may delegate its partner notification duties under this section to local health authorities unless the local authority refuses or neglects to conduct the partner notification program in a manner deemed to be effective by the department. . . .

Iowa Code Ann. §141A.5. Does the statute reach an appropriate balance between individual liberties and public health? What can or should be done if a person refuses to name his or her contacts? See also Lawrence O. Gostin & James G. Hodge, Jr., Piercing the Veil of Secrecy in HIV/AIDS and Other Sexually Transmitted Diseases: Theories of Privacy and Disclosure in Partner Notification, 5 Duke J. Gender L. & Pol'y 9 (1998).

Could email, social media, and forms of electronic communication be used to spur testing and contact notification? See David Tuller, After Hookups, E-Cards That Warn, "Get Checked," N.Y. Times, Jan., 20, 2009; Mary D. Fan, Decentralizing STD Surveillance: Toward Better Informed Sexual Consent, 12 Yale J. Health Pol'y L. & Ethics 1 (2012); Rachel Kachur et al., Reaching Patients and Their Partners Through Mobile: Text Messaging for Case Management and Partner Notification, 38 Sex. Trans. Dis. 149 (2011); and Summer McGee, Mobile Contact Tracing and Counseling for STI's: There's Not an App for That, 11 Am. J. Bioethics 3 (2011) (noting new mobile app for STD testing might increase testing while reducing use of counseling and contract tracing); but see Cornelis A. Rietmeijer et al., Evaluation of an Online Partner Notification Program, 38 Sex. Trans. Dis. 359 (2011) (finding low rates of use of Internet-based e-card notification program).

Problem: Reporting and Treatment for HIV Infection

States have gathered information for decades on persons testing positive for HIV infection. As a result, almost all states have information about positive test results along with information about the immunological status of HIV-positive individuals and their "viral load" (which, among other things, is correlated to the likelihood that the person would transmit the virus to others during, e.g., sexual activity). The emergence of therapies that seem to extend life for many people with HIV infection has created some controversy about whether and how surveillance data gathered for public health purposes could be used for clinical purposes. Should state reporting be viewed as a "one-way" process in which information is sent upward to the public health authorities or should the information collected at the state level be made available to clinicians providing care for patients? About half of all persons who know that they are infected "are not receiving regular HIV care." Amy Fairchild & Ronald Bayer, HIV Surveillance, Public Health, and Clinical Medicine, 365 New Eng. J. Med. 685, 686 (2011). Should confidentiality constraints governing information collected by public health authorities prevent using public health data to monitor and encourage follow-up care for HIV-infected persons? Should a state be permitted to link the public health database to clinical records so that "open[ing] a patient's electronic medical record in the state hospital system . . . triggers an automatic data query to the" public health authorities who could alert a caregiver via "an eye-catching 'point-of-care message,'" that the patient "tested positive for HIV but was not informed of the results or hasn't received a CD4 test within the past 12 months . . . [thereby] alerting the caregiver that the patient is HIV-positive and not receiving care and providing an opportunity to offer appropriate services." Id. Would the linkage have violated the privacy rights of HIV-infected patients, as those who know their status presumably should be able to decide whether or not to disclose their status to health care providers? Could the disclosure of information nonetheless be justified by the life-extending impact of appropriate HIV antiretroviral therapy? Could public health authorities justify the monitoring system by noting that antiretroviral therapy reduces the likelihood that an HIV-infected person will transmit the virus to others? See also Myron S. Cohen et al., Prevention of HIV-1 Infection with Early Antiretroviral Therapy, 365 New Eng. J. Med. 493 (2011); Stacy M. Cohen et al., Vital Signs: HIV Prevention Through Care and Treatment—United States, 60 MMWR 1618 (2011).

Problem: Reporting and Contact Tracing Under the MSEHPA

The MSEHPA also includes reporting and tracking provisions. The following sections are in effect whether or not a public health emergency has been declared:

ARTICLE III. MEASURES TO DETECT AND TRACK PUBLIC HEALTH EMERGENCIES

Section 301 **Reporting.**

(a) **Illness or health condition.** A health care provider, coroner, or medical examiner shall report all cases of persons who harbor any illness or health condition that may be potential causes of a public health emergency. Reportable illnesses and health conditions include, but are not limited to, the diseases caused by the biological agents listed in 42 C.F.R. §72, app. A (2000) and any illnesses or health conditions identified by the public health authority.

(b) **Pharmacists.** In addition to the foregoing requirements for health care providers, a pharmacist shall report any unusual or increased prescription rates, unusual types of prescriptions, or unusual trends in pharmacy visits that may be potential causes of a public health emergency. . . .

(c) **Manner of reporting.** The report shall be made electronically or in writing within [*twenty-four (24) hours*] to the public health authority. The report shall include as much of the following information as is available: the specific illness or health condition that is the subject of the report; the patient's name, date of birth, sex, race, occupation, and current home and work addresses (including city and county); the name and address of the health care provider, coroner, or medical examiner and of the reporting individual, if different; and any other information needed to locate the patient for follow-up. For cases related to animal or insect bites, the suspected locating information of the biting animal or insect, and the name and address of any known owner, shall be reported.

(d) **Animal diseases.** Every veterinarian, livestock owner, veterinary diagnostic laboratory director, or other person having the care of animals shall report animals having or suspected of having any diseases that may be potential causes of a public health emergency. . . .

(f) **Enforcement.** The public health authority may enforce the provisions of this Section in accordance with existing enforcement rules and regulations. . . .

Section 302 **Tracking.** The public health authority shall ascertain the existence of cases of an illness or health condition that may be potential causes of a public health emergency; investigate all such cases for sources of infection and to ensure that they are subject to proper control measures; and define the distribution of the illness or health condition. To fulfill these duties, the public health authority shall identify exposed individuals as follows—

(a) **Identification of individuals.** Acting on information developed in accordance with Section 301 of this Act, or other reliable information, the public health authority shall identify all individuals thought to have been exposed to an illness or health condition that may be a potential cause of a public health emergency.

(b) **Interviewing of individuals.** The public health authority shall counsel and interview such individuals where needed to assist in the positive identification of exposed individuals and develop information relating to the source and spread of the illness or health condition. Such information includes the name and address (including city and county) of any person from whom the illness or health condition may have been contracted and to whom the illness or health condition may have spread.

(c) **Examination of facilities or materials.** The public health authority shall, for examination purposes, close, evacuate, or decontaminate any facility or decontaminate or destroy any material when the authority reasonably suspects that such facility or material may endanger the public health.

(d) **Enforcement.** The public health authority may enforce the provisions of this Section in accordance with existing enforcement rules and regulations. An order of the public health authority given to effectuate the purposes of this Section shall be enforceable immediately by the public safety authority. . . .

Section 303 **Information sharing.**

(a) Whenever the public safety authority or other state or local government agency learns of a case of a reportable illness or health condition, an unusual cluster, or a suspicious event that may be the cause of a public health emergency, it shall immediately notify the public health authority.

(b) Whenever the public health authority learns of a case of a reportable illness or health condition, an unusual cluster, or a suspicious event that it reasonably believes has the potential to be caused by bioterrorism, it shall immediately notify the public safety authority, tribal authorities, and federal health and public safety authorities.

(c) Sharing of information on reportable illnesses, health conditions, unusual clusters, or suspicious events between public health and safety authorities shall be restricted to the information necessary for the treatment, control, investigation, and prevention of a public health emergency.

MSEHPA §§301-303, available at www.publichealthlaw.net (Dec. 21, 2001 version).

Evaluate the constitutionality of the Model Act's reporting and tracking provisions. Does the constitutionality of the provisions depend on the identification of a serious threat of bioterrorism or other public health emergency? Note that section 303 explicitly permits public health authorities to share information with public safety officials, before the declaration of a public health emergency. Does this entanglement of public health and police functions complicate your analysis? See Ferguson v. City of Charleston, 532 U.S. 67 (2001), supra at page 536.

Would the disclosures be permissible under the federal HIPAA privacy rule? See 45 C.F.R. §164.512; and supra at page 174; Julie Bruce, Bioterrorism Meets Privacy: An Analysis of the Model State Health Powers Act and the HIPAA Privacy Rule, 12 Ann. Health L. 75 (2003); Janlori Goldman, Balancing in a Crisis? Bioterrorism, Public Health and Privacy, 38 J. Health L. 481 (2005); Andrea Wilson, Missing the Mark: The Public Health Exception to the HIPAA Privacy Rule and Its Impact on Surveillance Activity, 9 Hous. J. Health L. & Pol'y 131 (2008).

Would contact tracing be a realistic option for contagious diseases like smallpox given the large numbers of potentially exposed people and the general hysteria that might accompany the discovery of the first case? See Edward P. Richards, III, The United States Smallpox Bioterrorism Preparedness Plan: Rational Response or Potemkin Planning?, 36 Wm. Mitchell L. Rev. 5179 (2010) (expressing skepticism). What does it mean to "counsel and interview" persons under MSEHPA §302(b)? Is the reference to enforcement powers in §302(d) meant to suggest that individuals might be compelled to disclose information about possible sources and contacts?

Compare the Model Act's provisions to the relevant public health statute in your own state. Which seems better from a legal or policy standpoint? Do health care providers in your state have an obligation to report diseases related to bioterrorism? What about pharmacists? How are these measures enforced? May public health authorities and law enforcement share information? If so, do you see any similarities or differences between your state law and the Model Act? If not, would you recommend the adoption of the Model Act's provisions? See also Lawrence O. Gostin, When Terrorism Threatens Health: How Far Are Limitations on Personal and Economic Liberties Justified?, 55 Fla. L. Rev. 1105 (2003).

3. Isolation and Quarantine

■ WONG WAI v. WILLIAMSON

103 F. 1 (C.C.N.D. Cal. 1900)

MORROW, Circuit Judge.

[A Chinese resident of San Francisco brought suit against various governmental officers, challenging the application of rules that (1) required persons of Chinese ancestry to undergo inoculation against the bubonic plague by a "serum known as 'Haffkine Prophylactic,'" and (2) prohibited uninoculated Chinese residents from traveling outside the city.] . . .

Upon the filing of the bill of complaint, together with affidavits supporting the allegations therein contained, the court issued an order to the defendants to show cause why an injunction should not issue, restraining the defendants from committing the acts and carrying into execution the threats set forth in the bill of complaint. To the order to show cause no return has been made as required by the rules of practice in equity cases, but in lieu thereof the defendants . . . . composing the board of health of the city and county of San Francisco, have produced a copy of a resolution adopted by the board on May 18, 1900, as follows:

> Resolved, that it is the sense of this board that bubonic plague exists in the city and county of San Francisco, and that all necessary steps already taken for the prevention of its spread be continued, together with such additional measures as may be required.

The defendant J. J. Kinyoun, the acting quarantine officer of the United States at the port of San Francisco, in response to the order has produced the following telegram:

> Washington, D.C., May 21, 1900.
> Surgeon Kinyoun, Angel Island, California: By direction of the president, secretary of treasury has promulgated the following regulations under act of congress March twenty-seventh, eighteen ninety: First, during the existence of plague at any point in the United States the surgeon general, marine hospital service, is authorized to forbid the sale or donation of transportation by common carriers to Asiatics or other races liable to the disease; second, no common carrier shall accept for transportation any person suffering with plague, or any article infected therewith, nor shall common carriers accept for transportation any class of persons who may be designated by the surgeon general of the marine hospital service as being likely to convey the risk of plague contagion to other communities, and said common carriers shall be subject to inspection. Inform transportation companies, and direct them, under above regulations, to refuse transportation to Asiatics, except on your certificate, and instruct bonded inspectors to inspect trains and prevent Asiatics leaving state without your certificate.
>
> Wyman, Surgeon General Marine Hospital Service.

No objections being offered to these documents as constituting the return of the defendants, they will be so considered. . . .

The defendants constituting the board of health of the city and county of San Francisco contend that they are justified in their action with respect to the matter in controversy under their authority as a board, acting pursuant to the resolution of the board of May 18, 1900. The charter of the city and county of San Francisco provides, in article 10, for a department of public health, under the management of a board of health. . . . Section 4 provides, among other things, that the board shall enforce all ordinances, rules, and regulations which may be adopted by the supervisors for the carrying out and enforcement of a good sanitary condition in the city and county, and for the protection of the public health; and the board is required to submit to the supervisors, from time to time, a draft of such ordinances, rules, and regulations as it may deem necessary to promote the objects mentioned in the section. . . . [The charter provides, however, that the Board of Supervisors is the legislative body of the city with the power to enact ordinances.]

It thus appears that suitable provision has been made in the city charter for the necessary legislation providing rules and regulations to secure proper sanitary conditions in the city and for the protection of the public health, but we are not advised that the board of supervisors has taken any action whatever in that direction; and the resolution of the board of health furnished to the court fails to disclose the method it has adopted for that purpose, under the conditions it has declared to exist. We need not, however, dwell upon the manifest lack of legislative authority to enable the board of health to deal with this important subject. It is sufficient for the present purpose to mention the fact, as one of the features of the situation to be considered in connection with the regulations which the complainant alleges have been imposed upon him and other Chinese residents of the city by the defendants.

It appears that there are about 25,000 Chinese residents in the city of San Francisco, and, while it is well known that a large number of these people are domiciled within the area designated as the "Chinese Quarter," nevertheless there are a great many scattered over the city, engaged in various employments. No restrictions have been placed upon any of the Chinese residents in passing from one part of the city to the other; nor has any house, block, or section of the city been declared infected or unsanitary. There is, therefore, no fact established by the board of supervisors or by the board of health from which an inference might be drawn that any particular class of persons, or persons occupying a particular district, were liable to develop, or in danger of developing, the plague. The restriction is that no Chinese person shall depart from the city without being inoculated with the serum called "Haffkine Prophylactic." The city has a population of about 350,000, but the restriction does not apply to any of the inhabitants other than Chinese or Asiatics, and the inhabitants other than Chinese or Asiatics are permitted to depart from and return to the city without being subject to the inoculation imposed upon the Chinese inhabitants. This restriction, it is alleged, discriminates unreasonably against the complainant and other Chinese residents, confines them within the territorial limits of the city and county, and deprives them of their liberty, causing them great and irreparable loss and injury.

The conditions of a great city frequently present unexpected emergencies affecting the public health, comfort, and convenience. Under such circumstances, officers charged with the duties pertaining to this department of the municipal government should be clothed with sufficient authority to deal with the conditions in a prompt and effective manner. Measures of this character, having a uniform operation, and reasonably adapted to the purpose of protecting the health and preserving the welfare of the inhabitants of a city, are constantly upheld by the courts as valid acts of legislation, however inconvenient they may prove to be, and a wide discretion has also been sanctioned in their execution. But when the municipal authority has neglected to provide suitable rules and regulations upon the subject, and the officers are left to adopt such methods as they may deem proper for the occasion, their acts are open to judicial review, and may be examined in every detail to determine whether individual rights have been respected in accordance with constitutional requirements. This proposition is too clear to require discussion. . . .

In the light of these well-established principles, the action of the defendants as described in the bill of complaint cannot be justified. The regulations they have adopted appear to be without legislative authority, but assuming that they have the sanction of a general authority under the resolution of May 18, 1900, still they cannot be sustained. They are not based upon any established distinction in the conditions that are supposed to attend this plague, or the persons exposed to its contagion, but they are boldly directed against the Asiatic or Mongolian race as a class, without regard to the previous condition, habits, exposure to disease, or residence of the individual; and the only justification offered for this discrimination was a suggestion made by counsel for the defendants in the course of argument, that this particular race is more liable to the plague than any other. No evidence has, however, been offered to support this claim, and it is not known to be a fact. This explanation must therefore be dismissed as unsatisfactory. . . .

It follows from these considerations that the defendants have failed to justify their action in the premises, and that an injunction must issue as prayed for in the bill of complaint.

Notes: Isolation and Quarantine

1. *Definitions and History.* "Isolation" and "quarantine" are technically different public health approaches, though the two terms are often used interchangeably to describe separating those who are or may be infected from those who are believed to be unaffected. Isolation is used to separate infected people with communicable conditions from others until the period of communicability passes. Quarantine is used to detain those who have been exposed to a disease for the incubation period of that disease so that contact with uninfected persons can be avoided.

However denominated, the concept of separation has ancient roots. In earlier centuries, the victims of disease who were believed to be dangerous to the public through some human contact (which then included most of the known afflictions of humans) were banished from the community and abandoned, beyond the campfire, the village, or the wall of the city. In urbanized areas in the Middle Ages, the practice of "quarantine" began. Voyagers were held on board ship; the local afflicted were confined to their homes. As hospitals and detention houses were developed, they were used for isolation or quarantine when other quarters were not available. With no available treatment, isolation for a temporary period until the person recovered and was no longer infectious, or until death, was the most humane alternative. In the nineteenth century and the early twentieth century, quarantine and isolation were the most common means of disease control. For a comprehensive historical analysis of the sweep of diseases and plagues from ancient times, see a wonderfully enlightening and exciting review by a leading American historian, William Hardy McNeill, Plagues and Peoples (1998), along with the excellent Norman F. Cantor, In the Wake of the Plague: The Black Death and the World It Made (2002). The plague can now be treated effectively with antibiotics. Modern contagious diseases that spark a similar level of fear include the Ebola virus and smallpox, see page 647.

2. Wong Wai. The public health measures adopted in *Wong Wai* combined a form of vaccination with a quarantine order restricting uninoculated Asians from leaving San Francisco. The court decision is relatively unique in its detailed examination and rejection of a measure asserted to involve protection of the public health. What explains the result?

Consider the large number of evidentiary and legal defects cited by the court. Should it matter whether there was evidence that the bubonic plague was present within the city? (The opinion casts doubt on this factor; others have suggested that cases of plague had been reported.) Were the quarantine and inoculation orders issued by the appropriate governmental authorities? The court suggests that the orders should have been passed as ordinances by the Board of Supervisors rather than issued by the city Board of Health. What should be the effect of finding the orders to be *ultra vires*? Why were the inoculation and quarantine orders applicable only to those of Asian heritage? What standard of review would a modern court apply to an order of this type? Cf. Jed Rubenfeld, The End of Privacy, 61 Stan. L. Rev. 101, 144-148 (2008) (exploring Fourth Amendment jurisprudence including implications for quarantine and civil commitment). What types of evidence would be necessary to support a public health measure applied only to persons of a particular racial or ethnic background? See also Jew Ho v. Williamson, 103 F. 10 (C.C.N.D. Cal. 1900).

3. *Isolation and HIV Infection*. Should persons with HIV infection be separated from the general population? Public health authorities uniformly reject the suggestion. See Lawrence O. Gostin & Zita Lazzarini, Human Rights and Public Health in the AIDS Pandemic 64-76 (1997). Segregation or isolation of persons with HIV within correctional facilities is nonetheless permitted but not required. Compare Onishea v. Hopper, 171 F.3d 1289 (11th Cir. 1999) (segregation of HIV-infected inmates does not violate Rehabilitation Act), with Glick v. Henderson, 855 F.2d 536 (8th Cir. 1988) (failure to segregate infected prisoners does not violate the Eighth Amendment's prohibition against cruel and unusual punishment). See also Annot., 162 A.L.R. Fed. 181 (2000); Scott Burris, Prisons, Law and Public Health: The Case for a Coordinated Response to Epidemic Disease Behind Bars, 47 U. Miami L. Rev. 291 (1992).

4. *Federal Quarantine Regulations*. The federal Public Health Service Act gives the Secretary of Health and Human Services authority over quarantines within federal jurisdiction:

(a) Promulgation and enforcement by Surgeon General
The Surgeon General, with the approval of the Secretary, is authorized to make and enforce such regulations as in his judgment are necessary to prevent the introduc-

tion, transmission, or spread of communicable diseases from foreign countries into the States or possessions, or from one State or possession into any other State or possession. . . .

(b) Apprehension, detention, or conditional release of individuals

Regulations prescribed under this section shall not provide for the apprehension, detention, or conditional release of individuals except for the purpose of preventing the introduction, transmission, or spread of such communicable diseases as may be specified from time to time in Executive orders of the President upon the recommendation of the Secretary, in consultation with the Surgeon General,

(c) Application of regulations to persons entering from foreign countries

Except as provided in subsection (d) of this section, regulations prescribed under this section, insofar as they provide for the apprehension, detention, examination, or conditional release of individuals, shall be applicable only to individuals coming into a State or possession from a foreign country or a possession.

(d)(1) Apprehension and examination of persons reasonably believed to be infected

Regulations prescribed under this section may provide for the apprehension and examination of any individual reasonably believed to be infected with a communicable disease in a qualifying stage and [who is a probable source of infection who is or will be moving from state to state] . . . Such regulations may provide that if upon examination any such individual is found to be infected, he may be detained for such time and in such manner as may be reasonably necessary. . . .

42 U.S.C. §264. The current executive order includes SARS and influenza viruses capable of causing a pandemic. See CDC, Legal Authorities for Isolation and Quarantine (with links to the current Presidential Executive Order). The threat of pandemic flu and the widely reported case of an international traveler who allegedly suffered from drug-resistant TB raised questions about the adequacy of federal rules governing quarantine. See, e.g., Symposium, The Dangerous Patient: Medical, Legal, and Public Policy Responses, 30 J. Leg. Med. 1-140 (2009) (including reactions to case involving traveler with TB).

5. *State Quarantine Law.* State quarantine laws were little used and little discussed for decades. The situation changed with the advent of drug-resistant TB and the threats posed by bioterrorism and resurgent strains of influenza. Professor Gostin notes, "While many existing state isolation and quarantine statutes are antiquated, 27 states have modernized their laws based on the [MSEHPA]." Lawrence O. Gostin, Public Health Strategies for Pandemic Influenza: Ethics and the Law, 295 JAMA 1700, 1703 (2006). The relevant MSEHPA provisions are discussed in the problem found at page 707.

6. *State Quarantines and Conflicts with Federal Law.* Where does the state's power to restrict the movement of people end? Is a state permitted to enact travel restrictions that hinder interstate commerce or immigration, two areas within the domain of federal law? Federal quarantine law specifies that: "(e) Nothing in this section . . . or the regulations . . . may be construed as superseding any provision under State law (including regulations and including provisions established by political subdivisions of States), except to the extent that such a provision conflicts with an exercise of Federal authority. . . ." 42 U.S.C. §264. Does this resolve the question?

In Compagnie Francaise de Navigation a Vapeur v. State Board of Health, Louisiana, 186 U.S. 380 (1902), the Supreme Court considered and upheld the validity of a board order barring entry of any "body or bodies of people, immigrants, soldier, or others" into cities where a quarantine had been declared. The asserted basis of this "reverse" quarantine was that the introduction of new, uninfected persons to an area would "add fuel to the flame." How would this case be decided today? What, if anything, has changed? Has Congress occupied the field more thoroughly than it had in the early 1900s? Has the Court changed its mind about the state's ability to enact public safety regulations that impede interstate commerce? Could a state pass a statute refusing to permit introduction of additional hazardous waste into its borders? See Chemical Waste Management v. Hunt, 504 U.S. 334, 346-347 (1992) (distinguishing permissible and impermissible state quarantine provisions that have an impact on interstate commerce, citing *Compagnie Francaise*). See also Annot., 86 A.L.R.4th 401 (1991). Federal laws prohibiting disability-based discrimination might also limit the permissibility of state quarantine rules in some situations. See supra at page 667.

7. *Responding to SARS.* The outbreak of Severe Acute Respiratory Syndrome (SARS) in Canada and other countries during 2003 provided a modern example of the use of quarantine and isolation. The crisis required the use of "in house" quarantine orders and sparked a number of important policy debates. See Lawrence O. Gostin et al., Ethical and Legal Challenges Posed by Severe Acute Respiratory Syndrome: Implications for the Control of Severe Infectious Disease Threats, 290 JAMA 3229 (2003); and National Advisory Committee on SARS and Public Health, Learning from SARS: Renewal of Public Health in Canada (2003) (the Naylor Report).

8. *A New Influenza Pandemic?* How should we prepare for the possibility of a new, deadly influenza pandemic? As noted above at page 652, a novel flu virus capable of rapid human-to-human transmission could cause millions of deaths worldwide. See also an online resource for avian and pandemic flu information managed by the Department of Health and Human Services: www.flu.gov/pandemic. Canada's experience with quarantine orders during the SARS outbreak suggests that isolation/quarantine might be important components of the public health response, although this will depend on the characteristics of the influenza virus. Neil M. Ferguson et al., Letter, Strategies for Mitigating an Influenza Epidemic, 442 Nature 448 (2006) (model shows that "case isolation or household quarantine could have a significant impact" on influenza pandemic). But see Wendy K. Mariner et al., Pandemic Preparedness: A Return to the Rule of Law, 1 Drexel L. Rev. 341 (2009) (contending that quarantine measures caused negative and counterproductive public reactions). Does the current legal framework in the United States permit the use of isolation and quarantine on the scale that might be warranted from a public health standpoint? See Note, Phase Six Pandemic: A Call to Re-Evaluate Federal Quarantine Authority Before the Next Catastrophic Outbreak, 44 Ga. L. Rev. 803 (2010); Lawrence O. Gostin, Public Health Strategies for Pandemic Influenza: Ethics and the Law, 295 JAMA 1700 (2006).

4. Civil Commitment and Mandatory Treatment

Should a state be able to promote public health by requiring medical treatment? In some sense, this form of state regulation could be viewed as the most direct and effective method of health promotion. So long as the state has correctly identified an affected individual and so long as an effective treatment is available, mandatory treatment would seem to promote both the health of the individual and of those with whom the individual interacts. The apparent simplicity of this approach is matched, of course, by the serious threat to individual liberties it entails. When should the state's interest in public health outweigh the individual's rights to freedom of movement, to bodily integrity, and to make medical treatment decisions free from state coercion? Should it matter whether the illness is mental or physical?

ADDINGTON v. TEXAS
441 U.S. 418 (1979)

BURGER, C.J.

[The appellant had a long history of temporary commitments as mentally ill (seven times between 1969 and 1975) to several Texas mental hospitals. In December 1975, appellant was arrested on charges of assault and threats against his mother. His mother filed a petition for indefinite commitment. A trial was held before a jury to determine whether the appellant was mentally ill and in need of treatment for his welfare and protection, or for the protection of others. The trial lasted six days. The appellant was found mentally ill and subject to commitment under the law based upon "clear, unequivocal and convincing evidence." The Texas Supreme Court upheld the commitment and the applicable standard of proof.]

The question in this case is what standard of proof is required by the Fourteenth Amendment to the Constitution in a civil proceeding brought under state law to commit an individual involuntarily for an indefinite period to a state mental hospital.

This Court repeatedly has recognized that civil commitment for any purpose constitutes a significant deprivation of liberty that requires due process protection. Moreover, it is indisputable that involuntary commitment to a mental hospital after a finding of probable dangerousness to self or others can engender adverse social consequences to the individual. Whether we label this phenomena "stigma" or choose to call it something else is less important than that we recognize that it can occur and that it can have a very significant impact on the individual.

The state has a legitimate interest under its *parens patriae* powers in providing care to its citizens who are unable because of emotional disorders to care for themselves; the state also has authority under its police power to protect the community from the dangerous tendencies of some who are mentally ill. Under the Texas Mental Health Code, however, the state has no interest in confining individuals involuntarily if they are not mentally ill or if they do not pose some danger to themselves or others. Since the preponderance standard creates the risk of increasing the number of individuals erroneously committed, it is at least unclear to what extent, if any, the state's interests are furthered by using a preponderance standard in such commitment proceedings.

The expanding concern of society with problems of mental disorders is reflected in the fact that in recent years many states have enacted statutes designed to protect the rights of the mentally ill. However, only one state by statute permits involuntary commitment by a mere preponderance of the evidence, Miss. Code Ann. §41-21-75 (1978 Supp.), and Texas is the only state where a court has concluded that the preponderance-of-the-evidence standard satisfies due process. We attribute this not to any lack of concern in those states, but rather to a belief that the varying standards tend to produce comparable results. As we noted earlier, however, standards of proof are important for their symbolic meaning as well as for their practical effect. . . .

Appellant urges the Court to hold that due process requires use of the criminal law's standard of proof—"beyond a reasonable doubt." . . .

There are significant reasons why different standards of proof are called for in civil commitment proceedings as opposed to criminal prosecutions. In a civil commitment state power is not exercised in a punitive sense. . . .

In addition, the "beyond a reasonable doubt" standard historically has been reserved for criminal cases. This unique standard of proof, not prescribed or defined in the Constitution, is regarded as a critical part of the "moral force of the criminal law," In re Winship, 397 U.S., at 364, and we should hesitate to apply it too broadly or casually in noncriminal cases.

The heavy standard applied in criminal cases manifests our concern that the risk of error to the individual must be minimized even at the risk that some who are guilty might go free. Patterson v. New York, 432 U.S. 197, 208 (1977). The full force of that idea does not apply to a civil commitment. It may be true that an erroneous commitment is sometimes as undesirable as an erroneous conviction, 5 J. Wigmore, Evidence §1400 (Chadbourn rev. 1974). However, even though an erroneous confinement should be avoided in the first instance, the layers of professional review and observation of the patient's condition, and the concern of family and friends generally will provide continuous opportunities for an erroneous commitment to be corrected. Moreover, it is not true that the release of a genuinely mentally ill person is no worse for the individual than the failure to convict the guilty. One who is suffering from a debilitating mental illness and in need of treatment is neither wholly at liberty nor free of stigma. See Chodoff, The Case for Involuntary Hospitalization of the Mentally Ill, 133 Am. J. Psychiatry 496, 498 (1976); Schwartz, Myers & Astrachan, Psychiatric Labeling and the Rehabilitation of the Mental Patient, 31 Arch. Gen. Psychiatry 329, 334 (1974). It cannot be said, therefore, that it is much better for a mentally ill person to "go free" than for a mentally normal person to be committed. . . .

The subtleties and nuances of psychiatric diagnosis render certainties virtually beyond reach in most situations. The reasonable-doubt standard of criminal law functions in its realm because there the standard is addressed to specific, knowable facts. Psychiatric diagnosis, in contrast, is to a large extent based on medical "impressions" drawn from subjective analysis and filtered through the experience of the diagnostician. This process often makes it very difficult for the expert physician to offer definite conclusions about any particular patient. Within the medical discipline, the traditional standard for "factfinding" is a "reasonable medical certainty." If a trained psychiatrist has difficulty with the categorical "beyond a reasonable doubt" standard, the untrained lay juror—or indeed even a trained judge—who is required to rely upon expert opinion could be forced by the criminal law standard of proof to reject commitment for many patients desperately in need of institutionalized psychiatric care. Such "freedom" for a mentally ill person would be purchased at a high price. . . .

We have concluded that the reasonable-doubt standard is inappropriate in civil commitment proceedings because, given the uncertainties of psychiatric diagnosis, it may impose a burden the state cannot meet and thereby erect an unreasonable barrier to needed medical treatment. Similarly, we conclude that use of the term *unequivocal* is not constitutionally required, although the states are free to use that standard. To meet due process demands, the standard has to inform the factfinder that the proof must be greater than the preponderance-of-the-evidence standard applicable to other categories of civil cases.

We noted earlier that the trial court employed the standard of "clear, unequivocal and convincing" evidence in appellant's commitment hearing before a jury. That instruction was constitutionally adequate. However, determination of the precise burden equal to or greater than the "clear and convincing" standard which we hold is required to meet due process guarantees is a matter of state law which we leave to the Texas Supreme Court. Accordingly, we remand the case for further proceedings not inconsistent with this opinion.

Vacated and remanded.

■ IN THE INTEREST OF J.A.D.
492 N.W.2d 82 (N.D. 1992)

Vande Walle, Justice.

J.A.D. appealed from an order of the county court of Stutsman County requiring that he be hospitalized and treated for mental illness for a period not to exceed 90 days. We reverse. . . .

Before a court can issue an order for an involuntary treatment, the petitioner must prove by clear and convincing evidence that the respondent is a person requiring treatment. NDCC §25-03.1-19. The determination that an individual is a "person requiring treatment" under the statutory definition is a two-step process: (1) the court must find that the individual is mentally ill, and (2) the court must find that there is a reasonable expectation that if the person is not hospitalized there exists a serious risk of harm to himself, others, or property.[1] NDCC §25-03.1-02(10). . . . We therefore focus on the evidence that J.A.D. was mentally ill and that there was a substantial likelihood of substantial harm to J.A.D. to determine if there is clear and convincing evidence to support the findings of the trial court. . . .

The record demonstrates that J.A.D. is suffering from a mental illness. The record also fairly indicates that without treatment, J.A.D.'s mental health would be

1. Section 25-03.1-02(10) reads:

> "Person requiring treatment" means a person who is mentally ill or chemically dependent, and there is a reasonable expectation that if the person is not treated there exists a serious risk of harm to that person, others, or property. "Serious risk of harm" means a substantial likelihood of: a. Suicide as manifested by suicidal threats, attempts, or significant depression relevant to suicidal potential; b. Killing or inflicting serious bodily harm on another person or inflicting significant property damage, as manifested by acts or threats; c. Substantial deterioration in physical health, or substantial injury, disease, or death based upon recent poor self-control or judgment in providing one's shelter, nutrition, or personal care; or d. Substantial deterioration in mental health which would predictably result in dangerousness to that person, others, or property, based upon acts, threats, or patterns in the person's treatment history, current condition, and other relevant factors.

at a substantial risk of deterioration. However, as we have previously held, the need for treatment alone is not sufficient to order hospitalization. The issue is therefore whether or not this likely deterioration of J.A.D.'s mental health will predictably result in dangerousness to himself, others, or property. . . .

The record is tenuous as to whether J.A.D. poses a danger to himself, to others, or to property. Testimony at the hearing indicates that J.A.D. may be a danger to himself, though most likely not a danger to others or to property. The concern over J.A.D.'s dangerousness to himself centered around his homelessness and his ability to take care of himself, such as his resourcefulness at getting food and proper nutrition, and his propensity to seek out shelter during the winter months. . . .

Dr. Kottke's testimony that J.A.D. was in need of treatment as defined by the statutes was not clear and convincing. Dr. Kottke's conclusion, that absent commitment to the State Hospital there exists a strong risk of harm to J.A.D., was also premised on his concern that J.A.D. would not seek appropriate shelter when winter came, as it surely will, in North Dakota.

All three witnesses expressed concern that because J.A.D. was a recent arrival from the deep South he was not aware of the severe cold which the winter season may bring to North Dakota and would not seek appropriate food and shelter. These concerns were essentially premised on isolated incidents in which J.A.D. did not take advantage of shelter the caseworker had arranged, the fact that J.A.D. took shelter in abandoned buildings, that he talked about obtaining a hotplate, and the fact that he once placed food he received from the private organization in a garbage dumpster because, according to the witness, he could not remember where he obtained the food and was afraid to eat it. . . .

Not all homeless people are mentally ill and in need of treatment. Homelessness may in some instances be a product of mental illness, but it may also be the result of economic hardship or simply lifestyle choice. We cannot categorize homeless people as people in need of compulsory mental therapy simply because they do without a traditional home, kitchen, plumbing, or electricity. Homeless people may be very resourceful in obtaining food and shelter, as evidenced by J.A.D. seeking out the Salvation Army and social programs offered by the various state and private agencies in the community. J.A.D. has been receiving food and meals, and has sought shelter. Because he did not make use of the shelter which he was offered during the summer months is not necessarily indicative of a propensity to not seek shelter in the winter months. J.A.D. had the wherewithal to travel to North Dakota, and we can presume that he has the wherewithal to leave. In the winter, he may seek assistance for shelter as he has in the past, or simply leave the state for warmer locations. There is no presumption that J.A.D., as a homeless person, will neither be able to fend for himself during the winter months nor be able to take care of his needs. . . . [The court also expressed its concern with the trial court's failure to adequately consider appropriate, less restrictive alternatives to commitment.] . . .

Accordingly, we reverse the order for hospitalization and treatment.

ERICKSTAD, Chief Justice, specially concurring.

I respectfully, reluctantly concur in the result of the majority opinion, with great concern that, in our effort to find clear and convincing evidence of J.A.D.'s need for treatment, we have actually tried this case anew and found that evidence wanting. . . .

Through our very careful review of the facts and our analysis of the possible consequences of the facts, we may have deprived J.A.D. of treatment crucial to his future welfare, without providing him with a safety net of any kind, at a time, considering the season of the year, when survival as a homeless person in North Dakota could be hazardous to say the very least.

Notes: Mandatory Mental Health Treatment

1. *Trends in Mental Health Treatment.* The *Addington* case in the Supreme Court represented a high-water mark in efforts to raise the standard of proof for compulsory hospitalization of the mentally ill. In large measure, the laws on commitment of the mentally ill came full circle in some 200 years in the United States. The nineteenth-century laws were essentially modeled after criminal procedures. The person who was believed to be mentally ill was "arrested" and "charged" with being "insane" and at large and was "committed" to a mental institution, usually for life. On any escape, the patient was hunted down like a criminal and returned to the institution in chains.

In the middle years of the twentieth century, the laws concerning mental illness were largely decriminalized, and compulsory hospitalization was made considerably easier as an administrative action without judicial intervention. This was the case all over the world. The movement away from the informal system back to a much more structured, judicially sanctioned review procedure for compulsory hospitalization began in the 1970s and continued into the 1980s. Michael L. Perlin, The Hidden Prejudice: Mental Disability on Trial (2000); The Evolution of Mental Health Law (Lynda E. Frost & Richard Bonnie eds., 2001).

2. *Clear and Convincing Evidence.* Why does the Court impose this higher burden of proof for civil commitments? Should the burden apply to all aspects of the state's case, including both the diagnosis of mental illness and the requirement of dangerousness? Most jurisdictions answer both questions affirmatively. In addition to *J.A.D.*, supra, see Colorado v. Stevens, 761 P.2d 768 (Colo. 1988); In re Richard A., 771 A.2d 572 (N.H. 2001) (reviewing standards); In the Matter of The Commitment of N.N., 679 A.2d 1174 (N.J. 1996) (discussing the constitutional constraints applicable to the commitment of minors). See also In re Jeffrey E., 281 P.3d 84 (Alaska 2012) (deferring to prediction of possible future grave disability). In most cases, the issues of commitment and treatment are intertwined. Will the same due process protections apply to "mandatory treatment," as an issue distinct from commitment? Yes. See Wetherhorn v. Alaska Psychiatric Institute, 156 P.3d 371 (Alaska 2007); Donaldson v. District Court, 847 P.2d 632 (Colo. 1993) (en banc); In re C.E., 641 N.E.2d 345 (Ill. 1994); In re W.J.C.A., 810 N.W.2d 327 (N.D. 2012). How do you reconcile this approach with the right to control one's own medical treatment described in Chapters 2 and 3?

A number of commentators have explored the law and policy governing mental health civil commitments. See generally Lawrence O. Gostin & Lance Gable, The Human Rights of Persons with Mental Disabilities: A Global Perspective on the Application of Human Rights Principles to Mental Health, 63 Md. L. Rev. 20 (2004); Nicholas Scurich & Richard John, The Normative Threshold for Psychiatric Civil Commitment, 50 Jurimetrics 425 (2009-2010); Alexander Tsesis, Due Process in

Civil Commitments, 68 Wash. & Lee L. Rev. 253 (2011); Bruce J. Winick, Therapeutic Jurisprudence and the Civil Commitment Hearing, 10 J. Contemp. Legal Issues 37 (1999); Annot., 97 A.L.R.3d 780 (1980). See also Symposium, Conundrums and Controversies in Mental Health and Illness, 38 J.L. Med. & Ethics 722-806 (2010).

The Americans with Disabilities Act (ADA) prohibits discrimination against persons with disabilities who do not present a direct threat to health and safety. Is this consistent with state law or does the ADA place any additional obstacles in the path of involuntary commitment? See, e.g., Shelton v. Arkansas Department of Human Services, 677 F.3d 837 (8th Cir. 2012) (medical treatment decisions not challengeable under ADA or Rehabilitation Act). In addition, courts will have to determine whether a specific claim for money damages under Title II against a state in matters involving mental health constitutes a valid exercise of congressional power under the Fourteenth Amendment. See supra page 667; Bolmer v. Oliveira, 594 F.3d 134 (2d Cir. 2010) (involuntarily committed patient's action against state mental health department and psychiatrist under constitution and ADA not barred by qualified immunity or Eleventh Amendment). See also Susan Stefan, Unequal Rights: Discrimination Against People with Mental Disabilities and the Americans with Disabilities Act (2001) (pre-*Garrett/Lane* analysis).

3. *Intellectual Disabilities.* Does commitment based on reduced intellectual abilities or developmental disabilities invoke the same constitutional concerns as commitment for mental illness? In Heller v. Doe, 509 U.S. 312 (1993), the Court considered the validity of a statutory scheme that imposed a lower burden of proof on involuntary commitments for persons who were "mentally retarded." The Court's analysis was based on a rational review standard because the litigants had failed to properly present their claim that a higher level of scrutiny should be applied. A divided Court upheld the lower commitment standard, in part because of distinctions between this form of disability and mental illness. Intellectual disabilities might be easier to diagnose, with less risk of error, for example. Similarly, Kentucky "could conclude" that persons with lower intellectual functioning were more likely to present a danger to themselves or others. In addition, treatment for this form of disability is "much less invasive" than treatment for mental illness. Justices Souter, Blackmun, and Stevens dissented, with O'Connor joining in part. See Susan Lee, Heller v. Doe: Involuntary Civil Commitment and the "Objective" Language of Probability, 20 Am. J.L. & Med. 457 (1994). See also Atkins v. Virginia, 122 S. Ct. 2242 (2002) (capital punishment of those with significantly reduced intellectual abilities violates Eight Amendment proscription against cruel and unusual punishment); People v. Barrett, 2012 WL 3064339 (Cal.) (no equal protection claim where different approach to requesting jury trials for mentally ill and dangerous persons as compared with "mentally retarded" and dangerous persons); Porter v. Knickrehm, 457 F.3d 794 (8th Cir. 2006) (only minimal procedural protections required for admission of intellectually disabled individual to state human development center when admission under voluntary authority of legal guardian); and Bryan Y. Lee, The U.N. Convention on the Rights of Persons with Disabilities and Its Impact upon Involuntary Civil Commitment of Individuals with Developmental Disabilities, 44 Colum. J.L. & Soc. Probs. 393 (2011) (comparing state civil commitment standards with emerging norms from U.N. Convention).

4. *Involuntary Treatment of Prisoners with Psychotropic Medications.* Do *Addington's* due process protections apply to prisoners? In Washington v. Harper, 494 U.S. 210

(1990), the Supreme Court analyzed the constitutionality of a state policy that authorized treatment of inmates with antipsychotic drugs without a judicial hearing. The Court held that prisoners do retain a protected liberty interest in avoiding unwanted treatment. It held, however, that this due process interest was subject to the reasonableness test of Turner v. Safley, 482 U.S. 78 (1987): Policies that infringe prisoner rights will be upheld so long as they are reasonably related to legitimate penological interests. Applying this standard, the Court held that "given the requirements of the prison environment, the due process clause permits the state to treat a prison inmate who has a serious mental illness with antipsychotic drugs against his will, if the inmate is dangerous to himself or others and the treatment is in the inmate's medical interest." Harper, 494 U.S. at 227.

The Court also considered whether Harper had been denied his right to procedural due process. See, e.g., Morrissey v. Brewer, 408 U.S. 471, 481 (1972). The state's procedure, which included determinations through administrative hearings before the institution's own mental health care personnel (although not those involved in the direct treatment of the prisoner), was deemed to be procedurally adequate. Harper, 494 U.S. at 232-236. The Court rejected contentions that the decision should be made before a judge and with the assistance of counsel. Justice Blackmun, often deferential to medical authority, concurred in the majority decision, while noting that use of a formal commitment procedure would render the debate unnecessary. Id. at 236-237. Justices Stevens, Brennan, and Marshall dissented, noting that the Court had failed to recognize and protect Harper's significant liberty interests. See also Foucha v. Louisiana, 504 U.S. 71 (1992) (person acquitted by reason of insanity who subsequently was found to be without mental illness could not be committed to mental institution based on dangerousness alone). For a discussion on forced medical treatment in order to stand trial, see United States v. Loughner, 672 F.3d 731 (9th Cir. 2012) (upholding involuntary medical treatment of pretrial detainee); Sell v. U.S., 539 U.S. 166 (2003); George Annas, Forcible Medication for Courtroom Competence—The Case of Charles Sell, 350 New Eng. J. Med. 2297 (2004).

5. *Outpatient Commitment.* In-patient commitment and mandatory treatment both involve substantial invasions of individual liberty. What standards should be applied to state laws permitting "outpatient commitment," under which individuals might be required to demonstrate continued adherence to medical treatment or therapy? Could outpatient commitment be used to ensure that mentally ill patients continue to take necessary medications while in the community, thus preventing relapses and the need for inpatient commitment? Cf. Miguel M. v. Barron, 950 N.E.2d 107 (N.Y. 2011) (excerpted at page 164; interaction between HIPAA and actions of physician accessing prior medical records in effort to secure court order authorizing Assisted Outpatient Treatment for patient); In re Luis, 99 Cal. Rptr. 3d 174 (1st App. Div. 2009) (court declines to reach constitutionality of probation condition that minor continue taking prescribed psychotropic medications). See Jeffrey Geller & Jonathan A. Stanley, Settling the Doubts About the Constitutionality of Outpatient Commitment, 31 New Eng. J. on Crim. & Civ. Confinement 127 (2005); Bruce J. Winick et al., Symposium, Preventive Outpatient Commitment for Person with Serious Mental Illness, 9 Psychol. Pub. Pol'y & L. 8 (2003). See also In the Matter of K.L., 806 N.E.2d 480 (N.Y. 2004).

Problem: Civil Commitment and Drug Abuse

Should persons addicted to drugs or alcohol be subjected to civil commitment and, where available, forced treatment? Under what circumstances would such a commitment be legitimate? Is addiction a "mental illness"? In E.P. v. Alaska Psychiatric Institute, 205 P.3d 1101 (Alaska 2009), the court considered whether a person who practiced "huffing" (inhaling gas and other fumes) could be involuntarily committed.

E.P. has a history of alcohol abuse and inhaling gasoline fumes and other substances to get high ("huffing"). These actions have led to several commitments, both voluntary and involuntary to the Alaska Psychiatric Institute (API). Huffing has damaged the frontal lobe of E.P.'s brain, resulting in dementia, personality disorder, and not otherwise specified psychosis. He has poor judgment and insight, and as a result cannot grasp the severe health consequences of huffing. E.P. is addicted to huffing. . . .

Alaska law permits involuntary commitment only of those who are gravely disabled or likely to harm themselves or others as the result of mental illness. Thus, the state may involuntarily commit E.P. only if he is "mentally ill" under the statutes. Alaska Statute 47.30.915(12) defines "mental illness" as:

[A]n organic, mental, or emotional impairment that has substantive adverse effects on an individual's ability to exercise conscious control of the individual's actions or ability to perceive reality or to reason or understand; mental retardation, epilepsy, drug addiction, and alcoholism do not per se constitute mental illness, although persons suffering from these conditions may also be suffering from mental illness.

E.P.'s organic brain damage meets the first part of the statutory definition: as found by the superior courts, E.P. suffers from organic mental impairments affecting his judgment, perception of reality, and rational decision-making capabilities. The evidence supported those findings. The question is whether the statute's specific exception of "drug addiction" from the definition of "mental illness" means that E.P. is not mentally ill. We believe that it does not.

E.P.'s organic brain damage is a condition apart from, and more than, his drug addiction. While it is the result of his addiction, it has led to greatly impaired ability to exercise judgment, loss of perception of reality, and impaired ability to communicate. E.P. is not simply a drug addict, he has lost the capacity to appreciate the dangers of his addiction. . . . [B]ecause of cognitive damage, E.P. had little or no insight into the fact that huffing gas hurts him. His continued desire to huff gas stems not only from addiction, but also from his cognitive inability to understand his situation. . . .

Although Alaska law allows commitment of mentally ill people "likely to cause harm to [self] or others," it does not define that term. . . .

We conclude that E.P.'s intent to huff gas constitutes intent to cause himself bodily harm, and that it results from his mental illness. The superior court's finding that huffing gas damages the brain is supported by the evidence. The finding that E.P.'s intent to huff gas if released is the result of mental illness, rather than just an addiction, because of the damage to his brain that prevents him from perceiving the dangers of huffing, is likewise supported by the evidence. We distinguish this case from one in which an addicted person with full mental capacity chooses to continue abusing harmful substances, no matter how unwise one might consider that choice. In such a case, the person's intent to harm himself by abusing substances results from drug addiction alone, which the legislature excluded from the definition of "mental illness." In this case, E.P.'s decision to harm himself by abusing substances results from his brain damage, and therefore meets the statutory standards. . . .

Id. See also Melanie B. Abbott, Homelessness and Substance Abuse: Is Mandatory Treatment the Solution?, 22 Fordham Urb. L.J. 1 (1994); Mara Lynn Krongard, Comment, A Population at Risk: Civil Commitment of Substance Abusers After Kansas v. Hendricks, 90 Cal. L. Rev. 111 (2002). Several states have enacted statutes providing for civil commitment of pregnant women who have habitually or excessively used specific enumerated controlled substances. See, for example, S.D. Codified Laws §34-20A-70; Wis. Stat. Ann. §48.193. See also the discussion of maternal-fetal conflict at page 532.

The deinstitutionalization of mental patients in the 1970s and 1980s added to the population of homeless persons. About one-third to one-half of the homeless are estimated to be coping with some form of mental illness or addiction. H. Richard Lamb & Leona L. Bachrach, Some Perspectives on Deinstitutionalization, 52 Psychiatr. Serv. 1039 (2001). Some jurisdictions have sought to institutionalize homeless persons on the theory that they are incapable of protecting themselves. What is your view? Are you concerned about the extent to which poverty might be misconstrued as mental illness? The Alaska statute discussed in E.P. established a different commitment standard for "the gravely disabled," defined as those who "risk[ed] harm from passive failure to secure their own basic needs." E.P., 205 P.3d at 1110. The legislation permits commitment of the "gravely disabled" only with evidence that treatment to improve the committed person's condition would be available. See id. at 1109-1110; and Wetherhorn v. Alaska Psychiatric Inst., 156 P.3d 371 (Alaska 2001). Is the distinction between the commitment rules for the gravely disabled and for those with mental illness rational? E.P. could not be committed as "gravely disabled" because the Alaska Psychiatric Institute was not a substance abuse treatment facility; E.P.'s commitment thus merely served to keep him from gaining access to inhalants. Does this affect your view of the court's reasoning?

Problem: Sexually Violent Predators—Treatment or Punishment?

Suppose that you are a legislator who is concerned about recent scientific studies that show high recidivism rates among sexually violent pedophiles. You understand public anxiety about the release of these persons into the community. Yet you also are concerned about protecting the constitutional rights of all citizens. A victims' rights group has proposed a new statute, called "The Sexually Violent Predator Act." Under the statute, the state health department could bring an action for the civil commitment of "sexually violent predators." The state would have the burden of proving, by clear and convincing evidence, that the person to be committed (1) had committed and was likely to commit in the future certain acts of sexual violence directed against persons under age 13, and (2) that the person had a "mental abnormality" or a "personality disorder." Persons committed under the proposed statute would be confined to a special unit, physically located within a correctional facility but separately staffed with trained, noncorrectional personnel. The individual's commitment would be subject to judicial review upon the motion of the individual or state but in any event on a yearly basis. Individuals housed in the special unit would be offered group therapy, although the legislation's proponents conceded that this therapy was unlikely to cure the committed person's underlying disorder. Do you favor or oppose the proposed legislation? What additional information do you need to determine the constitutional validity of the proposal?

Sexual predator laws have been widely enacted. In United States v. Comstock, 130 S. Ct. 1949 (2010), the Supreme Court upheld the federal power to enact the civil commitment provisions of the federal Adam Walsh Child Protection and Safety Act. This federal law requires proof by clear and convincing evidence that the "individual (1) has previously 'engaged or attempted to engage in sexual violent conduct or child molestation,' (2) currently 'suffers from a serious mental illness, abnormality, or disorder,' and (3) 'as a result of' that . . . [condition] is 'sexually dangerous to others,' in that 'he would have serious difficulty in refraining from sexual violent conduct or child molestation if released.'" See Note, Civil Commitment, 124 Harv. L. Rev. 279 (2010).

For information on state initiatives, see the National Conference of State Legislatures Web site, www.ncsl.org; Kansas v. Crane, 534 U.S. 407 (2002) (states must prove individual lacks control over dangerous behavior); Kansas v. Hendricks, 521 U.S. 346 (1997) (upholding state civil commitment statute for sexual predators); Lee v. Superior Court, 99 Cal. Rptr. 3d 712 (2009) (interaction of HIPAA's confidentiality provisions and court order to obtain medical records related to sexual predator law). See also Monica Davey & Abby Goodnough, Doubts Rise as States Hold Sex Offenders After Prison: Costly Efforts Keep Ex-Convicts Off Streets, but Mandated Treatment Often Fails, N.Y. Times, March 4, 2007; Annot., 96 A.L.R.3d 840 (2005).

Notes: Mandatory Treatment for Contagious Diseases

1. *Mandatory Treatment of Contagious Disease. Addington*'s principles have been applied to cases involving involuntary treatment of persons for contagious disease. Regulations adopted in the modern era tend to include elaborate due process safeguards. The ordinance in City of New York v. Antoinette R., 630 N.Y.S.2d 1008 (N.Y. Sup. Ct. 1995), provides a typical example:

> The issue presented at this special proceeding is whether the respondent, a person with active tuberculosis, should be forcibly detained in a hospital setting to allow for the completion of an appropriate regime of medical treatment. . . .
> Due to a resurgence of tuberculosis, New York City recently revised the Health Code to permit the detention of individuals infected with TB who have demonstrated an inability to voluntarily comply with appropriate medical treatment. . . . The prerequisite for an order is that there is a substantial likelihood, based on the person's past or present behavior, that the individual cannot be relied upon to participate in or complete an appropriate prescribed course of medication or, if necessary, follow required contagion precautions for tuberculosis. Such behavior may include the refusal or failure to take medication or to complete treatment for tuberculosis, to keep appointments for the treatment of tuberculosis, or a disregard for contagion precautions.

The statute provides certain due process safeguards when detention is ordered. For example, there are requirements for an appraisal of the risk posed to others and a review of less restrictive alternatives which were attempted or considered. Furthermore, there must be a court review within five days at the patient's request, and court review within 60 days and at 90-day intervals thereafter. The detainee also has the right to counsel, to have counsel provided, and to have friends or relatives notified. See Richard T. Andrias, The Criminal Justice System and the Resurgent TB Epidemic, 9 Crim. Just. 2 (Spring, 1994). . . .

In *Antoinette*, the city sought to apply its mandatory treatment regime to a 33-year-old woman who had repeatedly been diagnosed with TB but who had failed to complete her course of treatment after being released from the hospital. Court-ordered "directly observed therapy" (DOT) had failed when she refused to comply. The issue in the case was whether Antoinette would be forced to remain in the hospital for the estimated seven months it would take to complete treatment or whether she would be released for treatment in the home of her mother:

The mother of the respondent lives in a private home with four of her grandchildren and a newborn great-grandson, the grandchild of the respondent. The mother is willing to take the respondent into her home and provide cooperation should she be released from the hospital. Over the past two months the mother has visited her daughter on several occasions and talked with her over the phone on a daily basis. The mother has noticed a change in attitude in the respondent, that is, she is not as hostile. The mother attributes this change to the respondent's acceptance of religion. The respondent also contends that her attitude has been transformed and credits religion as her motivation. Since being detained at the hospital, she has joined various outpatient programs and attended parenting meetings. A nurses aide and the head nurse, who attend to the medical needs of the respondent, both verify that there has been an improvement in the respondent's demeanor. She is now cooperative while taking her medicines and on occasions has independently approached the nursing staff to request her medicines. Relying on her "change in attitude," the respondent opposes the order of detention and again requests the option of participating in Directly Observed Therapy to be conducted at her mother's place of residence. . . .

The petitioner's request for enforcement of the order of the Commissioner is granted. The petitioner has demonstrated through clear and convincing evidence the respondent's inability to comply with a prescribed course of medication in a less restrictive environment. The respondent has repeatedly sought medical treatment for the infectious stages of the disease and has consistently withdrawn from medical treatment once symptoms abate. She has also exhibited a pattern of behavior which is consistent with one who does not understand the full import of her condition nor the risks she poses to others, both the public and her family. On the contrary, she has repeatedly tried to hide the history of her condition from medical personnel. Although the court is sympathetic to the fact that she has recently undergone an epiphany of sorts, there is nothing in the record which would indicate that once she leaves the controlled setting of the hospital she would have the self-discipline to continue her cooperation. Moreover, her past behavior and lack of compliance with outpatient treatment when her listed residence was her mother's house, makes it all the more difficult to have confidence that her mother's good intentions will prevail over the respondent's inclinations to avoid treatments. In any event, the court will reevaluate the progress of the respondent's ability to cooperate in a less restrictive setting during its next review of the order in 90 days.

Accordingly, the respondent shall continue to be detained in a hospital setting until the petitioner or the court determines that the respondent has completed an appropriate course of medication for tuberculosis, or a change in circumstances indicates that the respondent can be relied upon to complete the prescribed course of medication without being in detention. The petitioner is further directed, pursuant to New York City Health Code §11.47 to apply to the court within 90 days for authorization to continue respondent's detention.

Assess the evidence in *Antoinette*. If you represented Antoinette, what evidence and arguments would you want to present at the next hearing? Do you think that you would be successful? See also In re Washington, 735 N.W.2d 111 (Wash. 2007) (upholding commitment of noncompliant patient with noninfectious TB found to be at "high risk of developing infectious tuberculosis"; court may take into account costs of confinement options in considering least restrictive environment; upholding commitment in jail).

2. *Due Process.* Should the clear and convincing evidence standard be used for commitment and treatment orders applied to persons with contagious diseases? In which ways are the consequences and proof disputes similar to those implicated in commitment for mental illness? Most jurisdictions that have considered the issue use the clear and convincing standard and provide other due process protections. See, e.g., Greene v. Edwards, 263 S.E.2d 661 (W. Va. 1980) (clear and convincing standard applied to commitment for TB treatment). See also Public Health Law at 444-445. Can these cases be reconciled with the "right to die" jurisprudence developed in Chapter 3? Patients with contagious conditions presumably are competent. What explains the state's ability to override their treatment refusals?

3. *Americans with Disabilities Act.* The ADA prohibits discrimination by public entities against persons with disabilities unless those persons present a direct threat to the health or safety of others. 42 U.S.C. §12131; 28 C.F.R. pt. 35, App. B. As noted above at page 667, there are substantial limitations on the ability to use Title II of the ADA to bring claims for money damages against states. The potential remains, however, to consider whether the ADA could be used to limit state control measures that "discriminate" against carriers of contagious diseases. In City of Newark v. J.S., 652 A.2d 265 (N.J. Super. Ct. Law Div. 1993), for example, the court construed the state's TB commitment statute to avoid due process and ADA claims. The court held that the city had presented clear and convincing evidence of the likelihood that J.S. presented a danger to others and approved his commitment. It rejected mandatory sputum tests and treatment, however, noting that J.S. could refuse these measures, although to do so would likely render his confinement indefinite. The court's analysis of the due process and ADA issues was heavily influenced by Professor Gostin's work. Lawrence O. Gostin, Controlling the Resurgent Tuberculosis Epidemic: A Fifty-State Survey of TB Statutes and Proposals for Reform, 269 JAMA 255 (1993).

4. *Directly Observed Therapy (DOT).* Directly Observed Therapy is similar to the "Outpatient Commitment" approach for persons with mental illness discussed above. DOT provides an alternative to commitment for persons with treatable, contagious conditions. In DOT, an individual is ordered to undergo treatment and is monitored to ensure that treatment is taken. A person's adherence to a drug therapy regime can be monitored by requiring the individual to appear at a health clinic daily or by daily visits from a public health worker. This strategy has some obvious

advantages for both the individual and the state: The procedure is less intrusive and less expensive. It still involves a significant liberty infringement, however, and, as in *Antoinette R.*, recalcitrant persons can evade monitoring. What are your views on the use of DOT? Would you object to a program of DOT designed to ensure that you take the entire course of therapy whenever you are issued a prescription for antibiotics?

Problem: Antiretroviral Therapy and the Risk of HIV Infection

Antiretroviral therapies for HIV infection are costly, can have significant side effects, and are not a panacea. These therapies nonetheless have played an important role in extending the lives and improving the health status of persons infected with HIV. Beyond the life-extending properties of therapy for the infected individual, antiretroviral therapies also been employed in some circumstances to reduce the risk of HIV transmission for decades. Antiretroviral therapies designed to prevent infection by HIV have routinely been made available to health care workers and emergency response personnel who have been exposed to potentially infected blood or body fluids, to survivors of sexual assault, and to pregnant women to prevent HIV transmission to their offspring. Should these drug therapies be provided to individuals who might have been exposed to HIV through a voluntary sexual or needle-sharing encounter? See U.S. Department of Health and Human Services, Antiretroviral Postexposure Prophylaxis After Sexual, Injection-Drug Use, or Other Non-Occupational Exposure to HIV in the United States, 54 MMWR 1 (2005) (RR-2) (yes, in specified circumstances). Should public and private insurers cover this use of antiretroviral therapy for uninfected persons?

Recent research suggests that antiretroviral therapy can reduce the risk of HIV transmission through sexual activity or needle-sharing in two additional ways. See, e.g., Myron S. Cohen & Lindsey R. Baden, Preexposure Prophylaxis for HIV—Where Do We Go from Here?, 367 New Eng. J. Med. 459 (2012); Scott M. Hammer, Antiretroviral Treatment as Prevention, 365 New Eng. J. Med. 561 (2011). First, HIV-infected persons who are able to access and adhere to antiretroviral therapy have lower viral loads and greatly reduced rates of HIV transmission through, e.g., sexual activity. Yet, as noted above, only about half of all persons who are aware of their HIV infection are receiving appropriate treatment. What factors might explain this rate of treatment, particularly given the evidence that antiretroviral therapy extends lives and reduces transmission risks? Leaving aside economic factors and social dislocation, should policymakers establish additional incentives for infected persons to access and adhere to therapy? For example, should persons with HIV infection who engage in sexual or needle-sharing activity be shielded from potential criminal penalties for exposing others to the risk of HIV-infection if they can prove faithful use of antiretroviral therapies?

Second, the risk of becoming infected with HIV through sexual or needle-sharing activity can be reduced if currently uninfected persons who engage in risky behaviors take antiretroviral therapies prophylactically. Should persons seeking to avoid HIV infection from voluntary sexual or needle-sharing activity be permitted to access antiretroviral therapies even though they are not currently infected with

HIV? Should the cost of these antiretroviral therapies be reimbursable for uninfected persons under private or public health insurance programs?

When, if ever, should the right of access to these therapies be transformed into a mandate that the therapies be used? Should women who refuse antiretroviral therapy for themselves or their newborns be charged with child neglect? Cf. Doe v. Division of Youth & Family Services, 148 F. Supp. 2d 462 (D.N.J. 2001) (complaint alleging improper HIV testing of pregnant woman along with effort to coerce perinatal antiretroviral therapy). See also In re The Termination of Parental Rights to Aaliyah W. v. Abigail W., 2011 WL 446866 (Wis. App. 2011) (noting detention of pregnant woman in hospital to ensure HIV treatment necessary to protect unborn child). Should HIV-infected persons who have engaged in conduct capable of transmitting the virus (e.g., through sexual activity or needle-sharing) be civilly committed or required to undergo DOT?

Problem: Public Health Emergencies, Mandatory Treatment, and Quarantine

The MSEHPA includes provisions giving state public health authorities broad powers to require treatment and to impose isolation or quarantine. These provisions undoubtedly are the most controversial in the Model Act. See, e.g., George J. Annas, Bioterrorism, Public Health, and Civil Liberties, 346 New Eng. J. Med. 1337 (2002); Lawrence O. Gostin et al., The Model State Emergency Health Powers Act: Planning for and Response to Bioterrorism and Naturally Occurring Infectious Diseases, 288 JAMA 622 (2002). See also Joseph Barbera et al., Large-Scale Quarantine Following Biological Terrorism in the United States: Scientific Examination, Logistics and Legal Limits, and Possible Consequences, 286 JAMA 2711 (2001). Review the following excerpts from the Model Act, which will only become effective when a state declares a public health emergency pursuant to the Act:

Section 603 **Vaccination and treatment.** During a state of public health emergency the public health authority may exercise the following emergency powers over persons as necessary to address the public health emergency—

(a) **Vaccination.** To vaccinate persons as protection against infectious disease and to prevent the spread of contagious or possibly contagious disease.

(1) Vaccination may be performed by any qualified person authorized to do so by the public health authority.

(2) A vaccine to be administered must not be such as is reasonably likely to lead to serious harm to the affected individual.

(3) To prevent the spread of contagious or possibly contagious disease the public health authority may isolate or quarantine, pursuant to Section 604, persons who are unable or unwilling for reasons of health, religion, or conscience to undergo vaccination pursuant to this Section.

(b) **Treatment.** To treat persons exposed to or infected with disease.

(1) Treatment may be administered by any qualified person authorized to do so by the public health authority.

(2) Treatment must not be such as is reasonably likely to lead to serious harm to the affected individual.

(3) To prevent the spread of contagious or possibly contagious disease the public health authority may isolate or quarantine, pursuant to Section

604, persons who are unable or unwilling for reasons of health, religion, or conscience to undergo treatment pursuant to this Section.

Section 604 **Isolation and quarantine.**

(a) **Authorization.** During the public health emergency, the public health authority may isolate . . . or quarantine . . . an individual or groups of individuals. This includes individuals or groups who have not been vaccinated, treated, tested, or examined pursuant to Sections 602 and 603. The public health authority may also establish and maintain places of isolation and quarantine, and set rules and make orders. Failure to obey these rules, orders, or provisions shall constitute a misdemeanor.

(b) **Conditions and principles.** The public health authority shall adhere to the following conditions and principles when isolating or quarantining individuals or groups of individuals:

(1) Isolation and quarantine must be by the least restrictive means necessary to prevent the spread of a contagious or possibly contagious disease to others and may include, but are not limited to, confinement to private homes or other private and public premises.

(2) Isolated individuals must be confined separately from quarantined individuals. . . .

(5) Isolated and quarantined individuals must be immediately released when they pose no substantial risk of transmitting a contagious or possibly contagious disease to others. . . .

(c) **Cooperation.** Persons subject to isolation or quarantine shall obey the public health authority's rules and orders; and shall not go beyond the isolation or quarantine premises. Failure to obey these provisions shall constitute a misdemeanor. . . .

Section 605 **Procedures for isolation and quarantine.** During a public health emergency, the isolation and quarantine of an individual or groups of individuals shall be undertaken in accordance with the following procedures.

(a) **Temporary isolation and quarantine without notice.**

(1) **Authorization.** The public health authority may temporarily isolate or quarantine an individual or groups of individuals through a written directive if delay in imposing the isolation or quarantine would significantly jeopardize the public health authority's ability to prevent or limit the transmission of a contagious or possibly contagious disease to others.

(2) **Content of directive.** The written directive shall specify the following: (i) the identity of the individual(s) or groups of individuals subject to isolation or quarantine; (ii) the premises subject to isolation or quarantine; (iii) the date and time at which isolation or quarantine commences; (iv) the suspected contagious disease if known; and (v) a copy of Article 6 and relevant definitions of this Act.

(3) **Copies.** A copy of the written directive shall be given to the individual to be isolated or quarantined or, if the order applies to a group of individuals and it is impractical to provide individual copies, it may be posted in a conspicuous place in the isolation or quarantine premises.

(4) **Petition for continued isolation or quarantine.** Within ten (10) days after issuing the written directive, the public health authority shall file a petition pursuant to Section 605(b) for a court order authorizing the continued isolation or quarantine of the isolated or quarantined individual or groups of individuals.

(b) **Isolation or quarantine with notice.**

(1) **Authorization.** The public health authority may make a written petition to the trial court for an order authorizing the isolation or quarantine of an individual or groups of individuals.

(2) **Content of petition.** A petition under subsection (b)(1) shall specify the following: (i) the identity of the individual(s) or groups of individuals subject to isolation or quarantine; (ii) the premises subject to isolation
or quarantine; (iii) the date and time at which isolation or quarantine commences; (iv) the suspected contagious disease if known; (v) a statement of
compliance with the conditions and principles for isolation and quarantine
of Section 604(b); and (vi) a statement of the basis upon which isolation or
quarantine is justified in compliance with this Article. The petition shall be
accompanied by the sworn affidavit of the public health authority attesting to
the facts asserted in the petition, together with any further information that
may be relevant and material to the court's consideration.

(3) **Notice.** Notice to the individuals or groups of individuals identified
in the petition shall be accomplished within twenty-four (24) hours in accordance with the rules of civil procedure.

(4) **Hearing.** A hearing must be held on any petition filed pursuant to
this subsection within five (5) days of filing of the petition. In extraordinary
circumstances and for good cause shown the public health authority may apply to continue the hearing date on a petition filed pursuant to this Section
for up to ten (10) days, which continuance the court may grant in its discretion giving due regard to the rights of the affected individuals, the protection
of the public's health, the severity of the emergency and the availability of
necessary witnesses and evidence.

(5) **Order.** The court shall grant the petition if, by a preponderance
of the evidence, isolation or quarantine is shown to be reasonably necessary
to prevent or limit the transmission of a contagious or possibly contagious
disease to others. . . .

(e) **Court to appoint counsel and consolidate claims.**

(1) **Appointment.** The court shall appoint counsel at state expense to
represent individuals or groups of individuals who are or who are about to be
isolated or quarantined pursuant to the provisions of this Act and who are not
otherwise represented by counsel. . . .

MSEHPA §§603-605, available at www.publichealthlaw.net (Dec. 21, 2001 version).

Evaluate the constitutionality of the Model Act's vaccination, treatment, and
quarantine provisions. Note that the "penalty" for refusing vaccination or treatment
under §603 is isolation or quarantine pursuant to §604. Is the threatened loss of
liberty more or less constitutionally problematic than the fine in *Jacobson*, supra at
page 654? Note that the Act anticipates that licensed health care providers might
not be available to care for all and merely requires states to use "qualified" persons.
Section 604 describes the conditions of isolation/quarantine, while §605 focuses
on the procedural prerequisites. Both sections take into account the possibility that
a massive public health emergency might preclude individualized determinations
and care. Public authorities are authorized to maintain "places" for quarantine, for
example, and notices may be posted if individual notice is impractical. The penalty for violating the Act's quarantine/isolation provisions is a misdemeanor. Would
this preclude criminal prosecution for attempted murder, for example, if a person
with smallpox escaped from isolation? Should it? Section 605 permits public health
authorities to impose isolation and quarantine without notice. A petition for a court
order must be filed within ten days. The Act also provides a mechanism for public
health authorities to secure a court order before implementing isolation/quaran-
tine. What standard of proof is required?

Compare the Model Act's provisions to the relevant public health statute in your own state. Does your state law permit public health officials to order vaccination or treatment? Does it include provisions for isolation/quarantine, with or without a court order? If your state has comprehensive public health laws covering these issues, do you see any similarities or differences between your state law and the Model Act? Which seems better from a legal or policy standpoint? If your state does not have such laws, would you recommend the adoption of the Model Act's provisions?

D. RESTRICTING CONSUMER CHOICE TO PROTECT PUBLIC HEALTH

The final section of this chapter explores a newly expanding frontier in public health law: the restriction of consumer choice to protect individual and public health. This form of public health regulation has long roots, extending back into the regulation of medicinal products and devices over 100 years ago. Yet public health measures that restrict consumer choices are increasingly important as public health officials seek to attack the consequences of behavioral choices that, while borne by individuals, create significant morbidity and mortality—and increased health care expenditures—across populations. How should the law treat public health measures such as restrictions on access to unapproved drugs, rules mandating the use of motorcycle helmets, or taxes focused on foods high in sugar or fat? While proponents argue that the protection of individuals and the reduction of health care costs provide more than sufficient justification for these forms of public health regulation, opponents argue that the initiatives are the precursor to the emergence of a "nanny state" in which individuals are no longer permitted to exercise autonomy in making decisions about the acceptance of risk. When, if ever, will constitutional limits be placed on these forms of public health policies? Given the broad constitutional authority governments have to protect health and safety and to use tax to shape behavior, the policy constraints may well be political rather than constitutional in many cases. How should health law and policy experts evaluate the range of options, risks, and benefits of policies in these areas?

1. The FDA, Pharmaceutical Regulation, and the Constitution

ABIGAIL ALLIANCE FOR BETTER ACCESS TO DEVELOPMENTAL DRUGS v. VON ESCHENBACH
495 F.3d 695 (D.C. Cir. 2007)

GRIFFITH, Circuit Judge:

This case presents the question whether the Constitution provides terminally ill patients a right of access to experimental drugs that have passed limited safety trials but have not been proven safe and effective. The district court held there is no such right. A divided panel of this Court held there is. Because we conclude that there is no fundamental right "deeply rooted in this Nation's history and tradition" of access to experimental drugs for the terminally ill, see Washington v. Glucksberg, 521 U.S. 702, 720-21 (1997), we affirm the judgment of the district court.

I.A.

The Abigail Alliance for Better Access to Developmental Drugs (the "Alliance") is an organization of terminally ill patients and their supporters that seeks expanded access to experimental drugs for the terminally ill. The Food, Drug, and Cosmetic Act ("FDCA" or "Act"), however, generally prohibits access to new drugs unless and until they have been approved by the Food and Drug Administration ("FDA"). See 21 U.S.C. §355(a). Gaining FDA approval can be a long process. First, an experimental drug's sponsor (e.g., a drug company) must submit an application for approval. Because no drug may be approved without a finding of "substantial evidence that the drug will have the effect it purports or is represented to have," an application must contain "full reports of investigations which have been made to show whether or not such drug is safe for use and whether such drug is effective in use," id. §355(b)(1)(A). Such reports rely in large measure on clinical trials with human subjects.

But before a sponsor can even begin human testing, it must submit for the FDA's approval an investigational new drug application ("IND") containing detailed information establishing that human testing is appropriate. Once the application for human testing has been approved, several phases of clinical testing begin. The Alliance's amended complaint alleges that this testing process is an extremely lengthy one, requiring nearly seven years for the average experimental [or "investigational"] drug.

Clinical testing for safety and effectiveness requires three or sometimes four phases. See 21 C.F.R. §312.21. Phase I involves the initial introduction of a new drug into human subjects. A Phase I study usually consists of twenty to eighty subjects and is "designed to determine the metabolism and pharmacologic actions of the [new] drug in humans, the side effects associated with increasing doses, and, if possible, to gain early evidence on effectiveness." Although gathering data on effectiveness may be part of Phase I, its primary focus is to determine whether the drug is safe enough for continued human testing. See id. Phase II studies are "well controlled" and "closely monitored" clinical trials of no more than several hundred subjects, used to evaluate both the "effectiveness of the drug for a particular indication" and its "common short-term side effects and risks." Id. §312.21(b).

Phase III studies are expanded clinical trials of several hundred to several thousand subjects designed to "gather . . . additional information about effectiveness and safety that is needed to evaluate the overall benefit-risk relationship of the drug and to provide an adequate basis for physician labeling." At any time during the clinical trials, a drug sponsor is required to notify the FDA of "[a]ny adverse experience associated with the use of the drug that is both serious and unexpected," and the FDA may order a "clinical hold" halting the trials if it determines that safety concerns so warrant, id. §312.42. To guide the clinical testing process, Congress has directed the FDA to establish "[s]cientific advisory panels" to "provid[e] expert scientific advice and recommendations to the Secretary regarding a clinical investigation of a drug or the approval for marketing of a drug." . . .

Terminally ill patients need not, however, always await the results of the clinical testing process. The FDA and Congress have created several programs designed to provide early access to promising experimental drugs when warranted. For example, under the "treatment IND" program, the FDA may approve use of an investigational drug by patients not part of the clinical trials for the treatment of "serious or immediately life-threatening disease[s]" if there exists "no comparable or satisfactory alternative drug or other therapy." . . .*

B.

Concluding that the FDA's current process for early access to new drugs was inadequate to meet the needs of its terminally ill members, the Alliance submitted its own proposals to the FDA. Those proposals culminated in a "citizen petition" to the FDA, arguing that there is a "different risk-benefit tradeoff facing patients who are terminally ill and who have no other treatment options." . . . Having thus been rejected by the FDA, the Alliance turned to the courts, arguing that the United States Constitution provides a right of access to experimental drugs for its members. In a complaint that mirrored much of its earlier submissions to the FDA, the Alliance argued that the FDA's lengthy clinical trials, combined with the "FDA's restrictions on pre-approval availability[,] amount to a death sentence for these [terminally ill] patients." Nor, the Alliance argues, are the FDA's exceptions to the clinical testing process sufficient to provide the terminally ill the access they need because they "are small, when they exist at all," and the ban on profits prevents many drug sponsors from participating.

"Terminally ill patients," in the Alliance's view, "are typically willing to assume risks. . . . " Before the district court, the Alliance argued that the Constitution guarantees them the right to do so. The district court rejected that argument, holding that "there is no constitutional right of access to unapproved drugs." A divided panel of this Court reversed, concluding that "where there are no alternative government-approved treatment options, a terminally ill, mentally competent adult patient's informed access to potentially life-saving investigational new drugs determined by the FDA after Phase I trials to be sufficiently safe for expanded human trials warrants protection under the Due Process Clause." Abigail Alliance for Better Access to Developmental Drugs v. von Eschenbach, 445 F.3d 470, 486 (D.C. Cir. 2006). We vacated that decision and granted rehearing en banc.

As framed by the Alliance, we now consider:

Whether the liberty protected by the Due Process Clause embraces the right of a terminally ill patient with no remaining approved treatment options to decide, in consultation with his or her own doctor, whether to seek access to investigational medications that the [FDA] concedes are safe and promising enough for substantial human testing.

*[The Court cited proposed regulations now codified as amended at 21 C.F.R. §312.300-.320. — EDS.]

Appellants' Br. at 1.[5] That is, we must determine whether terminally ill patients have a fundamental right to experimental drugs that have passed Phase I clinical testing. If such a right exists, the Alliance argues that both 21 C.F.R. §312.34(b)(3) (preventing access to experimental drugs for terminally ill patients where there is insufficient evidence of effectiveness or where there is an unreasonable risk of injury) and 21 C.F.R. §312.7 (prohibiting drug manufacturers from profiting on the sale of experimental drugs) must be subjected to strict scrutiny because they interfere with a fundamental constitutional right. We do not address the broader question of whether access to medicine might ever implicate fundamental rights.

II.

The Due Process Clause of the Fifth Amendment provides that "[n]o person shall be . . . deprived of life, liberty, or property, without due process of law." U.S. CONST. amend. V. The Supreme Court has held that the protections of the Amendment "guarantee[ ] more than fair process." *Glucksberg*, 521 U.S. at 719. The Court has stated that "[t]he Clause . . . provides heightened protection against government interference with certain fundamental rights and liberty interests," (citing Planned Parenthood of Se. Pa. v. Casey, 505 U.S. 833, 851 (1992)), including "the rights to marry, to have children, to direct the education and upbringing of one's children, to marital privacy, to use contraception, to bodily integrity, and to abortion," *Glucksberg*, 521 U.S. at 720.

As such rights are not set forth in the language of the Constitution, the Supreme Court has cautioned against expanding the substantive rights protected by the Due Process Clause "because guideposts for responsible decisionmaking in this unchartered area are scarce and open-ended." Collins v. Harker Heights, 503 U.S. 115, 125 (1992). There is an additional and substantial concern that courts must also consider: "By extending constitutional protection to an asserted right or liberty interest, we, to a great extent, place the matter outside the arena of public debate and legislative action." *Glucksberg*, 521 U.S. at 720. Thus, the Supreme Court

5. The dissent has recast the Alliance's proposed right away from the terms used in its briefs and oral argument—a right to access investigational new drugs—into a right "to try to save one's life," which has "its textual anchor in the right to life [expressed in the Fifth Amendment]." Dissent at 714-15. Regardless of how it is described, we must examine the proposed right under *Glucksberg*, which specifically cautions against the type of broad generalization the dissent now employs. See *Glucksberg*, 521 U.S. at 721 (requiring a "'careful description' of the asserted fundamental liberty interest"). If the asserted right is so broad that it protects a person's efforts to save his life, it might subject to strict scrutiny any government action that would affect the means by which he sought to do so, no matter how remote the chance of success. The Supreme Court rejected a similar attempt to broadly define the right at issue in . . . Reno v. Flores, 507 U.S. 292, 302 (1993). The dissent suffers from the same flaw in arguing that this is about the right to save one's life, because, in the end, this case is about the right to access experimental and unproven drugs in an attempt to save one's life, which we conclude under *Glucksberg* is not deeply rooted in our Nation's history and traditions. By describing too broadly at the outset a proposed right that will cover the Alliance's more narrow claim, the dissent fails *Glucksberg*'s threshold requirement of a carefully described right. We need not pursue the arguments that follow that initial misstep.

has directed courts to "exercise the utmost care whenever we are asked to break new ground in this field, lest the liberty protected by the Due Process Clause be subtly transformed into the policy preferences of the [courts' members]." Id. (and citing "history of the *Lochner* era").

In *Glucksberg*, the Supreme Court described its "established method of substantive-due-process analysis" as having "two primary features."

> First, we have regularly observed that the Due Process Clause specially protects those fundamental rights and liberties which are, objectively, deeply rooted in this Nation's history and tradition and implicit in the concept of ordered liberty, such that neither liberty nor justice would exist if they were sacrificed. Second, we have required in substantive-due-process cases a careful description of the asserted fundamental liberty interest.

We will assume arguendo that the Alliance's description of its asserted right would satisfy *Glucksberg*'s "careful description" requirement.[6] Looking to whether the Alliance has demonstrated that its right is deeply rooted in this Nation's history, tradition, and practices, the Alliance's claim for constitutional protection rests on two arguments: (1) that "common law and historical American practices have traditionally trusted individual doctors and their patients with almost complete autonomy to evaluate the efficacy of medical treatments"; and (2) that FDA policy is "inconsistent with the way that our legal tradition treats persons in all other life-threatening situations." More specifically, the Alliance argues that the concepts of self-defense, necessity, and interference with rescue are broad enough to demonstrate the existence of the fundamental right they seek—a right for "persons in mortal peril" to "try to save their own lives, even if the chosen means would otherwise be illegal or involve enormous risks."

. . . The Alliance argues that its right can be found in our history and legal traditions because "the government never interfered with the judgment of individual doctors about the medical efficacy of particular drugs until 1962," i.e., when major amendments were made to the Food, Drug, and Cosmetic Act. Appellants' Br. at 44. . . . The Alliance has little to say, however, about our Nation's history of regulating the safety of drugs. The Alliance's effort to focus on efficacy regulation ignores one simple fact: it is unlawful for the Alliance to procure experimental drugs not only because they have not been proven effective, but because they have not been proven safe. Although the Alliance contends that it only wants drugs that "are safe and promising enough for substantial human testing," i.e., drugs that have passed Phase I testing, current law bans access to an experimental drug on safety grounds until it has successfully completed all phases of testing. . . . Thus, to succeed on its claim of a fundamental right of access for the terminally ill to experimental drugs, the Alliance must show not only that there is a tradition of access to drugs that have

---

6. We nonetheless have serious doubt about whether the Alliance's description of its proposed constitutional right could ever pass constitutional muster. The Alliance's claimed right depends on a regulatory determination that the drug is safe for testing, prompting an obvious question: How can a constitutional right be defined by an administrative regulation that is subject to change?

not yet been proven effective, but also a tradition of access to drugs that have not yet been proven safe.

. . . [W]e conclude that our Nation has long expressed interest in drug regulation, calibrating its response in terms of the capabilities to determine the risks associated with both drug safety and efficacy. Drug regulation in the United States began with the Colonies and States when the Colony of Virginia's legislature passed an act in 1736 that addressed the dispensing of more drugs than was "necessary or useful" because that practice had become "dangerous and intolerable." Edward Kremers, Kremers and Urdang's History of Pharmacy 158 (4th ed. 1976). . . .

Nor were the States the only regulators of access to drugs. Although early federal regulation was not extensive, perhaps because "[n]ot until interstate commerce began its great expansion after the Civil War did the need for Federal rule-making become widely realized," Wallace F. Janssen, Outline of the History of U.S. Drug Regulation and Labeling, 36 Food Drug Cosm. L. J. 420, 425 (1981), there are early examples of federal government intervention. In 1848, the Import Drug Act, ch. 70, 9 Stat. 237 (1848), banned "imported adulterated drugs" after a congressional committee concluded that "this country had become the grand mart and receptacle of all the refuse [drug] merchandise . . . , not only from the European warehouses, but from the whole Eastern world." Wesley J. Heath, America's First Drug Regulation Regime: The Rise and Fall of the Import Drug Act of 1848, 59 Food & Drug L.J. 169, 175 (2004).

The current regime of federal drug regulation began to take shape with the Food, Drug, and Cosmetic Act of 1938, 21 U.S.C. §301 et seq. The Act required that drug manufacturers provide proof that their products were safe before they could be marketed. . . . We end our historical analysis where the Alliance would prefer it begin—with the 1962 Amendments to the FDCA. Undoubtedly, as the Alliance argues at length, Congress amended the FDCA in 1962 to explicitly require that the FDA only approve drugs deemed effective for public use. Thus, the Alliance argues that, prior to 1962, patients were free to make their own decisions whether a drug might be effective. But even assuming arguendo that efficacy regulation began in 1962, the Alliance's argument ignores our Nation's history of drug safety regulation. . . .

Nor can the Alliance override current FDA regulations simply by insisting that drugs which have completed Phase I testing are safe enough for terminally ill patients. Current law bars public access to drugs undergoing clinical testing on safety grounds. The fact that a drug has emerged from Phase I with a determination that it is safe for limited clinical testing in a controlled and closely-monitored environment after detailed scrutiny of each trial participant does not mean that a drug is safe for use beyond supervised trials.[11] FDA regulation of post-Phase I drugs is entirely consistent with our historical tradition of prohibiting the sale of unsafe drugs.

But even setting the safety issue to one side, . . . an arguably limited history of efficacy regulation prior to 1962 does not establish a fundamental right of access to unproven drugs. The amendments made to the FDCA by Congress throughout the twentieth century demonstrate that Congress and the FDA have continually

11. In fact, the FDA cites numerous examples in which drugs have been pulled from the market post-Phase I due to safety concerns.

responded to new risks presented by an evolving technology. Recent government efficacy regulation has reflected Congress's exercise of its well-established power to regulate in response to scientific, mathematical, and medical advances [such as the development of clinical trials during and after WW II]. . . . [C]reating constitutional rights to be free from regulation based solely upon a prior lack of regulation would undermine much of the modern administrative state, which, like drug regulation, has increased in scope as changing conditions have warranted. . . .[17]

Although it has not addressed the precise constitutional argument urged by the Alliance, we find it highly significant that the Supreme Court has rejected several similar challenges to the FDCA and related laws brought on statutory grounds. See, e.g., United States v. Rutherford, 442 U.S. 544, 552, (1979) ("we are persuaded by the legislative history and consistent administrative interpretation of the [FDCA] that no implicit exemption for drugs used by the terminally ill is necessary to attain congressional objectives"). And other courts have rejected arguments that the Constitution provides an affirmative right of access to particular medical treatments reasonably prohibited by the Government [citing, e.g., Mitchell v. Clayton, 995 F.2d 772, 775 (7th Cir. 1993) ("most federal courts have held that a patient does not have a constitutional right to obtain a particular type of treatment or to obtain treatment from a particular provider if the government has reasonably prohibited that type of treatment or provider")]. In keeping with those decisions, we conclude that the Alliance has not provided evidence of a right to procure and use experimental drugs that is deeply rooted in our Nation's history and traditions. To the contrary, our Nation's history evidences increasing regulation of drugs as both the ability of government to address these risks has increased and the risks associated with drugs have become apparent. . . .[19]

IV.

Because the Alliance's claimed right is not fundamental, the Alliance's claim of a right of access to experimental drugs is subject only to rational basis

17. . . . The Alliance can, of course, advocate its position vigorously before Congress and the FDA, and convince our Nation's democratic branches that the values the Alliance favors should be protected. In fact, within the last year, the political branches have responded to the concerns of the Alliance and others. The FDA recently issued a notice of proposed rulemaking [which resulted in the expansion of access to investigational new drugs for seriously ill patients outside of formal clinical trials, see 21 C.F.R. §312.300-.320].

19. As there exists no deeply rooted right, . . . we need not and do not address all of the Alliance's arguments regarding whether their proposed right is implicit in our Nation's system of ordered liberty, [but] we note a crucial difference between this case and one of the cases relied upon by the Alliance in making that argument, Cruzan v. Director, Mo. Dep't of Health, 497 U.S. 261 (1990). . . . Looking to *Cruzan*, the Alliance argues that "[i]f a patient has a fundamental right to medical self-determination that gives them the right to starve themselves to death, then surely they have a right to choose to fight for their lives even if that means taking a drug that has not yet met the FDA's full approval standards." . . . But a tradition protecting individual freedom from life-saving, but forced, medical treatment does not evidence a constitutional tradition of providing affirmative access to a potentially harmful, and even fatal, commercial good.

scrutiny. . . . [W]e cannot say that the government's interest does not bear a rational relation to a legitimate state interest. That conclusion is compelled by the Supreme Court's decision in United States v. Rutherford, 442 U.S. 544 (1979). In that case, terminally ill patients sought to prevent the FDA from prohibiting access to the drug laetrile, even though the drug had not been approved for public use. In rejecting a challenge by terminally ill patients claiming that the FDCA's safety requirement did not apply to them, the Supreme Court held that "[f]or the terminally ill, as for anyone else, a drug is unsafe if its potential for inflicting death or physical injury is not offset by the possibility of therapeutic benefit." See also id. at 558 (noting that history has demonstrated that numerous "resourceful entrepreneurs" might try to take advantage of an unregulated market, which "suggest[s] why Congress could reasonably have determined to protect the terminally ill, no less than other patients, from the vast range of self-styled panaceas that inventive minds can devise").

Although terminally ill patients desperately need curative treatments, as *Rutherford* holds, their deaths can certainly be hastened by the use of a potentially toxic drug with no proven therapeutic benefit. Thus, we must conclude that, prior to distribution of a drug outside of controlled studies, the Government has a rational basis for ensuring that there is a scientifically and medically acceptable level of knowledge about the risks and benefits of such a drug. We therefore hold that the FDA's policy of limiting access to investigational drugs is rationally related to the legitimate state interest of protecting patients, including the terminally ill, from potentially unsafe drugs with unknown therapeutic effects. . . .

Our Nation's history and traditions have consistently demonstrated that the democratic branches are better suited to decide the proper balance between the uncertain risks and benefits of medical technology, and are entitled to deference in doing so. . . . Jacobson v. Massachusetts, 197 U.S. 11, 30 (1905); see also Gonzales v. Carhart, 550 U.S. 124 (2007). Consistent with that precedent, our holding today ensures that this debate among the Alliance, the FDA, the scientific and medical communities, and the public may continue through the democratic process.

ROGERS, Circuit Judge, with whom Chief Judge GINSBURG joins, dissenting:

Today, the court rejects the claim that terminally ill patients who have exhausted all government-approved treatment options have a fundamental right to access investigational new drugs. The court's opinion reflects a flawed conception of the right claimed by the Abigail Alliance for Better Access to Developmental Drugs and a stunning misunderstanding of the stakes. The court shifts the inquiry required by Washington v. Glucksberg, 521 U.S. 702 (1997), by changing the nature of the right, by conflating the right with the deprivation, and by prematurely advancing countervailing government interests. The court fails to come to grips with the Nation's history and traditions, which reflect deep respect and protection for the right to preserve life, a corollary to the right to life enshrined in the Constitution. The court confuses this liberty interest with the manner in which the Alliance alleges that the liberty has been deprived, namely by denying terminally ill patients access to investigational medications under the narrow conditions described by the Alliance. The court conflates the inquiry as to whether a fundamental right exists at all with whether the government has demonstrated a compelling interest, when strictly scrutinized, rendering its restrictive policy constitutional.

These missteps lead the court to rely upon how rights and liberties have been limited and restricted—addressing regulations to prevent fraud in the sale of misbranded and adulterated medications or safety restrictions applicable to all medicines for any palliative purpose—which says little about the historic importance of the underlying right of a person to save her own life. . . . The common law doctrines [of necessity and self defense] remain good evidence of a history and tradition of protecting life and attempts to preserve life as a deep-seated personal right. That the right may be and has been denied in the face of compelling governmental interests is no reason for conflating the two stages of the analysis and looking only to the results of past cases in order to avoid the analysis prescribed by the Supreme Court in *Glucksberg*. . . .

In the end, it is startling that the oft-limited rights to marry, to fornicate, to have children, to control the education and upbringing of children, to perform varied sexual acts in private, and to control one's own body even if it results in one's own death or the death of a fetus have all been deemed fundamental rights covered, although not always protected, by the Due Process Clause, but the right to try to save one's life is left out in the cold despite its textual anchor in the right to life. This alone is reason the court should pause about refusing to put the FDA to its proof when it denies terminal patients with no alternative therapy the only option they have left, regardless of whether that option may be a long-shot with high risks. The court is on even weaker footing when it relies upon the risks entailed in medical procedures to wrest life-and-death decisions that once were vested in patients and their physicians. The court commits a logical error of dramatic consequence by concluding that the investigational drugs are somehow not "necessary." While the potential cures may not prove sufficient to save the life of a terminally ill patient, they are surely necessary if there is to be any possibility of preserving her life. . . .

[T]he history and traditions of this Nation support the right of a terminal patient, and not the government, to make this fundamentally personal choice involving her own life. Because judicial precedents and the historical record require strict scrutiny before upsetting rights of this magnitude, the FDA must demonstrate a compelling governmental interest before its policy restricting access can survive. Accordingly, I would remand the case to the district court to make the initial determination as to whether FDA has met its burden, and I respectfully dissent.

Notes: The Scope and Constitutionality of Pharmaceutical Regulation

1. *Federal and State Regulation of Pharmaceuticals.* The federal government has enacted a complex web of food, drug, and medical device regulations under the federal authority to regulate interstate commerce. The power to regulate interstate commerce includes the power to regulate commerce to protect public health. Federal law preempts many state law claims. See, e.g., Lawrence O. Gostin, The FDA, Preemption, and Public Safety, 41(5) Hastings Center Rep. 11 (Sept.-Oct. 2011). The regulation of drugs and medical devices is complex and detailed. See generally David G. Adams et al. eds., Food and Drug Law and Regulation (2d ed. 2011); Judith A. Johnson, Congressional Research Service, FDA Regulation of Medical

Devices (June 25, 2012); Kenneth R. Piña & Wayne L. Pines eds., A Practical Guide
to Food and Drug Law and Regulation (4th ed. 2012); and Susan Thaul, Congressional Research Service, How FDA Approves Drugs and Regulates Their Safety and
Effectiveness (June 25, 2012). For insights into the history, scope, and evaluation
of the role of the FDA, see, e.g., Daniel Carpenter, Reputation and Power: Organizational Image and Pharmaceutical Regulation at the FDA (2010); Philip J. Hilts,
Protecting America's Health: The FDA, Business, and One Hundred Years of Regulation (2003); Sharon B. Jacobs, Crises, Congress, and Cognitive Biases: A Critical
Examination of Food and Drug Legislation in the United States, 64 Food & Drug J.
599 (2009); Richard Merrill, The Architecture of Government Regulation of Medical Products, 82 Va. L. Rev. 1753 (1996). The Food and Drug Law Institute offers
programs and resources at www.fdli.org. The discussion here will focus on the intersection between the regulation of drugs and individual access to therapy.

   2. *The Drug Approval Process and Access to Experimental Therapies.* As noted in
Abigail Alliance, new drugs must go through at least three phases of drug trials to be
proven to be "safe" and "effective" in treating a particular condition. 21 U.S.C. §355;
21 C.F.R. §312.21. The fourth phase of drug trials alluded to in the opinion is the
post-market surveillance trial, which is used to identify any safety or efficacy issues
related to drugs across a broader population sample. See Barbara J. Evans, Seven
Pillars of a New Evidentiary Paradigm: The Food, Drug, and Cosmetic Act Enters the
Genomic Era, 85 Notre Dame L. Rev. 419, 476-485 (2010); Anna B. Laakman, Collapsing the Distinction Between Experimentation and Treatment in the Regulation
of New Drugs, 62 Ala. L. Rev. 305, 337-341 (2011); Laura B. Faden & Christopher-
Paul Milne, Pharmacovigilence Activities in the United States, European Union and
Japan: Harmonic Convergence or Convergent Evolution?, 63 Food & Drug L.J. 683
(2008).

   Under current federal regulations, patients with serious or life-threatening illnesses may be given access to certain types of investigational new drugs under some
circumstances. The court in *Abigail,* footnote 4, cites the "Fast Track" program,
designed to provide access to "drugs intended to treat life-threatening and severely-
debilitating illnesses." The court also noted that the FDA had proposed new regulations designed to enhance access to investigational drugs for treatment purposes,
which are now codified at 21 C.F.R. §312.300-320. These regulations apply to persons with life-threatening diseases or serious diseases or conditions "associated with
morbidity that ha[ve] substantial impact on day-to-day functioning. . . . Whether a
disease or condition is serious is based on its impact on such factors as survival, day-
to-day functioning, or the likelihood that the disease, if left untreated, will progress
from a less severe condition to a more serious one." See generally Benjamin R.
Rossen, FDA's Proposed Regulations to Expand Access to Investigational Drugs for
Treatment Use: The Status Quo in the Guise of Reform, 64 Food & Drug L.J. 183
(2009); Note, Expanding Expanded Access: How the Food and Drug Administration Can Achieve Better Access to Experimental Drugs for Seriously Ill Patients, 96
Geo. L.J. 2143 (2008). Could patients bring claims against drug companies demanding participation in these alternative access schemes? See Cacchillo v. Insmed, Inc.,
638 F.3d. 401 (2d Cir. 2011) (claim against drug manufacturer for failure to support
application for compassionate access).

   Access to investigational drugs under the regulations depends in part on a
determination that there are no other treatment options, that the patient benefits

outweigh the risks, and that "[p]roviding the investigational drug for the requested use will not interfere with the initiation, conduct, or completion of clinical investigations that could support marketing approval of the expanded access use or otherwise compromise the potential development of the expanded access use." 21 C.F.R. §312.305(a). Is there any constitutional problem with a regulatory regime that explicitly subordinates the needs of individual patients to the "greater good" that can result from the completion of clinical trials? See Elizabeth Weeks Leonard, The Public's Right to Health: When Patients' Rights Threaten the Commons, 86 Wash. U. L. Rev. 1335 (2009). If the *Abigail* plaintiffs had succeeded, would the need to preserve clinical trials have provided the compelling justification required to uphold the regulations in strict scrutiny review? Would this rationale apply to patients who are ineligible for clinical trials, who therefore could not be deterred from participating? See Abigail R. Moncrieff, The Freedom of Health, 159 U. Pa. L. Rev. 2209, 2243-2245 (2011).

3. *Pharmaceutical Choice as a Constitutional Right?* As noted in *Abigail*, the U.S. Supreme Court had not yet directly ruled on whether terminally ill patients had any constitutionally protected right to access unapproved potential therapies. The *Rutherford* decision cited in the opinion is almost solely concerned with the issue of whether the FDA's statutorily granted power to regulate the safety and effectiveness of drugs could be applied to drugs used to treat terminal conditions. On remand from the Supreme Court decision, the Tenth Circuit confronted and rejected the constitutional claim, holding that "the decision by the patient whether to have a treatment or not is a protected right, but his selection of a particular treatment, or at least a medication, is within the area of governmental interest in protecting public health." Rutherford v. United States, 616 F.2d 455, 457 (10th Cir. 1980).

The issue dramatically reemerged with the D.C. Circuit panel's initial decision in *Abigail Alliance*, 445 F.3d 470 (2006), which the decision above reversed en banc. The initial D.C. Circuit panel decision found that:

> where there are no alternative government-approved treatment options, a terminally ill, mentally competent adult patient's informed access to potentially life-saving investigational new drugs determined by the FDA after Phase I trials to be sufficiently safe for expanded human trials warrants protection under the Due Process Clause. The prerogative asserted by the FDA—to prevent a terminally ill patient from using potentially life-saving medication to which those in Phase II clinical trials have access—thus impinges upon an individual liberty deeply rooted in our Nation's history and tradition of self-preservation. . . . [W]e remand the case . . . to determine whether the FDA's policy . . . is narrowly tailored to serve a compelling governmental interest.

Id. at 486. Is restricting access to potential treatments for terminally ill patients consistent with the jurisprudence governing the termination of life-sustaining treatment? See Chapter 3. With case law on a woman's right to choose abortion? See Chapter 5.B.2. For more on the right to self-preservation, see Eugene Volokh, Medical Self-Defense, Prohibited Experimental Therapies, and Payment for Organs, 120 Harv. L. Rev. 1813 (2007). For additional commentary on the case and its controversial issues, see George Annas, Cancer and the Constitution, 357 New Eng. J. Med. 4 (2007); Richard Epstein, The Erosion of Individual Autonomy in Medical Decision-making: Of the FDA and IRBs, 96 Geo. L.J. 559 (2008); Elizabeth Weeks Leonard,

Right to Experimental Treatment: FDA New Drug Approval, Constitutional Rights, and the Public's Health, 37 J.L. Med. & Ethics 269 (2009); Seema Shah & Patricia Zettler, From a Constitutional Right to a Policy of Exceptions: Abigail Alliance and the Future of Access to Experimental Therapy, 10 Yale J. Health Pol'y L. & Ethics 135 (2010).

4. *The FDA and Drug Development Efforts.* The FDA has been criticized for unnecessary delays in the approval of important drugs. The laetrile dispute in the 1970s paved the way for vigorous protests by HIV/AIDS activists in the 1980s and 1990s. Congress sought to speed up the development of new drugs by providing additional incentives to pharmaceutical firms. Under the Orphan Drug Act, Pub. L. No. 97-414, 96 Stat. 2049 (1983), as amended, those companies are encouraged to develop and market drugs for rare illnesses, where the relatively small number of persons affected might otherwise not constitute a sufficient market to sustain the research and development costs of providing treatment. See also 21 C.F.R. §316.1-.40. In 1997, Congress also enacted the Food and Drug Administration Modernization Act, to provide a fast-track approval process and other measures designed to improve access to drugs that show real promise of substantial medical improvements. See Thomas Roberts, Jr. & Bruce Chabner, Beyond Fast Track for Drug Approvals, 351 New Eng. J. Med. 501 (2004); Eve Slater, Today's FDA, 352 New Eng. J. Med. 293 (2005). The Food and Drug Administration Safety and Innovation Act of 2012 includes additional provisions designed to free the FDA to implement fast-track procedures to provide access to life extending therapies.

Any effort to speed up the approval of new drugs inevitably creates the risk that truncated studies and review will result in the release of drugs with unknown hazards and uncertain effectiveness. The ongoing debate focuses on whether the reform of the drug approval process has gone too far or not far enough in providing consumers with access to safe and effective drugs. See, e.g., Daniel Carpenter et al., Drug-Review Deadlines and Safety Problems, 358 New Eng. J. Med. 1354 (2008); Jennifer Couzin-Frankel & Yasmin Ogale, Once on "Fast Track," Avastin Now Derailed, 333 Science 143 (2011); David Healy, Did Regulators Fail over Selective Serotonin Reuptake Inhibitors?, 333 BMJ 92 (2006); Anna B. Laakman, Collapsing the Distinction Between Experimentation and Treatment in the Regulation of New Drugs, 62 Ala. L. Rev. 305, 337-341 (2011); Mike Mitka, Oversight of Fast-Track Drug Approval by FDA Stuck in Low Gear, Critics Say, 304 JAMA 1773 (2010). Could greater public access to drug trial data benefit consumers? Aaron S. Kesselheim & Michelle M. Mello, Confidentiality Laws and Secrecy in Medical Research: Improving Public Access to Data on Drug Safety, 26 Health Aff. 483 (2007).

5. *Women and Minorities in Drug Research.* As noted in Chapter 2's discussion of human experimentation, at page 246, medical research has at least sometimes been advanced at the expense of minorities and other disadvantaged groups. Ironically, medical researchers have also been criticized for excluding women and minorities from research. For example, women were excluded from drug research trials because of fears that they could expose fetuses to potentially unsafe drugs during pregnancy. The exclusion of women and minorities from drug research meant that excluded groups did not have access to potentially effective (though possibly risky and ineffective) experimental treatments and that researchers failed to gather data on whether there were group-related variations in the effectiveness of the experimental drugs. Congress responded to these concerns with the NIH Revitalization

Act of 1993. The legislation requires researchers to include women and minorities in NIH-funded research and, where practicable, to include sufficient numbers to determine whether the studied drug is as effective in these groups. 42 U.S.C. §289a-2. The issue remains controversial, with some expressing alarm at the continued low rates of participation by some groups and others expressing concern about whether differences based on group classifications are meaningful. See American Health Lawyers Association's Advisory Council on Racial and Ethnic Diversity, Patient-Tailored Medicine, Part One: The Impact of Race and Genetics on Medicine, 2 J. Health & Life Sci. L. 1 (2008); J. F. Burke et al., Enrollment of Women and Minorities in NINDS Trials, 76 Neurology 354 (2011); Dan Bustillos, Limited English Proficiency and Disparities in Clinical Research, 37 J.L. Med. & Ethics 28 (2009) Lisa C. Ikemoto, In the Shadow of Race: Women of Color in Health Disparities Policy, 39 U.C. Davis L. Rev. 1023 (2006); S. S. Lee, Pharmacogenomics and the Challenge of Health Disparities, 12 Public Health Genomics 170 (2009); Marya Viorst Gwadz et al., Increasing and Supporting the Participation of Persons of Color Living with HIV/AIDS in AIDS Clinical Trials, 7 Curr. HIV/AIDS Rep. 194 (2010); and Symposium, The Responsible Use of Racial and Ethnic Categories in Biomedical Research: Where Do We Go from Here?, J.L. Med. & Ethics 483-558 (2006).

6. *Drug Labeling, "Off-Label Use," and the Learned Intermediary Doctrine.* Under the regulatory policy of the FDA, each prescription drug carries a package-insert label with quite elaborate information on the methods of administering the drug, conditions for which the drug is recommended, as well as warnings about contraindications for use and about known dangers and side effects. The package inserts have considerable, although not totally controlling, influence over the proper standard of accepted patient care related to the drug. Physicians may, and often do, prescribe drugs for "off-label" uses, see David C. Radley et al., Off-Label Prescribing Among Office-Based Physicians, 166 Arch. Intern. Med. 1021 (2006), although there has been controversy in recent years about physician discretion in this area and insurance reimbursement for such use. See, e.g., Michael Malinowski, Doctors, Patients, and Pills—A System Popping Under Too Much Physician Discretion?, 33 Cardozo L. Rev. 1085 (2012); Thomas v. W. Va. Office of Insurance Commissioner, 2012 WL 2865951 (W. Va.) (noting contention that off-label use unnecessary in workers' compensation case).

Should drug manufacturers be permitted to disseminate information about off-label uses to physicians? The FDA initially took the view that these communications should be severely restricted to prevent circumvention of the labeling process. Drug company off-label marketing practices have generated significant litigation and very significant judgments. For a sampling of parties and theories, see, e.g., Gardiner Harris, Pfizer Pays $2.3 Billion to Settle Marketing Case, N.Y. Times, Sept. 3, 2009; Krumplebeck v. Breg, Inc., 2012 WL 3241587 (6th Cir.) (analyzing possible liability claims related to off-label marketing in context of medical device); Thomas M. Greene, A New Weapon in Pharma Cases, Trial 40 (Nov. 2011) (RICO). See also Food and Drug Administration Safety and Innovation Act of 2012, 21 U.S.C. §379d-5 (directing development of guidance for promotion of regulated substances on the Internet, including on social media sites).

The FDA's rules restrict the freedom of drug companies to express their views. The Supreme Court historically has applied low-level scrutiny to governmental regulation of commercial speech. However, in Sorrell v. IMS Health, 131 S. Ct. 2653 (2011), the Court invalidated Vermont legislation restricting sale and disclosure of physician prescribing behavior under the First Amendment. The decision has suggested to some commentators that the Court may apply some form of heightened scrutiny to regulations restricting commercial speech, including the flow of information to physicians and to patients. See Jacqueline R. Berman, First Amendment Off-Label Promotion Cases Work Their Way Through the Courts, 14(2) J. Health Care Compliance 29 (2012); Margaret Gilhooley, Drug Safety and Commercial Speech: Television Advertisements and Reprints on Off-Label Uses, 47 San Diego L. Rev. 845 (2010); Lars Noah, Truth or Consequences? Commercial Free Speech vs. Public Health Promotion (at the FDA), 21 Health Matrix 1 (2011); David Orentlicher, The Commercial Speech Doctrine in Health Regulation: The Clash Between the Public Interest in a Robust First Amendment and the Public Interest in Effective Protection from Harm, 37 Am. J.L. & Med. 299 (2011); Symposium, Marketing Health: The Growing Role of Commercial Speech Doctrine in FDA Regulation, 37 Am. J.L. & Med. 203-421 (2011); Symposium, Commercial Speech and Public Health, 21 Health Matrix 1-230 (2011).

In the prescription drug field, the courts have quite uniformly accepted the package-insert warnings to physicians as meeting the drug manufacturers' legal obligation. The physician is expected to be a "learned intermediary" between the company and the patient in protecting the patient and in providing direct information about the drug to the patient. The retail pharmacist is also a source of advice for drug consumers. These assumptions have been shaken somewhat by the expansion of direct-to-consumer (DTC) advertising by pharmaceutical companies. See Prescription-Drug Advertisements, 21 C.F.R. §202.10; Jeremy A. Greene & David Herzberg, Hidden in Plain Sight: Marketing Prescription Drugs to Consumers in the Twentieth Century, 100 Am. J. Public Health 793 (2010) (tracing history of DTC advertising); Victor E. Schwartz et al., Marketing Pharmaceutical Products in the Twenty-First Century: An Analysis of the Continued Viability of Traditional Principles of Law in the Age of Direct-to-Consumer Advertising, 32 Harv. J.L. & Pub. Pol'y 333 (2009). For a discussion about DTC advertising in the context of the Vioxx controversy, see Ernst Bernt, To Inform or Persuade? Direct-to-Consumer Advertising of Prescription Drugs, 352 New Eng. J. Med. 325 (2005); Henry Waxman, The Lessons of Vioxx—Drug Safety and Sales, 352 New Eng. J. Med. 2576 (2005). As noted earlier, federal preemption of state claims related to disclosures made by drug companies remains an important issue. Compare Pliva v. Mensing, 131 S. Ct. 2567 (2011) (state warning claim preempted by federal law governing generic drugs when impossible for manufacturer to comply with both state and federal warning requirements), with Wyeth v. Levine, 555 U.S. 555 (2009) (state failure to warn claim not preempted by FDA labeling rule for non-generic drug where manufacturer could comply with both).

7. *The FDA and New Regulatory Challenges: Dietary Supplements and Genetic Tests.* The FDA regularly finds itself in controversies about the scope of its regulatory authority. One major controversy, involving the agency's attempt to regulate tobacco, resulted in legislation in 2009 giving the FDA the power to regulate tobacco products. See Lawrence Deyton et al., Tobacco Product Regulation—A Public Health Approach, 362 New Eng. J. Med. 1753 (2010) (Family Smoking Prevention and Tobacco Control Act, 21 U.S.C. §§387-387u).

The regulation of dietary supplements has been controversial, in part because of industry claims that the supplements are more like food than they are like classic pharmaceuticals. The FDA's suggestion that it might regulate supplements as though they were drugs drew congressional action in the form of the Dietary Supplement Health and Education Act of 1994 (DSHEA). The DSHEA gives the FDA the authority to "regulate[] vitamins, minerals, herbs, amino acids, and other dietary substances. Dietary supplements are generally regulated in a manner similar to food and the FDA is authorized to prevent adulterated products from entering the market." Nutraceutical v. von Eschenbach, 459 F.3d 1033, 1035 (2006) (interpreting DSHEA; upholding FDA ban on ephedrine-alkaloid dietary supplements). A dietary supplement is adulterated if it "presents a significant or unreasonable risk of illness or injury" under suggested or ordinary use. 21 U.S.C. §342(f)(1). Nutritional supplements are also subject to adverse event reporting requirements. 21 U.S.C. §379aa-1. See generally GAO, Dietary Supplements: FDA Should Take Further Actions to Improve Oversight and Consumer Understanding (2009); Ruth K. Miller et al., FDA's Dietary Supplement CGMPS: Standards Without Standardization, 63 Food & Drug L.J. 929 (2008); Lars Noah & Barbara Noah, A Drug by Any Other Name . . . ? Paradoxes in Dietary Supplement Risk Regulation, 17 Stan. L. & Pol'y Rev. 165 (2006); Institute of Medicine, Dietary Supplements: A Framework for Evaluating Safety (2005).

The regulation of genetic tests is another area of controversy. A quick Internet search will reveal several companies offering genetic tests and profiles to consumers, see www.23andme.com/. Are genetic tests best regulated as medical devices? Laboratory procedures and standards? Clinical practice? Ordinary consumer products? Consumer education? See GAO, Direct-to-Consumer Genetic Tests: Misleading Test Results Are Further Complicated by Deceptive Marketing and Other Questionable Practices (2010); Jessica D. Gabel, Redeeming the Genetic Groupon: Efficacy, Ethics, and Exploitation in Marketing DNA to the Masses, 81 Miss. L.J. 363 (2012).

2. Federal-State Conflicts: State Regulation and Medicinal Marijuana

Possession and use of marijuana have been subject to federal and state criminal sanctions for decades. See, e.g., Controlled Substances Act (CSA), 21 U.S.C. §§801-971. Despite this fact, patient advocacy and pro-marijuana groups successfully introduced "medicinal marijuana" laws beginning in the mid-1990s, for the most part through voter referenda. Proponents argued that the drug could be used to treat glaucoma and to reduce nausea and weight loss for persons undergoing chemotherapy. These state laws purported to shield from prosecution persons involved in prescribing, using, or possessing marijuana for specified medical purposes.

The California initiative is typical:

§11362.5. Medical use. . . .

 (b)(1) The people of the State of California hereby find and declare that the purposes of the Compassionate Use Act of 1996 are as follows:

  (A) To ensure that seriously ill Californians have the right to obtain and use marijuana for medical purposes where that medical use is deemed appropriate and has been recommended by a physician who has determined that the person's health would benefit from the use of marijuana in the treatment of cancer, anorexia, AIDS, chronic pain, spasticity, glaucoma, arthritis, migraine, or any other illness for which marijuana provides relief.

(B) To ensure that patients and their primary caregivers who obtain and use marijuana for medical purposes upon the recommendation of a physician are not subject to criminal prosecution or sanction.

(C) To encourage the federal and state governments to implement a plan to provide for the safe and affordable distribution of marijuana to all patients in medical need of marijuana.

(2) Nothing in this section shall be construed to supersede legislation prohibiting persons from engaging in conduct that endangers others, nor to condone the diversion of marijuana for nonmedical purposes.

(c) Notwithstanding any other provision of law, no physician in this state shall be punished, or denied any right or privilege, for having recommended marijuana to a patient for medical purposes.

(d) . . . [State criminal laws], relating to the possession of marijuana, and . . . relating to the cultivation of marijuana, shall not apply to a patient, or to a patient's primary caregiver, who possesses or cultivates marijuana for the personal medical purposes of the patient upon the written or oral recommendation or approval of a physician.

(e) For the purposes of this section, "primary caregiver" means the individual designated by the person exempted under this section who has consistently assumed responsibility for the housing, health, or safety of that person.

Cal. Health & Safety Code §11362.5; and People v. Mower, 49 P.3d 1067 (Cal. 2002) (interpreting key elements). For an update on state legislation, see National Conference of State Legislatures, State Medical Marijuana Laws, available at www.ncsl.org.

A substantial number of states now permit medicinal use of marijuana under some circumstances. Mark T. Smith et al., Recent Developments in Medicine and the Law, 47 Tort Trial & Ins. Prac. L.J. 393, 406-414 (2011) (16 states). These state medical marijuana initiatives are in profound conflict with federal criminal law. Controlled Substances Act (CSA), 21 U.S.C. §§801-971. In Gonzales v. Raich, 545 U.S. 1 (2005), the Supreme Court ruled that congressional authority to regulate interstate commerce included the power to prohibit the local cultivation and use of marijuana for medical purposes even in the states that permitted it. See Susan Okie, Medical Marijuana and the Supreme Court, 353 New Eng. J. Med. 648 (2005); George J. Annas, Jumping Frogs, Endangered Toads, and California's Medical Marijuana Law, 353 New Eng. J. Med. 2291 (2005); Lawrence O. Gostin, Medical Marijuana, American Federalism, and the Supreme Court, 294 JAMA 842 (2005); Note, 118 Harv. L. Rev. 1985 (2005).

After the Bush Administration's aggressive campaigns against the marijuana initiatives, the Obama administration initially announced a "non-enforcement policy" under which the federal government would refrain from prosecutions against individuals complying with state medical marijuana laws. Robert A. Mikos, A Critical Appraisal of the Department of Justice's New Approach to Medical Marijuana, 22 Stan. L. & Pol'y Rev. 633 (2011). In 2011, the Obama administration initiated an aggressive prosecutorial approach toward large-scale commercial operations, in part due to concerns that the medical marijuana laws were shielding substantial black market criminal activity. Erik Eckholm, Medical Marijuana Industry Unnerved by U.S. Crackdown, N.Y. Times, Nov. 23, 2011.

Problem: Drug Importation

Drugs approved for sale in the United States are often available at lower prices in other countries. Should senior citizens and the chronically ill be able to organize drug shopping trips to Canada and Mexico and to bring drugs back into the United States? What if the bargain hunters can demonstrate that they hold a valid prescription for the drugs and that the drugs have been approved for sale in the United States? Would state legislation authorizing or facilitating the importation be invalid?

The FDA Web site includes a page devoted to the topic, see www.fda.gov /Drugs/DrugSafety/ucm170594.htm. See also United States v. Rx Depot, Inc., 438 F.3d 1052 (10th Cir.) (disgorgement order related to reimportation profits upheld); and 21 U.S.C. §381(d)(1). For commentary on the reimportation issue, see generally Patricia M. Danzon et al., Commercial Importation of Prescription Drugs in the United States: Short-Run Implications, 36 J. Health Pol. Pol'y & L. 295 (2011) (concluding cost savings likely to be small and costs to foreign countries significant); Chang-fa Lo, Potential Conflict Between TRIPS and GATT Concerning Parallel Importation of Drugs and Possible Solution to Prevent Undesirable Market Segmentation, 66 Food & Drug L.J. 73 (2011); Abigail Zuger, Rx: Canadian Drugs, 349 New Eng. J. Med. 2188 (2003); Richard Frank, Prescription Drug Prices, 351 New Eng. J. Med. 1375 (2004); and Kevin Outterson, Pharmaceutical Arbitrage: Balancing Access and Innovation in International Prescription Drug Markets, 5 Yale J. Health Pol'y, L. & Ethics 193 (2005).

3. Clashes in Values and Jurisdictional Boundaries: Public Health Regulation and the Crushing Obesity Epidemic

■ PELMAN v. McDONALD'S CORPORATION

396 F.3d 508 (2d Cir. 2005)

RAKOFF, District Judge.

In this diversity action, plaintiffs Ashley Pelman and Jazlen Bradley . . . appeal from the dismissal, pursuant to Rule 12(b)(6), Fed.R.Civ.P., of Counts I-III of their amended complaint. Each of the these counts purports to allege, on behalf of a putative class of consumers, that defendant McDonald's Corporation violated . . . the New York Consumer Protection Act, during the years 1987 through 2002. Specifically, Count I alleges that the combined effect of McDonald's various promotional representations during this period was to create the false impression that its food products were nutritionally beneficial and part of a healthy lifestyle if consumed daily. Count II alleges that McDonald's failed adequately to disclose that its use of certain additives and the manner of its food processing rendered certain of its foods substantially less healthy than represented. Count III alleges that McDonald's deceptively represented that it would provide nutritional information to its New York customers when in reality such information was not readily available at a significant number of McDonald's outlets in New York visited by the plaintiffs and others. The amended complaint further alleges that as a result of these deceptive practices, plaintiffs, who ate at McDonald's three to five times a week throughout the years in question, were "led to believe[ ] that [McDonald's] foods were healthy and wholesome, not as detrimental to their health as medical and scientific studies have shown, ... [and]

of a beneficial nutritional value," and that they "would not have purchased and/or consumed the Defendant's aforementioned products, in their entire[t]y, or on such frequency but for the aforementioned alleged representations and campaigns." Finally, the amended complaint alleges that, as a result, plaintiffs have developed "obesity, diabetes, coronary heart disease, high blood pressure, elevated cholesterol intake, related cancers, and/or other detrimental and adverse health effects. . . ."

What is missing from the amended complaint, however, is any express allegation that any plaintiff specifically relied to his/her detriment on any particular representation made in any particular McDonald's advertisement or promotional material. The district court concluded that, with one exception, the absence of such a particularized allegation of reliance warranted dismissal of the . . . false advertising [claims]. As to the exception—involving McDonald's representations that its French fries and hash browns are made with 100% vegetable oil and/or are cholesterol-free—the district court found that, while the amended complaint might be read to allege implicit reliance by plaintiffs on such representations, the representations themselves were objectively nonmisleading. . . .

Plaintiffs' appellate brief . . . challenge[s] the district court's dismissal of the claims under §349 of the New York General Business Law, which makes unlawful "[d]eceptive acts or practices in the conduct of any business, trade or commerce or in the furnishing of any service in this state." Unlike a [false advertising claim], a private action brought under §349 does not require proof of actual reliance. Additionally, . . . §349 extends well beyond common-law fraud to cover a broad range of deceptive practices . . . [and] does not require proof of the same essential elements (such as reliance) as common-law fraud. . . . [T]he district court nonetheless dismissed the claims under §349 because it concluded that "[p]laintiffs have failed, however, to draw an adequate causal connection between their consumption of McDonald's food and their alleged injuries." Thus, the district court found it fatal that the complaint did not answer such questions as:

> What else did the plaintiffs eat? How much did they exercise? Is there a family history of the diseases which are alleged to have been caused by McDonald's products? Without this additional information, McDonald's does not have sufficient information to determine if its foods are the cause of plaintiffs' obesity, or if instead McDonald's foods are only a contributing factor.

This, however, is the sort of information that is appropriately the subject of discovery, rather than what is required to satisfy the limited pleading requirements of Rule 8(a), Fed.R.Civ.P. . . . So far as the §349 claims are concerned, the amended complaint more than meets the requirements of Rule 8(a). Accordingly, the district court's dismissal of those portions of Counts I-III of the amended complaint as alleged violations of §349 is VACATED, and the case is REMANDED for further proceedings consistent with this opinion. [In 2010, the district court refused to certify these claims as a class action.]

■NUTRITIONAL LABELING IN RESTAURANTS
21 U.S.C. §343

A food shall be deemed to be misbranded—[unless it meets the following requirements governing nutritional information] . . .

* * * *

(H) Restaurants, retail food establishments, and vending machines

(i) General requirements for restaurants and similar retail food establishments

Except for food described in subclause (vii), in the case of food that is a standard menu item that is offered for sale in a restaurant or similar retail food establishment that is part of a chain with 20 or more locations doing business under the same name (regardless of the type of ownership of the locations) and offering for sale substantially the same menu items, the restaurant or similar retail food establishment shall disclose the information described in subclauses (ii) and (iii).

(ii) Information required to be disclosed by restaurants and retail food establishments

Except as provided in subclause (vii), the restaurant or similar retail food establishment shall disclose in a clear and conspicuous manner—

(I)(aa) in a nutrient content disclosure statement adjacent to the name of the standard menu item, so as to be clearly associated with the standard menu item, on the menu listing the item for sale, the number of calories contained in the standard menu item, as usually prepared and offered for sale; and

(bb) a succinct statement concerning suggested daily caloric intake, as specified by the Secretary by regulation and posted prominently on the menu and designed to enable the public to understand, in the context of a total daily diet, the significance of the caloric information that is provided on the menu;

(II)(aa) in a nutrient content disclosure statement adjacent to the name of the standard menu item, so as to be clearly associated with the standard menu item, on the menu board, including a drive-through menu board, the number of calories contained in the standard menu item, as usually prepared and offered for sale; and

(bb) a succinct statement concerning suggested daily caloric intake, as specified by the Secretary by regulation and posted prominently on the menu board, designed to enable the public to understand, in the context of a total daily diet, the significance of the nutrition information that is provided on the menu board;

(III) in a written form, available on the premises of the restaurant or similar retail establishment and to the consumer upon request, the nutrition information required under clauses (C) and (D) of subparagraph (1); and

(IV) on the menu or menu board, a prominent, clear, and conspicuous statement regarding the availability of the information described in item (III)....

(vii) Nonapplicability to certain food

(I) In general

Subclauses (i) through (vi) do not apply to—

(aa) items that are not listed on a menu or menu board (such as condiments and other items placed on the table or counter for general use);

(bb) daily specials, temporary menu items appearing on the menu for less than 60 days per calendar year, or custom orders; or

(cc) such other food that is part of a customary market test appearing on the menu for less than 90 days, under terms and conditions established by the Secretary. . . .

Notes: Public Health Law and Obesity

1. *The Obesity "Epidemic."* News stories regularly decry the "epidemic" of obesity in the United States and other developed countries. Americans are allegedly

"addicted" to high-fat, high-calorie, processed foods that offer "empty calories" rather than balanced nutritional value. Food companies, restaurants, and TV cooking classes promote eating too many calories even as modern conveniences and sedentary pursuits such as Internet surfing have reduced our caloric needs. Advertisements for high-calorie foods and beverages, sometimes served in endless buffets, compete with media portrayals of the very thin and advertisements from companies selling amazing weight-loss solutions.

Numerous studies have documented the increasing prevalence of obesity in children and adults. More than two-thirds of adult Americans are either overweight or obese. See Committee on an Evidence Framework for Obesity Prevention Decision Making, Institute of Medicine, Bridging the Evidence Gap in Obesity Prevention: A Framework to Inform Decision Making (2010). One-third of children and adolescents over the age of two are overweight or obese. Id.; National Conference of State Legislatures, Obesity Overview, at www.ncsl.org; and Rachel Tolbert Kimbro et al., Racial and Ethnic Differences in Overweight and Obesity Among 3-Year-Old Children, 97 Am. J. Public Health 298 (2007).

While obesity is sometimes viewed as a health issue on its own, public health advocates typically target obesity and overweight because of associated negative health conditions. Obesity is correlated with specific diseases and conditions such as diabetes and cardiovascular disease. Committee on Progress in Preventing Childhood Obesity, Institute of Medicine, Progress in Preventing Childhood Obesity: How Do We Measure Up? (2007). Some types of foods, such as those containing "trans fats," carry specific risks. Valentina Remig et al., Trans Fats in America: A Review of Their Use, Consumption, Health Implications, and Regulation, 110 J. Am. Diet. Assoc. 585 (2010).

The obesity debate has a strong moral overlay: Overweight individuals are sometimes portrayed as morally blameworthy while efforts to prohibit or restrict unhealthy foods or to hold manufacturers or distributors of food products legally responsible are dismissed as the intrusion of the "nanny state" into unfettered consumer choice. See Rogan Kersh, The Politics of Obesity, 87 Milbank Q. 295 (2009). Despite the pervasive public accounts of crisis, there are critics of the medicalization of food and weight. See Michael Gard & Jan Wright eds., The Obesity Epidemic: Science and Ideology (2005).

2. *The Role of Public Health Law: Policy Options.* What should be the role of law and of public health law in particular in combating the "epidemic" of obesity? The "epidemic" is at least to some extent the product of individual decisionmaking about food consumption and exercise. Yet consumer choice occurs within a framework of complex environmental, economic, and market forces. See, e.g., Committee on Accelerating Progress in Obesity Prevention, Institute of Medicine, Measuring Progress in Obesity Prevention: Workshop Report (2012) (reviewing factors and initiatives).

A range of legal responses can affect this framework. Government policies can affect access to exercise in areas ranging from the tax treatment of gym fees, to the level of physical activity required in schools, to requirements for community sidewalks and parks. The foods available for consumer choice could be directly regulated to reduce exposure to substances like trans fats or indirectly regulated through farm subsidies that reduce the costs of healthy foods or tax policies increasing the costs of unhealthy foods, mirroring the familiar taxes on tobacco and alcohol. The decisionmaking environment for consumer choice could be influenced by requiring disclosure of the nutritional value of different types of food, such as in the restaurant nutritional labeling provisions found above, which were incorporated into the 2010 health care reform legislation.

What is the proper balance among (1) regulations designed to ensure that consumers have the information to make good food choices; (2) restrictive regulations diminishing access to certain types of foods; and (3) regulations designed to enhance opportunities for exercise? In addition to the sources noted above, see, e.g., Kelly Brownell & Thomas Frieden, Ounces of Prevention—The Public Policy Case for Taxes on Sugared Beverages, 360 New Eng. J. Med. 1805 (2009); CDC, Nutrition, Physical Activity, and Obesity, at www.cdc.gov/WinnableBattles/Obesity /index.html (materials on range of legal initiatives to combat obesity); Michael M. Grynbaum, New York Plans a Ban on Big Sizes of Sugary Drinks, N.Y. Times, May 30, 2012; Laura Kettel Khan et al., Recommended Community Strategies and Measurements to Prevent Obesity in the United States, 58 MMWR 1 (2009) (RR07); Katherine Pratt, A Constructive Critique of Public Health Arguments for Antiobesity Soda Taxes and Food Taxes, 87 Tul. L. Rev. 73 (2012); Special Issue on Physical Activity, 380 Lancet 188-196, 209-212, 219-229, 247-305 (2012); Symposium, Proceedings of the National Summit on Legal Preparedness for Obesity Prevention and Control, 37 J.L. Med. & Ethics 9-129 (2009) (special supp.).

Is there any role for tort law claims as suggested by the *Pelman* litigation, above? Sarah Taylor Roller et al., Obesity, Food Marketing and Consumer Litigation: Threat or Opportunity?, 61 Food & Drug L.J. 419 (2006); Joseph P. McMenamin & Andrea D. Tiglio, Not the Next Tobacco: Defenses to Obesity Claims, 61 Food & Drug L.J. 445 (2006).

3. *Restrictions on Trans Fats and Nutritional Information.* Some states and cities have attempted to ban harmful foods, with the focus on foods containing trans fat. See National Conference of State Legislatures, Trans Fat and Menu Labeling Legislation, available at www.ncsl.org; Susan Okie, New York to Trans Fats: You're Out!, 356 New Eng. J. Med. 2017 (2007).

What is the impact of nutritional labeling of restaurant food? Consumers might use the posted information to choose less caloric options and restaurants might have a clearer incentive to shift to lower calorie options. The preliminary evidence on the impact of restaurant labeling on consumer behavior is equivocal. See Marion Nestle, Health Care Reform in Action—Calorie Labeling Goes National, 362 New Eng. J. Med. 2343 (2010). As of late 2012, the FDA was working to provide proposed regulations implementing the nutritional labeling requirements for restaurants. See Gardiner Harris, White House and FDA Often at Odds, N.Y. Times, Apr. 2, 2012.

4. *Jurisdictional Conflicts.* The policy options for addressing obesity raise significant jurisdictional issues. International efforts are limited, with greater focus on providing access to food for those facing malnutrition than in addressing obesity. But see Joanne Stettner, International Obesity: Legal Issues, 24 Emory Int'l L. Rev. 210 (2010) (discussing WHO's global obesity strategy and initiatives related to food marketing to children).

What should be the roles of the federal, state, and local governments? Local initiatives may be easier to "pass" and can be tailored to local values and preferences but the result can be a patchwork of regulation that may be difficult for companies to negotiate while also leaving significant portions of the public in jurisdictions with no legislation. State or national policies can be more comprehensive but may offer lower protections. State or national preemption can reduce the flexibility of localities to adopt more stringent regulations. Paul A. Diller & Samantha Graff, Regulating Food Retail for Obesity Prevention: How Far Can Cities Go?, 39 J.L. Med. & Ethics 91 (2011) (special supp.); Sheila Fleischhacker & Joel Gittelsohn, Carrots or Candy in Corner Stores?: Federal Facilitators and Barriers to Stocking Healthier Options, 7 Ind. Health L. Rev. 23 (2010); Seth E. Mermin & Samantha K. Graff, Legal Primer for the Obesity Prevention Movement, 99 Am. J. Public Health 1799 (2009); Stephanie Strom, Local Laws Fighting Fat Under Siege, N.Y. Times, June 30, 2011.

These jurisdictional issues have been particularly important for the regulation of foods and labeling requirements. The nutritional labeling provisions in the Affordable Care Act, found above, were accompanied by a strong preemption provision:

§343-1. National uniform nutrition labeling

(a) Except as provided in subsection (b) of this section, no State or political subdivision of a State may directly or indirectly establish under any authority or continue in effect as to any food in interstate commerce— . . .

(4) any requirement for nutrition labeling of food that is not identical to the requirement of section 343(q) of this title, except that this paragraph does not apply to food that is offered for sale in a restaurant or similar retail food establishment that is not part of a chain with 20 or more locations doing business under the same name (regardless of the type of ownership of the locations) and offering for sale substantially the same menu items unless such restaurant or similar retail food establishment complies with the voluntary provision of nutrition information requirements under section 343(q)(5)(H)(ix) of this title. . . .

(b) Upon petition of a State or a political subdivision of a State, the Secretary may exempt from subsection (a) of this section, under such conditions as may be prescribed by regulation, any State or local requirement that—

(1) would not cause any food to be in violation of any applicable requirement under Federal law,

(2) would not unduly burden interstate commerce, and

(3) is designed to address a particular need for information which need is not met by the requirements of the sections referred to in subsection (a) of this section.

Would the *Pelman* litigation survive a preemption challenge? What better explains federal adoption of the restaurant nutritional labeling rules: a desire to bring the power of federal regulation to an important problem or the need to protect the food industry from uneven and uncertain regulation and the risk of tort liability at the state and local level?

See generally Lawrence O. Gostin, Law as a Tool to Facilitate Healthier Lifestyles and Prevent Obesity, 297 JAMA 87 (2007); Michelle M. Mello et al., Obesity—The New Frontier of Public Health Law, 354 New Eng. J. Med. 2601 (2006); Sarah Taylor Roller et al., Obesity, Food Marketing and Consumer Litigation: Threat or Opportunity?, 61 Food & Drug L.J. 419 (2006); Joseph P. McMenamin & Andrea D. Tiglio, Not the Next Tobacco: Defenses to Obesity Claims, 61 Food & Drug L.J. 445 (2006); Nestle, supra; Symposium, Childhood Obesity, 35 J.L. Med. & Ethics 7-157 (2007); Lindsay F. Wiley, Rethinking the New Public Health, 69 Wash. & Lee L. Rev. 207 (2012).

Problem: Helmets and the Law

Common sense suggests, and epidemiological data confirm, that motorcycle helmets can reduce dramatically the risk of injury or death associated with the use of motorcycles. Yet public debate about state helmet laws demonstrates that the reduction of deaths or injuries is not always sufficient to justify restrictions on individual liberty. What arguments can you marshal favoring or opposing the imposition of a mandatory helmet law? Are the issues similar for bicycle helmets? Should use of bicycle helmets be made mandatory? For all or just for minors? Would mandating helmet use protect public health by preventing head injuries or threaten public health by discouraging use of bicycles? Should it matter whether the law is designed to protect the safety of the rider or to reduce the costs of injuries in the health care system? Should this be a matter for state or federal lawmakers? What constitutional analysis would you apply to a law requiring cyclists of various types to wear helmets?

For an excellent survey of the issues related to motorcycles, see CDC, Helmet Use Among Motorcyclists Who Died in Crashes and Economic Cost Savings Associated with State Motorcycle Helmet Laws—United States, 2008-2010, 61 MMWR 425 (2012) ("Research has shown that when a state repeals its helmet law or opts for less restrictive requirements, helmet use decreases and motorcycle-related deaths, injuries, and costs increase"); Marian Moser Jones & Ronald Bayer, Paternalism and Its Discontents: Motorcycle Helmet Laws, Libertarian Values, and Public Health, 97 Am. J. Public Health 208 (2007); Melissa Neiman, Motorcycle Helmet Laws: The Facts, What Can Be Done to Jump-Start Helmet Use, and Ways to Cap Damages, 11 J. Health Care L. & Pol'y 215 (2008). See also Constantino v. Michigan Department of State Police, 794 F. Supp. 2d 773 (W.D. Mich. May 18, 2011) (upholding enforcement of state motorcycle helmet law); United States v. Bohn, 622 F.3d 1129 (9th Cir. 2010) (National Park Service had authority to require use of helmets).

For issues related to bicycle helmets, see Christopher S. Carpenter & Mark Stehr, Intended and Unintended Consequences of Youth Bicycle Helmet Laws, 54 J.L. & Econ. 305 (2011) (laws increase helmet use but decrease use of bicycles); D. L. Robinson, Bicycle Helmet Legislation: Can We Reach a Consensus?, 39 Accid. Anal. Prev. 86 (2007). See also State v. Portillo, 314 S.W.3d 210 (Tex. App.—El Paso 2010) (upholding city bicycle helmet ordinance against constitutional attack in state that allows motorcyclists not to wear helmets in some circumstances).

E. CONCLUSION

This chapter is a capstone in our focus on bioethical aspects of the treatment relationship. As you conclude this section, consider whether the rules developed in Chapters 3-6 consistently deal with the conflict between personal freedom and social interests. You may conclude that the chapters represent a progression of sorts, in which individuals' interests are measured against successively "weightier" social interests. In Chapter 3, the primary state interest is simply society's interest in preserving the life of the individual patient. Chapter 4 begins to look at situations where lives other than the patient's are at stake. In Chapter 5, the stakes are raised even higher on both sides of the conflict. On one side there is the notion that the individual herself owes an obligation of protection for the potential life of her fetus, and on the other side we recognize special constitutional protection for reproductive freedom. In this chapter, the state asserts the broadest interest, one that attempts to protect the health of the community as a whole. Do you think there is a matching pattern in the courts' rulings across these chapters? In other words, do individuals have consistently less freedom as the state's interests become progressively stronger?

Are the cases in this chapter united by any other common themes? Public health cases are often viewed in isolated groupings, identified by the specific public health strategy employed rather than by broader themes. Section C considered a wide range of state interventions into the treatment relationship. Does grouping these interventions together bring any clarification to your understanding of the law?

Public health challenges continue to elicit new strategies and new legal challenges to those strategies. These challenges may intensify in the future. Some scientists predict widespread outbreaks of highly lethal, antibiotic-resistant infections similar to the plagues that ravaged Europe centuries earlier. If this were to occur, would you predict greater or lesser recognition of personal liberty interests in public health matters?

This chapter also provides a useful jumping-off point for considering national discussion of health care expenditures and funding via payment for individual medical care by private and public health insurance. Professor Gostin and his colleagues have observed:

> Health promotion and disease prevention have a far greater impact on health than clinical services, in part because inadequate access to biomedical intervention is not the primary cause of premature morbidity and mortality. Evidence indicates that preventative interventions targeting behavior, the environment, and socioeconomic factors (including education, economic security, social support, and community safety) account for approximately 80% of the reduction in morbidity and mortality, whereas clinical care only accounts for 20%. This is because the burden of disease results from a combination of individual behavioral factors (e.g., smoking, diet, physical activity, and sexual behavior), the environment in which people live (e.g., environmental risk factors such as pollution, toxic chemical exposure, and contaminated food), and the social determinants of health (e.g., education, income, and housing). . . .
>
> Despite the value of health promotion and disease prevention in improving the public's health, they have limited political and financial support. Less than 5% of health spending is devoted to health promotion and disease prevention, even though [more than half of all deaths in the U.S. are from "preventable conditions"].

Lawrence O. Gostin et al., Restoring Health to Health Reform: Integrating Medicine and Public Health to Advance the Population's Well-Being, 159 U. Pa. L. Rev. 1777, 1792, 1795-1796 (2011). See also David Hemenway, Why Don't We Spend Enough on Public Health?, 362 New Eng. J. Med. 1657 (2010). Gostin and his colleagues argue that integrating public health promotion for populations with medical care for individuals can reduce costs (by, e.g., lowering the rates for obesity and its related health conditions) and improve outcomes (through, e.g., reducing hospital-acquired infections). See also Glen P. Mays & Sharla A. Smith, Evidence Links Increases in Public Health Spending to Declines in Preventable Deaths, 30 Health Aff. 1585 (2011). What is the proper balance between expenditures on public health—investments in the health of populations—as opposed to expenditures on health care for individuals?

Glossary of Organizational Terms and Acronyms

In previous generations, it was necessary to learn a specialized vocabulary to study law and medicine. This is still true, but in the past that vocabulary was purely medical. Today, it includes many obscure organizational terms as well. This is a selected glossary of organizational terms and acronyms, adapted from Prospective Payment Assessment Commission, 1996 Report to Congress.

ACA	Affordable Care Act of 2010
ACO	Accountable Care Organization
AFDC	Aid to Families with Dependent Children
AHA	American Hospital Association
AHRQ	Agency for Health Care Research and Quality
AMA	American Medical Association
CDHC	Consumer-Directed (or Driven) Health Care
CMS	Center for Medicare and Medicaid Services
COBRA	Consolidated Omnibus Budget Reconciliation Act of 1985
CON	Certificate of Need
DHHS	*See* HHS
DRG	Diagnosis-Related Group
ERISA	Employee Retirement Income Security Act of 1974
ESRD	End-Stage Renal Disease
FDA	Food and Drug Administration
HCFA	Health Care Financing Administration, now CMS
HHS	Health and Human Services, Department of
HIPAA	Health Insurance Portability and Accountability Act

HIV	Human Immunodeficiency Virus
HMO	Health Maintenance Organization
HRA or HSA	Healthcare Reimbursement or Health Savings Account (*see also* MSA)
IDS	Integrated Delivery System
IPA	Independent Practice Association
JCAHO	Joint Commission on Accreditation of Healthcare Organizations
MSA	Medical Savings Account
MSO	Management Services Organization
NCQA	National Committee for Quality Assurance
OBRA	Omnibus Budget Reconciliation Act
PHO	Physician-Hospital Organization
POS	Point of Service
PPACA	Patient Protection and Affordable Care Act
PPO	Preferred Provider Organization
PPS	Prospective Payment System
RBRVS	Resource-Based Relative Value Scale
SNF	Skilled Nursing Facility
SSI	Supplemental Security Income
TEFRA	Tax Equity and Fiscal Responsibility Act of 1982
UR/UM	Utilization Review, or Utilization Management

Accountable Care Organization (ACO)—An organization or network of physicians and/or hospitals that is able to receive payment from public or private insurers on a bundled basis that holds the provider group collectively responsible for the cost and quality of patients' care.

Adverse Selection—A term of art in insurance economics that describes the tendency of people who expect to have greater need for insurance to have more interest in purchasing insurance.

Community Rating—A method of determining an insurance premium structure that reflects expected utilization by the population as a whole, rather than by specific groups.

Consumer-Driven Health Care—An alternative to managed care, which seeks to activate patients to be cost-conscious consumers at the point of treatment, by requiring them to pay more out of pocket, and by providing better information about treatment options and costs.

Cost Shifting—Increasing revenues from some payers to offset uncompensated care losses and lower net payments from other payers.

Diagnosis-Related Groups (DRGs)—A system for determining case mix, used for payment under Medicare's PPS and by some other payers. The DRG system classifies patients into groups based on the principal diagnosis, type of surgical procedure, presence or absence of significant comorbidities or complications, and other relevant criteria. DRGs are intended to categorize patients into groups that are clinically meaningful and homogeneous with respect to resource use. Medicare's PPS currently uses 490 mutually exclusive DRGs, each of which is assigned a relative weight that compares its cost lines to the average for all DRGs.

Fee-for-Service—A method of reimbursing health care providers in which payment is made for each unit of service rendered.

Fiscal Intermediary—An insurer or other private company that the government contracts with to administer Medicare or Medicaid payments to providers.

Gainsharing—An awkward term referring to hospital arrangements that reward physicians for their participation in initiatives or programs that save costs or improve quality.

Health Maintenance Organization (HMO)—A managed care plan that integrates financing and delivery of a comprehensive set of health care services to an enrolled population. HMOs may contract with, directly employ, or own participating health care providers. Enrollees are usually required to choose from among these providers and in return have limited copayments. Providers may be paid through capitation, salary, per diem, or prenegotiated fee-for-service rates.

Health Savings Account (HSA)—A tax-sheltered account, similar to an IRA, and also known as a Healthcare Reimbursement Account (HRA) or Medical Savings Account (MSA), that is used to pay for medical expenses. It is coupled with high-deductible or "catastrophic" insurance, such that the HSA can pay for most ordinary expenses and insurance is used only for very expensive treatment.

Integrated Delivery System (IDS)—Any number of different arrangements among doctors, hospitals, other medical facilities, and insurers in which a full range of medical services is offered to employers, subscribers, or insurers. Includes conventional arrangements such as HMOs, as well as more innovative arrangements known as PHOs, PSNs, or MSOs.

Managed Care—Any system of health service payment or delivery arrangements in which the health plan or provider attempts to control or coordinate health service use to contain health expenditures, improve quality, or both. Arrangements often involve a defined delivery system of providers having some form of contractual relationship with the plan.

Moral Hazard—A term from insurance economics describing the fact that insurance makes people less concerned about the costs of their behavior for costs that are covered by insurance.

Peer Review Organization (PRO)—An organization that contracts with HCFA to investigate the quality of health care furnished to Medicare beneficiaries and to educate beneficiaries and providers. PROs also conduct limited review of medical records and claims to evaluate the appropriateness of care provided.

Physician-Hospital Organization (PHO)—A joint venture or affiliation among one or more hospitals and physicians or physician groups. The venture might encompass the full range of medical services, or only one or a few services.

Point-of-Service (POS)—A health plan allowing the enrollee to choose to receive a service from a participating or a nonparticipating provider, with different benefit levels associated with one or the other types of providers.

Preferred Provider Organization (PPO)—A health plan with a network of providers whose services are available to enrollees at lower cost than the services of non-network providers. PPO enrollees may self-refer to any network provider at any time.

Prospective Payment—A method of paying health care providers in which rates are established in advance. Providers are paid these rates regardless of the costs they actually incur.

Prospective Payment System (PPS) — Medicare's acute care hospital payment method for inpatient care. Prospective per case payment rates are set at a level intended to cover operating costs for treating a typical inpatient in a given diagnosis-related group. Payments for each hospital are adjusted for differences in area wages, teaching activity, care to the poor, and other factors.

Relative Value Scale — An index that assigns weights to each medical service; the weights represent the relative amount to be paid for each service. The relative value scale used in the development of the Medicare Physician Fee Schedule consists of three cost components, physician work, practice expense, and malpractice expense.

Risk Adjustment — A method to assess the relative severity or likelihood of medical conditions for different groups of patients, in order to adjust comparative measures of quality or cost. Risk adjustment is used, for instance, to increase or reduce payments to health plans to compensate for health care expenditures that are expected to be higher or lower than average. Risk adjustment is also used to determine whether differences in medical outcomes are due to patients' underlying conditions or instead to how providers treat them.

Uncompensated Care — Care rendered by hospitals or other providers without payment from the patient or a government-sponsored or private insurance program. It includes both charity care, which is provided without the expectation of payment, and bad debts, for which the provider has made an unsuccessful effort to collect payment due from the patient.

Utilization Review (UR) — A review of services delivered by a health care provider to evaluate the appropriateness, necessity, and quality of the prescribed services. The review can be performed on a prospective, concurrent, or retrospective basis.

Table of Cases

Principal cases are in italics. Cases cited in excerpted materials are not listed here.

Index